Eric Williams: The Myth and the Man seeks to
illuminate the political career of one of the
Caribbean's most elusive figures: Eric
Williams, the first prime minister of Trinidad
and Tobago. Selwyn Ryan uses a wide array
of primary sources, letters, interviews,
material from the Public Records Office in
the United Kingdom, State Department
records in the United States, and the Eric
Williams Memorial Collection in Trinidad
and Tobago, and demonstrates a strong
mastery of secondary sources to provide a
sophisticated political analysis of Williams's
role in Trinidadian and Caribbean politics.
Ryan focuses on Williams's entry into politics
and his tenure as prime minister from 1956
until his death in 1981. Ryan also provides an
interesting analysis of Williams's seminal
work, *Capitalism and Slavery*, and his role
as a scholar.

The book is a distillation of research and
writings that have spanned four decades.
Ryan brings a unique perspective to the work
as both a scholar and one who has studied,
criticized and been active in Trinidad politics
as chairman of the Public Utilities
Commission, Trinidad and Tobago, and as a
member of three national constitutional
reform committees.

ERIC WILLIAMS

Eric WILLIAMS

THE MYTH AND THE MAN

Selwyn Ryan

University of the West Indies Press
Jamaica • Barbados • Trinidad and Tobago • Open Campus

University of the West Indies Press
7A Gibraltar Hall Road   Mona
Kingston 7   Jamaica
www.uwipress.com

13 12 11 10 09   5 4 3 2 1

Ryan, Selwyn.

Eric Williams : the myth and the man / Selwyn Ryan.

p. cm.

Includes bibliographical references.

ISBN: 978-976-640-207-5

1. Williams, Eric Eustace, 1911–1981. 2. Political leaders – Trinidad and Tobago.
3. Prime ministers – Trinidad and Tobago – Biography. 4. People's National Movement.
5. West Indies (Federation). 6. Trinidad and Tobago – Politics and government.
I. Title.

F.2122.W5R83 2009   972.98'304'0924

Book and jacket design by Robert Harris.
Set in Adobe Garamond 11/14.5 x 29
Printed in the United States of America.

Contents

Acknowledgements

In the preparation and writing of this study, I was helped in various ways by several individuals whose contributions I wish to acknowledge. Thanks are due to Natasha Mortley, who served as my research assistant for a number of months during which she helped to identify some source documents that proved to be of great value. Deep gratitude is also due to my secretary, Mrs Gloria Lawrence, who patiently and without complaint typed and retyped the many versions of this manuscript that preceded the final product.

Thanks are likewise due to those who very kindly read and critiqued certain parts of the study where their expertise was particularly invaluable. Among them were Professor Bridget Brereton, Professor Anthony Maingot and Dr Anselm Francis. I also thank those who reviewed the manuscript at the request of the University of the West Indies Press and gave me the benefit of their frank academic judgement, from which I also benefited a great deal. The errors of fact remain mine. Given the controversial nature of Eric Williams's political personality, differences of opinion and interpretation as to who he was and what he really stood for are inevitable. Interpretations depend in large part on whether one accepts the authorized myths about Williams or whether one opts to reread and rescript the legends and narratives that have been associated with his name.

Over the years, I have had probing conversations with many who knew Williams well, both as prime minister and as political leader of the People's National Movement (PNM). Among those from whom I learned most about the Williams phenomenon were Ferdie Ferreira, Dodderidge Alleyne, Eugenio Moore, Gerard Montano, Winston Mahabir, De Wilton Rogers, Bernard Primus, Elton Richardson, Nicholas Simonette, Irwin Merrit and Cecil Dolly. It was a privilege to have had the opportunity to have them share their experiences as pioneers in the construction of the PNM and the modern state of Trinidad and Tobago. Those who pathologize and psychiatrize Williams's behaviour note that all of these men were very close to him professionally and emotionally, but eventually became victims of his inexplicable rage and seeming caprice amid great personal trauma. Their experiences are reflected in our narrative.

A number of other individuals and institutions were particularly helpful in the production of this book. Among them was the staff of the Sir Arthur Lewis Institute of Social and Economic Studies, which provided many of the services and courtesies that made this exercise possible; the West Indiana Division of the Main Library at the University of the West Indies, St Augustine, which houses the Eric Williams Memorial Collection; the editorial and production staff of the University of the West Indies Press, particularly Allyson Latta, who worked closely with me to improve the form of the manuscript, and Asha Claxton of the University of the West Indies Library, who assisted with the digitalizing and captioning of the images featured in the book. I wish to acknowledge my profound indebtedness to the Educational Foundation of the Royal Bank of Trinidad and Tobago, whose generous grant helped to defray the costs of sourcing research material as well as the expenses involved in preparing the manuscript for publication.

This book is dedicated to my wife, Jan Ryan, who provided the support, encouragement, environment and other intangibles that helped to sustain this project over the many years of its gestation.

Selwyn Ryan
October 2006

Abbreviations

ACDC	Action Committee of Democratic Citizens
BWIA	British West Indian Airways
CARICOM	Caribbean Community
DAC	Democratic Action Congress
DEWD	Development and Environmental Works Division
DLP	Democratic Labour Party
ECLAC	Economic Commission for Latin America and the Caribbean
EWMC	Eric Williams Memorial Collection
IRO	Inter-Religious Organisation
NAC	National Advisory Council
NJAC	National Joint Action Committee
OAS	Organization of American States
ONR	Organization for National Reconstruction
OPEC	Organization of Petroleum Exporting Countries
OWTU	Oilfield Workers Trade Union
PDP	People's Democratic Party
PNM	People's National Movement
POPPG	Party of Political Progress Groups
QRC	Queen's Royal College
TLP	Trinidad Labour Party
ULF	United Labour Front
WFP	Workers and Farmers Party

Introduction

As a professor, I tended to think of history as run by impersonal forces. But when you see it in practice, you see the difference personalities make.
– Henry Kissinger

This biography has, in a sense, been in gestation for a very long time. My interest in, and fascination with, Eric Williams began in 1955 when as a post-secondary school student, I listened attentively to his famous address "My Relations with the Caribbean Commission". That speech sharpened my motivation to further my education. Following that lecture, I attended every other that was delivered prior to the 1956 election at Harris Promenade, the San Fernando branch of the "University of Woodford Square". One lecture in particular, "Constitution Reform in Trinidad and Tobago", served to determine my vocational ambition. I would study history and then constitutional law. As it turned out, I did study history, at the University of Toronto, but switched to political science at Cornell University with the intention of returning to Trinidad and Tobago to get involved in politics. Happily, I gave up that ambition, and chose instead the academic vocation.

While at Cornell, then one of the major centres in the United States for the study of politics in the emergent states of Africa and Asia, I decided to give effect to my ambition to follow the lead set by Williams, who had written about the need to explore and document Caribbean history from a Caribbean perspective. Thus the choice of my PhD dissertation topic, "The Transition to Nationhood in Trinidad and Tobago". The early parts of that study dealt with some of Williams's precursors in the Trinidad nationalist movement – Alfred Richards, Andrew Cipriani, Tubal Uriah Butler, Albert Gomes, Adrian "Cola" Rienzi and Patrick Solomon. But the main focus of the thesis was the Eric Williams phenomenon, including the birth of the People's National Movement (PNM) and its struggle for Chaguaramas, constitution reform, federation and independence. Work on the thesis took me to Howard University, where Williams once taught, and to London, where I met and interviewed Learie Constantine, C.L.R. James, David Pitt and John La Rose among others. While in Trinidad doing fieldwork in 1963–64, I spent long hours at the West Indian Reference Library on Belmont Circular Road. I interviewed, and in some cases got to know quite well, PNM stalwarts such as De Wilton Rogers, W.J. Alexander, Irwin Merrit, Elton Richardson, Ferdie Ferreira, Gil Thomson, Nicholas Simonette, Ibbit Mosaheb, Donald Granado, Isabel Teshea, Winston Mahabir and several others who told me their stories. I also spent time in the Queen Street tailor shop owned by Hindu fundamentalist H.P. Singh, discussing the reactions of the Indian community to Williams, and interviewing Dr Rudranath Capildeo, who became political leader of the opposition Democratic Labour Party (DLP) in 1960. Many days were spent in the library at Balisier House, the PNM party headquarters, going through files and consulting the *PNM Weekly* (later the *Nation*), and I was given permission to attend several conventions of the PNM to see the party at work.

The thesis, which was approved in 1965, was in a sense the first instalment of the biography. The second instalment, *Race and Nationalism in Trinidad and Tobago*, published by the University of Toronto Press, was hailed by *Choice* as "one of the outstanding academic books reviewed during 1973", and was also included on its influential Outstanding Academic Book List (May 1974). The book is now out of print. I have often been asked to have it reissued, but resisted these invitations because I always regarded it as incomplete and in need of revision and updating. I never forgot Winston Mahabir's comment that *Race and Nationalism* was a very good book except that it sought to find a rational explanation for what Williams did. He advised that much was driven by tactical and personal considerations. Like Henry Kissinger, I also became more and more convinced that policy cannot be divorced from personality, and that history is not always determined by impersonal or structural forces.

Race and Nationalism was the first full-length study of the modern political history of Trinidad and Tobago. Its aim was to analyse the various processes and events that conduced to the making of the Trinidad and Tobago nation-state and the parties and personalities that helped to shape that development, the most significant being Eric Williams and the PNM. Williams's aim was to make one nation out of many and to fuse that creation with the state that he strove to build. Since the publication of *Race and Nationalism*, several other books and articles have appeared in learned journals and elsewhere to enrich our understanding of Williams and the impact he had on his contemporaries, admirers and political foes alike. Among the better known studies are those by Ivar Oxaal, *Black Intellectuals Come to Power* (1968), Ken Boodhoo, *The Elusive Williams* (2001), Ken Boodoo, ed., *Eric Williams: The Man and the Leader* (1986), Albert Gomes, *Through a Maze of Colour* (1974), E.C. Richardson, *Revolution or Evolution* (1984), Patrick Solomon, *Solomon: An Autobiography* (1981), Winston Mahabir, *In and*

Out of Politics (1978), Hamid Ghany, *Kamal* (1996), Ramesh Deosaran, *Eric Williams* (1981), Colin Palmer, *Eric Williams and the Making of the Modern Caribbean* (2006), and Lionel Seukeran, *Mr. Speaker Sir* (2006). Williams's autobiography, *Inward Hunger* (1969), and the unpublished versions thereof, were of great help to me in writing this book. I myself authored, edited or co-edited several books, articles and columns on Williams and the PNM, all of which have formed building blocks for this study. Among them are *Revolution and Reaction: Parties and Politics in Trinidad and Tobago 1970–1981*, *The Black Power Revolution: A Retrospective* (with Taimoon Stewart), *Trinidad and Tobago: The Independence Experience, 1962–1987* (as editor), and *Pathways to Power*, which deals in large part with the reactions of Indo-Trinidadians to Williams. I also wrote *Eric Williams: The Making of a Prime Minister*, a comic book in the Caribbean Leaders series.

As director of the Institute of Social and Economic Research at the University of the West Indies, St Augustine, I sponsored two extended symposia in 1990 and 1991. The first, "The Black Power Revolution 1970: A Retrospective", held in April 1990, revisited that revolution and provided a forum in which the *dramatis personae* of the 1970 "uprising" could tell their stories. Much was said about Williams's handling of the 1970 crisis during those discussions that proved invaluable to this book. The second symposium, "Eric Williams in Retrospect: The Williams Legacy Ten Years Later", held in April 1991, brought together academics and many of the key players in the political arena during the Williams years. The proceedings of these two meetings provided indispensable information about Williams from those who worked closely with him, opposed him, or merely observed him. Several other academic conferences dealing with Williams's classic study *Capitalism and Slavery* have been sponsored by the Department of History, the University of the West Indies, St Augustine, in conjunction with the Eric Williams Memorial Collection. Symposia have also been organized by Professors Barbara Solow, Selwyn Cudjoe and Colin Palmer. These academic meetings produced a wealth of data that were not available in 1967. Material relating to Williams in the Public Record Office in the United Kingdom, the US State Department Archival Records, and the Eric Williams Memorial Collection housed at the University of the West Indies, St Augustine, also became available and provided new source material.

I wish to record that my perspective on many of the issues discussed in this book was enriched by my experiences as a member of the Constitution Commission, to which Williams appointed me in 1971, and also by my chairmanship of the Public Utilities Commission, to which Williams appointed me in 1979. Both postings enabled me to observe Williams up close.

In this study, I sought to winnow as much of these experiences and the written material as possible, and bring them to bear on analyses first offered in *Race and Nationalism*. In a few chapters, some of what was said in the old study has been retained because little new material is available to alter the basic conclusions. In most cases, however, I wrote completely new sections or new chapters because these issues were either not dealt with in that book, or not adequately so.

The focus here is mainly on the public as opposed to the private Williams. My principal concern is with Williams as scholar, builder of the nation-state of Trinidad and Tobago, shaper of public policy, and political man. Yet a biographer could not avoid dealing with the personality issue and the various contested claims that Williams was psychiatrically challenged, and that his presumed illness is the key to understanding much of his contradictory and strange political behaviour, as well as some of the policy and personnel choices he made. Regretfully, one could not be faithful to the record without also dealing with the many allegations about sleaze that dogged Williams's regime and that he seemed unwilling or unable to address successfully.

Biographies, like obituaries, seek to tell readers something about the life and legacy of the person under scrutiny. They usually go beyond recitation of fact and detail to interrogate what was attempted by the actor, what was achieved or not achieved, and whether the failure was due to error, incompetence, wilful departure, defects of personality, or some objective constraint imposed by the physical, political or ideological environment. In doing so, biographers encounter a number of practical, methodological and epistemic problems, as well as issues relating to style and factuality. Questions arise as to what criteria should be used to judge the actor, especially if he (or she) is a controversial or a beloved and respected iconic public figure. Should he be judged by the heroic myths or legends that were officially constructed, the actions that were undertaken in seeking to fulfil the myth, or those that were contrary to those narratives? From whose perspective should the story be told, that of the actor and those who were within his charmed circle and who "spun" on his behalf, or those who were negatively affected by what was done? Whose narratives are to be privileged, those of the victor or those of the victim; the views of the educated elite and foreign critics or those of the inarticulate broad masses; those of individuals and groups who might have benefited by his programmes, or his rivals and his enemies? There are also those occasions when the lead actor is physically or psychiatrically ill and critical decisions are taken either by persons in the "throne room", or by the leader himself, who may be unaware that his vision and perspectives are affected by his illness.

There are also narratological considerations. Times change, as do paradigms, perspectives and orthodoxies. Should the actor, the action or the vision be judged in terms of what obtained and was deemed legitimate at the time, or by contemporary standards of what is right or wrong? If the narrative is being scripted long after the event, or even shortly after, whose memories or perspectives are being privileged? It is well known that memories are capricious, selective and mediated by ideology and demographic factors, including ethnicity and gender. We have likewise seen many instances of leaders who were vilified in the immediate aftermath of their time in office, but who were rehabilitated and transformed into mythologized heroes by successor generations whose experiences have led them to conclude that leaders who came later were worse, or because the difficulties faced were now better understood and appreciated. Kwame Nkrumah is one such leader. The reverse is the case with respect to Mao Tse-Tung. The official Communist Party line is that Mao was seventy per cent good and thirty per cent bad. A recent biography, *Mao*, by Jung Chang and Jon Halliday (2005), suggests that he was mostly bad. Biographies of Stalin, Mao's contemporary, have also come to diametrically opposed conclusions. Robert Conquest found Stalin to be a "vast dark figure looming over the century", a man who was defined by a "capacity for murder and deceit and for whom it was impossible to have a sympathetic relationship" (*Stalin: Breaker of Nations*, 1991). Robert Service (*Stalin: A Biography*, 2005), however, found him a "thoughtful man who was capable of kindness to relatives, a ruler of great assiduity and a delightful purveyor of jokes and mimicry". He was also, according to Service, "dangerously damaged".

Another problem biographers face is the question of the subject's speeches or policy papers and the extent to which he understood, modified or owned them. Most modern leaders have their speeches written for them by political specialists or public servants and sometimes deliver these without adding much value to the given text. Speech writers often force or slip ideas into such speeches without the leader fully understanding what message is being sent. Contradictory messages may also be sent if more than one person authors the speech. And finally, modern technology has compounded the problems that authors face: a great deal that was once committed to paper is now electronically transmitted, and remains unseen and unrecorded.

Biographers must also wrestle with whether they are writing mainly about the personal lives of their subjects, or about the times in which the subject lived. Questions arise as to what pedagogic or political purpose or lesson the study is intended to achieve. Is it meant to be merely descriptive and analytical, or didactic as well? Plutarch posed the questions starkly when he insisted that he was not writing history but about "lives". The writing of "history" he left to others who were interested in great and dramatic encounters. Plutarch's aim was to tell stories of great men that he hoped would serve as guides to action and character development. Given this aim, he preferred to focus on lesser events, since "It is not in the most conspicuous of a man's acts that good and bad qualities are necessarily best manifested. Some trivial act, a word, a jest often shows up character far more than [big] engagements" (Barrow 1967, 53).

Plutarch thus saw biography as portrait and not as photograph. Portraits were better able to capture the "real" hero. He was aware, however, that the "portrait" of a hero, to be a true likeness, must include that which might be unflattering. He agreed with Plato that "great natures produce great vices as well as great virtues", and that truth required that the full story be told. As Plutarch well put it,

> It is difficult, perhaps impossible, to exhibit a "life" which is blameless and pure; and so we must select its good elements and in these we must satisfy truth and present a likeness. The shortcomings and faults which run through a man's conduct owing to individual passion or political necessity we should regard rather as the defects of goodness than the misdeeds of wickedness; these our narrative should not display eagerly or gratuitously; rather it should show restraint out of regard for human nature, which produces nothing of unalloyed nobility, no character beyond the criticism of goodness. (Ibid.)

In this study of Williams, I have tried to follow Plutarch in his search for balance. I have focused on the good, the bad, and the very bad, and have found that Williams was not always the hero that the constructed myths made him out to be. Neither was he the wicked genius that some saw and still see him to be. The truth about him lies in the middle, as readers shall discover. Williams was capable of great human warmth as well as rudeness and insensitivity. That, and much else, remains puzzling.

I found it difficult to write about Williams's life without constructing the broad historical setting for that life. Indeed, whereas Plutarch focused mainly on lives, I found it necessary to focus on the times and the great and conspicuous encounters that Williams undertook in his heroic struggle.

Professional historians, both traditional and post-modern, have intensely debated the historiographic issues raised above. The post-modernists follow Nietzsche and Michel Foucault, who argued that "there are no facts in themselves", and that "it is always necessary to begin by introducing a meaning in order that there can be a fact". Post-modernists maintain that there are no "facts" or historical "data" that are "givens". "Facts" are ideologically elaborated, historicized, mythologized and processed by the culture before they become part of the historical edifice. Thus history is not about the past as such, but about ways of imagining and constructing the past from the "debris we find around us".

Language or "phrase regimes" are also important historical inputs. Language shapes perception and may in fact constitute the "infrastructural" imperative of history rather than its "superstructure". Interrogating the role of language in narrative is therefore an important aspect of what Kellner referred to as "getting the story crooked". I have looked at Williams through various analytic and narrative lenses – Grecian, Hegelian, Weberian and psychiatric – in the hope that by reading him "crooked" we will get to understand him "straight", or approximately so (see Kellner 1997, 127). I trust that I have succeeded in doing so. At the same time, I am aware that there are many Williams experts out there and that there will always be competing versions of what Williams said or meant when he spoke, and of who he really was.

In writing this biography, I have tried to steer a middle path in terms of documentation and footnoting. I wished to avoid over-referencing and over-footnoting while at the same time remaining faithful to my obligations to the scholarly community. I hope that I have not fallen uncomfortably between the two stools of readability and scholarly rigour. I may also have erred in the use of extended quotations when a summary would have sufficed. Using long quotations is a style that I have adopted over the years. My view is that letting the actors speak for themselves helps to authenticate the work and more effectively clinches the argument being made.

A word about the length of the work. My initial intent was to produce the study in two volumes. After writing and submitting what was conceived as volume 1, I came to believe that the work should be produced in two volumes simultaneously. In the end, integrating the two volumes seemed the best of the three options, notwithstanding what doing so would mean in terms of the size of the book. I trust that readers will concur that the choice made was the correct one.

PART 1

THE EARLY YEARS

1 The Frustrations of Genteel Poverty

The massas want to restore the old order with its social practices that have kept you and me where we have been with all our frustrations and inhibitions.
    – Eric Williams, *Massa Day Done*, 1961

"Some men are born great, some achieve greatness, some have greatness thrust upon them. Greatness Trinidad style was thrust upon me from the cradle." With this modification of Shakespeare's oft-quoted lines, Eric Williams began the third chapter of his autobiography, *Inward Hunger: The Education of a Young Colonial* (1960). Eric Williams was born in 1911, the first of the twelve children of Henry and Eliza Williams. Some siblings claim that his place of birth was 16 Dundonald Street, Port of Spain. Williams asserts otherwise. As he tells us: "I was born in a small house on Oxford Street, a typical house of the lower classes in a typical street in Port of Spain. . . . In the backyard were the kitchen, an indoor toilet, and servant quarters; the smallest West Indian middle class house has some sort of room for the servant, a visible and tangible ascent of the family in the social scale."[1]

Williams's parents were somewhat atypical of the lower middle class in those days. His father, who was thirty-three when Eric was born, was, he says, a "strong silent man, reserved, except in the company of close friends. On his father's side, he was Negro. On his mother's side, his father had some Scottish blood, which is found all over the West Indies, beginning first with the transfer of Jacobites in the English Civil Wars, ending with the stream of young bachelors – overseers and drivers brought in for the sugar industry in the 19th century."

Eric tells us that his grandmother, Onemia Hunt, was "high yallah", and not "the *café au lait* type so highly esteemed in the West Indies". Others felt "she looked like a white person". Williams in fact claimed "Scotch ancestry", among others. As he complained, "The dilution of my Scotch ancestry by other racial strains no doubt explains the marked inability which has characterized our family's failure to emulate the well known Scotch virtue of economy."

Williams also tells us a few things about his mother, née Eliza Frances Boissière. "My mother was much lighter in colour than my [father]. Her family bore a French name of which she and my father were proud, indicative of the social importance of the French creoles" who had fled Martinique and Guadeloupe during the radical years of the French Revolution. As a result of his racial mixture, Williams had what his family and friends called "good grass", that is, hair that was not woolly. His "grass" was the pride of his family. It was in fact often assumed that he had "Indian blood", and people were surprised to learn that he did not have a single drop of that "blood" in his veins. He claimed, however, to have had almost everything else. "Our family is typical of the miscegenation characteristic of the island's cosmopolitan population. The family runs almost the entire gamut of race and colour in Trinidad and Tobago." No mention was made of the fact that his great-grandmother was of Carib descent and that she had "straight long hair".[2]

In early versions of his autobiography, Williams takes time to comment at length on the issue of race and social class and hair types that resulted from mixed marriages in the West Indies. He notes that some offspring of those marriages were darker than their siblings but had "good hair", while others were fairer but had "bad hair". The latter were referred to as "shabeens" and "wire heads". West Indians, he noted, were "mortally afraid of bad hair, especially of the kinky variety maliciously compared in the local patois to 'goat dung' ". Like many black or mixed families, the Williams family was Afrophobic. They were mortally afraid of their African heritage. "My parents were adamant in their philosophy that one might come from Africa – that was one's misfortune, but hardly one's fault. But there was no point in going back to Africa. That would not only be one's misfortune, but one's fault."

In Williams's eyes, his family was made poor by the social system then prevailing, which ranked families and individuals on the basis of race, colour and other ascriptive social qualifications. As Williams complained, "In 1911, a young man in the civil service was denied the promotion he deserved and expected because, in the opinion of the head of his department, he lacked 'social qualifications'. The *Port of Spain Gazette* protested against the injustice. But the lack of social qualifications was an impediment to the progress of thousands of Trinidadians inside and outside the civil service. My father was one of them" (1969, 26). The Williams family was materially poor, as were a majority of the black families in Trinidad and Tobago in those years. There was, however, a dimension to their poverty that was not typical. They belonged to the aggrieved poor, the *déclassé* coloureds, that element which felt poverty was not their allotted condition but one thrust upon them by the structures of the social system. They were members of what Williams himself called the "genteel poor", victims of a vicious system of institutionalized racism and snobbery. As Williams himself tells us in the early drafts of his autobiography, "My mother and father had a profound sense of propriety and gentility. The house was always kept clean, and I can still recall my exasperation at having to assist with wiping off the dust from the myriad fine ornaments which decorated what were called the 'whatnots', full pieces of furniture about the height of a hat rack." Being neither "fish nor fowl" made their poverty less easy to bear, more shameful and humiliating than it was for their neighbours, from whom they barricaded themselves, not wanting to be seen or laughed at in their misfortune.

Henry Williams was not only without the appropriate social qualifications. He also lacked a good education and money. Williams makes a cryptic observation about his father's "three great expectations". One was that his wife's father, Jules Boissière, would be a beneficiary of the will of his father, Monsieur Jean Nicholas de Boissière, the French-creole baron of Champs Elysées, Maraval. Jules was the mulatto son of Jean Nicholas and a coloured Trinidadian woman. Eliza, Jules' second child, brought up her eleven brothers and sisters while still a teenager, and considered herself a member of the Boissière family. The story, as told by Gèrard Besson (1998; Besson and Brereton 1992) and Michael Pocock (1993), is that Eliza and Henry were "victims of the will", in that her father was not given the bequest (TT$4,000) that was left him by his father. Besson argues that this family event helps to explain the "chip" on Williams's shoulder and his political hostility to the white French-creole "massas".[3] In his mind, his family were "black French Creoles", dark-skinned descendants of one of the most prominent members of that aristocracy, and they had been schemed out of their inheritance, and their place in the family, much to their shame, chagrin and economic disadvantage.

Williams acknowledged that his father was disappointed in his hopes for a legacy.

> His three great expectations of money failed him. His mother, the daughter of a local white family of means, was disowned by them for eloping with and marrying a Negro employed by them in a menial capacity. This was deemed "unforgivable". The second disappointment was that his wife had the misfortune of knowing that a legacy allegedly made to her father went to another member of the family with the same initials, while my father's high hopes of a windfall on the death of her uncle resident in England never materialized. His third line of defence, my godfather, proved equally illusory. The estate was left to his common law wife. (Williams 1969, 26)

The principal source of the family's economic problems was that for reasons having to do with religion, birth control was not an option. As he reflected, "My parents' dilemma [was] to be faithful children of the Church and not to be poor parents. On my father's salary [approximately TT$60 per month], they couldn't be both" (ibid., 27). Henry was a devout Catholic, and birth control was an option he could not contemplate. "The school boy's joke that the Lord sent rain but did not tell you not to wear rain coats represented a philosophy that was unattainable by a practicing Catholic. In my father's house, we simply got wet."

The biennial appearance of a new offspring to feed and clothe imposed great strains on the family, not to say anything about the family matriarch, who became fat, querulous, and prone to headaches and nutritional deficiency. Eric had to help not only with routine chores, but also with the quotidian problems of family management. As he recalled: "My father desperately struggling to keep our heads above water in the struggle against the current; my mother borne down more and more by the rigours of child birth, the effort to stretch limited funds, and the strain of looking after an increasingly complicated household, the disciplining of the younger children fell increasingly on my shoulders."

While Williams stressed the role of his father in shaping his future and his attitudes, his mother was also pivotal. Many of his authoritarian traits seem to have derived from her influence. Williams's sisters tell us that she was a stern disciplinarian who insisted that things be done her way. She also considered herself a cut above those in the neighbourhood. As they told Boodhoo, "She had the French embedded in her, she had the French style. She had many French ways. She thought she was an aristocrat. She believed she was better than others. We called her 'Madam' [behind her back]. She was very proud. Everyone, including Henry, took orders from her. She was the boss, she gave the orders. You could not skylark! When she spoke, 'no dog barked' " (2001, 32). As we shall see, Eric would also insist that no dogs must bark when he gave orders. He would often repeat his mother's dreaded injunction to those who dared to challenge him. And it was a short step from helping to discipline his siblings to seeking to discipline his party and government. In respect of his inclination to be authoritarian, Williams claims that it was inborn As he tells us, when as children they played school, "I was always the teacher, always the disciplinarian, satisfying not only a pronounced trait in my character, but also, in the milieu I am describing, bearing rich dividends with pupils who, like most young girls of those days, wore short dresses and no trousers, and who showed no reluctance whatsoever to being benched in true Trini school fashion, smacked on the buttocks which I insisted on baring, and derived as much pleasure from being punished as a teacher derived from punishing [*sic*]" (ibid.).

The Williams family sought in various ways to overcome its perceived poverty. Eliza did so by making baked and crochet products for sale. Young Eric had to help her with the production and distribution process. As he tells us, "With a servant boy or girl carrying the basket [the $3 a month for whom the family could ill afford], I walked around to the various houses filling orders or getting new ones." Williams was a "reluctant *marchand*", and was mortally afraid that he would be seen by his school colleagues. "Ashamed of anything suggesting of work or poverty, I used to slink by in the streets, hoping that I would not meet any of my school mates. What on earth would I have done if I had to tote the basket myself, I do not know." Williams also resented the fact that deliveries had to be effected at the back or service entrances to the Queen's Park Hotel, and the fact that he was chastised when he failed to do so. Clearly, the Williams family did not suffer poverty gracefully. Henry sought to augment the family income by auditing the accounts of a number of friendly societies, but "it would have been necessary for my father to audit the accounts of all the Friendly Societies in the Island and my mother to supply cakes and bread to the entire population of Port of Spain in order to meet the fundamental family problem, which was the steady and inexorable gap between population and resources."

The fact that young Eric was forced to help his mother and father served him well in later life. Helping his father taught him to do complex arithmetical calculations in his head. He grew to love figures and to manipulate them easily. Working with his mother helped to provide him with kitchen skills that were useful to him in his bachelor days. He could not only cook and bake bread and cake, but frost the latter as well. Being the eldest, and his mother's principal assistant, he also helped with household chores and the purchasing of clothing for his younger sisters. "With my mother immobilized, and my father at work, I was obviously the man of the house." His boast was that the skills learned in buying lingerie, stockings and so on were later to serve him in good stead. The taste he developed for sweet meats may, however, have proved his undoing.

Poverty meant that the family could not afford medical care for Eric when he fell while playing football at school. "I was racing down the field with the ball. I was charged by an opponent, was lifted up in the air, and fell heavily on my head. No doctor was called in. The result was a progressive hearing impairment. I have grown more and more convinced that that fall had something to do with the deterioration of my hearing." Williams later argued that the impairment was a blessing in disguise. "A hearing aid is a powerful weapon against an opposition in parliament. One can always turn it off" (1969, 29). Interestingly, his lifelong friend and doctor Halsey McShine does not remember Williams having a hearing problem while they were at Queen's Royal College (QRC) or Oxford. He surmised that the impairment may have developed while Williams was in the United States.

Williams also had serious dental problems (pyorrhea), which he blamed on the fact that he did not see a dentist until he was sixteen years old. As he tells us,

> I paid my first visit to the dentist when I was sixteen. An enormous consumption of sweets, the use of coconut bark as a substitute for a toothbrush (a very common form of *ersatz* in my youth), and a total lack of instruction or advice in the field of personal hygiene – they all took their toll. . . . It is to this early neglect that must be attributed not only the bad condition of my teeth, but what is worse, that psychological outlook which allowed me to become so absorbed in my work that I had no time to visit my dentist until the gentle persuasions of my second wife, plus the kind ministrations of

my Trinidad dentist, a former student of mine and one of my closest friends, combined belatedly, three years ago, after several other unnecessary losses, to put regular dental attention first on my list of priorities.

Williams never overcame his "fear" of the dentist.

Providing food for the home was a continuing problem. Williams tells us that the Sunday table was good enough, but the rest of the week meant beef bones for soup, salt fish, tasso or dried beef, and "red" butter. Given the absence of refrigeration, one shopped in small quantities from the nearby Portuguese shop (mainly on credit), and as late in the day as possible in order to keep food fresh into the evening. On Sundays, however, the family sought to engage in the "gourmandizing which contemporary Caribbean society has inherited from the big house of the plantation economy".

The large family faced chronic difficulties in securing affordable but decent accommodation. Not being able to own a family home, they were peripatetic renters. As Williams tells us with biting wit:

> The housing problem was first in the list of evils which afflicted the family. We disputed our way all over Port of Spain, seeking living space at low rentals. In my first twenty-one years in Trinidad, we changed houses eight times, and it is possible to identify members of the family not only by name or by sex or by age, but also by the house in which each was born. The descending family fortunes were reflected in the descent from the water closet to the cesspit, and in one bad case the bailiff appeared. (Ibid., 27)

Williams tells us that the "the lowest point in the peregrinations was our transfer to Diego Martin in the midst of hardships occasioned by World War I". Diego Martin was then very different from what it is today. In those years, he had to contend with mosquitoes, alligators, bush fires, rickety cesspits as well as with the denizens of the night, *jumbies, soucouyants, diablesses* and other underworld characters of Trinidad's colourful folklore. Williams was particularly upset by the cesspits that faced the family, but observed that "the cesspit was not the only indignity to which genteel poverty exposed us".

The house that the family occupied in Woodbrook was not much better. Williams described it as a "chicken coop, but the rent was low and we had been given notice to move from the house we had occupied for some years in Newtown". Williams was unhappy in the Woodbrook home. It was in this house that the bailiff arrived one day to take away the family furniture because Henry had fallen into arrears on his rental payments. The levy was miraculously paid, but the problems remained. "The ordeal of removal, the horror of the cesspit, the dread of eviction, were only the external aspects of the increasing gravity of our housing problem. The domestic aspects were no less nagging." Williams was referring here to overcrowding in the home, the need for siblings to share beds, the quality of what passed for the bed and the boards on which it lay, the way in which one had to access the bed given the fact that the wooden frame and the room were roughly of the same size, and the routines that the family had to undertake to keep insects under control. Williams observed that the "bed bugs thrived more numerous than the stars on a beautiful tropical night, and more juicy than I have ever seen until I went to Harlem. The cleaning of the boards and the killing of the bed bugs were a regular Saturday morning chore."

Books and other educational material were hard to come by in the home, as were school clothes.[4] "The prayer book and the school text book represented the sum total of the literature in the home. . . . For the newspapers, we depended most of the time on friends and neighbours." McShine quipped that "there were more children around than books". Family poverty did not, however, prevent young Williams from pulling himself up by his bootstraps. Like thousands of other youngsters of his time, economic disadvantage served as a spur to effort. The need to escape poverty provided the incentive and the discipline that helped many to escape their pedestrian origins. Williams repeatedly referred to the role his parents played in equipping them to climb the social ladder. "My parents, like all good Trinidadians, passionately desired a higher status for their children. But this was not simply a material question, a matter of dollars and cents. They had all the complexes of the lower middle class, and status also involved for them questions of colour and hair."

Eric's siblings were not as fortunate as he and his brother Mervyn to get a good secondary education. His father's income was insufficient to meet the fees ($16 per term) that schools then charged. As he tells us: "It soon became an unspoken law in our family that a secondary education depended on the capacity of the child to acquire it, that is to say, by winning a college exhibition. Of the family of eleven, only four attended a recognized secondary school – myself and my younger brother who won college exhibitions and obtained our school certificates, my second sister, and my youngest sister who was given free tuition on my father's death." Williams felt that his success at school was in part due to his being the first born: "I am convinced by my experience in my family that as the eldest child, whether or not I was more pampered than the rest, I was able to acquire those habits and that foundation in an atmosphere of relative quiet and devoid of that pressure of living space which were totally impossible to my younger brothers."

What Williams lacked in material resources was compensated for by the encouragement provided by his parents, who saw that for children like theirs, education represented the only exit option from servitude and marginalization. As for the offspring of many other black or mixed families, getting ahead meant marrying well, securing a job or, for those who aspired to white-collar status, a place in one of the country's "good" secondary schools.[5] Such places were extremely limited in Williams's time. The options were St Mary's College, a Roman Catholic institution, or QRC, a state-funded school. Both were excellent schools, and competition between them for the few prized national scholarships was keen. Competition to gain entry was also keen. Many gained access because they had the right religious, social, economic, ethnic or chromatic qualifications, and above all the ability to pay, and those without such credentials had to win one of the state-financed college exhibitions. In 1922, the year in which Williams wrote the scholarship examination, there were eight such places. Prior to that, there were only four. In June 1922, when he was not yet eleven years old, Williams won one of the eight.

His success was no doubt due to native brilliance, but also to the intellectual discipline to which he was exposed at Tranquility School, Port of Spain's leading state-owned primary and intermediate school. Discipline was also supplied by his home environment. As Williams tell us,

> My father took the steps necessary for the realisation of the pious hope he shared with the majority of Trinidadians. The first was an unrelenting domestic pressure. It began in the cradle. He had read in a magazine about a nurse teaching a young child the alphabet and nursery rhymes. He promptly bought an alphabet card and began to put me through my paces. When I could recite the alphabet, I received a tricycle.
>
> I was never allowed to forget that I was the rising hope of my stern, unbending relatives. How my father sneered, for example, when on the occasion of one prize-giving day at the elementary school, he read out the title of the prize I had been given for having come third – Great Expectations! I should have come first. Poor man! Little did he suspect then how often I would come third before I came first or what hard times would have to precede the realization of his great expectations.[6] (1969, 31)

As in many black families of his time, extra lessons for their offspring were deemed essential. Williams's father paid the $1 per month ungrudgingly from his limited purse. Henry was so anxious to ensure that Eric and his brother were successful that he did what many other parents of his time considered to be absolutely necessary to ensure success: he took them into the hills of Laventille to an obeah woman. As Williams recalls,

> The practice [of obeah] persisted after emancipation, and it is astonishing how many West Indians, even the so called educated ones, still believe in love potions, or the efficacy of "stay at home coffee", or who would not pick up a coin in the street for fear that it may have been deliberately put there by an enemy with the intention of harming them. My younger brother and myself were dragged along with my father on his regular visits to the skinny mulatto woman (from St. Vincent I believe) living in the Laventille hills, and I seem to recall my father providing quite a number of chickens for the ritual occasions.
>
> My mother became increasingly restive under this dispensation, and the show down came one morning before my father went to work. Angry, with tears in her eyes, my mother deliberately smashed an earthen ware pot which the obeah woman had given

my father. I remember the incredulous look on my father's face, and how, always controlled and disciplined, he left without saying a word. Shortly after a priest began visiting the house regularly, and before I could fully realize what was happening. My father had become one of the prime movers in the building of a new church; far off in what was then the last street in Woodbrook, St. Theresa's Church. (EWMC folio 139)

Father Williams was justifiably proud of his sons' achievement. He was equally sensible in his choice of the secondary school to which Eric would be sent. As Eric wrote, "My father drew a distinction between religion and education." Though a staunch Catholic, he chose to send Eric to QRC, a decision which was "warmly approved" by his mother. In the earlier version of his autobiography, however, Eric gives no credit to his parents for the choice of QRC:

Why I chose QRC I cannot say. My father left the decision to me. The parish priest was aghast and even threatened to excommunicate my parents. I remained curiously unmoved. If anyone was to be excommunicated, it was me. Was it an early inability to see, as I still cannot see, any connection between education and religion, the school and the church? Or an early preference for state over private enterprise under West Indian conditions? Or the first faint glimmering of anti-clericalism? Or the first indication that religion was not profoundly to influence my life and thinking? I cannot say. I know only that the decision to enter the state school was my own, and neither my father or my mother ever tried to influence me one way or another. (Ibid.)

The choice of QRC, by whomsoever, would prove to be pivotal in Williams's odyssey. There he would meet W.D. Inniss, one of the two black teachers on the staff at the time, the other being C.L.R. James. Both would play critical roles in shaping his academic and political careers. The school's curriculum was then almost completely British. Williams would later recall that in his special subject, British colonial history, little attention was paid to the West Indian environment. "The British education of the young colonial was not distracted by the West Indian environment . . . there were some references to the West Indies, but they were in terms of European diplomacy and European war. What I learnt of slavery and the plantation economy came from Roman history."

The next step in Williams's "great ascent" was the Island Scholarship that was then the acme, the *summum bonum*, of the secondary school education system in Trinidad and Tobago. Winning that prize was the ambition of many a student. The same held for their parents because it was one of the pivotal escape routes from obscurity. Williams notes

One of the consequences of the system was to make the young child, particularly the boy, in the days of which I write, a potential economic and social asset, a possible future professional man. The only things that stood between him and the Elysian Fields were the Cambridge examination, the House Scholarship and the Island Scholarship. The

result was a premium on brains that nowhere else, except in another West Indian territory, affects the young child to such an extent – a pressure on him to do his studies and
a pathetic concern with the year of his birth.

Williams also had the following to say about how the society regarded the
Island Scholar: "The island scholar, around whom the entire school system
revolved, regarded himself and was regarded as a superior soul . . . cut out to play
a superior role in the goddam bourgeoisie. The coloured bourgeoisie, that is, but
not to be despised socially, with the public awe of the doctor, the "my learned
friend" salutation of the lawyer, the deference of the social climber, the salutes
of the policeman. The superiority consisted in the public eye precisely of the
British culture and the disparagement of the West Indian" (1969, 35).

Dr Patrick Solomon, one of Williams's political associates and also an Island
Scholarship winner, likewise commented on the role that winning the scholarship
played in the lives of those fortunate enough to secure it: "To scores of us, a scholarship was the only avenue of escape from the unsatisfying drudgery offered by
a civil service with severely limited opportunities, and the only door to a profession which brought independence and an income compatible with civilized
living. . . . To pass was in itself a good effort; to come first was to become a
national hero" (1981, 13). Another of Williams's political associates, Dr Winston
Mahabir, also indicated how important the winning of an Island Scholarship
was to his father. As he wrote in *In and Out of Politics*, "In my father's mind,
there was one burning ambition. One – any – of his four sons *must* win an Island
Scholarship, the *El Tucuche* of academic achievement in Trinidad and Tobago,
to which only a handful of Indians had climbed" (1978, 7).

Williams made a number of observations about life at QRC that are worth
restating. It was, he tells us, a grammar school based on the English model. Its *raison d'être* was to prepare boys for the external exams of Oxford and Cambridge
and through these for English university life. Ironically, only four or five boys ever
went to Oxbridge in any one year. Williams was also critical of the fact that the
school trained boys to be outstanding scholars and not to be good citizens when
they left its portals: "The burden of responsibility far beyond the weight of such
young shoulders has been borne by many before and after me, and will be borne
by many today, and will continue to be borne until that revolution takes place
in West Indian public opinion and social attitudes of which there is as yet no sign,
and the extensive production of good citizens is given precedence over the intensive cultivation of distinguished individuals." Here Williams was rejecting the
QRC educational model of which he was one of the most outstanding products.
One needs to bear this comment in mind when we look at what he did to the
school when he came to power. Unlike French universities, which regarded educated colonials as Frenchmen, the English regarded their "civilized" or enlight-

ened colonials as "coloured Englishmen in the West Indies". They were "tropical Englishmen" who played English games like soccer and cricket. In the end, they became veritable "Afro-Saxons".

While at QRC, Williams distinguished himself academically in Latin, French and Spanish, and in his later years, in history. As he himself tells us, "In contrast to my early flair for languages, I found myself in history relatively late. Thereafter, the distinctions came easily and without fail, the high water mark being reached with a distinction in the Higher Certificate in my third try. As compared with languages and history, I was never good or interested in geography or advanced mathematics. With the sciences, I had no problem whatever; I was a failure" (1969, 32).

Williams was regarded by his teachers and contemporaries as a "big brain" and a shining star, perhaps the brightest boy to have passed through the school's gates. As Victor Stollmeyer, the white creole who would rally to his political banner in 1956, recalled, "This man was far and away the most popular, charismatic and brilliant boy during my years at QRC. Most stood in awe of his achievements; a few were envious, but hardly dared show it." Williams won many class prizes over the years, leading Stollmeyer to wager "that his performance has never been bettered or even equalled. It may never be" (as cited in Boodhoo 2001, 47). C.S. Doorly, a master at QRC, shared Stollmeyer's view, noting that Williams's mark of 1,732 out of 1,800 was one of the best ever seen at the school.

Because he entered QRC at age eleven, Williams had three opportunities to try for the Island Scholarship. He won on his third try in October 1931. His anxious father was jubilant; his dream had been finally realized. As Williams tell us,

> His twenty-year-old-dream had come true. Under-paid, tired, demoralized by the sight of younger people promoted out of turn over his head because he lacked the necessary pliancy to ingratiate himself with the powers who controlled his destiny, he looked upon my victory as a decisive proof of his manhood. His bearing was more erect thereafter, his confidence in himself restored, and he often told me that, whatever his rivals had, they had not an Island scholar as their son. (Ibid., 33)

Young Williams and his father did not, however, agree about what career he should pursue. Traditionally, Island Scholars chose the professions of medicine or law, which, as Solomon noted, gave them a measure of economic independence. Some, like Nobel laureate Arthur Lewis of St Lucia, wanted to do engineering, but eventually had to opt for economics because it was assumed that he would not get a job as an engineer in colonial St Lucia.

Henry Williams did not approve of his son's choice of history because he did not feel that his son would secure a job as a teacher in colonial Trinidad. They disagreed bitterly. As Williams tells us, "On this question, the disagreement . . . was sharp, profound, persistent and destined to strain our relations almost to breaking point." The elder patriarch felt he had the right to decide. He wanted Eric (who once fainted at the sight of blood) to be a medical doctor. "My father looked upon his family circle as his domain, and his relations to it that of a crown colony Governor. As it was sedition to question what the Governor could do, so was it blasphemy to question what the father could do. He was to plan, we to obey. His conception of the *patria potesta* was nowhere more clearly indicated than in his attitude to the profession I should choose" (ibid., 38). Williams was determined, however, to follow in the footsteps of his mentors at QRC, particularly W.D. Inniss, J.J. Mitchell, C.E. Bradshaw, G.E. Pilgrim and Stokely Doorly. He wanted to be a teacher and would go to Oxford to read history. His father gave in "with poor grace".[7]

Eric's family life was not as joyless or as poverty-stricken as much of this account suggests. Williams tells us that his brother Mervyn bought a Victrola on which his father loved to play certain types of music – his favourites were "The Blue Danube", "My Old Kentucky Home", and "Oh, Donna Clara". Their entertainment also included drives around the Savannah, visits to "Sea View", and listening to the music of the police band in the botanical gardens. Williams himself enjoyed going to Carnival house parties and playing mas "with the best of them" – he played Robin Hood and his Merry Men, and Bedouin Arabs. He confessed that he "shuffled" rather than danced, since he could not dance. He also loved going to the races at the Savannah, where he paid more attention to card-sharps than to the horses. He had a passion for sports. He was in fact addicted to ball games and was what Trinidadian youth would call a "ball ho" (whore) or a "ball peong". He boasted of his soccer skills. "I became the wind ball king of Trinidad and Tobago, and specialized in magnificent left foot kicks from the touchline with the football."

Williams wrote much of what appears above while he was still at the Caribbean Commission. Then he clearly felt that it was necessary to tell the story of his early years in as frank and detailed a manner as possible, or as he remembered it. At the conclusion of one of the early drafts, he tells the would-be reader that "such were the circumstances of my birth, my lineage, such the family milieu which provided the background for the formative years of my life in this small West Indian community". It is also clear that he regarded some of what he was revealing about his education and his upbringing as having political significance, and as he told Norman Manley, then premier of Jamaica, he planned to use it when the time was right to fight the system. "*The fight takes the form of an autobiography, an account of my education. For years I have been biding my time with the autobiography*" [emphasis added] (EWMC folio 39). Clearly, Williams saw himself as a Homeric political "hero" in the making, someone who would one day fulfil his historic destiny by setting his people free.

Oxford

Williams was admitted to St Catherine's Society, which was not then a college of the university. The society, also called the Delegacy, was established in 1932 to cater to students who were admitted to the university, but who were socially and economically challenged and who could not afford the costs associated with membership in a college. Although Williams was a scholarship student, the factor of cost did apply since the scholarship allowance was not generous. One is not clear what other factors applied, and who was responsible for his placement, the authorities in Trinidad and Tobago, those at the Colonial Office, or those at Oxford. Williams himself says nothing about the matter in his autobiography.

Like many bright students, Eric attended few formal lectures while at St Catherine's and devoted most of his time to diligent reading and preparing for weekly tutorials. Lectures came a bad second. History came alive for Williams at Oxford. Unlike what obtained at QRC, it was no longer a record of battles, or a chronicle of key dates and events. History became a record of the development of humanity and civilization. As was the case with many a student from the colonies, Williams found that he could only now make sense of what he had learned by rote in colonial schools. Art and literature came together to illuminate the past. As he tells us, "My weekly tutorial hour at noon on Fridays – which grew longer and longer until it ran into nearly two hours – represented my sole connection as an undergraduate with the Oxford dons" (1969, 41).

Williams had good things to say about some of his tutors and little regard for some of the others. High on his list was Dennis Brogan, whom he described as "the outstanding social scientist at Oxford". He also enjoyed his history tutorials with the pipe-smoking Welsh cleric Trevor Davies, with whom he got on famously. Their only quarrel came when Davies sought to rationalize Aristotle's views on slavery. He got on well with his economics tutor, Hugh Jones, whom he says he had to thank for the contacts that eventually landed him at Howard. He had little use for his philosophy tutor, to whom he once submitted an essay in response to a question about the reality of sovereignty with two words only: "Ask Hitler." He also found Harold Laski (who was at the London School of Economics) "flat". Laski, he said, was not well thought of at Oxford.

Williams, a workaholic, did brilliantly at Oxford, achieving the much coveted first-class degree in modern history in 1935, placing among the top three in class. It was, he tells us, "the first college 'First' in History over a long period of years".[8] He had, as he boasted, "come, seen and conquered" (1969, 43). In doing so, he did not, as did some colonial students, focus only on books and exams. He distinguished himself at soccer and cricket,[9] as he had done while at QRC, and also found time to attend lectures that addressed the burning political issues that were on the agenda in Europe at the time. In these meetings, he came into contact with many political activists who would later lead movements on return to their native lands. Among them were Jomo Kenyatta of Kenya, Nmandi Azikiwe of Nigeria, and Kwame Nkrumah of Ghana. He also met outstanding Trinidadians, among them C.L.R. James, who had taught him at QRC, George Padmore and Learie Constantine.

James argues that being in Europe at this particular time was an important "accident" in Williams's political development and his training for political office. Williams was influenced by the great ideological debates that were taking place, and like others, James included, sought to locate and project the West Indies in that raging debate. Thus *Capitalism and Slavery*. As James observed in his *Convention Appraisal*:

> I remember the long discussion we had as to what the thesis should be and how it should be tackled. Those congenital idiots and backward people who talk about Williams having a chip on his shoulder on the race question should study all this, ponder over it and take a vow of silence for the rest of their days. West Indians and the West Indies were out of all that was going on in the thirties, and we deliberately set out to bring them in. When Dr. Williams speaks of West Indian nationalism, independence, it comes from the very roots of his being. He passed from studentship to maturity by projecting West Indian history into the surging stream of modern history and political theory from which it was absent. His nationalism did not begin in 1956. (1993, 336)

James also believed that Williams's experiences at Oxford and in England gave him a thorough grounding in the fundamentals of British parliamentary democracy. "Williams is as British as Mr Nehru. Williams's knowledge of British politics and history explains why he is so impatient with colonial bureaucrats." The idea of a Colonial Office official telling him what to do was intolerable. "As long as he was solitary, he had to take it. But the moment he had a majority of the people behind him, his present drive to independence was the order of the day. 1956 released a long-coiled spring" (ibid.).

All the evidence indicates, however, that Williams was not a political activist at Oxford. James tells us in *Party Politics in the West Indies* that, "He came to our meetings, read our magazines and pamphlets, took part in our discussions. He studied and wrote history. But he never joined anything" (1962, 158). Williams himself confirmed that he was not a joiner, a "Bolshie", or a fellow traveller. "I never had any connection whatsoever with any political organization at all, except that at Oxford, I attended regularly meetings of the Indian nationalist students in the club, the Majliss" (1955, 33–34). There was one exception. As Williams recalled thirty-four years after he left Oxford, "I had avoided all the wishy-washy political movements of the day, whatever their label. But Mussolini's attack on Ethiopia drew me into political activity. I led the fight at Aggey [*sic*] House against Italian imperialism, and advocated League of Nations support for Ethiopia." He claimed that that was his first entry into the political arena (EWMC folio 1914, 4).

On completion of his undergraduate degree, Williams wished to continue studying and sought an extension of his scholarship, which was initially refused by J.O. Cutteridge, then director of education. His college principal, K. Brook, wrote a letter to the Government of Trinidad and Tobago, recommending that he be given funding to pursue an academic career. As Brook wrote,

> Mr. E.E. Williams, who came to Oxford with a Trinidad Government scholarship in 1932, has just crowned a successful career there by getting a brilliant First Class in Modern History. The competition in that examination is very severe, but I have been told by one of the examiners that he was one of the best three men in. The examiners openly congratulated him on his work. That is a very distinguished performance, and the more so in that Mr. Williams has from time to time had trouble with his eyes, and also in that he has not been a mere book-worm, but has distinguished himself both in cricket and football. He plainly must be an exceptionally able man. I understand that the terms of his scholarship require that he should now proceed to the Diploma in Education. In my opinion, it would be a mistake if he were to do so, in that it would be rather a waste of his ability.
>
> He is plainly a man who is capable of advanced academic work, such as teaching teachers, not boys, and I strongly feel that, if it is at all possible, he should be encouraged to fit himself for that sort of work, either by taking another Honour School in Oxford or by taking a research degree there. Plainly, there may be difficulties about this from the point of view of the Government of Trinidad – but I think that if the matter is discussed, the Government ought to be appraised of the views of the Authorities in Oxford, that Mr. Williams is an exceptional man who deserves, if possible exceptional treatment. (1969, 43–44)

The principal's letter was pivotal in persuading Cutteridge to change his mind. Williams did have his scholarship extended, and he registered to do Politics, Economics and Philosophy (PPE). He also attempted the All Souls Fellowship examination in October 1935. He did not succeed at either, and deemed both initiatives "fiascoes", hopeless mistakes. He did not enjoy PPE generally, though he liked the politics component. He also did not do well at the fellowship examination, a failure which he blamed on racial and social discrimination. As he tells us, "I simply did not belong. No native, however detribalized, could fit socially into All Souls." Williams felt ill at ease in the dining and common rooms at All Souls, and confessed that he had always "lacked the social graces":

> The fellowship depended on correct choice at the right time of the knife, fork or spoon which one should take up – there were so many of them. The medieval verdict of trial by water seemed child's play compared with the trial by dinner at All Souls. After that came the ordeal of chatter in the Common Room. It was difficult to be polite to the

author of one of the wretched textbooks I had used in Trinidad when he defended the Hoare-Laval peace plan. It was not easy to show one's erudition in a discussion of sign-posts. I have always lacked the social graces, and had never cultivated – as good colonials must and do – the elegant art of balancing the coffee- or teacup whilst one's legs were crossed.

Gaucherie in the common room, incompatibility in the examination room. Either would have been sufficient to disqualify me; together they blackballed me. The Warden of the College took me aside later in the evening, complimented me on my perform-ance in the written examination – it seemed rather strange, as I had been told confiden-tially some hours before by a white aspirant whom I knew well and who had got the order of merit from an older colleague who was a Fellow, that I had been placed ninth out of some sixteen candidates – and advised me, in a paternal tone, that the greatest service I could render to my people who stood so sorely in need of it was to return to Trinidad. The entire episode, capped by the Warden's advice, convinced me that I would never get an All Souls Fellowship, and that the racial factor would dispose of me in 1936 as the examination factor had in 1935. I was very angry. It was not that I felt that I had won the fellowship. I knew I had not. (Ibid., 45–46)

The charge of racial and social discrimination was denied, however, by one of the then dons at Oxford who remembered Williams and felt he had not performed well.[10] Williams felt he was "blackballed", though he conceded that he had performed below his own expectations in that fellowship examination. He explained that he had only just completed his undergraduate finals, and the strain of the exams, including the oral examinations, was more than he had bargained for, though he claims that the strain was more mental than physical.

Williams was told by the director of education that a post of assistant master was becoming available and that he should consider it. Williams, however, had come to have other ideas about his future career. As he told Cutteridge, "The post of assistant master at a secondary school in the island comes up to my idea of perfect misery and drudgery. I want something interesting to do in later life. I want to lecture on history not to teach schoolboys and maintain discipline" (EWMC folio 033). He was able to persuade Cutteridge.

Instead of continuing with PPE, Williams abandoned it and switched to research for a doctoral degree, a decision that turned out to be one of the most critical in his academic and perhaps his political career. Williams regarded that "as the most important decision I had made in my life". As Carl Campbell correctly noted, "The economic connection between the imperial power and the colonies and the impact on British economic growth and the abolition of slavery was a good research position from which to develop into a radical spokesman on con-temporary West Indian colonial conditions" (as cited in Carrington 1991, 1). The product of that decision was a thesis submitted in 1938, "The Economic Aspect of the Abolition of the West Indian Slave Trade and Slavery", which dealt with the relationship between economics and the emancipation of enslaved Africans and would eventually emerge as the classic book *Capitalism and Slavery*.

Reflecting later on some of his experiences at Oxford, particularly the race question, Williams had the following to say:

> The racial question was very much in evidence in the Oxford of my day, though naturally, it was much less overt, much less vulgar than in the USA. Oxford, England can never be confused with Oxford, Mississippi. But one was made to feel it everywhere – on the cricket and football field, in the junior common room, and I felt it at much higher levels. Try to get a University Scholarship in my day? I had to fight every inch of the way. And hell threatened to break loose when I applied, by examination, for a fellowship. One day perhaps, I shall have to tell the full story. Some of the authorities were literally frantic at the thought that I would stay in England, as one put it quite frankly, to take a job that should be done by an Englishman.

Williams also reminisced on the battles he had in respect of his PhD thesis:

> All the dice were loaded against me, for at Oxford, I had committed the unpardonable sin – I had challenged the British interpretation of the abolition of slavery. I have not been forgiven for it – as if it is my fault that the British utilized and profitted from slavery and then threw the emancipated West Indians onto the rubbish heap. I still recall, how I was told, in unambiguous language, that if I persisted in my analysis of Pitt's policy in respect of slavery and the slave trade in the war with France, not only would my thesis be failed, but in the opinion of the spokesman, rightly be failed. (EWMC folio 1914, 4)

Following the completion of his doctoral dissertation, Williams was faced with the facts of life. He had to find a job: "England was clearly out of the question; there were too many senior people at Oxford, including the Dean of my College who was so impressed with my Latin background, who, on seeing me would say: 'Are you still here? You had better go back home' " (1969, 52).

Ironically, Williams tried to secure a job at QRC. The interviewer at the Colonial Office concluded that his qualifications were too high for the job. After trying and failing to secure an appointment at QRC, in India, Japan and Siam (Thailand), Williams sought out opportunities in the United States.

2   Scholar's Scholar or Nationalist Scholar?

A man is justly despised who has one opinion in history and another in politics, one for abroad and another at home, one for opposition and another for office.
  – Lord Acton

Having tried and failed to secure a fellowship at All Souls College at the "white" Oxford, Williams turned his attention to Howard University in Washington, D.C., which he dubbed the "Negro Oxford." Howard was the best of the historically black universities in the United States. The fact that war clouds were gathering ominously over Europe increased his anxiety to leave the United Kingdom. Virtue was being made of necessity.

With the enthusiastic help of Professor Ralph Bunche, head of the Department of Political Science, Professor Abram Harris, an economist with a special interest in American economic history, and Professor Alain Locke, an Oxford-trained philosopher who took a personal and "godfatherly" interest in him, Williams was able to secure an assistant professorship of social and political science at Howard, where he arrived on 7 August 1938. C.L.R. James noted that going to Howard, the "Negro Mecca" of learning, was one of the best things that Williams could have done to prepare himself for a political career. Williams, he opined, "was a lucky man. Nothing better for his future development could have happened than going to lecture at Howard, the Negro University in the United States" (Heyward 1998, 15). Heyward agreed: "Howard provided a sanctuary from racism and allowed him to mature intellectually and politically. Indeed, the Howard experience transformed him from a brash young colonial scholar into the mature anti-colonial warrior and Caribbean nationalist that he later became" (ibid., 15).

It is not certain that even Howard, situated as it was in the capital city, Washington, could be a "sanctuary from racism". But the connections that he made at Howard and the academic and political influences to which he became exposed did provide him with a valuable training ground for a political career. So too did the fact that he had to lecture to large classes, including veterans of the Second World War. Heyward was correct when she noted that the "Howard experience in no small way contributed to his racial awakening" (ibid., 23). That experience helped him to "decolonize his mind".

Williams's first assignment was to teach a new compulsory course on the history of modern civilization in the Faculty of Social Sciences, and a course on comparative politics with an emphasis on Latin America in the Faculty of Political Science. Ralph Bunche felt that Williams was well suited to fill those niches in the Howard programme. The course on modern civilization was a challenging task for Williams, who had to develop his own teaching materials. What was available assumed that civilization began with the Greeks and was the product of the white "races" and the Western world. His strategy was to develop an in-house three-volume anthology consisting essentially of original documents that widened the canon to include material more relevant to the interests and experiences of his mainly black charges. Attention was given, inter alia, to the works of Aristotle, especially as it related to the latter's rationalization of slavery, material about ancient Egypt, Mesopotamia, and the Aztecs and Incas of the Americas. Williams also included material that rationalized racial profiling and slavery by Thomas Carlyle, Lord Acton and Compte de Gobineau, the works of W.E. Dubois, Booker T. Washington and Marcus Garvey, as well as Adolph Hitler's writings justifying national socialism and pogroms against the Jews.

Heyward would later wonder why Williams did not include material relating to the ancient African kingdoms of Oyo, Ghana, Mali and Songhai, or to famous Africans or their descendants in the diaspora, including those in Haiti, of which he was definitely aware (1998, 24). Williams explained that some of this material had only just become available and he needed to assimilate it first. The compilation, which C.L.R. James helped him to assemble, was titled *Documents Illustrating the Development of Civilization,* and was available on sale only to Howard University students.

Williams tells us that at Howard he took a special interest in West Indian students, whom he coached in soccer and generally counselled. He also developed a good relationship with West Indians on the faculty. His relationships with the Black American faculty were in the main less than warm, though he was classified as being "on the left", and a member of the "Marxist clique". Some viewed him as an "outsider", particularly since he was from "white" Oxford and presumed to be superior in terms of academic attainment. The fact that he did not involve himself or take sides in conventional campus feuds and politics, especially those that involved bashing the university brass, also did not help. And he tells us that he avoided the politics of "fellow travelling", which was then a feature on

American campuses. "If they left me cold in Oxford, there was nothing about them to warm me in Washington, and I left them alone. . . . I concentrated on my work, and I soon came to be regarded as a worker doing his work and minding his own business" (Williams 1969, 62). Still, there were a number of faculty members at Howard for whom he developed a high regard. Among them were Locke, Harris, Rayford Logan, Sterling Brown, and Franklin Frazier, the distinguished sociologist whose work on the American Negro was internationally known.

Williams was regarded by students as a brilliant but atypical teacher who was always prepared, though from 1943 onward, he was often away from the campus "moonlighting" at the Caribbean Commission or giving lectures. Williams would himself say that "I put all that I have in anything that I do". His social sciences classes were large and well attended. Throughout this time Williams was careful not to become romantically involved with any of his students, as some of his colleagues were prone to do, though he must have been sorely tempted. As he tells us, "I maintained a rigid aloofness and an austere detachment from the shoals of women students with the aggressiveness of their breasts enhanced by sweaters, of their hips by tight skirts, and their legs by bobby socks, and the casual, easy way in which they sat, revealing their possessions, the beholder to enthral" (EWMC, folio 139).

One of his appreciative students was Ibbit Mosaheb, a Trinidadian who was later to play an important role in the founding of the PNM. Williams was also recognized as a brilliant and prolific researcher, and over time was able to secure funding for his research activity from the Rosenwald Foundation.[1] In 1940, he received a grant of US$2,000 to work on a project that was an extension and an amplification of his PhD thesis. The title of the proposed project was "The Rise of Capitalism in Europe and America and the Institution of Slavery". Following receipt of the fellowship, he boasted that "powerfully backed by Bunche, Harris, Locke, Ragatz, Vincent Harlow and my former principal of St. Catherine's, and fortified by my Oxford research in an area of great concern to America and Americans, the battle was not too difficult" (1969, 63).

This and other fellowships enabled Williams to travel through the region in the process of which he was able not only to source valuable historical documents but also gain first-hand knowledge of Caribbean societies such as Cuba, Haiti, the Dominican Republic and Puerto Rico. The latter he described as "a land of beggars and millionaires, of flattering statistics and distressing realities, Uncle Sam's second largest sweatshop" (ibid., 66). One might well wonder why he would later choose to emulate "Operation Bootstrap", as the Puerto Rican economic model was called.

The 1940 intellectual safari was critical for Williams's personal and professional development, without which his career might well have taken a different trajectory. As he himself reflected,

This most valuable summer expedition had widened my Caribbean democratic vistas, expanded my knowledge, and laid the foundations for my emergence as intellectual spokesman of the Caribbean peoples. I was in 1940 a West Indian who had more direct and closer contact, historically and actually, with the Caribbean area as a whole than any other. The subsequent years were to emphasise the flowering of a truly Caribbean vision which, in 1932 in Trinidad, had been limited to Trinidad and Tobago, and in 1939 had expanded at Oxford to embrace the British West Indies. (Ibid., 68)

One important by-product of this Caribbean sojourn was the book *The Negro in the Caribbean,* which Williams said "established my reputation":

Appearing in 1942, a little after two years after my first appointment, there was nothing like it in any language. It was an out-and-out attack on colonialism in the Caribbean. . . . The congratulations poured in. Lowell Ragatz congratulated me on a scholarly and interesting piece of work. Lewis Hanke of the Library of Congress expressed amazement at "the tremendous amount of factual material that you have been able to compress within the limits of a relatively small book". Arthur Lewis sent me his warmest congratulations on the "tremendous amount of research" and recommended it – unsuccessfully – to Penguin Books. . . . George Padmore described it as "the best overall survey of the Colonial problem in the West Indies which has appeared in this country". (Ibid., 69)

Appearing as it did during the war years, when European fleets were operating in Caribbean waters, it was of particular interest to the State Department, which was one of the "book's best single purchasers". As we shall see, the book would also land Williams in deep trouble with the West Indian plantocracy and British officialdom when he joined the Anglo-American Caribbean Commission.

The editorial foreword to the book was written by Williams's colleague at Howard, Professor Alain Locke, who opined that Williams had performed a "large service" by giving readers a "panoramic but not superficial overview of the Caribbean area, its islands and their people". He also expressed the hope that the study would provide a "sounder bond of understanding between the Negro-American and his brother West Indian who was known all too limitedly merely as a migrant". He likewise hoped that US policymakers would be instructed by Williams's analyses of Caribbean problems, and use them to promote the "constructive enlargement of Western democracy" (1942, ii).

The book was a radical critique of Caribbean society from emancipation to the late 1930s. Williams remarked that emancipation did not transform the economic circumstances of the former slaves in any dramatic way:

Emancipation was not an economic change. It left the new freeman as much dependent on and at the mercy of "king sugar" as he had been as a slave. It meant for him not the land, which was incompatible with the requirements of the capitalist sugar industry, but the Bible, which was not at variance with that industry. It meant a change from chattel slavery to peonage, or, as has been said in another connection, a change from the discipline of the cart-whip to the discipline of starvation. The slave was raised to the dubious dignity of a landless wage laborer, paid at the rate of twenty-five cents a day in the British islands. Sweet are the uses of emancipation! To free the Negro, it was necessary not so much to destroy slavery, which was the consequence of sugar, as to alter the method of production in the sugar industry itself. This simple point is essential to an understanding of the situation of the Negro population in the Caribbean today. The black man, emancipated from above by legislation or from below by revolution, remains today the slave of sugar. (1942, 16)

Williams was also savagely critical of the Caribbean plantocracy and the dividends that they appropriated without first ensuring that their workers were paid a living wage. He quoted the observation made by a white colonial secretary in 1937 that "an industry had no right to pay dividends at all until it pays a fair wage to labour and gives the labourer decent conditions" (ibid., 22). Monoculture also came in for pungent criticism, whether the crop was sugar, bananas or cocoa. But the most trenchant criticisms were reserved for the despotism of "King Sugar". As Williams complained, "The despotism of King Sugar is perpetuating another unhealthy feature of the slavery regime – a fatal concentration on a single crop. Monoculture is the curse not of nature but of man . . . where the absolute monarchy of sugar has been destroyed, it has been replaced, not by the liberal democracy of a diversified economy, but by another dictatorship" (ibid., 26–27). The answer to the plantation system and the many diseases that it spawned – malaria, hookworm, tuberculosis, malnutrition – was not to be found, however, in a radical distribution of the land to small farmers. Williams warned,

> We must not harbour the mistaken notion that the alternative to the plantation system with its army of landless blacks is a system of peasant proprietorship, the division of the large estate into small farms. The small-scale production of subsistence farming would be reactionary. The Haitian revolution was a mass revolt of the Negro slaves against their masters. The revolution achieved one fundamental result; it destroyed the plantation system and gave the land to the Negro masses. Today three-fifths of all Haitian peasants own their land. Land redistribution, however, is not everything. Peasant ownership, by itself, is not a solution, and by itself may even be an impediment to progress. But wisely encouraged, in conjunction with legal restrictions on the size of plantations, it forms a necessary part of any solution of the problem of the Negro in the Caribbean. (Ibid., 46)

Williams also had a great deal to say about the race problem and the middle classes in various parts of the Caribbean and the ways in which Caribbean patterns differed from that which obtained in Jim Crow America. He was himself a product of the system and much of what he says about the middle class anticipates his analysis of the Trinidad problem in *Massa Day Done* (1961a). Much also anticipates the work of Frantz Fanon in *Black Skin, White Masks*.

In his analysis of the political problems of the region, Williams's prescription was greater political freedom for the Negro. "There are for the Caribbean, as for the rest of the world, for the Negro as for the rest of mankind, only two alternatives: greater freedom or greater tyranny." Williams abhorred what he saw in the Dominican Republic. "The undiluted dictatorship [of Trujillo] in the Dominican Republic presses on all colours alike" (1942, 98). Williams's strong belief in the virtues and value of a pan-Caribbean economic and even political federation permeated the final chapter of the book, which he titled the "Future of the Caribbean". As he remarked,

> These islands have a common heritage of slavery, a labor base essentially the same. Burdened by the same curse, sugar, the dynamics of the different areas are the same, and it is time to pay more heed to fundamental identities than to the incidental differences. Too long has man been allowed to triumph over nature and geographical unity has too long been sacrificed to political and artificial divisions. An economic federation of all the areas will considerably strengthen their bargaining position in the world market. It would take a federation of democratic governments to settle the burning land question and introduce the program of diversification so necessary to a sound and healthy economic structure. If it be objected that the federation visualized is impracticable, it may be answered that the Caribbean, like the whole world, will federate or collapse. (Ibid., 104–5)

He would return to this theme following the collapse of the West Indies federation in 1962.

Williams also argued that the fate and future of the Caribbean was bound up with that of the United States. In a statement that he would make again in 1960 in the context of the Chaguaramas Base issue, he opined that "The Caribbean, in fact, is geographically and economically an American lake. It was in recognition of this fact that shrewd observers of American Independence declared that Britain had lost not only thirteen colonies, but eight islands as well" (ibid., 106). Williams in fact held the view that the United States had a responsibility to develop the Caribbean economically. As he argued, the United States cannot be a military friend and an economic enemy of the Caribbean. The burdens of hemisphere defence must be equitably distributed, and the American farmer made to bear his share" (ibid., 107).

In a little-known review of the book that appeared in June 1943 in *The New International* under the pseudonym "W.F. Carlton", C.L.R. James was ambivalent about its merits.[2] He described it as being "packed" and "incisive". The chapter titled "The Condition of the Negro Wage Earner" was said to be a "masterpiece of compression, a compendium of workers' misery and capitalist callousness" and a "must-read". James considered Williams's analyses "all the more valuable because he is no Marxist". He nevertheless found the work lacking in theoretical rigour and thought that the conclusions did not go as far as the evidence suggested.

> His mastery of his material forces upon him an inevitable pattern of economic necessity, class struggle and so on. He is sure of the past, clear as to the present, but the future demands more than Williams has. It needs a conscious theory. He is a sincere nationalist and a sincere democrat, but after so sure a grasp of historical development as he shows in this history of four centuries, he displays an extreme naiveté in his forecasts of the future. He seems to think that the economic forces that have worked in a certain way for four hundred years will somehow cease to work in that way because of the Atlantic Charter and the warblings of Willkie and Wallace. What makes the sudden slide downward so striking is that the whole book is a refutation of just such expectations. (1996, 118)

Williams had argued that whatever internal changes were made in the organization of the industry, the fact remained that it had to depend on the capitalist world market. James agreed, and argued further that without a socialist revolution, which was a remote possibility, sugar workers would continue to be strangled by the "monstrous octopus of American imperialism". The West Indian worker would continue to be a "miserable victim of a power which will grind the life out of him as the mills grind the juice from cane". Williams's whole book refutes the possibility of any peaceful change. "If America takes over, the labourer will change masters. Puerto Rico is the proof" (ibid., 123).

In the final analysis, James is dismissive of bourgeois idealism. He praises the book, but only faintly:

> Williams's immediate demands – federation, national independence, political democracy – are admirable, but he commits a grave error in thinking, as he obviously does, that these will end or even seriously improve West Indian mass poverty and decay. But for this lapse, his book is a little triumph, admirably planned and very well written. It should be read not only by those specially interested in the Negro problem or the West Indies. It is in this bourgeois way a short but instructive study of capitalist beginnings, maturity, decline; and, most important today, of the way in which it generates, out of is its own bosom, the forces which are to destroy it. (Ibid., 125)

Here one finds the seeds of that ideological disconnect that would lead to the parting of the ways between these two close associates in 1960, and the fatal encounter in 1966.

The Negro in the Caribbean may have established Williams's reputation among some of his academic contemporaries, but his magnum opus was *Capitalism and Slavery*, the elaboration and extension of his doctoral thesis in which he sought to establish that slavery and the rise of British capitalism were integrally linked. As he puts it, "Having demonstrated the fall of slavery as a part of the movement of mature British capitalism, I proceeded to trace the association of slavery in its heyday with the rise of British capitalism" (1969). Williams admitted that the idea was not originally his, and that he was encouraged to explore it by C.L.R. James, who had broached the argument with him orally and in his book *Black Jacobins: Toussaint L'Ouverture and the San Domingo Revolution*. Williams conceded that "the thesis advanced in this is stated clearly and concisely and, as far as I know, for the first time in English" (1966, 268).[3] He was also able to draw on the work of scholars such as Elizabeth Donan, whose anthology of documents on the slave trade he found remarkable, and Leo Stock's anthology of debates in the British Parliament regarding North America up to 1800, which he found equally valuable.

Also important, he conceded, was the master's thesis of Wilson Williams, one of Abram Harris's students, entitled *Africa and the Rise of Capitalism*. On reading Wilson Williams's work, William Darrity felt compelled to observe that there were passages in Eric Williams's book that "bear a strong resemblance in tone, phrasing and sentiment" with the other Williams's work. Darrity's comment was that "Eric Williams apparently seized upon Wilson Williams's thesis and ran with it to develop a far richer and more detailed analysis of the contributions of the West Indian slave plantation system to British Development" (as cited in Boodhoo 2001, 78). Williams was of the view, however, that the younger Williams had presented only "in a general way" the relationship between capitalism and slavery" (ibid., 78). Williams must also have been influenced by the work of Harris, who wrote *The Negro as Capitalist: A Study of Banking and Business Among Negroes* (1936).

Before submitting the manuscript to his publishers, Williams sent it to Lowell Ragatz, the celebrated author of *The Fall of the Planter Class*, asking that he review it. Williams told Ragatz that he knew he had "some excellent material, but since this would be his first major work, I do not want to spoil it by immature judgement or hasty conclusions". Williams told Ragatz that the "difficulty of being at Howard is that none of his colleagues knows the first thing about the Caribbean, and anything commonplace that he might say or write would pass for the highest wisdom".

He also advised Ragatz that he was being asked for yet another reason. He was hoping that Ragatz would write an introduction to the book, but "on the sole condition that you thought the performance of some real merit which would warrant your adding your name and prestige to it". Williams told Ragatz that he would not want him to use his name in a cause that was not worthy of it (Williams to Ragatz, 18 July 1942). For reasons that are not known to the author, the requested introduction was not forthcoming. Ragatz, however, wrote to thank and congratulate Williams when he received an autographed copy of the book:

"How you have laboured on it!" (Ragatz to Williams, 31 March 1944). Interestingly, the University of North Carolina Press required a US$700 subsidy to offset the costs of publishing. The book was priced at US$3 in 1945, and has since been translated into seven languages including Russian and Chinese (EWMC folio 96).

Williams's work was controversial from the moment of its appearance. It was widely acclaimed, and just as widely vilified. Praise came from Ragatz, the "master in the field" to whom Williams dedicated the book, Dennis Brogan, Gerald Johnson, Henry Steele Commager and C. Wright Mills. Ragatz described the book as a "corking good volume, one which makes a great and very, very important contribution to the literature of Colonial History. . . . There is certainly no one in the world better qualified than you, and you have rare ability both as an investigator and as a writer" (1969, 70). Johnson, writing in the New York *Herald Tribune*, described the book as "extraordinarily lucid" and a valuable addition to the literature on the subject (ibid., 70). Brogan, Williams's tutor in politics at Oxford, said of it that it was an "admirably written and argued original piece of work." Commager was equally full of praise. As he wrote, also in the *Herald Tribune*: "This is the most lucid, the most penetrating and the most original monograph that has appeared in this field of history. It would be cause for gratification if he were to turn his attention now to the economics of American abolitionism" (ibid., 71).

Professor Mills too was laudatory. As he told Williams, "With so much crap being printed, it is doubly refreshing to stumble onto something honest about a real problem. I found the book enormously good. Thank you for sending [it] and indeed for writing [it]" (EWMC folio 96).

The reactions of Professor Melville Herskovits to the book were more nuanced. Williams had sent the manuscript to Herskovits, author of the acclaimed *Myth of the Negro Past*, for his comment. Herskovits liked the document, but made some specific suggestions as to how it might be improved. He felt that sections of the text needed tightening, especially chapter 1. Some of his conclusions also had a "manifesto tone" about them. Herskovits expressed concern that Williams might end up antagonizing the very people whom he wished his arguments to reach, "as the phrasing he had would assuredly do". Herskovits further advised Williams about some of his propositions: "As a student of comparative culture, I do not think they have the universal validity which you assume for them. In their present form, they handicap your book, and give the opponents of your view a point of attack they would otherwise not have."

Herskovits also suggested to Williams that he should consider changing the title of the book to "Slavery and the Industrial Revolution", or "Slavery in the Development of Capitalism". Williams accepted Herskovits's suggestions about the proposed changes in the text and the comment about its "manifesto tone".

Williams told Herskovits that he had cut the text by a quarter and he was now more satisfied with it. He was reluctant, however, to change the title to Slavery and the Industrial Revolution. Doing so "would be a great mistake, and a change warranted neither by my conception of the book nor by the material presented". He was prepared, however, to consider the second title, and indicated that he would suggest it to the University of North Carolina Press. Williams thanked Herskovits for his kind review: "Your conclusions about the study, coming from such an authority, are highly gratifying." When the book was eventually published, Herskovits congratulated Williams for what he considered a "distinct contribution", and hoped its publication would open up the opportunity for further research along the same lines. (See the exchange of letters between Williams and Herskovits, EWMC, 8 and 19 December 1943 and 8 December 1944.)

The book attracted a great deal of critical comment. Critics focused their attention on Williams's methodology – his reliance on materialist explanations for human behaviour – and his de-emphasis of the role played by the humanitarians and human agency in the abolitionist movement. To many, this suggested that Williams was a communist or a Marxist, which of course he definitely was not. But he clearly had radical views as an academic, and was no doubt influenced by the Marxist perspective that was prevalent in those years. As one reviewer put it, it was "a book of the times written for the times".

Williams's main arguments in *Capitalism and Slavery* were threefold. The first was that African slavery was rooted in economic and not racial factors. Given his materialist approach to history, it is hardly surprising that Williams argued that racism was an invented by-product of slavery. "Slavery in the Caribbean has been too narrowly identified with the Negro. A racial twist has thereby been given to what is basically an economic phenomenon. Slavery was not born of racism: rather, racism was the consequence of slavery. Unfree labour in the New World was brown, white, black, yellow, Catholic, Protestant and Pagan" (1966, 7). The second argument was that black slavery and the slave trade generated the capital that helped to finance the industrial revolution in England, and the third was that capitalism destroyed the slave system when that system proved to be a fetter on the further development of that revolution.

The first thesis was accepted by many scholars, and challenged by those who argued that African slavery was driven by notions of the racial inferiority of Africans, who were seen as "animals" rather than as humans, and therefore enslaveable. Williams himself argued that these characterisations were advanced to justify and legitimize acts of greed and brutality:

> Here, then, is the origin of Negro slavery. The reason was economic, not racial; it had to
> do not with the colour of the labourer, but the cheapness of the labour. As compared
> with Indian and white labour, Negro slavery was eminently superior. "In each case,"

writes Bassett, discussing North Carolina, "it was a survival of the fittest. Both Indian slavery and white servitude were to go down before the black man's superior endurance, docility, and labour capacity." The features of the man, his hair, colour and dentifrice, his "subhuman" characteristics so widely pleaded, were only the latter rationalizations to justify a simple economic fact: that the colonies needed labour and resorted to Negro labour because it was cheapest and best. This was not a theory, it was a practical conclusion deduced from the personal experience of the planter. He would have gone to the moon, if necessary, for labour. Africa was nearer than the moon, nearer too than the more populous countries of India and China. But their turn was to come. (1966, 19–20)

Williams denied that the climate of the tropics was the factor that led to the replacement of the small white farmer by the enslaved black proletarian, noting that whites were the norm in many tropical countries where the plantation did not become dominant. As he continued, "Where the white farmer was ousted, the enemy was not the climate, but the slave plantation. . . . The climatic theory of the plantation is thus nothing but a rationalization. . . . The history of Australia clinches the argument" (ibid., 22–23).

Williams also noted that where the sugar plantation was not established, as was the case in Puerto Rico, Negro slavery was not as dominant as it became in Cuba. "Negro slavery blackened the [social] structure all over the Caribbean while the blood of the Negro slaves reddened the Atlantic and both its shores. Strange that an article like sugar, so sweet and necessary to human existence, should have accessioned such crimes and blood shed" (ibid., 27). Williams's conclusion was that "slavery in no way implied, in any scientific sense, the inferiority of the Negro. Without it, the great development of the Caribbean sugar plantations between 1650 and 1850 would have been impossible" (ibid., 29).

Williams's second thesis about the role of the slave trade and slavery in the industrial development of Europe was also extremely controversial. To him, his conclusion was obvious. As he wrote, drawing on the writings of Adam Smith and the Abbé Raynal in respect of Europe, "the triangular trade made an enormous contribution to Britain's industrial development. The profits from this trade fertilized the entire productive system of the country" (ibid., 105). Williams acknowledged, however, that the industrial development of England was also driven by other developments. His point was that some who capitalized these developments were key members of the West India Interest. As he explained, "It must not be inferred that the triangular trade was solely and entirely responsible for the economic development. The growth of the internal market in England, the ploughing-in of the profits from industry to generate still further capital and achieve still greater expansion, played a large part. But this industrial development, stimulated by mercantilism, later outgrew mercantilism and destroyed it" (ibid., 105–6). Williams's claim is a modest one compared to that advanced by some, namely that merchant capital generated in the triangular trade developed the New

World (America and the Caribbean), which development in turn fertilized the entire productive system of the mother country.[4]

Williams's arguments about the relationship between profits earned through the slave trade and slave labour and the growth of British industry have been challenged by several scholars, including Seymour Drescher, who claims that "the slave trade's primacy in funding British growth now has few defenders, even among those who argue for very high profits" (in Cateau and Carrington 2000, 83). Indeed, there are those who argue that slavery retarded the development of some European countries such as Portugal, and that the "periphery was peripheral" (see Patrick O'Brien, as cited in Drescher, ibid., 83). Drescher himself observed,

> The further one proceeds outside the British orbit, the greater is the evidence against a positive linkage between slavery and the rise of industrial capitalism. Case study after case study shows little sustained metropolitan economic development – let alone industrialization – arising from three countries of Continental European trading and slave labour plantations. Perhaps the most spectacular negative example is Portugal, which sponsored slaving, slavery and coerced labour systems for well over four centuries in areas as diverse as Asia, Europe, the Atlantic islands, Africa, and Brazil. As Eric Hobsbawm noted of Portugal at the end of its long legal toleration of chattel slavery: "Portugal was small, feeble, backward by any contemporary standard, . . . and only the eye of faith could detect much in the way of economic development. (Ibid., 5)

Joseph Inikori (2000) locates the controversy in the ideological and historiographical assumptions of Williams's critics and the period in which they wrote. He notes that *Capitalism and Slavery* appeared and gained its reputation in an era – 1940 to 1950 – when the "commercial revolution" thesis was dominant. This thesis argued that the industrial revolution in Great Britain was driven by the trade and commerce between the metropole and the periphery. Inikori quotes Williams's Howard University colleague Abram Harris to make the point that Negro slave labour helped to build the capitalist economy. Harris wrote,

> The shift in commerce in the fifteenth century from the Mediterranean to the Atlantic seaboard accelerated the disintegration of the feudal system in the Western European nations, especially England. This period from about 1500 to 1715, now known as the "Commercial Revolution", was one in which the accumulation of surplus wealth arising from the rapid expansion of trade and commerce led to the improvement of industrial technique, thus laying the basis of the industrial capitalism in the period of 1715 to 1815.

Despite the originality of Williams's contribution, his book appeared at a time when this thesis was dominant, and he must have been influenced by the prevailing neo-Marxist discourse. As Inikori notes, "His emphasis was on profits as the source of investible funds, profits from trade, profits from the production of traded goods and services" (ibid., 66).

This argument was popular among many Third World scholars from the Caribbean and elsewhere. It was rejected, however, by several Western scholars who were anxious to defend the moral foundations of British capitalism. The latter held that the Industrial Revolution was driven by "inward looking" endogenous human capital – research and development, inventions, improvements in agriculture, the Protestant religion and so on. As the "commercial revolution" thesis declined during the period, *Capitalism and Slavery* "went down with it" (ibid., 71). Scholars like P.T. Bauer (1981) insisted that Europe was neither guilty nor responsible for Third World poverty and misdevelopment. Colonialism and linkage with the metropole had helped to develop and not underdevelop Africa and other parts of the colonial world.

This rejection of the commercial thesis was reversed in the 1980s and 1990s, and had much to do with the climate of the times. The Soviet Union had collapsed, the Cold War was virtually over, and there was no pressure on the Western scholarly community to rally to the defence of the West in their historiography. "Export pessimism", the view that prevailed in the post-Depression era, that growth and development were driven more by the needs of the internal market than those of the export market, began to lose its dominance. The importance of trade to development was again recognized and with this recognition came a renewed appreciation of the role of the slave trade in the development of capitalism and Williams's thesis about that relationship. The scholarly consensus today among specialists in British economic history of the eighteenth and nineteenth centuries seems to be that overseas trade, including the sugar and slave trade, constituted *one* of several streams of capital accumulation that helped to foster the development of the Industrial Revolution.

Williams's third basic argument was that the enslaved Africans were not emancipated because of the philanthropic and moral activities of abolitionists such as William Wilberforce, Thomas Buxton, Thomas Clarkson, James Ramsay, Lord Macaulay, John Wesley, James Stephen, Lord Brougham and others, but because slavery had become economically dysfunctional and counter-productive as an institution. For Williams, abolition was not "God's work", as Reginald Coupland, one of his thesis examiners at Oxford, would have Wilberforce say in an "imaginary interview" (a sort of mock interview between Coupland and Wilberforce) that reeked of moral imperialism. "This misunderstanding springs, in part, from a deliberate attempt by contemporaries to present a distorted view of the abolitionist movement."

Williams's explanation of the motivation that lay behind abolition was more deterministic and materialistic. In his view, abolition was driven by impersonal forces that were not always perceived or fully understood by those involved: "The capitalists had first encouraged West Indian slavery and then helped to destroy it. When British capitalism depended on the West Indies, they ignored slavery or defended it. When British capitalism found the West Indian monopoly a nuisance, they destroyed West Indian slavery as the first step in the destruction of West Indian monopoly" (1966, 169).

Williams concedes that the "saints" waged a brilliant propaganda campaign against the odious institution, one of the most brilliant ever undertaken. "They raised anti-slavery sentiments almost to the 'status of a religion'. [Clarkson was one of Williams's heroes.] They agitated, pamphleteered and used parliament as it was meant to be used. The question that had to be answered, however, was why were they able to prevail in getting parliament to abolish an institution that had withstood so many other efforts to overthrow it" (ibid., 181).

Williams noted that it took the abolitionists years to come around to supporting full emancipation. Indeed, many of them, Wilberforce included, were initially opposed to the abolition of slavery. Slavery itself was supposed to merely wither away. Warning against rashness, Buxton opined in 1823 that "slavery will subside, it will decline, it will expire, it will as it were burn itself down into its socket and go out. We shall leave it gently to decay – to die away and be forgotten" (1966, 182).

Williams suggests, perhaps unfairly, that the true attitude of the abolitionists had to be seen in relation to the positions they took on the slavery issue in countries such as Brazil, Cuba, the United States and India. "Their condemnation of slavery applied only to the Negro in the British West Indies." Thus, when in discussing the bill to renew the East India Company's charter in August 1833, just hours before the bill to abolish slavery in the West Indies, it was proposed that slavery should also be abolished in India, the dominant view in the House of Lords was that that step was uncalled for and would in fact provoke insurrection. One argument heard in the House of Lords was that the British had inherited slavery in India from the Hindu and Muslim governments, and that it would not be prudent to interfere with the system without due caution. Basically, the abolitionists hoped to terminate slavery in India by exhortation and encouragement and not by legislation.

Williams wondered whether their caution was informed by the fact that some of them were shareholders in the East India Company. There was also the question of the West Indian monopoly. As Williams noted, "The real significance of the abolitionists' support of East India and later Brazilian sugar is that the issues involved were not only the inhumanity of West Indian slavery, but the unprofitableness of West Indian monopoly" (1966, 188). The abolitionist lobby, argued Williams, did not support programmes to end slavery in Brazil, the United States or Cuba in large part because the profitability of British factories depended on cheap sugar and cotton from these sources. The British did what was believed necessary to put down the slave trade, but not slavery itself. "The abolitionists were boycotting the slave-grown produce of the British West Indies, dyed with the

Negro's blood. But the very existence of British capitalism depended upon the slave-grown cotton of the United States, equally connected with slavery and polluted with blood" (ibid., 190).

Another argument advanced by some apologists was that slavery in the United States was more humane and also that most of the enslaved were born in the United States, which incidentally was also the case in respect of Jamaica. It was also argued that in a country such as the United Kingdom, it was not practical to boycott every product made with slave labour "unless one wished to take to the woods and live on roots and berries". Disraeli was less equivocal. He considered abolition "a mistake, the greatest blunder made by the English people. . . . It was virtuous but not wise. It was an ignorant movement . . . not easily paralleled in the history of mankind" (ibid., 195). Thomas Carlyle (*The Nigger Question*) agreed. In his view, the abuses of slavery should be abolished, but "indolent two legged cattle should be made to work for their living". It was right to compel them to do so.

On the question of compensation, Williams recalled that the slave owners were given the astronomical and extravagant sum of £20 million for the loss of their "property". What of compensation for the slaves? Buxton had a beautiful response, which Williams quoted with obvious relish:

> The Negro race are blessed with a peculiar aptitude for the reception of moral and religious instruction, and it does seem to me that there never was a stronger call on any nation than there is now on us to meet this inclination in them, to supply them amply with the means of instruction, to dispatch missionaries, to institute schools, and to send out Bibles. It is the only compensation in our power. It is an abundant one! We may in this manner recompense all the sorrows and sufferings we have inflicted and be the means of making in the end their barbarous removal from their own land the greatest of blessings to them. (1966, 192)

Christian evangelization was seen to be the ultimate and only radical cure for the vices and miseries of Africa and blacks in the Caribbean, which is what Buxton was concerned about.

Williams not only challenged the prevailing view that the enslaved were emancipated for purely philanthropic reasons. In the final chapter of the book, he sought to correct the view that the Africans were passive and not involved in promoting their own freedom. "The docility of the Negro slave is a myth", Williams argued, pointing to the *maronage* phenomenon in British Guiana and Jamaica. He also noted that whites in the Caribbean and mulattoes who owned slaves lived in mortal fear of another Haitian-type revolution, or some other form of insurrection. Indeed, the first decades of the nineteenth century were marked by several uprisings in Jamaica, British Guiana, Barbados and elsewhere, which were put down with ferocity. These insurrections were in part prompted by the slaves' belief that they had been freed by the Crown but that their freedom was being withheld by the planters. As Williams put it, all over the West Indies, slaves were asking, "Why Bacchra no do what King bid him?" The slaves were on edge, expecting to be freed immediately and not be patient as they were advised to be.

The Christmas rebellion of 1831 in Jamaica proved to be the decisive catalyst. Damage to property exceeded £1.5 million, and several rebels were hanged or whipped to death in the streets of Montego Bay. Freedom could no longer be withheld. As historian William Green opines, "it was the Jamaican rebellion, not the vigour of the anti-slavery movement that proved the decisive factor in precipitating emancipation" (1976, 112). Williams agrees, but puts the rebellion and its consequences in a systemic context:

> In 1833, therefore, the alternatives were clear: emancipation from above, or emancipation from below. But EMANCIPATION. Economic change, the decline of the monopolists, the development of capitalism, the humanitarian agitation in British churches, contending perorations in the halls of Parliament, had now reached their completion in the determination of the slaves themselves to be free. The Negroes had been stimulated to freedom by the development of the very wealth which their labor had created. (Ibid., 208)

This particular argument, which is to be found in "The Slaves and Slavery", chapter 12 of *Capitalism and Slavery*, was submitted while the book was already in press. Williams wrote the editor asking that she facilitate the addition. Williams told her that he was discussing the book with a friend, who realized that he had neglected to deal with the "root" cause of abolition, namely the "revolt of the slaves themselves as a reflection of the growing economic dislocation". The revolt of the weak was the precondition for abolition. The editor was asked to stop the press at chapter 11 to allow for the inclusion of this most important dimension of the problem. She readily agreed. Bridget Brereton has suggested that this chapter fits uneasily into the overall economic explanation of emancipation (communication to the author).

It is clear that it was C.L.R. James who urged Williams, his "star pupil" and "devoted admirer", to include the chapter that he felt would make the book even more brilliant than it already was. In a letter to his lover Constance Webb, James deemed the work a "superb master piece", and Williams "a most brilliant young man" (as cited in Boodhoo 2001, 160–61). James also insists that it was he who had inspired Williams to write *Capitalism and Slavery*. James told Williams the following when the latter asked for advice as to what topic he should explore: "I know exactly what you should write on. I have done the economic basis of slavery emancipation as it was in France. But that has never been done in Great Britain, and Britain is wide open for it. A lot of people think the British showed goodwill. There were lots of people who had goodwill, but it was the basis, the economic basis that allowed this goodwill to function."

James claims that he wrote the thesis proposal for Williams – not the book, as Selma James, C.L.R.'s third wife, argued. He also claimed he read the manuscript three or four times (ibid., 159). Williams's acknowledgement of James's support was parsimonious. In addition, no credit was given in the book to James for the chapter "The Slaves and Slavery". It is clear, however, that Williams's work was inspired by work that James had previously done on the Haitian revolution.

Williams's theses have been the subject of a great deal of academic comment, both favourable and hostile. The key criticism has been that they were too simplistic, materialistic and deterministic, and ignored the many other factors that were tributary to such an epochal event. As historian Thomas Holt puts it, "Williams made an easy target. His punchy, bold rhetoric did not concede much to the nuances and complexities of human motivation. But his fundamental insight was correct" (1992, 23). Drescher, for his part, claims that the abolitionists used economic arguments to cloak their humanitarian concerns, and that Williams got it all wrong. He also argued that there were certain specific groups that supported laissez faire and that the abolitionists mobilized them to help advance their crusade. Moreover, the West Indian planters were far from being a declining gentry with a commodity that was declining in value; sugar was booming in the years when the slave trade was abolished. Drescher in fact argues that the British abolished the slave trade *despite* their economic interests, not because of them! They were altruistic econocidists rather than hypocrites.

Williams, it should be noted, never denied the sincerity of the "saints", nor the importance of their humanitarian sensibility, which he readily conceded; nor did he argue that other factors were not operative in the rise of industrial capitalism. His claim was that those factors played a subordinate role in the process:

> The decisive forces in the period of history we have discussed are the developing economic forces. These economic changes are gradual, imperceptible, but they have an irresistible cumulative effect. Men, pursuing their interests, are rarely aware of the ultimate result of their activity. The commercial capitalism of the eighteenth century developed the wealth of Europe by means of slavery and monopoly. But in so doing it helped to create the industrial capitalism of the nineteenth century, which turned round and destroyed the power of commercial capitalism, slavery, and all its works. Without a grasp of these economic changes the history of the period is meaningless. (1966, 210)

Williams's argument was that one had to distinguish between general sentiments and the perspectives of the policymakers in the Colonial Office and the Whig ministry. What made the latter act? His view was that the latter acted because important capitalists saw abolition to be in their interest. As he argued, "The humanitarians, in attacking the system in its weakest and most indefensible spot, spoke a language that the masses could understand. They could never have succeeded a hundred years before when every important capitalist interest was on the side of the colonial system". The latter had long resisted abolition. When it no longer served their interests, they withheld their support, leaving the merchants and planters vulnerable to the abolitionists. "Even the great mass movements, and the anti-slavery movement was one of the greatest of these, show a curious affinity with the rise and development of new interests and the necessity of the destruction of the old" (1966, 211). The needs of the economy determined what was done at the superstructural level.

Williams's critics argued, however, that it was not the economic interests of the new capitalist elite alone that led them to support abolition, but their "bourgeois ideology". That ideology was not mere epiphenomena or "cultural decoration". By the early nineenth century, progressive people had come to see slavery as a moral aberration and an anachronism on both religious and economic grounds. Biblical endorsement was no longer an adequate defence. Moreover, given the prevailing religious economic orthodoxy, slave labour was seen to be less cost-effective than freely contracted labour, and also spiritually retarding for both slave and master. Abolition was thus a moral imperative whose time had come.

Ideology, religious protestation and economic calculation were reinforced by political considerations. The electoral reforms of 1832 eliminated several "rotten boroughs" and led to the creation of new urban constituencies that had within them many voters who belonged to dissenting religious sects. The 1832 election in fact changed the complexion of Parliament. The boom towns of the north and east of England were now represented at Westminster. The elections of 1832 registered the shift in the balance of political power in the United Kingdom. It marked the decline of the West India lobby in Parliament and their allies, the Tory landlords and those merchants who had an interest in preserving their monopoly in the sugar market. The House of Commons was virtually divested of members directly associated with the slavery interest. Still, the House of Lords had peers sympathetic to or connected with West Indian plantations. Fear was a precipitating factor that informed the reaction of policymakers. Drescher's point that Williams's view of the process of history was too linear and mechanical is well taken.[5] History cannot always be divided into neat stages as Williams suggested. Slavery was thus compatible with commercial capitalism as well as industrial capitalism. It was also important to consider the divisions within groups (the masses and the elites) as well as between them. What all of this suggests is that no single factor was responsible for abolition. The abolition movement was powered by many tributary and contradictory streams, among which were the new industrial capitalists who were opposed to monopolies and interested in free trade, moral imperialists, the abolitionists, the evangelicals, the artisanal classes, intellectuals, new voters, middle-class British women, practical policymakers, and above all, the slaves, especially the creole members of that element. The latter had absorbed Christianity, and like Caliban, had learned the slaveholders' language and how to "curse". Slavery and evangelization contained the seeds of its own destruction. Williams was right, however, to point to the critical underlying factors that helped to release these forces.

We have looked at the comments of a few of the many scholars that have debated the Williams thesis. Our aim here has not been to determine who was right, or more right than wrong, but to give those readers who are not familiar with Caribbean historiography a feel for what the debates have been about.[6] Williams authored several other publications, none of which achieved the status of *Capitalism and Slavery*. Among those for which there was either great acclaim or great controversy were *Documents in West Indian History 1492–1655* (1963b), *Education in the West Indies* (1955), *Inward Hunger: The Education of a Prime Minister* (1969), *History of the People of Trinidad and Tobago* (1962a), *British Historians and the West Indies* (1964a) and *From Columbus to Castro* (1970b). Unlike *Capitalism and Slavery*, which was directed to a scholarly audience, *History of the People of Trinidad and Tobago* was a "potboiler" written with a political purpose in mind. In the foreword to the book, which Williams tells us he began writing on 25 July 1962 and completed on 25 August 1962 "except for the index", we are told that it "originated in a personal conviction that it would be an unfortunate handicap in the field of international relations and a great mistake in respect of affairs and domestic relations, if Trinidad and Tobago were to enter on its career of Independence without a history of its own, without some adequate and informed knowledge of its past, and dependent solely upon amateur outpourings in the daily press" (1962, ix).

Williams tells us that in writing the book, his aim was "not literary perfection or conformity with scholastic canons", but to provide the people of Trinidad and Tobago on their Independence Day with a National History, as they have already been provided with a National Anthem, a National Coat of Arms, National Birds, a National Flower and a National Flag. It was, as he tells us, "the manifesto of a subjugated people", and a "Declaration of Independence of the united people of Trinidad and Tobago"[7] (ibid., ix). Williams was extremely proud of the fact that he was able to complete the work while in office. As he said, "I had proved that a Prime Minister could write a book while he was in office. This opened up untold possibilities for the wealth of research materials that I had in cold storage in my files. I followed this up the following year with the first volume of *Documents of West Indian History*, covering the period 1492 to 1655" (1969, 328).

Williams was aware of the book's weaknesses as well its strengths, and in fact sought to anticipate its critics. As he declared,

> Many will praise the book, and some will censure it. The author wishes to make it
> clear that he seeks neither praise nor blame, that his particular concern is with the peo-
> ple of Trinidad and Tobago with whom he is identified in aspirations and achievements,

and that he has always regarded it as his special responsibility to pass on to them the knowledge which would have been unobtainable without them and for which they in fact paid. If some do not like the book, that is their business. (1962, x)

The book was clearly not written in a month, and was in fact a collage of material that had been written over many years while the author was in the "wilderness". The book does, however, have a theme. It is a rhetorical reply to the aspersions that metropolitan scholars and policymakers had cast on the Trinidad and Tobago polity, whether intentionally or otherwise. It was also a reply to those who claimed that Trinidad and Tobago was too divided a society to be unified within the framework of one integrated political system. As he declaimed, possibly in response to those who were making claims for proportional representation or partition, "division of the races was the policy of colonialism. Integration of the races must be the policy of Independence. Only in this way can the colony of Trinidad and Tobago be transformed into the Nation of Trinidad and Tobago" (ibid., ix). It was a utopian paradigm that would land Williams in a great deal of difficulty during the run-up to Independence, and in the years immediately following.

The book had other weaknesses, the main one being what it excludes. It highlights what Williams and the PNM did on the "Road to Independence" and largely ignores the roles of other key actors such as Albert Gomes, with whom the PNM was in political competition. Although the book contains a chapter on the "Contribution of the Indians", that chapter deals mainly with Indian immigration. The Indians are largely invisible, as are the white creoles.

There have been many scholarly and political critiques of this book. The most comprehensive was written by Gordon Lewis of the University of Puerto Rico. Lewis, who was an admirer of Williams, described him as the "foremost economic historian of the region", and the book as a "noteworthy event in Caribbean society and literature". Lewis was full of praise for the volume, which he hoped, as did Williams, would be the first of several monographs on the Caribbean.[8] He notes that the book draws heavily on official colonial reports and that in doing so, Williams at times lets the document make his case. In Lewis's view, Williams was, in this book, the "nationalist intellectual and not the nationalist politician". "Far from the intellectual personality of the author dominating the argument, there is a real sense in which one loses that personality in the midst of the impressive documentation" (1963, 102).

Lewis in fact argues that Williams's historiographic style was similar to the tradition of the great English historians and men of letters who preferred "historical morality to historical scientism". They were "judge as well as witness", a tradition he claims Williams absorbed at Oxford. "The historian analyses the past in order to better comprehend the present and help shape the future. This is the inarticulate major premise of the Williams volume." Lewis noted that Williams had firmly rejected the "plural society" thesis advanced by Caribbean scholars such as M.G. Smith. Like Williams, he saw that thesis as being of "incalculable danger for Caribbean progressivism in that it emphasized the divisive elements of Caribbean society to the neglect of its emergent unifying elements; it takes racial and religious animosities as given permanent factors instead of seeing them as psycho-sociological accidents flowing from the character of colonial government; and it thereby mistakenly identifies those accidents as central essences of Caribbean society" (ibid., 104). Nationalism was the weapon to be used to unify the society. Those who were not prepared to come on board the nationalist train would be characterized as a "recalcitrant minority" who would be left behind by history.

Lewis was aware, however, that nationalism was a double-edged sword, and that the "black bourgeoisie" could use it destructively. He quoted Major Wood's report of his visit to the West Indies and Guiana of 1922 with approval. Wood had warned that there was a risk that the granting of responsible government might lead to the entrenchment of a financial oligarchy that would entirely dominate the colony and use its power for the sole purpose of benefiting one class instead of the community as a whole. He notes that Williams merely hints at the problem but was not detained by it, since he wrote, first and foremost, as the historian (ibid., 105). As we shall see, this is precisely what occurred within four or five years of the achievement of independence.

A more recent critic, Harvey Neptune, author of *Caliban and the Yankees: Trinidad and the United States Occupation*, complains that Williams's *History* omits much of what took place during the turbulent 1930s and 1940s in Trinidad, especially the American occupation, which radically changed the character of Trinidad's economy and society. In doing so, "it slighted and simplified mid-century Trinidad . . . and cast a shadow on Trinidad's historiography. . . . Almost inevitably, *History of the People* earned acceptance as a – if not the – landmark statement on the island's history. . . . A narrative authored with the post-colonical future in mind has captivated the scholarly imagining of Trinidad's past." Neptune goes on to accuse Williams and other nationalist historians from the region of telling "tall tales that vastly overstate the autonomy and the persuasive powers of the nation idea" (2007, 13).

Williams's scholarly works were also analysed by historians at the University of the West Indies. Some of the commentary was critical while some was full of praise. In most contexts, the evaluation was mixed. In her review of Williams's *British Historians and the West Indies* (1964a), which was based on lectures given in Atlanta on "British Historiography and the Negro Question" in 1946, Elsa Goveia praised Williams, whom she said had justly come to be regarded as one of the "prodigies of the contemporary West Indies". Goveia was impressed with the extraordinary energy and commitment that Williams displayed as he sought to combine the roles of scholar and active politician. Having said all that and more, she nevertheless found the book "disappointing and even somewhat irresponsible", and expressed the hope that Williams would "in future write no books like the one under review". She deemed it a piece of work that was quite unworthy of the brilliant reputation that still enabled his publishers to describe him as "the acknowledged authority in the field of West Indian history".

Goveia complained of the many critical omissions, distortions, dogmatisms and authoritative half-truths in the volume and suggested that the prime minister "no longer had the time necessary to undertake the kind of systematic critical investigation of sources which had to be undertaken before a detailed historical work on any subject can be written." Williams, claimed Goveia, was "discolouring history" and writing like a man who still believed that he was the only voice crying in the wilderness of an alien and hostile historical tradition. He seemed unaware that there was a new generation of historians "labouring in the vineyard". Williams was advised that his task now was to write a different type of book – perhaps a synoptic monograph reflecting on the role of those critics of slavery to whom he had dedicated the book. It would do no one any good to substitute "new shibboleths for old" (1964).

Williams was not amused by the review, and reportedly asked querulously, "Who is this Elsa Goveia" that had dared to chastise him? In his view, the book was an important contribution to the historiography of "the Negro Question":

> If the public does not share the author's view on this, he has perforce to fall back on another alibi, that his own part-time prosecution of his particular hobby is not inferior, in terms of his responsibility to his discipline, to that of the majority of the historians whose work he here seeks to analyse. And even if he is over sanguine in this respect, in the final analysis it is the heart that matters more than the head. The author seeks principally to emancipate his compatriots whom the historical writings that he analyses sought to depreciate and to imprison for all time in the inferior status to which these writings sought to condemn them. (1964, vi)

Bridget Brereton was also equivocal in her evaluation of Williams's scholarly output. In her critique of *History of the People of Trinidad and Tobago*, which she describes as a "brilliant, original, and polemical essay", Brereton observed, inter alia, that the book was "erratic in its selection and omission of topics and rather unbalanced in its treatment of the post-1937 period". Brereton was also mildly critical of *British Historians and the West Indies,* which she described as being "biased". She opined that "it failed altogether to meet the rigorous standards of professional academic history" and that "at some points, the anti-colonial got the better of the balanced scholar" (1999, 269). Much the same was said of *From Columbus to Castro* (1970b). The volume was deemed an "important book" and "an ambitious and original attempt to write a truly pan-Caribbean history". The book's weakness was said to be its failure to give a sense of the Caribbean people over time:

> We get an avalanche of figures, tables, statistics on economic developments, but very little on social history (chapter 26 being the only exception); we rarely glimpse the West Indian people as makers and doers, or indeed as anything except units of production. Thus chapter 19 on Asian immigration is a forceful argument that Indian indentured immigration was more or less a disaster which did not even "save" the sugar industry in Trinidad or Guyana; but there is not a word on the Indians themselves and their difficult struggle to adapt to a new and hostile environment. One can only conclude that Williams was, first and last, an anti-colonial historian. Caribbean history was a weapon in the struggle against the imperialists. The aim was to demonstrate the greed, the hypocrisy, the ignorance and the bigotry of colonialism and its agents, not to probe the way West Indians lived in the past. History provided the stick with which to beat the imperialists; the reconstruction of the victims' lives would have to wait. By no stretch of imagination was Williams part of the "new social history" movement with its focus on the lived experience of the ordinary people of the past. (Ibid., 270)

Much the same was said by Gordon Rohlehr in his trenchant review "History as Absurdity" (1970). Rohlehr observes that the book was supposed to be the intellectual climax of all that had gone before in Williams's work and career as a scholar and philosopher-king. Williams himself had indicated in the introduction that there was no history of the Caribbean area as a whole, and that "few colonials had extended their nationalism to the cultural field and dedicated themselves to the task of writing – or rewriting where necessary – their own history". *Columbus to Castro* was designed to fill the gap and correct the deficiency. "Its goal was the cultural integration of the entire area, a synthesis of existing knowledge as the essential foundation of the great need of our time, closer collaboration among the various countries of the Caribbean with their common heritage of subordination to and dictation by outside interests" (Williams 1970b, 12).

Williams believed that he had to rescue West Indian historiography, notwithstanding the fact that a great deal of work was being done by young historians at the Mona and St Augustine campuses of the University of the West Indies. However, he was either contemptuous of the work of the university historians or unaware of the substantial number of theses that had been produced by them but which remained unpublished in part because "their authors were not prime ministers".[9] In any event, argued Rohlehr, Williams's historiography had itself become obsolete. "His notion of writing history had hardly developed since *Capitalism and Slavery*. He still conceives of history writing as the gathering together of a stockpile of facts to be hurled like bricks against dead and living imperialists." In sum, Rohlehr's accusation was that *Capitalism and Slavery* was a book of its time, and that Williams ought to have moved on to produce a more nuanced historical product as befitting his status as the region's premier historian.

Rohlehr's extended review also attempted a psychiatric analysis of Williams, whom he compared with V.S. Naipaul, Joseph Conrad and Jonathan Swift among others, to make the point that Williams was in the final analysis the quintessential rebel, the polemicist who wrote to purge the poison from his soul, the proverbial Caliban who had learned how to curse, albeit with facts and statistics, and with a feeling of intellectual superiority and moral self-righteousness. As Rohlehr complained, "In order to counter the numerous damaging stereotypes which white people invented about black people, Dr Williams adopts a method of excessive factuality which in the end drains the Black experience of its humanity" (1970, 8). Rohlehr concedes, however, that Williams's excessive factuality was perhaps a "necessary defense against the accusation that as a black man, he was simply trying to write history as revenge". Williams was nevertheless chastised for having remained too long in the late nineteenth century, and of being too ambivalent towards the world of the colonizer. Like Naipaul, he seemed to "regard his position as a poor relation at the European feast".

Williams was also accused of representing Caribbean man as "nothing more than a rubbish heap of statistics about sugar". He was likewise criticized for having little to say about Caribbean nationalists such as Marryshow, Critchlow, Manley or Jagan, all of whom might never have existed. "Yet the book calls itself the *History of the Caribbean 1492–1969*." Rohlehr allows that it was probably meant to be the first volume of a serious study. In sum, *From Columbus to Castro* was dismissed as a non-book and not the pan-Caribbean historical bible that scholars were led to believe it would be.

Much of what Rohlehr said about the book was true. But just as the book was a period piece, so too was the review, which reflected the way young black academics at the University of the West Indies felt about Williams in 1970. There was little generosity, little acknowledgement that Williams was putting the volume together while an embattled prime minister on the eve of a major political crisis.[10] Williams himself tells us that the book was begun "some eighteen years ago", but that pressures of one sort or another militated against its completion.

Not surprisingly, and as befitting its title, *Columbus to Castro* focused on the Cuban development model and its appropriateness or otherwise for the anglophone Caribbean. Williams opined that the Cuban model constituted a tragedy in that in pursuing a particular path of development, it had to eschew democracy. As he put it,

> The real tragedy of Cuba is that she has resorted to a totalitarian framework within which to profoundly transform her economy and society. This is the real point about

the essentials of the political system in Cuba today. Perhaps over-simplifying, we may say that Cuba is essentially a highly nationalistic totalitarian society under a form of highly personalized rule, aiming at a complete transformation of previous economic and social structures through centralized planning and mass mobilization. (1970b, 510)

Williams admitted that the Cuban regime was still popular and the level of commitment high. He felt, however, that Trinidad and Tobago presented an alternative path that was between the Puerto Rican "Operation Bootstrap" model and the Cuban totalitarian model. He rejected the Puerto Rican model. While it had facilitated inward investment from the mainland, Puerto Ricans had lost their "souls". "Economic growth has been achieved, but national identity lost. What shall it profit a country if it gain the whole world and lose its own soul" (ibid., 511).

Trinidad, he felt, offered a better mix. The third five-year plan offered a less revolutionary and more gradualistic formula, one that was more democratic than the Cuban path but more self-reliant than the Puerto Rican path: "It involves continued reliance on outside investment and trade with the outside world; but it also involves steady and increasing assumption of control over the commanding heights of the economy by the Government and nationals, a determined attempt to promote racial harmony and social equality, and the conscious development of a national and cultural identity" (ibid., 512).

Williams regarded small size as a constraint that limited the scope of a less dependent and more open strategy of development. Ultimately, however, the answer lay in the economic unity that he had urged in *The Negro in the Caribbean*. Meaningful Caribbean integration was an imperative. What one needed was an economic union that would harmonize economic policy and present a united front to the rest of the world. As he put it,

> It should be possible to devise a form of Federalism which leaves the maximum amount of self-determination open to the units, whilst concentrating the power of dealing with the outside world in Federal hands. In fact, this principle may have to be applied in a wider setting should the present economic integration movement in the Commonwealth Caribbean ever develop into a new attempt at political union.
>
> For the real case of unity in Commonwealth Caribbean countries rests on the creation of a more unified front in dealing with the outside world – diplomacy, foreign trade, foreign investment and similar matters. Without such a unified front the territories will continue to be playthings of outside Governments and outside investors. To increase the "countervailing power" of the small individual units vis-à-vis the strong outside Governments and outside companies requires that they should aim at nothing less than the creation of a single centre of decision-making vis-à-vis the outside world. Everything other than external contacts can and should be left to the individual units which should be given the maximum autonomy and power of self-determination.

> Herein lies the resolution of the problem which plagued the former Federation so much – the division of powers between the centre and the units. (Ibid., 514)

This movement was also to involve Haiti, the Dominican Republic and Cuba, which he argued had to be incorporated into the inter-American family. "Once there was true integration among all the linguistically diverse units of the Caribbean (excluding Puerto Rico), and once all the vestiges of psychological dependence and racism had been removed, only then would the Caribbean take its place in the New World, and put an end to the inter-regional squabbles which from Columbus to Castro, had marked the disposition of Adam's Will."

The question that we will have to answer at the end of this study is the extent to which Williams helped or frustrated the process of regional integration. Williams once wrote that "Historians neither make nor guide history. Their share in such is usually so small as to be almost negligible. But if they do not learn from history, their activities would then be cultural decoration . . . useless in these troubled times". Yet Williams had two bites at the cherry. He was a writer of history and a maker of history. To what extent did the one fail the other?

The judgement made by Caribbean scholars that Williams was a "big picture" historian is a fair one. His strength was to grasp his pet themes, whether slavery, colonialism or the plantation system, and mine every document or event to make the case for his argument without allowing himself to be detained unduly to give the other side. In sum, in much of what he wrote, he was a polemicist trying to purge the "poison" from his system or to take a "particular line". He wrote as a warrior scholar for the victims of slavery and colonialism wherever they were in the wider Caribbean, and not for the masters. He would emancipate minds. He would use history and language to excoriate and crush his opponents intellectually and politically. He would use his formidable pen and oratorical skills to subdue the sword. He would educate the people in the intrigues that had saddled them with those monstrous burdens to the removal of which he had dedicated himself. Brereton puts it well when she said that for Williams, "History was not an intellectual pastime, nor an ivory tower pursuit of scholarship. It was a powerful tool which informed all his work, whether as scholar, public educator, party leader or statesman" (1999, 271).

Many wondered about Williams's failure to construct and equip a new National Archive, or rehabilitate the facility that he used extensively to write his books and papers before and after he gained office. It was a major contradiction.[11] The fault may have been partly with the academics who did not lobby hard enough for the project. It should be noted that when negotiations were taking place between Trinidad and Tobago and the Americans on the question of reparations for the use of Chaguaramas, Williams wanted provision made for an Americana library. This dimension of the settlement was never implemented when the John F. Kennedy Library at the University of the West Indies, St Augustine, was built. Williams also made provision for a national library in several of his budgets when funds were available in the 1970s. But not a "petro-penny" was spent on such a library in his lifetime.

Williams's role as a scholar extended beyond the formal classroom and publications in books and scholarly journals. His role as a public educator, political pamphleteer, and book reviewer for the *Nation* also has to be acknowledged. Williams boasted that between 28 August 1964 and 17 December 1965, he reviewed forty-five books. Since the population did not read books, he would do the reading and tell them what was in the books. It was also his way of keeping abreast of what was happening in the world (1969, 320). Norman Manley gave testimony to the bridging role that Williams performed between the academic and the political vocations. He was the charismatic political leader and the professor of the University of Woodford Square at one and the same time. As he told Williams in a letter written on 26 August 1955: "The Caribbean has, and will for a long time continue to have a tendency to endow one man with an almost magical significance at a particular moment in time. This must be the first occasion when a genuine intellectual like yourself and a person who's talking nothing but history and strait and good sense to the people, has found himself in something that resembles that position."

George Lamming, one of the Caribbean's outstanding novelists, recalls his intellectual encounter with Williams when he first came to Trinidad from Barbados. Williams's lectures in 1955–56 "turned history, the history of the Caribbean, into gossip so that the story of a people's predicament seemed no longer the infinite barren tract of documents, dates and texts. Everything became news: slavery, colonization, the forgiveable deception of metropolitan rule, the sad and inevitable unawareness of native production. His lectures retained always the character of whisper which everyone was allowed to hear, a rumour which experience had established as truth" (1998, 6).

To Lamming, Williams's achievement in the area of popular education was one of "genius". "His was an example, probably the first in our part of the world, of the teacher, in the noblest sense of teacher, turned politician and of the politician, in the truly moral sense of politician, turned teacher. The Woodford Square of Eric Williams has had no precedent or successor in any part of the English speaking Caribbean" (ibid., 6–7). Lamming also observed that one of Williams's characteristics as a public intellectual is that he took "the gravest of all political risks, the risk of refusing to talk down to an electorate". Williams had a profound effect on a generation of West Indians and not merely Trinidadians and Tobagonians. "His influence on me and my generation was profound and enduring. He taught us to see the history of any part of the Caribbean as the history of all. . . . Every novel of mine carried some trace of his research" (ibid., 7–9). Several other West

Indian scholars, the author included, could offer the same testimony to the influence that Williams had on them and their work, even when, as frequently occurred, they became sharply critical of their former intellectual master.

Scholar's Scholar or Nationalist Scholar?

Was Williams a scholar's scholar or a nationalist scholar? Opinions vary. Pemberton and Samaroo's (1998, xi) view that "Williams was a 'scholar's scholar' whose pioneering work in opening up new perspectives in Caribbean studies stimulated a rewriting of the region's history, now from the perspective of the ruled not the rulers" is certainly true. Williams chose, however, to be a popular historian who focused on a different audience than those normally found in the groves of academe. He spoke to the Caribbean people whom he believed identified with him in their aspirations. In the end, the judgements made would depend on the period of Williams's career on which the assessor focuses. The truth is that Williams sought to occupy two stools, the intellectual and the political, and in the end found himself caught between them. Whatever the judgement, there is no gainsaying the fact that Williams was a master scholar whose impact on Caribbean historiography will continue to be felt for a long time to come. Interestingly, Williams once confessed that it was the scholar's role he found most rewarding. As he wrote, "My chief interest in life is research in Caribbean history and the encouragement of others to undertake it" (1 January 1951).

Ironically, the man who would later challenge Williams's credentials as an intellectual and an original thinker was none other than C.L.R. James, who had in the past praised him fulsomely. As James said of Williams following his death,

> Many people feel he was the symbol of change from colonialism to freedom. That is not my view. Dr. Williams seemed reluctant or unable to provide a solution to the moral decline and malaise in the soul of the nation that cried out for a new quality of leadership and vision. I told him he was leading the country to catastrophy. You have departed from *Capitalism and Slavery*. I had to do with *Capitalism and Slavery*. I told him to write it. He had nothing to say of the crisis the country was facing. I taught him at QRC. When he was at Oxford, he spent his vacation with me. When I went to Paris to write "Black Jacobins", he went with me. He came to me often in the US for advice. He did nothing without consulting me. He was not an original thinker. He was, at best, a first class parliamentary secretary to a Political Leader who knew what he is about. (As cited in Seukeran 1991, 19)

James had said much the same when he was discussing his role in the production of the seminal address "Perspectives for Our Party", which Williams delivered to the PNM's third annual convention in 1958. James claimed that he prepared the draft notes and presented it to the party's general council and that Williams took copious notes that he then regurgitated "almost word for word" in his address to the party. James's comment was "Bill should be a permanent secretary. He takes so many notes!" (interview with Nicholas Simonette, as cited in Boodhoo 2001, 164)

While this judgement was informed by political pique and resentment about the way in which the erstwhile apprentice had treated the guru, James was making a distinction between "organic" reflective intellectuals who conceptualized new ideas and bold new visions for their societies, and research scholars who patiently and assiduously collect, pack, or repack information and ideas that they then rebrand.[12] One is a wholesale operation, the other is a retailing exercise. One is cerebral, the other is driven by a passion for factuality. There is little question that Williams had an enormous capacity to collect, assimilate and communicate ideas. Often he chose to let the facts speak for themselves, which of course they never do. Yet one cannot lightly dismiss James's claim, petulant and opinionated though it may be.

The question to be decided is just who or what constitutes an "original" thinker. There are few truly original ideas. Invention is almost always born of dissension. What invariably happens is that speculative philosophers and historians close their senses and trust their minds while social scientists claim that they do the opposite. The latter build incrementally on the works of their predecessors, seeing things and possibilities in ways they had not been seen before.[13]

The distinction made by Italian social theorist Antonio Gramsci (1971, 10) between "traditional" and "organic" intellectuals is relevant to James's characterization of Williams. Gramsci distinguished between professional philosophers and academics who regarded themselves as an independent and autonomous class, and those who were conscious defenders of the "common sense" ideas and beliefs that serve to sustain the interests of the ruling group, which he characterized as the prevailing "hegemony". The autonomy of the traditional intellectuals was, however, a myth, he insisted. They were, in fact, conservatives who assisted the ruling class to maintain their domination. The organic intellectuals, for their part, were those who were more openly and consciously linked to the dominant class and who supported their interests.

Radical social change takes place when the intellectuals switch sides and work towards the creation of a counter-hegemonic discourse in support of the masses. The latter could also create organic intellectuals of their own, persons who will work assiduously on their behalf. As Gramsci put it, "the mode of being of the new intellectuals can no longer consist in eloquence . . . but in active participation in practical life as constructor, organizer, 'permanent persuader', and not as simple orator" (ibid.).

Clearly, James did not consider Williams to be either an organic intellectual who was working on behalf of the Caribbean people or even a traditional intellectual of any greatness or worth. At most, he was an eloquent but simple orator.

It is worth recalling that James had expressed reservations about Williams's credentials as a radically conscious theorist. True, he had described *Capitalism and Slavery* as a "masterpiece" and had also boasted about "the quality of the work". But as we have seen in his review of *Negro in the Caribbean*, which he had described as a "masterpiece of compression", James complained that while Williams was "sure of the past", and "clear as to the present", "the future demanded more than he has. It needs a conscious theory." I suspect that what is at issue here is really an ideological disagreement. For James, "originality" would have pointed Williams in a more radical direction. Williams's empirical readings and factualism led him to adopt a more pragmatic stance.

Interestingly, James himself offers us a way out of this controversy as to who was an orgaanic, a traditional or an original intellectual. In a comment on what some "famous" historians such as Tacitus, Thucydides and Macaulay do, James noted that they were "more artist than scientist: they wrote so well because they saw so little". One is tempted to say that despite his own "practised vision which allowed him to see into the very bones of previous revolutions", James too was more romantic artist than scientist, and wrote like one.

What James had to say about the proper business of the historian may also be applicable to intellectuals generally, especially those who had the responsibility for administering states located in the American basin and who do not have the luxury of what James himself calls "infinite caprice and romanticism". To quote James, "Great men make history, but only such history as it is possible for them to make. Their freedom of achievement is limited by the necessities of their environment. To portray the limits of those necessities and the realisation, complete or partial, of all possibilities, that is the true business of the historian" (1980, x). Williams might have wished to do more, but felt constrained by his environment to be a trimmer. The Organization of Petroleum Exporting Countries (OPEC) revolution served to widen his horizon and to increase the possibilities for economic reconstruction.

My own considered view of Williams as scholar, and I speak as someone who used his books and speeches with great profit, is that one cannot proceed very far with any analysis of Caribbean (and not merely West Indian) political and social history without encountering Williams, and without taking a position for or against some aspect of his work. To be sure, there are many aspects of Williams's intellectual corpus with which one must take issue. At times, the political leader trumped the objective scholar. Yet his contribution overall has been monumental and indeed seminal, and he has clearly earned his place beside those greats who occupy the Caribbean Pantheon.[14]

Plate 1 Eric Williams's parents, Henry and Eliza Williams. (Photograph: Patricia Gittens)

Plate 2 Williams with young Erica. (Eric Williams Memorial Collection, University of the West Indies, St Augustine)

Plate 3 Williams autographing photo. (Eric Williams Memorial Collection, University of the West Indies, St Augustine)

Plate 4 Williams in 1970 autographing *From Columbus to Castro: The History of the Caribbean 1492–1969.* (Eric Williams Memorial Collection, University of the West Indies, St Augustine)

Plate 5 Graduation ceremony, University of the West Indies, St Augustine, 1966. Pictured in the centre are Princess Alice and Eric Williams. (Eric Williams Memorial Collection, University of the West Indies, St Augustine)

Plate 6 Williams in full flight at a meeting in Woodford Square. (Trinidad and Tobago Express Ltd)

PART 2

SEEKING THE
POLITICAL KINGDOM

3 Prometheus Bound
Williams and the Anglo-American Caribbean Commission

> If ever Western civilisation has anywhere had a chance to solve the world's problems, that place is the Caribbean. It is for this reason that seventeen years ago, I deliberately decided to make the Caribbean my special area of research. I had all the necessary equipment for that study, both psychological and technical.
> – Eric Williams

The Anglo-American Caribbean Commission was established in 1942 for the purpose of strengthening social and economic cooperation in the Caribbean between the British and the US governments and avoiding duplication of their research activities. The commission was a by-product of the "Destroyers for Bases" deal, which was negotiated in 1940 between the two governments to improve their capability to wage war against Hitler's Germany. The *raison d'être* of the commission was given in a joint communiqué issued by the two governments on 9 March 1942, which stated that the purpose was "[e]ncouraging and strengthening social and economic cooperation between the United States and its possessions and bases . . . in the Caribbean, and the United Kingdom and the British colonies in the same area. . . . Members of the Commission will concern themselves primarily with matters pertaining to labour, agriculture, housing, health, education . . . and related subjects" (as cited in Boodhoo 2001, 85).

In *Inward Hunger*, Williams gives us a running account of his relationship with the commission, which had hired him as a part-time researcher working four hours per week while he held a full-time position at Howard University. Controversies between him and the commission's official representatives developed early, and centred around some of his writings, especially *The Negro in the Caribbean* (1942) and his lectures on the Caribbean condition. Williams took the view that he was first and foremost a "teacher of political science" and not a civil servant, and that he should be free to write and lecture. He conceded, however, that it was prudent for him to submit whatever he proposed to say to both sections of the commission for prior approval. Williams tells us that it was he who proposed this formula "in order to protect himself from misreporting and distortion". Still, he stubbornly refused to have anyone dictate to him what he should say in his speeches or to serve as a mouthpiece for expatriate views. He would not allow "British words to be put into my West Indian mouth" (Williams 1969, 82)

There were numerous confrontations between Williams and Sir John Huggins, the commission's first British representative, who had come to Washington after serving as colonial secretary in Trinidad and Tobago. Williams was convinced that the British "never wanted to have me associated with the Commission at all". But he was warmly welcomed by Charles W. Taussig, the American representative, who knew his book and had no difficulty with the views he had expressed in the classic monograph. Nevertheless, the Americans changed their posture when Williams began making critical comments about racism in Puerto Rico and the US Virgin Islands.

Williams was particularly enraged with the comments (or "vapourings", as he termed them) made in July 1945 by the *Antigua Star*. The *Star* accused him of "misstatements, exaggerations and one-sided arguments" and claimed that he was painting pictures of the Caribbean that no longer existed. They were pictures of a "by gone day, but not today" (1969, 69). The *Star* and the West India Committee suggested that it was unfortunate and embarrassing that someone who had written such a document should be on the staff of the commission. Williams saw the hand of the planter class behind the criticism, and said that he was prepared for a "show-down" with such interests and with the British. As he told Sir John McPherson, "I find myself unable to reconcile freedom of speech and expression given me in 1945 with retrospective criticism of what I wrote in 1942" (1969, 89).

Williams noted that he had himself formally advised the commission in October 1944 that he had entered into an agreement with the African Bureau in London, of which George Padmore was a leading figure, to have an English edition of *The Negro in the Caribbean* published. Publication had been deferred during the war years owing to a paper shortage. Williams had formally advised the commission of its imminent publication, and in doing so went as far as disassociating himself from the radical views and policies of the African Bureau with which he said he had "never been identified", though he did know some of its members personally (1969, 85).

Williams reminded McPherson that he was not a civil servant and refused the suggestion that he should retire. He observed that much of what he had said about the condition of the peoples of the Caribbean had been drawn from reports of officially appointed commissions and was not invented by him:

> It is largely upon the opinions of these commissions that I have based the ideas that I now hold of the past, present and future of the West Indies. Every step that has been taken in the West Indies during the last ten years has been in the direction of the

strengthening of the freedom of opinion and free discussion so as to develop the masses of the people in the practice of democracy and to enable them to express their views, and if possible implement them, against the wishes of many of these very vested interests. (Williams 1969, 89)

Williams noted that his views were in line with current official thinking on the future of the West Indies and that resignation was unthinkable. "I do not propose to seek the post [of full professor that had been offered him] at that [Howard] University as a refuge from the hostility of West Indian planters" (ibid., 90). Williams claims that some of his critics had not even read the book.

Interestingly, Williams tells us that he considered leaving voluntarily in 1946. "I decided that the time had come to sever my connection with this collective colonialism [since] I had become increasingly convinced that my abilities and qualifications, such as they are, would be better suited and bear more fruitful results in scholastic work than in the particular administrative field in which I now find myself" (ibid., 91). The secretary general, an American, persuaded him to stay on and piled more work on him. "I thus found myself, from my Washington post, traveling frequently to Commission headquarters in Trinidad to assist the director of research, for whom I had been passed over on racial grounds, and because of political antipathy in carrying out the research which he was unable to do or to organize himself" (ibid., 92).

It was on one of these official trips that Williams found it possible to revisit his homeland for the first time since leaving for Oxford. While there, he gave two public lectures, one to the Literary Society of QRC, his alma mater, and another at the Public Library. Williams boasted that "all hell broke loose" when he was introduced by his old friend, Carlton Comma, the librarian. Comma noted that "Dr. Williams [had] come home, and [had] brought with him scholarship and learning of which anyone, anywhere, however talented, might be proud." Williams himself wrote emotionally of his "return to his native land", a phrase he borrowed from the Martiniquan poet Aimé Césaire:

These people were my own flesh and blood. I had been to school with them, played cricket and football with them, shared their sufferings, enjoyed carnival with them. We had grown up on the same food, the same drink, the same experiences. I had gone away, they had stayed home. I had come back with a University education, they had none. Now I, their former classmate, was their teacher, I who had shared their sufferings was explaining their sufferings. I who had been with them passive objects of British imperial history was telling them of their history. I who had suffered with them the tribulations of colonialism had come back as, so one called me, "the philosopher of West Indian nationalism." How they lapped up the lecture. The atmosphere was electric. (Ibid., 94)

Williams was so overwhelmed by the response to his lectures that he felt driven to proclaim that unlike the proverbial prophet, "The nationalist historian had his greatest honour among his own people. All their pent-up nationalist pride and West Indian dignity were caught up in my remark that 'two hundred years ago, we were sugar plantations. Today we are naval bases . . . .' One day, I knew, they too would assert the rights of man and rewrite the history it was my privilege to teach them" (ibid., 94).

Williams was never modest in terms of how he saw himself. As far as he was concerned, he was "one of the best known spokesmen of colonial peoples everywhere, and the champion of colonial nationalism, utilizing the Caribbean – and not merely the West Indies – as the exemplification of my thesis" (ibid., 100). He tells us further that he "deliberately sought to go outside the narrow British West Indian boundaries" to gaze and comment on what was taking place in Africa, India and other parts of the colonial world. The focus of his research, however, remained the Caribbean.

Williams clearly envisioned himself as a modern-day Caribbean Prometheus who would one day steal fire from the gods on Mount Caucasus and bestow upon his fellow Caribbean men, a fire that they would use to enlighten and emancipate themselves mentally and politically. At this point in his wanderings, he gave no thought to the fact that he would one day have to pay with his liver a price for defying Zeus and the lesser gods and vultures of the neo-colonial world.

Williams was posted to the commission's headquarters in Trinidad and Tobago in June 1948 to act as deputy chairman of the Caribbean Research Council, a post in which he was subsequently confirmed by way of a five-year contract after much pressure from Norman Manley and other West Indians connected with the commission. Williams tells us that the commission consistently tried to get West Indians appointed to the professional staff because they were more productive than the expatriates, some of whom claimed that the climate made it difficult for them to work afternoons. He also claims that he opposed the emphasis on "transient, temporary commuting experts who lack[ed] elementary knowledge of the Caribbean background, and who carry away with them at the end of their assignment, such experience, in the main valuable, as they may accumulate during their Caribbean peregrinations" (ibid., 107). He alleged some of the experts had a "Herrenvolk" mentality.

Williams likewise tells us that race prejudice was rampant at the commission, which selected French creoles and Chinese in preference to other locals. He also claims that during his tenure at the commission, there was a perennial conflict between West Indians and expatriates, with the governments fully on the side of the latter. He himself was to become a victim of this conflict.

C.L.R. James regarded Williams's stint at the commission as an important building block in his training for leadership. It helped to make him a "Hamiltonian" West Indian:

The work at the Anglo-American Commission filled one great void in Williams's equipment. It made him acquainted in the most comprehensive and intimate manner with the West Indian economy as a whole. That was his daily work for years. To us who grew up in the thirties, a strong central government and national economic developments as the indispensable basis of a successful Federation is second nature. We cannot think otherwise. But to these general ideas and his knowledge of West Indian history through the centuries, Williams now had an opportunity as no other West Indian politician ever had to constant study and coordination [*sic*] of the West Indian, in fact the Caribbean economy, taken as a whole. When he says West Indian nationalism, he speaks from deep down. When he says a strong Federation and a West Indian national economy, he speaks from roots almost as deep. He cannot think otherwise. For him to depart substantially from these principles would be to make a wreck of all his studies and the experience of a lifetime. (1993, 342–43)

As we shall see, Williams would soon disappoint James and many who looked to him to make federation a reality.

In 1951, Williams gave serious thought to leaving the commission, and wrote to Luis Muñoz Marin, whom he described as being, apart from Norman Manley, the Caribbean's only statesman, seeking his help in securing an appointment at the University of Puerto Rico that would enable him to undertake a programme of research on the Caribbean. Williams told Muñoz that he was not merely seeking a job:

I feel that any research programme for the area must consciously be oriented towards the development of the Caribbean people, economic and, therefore, intellectual also, but always with the practical goal in mind. Accordingly I do not wish to return to Howard, and Mr. Manley, for whose opinions I have the highest respect, is equally against it. Nor do I just wish "a job" in Puerto Rico. If I did, I would not waste your valuable time. I am anxious to undertake a programme which, whilst, from the intellectual standpoint, not unbefitting the University of Puerto Rico, is consciously motivated by the desire to provide the knowledge and data necessary for statesmen and planners all over the Caribbean, with a view to laying the basis for and facilitating Caribbean cooperation.

We have no record of Muñoz's response to Williams and have to assume that he did little or nothing to accommodate the latter's request.

4 Letting Down My Bucket

Whatever personal success may be associated with my name, I shall go down to our posterity as the architect of the University of Woodford Square.
  – Eric Williams

There are conflicting versions as to what Eric Williams did and stood for at the commission, but it is clear that he found it difficult to abide the incompetence that in his view passed for expertise on its expatriate staff. Given what we know of Williams's academic ability, his irascibility, the chip he carried on his shoulder, his inability to suffer intellectual mediocrity, and his tendency to be on the lookout for any sign of condescension or discrimination, it is hardly surprising that he should come into open and wrathful conflict with his colonial employers, who were ill at ease with the conclusions to which his scholarship led him. This was particularly important given the paranoia that obtained in both the Western and socialist camps in the era of the Cold War.

Williams was suspected of being a communist, in part because he had made some reference to the "abolition of private property" in one of the documents he authored. To some of his detractors, he was not only black, but red! However, he was neither a communist nor a Moscowphile, though he did espouse views that were radical. Williams himself tells us that at Oxford, he had no connection whatever with "any political organisation at all". He was the hero who was preparing himself in the wilderness of the empire for the historic mission to which he believed History had called him.

Williams had broad and profound differences with the secretary general of the commission, differences that were political and organisational. The secretary general felt that Williams was spending too much time on matters outside the scope of the commission's work, such as the adult education programme on which he embarked in Trinidad and Tobago in 1954–55. Differences also arose in respect of the relationship between the research and bureaucratic functions of the commission, as to which was more important. Williams told the secretary general that the core of the problem was the divergence between their views as to the status of the head of the research branch and the branch itself *vis-à-vis* the administrative staff. Williams clearly felt that the research function was more important than the administrative function and that this should be reflected in the hierarchical arrangements of the commission.

Williams enjoyed the comforts and perks that were associated with the job, however, and was not anxious to leave. He admitted that he considered the "travel and fieldwork associated with the commission the most attractive and valuable aspect of my connection with it". The job provided him with an unrivalled opportunity to become familiar with the entire Caribbean area, a facility that he clearly valued highly. As he explained, "I was in 1940, a West Indian who had more direct and closer contact, historically and actually, with the Caribbean area as a whole than any other." He was "Mr Caribbean" by birth, training, experience and mission.

At the end of his five-year contract, Williams was given a one-year extension, which in effect meant that he was on "probation". Williams viewed this as a veritable declaration of war. He saw dismissal as a distinct possibility. Angered, he began to canvass other possibilities. He wrote Norman Manley, then premier of Jamaica, to whom he was wont to turn for advice in matters relating to the commission and in respect of his political career. What was he to do? he whinged in his letter to Manley of 17 June 1954, quoted here at length:[1]

> I have, it seems to me only two alternatives: to bow down and worship, which means that the boots are waiting for me – this I could never do; or to leave things as they are, leaving it to them to decide next year, but should REC (Regional Economic Committee) materialize, just get to hell out. There is a third alternative, and this is the one that I am now pursuing: to fight them . . . I was denied a fellowship at Oxford – I have always been convinced it was on racial grounds – and every conceivable pressure was brought to bear on me to leave and return to Trinidad. . . . Taylor did not want me at Mona. McPherson tried to get me out of the Commission in 1945 because of the Negro in the Caribbean. . . . Now de Vriendt does not want me. What am I to do, cut sugar cane? They threatened to fail my doctor's thesis because they did not like my view; the British have never ceased attacking me for Capitalism and Slavery, very subtly, of course. Local representatives are always opposing my views. Hammond was distinctly rude about Education in the British West Indies. I am determined once and for all to put a stop to this impertinent persecution. They suspend the British Guiana Constitution and now they wish to suspend me. I am sick to death of it all. (1969, 113)

Williams evidently saw himself as a victim of colonially inspired disrespect and persecution, but not unwisely calculated that his dismissal could provide him with the platform he needed to launch his political career. As the frustrated would-be hero told Manley,

I may be out of a job in a year's time. There are elections here next year, and I have already been asked to come out and join the Independent Labour Party, and the suggestion has even been made that I should be Chairman. I do not rule it out. . . . If they do not want to deal with me at the level of an innocuous research worker, perhaps they prefer to deal with me as a legislator. If they insist on my being a hewer of wood and a drawer of water for a metropolitan boss, perhaps they prefer a colonial-metropolitan relationship at the level of my joining the demand for a complete responsible government and the complete West Indianisation of the Trinidad Civil Service. (Ibid., 113)

Edna Manley believes that Williams's decision to enter politics was largely determined by his friendship with her husband Norman. She believes that Williams's decision to throw his hat in the ring was made at a meeting the two men had at Piarco Airport. As she diarised, "It was a few weeks or even days before his fatal decision to go into politics, and he had come to the [Piarco] airport to 'put it' to NW. Should he or shouldn't he? – and Norman threw [his] full weight into the decision, urging him to do it. As usual when they got together, they talked till almost dawn." When dawn broke, Manley realized what he had done.

"Well, they won – I don't think it would have happened without Norman's pioneer work in Trinidad . . . . Just a year before, he had spoken at Woodford Square and had prophesied that they would enter party politics like the rest of the Caribbean. Trinidad, which later became so arrogant, was all those years [behind] everywhere else" (Manley 1989, 57–58).

Williams was aware that "throwing his hat in the ring would cause a sensation". He was equally aware that he would encounter "stiff opposition" if he chose to do so (EWMC folio 39). Thus his ambivalence and hesitation, even after the "Owl of Minerva" had already taken flight.

Williams decided to adopt three strategies to fight the commission. One was to write more. As he told Manley, "I am persecuted because of my writings; I think therefore I ought to write some more . . . and see if I can get a best seller which will allow me to retire and devote my time solely to scholarly writing". Williams told Manley that he could not go back to Howard, and the Trinidad government could not "offer him a job that would be of any interest to him". Williams told Manley that one of the arrows in his political quiver would be his autobiography, which, when written, would be a political embarrassment to the colonial establishment. He in fact gave Manley an outline of what would be the meat of the autobiographical statement. He told Manley he was not "down hearted" and that *"for years I have been biding my time with the autobiography"*. Williams went on to tell Manley that this planned *"autobiography will be a sort of party programme"* (emphasis added) if he was forced to take a political way out. He chose not to repeat this particular statement in *Inward Hunger*. The premeditation would have been too obvious to his readers.

His second weapon was an adult education campaign:

> If I could no longer stay in my administrative headquarters at Kent House in order to earn my daily bread, I would make the Trinidad Public Library my intellectual headquarters. If imperialism attacked from Kent House, nationalism would counter-attack from the Public Library. The Caribbean Commission was determined to do nothing to promote the cause of West Indian nationalism and the education of the West Indian people; then I would dedicate myself to the education of the West Indian people and the cause of West Indian nationalism and, by transmitting to them the fruits of the education I had received at their expense, I would repay their investment in me. The Commission wished a showdown; it would get one. (Ibid., 113)

In pursuit of this goal, Williams gave an extensive series of talks at the Public Library in Port of Spain, which was supplemented by articles in the *Trinidad Guardian* and lectures to groups that invited him to speak. The lectures were meant to inculcate the spirit of nationalism and the defence of national interests against colonialism. Some of the themes articulated were the importance of federation, nation building, and West Indianization of the school curriculum, themes that would recur following his separation from the commission. In his comment on the need for federation, we see glimpses of what would later be said in the *Economics of Nationhood*: "Only a Federal Government, working on a precise development plan for attracting outside capital and removing idle labour in various parts of the West Indies to the undeveloped resources of other parts, could hope to bring to St. Kitts–Nevis that economic and political stability necessarily lacking in a society dependent on a single industry resting on two foundations, a single factory and a single union" (ibid., 116). Williams also saw pan-Antilleanism as the only meaningful option available to the Caribbean. As he declared in one of his lectures: "A Federation based on participation by the French, Spanish, English and Dutch including 15 million people would enable the economy of the whole area to be organized. Industrialisation of Trinidad or Cuba or Haiti each in isolation is an absurdity" (*Trinidad Guardian*, 1 December 1954). He also argued that "any Federation is better than no Federation. . . . The Colonial Office should have imposed Federation on the West Indies!" (*Trinidad Guardian*, 7 December 1954).

On the question of nation building, Williams had the following to say:

> The task of building a West Indian nation is the decisive task of the present and future. . . . The school today in the British West Indies is the most potent force dividing up our communities. The school tomorrow in the British West Indies must be the most potent force bringing together our communities. The West Indian school today despises and disparages its environment. . . . The West Indian school of tomorrow must make a positive fetish of the West Indian environment. (Ibid., 116)

But Williams was careful to warn against the dangers of ultra-nationalism and exclusion of the cultural contributions of other peoples and civilizations.

His third weapon was to carry the fight to the metropolitan enemy. Williams noted that he had only months ago received commendations about his performance. The commission had in fact noted that the contracts of the deputy secretary general and the deputy chairman of the Caribbean Research Council would expire in July and September 1954 respectively and had recommended that the contracts be extended for a further five years on the same terms and conditions. Now he was being told, five months later, that because of "contemplated revisions of the Agreement of the Establishment of the Commission which is likely to call for a reappraisal of the Commission's Organisation in so far as its research activities are concerned", his contract would only be extended for the period of a year (ibid., 123). This decision left Williams "at a loss", and he saw the hand of colonialism in the plot. The decision, he said, reduced the status of research that West Indians associated with the commission believed should be emphasized. The commission was being bureaucratized. Williams was certain that the proposed restructuring of the commission was a way to avoid promoting him to the post of secretary general. The commission was accused of supporting the metropolitan representative against the West Indian at the least sign of friction (ibid., 124).

In responding to the commission's letter offering him a one-year contract, Williams was under no illusions as to what he was doing. "There were only two options available to the Commission – I had to be appointed Secretary General or I must be fired." As he also told the commission:

> It would not be possible for people to reconcile my role in the adult education movement with the dismissal by an organization established to promote regional co-operation in the Caribbean of the very person who has made the study of West Indian affairs the exclusive concern of his adult life and who is, in some eyes, "Mr. Caribbean". I would necessarily have to defend myself. I do not see how the Commission's prestige would be enhanced thereby or its possibilities of service to the area improved. (Ibid., 126)

On 26 May 1955, Williams was duly fired. "Your service contract with the Commission due to expire on June 21, 1955 will not be renewed," he was summarily told. Williams noted that he received the official notification of the commission's decision not to renew his contract on the very day the British Labour Party was defeated in the 1955 election. In Williams's view, this was not accidental. His enemies in the commission knew that he had lost his support base in the Colonial Office . There were no longer any British Colonial Office officials such as Stafford Cripps or Arthur Creech-Jones to advance his case with the bureaucrats who controlled the commission.

In January 1955 Williams wrote a curious letter to Manley that anticipates much that would happen when he eventually threw his proverbial hat into the political ring. Williams's letter indicated that he had already begun to assess the forces that would be arrayed against him if he were to let down his bucket in the Trinidad and Tobago political pond:

> The Catholics look upon me as their No. 1 enemy. . . . The position has not been improved by a controversy between myself and a Negro priest over Aristotle in which he was not spared and got much the worse of the exchanges. On the other hand, there have been clear overtures to me, based partly on the Indian Federation vote and the conclusions to be drawn from this vis-à-vis the denominational school. A recent lecture by me on Las Casas has pleased them very much, and in a reply I am making to various criticisms of my Aristotelian ideas, I shall go out of my way to indicate that I am not their enemy. . . . The Indians also were hostile, for I, apart from Nelson [a local journalist], did more than anyone else here to kill their opposition to Federation, or rather to cut the ground from under their feet. The most recent consequence is an open détente from the Indian Commissioner . . . [t]here is no doubt that throwing my hat in the ring will be a sensation. . . . Equally, there is no doubt that I can expect stiff opposition. Nelson will speak to you about assessing whether I should enter politics. . . . Elections are to be postponed until September 1956; this will give me more time. . . . I am immersed in a vast adult education programme . . . this will help keep my name before the public. (EWMC folio 39)

There is general agreement among Williams's colleagues as to what happened following his dismissal from the commission. Williams called on a few of them to discuss his next steps. Interestingly, he did not call John Donaldson and De Wilton Rogers, two "teacher friends" who had helped him in his quest to keep his name before the public and who had sponsored his historic lectures. Instead, he summoned the "Bachacs", Doctors Elton Richardson, Winston Mahabir and Ibbit Mosaheb and one of his brothers. As Mahabir recalled, "Dutifully and expectantly we complied. He resided then in a fairly posh residence on Lady Chancellor Road. . . . We talked until dawn. In psychiatric terms, we were administering conjoint psychotherapy to Eric during his spontaneous marathon abreaction" (1978, 18).[2]

Mahabir was not initially minded to respond to Williams's invitation. In fact he tells us that he was not at all sympathetic to Williams's plight:

> It is true to say that I felt no sympathy for Eric over his dismissal from the effete and stultifying Commission. Whatever machinations had occurred behind the scenes did not interest me. For my part a slave had been freed and this freed-man would in turn help us all to seek our just and rightful heritage as a free West Indian nation, the exemplar to the world of a society's ability to transcend the limitations of racial difference, economic disparity, religious intolerance and a heritage of colonial tokenism. (Ibid.)

When the question arose around 3 o'clock the following morning as to what Williams should do next, Richardson advised him to move from where he currently lived and find a home in the middle-class suburb of Woodbrook. Richardson also advised him to get rid of the Buick car that he was then driving and acquire something more appropriate to his new status as "just another poor Negro boy". Williams initially resisted this advice, and in fact burst into unrestrained laughter. As Mahabir remarked, "For him it must have been another ego-buster, but his basic sense of drama – always with him at centre stage and a concerned cast for supporting actors – allowed him to accept a temporary diminution" (ibid., 19). The Buick was duly sold. Williams moved to Woodbrook and bought a modest Vauxhall. Clearly, he had begun in earnest the struggle for power.

Richardson broadly agrees with Mahabir's version of what transpired after that all-night meeting. Williams did not communicate with them for quite a while, and it may well be that he was canvassing other constituencies. Once "it was decided" that he should go to the public, Williams began working on the speech that he would give to detail his relations with the commission. Williams's draft of the speech was read to the whole group before it was delivered to the public. Richardson's account of what occurred prior to the delivery of the historic speech bears retelling: "It was a beautifully done speech, but I felt that it lacked the quality of identification. I said that he ought to couch it so that all poor struggling folks could see their own struggles reflected in his experiences. Eric hesitated long before he accepted, but finally did" (1984, 131).

Following the successful delivery of the speech, Williams thanked Richardson for his suggestion, and told him to "go to the head of the class. . . . You were right. I should try to get people to see that my struggle was a replica of the struggles of others". The evening was an outstanding success, and Eric was safely launched.

Williams himself felt that the speech had accomplished its propagandistic objectives. He boasted that there were some ten thousand people in Woodford Square. "I got right down to brass tacks", following Richardson's advice to make a connection between his struggle and that which other black men were all experiencing in one way or another in colonial society. As he told the crowd, "I stand before you tonight, and therefore, before the people of the British West Indies, the representative of a principle, a cause, and a defeat. The principle is the principle of intellectual freedom. The cause is the cause of the West Indian people. The defeat is the defeat of the policy of appointing local men to high office" (1969, 131). He continued,

> I took them through a lecture of fifty-one printed pages – the whole sordid story of my relations with the Commission, the pressures on me, the efforts to remove me from my job or prevent my appointment to it. I put the story in language that was readily understood in Woodford Square of Trinidad in 1955. I was the nationalist victim of colo-

nial pressures. But I was also the trained national exposed to insults and pressures from relatively untrained expatriates. It was pure nationalist protest, and not personal pique. And all Trinidad and Tobago listened when I drew the inevitable conclusion from the story. (Ibid., 132)

Williams told his listeners that he had turned down many job offers that would have taken him out of the West Indies. He did not wish to "flee the imperialist enemy", or give in to the pressures of the West Indian plantocracy that was demanding his removal. Then came what Williams called the "grand finale". He "ramajayed", to use a Trinidad expression:

> The Commission had tried to get me out of Washington, being even willing to pay the price they had hoped to avoid at the outset, getting me back to Trinidad or even Jamaica. Then they tried to keep me away from Trinidad. Now that I was back in Trinidad, they tried to get me back to Washington. What was I, a blasted football of the Commission? Who the bloody hell were the Commission anyway? I let them have it. I told the Woodford Square audience:
>
> I was born here, and here I stay, with the people of Trinidad and Tobago who educated me free of charge for nine years at Queen's Royal College and for five years at Oxford, who have made me whatever I am, and who have been or might be at any time the victims of the very pressures which I have been fighting against for twelve years. . . . I am going to let down my bucket where I am, right here with you in the British West Indies. Woodford Square roared its approval, and the roar was heard in London and in Washington. I had crossed the Rubicon. (Ibid., 132)

The hero was now unequivocally launched on his history-making odyssey. There could be no turning back.

Following his departure from the commission, Williams sought to popularize Caribbean history and to build a political platform for himself. He told his audiences that his efforts were motivated by "national protest and not personal pique", a claim that many now challenge. A more likely explanation was that there was a fortuitous conjuncture of pique, a desire for revenge, nascent nationalism, and vanity and grandiosity on his part. The personal needs of the man and the needs of the people from which he sprang coincided to create one of those unique historical events that demarcate historical epochs. The partial autobiography had achieved its intended purpose. Williams had been anointed with the mandate of heaven. To many he was the messianic hero sent to lead the people out of Babylon to the promised land. He was to others the successor to Alfred Richards, Cipriani, Solomon, Butler and all who had gone before.

Would Williams have entered politics if his contract had been renewed? This is a question that continues to intrigue many who have followed Williams's career. Selwyn Cudjoe, correctly, in my view, argues that "Williams's entrance into the politics of the society was not as unplanned or as accidental as his initial speech 'My Relations with the Caribbean Commission' [June 1955] might lead one to believe" (1993, 51). Williams was clearly pulled in two directions, and, like many a general, was reluctant to "cross the Rubicon". Heroes always harbour private doubts about their invincibility and the authenticity of their calling and look to the "oracle" to give them a sign. Williams was no different, and hesitated a long time before finally deciding to enter upon a career of political activism. It is worth recalling that quite a few of Williams's friends, including Norman Manley, with whom he had discussed his interest in entering politics, had sought to discourage him from entering political life on the grounds that the masses were ungrateful and would reject him as they had done Captain Cipriani and Patrick Solomon. His indecision in fact angered some of his colleagues, who felt that for all his expressed concern for the people of Trinidad and Tobago, he preferred the cushiony comforts of his lucrative post at the Caribbean Commission. His dismissal from the commission, however, brought to a dramatic end his equivocation and his seeming reluctance to plunge into the uncertainties of politics. The hero had been given a sign and a ready-made issue with which to launch his political career.

If Williams had come to the conclusion that the commission was a do-nothing imperialist agency, it might have been wondered why he continued to associate with it, and why he had sought to be promoted to the vacant position of secretary general. Anticipating suspicions, Williams explained,

> I tolerated those conditions for over twelve years [because] I represented . . . the cause of the West Indian people. I also had more personal reasons. My connection with the Commission brought me into close contact with present problems in territories, the study of whose history has been the principal purpose of my adult life, while my association with representatives of the metropolitan governments enabled me to understand, as I could not otherwise have understood, the mess in which the West Indies find themselves today. (1955, 48)

The circumstances and sequence leading to Williams's decision to go to the people have generated much controversy. No doubt it was partly influenced by the concerted attempt of the Trinidad government, especially Minister of Industry, Commerce and Labour Albert Gomes, and Minister of Education Roy Joseph, to deny Williams the use of government buildings for his adult education programme. Pressure from his colleagues also provided him with the courage that he seemed to have lacked in those early months of 1955. It is certain, however, that had it not been for his dismissal from the commission, Williams would not have entered active political life that year. His friend and colleague Ibbit Mosaheb agrees that if Williams had been offered the job as secretary general, he would certainly have accepted, and that his dismissal was the historical trigger for his decision to enter politics. To quote Mosaheb, "If he was not fired from the

Commission, he would not have entered politics. I believe Eric was forced into politics by the firing. The position of secretary general rotated. Eric believed that when it was the turn of the English, he would be appointed secretary general. He wasn't, and was eventually fired . . . and decided to enter politics. He may have been planning this for years. He was an opportunist" (interview with Ken Boodhoo, as cited in Mohammed 2001, 33). Williams himself argued that he was certain he would one day enter West Indian politics, and that his dismissal from the commission merely affected the timing. There is no reason to challenge this assertion. His dismissal had served to resolve the dissonance he was experiencing. Thus his feeling of immense relief. Interestingly, his daughter Erica believed that if his wife Soy (her mother, whom he had quietly married in January 1951 in Reno, Nevada) had not died in 1953, Williams would not have entered politics, then or in the future.[3]

The enthusiasm with which Williams's speech was received made it quite apparent that the people had found a new hero. It is not only what he said that was important. How he said it was also important to what people heard.[4] Williams's cocky boastfulness and pugnacity elicited a ready response in the Trinidadian masses, who were also in search of a messiah. The perception that he was a brilliant academician, accepted and recognized as such in Britain and the United States, added to his legitimacy in their eyes, for to them, as to most colonials, the winning of recognition in status-defining metropolitan cultures was and still is a prerequisite for acceptance. His charisma derived largely from his intellectual achievements and his competence with the "word". He was "Mr Big Brain".

The address was repeated a few days later in San Fernando, where Mahabir was the evening's chairman. Mahabir introduced Williams as someone with a manifest prejudice – a West Indian prejudice. He also told the assembled crowd that in dismissing Williams, the commission "knew not what they did." Mahabir was full of praise for the landmark speech, which led to the growth of the halo that surrounded Williams, but noted that "his friends recognized his flair for drama and penchant for persuasive distortion" (1978, 19–20).

Despite the conflicts that he later had with him, Mahabir remained committed to the view that Williams's time had come:

> The time was ripe for such a man. Despite his personal faults and personality aberrations, he soon drove order into chaos, gave guidance and direction to vague impulse, synthesized the secret longings of lesser men, and finally brought a tremendous party organization into the 1956 election campaign, the exhilaration of which its participants can never forget. Eric Williams seemed to write the epitaph on the graves of previous political leaders and began his career as the oracle of Trinidad politics. (Ibid., 29)

5   **The Bastard Child of World Democracy**

The years following the end of the Second World War were characterized by a great deal of political agitation for electoral and constitutional reform in the colonial world. What was taking place in Trinidad and Tobago, and the Caribbean generally, was, however, somewhat different from what was in evidence in the countries of Africa, Asia and the Middle East, where nationalist elites were struggling for independence from colonial rule. In the latter areas, there was a greater degree of militancy and willingness on the part of the national liberation movements to use violent methods to achieve their goal of full independence.

This difference in terms of the strength of demand for independence and the stridency with which those demands were made was due in part to the nature of these societies, their historical antecedents, and the characteristics of the colonial rule to which they had to respond. In almost all cases, these were traditional or neo-traditional societies that had been ruthlessly penetrated and traumatized by the forces of imperialism and capitalism. Their populations were not, in the main, recent immigrants, as was the case in the Caribbean, where almost every group was a transplant that had been substantially deracinated and shorn of core elements of their "primordial" culture. Their nationalism was thus more confident, grounded as it was in a pre-colonial past to which reference could be made, sometimes with pride, even if the construction was mythical.

Caribbean nationalism by comparison was expressed in a demand for a more thorough inclusion in the culture of the colonizer rather than its repudiation. Williams was himself a moderate as a nationalist and as a constitutional reformer, despite the stridency with which he appeared to speak. He confronted the British, the Dutch and the Americans intellectually, but was not prepared to use the strategies and tactics of Gandhi, Sukarno, Nkrumah, Nehru or Nasser, all of whom he admired but would not imitate. His was the politics of intellect and not of the street and the prison. As he would later tell Uriah Butler, one of his predecessors in the vineyards of anti-colonial politics, the days of agitational street politics were over. Williams was an Afro-Britisher, or an Afro-Saxon as some like Lloyd Best called him, leading an essentially Anglo-centric population. Remarkably, Williams himself would declare that if the British Constitution "was good enough for Britain, it was good enough for Trinidad and Tobago".

Williams's views on constitution reform were systematically made public in a lecture that he delivered on 19 July 1955. He explained that previously he had been unable to make his views known because of the constraints of the job that he held at the Caribbean Commission. Since no member of the Constitution Commission asked him for his views, even if informally, "I necessarily had to remain silent. That restriction no longer applies" (1955c, 30).

Williams lecture drew a large and appreciative crowd from all strata of Trinidad society. He noted that he had been accused of speaking to an "uncultured mob". Not so, he boasted, and expressed the hope that the doctors, lawyers, dentists, civil servants, housewives and workers who were in the audience would take note of the vicious "canard". His was an attempt to bring university-type education to the public square where it properly belonged. As he told the cheering crowd,

> The age of exclusiveness in university education is gone forever, though our West Indian University College perversely refuses to recognize this. Somebody once said that all that was needed for a university was a book and the branch of a tree; someone else went further and said that a university should be a university in overalls. With a bandstand, a microphone, a large audience in slacks and hot shirts, a topical subject for discussion, the open air and a beautiful tropical night, we have all the essentials of a university. Now that I have resigned my position at Howard University in the U.S.A., the only university in which I shall lecture in future is the University of Woodford Square and its several branches throughout the length and breadth of Trinidad and Tobago. (1955c, 1)

Williams's lecture traced the history of constitution reform in Trinidad and Tobago from the time it was captured by the British to 1955 without ever attempting to be patronizing or to "dumb-down" his presentation for the benefit of the lowest common denominator. If anything, it could be said that the lecture might have been pitched at too high a level. Williams believed his historic mission was to raise the level of public education.

Williams explained to his listeners why Trinidad, not Tobago, was at the bottom of the British West Indian political ladder and how it came to have the type of constitution it did, one that differed from that of Jamaica, Barbados or the Leeward Islands. He noted that as in Jamaica and Barbados, whites were in a minority. Unlike the latter two, however, the people of colour and the mulattos made up the majority of those who were free. If one were to concede elected institutions to Trinidad, the free people of colour would dominate. Moreover, a majority of the white people of Trinidad and Tobago were French, and "ignorant of the British Constitution and unaccustomed to its operation". The British also did not want to have to deal with an assembly controlled by slave owners as they had to do in Jamaica and Barbados. As member of Parliament George Canning, a future British prime minister, had noted, "The government was averse to adding Trinidad to the number of islands where the introduction of every plan for ameliorating the condition of the slaves was uniformly opposed." They thus had to experiment with a new constitutional formula.

Williams observed that over the nineteenth century, some liberal Englishmen had argued that Trinidad's constitution should be patterned on that of Jamaica. The British government instead wished to reduce Jamaica's status to the level of Trinidad's. Among those who held this latter view were Bishop Thomas Carlyle, Anthony Trollope, the distinguished novelist, and James Anthony Froude, then professor of modern history at Oxford University. Their view remained dominant. The basic crown colony model thus remained in place until 1925, when provision was made for an element of representation, though it was limited to men of economic worth. Six of the twenty-four members of the legislature were to be elected.

Williams noted that whereas there was white creole support, however restricted, for representative democracy at the turn of the nineteenth century, there was a withdrawal of such support in the wake of the events following the First World War, which witnessed the emergence of political militancy on the part of the black working class led by Captain Cipriani and the Trinidad Workmen's Association. Whereas representative government was strongly supported by the black middle-class creoles and the working class led by Cipriani, the white creoles and the Indians now opposed it, the latter preferring either the nominated system or communal representation. Both feared that creole nationalism would emerge triumphant if the franchise were opened to all and sundry. Major Wood, who visited Trinidad in 1921 to inquire on behalf of the Colonial Office into the causes of the unrest that broke out in the post–First World War years, urged the Indians to eschew communal representation and identify themselves with the main currents of political life in the colony and assist in guiding its course (1921, 24). In the 1925 election, there were 15,632 registered voters. Only 6,832 persons voted. The total population of the electorate in the five constituencies in which elections were conducted was 244,551.

Williams proceeded to give his "class" a "history lesson" in British, French and American constitutional development, drawing on the work of the Greeks, and of Locke, Rousseau, Jefferson, Voltaire, Burke, Hamilton and the feminists in support of his argument about the need to have a system that left real power in the hands of the elected representatives of the people. Williams argued, however, that one did not need to go as far back as 1796 to make a case justifying the second chamber. One could in fact find ample justification in the 1951 Report of the British Guiana Constitutional Commission.

Williams chided the members of the Constitution Reform Committee, whom he said found Trinidad and Tobago the "outside child of world democracy" and who did nothing to make the child legitimate. The Trinidad and Tobago constitution remained, in his view, "democracy's bastard". Its defects, he said, were several. For one thing, it did not separate the legislative function from the administrative in that officials and elected representatives were both in the same chamber. Democracy, British style, required the separation of powers, or so Williams argued.

Williams took particular objection to the ministerial system that was put in place following the 1950 election, which he considered a "travesty" of democracy and which the Constitution Reform Committee proposed to continue. He noted that the ministers were not collectively responsible, and that it required a two-thirds majority of the legislative council to have any of them removed. Their behaviour was thus individualistic. "What you get is merely five people who behave like five people. . . . A system more absurd than the Ministerial system in Trinidad in the past five years cannot be found" (ibid., 28).

Williams observed that under the existing and proposed system, a chief minister could not discipline his colleagues because he would have no legal or political power to do so. The problem of course was that the system did not assume the existence of disciplined political parties and was in fact designed to abort their development. This was precisely what Williams hoped to see develop. He agreed that Trinidad lacked an effective party system. It would continue to do so until a constitution was introduced that would "encourage responsible people to join responsible parties to form a responsible government". To quote Williams further,

> Organised parties do not precede a sensible constitution. They did not in Jamaica or Barbados or Puerto Rico or Great Britain. So long as the travesty of the ministerial system is permitted, encouraging individualism, so long as the Government can depend on a block of official and nominated votes, for so long will the party system in Trinidad and Tobago remain a hollow mockery. As the British Guiana Constitutional Commission recognized, "the presence of a nominated bloc inevitably impedes and may stultify the growth of cohesive political parties". (1955c, 29)

What then did Williams want? In his own words, "a party around which all classes, colours, races and religions can rally for the constructive and uphill task of reorganizing the economy to provide jobs for the population" (ibid., 30).

Interestingly, Williams agreed with Butler that the commissioners did not need to engage in any extensive consultations before making recommendations as to what constitution formula they should propose, because there were any number of "foreign used" models they could recommend. In his view, the Colonial Office itself did not even have to examine its second-hand constitutions "since it had a constitution at hand which it could immediately apply to Trinidad and Tobago. That was the British Constitution!".

Williams went on to make a statement for which he will always be remembered and criticized by radicals who believe that the Westminster model is inappropriate in the context of the Caribbean: "If the British Constitution is good enough for Great Britain, it should be good enough for Trinidad and Tobago." Williams genuinely believed that what the broad population and the Afro-creole elements wanted was the installation of the Westminster model in Trinidad and Tobago. He in fact fully agreed with Lord Halifax that "[t]he whole history of the African population of the West Indies inevitably drives them towards representative institutions fashioned after the British model. . . . We shall be wise if we avoid the mistake of endeavouring to withhold a concession, ultimately inevitable until it has been robbed by delay of most of its usefulness and of all its grace" (1955c, 31).

Williams put the blame for the persistent failure of the nationalist movement in Trinidad and Tobago mainly on the inadequacies of the institutional framework. Unless Trinidad and Tobago were conceded British parliamentary institutions, political chaos and backwardness would continue to prevail. What was needed was the creation of a purely elective lower chamber, leaving the existing chamber to the nominated element. Here Williams turned his back on the whole radical tradition in Trinidad and Tobago, a tradition that was virtually unanimous in opposing a second chamber. His argument was that in the context of Trinidad politics, vested economic and religious interests must be given some say in the running of the country. "The nominated system is so essential that if it did not exist, it would be necessary to invent it" (ibid., 13)

Williams listed three defects of the system as it existed. In the first place, the nominated element had too decisive an influence in the system. One should take the nominated members out of the single chamber legislature where they could *determine* what the people of Trinidad and Tobago do, either by being in a majority, or by assisting ministers to get a majority, and put them in a second chamber. "Like Wordworth's perfect woman, nobly planned, they can warn and comfort, so long as unlike that estimable lady, they are not to command" (ibid.).

Williams also observed that the nominated system was not being used as extensively as it should have been. If the two-chamber system were to be introduced, it would then be possible to give representation to a greater variety of special interests such as those in cocoa, shipping, local industry, the clergy and the judiciary. Williams noted that the chief justice was in the legislative council up to 1866. He also argued that the clergy played critical social roles in the society, and that it would be in the public interest to have them represented. Williams noted that the clergy – the lords spiritual – were represented in the House of Lords. "An added bonus of having the clergy represented was that room could be made for representatives of non-Christian denominations. In doing so, a very important step will be taken towards fostering and encouraging unity in the community" (ibid., 33).

The third defect concerned the manner in which special interests were appointed. The fact that these appointments were made by the governor with the approval of the Colonial Office detracted from the legitimacy of such nominees. Inevitably, they had come to be regarded as the governor's stooges. Special interests must in future choose their own representatives, said Williams. "The second chamber must not be dominated by the Governor, by the Secretary of State for the Colonies, or *by the party in power*" [emphasis added] (ibid.). Somewhat contradictorily, however, Williams argued that persons of distinction who were to be nominated should be chosen on the recommendation of the chief minister because "West Indians must learn to appreciate that their political position depends on the confidence of the people and not on the confidence of the Governor."

Williams's constitutional proposals were a model of moderation. What was striking about them were the enormous concessions he made to the vested interests in the society, interests that on the surface he appeared to be attacking. Williams in fact conceded to his proposed upper chamber a greater delaying power than that enjoyed by the House of Lords after 1910. On non-financial matters the upper chamber was to be permitted to delay legislation for as long as twenty-four months! He defended this provision on the grounds that checks and balances were necessary in a society as politically inexperienced as Trinidad and Tobago:

> Checks and balances [are] necessary in a democratic society. Such checks and balances are doubly necessary when, as is always possible, one party might sweep the polls and find itself without effective opposition in the elected house, as has happened with Bradshaw in St Kitts, Bird in Antigua, Gairy in Grenada, Nkrumah in the Gold Coast and Muñoz Marin in Puerto Rico. To make assurance doubly sure, the delaying power of twelve months enjoyed by the House of Lords in Britain should be extended to twenty-four months in Trinidad as the system is new and as we have only a limited experience of democratic process. That experience dates back only thirty-two years, a short time in the life of man and an insignificant period in the life of a country. The second Chamber should be empowered to initiate legislation, except money bills which are reserved exclusively for the lower chamber. (Ibid., 35)

Two possible explanations might be advanced for Williams's constitutional moderation. It could be argued that the provisions demonstrated how conservative and Anglo-centric he really was despite his revolutionary rhetoric. The entire set of proposals was considerably to the right of those proposed by radicals in the 1940s. Williams appeared to be just as suspicious of dominant parties based on mass support as were the conformist middle classes. Indeed, he seemed to place himself in the republican rather than in the populist democratic tradition. It was to Alexander Hamilton, for example, that he turned for arguments to justify his proposals for a constitution that would include checks on the popular assembly. The appeal to vested interests might be viewed as a genuine attempt to offer them the opportunity to play a responsible and constructive role in the development of the region. These forces "can help run the country", he advised his followers.

But it is also possible to argue that Williams, though a committed radical, was deliberately casting himself in the role of the aggregator who, if given a chance, would unite all the disparate elements in the society. As such, he quite calculatingly designed a constitution that would appeal to all classes and all ethnic and creedal groups. Bouquets were thrown at every important sector of the society. As he confessed, "The proposals were designed to reconcile all conflicting points of view . . . to provide common ground for the widest possible measure of co-operation between all classes, races, colours and religions for the constructive work ahead of us in the field of economic and social development" (ibid., 35–36).

What Trinidad needed most of all, he argued, was a genuine multiracial party. That was the key. The creation of a proper constitution was, however, the *sine qua non* for the emergence of such a party. It was the door that must be opened if the dynamic energies of the people, now confined, were to be released. Williams observed that earlier attempts had been made to create a party that would cut across the vertical and horizontal interests of the society. Their weakness stemmed in part from the failure of those who led them to inspire the necessary confidence in their multiracial idealism. Andrew Cipriani, Patrick Solomon, Uriah "Buzz" Butler, Raymond Hamel-Smith (sometime leader of the TLP) and others never offered the minorities any constitutional safeguards with which they could defend themselves in time of need. This was Williams's unique contribution to the constitutional debate. He felt that with these constitutional safeguards, people of varying ethnic backgrounds would feel free to join a mass nationalist party. By implication, however, Williams was putting the blame for the failure of the attempts at multiracial unity on the political class in Trinidad and not on the Colonial Office. As he said later on (*Race Relations in Caribbean Society*), "The last apology or excuse for colonization will have been removed when Caribbean democracy can prove that minority rights are quite safe in its hands" (1957, 60).

Interestingly, Williams told the crowd that none of the existing parties, some of whom had invited him to join forces with them, appeared to meet his expectations in terms of what was needed. He had thus decided that if he did choose to enter the field, "not to accept any of the invitations extended . . . but to enter on the basis of a new party designed to offer the people of Trinidad and Tobago, whatever their race and class, colour, or religion, for their acceptance or rejection, the key which they have not yet found and for which they are so desperately searching" (1955c, 36).

Williams's constitutional proposal, embodied in a petition to the secretary of state for the colonies, was signed by 27,811 people from all over the country. Support came from all religious, ethnic and class groups, though the non-Indian community was heavily overrepresented. The marshalling of signatures to convince the Colonial Office that Trinidad was ripe for constitutional change provided the nucleus for the large volunteer network that was to take Williams to electoral victory in 1956.

Williams's constitutional proposals and the collected signatures were sent to the Colonial Office by the governor on 15 December 1955. Governor Edward Beetham told Lennox-Boyd that the proper course of action would have been for the petition to be presented to the Constitution Reform Committee, which was the proper body to consider it. If, as might have been the case, the proposals were not yet finalized while the committee was still *functus*, a member of the legislature could have been asked to introduce them for debate in the Council. "Neither of these courses has apparently been followed," wrote Beetham.

Beetham seemed to have been of the view that had the proposals been submitted to the legislature, some members of that body "would have been eager to align themselves with such a popular movement". Beetham was in fact full of praise for Williams. As he said, "It is difficult to escape the conclusion that this impressive memorial is at least as much a personal testimony to the regard in which Dr Williams is held as to the intrinsic worth of the proposals" (as cited in Ghany 1996, 76).

Beetham had other positive things to say to the colonial secretary about Williams and his lecture series, quoted here at length:

> Everywhere he has gone, he has had large attentive and intelligent crowds. I am told that he himself is surprised at the success which his appearance has had. In Woodford Square his crowds have varied between 3,000 and 5,000 men and women who have always listened with interest and appreciation. He has not at any stage used the tricks of demagoguery but has spoken in an academic style interspersing long lists of facts and figures with lively and racy quips in local vernacular often aimed against the Ministers. He has been applauded for saying that the Government should do a great many of the things that the Government has been trying to do for some time and for which it has only received criticism. For instance, he strongly urges the necessity of a depletion allowance for the oil industry – a matter with which the Government is proceeding but which we have expected will meet with considerable opposition. It is the fact that he has advocated such proposals which make them acceptable to many. There is no doubt at the moment he could be elected to the Legislative Council in many constituencies in Trinidad other than those dominated by East Indians.
>
> He has become, almost overnight, a political personality of first rate importance. But

it seems that he does not intend to join any existing Party at present and he will not speak under the auspices of any of the present political parties. I believe that he hopes to be able to create his own party but he has not so far made much headway. Although his ideas are generally sound, he is a marked individualist and does not easily co-operate with others. He has strong feelings on colour questions. He has been very sarcastic about the ability of Ministers, about the rates of their remuneration, and about their continual traveling abroad. While it is doubtful whether he would join with any of the present well-known politicians in Trinidad, he has a great admiration for Norman Manley and Professor Arthur Lewis. He, together with Hugh Wooding, might well form the Trinidad wing of a Federal party. (CO 1031/1804, Beetham to Lennox-Boyd, No. 771/55, August 19, 1955)

Beetham noted that the proposal for a bicameral house would require structural constitutional change that could not be addressed within the time available, even allowing for a moderate postponement of the imminent general elections. But the Constitution Reform Committee was not persuaded that the bicameral option should be pursued.

6 The Birth of the People's National Movement

The year 1955 saw the emergence of an entirely new brand of messianic political leadership in Trinidad and Tobago, a leadership that seemed to succeed in stimulating a fuller measure of political commitment on the part of the masses and the middle class. The political alienation of the middle class had been partly due to a crisis of confidence. They did not believe that the West Indies could long survive without the moral and physical presence of the imperial power. As one leading spokesman of the black creole elite, Henry Hudson Phillips, QC, opined,

> The West Indies can never stand alone nationally, economically, culturally or otherwise without the protection of a great power. Let British capitalism take flight from Trinidad tomorrow, and we face disaster; let British law and order and the much criticized British administration depart, and the West Indies would revert to barbarism within a year. Our plain duty, even self-interest and self-preservation, dictates that we continue to be part of the British Empire. We do ourselves a great injustice if we feel we can do without Britain and that we should not share the little we have with her sons and daughters, in return for the manifold blessing we receive. (*Port of Spain Gazette*, 8 August 1948)

The more conservative elements also feared that if political power were fully transferred, the hoi polloi and the demagogues who appealed to them would be the main beneficiaries. They were thus opposed to any exclusive reliance on the ballot box, and clung just as tenaciously to the nominated system as did Indians and white creoles. The fundamental problem, of course, was their unwillingness to compete on equal terms with "demagogues" for the suffrage of the masses. Politics was too sweaty, too ridden with graft and corruption for their taste.

To engage in politics successfully in those years, one had to have funds to pay professional canvassers, opinion leaders of the various ethnic groups, and enumerators to pad voting lists and ferret out the "dead vote". As Albert Gomes reminds us in his autobiography, *Through a Maze of Colour* (1974), would-be leaders had to be able to employ all the attention-getting artifices of the demagogue and make lavish promises to provide those little conveniences which meant a lot to the man in the street but which, to the middle class, were not objects of national concern. Politics in Trinidad was essentially parish-pump politics. Universal issues did not excite the masses in any fundamental way. They were concerned, in the main, with the immediate fulfilment of their deeply felt material deprivations. Their perspectives were short in range and quite parochial. In such an atmosphere, honest men had of necessity "to sacrifice reason to popular mass opinion". However well intentioned, inevitably and inexorably they became enveloped by the quagmire of Trinidad politics.

While most of the middle class remained aloof from the maw of politics, there was always a small element that was prepared to work actively for political change and social reform. Between 1950 and 1956 some of them met quite frequently to discuss the political ills of Trinidad and of the West Indies as a whole. One group that contributed significantly to the development of the nationalist movement in the colony was the Teachers' Economic and Cultural Association. The association, a cooperative formed in 1935 by a group of radical urban black teachers, was one expression of the widespread anger over the discriminatory manner in which the avenues of economic and social advancement were kept closed to Afro-Trinidadians. Frustration stemmed not only from the treatment meted out to teachers by the religious and state educational offices, which were staffed largely by foreign whites, but from the attitude of the established teachers' union, which they believed had become too accommodationist. The Teachers' Economic and Cultural Association was conceived with two goals in mind. It was primarily organized to cater to the economic, cultural and professional well-being of its members. In this role, it functioned both as a cooperative and as a ginger group around the teachers union. Its second goal was the "uplift of the people". The members saw themselves as a sort of yeast group that would later form the nucleus of a mass cultural movement. This aspect of the association's purpose was looked after by one of its subcommittees, which was established around 1950 and which later became known as the People's Education Movement. The People's Education Movement served as the political arm of the Teachers' Economic and Cultural Association.

Both bodies were fed by many streams coming from a wide cross-section of creole society. Among the more important were the literary, debating, choral and drama societies, which were then very much in evidence. Organizations such as the Thistle Debating Society, the Writers' Guild, the Nelsonians and Bara Juan were everywhere to be found. There were many other art, craft, choral and drama guilds as well as dance groups (such as the Little Carib, which Williams and others like H.O.B. Wooding patronized) in existence in an era that witnessed a virtual cultural renaissance in urban creole society. There were, however, two parallel cultural revivals. Inspired by what was taking place in India, which had recently won its political independence, many Indians in Trinidad, encouraged by the Indian commissioner, became smitten by nostalgia for the culture of India, particularly in the areas of drama, music, dance and film. The urban creoles were largely unaware of this development.

Williams often interfaced informally with some of these elements. Valda Sampson, a young teacher, credits John Sheldon Donaldson with "introducing" Williams to teachers. Donaldson was one of many black teachers who were victims of the Catholic school authorities. Punishment for not toeing the line often involved posting to a distant rural school. Donaldson got together with other teachers to form the Teachers' Economic and Cultural Association, which established a bookstore on Park Street geared to encouraging teachers to keep reading to broaden their horizons. An embittered Donaldson found in Williams the man whom he believed could help fulfil his purpose. Sampson characterized Williams as a walking library. She wrote:

> Dr. Williams lived up at Lady Chancellor Hill. His home was a library, and he had open house; all who had thirst after knowledge could go and read. I was a young inquisitive teacher and availed myself of the unique opportunity opened to us. Williams lived in a library; books, books and more books; books were his machine guns, books were his satisfying meal, books were his body guards. He wouldn't lend you a book to take away; go as often as you liked, read and take notes; books were his treasures laid up on earth. (*People Magazine*, September 1981)

Sampson also gave Donaldson the credit of having introduced Williams to the people of Trinidad and Tobago:

> Donaldson by this time had a bright idea. He could not be selfish and keep this material only among the teachers so he set about forming an association which he and his other associates aforementioned called the People's Education Movement which, apart from other things, organized lectures at the Public Library, Port of Spain. Yes it was John Sheldon Donaldson and the members of the People's Education Movement who exposed our nation's father to the people. Lectures and forums were organized. The library was packed to capacity each time. Dr. Williams was fearless, a sharpened little axe ready to chop down any supposedly big tree. He became the watchman for and the spokesman for the West Indian people. (Ibid., 42)

Other leading members of the Teachers' Economic and Cultural Association and the People's Education Movement were F.G. Maynard, Arnold Thomasos, three brothers, A.A., Cecil, and W.J. Alexander, and De Wilton Rogers, all of whom (except Maynard) were to play crucial roles in the nationalist movement that mushroomed in 1956. It is also interesting to note that all of these men, with the exception of Maynard, were "renegade" Roman Catholics. According to

Rogers, its director general, the aims of the Teachers' Economic and Cultural Association were: (a) to co-ordinate and synthesize all movements for the economic and cultural advance of the teacher, including literary, artistic and dramatic activities; (b) to establish an Institute of Cultural Studies; (c) to bring to the notice of the proper authorities such matters as concerned its members; (d) to reform the educational system in the West Indies as a whole; (e) to make the people aware of the legacies of slavery and the role of the Negro in the contemporary world; (f) to put an end to the philosophy of acceptance and passivity that affected the rank and file ("Out of this Womb Came PNM", *Nation,* 21 January 1966).

Williams was invited to serve as a consultant to the People's Education Movement, an invitation he readily accepted. In his acceptance letter, Williams told Rogers that he welcomed the opportunity to work with the group because it gave him the opportunity to become involved with the public, an involvement that he believed to be necessary:

> I have always had the view that the work of organizations such as the Caribbean Commission can very easily degenerate into a mere collection of papers and documents unless vitality is injected into it by the people whom it is designed to serve. In addition, as you know, I am consistently fighting against that West Indian complacency which is prepared to sit down and await official pontification, to applaud publicly and grumble privately, and I feel that whenever possible, the people, the ordinary people should be encouraged and stimulated to look for themselves into the problems of the area, discuss them, and develop their own point of view. I am prepared to work with any organization which has the same point of view. Within the limitation of my time therefore, the subject to my official responsibilities, I shall be very happy to work with you. (Rogers 1975, 15)

Rogers would later boast that the People's Education Movement was the foundation on which the PNM was built: "Unlike other parties, the PNM was not founded upon the rock of trade unions, but upon the granite of teachers." Rogers observed that unlike what obtained in other Caribbean islands, which were in a sense one large plantation, trade unions were a source of division in Trinidad.

One by-product of this renaissance was the debate organized by the People's Education Movement between Dom Basil Matthews and Dr Eric Williams. The debate between these two distinguished sons of the soil attracted thousands of people from all social classes. Matthews was described by Rogers in the following glowing terms:

> Dom Basil Matthew was considered the oracle, the God of Olympus. He was a Catholic divine standing over six feet in his socks, finely chiseled and considered the most learned man of his time. The PhD at that time was considered something not only extraordinary, but unordinary. As a priest, he wore a halo around his head; as a scholar [he] had produced a book, The Crisis of the West Indian Family which became a best seller as

soon as it was published. Eric Williams, PhD, was a mystery man buried in the Research Council of the Caribbean Commission. To bring these two together appeared to many a physical battle between David and Goliath. (Ibid., 38)

The two men debated Aristotle's view that state control of education was desirable. Williams had earlier delivered a lecture at the Public Library on 28 September 1954, entitled "Some World Famous Educational Theories and Developments Relevant to West Indian Conditions", in which he had quoted approvingly Aristotle's views about the role of the state in education. The Catholic Church was hostile to state control of education, and Dom Basil Matthews, an eminent churchman, sprang to its defence. Matthews delivered a lecture at the same venue in which he rebutted Williams. The stage was thus set for the head-to-head intellectual confrontation between these two distinguished black sons of the soil. Chairing the meeting was another brilliant black son of the soil, Ellis Clarke, who was later to become Trinidad's first black governor general, and president of the Republic. The title of Williams's lecture was "Some Misconceptions of Aristotle's Philosophy of Education".

Matthews, dressed in cap and gown, came with tomes on the Greek's writings. Williams reportedly came with "a little piece of paper barely visible in his hands". The consensus was that Williams got the better of Dom Basil, who, as a Catholic clergyman, was burdened with Catholic doctrines, especially those that were articulated by Thomas Aquinas and which drew on the writings of Aristotle, who had justified slavery and the subordination of women. In his account of the lecture, Williams noted that "There was not as much as a whisper about the slave basis of Aristotle's state. I had to drag it out of him with a question. What was his reply? [He said] that slavery was sometimes necessary to the common good, but that you could enslave men's bodies but not their minds." Williams told the crowd that the moral and religious excellence of the life of the Greek citizen that Dom Basil so extolled was "nothing more than the life of the slave owner" (*Trinidad Guardian*, 18 November 1954).

Williams's lecture was lapped up by the large crowd, which certainly felt they were in the presence of a very learned master. In the words of Rogers, Williams, buoyed by the enthusiasm of the crowd, "played on the heartstrings of the people. . . . From that night, he never looked back. He was said to be the sixth most learned man in the world." Ivar Oxaal likened the intellectual encounter to the famous Lincoln–Douglas debates, and assigned the role of Lincoln to Williams (Oxaal 1968, 104).

Other lectures given by Williams in the People's Education Movement series were "Constitution Reform in Trinidad and Tobago", "An Evening with Hansard", "The Bandung Conference", and "The Case for Party Politics in Trinidad and Tobago", the latter considered by Rogers to be "the gem of his lectures". The many who came to the lectures, including those from "Behind the Bridge", the so-called Bridgettes, learned a lot about who they were, and from whence they came. "Never before had the Negro such a champion", one man was heard to say. Another exclaimed, "That is man! He is the saviour of the Negro. He exposed those slave drivers!" People came with their benches, chairs and, in some cases, their infants. Many who did not want to be seen remained in the safety and anonymity of their cars. Some said the attendees were like "bachacs", a type of ant, only that they were "destroying mental bias rather than gathering food. They were in fact doing both" (Rogers 1975, 55, 72–73).

The People's Education Movement was an inchoate cluster of well-meaning individuals. Following Williams's historic speech about his relations with the Caribbean Commission, the core members felt that a committee should be formed to focus specifically on creating a political party. This body called itself the Political Education Group. W.J. Alexander tells us that the formation of the group itself was neither deliberately conceived nor planned:

> The Group rather grew out of the stimulation of private discussions in the aftermath of informal gatherings, and was to some extent inspired by the public lectures and talks delivered by Dr. Williams. Basically, its creation was at once a manifest symptom and an inevitable result of the reaction to the existing social and political situation. Its true inspiration was the need to find an avenue for expression, and to canalize thinking by the development of a new formula for the remedies for the prevalent social, political, and economic ills of the country. The Political Education Group was not a group of intellectuals or for intellectuals, though it was stimulated by a certain intellectualism. It was a heterogeneous group whose members were shocked with concern by their vivid realization of the social and political evils of the time. ("Birth of the PNM and Its Descent into the Political Arena", *Nation*, 21 January 1966)

The group often met at the Teachers' Economic and Cultural Association bookstore on Park Street.

According to Alexander, "There was a sharp division as to whether the crisis required the formation of a new political party or whether the situation could be met by the infusion of new life into one or other of the existing political parties." The Butler Party and the People's Democratic Party (PDP) were given consideration, but those options were rejected. "There was . . . a conscious apprehension that ideas which had been precisely hammered out in a small cohesive group may become swamped in the complexities which large membership brings with it" (ibid.).

Rogers's recollection of the reasons for creating the PEG was somewhat different from that of Alexander. For Rogers it was decidedly political:

> The Political Education Group was playing Chamber Music. The People's Education Movement had its full orchestra playing the Ninth Grand Symphony. Top members

of the People's Education Movement were top members of the Political Education Group but not necessarily the rank and file. The Political Education Group were members of the People's Education Movement. It is thought by many persons that the Political Education Group was formed to overshadow the People's Education Movement. The Political Education Group, as it were, was a necessary committee set up to perform with mechanical exactitude the transforming of the ready made People's Education Movement to a national political movement. There has been no evidence of chicanery or guile. The People's Education Movement prepared the ground culturally and educationally. The People's Education Group in its short existence directed the gaze of those specifically prepared towards the political channel. (1975, 56–57)

The foundation members of the twenty-two–member PEG included John Donaldson (Sr), D.W. Rogers, Elton Richardson, W.J. Alexander, Cecil Alexander, Felix Alexander, Mrs. Wong Shing, Donald Pierre, Donald Granado, Ibitt Mosaheb, Gerard Montano, Isabel Teshea, Kamaluddin Mohammed and Andrew Carr. Ibitt Mosaheb was appointed chairman of the group. The main criterion for membership was that the individual must be in broad agreement with the group's views, must have no political affiliation or political past, must be willing to accept the discipline of the party, sacrifice and work hard for it, and must be against racial discrimination. Individuals should also have some influence in the community. Worthy of note is that no reference was made to "socialism".

It was initially agreed, on Williams's suggestion, that the nucleus of the PEG should be limited to fifty hand-picked persons, a number that would allow for the formation of the broad social, racial, geographical and functional base needed for the proposed party to operate. Soon after it was decided that fifty was insufficient and that the base should be increased to one hundred. A motion to that effect was moved at one of its meetings: "That the present group be expanded to one hundred (100) members chiefly for the purpose of accepting the programme and the Constitution, but that the party be launched with a membership of not less than five hundred (500) members, this expansion to take fully into consideration the proposal from the Executive Committee relating to social, racial, geographical and functional representation and without prejudice to the criteria laid down."

The first one hundred members (who incidentally had to be screened and who had to give up their memberships in other parties if these existed), included persons from a wide cross-section of the population. The group was distinctly middle-class and professional. As Rogers tells us, "The first hundred consisted of college masters, teachers, druggists, accountants, civil servants, proprietors, architects, seamstresses, doctors, nurses, lawyers, engineers and trade union officials" (ibid., 59). Curiously, however, we are told by Rogers that "racially there were ten (10) West Indians of East Indian parentage in the first hundred [but] none in the first five hundred." One assumes that Rogers is referring to the second five hundred. Rogers also tells us that "Socially and functionally, [membership] was well spread, [but] no doctor, no lawyer, no engineer nor architect were [to be] found in the first five hundred" (Rogers 1975, 59). It may be that all of the professionals who were disposed to join were in the first group. It would seem that there was a great deal of jockeying to be included in the first one hundred. Williams also made a largely unsuccessful effort to recruit whites and representatives of other minority groups. As Victor Stollmeyer, a prominent white creole who had known Williams at Queen's Royal College, recalled, "Williams was begging the white people to come along. He wanted everybody" (interview with Boodhoo 2001, 114).

Several autobiographical accounts deal with how the PNM came onto the political scene. Many make claims as to who were the party's intellectual or organizational parents, who were founders and who were not, and where the party was incubated. Among the many who either laid claim to parentage or were said to have played foundational and pivotal roles (other than Dr Williams of course) were Kamaluddin Mohammed, Dr Winston Mahabir, Dr Ibbit Mosaheb, Muriel Donawa, Gerard Montano, De Wilton Rogers, John Sheldon Donaldson, Dr Patrick Solomon, Elton Richardson, Andrew Carr, W.J. Alexander, A.A. Alexander, and Donald Granado.

Mahabir, who knew and hosted Dr Williams while a student and vice-president of the British West Indian Society at McGill University in Canada, claims that he, Mosaheb (who was a student of Williams while at Howard University) and Williams met frequently in San Fernando in 1950 to discuss problems of the day. Mahabir tells us that "Williams, Mosaheb and I initiated a weekly study group which we named the Bachacs". According to Mahabir, "the small group was named after those fantastic ants whose characteristics include the ability to destroy apparently healthy plants by a team effort involving a sophisticated communication system. We saw ourselves nibbling at every plant – especially transplants in the socio-economic political order of Trinidad and Tobago" (1978, 17).

The Bachac group grew and later included Dr Halsey McShine, Elton Richardson, Norman Girwar, Telford Georges, Dr George Wattley, Dr Edward Lee, Gerard Montano, Donald Granado, Dennis Mahabir, Eustace Seignoret, and Claire Sloane-Seales, whom Williams allegedly fancied. Sloane-Seales told Mahabir that she had a preference for balance rather than brilliance. Wives were also invited to attend and contribute to the discussions that took place in various homes.

Mahabir tells us that Williams wrote McShine, Mosaheb and himself jointly whenever he was abroad, and speculates that together they must have a treasury of letters for a generation of would-be biographers and aspiring PhDs. Mahabir also tells us that as president of the Naparima College Old Boys' Association, he was instrumental in getting the association to sponsor Williams's lectures. As he writes, "Williams was pining for a large audience which our Association was the first to provide." Mahabir is certain that long before he was forced out of the Caribbean Commission, Williams was beginning "to sow his [political] seed and was using us to till the soil. He found in his audience many willing labourers for the amorphous estate of his ambitions." As Mahabir continued,

> I am certain that the political ambitions of Williams were latent for as long as I knew him. They were flogged into open activity by his dismissal from the Commission. They were injected with the venom of unmitigated hatred of Albert Gomes, his erstwhile friend whose personal cause he had espoused, only to be betrayed soon after the betrothal. Publicly he referred to Gomes as "that fat soucouyant." Had he been in power, he would have pinned on Gomes the order of the grand double-cross. (Ibid., 16)

Mahabir proudly notes that four members of the Bachac group became members of Trinidad's first "cabinet". Another, his brother Dennis Mahabir, became the first party mayor of Port of Spain, while another, Dr Ibbit Mosaheb, became the first party mayor of San Fernando.

Another "Bachac", Dr Elton Richardson, also reflected on his relationship with Williams in the years prior to the formation of the PNM. He too recalled the confused state in which the country found itself in 1950, when the governor and Gomes conspired to exclude Butler from office because the "respectable" elements in the society felt that they could not possibly have a government headed by Butler, even though his party had won the largest number of seats in the just concluded 1950 elections. Richardson felt that it was wrong for Butler to have been excluded as he was: "In 1950 I felt that if Butler had been given his chance, all the respectable people would have gotten off their fat fannies to rescue the country from what they called 'the dishonour of the Butler image.' It is wrong to try to save a people from themselves and democratic institutions are built on a respect for the votes of the majority" (1984, 23).

Richardson tells us that he met Williams in the years after 1950 and attended some of the lectures he gave. These he found to be "very good", so good that he felt that he ought to respond generously to Williams's appeal for donations to purchase books. He believes this response earned him an invitation to join the Bachacs. Richardson recalled that he tried unsuccessfully to get Williams to desist from attacking Dom Basil, who had angered him because of some comment that the latter had made in respect of his lecture on education. Richardson tells us that Williams was determined to attack Matthews, whom he assumed was speaking *ex cathedra* on behalf of the Catholic Church. "Williams was determined to attack the church. I argued against such an attack. He was adamant. He wouldn't budge. In desperation, I said if you must attack, attack the man. He loved this, and this is how the famous attack on the then good old Dom was launched" (ibid., 25).

Unlike Mahabir, Richardson did not believe that Williams was then interested in getting involved in politics, but he came to accept Mahabir's view that Williams had a long-term plan to enter the gayelle. As he writes, "Looking back now, it was not surprising that when Bill called us together to discuss his future [following his dismissal from the Commission], Winston at first declined. . . . It had dawned on Winston that Bill played his poker close to his chest, without letting the right hand know what the left hand was doing. Winston's behaviour, which appeared false to me at the time, was very much in place" (ibid., 26–27). Richardson notes that Mahabir was concerned even then about Williams's tendency to behave as though he had more brains than the rest of them (Mahabir was also an Island Scholarship winner), about his "bourgeois" orientation and life style, as well as his tendency to distance himself from his relatives. "He lived in an exclusive area where Negroes didn't live. . . . He drove a big Buick and looked neither to the right nor to the left" (ibid., 27).

Another foundation member of the PNM, Dr Patrick Solomon, also left us his recollections of these years. In his assessment of the factors that contributed to the success of the PNM, Solomon focused on Williams's unique leadership qualities as well as on the political and social conditions that led many to regard him as their political salvation. Williams, he sagely observed, was a beneficiary of much that had gone on before in the "wild west" that was Trinidad's politics in the post-war era:

> The success of the PNM was due to a combination of factors which occur not too infre-
> quently in some countries throughout the long course of history. A people may groan in
> bondage for a long time without relief – or even apparent hope of relief – and then sud-
> denly a door opens, almost by a direct intervention of Providence. What is not often
> realized is that during the long and weary years, events have been shaping themselves
> and only await the right person at the right time. So it was with Eric Williams and the
> People's National Movement. (1981, 135)

Williams's immediate political ancestors were Cipriani, Butler, David Pitt and the West Indian Independence Party, and Solomon himself who led the Caribbean Socialist Party to a surprising defeat in the 1950 election. Solomon was aware that Williams was seen by many as the political messiah who would redeem Trinidad's "anything goes" politics and put paid to the "rugged individualism" that characterized its politics at both the municipal and national levels. As he recalled, "The smell of corruption was heavy in the air. . . . Trinidad by this time had acquired the not underserved reputation of being the most corrupt society in the British Colonial Empire. . . ." (ibid., 132). Trinidad, then, was ripe for new leadership.

Solomon noted that the PNM differed from other parties. Whereas previous parties started out with the decided aim of capturing power, the PNM started out as an educational movement. Only after gathering momentum did the option of trying to capture power become an agenda item. Even then, the limited objective was to place Eric Williams in the legislature. Said Solomon, "It was only much later, when the actual election campaign had been underway for some time, that there was the realization that victory was possible by way of a majority of the 24 electoral seats" (ibid., 136).

When asked why he had joined the PNM after having vowed that he would abjure politics – having been rejected by the electorate in 1950 – Solomon indicated that Trinidad was on the cusp of a tidal movement that he felt he had to be a part of. As he wrote in 1956, "I should consider myself a poor citizen indeed if, at this most crucial and critical stage of my country's history, I did not make the maximum effort required of us all. Our objective should be nothing short of cleaning these Augean stables, which stink to high heaven and embarrass honest Trinidadians at home and abroad" (ibid., 140). A disillusioned Solomon would later wonder how a grown man could have been so naive. He had lost faith in Williams, though not in the PNM. Reflecting in 1975 on Williams's motives for "letting down his bucket", Solomon felt that pique, and a desire for revenge had much to do with it. He was annoyed with the commission and the *Guardian*, and felt that they must pay. He would rub their noses in the dust. He was a "grievance politician" par excellence.

Solomon, who broke with Williams amid much bitterness, went on to claim that Williams's concerns were always personal and not corporate:

> He never regarded Trinidad and Tobago as a corporate entity with a personality of its own, nor yet as his homeland to which he owed allegiance and loyalty. To the extent that he was proud of Trinidad and Tobago, it was merely as an extension of his own personality; and if he could not mould it to his own image and likeness, he would not stay and serve it. It had rather to serve him, to give him status and, above all, power. Should power be ever taken from him he would not remain in opposition. Equally, should he find the obstacles to his own personal ambitions being constantly frustrated despite his power, he would assuredly find an excuse to quit. (Ibid., 136)

Solomon's attack on Williams lacked balance and objectivity. Given what he saw and experienced personally, he could, however, be excused for the one-dimensional portrait he painted of Williams. We shall return to this issue later on.

Donald Granado's account of the early Williams years gives another view of the man. Granado tells us that Williams was academically brilliant, but a neophyte in dealing with ordinary people. He learned quickly, however. Like Mahabir and others, Granado claims that on occasion he had to rein in Williams, whom he says had a tendency to assume that he had sole ownership rights to the party. Granado tells us that he and others, including Eustace Piggott and Mahabir, often had to tell Williams that he was not the group, only its leader. In his unpublished autobiography (1987), Granado recalls that he got into trouble for opposing Williams's wish to bring young Ulric Lee into the party, and had to be quickly dissuaded by W.J. Alexander from continuing to oppose Lee's membership, which Williams was determined to have. Granado was advised that his opposition to Lee would not stand him in good stead in the future.

Kamaluddin Mohammed also claims parentage of the PNM. He tells us in Ghany's biography, *Kamal*, that the PNM was born in the Dil Bahar Restaurant at 55c Queen Street, which he owned. According to Mohammed, "It was out of the Dil Bahar Restaurant that the first major steps in the formation of the PNM were made." Mohammed got a telephone call from Dr Williams saying that he wanted to see him. They agreed on a time, and Williams came to the Dil Bahar Restaurant for lunch. They had *paratha* roti and curried goat and the meeting went well into the evening, and it was in that context that the idea of a political party was born. Williams promised Mohammed that he would call him within a few days.

One week after his visit to the Dil Bahar restaurant, Williams called Mohammed to invite him to a meeting with a few friends to continue the discussions of one week earlier. Mohammed arrived at Williams's home at Lady Chancellor at 7 o'clock on a Friday evening. There he met De Wilton Rogers, Wilfred J. Alexander and Donald Granado, who were already there. Later they were joined by Dr Elton Richardson and John Donaldson Sr. At that time, there was no discussion about forming a political party, but rather the need to mobilize the population by a series of public meetings. At the same time, there was agreement that it was necessary to widen the group. After a few meetings, the size of the group was increased by the addition of Tajmool Hosein, Felix Alexander, Isabel Teshea, Andrew Rose, Harold Duprey, Ulric Lee and A.N.R. Robinson. According to Mohammed, the Dil Bahar Restaurant became the first real headquarters of the PNM, and much political activity emanated from there. Six months later the headquarters was moved from the Dil Bahar to the Hajal Building further west along Queen Street (Ghany 1996, 70).

In a movement such as took place in Trinidad and indeed Tobago as well, there would of necessity be many channels of activity leading to the same hoped-for outcome. There were many circles, inner and outer, and it is not surprising that the narratives and versions of "what really happened" would differ in emphasis and the networks that would be involved. Suffice it to say that Trinidad was on the cusp of an exciting set of historical developments that ultimately led to the formation of the country's first seriously disciplined party.

7   The Movement Launched

We should openly be the party of inexperience, inexperience in corruption, inexperience in misgovernment, inexperience in changing our views and decisions, [and] inexperience in the determination to exclude reason and good sense from the conduct of public affairs.

   – Eric Williams to Michael Manley, 18 January 1955

The People's National Movement was formally launched on 24 January 1956 at a public meeting in the University of Woodford Square. It was an historic event. The behaviour of Trinidad's parties in the past had generated a great amount of cynicism in the community. As far as the public was concerned, parties were creations that appeared around election time only to fade into oblivion on the morrow of the election. The United Front, the Trinidad Labour Party (TLP) and the Butler Party were only a few, though perhaps the most notorious, of these electoral combinations. Williams and his colleagues were aware at the outset that the success of their new movement would depend on how well they managed to overcome this widespread anti-party feeling. As W.J. Alexander, one of the founders of the new party, recalled, "The decision to form a new political party . . . was approached with tremendous hesitation. . . . The political atmosphere was murky, the social conditions were forbidding, the initial reaction . . . expected to be chilling. . . . There were setbacks and defections, disillusionment and disappointments, but no lack of enthusiasm." However, by the end of 1955, the response to Williams had convinced all that to hesitate would be to "disappoint the legitimate expectations of the people" ("Birth of the PNM and Its Descent into the Political Arena", *Nation*, 21 January 1966).

    Dr Williams's awareness of the prevailing scepticism inspired him to go to the people with *The Case for Party Politics in Trinidad and Tobago*. In this 1955 pamphlet, Williams reminded Trinidadians that no individual politician, no matter how well intentioned, could successfully implement the glittering promises made before election day. He might, of course, be instrumental in obtaining a "standpipe" here, a school there and so on. But the problems that confronted the island could not be solved by parish-pump politics. What was needed was a *national party* with a *national programme* designed to cope with issues that were *national* in scope. Parties in the past had failed for essentially two reasons, he wrote. The first was the basic deficiency in the constitution, which worked in ways that discouraged party cohesion. The second was related to the nature of the parties that had been formed in the past. Strictly speaking, they were not parties at all, but "conglomerations of individuals around a certain man", with no programme that was collectively thought out and drafted.

Williams's approach to parties was somewhat Burkean. "Parties are nothing but an expression of the organized political opinion of the community or sections of it. Hence, before you can have party politics, you must have a public opinion to organize. The organization of that public opinion demands first of all education" (ibid., 11–13). Whereas Burke could assume that there was an existing opinion that individuals should unite to project, in Trinidad, national opinion had to be created:

> One of the fundamental deficiencies in the political life of Trinidad and Tobago is [its] low level of political intelligence. What Trinidad needed was a good democratic but highly disciplined political party which would dedicate itself to the satisfaction of the principal need of today – the political education of the people. All its activities must be subordinate to this, must draw sustenance from this, and must find their meaning in this.
>
> Williams envisioned himself as a Caribbean Pericles, and the Periclean ideal of a participant democracy was held out to the people. A party must not attempt to guide the people simply by lecturing to them. Political education, if it is to be effective, must entail much more: "Every step taken by the party must be a step calculated not only to do something in the interest of the people or for the good of the people, but rather designed to get the people to do things for themselves and to think for themselves. . . . The party is conceived of as a vast educational agency." (James 1962)

Williams agreed with Aristotle's view that "education was politics".

On the question of party democracy, Williams promised that, in contradistinction to the old "cadre" parties that had previously sought the people's vote, the party membership itself, in its various groups and divisions, would select the candidates for public office. Candidates would not be permitted to foist themselves upon the voters. The party must be a mass-based, dues-paying structure, organized from the bottom up. The regular payment of dues was the best guarantee that members had against the domination of the party by wealthy individuals or pressure groups. The public officers of the party would also be called upon to give an account of their stewardship to the membership at fixed intervals. These, then, were to be the basic organizational principles upon which the PNM would be based.

The Political Education Group, which had been created in July 1955 to transform the national movement into a political party, met for the last time on Sunday, 15 January 1956, and was replaced by the PNM. This inaugural meeting was preceded by a pre-inaugural meeting held on 12 January 1956.[1] De Wilton Rogers writes with feeling about the significance of the event:

> At this Inaugural Conference, the constitution and programme were adopted, discussed, and passed. This was due to the toil, self-sacrifice, blood, sweat and tears of the advance men who were thinking, accepting, discarding, rejecting and then refining the thoughts of hundreds of persons [including] the thoughts of the "Behind the Bridgettes" or the "Lamplimers" who knew that programmes were needed to alleviate ills and only wanted a medium of expression through which they could transmit their thoughts. Three of the leaders who had to deal with the Party programme, and one especially, who is the Father of the People's National Movement Constitution, are "Behind the Bridgettes." (1975, 60–61)

Rogers was referring to John Sheldon Donaldson.

One of the basic decisions made in advance related to the naming of the organization. It was felt that the term *party* was too limiting and suggested a mere electioneering machine. The term *movement* better described the aim of the group – the creation of an organization dedicated to radical social transformation. As the charter later declared,

> We are not another of the transitory and artificial combinations to which you have grown accustomed in election years, or another bandwagon of dissident and disappointed politicians, each out merely to get a seat in the Legislature. . . . Nor are we an ordinary party in the accepted narrow sense of the word. We are rather a rally, a convention of all and for all, a mobilization of all the forces in the community, cutting across race and religion, class and colour, with emphasis on united action by all the people in the common cause. (1956, 21)

The inaugural conference consisting of some two hundred persons met in an atmosphere of enthusiasm, optimism, collegiality and camaraderie.[2] The event was as historic as it was revolutionary. No other movement in the history of Trinidad and Tobago had ever succeeded in mobilizing such a varied collection of influential and dedicated people for such a specifically political purpose.[3] The main business to be settled was the discussion and adoption of a People's Charter, a constitution, and the election of officers. All the evidence indicates that these vital matters were settled without rancour or acrimony. Floor and platform were in basic harmony throughout most of the proceedings, a circumstance that disillusioned founding members would soon look back upon wistfully. This harmony was possible largely because the fundamental clashes over organization and ideology had already taken place within the drafting committees. Here, as

Wilfred Alexander recalled, "The clash of ideas and ideals, of isms and ideologies, of doctrines and philosophies . . . that went into the making of these documents . . . the fight over these things ended in creation of a nationalist party in which doctrinaire ideology [was] subordinated to practical philosophy" (Alexander 1966, 66). The opening statement to the conference was made by Learie Constantine, who was later elected to the chairmanship of the party.[4] Constantine declared,

> Our movement originated 8 months ago when 5 people met and decided that the time had come to organize a new and different party in Trinidad and Tobago. Some of the five have fallen by the wayside. Politics like cricket, is a stern game. Many are called, but few are chosen. The original number of members was then expanded to 26 out of which various technical committees were formed to draft a constitution and a programme, to prepare a programme of education to study the machinery and problems of elections, and to discuss the finance and economics of party organization. We studied the problems of politics, familiarized ourselves with the techniques of political organization in other countries, and sought advice from experts and sympathizers abroad.
>
> Three months ago – we decided to expand our membership to approximately 200 to broaden our geographic social and functional basis for the ratification of our constitution and programme and to provide the nucleus of party groups all over the country. On Sunday 15th, the child was born; we named it the People's National Movement, the very name signifying a decisive break with the past. Tonight it is 9 days old, and in the old Trinidad tradition, we have invited the neighbours to come in and celebrate its arrival.

Constantine told the gathering that the party had raised TT$1,200,000, of which all but TT$200 came from foundation members.

The motion for the formation of a political party was moved by Williams, who stated as follows:

> Whereas the long period of imperialism to which we have been subjected has stunted our economic growth, both by denying us the capacity to take part in the management of our own affairs and by the nominated system; whereas our political life has been as a result dominated by individualism, either in the form of the individual candidate who makes individual pledges to the electorate, or in the form of a political combination grouped around a particular personality without proper discipline, reorganized programme or democratic basis;
>
> Whereas many of the political parties which have emerged have not been able to survive the elections which they were principally established to contest;
>
> Whereas election pledges can only be fulfilled by a party so constituted that it can maintain sufficient discipline to command the adherence of its members to its stated programme; and whereas the situation in Trinidad and Tobago today calls for unity among its different races, classes, religions and colours on fundamental social and eco-

nomic objectives, be it resolved that we, these men and women assembled here this morning in the Good Samaritan Hall in Port of Spain proclaim the establishment of such a party, democratic, cutting across race, creed and colour, which shall hereafter be known as the People's National Movement of Trinidad and Tobago. (EWMC 543)

The adoption of the People's Charter was among the first decisions taken by the newly outdoored movement. The charter was conceived as a statement of three fundamental principles, discussed below.

Political Fundamentals

Under the category of things political, the charter came out with the demand for immediate self-government in internal affairs on the basis of Williams's proposals for constitutional reform. In addition, reform of the system of local government was proposed, with emphasis on the rationalization of fiscal relationships between the central government and the local councils. Expansion of the power of these councils, which were seen as vital training grounds for the exercise of civic responsibilities, was also advocated. Morality in public affairs was given special prominence. To the essentially middle-class conference, the decline in public morality seemed the most serious problem the country faced. Hitherto, as Williams had chided, "The middle class had for the most part been content to leave the corruption alone, to try to pass on the other side, rather than fight actively against it as the workers have done." Now they were willing to heed his warning that unless they made an effort to eliminate nepotism, favouritism and graft from the social system, they would be engulfed by it.

The charter also stressed the need to promote an enlightened and self-confident public opinion, West Indianization and inter-racial solidarity. Decolonization had to be integral, but it was not to be allowed to lead to the creation of a new cultural and political dominance by the Afro-creole majority. Respect must be had for all cultural contributions to the West Indian mélange. Since the ethnic configuration of Trinidad and Tobago made it "a microcosm of the new political grouping which emerged at Bandung", the movement, whose aim it was to mirror that microcosm, pledged itself to the "promotion . . . and to the cultivation of the spirit of Bandung on the sugar plantations of Trinidad" (1966, 23).

Williams told the gathering that the cause of the political problems of Trinidad and Tobago was the constitution, which, following Nkrumah, he described as "bogus and fraudulent. Paraded as a transition to self-government, the 1950 Constitution was an invitation to misgovernment. It was a bogus constitution, a damnable fraud. The 1956 constitution would perpetuate this fraud on an even grander scale. It would constitute an even more effective brake upon the will of the people."

Economic Fundamentals

The charter's statement of fundamental economic principles varied little from the ideas articulated in Williams's *Economic Problems of Trinidad and Tobago*, but it did give official endorsement to his view that a socialist ideology must be eschewed in the economic sphere even if the movement was to consist of people of "broadly socialist views". What sense did nationalization make in a community that lacked the basic skills to run a large enterprise? As one founding member reflected later on,

> The PNM avoided this common error and pitfall of West Indian parties. It refused to preach socialism in an island where there is no great accumulation of capital wealth and where poverty and ignorance alone abound. By not doing this, it is free to attract to its fold a wider following. More important than all this, however, is the fact that the mental horizon is left free from political labels and encumbrances which do not apply to the West Indian scene, and which only serve to clutter the mental faculties in its attempts to find solutions to the pressing political problems. ("The Significance of History in West Indian Affairs", *PNM Weekly*, 4 March 1957)

The general economic statement projected the image of an intensely concerned, science-oriented, efficient and puritanical organization equal to the task of clearing away the baneful effects of centuries of imperialist neglect.

Intelligence, assiduity, and a rational utilization of all the country's natural resources were its means. The charter confidently declared that "no difficulty in raising the necessary capital [for investment] was anticipated". Investors and loan agencies would be readily attracted by a "powerful political organization, a careful plan, an energetic people and a contented and well-trained labour force". No gloomy forebodings beclouded the pages of the charter. There was, however, a clearly nativist streak about the economic statement. Efforts were to be made to de-emphasize those areas of the economy that were dominated by the interests of external capital.

Social Fundamentals

The creation of a welfare state was the basic promise of the charter. The aim was to provide a "well-housed, well-educated, well-fed, healthy population. The provision of social services as a matter of right and not of grace is a fundamental feature of progress in the modern world." The problem of reconciling this consumptionist programme with the imperatives of economic development was postponed for later consideration.

Under the heading of "Labour Policy", the charter pledged to accelerate the development of democratic trade unionism that the crown colony system had frustrated. But workers were told that once they were given the right to choose their own representatives and to bargain as equals, "capital was nothing to be afraid of". By the same token, capital must be responsive to the legitimate democratic and nationalistic aspirations of the worker. As Williams had put it earlier,

> Capital must understand that the day when West Indians were content merely to hew wood and draw water for private investors is gone forever. The worker today requires inducements, incentives and guarantees, just as much as the investor does. The Party must be the defender of the workers, the political arm of the labour movement, providing particularly the information and data so urgently needed by the workers in their organizations. . . . It must not, however, actively intervene in the formation of management of trade unions; the people of Trinidad and Tobago are sick and tired of scheming politicians riding on the backs of the workers to gain the confidence of the Colonial Office and the Chamber of Commerce. (Williams 1955b, 10)

In its statement on education, the movement sought to assuage some of Williams's uncompromising hostility to the denominational school; it tried to do so without sacrificing any of its convictions as to what was needed to rationalize the general educational system. The charter made it clear that separate schools would not be abolished. It specifically declared that the "right of parents to send their children to a school of their own choice" should not be prejudiced. But it was evident that the movement intended the state to have a much wider authority over private schools than was previously the case. According to the charter, the current educational system had the following principal characteristics:

- uncritical imposition of alien standards and curricula unrelated to local needs, developed in a different climate for people with a different history and different traditions, and, as an inevitable consequence of this, the disparagement of the local culture, standards and traditions;
- concentration on the small group needed to fill the positions opened to them in the imperialist structure and subordination of the needs of the masses;
- abdication by the state of its educational responsibilities to the point where, had it not been for the Christian churches, the Christian population would have been neglected as the non-Christian population has, until recently been. (Ibid., 29–32)

The educational programme sought to alter this pattern. Educational opportunities must be widened to satisfy the legitimate demand of the people for education according to their capabilities, and not their social or economic class. As far as possible, education was to be free up to secondary school level. The emphasis on classical education also had to be altered; economic development required concentration on technical, vocational and business training rather than on the grammar school mystique.

Like nationalist parties in other newly developing countries, the PNM pledged to eliminate illiteracy. It also declared itself anxious to foster the development of

Caribbean art, literature and culture in order to correct the tendency in West Indians, encouraged by the old colonial system of which they were an essential part, to denigrate anything un-European as being primitive. As Williams had said earlier, "The West Indian school of tomorrow must make a positive fetish of the West Indian environment" (*Port of Spain Gazette*, 5 December 1965).

The Constitution of the Movement

The basic unit of the movement was to be the party group, and membership was open to any person who agreed to be governed by the decisions and discipline of the movement, provided such a person was "not a member of any other political party or organization whose principles . . . are inconsistent with those of the Movement". Membership was also declared open to organizations such as trade unions and friendly societies that accepted the principles of the movement, "provided [they] were not affiliated to any other political party or organization, or were not committed to the political support of an individual whose policy or programme was incompatible with those of the Movement. . . ." ("Major Party Documents", 1966, 14).

One of the key questions that had to be settled was the manner in which affiliate organizations, especially the trade unions, would relate to the movement. A few individuals proposed that the movement should be the political arm of the trade-union movement, just like the British Labour Party. This would mean that affiliate unions would subscribe heavily to the movement and enjoy substantial voting rights and privileges in the naming of candidates. Some trade-union officials (the names frequently mentioned include John Rojas, then boss of the powerful Oilfield Workers Trade Union [OWTU], Quintin O'Connor, and Simeon Alexander of the Federated Workers Trade Union) sought to colonize the movement before it was officially launched by attempting to seek guarantees of candidacies in return for the voting support of their union membership. This was vigorously opposed on the ground that the movement should make no deals, nor should it admit people whose political pasts constituted electoral and ideological liabilities. Moreover, the business of naming candidates was the primary responsibility of the party group, subject, however, to the approval of the central executive. The provision that gave the party group the power to nominate candidates was specifically inserted to frustrate the attempts of notables to capture the party. It was eventually agreed that in the case of trade unions, membership would be calculated only on the basis of those who agreed to identify with the movement and to pay a political fee. The unions would then pay an affiliation fee ranging from TT$5 to a maximum of TT$20 depending on the number of persons who "contracted in".

The "contracting in" stipulation was not relevant for other organizations. As far as voting at annual conventions was concerned, functional interests affiliated to the party were given one vote only. The conference felt that if the movement became too closely identified in the public mind with the predominantly black proletariat, the prospect of rallying the rest of the community would be impaired. Most of the trade-unionist foundation members endorsed this arrangement. They were also aware that it would have been unwise for any union to become organically linked with the movement. For one thing, there was no certainty that the PNM would form the next government; and even if this were the case, no labour leader wanted to be placed in a position where he had to accept directives from the unions. There was also the additional danger that the unity of unions with politically or ethnically differentiated memberships would be compromised. The PNM quite deliberately turned its back on the pattern of union-nationalist party fusion that had developed in the rest of the Caribbean after 1937. The different ethnic composition of the island was no doubt one of the most significant considerations. The fact that the unions were already well developed by 1955, with strong and ambitious leaders, also made it unlikely that the PNM would have agreed to pursue "united front from above" agreements with them.

Authority in the Movement

As with most mass democratic parties, the annual convention was recognized as the supreme authority in the movement. Its members were determined to reverse the normal pattern of party behaviour in Trinidad whereby political parties, such as they were, were dominated by those members who had succeeded electorally. Indeed, no party so far had ever really succeeded in maintaining for any length of time a fully autonomous party bureaucracy. The PNM sought to correct this by providing in its constitution that the legislative group of the movement would be responsible to the general council and ultimately to the annual convention. The convention was to have final authority over all policy issues and matters involving discipline, though the day-to-day business of running the movement was to be left in the hands of the central executive and the general council, the latter to be the governing body of the movement between conventions.

The democratic aspirations of the founders of the movement were somewhat tempered by their keen understanding of the harsh realities of Trinidadian society. While they essayed to create a democratic party, they were also determined to have a highly disciplined organization. To guarantee this, they took the far-reaching decision that members elected by the inaugural conference should be retained for the length of a legislative term. This provision was intensely debated among the inner core of the Political Education Group and was at one time strongly opposed by Williams, who felt it would compromise the movement's democratic ideals. Was it not possible that this rule might perpetuate in the top hierarchy a hand-picked leadership whose enthusiasms might have been keen in the early years, but who no longer served the movement with zeal and distinction? Might this not deny the movement the opportunity to recruit badly needed talent at the top level?

Those who argued for the provision insisted that it was important to keep the founding group together at the top so that the charter ideals of the movement might be zealously preserved. Most of the early foundation members were elected to the general council and central executive of the movement. Many of the later pre-conference recruits who felt that they should have been rewarded for their courage were later given positions on standing committees. Generally speaking, ambitions for office were not too openly revealed in the early period of the movement's history. It took a while for feelings of jealousy and pique to emerge. Many felt that it would probably take about five years for these ideals to penetrate deeply enough among the rank and file; until such time, the founders should retain control of the movement.

The democratic ideal was important, but it was equally necessary to prevent the movement from destroying itself because of yearly fights over leadership positions. West Indian history was replete with the skeletons of political parties that fell victim to the bitter struggles of the spoils men. It was quite a normal thing for defeated "bosses" and their followers to stalk out of parties – parties they had helped to create – amid the glare of newspaper publicity. These were powerful arguments to which Williams eventually gave in, though he succeeded in having the phrase "for a legislative term" substituted for the five-year provision.

The conference also sought to protect the movement from being undermined by the indiscipline of its members. The constitution stipulated that anyone who sought political office at any level outside of the party framework, or in defiance of the movement, would automatically forfeit his membership for a period of at least five years. Similar punishment was to be meted out to anyone who "publicly makes any pronouncement which in the opinion of the general council is contradictory to the principles, policy and programme of the movement, or who enters into public controversy with any other member of the movement thereon", unless that member could explain his conduct to the satisfaction of the general council (*Constitution of the PNM*, 1966, 14).

Members of the movement serving on public bodies were also required to vote in accordance with the directives of the movement, although it was not made clear who had the power to issue such directives. Any member who voted otherwise, or failed to vote, or who conducted himself in a manner contradictory to the principles and programme of the movement, was also subject to this "sudden death" provision in the constitution. These rules, stern though they were, were wise precautions, having regard to the buccaneering manner in which the Trinidad political class have traditionally conducted itself. Indeed, the real question was whether or not the medicine was powerful enough to cure the cancer.

Interestingly, Williams at one time considered naming the new party after the Jamaican People's National Party. Interestingly, too, some of the ideas and even specific words of the charter and the constitution were taken from documents that Williams had prepared while still on the staff of the Caribbean Commission for the Independent Labour Party, the United People's Movement and the People's National Party. All the words and ideas that were to become iconic to the PNM could be found in these documents. This was particularly true of the draft done for the United People's Movement, which found its rebirth in the charter and the mission statement of the organization. Wherever the letters *UPM* appeared, Williams simply scratched them out and inserted the letters *PNM*. The United People's Movement statement read as follows:

> We are not an ordinary party in the accepted sense of the word. We are a rally, a convention, a movement. We [are] a mobilization of all the forces in the community, not only racial but also social – cutting across class and creed, uniting all those who believe that certain things must be done to save all of us. Our emphasis is in unity, in the people, in united action by the people. Hence our name, the United People's Movement. (EWMC folio 543)

Ironically, the parties for which these were originally written did not accept them. What they had rejected became the PNM's cornerstone. The same applied in respect to the reference about the "Spirit of Bandung" (Bandung, Indonesia, hosted the first meeting of the Non-aligned Movement in 1955; the group included China, Ghana and India), which Williams used as a metaphor for his quest for Afro-Asian unity and solidarity in Trinidad and Tobago.

8 Professor of the "New" Economics

Despite Williams's strident criticisms of the constitutional arrangements that regulated political life in Trinidad and Tobago, he was always sensitive to the economic implications of colonialism. As he wrote, "The important thing in the history of the Negro in the Caribbean is not the political flag that floats over him, but the economy that strangles him." Prior to 1955, it was assumed that once self-government was achieved, reorganization of the economy would follow as a matter of course. Given this Micawber-like optimism, few of the earlier nationalists ever bothered to give any systematic thought to the problems involved in the transformation of the productive arrangements of the West Indian economy. Socialism, nationalism and federation were seen as the magical keys that would solve all West Indian problems. The focus was on distribution rather than production. West Indian reformers imbibed deeply, and quite uncritically, the socialist utopianism of Lord Beveridge and the British labour movement.

Eric Williams was the first would-be reformer in Trinidad to break openly with the socialist tradition. Whether his open disapproval stemmed from inner conviction or from sheer political opportunism is a question about which we shall speculate later. But his treatise *The Economic Problems of Trinidad and Tobago* (1955d) did show that he had a clear understanding of the inherent weakness of any socialist solution to the fundamental West Indian problem.

The core problem that faced any reformer in the Caribbean centred on the need to provide meaningful employment for a rapidly increasing population in an area that was considerably under-endowed in terms of conventional economic resources. Williams's key criticism of the 1950 ministerial regime was that it had made no real effort to reduce the colony's dangerous dependence on oil and sugar. The extent to which oil dominated the economy can be gleaned from the following figures. Oil was responsible for 72 per cent of the colony's export trade in 1946 and for 75 per cent from 1950 to 1954. In the period 1947 to 1954, sugar contributed a steady 10 per cent. Williams's argument was that these industries could not expand fast enough to absorb the vast numbers who were seeking employment. Indeed, the critical fact was that the continued expansion of these two industries, especially sugar, could be achieved only if they became more fully mechanized than they currently were.

Williams saw this tendency in the sugar industry as being both inevitable and desirable:

> This reduction of employment in the sugar industry is not an accident and is not due to malice. It is long overdue. The British West Indies have depended for too long on manpower in agriculture. The excessive and indiscriminate importation of labour, African slaves and Indian indentured immigrants, has been the principal cause of the technological backwardness of British West Indian agriculture. The reduction of labour going on today in the sugar industry in Trinidad and Tobago is a continuation of a process that had been going on for the past sixty years in British West Indian agriculture. (1955d, 66)

Even though the old regime had acknowledged the need to diversify the economy, its policies had reinforced the existing economic pattern by discouraging (even if unwittingly) agricultural rationalization. Instead of making bold and imaginative attempts to industrialize the society, the ministers had directed most of their attention to securing permanent protection for the colony's agricultural staples – especially sugar and citrus. Permanent protection depended on prolongation of the colonial relationship. "It was exactly the policy that has been pursued by the British West Indies sugar industry for the past two and a half centuries. It is the philosophy of colonialism. . . . Further protection should be asked for a specific period, twenty-five years, to set us on our feet in the early days of self-government" (ibid., 5). Those who argued that the West Indies should expand sugar as a crop with which to earn the desired wealth to pay for its imports from abroad were reminded that a monocultural economy is a precarious economy, always subject to the whims of world markets and the forces of nature.

Williams agreed with Dr William Arthur Lewis that "new forms must be created which will take the West Indian sugar industry 'out of politics' in the sense of earning general acceptance, or the West Indian community will sooner or later simply tear itself in pieces, and destroy the sugar industry in the process" (ibid., 7). He believed that "The Negro must be given a more equitable share of the wealth he produced. The sugar industry and the land that goes with it could no longer continue to be the monopoly of a few absentee companies." Williams was, however, aware that fragmentation of the land into two- and five-acre plots might be a political but not an economic solution. He warned, "We must not harbour the mistaken notion that the alternative to the plantation system with its army of landless blacks is a system of peasant proprietorship, the division of the large estate into small farms. The small-scale production of subsistence farming would be reactionary." Williams drew attention to the Haitian case to clinch his argument:

> Progressive opinion in the Caribbean today is looking inquiringly towards the Haitian example. That country points a moral which well deserves to be studied and heeded. If Haiti is the standing example of how the Negro can be driven to desperation, it is also the standing example of how a successful political revolution can be frustrated in some of its potentialities for progress by conservative economic practices. Haiti's wealth was sugar. Their revolution destroyed that wealth. Economic progress, political reform and social security cannot be achieved by destructive means. Sugar is the curse, but it is also the staple, of the Caribbean. The explosions in the British West Indies indicate the danger of continued exasperation and continued repression; there is still time to heed the signals and so correct, by democratic reforms, an unsound economy and the present abuses of the sugar industry. (1942, 105)

Williams noted that subsistence peasant-farming increased the numbers on the land, but was not the key to the emancipation of the peasantry. The small farm was not a viable economic unit. It would also be difficult for a family based on such a unit to make any dignified and meaningful contribution to the cultural and civic life of the community. As far as land reform was concerned, then, there seemed to be two alternatives. One might either create a twenty- to fifty-acre peasant class, which the state would have to subsidize heavily in terms of know-how and capital, or, if public capital could not be found, leave agriculture to large-scale operation by agencies that had the capital.

Williams preferred the former. He believed that a sensible programme of peasant proprietorship would have significant political, social and economic advantages. Politically, it was seen as contributing to the weakening of the power of the sugar barons over the masses. At the same time, it might very well help to ameliorate the potentially explosive relationship between the Indians and Africans on the plantation. It was also felt that a viable peasantry would help to clear up some of the social evils of the plantation system: the barrack system with all its attendant dangers to the health of the entire community, and the servile mentality of the peasant with his lack of drive and enthusiasm, as well as his dependence on the godfather figure. Williams believed that the acquisition of a piece of land would give the small farmer a sign of his ascent into a higher social class and engender in him the civic and personal pride he lacked. Economically, the intention of the programme was to transform African and Indian wage-earners into "petty bourgeois" farmers who would be encouraged to plant food crops. The country needed to import fewer of the basic food commodities, which, with some effort and initiative, it could easily produce.

Whether or not one chose to maintain the plantation system intact, the question of rural unemployment still posed enormous difficulties. But to Williams the answer was simple. One had to embark on a bold and dynamic programme of industrial diversification. Not only would diversification absorb labour surpluses from the land and new entrants into the labour market, but also it would be seen as a prerequisite to a meaningful existence for those who remained on the land. The agricultural and industrial revolutions were to reinforce each other.

Williams acknowledged that the old regime had begun a policy of encouraging potential investors by dangling the bait of tax exemptions, but believed that its failure was due to lack of effort on related fronts. He felt that more concessions had to be made to attract foreign investors. He also believed that greater emphasis on education could serve to alleviate the problem of joblessness. People who are better educated tend to have fewer children. One also needed to erect tariff walls, where necessary, to allow embryonic industries an opportunity to get on their feet. The state too might well take an initiative in establishing industries that did not seem sufficiently profitable to private investors. Williams was aware of the formidable costs involved in establishing new industries, and he was not very sanguine about state-sponsored industrialization. In his view, the solution to Trinidad's economic problem was a high-powered industrial development corporation with a dynamic programme aimed at attracting private capital. The strategy would later be ridiculed as "industrialization by invitation", but it was being pursued by several newly independent countries with some measure of success. Williams seemed immensely confident that an energetic, science-oriented and puritanically austere regime could successfully mobilize the energies of the community. He knew that the task would not be easy, and he noted the possibility that with a rapidly expanding population, economic development in Trinidad and Tobago might be a Sisyphean undertaking; but such doubts were not allowed to stand in the way of purposeful effort.

Albert Gomes was not as optimistic as Williams affected to be. Gomes, who had told Trinidadians that they must "industrialize or die", in fact despaired of the prospect of an industrialized Trinidad. "There was a school of wishful thinking economists who set up a picture of an ideal world and proposed that a diversification of the economies of countries dependent on plantation products would solve all problems. This policy had been tried in Trinidad but had not produced this miracle" (as cited in *PNM Weekly*, 13 September 1956).

Williams was aware of the political implications of an economic programme of the type he outlined. Any other strategy would have been explosive in a community as ethnically mixed as Trinidad. As Arthur Lewis had warned, "A community which is mixed racially needs, even more than other communities, to create for itself social and economic institutions which are broadly accepted." It is in this context that Williams's rejection of socialism must be considered. In his ability to perceive that socialism would divide rather than unite the community, he demonstrated a tactical superiority over those reformers who had preceded him.

If one were seriously interested in mobilizing not only have-not Afro-creoles, but Indians, Chinese and Europeans as well, one really could not make an appeal on the basis of class.

The only people in the West Indies who responded positively to the socialist creed were lower-class Afro-creoles and a sprinkling of intellectuals. The Indian masses, still largely a rural people with a passionate desire to acquire land and to succeed in the retail trades, would surely have been alienated by an economic strategy that, so they feared, would take from them everything for which they were struggling. It is true that no West Indian socialist had ever thought of collectivizing all forms of agricultural production or retail distribution, but the fear was there. The same held true for the small but economically powerful Chinese community, most of whom were anti-Peking, even though some took pride in China's emergence as a world power. Needless to say, the European business community and the established press were fiercely opposed to socialism, and, unless one was really prepared to resort to violence, it was pointless to attempt to "convert" them to it.

Despite what many thought at the time and have continued to believe, Williams was definitely not a socialist. It is true that he had written a study of the abolition of slavery from a neo-Marxist point of view, and that he occasionally used the language common to people of that persuasion. He had also written a radical account of the economic problems of the Caribbean in *The Negro in the Caribbean*. This led many to believe that he was a crypto-communist who had changed his strategy, though not his goals. It was argued that Williams, who was at one time suspected by the United States authorities of communist affiliations, was behaving like a trimmer in order to mobilize a mass following with which to strike later on. Others felt that his seeming orthodoxy was an overdone attempt to give the lie once and for all to the whisperings that he was a doctrinaire Marxist.

Such arguments showed a genuine misunderstanding of Williams's real motivations in those early years. There is little doubt that the driving impetus was his belief that he could, if given the chance, clear up the "mess" that the British had left in the West Indies, and do the job better than any imperialist bureaucrat. He was confident that he knew more about the West Indies than any colonial administrator, or any other West Indian for that matter. If anyone could cure the West Indian cancer, it was he, "Mr Caribbean". Williams was familiar with the abortive socialist experiment in Puerto Rico, and was not prepared to have it repeated in Trinidad. He was aware too that Trinidad, like British Guiana and Guatemala, would have had to face the full fury of the United States' cold war strategies if any such experiments were tried.

All these factors, however, merely served to reinforce Williams's own reformist tendencies. He was interested in nationalist and not class politics. "Operation

Jobs" was a rallying cry behind which such a national coalition could best be mobilized. As he phrased it,

> It is not a question of race, religion or colour; it is not a question of labour or capital. It is a question of jobs, schools, houses, water. It calls for the united effort of the entire population. . . . Puerto Rico has found the key to the door of this development pro-gramme. This is not only an economic question. It is also political. . . . Trinidad too must find that key which would open the door behind which the dynamic energies of our people are at present confined, to unleash the drive and enthusiasm which warm the heart in Puerto Rico and inspire confidence in the future. (1955d, 34–35)

That key was to be found in a new mass political movement that he aspired to lead. Williams was not entirely convinced, however, that the Puerto Rican way was the one that Trinidad should pursue. We note that he had earlier described Puerto Rico as "a land of beggars and millionaires, of flattering statistics and distressing realities, Uncle Sam's second largest sweatshop" (1969, 66).

It is worth recalling that Williams had argued on numerous occasions that any economic strategy, whether socialist or capitalist, that was not based on regional political and economic integration was an "absurdity" and doomed to fail. In an address to a conference held in Jamaica in 1955, he remarked,

> Jamaica by itself, Trinidad by itself, Barbados by itself, and if I might say Cuba and Puerto Rico by themselves, will always be entirely at the economic mercy of the more advanced and more powerful countries of the world. If the sugar industry is to be reor-ganized as every investigator realizes it must be; if the West Indian people are to develop some of their own foodstuffs on their own shores; if industries suitable to the islands are to be fostered; if West Indian education is to receive the attention which so important a subject deserves; then it must be done by the West Indian peoples as a whole, aim-ing always at an economic, social and political unity, first among themselves, and on that basis, with the rest of the world. (EWMC folio 135)

In another submission made during a conference that he organized, together with Franklin Frazier, on "The Economic Future of the Caribbean – The Economic Development of the Caribbean Up to the Present", Williams observed, "Trinidad by itself, Puerto Rico by itself, Cuba by itself can only continue at the economic mercy of the more advanced and more powerful countries of the world. Federation will make possible an economic development now impossible and give the Caribbean area a bargaining power in the world which its isolated units do not now have."

As we shall see, Williams continued to subscribe to this view intellectually, but his praxis often invited one to believe that he felt that capitalism or state capitalism in one country was a viable option, if not a perfect solution.

9 **The Old World versus the New**
The Elections of 1956

The first elections that William had to face, the elections of 1956, were beyond doubt one of the most exciting Trinidad and Tobago had yet witnessed. In Williams's mind, it was an historic encounter between two worlds: between the bright, brave, revolutionary new world of the PNM and the forces of the Old World, which had come to regard the movement as a threat to the privileged position they enjoyed in the society. To quote Williams, "The Old World is the corbeau declaiming against the brilliant plumage and graceful flight of the Scarlet Ibis; a conflict between obscene language and university analysis; a conflict between Patois and Latin, between the mauvais langue whispered from house-to-house, and the democratic, well-behaved, intelligent mass meeting of the age of political education dispensed by the PNM" (in Sutton 1981, 280).

George Lamming recalls what the public mood was like in the months and weeks that preceded the election, especially in the University of Woodford Square. There was, he tells us, "a revolution in political intelligence". As he wrote in August 1956,

> Woodford Square has become Mr. Everyman's Academy. The same people who used it appropriately or inappropriately, as you like, in the past, now assemble there to learn. It is this transformation of Woodford Square which is going to have the most profound effect on the forthcoming elections, and the forthcoming elections will most certainly be the most interesting, the most serious and the most historic Trinidad and Tobago will have experienced so far. This is precisely what I mean by the phrase, Trinidad and the revolution in political intelligence. It is the first time that the meaning of the machine, political party, has taken practical shape among Trinidadians, and it is certainly the first time that many a student of Woodford Square will have come to respect the importance of that powerful little weapon, the vote. It is the first time that many will be using that weapon with intelligence and effectiveness. (As cited in Cudjoe 1993, 323–24)

Eight parties and thirty-nine independents contested the election. What follows is an attempt to identify three of the more important parties and interest groups and the attitudes that they took towards Williams and the PNM, and vice versa.

The Party of Political Progress Groups

Formed in 1947, the Party of Political Progress Groups (POPPG) remained essentially what it was in the late 1940s – a relaxed and loosely articulated collection of squirely businessmen, professionals and members of the managerial and executive elite. Its centre of gravity was decidedly in the white or fair-skinned upper and middle class. Whatever success the party enjoyed in the past stemmed from the fact that its members, as individuals, were in a position to pay "influentials" to canvass for them among the basically uninformed electorate. Apart from Albert Gomes, the party did not have any leader with the mass appeal of Williams, nor did it include in its ranks anyone with his organizing competence. It did make an attempt to liberalize its image by bringing black professionals into its ranks, and by endeavouring to establish party groups and branches throughout the country; but it was congenitally incapable of any real expansion or democratization. The few branches that were formed in urban centres outside the capital city invariably came under the control of the same commercial and managerial types. The party remained a prisoner of its origins.

The difficulties that confronted the POPPG stemmed largely from its identification in the public mind with the Chamber of Commerce, the Roman Catholic hierarchy, and the French creole element in the society. Many of the party's leaders, such as Sir Gerald Wight, who was its chairman between 1947 and 1950, were members of the chamber. Others were pillars of the Catholic Church – "canopy boys", or *portes de l'eglise* as they were popularly known. The POPPG was thus constantly being accused of supporting only those people who could be expected to safeguard the interests of the church and the merchant community. Regardless of the liberal intentions of some of its officials, the party attracted many to its fold who were die-hard conservatives, people who saw it as the only remaining bulwark against the "subversive" forces at work in the society. The party, it should be noted, had the full backing of the US consulate in Port of Spain and the US State Department, who saw the election in cold war terms. The POPPG was their safe horse to back in the struggle for succession.

What the white creoles, especially those of Roman Catholic persuasion, feared most of all was Williams's approach to the school and birth-control issues. They refused to accept at face value the PNM's assurance that it had no plans to nationalize all schools or impose birth control. They were also extremely angry with Williams for "not letting slave history rest", for projecting onto them the blame for all the evils of the plantation system. It was strongly felt that he was using the guise of multiracialism to appeal subtly to latent black hostility against whites.

And, indeed, by condemning the social and economic monopoly that white creoles had on the society, and by advocating multiracialism, Williams was indirectly playing on sentiments latent in the black population who understood his message very well. Multiracialism for them meant a better deal for blacks – a status reversal *vis-à-vis* whites.

The POPPG's manifesto condemned communism in all its forms and the idea of class struggle, class oligarchy, dictatorship of the masses, and racial or religious intolerance, evils of which the party accused Williams.[1] Members boasted that their party was truly democratic, unlike the PNM, which they could not help viewing as a "one-man dictatorship". But there were many people, both inside and outside the POPPG, who believed that despite surface appearances, there were no fundamental differences between it and the PNM. Differences of style, tempo and rhetoric there certainly were, but on issues of policy there was no basic cleavage. Indeed, each party accused the other of copying its manifesto. One of the leaders of the party, prominent attorney-at-law Henry Hudson-Phillips, even went so far as to propose that the parties should enter into a coalition to ward off "the greater danger facing the country", that is, the PDP. It was feared that, given the fragmentation of the colony's party system, a weak and unstable government would emerge, and that in such a situation, the Hindu-based PDP might very well come to hold the balance of power (*Trinidad Guardian*, 3 July 1956).

The coalition manoeuvre was a disastrous failure, as neither party was prepared to entertain it. The POPPG maintained that though the two parties might share the same economic philosophies, they differed diametrically on basic principles. "The POPPG stands strongly for fundamental human rights and for the fostering of religion and spiritual principles. The party fails to find these attributes at present in the PNM, and a merger is therefore out of the question" (*Trinidad Guardian*, 5 July 1956). Interestingly, but not surprisingly, Albert Gomes was opposed to the alliance and chose to attack it on the ground that Williams was, among others things, a "fifth columnist" for Manley of Jamaica, whom he described as "the biggest myth of the Caribbean" and "a man of treacherous ambitions who wishes to dominate the British West Indian Federation" (*Port of Spain Gazette*, 6 May 1956).

Proponents of the alliance, who, like many others, had split loyalties, urged quite sensibly that a coalition was not a merger. The POPPG could easily refuse to go along with such policies as were inimical to its principles. The POPPG executive remained firmly opposed, however, its decision angering many who felt that the "national interest" was being sacrificed to parochial prejudices. There was widespread speculation that the coalition was indeed vetoed by the Roman Catholic hierarchy. Anglican cleric Canon Max Farquhar complained that "the POPPG has become the cat's-paw of influential religious direction, and thus become adamant in prejudiced hostility to the PNM. Thus, the politics would be abstractly precluded, not only on the ground of political impracticability, but in deference to certain vested religious interests" (*Trinidad Chronicle*, 15 July 1956). Another angry critic put it this way: "The PNM and the POPPG, too ignorant to recognize this danger [the Indians], treat coalition like a dread disease and will have nothing to do with one another. I suppose as the election approaches, both parties will unleash all the fires of hate at one another, allow Maraj to walk into power and then weep on one another's shoulder or blame each other" (*Trinidad Chronicle*, 11 July 1956).

In any event, the PNM expressed no interest in a "united front from above" coalition with the POPPG. Williams saw quite clearly that the POPPG was on the defensive, and that it was losing its supporters and paid canvassers, who, so it was rumoured, were accepting POPPG money while campaigning secretly for the PNM. Why should the PNM share leadership when the evidence indicated that it would sweep the urban areas where the POPPG might have been expected to gain its greatest support? The POPPG was thus left with the alternatives of facing the polls alone or merging with the five outgoing ministers. Many believed that the latter course was strategically necessary if the PNM was to be stopped. Others argued that any attempt to bring the ex-ministers into the party would contribute even more to the party's annihilation, since the PNM's fire was concentrated mainly on members of the old ministerial regime.

The POPPG's dilemma was that it could not make up its mind just what its policy should be towards the outgoing ministers. It was quite aware that it had become associated in the public mind with the old regime, yet it could do nothing to alter this image. Despite pressure from some of its members, the leadership could not agree to disavow Gomes, whom everyone expected to retain his seat in the legislature. In the end, the party adopted an attitude of passive support for the ex-ministers.

The Butler Party

When the party of Uriah Butler emerged as the largest political unit in the legislative council following the elections of 1950, Butler had expected to be called upon to form the government. This honour being denied him, he promised "agitation far surpassing anything in the history of this Council". But instead of remaining to do battle with the new administration as he had pledged, Butler spent most of the legislative term in the United Kingdom, "putting the case for the people of Trinidad and Tobago to the Colonial Office". There is no evidence that Butler ever had much opportunity to discuss anything with Colonial Office officials or that he made any consistent efforts to do so.

Butler's peregrinations in the United Kingdom remained a mystery to all but his fiercest supporters, who believed that he spent most of his time advocating the liberation of the West Indian peoples. It appears that he did manage to obtain a half-hour audience with the secretary of state for the colonies, whom he said had promised him home rule. According to Butler, he was told by the Colonial Office to "go to the people, preach unity as you did [in 1950] and return to the Colonial Office [victorious] and we will give you self-government, full and complete".

Butler seems to have felt that he could do in 1956 what he had done in 1950, return home triumphantly on the eve of elections and defeat his rivals. He was quite sure that his "ancient power" was enough to steal Williams's thunder. Butler was thus completely unprepared for the PNM phenomenon, and stubbornly refused to acknowledge that the messianic mantle had passed to Eric Williams. He in fact created a bit of a stir by declaring that he would challenge Williams himself as he had challenged Albert Gomes in 1946. He bragged that he was the only Trinidadian politician who had successfully bridged the gap between Indians and Afros, and that it was he, not Williams, who was the architect of Afro-Indian unity. Reflecting on the fact that two of his former Indian colleagues had bolted the party following the events of 1950, he added that "two traitors do not make a nation". He was not prepared, as he would be in 1958, to blame the Indians as a group for the treachery of a few ambitious politicians who had used him cavalierly in their quest for political power. Of the twenty candidates sponsored by the Butler Party, six were Indians.

Butler's failure in 1956 stemmed in part from his inability to perceive that his old "fire and brimstone" style of haranguing the masses was no longer legitimate. The hymn singing and chanting that typified Butler's meetings were completely absent from PNM meetings. The favourite party chant of the Butlerites was, "A happy band of Butlerites we are, oh we are / We never went to college, but Butler gave us knowledge, / What a happy band of Butlerites we are". The cold, brittle and unemotional style of Williams had captivated the country, and it was extremely difficult for people of the old oratorical school to get a hearing. Butler, at one time the undisputed "king of Woodford Square", could no longer hold court there without being subjected to vociferous heckling. Williams, now regarded as the logical successor to Butler, was not particularly happy about the humiliation to which Butler was being subjected. Butler had to be seen in proper historical perspective, he urged. The progress made in Trinidad and Tobago since 1937 stemmed from his opposition to the old colonial regime. As Williams observed in his *Two Lectures on Federation,*

> Some day in the future, when the people come to understand their history, they may even erect a monument to him, as the man who, whilst the middle and professional class, Cipriani always excepted, had abdicated their role as the natural leaders of the people for the mess of pottage handed out to colonials by the Colonial Office in the form of the nominated system, was the only one who dared publicly to challenge that

system and protest, notwithstanding privations, against the oppression inherent in that system. That is Uriah Butler in historical perspective. Had he died during his internment or from a bullet from the Marines, he would have gone down in history as one of the martyrs in the cause of the Caribbean people. (1965a, 35)

Butler had "outlived his usefulness", however. Political power could now be won, said Williams, without recourse to the barricades:

> The days of street fighting are over. Those of the parliamentary majorities have arrived. We are now on the road to self-government, and Mr. Butler underlines the Caribbean tragedy, of which Jamaica's Bustamante is another example. Beginning as trade union leaders, they found themselves catapulted into politics before they could even understand what a programme is. It is only now, after some twenty years that . . . Trinidad and . . . Jamaica . . . have begun to understand that agitation, militancy and graduation from jail do not equip a man for the tasks of government, legislation and planning. The problem of Trinidad and Jamaica today is to provide the political leadership in which both Butler and Bustamante, when tried in the balance, have been found wanting. (Ibid., 36)

Williams, always sensitive to the charge that he was a middle-class politician who did not really have the interest of the worker at heart, drew widely on his knowledge of the national revolutionary movement in the colonial world to reinforce his argument that it was no longer true that only a worker could represent the workers. Manley, Nehru, Nkrumah, Muñoz Marin, Gaitskell and Azikiwe were all intellectuals in politics. "All over the world, a new type of leader has been arising, especially in the former colonial areas, disproving the idea that only a man sprung from the working class can be trusted to do justice to the workers. . . . Mr. Butler is unsuited to the needs of our times and belongs to a pattern of activity from which the world outside has moved away" (ibid.).

Butler conceded that Williams might emerge triumphant from the elections; in fact he admitted defeat by deciding against contesting the constituency chosen by Williams. He warned, however, that should Williams win a majority and then turn traitor to the people, "so help me God, I will kill [him] with my own hands" (*Trinidad Chronicle*, 12 August 1956). Butler even threatened Williams on more than one occasion. Obviously put-out by the rough treatment he was encountering in the PNM strongholds, Butler warned, in an allusion to the burning of a black policeman during the riots of 1936, that if any of Williams's "stooges throw a stone at Butler, he [Williams] will end like Charlie King, burning like a lantern in the presence of all men" (*Trinidad Guardian*, 20 September 1956). It was clear that Butlerism was a spent force, even though Butler himself was still extremely popular in the oil belt.

The People's Democratic Party

There is a lot of mystery surrounding the immediate circumstances that led to the formation of the PDP, but there is little doubt that soon after its foundation, it became widely recognized as the political arm of the orthodox Hindu community, the vehicle of an Indian "nationalist" movement that paralleled the Afro-dominated PNM.[2] For the Hindu masses, though not for the intellectuals and the middle class, the leader of the PDP, Bhadase Maraj, filled the same role that Williams filled for the Afro-Trinidadians. Maraj was the man who had done most to lift up the Indian masses, both through his own achievements – many Indians believed Maraj to be the wealthiest man on the island – and through his activities on behalf of the flock.[3]

By his efforts to establish some forty-one Hindu schools and temples and by his carefully cultivated generosity (he contributed personally to school- and temple-building programmes and to funds for striking workers), he quickly gained a reputation as the foremost benefactor in the Hindu community. To the masses, he was the "Nehru of Trinidad" – a singularly inapt comparison – or, variously, the "chief", the "rajah", "babujii", or "baba". When he visited schools, children bowed and chanted as to a revered leader. Maraj worked closely with the Indian commissioner to Trinidad and Tobago, Mr Nanda, who was frequently accused by nationalists of surreptitiously promoting Hindu nationalism and separatism in both Trinidad and Guyana. Nanda also encouraged Maraj and Hindu elements to oppose federation, much to the chagrin of the British and American governments who were supporting it.

The PDP encountered extremely rough treatment during the election campaign. The fear that the PDP would control the country in 1956 was real to many people, and Maraj's statements did little to calm them. Maraj had called on all Indians to vote en masse to vindicate their forefathers who had not had the opportunity to vote. He openly boasted that the PDP would run the country after the election, a threat that Williams and creoles took quite seriously, even though the party only contested fourteen of the twenty-four seats. Maraj assumed that the PDP would win twelve of the fourteen seats and would be the lead party in a coalition with the Butlerites, whom he funded.

Having successfully crowded the POPPG and the former ministers out of the urban areas, it was now strategically necessary for Williams to isolate the PDP. Maraj had resigned his seat in the legislative council in protest against the decision of the executive council to postpone the 1955 elections, which he believed the PDP would win if they were held when due. The elections were postponed from 26 September 1955 to 24 September 1956. The reasons given for the postponements were the need to decide on and provide for the implementation of the new constitution and constituency boundaries, and the inadvisability of holding elections in the rainy season. It was also argued that postponement would make reaching the point of no return for the federation more certain, something the Indian community was expected to oppose. Maraj won the by-election handsomely, as well as fourteen of twenty seats in the County Council elections held that year, and demonstrated his powerful hold on the Hindu voter. Maraj also successfully claimed credit for sustaining and negotiating a critical industrial dispute involving recognition for sugar workers. Both events had combined to give his reputation a tremendous boost in the sugar belt and in the country as a whole.

Williams's strategy for dealing with Maraj was immaculately conceived and cleverly executed. He positioned the PNM as the embodiment of the Afro-Asian spirit of Bandung in Trinidad and Tobago. He himself had done much to focus the attention of the Indians on their social and economic plight by exposing the squalor of plantation life in the nineteenth and early twentieth centuries. In a speech on India's Republic Day in 1954, Williams endorsed the struggle of the Indian community to educate and improve itself:

> Every struggle by Indians or by Africans for the improvement of labour relations and for embracing the dignity of labour in the British West Indies is a step in the direction of the modernisation of Caribbean society. Every step in the education of Indians is a step in the production of that well-informed body of citizens on which British West Indian democracy depends; every Indian admitted to the professions and the Civil Service is a further victory in the cause of that full participation of local men in the administration of the British West Indies without which self-government is a delusion. (*Trinidad Guardian*, 28 January 1955)

Williams understood quite well why the Indian masses should want to elevate their co-ethnics to positions of leadership. If the orthodox Hindu masses could not be attracted to the PNM even though a few Indian professionals were identified with it, the Indian community as a whole had to be prevented from rallying behind the PDP. The strategy, then, was to drive a wedge between the orthodox Hindus on the one hand and the reformist Hindus, Muslims and Christianized Indians on the other, by portraying the PDP as an obscurantist communal organization. Williams's argument was twofold. First, he suggested that there was a link between the Maha Sabha of Trinidad (which ostensibly was a purely religious organization representing orthodox Hindus) and the intolerant and fanatic Hindu Maha Sabha in India, which both Gandhi and Nehru had vigorously denounced. Williams cleverly called in Nehru and Gandhi to fight his domestic battles. He quoted approvingly Nehru's statement in his *Discovery of India* that the Maha Sabha was "aggressively communal, but that it covers up its extreme narrowness of outlook by using nationalist terminology. It represents small upper class reactionary groups taking advantage of the religious passions of the masses for their own ends. Every effort is made to avoid and suppress the consideration of economic issues" (as cited in *Trinidad Guardian*, 1 August 1956).

The PDP was similarly represented as an economically conservative Brahmin party, having nothing in common with the modern Indian secular nationalism of Tagore and Nehru, whom the masses in Trinidad admired:

> The Maha Sabha is unrepresentative of Indian culture. The real Indian democrats and internationalists are something quite different. Its representatives are Gandhi in religion, Nehru in politics and Tagore in literature. When we look to India it must be to the India of Bandung. And here at home it is to the Indians whose blood and sweat and tears have helped to build up our country – Indians who are Moslems and Christians as well as Hindu, Indians who are democrats and not racialists. (*Trinidad Guardian*, 2 August 1956)

It was a clever broadside aimed at stirring up cross-pressures in the minds of reformist and progressive Hindus who identified with Nehru and Gandhi; he had made it difficult for Christianized Indians and Muslims to endorse the PDP. As far as the Muslims were concerned, this would have been even more difficult, because the Maha Sabha in India was a sworn enemy of Pakistan and the Muslim League. The complementary part of Williams's strategy was to place Muslims and Christian Indians in prominent positions within the PNM.

The second prong of the PNM attack on the PDP was the suggestion that the PDP was nothing more than the political voice of the Maha Sabha. The PDP in fact had never really functioned as an autonomous political party with a constitution and a grassroots organization. Unlike the PNM, it felt no real need to organize, because the branches of the Maha Sabha and the pundits were easily convertible into political instrumentalities. Apart from the role that the Hindu priesthood played in keeping the flock together, it had always been the source to which politicians turned for help in their political careers. Pundits were among the principal opinion leaders within the Hindu community, and a few of them used this advantage to seek political office.

There is considerable evidence to support the charge that many religious meetings in temples and in homes ultimately became political meetings, and that Hindus were enjoined to support their religion by ensuring that Hindus were elected to public bodies. Pundits were known to make individuals swear on the *lotah* (a holy Hindu vessel) to support candidates, and would threaten religious sanctions for broken pledges. Some Hindus were alarmed at the use to which religion was being put and appealed to Maraj in his capacity as president general of the Maha Sabha to call a halt to the prostitution of religion for political purposes: "This candidate is making the Maha Sabha the mainstay of his campaign and with a paid pundit is pushing the Ramayan in the homes of the Hindus night after night. After every *Ramayan Sat Sang*, which is just an excuse to get Hindus together, the wicked job begins. The pundit then begins to sow the seed of discord. Then it is that he tells the Hindus gathered that unless they vote in a certain way, the Ramayan is in danger. He begins a merciless attack on the Arya Samajists, the Muslims and the Negroes" (*Trinidad Chronicle*, 5 August 1956).

Islam, like Hinduism, was also undergoing a revival. The creation of Pakistan had served to sharpen Muslim cultural pride and feelings of separateness from Hindus. The revival movement came to the notice of the public during the celebrated "Ohrini" affair. The issue at stake was whether or not Islamic school boards could insist that teachers wear traditional dress if they did not wish to do so. The Islamic associations and leagues representing the various sects were also involved in a substantial school-building and cultural programme. Mosques became centres for a vigorous campaign of self- and group-improvement. In Muslim and Hindu communities, mosques and temples functioned both as places of worship and as schools, so urgent was the need for education.

Dr Kusha Haraksingh and Dr Brinsley Samaroo, two University of the West Indies historians, make a number of observations about Williams's discourses on "the Hindu question". Haraksingh argues that Williams did not, and possibly could not be expected to understand the cane field and "Lagoon" Indians and their cultural concerns and preoccupations. While Nehru and Gandhi were icons for whom they felt pride, they partitioned such feelings from what they did and thought in their everyday activities. Says Haraksingh, "For as far as the bulk of the Indian population was concerned, it was one thing to embrace an icon and to approach it with due reverence and even a feeling of pride for what it represented, but quite another to accept the message it crystallized and to shape one's life by the tenets contained therein" (1999, 63). One might say that their ethnic affiliations were situational. They were dormant in some contexts and volatile in others.

Like Nehru, Williams was agnostic and secular-minded, and assumed that Caribbean nationalism would ultimately prevail over communal consciousness. Williams described Nehru's *Glimpses of World History* as a "classic in the literature of intellectual decolonization". Nehru assumed that in the brave new world, the religious and cultural differences between the peoples of India would disappear. So too did Williams in respect of Trinidad and Tobago. Williams said as much in an address that he gave to the PNM in 1979, declaring,

> The essential point [is] that the Indians in the West Indies, however much they kept their religion and their priests, had abandoned the essence of Indianness – the caste system. The most significant characteristics of the Indian caste system were marital exclusiveness; ceremonial cleanliness (to avoid pollution by other castes and maintain food restrictions); economic position; hereditary caste occupation. But as someone said: in Trinidad the scepter of the Maharaj Brahmin had dwindled to the insignificance of a hoe handle. . . .
>
> A substantial measure of syncretism took place in religion, the most significant aspect being the full recognition, even if it was on days apart, of the feast of La Divina

Pastora in Siparia, the Black Virgin to non-Hindus; Siparia Mai to Indians. Indians participated in All Saints, as everyone else. It was their practice to dig their graves to face the Himalayas. Which direction would that be in Trinidad? In effect, the Northern Range became to Indians in Trinidad as the Himalayas were to India. The folklore-spirited world of the blacks was drawn on extensively by Indians.

In Haraksingh's view, Williams was mistaken in his view that Indians had abandoned the essence of their Indianness. "While there was some erasure, Indians wanted to retain their cultural differences. They believed that it was their positions that were being misconstrued or deliberately undervalued, and that an unthinking leap was being made to notions of disloyalty and lack of commitment to a national purpose" (1999, 67). Indians, he noted, did not endorse the nationalist struggle for self-government, independence, participation in Carnival, intermarriage, disavowal of Hindi as a language, or Hindu or Moslem schools in favour of state schools. The latter were seen as vehicles through which ancestral values would be taught, perpetuated and protected against the enveloping tide of creolization.

Haraksingh is disingenuous in his suggestion that Hindus and Muslims were anxious to have ethnic "others" join their respective faiths. In the view of most Hindus, only Indians could be Hindus. Many Indian Muslims also behaved as though the term African Muslim was an oxymoron. He is, however, correct in the way he evaluates Williams's strategy of dealing with the problem of Afro-Indian unity in Trinidad and Tobago:

> What was equally painful was the way in which Williams employed Nehru's arguments not only as a stick with which to beat down Indian opinion, but also as a peg on which to hang his own points. Thus Nehru as a torchbearer of the notion of Afro-Asian solidarity could be presented as impliedly advocating in Trinidad a domestic rapprochement between Asians and Africans in which all differences would be marked for extinction. And Nehru's famous advice to overseas Indian communities to identify fully with the country of their domicile could be interpreted in the same vein, and indeed Indians were often urged to read it as a kind of backhand slap for those who cherished ancestral ties not only with the geographical space of the subcontinent but also with its cultural heritage. It was also useful, incidentally, for keeping interfering Indian Commissioners at bay. (Ibid., 1999, 68)

Haraksingh further chastises Williams for not recognizing that Indians had made a positive contribution to the economic development of Trinidad and Tobago, in terms not only of the survival of the sugar plantation, but also its role in creating an artisan class. In Haraksingh's view, the plantation

> help[ed] to construct the basis for the region's first industrial revolution and for the rise of an artisan class, to enable peasant farmers to enter the cash nexus as consumers

and to propel labour relations, including those associated with female labour, onto a platform of modernity, while promoting renewable and sustainable agriculture, a bulwark against urban drift and city blight; . . . it sustained a countryside capable of delivering cheap food to the towns. Much of this was barely noticed; instead, the general argument was that Indian labour, degrading itself in the process, helped to sustain a plantation sector which in turn had truncated the development of the country. (Ibid., 71)

All this is of course true, though Haraksingh does not comment on the fact that the African artisan class that had emerged out of slavery and taken to the towns had led the way in this development. He concedes, however, that it would have been difficult for Williams to enter the Indian stream-of-consciousness because "the whole structure of Indian society was calculated to shut them [creoles] out and because, the Indians with whom he interacted were either de-Indianized or too concerned with the prospect of advancement or avoiding the removal of some privilege, to speak their minds truthfully" (ibid., 72). In sum, cosmopolitan Indians were prepared to pay an "ethnic penalty" that their successors were not minded to do in order to maintain their ancestral ethos. The PNM would in time be forced to move away from "New World totalizing" to accommodate the Indian presence as something more than a mere "oddity".

Dr Brinsley Samaroo agrees with Haraksingh that Williams misunderstood Indians:

Focussed [as he was] on the Africans' experience in the Americas, Williams failed to appreciate the rich civilisational heritage which Indians brought to their Caribbean homelands. He seemed to know little about the ancestral love for the land which they regarded as mother (Dharti Mata) or about the ways in which they had converted negative aspects of the plantation system to their own advantage, making the canefields a rich habitation rather than a place to be shunned. Williams himself, in the midst of his problems with the Caribbean Commission, had indignantly asked Manley, "What am I to do, cut cane?" Such a [question] would hardly have been expected to endear him to people who either worked in the fields or had ancestors who had been sugar workers. (1998, 20)

Williams's reply to the criticism that he did not know much about Indians in the diaspora was that he was working on slavery, but that "there was no reason why he should not do the story of Indian indenture". He promised to do so, and money was in fact collected to fund the research exercise, but eventually had to be refunded. Williams claimed that his schedule did not permit its execution.

The PDP reacted angrily to the charges made against it. Williams, they felt, was "a sawdust Caesar" who in his lust for power was willing to poison racial relations in the colony. First he had attacked whites, now Indians. Although loudly proclaiming his multiracial ideology, was Williams not appealing to black pride and feelings of animosity? The Maha Sabha denied that it was a political body like the Hindu Maha Sabha in India or the Muslim League in Pakistan. There was no connection between the movements, even though the term "Maha Sabha" was common to both. The words merely meant "great society" or "great council".

It was noted that there was a Sanatan Dharma Maha Sabha in India composed of High Sanatanist priests, which had the full recognition of the Indian government. Was it a mistake that Williams chose to associate the Maha Sabha in Trinidad with the Hindu Maha Sabha and not with the purely religious society in India? Williams's reply to the Maha Sabha on his supposed error was as interesting as it was politically devastating:

> The Maha Sabha now tries to draw the distinction between the Hindu Maha Sabha and the Sanatan Dharma Maha Sabha. I accept the distinction. But it is only a change of name involved. If the Maha Sabha insists on hearing what Mr. Nehru had to say specifically about the Sanatan Dharma Maha Sabha, then here it is . . . "Today the firmest champions of British rule in India are the extreme communalists and the religious reactionaries and obscurantists. . . . The Hindu Maha Sabha . . . is left far behind in this backward moving race by the Sanatanists, who combine religious obscurantism of an extreme type with fervent, or at any rate, loudly expressed, loyalty to British rule. . . . There is no more reactionary group in India both politically and socially." The Sanatanists in Trinidad, therefore, must attack Nehru, not me; unless of course, they wish to attack me because I know Nehru's works. (*PNM Weekly*, 23 August 1956)

Orthodox Hindus acknowledged that the Maha Sabha in Trinidad was a militant organization, but argued that there were reasons for this. The Hindu community had a substantial problem to face. According to the 1946 census, the Sanatanists in Trinidad were declining in number. Their ranks were being thinned out by the proselytizing activities of non-Sanatanists. The Maha Sabha was dedicated to recovering lost ground. Moreover, according to the 1946 Statistical Report, 50.6 per cent of the Indian population was illiterate. The Maha Sabha was merely trying to remove that blot by building schools, and using whatever facilities were available for educational purposes.

Williams was perfectly aware of the marginal status of the Indian community and why the Maha Sabha was so politically assertive. As he wrote in *Inward Hunger*,

> There was no question that the Indian occupied the lowest rung of the ladder in Trinidad. Cribb'd, cabin'd and confin'd in the sugar plantation economy, from which other racial groups had succeeded in large part in escaping, the few who did escape to the Mecca of Port of Spain were concentrated on the outskirts of the town in a sort of ghetto popularly known as "Coolie-Town" – today St. James, a bustling suburb of the capital – which tourists interested in Oriental scenes and ceremonies were advised to

visit in order to see "the Son of India in all his phases of Oriental primitiveness". (1969, 21)

Williams insisted that he was in perfect sympathy with most of the goals and objectives of the Maha Sabha, but that it could not make light of the fact that the president general of the Sanatan Dharma Maha Sabha was also the leader of the PDP.

The PDP's official position was that Indians were aiming not at domination but at cooperation. Cooperation with Afro-creoles was vitally necessary, since they controlled the police and other public services. Maraj also reversed himself by declaring that "East Indians will never gain power in Trinidad, nor do they have that ambition." The PDP also observed that it had sponsored three black candidates, a gesture that the black community dismissed as sheer opportunism. On the question of federation, the party insisted that it was a falsehood to accuse Indians in Trinidad and British Guiana of opposing federation because they felt they were about to attain political dominance.

The PDP made several attempts to escape the ghetto by seeking "united front from above" alliances with the TLP, the Butler Party and even the PNM. Afro-creole votes were crucial in a number of marginal constituencies, and the PDP wished to calm the fears of creoles that Maraj might be the country's first chief minister. It was openly bruited that in the event of a PDP victory, Maraj would not "seek the crown", but would give the leadership to someone more acceptable to the entire community. The PDP was unsuccessful, however, in its attempt to find allies in the urban areas and was forced to write off areas where Indians were not in commanding or near-commanding positions, except where Afro-Trinidadians could be found who "dared" to run on a PDP ticket in these areas.

10 The Glorious Morning Come!

The major issues at the centre of political debate during the post-war years were given exhaustive airing by Williams during the election campaign of 1956. Of major importance was the question of secularizing the educational system, family planning, the role of the press in the struggle for political reform, morality in public life and, of critical importance, the position of the various racial groups in the society.

The Denominational School System

Although Williams had conceded the right of parents to educate their offspring as they saw fit, loyal Catholics insisted on regarding his previously articulated secularist views as those of the party. It was difficult for many Trinidadians to understand that a political leader might hold and maintain views that are at variance with his party's. This was especially the case with the PNM, since for most people, Williams *was* the PNM. Thus a statement made by Williams in May 1955, "I see in the denominational school the breeding ground of disunity", was viewed as being representative of the party's thinking. His insistence that "the state school provided the opportunity for cultivating a spirit of nationalism among the West Indian people and eradicating the racial suspicions and antagonisms growing in our midst" was also seen as a clear threat that he would nationalize the educational system given the chance. Nor could Catholics accept his view that "denominational schools should be allowed to continue, subject to the cessation of state subsidies, certification of teachers and inspection of schools by the State" (*Trinidad Guardian*, 18 May 1955).

The possibility of a state-controlled curriculum alarmed the Catholic Church. To the church, the content of education in church schools was not a negotiable matter. The principles of Catholic education sprang from verities that were "supernatural and supranational". Nationalistic and utilitarian imperatives could not be allowed to subvert such principles. The hierarchy acknowledged that national integration was a legitimate ideal, and agreed that the church must "carefully avoid any action which would seem to encourage cleavages along racial lines or in any other way be divisive of the social unity of our emergent community" (ibid., 22 January 1956). But the answer was not to be found in the national takeover of all schools, or in an imposed uniformity.

It was an open secret, however, that Catholic schools were prone to discriminate against children who did not have the "proper" social or ethnic qualifications. Indians and Afro-creoles were the ones who suffered most from these invidious selection practices. The emphasis on religious instruction to the detriment of subjects that would provide the sort of technical skills needed for a newly developing community was also lamented by the more secularly minded. In an attempt to arrive at a sort of "concordat" with the church, Williams proposed five points as an irreducible "recipe for national education":

1. respect for the law of the land which provides for denominational participation in education with state aid;
2. enforcement of that law with respect to state control of buildings and building standards, curriculum and text books, the conditions of employment of teachers, and proper use of state funds;
3. the working out of a curriculum suited to the needs of the expanding economy which PNM will make possible;
4. integration of the various sections of the community;
5. raising of standards, especially academic, in all schools.

It was a package that was clearly unacceptable to the Catholic Church.

Note that the church was not the only religious group to oppose state control; Hindus and Muslims were also against it. While the Catholics were accused of using the denominational school to advance whites and near-whites, Hindus and Muslims were accused of using theirs as cells for the inculcation of a creedal nationalism that was inimical to the broader interests of the society. Williams tried to rally the Hindus by noting that Gandhi had been fundamentally opposed to state support of religious instruction; but the Hindus remained unconvinced. Only the Protestant churches, mainly Anglican and Presbyterian, rallied to the defence of the PNM.

The Birth-Control Issue

The question of the state's role in birth-control programmes was also a source of great conflict during the campaign. Williams's view that without family planning the economic goals of the country might never be fulfilled was widely shared among middle-class intellectuals. Williams also insisted that the problem of illegitimacy could best be solved by the diffusion of birth-control information throughout the population. As he wrote in a passage seemingly directed at the Catholic Church, "Anyone . . . and I say it with utmost deliberation . . . who opposes the provision of birth-control facilities in Trinidad today is in fact condoning . . . illegitimacy, is sacrificing the moral welfare of the entire community to group prejudices" ("Educational Problems of the Caribbean in Historical Perspective", *Trinidad Guardian*, 18 May 1955). To the church this was a frank invitation to sexual "promiscuity". There could be no compromise on this issue. Canon Max Farquhar, an Anglican cleric, felt that the Roman Catholics were full of cant and hypocrisy. He observed that notwithstanding the fact that Catholics were in a majority in the last administration, contraceptives entered the colony freely, and were sold in the shops of Roman loyalists (*Trinidad Guardian*, 23 September 1956).

Williams's views notwithstanding, the PNM declared in its manifesto that it considered the question of birth control a private and religious matter, and it was "absolutely false to say that the Movement has ever advocated birth control". PNM stalwarts explained that out of sheer self-interest it was impossible for a party with so many Catholics in its ranks to endorse birth control as part of its official policy. The Catholic hierarchy nevertheless insisted, as it did on the question of denominational education, that Williams's private views would sooner or later be adopted by the party. In vain did party militants explain that the decision-making process in the party was collegial. Events were to prove that the fears and suspicions of the church were not completely groundless.

The 1956 election thus found the church in a poignant dilemma. Should it assume a "*non-expedit*" position and urge its flock to boycott the elections? Should it openly recommend that Catholics withhold their suffrage from the PNM? There was the danger that if the church openly rejected the PNM, it might later become the target of the policies of a vengeful government, as occurred in Mexico and Haiti. It was also possible that the internal position of the church would be seriously undermined if it made such a recommendation.

The policy eventually decided upon was that Catholics as citizens had a duty to vote, but such a responsibility should be exercised only after careful personal deliberation, and not at the dictate of any organized body. The archbishop of Port of Spain enjoined in an official statement that, "At this *crucial* moment of our history, when for *weal or woe* we inaugurate a new era, every person, man or woman, who has a vote must use it with a sense of responsibility, *not at the mere dictate* of any party or junta (*Trinidad Guardian*, 8 July 1956; emphasis added). The meaning of this statement was clear. The archbishop was suggesting to Catholics that they should not be persuaded by the argument that party government was the prime goal for which Trinidadians should aim, though he was careful to add that he had no objection to any particular party. He did insist, however, that "any candidate or party that will not make a *clear and unequivocal* statement in regard to the recognition and defense of these rights [the basic rights conferred by God on every human person] is by the very fact, according to the law of the Catholic Church, 'suspect' and therefore unworthy of support by Catholic voters" (ibid., 2 September 1956).

The archbishop was hostile to the concept of party wherein members are expected to accept uncritically the directives of the party elite. Catholics could not support such a party or movement: "It is the duty of political parties and groups who seek to attract Catholics to their ranks to ensure that their programmes and policy agree with that of the Church, that they assure their members' complete freedom of action in matters of faith and morals as declared by the Church; and that they do not try to interfere with the members' right to vote according to their conscience. Catholics may not join or remain in any party that does not respect these principles" (*Catholic News*, July 1956). His view was that unless the PNM categorically stated that it was opposed *in principle* to birth control and state control of the school system, it could not expect to get the church's blessing. To the church it appeared that the PNM was temporizing for electoral reasons just as other totalitarian movements had done.

The church's anxiety stemmed from its fear that Williams's ultimate aim was to orient the PNM along totalitarian lines; that his insistence on discipline, organization and intensive social mobilization, his intolerance and declamatory rhetoric were part of a clearly recognizable totalitarian syndrome. There was also a basic conflict between the Aristotelian metaphysics of the church and Williams's secular rationalism and nationalism. In the church's view, Williams was making the "error" of which the nineteenth-century progressive had been guilty, that is, of giving the state a purely rational purpose and seeking to make all men uniform in their view of what the ideal state was to be. Unity and national integration need not be obtained at the expense of destroying idiosyncratic structures and values in the society. Nor should morality be made subject to the imperatives of class struggle.

Rather than openly name the PNM as the enemy to be destroyed, the church chose to wage its war by innuendo from the pulpit, a strategy that aroused tremendous hostility in the minds of many Catholics and non-Catholics. One outraged Catholic declared, "Every Sunday, instead of the long customary sermons, one has to listen to nothing short of a political meeting. . . . We should not thrash out a political issue under the skirts of divine ceremonies. . . . Anti-PNMism is forced into the heads of our unsuspecting school children in Catholic schools, colleges, and even convents. Why must the Church, in which I have lived for over 35 years, calumniate the PNM?" (*Trinidad Guardian*, 13 July 1956). Parish priests were also accused of telling the faithful that it was a mortal sin to vote PNM, and of using the young to reach the old.

There were a few radical "actionist" Catholics who felt that the church should make a bolder effort to fight the PNM. If victory was to be won, nothing short of an officially sponsored Catholic party would be adequate. As one of them wrote, "His Grace should form a party strictly comprised of the Catholic clergy, and officially campaign for the forthcoming elections. . . . This . . . is necessary since there is no party in Trinidad which is wholly Catholic enough – not even the POPPG. . . . We have a majority in the colony, and the time is ripe now, while we still have the nominated system with us. I see this as the only way to build a sound Catholic community" (*Trinidad Guardian*, 13 July 1956). It was this type of creedal exclusivism that stimulated the frenzied anti-Catholicism which prevailed during the election campaign.

The Catholic community was split right down the middle. Catholic organizations were openly divided in their reactions to the PNM. A few members of the clergy and nunnery were also partial to the PNM. There were not many, however, who shared the view that the church should sponsor its own political party. Never before had the church in Trinidad been so publicly flagellated by its own followers. Outraged, the archbishop declared, "Nothing can be more rash and scandalous than for Catholics to resist, attack or hold up to ridicule the authority of the Church voiced by the Pope, or the Bishops in their dioceses. . . . Such scandal must be corrected by every means possible" (*Catholic News*, July 1956). Many interpreted this as a clear threat of sanctions that might include interdiction or even excommunication.

As election day drew nearer it was evident that Williams and the forces of nationalism had considerably undermined the church's hold on its membership. The crowd had found a new messiah and a new political religion. Williams's embellishment of Nkrumah's commandment bears repeating: "We call on all those of little faith – seek ye first the kingdom of self-government and all other things shall be added unto you, for there shall be joy before the angels of Heaven for every nation that attaineth its independence." Human agency having proved unavailing, the church turned to prayer. A few days before the election, the *Catholic News* called editorially for prayer against the "threat of slavery". With an air of defeatism and despair, it declared, "The diabolical forces aligned against us are *too powerful* to be vanquished by any merely human means of attack or defence. The struggle finally will be won or lost, in so far as we use or neglect to use the irresistible force of the spiritual weapons at our command" (*Catholic News,* September 1956). The archbishop proclaimed a novena ten days before the election. Catholics were called upon to pray that "our elections may result in establishing . . . in our country the kingdom of Jesus Christ". Catholics were enjoined to repeat a special election prayer for the gift of true counsel. Part of the prayer read, "Show me how I ought to vote in the coming elections, so as to promote the true welfare of our country and the welfare of ourselves, our family and our children" (*Trinidad Guardian*, 14 September 1956).

It should be re-emphasized that the rabid anti-clericalism that prevailed in the urban areas antedated the 1956 election. Albert Gomes once complained that the Roman Catholic clergy was too powerfully entrenched in municipal politics: "The Roman Catholic Church wields a great deal of influence in the affairs of the municipality of Port of Spain. . . . There was a time when it was said that unless a man was a Roman Catholic, he could not be a mayor of Port of Spain. . . . You know that not one year would pass by without a request coming from the Church for a spot for a church or a school or a gift from the Council at a nominal rental, and they pull their strings. They are very interested to know that they have sympathizers in these bodies. . . . Many an important matter that has been decided by the Council was decided by certain caucuses in this particular organization" (*Report of the Franchise Committee of Trinidad and Tobago,* Council Paper No. 35, Port of Spain, 1944, 79).

It was also alleged that Catholics were opposed to federation on almost the same grounds as Indians. "In certain denominational quarters, Federation will always be anathema, since it poses for them a Trinidad merged into a larger West Indies, where certain entrenched rights and vested privileges now in being as a matter of course, may no longer remain acceptable without question of examination. Thus, whatever the species of objection raised, they were really a meretricious façade behind which lurked and flourished doubts and fears which it would not have been politic to stress publicly" (Max Farquhar, *Port of Spain Gazette,* 21 December 1954).

The creedal cleavages in the society were reinforced by class and ethnic considerations. Although many dark-skinned Afro-Trinidadians and Indians were Roman Catholics, a substantial number of urban Catholics were white or light-skinned. Many of them held status-giving jobs in the civil service and the commercial sector, and the feeling existed, however latently, that Catholics enjoyed occupational and social privileges that other creedal groups did not. For this reason many felt that national integration could not possibly be achieved unless all schools were required to recruit on the basis of universal competitive examinations.

The Anglican and Presbyterian clergy tended to resent the position of dominance that Catholics claimed for their creed. Some of this hostility exploded when one of the leading dailies, then dominated by Catholic interests, carried an unsigned feature article that declared: "According to Catholic doctrine . . . a state must accept the Catholic Church as the one and only true Church founded by God for the salvation of all men, and it must establish the Catholic religion as the official religion of the state. It can therefore allow non-Catholics to practice their religion only privately, not publicly; and it cannot give them freedom to propagate their erroneous doctrines and false practices. . . . The State must accept us as the official religion" (*Trinidad Guardian,* 17 September 1956). The fact that this statement appeared in bold black type led many to feel that powerful interests were behind it. The fact that it appeared during the heat of the campaign, and that no official disavowal was forthcoming, gave additional cause for suspicion. Williams attributed the article to a Catholic priest who was known to be hostile to the PNM.

In 1956, the church found itself in the unenviable role of defender of the old order, the major obstacle to social reform. Apart from a few intermittent references to the responsibilities of "employers to give a living wage to his employees", and to the "rights of individuals without distinction of race, colour, creed or social condition", the church had clearly ranged itself with those forces that wanted to maintain the *status quo.* This was its major weakness.

The Established Press

No treatment of this historic campaign can be complete without some mention of the role of the "established press", especially the powerful *Trinidad Guardian.* The *Guardian* and Williams were virtually at war from 1955 onwards. The *Guardian's* stand was one of almost continuous opposition to the movement. Its hostility to the PNM was in fact a continuation of the hostility that it had levelled at Cipriani, Butler, Solomon and Gomes (during his "red" period). Having regard to the ownership of the newspaper, this attitude was not surprising. Its major shareholders were a group of native white and near-white businessmen who had a vested interest in the status quo.

Williams's hyper-democratic political style did not appeal to the aristocratic-minded press barons. Woodford Square, which to Williams and his followers was both parliament and university, was to the *Guardian* nothing more than a "jungle . . . the stalking ground of an aspirant for political honours". The *Guardian* feared Williams even more than it did Butler. Williams had the ability, which Butler did not, to go beyond simple mass emotional appeal. He had shown that he could organize and discipline a mass movement.

The *Guardian's* attack on the "University and Parliament of Woodford Square" was bitterly resented by the PNM. Woodford Square was no jungle, Williams insisted; it was one of the finest experiments in mass political education anywhere in the world. The type of persons who attended "lectures" was viewed as evidence enough. Williams was not exaggerating when he declared, "Thousands have passed through its gates since my lectures began; those who dare not face the possible displeasure of their boss stay in their cars or on the adjoining sidewalks. People from all walks of life have come. . . . It is only at carnival or at some great international sport event that one can see a larger or more representative cross-section of our community" (1965a, 32).

Before the arrival of Williams's "discordant voice" on the political stage, the *Guardian* was the major influence moulding public opinion. The masses, who were by and large politically illiterate, took their cues mainly from the *Guardian.* If the masses were to be mobilized successfully into the nationalist movement, if the decolonizing revolution was to be integral, the legitimacy of the *Guardian* as a source of opinion on domestic issues had to be completely destroyed. Williams grasped this fact clearly and obsessively, and unrelentingly attacked the daily. Ridicule, "picong" and a vigorous party organ, the *PNM Weekly*, were his main weapons.

But as conservative as the *Guardian* was, it cannot fairly be said that it was pro-imperialist or "feudal". It was prepared to tolerate constitutional and social change that would limit the control of imperial interests without at the same time transferring power to the masses. The *Guardian* opposed British mercantilism and fought strenuously against metropolitan attempts to dissuade the country from pursuing a policy of industrialization (*Trinidad Guardian*, 17 May 1956). It was in fact a national paper, though it certainly opposed Williams's brand of messianic nationalism and did nothing to encourage the development of disciplined party politics. The paper openly urged its readers to ignore party labels and choose men of experience and integrity.

The *Guardian* placed such a premium on experience that it urged the public to "return without hesitation . . . the members of the last Council including Ministers who achieved an excellent record of progress" (*Trinidad Guardian*, 9 September 1956). It was particularly partial to Albert Gomes, whom it regarded as having provided Trinidad with the ideal type of political leadership that it needed at the time. By contrast, the *Guardian* attacked Williams as a dictator, and carried a portrait of him (captioned "Heil Williams") next to that of Adolf Hitler! It nevertheless endorsed him along with two of his colleagues. Williams, it advised, should be made "to win his spurs in opposition or in a ministry where his ability could be turned to good account".

Much of what has been said of the *Guardian* is also relevant to the *Trinidad Chronicle*. The *Chronicle*, formerly the *Port of Spain Gazette*, was also locally owned. But whereas the bulk of the *Guardian*'s directorate came from the English-creole community, French and Portuguese creoles dominated the *Chronicle*. A distinctly Catholic bias could be detected in its reporting, though the paper studiously refrained from commenting editorially on the school and birth-control issues. Its strategy was to open its Letters to the Editor columns mainly to anti-PNM Catholics.

The Politics of Integrity

Gordon Lewis of the University of Puerto Rico described Trinidad as the "Sodom and Gomorrah of West Indian politics". Similarly, the Mudie commission, which was appointed in 1956 by the British government to choose a capital site for the Federation, rejected Trinidad mainly on the ground of the corruptibility of its political life, which it feared might permeate the region as a whole. The cynicism of the politician whose premise was that "in politics anything goes" had penetrated deeply into the psychology of the masses. The alienation of the public from political life was graphically expressed in the widespread tendency to refrain from voting, especially in the major urban areas. The prevailing norm was one of civic incompetence; purposeful change seemed impossible. There was no such thing as a national purpose; the individual learned to manipulate the system as best he could, *chacun pour soi*. As V.S. Naipaul observed in *The Middle Passage* (1962, 72),

> Nationalism was impossible in Trinidad. In the colonial society every man had to be for himself; every man had to grasp whatever dignity and power he was allowed; he owed no loyalty to the island and scarcely any to his group. To understand this is to understand the squalor of the politics that came to Trinidad in 1946 when, after no popular agitation, universal adult suffrage was declared. . . . The new politics were reserved for the enterprising, who had seen their prodigious commercial possibilities. There were no parties, only individuals. Corruption, not unexpected, aroused only amusement and even mild approval: Trinidad has always admired the "sharp character" who, like the sixteenth-century picaroon of Spanish literature, survives and triumphs by his wits in a place where it is felt that all eminence is arrived at by crookedness.

But those who were struggling to forge a new national movement were not prepared to accept the argument that there was something inherently base about the Trinidadian personality that made it unsuitable for clean and disciplined political organization. To dramatize the fact that the PNM stood for a "new deal", Williams assumed a posture of uncompromising and puritanical electoral chastity. The PNM was making no deals, no alliances; it would be "PNM against the rest". To importuning parasitic parties, Williams had this to say: "If you really believe that there are too many parties and would like to reduce the number, then you must decide which of the existing parties have laid foundations worth building on. If you decide that our party is one of these, and you wish to join forces with us, then disband your own party, and join our party as individuals and take your chances on being nominated for elections and office on the same basis as all other members. . . . Too many people were too eager to change principles for the sake of party and not vice versa" (*Trinidad Chronicle*, 12 August 1956).

It was a clever strategy, and did much to reinforce the image of integrity and honesty that the party sought to create from its inception. Williams felt sure that it was precisely this image that attracted people and drove its opponents to despair. Alliances were unwise for another reason. By including in its ranks old machines and professionals, the party would be virtually committing suicide. Discipline and unity would become impossible. As Williams asserted, "Our policy on this matter has been simple and honest. We cannot agree to inheriting the prejudices and antagonisms of others. Arrangements of alliances with other parties, we have every reason to believe from the past history of this colony, are as dangerous as shifting sands, and will sink below our feet and possibly engulf us after the elections" (ibid., 1 August 1956). Williams underscored heavily the sad experiences of the Parliamentary Opposition Group, the United Front and the Butler Party to illustrate his point that mergers of progressive forces were inherently unstable. To bring so many notables under the umbrella of a single party would create immense difficulties when the time came for distributing the spoils of office. The coalition would splinter on the morrow of the election, causing it to collapse from within and undermining the confidence of the masses.

Williams was not averse, however, to cutting deals with old notables if he felt that doing so would advance his goal of winning power. Ashford Sinanan, one of the better known members of the outgoing legislative committee, reports that Williams at one time approved the suggestion that he should come in to the party and also undertake its organization in the southern part of Trinidad. Sinanan told the American consul, who was paying him a courtesy call, that he was putting Williams off because the latter "was seeking to organize the Indian and Negro populations on a racial basis for political gain. . . . Williams was attempting to incite discontent by quoting "ancient history" and recalling past equities affecting the Colony's coloured population" (as cited in Baptiste 2005, 44).

The PNM dramatically underlined its seriousness about discipline by dismissing several of its members, including a founding member, for fraternizing with the "enemy" or for campaigning as independents after failing to get party backing. As Patrick Solomon declared, "Party discipline in the PNM is no joke as some have already found to their cost. In all matters it is to be made crystal clear that the Party is bigger than the member whatever his status, record or individual value. No one is more insistent on this than Dr Williams himself" ("Why I Joined the PNM", *PNM Weekly*, 16 July 1956).

Williams did not even want legal luminaries like H.O.B. Wooding and Malcolm Butt (both of whom were blackballed) in the PNM as individuals. While he clearly hoped that the PNM would emerge from the election in a position of dominance, this was to be achieved without posing needless problems for the leadership. If notables came into the party with their followings, leadership would have to be shared; bases of factionalism would be institutionalized. To a man of Williams's temperament, this was intolerable. He wanted a united front policy, but it had to be a policy of united front from *below*, with the memberships of other parties over the heads of their leaders. And since the parties were already losing their followings to the PNM in the urban areas, alliances were not only undesirable but unnecessary.

Williams denied, as he had to, that there were no differences between the PNM and the other parties. The differences were not only stylistic but fundamental and spiritual. The PNM could not ally itself with the very forces it had been created to destroy. But to many people, including some in the party, it seemed unlikely that any party would emerge with a clear majority. Gomes chortled, "The only Government will be a coalition Government." But to Williams, post-election deals were just as objectionable as pre-electoral alliances. Anxiety for power must not be allowed to corrupt the movement, which could fulfill its goals without achieving power. In any case, it was only a matter of time before the people would give the party the opportunity to govern. As Williams advised, "If not now, then in five years' time; if not then, ten years' time. The PNM has time and youth on its side. It can wait. The PNM's . . . goal is the organization of one proper party in Trinidad and Tobago; it will arrive at this goal by political education of the people. There is no immediate hurry" (*PNM Weekly*, 16 July 1956). As one political commentator wittily declared, "PNM will have the whole hog or be violently anti-pork."

Multiracialism and Candidate Choice

In its choice of candidates, the PNM strove valiantly to be true to its multiracial ideal. But such a strategy, though commendable, went directly against the grain of the party's principles on race and elections, which implied that there should be no attempt to choose candidates on the basis of their acceptability to particular ethnic constituencies. The party, however, chose a European to contest one of the suburban areas of the capital city, and a Chinese creole to do battle against Albert Gomes in the European-creole fortress of Port of Spain North. The PNM tried to get a prominent white creole to carry its banner in the latter constituency, but failed.

The party did, nevertheless, obtain the public backing of some of the country's more powerful white families, much to the consternation of opposition circles. Party members welcomed these recruits enthusiastically, since they helped to give the movement additional respectability. The fact that a few people of social and economic prominence were prepared to risk loss of standing within their community to identify with the PNM helped to crystallize the opinions of many who were still wavering. One creole of German extraction, one-time West Indies cricketer Victor Stollmeyer, took the rather perceptive view that "if a movement such as the PNM fails to obtain a generous measure of active support from the type of persons referred to [white creoles], the possibility arises that the Movement will deviate from the path it now sets itself" ("Why I Joined the PNM", *PNM Weekly*, 18 June 1956).[1]

The breakdown of PNM candidates in terms of ethnic affiliation reveals that the centre of gravity in the PNM was in the black professional class, though only seven of the twenty-four candidates were graduates of universities or inns of court. Only one candidate could be seriously considered a worker in the sense in which that term is commonly understood.

The uniqueness of the PNM's campaign stemmed partly from the fact that it relied mainly on a corps of volunteer workers. Only in a limited number of cases did the PNM pay small sums to unemployed people to conduct door-to-door campaigns. The party and constituency groups were given the responsibility for raising money to pay for the election expenses of their representatives, the money to be sent directly to party headquarters, whence it was disbursed to responsible committees. Candidates were made to sign bonds to pay a fixed percentage of their salaries to the party treasury if elected. Both of these arrangements were substantial innovations to political life in Trinidad.

It is not clear just how much financial support the PNM got from the business community. Stalwarts insist that despite the impecuniousness of the party, it accepted no money from businessmen. But there are a few known cases where substantial contributions were made, though it was made clear that donors should not consider themselves specially privileged if the PNM came to power.

For the first time in Trinidad, party candidates were presented to the people en masse and required to repeat publicly pledges of dedication and fealty. The dramatic effect of these presentations can hardly be overestimated. During the campaign there were walkabouts, Freedom Train excursions, motorcades and even "cyclades". This constant crisscrossing of the community by people bedecked with balisier flowers and armed with chalk constituted a mass mobilization movement par excellence and attracted people of all social classes. As De Wilton Rogers recalled, "It was a pilgrimage, this ride on the Freedom Train; the 'marabuntas' were conscious that the journey was not merely a journey of pleasure, but a crusade." The male marabuntas wore white pants and black jerseys, and the women wore tangerine skirts and black jerseys (Rogers 1975, 65–81).

The multi-hued balisier is said to be native to Trinidad or at least the Caribbean, and is known botanically as *Heliconia bihai*, It was a metaphor for the party's multiracialism, but interestingly, has no black colour in it. It is also said to flourish luxuriantly, especially in the wet season and is also known to harbour one of Trinidad's deadliest snakes, the mapepire. Comments were made about these characteristics during the campaign.

It has been reported that Williams borrowed the idea of using the flower as a political symbol from the French Martinican leader Aimé Césaire, but this has not been confirmed. During the election campaign, it was everywhere to be seen. It was in evidence not only as a plant that decorated premises where meetings were held, but also on various items of clothing and accessories – shirts, blouses and ties worn by PNM politicians and supporters. The PNM had in fact become a cult and a way of life for many. Some parents also named their sons after Eric Williams, who was given the sobriquet "William the Conqueror" by the Mighty Sparrow, the calypsonian.

The efficiency, modernity and pervasiveness of the PNM's campaign convinced many of its invincibility. The party also tried to maintain its pledge to wage a clean campaign. Platform speakers were debarred from personal and family abuse; the public and not the private lives of opponents were attacked. When rebuked for the way in which its supporters heckled the meetings of its rivals, the party replied that the heckling occurred because the PNM had so raised the level of campaign rhetoric that the masses had now come to expect more than abuse and mud-slinging from political platforms. The intolerance of the masses was not inspired by the party elite. It was their own way of demonstrating that old-world politics had come to an end.

Of the three elections that had been held in the colony under universal suffrage, the 1956 election was unquestionably the most exciting. Wherever the PNM pitched its tents, it attracted crowds of people who were obviously aware that they were caught in the grip of a fundamental revolution. And though enthusiasm bordered on frenzy and hysteria, PNM open-air meetings were quiet and orderly. The magic of Williams's monotones hypnotized the urban masses. There were, however, several ugly features in the campaign. Racial violence always seemed imminent. "Never before has race been watching race as it is watching race now," moaned Albert Gomes. Threats of kidnapping and assassination, of impositions of religious and economic sanctions, were a standard feature of the campaign. As one reporter declared, "Never before was an election campaign so saddled with a mood of ugly savagery. Even to voice an opinion contrary to the man next to you was to invite a flood of threats and to incur deep-seated hostility. And in the rural areas, any candidate who runs into enemy territory must be prepared to vault walls and drains in order to decamp." Money and rum also flowed. Bhadase Maraj reportedly lavished money as he went from village to village. As Lionel Seukeran noted in his account of the election, "If a man was having a Bhagwat, he would leave two or three hundred dollars with him. If another was having a pooja or wedding, he would be the recipient of a hundred or two. To build a temple, he gave a five hundred or a thousand" (Seukeran 1991, 197).

As the campaign drew to a close, it was clearly Williams and the PNM against the rest. The press, the Catholic hierarchy, big business, the old government and members of the legislature, all came out in opposition to the PNM, while the Americans stood on the sidelines.[2] But the movement could not be stopped. By singling out Williams for persecution, slander and threats, the opposition had merely served to enhance the growing tendency to hero-worship him. They had completely misunderstood the phenomena that was Williams and the PNM.

Interestingly, the governor was apprehensive about the possibility that unrest might ensue during or following the election. He in fact asked the secretary of state for the colonies, the commander-in-chief of America and the West Indies, Station No. 22, and the officer-in-charge of troops in Jamaica, Station No. 19, to send troops to Trinidad, just in case. The following was the secret telegram sent by Sir Edward Beetham:

So far election campaign has been accompanied by surprisingly little lawlessness. I mistrust this unnatural calm and believe it may well be due to complete confidence in victory of supporters of the Williams party, the mass of whom are negroes.

1. Present indications are that this party will not (repeat not) achieve anything like the overwhelming victory expected, and practicability of results to this volatile section of population at the end of long and exciting day may lead to spontaneous disorders, particularly in Port of Spain [*sic*].

2. Elections take place on Monday 24th September and preliminary results will be announced between 20 and 24 hours in urban areas that day.

3. If disorders take place and are not (repeat not) put down immediately, trouble would spread like wild-fire and could be very serious. We are making our police dispositions, but if it could possibly be managed, visit by one of H.M. ships at that time would be of utmost help. The very presence might have the desired effect, and if emergency arises, naval personnel would be used to relieve police on guarding key points, e.g. power stations.

4. If at all possible, ship should arrive at Pointe-a-Pierre on the morning of Saturday 22nd September and at Port of Spain morning of 23rd September. She could leave, if all is quiet, afternoon of 25th September.

5. While in Pointe-a-Pierre and Port of Spain, all possible steps will be taken by means of sport and excursions to make incoming presence known.

Very much hope you can assist.

(CO 1031/1302, Beetham to Secretary of State, Top Secret Inward Telegram, No. 563, 15 September 1956, as cited in Ghany 1996, 89–90)

Contrary to Beetham's anxieties, the elections were peaceful and for the most part uneventful. Though the election served to sharpen racial and religious animosities, it did not create them. As Gomes (1974) observed,

The 1956 elections brought the racial question – indeed, the entire complex of racial questions – to the forefront in Trinidad. For the dismal fact is that exploitation of race had been the decisive factor in the elections, a fact which every one recognized, even though, as with a guilty secret, people hesitated to make public mention of its existence. Needless to say, the spectacle of black men in power evoked misgivings among the other racial groups. These were aggravated both by white and by Indian neurosis and the tendency among the black people themselves to become unsettled by their sudden rise to fame and prestige.

To the bulk of the urban African population, and a few detribalized Indians, the Glorious Morning had now come, *ambakaila*![3] The emancipation project had been further advanced. Williams remarked, however, that the PNM's victory was "not necessarily a blessing". The hero's historic tasks had only just begun. The obstacles in his path were many and complex and his enemies strong and determined to reverse the revolution. Success would depend on how skilfully he steered the state galley between Caribbean versions of the mythical Scylla and Charybdis.

11 Williams the Conqueror

Praise little Eric, rejoice and be glad,
we have a better future here in Trinidad,
PNM, it ain't got nobody like them,
for they have a champion leader,
William, the conqueror.
– Mighty Sparrow

The results of the election held on 24 September 1956 surprised the country, the governor and the Caribbean. For the first time in the history of Trinidad and Tobago, a political party had captured a majority of the elective seats in the legislative council. The PNM won thirteen of the twenty-four seats, a feat that many, including the PNM leadership, regarded as a veritable revolution. Even though the movement had won only 39 per cent of the popular vote, and five of the seats were won on a plurality basis, as far as its supporters were concerned, the "people" had given Williams a mandate to govern and to clean the Augean stables, which of course was not strictly speaking the case. Some 61 per cent of the electorate had in fact voted against the PNM. Of the other parties, the PDP won five seats with 20.3 per cent of the total vote; the TLP–NDP (National Democratic Party) and the Butler Party won two each. Of the thirty-nine independents who contested, two were returned.

One of the biggest surprises of the elections was the complete failure of the POPPG to gain a single seat in the legislature. Also puzzling to most people was the defeat of veteran politician Albert Gomes, whom everyone had assumed would retain his seat. Indeed, no PNM notable wanted to run against him, including Williams himself. Gomes attributed his defeat to his race:

> It would be an over-simplification to attribute Williams' success entirely to Negro nationalism. Our six long years of marginal government under a virtually impossible constitution undoubtedly were instrumental in guaranteeing his victory and our defeat.

Moreover, his campaign was a brilliantly executed affair. Shrewdly and imaginatively, he sensed the needs and grievances of the people and fed their hopes accordingly. Still, the campaign would have failed but for my skin complexion and race – and, of course, the threat of Indian communalism which was assiduously exploited. I was invitingly vulnerable in this regard, since all the auspices were favourable to a representation that I was unsuitable to occupy a position of leadership in a West Indian (coloured) community. (1974, 174)

To some, Gomes's defeat was a disappointment, since it would have been exciting and politically enriching to have both Gomes and Williams in the same legislature. But majority sentiment regarded Gomes's downfall as "Trinidad redeeming itself". The defeat of Gomes in Port of Spain North did not, however, mean that the upper- and upper-middle-class elements of that constituency had supported the PNM wholeheartedly. Gomes in fact won all the polling stations where such elements were concentrated. In the five polling stations that were in the high-status residential areas of Port of Spain North, the total vote for Gomes was 850, and for the PNM, 402. The fact that the PNM was able to win a little less than 50 per cent of the total votes in the five stations indicates, however, that the party did manage to win the confidence of some members of the European creole community.

Table 11.1   Election Results, 1956

	Number of Seats Contested	Number of Seats Secured	Total Votes Polled	Percentage of Electorate (Electorate 339,028)	Percentage of Votes Cast
PNM	24	13	105,153	31	39.0
PDP	14	5	55,148	16	20.0
Butler Party	20	2	31,071	9	11.0
TLP–NDP	11	2	13,692	4	5.0
POPPG	9	–	14,019	4	5.0
WIIP	1	–	446	<1	<1.0
CPDP	1	–	627	<1	<1.0
CNLP	9	–	3,864	1	1.5
Independents	39	2	40, 523	12	15.0
Subtotal			264,543	78	97.5
Rejected Ballots			6,991	2	2.5
Grand Total	128	24	271.534	80	100.0

Source: Report of the Legislative Council General Elections 1956, Table 4.

The geographical distribution of the party's support indicates that it triumphed mainly in the urban and suburban areas where nationalist feeling was more fully developed. As Oxaal noted, "The locus of charismatic authority is in the heart of the follower and the Trinidad public was far from unanimous in its adoration of Dr. Williams. The society was too highly differentiated culturally, and had lived too long under the traditional divisions to respond as one nation to the nationalist appeals of the aggressive Negro intellectual who burst into the political scene in 1956" (1968, 97).

In the rural areas, the complex of old loyalties to church, family, and political father images proved resilient enough to withstand Williams's charisma. The results also reflected the fact that although the PNM's campaign was islandwide, it was more intensely concentrated in urban areas and in the market centres of the countryside. The heartlands of the Hindu community were given only token stimulation. Then, too, the type of symbols that Williams manipulated in 1955–56 – nationalism, public morality, secularism, federation and administrative rationality – were marginal issues in the rural areas. Gomes's explanation of the weak receptivity of rural voters to PNM slogans was quite perceptive:

> They have very little of the sullenness of the urban types and certainly none of their truculence. Their psychology has been less complicated and corrupted by the teachings of their more learned compatriots whose frustrations they do not share. The racial chauvinism we have been experiencing in recent years in this country is almost entirely a product of urban middle-class life and conditioning. And the same may be said of our pseudo-nationalism which is so redolent of the inferiority complex. The rural type is not a disoriented type. (*Trinidad Guardian*, 13 July 1958)

It should be noted, however, that the PNM only narrowly lost Tobago and had run fairly well in the rural constituencies in the east of the island. It also gained a plurality victory in the southeastern constituencies. Predictably, the PNM failed to gain any seats in the sugar and water-crop belts where Indians were concentrated. Butlerism also proved strong enough to prevent the PNM from winning any seats in the oil belt. Some analysts believed that if the PDP and the Butler Party had worked together, the PNM would have won only ten seats and the history of the country would have been fundamentally different. Darius Figueria believes that Maraj was "delusional" in his belief that the PDP would win twelve seats. He believes that "the PNM's defeat was only assured with the unity of the PDP and the BP political parties" (2003, 3).

To most people it seemed obvious that Dr Williams would be called upon to form the government, but for a while there was uncertainty. The PNM had indeed won a majority of the elected seats, but the legislative council consisted of thirty-one members altogether – twenty-four elected, five nominated, and two appointed officials. To have a working majority, the PNM needed to control at least sixteen seats. Left-wing forces reopened their demand for the united front coalition that the PNM had earlier rejected. The PNM, they argued, should invite the two Independents into their ranks. Alternatively, the PNM were urged to work with the Butlerites or the TLP or both.

No one felt bold enough to propose a power-sharing coalition between the PNM and the PDP. Such a coalition, despite its inherent difficulties, might have done more than any other gesture to dramatize the multiracial purpose of the PNM. Failure to conclude an alliance of this sort was to involve the PNM in immense and perhaps unnecessary difficulties in the months ahead. What no one said aloud in these days of uncertainty was that a left-wing coalition of the type proposed would have been, quite literally, an anti-Hindu coalition. Christian Indians and Muslims would have been included in any of these combinations, but no Hindus, who were all in the PDP. There were Hindus in the PNM, but few in its elite strata. At the time of the election, only three hundred Indians of all creeds had become card-holding members of the party, a fraction of the total party membership. The possibility that a few Indians might have been included in the cabinet would have meant little to the Hindus, who regarded such Indians as "discontented" Muslims, or spoilers, and society-seeking stooges who were selling their birthright for a mess of pottage.

None of the proposals for a left-wing coalition materialized. The PNM insisted that it would govern alone or go into opposition. Declared Williams, "Time is on our side". Williams was perhaps speculating that no effective government could be formed without the PNM, unless PNM members broke ranks at the invitation of the governor or in response to some other coalition manoeuvre. Many indeed believed that the lures of ministerial office might have tempted some PNM members to leave the party, thereby disrupting it as had occurred with the United Front and the Caribbean Socialist Party in 1950. But to suggest this was to misunderstand the mood of the public in 1956. Such a breach of principle would have been unthinkable in PNM circles, and the public effectiveness of any such renegade would have been nil.

The liberal governor, Sir Edward Beetham, and, after some hesitation, the Colonial Office, eventually decided that the interests and the stability of the country would be best served if the PNM were asked to govern. To allow the PNM to form an effective government, the secretary of state agreed to vary the instructions relating to the neutrality of the five nominated members by allowing the PNM to name two of them.

The negotiations with the governor were conducted by Williams, assisted by Patrick Solomon and Clifford Inniss. The proposal to allow the PNM to name all five nominated members was initially rejected by the governor. Despite his favourable disposition towards Williams, Beetham opposed such a specific concession, which he believed was not necessary because nominated members normally voted with the government. Williams noted, however, that nominated members had on occasion voted against the government on matters of principle. It was a surprising acknowledgement to make, but a necessary one if his threat that the PNM would go into opposition, unless it could be assured of a working majority, was to be taken seriously. The governor was told that if the PNM could not have all five members, they should be allocated at least two so that they could count on a team of seventeen as opposed to fourteen for the "outs". Williams calculated that if he refused to take office, no one else could, and that this would cause a constitutional crisis. Solomon admits that the PNM could have gone ahead and formed the government with the threat of resignation if it was ever defeated on a vote in the House, "but neither Government nor Opposition could operate satisfactorily in such an atmosphere" (1981, 148).

The secretary of state for the colonies, Alan Lennox-Boyd, was eventually persuaded that the principles articulated in 1949, which provided that persons who were nominated by the governor should not be selected to represent any particular interest but to serve the broad and best interests of the Colony as a whole, should be suitably varied. The reasons for this policy shift were spelled out in a confidential telegram from the Foreign Office to its representatives abroad:

> Immediately after the election the Governor, Sir Edward Beetham, sent for Dr. Williams and offered him his cooperation in forming a Government. Dr. Williams then asked that his nominees should be appointed to fill the nominated seats, and this request at first threatened to give rise to some constitutional difficulty. The reason for this request was that the People's National Movement, holding thirteen out of thirty-one seats in the new Legislative Council, would, even with the votes of the two official members have to command the vote of at least one other member to give them an overall majority in the Council. Dr. Williams was not prepared to have to rely on the votes of independent nominated members to implement the Movement's programme which he claimed he had a clear mandate from the electorate to pursue.
>
> The revised constitution was designed by a Constitutional Reform Committee in Trinidad which included all the members of the previous Legislative Council to suit the continuation of a situation where the electorate had not returned a majority of one party. The basis on which nominated members are appointed remains as it was set out in 1949 in a dispatch from the Secretary of State to the Governor, namely that such members should "strengthen the experience and knowledge of the Council in dealing with the complex issues of Government" and should be appointed not to represent any particular interest, but "to serve the broad and best interests of the Colony as a whole."
>
> In one or two other colonial territories with advanced constitutions, it has, however, been recognized recently that nominated members could not be appointed to a Legislature to oppose the policy of the majority of the elected members, and in those

territories the Governors have consulted with the Leaders of the majority parties as to how the nominated seats should be filled.

In Trinidad, therefore, the emergence of a majority party was recognized as calling for some modification of the principles of the 1949 despatch. The Secretary of State therefore authorized the Governor to "take such steps by way of nominating suitable persons to the Legislative Council, after consultation with the leader of the majority party, as will provide a reasonable working majority for that party". (CO 1031/1301, No. 198 Intel, Confidential 18 November 1956; as cited in Hamid Ghany 1996, 99–100)

The Colonial Office in fact had little choice unless it was prepared to risk the possibility of throwing Trinidad into chaos. The events in Trinidad were not unlike those in the Gold Coast in 1951 when the Colonial Office was confronted with a triumphant Convention People's Party. As Arden Clarke, the governor, said on that occasion,

> Nkrumah and his party had the mass of the people behind them and there was no other party with appreciable public support to which one could turn. Without Nkrumah, the [Coussey] Constitution would be stillborn and nothing come of all the hopes, aspirations and concrete proposals for a greater measure of self-government. There would be no longer any faith in the good intentions of the British Government, and the Gold Coast would be plunged into disorders, violence and bloodshed. (Clarke 1958, 33)

The negotiators agreed not only that the two nominees would be subject to party discipline – that is, their status as nominated members would depend on their continued acceptability to the government – but that the other three nominations would not be given to people who were known to be openly hostile to the PNM. As an additional gesture of good faith, the governor declared that the votes of the two appointed officials would "normally" be available to the government as they had been to the colonial government in the past. The PNM was thus able to count on seventeen votes in normal circumstances. It was a brilliant coup, which showed that the Colonial Office was willing to redeem the pledge it had made in 1946, that it would respond positively to the development of effective party politics in Trinidad and Tobago. The irony of the PNM manoeuvre was not lost on many observers. The nominated-cum-official system that Williams had so vehemently attacked as being the "symbol of the island's arrested development" had now come to the rescue of the democratic movement.

The POPPG and the PDP vigorously opposed the concessions. It was argued that the governor's action was unconstitutional, since it was the legislature and not the governor who had the power to choose the government. The governor merely allotted portfolios; he had no knowledge of what the party configuration of the legislature would be. Moreover, was he not manufacturing a majority for the PNM that the country had refused to give it? The PDP was aware of the possibility that with the seven votes of the nominated-official bloc and those of the eleven non-PNM members, the PNM could have been prevented from holding office as the Butlerites were in 1950. The coalition might have been unstable, but it could have worked in the same way as had the Gomes regime.

The PDP also took the view that, by convention, nominated members should be free of party affiliation. By giving nominated members and officials "hidden instructions" that they should vote with the government, the governor was making it impossible to overthrow the government. But the governor had not really guaranteed the PNM an iron-clad majority; with just fifteen assured votes, the PNM had only a conditional majority. The additional two votes of the officials could easily have been withheld by the governor if the PNM departed too far from the framework of expectations. The constitution, in the governor's understanding, was thus a much more flexible instrument than the opposition imagined.

Interestingly enough, support for the governor came from the *Trinidad Guardian,* which, in the traditional spirit of post-election honeymoons, declared editorially, "A Party and leader, able to win 13 seats in a General Election, a feat never accomplished in Trinidad before, deserve an opportunity to show what they can do without petty spite or obstruction. If we have pointed to the Party's lack of experience, we do not intend to make it needlessly difficult for that same Party to acquire experience" (*Trinidad Guardian,* 30 September 1956).

Support also came from the Chamber of Commerce and the Catholic Church. In pledging its support to the government, the chamber invited it to make use of the experience and knowledge of its members. "All we ask is that we be given ample time to consider and comment on any matters, particularly those bits of legislation which might affect trade and commerce." The Chamber of Commerce as a pressure group was very anxious to ensure its access to the new centres of decisionmaking.

The Catholic Church was likewise anxious to heal the dangerous rift that had developed between itself and the PNM. The *Catholic News* observed, "The Catholic Church can live in peace and co-operation with any Government that will respect her own liberty in the sphere of faith and morals, and does not try to impose false ideas upon the people" (30 September 1956). The *News* noted strategically that His Grace the archbishop "never espoused or condemned any political party". At the same time it called on all Catholics to pray for moderation on the part of their representatives, and urged them "to co-operate loyally with the Government in all that was not opposed to the law of God" (ibid.).

Williams could not conceal his delight: "The undue influence of certain shades of religious opinion bordering on intimidation in some cases has boomeranged. If prayers were said against the PNM, far more prayers were said for the PNM" (*Trinidad Guardian,* 20 October 1956). Anglican clergymen also could not contain the glee they felt over the humiliation that the Catholic Church had suffered. The Muslim community was elated that Williams had included a popular Muslim in the Cabinet, since it was the first time a Muslim had been elevated to high governmental office. Muslims felt that their status in the community had been considerably uplifted. As the United Muslim League declared in its statement of congratulations to Williams,

> [E]ver since our forefathers came to these shores more than a hundred years ago, we have contributed with the other communities in no small measure to the economic development of our beloved island. Our political aspirations, however, did not meet with such salutary effects as it was only the late F.E.M. Hosein who succeeded in entering . . . the Legislature. Since his death more than a quarter century ago, Muslims did not and could not gain a single seat in the Legislative Council. (*PNM Weekly*, 1 November 1956)

The Muslim elite had calculated quite correctly that their chances of advancement were considerably better in the ranks of the PNM than in the Hindu PDP.

Left-wing forces were openly disappointed by the failure of the government to conclude an alliance with other elected members. It was felt that the PNM had concluded an alliance with POPPG types, if not with the POPPG itself. It was also noted that of the two candidates whom Williams had recommended for nomination, one was Cyril Merry, a prominent white member of the Chamber of Commerce. Merry was one of the "French creoles" who had joined the PNM. The cabinet also included two substantial businessmen of European extraction. So "respectable" did the Cabinet look that Albert Gomes was forced to note, "Within the Party itself, the middle-class elements are in the ascendancy. . . . The choice of certain persons for ministerial positions and other plums indicate quite clearly that while the rump of the Party remains proletarian, its entire personality is being controlled by elements from [the] higher social strata" (*Trinidad Guardian*, 11 November 1956).

Williams had moved strategically to the right to accommodate the very "old world" forces with which he had just done battle, or so it seemed. John Rojas, boss of the OWTU, noted that no genuine trade unionist was appointed to the Cabinet or given a nomination. The PNM had selected a "capitalist and a capitalist brief holder as its nominees even though these types were already represented in the Cabinet". But the workers themselves were in part to blame, since "they had indicated their determination not to be represented by labour". They had allowed Williams to condition their minds against the idea of working-class political leadership. Under Williams, the middle class had in fact seized power from the working class. To the radicals of the Caribbean National Labour Party, the PNM's victory was a counterrevolution, not revolution: "Right-wing indoctrination plus anti-socialism had paid off to the extent where the oil companies and the commercialists no longer need to rely upon nomination to protect their interest." The British Tory government was now very happy to relinquish power. "The workers of Trinidad were now just where they were wanted" (*Trinidad Guardian*, 28 September 1956).

The United States was pleased with the outcome of the elections. Williams had in fact sought a meeting with Stanley Schiff, the US vice consul in Trinidad and Tobago, which was held in June 1956. In the Memorandum of the Conversation, which was dispatched to Washington on 26 June (as cited in Baptiste 2005, 38), Williams was reported as having repeated what he had said publicly – that is, that the PNM was "pragmatic" and had no objections to the retention by the United States of the bases, but that he would expect economic and technical assistance from the United States in return if the PNM were to win power. Such aid was to come to Trinidad directly and not through the Caribbean Commission. He also expected certain tariff concessions on a bilateral basis. In terms of the British-owned oil company (Trinidad Leasehold Limited), Williams opined that it would be ludicrous for him to oppose its sale to Texaco when Trinidad and Tobago was seeking to attract foreign capital. He was of the view that the transfer of the company to American interests would benefit Trinidad, especially in respect of the petro-chemical industry.

Schiff reported that Williams had sought the meeting to rebut the charges of being communist, racist, and anti-American which had been hurled at him by Gomes and others. Gomes had in fact described Williams as an "unsavoury character, a megalomaniac seeking to gain power who should be immediately arrested on an outstanding charge of non-support of his divorced wife and children". Williams indicated that he was "anti-communist" but mischievously remarked that the "best way to get aid from the US is to have a communist problem or a threat". He did not, however, believe that aid should be conditioned on the existence of such a threat since "another party in power might find it expedient to manufacture a communist problem" (as cited in Baptiste 2005, 38–39).

The new American consul, Douglas Jenkins, also came to the conclusion that the Americans could do business with Williams, and that he was to be preferred to Maraj, who was viewed as Trinidad's "No. 1 gangster, someone who had a reputation for graft, corruption and even murder". Maraj was also seen as being Indo-centric. It was said that "if he [had] won 7 or 8 seats he would have introduced a new and dangerous element into Trinidad politics – a political party based on race. The growing fear that Maraj may succeed in winning a commanding position, with all the dire forebodings that implies, has caused many to stop and think" (ibid., 39). Douglas Jenkins noted that Williams had admitted that the PNM was an expression of "Negro Nationalism", but that this nationalism was "defensive and not aggressive". He felt that he would be able to "control it and blend it into a party seeking well defined political and social aims designed for the common good". Jenkins concluded that that was "probably the fundamental question to be answered by the forthcoming elections" (as cited in Baptiste 1999, 207–8; 2005, 42–43).

What seemed to radical leftists like a complete capitulation to vested interests was to Williams and his colleagues a statesmanlike gesture in the cause of community integration. The PNM's first responsibility was to heal the wounds that the bitter election had opened. If an "opening to the right" would achieve this goal, they were prepared to give it a try. In his first victory speech following the opening of the legislature, Williams declared that there would be "no chopping of heads, no victimization". The government would summon talent wherever it could be found regardless of race, class or creed. Everyone was to be permitted to make a contribution to the development of the society. The right of others to differ from the government was to be scrupulously respected; no attempt was to be made to silence opposition. There were sceptics who doubted that these gestures demonstrated a genuine willingness to take advice, but the country at large applauded Williams for his surprising display of political maturity.

The PNM's victory was hailed enthusiastically by West Indians everywhere. For many it heralded a new dawn. George Padmore, however, misread what occurred when he wrote that "the sweeping victory of the left wing People's National Movement in the Trinidad general elections is one of the most significant events in West Indian politics in recent years" (as cited in Rogers 1975). As we have seen, the PNM was a mass nationalist rally and not a class party. There were no trade unions or socialist organizations within its ranks. One English observer, John Hatch of the British Labour Party, captured the essence of the problems that Williams and the PNM faced on the morning of victory:

1. The difficulty of presenting a real nationalist front when so many different political views are held by members of the organisation.

2. The problem of overcoming racial divisions within the population. Negroes and Indians still hesitate to associate themselves in the same political organization (almost all the members of the groups which I addressed were of Negro origin).

3. The difficulties of party organisation and discipline . . . particularly with the intelligentsia of the country which Trinidad and the People's National Movement require as a first essential. (As cited in Rogers 1975, 94)

Plate 7 The hero and the crowd, 1956. (Eric Williams Memorial Collection, University of the West Indies, St Augustine)

Plate 8 On the campaign trail, 1956. (Eric Williams Memorial Collection, University of the West Indies, St Augustine)

Plate 9 Williams with the archbishop of Port of Spain, Count Finbar Ryan, 1961. (Eric Williams Memorial Collection, University of the West Indies, St Augustine)

Plate 10 Flag-raising ceremony, 1958. In the background: Governor Edward Beetham and the chief of the defence force. (Eric Williams Memorial Collection, University of the West Indies, St Augustine)

Plate 11 *Left to right:* Grantley Adams, prime minister of the federation; Sir Winston Churchill and Eric Williams. Back row: John Mordecai, deputy governor general; Mrs Mordecai; Lord Hailes, governor general of the federation; Mrs Grantley Adams and Lady Hailes, 1961.
(Eric Williams Memorial Collection, University of the West Indies, St Augustine)

Plate 12 State visit to Trinidad by members of the West Indian Federal Committee, May 1957.
(Eric Williams Memorial Collection, University of the West Indies, St Augustine)

PART 3

FEDERATION AND THE STRUGGLE FOR CHAGUARAMAS

12   Prometheus Unbound

Williams was elected Trinidad's first chief minister on 26 October 1956. He received the votes of nineteen members of the thirty-one-member legislature, four more votes than he could have counted on automatically. In the balloting, which was secret, nine persons abstained and two persons cast blank ballots. The other seven elected members of the executive council also received nineteen votes. They were Dr Patrick Solomon, minister of education and culture, Learie Constantine, minister of communications, works and public utilities, Dr W. Mahabir, minister of health, John O'Halloran, minister of industry, commerce and tourism, Kamaluddin Mohammed, minister of agriculture, lands and fisheries, Gerard Montano, minister of housing and local government, and Donald Granado, minister of labour. Victor Campbell, John Donaldson Sr, and Ulric Lee were appointed parliamentary secretaries in the ministries of communications, education and culture, and the chief minister's office respectively. Williams kept the Ministry of Finance and Tobago Affairs for himself. As was provided for in the constitution, the governor, Sir Edward Beetham, presided over meetings of the executive council and had the power to withhold assent to bills. The *de facto* arrangement, however, was quite different. As Williams tells us, "Ministers met privately before Executive Council so that we could provide a united front. I was normally the spokesman for the Ministers in the Executive Council. We called this meeting 'Cabinet'. So from 1956, Trinidad and Tobago had a *de facto* Cabinet. We set out to make it *de jure*" (1969, 168).

The months following Williams's assumption of power were almost barren of legislation, and many were becoming sceptical and restive. Sensing the mood of rising frustration, Williams had to remind his followers that he had not promised a new heaven. What he had promised was that under his leadership, with hard work by all the people, and with the application of knowledge, some improvement would be effected in the standard of living. The government had to be given time to plan its legislative schedule, since it had inherited from the last government a five-year development programme that was merely a collection of projects strung together without rhyme or reason. Before a rational development programme could be framed, committees had to be appointed to inquire into the state of the country. This was the scientific way to proceed. The committees were also seen by the new government as democratic workshops in which citizens could learn about the nuances of government, and as instruments through which persons initially hostile to the regime might be mobilized. They were seen as an essential part of the policy of national integration, though some party stalwarts did feel that in its choice of committee personnel, the government was rewarding its enemies and punishing its friends.

But opposition forces were determined to harass the government systematically. Motion after motion was introduced to embarrass the PNM, especially among its lower-class following. Proposals were introduced to increase old age pensions, to subsidize basic foodstuffs, to expand sugar welfare programmes, and so on. During 1956 and most of 1957 the opposition benches, which included some of the country's most experienced parliamentarians, were clearly in the ascendancy. Opposition propaganda was extremely fierce, and Williams was deemed "public enemy No. 1".[1] From the unforgiving pen of Albert Gomes, whose columns were carried in the *Guardian*, and from the *Guardian* itself, broadsides were fired at the fledgling government. Interestingly, the irresponsibility of the attacks was perhaps the most important factor in neutralizing much of the constructive criticism that was legitimately being offered against the government.

One founding member of the party, David Nelson (who had since been expelled), sought to explain the PNM's performance in terms of the constitutional structure:

> Because of the constitution, Government owes their existence and must depend for their week to week parliamentary survival on the guardians of vested interests; they are forced to respond to those very pressures which for 6 years prevented Mr. Gomes from being a proper Minister of Labour and which dictated his policy as Minister of Commerce.
>
> It is unfair to condemn Government's failure to launch a bold assault on the established bastions of vested interest when the guardians of vested interests in the Legislature, by virtue of being called upon to help Ministers get a majority, are in a position, not to "warn" and "comfort", but to determine what the Government can and cannot do. (*Trinidad Chronicle*, 2 April 1957)

It is possible to explain away the PNM's timidity in 1956 and 1957 on the basis of the inhibitions present in the constitutional framework, and to see its anxiety to change the constitution in this context. But the answer is really much simpler: Williams and the PNM saints were genuinely unprepared in those months to bring in the legislation that it was planning. Only one member of their team had had parliamentary experience. The boldness of its first development budget was to startle everyone.

The Rally of the "Outs"

The rally of the "outs", which is so typical a feature of the politics of newly emergent countries, was not long in crystallizing. Trinidadians, who are in the main opposed to the idea of a one-party state, took it for granted that an opposition party would sooner or later be formed; the two-party system was considered to be an essential part of a mature democracy. But there was some question as to what elements would combine to form this opposition. Many feared that if the Hindu PDP were to emerge as the main opposition to the Afro-dominated PNM, the stability of the community would be seriously endangered. The Democratic Labour Party (DLP) was, in a sense, "invented" to prevent this.

The DLP was a coalition consisting essentially of POPPG, PDP and TLP elements. The initial difficulty in the unification exercise centred on the problem of fusing the predominantly Catholic white creoles with Hindu elements. There were POPPG cadres who did not wish to form any alliance with a "pagan" element. They maintained that the POPPG should reorganize itself, perhaps under another name, and seek to improve its standing among the masses. In the view of this element, the PNM had to be destroyed.

Another wing of the party resisted this "bitter end" policy and warned that "a continuance of the misguided attempt to break or discredit Williams and the PNM at all cost" would only lead to the intensification of racial and religious differences. Such a policy would also lead to a repetition of the recent electoral disaster. "It was not the best way for a progressive conservative party to deal with the rising tide of West Indian nationalism." This wing of the party preferred to accept the PNM's olive branch. A third wing took the view that the Hindus provided the only alternative basis for a mass party. Whether one liked it or not, one had to accept the fact that if there was to be a two-party system, the second party must include the PDP. It would be unfortunate if Trinidad were to have an all-Indian opposition. The leading advocate of the PDP alliance was Gomes, who did not share the squeamishness of others about being in the same political bed with Bhadase Sagan Maraj.

The founding of the DLP was in fact largely the work of Albert Gomes. Gomes was looking for a base from which to stage an electoral comeback and found this in the PDP. He was aware, however, that doing so was risky. He would have to navigate through a "maddening" maze of race and colour. As he well put it,

> [I]f I wished to continue to be politically active, I would have to cultivate Indian support, for theirs were the votes I would need to get elected, and in the schizoid condition

of the country, once I was with the Indians, I would be assumed to be against the Negroes, for it was in the nature of the prevailing logic of a people riven by colour and race to reject all but black and white categories. (1974, 182)

Gomes was also aware that if Indians were to win power, there would be race-related difficulties. "The Indians would be no less chauvinistic in power than was the Negro, and would be equally discriminatory against the Negro once the role was reversed" (ibid., 182). He also feared that white-negro tension might increase if Indians gained power with the help of whites:

> While the Negroes ruled, anti-white feelings tended to subside, especially since foreign whites in particular and a fair number of local ones were genuinely eager to co-exist with a Negro regime and share a common heritage as West Indians. Among these there was profound suspicion of the Indian, whose image again was largely distorted by irrational prejudice. He was seen as the villain of the piece, a shifty oleaginous and untrustworthy fellow who might well consider himself the superior of the whites once he tasted power. The less hermetic, more extrovert Negro was cherished by such persons as the devil they knew. But the Negro was aware that the majority of local whites had made common cause with the Indian and were pivotal factors in the opposition that he was offering. Clearly anti-white feeling among Negroes would be inflamed if Indians ever assumed power with white support. (Ibid., 182)

Gomes tells us that a group of Indians invited him to join an underground movement to overthrow the PNM. "They had decided that constitutional methods were no longer adequate to the task of checking Williams' advance to absolute power" (ibid., 184). The group complained of discrimination in the public sector, in the award of scholarships and in other areas of the society. Gomes did not accept the invitation and in fact claimed that the Indian conspirators were overstating their case:

> In power, the Negroes were loading the dice in their favour, but certainly no more than the whites had done when it had been their turn or the Indians did in the business they owned. . . . As propaganda, the technique was positively lethal. I could imagine Indians responding by rushing for the nearest cutlass or gun and tearing into the first Negro who crossed their path. It was depressing to listen to the recital of inflammatory figures and reflect on their evil potentiality. (Ibid., 185)

The PDP, feeling its isolation in the Hindu "ghetto", avidly welcomed the possibility of a merger with the elements that Gomes represented. Unless its image was updated, power would forever escape it. The Muslims – at least the urban ones – and the Christian Indians would never identify with it; nor could it expect to obtain any significant African support. The PDP leaders at first insisted that they would keep their party intact, and that, being the most powerful unit, they should lead the coalition. But this requirement was later abandoned. The PDP seemed to have realized that the new party would be more viable if all units were completely dissolved.

The PDP itself was in fact already having leadership difficulties. Maraj startled everyone in the early months of 1957 by declaring that he was no longer a member of the PDP. "I want the public to hear that I do not enjoy the confidence of the four members [of the parliamentary PDP] and I will like to be addressed in future, not as leader of the Party but as an individual" (*Trinidad Chronicle*, 9 March 1957). The struggle in the PDP arose over the attitude the party should take on the federal issue. Maraj was willing to cooperate with the PNM, while his colleagues preferred to maintain their attitude of non-cooperation.

The imminent federal elections provided the catalyst for solidifying the opposition. The launching of the DLP had been continually deferred because no leader could be agreed upon; every notable felt that he had ample qualifications for leadership. It took the intervention of Jamaica's Alexander Bustamante to get the DLP to agree to be led provisionally by the TLP president, Victor Bryan. It was felt that the image of the DLP would suffer if either Gomes or Maraj were given the leadership. It should also be pointed out that the DLP as constituted in 1957 was a *federal*, and not a territorial, party. The leadership issue in the territorial party was not to be settled for a long time.

With the Labour Party finally launched, the opposition intensified its policy of systematically opposing Williams and the PNM by introducing its first no-confidence motion on 9 September 1957. In terms of substantive policy, the opposition criticized what it viewed as part of the government's plan to subject the public service to political control and partisanship, and there is indeed evidence to indicate that conflicts were beginning to arise between the newly elected government and senior civil servants. Many of these were persons whom the nationalists considered holdovers from the old order, persons of a different social class committed to values, policies and ways of doing things that were quite at variance with those of the new political elite. Charges that civil servants were sabotaging the government's development plans, and counter-charges that politicians were muzzling or victimizing senior officials were frequent. The fact that many senior civil servants were white creoles only served to complicate some of the crucial issues involved. Quite a few resigned and went into business rather than work under a "black" government. There was a general fear among white civil servants that sooner or later they would be victimized. Resignation was considered a more prudent course of action. As it turned out, very few were openly victimized in any way, much to the disappointment of party stalwarts.

The new government insisted that the civil service must recognize the new masters. The PNM – not senior officials, as was the case in the colonial period – must make laws, and form and state government policy. Party politics and a rationalized administration implied that the organs that executed the law should be subordinated to those that made it. Williams also angrily refused to counte-nance the view that civil servants should have direct access to the governor when they disagreed with ministerial policies. That practice was dismissed as being absurd. As the *PNM Weekly* (2 September 1957) bluntly stated,

> The PNM Government will, in its constitutional changes, see to it that . . . matters per-taining to the Civil Service will be regularised. When this is done, there will be little doubt as to whom and in what direction the Civil Service will have to turn for direction and guidance. . . . Many senior civil servants still think in terms of independence and an independent appeal to the Colonial Office. These officers cannot realize that full self-government is around the corner. . . . The Civil Service should be there to serve any gov-ernment the people elect. It is no longer possible to tolerate officials who can embarrass the Government and maintain their standing in that service.

Efficiency and harmony of action demanded that all organs of the administra-tion function as a united team, with one public voice.

Another major area of disagreement concerned the question of conditions under which foreign capital was to be allowed to come into the country. A defi-nition of policy had been forced upon the government by the actions of a US firm assembling office equipment in Trinidad. Faced by a union demand for the right to organize workers in its employ, the management took the position that it was not prepared to tolerate "outside interference" by any union, since its workers were well cared for and their wages were above the prevailing wage structure for persons in that classification. Factory conditions were also said to be optimum, and the extra-vocational welfare of workers was looked after by the company.

Williams, who was particularly sensitive to the suspicion with which the party was viewed by the trade union movement, chose to support the demands of the union. The minister of labour advised that the government would not allow industrialists to come into the country – especially under the Pioneer Industries Ordinance, which gave them exemption from certain forms of taxation – and do exactly as they pleased. The island was in need of foreign capital and welcomed it, but not at any price; self-respect and national pride would not permit it. Moreover, such a policy could only lead to industrial unrest. Williams took a much more belligerently nationalistic attitude. "Any industry coming in here and behaving decently will be given decent treatment. If they do not like our action, let them pull out" (*Trinidad Guardian*, 23 March 1957). The company in its turn warned the government that if it continued in its policies, US compa-nies would indeed "bail out and go", to the ultimate detriment of the people of the country. While both sides were guilty of lack of good judgement and restraint, the government was right in condemning the paternalism that was so evident a feature of industrial relations in Trinidad. White employers believed that they understood and represented the interests of their employees much better than union leaders, some of whom, it must be admitted, were still extremely immature in their bargaining techniques. The composition of the society and its system of job allocation made what was normally a class issue also a racial one.

Trade unions, both in Trinidad and throughout the Caribbean, applauded the government's boldness. The incident in fact marked the beginning of that fundamental alliance between the trade union movement and the PNM that was to bear such rich fruit in the 1961 elections but which was also to lead to some of the bitterest outbreaks of industrial unrest the country had witnessed thus far. As far as the trade unions were concerned, it was up to them to deepen the basis of the national revolution to make it meaningful to the worker.

The business community, it should be noted, had already begun to withdraw its confidence from the government. The commercial banks, bastions of the old order, refused to make loans available to the government on the basis of promissory notes. The government was warned by B.S. Maraj of the DLP that its behaviour was damaging the country's reputation:

> The Chief Minister ought to be more guarded in his expressions. . . . He is preventing people from coming to invest money in Trinidad. . . . [T]he Colonial Office has refused to grant him assistance and we now have to pay the "cake" by way of higher taxation. It is not right for the Chief Minister to adopt this attitude in a small two-by-two colony like Trinidad. We cannot do that to our bosses in the Colonial Office, or act as we want with them. (*Hansard*, 9 September 1957, 2301)

The opposition also noted that although the PNM had pledged in its manifesto that it would honour all international agreements, especially the one relating to the Bases Agreement of 1941, the government had allowed Jamaica and Barbados to force it into making a claim to the territory at Chaguaramas, leased to the United States, on the ground that it was the only satisfactory site for the federal capital. Williams, insisted Maraj, had fallen for a trick that would lead to a reopening of the capital site issue. "The Americans will not stand for petty bullying even if it is true they occupy part of our territory. You may speak to Woodford Square as you want, but you cannot speak to the Americans as you want. They partly control the entire globe" (ibid., 2303).

The final issue raised by the opposition was the question of the government's "violation of our parliamentary institutions". The government, said the DLP, was emphasizing Whitehall and forgetting Westminster. It was bypassing standing committees, including the Finance Committee, suspending the business of the House to avoid private members' motions, bypassing the Tenders Board, and generally infringing on the rights of the minorities. Alarm was also expressed at the growing "Caesarism" and intolerance of Dr Williams. Williams was criticized for his statement that, given a chance, he would prevent other parties from using Woodford Square, for politically assassinating his enemies and rewarding friends of the PNM, for declaring "war" on the opposition, for using committees to confront the opposition with *faits accomplis,* and for discriminating against rural areas that had not supported the PNM. The PNM also provoked concern when it expelled two of its members serving on local bodies for breaking party discipline. Williams declared publicly, "we helped to make these people, and by God, if they play the fool, we will break them" (*Trinidad Chronicle*, 3 October 1957). The opposition attacks were ferocious and devastating, and Williams himself was forced to admit that "some of the points were really good", even if twisted. One of the most articulate spokesmen of the opposition was Simbhoonath Capildeo, who had been a member of Dr Solomon's Caribbean Socialist Party before joining the PDP–DLP.

The leader of the House, Dr Patrick Solomon, reassured the opposition that the government would not restrict or oppose its right to function in the legislature, but warned that the PNM could not be expected to say thank-you for harassment. "Mere self-defence demands that we use a reasonable degree of force ourselves" (*Hansard*, 13 September 1957, 2363). The honeymoon was clearly over and Trinidad was being readied for a period of bitter party warfare in which racial tension would mount beyond the limits previously considered tolerable.

The Formation and Consolidation of the DLP

The consolidation of the DLP was a development that Williams and the PNM had not envisaged. As the PNM organ observed, "Bustamante's unification of the fragmentary groups in Trinidad was a fortuitous circumstance we never realized" (18 August 1958). At the second annual convention of the PNM in September 1957, Williams told assembled delegates that "the Party runs this great danger – that as the strongest Party ever organized in Trinidad, it has brought together some of the worst characteristics of the political life of the old world which it was pledged to destroy". Though recognizing the danger, few people in nationalist circles believed that the DLP would survive for any length of time. To the PNM, the DLP was not an opposition in the parliamentary sense of the word. "It had no programme or philosophy but was merely a collection of individuals with some personal following." There was also a great deal of confidence that the PNM could not be beaten in twenty-five years. Williams himself maintained that the PNM faced no real threat except from within its own ranks – from the ill-discipline, ambition, intrigue and inertia that were already manifest.

Despite the PNM's conviction that opposition was desirable and necessary in the democratic society to which it was committed, nationalists were extremely intolerant of such opposition whenever it presented itself. After 1957, Williams practically declared war on the DLP, the press, the Chamber of Commerce, and the European community. As Williams announced, "From now on we shall attack 'black is white' all who take PNM's name in vain." Williams's solicitude for opposition was intellectual and abstract. His intolerance of actual opposition forces was rendered all the more acute because he and his colleagues were convinced of the righteousness of their cause, and of the treasonableness and irresponsibility of their opponents.

Reflecting later on his first years in office, Williams was eminently satisfied. He notes that the major burden for fashioning the new regime fell on his shoulders:

> As Chief Minister (later Premier) and Minister of Finance, Planning and Development, I necessarily had to carry a heavy burden in the Legislative Council. The head of the government spoke with an authority that his cabinet colleagues obviously lacked. The Ministry of Finance was an innovation in the 1956 constitution, and it had to be built up bit by bit. The annual budget was my responsibility, and the whole field of taxation and expenditure necessarily devolved upon me. (1969, 246)

He also boasted that the PNM had introduced the country to planning and had popularized the concept of the development programme. The first development programme, which was part of the 1958 budget, was prepared with the help of Arthur Lewis and Teodoro Moscoco of Puerto Rico. "To the great wrath of the opposition, it was called 'the Peoples' Charter for Economic Development'." That budget speech, incidentally, lasted for six hours, and was described by the opposition as a "vast travelogue". To Williams, the speech was epic and the "fruit of long years of study and historical scholarship. This was really the first PNM budget, so I was concerned with the education of the population, the elucidation of the complexities that faced our economy, and with putting our small country in the international context" (ibid., 247).

Williams was scornful of "opposition economics", which he claimed was dominated by the view that one should not tax the population but borrow instead. He argued that if the population wanted development, they had to pay for it. The PAYE system, which was introduced in 1957, was designed to make defaulters meet their obligations. Something had to be done about the fact that there were more owners of private cars than taxpayers. Williams was pleased when the Mighty Sparrow endorsed his tax policy in calypso.

> The public reaction to PAYE was quite different [from that of the opposition and the media]. It gave rise to one of the best calypsos in Trinidad's history, the work, as always, of Sparrow. I can still recall the 1958 Carnival when all over the place people were singing:
>> The Doctor say, to pay as you earn,
>> But Sparrow say you paying to learn,
>> And me father say he sharpening the axe,
>> For when the collector come, to pay off the income tax
> (Ibid., 248)

In another verse, Sparrow, who emerged as the calypsonian laureate of the PNM, told well-to-do men "like de Freitas and Fernandez" to stop blaming "the Doctor", and that "jump high or jump low, they can't get away from the tax":

> I would like to know, why they blaming the Doctor so,
> Tell me, I would like to know, why they blaming the Doctor so,
> One class of people, while the other class cussing,
> Running they mouth like they take Brooklax,
> Only blaming the Doctor for they income tax,
> That's the law now in Trinidad,
> If you don't like it, that's too bad,
> Take your things and clear out today,
> For all who working must pay.

Williams argued too that spending priorities had to be determined. Subsidies on consumption goods and services had to give way to subsidies on capital goods.

It is difficult, however, to describe the development programme and the 1957 and 1958 budgets as either scientific or far-reaching, since they were little more than a collection of desirable infrastructural projects that the PNM had pledged to introduce in 1956. These projects included subsidies to cane farmers, peasants and fishermen; hospital and housing construction; better access roads for agricultural areas; rural electrification; harbour improvement; and increased expenditures on Tobago and on education with the ultimate prospect of free education. Many of the projects had been begun by the old regime.

To finance the development programme, which was expected to cost TT$191 million, funds had to be obtained from somewhere. The government had already failed in its bid to obtain assistance from London or to raise loans locally and on the US and London markets, and the only alternative source was public revenue. Increased taxes were thus imposed on commodities such as rum, tobacco, gasoline, automobile licences, legal transactions and the like. But the major anticipated source of new revenue was oil. The government declared that it would renegotiate its tax arrangements with the oil companies so as to secure a 50–50 split in oil profits. Williams, who was minister of finance, noted that Venezuela had such an arrangement, and that in some Middle Eastern areas the arrangement was 75–25.

Williams also did a complete somersault on the question of depletion allowances for the industry, which he had earlier criticized the Gomes regime for not conceding. "The case for the special concessions in marine drilling to Trinidad was simply overdone," he maintained. "It is not possible to see how anyone could have taken seriously in 1954 the old claim of probable exhaustion of reserves in a few years." He now saw Gomes's subsequent decision to grant them as "the worst example of political irresponsibility, the greatest sell-out in the history of Trinidad. It was the legacy of a Government which during the extension of its life beyond its legal term, gave away for 25 years, the birth-right of the people . . . it was a ghastly illustration of colonialism and the lack of respect for colonials."

Williams qualified his rejection of the allowances by saying that the concessions given were too wide. He also claimed that the government had not followed the advice of those who had warned that the concessions should await further geological study, and that they should not be given for operations that had not yet commenced. Provisions permitting review of the agreement in cases where prolific wells were struck should also have been inserted. Williams noted that such allowances were not given for operations in Lake Maracaibo or in the Persian Gulf (*Hansard*, 9 September 1957, 556). Williams's basic argument in these two budgets was that if the country wanted improvements in social amenities, it had to pay for them. It was better for Trinidad to pay for its development programme out of its own revenues, since high interest on loans from abroad would only add to the cost of the total programme. Virtue was being made out of necessity.

The opposition strongly criticized the government for planning to exhaust the colony's reserves on projects which, they argued, were aimed mainly at helping the urban population. Indian legislators were especially angry about the new taxes on licences, fuel and alcohol, which, they maintained (quite unjustifiably), were directed specifically at the Indian community. They even declared that the government was mobilizing support for the new tax structure by claiming that it was directed mainly against Indians. Butler's hostile anti-Indian outburst that the traitorous Indians should be taxed "more and more" also served as an irritant to the Indians. Stung by the defection to the DLP of one of the Indian members of the legislative council from his party, Butler had declared that he was finally convinced that all Indians were traitors, and that he would never again sponsor another Indian candidate. He even warned Williams that very soon he would be "deserted by all those Indians whom he is now putting into power – they are all traitors – one and all of them" (*Trinidad Chronicle*, 17 December 1957).

The urban community took the tax increases stoically, even if sullenly. The fact that the protests of the Indian and European communities were so extravagant, however, did much to rally them behind the PNM banner. But the budget, together with the issues described above and those relating to morality in public affairs, had helped to solidify the DLP, which won the 1957 local government elections and had already begun its campaign for the first federal elections, to be held early in 1958.

13   The Recalcitrant Minority and the Federal Elections of 1958

The first stage of the protracted struggle to achieve political unity among the English-speaking Caribbean peoples came to an end in July 1957 when the British Parliament approved an order-in-council establishing the Federation of the West Indies. The elections to the first Parliament of the West Indies, which were scheduled for April 1958, provided the first opportunity for a country-wide electoral confrontation between the DLP and the PNM. Since its formation in 1957, the DLP had shown elements of strength as well as weakness. The weakness stemmed mainly from the excessive individualism of its members. Alexander Bustamante, who had been made life leader of the Federal Party, urged Trinidad DLP politicians to discipline themselves, to put party above self as a condition of effectiveness. "No member must believe that because he has some following he is greater than the Organisation. The Organisation always comes first, the country and the members after" (*Trinidad Guardian*, 1 January 1958). But Trinidad's DLP chieftains were congenitally incapable of organizational fidelity. There were resignations and threats of resignations within weeks of the party's founding. Maraj himself, conscious of his power as the party's main vote-getter, threatened to resign and form a new party whenever he did not get his way. The fight over the selection of candidates for the federal elections almost split the party wide open.

Younger elements were disgruntled about the party's electoral preference for established notables and its seeming inability to present a positive image to the public. Even the *Trinidad Guardian,* the *de facto* organ of the DLP, found it necessary to criticize the DLP's political immaturity: "An opposition, to be effective, should not concern itself merely with the strategy of keeping the Government extended on all fronts, useful as this might be. It should offer the electorate a positive programme which will carry conviction of its readiness to take over the administration of the country should the logic of events some day put it in a winning position" (ibid., 11 November 1958). But try as it did, the DLP was never able to take advantage of this advice. It remained imprisoned by its origins.

The PNM contested the 1958 election as part of a coalition of what were then considered to be the progressive forces of West Indian politics: the People's National Party of Jamaica, the Barbados Labour Party, and other labour parties that were in power in the smaller units of the federation. The fact that the West Indian Federal Labour Party, as the coalition was called, was conceived as a socialist united front posed ideological difficulties for the PNM. Some members insisted that the party must continue to "fight shy of 'isms'". Williams himself refused to entertain suggestions that PNM should "go socialist":

> The PNM should be chary of 18th century political labels and categories, especially those with an emotive appeal that have no relevance for a 20th century world, let alone a West Indian environment. In every case, the test must be which [economic strategy] is best designed to improve the living conditions and promote development of the people of the country as a whole. Placed against this background, nationalisation and private enterprise, public and private capitalism, become mere techniques to be used at one time or another for a larger end, and not merely as ends in themselves. PNM's sole aim is the removal of the political and economic barriers to the full development of the West Indian personality. (*PNM Weekly*, 27 May 1957)

But the fact that the West Indian Federal Labour Party was socialist did not deter the PNM from joining it. Williams observed that in spite of the socialist label, Jamaica and Barbados were pragmatic in their development strategy – no nationalization, no expropriation, no revolution. What is more, the West Indian Federal Labour Party had agreed to create a separate category of "associate members" for the parties that were not socialist, but nationalist and progressive. The manifesto of the party itself said nothing that gave one the impression that it was a revolutionary socialist party. The economic strategy that it endorsed for the federation was no different from that being followed by the PNM in Trinidad, and the People's National Party in Jamaica.

The campaign in Trinidad, though on the whole not as fierce as in 1956, was much more racially tinged. Every issue was twisted to fit the racial cleavages in the society. Each party nevertheless strove to buttress its claim of being genuinely multiracial by wooing as candidates notables whose ethnic identification differed from the dominant one in the party, even if this meant sacrificing the claims of some dedicated workers. The results were quite satisfactory. Of the ten candidates sponsored by the DLP, only three were Indian; four of the PNM's were Indian. But the value of such ticket-balancing strategies was severely compromised by the tendency of both parties to "type" the other in racial terms. PNM followers promptly re-baptized non-Indian candidates in the DLP with Hindu or Muslim names such as "Bryan Singh" or "Gomes Maharaj". Creoles who appeared on DLP platforms were invited to "show us your capra". PNM followers also tended to view such persons as "enemies" and "traitors", persons who could not see that a vote for the DLP was in effect an anti-African vote. The Indian element in the DLP leadership also contributed to this unfortunate circumstance. One of their main talking points in the campaign, especially in the rural areas, was that a victory for the DLP would mean that the first prime minister of the West Indies would be Indian. The DLP had in fact designated Ashford Sinanan, a Presbyterian Indian, as its candidate for the prime ministership.

No party was blameless; there was instead a balance of blame. As the nationalist movement became more fully developed, the irresistible tendency was for race and nationhood to become interrelated. Both ethnic groups interpreted nationhood and emancipation in terms of their own communities and symbols. Even the party leaders, committed though they were to universalistic norms, could not resist the temptation to manipulate sectional symbols, sometimes subtly, sometimes quite unashamedly, in their pursuit of political advantage. To the DLP, the election presented an opportunity to use a federal base of power to neutralize the PNM at the territorial level.

Many of the issues raised during the campaign were hangovers from the 1956 election. The criticisms levelled at the ruling party during the debate on the 1957 no-confidence motion were also given further airing. As far as Chaguaramas as the site for the federal capital was concerned, it was obvious that Williams had deliberately seized upon it as *the* historic issue with which to mould an emotional West Indian nationalism. Williams also sought to use the controversy as a lever with which to negotiate a *rapprochement* with the Indian community following the 1956 election. The British commissioners who had been retained in 1956 to recommend sites for the location of the capital had rejected Trinidad because of the "disruptive" influence that the Indian community was said to have had on its political life: "We consider it would be better to put the capital in either Jamaica or Barbados than in Trinidad. Our reasons are the instability of the island's politics and the low standard accepted in public life. To put the capital near Port of Spain would, in our opinion, be to run a great risk which need not be run"(1956, 22; see Report of the British Caribbean Federal Commission [London: HMSO, Col. No. 328]).

Williams's vigorous condemnation of this slur on the Indian community won him the support of many Indians whom he had alienated by his Maha Sabha addresses in 1956. This gain was reinforced by the clever decision, encouraged by Winston Mahabir, to invite the leader of the PDP to join the government's delegation to the federal conference held in Jamaica in 1957, at which the capital site issue was to be settled. Maraj viewed his acceptance of the invitation in the face of opposition from some of his party colleagues as the final reproof to those who insisted that he was anti-federation. Mahabir writes that the recommendation to invite Maraj was his: "Williams wanted me to go to Jamaica with him when the issue of the Federal capital was to be decided. I suggested that Bhadase

Maraj would be more appropriate, since he was not only a shrewd bargainer, but his presence would represent a more widely based Trinidad consensus. In addition I knew that Bhadase and Williams admired each other in peculiar ways" (1978, 77).

Williams's decision to go back on his pledge to respect the agreement between Britain and the United States concerning the terms under which a naval base was to be established in Trinidad neutralized all the advantages that had accrued as a result of Maraj's participation in the conference. Maraj's revelation that the government had earlier decided on an alternative site outside the base area further hardened the differences between him and the PNM. The charge of "treasonable betrayal of confidential secrets" was frequently thrown about during the campaign. As far as Patrick Solomon was concerned, the Indian elite was putting a knife in the back of the new West Indian nation, something nationalists could not tolerate. There had to be a "fight to the finish" between the two parties. "One or the other party had to go to the wall because we can no longer tolerate this odd conglomeration of people who call themselves the DLP" (*Trinidad Guardian*, 4 March 1958).

The DLP were similarly convinced that they were the true West Indian patriots. The question at stake was not whether the West Indies could lay claim to Chaguaramas, but whether they should. The true interests of the West Indies, they charged, were being sacrificed to satisfy the vendetta of one man. The DLP in fact alleged that Williams's *volte face* had to do with his conflict with American authorities for his alleged negligence in meeting alimony obligations to his first wife. The party felt it was idle and unrealistic to talk about a neutral West Indies joining the Bandung bloc, since the hard facts of geography and economic dependence ruled out all prospects of neutrality being practised by the West Indies. The DLP felt that the Bases Agreement should be re-negotiated in such a way that United States funds would be forthcoming to assist the federation in solving its economic problems. Welfare issues should be placed before status issues. The DLP also claimed that talk about socialism, capital gains and other punitive taxation measures, and insistence on the rights of trade unions, would scare away foreign capital. As the party warned: "a socialist government dealing with taxation cannot win the full confidence of external or local capital and therefore must resort to increased taxation to maintain normal services. A policy of high taxation now in the West Indies would defeat its own aim because of its deterrent effect on investment. . . . We are inflexible in our advocacy at all times that the only hope of the entire West Indies is the belief in private enterprise" (*Trinidad Guardian*, 12 January 1958).

The DLP also underscored their contention that the PNM had a distinctly urban and middle-class bias, and that its development programme was prejudiced in favour of the urban bourgeoisie. It was noted that while increased cost-of-living allowances were given to civil servants, no basic foodstuffs were subsidized; nor were pensions for the aged increased. And there were indeed protests from lower-class elements that the PNM had not relieved them from the yoke that they had had to endure under the Gomes regime. They were still the forgotten pariahs from "behind the bridge".

These accusations were not entirely just, though many of them were. While it is true that there was an urban middle-class bias in the PNM, the government had not completely ignored the rural citizen. Its first provisional budget in 1957 had assigned funds to relieve the hardships of seasonal workers in the sugar industry, and had provided funds to create supplementary jobs for intermittent workers in both the rural and urban areas. Money was also provided to construct outdoor privies in the rural areas to combat the incidence of hookworm, and contributions were made to the Sugar Industry Welfare Fund for the servicing of lands made available for worker housing by the sugar estates. In the development budget, modest sums had been allocated to help the farmer, fisherman and other small proprietors. Williams had also declared that his government was anxious to stimulate a "back to the land" movement and to ensure that the countryside was not subordinated to the urban areas as far as the normal amenities of civilization were concerned. The stated aim of the development programme was to lay the foundations of the national community. But the effects of the modest programme had not yet begun to be felt, and the DLP had proven to be a much more effective propaganda machine than Williams had given it credit for.

Election Results

The results of the federal elections came as a complete surprise to Williams and the PNM. The party had become so used to easy victories in municipal areas that it had anticipated no difficulties in the federal elections.[1] It had in fact ruled that no member already elected to public office would become a candidate for the election, on the grounds that this would dislocate the development programme. It was also explained that by-elections to vacated positions would again involve the country in disruptive political strife. Moreover, Williams had decided that for the next five years, the PNM's role would be to concentrate not on federal politics, but on its development programme as a prerequisite to a more effective participation at the federal level in the years ahead. As Williams declared, "If there is one party in the West Indies which cannot be expected to accept any excessive responsibility for the operation of the federal machine in the early years, it is the PNM" (*Trinidad Guardian*, 12 January 1958). The PNM needed time to consolidate itself. The party was still too young and too unformed to risk losing the concentrated attention of its best talent.

Despite their unwillingness to participate actively in federal politics, Williams and the PNM were stunned with disbelief when it was revealed that the DLP had won six of the ten seats allocated to Trinidad. Everyone agreed that it was a tremendous triumph, not so much for the DLP, but for Bhadase Maraj, who proved to be his party's principal vote-getter. His supreme achievement was the political resurrection of Roy Joseph and Albert Gomes, two ministers of the old order who had been buried by the PNM in 1956. DLP supporters regarded the results as a welcome rebuff to the PNM, whose "goose-stepping" and intolerant exclusivism had driven many to anger and frustration. Gomes, who had a genius for exaggerating the "crimes" of the PNM, was not unfair when he observed that "the attitude of the cohorts of the new cult was insufferable. . . . Decent citizens were the victims of vulgar abuse on the streets, for no other reason than that they did not *look* like the sort of people who would be PNM supporters. A section of the community interpreted the victory [in 1956] as establishing their right to dominate the country even to the extent of subscribing to the belief that other elements were trespassers" (*Trinidad Guardian*, 13 April 1958).

Gomes saw the victory as "a welcome Thermidorean reaction, a successful rally of decent people against a dictatorship of hooligans". The age of persecution hopefully was over. The DLP also claimed that since Chaguaramas and government taxation policy were the main issues during the campaign, Williams should, in fact, resign. The public had shown a lack of confidence in the government. An Anglican cleric, Canon Max Farquhar, spoke for many former PNM supporters who had become thoroughly disillusioned with the PNM when he declared that he hoped the defeat would have a sobering effect on "fanatical nationalists whose minds had begun to lose touch with reality":

> The defeat could, at the very worst, invoke only the spur of wholesome embarrassment, or else [the] timely corrective of humiliating disillusionment to a government whose chief besetting sin has been the familiar nemesis of being "power drunk." The most recent outburst of the Chief Minister, "Don't get me blasted vex", follows in a sequence of hysterically unbalanced statements, which have too long pointed to flagrantly overweening conceit. Another favourite slogan, "Heads will roll", used persistently in brandishing threats, is further indication of an attitude of mind dangerously out of hand. (*Trinidad Guardian*, 16 March 1958)

But the hoped-for peace that the results had led DLP circles to expect was not forthcoming, since Williams puzzlingly chose to interpret the election results not as a rebuff, but as an impressive vote of confidence. The interpretation was based not on numbers of seats won – which they attributed to the mischance of electoral geography – but on the size and distribution of its popular vote. PNM psephologists noted that although the total vote cast was 20,379 less than it was in 1956, the party had increased its take by 12,379. By winning 117,432 of the 251,739 votes cast, they had in fact captured roughly 48 per cent of the electorate, compared to 38.9 per cent in 1956. This was especially significant in that the vote in the urban areas, where the PNM was entrenched, had declined, while that in the rural areas had increased. The claim was that PNM urban members were sure of victory, and had stayed home.

Williams was also proud of the fact that the PNM had made substantial inroads into former "enemy" territory. The party had improved its position among rural Afro-creoles, especially in Tobago and the eastern counties. And it had been giving substantial attention to Tobago, which they had narrowly lost – by 342 votes – in 1956. The DLP claimed that the PNM had used the treasury to wage its campaign in the island ward. While the political significance of Tobago was not lost on him, Williams was genuinely interested in correcting the neglect with which the island had been treated in the past. The party's performance in Indian-dominated areas had also improved over that of 1956; 950 additional votes were won in Caroni, 1,200 in Victoria, and 2,950 in St Patrick. This suggested to the PNM that although they were not winning these areas outright, and probably never would, they were at least winning some adherents among the Indian community.

It did not follow, however, that all the additional support that the PNM obtained in these areas came from Hindus. In 1958, as racial polarization increased, many non-Indians switched to the PNM. Moreover, the PNM was represented by Indian candidates in two of these areas, and it is difficult to determine whether Indians who voted for the PNM gave their support to the party itself or to these representatives. The overall increase of voting support for the PNM in 1958 could be easily explained as a displacement phenomenon. The withdrawal of independents and small parties from the electoral fray released a substantial number of voters, many of whom were not necessarily anti-PNM in 1956. Some who had been intensely cross-pressured in 1956 had resolved their indecision in favour of the Catholic Church. Now that the church was no longer openly hostile to the PNM, many were available for mobilization by the party.

Catholic authorities had in fact warmly approved Williams's move to squash the zeal of those who wished to erect a monument to him in commemoration of his contribution to the political emancipation of the community. As the *Catholic News* (23 March 1957) declared editorially, "His action comes as a virtual tonic to those who have been languishing for this sort of spirit among public leaders. . . . It is a sign of true greatness when a leader does not lose sight of his mission, which is to strive for the welfare of those he leads and represents, even at the expense of self."

Similarly, a substantial number who had supported patrons and parties that had since merged into the DLP had refused to follow their leaders, and had switched to the PNM. While the non-PNM vote in the capital city was 18,851 in 1956, in 1958 it fell to 12,474 – a significant shift. The PNM's total vote in these areas declined by about 2,000, but this can be explained by the lower voter turn-out in these constituencies, averaging 60 per cent in 1958, compared to 78 per cent in 1956. The unattractiveness of PNM candidates might also have affected the election voting figures. The contention that the DLP's vote had decreased was invalid. The DLP did not exist in 1956, and it was sheer statistical chicanery to argue that all or most non-PNM votes in 1956 were "potential" DLP votes. Only on the basis of such an assumption could Williams have maintained that the DLP vote had decreased by over 14,000.

Williams and the Appeal to the "Indian Nation"

One of the more dramatic but unfortunate sequels to the election was the historic and far-reaching address delivered by Williams on 1 April 1958. The address, enti-tled "The Dangers Facing Trinidad and Tobago and the West Indian Nation", was an attempt to account for the defeat of the PNM in the federal election. The reason, declared Williams, was "race, pure and unadulterated". In certain areas where the PNM was decimated, the correlation between ethnicity and voting was almost total. A breakdown of the vote in certain polling divisions "chosen at ran-dom" by Williams revealed the pattern shown in Tables 13.1 and 13.2. The fig-ures spoke for themselves, said Williams, who charged that "by hook or crook, they brought out the Indian voter, the young, the old, the literate and illiterate, the lame, the halt and the blind" (*PNM Weekly*, 21 April 1958). Williams also argued that the results showed the effects of the promises that had been made to the Indians that victory would mean an Indian prime minister and governor general.

Table 13.1   Ethnicity and Voting in the 1958 Federal Election: Selected Electoral and Polling Divisions

Division	Number of Indians	DLP Vote
Tunapuna	3,427	3,402
Curepe and St Augustine	3,140	4,284
Tacarigua	948	911
Arouca	1,567	1,454
D'Abadie	313	272
Piarco	277	300
Caroni	1,272	1,313
Total	10,944	11,936

Source: PNM Weekly, 21 April 1958.

Table 13.2 Ethnicity and Voting in the 1958 Federal Election: Selected Polling Booths

Polling Division	Indians	DLP Votes
52	135	135
53	20	21
54	169	170
55	235	228
56	184	204
57	245	249
60	315	313
63	56	52
25	54	54
26	51	54
29	49	50
34	106	103
36	306	298
39	117	116
40	117	115
17	206	206
122	243	241

Source: PNM Weekly, 21 April 1958.

Williams likewise disclosed that during the campaign, a letter addressed to "My dear Brother Indian", and signed, "Yours truly Indian", had been circulated throughout the countryside. The letter accused Williams of favouring his own kind in the Cabinet, and of selecting a few Indians merely to mislead other Indians into supporting his movement in order to have a majority. It concluded, "If, my dear brother, you have realized these occurrences, and the shaky position in which our Indian people are placed, woe unto our Indian nation in the next ten years" (ibid.).

Williams saw this appeal to the Indian "nation" as an insult to the people of the West Indies. "The Indian nation is in India," he snapped, "it is the India of socialism, of Afro-Asian unity, the India of Bandung." Indians in Trinidad, far from being genuine Indians, were a "recalcitrant and hostile minority masquerading as the Indian nation, and prostituting the name of India for its selfish, reactionary political ends" (ibid.). The growing tendency towards racial chauvinism, towards the exploitation of race as the basis of political power, was the "great danger facing Trinidad and the West Indies".

Whether deliberately or not, Williams misrepresented what was meant by the term *nation*. The term, a translation of *jati*, did not mean what the term means in occidental discourse. It means no more than tribe or kin group. As Haraksingh observes, "The word 'nation' in this context was a somewhat loose approximation of the Hindi term of community or people, and certainly not an allusion to nation in the sense of a state and its institutions. In fact, the pamphlet was simply a rendering of the traditional battle cry, which had been raised in Trinidad before and most pointedly in the prelude to the 1884 Hosea Riots, of 'dharma in danger'." But Williams saw red, and as he himself explained, "I let them have it" (*Caribbean Issues* 8, no. 2 [1997]: 67–68).

Politicians such as Victor Bryan and Albert Gomes also came in for their share of public excoriation. It was noted that while they had once bitterly attacked the Indians, they were now prepared to become "Maraj's lick-spittles" in order to hold on to power. "Thus do men sell their soul to gain their political world." These men had talked loudly about federation, and yet had forged an unholy alliance with a party that was determined to destroy the federation. Williams, in fact, now put himself on record as believing that a substantial sector of the Indian elite was still opposed to federation: "Many of them are opposed to Federation . . . and who will forget the fanatical Indian stand against freedom of movement in Trinidad?" (ibid.). No one who heard Williams's speech could doubt that it would have significant political consequences.

But the fundamental question is, why did he, as chief minister of the country, make such an address? Was it merely the rash speech of a man motivated by anger and pique, a man and a party who could not accept defeat gracefully? Williams explained why he made the speech:

> Tonight's analysis is not an attempt to juggle with election statistics. It is a factual, cold-blooded analysis of a situation which poses a dangerous threat to the stability and progress of our country and the new nation. As the party responsible for the initiation of an attempt to bring sanity, political morality, decency and self-respect to this country, it is our duty to warn the electorate and the people of this country of the situation which threatens to engulf the progress that has been achieved. (*PNM Weekly*, 21 April 1958)

Certain members of the party insisted that the attack was not racially motivated at all and that Williams's only purpose was to bring the issue of ideological recalcitrance out in the open so that the country might face it in a mature fashion. But it was clear that behind the glitter of cold statistics, there were also hidden propaganda appeals to the Afro-creole population, both in Trinidad and the West Indies. Williams betrayed his purpose openly when he declared,

> We sympathize deeply with those misguided unfortunates who, having ears to hear, heard not, having eyes to see, saw not, who were complacent, for whom everything was in the bag, who had the DLP covered, who were too tired or busy to vote, who wanted a car to take them to the polling station around the corner. . . . They will understand hereafter that he or she who stays home and does not come out to vote PNM,

in effect votes DLP. They have learnt their lesson. Today they regret it bitterly, and they are already swearing that *it must never happen again.* (Ibid.; emphasis added)

It was a clever attempt to rouse the black population from their apathy and lethargy. They were fighting among themselves and treating the vote irresponsibly while the Indian community was mobilizing all its energies to capture power. Sympathy for the Movement was not enough. As Williams advised, "It is only the actual votes that matter in the long run! Nothing else!" Many party members in fact wept bitterly when the results were known. The DLP victory was a shocking affront to their pride. As the party organ admitted, "Tears flowed freely that night, and the following day, there were thousands whose spirits were droopy. . . . Since then, there has emerged the will and confidence that never again will a PNM victory be taken for granted" (*PNM Weekly*, 21 April 1958).

Even if one were to be charitable and absolve Williams from the charge of openly inciting racial counter-mobilization, one cannot condone the tactlessness of the address – especially when racial passions were already so inflamed. Williams spoke in his capacity as leader of the PNM, but he was also the country's chief minister. It would have been more prudent for an address of the sort to have been given by another official of the party. It was one thing to be a psephologist in an academic treatise designed for a limited audience, but quite another to make that type of appeal in the public squares. The unsophisticated man in the street was bound to interpret it as a declaration of racial counter-exclusivism. When DLP parliamentarians in 1960 attempted to do the same thing, use sociology to make political appeals, Williams would accuse them of being "stink with racialism".

Indian members of the party elite were deeply embarrassed, and two ministers recorded their views as to what happened. Because of the pivotal nature of the event, their views are quoted here at length. Mahabir tells us,

> Montano, Mohammed and I were worried about his planned exposition in Woodford Square. We confided our fears to Solomon, requesting him to ensure as far as possible that Williams would say nothing to ignite the sub-surface sparks of racial antagonisms. Solomon assured us that he had read the script of Williams' report to the people. He had approved everything in it. We should stop worrying. My prognosis, he said in his superior clinical wisdom, was totally wrong. Our fears were quite unjustified. Solomon had [however] completely concurred with what Williams was to say that evening.
>
> Woodford Square – the University of Woodford Square – in the evening. Huge, expectant crowd. My wife and I arrive late. Air of tension. Williams in mid-sentence. Unusually perfunctory, almost timid applause greets our arrival on stage. Williams continues to read his script after making some "ad lib" remark to the effect that I was not to be grouped in the category of those he had been describing. It did not take long to realize that we had arrived in the middle of the main course. It contained generous ingredients of abuse of the Indian community which was deemed to be a "hostile and

recalcitrant minority." The Indian community represented the greatest danger facing the country. It was an impediment to West Indian progress. It had caused PNM to lose the federal elections.

There were savagely contemptuous references to the Indian illiterates of the country areas who were threatening to submerge the masses whom Williams had enlightened. He reproved the Indians for having brought to the polls the lame and the halt, the blind and the deaf. He referred derisively to an Indian from Coon Coon village, evoking peals of laughter with his scornful tone. My wife was appalled after the first few sentences she heard. She wanted us to leave the platform. I prevented her – fearing to precipitate any disturbance in an atmosphere which Williams had charged with hate.

There were other Indians on the platform – Martin Sampath, Ibbit Mosaheb, Walter Annamunthodo. We all exchanged horrified glances. We experienced a sudden shattering of all the ideals for which we thought we stood. We felt guilty of the lies we had preached to the Indians about the genuineness of Williams and our Party. At the end of the meeting we decided to proceed to Williams' home to tell him precisely what we thought of his speech. When we arrived we succeeded easily enough in penetrating the barrier of policemen and got past the second phalanx of sycophants, arriving ultimately to Williams himself. There he was, the conqueror, in an exuberant, gloating, hypomanic mood of triumph. He had obviously gained exquisite emotional satisfaction from his diatribe against the Indians. Sampath, Mosaheb, Annamunthodo and I all expressed in our own way the surprise, disappointment, disgust we felt. Williams was due to repeat the same speech in San Fernando the following evening.

Montano arranged a private meeting of Mohammed, my brother Dennis and me at his home prior to the public meeting. We decided that both Montano and I should speak before Williams; that we should plead for interracial solidarity; that we should interpret the election results in a more objective manner. We made an assumption that we could jointly take the winds out of his sails and diminish the impact of his racial slurs. Perhaps we did to a limited extent. But he delivered the same speech none the less.

The days that followed placed me in a peculiar plight. My family, especially my father – a consistent admirer of Williams – was bitterly resentful. Phone calls and letters gave all kinds of directions on how I should react in this "crisis." Some took the line that I should resign. Others stated that I would then become yet another scapegoat for Williams' fury with further deterioration in race relations in the country. (1978, 78–80)

Mahabir consulted with Sir Solomon Hochoy, whose views he respected. Hochoy advised him to swallow his hurt silently, since in the long run, the party was greater than one man and the country more than the party (ibid., 80). Mahabir also noted that when a no-confidence in Williams motion was brought to the legislature, he, Mohammed, Montano and Ashford Sinanan of the DLP persuaded the DLP to drop the motion "in the interest of national peace". As he writes further,

Williams was visibly nervous about this no-confidence motion. He was led to believe by his hangers-on that Montano, Mohammed and I were going to vote against him. He must have discovered later that Mitra Sinanan and the three M's had saved the day for him. What lessons did I learn? First, I recognized more clearly than ever the gross emotional instability of Williams. In the moment of defeat, he had disgorged dangerous half-truths and was grappling with endless shadows. He would trample relentlessly upon the feelings of friends, impassively exploiting the baser emotions of his supporters, repudiating our Party's written philosophy while reflecting his personality's deficient ability to accommodate set-backs of any kind. The second lesson, that Solomon was an accomplice, appeared in a worse light even than Williams. At least Williams dared to say publicly what he felt and thought. (Ibid., 80)

Mahabir nevertheless felt that the unfortunate effects of Williams's address had to be corrected, if possible, lest the community become enveloped by violent racial strife. As he warned the PNM,

The challenge . . . now is to stand firm . . . against the temptations to fight racialism with racialism, because if we choose to fight racialism with racialism, the only possible result will be death, destruction and despair in this little country of ours, whose greatest boast to the outside world has always been the ability of our many races to dwell together in unity.

Let us all pledge jointly now, as a first step in the amelioration of an increasingly tense situation, that the two obscene and obsolete words "nigger" and "coolie" will be herewith banished from our vocabulary. . . . Let us learn the lessons from our election experiences, but let us be forever mindful of the fact that PNM is something more than an election-winning machine, that it is, as I have said before, a way of life in which I firmly believe. (*Trinidad Guardian*, 23 April 1958)

Ibbit Mosaheb was also deeply upset by Williams's broadside. As he recalled, "After he lost the Federal Elections to Bhadase Maraj, he became very hostile. . . . Many of us went to his home after and told him it was a political blunder. He was hurt by the outcome of the elections. He had to place the blame somewhere" (interview with Ken Boodhoo, as cited in Mohammed 2001, 29).

Mohammed was more diplomatic in his account of the incident. Mohammed's official statement as related by his biographer was that he had "never known Dr. Williams to be a racially prejudiced man". He concedes that the statement caused hurt, but explained that there was a "great deal of bitterness and hostility coming from certain sections of the community at the time in the most derogatory forms against the person of Dr. Williams and certain members of the PNM, and that history should record that the statement was made in the heat of the aftermath of a bitter Federal election campaign" (Ghany 1996, 104).

Williams's address elicited frenzied outcries from the Indian community and the press. He was accused of using race to maintain his slipping power, of "soiling other people's clothes while licking his wounds", of "unleashing the mad dogs of racial strife". Maraj declared that Williams would have to "destroy every East Indian in Trinidad because we do not intend to sit with our arms folded and let him do what he wants". What galled Maraj was the fact that the PNM had selected the Indians as the acceptable social target rather than the Europeans, who had rejected the PNM just as completely. Why not attack them? As Maraj thundered, "The plain truth is that he is afraid to tread on the corns of the white people. But he is trying to sow the seeds of dissension between Indians and Negroes. We must not allow that day to come when we have to go into civil war because one man wants to keep at the height of his power" (*Trinidad Guardian*, 23 April 1958). The fact is that the statistics could also have been used to show that the DLP was defeated by a racial vote in the urban areas. The Indians were indeed clannish, but their behaviour had to be viewed as a natural urge on the part of a minority to preserve its religion and culture, and to advance itself as a group.

The defeat of the PNM in the 1958 federal elections and in the two by-elections that followed could be ascribed to a number of factors apart from race. The party began its campaign late – approximately one month before the election. The fact that it ran a weak team also strained the loyalties of its followers somewhat. The PNM candidates proved unable to hold their own against the old chieftains whom they believed had been buried with the "old order". It is also clear that the government's "tax like fire" budget, just four months before the election, was extremely injudicious, even if indicative of its honesty. Many lower-class urban and rural voters especially were alienated by the new taxes, since they generally lacked the perspective to integrate needs for social improvement with the corresponding necessity to pay increased taxation. Many who expected dramatic evidence that their aspirations were being fulfilled were already expressing disillusionment. The promised jobs, schools and houses were still only being talked about. Even the Mighty Sparrow felt driven to criticize Williams:

> After promising to give so much tender care,
> They forget me as they walk out of Woodford Square,
> They raise up on the taxi fare, no doctor no,
> And the blasted milk so dear, no doctor no,
> But you must remember, we support you in September,
> You better come good,
> Because I have a big piece of mango wood.

It also seems fair to say that the verbal and other excesses of Williams and the PNM alienated many who ordinarily would have identified with it rather than with the DLP.

In the final analysis, however, there is no escaping the fact that the DLP defeated the PNM principally because of the way in which the constituency boundaries were drawn. Anyone who had taken time to look would have seen that the PNM could not possibly have won more than five seats, unless they had assumed that the PNM's magic had exorcised the racial monster. A little less than half of its voting support was bottled up in the three urban and suburban areas of the capital city, and the remainder was so distributed that it could easily have been swamped by the Indian vote. It should also be recalled that the PNM had won four or five seats in 1956 because of splits within the Indian electorate. With many of these votes now largely solidified behind the DLP in enlarged constituencies, the results were predictable. The PNM vowed that never again would it leave the business of drawing electoral boundaries to a neutral electoral commission. The party was also determined that the rural voter must in the future be more resolutely wooed.

14　The "War" for West Indian Independence

We of the PNM are the voice of West Indian Independence. We are the writers of the New West Indian history. . . . We are, and we set out to be a living protest against colonialism and all its works, a living symbol that notwithstanding our slave past, we too want a place in the sun, we too belong to the aspirations of the twentieth century.
– Eric Williams, 1960

During the latter months of 1959 and the early part of 1960, the struggle for the return of the base areas leased to the Americans in 1941 reached a new intensity. The issue became the focus of an intense war of nerves between Williams on one side, and the federal, British and American governments and the DLP on the other. To understand the many twists and turns that attended the Chaguaramas issue and the bitterness associated with it, it is necessary to take note of a few antecedent developments. It is relevant to recall that the Federal Capital Site Commission had received representations that Trinidad and Tobago should not be the chosen site of the federal capital because of the presence in Trinidad of elements whose political culture and behaviour could contaminate the politics of the federation, and that the commission recommended that the capital should preferably be located in Barbados or Jamaica.

At a meeting of the Standing Federation Committee held in Jamaica in 1957, Trinidad was nevertheless chosen as the site of the new capital. Williams, it should be noted, took no part in making this decision (Lewis 1991, 10). The final vote on the question was Trinidad, eleven, and Barbados, five. At a subsequent meeting of the committee held in Trinidad in May 1957, it was decided by majority vote that the capital should be in the North West peninsula and that the UK and US governments should be apprised of that decision and urged to meet with a delegation of the committee to discuss the terms and conditions under which the US base would be handed over to the West Indies federal government.

According to Williams, this decision put him in a quandary. The PNM had agreed in its 1956 manifesto to respect international obligations with particular reference to the Anglo-American Bases for Destroyers Deal of 1941. By the same token, a PNM government could not resist its federal colleagues or inflict on the federation a capital site of its own choice (1969, 205). Williams explained his dilemma to the US and UK authorities and secured their agreement that Trinidad's participation in the federal delegation and also in its own right would not be considered a breach of its international obligations. At the meeting, which was held in London in July 1957, the West Indian case was put by the premier of Jamaica, who urged the United States to consider the need to preserve and enhance its good relations with the new state that was in the making. The United States took the position that it could not cede Chaguaramas, and that there was "a conflict over mutual defense interests and our mutual political interests" (ibid., 206).

Williams intervened in the discussions, making use of files that he had previously not seen, which indicated that the then governor of Trinidad and Tobago had strongly opposed the 1941 agreement and that the Trinidad government had not been consulted on the matter. The governor had in fact suggested that the Caroni Swamp be reclaimed and used for the proposed base. Williams also noted that the then American attorney general had indicated to President Roosevelt that the fifty overage destroyers would have fetched only an average price of US$300,000 – US$40,000 of which would have been in respect of the acquisitions in Trinidad. Williams's reaction to this discovery was to say that "no Trinidad representative would have accepted such an arrangement. . . . We never consented to be sold for scrap" (1969, 210).

In his *History of the People of Trinidad and Tobago* (1964a), Williams provided additional documentation on the exchanges and opinions expressed on the merits and demerits of the proposed bases deal. Noted is Roosevelt's view that the United States should steer clear of assuming political control over the identified territories, which he feared might well become a two-million-citizen headache for the United States. As he wrote to Secretary of State Cordell Hull,

> There is always the possibility of their putting up their sovereignty to and over certain colonies, such as Bermuda, the British West Indies, British Honduras and British Guiana. I am not yet clear in my mind, however, as to whether the United States should consider American sovereignty over these islands and their populations and the two mainland colonies as something worthwhile or as a distinct liability. If we can get our naval bases, why, for example, should we buy with them two million headaches, consisting of that number of human beings who would be a definite drag on this country, and who would stir up questions of racial stocks by virtue of their new status as American citizens? (Williams 1964, 267)

Williams noted that the British government and British officials were unhappy about the arrangements, and had put up what resistance they could, which was not much, to American demands that seemed far in excess of what was required for military defence. The British, he noted, agreed with the US position with the greatest reluctance, and only Churchill's personal intervention allowed it to go through.

The British Embassy in Washington sent a memorandum to the US Department of State, urging that

> fullest consideration should be given to the interests and feelings of the local inhabitants, and that the existing administrative and jurisdictional arrangements should only be disturbed if this is really essential for the proper defence of the American bases. While the British authorities are naturally particularly concerned to protect the interests of the local inhabitants for whose welfare they are responsible, it is felt that it is equally to the advantage of the United States authorities to see that the leases are drawn up in such a manner as to reduce to the minimum the possible causes of friction between the various parties concerned. The leases are to run for a period of 99 years, and that being so, it is clearly necessary that their long term effect upon the well being of the local inhabitants should be taken into account. (Ibid., 269)

Churchill felt that if the US demands were excessive, the British government would encounter opposition in colonial legislatures, and would require the British government to override these legislatures – which could well prove difficult to defend in the British Parliament. Churchill was anxious that the agreement appear like one between "friendly powers" and not as if there was a "capitulation".

The Americans, however, argued that the agreement was a fair one from which the territories would ultimately benefit. The American ambassador in London was eloquent and condescending in his assessment of the agreement:

> The Base Agreement has been signed. I think it contains everything we need to use these bases effectively. The rights and powers it conveys are far-reaching, probably more far-reaching than any the British Government has ever given anyone over British territory before. They are not used to giving such concessions and on certain points they have fought every inch of the way. While they have intended all along to give us everything we really needed – they could do no less, and had no desire to do less – it was a real struggle for them to break habits of 300 years. The Prime Minister has been generous throughout. Certain powers, notably those in article XII, are so sweeping that the British would never have granted them except as a natural consequence of the original agreement and the spirit which it embodies. It is important that the agreement be carried out in that spirit. The Colonies have been lightly touched by the war; their point of view is local and their way of life will be greatly changed by the bases. In the main, the changes will benefit them, but it may take them some time to find it out. In the negotiations, both sides have tried to avoid anything which would wall off the bases from the local communities. Our people and theirs are to live together without even a fence, much less a frontier, between them. The character of the men in command of the bases is of tremendous importance, especially in the beginning. If they are the right kind

and ready to carry out our part of the agreement in a friendly and understanding spirit, they can do much to inaugurate 99 years of good neighbourliness. (Ibid., 270–71)

Opposition in Trinidad to the "bases deal" was led by the governor, Sir Hubert Young, who stressed the future importance of Chaguaramas to Port of Spain and suggested that the United States should instead develop an area that would add value to the country's developed assets. He also noted that some of the country's best beaches were to be found in the Chaguaramas peninsula. Young went so far as to journey to Washington to lodge his protest, and to warn of the unavoidable conflicts that would ensue between the US and emergent nationalist forces. The Americans were unimpressed and felt that the indicated site in the Caroni Swamp would take too long to develop and would cost too much.

Williams complained that the Government of Trinidad and Tobago was not consulted on the terms of the agreement, nor on the precise location of the bases. As he noted,

> The Governor and Executive Council of Trinidad and Tobago of that day led the fight against the decision to take over Chaguaramas. The United States was however, inclined to pooh-pooh any suggestions of political difficulties if US soldiers and sailors were dotted all over the island. The Governor complained that the American attitude was all take and no give. The Governor was of the opinion that the United States was seeking not a naval and air base for the United States in a part of the British empire, for the security of which the British Empire was and would remain responsible, so much as a naval, military and air base in an outlying island of the South American continent, for the defence of which the United States Government would assume responsibility and which was to serve if necessary as a jumping-off ground for operations by the United States Army in South America. (1969, 210)

The governor's views were endorsed by the executive council, which also warned of the possible consequences of a lease with a life of ninety-years – close to a century. The governor warned too of the constitutional dimensions of the problem. Might it not conflict with the constitutional reform agenda implied in the Moyne Commission report? The governor warned not only about tying the hands of the then legislature of Trinidad and Tobago, but of future legislatures. "On every point the British Governor was overruled." "The US Government was prepared to exert pressure on the West Indian Governments as well as on the British government. Their attitude indicated that American Service interests were put first, second and last with disregard of West Indian political conditions, constitutions and outlook" (ibid., 211).

Williams suggested that the British prime minister, Winston Churchill, was unhappy with what had been negotiated, and that he might have had the agreement in mind when he stated in his memoirs that his government often did things that were "harsh and painful". As Churchill himself complained, "For the sake of the precise list of instrumentalities [50 destroyers] mentioned, which in our sore need we greatly desire, we are asked to pay undefined concessions in all the islands and places mentioned . . . as may be defined in the judgement of the United States. Your commitment is limited, ours is unlimited." On another occasion, Churchill noted that "deep feelings were aroused in Parliament and the Government at the idea of leasing any part of these historic territories, and if the issue were presented to the British as a naked trading of British possessions for the sake of fifty destroyers, it would certainly have encountered violent opposition" (see E.C. Richardson, "Churchill and the Destroyers", *Trinidad Guardian*, 29 June 1959).

Williams noted that he could not in 1957 and 1958 take positions that were less progressive than those taken by a colonial governor or a British prime minister. He also noted that many of the terms of the lease were obscure and were left hanging because it was impolitic to bring them before the legislative council. They involved matters relating to customs and immigration law as well as matters relating to offences against Trinidad and Tobago law committed by American personnel. "Such legislation has not been implemented out of fear of the wrath of the population of Trinidad and Tobago."

Following the 1957 London conference, Williams proposed in the name of the Trinidad government that the matter be reexamined by a joint commission consisting of the four interested parties – the United Kingdom, the United States, the West Indies federation, and the Trinidad government – to revise the 1941 agreement and to find a new site for the base. The joint commission, which met under the chairmanship of Sir Charles Arden-Clarke, a former governor of Ghana, decided that Chaguaramas was the most suitable site for the base, but its partition was impractical. Williams challenged this decision, claiming that it was in fact made unilaterally by the naval representatives of the UK and US governments and not the full commission. Moreover, it was his understanding that the Report of Joint Commission would be referred to a political conference of the four parties. Instead, the UK government accepted the report. Williams was furious:

> The Commission found five alternate sites. . . . How can you, in spite of these five alternative sites taking different periods of time to develop, costing different sums of money – how can you sit down at somebody's desk and say, "We accept the Report"! What do you accept in the Report? The Report said that you have certain requirements for a base. The Report said that Chaguaramas can meet those requirements. The Report said that there were five alternatives sites which fulfilled or could be made to fulfill these requirements. . . . I am absolutely convinced that the Chaguaramas Joint Commission and in particular the United States Naval Representatives left themselves a line of retreat from Chaguaramas to Irois Bay should it be found necessary for them to vacate Chaguaramas. . . . The Government of Trinidad and Tobago say today it is quite

possible to accommodate the Base at Irois Bay and the Capital at Chaguaramas – far more than to accommodate the Base at Chaguaramas and the Capital at Irois Bay. (1969, 209)

On his return from the London conference, Williams reported to the party on what had happened. As he told the party meeting held on 7 August 1957, "the matter of the Federal capital is settled. . . . If the Federation wants Chaguaramas to be the federal capital, then the capital will be Chaguaramas." He later told the legislative council, borrowing from Churchill, that he did not "have the honour of becoming the Queen's first Chief Minister of Trinidad and Tobago to preside over the perpetuation of colonialism" (ibid., 214).

Some members of the parliamentary opposition objected to the capital being located in Trinidad and Tobago because building it would impose a heavy economic burden on tax payers. It was noted that the commission appointed to consider the cost of building the capital had estimated that it would cost TT$225 million to do so at Irois Bay, and TT$425 million at the Caroni Swamp. The latter exercise would take seven years while the former would take 30 months. Opposition spokesman L.F. Seukeran also criticized Williams for going back on his solemn undertaking to respect an international agreement. Seukeran felt that the value of the destroyers had nothing to do with the matter. What was relevant was the government's word. The fact that Trinidad belonged to the Commonwealth also made it imperative that the government should honour commitments made by the British government on Trinidad's behalf. Williams was disdainful of the stance of the DLP.

The American and British governments declared the issue closed, and the federal government, to the consternation of Williams, agreed with the American proposal to allow the matter to remain where it was "for say ten years". According to Williams, federal prime minister Sir Grantley Adams gave him only a "couple of hours' notice that he had accepted the American assurance that it would review the matter in ten years time. . . . I knew that it was only a question of time before the final nails were driven into the coffin of West Indian nationalism on a federal basis" (*Nation*, 8 October 1965). The federal government later denied that it had agreed to any such proposal. It is clear, nevertheless, that Adams did in fact agree to the ten-year moratorium, but later sought to escape the embarrassing corner in which he found himself. His new proposals were: (a) that the base eventually be handed over for use as the capital; (b) that *three-cornered* talks between the West Indian, US and British governments be called to decide on the timing of the transfer, with the West Indies having the final word. The West Indies, he declared, did not wish to jeopardize the defence systems of the Western world, but as part of that world, it demanded that it be consulted. Adams also agreed that the report of the commission, which ruled out handing over Chaguaramas, was a subcommittee's report and was therefore not binding on the West Indies (Adams to US Consul Orebaugh, *Trinidad Guardian*, 21 March 1959).

Williams never forgave the federal prime minister for what he considered to be an abject betrayal, especially since it was at the request of Adams, Manley and others that he had made his first demand for return of the base. Adams was accused of cutting the ground from under his feet. Williams was also angry that other West Indian governments had not raised their voices in support of Trinidad's fight for Chaguaramas, and accused them of bartering their national souls for a mess of American pottage. As Williams complained, "the support we received from West Indian governments . . . was infinitesimal . . . here and there they sought to bargain support for our stand on Chaguaramas in return for some other concession. . . . Our stand on this matter, as on so many other was no deals" (*Nation*, 8 October 1965). The federal government, he insisted, was nothing but a stooge of the Colonial Office. Instead of carving out a role for itself that would give it dignity, it had simply joined the State Department and the Colonial Office in harassing the Trinidad government. Whinged Williams, "If the Federal government wants to establish rights, it seems to me that it has a lot of foreign governments that it could take a firm attitude to. I'm getting a little tired of all these arrows constantly pointed at the heart of Trinidad" (*Nation*, 6 June 1959).

This view was further strengthened when a visiting US congressman Walter revealed that conversations with Adams and other federal officials had led him to believe that the federal government was opposed to Williams's stand on Chaguaramas. That the federal government did not deny the revelation further incensed the Trinidad premier. Williams also complained about the way in which the British government represented West Indian interests with other countries, and about the way in which it had used the federal government to embarrass the Trinidad government in its dealings with Venezuela and Curaçao on matters relating to Trinidad alone. Williams was especially angry that Britain had done nothing to pressure the Venezuelan government to remove the 30 per cent surtax that had been imposed on goods entering Venezuela from Trinidad, and was annoyed at their failure to prevent the Americans from establishing a missile-tracking station at Chaguaramas. The British government replied that by the terms of the 1941 lease, the Americans needed no permit to establish the station.

It is clear that there was a fundamental difference of opinion between Williams and the Colonial Office as to what Trinidad was "entitled" to claim constitutionally. The Colonial Office held fast to precedent and insisted that, as a colony, Trinidad had no international status and thus could participate in diplomatic negotiations with foreign powers only through British governmental channels or in the presence of British observers. The same held for the federal government, which in Britain's view was not a sovereign power. Williams was impatient with these juridical niceties. Independence was imminent, and the West Indies should be treated with the equality and courtesies that befitted its status. "The only conclusion . . . that can be drawn from the attitude of the Colonial Office is that it does not envisage the early attainment of Independence by the Federation" (*Nation*, 8 October 1963). Either that, or it conceived of independence as a juridical masquerade behind which influence would continue to be maintained.

Williams could not understand why the British government was so stubborn in its refusal to pressure the Americans into sitting down to renegotiate the Chaguaramas lease. Britain was either a "pusillanimous third-rate power" completely under the American thumb, or she had in fact abandoned the West Indies to the American sphere of influence – except insofar as it could be used as a "valuable pawn in British diplomatic moves in other parts of the world" (see Williams 1960b, 13). Britain and the United States were so contemptuous of the West Indies that they believed they could ignore it at will. As Williams repined, "Bad habits die hard; and the long tradition of metropolitan equation of the West Indies with naval bases and military outposts sub-serving metropolitan interests dominates metropolitan attitudes today with respect to the independence of the West Indies" (*Nation*, 8 October 1963).

Williams admitted, however, that the US reluctance to reopen the Chaguaramas issue might have been due to its reluctance to endanger base arrangements in Panama, Guantanamo and other parts of the world. He nevertheless believed that the strategic importance of the base was not as great in the context of changes in military technology and naval warfare as was being claimed. It was a case of malice towards the PNM and contempt for the general population. Even if the base was really needed, the conditions under which it was to be occupied had to be renegotiated with the Trinidad government, which had the right to determine what commitments it would assume in the global nuclear struggle. Capital site or not, Chaguaramas was "the principal hydra-head of colonialism . . . the crux of West Indian Nationalism, the symbol of West Indian Independence" (*Approach*, 1960b, 4).

The "war" for West Indian independence thus had to be waged on three fronts – against the State Department, the Colonial Office and the federal government. The struggle between the Trinidad and federal governments reached a point where verbal communication between West Indian leaders had literally broken down. Williams quite explicitly declared: "We have now reached a stage where we have to examine with utmost care and suspicion, any action that the Federal Government takes or does not take on any issue . . . Trinidad and Tobago is not going to support any West Indian Federal Government which starts off by being the stooge of the Colonial Office" (ibid., 5). Williams saw the federal government as the weakest link in the chain of West Indian independence, as the medium through which foreign influences would seek to operate to keep the West Indies joined to Western economic, political and strategic interests. Such a situation endangered not only the West Indies as a whole, but the PNM in Trinidad as well: "The whole life of the Federal Government was [thus] a conflict between the nationalist West Indian forces, with the PNM in the lead, and foreign influences which sought to control the Federal Government in general, with the specific aim thereby of controlling the PNM. . . . We in the PNM had to fight against this all-pervasive foreign influence" ("Reflections", *Nation*, 8 October 1965). Williams in fact still believed strongly that outside interference was one of the principal reasons for the collapse of the federal experiment.

Stung by Williams's public insults, the prime minister of the federation took to the airwaves to reply in kind to the Trinidad premier, whom he accused of being a "slanderer". Adams denied that the federal government was selling out to US and UK interests, and that it did not wish to have the Trinidad government participate in the discussions about the base. Adams maintained that the position of the federal government was that the West Indies must go to the talks as a single delegation consisting of representatives from all units. The Trinidad government would be free to pursue matters that affected Trinidad alone and would be supported by the federal government. On all other issues the federal government had suggested that there should be cooperation between the two levels of government.

Whatever the justice of this contention, it is clear that the federal government was worried about the strong line that Williams was taking on Chaguaramas. It was inconceivable, declared Adams, than anyone who wished a strong federation should deny the federal government the sole right to deal with external affairs. Adams was of course correct, and Williams was caught on the horns of a dilemma. He wanted a strong federal government, but was not convinced that the existing one had distinguished itself in the cause of West Indian nationalism. It had not defended the Trinidad government in its struggle for constitutional reform or for Chaguaramas. He thus refused to participate in any three-power conference as part of an all–West Indian delegation until the federal government had stated more unequivocally what its stand was on the burning issues of the day. He did not want to find himself saddled with a decision to which the federal government agreed over Trinidad's objections.

In his fanatical hostility to Adams, Williams was thus driven to take stands that conflicted with his basic federalist orientation. He even put himself on record as believing that his government's "procedure was perfectly normal": "It may well have to be one of the principal features of the conduct of foreign relations by a Federal Government where you have an Island Federation stretched over a long expanse of sea, with one particular island having interests in foreign affairs that another island did not have." Williams maintained that the federal government knew nothing of Trinidad's problems, but he refused to permit the federal government to see the relevant files: "The land is our land, and the problem is ours."

But he nevertheless maintained that the action of the Trinidad government in the external sphere would always be subject to the approval of the federal government. Still, Williams was not even sure whether the federal government should attend the conference by right or out of courtesy. He seemed to lean to the view that the role of the federal government should be to speak for other units, and to look for clauses in the agreement that might later tie its hands. At one point, however, he did propose tripartite talks, provided they were preceded by bilateral talks between the US and Trinidad governments; the substance of these talks was to form the basis of Trinidad's position at the conference. The United States refused.

What alienated Williams still further was the reluctance of the federal government to agree to set a date for the achievement of West Indian Independence. As early as November 1958 Williams had decided on a date himself: "The PNM is working for a powerful, healthy, economically viable West Indies, with Independence for Trinidad and Tobago by April 22, 1960 [eleven o'clock in the morning]. We want to be represented, and we want to take our place in the councils of the world" (*Trinidad Guardian*, 26 November 1958). Conservative forces in the Caribbean opposed this on the grounds that too many issues had to be settled *within* the West Indies before independence talks could begin. The small units, for instance, were anxious to know what their fate would be if British subventions to their economies were terminated. It was also felt that the money spent on financing the responsibilities of independence "could usefully be spent on improving the economic conditions of the West Indian people. [The demand] is traceable to overweening political ambitions" (*Trinidad Guardian*, 14 September 1959).

But nationalist forces in Trinidad took a different view. It was necessary to establish firm guideposts and direct one's energies towards their achievement. The terminal colonial period in Trinidad was too full of uncertainties, too open to conflict, too time-wasting. The sooner it was brought to a close, the better for all concerned. Only then could energies be directed towards the building of the "national community". As C.L.R. James complained, "London is still the capital of the West Indies, and, as long as West Indian politicians carry that millstone around their necks, they will never be able to mobilise the full power of the West Indies to meet the grave problems that they have to overcome" (*Nation*, 16 September 1959). Williams was delighted then with James. As he declared, the *Nation* was the "established spearhead of the militant, the textbook of Independence".

If the federal government was not prepared to seek independence at an early date or back Trinidad's demand for Chaguaramas, Trinidad would take matters into its own hands. There was indeed concern that Williams might unilaterally declare independence. Williams also strongly considered breaking with the West Indian Federal Labour Party, which had not supported him in his struggle. He would emancipate the West Indies against its will. This was the prevailing sentiment at the PNM convention that met in March 1960 and made the historic decision to step up the campaign and take to the streets to dramatize its demand for the return of Chaguaramas. The "war-hawks" in the party wanted to march on the United States base, or to assemble a fishing fleet to "invade" Chaguaramas and plant the Trinidad flag. But saner heads warned that the party must avoid any accidents that might result if the march got out of hand. One could not be sure of controlling the politicized masses once they were turned loose.

Williams himself discussed the options, including unilateral declaration of independence, with his mandarins. In the end, he opposed the notion that they should march to the gates of Chaguaramas. As he said in his autobiography, "I had not the slightest intention of proposing any march on Chaguaramas, and the PNM would never have agreed to that; but we saw no reason why we should broadcast that fundamental decision all over the place long before the appointed date" (1969, 227). The convention agreed that the proper thing to do would be to march around the Queen's Park savannah to the US consulate, the legal representative of the American government in Trinidad, and not to the governor general of the federation who was the highest authority representing the British government in the region. The date chosen for the march was 22 April 1960, the day on which Williams had threatened to declare Trinidad and Tobago independent. (April 22 was the anniversary date on which the federation was established in 1958.) Williams was thus about to make good his boast that "the Trinidad flag will fly over Chaguaramas before many of us are many days older". If the Americans refused to renegotiate the agreement, it would be repudiated after independence was achieved. The "War for West Indian Independence" was to be bloodless, however. One had to be careful to avoid the sin of hubris and in so doing invite retribution. Williams's formula was to make a strategic retreat even while pretending to be moving his political troops forward. As he told his followers,

> Ours has been a peaceful and bloodless revolution. Keep it so. But precisely for that reason, it is a revolution that is far more dynamic, far more significant than all the revolutions that have taken place and are taking place in the world today. . . . We have no [physical] weapons, we can't fight any battles, [but] we have the most powerful weapons of all. . . . Our weapons are intellectual and moral arguments, and we will not hesitate to use them. ("From Slavery to Chaguaramas", *Nation*, 20 July 1959)

> Our "base" is the University of Woodford Square, our "army" is the citizen body; their "arms" are the banners proclaiming Independence and their placards denouncing colonialism. . . . The world history of the last ten years is there to

tell us the outcome of this struggle. . . . What counts is power. . . . The British Government has many divisions, but dares not use them. (*Tribune*, Organ of the PNM Legislative Group, vol. 1 & 2, 25)

Williams was determined, however, to show the DLP, the Colonial Office and the State Department – and indeed the rest of the West Indies – that he was not a lonely embittered agitator who had gone too far out on a shaky limb to satisfy a personal and pathological grudge against imagined "devils". Williams denied vigorously that his "struggle" was a personal one. He was "only the mouthpiece of the aspirations of the West Indian people", and in that role, he would fight for a dignified settlement, "with the last ounce of strength in my body. I today have more power in Trinidad and Tobago than any Trinidadian has ever had – any! All of us [in the cabinet] derive our power, the power that we have for good or evil, from people like you here tonight. . . . No power on earth can make a crowd, and a highly politicized crowd cheer and applaud unless it felt an inner compulsion to do so" (1969, 237). C.L.R. James argues that Williams was in fact restraining the party.

The minister of health, Dr Winston Mahabir, also testified to the support that Williams had from his ministerial colleagues:

> Do not for a moment believe that in this issue, the Political Leader has been a lonely genius out on a fragile limb. In the matter of Chaguaramas, he has had the *constant and unanimous support* of his cabinet colleagues. It is true that we shall never be able fully to control his occasional wicked turn of phrase, or to curb his propensity for provocative *picong*. But on the basic principles relating to Chaguaramas, there can be no compromise, and our principles are neither for sale nor for barter. The presence of an American Base on Trinidad soil without Trinidad's consent in an age of independence is a callous anachronism. . . . We are bound to emerge victorious, the victory will include a greater respect by the Americans for us, and a closer friendship than ever before. (*Nation*, 1 April 1960)

The resounding success of the march, despite torrential downpours, established that once and for all. Crowds – estimates of those participating varied from fifteen thousand to thirty-five thousand – marched in the rain to Woodford Square, where the Trinidad flag was raised and "the seven deadly sins" ritualistically consigned to the flames by Williams. The documents burned included the 1941 lease agreement, the 1956 Trinidad constitution, the DLP statement on British Guiana, the Mudie report on the capital site, the telephone ordinance of 1939, and, of course, a copy of the *Trinidad Guardian*. Memoranda were sent to the British as well as the American government, requesting independence, federation, the return of Chaguaramas, and a conference on West Indian bases at which Trinidad was to be represented as an equal principal.

Williams had made his point; the ball was in the court of the Americans. As

C.L.R. James, editor of the *Nation*, commented, "If the Americans are not now able to come to terms with us as to the details of the eventual return of the Base, then you have made it clear that our Independence will restore our rights to do as we please with our territory. . . . Independence is just around the corner. Everybody knows that now. So that one way or another, the eventual return of Chaguaramas is safe." James also warned the Americans that if they did not give up Chaguaramas, "steps would be taken to make life impossible for them there. These steps are legal and constitutional" (*Nation*, 18 April 1960, 50).

The success of the march was eminently satisfying to Williams, for whom it came as a tonic, a purge, a sort of catharsis: "A demonstration such as this is not only a political leap forward, it is also a spiritual purification." Trinidad had at last done something "revolutionary", and had matured under his stimulation. The national community was now in the process of taking shape. The report of the PNM general council to the fifth annual convention in September 1960 boasted, "This demonstration, its magnitude, its orderliness and its tremendous success, both in itself and its purpose, will go down in the history of Trinidad and Tobago and the West Indies as the Great Divide between Colonialism and Independence." So reinforced did Williams feel that he proclaimed Trinidad sovereign and independent, "in fact if not in law". A firm attitude was extended to the federal government as well. When Chaguaramas is returned, Williams noted, if the federal government is still interested in using it for the capital, "they can come in and we will sit down with them and bargain about it". Williams himself sent an ominous message to the Americans when he declared that "with independence, if no agreement is reached, the 1941 agreement lapses" (1960b, 13). He even warned that Trinidad might have to go it alone to independence against its own will.

Conservative forces were alarmed at the new turn of events. The *Guardian*, which again made a pictorial comparison between Williams and Hitler, declared that Williams was pushing at an open door. Williams was accused by Gomes of *caudilloism*, of paranoia, of being so desperate for an election issue that he was ready to destroy the West Indies in the process. "Williams is trying to keep the West Indian revolution alive. . . . He is badly in need of something about which people can get excited. His is the dilemma of every loud-mouthed demagogue during this period of history" (*Trinidad Guardian*, 19 May 1960). Since the West Indian economy did not permit him to take a radical stand on class issues, he found it necessary to create devils by establishing historical lies against colonialism. The politics of heroism required that colonialism be portrayed as an unmixed evil, and that the leader present himself as the symbol of that protest.

Williams argued, quite incorrectly, that it was "we [the PNM] who first started the tradition of West Indian nationalism . . . we who for the first time in West Indian society raised the question of federation meaning the integration of the isolated economies" (*Speech on Independence*, 1962b, 18). West Indian economic integration had, however, been preached since the end of the First World War by several people, including Cipriani. After the Second World War, it was one of the key planks in the platform of the West Indian National Party and the Caribbean Congress of Labour. Williams's contribution to the West Indian national tradition, though substantial, was not as unique as he affected to believe. Indeed, Williams and the PNM were latecomers on the scene of West Indian nationalism.

Leaders of opinion in other parts of the Caribbean often had to remind Williams that Cipriani, Marryshow, Adams and Manley had been preaching nationalism long before he entered political life. Manley himself declared by way of rebuff to Williams that "it is a fact that the West Indies can have Independence as a Federation as soon as the West Indies wishes it. There is no problem about Independence – except the working out of the sort of Federation we want when we get Independence. I do not think there is any point in fixing a date for Independence until we have settled the future of the Federation which is our business" (*Sunday Guardian*, 17 April 1960).

The presence of known Marxists such as Lennox Pierre on the PNM platform also worried conservative forces, who were concerned too about the presence of self-confessed Trotskyite C.L.R. James in the PNM leadership circle. James had returned to Trinidad and Tobago in 1958 as a guest of the federal government and was subsequently made editor of the PNM party organ. The influence of James on Williams was seriously deplored. James did not conceal the fact that he was a Marxist, but denied that he was pushing Williams further than he would normally go. James insisted that he was *following* Williams: "I was aware of a certain tone in the recent speeches of the Doctor; I followed that tone. If the Doctor changes his tone, I shall change mine also." James reminded his critics that he was "not a member of the General Council. I am not a member of any committee. I read the government documents. I listen to the Political Leader and I guide the paper according to these. If I am in a difficulty or I am uncertain, I consult him" (*Nation*, 8 April 1960). But orthodox party cadres were worried. Cabinet ministers were also known to be concerned about the pervasiveness of James's influence over Williams, which they believed threatened their own position. As we shall see, Williams soon came to the conclusion that James was also a threat to his own position. James had seen the Battle for Chaguaramas as "one of the greatest in the history of the West Indies" and was mortified when Williams chose to retreat strategically on issues that he had once considered fundamental. James conceded, however, that the Trinidad population displayed no anti-British or anti-American sentiment whatsoever, or any support for non-alignment during the campaign for Chaguaramas (see James 1980, 412–413).

It is perhaps worth noting here that in Williams's narrative about the American occupation of Chaguaramus between 1941 and 1947, several omissions were deliberate, understandably so given the "war" that he saw himself waging and the evil that he believed he had a historical responsibility to exorcise.

There is, however, another way of scripting the Chaguaramus interlude. It can instead be regarded as a dramatic event that accelerated the social, economic and cultural transformation of the country, a dimension of the nationalisation process that had begun in a serious way in the 1930s with the Butler riots (Ryan 1972a). The presence of thousands of American servicemen, both black and white, in the urban east–west corridor had an explosive impact on the economy and the society in ways that were tangible and intangible. Wage rates shot up in response to the demand for labour in the construction sector, and labour in fact had to be imported from Barbados to fill the gaps that were created in virtually every sector of the economy. Trinidadians never had it so good. Money was no longer a problem. As C.L.R. James himself observed, "Trinidadians freely admitted that [they] had never enjoyed such financial opulence as when the Americans were there during the war" (James 1980, 412–13). In sum, the occupation was not universally regarded by the broad masses as being oppressive. Thus their ambivalence to Williams's campaign.

The occupation helped to democratize the society. It transformed the way in which calypsos were composed and sung; it changed patterns of dress, relationships between worker and boss, between the sexes, which became more commodified and "colour blind", and between the various ethnic groups. When Williams declared "Massa Day Done" in 1961, he could easily have acknowledged that that social death had been effected by the Americans and not by him. What took place in the community was effectively captured by Harvey Neptune in his book *Caliban and the Yankees: Trinidad and the United States Occupation*:

> This sweeping array of change, not surprisingly, sparked a response within the establishment and broadly among those invested in the status quo. Throughout the occupation, Trinidad's white plantocracy, its respectable, Anglocentric types, and more generally, its male population, maneuvered to pre-empt, counter, and manage what they experienced as a period of electrifying disorder. The colony was a veritable theatre of social battle in these years. By the time the dust cleared, the result was indisputable: those groups fighting to turn back the hands of time, to restore the society to its pre-war mores and conditions, ended on the side of futility. . . . Such was the decisiveness of the upheaval that by late 1943, ubiquitous social observer Albert Gomes, could declare that the old Trinidad "will never return". (2007, 10)

 **15 Chaguaramas and the Promised Political Kingdom**

The Chaguaramas issue became inseparably entangled with the constitutional issue that Williams had agitated in 1955 and 1956, as well as with the federal issue. Given the intensity of racial feeling that the federal election had evoked among the population, it was to be expected that any attempt to alter the 1956 constitution would be fiercely opposed by those who stood to lose by the proposed changes. Williams had attacked the constitution as being "bogus and fraudulent", but had promised to work with it until change became feasible. Within a year after he assumed power, however, proposals were submitted to the Colonial Office for reform, the stated aim being to bring Trinidad's constitution into line with constitutions of other units of the federation, mainly Jamaica and Barbados. Proposals were made for the recognition of the conventions of party government in the appointment of the chief minister and his ministers, the introduction of the cabinet system, and the remodelling of the public and police service commissions. By the middle of 1958, however, the Colonial Office had not stated publicly whether it approved or disapproved the submitted proposals.

Williams did not seem anxious to agitate the constitutional issue while the party's affairs at the governmental and party levels were still disordered. But with the budget and the federal elections out of the way, he was ready to force the hand of the Colonial Office. In June 1958, the government brought proposals before the legislature aimed at eliminating the power of the governor and the Crown to disallow laws passed by the people's representatives, insofar as these related to the internal affairs of the colony. Other major requests were for the creation of a Ministry of Home Affairs to control, among others, the police, and for the introduction of cabinet government based on the Westminster model.

These were far-reaching changes, and Williams's opponents believed that he was seeking to consolidate himself as Nkrumah had done in Ghana. Nkrumah was in fact the bogeyman of the Caribbean anti-colonial movement. The government was accused of "stampeding the country into constitutional change" when the Colonial Office had not made up its mind about the initial requests, and of employing "salami tactics" to create a party–police state. The government's failure to ventilate the constitutional issue before it was brought before the House also aroused resentment. It was maintained that the government had a responsibility to take the public and the opposition into its confidence. The DLP argued that it should have been not only consulted, but also invited to participate in discussions with the Colonial Office, since the issue was not purely a party matter.

Williams's claim that Trinidad and Tobago had to keep abreast of constitutional changes in Jamaica was not acceptable to the opposition. Jamaica, they argued, was not the proper yardstick to use. Jamaicans were a homogeneous people; the parties, though highly critical of each other, represented the same ethnic interests, and the constitutional issue could thus be debated without involving ethnic conflict. In a plural society, it was not possible to apply bookish theories about what a democratic constitution ought to be. The problem, however, was that Williams had not conceded that Trinidad and Tobago was unalterably a plural society.

The proposal to remove the police from under the control of an official representing the Colonial Office alarmed the opposition. When this request was conjoined with the demand for a politically appointed attorney general, suspicions were further aroused. The PNM denied that a politically appointed attorney general was part of any plan to establish a police state: "We advocate this because we feel that the Government, as distinct from the Governor, is entitled to have official political advice, not merely legal advice – political advice in a legal sense or legal advice in a political sense. . . . That advice should be available to the party in power and to the Government through a legal man chosen by it, who represents the political views of the party, and can advise on the political issues, or the legal issues involved in the political activities of the Government" (*Nation*, 4 December 1959). The opposition feared, however, that with the power to initiate prosecutions in the hands of a politically appointed justice department, the predominantly black police force would be used against minority groups.

Some of the opposition's fiercest attacks were trained on the government's proposal to remove the Crown and its local representatives from the internal politics of the country. To the "royalist–loyalist" element, this was rank disloyalty and decidedly revolutionary. "The Governor is the symbol of colonialism in this country. Remove him and you remove the first block. We do not want power taken from the hands of the representatives of the Queen and put in the hands of a modern *Fuehrer* in Trinidad and Tobago. We want to save this country from the fate of Haiti, and from what is happening in Ghana." As Lionel Seukeran, the member of the legislative council who argued thusly, had asserted earlier, "We are trying to remain a colonial territory, and we do not intend to take the gates that would lead us to Moscow. We are heading for the gates of London to bring security to the West Indies" (*Trinidad Guardian*, 3 March 1958). If the power to disallow legislation were to be withdrawn, there was nothing to stop the government from passing a punitive bill to deal with its political opponents. Williams was scornful of the opposition, and as he said, "I let them have it":

> If the United Kingdom traditions, one thousand years old, were too much for us to aspire to, what of Malaya, where the traditions were only three weeks old? I place particular emphasis on the provision in the existing constitution which allowed any civil servant who disagreed with his Minister to send a statement in writing to the Executive Council which would dispose of it. I tore up the constitution in their faces. It was a symbolic act. Trinidad and Tobago would proceed under my leadership to full internal self-government in a fully independent Federation. (1969, 169)

Williams's growing intransigence over Chaguaramas also gave rise to additional fears that the PNM was "eastward bound". What would the government do if the United States and the Colonial Office refused to retreat on the bases issue? Would they proceed unilaterally and revoke the treaty, thereby confronting the Crown with open rebellion? Was this not part of a plan to take Trinidad out of the Western defence system? Was the chief minister not being treasonable when he declared that his loyalties were to the people of Trinidad and Tobago, and not to the Crown? Had he not taken a loyalty oath to the Crown? What frightened this element most of all was the threat to the country's economic prosperity. As Neal Fahey, a nominated member of the legislative council and a planter, thundered, "[W]e depend absolutely for our prosperity on the arrangements made with Great Britain in regard to sugar and citrus, and if these powers asking for the severance from the British Empire are obtained, then we would find ourselves in the most miserable position we have ever been in. You will not get any money from abroad" (*Trinidad Guardian*, 14 June 1958).

The European business community was seething with unrest. The Chamber of Commerce complained that the PNM had given scant evidence of its willingness to tolerate opposing views, however well intentioned, and advised the government to pause and review the colony's situation before making further attempts to secure rapid constitutional advancement, lest investors be frightened away. In its haste to establish a "modernized system of party government, the PNM appears to have put on blinkers, and [is] therefore missing or ignoring . . . side issues of varying importance that cannot be and should not be ignored" (*Trinidad Guardian*, 20 March 1959).

The government's reply to the Chamber of Commerce was that its views represented those of a minority; democracy implied that the government should represent the will of the majority. The minister of industry and commerce (himself a successful white businessman) likewise pointed out:

The members of this Chamber are perhaps one of the smallest minority groups in this country, and therefore it could hardly be expected that the Government should express the will of your minority. It may be that the feeling on the part of those members of your Chamber to which you have made reference, derives from a sense of disappointment over the fact that the majority view which the Government is constrained to follow, does not, in all cases, agree with the minority view of the members of your Chamber. (*Trinidad Guardian*, 20 March 1959)

It was this majoritarianism that minority communities in Trinidad found so frustrating; and, interestingly enough, it was on this very issue of democratic majoritarianism that the DLP tried to entrap the government.

Some members of the DLP were beginning to feel that it was politically unwise to make a blanket objection to constitutional reform: agree to change, they argued, but insist that new elections be held before the changes could be introduced. The issue on which they based this new stand was the nominated system. The PNM, they argued, was using "undemocratic" methods to give it the majority position that it did not secure at the polls. As Lionel Seukeran put it, "A prerequisite to cabinet government is to have a fully elected House. . . . The first reform needed in this country is the removal of the nominated element from the single chamber legislature" (*Hansard*, 21 November 1958, 31). It was a clever strategy. The DLP knew that the PNM would be embarrassed by this offer of cooperation to abandon the nominated system, as the PNM itself was pledged to do. The government was urged to go to the country and ask for a mandate to introduce full responsible government. The DLP, buoyed by their success in the federal elections, were confident that they would win a general election if one were called, and their strategy from 1958 onward was to try to get the Colonial Office to help them overthrow the PNM.

Williams agreed that a change of the nominated system was a fundamental issue that would require electoral approval, since it necessarily involved the creation of a second chamber, but he refused to go to the polls until the PNM's promises to the electorate were fulfilled. Nevertheless, the PNM was clearly on the defensive. The changes they were proposing were substantial enough to take to the country. It is true that their manifesto had pledged to introduce internal self-government, but they had also pledged to eliminate the nominated system and introduce a second chamber. What Williams was now proposing was that the Colonial Office institutionalize the precedent established in 1956 whereby the leader of the largest party in the House would have the right to choose a certain number of nominated representatives whom, technically, the governor was still free to appoint in his own right. This was demanded as a safeguard against the possibility that the Colonial Office might reverse its instructions to the governor, who could then nominate non-party people. By the use of such a legalistic *coup,* the Colonial Office, encouraged by the United States, could in fact have brought down the government.

While it is true that the Hindus, the Europeans, the established press and the business community at times assumed an "anti-nationalist" stand that Williams could legitimately describe as "obscurantist, recalcitrant and reactionary", minority groups did have reason to be alienated from the PNM. Williams would certainly have had less difficulty in mobilizing the entire community behind the PNM if its leaders had displayed a greater degree of patience and tolerance, provoked though they admittedly were. But by 1958 Williams had become even more abusive and righteous. He attacked the white creole community when it stopped the PNM's winning streak in municipal elections by winning one of the thirty-two seats. He warned them that "we will be coming for you next time. . . . PNM bulldozers will be digging into the hillsides and God help any minority groups that stand in the way" (*Trinidad Guardian,* 5 November 1958). The DLP's victory, said Williams, posed a fundamental problem for the white community. Were they going to oppose to the bitter end the PNM's inter-racial progressive nationalism, or were they going to accept the invitation to come in as equal citizens?

Williams was galled by the fact that the white upper class had now categorically turned against the PNM. Many of the younger members of the white community who had earlier rebuked their elders for being so resolutely opposed to the PNM had by now gone over into hostile and sullen opposition. Polarization was becoming complete. Many, including PNM partisans, were fearful that if some real effort were not made to adjust group differences, the community would soon be engulfed in serious ethnic strife. Through the medium of the *Nation* (which up to 1958 when C.L.R. James took over as editor was known as *PNM Weekly*), James strove to woo the white community out of its hostility to the PNM. He urged them to view the party in proper historical perspective:

> The PNM is not some monstrous misfortune which has overtaken the unfortunate upper class in Trinidad and Tobago. Something like the PNM was due in Trinidad sooner or later. It is one of the features of modern society. . . . It must be understood that political awakening and party politics came late to Trinidad after years of failure. Twenty years of nationalist and democratic development were accumulated underground in frustration and suppressed anger until it burst out in 1956. It is in full tide; it will not be halted nor diverted into frivolous or dead-end channels by the reckless plots and manoeuvres of political desperadoes. ("Our Upper Classes", *Nation*, 28 February 1959)

James urged the white upper class to detach itself from DLP extremism and participate in the political process in a constructive way. Instead of hoping in silence for a crash that would invite colonialist intervention, he said, they should try to understand that the nationalist movement was going through a necessary phase that had to be accommodated. The upper class should try to provide a sobering influence on the community, rather than pretending "not to notice":

> Frightened by the power of the PNM, and with an instinctive repulsion from its mass support, disappointed that the DLP has not developed into the conservative opposition that they hoped for, they think or behave as if they have no interest in politics. . . . In the perpetual lies and scandals with which the opposition press bombards the PNM, your voice is silent. No elder statesman, no prominent industrialist, no distinguished social figure, no member of an old and well established family . . . raises a single word in protest. . . . Is all of Trinidad, which has what is called a stake in the country, so sunk in cynicism, in mean self-interest, in indifference to the public weal, in this stupid belief that "anything goes" if the PNM is somehow defeated? Do they believe if this happens, the good old days will return? ("The New Desperadoes", *Nation*, 22 May 1959)

James, however, understood the reason for the frustration and desperation that had overtaken the Indians and the white upper class. The activities of the opposition were not all due to spite, obscurantism, malice and recalcitrance. Fear, mistrust and reciprocal hostility were basics of the unfurling oppositionist drama. As James would concede in 1965, when he too was in opposition to Williams and the PNM, there were many racial fanatics in the PNM, "chiefly some leaders and a portion of the rank and file, the lowest gangster types whom the gangster leaders have miseducated" (1965, 7).

The Cabinet Crisis

The Colonial Office went a long way towards meeting Williams's demands on the constitution. Cabinet government and most of the conventions associated with it were conceded. The Colonial Office had not, however, made up its mind about the request for the transfer of the police; nor did it agree to take away altogether the power of the governor to withhold his assent to legislation. The governor was to be advised that henceforth this power was to be used only on advice from the Crown, whose power to legislate by order-in-council was left intact. The constitutional arrangements were scheduled to take effect in June 1959. Williams decided at the very last minute, however, that he would not accept cabinet government without control of the police.

The Colonial Office had given the DLP firm guarantees that it would not agree to Williams's request for the appointment of a ninth minister to control the police. Williams took the view that there was no reason why the police should not be transferred. For the Colonial Office to withhold this was to say, in effect, that the police had no confidence in the PNM. As he declared, "The Colonial Office would not want to be in a position to say that it would give control of the police to Bustamante and the JLP and will deny it to Williams and the PNM. They could not say it. . . . Trinidad is not British Guiana. Trinidad is not tainted with any dangerous ideology. . . . Law and order are the last bastions of colonialism and it is necessary for the PNM to control it" (*Nation*, 10 July 1959). In reply to the DLP observation that Trinidad was not Jamaica, he noted that control of the police had been handed over to elected ministers in multiracial Malaya and Singapore.

Williams's extreme and uncompromising anti-colonialism drove Gomes, who was at one time one of the stoutest opponents of colonialism, to assume the role of defender of imperialist intervention:

> There are times when the popular will can be so egregiously wrong as to justify redressive intervention by the extraneous authority. . . . PNM has compromised itself and the popular movement in the West Indies. It has established the need for continuing the presence of the British Government in the West Indies. Opposition movements in particular have to thank their stars that they still have the parental shelter of the British authority to whom to look in their hour of travail. (*Trinidad Guardian*, 1 April 1959)

Williams was insistent, however, that control over the police was a non-negotiable demand, a deal breaker, and he cancelled planned celebrations to mark the inauguration of Cabinet Day, scheduled for 26 June 1959. The Colonial Office responded by sending Julian Amery, the undersecretary of state in the Colonial Office, to Trinidad. Williams told Amery that he would not discuss Chaguaramas on any terms while the constitution issue remained unsettled. "When he settled the issue . . . I let him have my views" (*Nation*, 8 October 1965).

There was yet another dimension to the Cabinet Day issue. Winston Mahabir tells us what happened:

> It was April 1958. Cabinet Government for Trinidad and Tobago was about to be "granted" with fanfare and trumpets. Last-minute hitch! Ian McLeod, the Secretary of State for the Colonies, is playing the ass! He refuses to give us control of the police! Urgent telegrams back and forth. O.K., we say. No control of police, no Cabinet Government. McLeod decides to send Julien [*sic*] Amery to Trinidad for an on-the-spot report. Williams in turn will turn on the heat. What kind of heat? A new and dangerous kind! He announced in highly dramatic fashion that he had substantial evidence of radiation being used by the Americans at Chaguaramas. I was on the platform and did not know whether to laugh at him or cry for the gullible crowd which was being ultra-violated. (1978, 83)

The British government sent an expert to investigate the claim. He found that the only radiation at the base was electromagnetic and non-nuclear. He also concluded that there was no danger to either US or Trinidad personnel. Patrick Solomon, however, was of the view that the Americans had dismantled the equipment that was causing the problem before Dr Evans arrived.

By calling off the Cabinet Day celebrations, Williams had forced the hand of the Colonial Office, which was becoming aware of the massive popular backing that the PNM could mobilize on almost any issue. DLP members were encouraged to endorse the police transfer in return for a firm promise that the Colonial Office would insist on an independent boundary commission before the next general election. The hand of the Colonial Office was also in part forced by the fact that the governor, "the man on the spot", had admitted that there was no reason why the police should not be transferred. With the governor giving the PNM full support on most of the issues that arose during the period, the DLP had little hope of outmanoeuvring the PNM. The DLP, betrayed and outfoxed, could do no more than accept the assurances of the Colonial Office that there were still enough existing safeguards to prevent the PNM from misusing its newly gained prerogatives. Once the Colonial Office decided to concede, the DLP, which never functioned as a cohesive unit, showed itself completely bankrupt.

The Colonial Office had in fact already agreed in principle to transfer the police but had hoped to extract some concessions from the PNM on Chaguaramas. But the chief minister was not in a compromising mood. As Williams stated, "I was not going to sacrifice my fundamental principles for a little power. The fundamental purposes were to eliminate the influence of Downing Street from the politics of the country and to get the Americans out of Chaguaramas" (*Trinidad Guardian*, 22 July 1959).

On another occasion, Williams signalled that he would not be seduced by offers of money, much as he needed funds to effect his development programme. "I want everybody to know that the Government of the PNM of which I have the honour to be the leader, is not at any time going to be bought for $766,000 or for that matter $760 million. I am afraid the issues involved are worth far more than a few thousand dollars" (*Nation*, 8 July 1959). Williams made it clear that full independence was now the goal of the PNM. "Cabinet Government and the Premiership are . . . but additional instruments for the constitutional but relentless achievement of this aim." He deliberately threw down the gauntlet to the DLP. The central issue was treasonable colonialism or independence with dignity: "The only alternative to the road to Independence is the road back to colonialism . . . the issue has nothing to do with race at all, though race might complicate the objective social, political, and economic issues that are involved." And the road to independence lay through Chaguaramas!

Reflecting later on Amery's visit, Williams had the following to say:

> Amery was as rude as possible. He saw the Chief Minister only after he had seen the Chief Secretary and the Commissioner of Police. We had decided we were not backing down. So I did not spare him. I accused him of using the constitution reform issue as blackmail on the Chaguaramas issue, where we had recently been led to suspect that radiation was involved, and I declined to argue the matter. I stood on my rights. He

went around meeting people, including members of the opposition, and eventually capitulated. I promptly went to the University of Woodford Square to report to the people on July 31st. I said in part: "There was a crisis, ladies and gentlemen, true enough. The central issue had nothing to do with police, it had nothing to do with elections, it had nothing to do with the Police Force, it had nothing to do with the ninth Minister, it had nothing to do with dictatorship. The central issue in the crisis was Chaguaramas (loud applause)." It was a great triumph for us. The Party and the population stood firm, shoulder to shoulder with the Government. (1969, 170)

Chaguaramas had now become the central issue in the political struggle between the parties. To Williams and James, the reluctance of the Americans and the British to sit down and renegotiate the bases agreement was symbolic of an unwillingness to recognize that Trinidad in 1959 was vastly different from Trinidad in 1941. As James phrased it, "What hangs in the balance is whether this territory must submit to a new colonialism just at the time when it is making every effort to free itself from the old" (*Nation*, 8 August 1959). The struggle was being waged not only on behalf of Trinidad alone, but for the West Indies as a whole. "Trinidad, as the 'spinal cord' of the West Indian national movement, is going to lead in giving the West Indies some conception of dignity, some conception of importance, some conception of self-reliance as the PNM has given to Trinidad and Tobago" (*Nation*, 8 August 1959).

Constitutional Imbroglio 1959–60

The country was given little time to digest the constitutional changes that had recently been introduced. In keeping with its promise that proposals for future constitutional changes would first be subjected to public and bipartisan parliamentary scrutiny, the government appointed the Select Committee on Constitutional Reform in June 1959 and invited the public to submit memoranda on the question of political reform. The PNM's new proposals were far-reaching. The most controversial demands were for a bicameral system, for a redrawing of the electoral boundaries to permit an increase of six seats in the legislature, and the appointment of a West Indian governor on the advice of the cabinet. The most crucial demand of all was that a two-thirds majority of the Lower House be given the power to amend the constitution.

The DLP, strangely enough, refused to submit a prepared memorandum, and it was difficult for the public to know what specific proposals (if any) they had on the question of reform. This irresponsibility was compounded by the decision of the party to boycott the debate on the committee's report because of the government's unreasonable refusal to allow the opposition the freedom to choose its own delegation to the Colonial Office. The PNM took the view that if the DLP was not sufficiently alert to its proper role as a responsible opposition, it should not expect the government to treat it as such. The DLP had forfeited the right to name its delegates. The *Guardian* correctly took the opposite view. A tutelary government had a responsibility not only to govern, but also to ensure that a responsible opposition was cultivated: "However ineffective the present Legislative Opposition, the correct procedure should at all times be followed if the Government is sincere in its desire to encourage the development of a functioning two-party system. The very weakness of the present Opposition furnishes grounds for special care in observing all the conventions of parliamentary usage" (*Trinidad Guardian*, 10 October 1959).

The position of the DLP became clear at the negotiations in London. They strongly opposed the proposal to alter the electoral boundaries on the ground that it was a palpable attempt on the part of the ruling party to obtain a virtual one-party system by electoral gerrymander. The PNM, it was argued, had seen the voting trends in the 1958 federal and 1959 county council elections, and were seeking to carve out new constituencies that would entrench them indefinitely. Maraj warned that any such manoeuvre would lead inevitably to national convulsions. If the boundaries had to be redrawn, an independent commission, recruited from either the United Kingdom or the United Nations, must be assigned the task.

Williams flatly opposed the idea of an independent boundary commission, whether externally or internally recruited. This was a chance that the PNM could not afford to take. To accept this was to commit political suicide, though Williams could not phrase the issue in these terms. Instead he noted that it would be difficult to get independent men, and that deadlock might arise between principals on the acceptability of nominees. A crisis might also arise if one party refused to accept the decision of the commission. The government would accept nothing less than the method used in Jamaica – a select committee of the legislature with the Speaker as chairman. For the Colonial Office to refuse this was to declare that it had no confidence in the government elected by the people. Or so Williams argued.

The demand for a locally appointed governor was also bitterly opposed. The DLP had been extremely unhappy with Sir Edward Beetham, who, generally speaking, tended to sympathize with nationalist forces. Apart from his apprehensions about punitive taxation of the oil industry, and the PNM's "extremism" on Chaguaramas, Beetham had few difficulties with his cabinet. The farewell address made by the premier to Beetham testifies to the warmth of the relations between them. Beetham was later to take up an ambassadorial position with the Trinidad government. He also became a director of one of the Trinidad-based oil companies (*Trinidad Guardian*, 10 March 1959).

Beetham was, however, a nightmare to the DLP. By refusing to intervene against the PNM, he "was out of harmony with the rights and prerogatives he enjoys by provision of the Constitution". The governor was not yet a "constitutional monarch", as Beetham seemed to imagine. If a Crown-appointed governor was so partial to the PNM, the situation could only worsen if the PNM were given the right to name the next governor. But Williams was determined to make the governor a constitutional monarch who would act only on the advice of his ministers. Williams had no patience with legal niceties about the differences between the roles of the heads of state in dependent and independent territories. As far as he was concerned, a Crown-appointed governor no longer had the right or authority to speak on behalf of the West Indian people.

The request to allow the legislature to amend the constitution by a two-thirds majority in the Lower House was greeted with a storm of objections from opposition elements who claimed that if this recommendation were accepted, there was nothing to prevent a party commanding such a majority from amending the constitution as it wished. The proposed second chamber also provoked a great deal of controversy. The DLP denounced the second chamber idea as being "reactionary and unprogressive", and as a "departure from one of the avowed purposes for which the Federation was established, the reduction of the size and cost of the apparatus of Government in the territories" (*Trinidad Guardian*, 12 November 1959). A senate nominated in the manner proposed by the PNM would almost certainly become a means whereby the ruling party would be able to endow certain of its supporters with the elegant trappings of high political office, while remaining mere puppets of its overriding control and authority. This was a valid observation, since the PNM had altered its basic position on the manner in which senators were to be chosen. In Williams's 1955–56 constitutional proposals, senators were to be appointed by vested interests. In the proposals that Williams put on the table, the senate of eighteen was to be nominated by the governor on the advice of the premier, though seven were to come from the economic and religious interests in the community.

Interestingly enough, the Colonial Office initially came out in support of the DLP on the senate idea. The PNM was aghast. Williams let it be known that if vested interests, to whom the concession was principally directed, did not want the second chamber, he would not "stick his neck out" to force the hand of the Colonial Office. He also expressed dissatisfaction with the fact that vested interests had retreated into silence even though the government had appealed to them to speak out on national issues. The *Guardian* was, however, quite just when it maintained that the "silence and cringing aloofness of the Chamber and other responsible organizations and individuals" was due to fear (*Trinidad Guardian*, 23 September 1959). The premier had shown himself so intolerant of views that from his perspective seemed "anti-national" that many who would normally have voiced a critical opinion had retreated into fearful silence. As an economic interest group, the Chamber of Commerce was reluctant to go on record on any issue with which it was in fundamental disagreement with the PNM.

These issues were ventilated during a constitutional conference held in London, which lasted from 27 October to 25 November 1959. The government's delegation was led by Patrick Solomon, and included Ellis Clarke, W.J. Alexander and Arnold Thomasos. The DLP delegation was led by Lionel Seukeran, and included Albert Gomes and Stephen Maharaj. Tubal Uriah Butler represented the Butler Party.

The colonial secretary, Ian McLeod, reiterated the view that some of the demands being made by the PNM were fundamental and should only be incorporated in a new constitution after they were ventilated in a general election. This was also the view of the DLP, which argued that changes in the number of constituencies should be made by a neutral and independent boundaries commission and that the new boundaries should await the 1966 elections. The DLP in fact argued that there should be no constitutional changes until the issues were fully ventilated in the 1961 elections. The party that emerged victorious in that election would determine what proposed changes would be on the negotiation table.

Interestingly, Solomon believed that McLeod had agreed to all the PNM's proposals and informed Williams that this was the case, leading the DLP to accuse McLeod of duplicity. Embarrassed, McLeod felt driven to write to Solomon accusing him of misrepresenting what had been agreed to. As he wrote to Solomon on 25 November,

> We are now for the first time considering a constitution giving Trinidad and Tobago full internal self-Government, and as I emphasized at the beginning of our talks, this aim is not in dispute. The parts in dispute, principally the creation of a Senate, are an issue between political parties as to what form the advance should take, and not between any or all of them on the one hand, and Her Majesty's Government on the other. I am willing to accept either a bi-cameral or unicameral legislature, which ever is endorsed by the electorate. It is therefore a local, political party issue in which it would be quite wrong for me to take sides.
>
> If the constitution were to be generally accepted by the political parties in Trinidad, no problem would arise. If on the other hand, the constitution is not generally accepted either in whole or in part, then their differences must inevitably become an issue at the general election. I do not see how it could be considered compatible with democratic procedure to insist on the introduction of a constitution after the general election, if the electorate had decided in favour of those who oppose it.
>
> So long as parts of the constitution are in dispute between the political parties in Trinidad and involve a general election there is always a possibility that the electorate may decide against the party which supports the present proposal. It is clear to me that in the context of full internal self-Government in which we all agree, the only democratic course is to provide for this emergency. I see no way of doing so other than the one described above. (Solomon 1981, 167–68)

Solomon flew home to get further instructions from Williams, leaving Thomasos and Clarke behind. He never returned, because the government chose to break off the negotiations. Williams decided that "if McLeod had anything to say, he would have to come to Trinidad to say it". Williams was fed up with the to-ing and fro-ing with the Colonial Office. The next round would have to be settled in Trinidad (1981, 169).

The constitutional issue dragged on for the remaining months of 1959 and into 1960. Neither party budged from its basic position. The leader of the DLP maintained that had it "not been for the special circumstances which exist in the country today, we . . . would surely be further on the road to Independence", and further stated,

> The actions of the Government over the last three years . . . could not possibly inspire confidence. We have witnessed the Government's high-handed dealings with statutory boards and local bodies; their infiltration of the Civil Service; their tampering with the trade unions; their litigation with the Telephone Company; their intemperate attacks on individuals and concerns whose only fault would seem to be in their own power and prestige which they now enjoy. It would seem that the Government does not like opposition whether from political parties or from individual persons, and that they are determined to destroy every possible centre of opposition and resistance. We have registered increasingly that there exists in all of this a sinister pattern from which there emerges only the desire for power and more power, irrespective of any other consideration, even of the strangling economy of the country; and we have reluctantly, for some time now, come to the sad and unavoidable conclusion that in all of this there is a dictatorship in the making, and conditions are coming about in which freedom will not flourish. We stand by our declaration that there must be a general election before effect is given to reforms. (*Trinidad Guardian*, 2 December 1959)

The Colonial Office urged both parties to accept a compromise. The DLP was urged to agree to the proposed increase of seats, the new boundaries to be determined by an independent boundary commission. The Colonial Office, as we have seen, advised the PNM that it should be left to whichever party formed the government after the election to determine whether to accept fully or partially, or indeed reject, the constitutional changes to which the colonial secretary had agreed in principle. This gambit was extremely clever. It seemed a perfectly democratic and fair issue on which to take a stand: "No reforms before the people have spoken." McLeod was either gambling that Williams would accept, and perhaps lose the election, or refuse, thereby making it possible to hold up further reforms indefinitely. The PNM was trapped because it did not feel confident enough to call a snap election.

Williams maintained that the people did not want an election at this time, and that given the tension in the country, elections would only lead to violence. The country had already witnessed three elections in a short space of time (1956, 1958, 1959). Another election would only disrupt the government's development programme. He denied, however, that the PNM was afraid of being rejected at the polls. But as we shall argue later on, Williams was anticipating a very close battle with the DLP. Williams dispatched a strong letter to the colonial secretary, whom he accused of conspiring to bring down his government, asserting,

> Your proposition will only strengthen the prevailing impression, nurtured by the "crisis" which attended the inauguration of the Cabinet system, that every effort is being made to force upon us at all costs an election at the earliest possible moment, to give the Opposition an election issue, and to set back the movement for self-government to the degree that it is associated with the PNM. The proposition can serve only to maintain the suzerainty of the Colonial Office with all the restrictions therein entailed on colonial emancipation and colonial development. You will appreciate that this is a situation which cannot be allowed to continue. (*Nation*, 18 December 1959)

There was no need for an election to decide the issue of bicameralism, added Williams, since the electorate had endorsed it in 1956. This was a rather weak claim to make, since Williams was prepared earlier to abandon the second chamber that he had insisted was a "gratuitous concession" to the vested interests. Moreover, the type of senate now being advocated, along with some of the other recommendations relating to the size of the chamber, was quite different from that proposed in the Williams petition on constitutional reform.

In the 1955 proposals, the emphasis was on representativeness. Now the concern was with political stability. Williams had come to understand the importance of this consideration, since the matter had generated a great deal of confusion when appointments to the federal senate were being made in 1958. On that occasion, the governor general and the premier of Jamaica had fundamental differences of opinion as to who should be appointed, and on whose advice the appointments should be made.

Williams also recalled how important the nominated element had been in 1956 when he needed the support of at least two of them to enable him to form his government. As Ghany notes, "Whereas his 1955 proposals were somewhat idealistic, those in 1958 reflected the ideas of a man who knew the importance of ensuring a government majority at all times in a nominated House. This could be combined with a judicious use of political patronage which would ensure the entrenchment of the PNM as a major political force in Trinidad and Tobago" (1999, 116). The Colonial Office at times gave the impression that it was sympathetic to the DLP's opposition to bicameralism. The available evidence indicates that the Colonial Office was open-minded about the options and would have preferred both sides to reach a compromise on the matter. As it turned out, it was the PNM and the Colonial Office that, unknown to the DLP, had reached a compromise on the issue. In a briefing paper entitled "General Tactics", the Colonial Office advised undersecretary of state Julian Amery as follows:

> . . . the unexpected breaking off of the talks by the Government meant that we never reached the stage of telling the Opposition officially how far the proposals had been modified in discussion with the Government. We gave them some broad hints, and their ignorance of how far the original proposals had been modified may have been more apparent than real; but to some extent the Opposition may still at the end have been opposing proposals which, unknown to them, no longer held the field. (As cited in Ghany 1999, 125–26)

The briefing paper went on to note:

> At the time the talks were suspended, it had been agreed with the Government delegation that the Senate should be co-terminous with the Lower House and its membership as follows:
> 12 members appointed on the advice of the Premier;
> 2 on the advice of the Leader of the Opposition; and
> 7 after consultation with the Premier to represent the main religious and business interests (it being understood that the Governor would be free to consult with others as well as the Premier regarding these appointments). (Ibid., 126)

Reflecting on this briefing paper, Ghany concludes that both the PNM and the Colonial Office had shifted their positions on the bicameral issue (ibid., 126–27).

The McLeod Formula

The colonial secretary, Ian McLeod, visited Trinidad and Tobago in June 1960 and brokered a settlement of all the outstanding constitutional issues as well as matters relating to the federation and Chaguaramas. Williams seemed to believe that McLeod's visit and capitulation was a result of the success of the march that he had organized in support of the return of Chaguaramas. He boasted,

> After our famous April 22 march from Chaguaramas, the Secretary of State decided that since Mahomet would not come to the mountain, the mountain must perforce come to Mahomet. He decided to visit Trinidad himself in June 1960. We met, discussed pleasantly, settled all outstanding problems in one or two sittings of a few hours, and Trinidad and Tobago had its full internal self-government with a bicameral legislature which came into effect after the General Elections on December 4, 1961. (1969, 172)

It is possible that McLeod's visit was a response to the suggestion made by the governor general of the federation that such an unprecedented gesture would be welcome as well as being good tactically. Williams would himself argue that McLeod's visit had little to do with the constitution or with Chaguaramas and was in fact prompted by Britain's wish to hurry the Caribbean to independence.

Williams had been told as much by Winston Mahabir, whom he had sent to London to get a feel for McLeod's position. As Mahabir reported,

> There was no serious battle against McLeod and Britain for independence of Trinidad and Tobago. This was the essence of the detailed message I sent to Williams after my long, enlightening meeting with McLeod in England. McLeod was about to visit Trinidad personally, the first Secretary of State for the Colonies to do so while still in office. McLeod assured me that there was no impediment to independence. My letter to Williams paved the way for a different reception of McLeod than might otherwise have occurred if Williams had continued to harbour suspicions of resistance. When I returned to Trinidad, Williams greeted me with a warmth reminiscent of our earlier friendship. "That letter," he said. "That letter."
>
> As a footnote I would add that when I asked McLeod where in the spectrum of political ideology he would place the PNM, he replied, "In the right wing of the British Conservative Party!" (1978, 86)

The McLeod formula for constitutional reform can be described briefly. The new constitution, which was to come into effect after the elections of 1961, provided for a senate of twenty-one members of which twelve were to be appointed on the advice of the government, two on the advice of the opposition, and seven by the governor in consultation with vested interests. The senate was to be given the power to delay for a year all bills save those deemed to be money bills. A cabinet of twelve ministers, a politically appointed attorney general, and a solicitor general to advise the governor were also conceded. The colonial secretary did not, however, agree that the new legislature should be given full sovereignty. The power to amend the constitution was still reserved to the Crown and its agents, as was the right to withhold assent to legislation that appeared to be inconsistent with the constitution, Her Majesty's international obligations or royal prerogatives. The notion of an independent boundary commission was abandoned, much to the consternation of the DLP. But despite all constitutional niceties, the arrangement meant that for most purposes Trinidad would become internally self-governing in 1961.

Ellis Clarke as attorney general played a crucial role in negotiating and sorting out the differences between Williams, the governor and the Colonial Office. As Clarke's biographer, Timothy Seigler, observed, "The providential collaboration of Williams's scholarship and charisma and the legal expertise of Clarke, would direct the destiny of Trinidad and Tobago." As Seigler further noted, "Attorney General Clarke assisted the Governor in drafting the telegram that went to London, helping them to assess the situation. The moderate loyalist Clarke saw the inevitability of such a transfer of power and brought reason to the decision-making process. Police powers, with his help, were eventually transferred to the administration of PNM ministers" (2001, 46).

The fact that the British government had already become committed to independence for the West Indies did not of course mean that it was not concerned about the outcome of the Chaguaramas or the constitutional issues. McLeod had tied the constitutional settlement to a "deal" on the Chaguaramas and federation issues, even though he denied that he had done so. "There was no bargaining; Chaguaramas in no way, directly or indirectly, came into these constitutional discussions" (*Trinidad Guardian*, 19 June 1960). But it can be reasonably surmised that McLeod's concessions were designed to disarm Williams and to persuade him to refrain from publicly criticizing Jamaica's decision to hold a referendum to determine whether or not the Jamaican people wanted to continue in the federation. Williams was bitterly opposed to Jamaica's being allowed to hold this referendum. It was clearly unconstitutional, as British authorities have since admitted. McLeod had also blundered into making it known that no sanctions would be imposed on Jamaica if she left the federation. He must have feared that, if Williams spoke out against the right of Jamaicans to vote on the issue, it would only serve to weaken Manley's chances at the polls. Williams confessed, "I intended to attack the [referendum] decision, but was persuaded not to do so by the Secretary of State" (Mordecai 1968, 236).

It is also evident that McLeod wanted to induce Williams to take a moderate stand on Chaguaramas. As Sir John Mordecai, former deputy governor general of the federation, noted, "McLeod adroitly ordered his programme, making a virtue of necessity in his first move. . . . Advanced securement of Williams' good graces [on the constitutional issue] served well the major purpose of McLeod's visit – to get agreement upon a means of settling the Chaguaramas issue" (ibid., 227). The DLP were the net losers in the negotiations; but short of threatening physical resistance, the DLP could do little to force the combined hands of the PNM and the Colonial Office. The leader of the DLP insisted that he had little choice since it was obvious that the Colonial Office was prepared to dictate a solution. The PNM, he notes, had convinced the Colonial Office that the DLP was not a viable party to which power could be entrusted.

Williams was ecstatic over his victory. In a speech full of messianic symbolism, he told his followers that they "can now see the promised political kingdom". As far as he was concerned, Trinidad was free to pursue its own career in the international sphere: "Regardless of British reserve powers, arrangements are going to be made in the field of external relations involving the full and direct participation of the representatives of Trinidad and Tobago." To underline his determination, an office was established in London to "promote the financial and economic independence of Trinidad and Tobago" (*Nation*, 11 July 1960). Williams also began negotiations with the World Bank for a loan for the expansion of the island's electricity network. The agreement, when concluded, was formally endorsed by the British government.

But Williams also sought to reassure those who were still watching apprehensively. He not only reassured his hearers that Trinidad would not seek independence alone as he had once indicated it would do, but also promised that independence, when it came, would not mean that Trinidad would follow the path chosen by some new states: "We have seen that the coming of Independence sometimes results in the weakening of democracy. I am confident that we can avoid that." Williams's statement on the question of independence alone is worth noting for its irony and historical significance:

> The very fact that considerations of this sort [going it alone] could, in 1960, be allowed to become fundamental political issues is an indication of the heritage left behind by colonialism, the parochial outlook, the inadequate preparation for self-government, the ignorance of our historical past, the congenital inability to see beyond the confines of our own puny territories, the obsession with ancient traditions of West Indian glory and importance. Everywhere the movement is towards unity and away from division; everywhere save in the West Indies. We in Trinidad and Tobago will be reducing ourselves to this lower political West Indian level if we too should try to talk of going it alone. (*Nation*, 1 July 1960)

16 Slavery to Chaguaramas

I shall break Chaguaramas or it will break me.
– Eric Williams

During the agitation over Chaguaramas, a number of extreme statements had been made by nationalist spokesmen, which had led many to believe that the position of the PNM was that the Americans must withdraw from Trinidad completely. As Williams had himself asserted, "Every West Indian island has been a base at some time or another. The development of every West Indian island has been subordinated for four and a half centuries to the strategic and military considerations of Europe. It is time to finish up with that sort of thing and allow us to live our lives in peace" ("The Road to Independence", *Nation*, 24 July 1959). But the substantive position of the party as approved in convention was much more moderate. The proposals made to the Americans as early as 1959 included the following requests: (1) that they give up such portions of the leased area as were not being utilized for defence purposes to permit the beginning of construction work on the federal capital; (2) that they indicate when they proposed to leave Chaguaramas – the departure date to be no later than 1967, ten years after the first request for Chaguaramas had been made; (3) that if a base were still needed in Trinidad, it should be built at Irois Bay, the Chaguaramas area being too vital to the economic and recreational needs of the community to permit its continued alienation; (4) that the United States make "reparations" for the contribution that Trinidad and Tobago had been forced to make towards American defence during the past eighteen years (suggested compensation included the construction of a college of arts and sciences at the university, with a suitably endowed library, the building of a jet runway at Piarco airport, and the training of local military and technical personnel on the base); and (5) that the base should be operated jointly by the governments of Trinidad and the United States.

Nationalists were concerned about the amount of arable land that was tied up in the agreement with the United States, land that was known to be suited to the growing of citrus, cocoa, green beans and tobacco. The agreement also tied up some of the island's best beaches and deep-water harbours – harbours that were said to be necessary for the expansion of the current overused docking facilities. The contribution that the United States presence was making to the economy was not considered large enough to offset these handicaps, since most of the material consumed from the base was imported from the United States without reference to local customs authorities.

Williams repeatedly stated that his stand was not based on anti-Americanism, but on principles. The continued presence of the United States in Trinidad was something that had to be negotiated between the two countries. For Williams, the fact that Trinidad was not legally independent was irrelevant. What was important was the right to have some say as to whether bases were to be on Trinidadian soil, what power or powers should possess them, their location, and the conditions relating to their establishment and operation. It appears that the Americans had indicated their willingness in 1959 to sit down and bargain on these terms; however, for reasons that are not clear but which seem to do with conflicts between the Trinidad and federal governments, with the internal political struggle, and with American uncertainty about what sort of deal could be extracted from the PNM, the plans for the meeting collapsed.

Beetham, McLeod, Williams and Chaguaramas

The Chaguaramas controversy imposed strains on the normally cordial relations between Williams and the governor, Sir Edward Beetham. At the height of the crisis, Williams wrote Beetham telling him that "on this matter of Chaguaramas, you and I, Governor and Premier, are on opposite sides". As he later said: "He and I had worked reasonably well together for over three years. But I was fed up with the shilly-shallying and the bad faith that had been demonstrated for many weary months" (1969, 227). Beetham was not aware that Williams did not intend to lead a march to the base. Williams complained that the governor was taking his instructions from the Colonial Office and not from the premier, and resented Beetham's attempts to interfere in decisions that as far as Williams was concerned were "party decisions". Acting in response to concerns expressed by the American consul general about what could happen if Williams led a march to Chaguaramas, Beetham wrote Williams seeking assurances. Williams "let him have it". Reports in circulation said that the Americans were giving thought to destabilizing Williams's regime.

As we have seen, the visit to Trinidad and Tobago in 1960 by Colonial Secretary Ian McLeod reflected the fact that the Colonial Office was becoming more and more concerned that the crisis in the West Indies was delaying the granting of independence. It had now become clear that the constitutional and Chaguaramas issues had to be settled and that British intervention was necessary to help West Indian politicians compromise on the outstanding issues in the protracted federal negotiations. McLeod in fact disclosed that West Indian independence had been conceded by Britain for the past two years, and that provision in the parliamentary timetable had even been made for it. The West Indies were told to "hurry up" and take the freedom that was there for the asking. Britain needed "no lecturing on the issue"; she was prepared to admit the West Indies to the Commonwealth and to sponsor her in the councils of the world.

It was felt at the time that McLeod made this statement to save the face of the Colonial Office and steal the thunder of the PNM. Williams was in fact somewhat ambivalent in his explanation of the "capitulation" of the Colonial Office. His first impulse was to credit Britain's new *démarche* to the 22 April demonstration. "Our tremendous . . . demonstration . . . made it impossible to deny the PNM's claims for renegotiation of the Treaty, and it laid the foundations for West Indian nationhood." Williams desperately wanted to claim that he had forced the British and the Americans to capitulate. But he hastened to concede that the capitulation was "in theory, if not in practice, for by April 22, 1960 the British Government . . . was more anxious than the federal politicians to give the West Indies Independence. They wanted to join the ECM [European Common Market], and one essential step . . . was to rid themselves of the West Indian millstones. So McLeod . . . came down to settle outstanding issues with the PNM, to concede full internal self-government, and to urge West Indian slackers: "Hurry on to independence" ("Reflections", *Nation,* 15 October 1965).

The premier of Jamaica, Norman Manley, conceded that it was only timidity that was preventing the West Indies from gaining its independence. "The British Government is not withholding self-government from the West Indies. We can have [it] whenever we ask for it" (as cited in Mordecai 1968, 237). This was true, but Britain was anxious to ensure that, while rid of her Caribbean burden, her strategic and economic interests in the area were nevertheless well served. Williams was made to fight for every concession that was finally made, though the Colonial Office was not unaware of the basic orthodoxy of the PNM.

Britain's offer of freedom, however, was still conditional. Independence was to be granted subject to the provision that "the essentials of sovereignty were satisfied". This was interpreted by some to mean that an independent West Indies would have to cut its ties with the British treasury as well. McLeod had earlier promised that Britain "recognises that the West Indies may not be able to assume the whole weight of the financial burdens which would normally fall to an independent member", but he had also added, "*if this proves to be so,* HMG will . . . consider . . . ways in which help might be given over a transitional period" (ibid.; emphasis added).

For many, this assurance was not "hard" enough. It left a way out for Britain to claim, *after* independence was granted, that the West Indies was better equipped to deal with problems of independence than many other independent countries. This argument was in fact made during subsequent negotiations (ibid.). Grantley Adams put his finger on the essential problem confronting the West Indian nationalist movement when he noted that the West Indies feared to seek independence because in London political independence was interpreted to mean economic independence as well. This was the core of the difficulty between Trinidad and the rest of the West Indies.

Williams believed that Trinidad was reasonably well off and could afford to take a tough stand against diplomacy by bribery. Many Trinidadians did not agree, however, that Trinidad could afford to turn its back on financial bribes from the United States and United Kingdom governments. The plantocracy and the *Guardian* were especially sensitive to the vulnerability of the dependent Trinidad economy. But nationalist forces refused to accept any bribes. Williams noted that the secretary of state had said to him, "If you want Independence, you must have economic independence, you must pay for it." Williams's reply was, "Fine. We don't want a penny from you. We are not getting any grants from you. We'll pay for our development ourselves. . . . We must be free to make mistakes. We may make mistakes in 1956 but we will not make them in 1960, and in the history of self-government 10 years is a very short time in the life of a country." ("From Slavery to Chaguaramas", *Nation*, 20 July 1959). Jamaica up to 1959 had received about WI$45 million from colonial welfare and development grants, whereas Trinidad had received only WI$7 million. Williams sought to convince West Indian leaders that what they would lose in colonial subventions when the West Indies became independent, they would receive from the Commonwealth or from other developed countries.

Jamaica and the rest of the West Indies were not prepared to risk any cuts in aid. The issue was not treason or colonialism at all, but a crisis of confidence. Chaguaramas was not worth the sacrifice to those who thought in terms of welfare rather than status. Williams, however, had the vision to see that the two things were not necessarily alternatives. The West Indies should struggle to obtain both dignity and economic aid out of the bases issue as other nations like the Philippines and Morocco were doing. And in the course of that struggle, he had made his voice, and Trinidad's, the strongest and most respected in the Caribbean area.[1]

By the end of 1960 all parties had agreed on an acceptable compromise. Formally, the talks were still to be "tripartite", that is, the United States, the United Kingdom and the federal government would be the principals at the final stage of the negotiations, but the Americans agreed to negotiate first with the government of each territory on which there were installations. Indeed it was at this stage that the material decisions were taken. The United States set aside its earlier stand that it would not negotiate with non-sovereign powers. The leader of the United States delegation, John Hay Whitney, asserted that, "The United States Government was conscious of the aspirations of West Indians who were taking the road to freedom which Americans themselves took not long ago, and wished therefore to conclude agreements conforming and contributing to those aspirations and acceptable to the people and their political representatives" (*Trinidad Guardian*, 6 December 1960). It was a rather belated recognition, encouraged by diplomatic assurances that the PNM was not committed to neutralism or American withdrawal. Moreover, the Americans were obviously becoming more and more embarrassed at having to "bear the ugly image of an unwelcome giant straddling the front garden of a small, poor country" (Mordecai 1968, 190).

At the negotiations held in Tobago, Williams argued that Trinidad had contributed freely to the preservation of the American way of life, and that in the new agreement, the United States should undertake to contribute to the preservation of the Trinidadian way of life. Williams was explicit about his primary motivations in respect of the negotiations. As he declared, Trinidad went to the conference with the problem of the economic needs of Trinidad and Tobago dominant (*Trinidad Guardian*, 17 December 1960). At the Tobago meeting, five projects were proposed:

1. The construction of an alternative road from Diego Martin to Chaguaramas to ease existing congestion which would obviously be enormously aggravated in time of emergency if the base were to be called upon to perform the functions for which its retention was requested by the United States Government.

2. The reclamation of the Cocorite Swamp as an integral part of the new road to Chaguaramas, which would incidentally make available a large area of land for low cost and middle class housing for the benefit of the people of Trinidad and Tobago.

3. The improvement of the port facilities in Port of Spain, not only to assist the Territory, but also as an insurance in the event of war in the light of the experience in 1941 when the port was almost entirely taken over for United States military purposes.

4. The rehabilitation of the Trinidad Government Railway which had been taken over by the military authorities in 1941, which would serve conceivably a similarly valuable purpose in the event of another emergency, and whose notorious deficits originated with American control during the Second World War.

5. The establishment of a College of Arts with an excellent library endowed with a collection of *Americana* as the most appropriate contribution that

America could make to Trinidad and Tobago and which Trinidad and Tobago would always want to associate with America.

The delegation also raised the question of a sugar quota for Trinidad and Tobago in the United States market, on the principle that America cannot be the military friend and the economic enemy of Trinidad and Tobago.

Back-channel negotiations played a critical role in facilitating the post-Tobago negotiations. J. O'Neil Lewis recalled the following incident involving Williams and President John F. Kennedy:

> After we became independent we had no money, and this became known. President Kennedy sent a man called Prowler Hamilton to see Dr. Williams at the Hague. Prowler Hamilton had been a very distinguished lawyer and had been the Head of the US Aid Agency, and he met with Dr. Williams one Saturday morning. I remember that I was there because he said that on these visits that I should take the notes. We [later] met the late Richard Alexander, who said, "Well, Mr. Prime Minister, President Kennedy has asked me to come to see you." He told Prowler, "if it is the last thing you do, for heavens sake, go and see that man Eric Williams and try to settle the Chaguaramas business." So I have come Mr. Prime Minister to see what I could do to settle. He said, "Well Mr. Hamilton, I am glad to see you, but that is one way of dealing with the matter. You think that you could just say get out and forget all about your obligations? Your Government has had this country for a long time." He said: "I didn't mean to get out. I mean I have come to negotiate. And in fact the negotiations were finalized in London, I think in the following year." (Lewis 1991)

Kennedy also sent Williams a gift on the occasion of Trinidad's achievement of independence, which was in his baggage as he travelled to Berne. Much to Williams's consternation, the bag containing the gift was misplaced – there were thirty-two other pieces. Lewis and Williams's bodyguard, Constable Bridgeman, searched for the missing gift in vain. It turned up three months later. Kennedy, who had only recently had to deal with the Bay of Pigs and the crisis relating to the Soviet attempt to deploy nuclear weapons in Cuba, was anxious to ensure that Trinidad remained firmly in the Western camp and that the naval facilities at Chaguaramas were readily accessible to the US navy.

Only a broad description of the settlement can be attempted here. By the terms of the accord, the United States agreed to release unconditionally most of the unused land surrounding the base at Chaguaramas and other locations in the northwest peninsula, and to release all lands outside of that peninsula. Certain parts of the base area were to be used jointly by United States and local defence and security forces. Facilities were also to be made available for the training of local personnel in certain technical and military fields. The United States was, however, allowed to retain its facilities at Chaguaramas until 1977, though provision was made for review in 1968, and at five-year intervals thereafter, to determine whether modifications to the lease were necessary. Withdrawal in 1977 was not automatic, however; it was contingent upon the state of global tension. This meant that the demand for Chaguaramas as the site of the federal capital was to all intents and purposes dropped. In return for Trinidad's agreement to a partnership role in the defence of the hemisphere, the US delegation agreed to recommend American participation in the improvement of the country's port, road, airport and railway facilities, and to participate in the construction of an arts and sciences faculty at the Trinidad branch of the University of the West Indies. According to Williams, the conference almost broke down over the question of the proportion of the costs that would be borne by the two parties on all the projects. The US spokesmen wanted Trinidad to pick up the local costs and to make the US contributions subject to the availability of US funds and Trinidad's national income. Williams was bitterly opposed to these proposals. As Williams told the Americans,

> Our Government considers this to be a matter of fundamental principle, on which it will not be possible to compromise, the population of Trinidad and Tobago would find it difficult to understand such an interpretation of the Tobago Agreement. Eventually the Cuban missile crisis intervened and the problem had not been solved. I was in London at the time, and I made it clear in a press conference that the Chaguaramas question was a domestic issue which I did not wish to get embroiled in extraneous considerations. Shortly after, President Kennedy sent a special emissary to me in London to make an offer of US$30 million – $51 million of our currency. I accepted. (Williams 1969)

Though the premier later admitted that the British government forced him to compromise on "important issues", he affected to be "extremely pleased" with the settlement. He had gone into the conference determined that any new agreement must recognize the fundamental political fact that the political situation in Trinidad and Tobago in 1960 was quite different from the one existing in 1941, and this he had forced both the United States and British governments to acknowledge. Both governments had, for practical purposes, recognized the "independence" of Trinidad and the West Indies. In the words of Ambassador Whitney,

> Your period of transition has served its purpose. The mantle of Independence is justified by the progress which you have made. We have great expectations of the role which a politically stable independent West Indies can play in world affairs. We want that kind of neighbour on our doorstep, using its helpful influence also in affairs of this hemisphere. If there was any doubt of our interest in West Indian Independence, our presence here today should dispel it. We have concluded this venture in what has been called "anticipatory diplomacy" dealing with a nation as though it were fully independent. We hope it is soon. (*Trinidad Guardian*, 11 February 1961)

Early in 1961, British prime minister Harold Macmillan visited Trinidad, which he referred to as the "Athens of the Caribbean", and again urged West Indians to "hurry to independence". His remarks on Trinidad were especially flattering to Williams:

> Though one of the youngest legislatures in the Commonwealth, I feel at once the strength of your parliamentary traditions. . . . We in Britain recognize how deeply you treasure the traditions and safeguards which are of such vital importance in the world if democracy is to survive. . . . The negotiation of this Agreement was an act of real statesmanship. By it you made solemn recognition of the responsibility which you will soon assume in international affairs. . . . You are not without material resources. You have greater moral and intellectual resources than many countries already playing a role in world affairs. You have powerful friends. Now that your moment of decision [to enter federation] is upon you, you must not fail the outside world. (*Nation*, 31 March 1961)

For Williams this aspect of the negotiations was perhaps worth most, since he must have felt at the time that, in terms of material gain, the agreement left much to be desired. Only about US$30 million were involved, in addition to any funds already spent in connection with the construction projects included in the Tobago Agreement. Williams was not entirely happy about the settlement. As he said much later, "The arrangement is a reasonable one. I had certain reservations but [agreed to it] in the interest of a general settlement. . . . By and large, however, it is quite satisfactory" (*Trinidad Guardian*, 30 November 1962).

The DLP argued that the settlement did not represent any considerable advance over offers the Americans had made in 1954 to 1956, and was much less than the PNM had led its followers to expect. The DLP also claimed that the premier had done exactly what they had suggested in 1957–58. He had made Chaguaramas pay for the economic development of Trinidad and Tobago. What was once attacked as neocolonialism was now being accepted enthusiastically by anti-colonialist forces. DLP politicians dismissed the whole settlement as nothing more than a desperate electioneering manoeuvre.

Most PNM supporters did not agree that the settlement was of the same nature as that urged by conservative forces. They noted that even though conservative elements initially might have been disposed to revision, they had given no support whatsoever to PNM demands after 1957. Either their national feeling had been slumbering after 1957, or it had been deliberately sacrificed for the "greater good" of discrediting the PNM and its leader. And it is true that established elements behaved as though it was sheer impudence on the part of Williams to demand that the Americans leave Chaguaramas once they had indicated their unwillingness to do so in 1957. Williams was quite fair when he accused the established press of being ready to "hang" him "for treason against the U.S. government" ("Reflections", *Nation*, 15 October 1965).

PNM supporters also noted that it was only in 1960 that the DLP had shifted away from the stand that the Americans should be left alone. DLP politicians might have been predisposed to negotiation on Chaguaramas, but in their desire to break the PNM they had taken stands that, in effect, would have allowed the Americans to stay under the terms imposed in 1941. The difference between the two parties on the issue was essentially one of temper. The DLP was prepared to accept dictation from the State Department and the Colonial Office. Williams was not. He would "break Chaguaramas" or Chaguaramus would break him. It was a fight to the finish.

Although most people in the PNM seemed gratified with the agreement, a sizeable number were vocally dissatisfied. They complained bitterly that Williams had conceded more than the party had agreed to in convention, that he had sacrificed the left in the party at the virtual dictation of the State Department. Even more shocking to them were the statements concerning foreign policy commitments that Williams and Manley made after the signing of the agreement. Both men had put themselves on record as being "with the West". Manley observed that Chaguaramas posed the question "What role would the West Indies play as an independent nation?". His personal conviction was that "we have done wisely . . . in deciding that neutrality serves no purpose" (*Trinidad Guardian*, 11 February 1961). Williams was even more expressive:

> Trinidad and Tobago are not immune from those subversive tactics, rooted in treachery and intrigue, which seek to duplicate in the West Indies situations that have developed elsewhere. . . . We face a recrudescence, as exasperating as it is unnecessary, of that disruption of our lives by tensions imported from outside which have weighed on the entire Caribbean for over four and a half centuries. So long as I and my colleagues, both Government and Party, have any responsibility for the affairs of Trinidad and Tobago, and through it, of the Federation, we shall continue to work for the achievement and maintenance of a stable democratic society which, insofar as there is any curtain dividing the world, is, as I have more than once unequivocally stated, . . . West of that curtain, and not East of it. . . . I am for the West Indies taking their place in the Western Hemisphere and for membership in the Organization of American States, without any loosening of ties with the Commonwealth. (Ibid.)

Left-wing forces, most notably C.L.R. James and Winston Mahabir, were chagrined by the direction in which the party was now moving. As Mahabir publicly stated,

> Trinidad and the West Indies had compromised their independence by entering into such an agreement. What would the leaders of the West Indies tell Ghana, India, and the rest of the Afro-Asian neutralist bloc? Why should West Indian delegates agree to tie the hands of the future independent West Indian Government, which might have different views on foreign policy? Moreover, the Party had never been given the opportu-

nity to discuss the whole question of alliances. Williams was arrogating to himself the right to make Party policy in this field.

Radical West Indian intellectuals were also vocally annoyed at what they were convinced was a palpable "sell-out". It was aid with strings.

But by agreeing to respect the bases agreement in their manifesto in 1956, the party had in fact declared for the West. It was also not the first occasion on which Williams had publicly declared Trinidad on the side of the West. He had done so in a speech in May 1960. Following that particular speech, a US official remarked that "the Speech marked Williams' break with James. After that speech, we knew we could do business with him" (as cited in Oxaal 1968, 134). Throughout 1961, Williams continued to signal that it was "Westward Ho" for Trinidad and Tobago.

At a party convention in September 1961, Williams listed communism as one of the five dangers facing the PNM, the others being racialism, reversion to colonialism, unemployment, and trimmers and wagon-riders. Communism was singled out because of the disruptive effect it has on economic planning and development. He cited the case of Venezuela, "where serious planning for the reorganization of the society has become virtually impossible because of the permanent uncertainty and constant disorder". Williams, it should be noted, had at first welcomed Castro's takeover of Cuba and some of his nationalization measures. When he met Castro in 1959, he declared that he sensed that he was meeting "in the flesh the centuries-old frustration of the Cuban people for autonomy and democracy. . . . Castro's revolution brings one step nearer the realization of the old dream of a Caribbean Confederation and also the goal of the ownership of the West Indies by the West Indian people themselves" (*Nation*, 8 May 1959).

Williams was determined to avoid the entanglement of the West Indies in Cold War disputes, though he admitted that he tried without much success to get Nkrumah and Nehru to give him support. He felt proud, however, that he had achieved a "decisive victory" by settling the Chaguaramas issue without bringing it into "the entanglement of the cold wars in the outside world" (*Nation*, 28 January 1966).

The intemperate language used in public by Williams to excoriate his critics was indicative of the private needling he was receiving from elements within his circle of advisers. Williams may have sought to whip up a public scare about communist infiltration to cover up his capitulation, but he was also genuinely seeking to disabuse the population of the myth of West Indian exceptionalism. He observed on one occasion, "Let us above all not be deluded into the smug complacency that it cannot happen here. There are communist parties in Martinique and Guadeloupe, not far away from us. Communist sympathizers are associated with other West Indian territories. We have some in our midst, and like elsewhere, they seek to infiltrate our trade-union movement." Williams lashed out mercilessly at the "comsymps", who he claimed were trying to lead him along the path that the Fidelistas had taken:

> Chaguaramas is becoming involved in a mess of intrigue. Communists and fellow travellers wanted me to pull their chestnuts out of the fire. I am not going to do it. If anybody tries to mess up this Chaguaramas issue as they are trying to do now, God help them when I talk publicly. . . . If anybody tries to interfere with the national interest for the sake of pursuing a vendetta against me, or his hostility to the PNM, I am going to be sorry for that man. Anything short of crucifixion, that is what I promise. And I am not making any joke about it. The nation's interest comes first. (*Trinidad Guardian*, 11 February 1961)

While there were a few Marxists in Trinidad, there was no real evidence to give rise to fears of a communist coup. The West Indian Independence Party was quiet, and, as its leader Lennox Pierre declared, the party had no plans for building membership. "We are waiting to see what develops. Independence will be the time for considering whether the territory wants a socialist party" (*Trinidad Guardian*, 1 October 1961). But fears of communist infiltration were being vocally expressed in 1961, and security forces were requested to search files and offices of trade unions and suspected individuals.

Though Williams was deeply concerned about events in Cuba, the man he was most worried about was his erstwhile friend and confidant, C.L.R. James. James denied that he was plotting any coup, but it is well known that he was chagrined about the rightward thrust of the PNM in 1960, and that he was trying to build up internal support to force Williams and the party to "go forward". Williams was apprehensive that James might attempt to split the party and also that he might expose many of the confidences they shared.

It is clear that James was the "Mr X" who, according to Williams, opposed the compromise because he "wanted to be Political Adviser to the West Indian Prime Minister" ("Reflections", *Nation*, 15 October 1965). Among those familiar with what was taking place, there was a strong suspicion that the Americans demanded James's "scalp" as part of the Chaguaramas settlement. There were other understandings, it is clear, that were not made public at the time. It appears, for example, that the Americans agreed to help the government to obtain loan and investment capital for its islandwide sewerage and electrification projects, both of which were considered crucial for the winning of the 1961 elections. If James constituted an obstacle to the "national interest", as it was now being defined, he had to go. James insisted, however, that Williams had taken the wrong fork in the historical road and that his decision would have fatal consequences for the region. As he told Jamaicans,

It is my firm conviction that if the West Indian politicians had put forward to the West Indian people a programme, or even a perspective, of economic development and made the people the centre of what they were thinking and doing, Mr. Manley would have won the referendum and the general election. If the premier of Trinidad and Tobago had not sold out over Chaguaramas, if he had kept to the widely publicized aims of his campaign, his voice would have been the most powerful in the West Indies for a Federation. Tens of thousands in every island would have poured out to see and hear and welcome the West Indian politician who had fought and won against the all-powerful Americans. (*Federation: We Failed Miserably,* 1961, 10)

Winston Mahabir believed that some of Williams's remarks also referred to him, and warned the country that freedom to think and to voice contrary ideas had to be protected against those who believed that party unity was more important than anything else. But such discontents and warnings were lost on the general population, for whom there was no doubt that "the courageous Doctor" had scored a smashing triumph over the *Guardian,* the DLP, and the American colossus, and had taught Trinidadians how to be independent in spirit and in fact, if not in law. He had brought them pottage, but without any loss of national dignity. As Lynn Beckles, a leading party member, phrased it, "What made Trinidadians – and in fact all West Indians – so happy was the fact that the chief mover in this whole issue, could, with such skill, utilize local sentiments within the prescribed limits, and in a comparatively short space of time, steer the West Indies to a point so eminently satisfying to national pride" (*Nation,* 21 April 1961).

Writing in *Inward Hunger,* seven years later, Williams had the following to say:

It became fashionable in certain quarters – particularly by James, former editor of our party weekly – to criticize me and our delegation for agreeing to the continued tenure of Chaguaramas for seventeen years. I acted on the instinct that the Americans did not want Chaguaramas at all, not even for seventeen months; what they were concerned with, in my opinion, was in not supplying ammunition for the Panama Canal and the Cubans in Guantanamo Bay. My instinct proved to be sound. Before even the first period of review arrived in 1968, the Americans decided to leave the greater part of Chaguaramas, retaining only the Missile Tracking Station and a new navigational station. The evacuation began on July 1st, 1966, and a large area was returned to us in a simple ceremony on June 9th, 1967. (1968, 244)

This did not mean of course that the struggle had not been worthwhile, and that the "victories", such as they were, were not of heroic proportions. They were milestones on the path to independence and self-determination.

17 The Federal Collapse
"An Absolute Blessing in Disguise"

The federal constitution agreed upon in February 1956 had been a temporary settlement. The key issues that had never been satisfactorily settled were the sources of revenue for the federal government, freedom of movement of people and goods, and the question of the division of responsibility for the economic development of the units of federation. A conference to review the constitutional document was expected to take place sometime in 1961 or 1962. The decision to convene the meeting in 1959 grew out of party and island competition within the federal parliament during its first session, and out of a general sense of frustration about the limitations of a constitution that had left a variety of discretionary powers to the Crown-appointed governor general, and that had provided for revenues which were grossly inadequate to meet the needs of the federal government.

This unexpected development met with Williams's approval. Williams had always complained that the federal constitution was totally unrealistic in light of the needs of the West Indies. His position, one that had been articulated in earlier statements that he prepared prior to entering the political arena, was enunciated in a radical document put out by the premier's office entitled *The Economics of Nationhood:*

> The . . . economics of nationhood . . . in the West Indies demands a Government absolutely and completely independent. A Federal Government, in attempting the profoundly difficult task of laying the foundation of a national economy, must have complete command of all its material and other resources, including its perspective for the future. . . .
>
> These islands have a long history of insularity, even of isolation, rooted in the historical development of their economy and trade and the difficulties of communications for centuries. No amount of subjective, that is to say historical, cultural or other activity of the time can be expected to overcome this heritage. Only a powerful and centrally directed economic co-ordination and interdependence can create the true foundations of a nation. Barbados will not unify with St. Kitts, or Trinidad with British Guiana,

or Jamaica with Antigua. They will be knit together only through their common allegiance to a central government. Anything else will discredit the conception of Federation, and in the end leave the islands more divided than before. (1959, 3)

Williams's argument was that the poor showing of the federal government was in part due to the straitjacketed system of fixed grants from unit governments for which the 1956 constitution had provided. He thus proposed that the federal government must be given sole power to raise external loans as well as extensive revenue-raising authority. "An independent West Indies [Government] will be considered credit-worthy by foreign investors . . . only if it has large independent sources of revenue. The Federal government must also be given the main responsibility for central banking and the manipulation of finances to counteract economic fluctuations. This power could not possibly be exercised properly unless the central government had flexible taxation powers." In fact, what Williams was proposing was that the central government be given the power to "impose any kind of tax" in the interest of economic rationality and equality. *The Economics of Nationhood* declared quite bluntly:

[The] rationale of Federation [does not] lie in the opportunity it provides for the "better off" members of the Federation to narrow the gap between themselves and the "better off" countries outside the Federation. To argue that the "better off" territories within the Federation must be aided to get still "better off" so that they will, eventually, be better able to assist their weaker brethren is to ignore the harsh fact that, meanwhile, the gap will be growing steadily wider; so that, the longer the delay, the greater the amount of assistance that will be needed. (Ibid., 10)

Only by the equalizing principle could the federal government inhibit excessive migration from the poorer to the better-off units, migration that would bleed the small units of their skilled and semi-skilled personnel, thereby rendering more difficult the cost and problems of future development. The absorption of migrants would also prove to be an expensive undertaking. "In their own interests, the 'better off' territories would wish to do all in their power to ensure for their 'poorer' brethren immediate and adequate assistance. One way of ensuring this would be to accept the principle of equalization as the basis of distribution of development funds" (ibid., 11).

The Economics of Nationhood embodied a new and radical Hamiltonian approach to the question of West Indian nationhood. It broke decisively with the earlier tradition of federation as a mere instrument of administrative rationalization and cooperation in defence and external affairs, which had been endorsed by the British and other West Indian governments. Williams placed the *people* of the West Indies at the core of his thinking. The West Indian people interacting with a dynamic central government would be the bedrock on which federation would succeed. Only a perspective such as that embodied in *The Economics of Nationhood* was adequate to stimulate the idealism and dynamism that would be needed to overcome the disunity and insularity inherited from colonialism:

> We are confident that given a clear and elevated perspective, the people will guarantee the success of what is proposed here by their readiness to double their efforts, their willing patience under the inevitable difficulties of readjustment, and the sacrifices of immediate needs for ultimate aims which will periodically be needed. In this atmosphere, with the further stimulus created by freedom of movement, we can confidently expect an increase in social discipline, an outburst of creative activity directed to the improvement of the economy, and a general increase in the productivity of labour which will be one of the most powerful forces working towards the raising of the material standards and cultural levels of the new West Indies nation. The concept of nationhood and the national economy can do this. Nothing else can. (Ibid., 6)

The Economics of Nationhood was the most explosive document that had so far been injected into the federal debate. The Jamaicans reacted to it as if it were a red flag waved in front of a maddened bull. The premier of Jamaica dismissed it as "childish"; so too did the DLP and the British government, which feared that by demanding a "classical" federation, Williams was destroying the chances of any kind of federation at all. Indeed, the DLP believed that Williams's advocacy of a federation with a strong centre was clearly intended to destroy the union and pave the way for independent statehood for Trinidad and Tobago. This was far from the case.

To understand the hostile reaction that *The Economics of Nationhood* created, it is necessary to relate briefly what had happened in Jamaica since the federation had come into effect. Before the crystallization of federation, there was a fairly widespread belief throughout the West Indies that federalism was the only instrument through which independence and economic viability could be achieved. After the federation was inaugurated, a number of factors led to the re-examination of this assumption and to the strengthening of the anti-federal sentiment that had always been latent in Jamaica. That the federal capital was situated in Trinidad represented the first serious challenge to the ascendancy that Jamaicans had always assumed. Of even greater importance was the fact that the new federal government was controlled not by Jamaicans, but by politicians from the eastern Caribbean. The prime minister, Grantley Adams, was a Barbadian. Manley and Bustamante, for reasons having to do with the exigencies of local politics, had both chosen to remain in Jamaica rather than go to far-off Port of Spain, with the inevitable consequence that as far as Jamaica was concerned, there was no transfer of loyalty to the federal government; for them it would always remain something alien and potentially mischievous.

These two factors alone would have been sufficient to generate tensions that could have endangered federation. Jamaican pride and apprehensions were further provoked by the extremely ill-advised remark made by the federal prime minister in mid-1958 that the federal government needed the power to impose taxation on income and profits, and that it might do so in future with retroactive effect. In retrospect, it is fair to say that *this* statement was the most damaging blow that had been delivered to the fledgling union. Williams compounded the difficulty by opposing the establishment of a proposed TT$25 million oil refinery in Jamaica because of the negative impact that it was likely to have on the oil industry in Trinidad and Tobago. The Jamaicans took the view that the economic advantages that would accrue to Jamaica outweighed any foreseeable adverse effects on the existing industry in Trinidad and Tobago.

A land-acquisition ordinance passed by the federal government in 1958 also intensified fears about federation:

> The realization that the Federal Government was a separate entity which might do things that would affect Jamaica was a shocking experience for a large number of Jamaicans. . . . Until the Federal Parliament was actually functioning, very few Jamaicans had paid any attention to the . . . meaning of federation . . . outside of the small circle of those involved directly or indirectly in the making of government policy. . . . Until . . . the reference to retroactive taxation . . . the firm assumption [was] that nothing in Jamaica's position would be changed. (Springer 1962, 20)

Keen political rivalry between two evenly matched political parties, and an imminent election, made it almost inevitable that politicians would compete fiercely to defend the "Jamaica first" principle. It was the Jamaica Labour Party under Bustamante's leadership that seized the initiative and began a systematic policy of manipulating the insular nationalism that had been awakened in the 1930s. The party went on record as being in opposition to any revision of the constitution that would give the federal government the power to impose retroactive taxation or interfere with the tax or tariff structure of the units without their consent. It also raised the demand for representation by population, which so far had not been applied in the division of elective seats at the federal level. Bustamante also made it clear that he would never accept the principle that Jamaica should subsidize the poorer units.

All this took place before the end of 1958, and it was into this atmosphere that the Trinidad document was thrown. Manley, who had always been an ardent federalist, found himself on the defensive both in the country and within his party, which had always harboured a powerful anti-federal wing. When the review conference assembled in 1959, it was clear to almost everyone that Jamaica had to be placated at all costs if she was to be persuaded to remain in the federation. Manley admitted that Jamaica had much to gain from federation. Although

Jamaica could become a dominion by itself, it would not enjoy the same inter-national status as would a united West Indian nation. From an economic point of view, a united West Indies would also prove more attractive to investors and loan agencies and would be able to bargain more effectively in the trade marts of the world. It would also be more economical to administer public services for a pop-ulation of 3 million than one of 1.5 million.

Manley insisted, however, that the West Indies should seek to enjoy these advantages within a confederal framework. Jamaica had certain unique economic problems that made it absolutely necessary that she retain maximum freedom to control the direction of her own economic development:

> The beginning of Federation has coincided almost with the climax of the combina-tion of activities which have been undertaken by Jamaica with a view to a transition to a higher level of economy. . . . For this reason, the Federation must proceed more slowly than other Federations in the past. Jamaica has the highest percentage of unem-ployment of any country in the West Indies [18 percent for males and 38 percent for females in 1961]. . . . Consequently, there is no part of the West Indies in which any disruption of the forward progress would be more damaging and disastrous . . . to the whole future of Federation. (As cited in Springer 1962, 25–26)

Manley did not agree with Williams's argument that the poorer units should be developed industrially *pari passu* with Trinidad and Jamaica. He felt that these islands should concentrate on agriculture, since industrial development would yield only marginal returns. It was also clear that, unlike Trinidad, Jamaica believed it had less to gain from developing the economies of the eastern Caribbean, since Trinidad and not Jamaica would have to bear the brunt of pop-ulation movements from these islands.

The 1959 conference was a dismal failure; it settled nothing and had to be adjourned prematurely. Confusion and frustration developed over the formula for parliamentary representation, over the timing of independence, over the question of finance, and over the terms of reference of committees that were to report back to the conference at a later date. As Williams observed in his *Report on the Inter-Governmental Conference* (1961, 12), "Behind the turmoil . . . lay the uncom-promising assertion of Trinidad and Tobago of the two fundamental West Indian truths of economic integration and Dominion Status as against the position of Jamaica that [was] neither truly Federation nor truly Confederation." Williams would later concede that he had never expected that the acceptance of *The Economics of Nationhood* would be a "pushover". "We anticipated difficulty, but we were by no means inflexible in our approach" (*Nation*, 1 October 1965).

Though hoping that some acceptable formula could be found to ensure Jamaica's continued participation in the federation, Manley was clearly beginning to have doubts. In January 1960, he sought and was given the assurance of the

Colonial Office that Jamaica could achieve independence on her own if she left the Federation. In June, Manley made another move that would finally prove fatal to the cause of West Indian political unity: he announced that the Jamaican people would have to decide by way of a referendum whether or not they would remain in the federation. Manley, who had earlier dismissed the referendum proposal as a "betrayal of responsibility and leadership", insisted that the decision of the Jamaica Labour Party to come out openly against federation left him with no alternative. As he told his federal party colleagues, "When the West Indies achieves independence, there should be no talk of any unit seceding. . . . Neither Jamaica nor the Federation can proceed into the future on a basis of uncertainty" (as cited in Mordecai 1968, 226).

When the conference resumed its deliberations in May 1961, the Jamaican delegation was in an extremely strong bargaining position and the conference had little alternative but to accept its version of the federal arrangement. Williams conceded reluctantly that Jamaica's position would prevail. "If there was to be a Federation, there had to be an accommodation between . . . Trinidad and Jamaica . . . for Jamaica, referendum or no referendum, would walk out of the Federation if it failed to secure some of the safeguards which rightly or wrongly it demanded; . . . we . . . decided that Jamaica was not to be pushed to the wall . . . and the growth of Federal power would be more gradual than in our hearts we had originally anticipated" (*Report on the Inter-Governmental Conference, 1961, 27*).

The only serious point of difference concerned the timing and the formula for transferring the vital issues of industrial development and income tax from the reserve list to which they had been assigned to the federal list where Williams agreed they ought to be ultimately. Jamaica wanted to make any transfer subject to approval by the unit governments and the federal parliament in which she would be in a commanding position. Williams conceded that Jamaica's economic position was precarious, but argued that a more flexible amendment procedure should be agreed upon. Jamaica should not make the mistake of confusing federation, which she would inevitably lead, with the existing federal government, which was everybody's nightmare:

> We of the Trinidad and Tobago delegation urged the Conference to appreciate Jamaica's difficulties and understand, even if it did not accept, Jamaica's fear that these difficulties might be aggravated by Federal lack of experience. We stated publicly that it was because we recognized these difficulties that we would accept Jamaica's stand on representation, the Council of Ministers, the Reserve List, and the phasing of Customs Union over nine years. But we indicated to Jamaica that, in our opinion, it did not sufficiently emphasize the advantages it would gain from Federation. . . . We asked Jamaica, in return for our recognition of her present difficulties and our readiness to agree to a ten-year moratorium on the subjects on the Reserve List, not to subject the Federation after ten years to the veto of a single territory in circumstances that could

conceivably be quite different and not as unfavourable to Jamaica as they are today. (Ibid., 28–29)

Trinidad made it clear that economic development also involved freedom of movement, and that Jamaica's demands could not be considered in isolation. Though the Trinidad delegation agreed to leave freedom of movement on the exclusive list, it insisted that the power of the federal government in this area remain inactive "until such time as it assumed jurisdiction over the subjects on the Reserve List". It was also noted that industrial development involved the raising of external loans and participation in the field of foreign affairs.

The issue of transfers from the reserve list was not settled until the final conference on federation, which was held in London at Lancaster House in June 1961. With the support of the British, federal, and other unit governments, all of which were unwilling to see Manley lose the forthcoming referendum, Jamaica was able to gain acceptance for all of her demands. On 19 September 1961, the Jamaican people nevertheless stunned the West Indies by voting against federation by a 54 to 46 per cent majority, finally putting an end to any immediate hopes for West Indian political unity. The vote (256,261 to 217,319) was perhaps more indicative of the decline in popularity of Manley and the People's National Party in the rural areas than it was of a basic hostility to federation. The urban voter remained faithful to the People's National Party by a four-to-one margin.

Dr Williams has argued that the Jamaican referendum was only the ostensible reason for the collapse of the federation, which he referred to as "an absolute blessing in disguise". As Sir Ellis Clark agrees, Williams was "delighted" at the outcome, which in effect allowed him to achieve a desired outcome without having to bear the historical burden for having been personally responsible for mashing up the federation, which he would have done had the outcome been different. As Williams confessed,

> I say it openly to the Party, that if Jamaica had won the referendum, I was going to come to the PNM and propose that they reject the Lancaster House Conference. I was going to propose to the Party that they should not join the Federation. . . . The Party would have had to decide. The Party would have been free to go into the Federation. They would have gone into Federation with another political leader. I would not have been false to my conscience. I would not have agreed to take on the responsibilities for putting that rope around the neck of the people of Trinidad and Tobago by accepting that bastard Federation that was created in Lancaster House. (Williams 1962b, 19–24)

The Trinidad delegation had been extremely angry about the treatment it received, and had made it clear to the conference that it would not accept the results. It was defeated on every issue that it considered fundamental – in particular on the questions of freedom of movement, unit conduct of external affairs, and the formula for British Guiana's accession to the union. "The Lancaster

House formula in their view was merely a concession to the smaller units [who wanted freedom of movement], and to Jamaica at the expense of Trinidad. [It produced] a Federation that was merely an administrative superstructure. . . . It had nothing to do with economic realities."

J. O'Neil Lewis provides an interesting anecdote relating to the issue of the reserve list. During the intergovernmental meeting held in Port of Spain in 1959, acute controversy surrounded what should be done about the power to levy income tax, industrial development and freedom of movement. Trinidad wanted all three placed on the exclusive list. Jamaica, Barbados and Antigua disagreed, while some of the other islands such as Grenada sided with Trinidad and Tobago. At a subsequent bilateral meeting between Manley and Williams held in Antigua at the Anchorage in 1960, Manley proposed and Williams agreed that the items should be put on a reserve list for nine or ten years. There the matter lay until the 1961 Lancaster House Conference. When the issue of the reserve came up for discussion, Ian McLeod raised the question as to the formula that was to be used to allocate matters from the reserve list. To Williams's surprise, most delegations, including Jamaica, insisted on "unanimity". Williams asked Manley to confirm that unanimity was not specified in their agreements. Manley evaded the issue, whereupon Williams insisted that freedom of movement also had to be subject to the new unanimity rule. Trinidad was not going to accept the burdens that would be involved in free movement if the federal government was not given the power to put in place the necessary policies to address the problems that could trigger unimpeded movement. Trinidad was outvoted, whereupon Williams told the conference that "what they had done today had destroyed federation" (Eric Williams in Retrospect symposium, April 1991).

The recollections of Patricia Robinson, a young economist who worked closely as a personal assistant to Williams, are worth noting because of the light they throw on what was taking place during the conference. Robinson recalled the atmosphere that prevailed among the technocrats and their relationships with Williams. As she noted, "We worked incredible hours to prepare *The Economics of Nationhood,* and he would say how marvelous we were, you know, that whole atmosphere." Robinson gives us glimpses of how the personalities of Manley and Williams impinged on the negotiations, and the way in which Williams negotiated, led to Manley's decision to invite the Jamaican people to vote on the issue:

> I don't think he perceived Manley's problems fully. . . . I wouldn't say he had a love hate relationship with Manley, but he both idealized and idolized Manley. He just could not see how this great federationist could be pussyfooting now that they had a federation. . . . In his mind, he and Manley would fashion this perfect federation. . . . He felt very betrayed by Manley. You see he just assumed that Manley was *ad idem* with him on the Economics of Nationhood that was intended to be the blue print of Federation. (*Sunday Express,* 20 July 1986)

Robinson was of the view that Williams was a poor negotiator who lacked subtlety and flexibility, and that this might have been the trigger that led Manley to decide that the question of whether Jamaica would remain in the federation should be decided upon, once and for all, by the Jamaican people. "Some would say that Williams was immature. He posited an all-or-nothing position and sharpened every issue; he intensified every conflict. He would make these intellectually thought-out speeches. Now that I am older, I realize that you don't negotiate that way. Williams brought everything down to black and white. You couldn't gloss over anything with him. There was no leaving things to be done behind the scenes in smoke filled rooms behind the conference room. The Jamaicans were consummate at that" (ibid.).

Robinson tells us that when Manley declared that he was going to seek a mandate, she felt sadness and gloom. Williams too felt that way, and tried frantically to avert a referendum. But it was much too late. Williams's inflexible approach had backed Manley into a corner and the latter felt he had no alternative but to take the matter to the electorate.

> The decision to hold a referendum was really the bottom of the barrel for Williams. I think he realized that he had gone too far. And of course he began to blame the British and see signs of some plot. He believed in plots between Manley and the British, who were never sure of Williams. . . . Manley spoke their language. . . . Manley was really their candidate, and to reassure Manley, they were prepared to agree to anything. They were really darned irritated when Manley was forced into a corner as they thought. (Ibid.)

Williams denied that Trinidad was responsible for breaking up the federation, as many people, including C.L.R. James, asserted. Despite the seeming inflexibility in his demands for a strong union, he believed he went a long way to conciliate Jamaica. The federal and British governments must accept some of the blame, the former for provoking Jamaica and not inspiring her confidence in federation, and the latter for making it easy for her to break the federal pact. Had Manley come to the centre, of course, the crisis might never have developed, though it is arguable that if he had done so, he and Williams would have quarrelled sooner or later. It is also possible that if he had come to the centre, the People's National Party might have lost power to the Jamaica Labour Party in 1959, and that might have wrecked federation. It is difficult to apportion blame in this unfortunate affair. Everyone blundered. It may also be that the idea was premature.

Arthur Lewis ascribes blame for the collapse of the federation to the "awful" leadership of the West Indian politicians, and Williams in particular.[1] Among the costly errors Lewis cites was the politicians' tendency to rely on "open diplomacy" rather than on informal negotiations. As Lewis complains,

Their . . . big failure was . . . [that] they adopted a standard pattern for communicating with each other . . . based on "open diplomacy", which in practice meant shouting at each other by press or radio, or by issuing Ministry Papers or obtaining binding resolutions in their legislative assemblies before setting off to meet each other. . . . This neglect of the elementary rules of diplomacy soon poisoned the personal relationships among the three men [Williams, Manley and Adams], and between them and the federal leaders on the other islands, with the result that by the middle of 1961 the chief champions of the Federation were hardly on speaking terms with each other. (As cited in Mordecai 1968, 455–62)

Lewis believes that "the Federation was destroyed by poor leadership rather than by the intractability of its own internal problems", though he was not confident that "wise leadership could have put it together again".

18   One from Ten Leaves Nought

The anti-federation vote in Jamaica on 19 September 1961 posed a crucial dilemma for Williams. The diplomatic traffic that followed the Jamaica decision to turn its back on federation provides interesting bits of information about the process by which Williams came to his conclusion that "whatever might be true in the world of mathematics, in the world of politics, one from ten leaves nought."[1] Williams was clearly equivocal as to whether he should work towards an eastern Caribbean federation with a strong centre, a unitary regional state, or whether Trinidad and Tobago should go it alone. Given all that had occurred, his basic instincts drove him to the third option, but there was the question of how to finesse that approach.

Not surprisingly, several efforts were being made to salvage what could be secured out of the crisis. The federal government, the British government and some of the chief ministers of the eastern Caribbean islands were hard at work. In his letter to the Colonial Office, acting governor general John Mordecai advised that Williams did not seem to have made up his mind as to what he would do. He observed that Arthur Lewis had been formally retained as an adviser by the federal prime minister for three months and that Williams, "while still non-committal, personally, welcomed this arrangement" (Mordecai to Secretary of State, 21 September 1961, as cited in Ghany 1996, 135).

Mordecai urged the secretary of state to avoid making any public statement that Jamaica could proceed to independence, since this could well serve to provoke Williams to say that Trinidad and Tobago would follow suit. The governor of Trinidad, Sir Solomon Hochoy, agreed with him: "Hochoy is apprehensive lest his premier reacts to an announcement demonstrating the Colonial Office 's willingness to tackle Jamaica's independence by launching a campaign in Trinidad also" (ibid.). In sum, Hochoy was conspiring with Mordecai when both knew that Britain had already decided to cede independence to Jamaica. The secretary of state, Ian McLeod, had in fact briefed Prime Minister Macmillan to that effect.

McLeod's letter to Macmillan is worth quoting at some length since it provides an excellent view of the attitude of the Colonial Office. As McLeod told Macmillan,

The Jamaica referendum has resulted in a defeat for Manley on the Federation issue. We expected and hoped for a narrow but clear affirmative. The result is a narrow but clear negative.

This is a most grievous blow to the Federal ideal for which we and enlightened West Indian opinion have striven for so many years. It is certain that the Federation cannot continue in its present form and it must be doubtful whether it can survive at all.

The decision of Jamaica to quit the Federation must be taken as final. We may expect a demand that they should be allowed to go forward into Independence as a separate member of the Commonwealth. In view of the size, population (1.6 million) and economic viability of Jamaica this will be a demand which, with the precedents of Sierra Leone and Cyprus before us, we could not resist. Whether there will have to be a General Election in Jamaica or whether Manley will successfully maintain that an adverse vote on this single issue does not constitute a vote of no confidence in his Government remains to be seen.

The question whether a Federation of most or all of the East Caribbean Islands can survive the defection of Jamaica depends more on the attitude of Trinidad and Tobago than on any other single factor. Dr. Williams (Premier of Trinidad and Tobago) made it clear during the West Indian Conference that if Jamaica left the Federation, Trinidad would follow suit since she would not be able or prepared to take on the financial burden of "carrying" the Federation. (Jamaica and Trinidad contribute about 85 percent of Federal revenues in roughly equal shares). If he maintains this line, we can expect a demand from Trinidad and Tobago that they too should be allowed to "go it alone" into independent membership of the Commonwealth. This would be as difficult to resist as a similar demand from Jamaica.

If Trinidad takes this line, it is difficult to see a "rump" Federation of Barbados and the smaller islands surviving. Antigua has always taken a pro-Jamaica line and is unlikely in any case to continue in a Federation that does not include Jamaica. She may well seek some form of association with Jamaica (though whether Jamaica after the referendum would be in a position to accommodate her is doubtful). Barbados is not very likely to press for independence and is more likely to want to continue as a separate self-governing Colony, possible with some special status. This would leave us with six small Windward and Leeward Islands which have no prospect of "making independence" alone and all but one of which are budgetarily in the red and supported financially by the U.K. – a most dismal prospect.

It is, however, just possible that Trinidad might be prepared to lead an East Caribbean Federation – on her terms. Eric Williams has always disliked the present loose form of Federation which has been a condition of Jamaica belonging. The defection of Jamaica will give him the opportunity to press for the tighter form of Federation which he has always advocated, with strong central powers over taxation, development planning, etc. In return for that he might be prepared to make a concession over his earlier stand against the early introduction of freedom of movement. This might overcome the prejudice of other Islands against continuing in a Federation dominated by Trinidad, since it is on this issue that they have been most bitterly critical of Trinidad. On this hypothesis we might salvage a viable Federation which could go forward to independence without Jamaica – and relieve us of the prospect of having the smaller islands indefinitely on our hands. But Eric Williams will in that case make full use of his strong bargaining position and no doubt demand a handsome financial contribution over the early years from H.M.G. On balance, however, it seems more probable that he will want to "go it alone".

We cannot, of course, express publicly our regret at the result of the referendum since that could embitter our relations with Bustamante if he returns to power in Jamaica. Our immediate line with the Press is that it was recognized that the Lancaster House Agreement was dependent on the Jamaica referendum and the endorsement by Legislatures in other Islands; that we have always regarded the form of Federation as a matter for West Indians themselves to settle; and that the referendum result is a new factor in the situation the effects of which we are studying. (McLeod to Macmillan, Secret, 22 September 1961, as cited in Ghany 1996, 130–42)

Reginald Maulding, McLeod's successor at the Colonial Office, also agreed that the Jamaican decision had to be regarded as the final verdict, and that Jamaica would be allowed to proceed to independence sometime in 1962.

Williams said that he had made up his mind that Trinidad would follow Jamaica if the referendum failed. Arthur Lewis's account, however, suggests that the process was complex and that Williams zigzagged and slalomed, or at least appeared to. Lewis saw him four times, he tells us. On 22 September, three days after the referendum, he was "full of venom and insisted that he wanted the whole Federation to mash up".

Only then would he consider starting a new federation, on Trinidad's terms. I then switched to persuading him not to say anything at all, and he said he would propose to his party that it keep federation out of the election. Trinidad's terms would be strong federation, on the lines of *The Economics of Nationhood*. He welcomed the proposal that I sound out the other governments. He repudiated any immediate intention of declaring for the independence of Trinidad. (As cited in Ghany 1996, 148)

When Lewis again saw Williams on 3 November, he detected an "alarming shift" in his thinking towards a unitary state, though his mind still seemed open. Was Williams game-playing? Lewis gained the impression that destroying the federation had become "an obsession, and his desire to bring off this coup was his main reason for elaborating a programme of public education". By 8 November, Williams appeared a "little less open, but he still argued in a friendly way". He was, however, hostile to any meeting called by the federal government, which he assumed would be *functus* by March 1962.

Williams told Lewis that the "Colonial Government had gotten the West Indies into the mess, and had the duty to take the initiative to get us out". However, he would attend a conference if it was clear that the federal government would not keep interfering in the discussion. Williams also indicated that he was anxious to enter into some arrangement to keep certain common services such as the university going. Told that he was creating an impression of a "big bad wolf waiting to devour the little islands", he promised to "mend his ways" (note by Lewis, 9 November 1961, as cited in Ghany 1996, 148–49). Lewis also noted that Vere Bird of Antigua and Errol Barrow of Barbados had already started signalling that they were suspicious of Williams and did not want to be "little Tobagoes" in a unitary state, or even a federation. Antigua indicated it mistrusted any federation that did not include Jamaica, since it feared that Trinidad would overwhelm them. Antigua wished to "retain its identity and to have freedom of initiative in respect of schemes for Antigua" (Antigua Monthly Intelligence Report, September 1961, as cited in Ghany 1996, 139).

Barrow, who had come to power in Barbados on 4 December 1961, was persuaded by Lewis to visit Williams to try to persuade him to reconsider his position on federation. Williams was not willing to reconsider, and in fact told Barrow, who as a newcomer had not participated in the federal negotiations, that Barrow did not know what he was getting into. "Williams refused to bend, and this left Barrow very disappointed. It was to be an event that discoloured relations between these two Caribbean leaders for a long time to come and may have helped Williams to make up his own mind about what he should do" (ibid., 150).

My own view is that Williams had made up his mind way in advance of these meetings and was playing a cat and mouse game with the Colonial Office, Caribbean leaders, the Caribbean diaspora and, just as importantly, the opposition in Trinidad and Tobago, which accused him of being responsible for the collapse of the federation. DLP parliamentarians charged that Williams's constant pin-pricking of Adams, and his precipitate haste for customs union and for freedom of movement all contributed to the destruction of the federation. Williams, however, was anxious to ensure that he would not have to shoulder the historical blame for mashing up the federation, something that he had once passionately endorsed.

Although Williams had decided that federation should not be made an issue in the general election, numerous statements made during the campaign provided clues to his thinking on the issue. On one occasion he declared,

> We of the PNM don't know if we should go along in any association at all; and if we are
> to go in an association, we don't know if it is to be a Federation. . . . I for one, and I
> am sure the PNM, will not go in for any Federation at the sacrifice of the people of
> Trinidad and Tobago just for the sake of supporting British or American policy, what-

ever it might be. You and I have not fought for West Indian nationhood . . . merely to find ourselves a little pocket on a string held by Britain . . . or America which might want another banana republic in this part of the world. We are going to have Independence by ourselves without their help. Let us have something that everybody can respect and understand, especially . . . when it costs a lot of money. (Williams at Arima, tape, n.d.)

On another occasion he seemed less uncertain, and warned,

People will come here to take up land we don't have, possibly to take up jobs at rates of wages lower than the workers of Trinidad and Tobago would work, come in here perhaps to be strike breakers, . . . come in here looking for houses that don't exist and create shanty towns, while we are at present and at an enormous expense cleaning the shanty town on the outskirts of Port of Spain. *That is the type of argument the DLP brings.* (Williams at Arima, tape, n.d.; emphasis added)

Williams admitted that he was "sorry" for the smaller units, and promised that Trinidad would help fight to get Britain to acknowledge her responsibility to them, but not at "our expense" (Williams at Woodbrook, tape, n.d.). As he declared further, "We . . . were not imperialists; we had not exploited other territories, and whilst we are willing to help our neighbours achieve nationhood if only because we did not want colonialism perpetuated next to us, we could not undertake that at the cost of our own economic stability. . . . If Jamaica left, Trinidad and Tobago . . . would not undertake to carry the rest of the Federation" (*Report on the Inter-Governmental Conference*, 1961, 19–30).

Williams was clearly hinting at what his own decision would be, or was at least sounding for response. He openly rejected the DLP's suggestion that Trinidad should go into a new federation that Britain and the United States would help to finance. He noted that neither country had given any indication that it would offer substantial aid to the West Indies, certainly not in terms that bore any relationship to the economic realities of the situation. As far as he was concerned, the DLP, vested interests, and outside forces were supporting the federation only because they saw in it an opportunity to break the PNM's hegemony in Trinidad. Williams had nightmares about a federal government controlled by a coalition of the DLP and other Caribbean politicians: "Imagine what will happen if this vindictive and ferocious Opposition that we have . . . could, with some backward politicians, get control of the *PNM's treasury.* All of them want to get control of Trinidad's revenue from oil" (Williams at St George County Council, tape, n.d.; emphasis added).

During the negotiations on federation, Williams and other Caribbean politicians had come to dislike one another intensely, and verbal communication between them had often broken down. The "mendicant mentality" of the politicians from the eastern Caribbean, born of necessity rather than predisposition, infuriated Williams. As noted above, Arthur Lewis found him implacably opposed to working with the eastern Caribbean politicians: "He would have nothing to do with a federation run by Sir Grantley Adams and his company. The existing Federation must be wound up." Lewis also found that while Williams was inclined towards a unitary state arrangement rather than a federal one, other PNM politicians were not anxious to continue in any form of association with the other units and were encouraging Williams to take Trinidad to independence alone (Lewis 1965).

In an attempt to get a consensus on the issue, the PNM executive established a committee to study the problem and report back to a special convention to be held on 27 January 1962. Before the convention met, however, it was announced that the secretary of state for the colonies, Maudling, would pay a visit to the West Indies. Williams suspected that Maudling's aim was to force Trinidad to continue in the federation. To forestall this, the committee procedure was abandoned and a meeting of the party's general council summoned to decide the issue. Under Williams's leadership, the council recommended that Trinidad should go to independence alone, but that any other island wishing to join it in a unitary state would be welcome to do so. The pro-federalists in the party were decisively outmanoeuvred. According to Mordecai, this new arrangement allowed Williams to "marry his own inclinations towards association in a unitary state with his colleagues' yearnings for Independence now. . . . This dilemma resolved, the proposed elaborate consultation of public opinion so repeatedly announced, was no longer considered necessary, and was simply set aside" (Mordecai 1968, 416).

When the PNM convention met to settle the issue, the prevailing mood was clearly against federation. Williams argued that Trinidad had wasted too much time and money on federation (TT$20 million in four years) and could not afford such waste any longer. Important decisions affecting Trinidad's economic position were being taken in the councils of the European Economic Community, and it was felt that Britain was not to be trusted to negotiate the best agreements for Trinidad. No one knew how long it would take for a new federation to come to fruition, and Williams was not anxious to go through the exasperating and interminable rounds of discussions that the establishment of a new structure would involve. Decisions in the context of the modern world had to be made fast, and efficiency could not be expected from the ministries of the "smaller islands".

Williams made it clear that he was not going to participate in any more discussions with Caribbean politicians. As he said, "If you have to continue [negotiating federation], for God's sake leave me out of it. These negotiations that have been going on for three years! To sit down again! Must we negotiate thirteen years more to end up with another fiasco? . . . I never want to attend another conference of Governments to discuss the question of a federation . . . to go through the ordeal . . . beat your head against a concrete wall . . . to have people tell you absolutely cavalierly, man we ain't interested in . . . principles, all we want to know and talk about is economic aid and freedom of movement" (*Speech on Independence*, 1962b, 20, 39).

It was no surprise that the convention overwhelmingly approved (subject to a few changes in phrasing) the resolution of the general council that "Trinidad and Tobago reject unequivocally any participation in a federation of the Eastern Caribbean, and proceed forthwith to National Independence, without prejudice to the future incorporation in the unitary state of Trinidad and Tobago or any Territory of the Eastern Caribbean whose people may so desire, on terms to be mutually agreed, or to the future establishment of a Common Economic Community embracing the entire Caribbean Area" (*Nation*, 15 January 1962).

The basic arguments made on behalf of the general council's proposals fell under two main categories, economic and political. The economic case was convincingly made. It was noted that in an eastern Caribbean federation, Trinidad would have as much as 55 to 60 per cent of the population and contribute 75 per cent of the total revenue. It was also noted that Trinidad's trade with the eight other units was minimal – TT$16 million of a total external trade of $897 million. These units also had a net public debt of TT$46 million, which it was felt Trinidad would have to absorb. For an additional market of 670,000 persons, these burdens were not considered economically worthwhile. There was some question as to how valuable this limited market would continue to be, since the "Little Eight" were still maintaining "a proud insistence on new industries which constitute half of our exports to them". The "injudicious" duplication of industries such as cement, beer and oil-refining threatened to reduce even more the value of these units as markets for the Trinidad economy.

The cost of sustaining the elaborate administrative structures of the eight units, once grants-in-aid from the British treasury for recurrent expenses were cut off, was also cited as reason for pause. The problem of migration to Trinidad was starkly documented. In 1958 and 1959, some ten thousand migrants from these islands came to Trinidad, while thiry-seven thousand went to the United Kingdom. With the closing of the United Kingdom "border", Trinidad was expected to be the prime focus of population movements in the southern and eastern Caribbean. The social services of the community were considered inadequate to sustain such pressure. Problems were also expected to arise from the disparities in the levels of economic development in the various units. The gross domestic product at factor cost per capita (in TT dollars) was $822 in Trinidad, $443 in Barbados, $259 in the Leewards, and $240 in the Windwards.

To combat the anticipated charges that Trinidad was too small and too weak economically to sustain independence, a battery of comparative statistics was adduced to show that Trinidad was much better positioned to do so than most of the independent Afro-Asian states. With a per capita income in 1960 of

US$500, Trinidad was, next to Cuba and Puerto Rico, the wealthiest of the underdeveloped states. World Bank data was also cited to establish the argument that Trinidad and Tobago "enjoy[ed] one of the highest standards of living in any Afro-Asian Community" (*Nation*, 15 January 1962).

The case was powerfully argued, and most doubters – at least within the party – seemed convinced, especially when it was shown that the cost of independence in terms of new commitments would not exceed the costs (to Trinidad) of the federal agreement worked out at Lancaster House in 1960. But the case for independence in political terms was much more difficult to make. The general council's resolution made no mention of political considerations at all, except to say that the federation afforded too many opportunities for "foreign intrigues in West Indian affairs". The political justifications were left to the speeches of the party elite. Williams's arguments were quite familiar. He complained of the time lost on bargaining, which involved a sacrifice of the 22 April 1960 deadline for independence that he had set, and "the narrowness of vision and unwillingness to change old patterns" that characterized the politicians of the eastern Caribbean. Williams argued, however, that the general council's proposals – a unitary state with those who wished to join Trinidad, and a Caribbean Economic Community – were revolutionary initiatives, which, in the long run, would provide the solution to the West Indian dilemma: "What the General Council . . . proposes to you . . . is nothing short of a revolution in Caribbean society with its history of disunity and separation, metropolitan domination and outward looking. . . . The temporary partial disappointment itself contains the seed, itself lays the foundation for the larger permanent hopes of the West Indian area in the world" (*Speech on Independence*, 22–30).

For Williams, a Caribbean Economic Community had now become the method whereby the whole of the Caribbean would be reunited. The failure of the political federation of the British Caribbean was not to mean the end of the pan-Caribbeanism that he now confessed had always been his ultimate goal. Economic integration and cooperation in the use of certain vital common services should now be viewed as the principal means to break down the linguistic, cultural and historical barriers that divided the West Indies. It was time for the Caribbean to look inward and depend on its own resources. The Papal Donation of 1493 was dead, but there was no reason to continue accepting as permanent the divisions that were the result of four and a half centuries of European rivalry and domination. As Williams perorated, "If somebody in Africa can talk about Pan-Africanism . . . somebody in the West Indies has to raise the call for some larger unity, something that makes sense, something that can represent a certain amount of intellectual dignity and economic perspective for the people of these frustrated areas who don't know where to go" (ibid., 23).

It was a bright dream, and one that West Indians before Williams had entertained. But one wonders whether Williams seriously believed in the possibility of bringing the viciously competing economies of the Caribbean into any sort of single market and economy. He was fully aware that it would not be easy to overcome the colonially derived obstacles in the path of unity. With Cuba excluded for ideological and practical reasons, Williams's proposals seemed even more visionary. If it could be argued that the uneven economic development of the anglophone West Indies was one of the main obstacles to federation, then it seemed all the more difficult to visualize any meaningful Caribbean economic unit, however much one might agree on its desirability and necessity. Williams was certainly aware of the difficulties that his proposal involved, but seemed to view it as an ideal to which all West Indians should bend their energies in the future. It was, he believed, the only medium through which the economic viability of the area could be achieved. And political unity might indeed grow out of successful economic cooperation.

Williams remained optimistic, and Europe offered him reason to believe that his vision could one day become a reality. As he said, "If Europe could overcome its division, so could the West Indies. If the Caribbean gets together, there might not be any great scope for interchange. But are we sure there would not be? Isn't the economy of Belgium to a large extent competitive with the economy of Germany? The Europeans have been able to work out some sort of rational division of the market. . . . Why should we assume that . . . we couldn't get together and work out some sort of common policy as producers interested in markets . . . ?" (ibid., 28).

But there seemed one fundamental flaw in the unitary state thesis that the general council had proposed for the immediate future. The very arguments that were made against the idea of an eastern Caribbean federation were even more powerful when applied to the idea of an expanding unitary state, and it would appear that some of the isolationists in the cabinet accepted the latter because they knew it would never be realized. Williams was not that certain, however, and argued that the unitary state would be more rational and more efficient from the point of view of administrative organization and social and economic planning. If the Philippines and Hawaii could make a unitary system work, so could the West Indies. Distance was no longer the problem it used to be.

As true as this might be, the decision still meant that Trinidad had to jeopardize its economic development by diverting time, energy and resources for the development of the eastern Caribbean. And if the suggestion that the British and US governments should help finance the federation was to be rejected as being unrealistic and beggarly, the same held for arguments that Britain should underwrite the costs of developing the "depressed areas" of the unitary state that Williams insisted was still Britain's responsibility. It was Britain that had "sucked the orange dry . . . and we would never allow Trinidad and Tobago's stability and economic progress to be endangered by pulling Britain's chestnuts out of her own fire". The British nevertheless made it clear that Trinidad would have to foot the bill for developing those islands that chose to join it. According to Williams, "the British attitude . . . is that if Trinidad is so upstart as to want Grenada [who alone opted for the unitary state] to join it, Trinidad and Tobago must pay the cost" (ibid.).

The only argument that made any sort of sense was the political one. Williams told the convention that there was a "solid political factor" that must be considered if the party opted for federation.

> Could you be sure, Ladies and Gentlemen, that in a Federation, where the other places must get a number of seats . . . that a Federation does not expose you to having a Federal Government constituted of an Opposition minority in Trinidad buying fluid votes in other territories and able to control the Trinidad economy through controlling the Federal Government? The question is not an academic issue at all . . . the last Federal elections produced a government that has given the PNM more trouble than even the DLP. (*Speech on Independence*, 1962b, 38–39)

Williams felt that "jealousy" and "malice" towards the PNM and to him as its leader were so strong among Caribbean politicians that they would do anything to undermine its strength, even if the interests of the West Indies were sacrificed in the process. They preferred to remain colonies and be "tupenny" rulers in their own little bivouacs, rather than be led by the PNM, "the undisputed intellectual leaders of the colonial nationalist movement in this part of the world" (ibid., 38–42). What Williams was demanding, in his typically monopolistic "zero-sum" approach to party politics, was "one single state ruled by one single party, the PNM, which lays down the blueprint for legislation and development" (ibid., 34). The only way to save the eastern Caribbean was for Trinidad and Tobago to expand, absorb and socialize its population into the norms that the PNM had defined for Trinidad. It was the very sort of missionary paternalism that the minorities in Trinidad were not prepared to accept, even though often it was the methods chosen to define and impose those norms, rather than the norms themselves, that were the main source of alienation. Williams was accused by DLP spokesmen of wanting to go it alone; a lone star was always brighter and more conspicuous than when there were myriads in the firmament. Williams, it was argued, preferred to shine alone rather than in the company of equals in a federation.

A small element within the PNM felt that the political dangers Williams cited were real but certainly not insurmountable. There was no reason why the party could not expand within a federal system and undermine the old-line leadership in the eastern Caribbean just as easily as it assumed it could do in a unitary state. Was the PNM not confusing the people of these islands with their current leaders? PNM pro-federalists felt that a great deal of administrative rationality could be achieved within a strong framework. Williams was nevertheless right when he insisted that a unitary government would be less inhibited in its economic and social planning than would a federal government, though it was perhaps deceptive for him to suggest that a unitary government would be much better able to prevent inter-territorial migration. Williams argued disingenuously that "it is much easier for a unitary state to control the . . . factors involved in migration than it is in a federal government, where you must have, if it is a proper federation, the right of freedom of movement, with the territory that is affected by the migrants having no effective economic power over the territories that supply the migrants" (*Speech on Independence*, 1962b, 47).

Supporters of the federal proposal included Senators Wilfred Alexander, Hamilton Maurice and the Honourable Andrew Rose, minister of communication in the defunct federation. Rose was suspected of having had hopes of becoming the governor general of the federation. It should also be noted that a subcommittee of the party's policy committee, which had been appointed to study the question of migration within the eastern Caribbean, had come out in unanimous support of federation. This document was not circulated at the convention. The author, it is reported, was discouraged from defending it at the general council meeting. So far as can be discerned, Williams was never defeated in the general council, which he easily manipulated. Few general council members could resist the dazzling round-the-world and historical analyses of Dr Williams. Top party and cabinet ministers in fact complained that Williams played the general council "card" whenever he was having difficulty in the cabinet or executive.

A large number of delegates at the convention accepted Williams's arguments, but felt that the tone of the general council resolution was harsh and an affront to the pride of the people of the eastern Caribbean islands. Williams accepted this observation and agreed that "particular attention would have to be paid to the sensibilities of a territory like Barbados, which has a long history of struggle for self-government, [and which was] the first place in the British Empire . . . to demand self-government, 125 years before the mainland colonies in . . . America". A few delegates also objected to what they believed was an attempt by the party leadership to force them to go along with the general council's resolution. They objected to what they believed was the political leader's suggestion that if the party wished to go into federation, it would have to do so without him. Williams correctly noted that this remark had been made in the context of his discussion of the Lancaster House constitution. Even so, the party could not fail to notice that he had restated the principle that the "political leader [of a democratic party] must go . . . if [he] takes a particular stand on an issue on which he is not supported by his Party" (ibid., 50).

The convention did have a chance to consider the alternative motion: "That

Trinidad and Tobago should agree to participate in a Federation of the Eastern Caribbean having the strongest possible central powers on condition (i) that adequate financial assistance will be forthcoming from the United Kingdom, the United States of America and Canada, (ii) that adequate representation for Trinidad and Tobago is assured in such a Federation, and (iii) that such participation will not delay the achievement of Independence for Trinidad and Tobago." Andrew Rose took his political life in his hands to propose the motion. The political leader was known to be quite displeased, and it took a bit of persuading to have him agree to allow Rose to withdraw the motion after it was clear that it would have been decisively defeated on the floor. Many felt that Rose's political career in the PNM was finished.

There was no doubt that majority sentiment in the party was in favour of the general council's proposal, which was eventually accepted with an amendment to the effect that a maximum degree of local government would be provided for those territories wishing to associate with Trinidad and Tobago. Trinidadians might very well have chosen to stay with the eastern Caribbean in a new federation if Williams had given them a lead in that direction. But it was quite obvious that the majority were not anxious to share their jobs and growing affluence with their "have-not" neighbours. There was nothing to gain and everything to lose, at least in material terms, and the man in the street, and increasingly the middle class, had begun to renounce whatever little idealism they had once had. With the Jamaican decision to "go it alone", the appeal of federation had lost its magic. Trinidadians were no longer willing to be inhibited or restrained. The primary stream of insular egoism, which had always been latent among the non-Indian population and which Williams shared and had whipped to a frenzy during the Chaguaramas "crisis", was at full tide. The remark of a delegate to the PNM convention – "Mr Political Leader, to hell with Federation" – was one that found a responsive echo in many elements of the population for whom the difference between the federal and unitary proposals was scarcely intelligible. They wanted neither. Williams's dream of a "wider Caribbean community" was lost on all but a few.

Reaction to the Unitary State

The Indian community was concerned about the possible racial significance of the PNM's decision to work for a unitary-state settlement. One could not really blame them for believing that it was just another plot to swamp them. To them it seemed logical that Afroids would neutralize them more easily in a unitary than in a federal state. As one of their pamphleteers expressed it,

> It is not so much the welfare of these little islands that the PNM is interested in, but the votes which they believe they will receive from them, and which they hope will abrogate the voting capacity of the Indians in Trinidad twenty or thirty years from now. The con-

cept of a unitary state, therefore, is founded on racialism. We protest against any
attempt to swamp Trinidad with Grenadians or any other people for no other reason
but for vote-catching. . . . We were in a Federation with these islands, and mainly
through PNM connivance this Federation is now defunct. We are still prepared to
consider the question of a Federation of the nine units, but we will not have any of
them in any unitary state with Trinidad, it does not matter who says that we should.
(Singh 1962b, 11–12)

The argument was that in a federation, the votes of the black population in the
"Little Eight" would not be of any assistance to the PNM in its aim to nullify
Indian voting-strength twenty years hence. In a unitary state, the black vote in
these islands would provide the PNM with the voting strength they needed to
establish a one-party racial dictatorship against the Indian community. But in
view of the general agreement that any recreated federation would have had to
be a strong and highly centralized one, would it really have been any less difficult for the PNM to manipulate the system against the Indians, if indeed this
was their true aim?

One could not help speculating that the harsh terms which Williams proposed
for such a union were meant to discourage anyone from taking them seriously.
It seemed to be a new form of imperialism located in a new metropolitan centre, with the smaller units abandoning all hope of economic development based
on industry. In fact, they would become tutelary wards of Trinidad, as was
Tobago, a prospect that few eastern Caribbean politicians were likely to find
attractive. Their response was almost predictable. The chief minister of Grenada,
Eric Gairy, declared, "The smaller units will not agree to any unitary state. They
have their national aspirations and would not give in easily" (*Trinidad Guardian*,
9 December 1961). R.A. Bradshaw, chief minister of St Kitts, was even more
expressive: "Federation has been brutally violated. It lies prostrate, frightfully
dismembered and torn for all the world to see the destructive capabilities of some
learned West Indians. . . . The culprits are known, and the memory of what
they've done will ever haunt them. They take a sadistic pride in their destructive
achievement. . . . They have disgraced and made the West Indies the classic laugh-
ingstock of the twentieth century" ("Debate in the Federal House", *Trinidad
Guardian*, 11 April 1962).

The premier of Barbados, Errol Barrow, who as we have seen had offered to
work closely with Williams in the new federation, saw the PNM's offer as "the
most gratuitous insult that could ever have been extended to any group of
people – an even more gratuitous insult than was offered by Verwoerd to native
peoples in South Africa" (*Trinidad Guardian*, 23 June 1962). Sir Grantley Adams,
now an embittered man, simply urged that "the feelings of the people of Trinidad
should be tested"; Adams felt, quite mistakenly, that the average Trinidadian still
wished to remain with the other units. "Williams is fast becoming a little Castro",

he complained (ibid., 27). Trinidad's premier calypsonian, the Mighty Sparrow, himself a native of Grenada, used the medium of the calypso to express his belief that "this ain't no time to say we ain't federating no more". Sparrow captured the mood of the pro-federalists when he sang the following stanza:

> Federation boil down to simply this
> Is dog eat dog and survival for the fittest
> Everybody fighting for Independence, singularly;
> Trinidad for instance
> But we go get it too, don't bother
> But ah find we should all be together
> Not separated as we are
> Because of Jamaica

Sir Arthur Lewis, a native of St Lucia, also lamented, "To most West Indians, the disintegration of this group [of islands] into two independent states whose peoples would be foreigners to each other would come as an immeasurable personal tragedy, and the authors of such a break would have a sad niche in History." As Lewis further added, "The main economic reason for Trinidad's refusing to continue in Federation in 1962 or to start a new Federation was that the Trinidad blueprint *The Economics of Nationhood* was now generally acceptable" (Mordecai 1968, 460).

West Indian intellectuals, especially those in the diaspora, were deeply shamed and embittered by what seemed to be a cynical wrecking of the only real chance of Caribbean integration and nationhood. Their hopes for a meaningful economic and political base for West Indian independence were now dashed. The wave of disillusionment following Jamaica's decision to withdraw had merely served to make them even more determined to salvage what was left of the truncated union. They were convinced that Williams had quite irresponsibly allowed his partisanship and his animosity to the old-line leadership in the Caribbean to frustrate the long-held dream of a Caribbean commonwealth. They were shocked to find that their intellectual leader had proven to be every whit as insular as those whom he had once chastised.[2]

In Trinidad, there were angry cries that the PNM had betrayed the solemn commitment it had made to take the issue to the public after the general elections. Some were more opposed to the method by which the decision was made than they were to the decision itself. A fairly typical comment came from the president of the Southern Chamber of Commerce, who condemned what he viewed as a serious breach of public faith:

> Was the Party Convention the proper forum for the final consideration of a matter which was obviously of national and not only Party importance? . . . Why wasn't the House of Representatives given an opportunity, at least similar to that given to the

Party, to decide whether Trinidad should "go it alone", or continue in a Federation? What has become of the Party's promise to consult responsible organizations in the Territory – political, economic, social, civic, cultural and fraternal, with respect to "going it alone"? Is the public correct in assuming that the Party's opinion is all that must be taken into consideration? If so, is there any need for a House of Representatives where opposing views are expressed? (*Trinidad Guardian*, 3 April 1962)

The basic complaint of a large section of the population was that no political party, no matter how large its majority, had any right to take a decision of such magnitude without consulting the people. The DLP was similarly anguished that its offer of a bipartisan approach to the questions of federation and independence had been contemptuously refused. The DLP had offered to take the issue out of the elections if it was agreed to establish a bipartisan parliamentary committee to work out a consensual approach to the political future of Trinidad and the federation. There was a decided air of partisanship about the way the decision to reject federation was arrived at. Williams himself told the party that the government was not "responsible to anybody except to [the] Party which put [them] in power and the voters that voted for [them]. . . . We [do not] have to answer to the DLP for anything." Williams had promised, however, to take the matter to the population. As he had pledged, "We will study Federation . . . we will get all the necessary documents and put them together, take them to the Party, let our Party decide, and when our Party has decided on a particular line, we go to the population (Williams to St George County Council, tape, n.d.). Whether this implied a referendum is difficult to say. It was likely, however, that after the Jamaican referendum, Williams was not anxious to see the people, in all its "virtue", make another "mistake".

Williams was visibly annoyed by complaints that he should have sought a broader consensus, and lashed out quite pugnaciously, and often contemptuously, at his critics. He declared in Woodford Square, "We marched from here . . . for Independence . . . and whoever don't like it can go to hell. We educated the people for Federation, we promoted Federation. . . . We are not going to be forced to stay in a truncated Federation. It is going to be legally dissolved as it was politically broken by Jamaica's action." But the question was not whether Trinidad and Tobago was under any legal obligation to continue in any form of federation, but whether or not it *should* stay. The people and their representatives in parliament had to decide this, and not the PNM. Many people, especially recent immigrants from the islands, had supported the PNM during the elections on the assumption that it would support federation. Though Williams had given open hints during the campaign as to the line he would take, it cannot be said that he had any mandate from the country to "go it alone", or to take any other course. The premier had proceeded in a very high-handed fashion to ignore political forces that were not associated with the PNM. Some top-ranking party members were known to have been quite embarrassed by Williams's bad political manners, regardless of their own position on the substantive issue. By failing to establish truly national machinery for settling the federation issue, the PNM had needlessly plunged the community into bitter turmoil on the eve of independence.

Williams later put other proposals on the table. In two documents written in 1964 and 1965 respectively, he revealed that he was asked by the British to indicate the practical implications of the position he had taken at the convention. Williams's response was that there were four or five options. One was that the eight islands should remain colonies, an option that he said no one would now accept. Another was that they should form a federation, which he did not think would work. The third option was that they should all go to independence on their own "which to be polite as possible, does not seem to be realistic or practicable". The fourth option was the unitary state *demarche* that Grenada had accepted.

Williams argued that federations had not worked anywhere and sought to clinch this argument by reference to Nigeria, East Africa, Canada and French West Africa: "The simple fact is that federations, the world over are not working." In his view, they were all vehicles of neo-colonialism. He preferred the unitary state option, which seemed to have done better. His examples were the Philippines, Indonesia and Hawaii. He also indicated that the unitary state option was not original to him, and that it had been put on the table some forty years ago when it was suggested that Trinidad and Tobago should forge such a union with the Windward Islands. The British gave it consideration and even sent out an official to explore its feasibility. Trinidad, however, declined.

Williams made another novel suggestion to the British – the formation of a West Indian Confederation that could bring together associate states based on Trinidad and Barbados, that would then be yoked to Jamaica, British Guiana and Belize. The Associated State of Trinidad and Tobago and the Windward Islands would have centralized services in foreign affairs, external representation, economic planning, and fundamental legislation such as income tax and import duties, but with the Windward Islands retaining full internal self-government in a single parliament bearing the same relation to the parliament of Trinidad and Tobago as the parliament of Northern Ireland bears to Westminster.

A similar arrangement would obtain in respect of Barbados and the Leeward Islands. Williams recommended that a West Indian Confederation, as defined above, should have a common foreign and defence policy with single external representation and other common services and policies to be agreed upon. All this would be a prelude to a wider Caribbean integration. Williams said he got no response from the British on his proposal. He was aware that "many would sneer at the proposal, and that many would criticize it". Those who were privy to it seemed to ignore it. But it was not immediately clear why federations would fail and confederations prevail (see EWMC folio 660).

Plate 13 State visit to Jamaica in 1963. Also pictured are Robert Lightbourne, (*left*) and Alexander Bustamante, prime minister of Jamaica (*centre*). (Eric Williams Memorial Collection, University of the West Indies, St Augustine)

Plate 14 Williams and delegation leaving for London. *Left to right:* Learie Constantine, George Richards, W.J. Alexander, Saied Mohammed, Donald Pierre and Patrick Solomon. (Eric Williams Memorial Collection, University of the West Indies, St Augustine)

Plate 15 Williams marking the formal end of US occupation, 1977. (Eric Williams Memorial Collection, University of the West Indies, St Augustine)

Plate 16 Williams chatting with Attorney General George Richards, *c.* 1960. (Trinidad and Tobago Express Ltd)

Plate 17 Williams with Patrick Solomon, being welcomed by constituents, 1956. (Eric Williams Memorial Collection, University of the West Indies, St Augustine)

PART 4

SECURING THE POLITICAL KINGDOM

19 **The Elections of 1961**
Consolidating the Power Base

At the end of his first five years in office, Williams surveyed his handiwork and declared himself immensely pleased. As he stated on the eve of independence, "a political party, a relatively new phenomenon in the history of Trinidad and Tobago, drawing a considerable measure of mass support, had released the latent capacities and pent-up energies of the people of Trinidad and Tobago and was leading them inexorably on the road to independence" (1962, 248).

Williams itemized what he considered to be the achievements of his first government. At the political level, there was the party, which had maintained a level of stability and discipline that no other party in Trinidad's history had ever achieved. "The Movement", he said, "had established the system of party politics in the traditional land of unrestrained and undisciplined individualism" (ibid., 244). It had also done what no other party in the region had, that is, provided a sustained level of political education in the public square.

At the level of the state, Williams's boast was that his government had introduced the concept and techniques of planning in the nation's life:

> Within one year of assuming control of the Government, the new Government had ready for general discussion a five-year plan of the order of $191 million, providing for the extension of roads, the increase in hospital accommodation, the construction of new schools, the expansion of the Airport, the development of neglected and maligned Tobago, the construction and encouragement of hotels, the organization of new markets, the expansion of electricity, the modernizing of the sanitation system, and a vastly extended water supply.
>
> Subsequent revisions raised the cost of the five-year programme to $248 million. . . . The success of the programme has been obvious to all. Its greatest achievement [was] that it has been financed to the extent of 98 percent from purely local resources, surplus revenues or local loans, without assistance from outside. (Ibid., 244–45)

Williams listed a number of projects that had been initiated and completed in that period. The entire population had been able to hear, to touch and to feel these and other kindred developments. Where Spanish and British colonialism had failed, Trinidad nationalism had been able to achieve where the others had not yet dared to aspire (ibid., 245). Williams likewise bragged about what had been done to restructure the public service and the ministries, the tax system, and the various mechanisms that had been initiated to introduce transparency and accountability in the financial management of the country by the new Ministry of Finance. Whereas before, Trinidad and Tobago's financial system was dependent on the approval of the Colonial Office, it was now the responsibility of the people acting through their elected representatives. Also itemized were the acquisition of the telephone company from its private owners and British West Indian Airways (BWIA) from British Overseas Airways Corporation, and reforms in the electoral system. Williams felt that gains had been achieved as well in the area of race relations. Indians were no longer, "as the saying went, either in the field, in the hospital or in jail" (ibid., 248).

Having settled the Chaguaramas and the constitutional issues to the satisfaction of the greater part of the population, Williams turned his attention to the 1961 elections, the outcome of which he viewed as critical to the future of Trinidad and Tobago and to his political career and historic mission. The opposition was also aware that a victory by Williams would determine Trinidad and Tobago's future development for many decades to come. Both sides thus had to take extreme positions. The basic elements of Williams's strategy involved the introduction of a permanent voter-registration system, voting machines, limited transportation for voters, and the drafting of new constituency boundaries. The latter was particularly critical.

Electoral Boundaries

The Colonial Office had agreed to the creation of a Boundaries Commission, which would be drawn largely from members of the legislature instead of from among neutral persons from the West Indies or the United Kingdom as had been demanded by the DLP. The commission established under this ruling consisted of the Speaker of the legislative council as chairman, a judge, two members chosen by the government, and one member chosen by the opposition. The DLP, which believed that it had been betrayed by the Colonial Office, claimed that the commission had been rigged by the PNM. With three party members on the commission, and a judge who was allegedly a party sympathizer, the one-member opposition team did not have a chance.

The debate on the report of the commission provides rich evidence in support of our fundamental thesis, that is, that *ethnicity is the dominant variable in the political life of Trinidad and Tobago*. Whatever the issue, sooner or later the trails led to the ethnic configuration of the community. The DLP complained that the commission had violated its terms of reference, which stated that constituencies should represent approximately 12,000 voters, and that any substantial departure from that figure was to be applicable only in the case of sparsely populated areas "which, on account of size, isolation or inadequacy of communications", could not adequately be represented by a single member. The DLP member of the commission maintained that while he agreed that Tobago should be given two seats on this basis, even though the total voting population of the island was around 13,500, the PNM delegation refused to do the same in other sparsely populated areas in Trinidad. Instead of overloading the urban areas, they did just the reverse. Most of the urban seats were 300 voters under the 12,000 pilot figure, while most of the rural areas exceeded it by 300, a discrepancy of some 600 voters. One seat in the capital city carried as few as 11,492 voters, while seats in the rural Indian belt carried as many as 12,735, 12,467 and 12,589, resulting in differences of more than 1,000 voters.

During the debate, the PNM did more to point up the indiscretions of the former regime than to correct the impression that it had used the returns of previous elections to create majorities for itself. Six additional seats were given to the county of St George, which, admittedly, was the fastest growing in terms of population. But it was precisely in this area that the PNM had shown itself strong. The county, if Port of Spain were to be included, now had thirteen of the thirty seats, all of which were expected to, and did in fact, go to the PNM.

Williams took no chances, even in Port of Spain where the boundaries were redrafted to make sure that all potential DLP areas, that is, the upper-class and upper-middle-class residential areas, were attached to heavily working class areas where the PNM had been consistently strong. The DLP was not given an outside chance to gain a seat in the capital city as they had done in the 1958 and 1959 municipal elections. The PNM refused to accept the suggestion that they should have gone beyond the Port of Spain city limits, as they had done in San Fernando, to include part of the suburbs of St George, which might then have been given eight seats, all of which would have had a potential electorate closer to the 12,000 mark. In the countryside, there was strong evidence to substantiate the DLP's claim that the PNM had herded as many Indian voters as possible into constituencies that they could not possibly win, and had extracted from such areas large blocks of Afro-Trinidadian voters who were then recombined into new constituencies. With much justification, the PNM was accused of having committed "territorial murder" and of having shoved aside the concept that roads, rivers and natural landmarks should define boundaries.

Ten of the thirty constituencies contained populations that were more than 50 per cent Indian. The DLP would win them all. One minister reportedly boasted that the constituencies were "scientifically gerrymandered", and the evidence certainly suggests that the cartography was undertaken with the electoral returns of the previous elections in mind. The government's delegation on the commission had been advised by a PNM constituency delimitation committee, which included some of the best surveyors in the country. As the Report of the General Secretary to the Special Party Convention, held in September 1961, declared, "The committee carried out its assignment wonderfully, and advised the PNM members on the commission accordingly, the result of which is well known to all party members" (Files of the PNM, PNM Party Headquarters). The DLP, it was noted, had no comparable backroom boys.[1]

Williams made a spirited defence of his party's handling of the Representation of the People Bill in the legislative council. As he recalled in *Inward Hunger*, the "Opposition was furious. Day after day, night after night, it went at us, hammer and tongs. . . . They claimed that we followed the precedents of the southern states of America". Williams claimed, wrongly, that literacy tests had nothing to do with the South or with Negroes. "I showed that it was an integral part of American democracy" (1969, 253). Williams also defended the PNM against changes of gerrymandering and of crowding Indians into constituencies that caused them to waste votes. He likewise tried to justify the use of voting machines. He claimed that he had made a special study of the 1956 elections and found that the boundaries for those elections had been gerrymandered.[2] Urban constituencies such as Laventille were overloaded by 35 per cent above the national average while rural constituencies such as Caroni South were 28 per cent below the national average. In Williams's view, "that was gerrymandering as compared with the 1961 boundaries where the largest constituency was 124 percent of the size of the smallest, and the smallest was 82 percent of the largest" (ibid., 254).

Williams also noted, disingenuously, that the composition of the Boundaries Commission was not his "handiwork" but that of the secretary of state for the colonies, Ian McLeod. The opposition had insisted on a neutral Boundaries Commission. "I attacked this unmercifully as representative of the last refuge of the obscurantist politicians in this country at this late date in our history seeking to hide behind the coat tails of the Secretary of State for the Colonies who has told him a million times, and is likely to tell him again, that he has no use for colonialism, and he is determined to be the last Secretary of State for the Colonies" (1969, 254). Williams was confirming that the Colonial Office had abandoned the DLP.

The Parties

The PNM

As an electoral machine, the PNM was in excellent condition on the eve of the 1961 election. The party had 370 actively functioning party groups and a financial membership of approximately 16,395, which formed the nucleus of a slick and highly disciplined electoral unit. From 24 September 1960, the fourth anniversary of its first victory at the polls, Williams busily began putting the party in shape for the coming "cataclysmic" encounter. He gave the party a six-point code of responsibilities to guide it in the months ahead. The first was loyalty and discipline. Absenteeism and general delinquency in the execution of party responsibilities at the pedestrian level, individualism, faction, intrigue, shoddy emotionalism in the selection of candidates – all had to be resolutely combated. But discipline was not to be blind and unquestioning: "Party democracy means the fullest opportunity for expression of your views on the policy when it is to be decided, and on the implementation and details of that policy, which, once a decision is arrived at by majority vote, must be supported and carried out by all (Williams 1960a, 3). This was of course a classical restatement of the Bolshevik concept of "democratic centralism", and was an input from C.L.R. James, who inspired the document and possibly ghost-wrote most of it.

The second responsibility was to the treasury of the party. Williams complained that members were not disciplined in their financial responsibilities to the party. Dues were paid intermittently, and insufficient support was being given to the press organs of the movement. It was noted that "donations from well wishers constitute by far the largest part of our revenue. There are times when we have had to solicit gifts to pay our debts, to pay wages and salaries, to meet rent, light, and telephone bills. We are a poor Party." The party, it was also noted, had support in some business circles, but there were some who did not wish to run the risk of being identified with it. But if the PNM was to remain a mass party, unfettered by obligations to "pressure groups" and individual lobbyists, if it was to continue to engage in successful political struggle, the membership had to do more to finance operations. "The sinews of war is money. Our opponents have money to fight us. We must have money to fight them" (*Our Fourth Anniversary: The Last Lap*, 1960, 13). The committee appointed to raise funds consisted of five businessmen of whom four were of European extraction. The appeal grossed approximately TT$180,000, a phenomenal achievement for a political party in Trinidad and Tobago in those years.

The number of propaganda battles that the party had waged during its period in power had put an enormous strain on resources. Despite the massive propaganda output, the offices of the movement were cramped, its officers underpaid, its printing press almost obsolete, and its files and finances in chaos and disorder. It was ironic, Williams noted, that a party that had produced a government which had done so much to rationalize administration at the public level was so undisciplined in the ordering of its own affairs. It was said by some concerned party members that the PNM had won the government but had come close to losing itself as a party.

The third responsibility urged on the party rank and file was agitation and propaganda. Members were advised to take propaganda and agitation into every sphere of their daily rounds, "in taxis and buses, at work, in clubs, friendly societies, and fraternal organizations, on and off the playing fields, at fetes and functions of all sorts" (Williams 1960a, 5). The whole community must be politically mobilized. The faithful had to be strengthened, and the uncommitted persuaded. The "enemy" had to be attacked everywhere and put on the run. Members were advised to read *Hansard* and party publications for the necessary ammunition for counter-propaganda. A research group was also established to feed information to party cadres and to provide dossiers on the "enemy".

The fourth responsibility of the party member was interracialism. The PNM, declared Williams, was not a mere electioneering machine, but something larger than itself, the function of which was the creation of a "national community". Members of the party must be living exponents and symbols of its multiracial and nationalist outlook. Williams warned party members against the fallacy of assuming that everyone who was not Afro-creole was anti-PNM, against the well-known tendency on the part of Afro-creoles to make fun of Indians who accepted and displayed the symbols of nationalism: "There are Hindus, Chinese and whites in the Movement." Muslims, especially, "are satisfied that they have equal status in the party". Party members must "stop once and for all this infuriating nonsense that every Indian is anti-PNM. . . . Some of the worst enemies of the PNM are as black as the ace of spades. Reaction knows no colour. . . . A PNM Indian, trustworthy, loyal, devoted to the PNM, is a thousand times a better citizen than an anti-PNM African" (ibid., 7–9). No attempt must be made to impose cultural uniformity on minorities. What must be demanded, however, is that they accept certain fundamentals – the national community, West Indian Independence, and the return of Chaguaramas. Other groups had their legitimate cultural pride and affiliations. "If we take pride in Ghana and Nigeria, we are strengthened as a new nation by being able to take pride also in India, Pakistan, China and Europe. Other groups too have their national pride. . . . We ask these groups to accept the national community, that is all" (ibid., 8).

Williams admitted that the party had not always lived up to its multiracial ideal:

> You cannot expect that you just proclaim interracial solidarity from the housetops, and, lo and behold! in four years, you break through all the tactics of divide and rule practised by imperialism for four centuries in our territories, you abolish the aristocracy of skin and colour which grew up within the imperialist framework. It takes time for some at least of the perspectives of the new society to be appreciated, and to become the conventions, of the new day. (Ibid., 7)

The hope was that after independence had been achieved, and the tension inherent in a period of rapid transition had been reduced, positive steps would be taken to fuse and solidify the constitutive elements of the society.

The fifth obligation enjoined upon party members involved the selection of candidates who would carry the movement's standard in public. The cavalier manner in which some candidates had been selected in the past, Williams complained, had saddled the party with a number of incompetents who could not face up to the onerous responsibilities of office. The party had to discipline too many persons for disloyalty, financial irregularities, failure to follow directives, and lobbying, all of which had served to reduce the prestige of the PNM in the eyes of the public. In choosing candidates for 1961, party groups were advised to "think well whether you are enthroning factions, whether you are strengthening disloyalty, whether you are putting someone in power who will use the Party for his ends and move heaven and earth to evade his responsibilities, including financial, to the Party which takes him out of obscurity and puts him in the limelight of public acclaim" (ibid., 12).

The last appeal made to the party related to the tremendous burdens that were devolving upon their political leader. This was perhaps one of the greatest problems the party had to face. Everything seemed to require the personal attention of Williams. The party held that view, as did members of the public. And although Williams made numerous appeals for mercy, it was difficult for party members and citizens to appreciate that by bypassing other channels and demanding to see the "boss" on every issue, they were contributing to the substantial administrative bottleneck that was already bedevilling the party and the government. Williams himself was guilty, perhaps unwittingly, of encouraging this sort of dependence.

During 1960–61, the party's electoral machinery was drastically overhauled. Operations committees and transport pools were established at all levels to ensure that supporters were registered and photographed. Speakers, party workers and potential candidates were trained in the arts of campaigning in weekend schools established for this purpose. Instructions were given on the meaning and scope of party politics, the constitution, the elements of public speaking, the responsibilities of a good legislator, and the relationship between the central government and local and statutory bodies. It was a tremendous achievement that bore ample testimony to the organizing and inspiring genius of Williams. This was by no means a one-man show, but the inspiration that galvanized the party into such frenzied enthusiasm came from him as much as it did from fears of a DLP takeover. The machine was not allowed to relax until the last vote was counted. Despite its glaring imperfections, which had less to do with the framework itself than with the human element in that framework, there is no doubt that the party was in superb shape as an electioneering machine in 1961. There had been no open splits or factional struggles of any major significance in the party's five-year history, a remarkable performance under any circumstances, but one of revolutionary proportions in anarchic Trinidad.

The DLP

Reference has already been made to the numerous splits and fissures that bedevilled the efforts of the DLP to forge a cohesive organization capable of coping with the PNM. The party's basic need was for a leader who would command the type of loyalty and respect that PNM followers had for Williams. The party spoke with too many voices, none of which was authoritative. The DLP was also not attracting the younger and more progressive people in the community, the professionals, the white-collar workers, and people who for one reason or another were alienated from the PNM and looking for a home. To attract these people, the DLP would have had to project a new image. There was need for a party that had a challenging programme, one that was thinking seriously about the possibility of forming an alternative government, a party that was ready to get down to the time-consuming task of organizing a mass following into groups that would function with some degree of autonomy.

The seeming imminence of a general election during 1959 and 1960 had given special urgency to the need for a new DLP leader. All efforts to form a third political force that would be truly "non-racial" or "all racial" having failed, it was agreed that the only real hope for a viable, competitive two-party system in Trinidad lay in reforming the DLP. Most people were convinced that Dr Rudranath Capildeo, a young mathematics lecturer at London University, was the man who could accomplish this. He was expected to lead the DLP out of its stubborn opposition to the People's Nationalist Movement. With the parties agreeing on the fundamentals of the national community, they could then compete on political rather than on racial issues.

After some hesitation, Capildeo succumbed to the pressures of party and public and accepted the leadership. But the transfer of leadership from Bhadase Maraj to the new Indian hero generated a bitter power struggle that almost wrecked the party. While most militants seemed willing to accept Capildeo, DLP chieftains were divided among themselves as to whether he was the right man for the job. Some felt that he had been away from the country for too long and was not sufficiently aware of the pitfalls of Trinidad politics. Others did not want to see Maraj pushed out if it meant a recurrence of the crisis of 1958–59, when a similar leadership dispute caused Maraj to walk out of the party with the bulk of its Hindu membership. And party professionals were anxious to retain Maraj because he was a proven vote winner and easier to manipulate. With Capildeo as the new leader, there were too many uncertainties about candidacies, policy and authority in the party.

The need to keep Maraj out of the forefront of DLP politics grew out of the party's valiant attempt to woo both the white creole element and the uncommitted voters whom it was believed Maraj would alienate. The urgency of the electoral struggle stimulated a mass rally of minorities behind Capildeo. Substantial numbers of prominent English, French, Syrian and Chinese creoles decided to come off the fence to join the "crusade of respectable people" against Williams and the PNM. Several established families publicly identified with the party, and the hand-picked executive was crowded with businessmen from the Chamber of Commerce.

The DLP was enthusiastic about the response to its appeal for a "crusade" to stop the march of the PNM into a "Castroite version of totalitarian dictatorship". Members were especially delighted that Sir Gerald Wight, a progressive white creole "patrician" who had once headed the POPPG, chose to return to politics under the DLP banner. This, perhaps one of the most significant events of the entire campaign, gave the campaign its tone. And it was a significant coup for the DLP. Wight's decision to enlist helped legitimize the party, and brought many of his type – "the massas", as Williams promptly dubbed them – out in the open.

It was clear to the DLP leadership, however, that the party could not defeat the PNM without the help of non-Indian elements. The party needed the financial backing of the European business community as much as it needed the voting support of Muslims, anti-PNM blacks, and others who were currently uncommitted. Capildeo made it quite clear to the Hindus that alone they could win only thirteen seats. They needed black votes, especially those in the two Tobago seats, and it was mainly for this reason that the party endorsed the proposal that Tobago be given independent status in the federation. The major premise that guided the reorganization of the party and the selection of notables was that it would take nothing short of a grand coalition of all "out" groups to overthrow the PNM, an outcome that would not materialize before 1986. DLP faithfuls talked glibly of the new formation as a "way of life", something that would last beyond the noise of election battle, but few were misled. It was a fragile house of cards, a rally of convenience, which almost disintegrated before election day.

The Trade Unions

The street marches sponsored by the trade unions in favour of the PNM were huge, noisy, and at times disorderly. The atmosphere of many was carnival-like, complete with steelbands. The *Guardian* and the DLP, which referred to the marchers as "rabble parading under the banner of a trade union", called upon the government to ban the marches. Williams's only reply was that the *Guardian* had the freedom of the press, and the workers the right of assembly. To the unionists he said, "March where the hell you like." Williams was openly grateful for the impressive display of support that the PNM had received from the workers. As he declared, "If there is any group in the community which is going to defend democracy and self-government, that group is the workers. . . . If any group is the repository of patriotism, that would be the workers of the country. No Government will survive without the point of view of the labour movement behind it . . . and we have it. . . . No one else could defend us, you know. . . . The workers are the force of the future. . . . After the elections I recognise my friends" (*Trinidad Guardian,* 28 November 1961). Williams was particularly solicitous of the Seamen and Waterfront Workers Union, which in fact became a bastion of PNM support. The Sugar Workers Union, in its turn, functioned as the base of the DLP.

Although Williams had opposed any representation for labour in the senate in his 1955 constitutional proposals, he now made it quite clear that he intended to nominate unionists to the upper chamber. He also promised to establish a labour college to teach unionists economics, sociology and politics so that they might not be at a disadvantage at the bargaining table. While there is little doubt that the PNM could have won without the marches, the margin of victory was substantially affected by the zeal with which labour's support was manifested. The workers had started a movement that caught on and spread to other groups as well.

The success with which the PNM had handled labour between 1956 and 1961 was quite unique in the history of the nationalist movement in the West Indies. The party was able to mobilize and retain the support of the working class without having to organize it in affiliate unions. As C.L.R. James observed, 'Whereas it is the standard practice in the West Indies for political parties to create unions, or vice versa, here the TUC is independent. The fact that an independent body has endorsed the PNM was very significant. It testified to the confidence which the unions had in the PNM (*Trinidad Guardian,* 27 November 1961). The unions had translated the "massa day done" spirit into terms meaningful to them. But they had also created tremendous problems for the PNM on the morrow of the elections.

The Chamber of Commerce

Unlike the Trade Union Congress, the Chamber of Commerce, as the major voice of the business community in the territory, preferred to retain its official position of political neutrality. The chamber in fact took the view that, by its articles of association, it could not support any political party directly or indirectly. As an associational body that included individuals and firms which identified with both political parties, it could not take any partisan action (*Trinidad Guardian,*

I December 1961). Many refused, however, to take the chamber's protestation seriously. As in 1956, PNM supporters were convinced that the chamber was against them, and that it was giving financial and organizational support to the DLP. Williams himself complained that business, "which never had it so good", was pouring enormous sums of money into the DLP war chest. Williams even threatened to reveal the names of the firms involved, and subtly encouraged his supporters to patronize selectively. There were good enough reasons to suspect that business was partial to the DLP, since many prominent businessmen were on the DLP executive; but this is to simplify grossly what was in fact a much more complex issue.

Many businesses concluded that regardless of their personal dislike for Williams and the PNM, it was suicidal to oppose them frontally. A few of them entertained positive feelings of allegiance towards the PNM. Whether out of love or opportunism, the fact remains that business gave as much money to the PNM in 1961 as it did to the DLP. DLP executives even contended that the PNM received more. All the firms interviewed reported that they divided their contributions equally between the two parties regardless of what employees might have felt or done as individuals. This was true of both native and foreign firms. Chinese businessmen were quite emphatic that they gave equally to both groups, though there is a strong suspicion that they were more partial to the PNM. One prominent member of this group, in an unguarded remark to the author, intimated that he did not really care which of the two major ethnic groups destroyed the other, just so long as he was left free to make his profits. The impression conveyed was that this was not an uncommon view in his and other business circles.

The business community had apprehensions about both political parties. Cross-pressures were intense for many, especially for native elements. Capildeo's threats of violence (see below) sent business into a tailspin. The Chamber of Commerce was quite explicit about its fears:

> The ripple of violence which has appeared on the scene and which threatens to develop into a wave, is deplored by the Chamber, not only for the death or injuries to persons and the destruction of properties, but also for the crippling effect which it will have on the economic development of the area.
>
> This Territory, noted in the past for its stable and responsible Governments and for its peaceful and tolerant people, is in danger of losing that reputation. Once lost, it will be many long years before investors from overseas can be convinced that it is safe to bring their capital and their technical skills here. (*Trinidad Guardian*, I December 1961)

The chamber only hesitated at the last moment and did not name Capildeo as the principal threat to social peace.

Another unspoken (at least in public) objection that the European business aristocracy held against Capildeo was his "Indian-ness". If it was clear that many of them did not want a "black" prime minister, it was even clearer that they preferred that unhappy fate to the prospect of a "coolie" prime minister whom they felt they could trust even less. This preference held as much for the social groups they represented. Capildeo was quite aware of this, and in fact bitterly denounced the chamber for what he felt was its egregious failure to overcome ethnic prejudices and come to the rescue of democracy in Trinidad. This to him was the real issue. He warned them against the illusion that they were sufficiently entrenched in their hillside bivouacs and could stay out of the arena of politics. It was a phantasmagoria that they would soon come to regret.

But as alienated as big business was from the DLP, it was also afraid of Williams and the PNM, and deeply concerned about the damage that Williams's "Massa Day Done" campaign strategy might do to the social order as they knew and preferred it. Business was also concerned about the "dangerous" alliance between labour and government that the elections had solidified; and it was for this reason that many businessmen who had no love for the PNM contributed so heavily to its appeal fund. This was the least they could do to weaken the feelings of dependence that nationalist forces were beginning to feel for labour. The dilemma of the business community in 1961 was real and poignant, and this should be borne in mind as the campaign strategy of the PNM is examined. One gets an entirely different impression from the loaded and inflammatory rhetoric of Williams.

The Catholic Church and the Concordat

A considerable amount of attention has already been given to the positions taken by Williams and religious groups on the explosive subject of education in the 1955–56 period. The issue, which had disappeared from public notice following the 1956 election, had again appeared on the political agenda in July 1960. An important event that formed the essential backdrop for the heated discussions of 1960 was the publication of the report of the Committee on General Education, which made recommendations for overhauling the educational system with a view to the "integration of the diverse elements which comprise our cosmopolitan population" (Maurice 1960, 32).

The recommendations of the Maurice Committee contain the essence of the spirit that agitated the minds of nationalists in 1955–56 insofar as they related to the creation of a national multiracial community. The committee included representatives of most religious groups, but nevertheless contained a majority of PNM stalwarts and sympathizers. It gratefully acknowledged the contribution that the churches had made to the educational development of the community, but noted that the system had created a number of difficulties and problems that had not been anticipated when education mushroomed in the nineteenth century.

Observing that there were now fifteen denominational school boards in existence, the committee felt that this fragmentation had contributed a great deal towards the creation of "an unfortunate division of plural and parallel societies in Trinidad and Tobago" (ibid., 48–49).

Analysis of the ethnic distribution of certain schools revealed the alarming fact that in some of them, even those in racially mixed areas, as much as 97 per cent of the school population belonged to one ethnic group. "This," the committee observed, "is not a healthy prospect in so mixed a racial population, and does not envisage the harmonious mixing of the society outside school. Nor should this harmony be taken for granted." The committee felt that a system of state schools could combine the best elements of all the various systems, while at the same time permitting the elimination of the glaring drawbacks of the existing system. A strong case was made for a system of localized school boards that would consist of both state and denominational authorities. This would permit the development of a school system that would serve the needs of the community as a whole, omitting at the same time the jealousy and rivalry that obtained among religious groups in terms of building construction, personnel recruitment and management. And most important, such a system would achieve the stated aim of having most of the school population pass through the crucible of a common school system with a common curriculum and examinations. Those who resolutely refused to be absorbed into the new system should, however, be left free to maintain private and independent schools. The committee did not recommend that all schools should be nationalized, or that further construction of such schools should be prohibited. It did recommend that in order to qualify for state aid, both primary and secondary schools must agree to come under the jurisdiction of the local boards and ultimately the Ministry of Education.

The report, and the government's proposals based on it, had an extremely rough passage in the legislative council. Lionel Seukeran, DLP member of the legislative council, declared that the committee had interpreted its terms of reference to mean not integration, but "subordination and subjugation of the several denominational authorities to the will of the PNM" (*Hansard*, 27 July 1960, 2999–3040). Opposition from Hindu and Catholic groups in the country was intense. Catholic authorities noted, by way of justification for particularistic recruitment policies, that Catholic schools depended largely on endowments from Catholic benefactors. The church schools had their own traditions and obligations to their own people. Many parents sent their offspring to Catholic schools because they wished them to have a religiously influenced education. All this was threatened by the proposed new arrangements.

The announced aim of the government to make education free was also opposed on the ground that "Catholic social doctrine disapproves of the welfare state in which Government provides all social services free of charge to its citizens indiscriminately" (*Trinidad Guardian*, 27 July 1960). It was nevertheless admitted that until the community as a whole had sufficient means to pay for such services, the government had an obligation to provide for those unable to pay. But parents should not be coerced by the state because they did not have the economic means to sustain their private choice.

While the Protestant churches seemed prepared to back most if not all of the government's education proposals, the Catholic Church was prepared to fight the "schoolmaster government" that was seeking to invade the schools to purvey its "abominable totalitarian ideology". Through its press, forums and pulpits, the clergy resolutely sought to incite Catholics to put pressure on the government. Fears were aroused that Hindus and Muslims would be in charge of Catholic education institutions, and that party cells for indoctrination would be established in the schools. In a pastoral letter that was read and explained in every church and oratory in the community, Archbishop Finbar Ryan contested the view that "education is essentially a national affair". This postulate clashed with "the law of nature as well as the positive law of God". Responsibility for the education of children belonged primarily to the family:

> Those who govern the State and administer its resources must not think, nor act, as though children belonged to it, before they belong to the family, and that, consequently, the State has an absolute right over education. The State and the teachers it employs exist to supplement the insufficiency of the family and the Church. It acts in loco parentum, and not on its own authority. . . . Ministers of State are not the owners of the monies they administer; they are trustees. Catholics of this territory contribute indirectly and/or directly, to the taxes; they have, consequently, a right to demand an equitable share of the monies set aside for education so that their teachers and their schools shall be able to function in conformity with Catholic principles; and without any "string" other than that they render an account of the use made of monies disbursed to them. (Ryan 1960, 8)

The church, it was maintained, had no objection to its followers being good citizens, and in fact encouraged it. It agreed that they should have a suitable knowledge of their civic and national duties, and applauded the state's attempts to "mobilize all the people's human resources" for the development of national pride and nationhood. But man also had purposes that were not earthbound. Temporal ideals must be sacrificed to eternal ideals. The church would therefore "never assent" to any arrangement that would subject the government of schools to the civil and political powers, whose seeming aim was to encourage communal interdenominational worship and "bowdlerized" religious education. The purpose of religion in the schools was not to give children "a tremendous emotional experience of love and fellowship", but rather specific indoctrination.

The church also expressed itself sympathetic to the need for the racial integration of the community, but argued that this goal could best be achieved by "the acceptance of the supra-national ideal given the Catholic Church by its founder Jesus Christ". Not a word was said about correcting the type of ethnic exclusivism for which some of its schools were known. The archbishop presented what he believed to be the "irreducible minimum" that the church was prepared to accept in its negotiations with the state:

1. While prepared to cooperate as far as possible with the "Proposed Machinery of Administration" . . . the Catholic Church cannot cede its ownership nor the right of direct control and management of her primary and secondary schools. The existing managerial system may be modified and its working clarified, but the authority of the Church . . . must be retained and safeguarded.

2. In Catholic schools, no books, lessons, nor apparatus to which the competent Catholic Authority formally objects may be introduced and imposed; nor in non-Catholic schools may Catholic teachers or children be compelled to use them.

3. No teachers, including especially head-teachers, to whom the competent Catholic Authority objects on grounds of faith and/or morals, shall be appointed to Catholic schools.

4. The pluralist composition of the pupil-body in Catholic schools and colleges is a natural and largely inevitable consequence of the pluralist composition, national, racial, linguistic, and religious, of our Trinidad and Tobago society. But . . . disproportionate mixing of Catholic and non-Catholic children, must as far as possible be avoided, and the clerical manager's right to supervise the entry of non-Catholic pupils and their conduct after admission must be recognized, as well as his right to demand their withdrawal should their creedal or moral influence be injurious.

Concluded the archbishop, "We trust that a Government which professes to be democratic will modify the recommendations in a manner satisfactory to the Catholic Church and Catholic parents. . . . The Church is not raising a question of party politics . . . but all should note that Catholics are roughly one-third of the population and include representatives of every section of our cosmopolitan community. *Their suffrage is no small power*" (ibid., 15; emphasis added).

As in 1956, the church was again prepared to engage its authority on a fundamental issue. PNM stalwarts in their egalitarian zeal were also prepared, as they were in 1956, to take up the gauntlet thrown down by the hierarchy. But not so Williams. With an approaching key election, Williams was anxious to remove all issues around which anti-PNM groups could forge a united front. The Chaguaramas and constitutional issues were already out of the way, and only the church remained to be accommodated. On Christmas Day, 1960, it was announced that church and state had reached "complete accord" in their negotiations on the school issue (*Trinidad Guardian*, 25 December 1960). Williams had again made a strategic retreat on an issue that had been assumed to be non-negotiable.

By the terms of the concordat, the churches were confirmed in their proprietary rights to their schools. The right of the church to veto the introduction of books, apparatus and changes in the curriculum in their schools was also conceded. The churches also retained the right to insist that their religion be the only one taught in their schools by teachers who belonged to their denomination, though pupils of other faiths were not to be compelled to take such instruction. Churches were to be allowed access to state schools at given times to give instruction to children of their flock.

The rights of appointment, retention, promotion, transfer and dismissal of teachers were to be vested in the Public Service Commission as was the case with other civil servants, but denominational boards were given the right to refuse to accept or retain a teacher whose moral or religious conduct did not meet with their approval. Any disciplinary matter short of expulsion was to remain solely with the boards, which were also allowed to maintain teacher training schools subject to the provision that the state had to approve selection to them. On the question of recruitment of pupils, the church made its biggest compromise. On the basis of a common entrance exam, the state was to determine 80 per cent of those who entered the first form of the secondary schools. The principals of church schools were left free to allocate the remaining 20 per cent *"as they saw fit,* provided that *normally,* the pass list of the common entrance examination serve to provide the pupils" (emphasis added). Church schools remained eligible for state aid.

The government had capitulated to the Catholic Church. While some of the drawbacks of the old system were corrected, especially in regard to teacher and pupil recruitment – because the state could now use its control of the 80 per cent pupil quota to change the complexion of the schools – the churches were left relatively free to carry on as before, with only a minimum of government supervision or dictation. Moreover, despite the assumption that the state would use the examination pass list as the basis for recruiting the churches' quota, in fact the churches were free to assign scarce school places at state expense to pupils who need not possess the achievement criteria for admission, while qualified pupils were allowed to go unplaced. With twenty-five thousand pupils competing for four thousand places, this was a substantial concession to make. The egalitarian purpose of the PNM was seriously compromised.

Many party stalwarts, especially those who were teachers, were infuriated, especially since the party had not been consulted. The party was split on the issue, as was the cabinet. Some ministers felt that it was not "safe" to take the matter to the party. The author of the report, Senator Hamilton Maurice, remained outspokenly convinced that "in a society of competing ethnic groups, a society where religious dogma combines with racial differences, the existing educational system poses the greatest threat to national unity". Only a unified state system could contain the strife potential of the community. "No system that is the servant of any one particular class, race or creed can achieve this goal" (*Nation*, 2 December 1960).

The Protestant churches were quite pleased with the settlement that the Catholic hierarchy had been able to force on the PNM, though they might very well have been chagrined that the government had bargained mainly with the Catholic Church. Between 1960 and 1965, when the issue was reopened, the Catholic Church gave open support to the PNM regime. The "opening to the right" strategy had been given additional thrust. With the church, the Colonial Office, and the State Department neutralized, Williams could declare to the nation that the government had now cleared the road of all the obstacles that had inhibited the creation of the national community.

But the consolidation of the power of the PNM was a prime prerequisite for effecting this goal. The party that had initiated the "revolution" had to be allowed to complete it, even if this meant that some of these revolutionary goals had to be sacrificed in the short run. As Williams told the sixth party convention in January 1961, "I for one intend to play politics. Let everybody understand that. I have been accused for four years of playing politics. Well by God, they are going to get politics now, and I hope they recognise it." The "no deals" era had come to a close.

20   **The Elections of 1961**

Massa Day Done

> My opponents were always playing into my hands, giving me opportunity after opportunity to develop my specialty.
>   – Eric Williams

The general elections of 1961 were the most pivotal that the country had faced in the post-war era. The 1956 elections had been important as well, as we have seen, but those of 1961 were more so because their outcome would determine the question of which of the two ethnic groups and their respective heroes would rule Trinidad and Tobago for the foreseeable future. Would Eric Williams, the Afro-creole messianic leader, and the PNM be confirmed in their hold on the country, or would Dr Rudranath Capildeo, the Indo-creole challenger, and the DLP succeed in arresting and reversing what had been indicated by the results of the 1956 election? Were the federal election of 1958 and the county council elections of 1959 any indication that Williams and the PNM were not invincible, or had those results been achieved against the run of play, so to speak; or had the DLP been neutralized by what had been done in parliament in respect of the new electoral rules that the PNM had put in place even before a single vote was cast? The country and the region looked on in awe and anxiety as the two formations struck mightily at each other and at the foundations of the social order.

Capildeo had been recruited in 1960 as the Indian equivalent to Williams and he sought to play the role. He was quite persuaded that the rule of law was no longer a meaningful principle in Trinidad and Tobago, and that the PNM, or at least its spirit, was enthroned in the judiciary. His thesis was that in the modern parliamentary state where power was held by the prime minister, the only real restraint was an alert public opinion. What Williams had done, he argued, was to divide public opinion by manufacturing crises and subtly exploiting racial differences. In the process, Williams had silenced critical opinion; frustrations, which would normally be focused on the government, were directed to minority elements, who were made the acceptable targets of blame. By posing as the redeemer of the Afros, Williams had put himself beyond the pale of effective critical intelligence. To dissent was to split the ranks, to be treasonable. Whether the population was aware of it or not, Williams had used race and the symbols of democracy to establish a dictatorship, unchecked and unbalanced, and to camouflage a naked will to power and dominance. Trinidad society had been "murdered" by a revolution that had been carried through under the cloak of democratic and legal theory ("The Rule of Law", *Trinidad Guardian*, 3 August 1961).

Capildeo admitted that Indian leaders had also used the issue of race for political purposes; he even suggested that this was the reason why they never produced an outstanding national leader. "Dr Williams," he said, "took a leaf from their book; that is the big disappointment about him. If people think I am going to be a racial leader, they have the wrong man" (*Trinidad Guardian*, 30 April 1961). Capildeo disclosed that he had voted for the PNM in 1956.

But race was not the only tool used to silence dissent. Williams, the DLP argued, had destroyed the local press and had intimidated individuals who might have been disposed to criticize the performance of the regime. There were indeed many people who were alienated by the PNM but who feared to come out in the open. Self-interest and cowardice reinforced each other. Capildeo put the blame squarely on the middle classes for their "spiritual flabbiness".

On the question of public morality and financial integrity, Capildeo had much to criticize. He claimed, with good justification, that the PNM was using the treasury to finance the election. He held that the government had used special warrants to hand out TT$6.5 million to daily paid workers in retroactive pay, $4.5 million to the unemployed in an uncoordinated "boondoggling" crash programme, the benefits of which went mainly to PNM areas and supporters, and $2.5 million for a job-evaluation scheme to hold civil servants in line. As in the old order, he said, sections of the population were being extravagantly bribed. The DLP also complained that deficit financing had depleted the country's reserves. According to figures released by the Central Statistical Office, expenditure consistently exceeded revenue in 1959 and 1961 (*Annual Statistical Digest*, 1962, 159).

The government's handling of the financing of the islandwide sewer programme also came in for a merciless muckraking. The details of the "sewerage scandal" cannot be told here. Suffice it to say that the circumstances surrounding the negotiations between the government, the Swiss West Indies Bank, and the Compagnie Française de Transactions Internationals left many people wondering just how seriously they should take the PNM's claim to be the restorer of public morality. According to the evidence presented by the DLP press, evidence that included photographic copies of letters, notes, official communications and ministerial bank accounts in Switzerland, all of which were leaked, international financiers offered to provide a press for the PNM, shares to four or five ministers in a projected metal-works company, huge overdrafts and other privileges, in return for franchises to operate a number of concerns and, above all, to serve as the government's agents for financing the sewerage project. Because of indiscretions on the part of principals, news of the negotiations began to filter to the informed public, and before long mushroomed into one of the biggest public scandals the country had yet faced.

Williams, who was not personally named in any of the transactions, made a brilliant defence of the integrity of his administration, which seemed to satisfy most of his party followers and those who refused to believe that the PNM could ever be guilty of such shady practices. But a large bloc of opinion remained suspicious. If the DLP had concentrated mainly on its published programme and on the record of the PNM administration, perhaps the "sewerage scheme scandal" would have swayed more floating voters. The outcome might not have been significantly different in terms of seats, but the popular vote might have been considerably affected, especially in the urban areas. By introducing the spectre of armed violence into the campaign, however, the party alienated and frightened away much of the support that might have been attracted to it.

For a while the DLP was quite undecided whether it should contest the election. Party officials complained not only that they were not properly consulted on the decision to use the voting machines, but that they were not even given adequate opportunity to examine them. The veil of secrecy surrounding the machines made the party suspicious that the PNM was tampering with them while they were in storage. Members could not understand why they were not allowed to import one privately so that they could satisfy themselves that it was tamper-proof. The DLP organ, the *Statesman*, reported (8 December 1961) that the minister of home affairs had told a DLP businessman, "If you bring down voting machines and give them to the so-and-so DLP in order that they may teach their supporters how to vote, I shall break you socially, politically and economically." The DLP feared that many "DLP voters" – a euphemism for Indians – would not be able to complete all the procedures involved in casting votes on the machine, especially when, for lack of proper electrical facilities, the machine had to be manually operated. It was also feared that partisan machine attendants would give false guidance to such voters. So desperate had Capildeo become, in fact, that he issued a clarion call for a thousand of his followers "to come forward on election day and smash up a thousand voting machines" (*Trinidad Guardian*, 10 September 1961). He assured his followers that if the PNM won the election, only a revolution could dislodge them in the future.

Capildeo insisted that he had threatened violence against machines and never against persons. But in the same speech, we find him declaring, "Today I have come, but I have come not to bring peace, but to bring a sword. We have brought peace long enough and they cannot understand." Capildeo explained later that his threats of violence were meant to dramatize the plight of the opposition and force the community and the media to listen to it. He bitterly complained that the communications media were opposed to the DLP, and that the government had also refused to grant them time on the radio network to state their case.

But it was over the question of PNM "hooliganism" and the partisanship of the police that the temper of the DLP really exploded. The DLP complained that their "people" had become the principal targets of Afro vandalism. Items on the catalogue of woes related by the DLP press included the stoning of mosques and temples, the looting of Indian homes and retail establishments, the beating of Indian vendors, the slashing of tires on the cars belonging to Europeans, the pulling down of DLP streamers, the breaking-up of DLP election meetings, police brutality, and the use of insulting expressions, for example, "We don't want no roti government", and "Coolie must feed nigger".

The DLP organ was replete with bold headlines: "Dark Times Ahead", "Floods of Strife", "The PNM, the Police, and Violence", "Rule By Force", "Sleep No More", "A Nightmare Reign of Terror Is Upon Us", "Towards a Crisis", "Congolese-Type National Guard". There is no doubt that the Indians felt themselves a persecuted minority. They were convinced that the PNM elite was not really making more than a token effort to contain their followers. Williams's invitation to his followers to "march where the hell you like" was seen as an open invitation to attack the Indian community. Woodford Square had become a shrine of hate where minorities were offered up for sacrifice, they complained. So tense had the situation become that Indians were ready to believe that a programme of inoculation in the countryside was the beginning of mass genocide. Wild but groundless rumours began circulating that six hundred Indian children had died following the inoculations. Similar reports said that Indians planned to retaliate by attacking police stations and schools in Port of Spain.

In the last two months before the elections, DLP politicians were becoming increasing desperate and seemed ready to plunge the community into open strife, which to them now seemed the only redressive measure at hand. The DLP appealed vainly to the governor, who refused to overstep what he felt were his constitutional limitations. The DLP disagreed with this interpretation of the governor's role. It argued that he was still the representative of Her Majesty the Queen, and should, therefore, grant an audience to the party. It is in this context that the question of consultation must be viewed when the independence constitution is discussed. On 8 October, Capildeo told his constituents, "The day we are ready, we will take over this country and not a thing will stop us. . . . If [the Governor] is so misguided as to tell us no, we are going to McLeod, and if he is stupid enough to tell us no, then we will come back and take over. It is as simple as that" (*Trinidad Guardian*, 8 October 1961). On 10 October, the statements became even more extreme. "The only remedy to PNM persecution is to adopt the South American method of bloodshed and riot, revolution or civil disobedience, until you grind Government operations to a full stop, and then you get possession" (Capildeo, 10 October, 1961, Port of Spain, to a group of businessmen). Capildeo was well aware that this was an idle threat and that Caroni, a predominantly Indian county, was perhaps the only area where he could make a successful "stand". As he told a prayer-meeting in Caroni, "We shall not rest until final victory is achieved . . . even if Caroni alone is left. The fight will be carried on and we will make people outside feel the force of our arms, the strength of our intellect and the breadth and vision of our character."

The racial bloodbath that many were beginning to fear seemed more imminent on Sunday, 15 October. One of the largest multiethnic crowds to assemble for a political meeting began dispersing in alarm when they heard Capildeo tell his supporters in a screaming voice to "Arm yourselves with weapons in order to take over this country. . . . Get ready to march on Whitehall; get ready now. Get ready to march on Government House . . . that is what I am asking you to do" (Siewah 1994, 97). The meeting, which was held on the Queen's Park Savannah, not far from the governor's residence, was viewed by the DLP as a test case to determine whether they would be allowed to conduct their meetings in peace. There had been a lot of heckling at their meetings and they claimed that they had deliberately avoided Woodford Square for the serene atmosphere of the greens in front of the governor general's home. Alarmed the *Guardian,* which appealed for an "armistice" between the two "warring" groups, warned the leader of the DLP that it would not support him or anyone else who threatened the flouting of the law. "Force," declared the *Guardian,* "was alien to our tradition. . . . An Opposition is expected to conduct itself with the restraint of an alternative Government" if it expects to enjoy public confidence (*Trinidad Guardian*, 16 October 1961).

Reports vary about how much heckling there was on that Sunday, but Capildeo felt that despite Williams's advice to his supporters that they should *not* heckle, there was too much of it, the police presence notwithstanding. If the police and the government could not or would not restrain the crowd, there was no alternative but to turn crowd against crowd. Capildeo sought to do so at another election meeting at Streatham Lodge on 19 November 1961:

> If the police will not protect us, I shall call upon my supporters to arm themselves. . . . If the PNM continues to organize hooligans, to disrupt our meetings, . . . you will be called to arms.
>
> Wherever PNM holds a meeting, you will have to break it up; wherever PNM holds a meeting, destroy them. Do not give them a chance. Those are my instructions to you today.
>
> Wherever Dr Williams goes, run him out of town; wherever Dr Solomon goes, run him out of town. From now on, the chips are down, and I expect you to stand with

us, and free this country from this type of hooliganism once and for all.

I am asking you to arm yourselves with a weapon in order to take over this country. I have stood as much of this nonsense as I can stand. . . .

I thought I was leading men, not women. I thought you had red blood in your veins. You don't have. Which of you would slap Dr. Williams in his face? . . . Not one of you.

Capildeo's outburst was blamed on the unwillingness of the police to stop vandals from breaking up their meeting. The official police report maintained that there was no more heckling than was normally associated with meetings of that size. Trinidad seemed poised on the brink of racial war; security forces were immediately alerted.

Capildeo also accused the PNM of contriving to steal the coming election via voting machines:

> [W]hat of those voting machines that have been brought in by the PNM for the general elections? These machines are one possible means by which the PNM government can stop the DLP from winning elections after what happened in 1958. The PNM lost the Federal Elections in 1958 to the DLP. We are asking again for the right to vote by the ballot box. We had asked for a referendum, but the Government turned down our petition. I appeal to you, therefore, for a mandate to petition the Governor, Sir Solomon Hochoy, and the Governor General, Lord Hailes, for the ballot box system of voting to be retained. If they refuse, we must go to London to seek an audience with Mr. Maulding, the new Secretary of State for the Colonies. God help the Colonial Office if he refuses this reasonable request. (In Siewah 1994, 106–7)

Williams was convinced that the aim of the DLP leadership was to incite violence as a method of forcing the Colonial Office to intervene and postpone the elections. But the government itself was taking no chances. Minister of home affairs Patrick Solomon, who was given the sobriquet "Minister of War", warned Capildeo that "anyone who adores the guillotine must be equally ready to caress its cold steel". When Capildeo showed no willingness to recant, but in fact reprimanded his followers for their cowardice and irresolution, Solomon again warned, "If Capildeo incites violence, I will slap him in gaol fast . . . and he would not get out again. Nobody will be able to bail him out. . . . No tuppeny hapenny dictator [is] going to walk through this country and tell people to take up arms." Belatedly remembering that there was "due process of law", Solomon added, "I would take him before the Judge, and the Judge would impose the necessary sentence" (*Trinidad Guardian*, 23 November 1961).

As a precautionary measure, the government declared a state of emergency in a number of areas where gunplay had led to fatal violence involving PNM party workers. (One person was killed and four wounded.) The office of the DLP political leader was also raided for evidence of sedition. The DLP protested that emergencies were not declared in areas where violence directed at them had erupted.

They also complained that during the search for hidden arms, Indian women were indecently frisked by black policemen. The emergency was said to be designed to pre-empt violence, but the precautionary measures served to harden the hostility that embittered both sides. They had the effect, however, of shocking the community out of its complacent feeling that "it could never happen here". It was to the credit of both parties that they chose to hesitate at the brink. Capildeo himself suspended all open-air meetings temporarily in the hope of forestalling the spread of violence, and called upon the population to pray for racial peace. The DLP also declined to contest the municipal elections in November 1961 on the grounds that it would only disturb the territory more than was necessary. Had Capildeo been preventively detained, as some PNM supporters demanded, his "martyrdom" would most certainly have been the signal for racial war. But Capildeo had clearly proven to be the DLP's greatest liability during the campaign, provoked though he most certainly was. Many DLP stalwarts in fact felt that Capildeo had "done Dr Williams's work for him". L.F. Seukeran subsequently wrote about Capildeo's speech on the Queen's Park Savannah,

> If he expected deafening applause he was mistaken. No one took him on, no one responded to his call. Instead one by one, I saw people moving out. First the whites then the Chinese and Syrians and business people whom I recognized, and the Savannah began emptying. As he sat, a dejected, defeated man, I told him that he had done us the greatest disservice by losing the election that day. He was a greater enemy of the people than the PNM was. He asked me to speak. I refused. We did not have to go to the polls to lose. He had done Williams' work for him. (Seukeran 1991, 256)

Oxaal agrees that Capildeo's outburst and his call for violence led to a loss of support. As he opines, "his call to violence, designed to end forever the ancient stereotype of the weak and fearful coolie which had made Indians the prey of Negro bullying and arrogance, went unanswered. Rather than gaining support, the DLP now lost support. Intended by some business interests to serve as the party of order, it became a party of disorder" (Oxaal 1968, 172). Oxaal agrees, however, that Capildeo was heckled and harassed by Afro-Trinidadian voters, even in staid Woodbrook. "As I looked on incredulously, his Negro antagonists howled and raged like crazed animals against the cast iron fence which fortunately separated the house from the street. It was a hideous ordeal, but he bore it with fortitude. Somehow sensing his vulnerability, the mob, under the eyes of the alert but inactive police, redoubled their taunts: Mad Scientist, Mad Scientist. The DLP campaign soon withdrew from the streets altogether and was conducted indoors, chiefly in private homes" (ibid., 172).

Winston Mahabir offered another explanation for Capildeo's erratic behaviour. Capildeo suffered from rheumatic fever and knew that he did not have long to live. To quote Mahabir,

Rudranath recovered but his heart suffered further damage. He knew his time was limited and this might well have determined to a large extent the almost frantic nature of his activities during his latter years. He was like a doomed giant looking for a cause – and an opportunity. He found both.

After Bhadase handed him the leadership of the DLP, Rudranath's ambitions seemed to grow exponentially. He would be Prime Minister at any cost. Nothing less would do. This is not hearsay, but is precisely what he told my wife and me at our home while I was still a Minister in the PNM Government. He would join the PNM on one condition – Williams must step down! At a subsequent gathering he said openly to us that he was prepared to have a blood bath if such became necessary to achieve power! He became obsessed with the idea of power. After I decided not to continue in politics, he telephoned me repeatedly, at first entreating me to join him in his relentless pursuit and reminding me of his accuracy in predictions.

In his personal conversation and public pronouncements his bombast became increasingly offensive. As the campaign progressed and one measured his leadership against that of Williams, he was a loser all the way. Both Capildeo and Williams exhibited signs of sporadic emotional imbalance. (1978, 110–11)

It is worth noting that, fearing a crisis, Williams requested the federal government to release the Trinidad contingent of the West Indian army, a request that was refused, much to the anger and dismay of the Trinidad government. The federal government took the position, a correct one, that the army was a federal unit, and as such no island had the right to request specific elements of it. And in the context of this crisis demands for a national guard began to be heard.

The PNM on the Eve

The major themes of Williams's campaign in 1961 were national independence, equality and interracial solidarity. These were to be the essential pillars of the "new society". On the question of federation, Williams's view was that Trinidad's future role in the Caribbean should not be discussed during the campaign as the DLP had suggested. At a special election convention held on 23 September 1961, Williams told the party that the issue was still very "unsubstantial", too filled with uncertainties for a decision to be made at that time. Williams warned non-Trinidadian politicians against coming to campaign for federation in Trinidad: "If there is any interference from any outside quarter in the Trinidad and Tobago elections, I will call a meeting in 24 hours and blow up the whole damn scandal of the Federation" (*Trinidad Guardian*, 6 October 1991). The remarks may have been directed to the Colonial Office as well.

The party agreed enthusiastically to go along with this advice, and voted to leave the matter in the hands of the leader and his close advisers, who assured them that following the election, the country would be given the opportunity to make its views known on the subject. Williams promised that before the federation issue was negotiated, the PNM would educate and take the general feel of the population. But it was also noted that, legally, the federation no longer existed. There was no federation to stay in: "one from ten leaves nought" in constitutional law. As we have seen, this clever remark caused a great deal of anguish in the Caribbean and the Caribbean diaspora.

The reaction of the public to the decision to take federation out of the campaign was mixed and did not necessarily follow party lines. The *Guardian*, which under its new foreign management was basically pro-government, endorsed the PNM's stand: "The electorate should not be asked to pass judgment on issues, the full implications of which the politicians themselves have not yet been able to grasp" (*Trinidad Guardian*, 27 September 1961). The DLP took a different view: parochial issues should not have precedence over a vital issue like federation. Williams was unreasonably contemptuous of the DLP's demand that the issue be debated:

> What business is it of the DLP if we are opposed to [discussing the idea] . . . of Federation? When we are ready to come and tell the population what they should do, [we will do so]. . . . We know that we enjoy the confidence of the population to such an extent that we merely have to explain the issues, the pros and cons, argue this and argue that, and the whole population, when it sees the issues . . . would go along as one united nation on this issue. . . . They tell me that 99 percent of the people in the country would follow blindly whatever I say on Federation. If that is so, then that only puts a greater responsibility on my shoulders not to play the fool and go leading the people up the garden path. (Williams at Fifth Street, Barataria, tape of speech, n.d.)

The manifesto of the PNM was in large part an attempt to make the public aware of what the party had achieved during its term of office. The PNM took credit for the creation of approximately forty thousand new jobs, though they admitted that these gains were offset by a reduction of 8 per cent of the labour force in the oil and asphalt industries, 50 per cent in the sugar factories, and about 20 per cent on the sugar estates. Mechanization had eliminated as many jobs as had been created by new industries. The PNM also took it as a vote of confidence that thirty-two new industries with an investment capital of TT$33 million had been attracted to the island since 1956, to create jobs – when completed – for an additional 3,375 persons. As of 1961, only 1,540 persons had actually been employed in these industries. It was boasted that in 1961 alone, as many as fifty-three applications had been received for pioneer status, a provision that allowed firms to secure tax relief and access to state-provided facilities designed to attract their investment. The party manifesto seemed quite optimistic that the job problem could be solved by the methods that had been pursued in the past.

The party boasted too about its efforts to expand the supply of water to all areas of the community, though admitting needs continued to outrun facilities. Credit was also claimed for the construction of thirty-three thousand outdoor privies, which had helped to eradicate hookworm disease; for the new Workmen's Compensation Ordinance, which had given increased and wider protection to the worker; for the Hire-Purchase Ordinance, which had made it more difficult for firms to repossess purchases after a fixed percentage of the amount owed was paid; for the Agricultural Small-Holdings Ordinance, designed to give peasants greater security of tenure; and for efforts in the field of housing for people of all classes, including the Indian estate-worker, who no longer lived in barracks.

The fiscal reserves were indeed low, but they had gone into the creation of much-needed welfare services and social overhead capital. The government made no apologies for its crash programmes, which it claimed were designed to give the small man a job. Preoccupation with classical economics must not be permitted to obscure the needs of the "forgotten man", who in the meantime had to live. As he surveyed the achievements of the past five years, Williams boasted that nothing had been accomplished in Puerto Rico under Muñoz Marin that had not been accomplished by the PNM in its first term.

But no one was more aware of the incompleteness of the PNM revolution than Williams himself. And as the PNM Manifesto reminded people, "A national revolution cannot be expected, in a mere five years, to correct the neglect and deficiencies of centuries." In terms of legislation introduced and passed, the PNM had indeed created a fundamental social revolution. But by 1961 much of the legislation was still on paper, awaiting administrative machinery to give it significance. The PNM was demanding, then, a chance to finish the job that it had begun in 1956.

Massa Day Done!

Williams chose to make the black–white issue the basis of most of his campaign speeches. In speech after speech on the theme "Massa Day Done!", he poured scorn on the European creole community and even accused them, rather unfairly, of supporting the DLP's call for violence. "These vagabonds . . . these people whose hands are at your throats, see your rising dignity and economic progress as something to be destroyed so that they may enter and rule." He warned that he would use his knowledge of West Indian history to put their counter-revolutionary attempt in perspective:

> They cuss me out because I know the history of Trinidad and Tobago. I didn't go into politics to forget what I used to teach in the University where I paid the price of my judgment. . . . If I started to use history as the murderous ruthless weapon that it could become in my hands, boy I am sorry for them. After all, I did not write that history. They wrote it; I only analyse it.

Williams told the masses that whatever history he knew, he had learned at their expense: "Everything that I learned, I will pass on to you. By giving you information about your past, I am giving you the weapon which you can use to defend yourselves. The education of the people has been the popular rock on which I built the PNM, and the gates of the DLP hell will never prevail against it" (Williams at Woodford Square, 9 November 1961). Referring to Capildeo's threats to use the sword, Williams replied, "Anyone can come to you with the sword. I come to you with the pen. The pen is mightier than the sword. I bring to you the pen to analyse, the pen to write the history of the future, the pen to organize society" (Williams, *Trinidad Guardian*, 18 October 1961).

He reminded the masses of the Water Riots of 1903, during which the upper class used the masses to fight their battles while they enjoyed all the benefits:

> Violence is nothing new to the history of Trinidad and Tobago. History has shown that it is the traditional weapon, the traditional tool of the privileged. . . . The call to arms is not merely the frothings of a mad scientist, but something familiar to West Indian history. This call to arms is the last dying attempt to strangle the national movement. It is up to you to decide what you do with the freedom given you by the PNM. *You can cut their throats if you wish; the future is in your hands.* (Ibid; emphasis added)

Williams accused the whites of being opposed to him because he was black. PNM canvassers were being insulted in the "European belt" as they were in 1956:

> Hundreds of people are saying that they don't want any black Premier. . . . Pure blasted prejudice, social prejudice is the issue in this election. They don't like the PNM because the PNM stands for equality, and because the PNM takes the humble person in this country and says "hold your head high, damn you, don't hang it down any more". This is the age of self-government. It is Massa whose head is knocked down, that's all. Ours is a very simple philosophy. You take from those who have had too much for too long, and distribute it among those who have had too little for too long.

Williams accused the whites of rejecting the conciliatory hand that had been offered them after 1956. Numerous appeals had been made for their cooperation, for their understanding; yet they turned to the DLP. This was especially true of the creole Europeans:

> The local business big-shot families, French creoles in particular, determined to control this country as they controlled it for several years, are going all about the place irritating PNM members, saying they don't want any black Premier. For five years we have tried to make a national community of this whole people . . . it didn't matter who attacked us in 1956. We invited all and sundry to work for the benefit of the country as a whole, and after five years to have this offensive campaign, sparing no effort or money to destroy the PNM and push the country back into the slavery and domination that we of the PNM have brought it away from. . . . We didn't cut anybody's head off.

> . . . I would like to send some of them over to Cuba for Castro to do a little purging and
> see what happens when they come back. Ladies and Gentlemen, they have it good here.

The "massas" were also accused of being opposed to the government's decision to introduce free secondary education. All the old arguments against the ascriptive bias of the old school system were again aired. In spite of the new concordat between the government and the Catholic Church, negotiated and signed in December 1960, Williams still pointed the accusing finger at the Catholic school system. "Even if you could afford to pay, they gave preference to the Venezuelan child." The "massas" were up in arms against the new education system because such a system made it more difficult for them to bribe their way into the island's best schools. "But they can't do that any more. Nobody is getting in unless they pass the Common Qualifying Examination." The Honourable John O'Halloran, himself a European, also declared that whites were opposed to the new system because they knew that their sons could not compete equally with the achievement-oriented sons of lower-class parents; nor did they want to send their children to school with coloured "rabs". There was much truth in this accusation. Some white creoles, and even the brown middle-classes, were opposed to an education system in which children of black lower-class families were permitted to socialize with their offspring.

The PNM's proudest boast during the campaign was that it had now freed the educational system of the virus of influence-peddling. Education was no longer open only to the privileged aristocracy of the skin. It would soon be free. In 1961, the number of free school places was increased from one hundred to four hundred. Williams warned parents that they should avoid giving their ingrained prejudices to the young: "Set the children free. Let them show their talent and make their contribution to the building of the national community."

Williams also accused French creoles of seeking to mount an economic counter-revolution: "They are trying to get their blasted hands back at your throats after we, the PNM, have moved them. The exporters wanted to be free again to defraud the cocoa farmers, to pay them unfair prices based on quantity rather than quality. They wanted the Telephone Company handed back to the old Company. They were also planning to restrain labour, to fix wages, and return to the old practices whereby troops and scabs were used to break strikes." This was the programme that the DLP – "the shoe-shine boys for the planters and merchants in Port of Spain" – had endorsed. The DLP, Williams claimed, was waging a last-ditch fight because they knew that if they lost in 1961 they would be saddled with the PNM for another three decades. They wanted to stop the revolution, and "restore the old order with its social practices *that have kept you and me where we have been with all our frustrations and inhibitions*. But if there is one thing I am going to do in this election, it is to mobilize the whole force of national dignity and national decency to defeat once and for all the DLP and their reactionary tendencies" (emphasis added). Here perhaps is the "smoking gun" that links Williams's status as a frustrated black French creole to his political and social war against the white French creoles who had refused to treat him and his immediate family as part of the kin.

It should be noted that Afro-creoles were not the only ones to whom this type of appeal was made. Indian proletarians and cane farmers were reminded that they too were the victims of the "massa" system. "Sahib day done"; "yes suh Boss Day done," he told them. Williams informed the Indians that he had concerned himself with the history of their degradation as much as he had with that of the Negroes. "I know the history of every one of you here better than anyone else in Trinidad," he boasted. "I have made that my business, and knowing that history, I know the road we have to go. The only alternative to that road is the road we have come from, the road of the planters and the road of the merchants in Port of Spain." The government's health programme in the sugar belt, the new bargaining status given to the independent cane farmers, the tractor pools, and the new tenure arrangements were all designed to correct the neglect of the sahib era. Free education was for Indians too, he reminded them, "We don't have any segregation in the PNM. You have to understand that this is a social revolution at work in Trinidad and Tobago that knows no colour, that knows no race, that distinguishes only between the depressed and the disinterested, and those who have always had too much. The election issues are social not racial. Race has only confused and complicated the issue. We can't work miracles, but our goal is racial integration."

Williams was trying to appeal to the Indians over the heads of their leaders, who he said had done nothing in the pre-1956 period to help the people's economic plight but had merely ridden on their backs into power. They, the sons of the sahibs, had now joined the plantocracy to keep the masses where they were. The PNM's aim was to forge a revolutionary front of the "have-nots" against the "haves".

Williams considered it strategically necessary to win at least one seat in the Indian strongholds and in the oil belt, which was once the preserve of Butler. It was the evidence that he needed to show that his movement could cut through the inherited prejudices of the colonial past. In 1961, however, he was not too sanguine about the possibilities; nevertheless he felt sure that, if not in 1961, certainly in the near future, once the revolution had begun to see its full impact, "DLP fathers would produce PNM sons". Williams was also anxious to win Butler's following in the oil belt. To do this, he found it necessary to play down Butler's role in the 1937 riots. He told the residents of Strikers' Village,

> When you the people decided to fight for your emancipation, you did it, not Butler. He
> led you. You created your own traditions then. If you feel ashamed of what your erst-

while leader of yesterday is attempting to do today, move away from him, hang your head in shame. The old man led the movement, your movement. Today you must lift it higher than it was in 1937. . . . We the PNM will continue what you started. Leaders have come and gone before. Any national movement will also throw up its own leader. . . . Mr. Butler is a national figure and as such should have been left to glory in his past actions. (Tape, n.d.)

In response to the criticism that his "calibanistic anti-massa" raving was sheer racialism, the purpose of which was to turn blacks against whites, Williams repeated what he had often said before, "Not all Massas were white, nor were all whites Massas", though the majority of them were. "Massa is not a racial term," he corrected. "Massa is the symbol of a bygone age. Massa Day is a social phenomenon; Massa Day Done connotes a political awakening and a social revolution" (*Massa Day Done*, 1961a, 2). He drew attention to the number of whites, in both Europe and the West Indies, who had opposed the plantation system.

Williams also made reference to the West Indian *café au lait* society, which had constituted itself a new caste on the periphery of the white establishment. These people were still opposed, as they had been in the past, to any social progress that threatened to displace them from their preferential positions. Williams, who was himself a "black French creole", never really trusted the mulatto middle class, whom he accused of identifying with the DLP. He reprimanded the "so-called respectable people" for their lack of patriotism, for their abdication to the masses: "You have today a curious picture in Trinidad and Tobago. Where one was forced once to associate political power and prestige with people who were considered respectable, today one has to go down to the mass movement . . . for the expressions of patriotism, decency and self-respect." Middle-class blacks also came in for their share of abuse. They too were social climbers, anxious to get close to the "massas", and unconcerned about the needs of the masses.

The hostile reaction to Williams's "Massa Day Done" electoral strategy did not come from whites and near-whites alone. Some of its most vocal critics were blacks who insisted that it was either mischievous or misleading in terms of fact. One such critic, Canon Max Farquhar, expressed concern that Williams seemed unable to settle into the role of a national statesman. While applauding Williams for his "rousing evangelism", which had hastened the coming of responsible government, he nevertheless felt that it was time for him to shift his image from that of the protest leader to that of a sober and responsible statesman.

Criticism of Williams's analysis also came from the small African National Congress. John Broome, its founder and leader, noted that despite the PNM's proud boasts, the African population still did not have any significant economic or social status. The majority were still employed in menial occupations. Given this situation, it was surprising that there had been no open revolt against the system. Using idioms similar to those used by Black Muslims in America, Broome urged Africans to begin doing business on a racial basis. Africans should "buy black" and strive to build up an economic empire of their own.

Broome was aware of the dangers of this programme in a close society such as Trinidad's: "The question lurks in one's mind as to how it is possible to achieve this aim without endangering racial relationships." But he believed that with tolerance and understanding no problem need arise. He felt sure that everyone "agrees and sees the necessity for collective security among Africans in the West Indies. Once it is conceded that this is necessary, and once it is agreed that the strategy is not anti-white or anti-Indian in its bias, but rather pro-black, there should be no hostility" (*Trinidad Guardian*, 17 October 1961). Broome's criticism was that Williams talked a lot about African dignity, but had done little to give it economic significance. Williams, in truth, had reminded the masses of the economic power that they held in their hands to punish anti-national merchants, but on no occasion had he ever publicly urged pro-black purchasing strategies. Given the ideology of the PNM, he simply could not, though he must have thought about it quite frequently.

Broome's criticisms about the failure of the PNM to do much by way of integral West-Indianization were correct, though they were somewhat unfair. Williams had always expressed himself determined that the West Indies must be run by West Indians. But at the same time he was not anxious to farm out strategic jobs to West Indians simply because they were West Indians. Nevertheless, over the five-year period, the top levels of the administration, both in the civil service and on statutory boards, had been almost fully West-Indianized, and the bulk of the appointees were mixed or fully Afroid.

It was in the private sector that the problem presented real difficulties. Except for a limited number of cases, there were few Afro-Trinidadians or Indians in the senior offices of the industrial and commercial establishments of the community. Many of these firms still imported Europeans to fill positions that, with a little training, locals could have filled. As one PNM city councillor, Dennis Mahabir, complained,

> Looking around in several Port of Spain offices, there sit comfortably behind executive desks third raters from abroad, doing jobs from which Trinidadians have been kept out and which our people can do much better. And what is more, jobs are found for their wives. These people should never have been allowed to enter the country for the purposes for which they came and remained – doing jobs of no particular importance and requiring no particular skill, and what is more, depriving Trinidadians of a job. Heed must be paid to our national aspirations, and our people must be allowed to grow to the full height of their stature in their own country. Gone must be the days when a linesman from Yorkshire can pose as an engineer in Port of Spain. (*Trinidad Guardian*, 3 February 1961)

Some firms had made efforts to promote to managerial positions locals who had long been stagnating in their employ, but these were essentially mixed *café au lait* people, not Indians or Afroids, who had only marginal representation in the business-managerial elite. One journalist complained, "The shade complex is the curse of Trinidad society. It makes a hollow mockery of the words 'local man'. How many 'local men' of a certain colour and race make the progress in the sphere of private employment to which their ability, conscientiousness and integrity entitle them? The square deal and fair shares principle must be extended to private industry" (*Trinidad Guardian*, 24 November 1957).

Some employers were anxious to bring in skilled persons of any colour to cope with the increased volume of business and to maintain their competitive positions, but resistance within firms, especially family establishments, proved too strong. Williams complained about these discriminatory practices, but not until 1963 did he attempt to impose curbs on the importation of alien personnel. Even this did not go very far in altering the complexion of offices in the private sector, which were still largely owned by European and North American capital. There were many radicals who wished that the PNM as a party, if not as a government, had done more to organize sanctions to force employers to give equal opportunity to talent, irrespective of its ethnic identification.

But such considerations were not very relevant to the campaign of 1961. If blacks worried about them, the general feeling seems to have been that before long in Trinidad and Tobago, it would be "Please, Mr Nigger, please!", to use the Mighty Sparrow's phrase. Certainly this is what Williams seemed to have been promising when he advised the "disinherited and the dispossessed" to hold their heads high because they were about to come into their kingdom. As he exhorted,

> Hold up your heads high, all of you, the disinherited and dispossessed, brought here in the lowest states of degradation to work on a sugar plantation or a cocoa estate for Massa. All of you, don't hang your heads in shame. You are today taking over this country from the Massa's hand. . . . In the last five years I have symbolised, as the head of the Government, the determination of PNM and the majority of the people of the country never to allow Massa to have the privileges that he has had in the fifty or a hundred years before.

Borrowing another phrase from the calypso, he advised the masses to "Clear the way, and let the people make their play".

Williams warned the DLP against speculating on intervention from the Colonial Office to delay the movement to independence. He unequivocally rejected the charge that he was pro-Castro and made it quite clear that he was not in sympathy with what he referred to as Castro's "extravagance":

> We will tolerate no interference from the United Kingdom in the electoral laws of Trinidad and Tobago. Trinidad wanted neither intervention from the right nor from the

left; it merely wanted to be left free to build its own national community now that some of the major struggles against colonialism were behind. That revolution has been peaceful . . . no blood flowed in Trinidad. . . . Some people are opposing this. If they do not like it, they can go to Castro, or they can go to Jagan. (*Trinidad Guardian*, 6 October 1961)

Williams was referring to C.L.R. James, who was expelled from the party in September 1961 on a controversial charge of embezzling party funds; but it was an open secret that James wanted to push the revolution further to the left.

The PNM campaign in 1961 was an enormous success and few objective analysts doubted that the party would be returned with an increased majority. It was also clear that despite the extremely radical tone of Williams's campaign speeches, the party was planning no radical swing to the left. Williams's supreme achievement in 1961, with considerable help from the calypsonians who told the masses to "shake their balisier", was to convince his followers that independence would mean a new deal for the small man, while at the same time maintaining Anglo-American confidence in his party's orthodoxy.

There was a view that Williams had deliberately cleaved to the right in 1960–61 in order to counter the image that he was a radical. Others held the view that Williams was never a social radical and only pretended to be so when it suited his purpose. Albert Gomes comes close to my own view as to what happened in 1960 to Williams's so-called social revolution, and the move to counter it. As he wrote,

If counter-revolution it is, who is responsible for it? Did the PNM scuttle its own so-called revolution, or is the Opposition, as Williams now alleges, making the attempt to do this? The truth is that Dr. Williams and his Party had been zig-zagging along the political road since 1956, alternately driving to the Left and to the Right – until 1960, a year that marks a definite turn to the Right with the ruthless unloading of Mr. C.L.R. James and the détente with the Americans over Chaguaramas . . . any suggestion that the election is a battle between the forces of progress (PNM) and those of reaction (DLP) is a convenient fiction invented by Dr. Williams. . . . In an ideological sense, this is a battle between Tweedledum and Tweedledee, both of whom are driving hard on the Right. If Dr. Williams sees capitalist ghosts in the Opposition camp, he has only to be reminded of the capitalist phantoms in his own camp. . . . No doubt Dr. Williams has justifiable grounds for accusing many of his opponents of opposing him and his Party because they do not like to see persons like himself in prominent positions, nor are such persons at all willing to bend to the winds of change.

But Dr. Williams would have been indulging in dangerous self-deception if he believed that that was the entire story. The truth was that thousands of people in Trinidad and Tobago, who desired the same change that he did disagreed entirely with both the methods by which he introduced such changes and the venomous character he imparted to the actual changes. . . . To them, the election was a fight not to establish the status quo ante but to retrieve some of the order and the goodwill and the ordinary decency without which, no matter the ostensible gains, progress was not worthwhile. ("PNM Counter-Revolution", *Trinidad Guardian*, 19 November 1961)

Election Results

Both the PNM and the DLP were confident of victory. Both parties were sure that they would win a minimum of ten seats and a fair share of those in which the two major ethnic groups were relatively evenly balanced. Though Williams "ran scared", he nevertheless felt certain that the PNM would win twenty of the thirty seats. The DLP, fooled by the large crowds that followed its meetings, perhaps out of curiosity and the expectation of excitement, widely anticipated that it would win twenty-three to twenty-five seats. That the party won only ten seats came as a shock to many. One DLP candidate, Lionel Seukeran, on the morrow of the election, declared, "Surprise more than disappointment agitates me at the result of this election. All of us believed we had an excellent chance to form the Government. We worked ceaselessly as a team to achieve this aim. Now, in retrospect, I can visualize that we were not as well organized as we thought. Perhaps, too, we made tactless mistakes and underrated our opponents" (*Trinidad Guardian*, 5 December 1961). Seukeran placed a great deal of blame on Capildeo for the DLP's defeat.

Other members of the DLP were not as graceful. They noted with chagrin that the PNM had won all six of the newly created seats, and were frankly puzzled by the showing that the PNM made in Indian strongholds. The political leader of the DLP declared, "We did not fight an election. We simply went through the motions of a monstrous farce. We were given certain seats by the PNM and we wrestled two from them – Point-a-Pierre and Fyzabad." Far from providing a method which would ensure free elections as far as human ingenuity could guarantee, as Williams had claimed, "the PNM has found a way to win elections without popular support" (*Statesman*, 8 December 1961).

Williams was jubilant over the PNM's victory and the fact that by winning 58 per cent of the popular vote it could no longer be accused of being a minority government. The party was also enthusiastic about the wide distribution of support. It had won two of the three rural constituencies in the eastern counties and ran very well in the third. It had also won the two St Patrick constituencies that had given birth to the revolutionary nationalist movement in the 1930s and which, until then, had remained relatively faithful to Butler. Butler himself was decisively defeated, gaining only 617 votes, or roughly 6 percent of the votes, in his constituency. Both Tobago constituencies went to the PNM. Victory in Port of Spain North was especially satisfying to Williams, though the white and near-white upper and middle classes of that constituency had again rejected him and the PNM. Williams himself was rejected in those polling divisions of his constituency in which this element lived. In the three sugar seats of Caroni, the PNM ran fairly well, gaining an average of 33 per cent of the votes, with a 40 per cent share in Caroni East, which it had been accused of gerrymandering.

A number of observations can be made about the results. The PNM improved its hold on the voters in the four Port of Spain constituencies. Whereas in 1956 the party had received roughly 67 per cent of the votes, in 1961 this figure increased to 74 per cent. But considering the assumed omnipotence of the party in the urban areas, it is perhaps surprising that the DLP did so well. When the figures for the city as a whole are compared with the returns from the lower-class constituency of Laventille, where the PNM gained 93.53 per cent, the only conclusion that can emerge is that the DLP vote in the city came mainly from the upper and middle classes. The "Massa Day Done" slogan had achieved its desired effect. If one looks at Port of Spain North and West, where the middle- and upper-class elements represented a fair proportion of the population, the DLP performance appears decidedly better. Here the party gained roughly 33 per cent of the vote. Given the extremely unimaginative campaign that the DLP waged, this percentage is even more surprising. The argument that the PNM was rejected by large sections of the middle class, including the Indian middle class, is given further support by the figures from San Fernando West, where the DLP won an impressive 42.59 per cent of that electorate. The PNM had only improved its position there by 3 per cent since 1956. The result, however, mirrored the ethnic composition of the constituency.

One can conclude two things from the analysis of these selected urban constituencies. First of all, it appears that Williams's style of governing had not appealed to a large number of people in urban Trinidad, especially those who were not members of the black majority. The middle class was predominantly mixed racially. It can also be argued that, had the DLP not suffered as much in the past from leadership crises, and had Capildeo not frightened the population to such an extent by his call to arms, the results might well have been different in terms of popular votes, if not in seats. There are those who believe that the DLP could have won the election had Capildeo proven himself equal to the expectations that many held in 1960. The argument of this study, that ethnicity was more relevant than cognitive evaluations, leads me to reject this contention. The figures are eloquent in their support of this assumption: the DLP won only those areas where the total Indian population exceeded 50 per cent.

The DLP, however, was convinced that the election results were fraudulent, and that the voting machines had been manipulated to produce the desired percentages. It felt that the PNM's margin of victory was too nearly identical with its pre-election predictions to be accidental. The DLP claimed too that there was an evident pattern in the way in which the machines malfunctioned. Most of the mechanical breakdowns and delays occurred in heavily Indian areas. Officials were late or else were unfamiliar with the apparatus, and nothing had been done to ensure that polling booths were properly equipped with electrical outlets. This was regarded as part of a deliberate attempt to slow down the voting procedure so as to reduce the DLP's popular vote and, if possible, to deprive late-arriving rural field workers of the franchise. It was also noted that there were frequent discrepancies between the figures recorded on the machines and those proclaimed by officials.

The DLP claimed that in fact it had won twenty-two seats. It was especially sure that it had won the Barataria constituency where the Indian population was substantial but not larger than the Afro and mixed element combined. Many of the Indians were Muslims loyal to PNM stalwart Kamaluddin Mohammed. The DLP was convinced that it had been defrauded at the polls and decided to boycott the legislature and seek redress in the courts. As Capildeo told his followers, "The DLP will not offer themselves as any prisoners tied to the triumphant chariots of the PNM" (*Trinidad Guardian*, 14 December 1961). At the same time, he rejected the claim of some DLP extremists that they should resign their seats and petition the British government for partition. Capildeo was sensible enough to know that partition would never be conceded, even if it was a desirable solution to the problem; neither would he resign: "If we resigned, the PNM would get the *usual stooges* to come forward to fight the vacant seats. We have no intention of resigning to allow them to do what they like. We will seek to put into effect the DLP Manifesto as far as possible within the limitations imposed by the House. We will not let the PNM have everything to itself in a one-party State" (ibid., 8 December 1961; emphasis added).

The DLP was still hoping to invite British intervention. As the party organ warned, "Now that the constitutional struggle was coming to a close, foreign policy would be used to create crises. Democracy will be struck on the head with a heavy hammer while the grass under our feet will be cut by a sickle. Let the Colonial Office play Pontius Pilate" (ibid.). But the Colonial Office was not disposed to listen to the entreaties of the DLP. As far as the colonial secretary was concerned, Trinidad was internally self-governing, and he had no intention of telling it how to run its affairs. His main hope was that the PNM would agree to remain with the rest of the southern Caribbean in a new federal unit. The Colonial Office had long concluded that the DLP was not a genuine alternative to the PNM government and that it had nothing to fear from the PNM.

Forming the Government

In staffing the ministries and the senate, Williams tried as far as possible to give expression to the PNM's multiracial philosophy. Of the twelve cabinet places, two went to Muslims, two to persons of European stock, and eight to Afros, including one female. There were no Hindus among the PNM legislative team, and for the second time the Hindus remained unrepresented in the government. This deficiency was somewhat compensated for in the senate by the appointment of a Hindu party member. One seat each was given to Syrian and Chinese creoles. The remaining nine senate places that the government had at its disposal went to Afro and mixed elements. The governor's senate appointees (that is, the independents) redressed the ethnic balance somewhat. There were three white-creole businessmen, one trade unionist, one solicitor, one musical director and one Hindu businessman. Three of the governor's appointees were Afroids. The DLP refused to make any nominations.

The composition of the senate made it obvious that the government would have no trouble there. The complexion of the new body also symbolized that a new type of man had come to inherit the seats of the once-mighty plantocracy. Williams was frank about the significance of his selection of senators. From now on it was "down with the big boys". As he put it, "You can't trust the people at the top. The small people are going to come up and forward: the lines are drawn. We want the people on Statutory Boards and other adjuncts of Government."

Whites and near-whites did not take kindly to their displacement. Although the Roman Catholic Church reaffirmed its pledge of loyalty to the government, it reminded the PNM that "the furtherance of the common welfare implied that the Government fosters the well being of all classes and sections of the people. Fidelity to this trust of safeguarding the rights of minorities is the test of high-mindedness and is the hallmark of true statesmanship" (*Catholic News*, 9 December 1961). Even Albert Gomes, who had once identified himself with the black proletariat, complained that he had been displaced from political life because he belonged to neither of the two dominant ethnic groups. Gomes in fact elected to go into exile in the United Kingdom. Hindus and Muslims were equally dissatisfied with their representation in the senate. Given that together they constituted roughly 37 per cent of the population, they felt they deserved far more than the token two places they received. This, they claimed, was a shocking denial of the vaunted multiracialism of the PNM regime. Demands for parity were already being heard in certain places.

21 The Approach of Independence
From Queen's Hall to Marlborough House

On 9 May 1962, one month after making its historic and revolutionary decision to take Trinidad to independence alone, the Williams government published a draft independence constitution. The initiative on the part of the government to publish a draft constitution provoked a heavy storm of public criticism. The preparation of this draft was the work of the attorney general, Ellis Clarke, who at a conference organized to mark the twenty-fifth anniversary of independence, told the following story about how he came to prepare the foundation document that was discussed at a constitutional conference held at Queen's Hall and later became the independence constitution.

Clarke's initiative in preparing the draft was prompted by J. O'Neil Lewis and William Demas, both of the Ministry of Trade, Industry and Commerce. When the two permanent secretaries learned of the outcome of the Jamaican referendum, they sought out Williams, who was then in attendance at a political meeting. Williams was not pleased to see his senior public servants in such a context and asked them whether they had no work to do. To which Lewis replied, "You are our work." Lewis then indicated to the prime minister that they were seeking his instructions as to what they should do, given his "one from ten" aphorism. Williams authorized Lewis to form a committee consisting of himself as chairman; David Weintraub, general manager of the Industrial Development Corporation; and William Demas. When legal problems later arose, Lewis again approached Williams to secure his agreement to have Ellis Clarke co-opted. Williams agreed and Clarke was made a member of the working group. What happened next is best told by Clarke himself:

> J. O'Neil Lewis, with his clear, very precise mind said: "Shouldn't we have something before us indicating what we are talking about? What sort of Constitution are we thinking about?" I then put it to the group: "Do you really want this?" They did, and I said: "And then who should do it?" and they laughed; so it became my responsibility, and

in due course I began to work on a document for the purposes of this little group. Dr. Williams discovered early in February 1962 that this was being done, and spoke tome about it and said, "I want that Constitution; I want it right away. I want it yesterday." So the Draft Constitution was submitted to Dr. Williams and was considered by the Cabinet. It was thereafter published for public comment.

Clarke, concerned, was approached by a businessman, Ray Lange, who invited him to meet privately with business and religious groups that wanted him to explain the constitution to them. Clarke agreed, and met with two such groups. A larger meeting was proposed, which Clarke also agreed to. He was urged by his secretary, however, that he should first clear it with the prime minister. This was done and Williams objected strongly:

> Not on your life are you going to speak to these people. Why should they have the privilege of an explanation that nobody else has? People have commented and people have written in; let them write in their comments; gather all the comments together; you can reply, in writing, to them and out of this we can convene everybody who has sent in comments and not have it limited to any privileged class. And so came about the Queen's Hall Conference – all because of the wisdom of my then Secretary, Patricia Hovell! (as cited in Ryan 1988b, 168)

Objection was taken by various groups, both to the method of handling the constitutional issue and to the substantive provisions of the draft; in some sinister way these things seemed integrally related. Organizations and individuals vociferously condemned the government's "indecent haste" in putting the independence constitution on the political agenda with only six weeks allotted for comment, especially since nothing had as yet been done to consult the people on the proposed unitary-state option. The substantial criticisms of the bill were directed mainly at the sections on civil liberties, the provisions for entrenchment, the composition of the senate, the question of consultation, the appointive power of the prime minister, and the machinery for the conduct of elections.

The Queen's Hall Conference

In a broadcast on 10 April 1962, Williams replied to some of the criticisms and announced that the government would establish consultative machinery to mobilize agreement on the constitution. He denied that the time given to the public was too short for proper study of the draft. He noted that 432 typewritten pages of comment had been received from eighty-four organizations and fifty-two private citizens. He revealed that the government intended to collate and distribute the memoranda to individuals and organizations who had submitted comments and that those parties would then be invited to a constitutional convention, to be held at Queen's Hall, where the issues raised would be discussed. The compromises agreed upon would then be discussed by a select committee of the legislature before the British government was approached. According to Williams, this was being done in an honest and sincere attempt to achieve a democratic consensus on a matter of national concern. He boasted that "no other country had adopted the course Trinidad and Tobago had decided upon in gathering response to constitutional proposals" (*Trinidad Guardian*, 8 April 1962).

But the government had been forced into a constitutional conference that Williams in fact termed a "luxury" in the context of the extreme fluidity of discussions on the European Common Market. He seemed to be suggesting that the ideal of having popular participation on the constitution was less important than the need for an independent Trinidad to participate in negotiations that affected the future market of its basic products. As he declared later on, disingenuously,

> It may surprise you to know that the greatest danger we had to face was not really the type of Constitution we should have. We can always let the citizens discuss and help us to change those parts of it that do not seem to meet requirements. The greatest trouble is how soon this tremendous disorganization . . . involving Britain's . . . going into the European Economic Community [is going to take place]. We did not know in January when that would take place. We knew it was coming soon. You can see it a little more clearly in May. . . . And, if we seem more prepared now . . . it is because of the action the Government took in January to prepare for the worst. The best Constitution in the world would be simply wasted paper if we were to disrupt and make unstable present trading arrangements with other territories, and we must move to protect the economic position of Trinidad and Tobago. (*Trinidad Guardian*, 19 May 1962).

Williams was clearly apologizing for what seemed to be the PNM's bad political manners, but he genuinely believed that the constitutional settlement was less important than the economic threat posed by Britain's entry into the European Common Market. As C.L.R. James remarked in a lecture given in Jamaica as early as November 1959,

> Dr. Williams made it absolutely clear that his immediate and undeviating demand is for a declaration of national independence on April 22nd – it is not a mythical date, it is the anniversary of the inauguration of the Federation. But he goes on to say that after that declaration, the Constitution, the question of customs union, the question of fiscal problems, the questions of the powers of the centralized government, all the questions which we are debating, can then be discussed. He says that all this will take two or three years and so at the end of the five years of the present Federal Government we shall then be in a position fully to embark upon the new stage of our independence. (James 1961, 25–26)

Before the constitutional convention met at Queen's Hall, Williams disclosed that his government was willing to accept many of the suggestions incorporated in the memoranda, but there were issues that he was reluctant to concede.

Though admitting that hostility to the composition of the senate was fairly widespread, he was unwilling to embarrass the individuals who had been asked to serve in that body: "The Government refuses to associate itself with any suggestion that, within two months of the appointment of these citizens, . . . after the issue had been debated for five years in the community, the system should be changed before anybody has had an opportunity to assess the value of what constituted an innovation on our part. . . . If the community wishes to change it, that is another matter." This was an unmistakable hint that the government might give way on this point if pressed (*Trinidad Guardian*, 18 April 1962).

With respect to the proposal that provision should be made for a referendum to amend the constitution, he simply took the Afro-Saxon line that a referendum was not a very British practice. The same type of observation was made to criticisms that the prime minister was being given too much appointive power. This was quite normal in parliamentary democracies, he asserted. It was a rather strange reply coming from the head of an anti-colonial government that always insisted on its right to choose that which suited the particular needs of a cosmopolitan society.

Williams also turned his back resolutely on all proposals for proportional representation, which in fact meant racial or communal representation. He expressed himself as being opposed to any suggestion that minority groups be given special constitutional standing:

> There are those who would like the Trinidad and Tobago Independence Constitution to be patterned on that of Cyprus which means that the Constitution will emphasize, and in fact establish sharp lines of division between the various racial groups. . . . I would far prefer to have a Government of Trinidad and Tobago accused of not dividing up the community into racial groups rather than have it accused of constitutional provisions which would establish a Negro President and an Indian Vice-President of a Republic, with a fixed proportion of seats or places to the various racial groups in the Cabinet, in Parliament, in the Judiciary, in the Police Service and in the Civil Service. As far as I am concerned, that way madness lies. (Ibid.)

While the concessions initially made went a long way towards dispelling the suspicions of most critics, there were some who remained dissatisfied. It was observed that the number of memoranda submitted was not indicative of the adequacy of the time given for study of the draft. Most associations were only able to discuss those issues that concerned their clientele and were not as satisfied with other sections as the premier had implied. Others noted that the fact that certain items in the draft were also found in other countries or in existing statutes was no particular recommendation for an independent Trinidad. "The Government should use its good sense rather than its research abilities." Objection was also taken to the premier's reference to popular deliberations as a "luxury".

The Queen's Hall Conference was perhaps one of the finest democratic exercises that Trinidad had yet witnessed, despite its shaky beginning. Quite accidentally, Williams had hit upon a method of obtaining popular participation in the constitution-making process. But he did not tell the delegates attending the conference how he had come to decide that it should be held. He took full credit for what happened, and in his opening remarks to the conference stated,

> The presence of some 200 citizens from all walks of life including representatives of religious, economic, labour, civic, professional and political organizations as well as governmental agencies, constitutes a landmark in the history of our Territory. Today's meeting represents the closest approximation we have yet achieved towards the national community. . . . All of you added together, with your collective views however divergent or contradictory, constitute a citizen's assembly the like of which has seldom been seen in the world. . . . You are all here this morning . . . the nation in conference, an educated democracy in deliberation, a Government seeking advice from its citizens. (Queen's Hall 1962, 3)

The utility of the conference as a consensus-building mechanism was seriously impaired, however, by the refusal of the leading representatives of the Hindu community to participate. The president general of the Maha Sabha, who claimed to speak for 250,000 Hindus, observed that since his organization had not been consulted before the constitution was drafted, and had in fact rejected it in its entirety, he could not possibly cooperate. The fact that there was no mutually agreed agenda for the conference also made it difficult for him to participate.

Bhadase Maraj still believed that it was the duty of the government to call a referendum on the question of federation. He strongly condemned the leadership of the DLP, which had agreed to participate: "Where is the consistency when the DLP refused to nominate their Senators, when the DLP has two serious matters before the Privy Council, and three others pending in the Supreme Court, all alleging malpractice on the part of the Government, and all challenging the very life of the Government? Participation . . . automatically vitiates all arguments as to who are the rightful government" (*Trinidad Guardian*, 25 April 1962). He warned the DLP that by participating in the conference, it ran the risk of legitimating the PNM government and the decisions of that conference, which would likely not be in accord with those that the party was demanding. Maraj maintained that there was no question of his not being in favour of independence, which he considered imperative. What he wanted was a constitution in which minorities would be given adequate safeguards. Until the government was "prepared to sit down with minority groups for a full and frank discussion leading to a completely new draft constitution", the Indian community would have to dissociate itself from the constitution-making process (ibid.).

Whether or not the DLP agreed to participate merely to obstruct the proceedings and destroy its effectiveness is indeed difficult to determine. The behaviour of its spokesmen and some of its supporters certainly created that impression. The party took issue with the tight security arrangements surrounding the conference hall, the exclusion of the press and the members of the select committee, the five-minute speaking limitation, and the agenda that the government imposed on the conference. The DLP delegates further objected to the ruling of the chairman that delegates would be permitted to speak only once, and then only on issues that had been raised in their memoranda. This ruling was rejected on the ground that it presumed acceptance of the general principles of the draft. It would also silence persons who did not make detailed criticisms, but who had in fact rejected the entire draft. The Hindu Youth Association and the African National Congress were in this predicament, and had no alternative but to accept the invitation of the chairman to leave the conference. After some heated exchanges and threats, the DLP also walked out of the conference, such behaviour doing much to destroy the sympathy that some delegates might have had for the party's point of view. The walkout coloured much of the proceedings, especially those relating to the question of consultation with the leader of the opposition.

Williams later advised that the government planned to make arrangements for broadcasting the full proceedings of the meeting. The opposition feared that the public had been given edited information releases. The government was probably hesitant at first to hold an open meeting, uncertain as it was about how the conference would deal with the draft, and unwilling as it was to have it appear that the draft had been repudiated by the conference. Clearly the government did not trust in the competence of the press.

The conference helped to dissolve much of the tension that the publication of the draft had created. Participants were enthusiastic about the device that the government had arranged to obtain the public's views. The spokesman of the Employers Consultative Association described the conference as being "absolutely unique". The representative of the Muslim Anjuman Sunnatul-Jamaat felt that the meeting was the "most admirable step taken by a Government to satisfy all sections of the Territory. . . . The greatest piece of democracy ever to be displayed by a Government of the Territory". Even His Grace the archbishop of Port of Spain felt moved to invoke God's blessing "upon the Government and its Works" (ibid., 275).

Williams himself was particularly proud of the "novel" way that the community had found to create consensus on the constitution, though he had a mild rebuke for those who "congratulated the government" on the "privilege" they had been afforded. Participation was a right and an obligation, not a favour, he reminded them. Williams also disclosed that the draft had been prepared in only three and a half weeks. They were men in a hurry, he explained:

> If there has appeared to be a certain amount of haste in this procedure, ladies and gen-
> tlemen, please understand that anybody who is a representative of the Government
> today, responsible for improving as rapidly as is humanly possible the material condi-
> tions under which our citizens live, [doesn't] have a great deal of time. We have to
> work to our time-tables. . . . We are now in a twilight zone. . . . We cannot afford to
> remain in this particular period for too long, where we have nobody to speak for us
> on this question of the European Common Market. So if there has appeared to be a cer-
> tain element of haste, I give you the assurance that the sooner we could get this thing
> done, as far as the members of the Government are concerned, without in any way
> detracting from the participation of the widest possible number of the population in
> this exercise, then a lot of us would sleep a little more peacefully at night. (Ibid., 284)

He was also frank in admitting that the conference was "accidental". The cabinet had intended to study the memoranda before agreeing upon a stand, but later
agreed, on his suggestion, that the citizenry should be made to do the homework. Williams declared himself extremely satisfied with the way in which the
conference had performed. Delegates had made it their business to study the constitutions of a number of countries, both new and old, in order that they might
construct something worthy of admiration and respect. Williams asserted,

> This meeting is a tribute to the citizens, not to the Government. It shows how you have
> done your homework, and I believe, at this moment of national pride, I may be par-
> doned the statement: that I doubt that there is any country in the world in which there
> has been such a demonstration of civic pride and civic responsibility on the part of
> citizens from all walks of life. It is your success and not ours. Our success, I take it, is
> in being able to stimulate response from the citizens. We as members of the
> Government have benefited from this meeting of the minds of the citizens. (Ibid.,
> 282–83)

Other voices were not as sanguine about the usefulness of the conference.
C.L.R. James referred to it as a "phony conference" that was not representative
of all the people (1962, 163). In the view of the DLP, the whole thing was a circus from start to finish. Opposition elements described it as a "citizen's committee to cover a dirty dictatorship", a "mahogany casket to hide a rotten corpse".
Others contended rather unfairly that it had been packed with PNM supporters. Critics also justly rejected the government's arguments that the country had
to hurry to independence, and thus could not allow the citizenry more time to
debate the issue. One participant, Cyril Henry, noting the fawning attitude of
some delegates, made the rather apt comment that the "people of Trinidad and
Tobago have been so accustomed to treat colonial governments with awe that now
that representative government has been established, many of them regard the
Premier as inviolable as they once regarded the colonial governor; any rebuff to
the Premier's expressed will is regarded not by them as an assertion of the demo-

cratic right to protest . . . but as an illustration of an unreasonable determination to be as uncooperative as possible" (*Trinidad Guardian,* 8 June 1962). New premier was but old governor writ large. It was a devastating and somewhat correct analysis, not only of the conference, but of many other aspects of the territory's political life as well.

The failure of the two parties to settle their differences before going to the Colonial Office must in part be ascribed to the unfortunate procedure that Williams chose to adopt in framing the constitution. As Dr Capildeo himself argued at Marlborough House in London,

> Wider measure of agreement would have been achieved if an attempt had been made to secure our co-operation from the outset. . . . The Government however chose to ignore us and proceeded to prepare a draft on its own, so that when the joint select committee was belatedly appointed, the Government members of the committee had already closed their minds, and in committee they were not disposed to discuss issues but were determined to defend a draft to which they appeared to be irrevocably committed. The joint select committee, was, therefore, prejudiced from the beginning. (*Trinidad Guardian*, 29 May 1962)

While it is clear that Williams blundered in not consulting the opposition, it is to be wondered whether any cooperation was possible with the DLP in the climate that prevailed after the 1961 election. This does not exonerate him, however, from the crassness of the methods he adopted to terminate the colonial period.

The Marlborough House Conference

At the opening of the Marlborough House Conference on 29 May 1962, the last of those frustrating pilgrimages to London, the leader of the DLP stated succinctly but emphatically what his delegation was after:[1] "We want a judiciary which is independent; we want provisions which really guarantee effectively the rights and freedoms which ought to exist in a democratic society; we want Parliament democratically constituted; we want a procedure for the amendment of the Constitution which effectively protects us from the arbitrary exercises of the power to amend; we want the various commissions so constituted as to ensure that they function effectively and impartially" (ibid.). He was also insistent that elections be held before independence to determine which of the parties would be the immediate beneficiaries of the transfer of power. This, he observed, was a vital precondition of harmony, unity and confidence.

The demands of the Indian National Association went even further. They wanted "parity or partition"; they did not believe that the DLP, committed as it was to other ethnic groups, was in a position to make an effective case for the Indian population. As H.P. Singh, the president of the INA, stated,

The Indian community must spear-head the demand for proportionate representation for all the ethnic groups in the councils of the nation. If, perchance the "obscurantist" minorities are not interested in protecting themselves in this way against PNM racialism, then we, the Indians, must demand parity with the Negroes in government, in the Civil Service, in the Police and every aspect of government. If there are thirty seats in the House, we insist on having fifteen. If there are twelve ministers, we demand six. We demand that 50 percent of the jobs in the Civil Service be given Indians, and 50 percent of the men in the Police Force be of our community, as well as 50 percent of the officers. (Singh 1962a, 9–10)

Singh, who was supported by the All Indian Youth Association, believed that these stark alternatives could be avoided only if the "dishonest machinery for election" was eliminated. The Trinidad Partition League also supported this claim in a cable to the colonial secretary.

None of the principals, including the DLP, endorsed the demands of what was considered an extremist minority of the Indian community. The DLP strongly rebuked the INA for its extremism: "The Indian Association is a many-sided thing. Cranks who have weird ideas of removing governments, communist sympathizers, frustrated people who would have liked to be candidates in the last elections. . . . They are prepared to destroy left, right and centre if they do not get what they want. They conspire, intrigue and undermine. They, most of them, have chips on their shoulders" ("The Indian Association Makes a Mess", *Statesman*, 30 November 1962). The colonial secretary, Reginald Maudling, also rejected partition quite firmly. As he advised, "The last vestiges of external control, for better or worse, are about to be removed, and a heavy responsibility therefore lies upon those attending . . . to ensure that the new Constitution they are devising will be one under which the peoples of a former dependency can emerge and govern themselves as a single nation" (*Trinidad Guardian*, 24 May 1962). Since both the PNM and the DLP were in agreement that partition or proportional representation was undesirable and, in the case of partition, meaningless, the negotiations did not give consideration to such proposals.

The proceedings of the conference were unduly long and frustrating. Neither side was anxious to concede, even though Maudling made it clear that differences would have to be narrowed before independence was granted. The DLP insisted on new elections first. The Maha Sabha even wanted the conference abandoned completely until such elections could be held. Those elections, moreover, would have to be held after an independent boundaries commission, consisting of representatives from either the United Kingdom or the United Nations, had redrafted the constituencies. Reintroduction of the ballot box was also demanded: Capildeo admitted that both methods were open to fraud, but he felt that abuse of the machines could be more "total".

Williams angrily rejected these demands. The appointment of such a commission would be harmful to the reputation of the country. Moreover, the country could not afford the luxurious delays that these proposals would involve – he estimated that independence would be delayed for at least four months. The DLP felt this was a small price to pay for social peace. Williams feared, however, that rather than promote harmony, new elections would only serve to disrupt even further the tattered fabric of the society. Before leaving for London, Williams warned about the disruption that would be caused by holding another election and swore that he would be ruthless with the opposition if they should force on the country another pre-independence election.

On the question of entrenchment, the DLP demanded a three-quarter majority in both houses, and an entrenched right of appeal to the privy council on all issues relating to the interpretation of the constitution. Capildeo declared that he had no faith in the integrity of Williams, and could not accept his pledges or those of his party. Williams had "torn up" the federal constitution and the old Trinidad constitution, and there was nothing to stop him from "tearing up" the new constitution and making Trinidad a republic, as Nkrumah had done in Ghana. The DLP also wanted a firm guarantee that the civil service, the police force and the national guard would be more representative of the ethnic physiognomy of the community. Capildeo complained that at present, "one section of the community was armed against the other".

Deadlock in London only served to aggravate tensions in Trinidad. According to the president of the INA, he had to restrain extremists in the Indian community who were already arming themselves in preparation for any emergency that might arise in case of an unfair imposition. It was the INA, its president later asserted, that brought home to the Colonial Office the gravity of the crisis in Trinidad. The DLP organ in fact accused the *Guardian* of deliberately suppressing news of violence in the territory in the hope of strengthening Williams's hand. "Dr Williams," the *Statesman* declared, "could not afford to let the Colonial Office know that Trinidad was sitting on a volcano of racial hate . . . a volcano which may violently blow up at any moment." The PNM was warned that racialism would develop into a monster that it would not be able to control: the PNM "have whipped racialism to such a pitch that it now threatens to become an inferno consuming everything. The schism between blacks and other minorities, East Indians in particular, has become a yawning unbridgeable chasm. . . . The white heat of anger is spreading" (*Statesman*, 25 May 1962).

The Marlborough House Compromise

Whether at the instance of reports from Trinidad, or intuition that Trinidad might indeed witness a bloodbath, Williams finally agreed to compromise. The conference seemed on the verge of complete collapse when Williams decided that he would make a statement that he hoped would meet some of the objections of the DLP. The concessions were the following:

- Special entrenchment of an increased number of provisions by a three-fourths majority of the members of the lower house and a two-thirds majority of the members of the upper house.
- An independent boundaries commission which would delineate new constituencies which would vary by no more than a margin of 20 percent.
- An elections commission which would be responsible for the conduct of elections and the registration of voters. The commission was also to be responsible for ensuring the accuracy and competence of voting machines and for seeing that these were fully tested and sealed in the presence of representatives of political parties. The commission was to be completely free of any direction or control from the executive or any other authority.
- Widening of the right of appeal to the Privy Council in matters other than constitutional rights.
- Limitation to six months of the period during which a proclamation of a state of emergency could remain in force without being extended by parliament.
- Strengthening of the provisions for the independence of the auditor general.
- Entrenching of the provision that Trinidad and Tobago remain a constitutional monarchy.
- Entrenching of provisions relating to the independence of the judiciary from partisan political pressure.
- Consultation with the leader of the opposition on important appointments including the chairmanship of the elections and boundaries commissions, and on all the important national issues.

This last concession was not promised as a part of a constitutional requirement. The colonial secretary indicated that he was of the view that it should not be written in but should be treated as an indication. A promise was also given that a bipartisan committee of national integration would be appointed to examine the methods by which the community could be more satisfactorily integrated.

Williams had at first planned to have Colonial Secretary Maulding serve as a liaison between himself and Capildeo, but later decided to inform the opposition leader personally that he planned to make some new proposals. During the tea break, Williams pulled Capildeo aside and told him that the two leaders should settle the outstanding issues rather than leave it to the British to resolve. Capildeo made his reply contingent upon the content of the proposals. According to Capildeo's version of the event, "Dr. Williams came to me and said, I intend to make a statement that we shall co-operate, that we shall meet and that we shall discuss our differences. I replied, that statement is very good to make under any circumstances. Go ahead and make it by all means. If you make that state-ment, I would underline it" (*Statesman*, 21 August 1962). Williams, who had kept his hearing aid switched off for most of the meeting while Capildeo hurled impre-cations at him, turned it back on and sought to charm Capildeo.

Somewhat surprisingly, Williams claimed that he had made no concessions. Even the 75 per cent provision, which he agreed was a "stiff measure of entrench-ment", was not one he viewed as a concession. He noted that he would have noth-ing to do with a police state, and had no objections to any safeguards that would strengthen the independence of the judiciary. The DLP, for its part, accepted these promises and agreed to drop its demand for pre-independence elections and for the constitutionalizing of the principle of consultation. It also agreed to the use of voting machines on the understanding that every machine would be fully exam-ined before use and sealed in the presence of representatives of the political par-ties. According to Williams, "Capildeo thanked me and withdrew all opposition to the date of independence. The conference ended, catching the British flat-footed, without the reporters and television being on hand. The British never knew what hit them, and I never presented my letter to Maulding" (1969, 285). Interestingly, Ellis Clarke reports that in his capacity as constitutional adviser, he had gone up to London a week before the meeting to hold talks with the colo-nial secretary, with whom he had settled certain matters even before the confer-ence began. Williams's initiative pre-empted those agreements.

Williams, who was extremely anxious to attend the prime ministers' conference in September, which would deal with the question of Britain's role in the Common Market and Commonwealth, declared that he was not surprised that DLP negotiators agreed to his proposals and that there was a meeting of minds on the essential outstanding questions. This was a rather curious statement, especially since Williams disclosed that one or two of the proposals were a little hard to take, but he agreed to them. Williams later claimed that the need for him to attend the prime ministers' conference was crucial to the setting of the date for inde-pendence. As he declared, "We are not free to fix the date for Independence. The September 10th meeting of the Commonwealth Prime Ministers' Conference fixes the date" (*Trinidad Guardian*, 31 May 1962).

In his post-conference broadcast to the people of Trinidad, Williams declared, "We on the Government side approached the Conference from the point of view that . . . if there was any particular safeguard that we could introduce for the benefit of the community as a whole, no matter what the origin of the proposal, we gave it the most serious consideration." This was an obvious attempt to con-ceal defeat, but a useful one in the circumstances. Williams quite rightly sought to convince the people of Trinidad and elsewhere that agreement was achieved on a "happy note". "The Conference involved this question of inspiring confidence in the community and removing tensions. So, at the end of the Conference, as the leader of the delegation, I made a clear statement indicating that we of the Government Party intended to extend an invitation to the opposition to discuss all issues on our return to Trinidad which might retard or could retard the promotion and development of national unity" (ibid., 9 June 1962).

It is worth noting that DLP spokesmen were convinced that Capildeo had triumphed over Williams. As one member of the legislative council exclaimed, "You [Capildeo] outfoxed Williams and he knows it. They are happy and so are we!" Another member of the DLP delegation observed that "the Constitution . . . contains all the safeguards that it is possible to build into a constitution. If this Constitution fails to achieve the objective of safeguarding the democratic rights of the people, it will not be the fault of the Constitution, but of the men who have failed to exercise the eternal vigilance without which no constitution, however cleverly drafted, can prevail" (*Statesman,* 19 June 1962).

Capildeo was not as happy as some of his followers, but he was honest enough to admit that the DLP was as much to blame for its defeats as was the PNM: "The DLP could have achieved a great deal more, but had to struggle against the history of its own past leadership, with its internecine conflicts; but their defeat [especially on the elections issue] was also due to the fact that the assiduous propaganda of its opponents, that the country had no genuine alternative to the present Government, had been swallowed by the Colonial Office" (ibid.). Capildeo also argued that Williams did not want to "knock out" the opposition completely; he preferred to retain the mirage of a democratic two-party system while at the same time enjoying functional one-party control. He also ascribed his party's reverses to the fact that the communications media and the upper classes had turned their backs on the DLP, regardless of how they felt about the PNM:

> Whatever purpose the Queen's Hall Constitution exercise may have served, it revealed one unpalatable fact, that the loudest well-to-do critics of the Government and those who criticized from what they fondly believed were well entrenched positions, did not want the DLP to form the Government. . . . The sources of public information were also arrayed and marshalled against us. This is a grave defect in the body politic of Trinidad, and, in my opinion, constitutes a far greater danger, in that it creates the atmosphere conducive to a one-party state, and so encourages such results even if the direction of political leaders were otherwise oriented. (*Statesman,* 24 August 1962)

He also disclosed that he, like Williams, was driven to compromise because of fear of the consequences for Trinidad, both internally and in terms of its reputation abroad, if racial war should break out. To quote Capildeo, "At the start of the . . . Conference, the decision confronting the leaders of the DLP was whether they should plunge the country into chaos with civil commotion and strife, or try to explore whatever reasonable avenues may be presented to us as the Conference developed. . . . It is easy to let slip the dogs of war; it is impossible to return to the positions before they were unleashed" (*Statesman*, 19 August 1962).

Capildeo was being less than frank, however, in his depiction of the role that he played at Marlborough House, if the recollections of Lionel Seukeran are to be believed. Capildeo, who was suffering from an injury that he sustained in a car crash some three weeks earlier, was moody and intemperate and often had to be restrained and bullied by others on his team. As Seukeran recalled,

> I was well aware of his idiosyncrasies. He was volatile by nature, incapable of compromise, resentful of counsel, unaccustomed to diplomacy, possessed of an over-sized ego, and steeped in demagoguery. I pondered this phenomenon of a man. Brushing aside his tantrums and moods, and realizing the sacred trust reposed in us by the minority groups at home to win for them every advantage, we examined every aspect of the draft. (Seukeran 2006, 291)

Seukeran also noted that Capildeo at one point proposed incorporating the extremist views of the Indian National Association in the constitution. Seukeran told Capildeo that he had heard people say that he was "mad", and that he now believed it to be true. Others in the DLP delegation told him that they would not be party to any such proposal and forced him to take a more conciliatory line.

It would seem that Williams learned about this development and was thus encouraged to moderate his own positions. According to Seukeran, Williams thanked him for "saving the day" (ibid., 292). Seukeran boasts that it was the negotiating capacity of the DLP team, and in particular that of Tajmool Hosein and Seukeran himself, that was responsible for the democratic safeguards eventually inserted in the constitution – not Williams and his team, who were strict majoritarians who kept insisting on practices that obtained in the United Kingdom without appreciating that Britain was a homogeneous society in which conventions had force of "lore", if not law.

> When future historians chronicle our achievements, it will be noted that the negotiations we spearheaded at Marlborough House constitute our greatest gift to the nation. The freedoms we have written into the Constitution of Trinidad and Tobago constitute our greatest legacy to posterity. We were uncompromising over the freedom of the Press and the Independence of the Judiciary. We made sure that Trinidad and Tobago acknowledged the supremacy of God, hence a prayer by the Speaker before each session of Parliament; we made sure that there would be no discrimination by reason of race, colour, origin, religion or sex; we wrote into the Constitution the individual's right to life, liberty, security of person and enjoyment of property; we secured the individual's right to show affiliation to the political party of his choice and to express himself freely and openly.
>
> The Government delegates had no objection to our stipulations, though Williams had been at war with the Press for some time. I was adamant, however, that an avowal

of agreement was not enough. Our team fought to have these written and entrenched into the Constitution, so that there could be no amendment or withdrawal of any of the provisions without a three-quarter majority in the House. (Ibid., 293)

English observers were surprised and pleased about the outcome of the deliberations. Maudling himself confessed that he was pleasantly surprised by the developments after a day that had begun so unpromisingly. "We have been very worried," he admitted. "There were so many fears and suspicions, and the trouble with fears and suspicions is that they build on one another." The *Times* was also pleased with the settlement, and in fact, hailed it as a "model of textbook perfection". The constitution was "as sound and water-tight a unitary constitution, safeguarding human rights, as yet has been put on paper". It was not overwritten, like Jamaica's, nor underwritten, like Ghana's or Tanzania's, both of which were too easy to change. According to the view of the *Times* analyst, the fault of Jamaica's constitution was that it depended too much on a competent and cooperative opposition to function well. The weakness of underwritten constitutions like Tanzania's was that they "presuppose the perpetual existence of a reliable governing body which will never be tempted to abuse freedom". Trinidad's avoided these extremes. "It ensures freedom of action of government within the framework of British democratic traditions. It contained a full guarantee of individual rights and at the same time permitted the executive to govern freely without possibly being hamstrung by a malintentioned opposition. It left the business of governing to the government, and not to both government and opposition, as the Jamaican constitution did" (*Trinidad Guardian*, 17 June 1962).

Trinidadians were immensely relieved that what had begun on so ominous a note had at last been brought to a happy conclusion. Generally speaking, the majority of the population was pleased with the settlement. They were also proud that their respective heroes had been able to rise to such levels of statesmanship. If there were persons who had reservations about independence, they were quite mute in the months of July and August 1962, when the umbilical cord that had bound Trinidad and Tobago to the British Empire for 165 years was finally cut.

Rendezvous with Destiny

Williams had looked forward to 31 August 1962, notwithstanding his comment in 1960 that those who wanted "independence alone" were "victims of the heritage left by colonialism, persons who were unable to see beyond the confines of our puny territories and their obsession with ancient traditions of West Indian glory and importance". He too had now become parochial. Preparations had been in process since weeks earlier to put in place the symbolic paraphernalia of independence – a national flag, an anthem, a defence force that he said he was not eager to have but that the British insisted upon, an order of precedence for state offices, arrangements for the formal hand-over of power by the Crown, and much else. He also had to decide and compose what he was going to say to the nation on the historic occasion of his first speech as prime minister of Trinidad and Tobago.

One of the most important of the pre-independence events was his "conversation" with schoolchildren at a rally held in Port of Spain on the day preceding independence. Williams told the children that they must practise what they were affirming in the national anthem – "Let every creed and race find an equal place." He also advised them that on their young shoulders would rest the future of the nation, and that each and every one of them "carried the future of the country in their school bags".

The night of 30 August was another important milestone for Williams. As he recalled in *Inward Hunger,*

> At midnight the Union Jack was lowered in dead silence, and our red, white and black flag went up to the deafening roar of the thousands who had assembled to witness the historic ceremony. At the formal opening of the first Independence Parliament, the Princess Royal read the Queen's speech which pledged: My government undertakes to govern the country in the spirit which marked the Independence Conference in London. It will seek the co-operation and invite the participation of all groups in the country in its approach to National questions. (1969, 286)

Independence Day found Williams lecturing to the population as to what the day meant then and what it could mean five years hence. He was painfully aware of the risks associated with independence. The people were now masters "*chez nous*", but as he asked them with a perceptible sense of lurking danger, "What use will you make of your independence? What will you transmit to your children five years from today?" He observed that "other countries had ceased to exist in that period. Some, in much less time, had become totally disorganized, a prey to anarchy and civil war" (1969, 286). Williams proceeded to lecture the population as to what democracy meant and did not mean. It involved, at a minimum, the right to vote, recognition of the rights of others, equality of opportunity in education, employment in the public service and in the private sector (the latter was emphasized). Pointedly, it also meant the obligation of the minority to recognize the right of the majority and the responsibility of the government to protect the rights of citizens from arbitrary power and other conventional abuses.

But just as the state was obligated to its citizens, so too citizens had to recognize their obligations to the state and to the national community. Citizens were thus called upon to heed the watchwords that he gave to the nation "for all times": Discipline, Production and Tolerance. Without these, the new state and its economy were at grave risk of anarchy, impoverishment and ethnic conflict. Williams also recommitted himself and the PNM to inclusive parliamentary democracy. As he told his national audience,

> The Constitution recognizes [that] the position of the Leader of the Opposition and the normal parliamentary conventions of consultation between Government and Opposition are being steadily developed and expanded. The Constitution itself, Independence itself, represent the agreement of the two political parties on the fundamental question of national unity. The ordinary citizen must recognize the role of the Parliament in our democracy and must learn to differentiate between a Member of Parliament, whom he may like or dislike, and the respect that must be accorded to that same Member of Parliament *ex-officio*. (1969, 286)

In the final analysis, however, democracy would only flourish and be sustained if it was buttressed by an informed civil society, which Williams himself had done so much to empower. As he perorated, "Democracy, finally, rests on a higher power than Parliament. It rests on an informed and cultivated and alert public opinion. The Members of Parliament are only the representatives of the citizens. They cannot represent apathy and indifference. They can play the part allotted to them only if they represent intelligence and public spiritness" (ibid., 268).

C.L.R. James remarked that the population marched to independence "as if they were going to a funeral", so disappointed were they about the collapse of federation and the retreat from confrontation with Americans over Chaguaramas. Some were no doubt disillusioned, especially over federation. Some were also fearful of the future now that the Colonial Office and "the Queen" were no longer there to serve as political long stops. This was particularly true of the French-creole and the Indo-Trinidadian communities as well as the other ethnic minorities. Williams sought to reassure them in his Independence Day address, but many remained doubtful, watchful, but nevertheless hopeful that the era of good feeling that had developed following the Marlborough House compromise would last. Bhadase Maraj spoke for many of his co-ethnics when he telephoned "Bill" in London to tell him that he had always maintained that "you had more brains than the rest of those fellows put together" (as cited in Oxaal 1968, 174–75).

The creole majority, for their part, were satisfied and thankful that the long journey to independence had come to an end and that the "Port" and not the "Plantation" had emerged as victors in the struggle for succession to the imperial power. "Williams the Conqueror" had prevailed, and most had confidence in his capacity to steer the ship of state into the new dispensation. Williams's self-appointed task was to control and transform the "Negro Nationalism", which he had fired but which he insisted was "defensive rather than aggressive", into a movement seeking well-defined political and social aims designed for the common good. He warned that Trinidadian identity must now displace and prevail over other constituent identities. As he told the nation in his anaugural address on the eve of independence,

> There can be no Mother India for those whose ancestors came from India . . . there

can be no Mother Africa for those of African origin . . . there can be no Mother England and no dual loyalties; . . . there can be no Mother China even if one could agree as to which China is the Mother; and there can be no Mother Syria or no Mother Lebanon. A nation, like an individual, can have only one Mother. The only Mother we recognize is Mother Trinidad and Tobago, and Mother cannot discriminate between her children. (*Trinidad Guardian*, 1 September 1962)

Interestingly, the Americans were very much in evidence on Independence Day and even hosted a function to mark the event. The Americans had also signalled their disposition by offering to display manoeuvres involving an aircraft carrier. The flip side of this show of enthusiasm was an attempt on the part of the consul general to discourage the Trinidad government from inviting Cuba to the celebrations on the ground that the United States did not recognize Cuba. The Trinidad government refused to genuflect. It was not a satellite, and saw no need to offend a regional neighbour with whom it had no quarrel (Solomon 1981, 218). The Cuban missile crisis, however, helped to bring home to the governments of both countries the need for mutuality. "They [the US] must have realized that if our grievances were not met, there could well be a change of orientations" (ibid., 218).

One of the many interesting and perhaps surprising developments that followed upon the Marlborough House negotiations and independence was the rapport that developed between Williams and Capildeo. Writing eight years later, Williams was nostalgic about this relationship. The statement is important and worth quoting at some length:

We started off our Independence career on the basis of as healthy a relationship between Government and Opposition as has been developed anywhere. The Marlborough House Independence Conference reached a happy conclusion on the basis of personal accord between the Prime Minister and the Leader of the Opposition, the late Dr. Rudranath Capildeo. The Prime Minister, at his first Commonwealth Conference, had a powerful team of advisers which included the Leader of the Opposition and representatives of several key organizations.

In our first approaches to the European Economic Community in Brussels, the Prime Minister was associated with the Leader of the Opposition. The Prime Minister and Leader of the Opposition listened together to President Kennedy's missile speech and viewed together the Berlin Wall, understanding together the formidable difficulties facing a minute country like Trinidad and Tobago in the world of the super powers. On two occasions in Parliament, on the representations of the Leader of the Opposition, the Prime Minister intervened to make fundamental modifications in the original Government Budget proposals.

With the death of Dr. Capildeo, this *modus vivendi* has broken down, fragmentation and individualism have become more rampant, and the Opposition has become a mixed group of dissident factions uttering slogans imported from other countries, other times and other situations. (As cited in Boyke 1972)

22 The "Hindu Question"

In the pre-independence period, neither Williams nor his followers understood the political psychology of the Hindus in Trinidad. If they had, they would never have assumed that a few urban assimilationist Hindus could rally the Hindu masses behind the nationalist movement. In the 1956 elections, the PNM was unable to attract more than a few Hindus who had any legitimacy among their community, and those who were so attracted rapidly lost most of their supporters. A count of delegates at the seventh annual convention of the PNM in 1963 revealed that only 7 per cent were Indian.

Williams's attacks on the Hindi linguistic movement, the Hindu school-building programme (he described the Maha Sabha–constructed schools as "cow-sheds"), and the Maha Sabha during the 1956 election campaign had effectively destroyed whatever chances the PNM had of mobilizing the Hindus, who viewed the attacks as gratuitous insults to the community as a whole. Some of the damage was rectified by Williams's success in getting Maraj to go to the federal conference in Jamaica in 1957, but the renewed attacks on Hindu nationalism following the federal elections of 1958 and his description of Hindus as a "recalcitrant minority" were deeply resented. From 1958 onward they were in open and systematic revolt against the PNM. The events leading to independence showed to what extent the community had become dangerously polarized. The fact that the society was small, dense, claustrophobic and without either privacy or viable cultural outlets only served to sharpen the inevitable confrontation between the groups.

In his well-meaning attempt to create a programme of social action that would establish dominance over the divisive forces in the community, Williams did not realistically evaluate the extent to which the society was fractionalized. Urban dreamer that he was, he seemed to assume that the People's Charter was attractive enough to cut through the fear, hostility and misunderstanding that had kept the groups socially distant for more than a century. He did not see that the withdrawal of the imperial power would activate latent conflicts, because it was his premise that the blame for such antagonisms rested solely on the ruthlessness of the imperial system. He apparently presumed that once the imperial system was withdrawn, the divisive forces of the community would be harnessed by the effort to clear up the "mess" that the imperialists had left behind. His was the characteristic mistake of middle-class reformers who believe that the appeal of reason is powerful enough to dissolve prejudices.

In his proposals for constitutional reform in 1955, Williams did seem to recognize that Trinidad was a plural rather than a homogeneous society. His proposals relating to the composition and powers of the upper chamber had been designed to accommodate the ethnic and creedal divisions in the society. But once in power, Williams became a strict and uncompromising majoritarian; any ethnic group that did not rally behind the PNM was recalcitrant, treasonable or obscurantist. Despite his genuine intellectual commitment to multiracialism, he refused to concede minority communities the right to elect their own kind, or to articulate their own version of the national community. The majoritarian thesis implicitly promised a homogeneous society, a non-racial rather than a multiracial society.

Winston Mahabir was correct when he noted that Williams did not fully understand that the issue in Trinidad was race and not class. In a letter written to Mahabir in 1948, Williams admitted that he did not "give a rambling damn about the whites. If they wish to come in well and good, but if coming in means the principle of white supremacy, then is hell with them. The Indians are an entirely different problem. . . . The political line for the society . . . must be economic and political equality and cultural autonomy for any minority that wishes it. . . . The whole future of the West Indies hinges on the labour movement; that is a class, not a race issue. . . . The Chinese will follow the Indians, and if they don't . . . they don't" (*Vanguard*, 1 April 1966).

Two hypotheses might be adduced to explain Williams's handling of the "Indian problem". It may be that he recognized the composite nature of the society, but nevertheless deliberately ignored it on the grounds that the anti-colonial struggle and the social revolution had to be given priority, even if it meant a temporary postponement of the goal of establishing a loyal national community. One might argue that Williams was driven to this position by his recognition that it was not possible to bring the period of metropolitan tutelage to a quick end and achieve inter-ethnic consensus at the same time; one goal had to be temporarily sacrificed in a deliberate risk. Perhaps also Williams believed that he had a responsibility to emancipate the African, to stimulate in him pride, dignity and a feeling of independence, and that this goal necessitated an attack, however subtly concealed, on the European and Indian communities. The post-federal election and "Massa Day Done" speeches might be viewed in this light. If the Indian leadership was doing the same for the Hindus, and using the Europeans in the quest for power, why should he not alert the Africans? Power considerations may have reinforced this line of thinking. A combination of Hindus and other minorities might again displace the PNM, as had happened in the federal elections of 1958.

The second hypothesis centres on the question of the accuracy with which Williams and the coloured middle class had defined the problem. There is evidence that they took for granted that the Indians had been assimilated into the society, and that the common experiences they shared with Africans on the plantation predisposed them to follow a national movement dedicated to an overthrow of the plantation system. The fact that they did not do so was perceived as the fault of their leaders, first in the PDP and then in the DLP, who in their quest for power deliberately exploited the residual differences that existed between Indians and Africans. Williams remarked, "[W]e must not do the Indian people the gross injustice of believing or even pretending to believe that those Indians who claim to speak in their name are the genuine political leaders. The 1956 election showed that a large section of the population was waiting for people to come forward so that they could turn their backs on those who had led them for so many years" ("Perspectives for Our Party", 17 October 1958, 19).

It was not the Indian masses, then, who were treasonable, subversive, antinational and recalcitrant, but the Indian elite. The PNM's stubborn refusal to cooperate with the DLP necessarily followed from this conclusion. Anyone who advocated cooperation with the opposition, or identified with it in any way, was disloyal and anti-national. The DLP was not a genuine or legitimate opposition. The PNM would then have to appeal over the heads of the Hindu elite, as Williams in fact attempted to do during the 1961 election campaign.

It is true that PDP and DLP politicians were extremely irresponsible during this period; but their behaviour cannot be ascribed entirely to spite, malice or a lust for power. Their desperation was just as much a reciprocal product of the hostile provocations of Williams and his supporters. Prominent party members do not dispute this:

> The longer sections of the electorate believe they are unfairly and unjustly treated by reason of race, the easier it is to organize such resentment under the guise of a political party. I am far from satisfied that the PNM is entirely blameless for this unfortunate state of affairs. Living in harmony is, after all, a two-way process. And every member of the PNM has his part to play in ensuring that we here do in fact live in unity. (Lynn Beckles, *Nation*, 9 February 1962)

C.L.R. James, once a leading activist in the PNM, also accused the PNM leadership of fanaticism and gangsterism on the racial question (James 1965, 7). James himself was not blameless on this issue, though he always took more of a class attitude to the pre-independence crises than did others in the PNM. James found it perfectly natural that a formerly oppressed group should want to raise its status by elevating one of its members to political leadership ("Why Abuse Him?", *Nation*, 28 February 1969).

The pre-independence compromise worked out at Marlborough House in 1962 did seem to mark the introduction of a new chapter in race relations in the nation. After independence, Williams showed great willingness to consult with the leader of the DLP and sought his cooperation on a variety of projects. DLP supporters and parliamentarians in fact complained that Capildeo worked much too closely with the prime minister and that his freedom to criticize had been severely inhibited. By way of apology, Capildeo explained that if he had been an active opposition leader, Afro-Trinidadian elements would have viewed his actions as being racially motivated. It would have been said that Indians were again "harassing" the PNM, preventing it from getting on with the development programme. This, he felt, would have consolidated the PNM, which he believed would collapse under its own weight.

The PNM also made efforts to recruit Indians to the police and defence forces, though these remained overwhelmingly black. The same was true of the senior ranks of the civil service. Muslims, three of whom represented the PNM in the legislature, improved their status more rapidly, and some of their spokesmen proudly referred to Williams as "the Father of the Nation and Defender of All Faiths". Hindus, however, still felt that the promise of cooperation had not been adequately fulfilled. "The Independence of the country itself was not celebrated together," complained the president of the Indian National Association. "It was a PNM Independence Committee which made the preparations. . . . The very national flag was not the result of our [working] together." Hindus complained that members of their community were not being appointed to ambassadorial and other important positions, most of which were being given to members of the PNM.

In response to this accusation, the government appointed a Christian Indian, the former deputy leader of the DLP, to the high commissionership to India, a move that was highly acclaimed within the Indian community. The creation of a post in India was no doubt a belated signal to Indians that India was as important in the PNM's diplomatic pecking order as was Africa. Hindus also pressed successfully for the establishment of publicly supported Hindu secondary schools and official recognition of their religious festivals on the grounds that Christian religious groups were allowed similar privileges.

There were also complaints that the cultural contributions of Indians were not given the same measure of support and public recognition as other groups, that secondary schools still discriminated against Indians, and that most of the public resources were allocated to areas that were predominantly Afro-creole. The government denied these charges, but some contained an element of truth.

Demands continued to be made for the teaching of Hindi in the schools, and complaints were often heard about the anti-Indian bias of the communications media. There was indeed a prevailing feeling among Indians in general and Hindus in particular that they were still discriminated against by creole society, and that the national motto "Together We Aspire, Together We Achieve" was not a reality. Until March 1970, however, there was general agreement that the fears of head-on confrontations between the two groups had receded considerably, and that conflicts had returned to the state of latency that prevailed in the pre-1956 period. Williams's "meet the people" tours and the government's Better Village and Community Development Programme did a great deal to reduce feelings of hostility and alienation among Indians. Hindu groups began garlanding Williams, and pundits blessed him with "water from the Ganges" (*Daily Mirror*, 12 May 1966).

Plate 18 Williams with Chief Justice Hugh Wooding, Senator Hamilton Maurice, Gerard Montano, Kamaluddin Mohammed and Solomon Hochoy. (Eric Williams Memorial Collection, University of the West Indies, St Augustine)

Plate 19 Williams with Ian McLeod, colonial secretary; John O'Halloran, minister of industry and commerce; and Hugh Gaitskell, leader of the opposition in the House of Commons at the opening of the Trinidad and Tobago office in London, 1961. (Eric Williams Memorial Collection, University of the West Indies, St Augustine)

Plate 20 Williams with Sir Learie Constantine and Winifred Atwell at cocktail reception in London, June 1962. (Eric Williams Memorial Collection, University of the West Indies, St Augustine)

Plate 21 Williams with minister of health Winston Mahabir and Minister Gerard Montano. (Eric Williams Memorial Collection, University of the West Indies, St Augustine)

Plate 22 Williams with minister of labour Donald Granado and Solomon Hochoy at cocktail reception, June 1962. (Eric Williams Memorial Collection, University of the West Indies, St Augustine)

Plate 23 Williams with Sir Winston Churchill during state visit, March 1961. (Eric Williams Memorial Collection, University of the West Indies, St Augustine)

Plate 24 Williams sharing a joke with (*left to right*) Errol Mahabir, Boysie Prevatt and Kamaluddin Mohammed. (Trinidad and Tobago Express Ltd)

PART 5

THE REALITIES OF INDEPENDENCE

23 Cabinet and Party in Independence

The Prime Minister is Prime Minister only because of his party. His responsibilities as party leader are therefore basic and cannot be subordinated to his Government obligations.

– Eric Williams

The democracy that Williams gave to the country, he never gave to the Party. He kept the Party as if it was his. It was the most offensive thing for you to be critical of Dr. Williams in the Party.

– Ferdie Ferreira

In the years that followed his electoral victory in 1956, Williams made a valiant attempt to create an educated and participant democracy. At public rallies throughout the country, at weekend schools, and at seminars, Williams tried to give the people a wider perspective on the problems that faced the community. He also made a careful attempt to work closely with the party's Policy Advisory Committee, which in turn was fed by a number of sub-committees. But there is little evidence that the people, or even the membership of the party, were ever allowed to decide anything. The party quickly became an electioneering machine, a sounding board, and a legitimating agent for decisions taken by the leadership. The flow of traffic was almost always from the cabinet to the party, and rarely the other way around.

Several explanations have been offered as to why this imbalance occurred. One view held that the extra-governmental party lacked the competence and experience to function autonomously. The speed with which it came to power also prevented it from developing a personality of its own, independent of the government. Williams recognized this weakness: "The difficulty with which the party is faced has been its repeated successes and the speed with which it has been built up. In other countries, other parties have been built more slowly, and they have had time to build up their foundations more securely. The task that lies before us is to ensure that the gains are not dissipated by hasty action or complacency" (*PNM Weekly*, 1 July 1957).[1]

Many did not agree with these explanations. They claimed that there was talent outside the government, but that there was a sort of tacit agreement that in the interest of unity, there should be no opposition to the political leader. The first chairman of the party, Sir Learie Constantine, took the position that Williams was a "god-send" to the party and the country, and that he should be allowed to "soar" without constriction. Williams was to be warned and advised, but was not to be openly fought if he insisted on a particular course of action. He was also to be shielded from attacks from the rank and file lest the party become enveloped in internecine strife. Party leaders went along with the Constantine thesis, but some were of the view that it was a mistake to allow the party to become little more than an extension of Williams's personality.

A number of factors contributed to the ascendancy of the political leader and the governmental bureaucracy over the party and the public: the nature of the political system, the personality of the political leader, and the deferential orientation of the party rank and file and of the masses generally.

Nature of the Political System

Williams took it for granted that Trinidad and Tobago should operate according to the canons of the "pattern state" at Westminster. Inevitably, this meant that the party in the country had to play a secondary role in relation to the party in government. It was easy for the cabinet to establish dominance over the party, since it could always be argued that key decisions had to be made in cabinet and announced in the legislature before they came before public and party for scrutiny. The requirements of official secrecy could also be invoked to exclude the party from the crucial periods of decision-making process.

It did not follow, of course, from the mere acceptance of the Westminster model that the party would be pushed into the background. It was quite possible for the new elite to institutionalize methods for the communication of party opinion to arenas of public policy-making before the cabinet had taken a stand on any issue. All that is being said here is that the adoption of the Westminster model made it easy for the new elite to slip, perhaps unconsciously, into the bureaucratic methods of the old colonial system. The output structures of the system quickly gained ascendancy over input structures in the nation and within the party, although the leadership had created an elaborate network of safeguards to ensure against this very possibility.

Whereas the old ruling class had been able to use the authority of the imperial power to control, directly or indirectly, the entire system, including the structures of local government, statutory corporations and other quasi-independent agencies, the new elite invoked the authority of the party and the people to do the same thing. In the name of administrative efficiency and financial rationalization, the system became even more centralized than it was before. But these developments cannot be properly understood without reference to the charismatic style of the political leader himself.

Personality of the Political Leadership

Two views struggled for dominance within the PNM and very often within the minds of the same people – the one ultra-populistic, the other elitist. The first view held that the masses in Trinidad were, "like the Athenians", highly sophisticated politically; given the necessary stimulation and opportunity, they could make public policy for themselves. To quote Williams, "I can say without fear of contradiction, except by those who stand to lose by it, that the political intelligence of the masses of the people is astonishingly high, their political instincts astonishingly sound, and that they are the best and most vital students I have encountered in any university in my experience" (1955b, 12).

The second view, and the one that gained dominance, held that the Trinidad masses were inert and politically uneducated. There was no public opinion in Trinidad. What was needed was a new intellectually oriented regime that would educate and organize public opinion through mass educational meetings, pamphlets, newspapers and other media of propaganda. The elite would emancipate the masses. It was an essentially Marxist-Leninist image of the political party to which, according to C.L.R. James, Williams had become exposed during his student days in London and Oxford during the 1930s.

But it is not necessary to go that far to explain Williams's political methods; his own intellectual gifts and his personality were more germane to the issue. Williams was a man driven by an overweening belief in his rectitude, wisdom and historical mission. Because of his prodigious research talents, his amazing capacity for analysing, organizing and articulating information, and for manipulating people, he easily dominated the political stage. His essentially monopolistic personality also made it difficult for him to share leadership readily. Williams had an inordinate capacity for inflicting deprivations upon himself, though he complained bitterly that it was the party and public that mercilessly forced him into playing so many roles.

Intellectually, Williams was firmly committed to the democratic ideal, and he often went to great lengths to conceal the fact that he was the chief decision-maker. His political methods were designed to keep everyone off guard by a seemingly deliberate confusion in the lines of authority. Persons and instrumentalities were manipulated as the situation demanded; sometimes it was the cabinet, at other times the planning commission; sometimes the policy committee of the party, at times the general council or the convention. In the process, the masses were left out, except insofar as they were required to provide logistic support for the high command. Some cabinet ministers also complained bitterly about what one referred to as "smokescreen government". As Winston Mahabir noted, he, like many other ministers, was in a kind of political indentureship relationship with Williams ("The Real Eric Williams", *Trinidad Express*, 5 January 1969).

Every cabinet member was aware that it was the political leader who commanded the mass following, and no one interested in political survival or popular legitimacy really dared to push opposition too far. This is not to say that there was no opposition to Williams in the cabinet or in the party, but such opposition almost always functioned within well-defined limits. If the leader was known to feel strongly enough about a particular issue, the party and cabinet usually went along. The need for loyalty, sincerity or discipline was readily invoked to silence "recalcitrants" or "individualists". Williams also had a tendency, not uncommon among leaders of movement regimes, to threaten resignation whenever he felt thwarted or harassed. The community or party was reminded that he was performing an indispensable role that he was only too anxious to give up so that he might return to writing his delayed history of the West Indies.

David Nelson, a former party colleague of Williams who was himself an early casualty, remarked that "fear of the personal consequences of open disagreement with, or efforts to control, the political leader is today the only neutralizer of the poison which is slowly eating into the PNM system". Williams was a genius at alternating bluster and charm to hold cabinet and party members in line, and often applied the knife to ministers who crossed him. Exile to embassies or to less important cabinet or civil service positions were effective parts of his armory (*Trinidad Guardian*, 25 January 1959). Other critics accused Williams of instituting a personal "monarchy" and of deliberately creating an image of an omnipotent superman, one who could keep all the levers of the system going effectively. In their view, however, it was activity without purpose.

Founding member and one-time general secretary of the party D.W. Rogers made much the same complaint with a great deal of bitterness. There was grumbling from the outset among some stalwarts. Rogers complained that some who were allowed to stand as candidates were not supporters of the party. Some were not even members.

> The compromising of principles was one of the first mistakes of the political leader; a short-term glory for a long-term disaster. This was felt early in the game. Hard-working members with the highest qualifications, unimpeachable integrity, and undivided loyalty, who gave unstintedly of their time, energy and money were thrown on the scrapheap and instead, swashbuckling dilettantes and quacks jockeying successfully for places of honour and remuneration were exalted beyond all reason. (1975, 102)

Rogers revealed that J.S. Donaldson, who had done more than anyone else to build the People's Educational Movement, the Political Education Group, and ultimately the PNM, "had to fight for his life to get the nomination to contest the 1961 election though he was named by his constituency". Rogers does not tell us who sought to block Donaldson, but invites us to conclude that Williams was behind it. As he writes suggestively, "This ingratitude was very noticeable early, very early in the game" (ibid.). Williams believed, however, that he had to find room in the party for minority groups who were underrepresented there.

Williams was accused of using all sorts of tricks to get those whom he endorsed or opposed included or excluded as candidates. Ulric Lee, who fought Albert Gomes in 1956, was a case in point. He was unwanted by the constituency, but Williams insisted on his selection (Granado 1987). One of Williams's strategies was to over-quiz those he did not want. Some were quizzed for hours while others were questioned only for minutes. Rogers claimed that in 1966, he was quizzed for two hours and five minutes! He was endorsed by his constituency and the executive committee, but rejected by the "all powerful" (ibid., 129).

Following the September 1956 victory, Williams devoted much of his time to organizing the new state and the budget and to working out modalities for the federation and constitutional reform. Little time was left for the party, even though he tried to visit party headquarters after leaving his office. As he told the party on 17 October 1958, in "Perspectives for Our Party", his address to the third annual convention,

> From January to November 1956, we concentrated on the island-wide dissemination of our principles, ideals and programme. All efforts, all energies were concentrated on this goal. The [next] phase began with the approval of the 1958 Budget and the Five-year Development Programme. . . . Thus, for two years and nine months the party had to play a subordinate role to the Government. . . . So that when we ask in October, 1958, the question, "Where do we go from here?"
>
> The Party, left to fend for itself for two years and nine months, became automatically and necessarily the number one priority.[2]

The fact that the party was left to fend for itself upset Rogers. As he whinged,

> [T]he fending of the party for itself in these two years and nine months brought disastrous results. There began a subtle [and] confused scramble for individual gain. It did not take long to see the selfishness, venality, and even undisguised chicanery dripping down. Loyalty to the Party meant loyalty to the Political Leader of the Party exclusively. One word, one gesture from the political leader, one look from him meant "off with his head." One cannot divine if the political leader loved it so, but it was forced on him from all sides. It was not the ordinary hero-worship. Self-confessed crooks were promoted. And while [Williams] would justly rebuke in no uncertain terms – graft, corruption and bubohl, and while his action upheld his utter disgust over Trinidad's life

with its patronage, and drink-a-rum friendship, and while he took a delight in "bouff-ing" those who played "Big Shot", yet he had a penchant for drawing around him intel-lectual nitwits who were incompetent as well. (Rogers 1975, 189–90)

Rogers complained that Williams's political style had implications for the party, which became a veritable morgue: "Something even more dangerous was cropping up, not only [in respect] of the rank and file at conventions – the rep-resentatives of mass support for the party – not only in these was there blind obedience, but also at the General Council and Central Executive; there was a numbness, a freezing of speech" (1975, 115–16). While there were "ministers of silence", many ministers and other party members were silenced. "The history of the PNM is replete with instances where innocent men of action have been destroyed because of suspicion, haunting suspicion." Rogers himself was sus-pended from his post as general secretary, though he never received a letter of suspension. His name, however, appeared both in the dailies and in convention documents indicating that he had been suspended. More than three years passed without an investigation or trial.

Another tendency that Rogers found disturbing was that of people to fawn on Williams. Everything had to be dealt with by him. Ministers were routinely bypassed:

> At the constituency level, ministers complained that the electorate looked upon them as minions. Constituents by-passed their representatives and carried delegations straight to the Prime Minister. In the midst of a conference for redress of real or imag-inary ills held before a minister, one will hear the leader of the delegation say to the minister: "We want to see Dr. Williams. You can't handle this." And they do see him. This has happened more than once. This veneration, this awe-inspired aura, this potent prestige was more ascribed than achieved. He came into the party as a celebrity. To speak to the celebrity was an honour; to be spoken to by the celebrity, more hon-our; to submit to the celebrity, most honour. Even to be kicked by the celebrity was a kiss on the cheeks of the political buttocks. I have seen a councilor cry tears for more than an hour because the latter was pulled up by the Political Leader. Men grouped around Williams more than they did around the party. . . . Men became "macosychopants". (1975, 116)

Rogers complained that "not even a blurred photo of the pioneers hangs any-where". Founders were erased from the historical record. The ghost of Caligula was restored. "Let them hate so long as they fear."

The Deferential Nature of Party Opinion

It must be noted that Williams was virtually allowed to monopolize the political system. For the most part this was not a case of a leader seizing power from popular elements, as discontented intellectuals and some party members like to claim. The documents of the party are full of evidence to indicate that the awe-struck rank and file deferred to the superior judgement of the charismatic hero. Time and time again, the party simply abdicated its authoritative role with the declaration that the leader could be entrusted to make the best possible settlement on behalf of the nation and the party. As one senior party member wrote, "The PNM rank and file have not yet reached the stage where the desire to participate in top level discussions is extremely pressing. Party members are satisfied so far with the conduct of Government business."

A good example of this was the resolution on federation approved in September 1961:

> This Special Convention expresses its complete satisfaction with the handling of the question of a West Indian Federation by its Political Leader up to the present moment, and entrusts the future handling of this matter to its Political Leader in consultation with such units of the Party as he may see fit, and requires him to report to the Party on this matter as soon as it is politically proper and wise or in the best interest of the country to do so, and further that there should be no discussion on the topic of Federation until after the General elections. (Files of the PNM Special Convention, 1961)

One is certain, however, that this resolution was authored by the political leader himself.

Generally speaking, annual conventions were not times of serious business, but occasions when the faithful from all parts of the country met to exchange gossip and greeting. Even small bodies like the general council invariably just listened to the political leader and other leading members of the party and ratified what had already been decided in the corridors of power. One cannot understand decision making in the PNM without appreciating the strong moral influence that Williams had over the membership.

But while it is generally true that the rank and file willingly deferred to party and government specialists, there was always a small element, usually "out" members of the elite, who were critical of the "leave it to the Doc" attitude. They felt that such a development was destroying the vitality of party organs and that groups were growing atrophied for want of purpose; this was especially true in party strongholds. They were also concerned about the leadership's cavalier treatment of party opinion. And there were occasions when party abdication was not spontaneous, but came as a result of manipulative persuasion by the party elite, who argued that some things needed to be done with dispatch and secrecy, and with room to manoeuvre. At such times the party was treated as though it were a hindrance, especially when action involved the compromising of ideological goals. And frequently, when consultation was conceded, it was either ceremonial or made imperative because the leadership felt it was strategically necessary to obtain mass support for new policy departures.

There were frequent complaints about the dominance of ministerial elements in the major policy-making organs of the party, that the general council was too large and unwieldy as a democratic instrument, too satellitic and pliable, and that those who disagreed with the leadership were not permitted to bring their differences out into the open. Rebels in the party, such as Gil Thompson, felt that its hierarchy, elected for five years, had become fossilized, self-satisfied and timid. They were accused of caring more for their own standing with the leader than for the real problems of the mass party. Members were unhappy about the failure of the hierarchy, deliberate or otherwise, to provide the party with important documents that were expected to form the basis of policy decisions in sufficient time to allow for proper study and thought. The author often witnessed the extent to which this strategy made it possible for the platform to seize the initiative from the floor of the convention, which was invariably forced to accept the manipulative interpretations of the political leader without much chance of "answering back". The short time given to the consideration of policy issues, especially resolutions from the rank and file, made it difficult if not impossible for the party to maintain a sufficient degree of self-direction.

The same complaint was made by a member of the general council about the proceedings: "So packed becomes the agenda, and so protracted the meetings, that intelligent group participation throughout an entire meeting is barely possible. General council members are held responsible for decisions which they did not really make, and this leads to frustration." At the third annual convention, for example, the party passed a motion to the effect that the annual convention was the supreme body of the party, and as such its directives were to be complied with, with all due speed and attention. In most cases, opposition elements waged their struggles around constitutional issues or over the standing orders that were the ruling of the platform and not of the convention. Provisions such as the five-minute speaking rule at conventions and the finality of the chair's ruling were always opposed by this element on the floor. It was felt that the chairman of the party should not be a minister and that the general council and the policy advisory committee should be able to convene without ministerial initiative. There were also complaints that ministers were not attending general council meetings or giving sufficient attention to the affairs of their constituency groups. One member warned that

> the strength of the Party lies in the thousands of little people who have laboured to build up, in the name of the PNM, small voluntary groups engaged in community activity. . . . It is at this level one finds the hopes, aspirations, fears and frustrations of Trinidad and Tobago. . . . In every sense it is a world in itself and it is not surprising that representatives who become PNM representatives without a period of work among

groups, become bored with the trivialities of this level in contrast to "important" Government business [and] find themselves divorced from the hearts and minds of the people they represent. (Lynn Beckles, *Nation*, 7 July 1961)

Many members were unhappy about the weakness of the party's information services, about the fact that often they learned of new policy from the public news media, and consequently had no superior information with which to combat distortions that might appear in such reports. Party groups, especially in the rural areas, remained inert due to a similar lack of information and stimulation. This discontent was easily detected in numerous resolutions submitted to conventions, one of which read, "Whereas it is found that too many important party matters, when discussed at hierarchy level, are kept secret, and whereas party members are never in a position to discuss these matters authoritatively, be it resolved that this Conference recommends to the Annual Convention that this Policy be abolished immediately, and plans made to familiarize party members with information before it is made public" (Party Group #17, St George West, to the Fourth Annual Convention, 1960).

Williams himself was often a stern critic of the PNM. He complained of the corruption, nepotism, factionalism and individualism that strangled the party, as well as the "lack of training . . . political immaturity, complacency, and gross absenteeism of some of its principal representatives. The weakness of [its] organization weakens our efforts in every sphere of government and social life" (Williams 1960a, 11). To enhance its operational effectiveness, the party had to rely less on its legislative arm and more on its own resources:

> The Party must have its own "Cabinet" and its own "Ministers" . . . who in caliber and in status must be on par with the legislative representatives of the Party. . . . Building . . . the Party cannot be carried out by legislators. If they attempt to do so, the only result will be that the scope and possibility of the Party will be cut down to the size which suits such time and energy and thought as the legislators can spare for it, and you know how precious little time and energy and thought some legislators have spared for the Party. (Ibid., 9–10)

Williams also urged that greater effort be made to develop powerful press and propaganda machinery, and exhorted party members to function as leaders of all progressive causes and movements in the community. In the pre-independence era, the party was never able to summon the resources to reform itself, because most of its top officials were members of the governmental network and fully preoccupied with the anti-colonial struggle. The lower political temperature that followed independence made possible a serious attempt to restructure and reinvigorate the party. In 1963, its constitution was revised substantially and a sizeable core of new officers was returned to the central executive and policy committee. With Williams's encouragement, this element made a praiseworthy attempt to inject some dynamism into the life of the organization and to make it an initiating agent. The party organ, which was under its control, became somewhat more aggressive, and legislators began taking a greater interest in party activity. Greater emphasis was also to be given to political education through lectures and seminars, and Williams found time to write informative book reviews and commentaries on national and international events for the benefit of readers of the party weekly. Several important policy issues were also referred to the party for study and recommendation, and some of the reports were remarkably competent.

Despite all this activity, the PNM remained an essentially bureaucratic organization. Williams himself felt driven to distraction. In an address to a party convention on 5 September 1962, he noted, "You have all the confusion in Trinidad concentrated in the PNM. The PNM instead of being representative of the best in the country, instead of blazing the trail for the rest of the country, becomes nothing more than a gigantic conglomeration of all the vices in the country. You have too much in Trinidad concentrated in too few hands, too much responsibility placed on the too few shoulders."

In a comparative comment on politics in Cuba and Trinidad, Williams agreed that "the capacity to enthuse thousands of people . . . presented one of the most decisive advantages which the Castro movement has had over the PNM", though he noted that the comparison was not quite fair, since "Castro's procedures" and a "one-party dictatorial state" gave him decisive advantages in organizing the society. The type of orthodox, pragmatic and bureaucratic politics to which the PNM was wedded made it difficult for the party to appeal to the population for idealism and sacrifice. This indeed was the major criticism of radical intellectuals who for the most part remained completely alienated from the PNM.

During the latter months of 1964, Williams embarked on a dramatic "Meet the Party" tour in a determined attempt to reinvigorate languishing party groups. During the meetings, party members complained that the leadership provided no incentives to encourage dynamism, that party members got no special privileges, patronage or information. Nothing was ever done to give them a distinctive role in the community. Williams admitted that liaison between party and government left much room for improvement, but noted that in many cases party members themselves were to be blamed. Members, he said, were not sufficiently vigilant, and, judging from their complaints, often seemed less informed than the public on policy issues. They were urged to make a greater effort to follow the activities of their legislators through the medium of the daily and party press, and through government announcements. If party members felt that certain information was not being revealed to them, they should be alert enough to infer that political strategy or parliamentary protocol prevented disclosure. No government was completely free to reveal everything it had in mind at a particular time.

Williams also defended the record of members of government, saying that many of them were genuinely bogged down with affairs of state and were unable to make monthly oral reports to their constituency groups, as the party's constitution prescribed. He suggested that a written report be acceptable when visits were not feasible, or that a party senator be accepted as a substitute. It was also agreed that there was a pressing need for constituency offices on a non-partisan basis, through which citizens could make representations to the proper authorities.

Despite promises that greater efforts would be made to reinvigorate the party, very little progress was made. Williams confessed to the eleventh annual convention that he was "deeply disturbed by the inactivity of many party groups and the unfinancial status of many party members. . . . It is clear that many groups come to life only to select candidates for elections." The political leader made the same promises he had made in 1964 – to encourage greater stimulation of group activity, more training and involvement for youth and women members, and closer liaison between elected representatives and constituencies – and pledged to get "very rough with those who do no more than use their positions for intrigue and self-aggrandisement" (*Trinidad Express*, 29 September 1968).

In Williams's view, the fundamental difficulty affecting the party was the passivity of the individual member, who, like the rest of the community, was more interested in what the party could do for him than in what he could for the party or the community. The problem, he believed, stemmed from the laziness of the Trinidadian, his general lack of responsibility, his tendency to say "man, I can't be bothered". Whereas in the pre-independence period belief in the new world and the legitimacy of the PNM was enough to stimulate militancy, enthusiasm was at an extremely low level. Attendance at unit meetings was scanty and the same held true for public meetings. The "University of Woodford Square" in fact did not hear from its once popular professor for many years.

Despite the criticisms, the PNM remained an empirical, fairly efficient (in a bureaucratic sense) and disciplined organization, at least when compared to parties in the Caribbean and other developing areas. It avoided one of the weaknesses that bedevilled the opposition DLP, squabbling in public. Individuals who disagreed with the leadership left, or were led out of the fold, but the public remained largely unaware of the internal crises, which on occasion were very serious. It was not an incorrupt organization, as Williams himself admitted, but the level of corruption was much lower than one would expect from a party that had been in power for so long. Williams was on solid ground when he boasted that the PNM had managed to bring some decency, some order, some good sense and some rational outlook to political activities in Trinidad. It was an achievement of which he, as its principal author, could be justly proud. Few dominant parties in the Third World could match its record. As one minister, Patrick Solomon, boasted, "Only two organizations have the discipline of the PNM – the Catholic Church and the Communist Party." It was a discipline based not on physical violence or the threat of it, but on the persuasive and manipulative ability of Williams as well as a widespread fear of incurring his displeasure.

The Deferential Orientation of Public Opinion

The deference of members was a reflection of similar attitudes among the general population. The prevailing norm was civic incompetence, a feeling of powerlessness to affect the direction of public policy. The old metropolitan bureaucracy that revolved around the governor and the imperial civil service had simply been replaced by another bureaucracy. Except perhaps where public utilities, educational issues and social services were concerned, few people organized themselves into pressure groups, wrote letters or petitioned their members in the legislature. They were more likely to go over the heads of their elected representatives to the prime minister, who to them was the real source of power; and when such efforts were made, there was, on the whole, little continuity or follow-through. People sulked or withdrew support; hardly ever was discontent translated into continuous political activity.

Apart from the leadership of organized labour, which openly challenged the government, the organized political opposition, and the small radical group at the university, there was little vocal political opinion on general issues. There were substantial pressure groups that made their influence felt when the interests of their clientele were affected, but the middle class was extremely inarticulate in public. There were grumbles in private, but rarely did one hear voices of protest against violations of civil liberties, public immorality or arrogance on the part of the bureaucracy or the political elite. The same passivity that was typical of the middle class in the colonial period continued in the era of self-government.

Part of this attitude can certainly be explained by the fact that many were public employees and as such could not criticize the regime in public. C.L.R. James, who was at times unfairly harsh in his criticisms of the middle class, just the same understood their plight: "One of the most precious heritages – the most precious heritage of the British connection is their . . . instinctive, not merely legal, recognition of the right to differ without being penalized. Even before Independence, that is fast disappearing; you bend the knee, and keep it bent, or you are offered the choice, blows or a Government position" (James 1961, 3).

Williams's "if you don't like it, get to hell outa here" attitude terrified many into silence, especially those whose economic existence and future well-being depended upon the grace of the political elite. The smallness of the community, which made authority close, and the limited number of job outlets in the private sector only served to reinforce this timidity. It was an open secret that the ostensibly neutral Public Service Commission was manipulated by the prime minister.

But fear and timidity, and the requirements of the civil service, do not entirely explain the attitude of many who did not really stand to lose much by voicing criticism. The fact is that among a large section of the black and mixed population, there was an attitude of "leave the Doctor alone". This was especially true in the pre-independence period; in public as in private, criticism of the Doctor was recognized not as the right of the citizen, but as an expression of a fractious and unmannerly spirit. The Mighty Sparrow, Trinidad's calypsonian laureate echoed the mood of the black masses to their beloved "Williams the Conqueror" when he sang,

> Leave the dam Doctor
> He ain't trouble all you.
> Leave the dam Doctor;
> What he do, he well do.

The prime minister inherited the "institutional charisma" of the old colonial governor who was to be congratulated and flattered but not criticized; those who did not share this point of view, the people of European or Chinese stock in particular, either stayed aloof and sullen or compromised the legitimacy of their contributions by open partisanship to the opposition DLP. The absence until the late 1960s of a vibrant daily press and university community, and the almost total absence of any journals devoted to serious political analysis only added to the general political blandness of the community. Williams himself agreed that people behaved towards him as they did to the old colonial governor. This was particularly manifested in the practice of seeking his intervention on every grievance or his "grace" on every social occasion. As he wrote, "In the colonial period, one wrote to the Governor for all manner of things. Today, in Independence you have the mentality unchanged, [people have] merely substituted the Prime Minister" (*Nation*, 5 March 1965). The Mighty Striker captured the dependent disposition of the black underclass when he sang the following:

> Annabella stocking want patching.
> She want the doctah to help she wid dat
> Johnson trousers falling.
> He want the doctah help he wid that
> Some want a Zephyr motor car
> Others want piece of land
> Dorothy lose she man
> She want to complain to Doctah Williams

24 Operation Jobs

Restructuring the Trinidad Economy, 1956–1966

Fear of "confronting" the structural underpinnings of the colonial economy was one of the many stumbling blocks that retarded the development of a successful nationalist movement in Trinidad during the 1940s and early 1950s. The meagreness of the territory's economic and human resources, the smallness of scale on which it operated, and its dependence on the United Kingdom had convinced many would-be reformers that self-propelled economic development was not a genuine possibility. It was in this context that a Puerto Rican–style programme of "industrialization by invitation" was begun by the quasi-ministerial regime that governed Trinidad between 1950 and 1956. That programme had resulted in the establishment of about thirty-five industries, the creation of 2,195 jobs, and investment totalling TT$35 million.

Perhaps the most worrisome feature of the economy was the performance of the critical oil industry, which was responsible for 30 per cent of government revenues, 30 per cent of GNP, 80 per cent of total export value, but only 5 per cent of total employment. Despite increases in indigenous crude production due to secondary recovery techniques and successes in marine drilling, it was feared that time was running out on the Trinidad industry. Unless new sources of indigenous crude were found soon, it was feared, the industry would likely go into liquidation or be forced to rely on refining capacity alone.

Needless to say, reduced economic activity in the private sector was forcing contractions in the public sector, which had retrenched around eight thousand daily paid employees since the end of 1966 (an election year). Pay increases for monthly paid government employees in 1966 no doubt exacerbated the difficulties being experienced by the private sector. The country and Williams began to panic over the crisis, and everywhere one heard the complaint that "an air of depression and worry has settled over the nation. The economic outlook is gloomy".

The wisdom of continuing dependence on the Puerto Rican "branch plant" model was being seriously questioned, especially since the experience of Puerto Rico itself was not heartening, as Williams himself acknowledged. In Puerto Rico, as in Jamaica, "industrialization by invitation" resulted in the development of a small, relatively well-paid unionized working-class elite co-existing with a growing pool of unemployed people who were worse off because of the inflationary pressures on the economy. Williams refused, however, to countenance any departure from the Puerto Rican system and deliberately turned his back on the Cuban model, which he believed had not yielded any solutions that were practicable in an "orthodox" political system. Discussing the alternatives presented to Trinidad, Williams declared, "The Trinidad and Tobago Government and people have sought, and believe they have found, a middle way between outright nationalization and the old-fashioned capitalist organization backed by the marines and the dollars of the United States of America. That middle way is an active partnership between Government and major foreign investors in both the formulation and the achievement of the Government's development targets and the Government's social objectives" (Williams 1963).

Williams was of the view that it was impossible to nationalize an economy that depended on foreign trade more than most countries did, and whose limited domestic market of nine hundred thousand people could not possibly absorb the total production of large-scale industries such as petroleum and sugar, which, combined, contributed more than 90 per cent of the total export trade. The inefficiency of much more modest efforts in the field of public ownership of public utilities was, in any case, an inauspicious beginning to public ownership of basic industries, the capital needs of which would seriously interfere with the requirements of government financing of the public sector of the economy (1964c, 333).

Agriculture and Land Reform

In the years after 1964, Williams gave increased attention to the agricultural sector, which between 1951 and 1961 grew by 4.2 per cent per annum, and which contributed 12 per cent of the real total output in the latter year. Agriculture, which employed about 22 per cent of the total workforce, was enthusiastically regarded by all as the critical hinge in the programme of job-creation and national community-building. The programme, one aspect of which involved the preparation and distribution of 20,000 acres of public land in varying sizes (five to fifteen acres depending on the kind of economic activity), was designed to absorb surplus manpower, slow down the drift to the towns, and cut down on the import food bill – TT$90 million in 1966 – which was a serious irritant to the balance of payments problem. The programme also had political and racial implications: the

Indian community represented the PNM's previous lack of interest in agriculture as an attempt to "suppress one section of the community".

Williams claimed that the programme was agro-technical rather than agrarian. The latter, which he imputed to his radical opponents, involved the mere distribution of appropriated land. The one was economic, the other political. Agro-technical reform was costly and complex. It implied the creation of viable, stable and contented farming communities, and meant, among other things, irrigation (only 10 per cent of the arable land in Trinidad was irrigated), housing, electricity, water, road and transportation facilities, cooperatives, mechanization, refrigeration and storage, pest controls and fertilizers, market intelligence, risk capital, subsidies, guaranteed prices, a rational land-tenure system, and skilled officers to disseminate and supervise new agricultural methods. Moreover, the farmer had to be systematically persuaded to begin using the scientific agricultural techniques that had lain at his doorstep on the plantations for so long. Links also had to be forged between agriculture and the growing manufacturing sector. All this took time and a capable infrastructure. Williams argued that the major bottleneck in its agricultural programme was not land, or even capital, but an insufficient number of entrepreneurial farmers, soil analysts, land surveyors, and dedicated agricultural officers. Criticisms were frequently heard that agricultural officers were not doing enough to inform farmers of the new facilities that had been made available. Indeed, because of difficulties of one kind or another, only 6,500 acres of the planned 14,000 acres were distributed by the end of the 1963–68 plan period, and only $50 million of the $61 million planned budget was used.

The Politics of Sugar

One of the most controversial issues that Williams had to address in the early years of independence was the future of the sugar industry. Opinion was sharply divided as to whether the industry should be maintained or destroyed. Some radicals argued that the land being distributed by the PNM was not the best and that the sugar lands were more arable, more accessible, and, equally important, already developed. These lands should be taken out of sugar and converted into cash crops and livestock for the domestic market. This policy, it was felt, would increase agricultural employment as well as agricultural incomes. Others believed that sugar must be maintained, but on a new basis. In their view, the lands should be divided among sugar workers and cane farmers, leaving processing to the companies, as was done to a great extent in Puerto Rico. It was claimed that, properly supervised, the peasants would be even more productive than the estates were. Williams himself had endorsed this stand in 1961. As he argued, "Even if the cane farmer was not as efficient as the planter, the issue is not solely an economic one, and you may pay a certain price in terms of economic efficiency for the greater social stability and advantages that are associated with a widespread ownership and on a small scale" (*Hansard*, 17 May 1961, 21).

Those who recommended the phasing out of sugar did so on political, social and economic grounds. The basic economic argument was that land use must not be determined purely in terms of private returns, but from the standpoint of the social and economic returns to the country as a whole. If this were done, sugar cultivation would be seen to be inferior to other available alternatives. Concentration on new domestic crops, it was felt, would have more effective backward and forward linkages with the rest of the economy. Whereas most raw sugar was refined abroad, new crops could form the basis of a new industrial complex, especially if the incentives now given to foreign industrial capitalists were given to peasants and local entrepreneurs who wished to go into food processing, preferably on a cooperative basis. With the de-emphasis of sugar, local financial resources that were now channelled into the industry through foreign banks would be available for other uses.

In response to the observation that foreign exchange earnings were an important consideration, as the experience of Cuba showed, it was noted that the situation was somewhat different with respect to Trinidad, which had a major foreign-currency earner in its petroleum, petro-chemicals and asphalt industries. Also, while sugar exports earned foreign exchange, there was also a foreign-exchange leakage in terms of exported profits and imported materials. Moreover, diversification, by cutting down the food-import bill, would lead to savings of foreign exchange.

Confronting sugar was also seen as the only medium through which the mal-integrated rural Indian population could be brought into the mainstream of the larger society. Unless something radical was done to reorganize agriculture, there was no hope that they would ever become first-class citizens in a genuinely multiracial national community. Racial animosity between Indians and Africans would continue to plague the island unless sugar was destroyed and the rural population harnessed for agricultural reconstruction.

Relying on sugar also had significant political costs. In the first place, the need to secure favourable quotas and preferences contributed to the maintenance of that attitude of dependence that was a hallmark of colonial plantation society. It also perpetuated in a disguised form the old colonial political system in which planters and politicians worked closely together to maintain the hegemony of sugar while neglecting to exploit other alternatives fully. It was felt that a new and radical agricultural policy would lead to involving the people in achieving national goals and would also help to break down the polarization of the two major ethnic groups into racially based political parties, a division that made it difficult for the society to undertake the radical policies that were needed to repatriate and close the economy.

Even if the seizure of the sugar estates was considered an economically worthwhile policy, Williams rejected it on political grounds. As he once declared, "We are not going to nationalize and take people's lands to have it owned by the state and then have people work for the state. Let them work and develop their own lands. The state is giving away land instead of taking it away as in communist countries." Williams accused the radicals of being Castro-inspired and of pursuing a Bolshevik land-reform strategy, promising land to the peasants only to collectivize or nationalize it as Castro had done, with results that were disastrous economically as well as politically. In his view, the test of statesmanship in new countries is "to avoid the Charybdis of critical underdevelopment as well as the Scylla of chaotic rebellion or totalitarianism". The PNM, he boasted, had given Trinidad "the finest agricultural programme in the West Indies" (*Trinidad Guardian*, 20 July 1966).

Nationalization was said to be irrelevant in Trinidad, where the government owned about 35 per cent of the land and small farmers (owning under fifty acres) held about 43 per cent of the remainder. Unlike Cuba and Brazil, opined Williams, "Trinidad is a paradise for the small farmer." He noted that the sugar estates held just over 16 per cent of the private lands compared to Cuba where about 20 per cent of all lands had been owned by absentee sugar interests.

But while it was true that land-owning was more monopolistic in Cuba than it was in Trinidad, it was nevertheless true that 1.6 per cent of the holders of land owned about 40 per cent of the total private acreage. Just the same, Williams was not convinced that fragmenting sugar-estate holdings among cane farmers would yield viable units for cane farming. "To divide up the estate lands among tens of thousands of cane farmers is to destroy an industry which in 1965 earned us $42 million in foreign exchange out of a total of $673 million." Williams had observed as early as 1942 that "Haiti's . . . revolution destroyed [her] wealth. Economic progress and political reform cannot be achieved by destructive means. Sugar is the curse, but it is also the staple of the Caribbean" (1942, 105). Developing public lands represented the best and ultimately the least "costly" line of attack on the employment and foreign exchange problems, everything else being considered. The key difficulty was to find enough money and skills to do the job properly.

The Radical Critique

Williams's economic policies drew stormy criticism from intellectual radicals and trade unionists in the country. The PNM was accused of stabilizing and standardizing the age-old exploitation that kept sugar workers poor. Like the oil companies, the sugar companies were accused of hiding profits, padding operating costs, bribing governments and union leaders, and paying ridiculously low wages to native workers (despite increases in productivity of 40 per cent between 1956 and 1963), while paying astronomical salaries to expatriate staff and making as much profit as possible before "the flood". "If sugar is uneconomic to produce, it is so at least in part because the owners are taking too large a share of the wealth produced and the staff too large a share of wages" (*Vanguard*, 5 August 1966). Radicals were convinced that Williams's reformist strategy would not solve the country's economic problems. They observed that as a "semi-developed" country with a fairly high per capita income – US$815 in 1970 – Trinidad did not receive any significant aid from the West, and when such aid was forthcoming, the terms were unfavourable and burdensome. They argued that the attempt to transform the economy "structurally" had to begin immediately and that only a decade or so remained before the economy would cease to be viable ("Viewpoint on Sugar", *New World* 5, nos. 1–2 [1969]: 51).

Williams's "pioneer" industrial policy was also roundly condemned. Critics felt that the tax concessions made to these "fugitives from the law of diminishing returns on the mainland" were too generous and unnecessary, and many expressed fear that they would migrate once the "tax holiday" period was over, thus making the sacrifices in terms of revenue losses worthless. The number of jobs the tax concessions generated was also deemed to be inadequate and well below what the businesses promised when making claims for exemptions. Moreover, the industries did not break into export markets to any great degree; nor were the high-priced materials they offered on the domestic market, in which they had protection, of good quality. In short, the radical left had strong doubts about the advisability of the programme, especially because it strengthened the dominance of Anglo-American economic and cultural influences and manipulative bureaucracy, and postponed efforts to create an ethnically integrated society based on popular participation, self-reliance, social equality and cultural autonomy.

The New World Group was severely critical of Williams's unwillingness or inability to undertake the sort of radical reform programmes that they believed to be necessary if the people of Trinidad and Tobago and the West Indies generally were to inherit the Brave New World that he had so brilliantly envisioned in 1955 and 1956.[1] Much of what the New World ideologues said was informed by the ideas of C.L.R. James, Frantz Fanon (*Black Skins White Masks*), and André Gunder Frank, whose *Capitalism and Underdevelopment* was a must-read for the left. Lloyd Best was the principal guru of the regionally based group. His criticisms of Williams were articulated in a brilliant polemic, "Chaguaramas to Slavery?" which was published in 1965 and which was a riposte to Williams's equally brilliant polemic "Slavery to Chaguaramas". Best opined that the choices Williams made in respect of Chaguaramas and the federation were crucial in determining the social and economic policy choices that he made in the aftermath of independence. He argued further that Caribbean reality was tragically mired in slavery, colonialism and monoculture. That reality was seriously challenged by the popular explosions of 1933 to 1938, which cleared the way for self-government. Williams's campaign for the return of Chaguaramas and for political independence was the next major challenge, one that placed a "wedge in the door of economic independence". Whether rightly or not, many felt that those campaigns were intended to shift responsibility for the future of the Caribbean from outside to the people of the region. Williams, however, chose to avoid confrontation with Anglo-American imperialism out of fear for what such a choice would cost:

> If the American base had to go, or even merely to be re-located according to the dictates of West Indian interests, it could have meant a drying up of the largest single potential source of economic aid and a degree of dissociation from the most influential purveyor of North Atlantic ideas. For the Caribbean, such a development would have been revolutionary. The people of the West Indies would have been forced back onto their own resources for the first time. West Indians might have been led to discard the constitutional instruments which the Colonial Office [was] inclined to impose upon its Commonwealth partners-to-be and impelled to define institutions more appropriate to their own specific needs. This development would have brought the conservative, creole, outward-looking culture of the dominant groups into more open conflict with the natural aspirations of the population at large. (Best 1965, 44)

Such a *démarche* would also have required the PNM to attempt to alter the realities of the countryside by confronting "King Sugar" and the relations of production to which its hegemony gave prominence. Confrontation would likewise have involved a serious effort at racial integration in the countryside and the creation of a party system that did more than mirror the existing divisions between Afro- and Indo-Trinidadians. Instead, the transfer of political power took place within a neo–crown colony framework and an economy that left the commanding heights and decision making in imperial hands. As Best complained,

> [The PNM] never built up the [sugar] issue in such a way as to secure the support of the large, rural, racially distinct subculture. . . . This omission made the essentially urban creole party vulnerable by keeping the door open to another power grouping based on the rural subculture. Thus unless the sugar issue and all the attendant issues of rural reform to which it was central were brought into the arena . . . the PNM could chance no programme involving the people without risking a defection of the elitist wing of its own "nationalistic" support, uncompensated by converts from the countryside. (Ibid.)

The by-product of all that had happened or had not happened was that the University of Woodford Square soon lost its *raison d'être*. The PNM had also become a "morgue" rather than a dynamic modern political force for meaningful change. The civil service and the trade unions had been co-opted and transformed into clients of the party leadership. Disenchantment bordering on disaffection and in some cases rebellion was met by exhortation, intimidation and political bribery. Trinidad and Tobago had in fact turned backward from Chaguaramas to slavery, or so it seemed (ibid., 44–45).

Best was severely critical of what later became popularly known as "doctor politics", the dominance of a charismatic hero whose "brain" was deemed to be so "big" and "long" that it was virtually all that was needed to effect the kind of basic transformation required by the society.[2] Williams was for many the messiah who had been sent to take the downtrodden from Egypt to the Promised Land. As one party member exulted, "God could not come himself so he chose instead to send his political son in whom he is obviously well pleased."

The other side of doctor politics was a deferential, reverential and awe-stricken mass mind, willing to leave everything to the "doctah" who was saviour, teacher and deliverer of all material and symbolic things that were in the gift of the state. One recalls the advice given by Kwame Nkrumah to the Ghanaian masses: "Seek ye first the political kingdom and all else would be added unto you." Doctor politics thus meant that the PNM was never allowed to have a personality and institutional integrity of its own and instead became an extension of the charismatic leader, tied to his agenda. Williams owned the party lock, stock and barrel. "Intellectual demagoguery and charismatic leadership did help for a time to rally a following, but they also served to disguise real deficiencies in the Movement in its role as an agent of social and economic transformation" (Best 1965, 47).

Williams's decision to go it alone after the collapse of the federation was seen to be a logical sequel to the decisions that he made in respect of Chaguaramas. That decision "put a premium on the metropolitan rather than on the regional connection". Best also argued, disingenuously perhaps, that the demoralization caused by the decisions made in respect of Chaguaramas so traumatized the population that the leadership felt that it had to exercise political and electoral caution on the eve of the 1961 pre-independence elections:

> The demoralisation of the popular forces deprived the Movement of the energies required to face the difficulties inherent in modernising the regional economy. The waning of popular enthusiasm for the PNM which followed the ending of the Chaguaramas campaign made the Party so insecure that it began to adopt an attitude of "play for what you see." And decisively, the basest perspectives now being operative, it was the general fear that the Indians might have forced an unmanageable crisis over any attempt by the PNM to link up with potential Negro support in the Eastern Caribbean. Thus it was decided to debar PNM candidates from discussing the Federal issue on their election platform. (Ibid., 52–53)

Best regarded the decision to offer the states of the eastern Caribbean unitary state status with Trinidad was a device employed primarily to "satisfy the lingering Federal sentiment", and was never meant to be taken seriously. The terms offered were so insulting that they could only have been meant to provoke the derision that was forthcoming. "A different perspective would have led them all to accept Dr Williams' offer and to force a debate about real issues" (ibid., 53).

Several economic consequences followed from the choice of the Puerto Rican model. Best noted that there was a large gap between GDP and GNP, the difference going as income to the metropolis. The second and perhaps more critical consequence was that policy making in respect of taxation and exchange controls had always to take investor confidence into account. Planning was "phony" and limited to the indicative variety; state activity was likewise limited to facilitation in support of such investments as private individuals chose to make. One was also limited in terms of what could be done to mobilize and redirect resources to level out inequalities. Investor confidence was thus bought at the price of greater inequality and greater waste of national resources. A concomitant feature of the model was the need to restrain trade union activity to what was deemed "responsible". Any challenge to the elite or the system became ipso facto "romantic, obscurantist or subversive." Stability was an imperative.

The dynamics of the model had other serious implications. For one thing, it proved difficult to satisfy both the metropolitan constituency and the local one on which the party depended for its electoral survival. The model also ruled out certain radical options. Given the context in which the party had been conceived, this submissive posture presented the leadership with a dilemma. Williams was not content to be a "cuckoo" politician and always seemed at "wits' end to find ways to rally a disenchanted people".[3] Thus the reliance on "meet the people" and "meet the party" tours, on exhortations to do this or that, or at times on the abuse of imagined or created enemies. "The end result was constant 'zigzagging' between a radical modernity in statement and a tame accommodation with traditionalism in fact . . . which brought in the end the worst of both worlds" (Best 1965, 53).

Best's critique of Williams was brilliant, but one wonders just how practical it was given the conjuncture that then prevailed. While he was aware of the likelihood that the United States would move heaven and earth to prevent the emergence of another Cuba in its backyard, he downplayed the threat. Events in the hemisphere and elsewhere, however, made it clear the United States would sedulously undermine and if necessary smash any radical movement that threatened its Cold War strategies. One recalls that the US landed marines in Santo Domingo to forestall the coming to power of Joaquim Balaguer in 1965. The United States also reportedly put pressure on Norman Manley to get rid of socialists in his party. They likewise subverted the Arbenz regime in Guatemala, the Quandros regime in Brazil, and collaborated with the British to force Cheddi Jagan from office in British Guiana. Following the Bay of Pigs fiasco, Kennedy became obsessed with the spread of communism in the Caribbean and Latin

America, which he described as "the most dangerous area in the world. The effect of having a Communist state in British Guiana in addition to Cuba in 1964 [the year of the next presidential election] would be to create irresistible pressures on the US to strike militarily at Cuba" (Seeteram 2005, 537). Kennedy did not want to appear weak or indecisive in the face of a communist threat or to be accused of "losing" British Guiana. British Guiana, though small, thus had great symbolic importance in US foreign and domestic policy. One assumes that Kennedy would also have brought pressure to bear on Trinidad and Tobago if Williams had shown any disposition to rock the hemispheric boat. Given the presence in Trinidad and Tobago of Texaco and the Chaguaramas base, one can only assume that Kennedy would have done more than he did to pressure the British to block the emergence of an independent British Guiana under Jagan.

Answering the Radicals

Williams acknowledged the genuineness of some of the criticisms that were levelled at his policies, but was convinced that any strategy that might entail violent ethnic or class confrontation was undesirable, and that economic rationalization must stop short of this. He did not believe that people voluntarily renounced present consumption in favour of future generations, and he had no intention of coercing them by an authoritarian system of rule as Cuba or other countries in the Soviet Bloc had done. Williams believed that "unorthodox" economic strategies would sharpen rather than reduce racial conflict and would force the PNM to use dictatorial strategies to contain it. As he told a group of British members of Parliament in 1962, "We are particularly concerned with demonstrating the fallacy . . . that despotism is normally associated with hot countries and that democracy is impossible in a multiracial society" (*Trinidad Guardian*, 15 June 1962).

Williams was not really coerced into orthodoxy. He was always an orthodox pro-West intellectual who at times used the language of radicals for tactical reasons. The economic strategy of the party remained essentially as it was conceived in 1955–56. The difficulties that the PNM was encountering with the Colonial Office and the Americans made Williams sound more revolutionary and anti-American than he had ever anticipated. In 1960, he merely returned to the orthodoxy that he had adopted in the People's Charter. As our analysis has shown, he "zigzagged" on Chaguaramas, but never sought to push the Americans out of the western peninsula. He wanted the Americans to recognize that the world had changed since 1941 and that they now had to negotiate with him, the "Father of Caribbean Nationalism." Even before the 1956 elections, as we have seen, Williams had called on the US vice consul in Port of Spain to assure him that he was not a communist as alleged, and that the United States would be allowed to keep their military installations in Trinidad provided they compensated Trinidad for the privilege (Baptiste 1999).

Williams's political cautiousness was also evident in his consistent refusal to commit the party to a socialist ideology, his refusal to endorse proposals for the state to buy into the oil industry when it was being sold to Texaco in 1955, and in his reluctance to take over the telephone and public transit companies. As he told a public meeting in San Fernando in 1965 in a speech, quoted here at length,

> You have people around you who say that you shouldn't follow the West now that you are independent. Every now and then the half-wit advocates you should go and follow the communist method. Go and follow what communist method? What communism are they talking about anyhow? Russia? China? Castro? Tito? African socialism? But they have stopped following their own communism. The Russians suddenly discover what everybody knew all these years, that their economy operated on the basis of the ordinary principles, but in a different way, perhaps with different terminology. They have just discovered that they have a lot of unemployment, they have a lot of teenage problems, they have got to modify some of the strict controls and allow free market arrangements, and let the peasants sell stuff on the free market instead of giving it over to the state.
>
> All Castro's economy is in a hopeless mess because of that. We in Trinidad and Tobago don't control labour or fix wages or put them in a labour force or put them in the army. Castro has all that and he can tell them go and do this, and come out as volunteers to go and cut the sugar crop, and if you don't volunteer, boy, they report you and the police come for you. You think this is what you could do in Trinidad? You fellows in San Fernando would stand for that? And if you absent yourself from work, you have one labour law there; you get a warning and the first thing is that you get a cut of so much percent; and then the second offence is so and so; and the third offence is so and so, leading ultimately to dismissal. Oh boy, that is control. And then they say the money is to go here and it is to do that, and you take away people's land. And the state puts the bureaucrat to organise, and they make a hopeless mess of the blooming thing. If anybody so likes what Castro is doing, boy, take a boat from Trinidad and go to Cuba tomorrow, and stay there!
>
> People are running from there now. If you want to run there, okay, but don't bring it here. We have difficulties enough of our own. The Yugoslavs have their own communist development. They have just said that in future every state farm has to pay its way. What they had before is that they used to give it so much money and if it lost, it just lost and the state paid some more. They have to adopt the ordinary, conventional, western principles of operating a state enterprise which we are going to have to do in Trinidad and Tobago. (Williams 1965b, 89)

Williams also claimed that he was concerned about the security situation in the country and that he had to do something about it. As he said in March 1965,

We have been made aware of the fact that we are part, however small, of the cold war, and we have become more national-security conscious in the process. A government which is responsible for the security of the nation must necessarily act on information available to it even though that information is not of a nature which in the public interest can be made public, and it cannot possibly be expected to be influenced by sentimentality. ("The Reality of Independence", 1965, 76, EWMC folio 136)

Williams was also aware that just as "socialism in one country" was certain to fail, so too was any significant attempt to experiment with serious economic restructuring involving planning in the absence of the economic and political unity of the Caribbean. As he had warned in 1942, the "industrialization of Trinidad, or Cuba or Haiti, each in isolation, is an absurdity. A federation based on participation by the French, English, Spanish and Dutch, including 15 million people would [however] enable the economy for the whole area to be organized. A Caribbean federation would solve industrialization problems that small countries are unable to handle" (1942, 57–58).

Economic Nationalism

In the mid-1960s, however, Williams began showing greater boldness in devising new economic strategies that alienated labour, capital and other vested interests. The party gradually began to leave behind the era of economic innocence, though it did not depart very far from the fundamentals of the Puerto Rican model. The major new policy instruments were the Industrial Stabilization Act, new finance, insurance and banking acts, and an officially endorsed birth-control programme. Faced by growing labour militance – between 1960 and 1964 there were 250 strikes involving 74,574 workers and the loss of 803,899 man-days, mainly in the oil and sugar industries – Williams embarked on a policy of disciplining the labour movement, which he had vowed he would never do. The government declared a state of emergency in the sugar belt in March 1965, under cover of which it steamrollered a bill that circumscribed the freedom to strike. The bill, which obviously had been in preparation for some time, was pushed through the legislature in one day, with vested interests given almost no time to study it. The Trade Union Congress, which had marched in support of the PNM in 1961, was not consulted at all, though party-connected trade unionists may have been.

Williams argued that there was now need for greater discipline. If the people would not do it themselves, he would have to do it by legislation:

The events of the last fortnight, culminating in the ISA [Industrial Stabilization Act] bill, have brought to the fore the urgent need for discipline in our community. We have made remarkable progress in respect of tolerance since Independence. Without becoming complacent on this matter, or without seeking to push it now into the background, it is obvious that priority must now be given to discipline. The ISA is only the first step towards the development of a national discipline which needs to be extended to other fields. ("The Reality of Independence", 79)

Anticipating the events of 1970, Williams also declared: "We need a Public Order Act which will allow our protective services to maintain law and order without having recourse to the declaration of states of emergency to control demonstrations, marches, meetings and even false news calculated to incite dis-affection." Williams further argued that there was also need perhaps for compulsory military training. This he felt could have a positive effect on the rate of unemployment. As if to make the point that these legislative mechanisms were not only founding dictatorships, Williams noted that some of the provisions of the Industrial Stabilization Bill were drawn from Australia, New Zealand, Singapore, Malaysia, and even Canada (ibid., 81).

The timing of the bill reflected Williams's determination to prevent the "freedom fighters" in the sugar industry from seizing the leadership of the All Trinidad Sugar Estates and Factory Workers Trade Union from the accommodationist executive and linking up with the radical OWTU. The fear was that a juncture of these forces would upset the political and ethnic balance and pave the way for a new, genuinely radical multiracial regime. The hypothesis is a plausible one, but there is no evidence that Indian sugar workers were ready to follow black political leaders, whatever they might do in the field of industrial relations. Black workers had consistently refused to return labour leaders to the legislature.

The conditions under which strikes, go-slows and lockouts could be initiated were circumscribed, and penalties for breaches were quite severe under the Industrial Stabilization Act; it also provided a formula for the recognition of trade unions by employers – a 51 per cent vote by the workers – and for an industrial court, the adjudications of which were to be binding on all parties subject only to appeals on points of law. The court was enjoined to ensure the workers a fair share of increases in productivity and to keep in mind the need to maintain and expand the level of employment, domestic capital formation, economic growth, and the competitiveness of Trinidad's industries in export markets. The court was also charged with the responsibility for ensuring the continued ability of the public sector to finance development projects and for maintaining a favourable balance of trade and payments. These were heavy responsibilities to impose on a quasi-judicial body, as the unions consistently pointed out.

Williams denied that he had sacrificed labour to capital. Rather, he wanted to change the "old-fashioned loudmouthed" style of industrial bargaining by reducing the number of trade unions (there were 165) and by helping to upgrade the bargaining skills of unionists through the newly created Cipriani Labour College and the research facilities of the industrial court. He also hoped that the court would allow labour leaders to accept settlements in the national interest without running the risk of alienating their following. "The days of agitation are over," declared Williams. He claimed that labour was now part of the establishment and had a responsibility to respect the needs of the national interest. The PNM admitted that the distribution of income in Trinidad was not as satisfactory as it might be, but blamed organized labour as much as business, if not more. The then minister of finance, A.N.R. Robinson, complained that "the increases in the proportion of income accruing to persons was at the expense of Government income and company savings" (87.2 per cent in 1956 compared to 88.4 per cent in 1962) (*Trinidad Guardian*, 17 June 1965).

The Industrial Stabilization Act was welcomed by employers and initially by the general population. But radical unionists and intellectuals bitterly condemned it and vowed to have it repealed by constitutional means or, failing that, "from below". The OWTU and radicals belonging to the Workers and Farmers Party (WFP) led by C.L.R. James saw the act as a return to the pre-1937 situation, which it clearly was not; as a restraint on free collective bargaining, which it was; and as the PNM's main instrument for maintaining stability and restraining the "just" demands of labour for internationally comparable wages, in the interest of encouraging capital from outside. The radical unions claimed that they and not the PNM were the true guardians of the dignity of the worker and the national interest, since they were the ones leading the fight against mechanization and for the retention of profits in the country via increased wages for workers. Williams dismissed their claims and described them as a recalcitrant minority, a term he had previously used in 1958 to describe the conservative Hindu community (Ryan 1972a, 192).

The complementary aspect of Williams's 1965 labour policy was an attempt at far-reaching fiscal reform. The reform programme, which began with the introduction of the pay-as-you-earn system of taxation in 1957, was expanded in 1963 when higher income and company taxes were levied and a comprehensive tariff reform introduced to restrain (unsuccessfully) the consumption of unessential imports. In 1966, three major pieces of legislation were introduced in the fields of banking, insurance and investment policy. The least controversial of these was the Central Bank Act, the aim of which was to provide the nation with instruments to regulate its money supply. The Central Bank was given wide powers to regulate the commercial banks, hire-purchase credit, and interest rates in general, but the bank made it clear that its policies would be conservative.

More controversial than the new banking legislation was the Insurance Act, passed in December 1966. The main aim of the act was to regulate the conditions under which insurance firms were to operate in Trinidad and Tobago, and above all to force them to invest more money domestically. It stipulated that 36 per cent of the assets of registered companies must be locally invested, and provided for annual increases of 6 per cent up to a maximum of 60 per cent. Companies were required to make guarantee deposits of TT$250,000 in government issues. Three Canadian insurance companies found the terms of the long-overdue act unacceptable and stopped selling new policies in the country.

By far the most controversial of the acts was the Finance Act, and in fact attempts to introduce it gave rise to a veritable crisis. The draft bill was an ambitious attempt to plug loopholes against tax evasion by both domestic and foreign businessmen, to discourage repatriation of profits, or alternatively to cream off some of these before they were sent abroad. It was argued that businessmen should pay some compensation for the "benefits of the ISA". Writing some years after leaving office in 1970, A.N.R. Robinson recalled what occasioned the crisis. He explained that the Finance Act represented an attempt on the part of the government to restructure and modernize the country's tax regime in the era of independence. He observed that the reform was undertaken at a time when there was considerable pressure on sterling and on the dollar, and that the UK and US governments were taking steps to defend their currencies by taking measures to reduce capital outflows. In seeking to achieve this goal, they were encouraging overseas branches of metropolitan firms to repatriate all possible profits and even working balances.

This helped to create major balance of payments problems for developing countries, problems that were aggravated by the fact that loans were expensive and aid tied to the economies of donor countries. Existing double taxation treaties also favoured the developed countries. In the case of Trinidad and Tobago, the problem was acute because foreign companies accounted for 85 per cent of the profits subject to the tax laws. The intent of the proposed reform was to secure more by way of taxes for the Trinidad treasury. The draft bill also aimed to improve on the efficiency of tax collection, to minimize tax evasion, especially by foreign companies, to reduce inducements to distribution and consumption, to replace them with incentives to reinvestment, to introduce a tax on capital gains formerly untaxed or evaded, and to provide relief from double taxation (Robinson 2001).

Robinson noted that the tax system encouraged companies to remain private. Of the 567 resident companies in Trinidad and Tobago, as many as 547 were private. More significantly, "all of the country's 640 registered firms, which included foreign firms, together paid only TT$50m in income tax, and 95 percent of that amount came from 25 percent of those companies. Seventy-five percent of the resident companies paid only TT$2m in tax." The tax regime also gave rise to "tight control of the economy of the country by an oligarchy made all the more limited through interlocking directorships" (2001, 66). This made it difficult for the government to promote anything resembling natural economic development.

The reaction to the draft bill was fierce. Business elites complained that the proposals, which introduced the concept of corporation tax for the first time, completely upset all the accepted principles of taxation on which the financial and business structure of the country had been built. The chambers of commerce called for a "complete withdrawal" of the bill and warned that existing investments would dry up. The old company tax system permitted shareholders to mix up their personal affairs with those of the company, with the result that it was easy to obscure transactions that should have been subject to taxation. Corporate taxes were set at 44 per cent, 1.5 per cent higher than the company tax rate set in 1963, and the act disallowed the old practice of claiming company-paid taxes against personal income taxes.

A wider range of transactions previously entered as costs – for example, fees for patents or management services of foreign head-office representatives – were also brought within the tax net. The operating principle was that all income earned in Trinidad must be taxed in Trinidad; otherwise its forbearance would result in a straight gift to a foreign treasury. The act also provided incentives to domestic firms engaged in export creation. Double taxation treaties were also proposed with the US, UK and Canadian governments, which in effect meant that profits taxed in Trinidad would be exempt from taxation in these countries.

Many of the tough provisions of the act, such as a capital gains tax of 20 per cent and a withholding tax of as much as 30 per cent in addition to the corporate tax, were withdrawn or modified because of strong pressure from business elements, the opposition parties, certain labour organizations, and even PNM elements. A fiscal review committee, consisting of labour, business and government representatives, recommended that withholding taxes should be lowered from 30 per cent to 15 per cent in respect of remittances of dividends from subsidiary to parent companies, and from 30 per cent to 25 per cent in respect of dividends to non-resident investors other than parent–subsidiary relationships. The capital gains provision was also dropped.

The cabinet was openly split on the foreign capital issue. The business wing, led by Gerard Montano and John O'Halloran, urged Williams to withdraw the bill. They feared that its provision would lead to capital flight and a drying up of investment, which would negatively affect the job creation programme. Corporate interests in Trinidad, both local and foreign, but especially Texaco, successfully lobbied the US Treasury Department, which made it clear to the Trinidad government that the bill did not have the blessings of the US government. The sticking point was the withholding tax. The Treasury Department knew that the Trinidad cabinet was badly split on the matter and so exploited the division. They in fact refused to discuss the matter with a delegation (led by Patricia Robinson, wife of the finance minister), and only did so after bilaterals were held with Texaco to which concessions were made. Once Texaco was appeased, negotiations resumed. Williams supported the draft bill aggressively at first, but chose to play a cautious game. As he reflected,

When I indicated that the Minister of Finance while not increasing taxes would collect his taxes, and that that was "the sting in the tail" in the 1965 Budget, I was promptly attacked by a local capitalist who behaves, as usual, as if it is a crime for a country to tax people who can pay to provide the revenues for its essential services. . . . This dependence on foreign sources of finance, apart from being psychologically prejudicial, is practically dangerous. Many of the foreign interests behave as if they have some God-given right to be exempt from paying taxes to a national Government and as if private investment from overseas is entitled to any privilege which it demands.

What is more serious than this, however, is the possible worsening of the United States balance of payments problem. One already hears rumors in-so-far as restrictions on tourist travel are concerned, and there are even more disturbing rumors about possible future investments overseas in the oil industry. ("The Reality of Independence", 44)

In response to the pressure mounted by the business community, Williams was minded to withdraw the draft bill, but was blocked by the party, which backed A.N.R. Robinson in his stubborn defence of his ministry's project. The party committee was chaired by Francis Prevatt. Robinson strongly opposed many of the concessions that were made. As he told the party, "In politics as in business, the hard decisions must be taken if you are to deal with the underlying situation and not just postpone the problem until you create an unholy mess" (*Trinidad Guardian*, 25 August 1967). Robinson was scapegoated, however, and offered up as a sacrifice to the business community. Williams sought to give the impression that he was not privy to what was in the original bill – which of course was not the case. But Williams feared that if he pushed too hard, investment would dry up, and that the industrialization and job-creation programmes would be affected even further than they had been by "normal" capital outflows and shrinking inflows. It is worth noting that the extremely consensualist approach pursued during the enacting of the Finance Act was vastly different from that followed in regard to the Industrial Stabilization Act, and labour elements did not hesitate to draw the logical conclusions.

Gerard Montano tells us that Williams was extremely depressed when he listened to Robinson present the 1966 Budget, which followed upon the election victory of 1966. As Montano recalls,

When Robinson was presenting his budget, he was slumped in his chair – Williams that is – and as leader of the House I sat next to him. Robinson was reading the budget speech, and he kept sort of going lower, lower, and I turned to him and said: "Bill, you're very depressed, do you know why?" And in his usual little gruff manner, he said: "Go on", I said: "you know, you just won your third election with a bigger [parliamentary] majority than ever, you should be riding very high, but you're not. The reason for it. Listen to your Minister of Finance; he is announcing a recession. He is announcing severe cuts in public employment. What do you think will happen as a result? If you start to cut back, the private sector will follow. You can already see a downward spiral in the economy and an upward spiral in unemployment and you know as well as I do the social upheaval that we are heading for: but there is no need for that. Your economy is basically sound.

I warned you a little over a year ago, when we introduced our Finance Act, that there were measures being introduced in that Finance Act which would cause a loss of confidence among the business community. A loss of confidence would mean a lack of expansion, a lack of expansion would eventually lead to a downward spiral and that downward spiral would eventually lead to recession, which in turn would lead to social upheaval, and I strongly urged you and the Cabinet at the time not to approve that Act and to have much more time to consider it and listen well to the comments made by the business community. But I was completely overruled.

The truth of the matter was that in the Cabinet, I was really the only voice which could appreciate the businessman's point of view. The others didn't. As far as they were concerned, the businessman was a rascal and therefore any way you had of extracting more money from him was good in the public interest and legitimate. No thought was given to the effect on the economy and in fact nobody but me contributed to the discussion on the Act. The only other person who supported it . . . who supported my point of view was O'Halloran. (Interview with author, 1991)

Williams refused to beat a full retreat as Montano had advised him to do. As he declared in *Inward Hunger*,

Our banks, insurance companies, hire purchase arrangements, advertising, external telecommunications and mass media are all in foreign hands, together with a large portion of our lands, especially the lands devoted to sugar cultivation. We have to think in terms of some form of control of this arrangement, by restricting the sale of lands to foreigners, by opposing exclusive beach rights (and casinos) in tourist development, by the control of work permits to expatriates, by the requirement that foreign companies must re-invest a portion of their profits in local enterprise, by establishing a commercial bank of our own and a National Petroleum Company, by assuming some control over radio and television, by encouraging private companies to go public and issue shares to the Trinidad and Tobago community, and by government partnership in industry and tourism where the national community is not yet prepared or ready to participate. All this will raise in an acute form the problem of management. (1969, 340)

Williams had long since come to the conclusion that the Puerto Rican model had failed. Puerto Rico had become the quintessence of dependence, the "world's greatest welfare state". The model had also produced too few jobs – six thousand and not the thirty-five thousand anticipated. As Williams admitted, "the bootstrap broke". Williams felt that the Trinidad state had to become directly involved in other kinds of economic activity to diversify the economy and reduce dependence on foreign imports, though he recognized that this strategy would also put pressure on the country's balance of payments. This orientation towards greater economic nationalism would become more marked in 1970.

It is worth noting, however, that the "industrialization by invitation" model that was so heavily criticized and demonized in the 1960s and 1970s by Lloyd Best and the radicals at the University of the West Indies is now being reappraised positively. Kari Levitt, a close collaborator of Best, is of the view that "while the failures were real, much of the criticism was misplaced. . . . Industrialisation policies which established import substitution industries, with all their shortcomings, were important in upgrading technical and managerial skills. They have served Trinidad well in the development of a diversified manufacturing sector, now strong enough to expand into regional and overseas markets" (2005, 335).

25   **Heroes in Conflict**

James versus Williams

> The race question is subsidiary to the class question in politics and to think of imperialism in terms of race is disastrous, but to neglect the racial factor as merely incidental is an error only less grave than to make it fundamental.
> – C.L.R. James

The relations between Eric Williams and C.L.R. James had all the makings of a Greek tragedy – friendship, betrayal, hubris, revenge, mortal political combat and intellectual "parricide". As we have seen, James did a lot to shape the young Eric Williams into what he later became, both intellectually and politically, a debt that Williams acknowledged, even if grudgingly at times. James was a father figure and guru to Williams, and the latter regarded himself as disciple and "god child" and in fact described himself as such in his letters. (These relationships have been described in chapters 2, 14 and 16.) Despite their closeness, it is clear that these two heroic figures did not always sing from the same hymn book, let alone from the same page, and that the need to make real world political choices would either force one to give way to the other or drive them apart. The latter is what occurred. In a real sense, the clash between the two in 1960 and again in 1966 symbolized the contradictions that characterized and constrained the search for epistemic, political and economic sovereignty in the post-colonial Caribbean.

James returned to Trinidad and Tobago in April 1958 after an absence of some twenty-five years, as a guest of the governor general of the West Indies, to witness the opening ceremonies of the federal parliament. The decision to invite James was approved by the executive council on Williams's recommendation. Montano, who distrusted James's ideological credentials, was the sole objector. Williams also foisted James on the party as editor of the party organ, the *PNM Weekly*, and contrived to have him chosen as the general secretary of the West Indian Federal Labour Party. The alliance between mentor and mentee, however, proved unworkable, and lasted less than two years. James was sharply critical of the manner in which the party was allowed to atrophy, and sought to persuade Williams to pay attention to its organizational needs. James also felt that the party organ, which was renamed the *Nation* in December 1958, should be published twice weekly, or even daily, which of course would have taxed the party's meagre human and financial resources.

For a while, Williams accepted and sought to put into place James's ideas as to what should be done with the party, and also the *Nation*, which he described as "the spearhead of the party militant and the text book of independence". James, however, saw the role of editor differently from Williams. He argued that a serious party needed a serious party organ, and that the editor of that organ "should by rights be a member of the General Council and an active participant in the leadership of the party". James also seemed to covet the role of PNM party secretary, and argued that "the General Secretary and the editor of the party press should be elevated to a status not inferior to any legislator". Even though James had long abandoned the Leninist model of the revolutionary party, he advised Williams that a serious party should have a theoretical leader in addition to its political leader. He likewise recommended that the party should set out to raise an annual fund of, say, $100,000 to purchase its own press and party headquarters (*Party Politics*, 1962, 41). Williams no doubt saw all of this as a threat to his ownership of the party, which he clearly regarded as an extension of his person.

James was also critical of the elected elements in the party, whom he accused of concentrating too much on their official duties and of paying no attention to the needs of the party. He warned them that the *Nation* would not "put forward consistently the work of the government, but the problems of the people as seen by the people". They were also told that the *Nation* would view the behaviour of the state elite critically, that is to say, from the point of view of the public and not from the point of view of the party or the government ("Without Malice", *Nation*, 17 April 1959). Needless to say, these views did not endear James to the legislative element. Some, such as Gerard Montano, John O'Halloran and Kamaluddin Mohammed, were concerned about James's ideological leanings, which they broadly labelled as communist, and his presumed influence on Williams. As one member of the party complained, "For over one year, Nello was No. 2 in the Party. In fact, there were times when he thought he was number one" (as cited in Oxaal 1968, 120). The general view among most party members was that James had revolutionary delusions and was attempting to seize control of the party.

James, who was at odds ideologically with Williams on many issues, was, however, not an "irresponsible" ultra-leftist during his stint at the *Nation*, although Williams would complain about the "absurdity of his commitment to world revolution". James had promised Williams that in the interest of party unity, he would "curb his political rhetoric and anti-leadership tendencies". He insisted that he followed Williams's tone and did not attempt to push him further than he would have wished to go himself. He claimed that he discussed the question of socialism with Williams for at most three minutes. As one of James's biographers, Kent Worcester, observed, "as an anti-Stalinist and a Marxist, he dismissed the possibility of 'socialism in one country', and did not foreground the transition to a pan-Caribbean or global socialism in his political propaganda. There was a sense that his ideas concerning the future of the West Indies had a decidedly modest character. If his conception of independence was at all ambitious or radical, it was in the way James saw social and cultural matters as integral to the construction of a viable model of post colonial development"(1996, 148).

While it is not clear who was leading whom, the PNM did take a leftward lurch between 1958 and early 1960, leading many, including the Americans, to fear that the party was falling into the communist orbit. The American consul general in Port of Spain felt driven to report to his superiors in Washington that "although there is no evidence, there is the possibility that James is under international communist discipline, and continues to use his Trotskyite identification as a cloak. It is rumored locally that James has access to communist money" (*Ambivalent Anti-Colonialism*, as cited in Baptiste 2005). As we noted in chapter 23, the radical document "Perspectives for Our Party" (1958) was largely ghostwritten or inspired by James.

By 1960, Williams had what he wanted from the Americans, that is, an agreement that they would negotiate directly with him. On 30 May 1960, he openly signalled *(Perspectives for the West Indies)* that the "War For Independence" had been won and that Trinidad was now ready to take its place in the western hemisphere and the Organization of American States without loosening ties with the Commonwealth. Trinidad and Tobago, he said, saw itself as being on the Western side of the "Iron Curtain". An American official in Trinidad, on hearing the speech, remarked that "the San Fernando speech marked Williams' break with James. It is a part of Williams' political style to telegraph his punches. After that speech, we knew we could do business with him" (Oxaal 1968, 134).

Following Williams's decision to negotiate an accommodation over Chaguaramas, James came to the painful conclusion that Williams had capitulated, and that he had no further use for him. There was in fact speculation in the party that it was James who had encouraged Williams to demand the return of the base. What seems to have happened is that the right wing element in the party, and more than likely the Americans, leaned on Williams to get rid of James as editor of the *Nation*. James's enemies in the party accused him of "mismanaging" the affairs of the *Nation*, and imputed that funds were being misappropriated. With Williams's concurrence, James was summoned to appear before a disciplinary committee to answer charges of mismanagement. Needless to say, he refused the invitation, and left the party in October 1960. Williams claims he was expelled. In his resignation letter, James told Williams,[1]

You have had a very easy time in politics, Bill. You don't know what political struggle is at all in the internal party sense. That is what makes me now so nervous. . . . I doubt if you are in any position for a variety of reasons to undertake the reorganization of your party. If you do, you will do it under a sense of pressure. You are, I think at present, temperamentally disinclined to it. . . . I do not want to be in that position where I will be one of the main advocates of a course that you will either refuse to take or undertake, I am sure, with a sense of grievance and great irritation. . . . I want to be out of this business. (Buhle 1988, 148)

James wrote to Williams in March 1960, prior to going to Ghana (a trip that Williams encouraged, probably to get him out of the way), asking to be relieved of his position as editor of the *Nation*. As he told Williams, "Too many people seemed to have forgotten or never knew that I am a person with definite political principles and attitudes. I have subordinated myself to the PNM completely. I can do so no longer." In July 1960, he sent Williams a final letter telling him that he was not prepared to work at the *Nation* any more. "I couldn't carry on there if I wanted to" (Worcester 1996, 159).

Following his expulsion (or resignation) from the party, James produced *PNM Go Forward*. The pamphlet, which was submitted to Williams and a small group of supporters in April 1960, later became *Party Politics in the West Indies* (1962), which was meant to educate members of the party as to what had gone wrong and what had to be done to put it right. James repeated his complaints about the under-resourcing of the *Nation* and the neglect of the party, and its annual conventions, which he described as being "defective". James was of the view that the PNM as a political organization was lagging behind the development of the masses and the needs of the day.

Like most progressive West Indians, James felt that the West Indies could only become a meaningful nation state with a planned economy in the context of federation. As he told audiences in British Guiana, Jamaica, and Trinidad and Tobago, "Federation is the means whereby the West Indies and British Guiana can accomplish the transition from colonialism to national independence, can create the basis for a new nation; and by reorganizing the economic system and the national life, give us our place in the modern community of nations." James was mortified when Williams proclaimed that "one from ten leaves nought" and proceeded to administer final rites to the comatose "patient". James believed that Williams's climb down on Chaguaramas and Manley's lack of resolution were responsible for the collapse of all that he and others had struggled to achieve, including federation. As he wrote in 1960, with a touch of naïvety,

It is my firm conviction that if the West Indian politicians had put forward to the West Indian people a programme, or even a perspective, of economic development and made the people the centre of what they were thinking and doing, Mr. Manley would have won the Referendum and the general election. If the Premier of Trinidad and Tobago had not sold out over Chaguaramas, if he had kept to the widely publicized aims of his campaign, his voice would have been the most powerful in the West Indies for a Federation. Tens of thousands in every island would have poured out to see and hear and welcome the West Indian politician who had fought and won against the all-powerful Americans. (1961, 10).

James argued that after 1960, Williams was confronted with a terrible dilemma: "Williams now came face to face with the economics and the social relations of Trinidad and Tobago. I suspect that he now saw, 'Either I go the whole way, organizing the party, getting a local daily paper, and tackling the economy, which means a fight even more merciless than all I have just gone through, and a mess of trouble with my Cabinet; either that, or I give all up.' " (1962, 160). Williams, he said, chose to give it all up; he "turned round, ran, and has been running ever since". According to James, "Williams' decision was a property of the colonial past and existing class relations in the West Indies. West Indian middle-class political intellectuals all began as radical social reformers, but sooner or later were strangled by the West Indian environment." Williams's uniqueness was that he took "a mere five years to become just another West Indian politician":

> Little by little, they were worn down until today they are busy building schools, build-ing roads, West Indianizing, and begging for grants, loans, investments. . . . Dr Williams . . . was going to show the oil companies where to get off. He was the mor-tal enemy of the American State Department and the Colonial Office. But now he is finished with all that. He has followed the same course as Manley, Adams, Jagan. The question of political personality limited to personal characteristics sinks into total insignificance. The more highly placed a politician is, the more you can expect his per-sonality to have historical attributes or express the pressure of social forces. (James 1962, 160)

James believed that what was needed was a genuinely national and properly organized mass party that would force the new West Indian nation to be econom-ically self-reliant and to lift itself up by its own bootstraps. He believed that such a solution would not "imperatively and inescapably demand revolutionary meas-ures as took place in Cuba in 1958". James, unlike some radicals, however, explic-itly rejected demands for nationalizing the oil and sugar industries or the banks:

> Young West Indians . . . talk of nationalization, even of revolution. They . . . are either ignorant or crazy. Nationalize what? Oil? That is insanity. . . . We should leave the sugar factories just where they are. . . . To talk nationalization is to start a fight you are bound to lose: you thereby advertise your immaturity. Little countries . . . must know their lim-itations, how and when to fight. We clarify the national purpose by discouraging any belief in nationalization as a panacea.

He believed, however, that the West Indian masses, with their strange historical past – no native language, no native way of life, not even any native religion – must feel an organic link with the country. The party thus had to be "the life and death of an emergent West Indian society". It had to serve as the functional equivalent to the indigenous institutions that could be taken for granted in certain other societies in Africa and Asia:

> [The] political temper of [the] West Indian masses is at an extremely high pitch. The masses assemble in numbers of 15, 25, 35,000, because they are aware of a profound change in their society and are looking for new foundations. This is the key to the whole situation. . . . The West Indian masses are on a broad road and traveling fast. Everything pushed them forward. Nothing holds them back . . . [and so] the mass democratic party must see itself as first of all a social as well as a political organization operating in the community, as the vanguard of a new regime . . . . India, Burma, Ceylon and Africa have an indigenous civilization and culture. They adapt and modernize this, but in the period of transition this civilization serves as a rallying-point and a basis of solidarity. West Indians have nothing of the kind. Politics, economic development, art, literature, history, even social behaviour, these have to be recreated. Everything. What is to be preserved, what rejected? . . . If we do not produce new conceptions, organizations, etc., the old ones remain in bastard form, creating confusion and disorder. . . . A mass party of this kind is the sole means by which the developing consciousness of the people can be translated into such forms as to make the people themselves conscious of what it is they want, of the possibilities and the limitations of their desires.

James also argued that the party had to give the population specific tasks. Development also had to be planned: "It is no use lecturing people on the plane of public morals and duty. You have to give the morals and the duty an objective base and a stimulating but realizable perspective. . . . A government of national purpose can make demands on the population instead of continuous demands [being made] by the population on a government which cannot supply [them]" (*Sunday Guardian*, Independence Supplement, 30 August 1964, 4, 5; see also the foreword to James 1961). James believed that native whites recognized that "something must be done, and can be done" and that they could be persuaded to accept changes that would still allow them a strategic role in the system:

> The governments of these territories have got to sit down and plan and decide, in view of the general level of social life and economic life, in view of the special situation in the countryside, in view of the dangerous political pressures which the unemployment and other problems are bringing to bear upon the government, they will have to decide what industries it will be necessary to establish . . . irrespective of the traditional profit motive. If we had 150 years . . . there would be no need for this telescoping of economic developments. But I see no possibility of individual entrepreneurs, either inside

the West Indies or from outside the West Indies, developing the economy to a pitch at which it will be possible for us to feel that the economy is now a going concern and sure to move forward, taking up the increases in population as time goes on. I cannot see it being done by private enterprise in the old sense of the term. There has to be a set plan, in which the State, taking all needs into consideration, not merely the ordinary economic demands but the social necessities of the population, will decide on a programme . . . to satisfy the urgent needs of the people and, this is very important, because this is the political issue, to make an impatient people understand that some serious, tremendous, new and sustained effort is being made to satisfy the demands which are increasing every day. (1961, 21)

James believed that this sort of initiative would prove attractive to international financial organizations as well as Western governments to whom it could be sold with the warning that the alternative was Cuba. He felt that in the event that "some misguided people" refused to support the effort, "We can fight them and we can win. There is irrefutable proof of this." He (in conversation with the author) opined that the United States would not dare to intervene since "we licked them on Chaguaramas", a view that is hard to reconcile with his analysis of that event. James was deeply chagrined about what the West Indian leaders seemed unwilling to do, that is, articulate a plan to create a genuinely self-reliant nation. "They seemed too willing to settle for flag independence, a national anthem, and an enormous number of individuals running up and down and in and out while remaining essentially colonial with the colonial mentality remaining with us on every side" (James 1961, 28).

Williams's version of the controversy with James is quite different, as was his assessment of what he had done in respect of party organization. Williams boasted that he had made it his "conscious duty to develop the party organization and to encourage it to live a life of its own" (1969, 260). He claims that he had long become aware that it was important to prevent the party from being encrusted with red tape and dominated by bureaucrats and the governmental elite. Given this, he had outlined "Perspectives for Our Party" at its third annual convention in 1958. In doing so, Williams took ownership of the paper that James claimed he had authored or at least inspired. That document, as we have indicated, expressed the view that there was need to create an organization that would develop in such a manner that the island would be aware that its future lay with the party and the functioning of the party. "On such a basis, legislators can introduce the boldest and most far-seeing legislation, confident that there can be no serious resistance because all reactionary and disruptive elements will be aware of the strength of the Party in the population surrounding them."

Williams claimed that he had committed the party to doing a number of things to raise its profile and to increase its capacity for carrying out mobilization and educational activities. These tasks included the raising of funds to buy a building to house the party, the establishment of a party library, a properly functioning secretariat, and a press to publish documents, including the party organ. Williams also claimed that he caused a policy advisory committee to be established to which many important matters were referred before policy was determined. Williams was thus claiming, even if by indirection, that he had done everything James accused him of not doing in respect of the party.

Williams blamed James for getting the *Nation* into serious difficulties with the party. James had in fact "made the situation worse" by making statements that were "off message". According to Williams,

> His comments before McLeod's arrival were deprecated by the General Council which had been summoned to decide on the line to take. He used the Party paper to build up himself and his family, and his personal articles on George Padmore and the James family were widely resented. Whilst party members generally supported his stand that Frank Worrell should be made captain of the West Indies cricket team, more than one looked askance at his methods. (1969, 268)

Williams tells us further that the fourth annual convention, presumably at his instigation or with his concurrence, had appointed a committee to examine the relationship between the party and the publishing company and to ascertain the financial position of the company. "The Committee's Report (October 1960) revealed a situation that bordered on chaos. It condemned administrative confusion and disclosed a very real absence of liaison between Paper and Party." The report also had the following to say: "The whole question of management during Mr. James' term of office could be written off quite briefly as a period of mismanagement. Given a free hand, he appeared to use it freely without regard for his own or the Company's responsibilities." According to Williams, when summoned, James became abusive and accused him of being a "gangster" for refusing to discuss the convention's actions with him. James also accused Williams of having sold out to the Americans at the Tobago Conference on Chaguaramas (Williams 1969, 268). Williams said that he refused to be party to bypassing the actions of the convention.

Williams was generous, however, in his praise of James's role in the struggle for Chaguaramas, a viable federation, and independence, when he announced to the fifth annual convention held in September 1960 that James had resigned from the party. As he told the convention, seemingly with utmost deliberateness and a great deal of irony,

> I say, as Political Leader, that James' pronounced intellectual gifts, with which I have been personally familiar at close quarters for some thirty years, and his political sagacity contributed immeasurably to that successful vindication of our claims and position in respect of self-government the return of Chaguaramas, a strong and viable federation and the achievement of independence which has in the past twelve months, so stimu-

lated party morale and increased the confidence of the public. My only regret is that he did not stay long enough with us to introduce the great need of our time, a decent, modern daily newspaper. (Williams 1960a)

The truth is that the two old friends had different notions about what was necessary to move the country forward at that particular conjuncture, and who should be responsible for heading that forward movement. Oxaal was correct when he observed that

> The estrangement which developed between James and Williams partly resulted from the fact that each man had placed himself in a false position. For all his early regard for Nello James, Eric Williams was no revolutionary: and James, although he had curbed his radical instincts, was no bourgeois reformist. There was, however, more to the Williams-James split than that. . . . Political parties are sociological phenomena, groups in process, and the surface drama of the Williams-James estrangement had a structural cause. (1968, 136)

Presumably the structural cause was to be found in differing notions as to what was possible in the Caribbean region as well as in terms of who would control the PNM. Williams, who was extremely credulous, openly accused James of subversively seeking to build a base to capture the party and even brought charges to that effect. These were subsequently dismissed.

Ironically, one of the most positive diagnoses of the Williams phenomenon was penned by James in May 1960, the same month in which the two men clashed openly. James sought to explain to the Trinidad population why Williams behaved in the manner he did. His *Convention Appraisal* was in part intended to counter the analyses forthcoming from the *Trinidad Guardian*, which James described as "that ball and chain on the feet of the new nation". James saw Williams as a postwar nationalist who was faced with a society in a state of arrested development. The system was so bad that it had to be radically changed if one was not to be worn down, demoralized and defeated as others before had been. Williams sought to change the system, and in so doing brought his own special intellectual gifts and experiences to the battle. One of his unique characteristics was said to be his abiding faith in the power of the intellect. Thus the unique creation, the University of Woodford Square.

James noted that Williams was among the first to break out of the mould that colonialism had defined for the man of colour. Unlike other Island Scholarship winners, he chose to study history rather than law or medicine. He was also fortunate to have gone to the United Kingdom when Britain and Europe were in ferment with various ideologies contesting for supremacy. His sojourn in America too served to sharpen his awareness of racism and augmented the energy that he brought to problem solving. His stint at the Anglo-American Caribbean

Commission likewise helped to broaden his knowledge of the Caribbean and his sensitivity to the need to frame policy within a regional context. With respect to federation, James said that Williams believed in it as an article of faith: "He cannot think otherwise." In terms of his determination to do certain things, he was said to be "inflexible" (1993, 347). Much of Williams's behaviour was explained in the context of objective reality and the accidents that shaped his relationship to that reality.

James chastised the *Guardian* for focusing too much on the "angularities of Dr. Williams personality, and on slanders, scandals, suppression of facts, and analyses always on the level of the lowest attributes of human character" (ibid., 350). Some six months after he had praised James (22 March 1961), Williams attacked him viciously in his "Massa Day Done" speech:

> [T]he PNM, having won power in 1956 after a mere nine months, was faced with ever increasing pressures in the four and a half years that followed. It was inevitable that the scamps, vagabonds, and individualists should hop on the band wagon and seek to corrupt the party for their personal ends. We are now finding out those who pretended to support us on Chaguaramas because they thought we would not succeed in our declared policy to tear up the 1941 Agreement. They applauded loudly when I said that I would break the Chaguaramas problem or the Chaguaramas problem would break me; they saw me broken already. Now that I have broken the problem, low [*sic*] and behold, all the scavenger birds of the PNM suddenly suggest that I changed my direction and they don't like us West of the Iron Curtain. All those who see in Castro a precedent for a few persons lusting for power to take control suddenly begin to attack us for not emulating Castro; they forget we took power peacefully and did not take it from a fascist dictatorship. All such who wish to confuse, who seek to climb on PNM's back to achieve their own mental aberrations, who want to abuse me because I refuse to condone corruption in any quarter, all these imps of Satan will be dealt with in due course. CLR James' case has been sent to our Disciplinary Committee for action; when it is no longer sub-judice, I shall deal with it fully and publicly, and with all those who seek to use him in their struggle to defeat the PNM and to destroy me (1961, 16–17).

There were some heavy messages in this discourse. James was clearly being accused of corruption, of political back climbing, of being mentally aberrant, of being "an imp of Satan", and of ignoring the context in which power had been contested and won. Williams was suggesting that since the enemy was not a fascist dictatorship, he did not have to resort to the type of violence that Castro used after the capture of power in 1959.

Williams went on to boast that it was he alone who was responsible for all the goals that the nationalist movement had recently converted, though he was careful to use the phrase "we of the PNM".

It is we of the PNM who brought the United States Government to you to renegotiate in Tobago a treaty negotiated for you in London twenty years ago. It is we of the
PNM who gave you your flag and ran it up at Chaguaramas to do the saga thing everyday in the breeze. It is we of the PNM who will shortly renegotiate the basis of your
relations with Venezuela with a view to removing the discrimination against you that
is sixty years old. It is we of the PNM who brought the Secretary of State for the
Colonies for the first time in your midst to appreciate at first hand that the future destiny of the West Indies depends on you. With the new Agreement on Chaguaramas,
we of the PNM have been able to welcome Sir Winston Churchill to Trinidad. It is
we of the PNM who will take the United Kingdom Prime Minister around when he
comes on Friday on his historic visit, and I hope hundreds of you will be at Piarco to
welcome him. It is we of the PNM who will show him around some of our development projects, who will take him to Chaguaramas, who will take the lead in making
representations to him in respect of West Indian migration to the United Kingdom,
protection for West Indian products and economic aid to the West Indies in order to
assure economic stability as the foundation of our political democracy. (Ibid., 18)

Ironically, Williams would end his speech with a genuflection to the imperial
connection that he had once done so much to lampoon. As he said, "It is only left
now for Her Majesty the Queen to visit us. After all, we are an important part
of the Commonwealth, and if her majesty can go to Australia, to India, and to
Pakistan, Nigeria and Ghana, she can also come to the West Indies." Gordon
Rohlehr pointed to the ironies involved in Williams's remarks about Churchill
and Sir Harold Macmillan: "Chaguaramas was not a PNM victory. Everyone
recognized it as Dr. Williams' personal triumph. Everyone, that is, except CLR
James who saw it as primarily the people's, whose spokesman Dr. Williams was.
To show Churchill Chaguaramas, then, was the last thing necessary to assure himself of his achievement. The achievement could not be real until it had received
the applause of the right people" (1970, 11).

The 1966 General Election: Mixing Sugar and Oil

Given the bitter antagonism between the two Caribbean titans, it was hardly
surprising that they both felt they had to engage in a definitive "fight to a finish", to use Williams's term. James, who had left Trinidad in August 1960, was also
anxious to settle scores with Williams. At a meeting in Edinburgh, Scotland, in
February 1964, he openly signalled his desire to do battle with his former mentee.
As he said to the group in words that were clearly intended for a Trinidad
audience,

If you want me, send for me. You sent for George Headley because you wanted him
to play against the Englishmen. If you want me to come and enter politics, then make a

public subscription and send for me. I will come. Furthermore, I don't want a seat. My people have been living in Tunapuna for 150 years in the same spot. Everybody knows them, and it would be the general opinion that if I ran in Tunapuna, I am hardly likely to be defeated. I will not run in Tunapuna. If I go, I am running in the constituency that the Premier has chosen for himself – which ever one he likes, that's up to him. If he says he's going to run for this one, I will oppose him there. The whole of the West Indies will see it. . . . If he wins, well, he wins. I am not dying to be any minister in any West Indian island. But if I win, that is clear notice to everybody that the people want a change. And even if I lose, the alternative position would have been put before them. And that is what I am prepared to do. I don't want anybody to give me some money. Not at all. Public subscription. Put it down for everybody to see: "We want James to come back." I say if you do that, I will come. (As cited in Millette 1995a, 339)

James was no doubt assuming that the electoral rumble would take place during the 1966 elections and he returned home in early 1965 ostensibly to cover the cricket series between the West Indies and England for the *Manchester Guardian*. The country was at the time seething with industrial unrest. There was much talk about communist or Marxist conspiracies, and about plots to seize power by the radical unions in the oil and sugar industries, the perennial holy grail of the radical left in Trinidad and Tobago. Trinidad seemed ripe for revolution. The honeymoon that the PNM had enjoyed with the black masses and the intellectuals appeared to be over.

University radicals and trade unionists were in the vanguard of this anti-Williams movement, but public-spirited individuals and religious and professional groups were also becoming more concerned about the increasing tendency towards PNM authoritarianism. The establishment of a locally owned daily, the *Express*, and radical weeklies like the *People* (now defunct), the *Vanguard*, *Tapia*, *Moko* and the *New World Quarterly* were also doing a great deal to raise the level of public awareness and debate. The radical press forced the PNM on the defensive and gave an outlet to currents of opinion that the foreign-owned press had hitherto neutralized. The *Vanguard*, the organ of the powerful OWTU, took the line that the PNM had sold out to Anglo-American imperialism. The president of the union, George Weekes, argued that the real rulers of Trinidad were "the big American and English oil and sugar companies who made loans to help the Government out in emergencies, advance income tax and . . . offer inducements to politicians such as directorships that carry little work. They thereby get an altogether overwhelming political power which more than offsets that of the electorate." Weekes argued that "the goals which people hoped would follow Independence seem even further away than ever. People are disillusioned with democracy and are searching for other means to get what they want" (Kambon 1988, 121).

Williams's political enemies saw him as a *vendu* who had betrayed everything he stood for between 1955 and 1964. In their schema, he had become the "Negro" poster boy for the foreign multinationals and their white associates in Trinidad and Tobago. The unions argued that the problem was not that wages were too high but that foreign firms received too many tax concessions. They were taking out far more than they brought in. Williams saw the matter differently. As he said during an interview, "Now that we are independent, we have to save Trinidad from Trinidadians." The unions were the enemy and not the multinationals.

Williams was clear in his mind that his "range of choice", and his freedom to operate were limited by Trinidad's size and its location in the Americas. Williams's earlier hope was that he could play the role of honest broker to both capital and labour. He told workers that the country needed capital to invest and create jobs and that this could come only from foreign private sources. Capital had to be induced and seduced with incentives and guarantees against nationalization without compensation. As Williams opined in the course of a parliamentary debate in 1963,

> Guarantees to investors cannot be less than other countries offer, possibly more. The workers must understand that this is necessary if jobs are to be provided for them. They must understand that once their organizations are secure, capital is nothing to be afraid of. . . . But capital must co-operate in all this. The jobs it provides must be adequate jobs, well paid, with conditions of labour associated with a modern democratic society. *Capital must understand that the day when West Indians were content merely to hew wood and draw water for private investors is gone forever. The worker today requires inducements, incentives and guarantees, just as much as the investor does.*
>
> The party must be the defender of the workers, the political arm of the labour movement, providing particularly the information and data so urgently needed by the workers in their organizations. The party must give every encouragement to effective trade unionism, and must make it clearly understood that this includes the right of the workers to choose their own representatives. *We must repudiate unambiguously the indefensible efforts of Ministers to intimidate the trade unions, split the workers' ranks and set themselves up as little demigods recognizing only those they consider amenable. That road leads straight to totalitarianism.* (Hansard, 1962–63, 563–67; as cited in Parris 1976, 105; emphasis added)

In one of his first official acts after coming to power, Williams had urged the British government to sign a treaty with American investors guaranteeing against expropriation: "We will have no objection to its being extended to Trinidad and Tobago" (*Hansard*, 1961–62, 79). Williams also told W.R. Grace and Company, who owned Federation Chemicals, that they were free to tell the State Department and any agency of the American government that the Government of Trinidad and Tobago had given them the full and unqualified assurance that it would guarantee the repayment that they were seeking against expropriation. Williams made it clear, however, that he would not countenance anything that smacked of strike breaking, since "industrial democracy is based on the right of workers to withhold their labour by way of a strike even though the community is thrown into turmoil" (*Sunday Guardian*, 24 July 1960). By 1965, he was forced to eat these words because strike activity was occurring with increasing frequency.

Williams convened a tripartite conference in 1965, during which he urged the oil and sugar companies to get involved in establishing industries other than those in which they were then specializing, including petrochemicals and a steel mill as an alternative to retrenchment. The companies all refused, indicating that they preferred to remain in the areas of their core competences. They would stick to the industries they knew in the interest of their shareholders (see Ministry of Planning and Development, Tripartite Conference on Employment in Sugar and Oil, Trinidad and Tobago, 1965).

Williams, as we have seen, responded to the perceived or imagined threat from those whom he deemed a "recalcitrant minority" by appointing a commission of inquiry to investigate and report on the existence of subversive activity in Trinidad and Tobago, under the chairmanship of Sir Louis Mbanefo, a Nigerian jurist. The commission, which was established in 1963, reported in 1965, and its findings were made public on the day that the Industrial Stabilization Act was debated and passed in parliament. As Millette rightly observed, "Mbanefo was part of the theatre that accompanied the hurried enactment of the first overtly hostile piece of legislation by the PNM in the post-independence era" (1995b, 64). Williams linked James's arrival to all that was said to be ongoing. As he alleged, "The subversive elements in the society, with James in the forefront, were at work; the background was an open attempt to link the trade unions in oil and sugar." Williams warned the radicals that it would be a "fight to the finish". James was put under house arrest, much to the chagrin of the radical element in the country in general and the university dons in particular, many of whom had become increasingly radicalized as a result of the government's handling of the labour crisis. James was not prevented from receiving visitors, and many who came urged him to do as Williams had done in 1955, that is, let down his bucket in Trinidad's turbulent politics. Williams contemptuously dumped it before James could let it down. He was kept in detention for six weeks. Once the ISA had been passed, and Williams sensed that the danger was over, he had James released. His embarrassment must have been keen, having regard to the nature of the relationship that he and James once shared.

James believed he had a formula for winning power. The strategy, which was outlined in a pamphlet titled *West Indians of East Indian Descent* (1965), involved "mixing oil and sugar", getting Indo-Trinidadians to coalesce with Afro-Trinidadian oil workers. James's analysis led him to believe that "East Indians" were fast becoming "West Indians", and that they were beginning to see that their interests would not be well served by an East Indian party, but by one based on class and a common creole culture. As he told them, "Sugar and oil workers together can make a new Trinidad. Some will fight to keep them divided. . . . [But] nothing can stop it. But blood can flow and hold it back. *Blood must not flow*. Politics, generous but firm, can prevent it. History can help" (1965, 3; emphasis added)

James advised the Indians that they had "to fit themselves into the historical movement of the country". The strategy of relying on an East Indian party had isolated them "and had created more disharmony, disorder, suspicion, even hatred than ever before". Reliance on the PNM was equally obsolete, historically. The PNM's "sawdust Caesar" had "ruined the party and was leading the country God knows where". Williams was a "gangster leader" who had "miseducated lower gangster types", making "the country sick with fear". In this environment, Indians were marginalized and excluded. As James told them, "Let us face the fact that the middle class West Indians of African descent feel that this island, as part of the Caribbean, is predominantly their field of operation."

Trinidad could, however, be transformed into "a tropical paradise" if both ethnic groups eschewed race and conducted their politics on the basis of class: "It is this miserable division into racial parties that had helped to bring this country in the mess that it is. The clean up will be a gigantic job. Come in and help. It cannot be done without you. You do not wish to go back to India. Make your Trinidad into something" (ibid., 7–8).

James made an open appeal to the Indian business class for financial support and also for their political endorsement: "A party cannot be built without finances. Send us your cheques or bring your cash. We need tens of thousands of dollars to build a real party, to employ organizers, to publish material, to educate the public, the whole public – the whole public, for history has made us into one people. Do not hesitate. Do not fumble. It will be the best investment you have ever made" (ibid., 8).

Anticipating that he would be told that he had never shown any solicitude for Indians when he was in the bosom of the PNM, he noted that he had been making these appeals since 1962, and quoted the foreword, which he had written to his pamphlet titled *Federation*: "The East Indians have contributed far beyond their numbers to the economic development of the territory. A heavy burden is placed on them. They more than all others have to break the racial stranglehold which both DLP and PNM are using in common against the political instincts and social aspirations of the people."[2]

James needed a political instrument to mount his electoral challenge to Williams. First a few dissidents made efforts to get James to take over the leadership of the DLP in order to help the party escape its racial origins. The effort, spearheaded by Stephen Maharaj and Jack Kelshall, failed. Another vehicle thus had to be found. The result was the Workers and Farmers Party, which brought together the leaderships of the radical OWTU, the embryonic Transport and Industrial Workers Union, and members of various Marxist parties whom James Millette described as "determined, but small and weak" (1995a, 432).[3] At the party's inaugural conference, James, noticing that few were present, quoted Shakespeare's line: "We few, we happy few, we band of brothers." Quite sensibly, but ominously, James declined the invitation to serve as chairman of the new party. He instead accepted the post of second vice-chairman.

The officers and candidates who offered themselves to the electorate constituted a virtual who's who of the Trinidad left. Among them were George Weekes, Joe Young, Stephen Maharaj, Clive Nunez, Max Ifill, Lennox Pierre, Eugene Joseph, Roderick Thurton, M.A.S.A. Trevor Sudama, Krishna Gowandan, Walter Anamunthodo, Leon Alexis, Joseph Dube, Jack Kelshall, George Bowrin and Clive Phill. James Millette, who did not run, expressed regret that his university colleagues in the New World Group did not join the struggle. As a result, "the political challenge promised by James was not quite what either he or the public expected" (ibid., 343). It was not the proverbial "mother of all political wars".

The party went up and down the countryside targeting industrial and sugar workers, though principally the latter. The meetings, many of which the author attended, were never large, and it was evident before a single ballot was cast that the party had failed to set the working class of either ethnicity on fire. The manifesto of the WFP constituted a compromise between radical ideology and the practical needs of the moment. It thus talked of the need for "national purpose". It also promised to break up large agricultural holdings and to develop an efficient peasantry capable of achieving a high standard of living. Farmers would be encouraged to produce food to help reduce the country's food import bill. Holdings were to be limited to 250 acres. Following James, the party eschewed nationalization and promised to give the "national bourgeoisie" (the local business and commercial interests) opportunities to create a national economy. There were elements in the party, however, who wanted to nationalize the oil and sugar industries.

The WFP neither performed nor behaved like a conventional party. It refused to identify a leader or to do some of the things that electoral parties feel they must do if they are to be deemed serious contenders for parliamentary power. Indeed the party could not seem to decide whether they were a class party or a conventional party, and thus got caught between two racial blocs. As Khafra Kambon correctly notes, "The ideology of the WFP embraced an important aspect of the natural reality, class contradiction, but treated it as the only political significant reality if not the whole reality" (1988, 160).

One of the leading members of the party and of the radical opposition was George Weekes, who considered Williams his mortal political enemy. As Weekes said of Williams, "Instead of using the power vested in him for the destruction of foreign exploiting interests, Dr. Williams has preferred to side with those foreign exploiting interests and stabilise them, to use a word now popular" (ibid., 154). Weekes accused Williams of seeking to divide and destroy the trade union movement by offering opportunists all sorts of diplomatic appointments. Weekes saw it as his historic responsibility to prevent Williams from doing so even if it meant joining the traditional DLP. Weekes argued that trade unions could not limit themselves to the struggle to increase wages. They had to get involved in politics. Weekes knew of course that Williams had a great deal of political support among the members of the OWTU. He believed or hoped that workers would "see off" Williams's challenge to their economic well-being.

James, knowing Weekes's ambivalence about entering the political arena, encouraged him to assume leadership of the working class. Quite bizarrely, James claimed that Weekes had "knocked out Eric Williams flat". James was either being naive or overoptimistic when he claimed that the working class had now seized the moral high ground from the middle class, and were now poised, under Weekes's leadership, to seize "preponderant political influence" and power from the middle class (Kambon 1988, 158). James and other radical intellectuals misread the political equation completely when they claimed that the struggle that the workers put up against the Industrial Stabilization Act was evidence that Williams and the middle class had "suffered a telling defeat" (*Vanguard*, 27 August 1965). Either that or they were telling political "noble lies". Kambon, Weekes's biographer, speculates that James was not so much interpreting the political situation as trying to influence it by an ideological intervention. "He was after all writing not as an academic observer, but as a political activist" (1988, 158–59).

What James failed to recognize was that workers in Trinidad, unlike what obtained elsewhere in the Caribbean, did not automatically support their union leaders, and that race was a more critical variable than class. Workers supported their union on economic issues, but absolutely refused to vote for union leaders who belonged to the "wrong" political party. The result was that Afro-Trinidadian workers did not support their co-ethnics like Weekes, and Indo-Trinidadian workers turned their backs on people like Stephen Maharaj and Basdeo Panday. As one Indian sugar worker told Weekes, "Workers in oil are not voting for you: why should I vote for you?" This despite the fact that Weekes had supported sugar workers in their conflict with Tate and Lyle and the leadership of the Sugar Workers Union that had been compromised by Tate and Lyle and the PNM.

The government had further weakened Weekes's hands by submitting a statement to the industrial court (to which negotiations between OWTU and Texaco had been referred) that the days of substantial wage increases were over, and that any substantial wage increase would not be in the national interest. The statement claimed that increased wages could "adversely affect the growth of Government revenues derived from the industry or the ability of the companies to maintain a high level of local investment". It was also indicated that those effects would impact negatively on the goal of the Second Five- Year Plan to create jobs, and "could in fact lead to further retrenchment in the oil industry". The statement further argued "that wages and conditions of work in the oil industry exerted considerable upward pressure on wages and other conditions of work in other industries, both in the private and public sectors", with negative effects on employment and other important economic variables (ibid., 141). The industrial court's award in December 1965 was less than the OWTU had hoped for, but the union conceded that it was what they would have secured if the government had not intervened (*Vanguard*, 23 December 1965).

Williams was aware that Trinidadians were "allergic" to Marxism, communism or anything associated with Cuba, and during the election campaign, constantly harped on Weekes's links with Castro and international communist groupings. As he wrote in the *Nation* (15 July 1966),

> A specter is haunting the trade union movement, especially active among the Oilfields Workers Trade Union, and concentrating in the sugar belt. The specter is the political ideology of MARXISM dressed up in the white robes of purity. The Oilfield Workers Trade Union has already been bought and sold in the auction without a murmur at the cheapest price. Cheaply, because they have allowed themselves to be drugged into believing that the activity of their Executive, or a section of it, is honestly and truthfully directed against the Industrial Stabilisation Act.

Williams told OWTU workers that they were being used by their leaders and other "ambitious Marxists" to bring Trinidad and Tobago "under the boot of the Russian soldier and the tracks of Russian tanks".

Weekes had played into Williams's hands by attending the tricontinental conference held in Cuba in January 1966. On his return, he crowed that the visit had given him "added enthusiasm for my own just cause". Williams accepted the opening offered by Weekes. He was ably supported by Gerard Montano, the minister of home affairs, who suggested that the prime minister should pay Weekes's passage to allow him to return to Cuba, provided he stayed there. Montano's secret agents (Special Branch) had infiltrated the OWTU, the WFP and other radical institutions and were bringing information to him as to what was being said by whom, both in Trinidad and Tobago and in Cuba. In his mind, James was the architect of the WFP and was clearly plotting insurrection: "James was well known for his Marxist outlook, philosophy and drive, even though he was a Trotskyite rather than a Stalinist. Same breed of dog as far as I was concerned. Both frequently burrowed into left-wing movements that were not necessarily communist, and they would confuse supporters who were left wing in orientation – babes in the wood" (interview by the author, April 1991).

Montano attacked the WFP's policy of not indicating its leader. His platform strategy was to warn the audience that this was a formula designed to foist either Weekes or James or both on the country. "The child of that marriage bound to be Marxist. So I would sell it that way. Make them lose their deposits and in truth they did. Every man jack lost his deposit" (interview with author, 1990). Williams himself threw down the gauntlet to Castro and his followers in Trinidad and Tobago. Ignoring that he had hugged and kissed Castro when the latter visited Trinidad and Tobago, and that he too had once been wrongly labelled as Marxist or a communist, he told a large audience in San Fernando on 14 September 1966,

> Go out and finish up with this Marxist ideology which goes to Havana, Cuba and dares to sit down and take part in subversive resolutions against the lawful Government of Trinidad and Tobago. To hell with Castro. San Fernando put PNM in power, not Castro. Castro has no right to interfere with Trinidad and Tobago Affairs. We don't interfere with Castro's affairs, and Castro has no business setting up any revolutionary organization to interfere with and disrupt the normal development of Trinidad and Tobago. (1969, 335)

Williams was also equally critical of right-wing elements represented by the Liberal Party, a breakaway element from the DLP that was congenitally unable to keep its key members from tearing at each other's throats. Indeed the DLP leader, Rudranath Capildeo, directed most of his salvos towards the Liberals whom he accused of being *nemakharamas* (ingrates). Given the racial polarization that continued to prevail in spite of all attempts to define issues in terms of class, the Liberals were electorally smashed. The party did not win a single seat. The WFP also failed to win a single seat, and all its candidates lost their electoral deposits, which had been paid for by a single donor. The party had no resources and failed to raise much.

The WFP's failure also had to do with its failure to reconcile the contradictions of race and class and to the fact that it sought to be a class-based party in a society where race trumped everything. As Millette observed,

> What was to have been the "war of wars" turned out to be little more than an ill-matched confrontation between a prime minister and national party political leader on the one hand, and a highly intelligent, highly developed Marxist politician with few real resources at his disposal on the other hand. The WFP was doomed from the start. It was in fact the alter ego of the DLP which Stephen Maharaj had failed to capture and bring with him into the camp that James had fashioned out of radical trade union and political activists. It was like the DLP in that it aimed to win prime political support among the organically alienated Indian population; but it was different from it in that its appeal was not couched in racial or sectarian language but rather in a work-

ing class discourse intended to reach out across racial lines to the organized workers, the unemployed and the under-employed of the two main ethnic groups. (1995b, 75)

The WFP was in a sense ahead of its time. Its potential support was spread thinly, even in south and central Trinidad, and was poorly organized. It had no base in the north of the island and no leadership with the charisma of Williams. As Millette observed,

> As is usual in parties of the Left, elections were regarded with great scorn, as an unnecessary diversion from the real business of "mobilizing the people." And so it was that some of the greatest ideologues of radical politics contented themselves with articulating the issues and ignored the vital task of seeking the suffrage of the electorate in any seriously organized manner. The story is told of one such candidate whose entire programme of electoral persuasion in the constituency of his choice amounted to a single open air political meeting and a frenzied round of households on the night before the polls, desperately throwing election propaganda onto the verandas of the sleeping voters. (Ibid., 77)

James himself conducted the elections in large part from a reclining position in an apartment provided for him on Richmond Street. This is not to say that he was inactive. He edited the party newspaper, *We, the People*, from there. And he emerged from time to time to address private and public political meetings held by the party. He was in every sense the party's main asset, and its principal platform spokesman, but he was already quite frail, did most of his speaking from a sitting position, and seldom spoke at any great length. As he himself said, "If you couldn't say what you had to say in an hour, then something was seriously wrong." The fact was that James had been ailing for years. He had been seriously hurt in an accident in Jamaica in 1958 while fulfilling a programme of lectures at the University of the West Indies. This had seriously impeded his intellectual work and he was never thereafter able to write with his accustomed ease. All his original work virtually came to an end and, for the rest of his life, as one of his closest associates was later to point out, his publications were limited to the re-issue of material already written before his injury. To put it mildly, that fooled a lot of people (ibid., 77).

Following the election, Williams treated James with studied derision. As he said in his autobiography, "James, like a flushing of the WC, ran with the rest" (1969, 336). In terms of seats, the PNM won twenty-four and the DLP won twelve. In terms of percentages, the PNM won 52.4 per cent of the votes cast, the DLP 34 per cent, the Liberals 9 per cent, and the WFP 3.5 per cent. Some two-thirds of the electorate cast their votes despite machine malfunction and incompetence on the part of the returning officers. Eighty-two candidates failed to get 8 per cent of the votes and thus lost their deposits; none belonged to the PNM.[4] It is worth noting that the PNM got 52.4 per cent of the votes cast compared to 57

Table 25.1   Parliamentary General Elections: Total Votes Cast for Each Political Party

1966	Votes Received	Percentage
PNM	158,573	52.41
DLP	102,792	33.98
Liberal Party	26,870	8.88
WFP	10,484	3.46
PDP	943	.31
Butler Party	704	.23
Seukeran Independent Party	569	.19
Independents (No Party Affiliation)	1,476	.49
Rejected	146	.05
Total Votes Cast	302,548	

per cent in 1961. It also received 31,425 votes fewer than it did in 1961. Indeed, in the 1961 pre-independence election, 88 per cent of the electorate cast their votes. A huge chunk of the electorate had clearly become disenchanted with the PNM.

The WFP candidates were humiliated. A dejected James took the next flight out of the country. Weekes vowed he would never face the polls again. James Millette, a stalwart supporter of James, claims that the WFP manifesto anticipated a great deal of what Williams would put on the policy agenda following the Black Power revolution of 1970. As he argued, "The WFP Manifesto of 1966 was a more enduring achievement than the WFP campaign for political power, and was one of the legacies left by C.L.R. James to the politics that emerged in the ensuing period" (1995a, 342). Pity so few people read it! Millette also claimed that the WFP left another enduring legacy: it had formalized the radical dissent against Williams. From that time on, politics proceeded on three distinct tracks, the parliamentary track, the unconventional track taken by the Marxist and non-Marxist radicals disenchanted with elections, and another stream that was actively involved in undertaking revolutionary insurrection under the guidance of C.L.R. James (ibid., 344). This latter element was to come into its own in the period between 1966 and the rise and fall of the United Labour Front (ULF) in 1976 and thereafter.

To hide their embarrassment, the conventional opposition claimed that the PNM had rigged the elections by using the voting machines, and they refused to speak in parliament when it reconvened. They also vowed that they would never again contest an election using the voting machines. Circumstances forced them to reconsider their strategy. Rudranath Capildeo, whom Williams had cultivated by allowing him to continue teaching in London while leader of the opposition, found that Williams had no further use for him. He was denied additional leave from parliament by the Speaker and thus made to forfeit his seat. He had previously missed seven consecutive sessions of parliament. In the by-election that followed in 1968, his seat was won by the old warhorse Bhadase Maraj, who sought to resurrect the PDP. Maraj had, however, come to terms with Williams, who propped him up financially and otherwise, in part by acquiring lands which he owned. The DLP urged its supporters to boycott the election, but many disobeyed that advice. The DLP eventually abandoned the policy of silence and contested the local government elections with the voting machines. The PNM won sixty-eight of the one hundred seats and controlled all three municipalities – Port of Spain, Arima, and San Fernando – and four of the seven county councils. The PNM hegemony was complete, or so it seemed on 7 November 1966.

As if to rub salt in James's wound, Williams boasted of the role of the *Nation* in the election. He was in effect telling James that he was not indispensable. Crowed Williams,

> *The Nation* had done a magnificent job during the election campaign; under its young editor Irwin Merritt, it had brought political reporting to heights never before achieved in Trinidad and Tobago. It had kept the issue of subversion before the electorate, challenging the WFP week after week. It had dissected, to the point of damning them, the parliamentary records of the leaders of the Liberal Party and the WFP. I set out to work to give *The Nation* a home of its own, with improved equipment. The new headquarters was opened in June 1967. (1969, 337)

One wonders if Williams, in the quiet of his mind, ever regretted how badly he had treated James as a human being, former friend and mentor, if not as a political rival. If Williams was not depressed about James, he was certainly depressed about the state of the economy. He clearly saw the writing on the wall and was no doubt aware that politically, he was trying to re-cross the Rubicon. He must also have been aware that the ideological ghost of C.L.R. James was still hovering over the country and that it would seek materialization in some form. The WFP had died but it was not churched. Williams did not have long to wait for the toll of the bell that would signal the beginning of the definitive historic round of the epic war that had to take place before one or the other of the tragic heroes could declare victory, and claim to be the true son of the lord of Olympus.

26   **The Roaring Seventies**

Do you know how difficult it is to be the Prime Minister of a country where people believe, that like a conjurer, I can wave a wand and get rid of all their problems?
– Eric Williams

The Gathering Storm

The years between 1965 and 1973 were marked by acute social and economic crises. Whereas in the period 1956 to 1965 the challenges to Williams came mainly from what he termed the "recalcitrant" or the "obscurantist" minorities – the Indians, the white creoles, and the small commercial minorities – in the latter period, the threat came principally from the radical trade unions, black youth, and neo-Marxist revolutionary elites, all of whom had come to the conclusion that Trinidad and Tobago had secured "flag independence" in 1962 but that the moorings of the old social and economic system remained firmly in place. Such changes as had taken place were cosmetic and concealed the fact that colonialism had been replaced by neo-colonialism.

The radical elements were impatient with Williams and linked the struggle for structural economic change with demands for the exercise of greater social and political power by "oppressed" black people of Indian and African ancestry. They campaigned against tokenism, and against the continued ownership of the principal means of production and distribution by foreign and native whites and their mixed allies. The Guyanese historian Walter Rodney well expressed the mood of the radicals when he proclaimed that "the myth of a harmonious multiracial society must be blasted into nothingness". President general of the OWTU George Weekes also remarked that "our struggle for economic liberation must mean one thing, 'Black Power'. When we advise the Government to acquire British Petroleum's holdings, what we are actually advocating is the transfer of power, white power, into the hands of black people, Africans and Indians" (*Vanguard*, 19 October 1968).

Notwithstanding all that had taken place since 1956, whites retained a great deal of the influence that they had in the colonial period. This influence was not as unquestioned as it once was, nor was it exercised in the same crude forms, but it was nevertheless abiding. Whites still enjoyed most of their social and economic privileges, which were reinforced by the increased incursion of Anglo-American capital and technological expertise. The government's fiscal initiatives, its restrictive policy towards the importation of managerial personnel, and its educational policies were constant sources of irritation, but they did not amount to any fundamental disruptions of the established socio-economic order.

Outside of the public bureaucracy, colour, kinship and other particularistic ties remained dominant considerations that affected vocational opportunities and primary social contacts. Improvements in recruitment policies came about as business concerns felt the need for "window-dressing", or as economic expansion and immigration policies dried up the available supply of white and fair-skinned personnel; but the pace of social change in this area was painfully slow. Progress was made in the oil and petrochemical industries, and in some foreign-owned industrial and financial establishments, but in the native commercial sector, the older banks and the sugar industry, ascription was still widely prevalent as a basis of recruitment, especially in family-owned firms.

To the protesters, something was fundamentally wrong with the system that more foreign investment could not eradicate. The yawning credibility gap that had gradually been developing between Williams and the black elite on the one hand and the black urban masses on whose behalf they were supposed to have been governing for the past fourteen years, had become dramatically obvious by 1969–70, and revolutionary regime change appeared imminent. Much of the consciousness raising was the work of Geddes Granger and the National Joint Action Committee (NJAC).

The National Joint Action Committee

The NJAC was formed in 1967 as a coalition of radical trade unions, student and youth groups, and several cultural and sporting organizations, all of which were concerned about the need for a more vigorous public opinion in national politics. The movement gained prominence in 1969 when student elements physically confronted the governor general of Canada while he was on a visit to the University of the West Indies in Trinidad over the question of the treatment of their "black brothers" who were accused of smashing and burning the computer centre at Sir George Williams University in Montreal, Canada. The NJAC put pressure on Williams to intervene with the Canadian federal and provincial authorities on behalf of the Trinidadian students who were on trial for that incident. As part of the campaign, the NJAC also began questioning Canada's economic role in the Caribbean. Canadian banks, insurance companies and industrial firms came in for strong condemnation, as did Canada's sugar-purchasing policy in the region. Almost overnight, "Canadian imperialism" became a formidable bogeyman. Canada was now seen not as the friendly neighbour to the north, but as a country that had exploited its native Indians and blacks as well as people in the Caribbean with which it had been economically related for centuries.

Although the Trinidad government did provide legal, diplomatic and financial help for the students in Canada, radical elements in the NJAC were dissatisfied with Williams's apparent low-profile stance during the controversy, and began to assert not only that the government was in collusion with Canadian authorities but that it had done nothing to break the control of Canadian economic imperialism. Protests in support of the students soon escalated into demands for "black power" in Trinidad and Tobago. A street march in support of the students, which began in front of the Royal Bank of Canada on Independence Square on 26 February 1970, grew into demonstrations protesting Canadian racism and economic exploitation, and progressively transformed into massive rallies protesting the entire social and political system.

The charismatic eloquence of Geddes Granger, who emerged as the major spokesman of the NJAC, attracted the attention of thousands of Trinidadians – the young, the unemployed, the people of the slums of Shanty Town, on the periphery of Port of Spain – in a way that was curiously reminiscent of Williams in 1955–56. The University of Woodford Square, having done its job of training a new generation of political activists, had now given way to the People's Parliament. Granger, who took the name of Daaga, had become the new king of Woodford Square. Granger swore that he would "bring Williams to his knees". (Granger's transformation to "Makandal Daaga" is told by Roy Mitchell in Ryan and Stewart 1995, 97–132.)

The arrest without bail of the leaders of the demonstration for unlawful assembly and behaviour, which was calculated to cause disorder, helped to escalate the protest movement, and for sixty days the pounding feet of thousands of black marchers were heard all over Trinidad and Tobago. As Granger shouted, "We shall walk without speaking, without shouting, without smiling, but we shall walk with anger." Referring to the red, black and green flags carried by the marchers, Granger declared that "the red flags are a declaration of war, black is for victory and black unity, and green is for peace after we have achieved victory".

As the NJAC saw it, "white power" and the collusion of "Afro-Saxons" with it was the root of the problem in the Caribbean:

> Too many of us are blinded by the constitutional disguises which give the appearance of Black people being in control. This is the way the white power structure wants us to see it. The economic control which white people have, gives them political control. Our politicians are turned into mere puppets. Once in every five years Black people get a lit-

tle (very little in the set up) political bargaining status as election comes around. We are fed crash programmes and promises. Then the rest of the time is spent by the politicians bootlicking for the white power structure. The white imperialists used their control of the economic system to divide Black people, African against African, African against Indian, Indian against Indian. In fact, divisions of race and class are embedded in the structure of the whole society. (*NJAC* 1970, 11).

Kafra Kambon, one of the NJAC leaders, indicated that Williams did try a strategy of co-optation. He not only capitulated on several occasions to outrageous demands for money and property made by black militants, but also sent many messages indicating that he was prepared to engage in dialogue with the NJAC to implement, where possible, some of their specific programmatic concerns. Indeed, Williams saw the NJAC as providing him with the leverage that he needed to further his social agenda, including taking over a section of the banking sector. Some of the militants were prepared to sit down and talk with him, but the organization took a formal position that there should be "no dialogue with the enemy". To quote Kambon, "There was the effort to co-opt what was seen as the type of programmatic thrust of NJAC and the Black Power Movement, the kind of things that they wanted in terms of changes in the economy and that sort of thing. So you had a concessionary response but you also had the response of a great deal of repression" ("The Black Power Revolution 1970", symposium, April 1990).

As the protest movement gathered momentum, the PNM and its middle-class supporters began to panic, as did the police, who reacted by using tear gas, horses, guns and night-sticks to disperse the demonstrations. Overnight, phrases such as "pigs" and "police brutality", familiar in North America, became part of the radical vocabulary in Trinidad. During a court hearing, Kambon, who was one of the nine demonstrators arrested, urged black policemen to join the crusade: "You police should be on our side. The army is on our side. All we need now is your help to seize power. We have suffered too long at the hands of those Canadian bastards."[1]

Williams was in a quandary about what steps should be taken to quell the unrest. Some ministers wanted him to declare a state of emergency immediately. Others argued that it was only a matter of time before the protest movement collapsed. Yet others, like the minister of commerce and industry, John O'Halloran, and the minister of home affairs, Gerard Montano, were not so optimistic. O'Halloran opined that "the present black power demonstrations have been engineered by communist agents trained and paid by Fidel Castro" (ibid., 10). Williams, who perhaps knew better, built a wall around his house and isolated himself for a full month before he finally spoke to the nation, a delay that angered middle-class elements, some of whom had begun to organize protective vigilante groups. There were strident demands that he crush the Black Power movement as the Government of Jamaica had done in October 1968.

As someone who had begun his career as a black "militant", Williams was aware that he was in large part responsible for what was taking place. The NJAC was only trying to complete what he had written about in his years as a nationalist scholar and had begun to do between 1956 and 1960. Williams understood the historical antecedents of the protest movement, as well as its relationship with the worldwide revolution of youth against authority, cant and hypocrisy. According to Williams, who boasted that he was the "biggest black power",

> the fundamental feature of the demonstrations was the insistence on Black dignity, the manifestation of Black consciousness, and the demand for Black economic power. The entire population must understand that these demands are legitimate and are entirely in the interest of the community as a whole. If this is Black Power, then I am for Black Power. . . .
>
> Anyone who wishes to continue to march and demonstrate, by all means let him do so. The Constitution guarantees this as a fundamental right. But I urge that this should be done without violence, without trespassing on the constitutional rights of others, without interference of any sort with the freedom of worship equally guaranteed by the Constitution. There must be no interference with the churches, no interference with the temples, no interference with the mosques, no interference with any place of worship.
>
> Our young people are a part of the general world malaise, seeking something new and something better, and seeking it with a sense of urgency. They are restless, trusting, possibly a little exuberant. But let there be no misunderstanding about this. It is a horse of a different colour if what is involved is arson and molotov cocktails. In that case the law will have to take its course. (Nationwide broadcast, 23 March 1970)

Williams's strategy was to wait until the Black Power movement had either exhausted its welcome, or overreached itself and thereby provoked a "backlash" to his benefit. There was, however, growing restlessness in the labour movement and the Trinidad and Tobago Regiment, and it was well known that there was sympathy for the militants among enlisted men and elements in the junior officer corps. A.N.R. Robinson's resignation from cabinet on 19 April also led to wild speculation that he was closely tied up with the NJAC, and that he would be its choice to replace Williams. There were also rumours that Trinidad-born US-based Black Power activist Stokely Carmichael was due to arrive in Trinidad (he was in fact not allowed to board any aircraft bound for Trinidad); that mystery vessels had begun to appear in Trinidad territorial waters; and that money was being channelled from outside to the marchers, who were growing more daring and confident each day.

On 20 April 1970, the NJAC made a dramatic and symbolic march into the sugar areas in an attempt to link up with "the brothers in indenture". This was preceded by efforts to unite the two races – not particularly successfully, since

Indians feared that they would become victims of Black Power. Black cultural assertiveness in fact led to counter-mobilization on the part of Indians. On the campus of the university, this phenomenon gave rise to the creation of SPIC, the Society for the Promotion of Indian Culture, and SPAN, the Society for the Propagation of African Nationality. The march into Caroni was also not as successful as the NJAC activists like to claim. Indians were curious and courteous, but did not embrace the marchers with open arms and open homes. Some sugar workers were, however, willing to invite radical urban union leaders to use whatever leverage they had to help them with their industrial grievances.

During the march to Caroni, protestors passed in front of the home of Bhadase Maraj, boss of the Hindu Maha Sabha and the All Trinidad Sugar Estates and Factory Workers Trade Union. With Remington gun in one hand and revolver in the other, Maraj sought to intimidate the workers. He also circulated pictures of four children who had been burned when fire broke out in a nearby Indian-owned barber saloon. The pictures bore the caption *burn baby burn* and the imputation was that Indians were being targeted. All this served to frustrate the NJAC's coalition-building exercise. Williams would later thank Maraj for having helped to contain the marchers and generally for the fact that the Indian community had once more served as a counterweight to black radicalism. Incidentally, this was a role that they had played in colonial times (related to the author by Lionel Seukeran at the symposium "Eric Williams in Retrospect", April 1991).

The Eye of the Storm

By late April 1970, political hurricane winds began to blow fiercely over Trinidad and Tobago. Sugar workers, who had struck over their own industrial grievances, planned to march into Port of Spain on 21 April, and there were reports that a general strike was being planned for 22 April or 1 May. At this point Williams concluded that the confrontation could no longer be avoided, and that a state of emergency had to be declared. The feared hurricane had struck. As he told the nation,

> For some years now we have been aware of dissident elements in the society, especially among a minority of trade unions, seeking to displace the Government. At first they tried to do so by the electoral process; no one can have any quarrel with that. When that failed, however, they turned increasingly to unconstitutional means and armed revolution. . . .
>
> The first date selected for the contemplated overthrow of the Government was foiled by developments which I do not wish to discuss tonight. The alternative date selected was ruled out by the declaration of the State of Emergency.

During the weekend before the declaration of the State of Emergency, after weeks and weeks of demonstrations, a new factor was introduced into the situation. This was the total repudiation by certain workers in one of the statutory boards of all recognised trade-union practices and procedures. In the process, all the agreements reached by the Government as employer with the union involved in respect of classification and compensation were thrown out of the window. This had enormous implications for the entire Public Service. This was in the context of public statements by the dissident element in the society that the sugar workers and the workers in water were to march on April 21 to link up with transport workers, to be followed on Wednesday, April 22, by some action in the oil industry. (Nationwide broadcast, 3 May 1970)

Williams noted that the Black Power movement had enlisted the sympathy of a number of people, especially young people, who bitterly resented discrimination against black people at home and abroad:

This is a legitimate grievance, and I would have been no party [*sic*] to any attempt to repress this. I knew that much more was involved. But these young idealists had to see for themselves the ulterior motives of those who were seeking to use slogans of Black dignity and Black economic power as the basis of enlisting mass support. They had to see for themselves how the Black Power slogan degenerated into race and hatred and even to attacks on Black business in Tobago and Point Fortin. Moreover, if I had told the general population of the larger plan I have indicated to you tonight, 75 per cent of you would have been skeptical and would not have believed it. You had to be made to put your finger in the wound in order to believe. It was only when the total breakdown of the trade-union movement was imminent that I decided to act.[2] (Ibid.)

As in 1965, when a similar coming together of sugar and oil appeared imminent, Williams declared a state of emergency. He did so on the night of 20 April. In a pre-dawn raid, security forces, casting a wide net, arrested the leaders of the Black Power movement. The move had been expected, and the NJAC had called on its followers to defy it. As Granger had declared on the night of 14 April,

From the time the Emergency is declared, come to town to demonstrate. By God, we will fight fire with fire. If you bow to the State of Emergency, mark my word here tonight, your children will curse the day you were born. Your children will not respect you, your wives will turn against you. . . . We will not retreat one single inch. This is war. We are going to show them that the will of God is the will of the people. Come to town. If they want to lock you up, let them lock up all "ah we". . . . No rum drinking. From tonight do not buy anything except food.

The stealth with which most of the leaders of the movement were picked up – the arrests were made at night and not during the early morning as expected – did not prevent the anticipated confrontation with the police. But in the short run, at least, it was a futile confrontation. In the words of Lloyd Best, "On the morning of the 21st, the population assemble[d] in the public square, smash[ed] up all the store fronts in Port of Spain, every one . . . a final grand romantic gesture, finish[ed] and [went] home. No leadership left. All the terror in the system is police terror, official terror" ("The February Revolution: Its Causes and Meaning", *Tapia*, 20 December 1970).

An important dimension of the timing of the decision to declare a state of emergency was revealed in a heated public exchange between the prime minister and Clive Spencer, a former senator and president of the Trinidad and Tobago Labour Congress. According to Williams, on the morning of 20 April, the president of the Labour Congress issued an "ultimatum" to the government:

> If immediate action was not taken by the Government to bring the whole situation under control, then the Labour Congress, which controlled the responsible unions, would bring the whole community to a standstill by calling out the workers in the Port, the Airport, external and internal communications, the Civil Service, and the daily paid workers.
>
> It was clear to the Ministers present and particularly to the Prime Minister that the time had come for decisive action; it was no longer a problem of aimless marches and wild public statements; the whole Labour Movement was threatened. An emergency Cabinet session was summoned three hours later and the decision taken that a State of Emergency should be declared at such time as the Prime Minister thought it fit. (*Trinidad Guardian*, 25 September 1971)

Williams claimed that Spencer thanked him for declaring the state of emergency, and requested him to intervene to get the police authorities to issue arms to a vigilante group that he had set up for the protection of one of the most important public utilities.

Stung by Williams's disclosures, which in Spencer's view were designed to make him an object of hate and disaffection among the left, Spencer gave his version of the story. He agreed that he had given the prime minister an ultimatum, and that he had agreed to help mobilize volunteers "twice the number of the Army if it becomes necessary" to contain the army rebellion and the militants in Port of Spain. Spencer said he was forced to do this because NJAC elements were poaching on union affiliates, had called workers from the Water and Sewerage Authority off their jobs, and were making violent threats to union leaders: "I told him further that whoever survived after that will rule as it appeared that although he was reigning, he was afraid to rule, and that the Congress was not prepared to tolerate the Government's 'wait and see' attitude anymore. The Prime Minister replied that he had heard me 'loud and clear,' and that his Government was watching the situation, and would not allow it to deteriorate any further, but that he was not aware that it was as serious as I had indicated" (ibid.).

Spencer was concerned about what might happen during the massive demonstrations that the militants had planned for 21 April. "With all these workers on the streets, and with WASA [Water and Sewerage Authority] pump attendants having been told to lock off all supplies of water . . . the smallest spark could burn the city, and what may have to be done then could result in serious bloodshed and loss of lives and property" (ibid.). Spencer further claimed that he warned the prime minister that three officers of the army and about sixty dissident soldiers might obstruct the regiment from coming to the assistance of the government, and that he ought to recheck the loyalty of the army before taking any action. The prime minister, who had been assured that there were just "a few dissatisfied soldiers whom there would be no trouble in controlling", was, according to Spencer, "on the verge of tears" when he later learned that the army had revolted. Other cabinet members were also in a state of panic and hysteria, and there were reports that helicopters and BWIA aircraft had been ordered to stand by to fly members of the government to Tobago or farther afield if necessary.

Mutiny or Failed Coup?

The crisis in the armed forces indeed created a dramatic complication that led Williams to hesitate about declaring a state of emergency. Evidence suggests that in spite of all that had been happening, the military uprising took him by surprise. The army had been in a state of severe unrest for several months and morale was extremely low. No one had given much thought to the role of an army in Trinidad and Tobago, and there was a great deal of purposelessness and boredom among enlisted men. Mental health problems were also serious. Senior officers were being accused of nepotism, womanizing, establishing brothels, corruption, stealing food and army supplies left by the Americans, professional inefficiency, condoning the perpetuation of racially discriminatory practices in the use of beaches and mess facilities, and misusing the army band and army personnel for private purposes. Senior officers, many of whom were not professionally trained, were also accused of being party hacks who encouraged spying on officers suspected of being hostile to the PNM and sympathetic to Black Power. The newly trained officer corps also felt that the command structure had broken down and that their career paths were being blocked by incompetent old-timers, many of whom were holdovers from the federal army and the public service, from whence they were recruited on terms that were superior to those of the more recent recruits who had to retire at age forty-five. The older officers had negotiated to remain in the army until they were sixty, the age at which they would have been required to resign if they had remained in the public service.

On the morning of 21 April, a group of rebel soldiers seized the opportunity to try to force the government to deal with their internal grievances. The soldiers claimed that they mutinied for sound reasons. At a symposium in 1990 which rensited the events of 1970, Lieutenant Raffique Shah, one of the key officers involved, declared that "we acted because of corruption and inefficiency at the Regimental level". Shah and his colleagues claim that they felt it was unwise to take a restless army that had no confidence in its senior officers into a crisis situation, where there was no telling what the officers might do. They denied the accusation that they were leading soldiers into Port of Spain bent on arson, rape and looting, or that they ever had any plans to seize the government, either independently or in collusion with the NJAC or any other organization. Also denied were reports that they were going into "town to help their black brothers", or to engineer the formation of a national government, possibly led by A.N.R. Robinson, who had resigned from the government.

Whatever the soldiers' intentions – and there were differing views among the enlisted – there is no telling what might have happened if the rebel army had succeeded in their march to Port of Spain. As fate would have it, the convoy was intercepted by loyalist elements of the coast guard, which shelled and blocked the only road linking the army base with the city. The unexpected intervention of the coast guard threw the soldiers into a panic and forced them to retreat. Promises of negotiations and hints of amnesty gave Williams the breathing space he needed to deploy arms to the loyalist police. The soldiers were able to hold out for five tension-filled days, but in the end were completely outmanoeuvred by Williams.

Shah has consistently denied claims that there were plans for the soldiers to link up with the NJAC or anyone else. He insisted that mutiny was the immediate objective, but conceded that an overthrow of the government was "on the cards" if their demands were not met:

> We had graduated from being rabid nationalists to something akin to utopian socialists, maybe even romanticists. But we were still fired by the decisive actions of legends like Che Guevara and Patrice Lumumba, by then both deceased. We had established loose ties with certain political activists on the outside – not NJAC, I must stress, and the overthrow of the military establishment, and if it came to that, the government was on the cards.[3] (Ryan and Stewart 1995, 514)

Shah claimed that if the army had decided that it was going into Port of Spain to overthrow the regime at any cost, there was really nothing to stop this from happening, because the army could have blown the coast guard vessels that interrupted their march into Port of Spain "out of the water" with their Gustav 84-mm anti-tank weapons. He also insisted that the police were no match for the highly trained rebel army and could not have saved the government. In sum, the regime was saved because the leaders of the mutinous soldiers had not planned to overthrow the regime and the majority had no wish to kill their colleagues who were on the coast guard vessels.[4] After the rebels were apprehended and arrested, the government insisted that they were guilty of treason. The charge was later reduced to mutiny, a change that Shah conceded they were guilty of. The soldiers, however, claimed that their commanding officer had condoned their activities. The military tribunal did not accept this claim and the three ringleaders, Raffique Shah, Rex Lasalle and Michael Bazie, were sentenced to twenty, fifteen and seven years in prison respectively. The appeal court later upheld their appeals. The court held that the condonation defence was not given a fair hearing. The privy council upheld the judgement of the appeal court without even hearing arguments from the defence. Shah felt that he and his colleagues had triumphed over Williams and his team: "We remain proud of our role in one of the most significant events in the history of this country, the Black Power Revolution." (For a fuller discussion of the mutiny and its aftermath, see Ryan and Stewart 1995, 419–616.)

Inside Williams's "Bunker"

The most comprehensive insider account of what took place inside Williams's "bunker" during the events of 1970 was that given by Gerard Montano, minister of home affairs at the time of the uprising. In his view, the crisis was partly due to mismanagement by the Ministry of Finance of the affairs of the army and the police, as well as Williams's unwillingness to act promptly to contain the enveloping crisis when it began to mature. There were also factors over which the government had little control. Montano claims that the crisis began to bubble in 1968 when radical elements in the Trinidad and Tobago Regiment began to link up with radical elements in the United States and elsewhere, and when these elements began to link up with Marxist groups in the hemisphere in general and Cuba in particular. Much of this activity was being monitored by Special Branch personnel within the police.[5] Welfare issues in the protective services were also fuelling discontent, much of which was being ignored by the management of the services and by Williams. As Montano complained,

> Williams was told of these developments and warned that if there was an uprising, there was no way it could be put down easily since the conspirators were heavily armed – big guns, automatic weapons and the police were armed with 1914/18 rifles. There were 3000 policemen, and there were 746 or 756 men in the Regiment. They could take only about a half-hour to come into Port of Spain, surround the police, and the whole game was up. (Ryan 1995, 585)

Montano claims that he tried and failed to get Williams to promulgate laws to prevent the use of racial epithets and slurs that could stir up blacks against whites and ultimately Indians. He also complained that many of the demonstrators were often high on marijuana and that some resorted to arson: "Business places were being burnt every night. The fire brigade services were overwhelmed with the need to put fires out." The NJAC spokesmen denied allegations that the fires were directed at Indian business firms. They claimed that two major fires for which militants were blamed were not set by anyone associated with the movement and may well have involved arson. But it is true that many firms and residents of upscale neighbourhoods were shaken down by elements who used the crisis as a pretext for predatory activities. Many white and fair-skinned citizens, and persons with artificially straightened hair, were also harassed and told to adopt Afro styles of coiffure and dress.

With respect to the events in Canada, Montano believed that Williams did not have any options, and that he did the prudent thing in appealing to Prime Minister Pierre Trudeau to use his influence to give the students the option of a fine and repatriation. Had he not done so, the Black Power elements would have targeted whites, and Canadian interests in particular. The return of the students, however, served to fuel the crisis.

Montano had some interesting things to say about the relationship between Williams and A.N.R. Robinson, who was the PNM's deputy political leader, deputy prime minister, and minister of external affairs:

> There were disturbing reports that people who were sympathizers with the Black Power movement were meeting with Robinson from time to time, whether at the university or at his house. But there were meetings taking place and there was concern that government decisions were being leaked to the militants. It was therefore agreed that steps had to be taken to ensure that sensitive information would only be shared by a limited number of trusted ministers. There was also concern as to what Robinson might do if he was appointed to act as Prime Minister during Dr. Williams' absence from the country to attend the Conference of Commonwealth Caribbean Heads of Government on April 12, 1970, in Jamaica.
>
> It was thus decided that Dr. Williams would not go to Jamaica, but that this would not be publicly announced. It was agreed that Minister Kamaluddin Mohammed would go instead. Normally, when Robinson acted for Dr. Williams, he would send for the big Princess – you know the car? And he would drive up to Whitehall in the Princess. He did so on this occasion and called on his secretary to say that as soon as she got the warrant from the Governor General, she was to bring it to him. But the warrant never arrived: every half hour or every hour on the hour, he kept asking for it. It never arrived, and he was blue; he was angry. Eventually, at about midday, the lady brought the report that Kamal had gone to Jamaica instead of Williams. Robinson was angry and that evening or sometime later, he resigned his office. I cannot altogether blame him, but his behaviour before that certainly left a lot to be desired. But now it was fairly obvious that he was not being trusted. Therefore, if he chose to resign, one could understand his feelings.[6] (Ibid., 592–93)

Robinson has since claimed that given what was taking place in the society, he did not want the responsibility of having to act as prime minister, and that he was libelled by those who accused him of planning to seize power during

Williams's absence. He told this author that on the day that he was said to be in Williams's office, he was on a "beach in Castara, Tobago, drinking fish soup". Checks with three of Williams's secretaries confirmed that Robinson did call the prime minister's office from time to time to inquire about the warrant and was told that it had not yet been received. Williams's secretaries also pretended to be busy. When it became clear that he had been duped and distrusted, he submitted his resignation from cabinet, though not from the party, and left the country for several months. He expressed fear that he was a target for assassination. Williams called W.J. Alexander to inform him of Robinson's resignation.[7]

Montano's account of Williams's handling of the declaration of a state of emergency is also worth recounting. He notes that elements in the private sector, the diplomatic community and the cabinet were urging Williams to declare a state of emergency pre-emptively. Panic was beginning to set in as reports filtered in about arms being taken from the bunker at the regiment base at Teteron, along with rumours that thousands of yards of khaki material identical to that used to manufacture uniforms for the regiment were being imported. Members of the cabinet, who were all holed up in the Hilton Hotel, believed that they were to be strung up and killed once the army moved into Port of Spain.

Williams argued that timing was of the essence, and that it was important to wait until the protesters had overreached themselves and the public had begun to tire of them. He did not wish to make martyrs of them or provoke a confrontation between them and their kith and kin in the regiment. He was also calculating that once the emergency was declared, Granger and his followers would "run like rats". Montano conceded that Williams might have been right:

> Williams was a master of timing politically. No question of it, and in retrospect perhaps he was right, perhaps. Many still believe that he should have put it down long before and introduce the legislation which was brought in afterwards. He should have done it then and eased the situation. Cabinet eventually decided on April 20th to call the State of Emergency. It was decided that it would be declared at 6.00 p.m., and that the Nigerian Government would be approached for help. (Author interview, April 1990; see Ryan and Stewart 1995, 579–606 for fuller transcript)

Montano told Williams that getting help from Nigeria would involve all sorts of logistical and diplomatic difficulties, including having to work through the British government, which would be time consuming. He estimated that this option would take some two to three weeks, by which time the government could be overthrown. Interestingly, the British prime minister, Harold Wilson, was puzzled by Williams's request that the British government serve as the go-between among Williams and the Nigerian and Tanzanian governments, from whom one thousand soldiers were being sought. Wilson told Williams that he was prepared to facilitate, but that it would be wiser to have the request conveyed through

Trinidad's high commissioner in London to the Nigerian and Tanzanian high commissioners based in London. Wilson sagely advised Williams that the Nigerians were "very conscious of their reputation as an independent African state" and were "very likely to be more receptive to a request that did not pass through our channels" (Palmer 2006, 300).

One wonders why this did not occur to Williams, the erstwhile rabid anti-colonial. Williams was aware that the Tanzanian army had mutinied in 1964 and that Nyerere had gone into hiding on a British ship. How could Williams have come to the conclusion that the Tanzanian army would rush to his assistance? But Williams wanted black troops in a hurry and was not squeamish about how and where he sourced them. He had tried and failed to get help from Jamaica, Guyana or Barbados. Burnham of Guyana, who did not really care much for Williams, reportedly did not want to "back a loser", and was not readily forthcoming with offers of assistance. He also did not want to alienate black radicals in Guyana. Neither did Hugh Shearer, though he had earlier put down the "Rodney riots" in Jamaica. There were some discussions with the Jamaicans, but these were not productive.

During the discussions that took place among members of the cabinet, some ministers urged that help should be sought from the Americans. Others plumped for the Venezuelans. According to Montano,

> One Minister said: "you sons of bitches are always cursing the goddam Yankees, and the first time your arse is on fire, it's the Americans you turned to." There was one other avenue open, and that was the Venezuelans. But some believed, all things being equal, that the Americans would probably get here more quickly. Williams was told that it was not necessary to have American soldiers land. All that was required was an American presence in our waters or just outside our 12-mile limit, so that the revolutionary boys would know that in the event that they made their move, the Americans were waiting right there. Williams agreed, and said, "On no account are they to enter our waters." We also needed weapons since we could not keep the loyalist soldiers barely armed, and our police without weapons. Help was needed and the only people who could provide that help quickly would be the Americans. Williams agreed with these assessments. (Ryan and Stewart 1995, 597)

The American ambassador was asked to procure a supply of weapons and urged to have them delivered in forty-eight hours. He agreed to source them, but could not guarantee timely delivery. He also made it clear that they would have to be paid for. In terms of warships, the idea was to get them positioned where they could be seen from Chaguaramas. It was known at the time that they were anchored not too far off Trinidad's waters, in order to evacuate American citizens if necessary. The Americans, however, refused Williams's request for help in putting down the uprising. Officially, their position was that democracy would be allowed to take its course.

Interestingly, Williams had made up his mind long before the events of 1970 that if he ever had "army trouble" such as Nyerere had to face in Tanzania in 1964, he would not hesitate to call on American marines to rescue his regime, nor would he run like Nyerere did. Williams reportedly told the British ambassador to Ethiopia that if there ever was a threat to the welfare and integrity of Trinidad from an unrepresentative and determined group such as there had been in Tanzania, he would not have the slightest hesitation to call on US troops based in Trinidad. "Why for a paper scruple and his personal face, should he hand over his country to foreign subversion?" (Palmer 2006, 292–93). Williams felt that Cuba was to Trinidad and Tobago what Zanzibar was to Tanzania.

Williams also negotiated with the Venezuelans. The Venezuelan ambassador, Carlos Irrazabal, who was new in his post, was called at all hours of the day and night and told what was needed. Irrazabal informed Williams that the Venezuelan government was already discussing various options. The Venezuelan foreign minister, who was also contacted, told Williams that the Venezuelans had decided that its fleet would come into Trinidad waters and that Venezuelan military aircraft would overfly Trinidad's airspace.[8] He was also told that troops were ready to land any minute. Venezuela was concerned about the prospect of a hostile Cuban-inspired revolutionary government on its doorstep, and was taking no chances. Air force, navy units and other troops were dispatched to the northeast of Venezuela, just in case.

Williams, who believed that Venezuela harboured imperialistic designs on the Caribbean, was unwilling to embrace the Venezuelans too closely. As Montano tells us,

> The Venezuelan envoy, Captain Gomez, was told that those overtures were unacceptable and that what was required was for Venezuelan warships and aircraft to remain just outside Trinidad's territorial air and sea space as a deterrent to the insurgents who would know that if they made a move, help would be available. The Venezuelans were also told that help would be forthcoming "today or tomorrow." To cut a long story short, their weapons arrived in 36 hours; the American weapons arrived in 48 hours, and we were now armed and we quickly used the soldiers we had outside to demonstrate the weapons to the police. We were now better armed and protected. (Ibid., 599)

The Venezuelans were puzzled by Williams's behaviour during the crisis. Irrazabal told the American ambassador that Williams was "*loco*" (insane). Williams, he said, was calling him at all hours. According to the Venezuelans, Williams had formally requested two warships, one to be positioned in Port of Spain harbour and the other in Teteron Bay, Chaguaramas. When one of the warships arrived in Trinidad waters, Williams, acting on the basis of requests from the coast guard and soldiers who were involved in the negotiations taking place between radical soldiers and representatives of the government in respect of an amnesty at the Chacacabana Hotel in Chaguaramas, promptly asked it to leave (see Ryan 1995).[9] The Venezuelan ambassador was also upset that Williams refused his request to permit twenty Venezuelan guards outside Williams's residence. The armed Venezuelan guards were eventually posted.[10]

The British, whose help was also sought, as we have seen, were reluctant to send troops and warships to Trinidad as Williams requested. Some members of the British government were opposed to any interference in the internal affairs of a fellow Commonwealth member. But Britain had significant investments in Trinidad and Tobago and some two thousand British citizens resident in the country. Britain eventually decided to safeguard those interests and sent two frigates, HMS *Jupiter* and HMS *Sirius*, into Trinidad waters, ostensibly to protect British citizens and property. Williams had also asked for machine guns, mortars, rifles, hand grenades and scout cars. The British were minded to comply, but Williams withdrew the request for these a day after he had made it, telling the British that he had sourced the supply elsewhere (Cabinet minutes of meeting held 23/4/70 FCO 63/593; as cited in Palmer 2006, 299).

Following Williams's death, Robinson made public the fact that Williams had appealed to the former imperial power for guns and warships to subdue unrest. According to Robinson, "Williams the Great" was so terrified in 1970 that "he sent telegrams to no fewer than five foreign governments for help".[11] John Donaldson, who was stationed at the Trinidad high commission in London, denied that any such approach was made. Donaldson said that he would have known, because he represented the government in London. However, it is well known that Williams often bypassed his high commissioner to London and dealt directly with the British government (*Trinidad Express*, 4 November 1981).

It is worth noting that Robinson had previously been openly critical of Williams's decision to call in foreign troops even before the latter's death. In a speech given in November 1972, he accused Williams of having "performed one of the greatest acts of betrayal in Caribbean history. . . . In the context of Caribbean history, it is a supreme act of treachery." Robinson said that he wanted to "lay bare the shameful and sordid episode so that it would not escape the historian" (1986, 155–56). The regional press was all of the same view. The *Barbados Advocate* (5 May 1970) considered the call to the United States for help "the most damning thing the diminutive Doc has done". The *Daily Gleaner* in Jamaica opined likewise: "It is somewhat ironic that the Government of perhaps the Caribbean's foremost intellectual analyst of the dynamics of imperialism, of the historicity of black frustration, and of the disrepute of foreign intervention should now find itself the object of mass demonstration and calling for assistance from the United States and the United Kingdom" (as cited in Robinson, 1986). The *Guyana Graphic* (23 April 1970), the *Financial Times* (23 April 1970) and the *Economist* (25 April 1970) also carried reports of ships, helicopters and troops headed for Trinidad and Tobago.

Williams was embarrassed by these reports, and issued a press release that all ships and aircraft had been asked to leave Trinidad's air and sea space. There was no condemnation of foreign intervention. Interestingly, one of Robinson's concerns was that by inviting Venezuelan military help, Williams was creating a precedent that could have future implications not only for Trinidad and Tobago, but for Guyana, a large part of which Venezuela claimed. Others raised the spectre of Venezuela and the United States becoming embroiled in a military struggle for control of Trinidad and Tobago if Williams had been overthrown (Baptiste 1976, 26–27).

There is much controversy as to whether Williams panicked in 1970 or was always in full control of events and emotionally stable. Two pictures have emerged. One has him calm and calculating while the other has him "manic" and panic stricken. One close observer, Bernard Primus, who was based at the Industrial Development Commission, formed the opinion that Williams was a "coward" who was desperately afraid of unions and Black Power militants. He always sought to appease them. In one case, he instructed Primus to give a group of protestors the bottom floor of the newly built IDC headquarters to establish a cooperative. Primus advised against capitulation to the group, which was using intimidatory tactics and seeking to feather their own nests. Williams advised Primus to give the protestors the whole building and have the IDC rent a floor from them! Primus advised Williams that the plan would backfire, because other groups would also demand a piece of the action. Williams eventually conceded that Primus was right (author interview, 30 May 2006).

Williams also bought an old colonial bungalow and an estate in Tacarigua that was formerly owned by the Milneholme family. The property was acquired by member of parliament Lionel Seukeran and others for TT$710,000. Williams sought to appease Granger and others by literally giving them the property. He paid Seukeran TT$1 million, much to the delight of the latter and his business colleagues, who celebrated with champagne. Seukeran had asked for TT$3 million, but Williams pleaded that the treasury could not afford it, and that he would not be unmindful of Seukeran's "sacrifice" (related by Seukeran at the symposium "Eric Williams in Retrospect", April 1991).

Montano claims that Williams never panicked: "He was calm, collected, and listening. The other members of Cabinet lost their nerve. One of those in particular who lost his nerve was Hudson-Phillips. The other chaps were scared as hell, perhaps because they did not have the authority, the insight, or the knowledge of what exactly was going on" (Ryan and Stewart 1995, 605).

Montano also dismissed as a "nasty lie" Attorney-General Karl Hudson-Phillips's claim that a BWIA plane had been put on standby to fly Williams, the cabinet, and a few trusted aides out of Trinidad and Tobago if a coup did take place. As Montano declared,

That was a nasty, willful lie. Karl knew very well what had happened. In any such uprising, a principal feature is to keep your airport open. So the airport had to be kept open
and not destroy your communications. Then, since it was possible that the Government
might ask Barbados, Guyana and Jamaica for troops if necessary, and they didn't have
an airline, BWIA would have to transport them. So instructions were given that one
plane should be kept there. Karl was party to that decision. So when he came out and
said what he said, that was a nasty, wicked lie. (Ibid., 602–3)

Inquiries have led me to conclude that there was a plane standing by which
was fuelled, provisioned, staffed and ready to evacuate ministers and other key
players. The pilot insisted that his family would also have to be accommodated.
The arrangements were probably made by the party chairman, Francis Prevatt,
and it is possible that Williams and Montano were blindsided on the issue.
Conversations with the late Carl Tull, one of Williams's trusted aides, also
yielded information as to how some of Williams's men behaved, and which of
them had suitcases with US dollars. According to Tull, Williams's security guard
was told to make sure that Williams was bundled onto the helicopter that was
to land on his lawn to take refugees to Piarco or to an Amoco offshore platform
if negotiations with the regiment at Chacacabana broke down.[12] Williams
insisted that he was not going anywhere, and was reportedly angry with those
who were panicking and planning to abandon ship.[13] (See Ryan and Stewart
1995, 607–16.)

"I Am Not Losing My Head!"

Williams himself denied that he panicked and lost his nerve. He in fact found
time to write almost daily to his daughter Erica while she was in London and later
when she was brought to Barbados at the height of the crisis, updating her on
what was happening, at least from his perspective. He assured her that all was well
and that he had the situation under control. He also told her that he was glad that
he did not go to Jamaica, but did not accuse Robinson of being involved in any
plot to overthrow him. Williams correctly speculated that Robinson saw crisis
ahead and did not want to be part of it. This was the version that Robinson gave
when denying that he wanted to be appointed acting prime minister during
Williams's planned absence to Jamaica in order to effect a coup. Williams was
happy that Robinson had resigned from the cabinet, but insisted that he would
not fall into the trap of dismissing him as deputy political leader as some were
calling on him to do. "In terms of strategy, we should not at this stage give
Robinson an opportunity or an alibi to move from the PNM. He must make
the jump himself" (as cited in Palmer 2006, 294).

In terms of the mood of the "crowd", Williams assured Erica that the tide was swinging away from the protesters and that the police had things well under control. He thus did not agree with those who were urging him to bring out the regiment. Ironically, as we have seen, Williams did not initially regard the army as a threat to his regime and seemed to be more anxious to avoid a confrontation between the protesters and their kith and kin in the regiment. Such a clash, he felt, might make martyrs of the Black Power leaders. It was better to wait until the latter had exhausted their legitimacy. Williams also expressed concerned about the planned march into Port of Spain on 19 and 20 April, and also about the possibility of a general strike on 1 May that would paralyse the country. On 18 April, he told Erica that the declaration of a state of emergency that he was contemplating "would allow us to detain all the leaders, including Weekes, and that [that] would assist in creating a climate of order and quiet in which one could pass essential legislation, including a Public Order Act to control demonstrations and an amendment to the Trade Union Act limiting any union to one particular industry" (ibid., 296). Clearly Williams was already contemplating introducing the draconian Public Order Act for which Hudson-Phillips would subsequently be made to fall on his sword.

Williams's letters to Erica also seem to provide confirmation that he did not panic during the crisis of mid-April. As he told her in one letter, "The heaviest cross I have to bear is the panic among the Ministers, especially after Robinson's resignation and the call up of the reservists. They can't see that [the call-up] is just a show of force to let the Black Power boys know what they are up against and to reassure the general population. . . . Whoever is losing his head, I am not one of them" (ibid., 295).

The American ambassador had a slightly different assessment of Williams's behaviour. As he wrote, "We cannot overlook [the] possibility that Williams, in normal times a moody person, may have been pushed by tension which he is under, dangerously close to irrationality." He found Williams and Montano "fluctuating between war panic and optimism". The ambassador complained that Williams had not appealed for public support, but instead had "holed himself up in his residence" (US Embassy to US Department of State, 30 April 1970, as cited in ibid., 298).

Restoring Public Order

Between the months of April and November 1970, Trinidad's jails were crowded for the first time with political prisoners. Eighty-seven soldiers and fifty-four militants were arrested and charged variously with treason, sedition and mutiny. The arrested included trade union leaders, university students, graduates and lecturers, not all of whom were centrally involved in the demonstrations. The police, who unlike the soldiers remained loyal to the government, were hastily equipped with the arms that Williams had obtained from the Americans on 22 April, ten years to the day after he had threatened to force them out of the Chaguaramas peninsula that the regiment had come to occupy. During those tension-filled months, there were dramatic manhunts, seizures of documents, reports of hidden weapons being found, charges of harassment in the prisons, and clashes between soldiers and prison officials. Four persons were killed in skirmishes with the police, who, feeling threatened, began making demands that guns be made a regular part of their uniform. A dusk-to-dawn curfew was also imposed, though subsequently relaxed on 1 May.

The intensity of the crisis was heightened considerably on 7 August, when the government introduced the Public Order Bill that it had been threatening since 1965. A draconian piece of legislation, it was a compilation of some of the most repressive colonial laws and a few new ones tailored to suit the contemporary situation in Trinidad. The outcry against the bill was vehement and overwhelming, with criticisms coming not only from radical militants, but also from establishment lawyers, doctors, the unions, the official opposition, university students and the established press. The only major body to endorse the bill openly was the Catholic Church, which spoke through an editorial in the *Catholic News*. A great deal of the support that the PNM had rallied after April evaporated, and on 13 September, Williams withdrew the bill, much to the chagrin of Hudson-Phillips, who offered his resignation. Williams did not accept it.

Williams and his attorney general (who took the blame for the bill) had clearly miscalculated. The bill should never have been introduced in the form in which it appeared, let alone during the last months of the government's life. Even assuming that the government wished to take precautionary measures to prevent a recurrence of the February-to-April crisis when the state of emergency was lifted, it did not take the trouble to explain to a frightened public why it was resurrecting old colonial laws, or why it was felt necessary to set aside basic constitutional freedoms, of which Trinidadians had assumed they would never be deprived. The fact that such laws existed in England or had been used in colonial days was no justification for making them the cornerstone of the Trinidad nation-state. Many people feared that Trinidad was on its way to becoming a typical repressive Third World dictatorship.

Williams was fortunate that the radical opposition was weak and divided. The problem was that its skills were essentially destructive. Its strength lay in its ability to define problems, to lay bare contradictions in society and to mobilize the frustrations that were so widespread at all levels of society. Yet the NJAC lacked the organization to channel into constructive outlets the consciousness and the energies that it had roused so dramatically. Intoxicated by its spectacular but unexpected success, it sought a premature confrontation, hoping to bring the establishment to its knees. As Lloyd Best rightly noted, "NJAC was trying to win by 'knockout' instead of on points when it lacked the capacity to do so. But you can't provoke a revolutionary situation unless you have the resources to take the power – and we did not have them." Best argued that unconventional politics is not necessarily the politics of violence, that it could be a politics of participation and involvement.

Best accused NJAC of simplifying the issues and of refusing to do their intellectual homework:

> The weakness of the Black solidarity movement here is its tendency to over-simplify the issues and to see things in terms of black and white, we vs. they, capitalists vs. workers, intellectual discussion vs. direct action. . . . It is crucial that in the ranks of the dispossessed there [were] no white, but the real war is still between the dispossessed and the over-privileged. . . . To define the issue this way is not to underplay the significance of blackness, but to guard against the danger of racism in reverse. . . . Blowing up Kirpalanis and slapping up white people out of a sense of outrage and resentment will never destroy tyranny. We cannot risk destroying more than we create. We cannot even risk threatening to do so because that would be playing into the hands of reaction. . . . We [must] seek to avoid the kind of "revolution" which by taking a "leap in the dark" succeeds only in replacing one tyranny by another. ("National Crisis", *Tapia*, special issue no. 1, n.d.)

In pursuit of its maximalist strategy, the NJAC failed to realize that only a few of its supporters were ready for revolution, and that the bulk of its support came from people who wanted jobs, better economic and social opportunities for the dispossessed, and black dignity, but wanted this to be achieved short of total revolution. Thus, when the demonstrations began to turn into "Molotov cocktail parties", and began to have the effect of driving away investment and destroying existing plants, many abandoned them. NJAC might have been correct in pointing out that certain kinds of investments should not be encouraged to remain in Trinidad at all, but this was an intellectual viewpoint not shared by those who wanted a job at any cost. As the *Nation* noted, "NJAC refused to recognise the basic facts . . . when they appealed to the masses not to take up the 'bribes' of the Government by accepting jobs on the Special Works Programme. The isolation of the hard-core NJAC elements began when the unemployed registered heavily at the various registration centres" (29 January 1971).

NJAC refused to contest the 1971 election because it associated parliament, elections, parties and other conventional political institutions and processes with "the frequent frustrations felt by our people". What was needed, it believed, were new institutions and processes that genuinely involved the people. They were not bothered by the rising tide of reaction among the middle class and the middle-aged, because its strategy was based on the fact that the bulk of its hard-core support came from the young who had shown a marked contempt for "conventional politics". By the end of 1970, however, the NJAC had become a spent political force.

The White–Black Question

Williams smashed the Black Power movement, but the crisis left deep scars. The population became more racially polarized than it had been, with most of the middle class demanding extreme punishment for the militants who were charged with treason and sedition against "Her Majesty's Government". Middle-class elements accused the radical blacks of being envious of their success, of wanting things for nothing, of being disrespectful towards age and authority, and of mindlessly aping American styles and political techniques that had no relevance to Trinidad, where "after all, power *was* black".

Williams was aware that there were some aspects of the ideology that were indigenous to the region and consequently had authenticity. As he wrote,

> It is immediately obvious that the issue of the constitutional inequality of the blacks has no relevance for the West Indies. But it is absurd to expect black West Indians not to sympathize with and feel part of black American movements for the achievement of human rights by black Americans, or the emancipation of black Africans from white tyranny in Rhodesia, Portuguese Africa, and South Africa, or pride in the historical and cultural past of the peoples of the African continent.
>
> It is also absurd to expect younger people of one of the non-white historically dispossessed groups in the Caribbean not to become, as a result of this impact, more conscious of their cultural deprivations and of the economic and social disabilities still affecting many members of both groups in contemporary Trinidad and Tobago and other parts of the Caribbean. ("PNM Perspectives in the World of the Seventies", *Nation*, 25 September 1970)

He noted that Black Power could not be accepted indiscriminately in a society that consisted of other ethnic groups with equal claims to being treated as full citizens. But he welcomed the new emphasis on Africa and pride in blackness:

> Black people, culturally deprived and insulted for centuries, are now taking pride in origins that they dimly suspect, and are happy to have confirmed. In the last few years there has been an enormous interest in African drumming. At this moment there is a growing revival of interest in African religion and religious practices, with particular emphasis on Shango. There has been for some time a group whose special interest is in Yoruba culture.
>
> It is very certain that the next few years will see a tremendous interest in the study and analysis of African survivals and influences in the entire Caribbean.
>
> Thus all of us had better get used to the idea that African culture is here to stay. It is intellectually constructive and psychologically legitimate. It has its possible dangers

if it is overplayed, if it seeks to impose the very apartheid of which it has been a victim in the past, and if it seeks to dominate and denigrate other cultures which have contributed to Trinidad and Tobago. (*Sunday Guardian*, 29 November 1970)

While black militants did not question Williams's understanding of the historical roots of the Black Power movement in the Caribbean that he himself had done a great deal to stimulate, and that he did do and say "some black things", they complained that he did not do enough during his long ministry to alleviate black oppression. Williams denied that this was the case. As he declared in a nationwide broadcast on 23 March 1970,

> We consciously sought to promote a multiracial society with emphasis on the economic and social upliftment of the two major disadvantaged groups. Our goal has always been Afro-Asian unity. We have consciously sought to promote Black economic power. We have in five years created 1,523 Black small farmers over the country; we have encouraged small businesses in manufacture and tourism; we have, without too much success, sought to promote fishing co-operatives. We have brought free secondary education within the reach of thousands of disadvantaged families who could not dream of it in 1956. We have sought to provide further training for the youths in youth camps, youth centres and trade centres. Our Public Service, at all levels is staffed today almost entirely by nationals, mainly Black. (Nationwide broadcast, 23 May 1970)

The militants conceded all this, but insisted it was not enough for a government that had been in power for fourteen years.

But it is true that Williams and the middle class that brought him to power had in a fundamental sense betrayed the black masses in whose name they governed. The middle class had adopted a lifestyle that was for the most part imitative of whites during the colonial era, a style that had the effect, perhaps unintended, of excluding the bulk of the black masses from a meaningful share of the material wealth in the society. Novelist Earl Lovelace drew attention to the psychological fears that the brown and black middle class had about blackness: "What Afro-Saxons are afraid of is not violence or Black Power. It is blackness. Their blackness frightens them, embarrasses them. Most of their lives have been spent atoning for their black skins. . . . Black Power threatens to upset the psychological adjustment we have made to blackness" (*Trinidad Express*, 21 January 1969).

But while the psychological difficulties that Black Power presented were real, they were reinforced by powerful material considerations. In a society of scarcity, people discriminated, and connections ("contac", to use a local expression) remained important in resource allocation. Mixed bloods who claimed that Black Power was irrelevant in Caribbean society realized that if it were to become the guiding philosophy, the privileges that they and their children enjoyed would have to find a new basis of legitimation and might in fact become untenable.

Access to scarce jobs, educational opportunities and a variety of services was easier for those who were not obviously black. If significant numbers in the society were to accept the fact that "black is beautiful", fundamental revisions would have to be made in the way that status was conferred and legitimized. Blacks who managed to rise despite the restrictiveness of the system and who were anxious to preserve their gains also realized the revolutionary potential of the Black Power movement.

While it was a gross exaggeration to say that all those who had well-paying and status-defining jobs had acquired them because of colour, race or connection, there was a pervasive feeling among many unemployed or lowly placed blacks that this was so and that their own deprivation was due to blackness rather than to laziness or lack of entrepreneurship. The privileged, however, were firmly convinced that what they enjoyed was legitimately acquired, and were genuinely perplexed when they were accused of being "racist" or exploiters of black people.

It is true, however, that the social system had certain built-in behavioural mechanisms that gave a premium to lighter complexions. There was an unarticulated but generally held assumption that it was not tragic if the unemployed and the underfed, the poorly schooled and those with poor health and poor housing were blacks. It was assumed that blacks had a greater capacity to tolerate deprivation; either that, or their level of expectation was so low that they could safely be ignored, while the bulk of the resources were allocated to those who already had privilege, the "haves" and the "have mores".

The Black Power movement helped to increase race and social consciousness in Trinidadian society. More than half of the calypsoes sung during the 1971 carnival were on the theme of Black Power (both for and against), and a significant proportion of the carnival bands portrayed African themes. The 1971 carnival queen was also unambiguously black, as was her runner-up, a circumstance that was unprecedented in the history of the competition. Reports are that militants had threatened to "smash up" things if a black girl was not selected queen, and there is evidence that the competition was rigged to ensure that result. The newspapers also began to give far more coverage to Africa and black struggles in the Americas than had been the case earlier. Beneath the joviality and cosmopolitanism that normally characterized Trinidad society, one sensed that economic and cultural decolonization had been taken a step further as a result of the "February Revolution". The politicians sensed it and were busily trying to cater to the new mood. No political party in the 1971 election – not even the PNM – sponsored white candidates as was the case in 1966, when four were returned to the legislature. Public policies also began to reflect the new emphasis on blackness in Trinidad society.

27 The One-Horse Elections of 1971

There was much uncertainty as to whether the events of 1970 had mortally wounded Dr Williams and the PNM as a political force. Some felt that the opposition elements would succeed in their attempt to dislodge the PNM, this time using conventional strategies. Others felt that a thermidorean reaction had set in, and that the revolution had revolutionized the counter-revolution. Two political parties mounted serious challenges to Williams in 1971. They were the Action Committee of Democratic Citizens (ACDC), a group formed by A.N.R. Robinson, and the DLP. There were several other small radical parties and movements, some with a Marxist flavour, that sought to continue the struggle. The most significant of these were Tapia and the National Union of Freedom Fighters. The latter chose to adopt a "guerilla" strategy then prevalent in Latin America and other parts of the so-called Third World.

Robinson, who until April 1970 was regarded as the logical successor to Williams, complained publicly that "there were definite signposts to danger" in the community: "There are many people who know of wrongs being committed . . . but are afraid of victimization of one kind or another. In fact, there are many people who will not do their jobs for fear of losing their jobs." Robinson lamented the "epidemic of silence" that prevailed, and warned that fear to speak was one of the major causes of the breakdown of democratic regimes in newly independent countries. Robinson expressed concern that the PNM was playing the fool in parliament and "was heading straight towards a military *coup d'etat*". Corruption and the unwillingness or inability of the prime minister to do anything about it was also said to be a serious problem, as was his tendency to zigzag on basic policy issues. This was particularly evident in his handling of the economy:

> Today it is sell wholesale, tomorrow it is buy wholesale, and hardly anybody seems to know the full details of the transaction. All these causes have combined to produce a national crisis of the first dimension. They continue up to today, in most cases in even

more exaggerated form. The gap between the government and people is wider than ever. Junior civil servants are catapulted into ministerial positions without any reference to party or people. The unemployment grows and the waste increases. While the population increases, the voters' list decreases. (*Trinidad Guardian*, 12 February 1971)

Robinson, as we have seen, also bitterly opposed the detention without charge of Black Power militants and the Public Order Bill introduced in August 1970. He described the bill as a "series of prohibitions and penalties all of which give power to one man", the minister of national security:

> It is a shameful declaration of no confidence in the people of Trinidad and Tobago. If it goes through, Trinidad and Tobago will become the private family plantation of one man. The rest of us will be half slave and half free. The Bill is worse than any colonial legislation; it is insulting, divisive and abominable. Nothing will entrench division and hatred in this community more than that Act. It must be withdrawn, destroyed and thrown into the waste-paper basket of history. (*Trinidad Guardian,* 12 February 1971, 12)

Williams was at the time minister of national security, minister of finance, minister of planning and development, minister of local government, minister of Tobago affairs, and minister of external affairs.

Robinson argued that the only solution to the problem facing the country was for the government to resign and make arrangements for the formation of an interim government that would prepare the country for elections: "The electorate must be permitted to determine, in a free and fair election, at the earliest opportunity, whether one who has led us into the present situation can lead us out again. This has not been the experience in other countries, particularly newly independent countries. It is not likely to be the experience in Trinidad and Tobago. The Public Order Bill is testimony to this. . . . No more substantial measures should be attempted by this Government" (*Trinidad Guardian*, 12 February 1971).

Robinson claimed that the PNM could be defeated in the 1971 elections, and that Williams himself would be beaten. He pointed out that Williams only received 5,478 votes out of a possible 13,800 in his Port of Spain South constituency in the 1966 elections and assumed that about 2,000 of these had either defected to other movements or did not bother to register. Indeed, according to figures released by the Elections and Boundaries Commission, Williams's constituency recorded the highest drop in electoral registration between 1966 and 1970 – from 12,801 to 7,728. Said Robinson, "That is why there has been tinkering about with the boundaries, why the boundaries [of Port of Spain South] had to be extended to include parts of Barataria." Drawing attention to the fact that the PNM's share of the popular vote had also been falling dramatically since 1956, Robinson concluded that "the PNM [was] not truly representative of the population" (Ibid.).

The PNM's percentage of the total vote did in fact drop from 57 per cent in 1961 to 52 per cent in 1966. Disaffection was even more evident during the local elections held in June 1968, after a lapse of nine years. Only 32 per cent of the registered electorate went to the polls, and in some urban areas, such as San Fernando, the turnout was as low as 20 per cent. Although the PNM won sixty-nine of the one hundred seats (fourteen were uncontested), it got the support of only 50 per cent of these hard-core voters. It is also worth noting that for the first time, a rebel PNM candidate was able to defeat a regular who had the active backing of the party high-command. And there was of course the possibility that Williams could be defeated. And the question that many asked was, "Who would replace him?"

But Who We Go Put?

Lloyd Best founded the Tapia House Group in 1969. Its party emblem, the tapia house, symbolized Best's belief that genuine reconstruction must begin from the bottom up, using material such as mud and palm leaves with which the folk were familiar. Establishing the group was regarded as a gesture of protest against some of Best's colleagues in the New World Group who had opted for conventional political activity. Best expressed disdain for what he referred to as "doctor politics". He argued that all the movements that had appeared in the Caribbean failed because they were based on devotion to a single leader. In Trinidad, Cipriani, Butler, Solomon, Williams, Capildeo, Millette and even Granger failed because they did not organize genuine grass-roots movements; they assumed that all that was needed to transform Caribbean society was to capture and manipulate existing institutions of the state. Best felt that "we have to stop being duped by personalities into forming now-for-now political parties. We have to discard the Westminster parliamentary model and design a form of government appropriate to our needs" (*Tapia*, 9 August 1970).

Best asserted that the system of government established in Trinidad and Tobago had no roots in the people. But it was not true to say that the independence constitution was imposed by the Colonial Office. It is far more accurate to say that Williams and others borrowed metropolitan institutions uncritically, and that the bulk of the population simply assumed that these were the only acceptable alternatives – they knew about nothing else.

Best and the Tapia Group were scornful of Williams and the PNM: "The Little King cannot even organise a dance. He has promised at least six re-organisations of the civil service and countless reorganisations of the PNM. But his overriding need for sycophants, flatterers and news-carriers and his insistence on perpetually demonstrating who is head-boy have made any serious improvement impossible. . . . No Afro-Saxon King can afford any real decentralisation of power" (*Tapia*, 9 August 1970).

Best accused Williams of having become a traditional Caribbean *caudillo*, a "Papa Doc" who relied on bribes, intimidation and terror to maintain control, now that he had lost the "mandate of heaven". But he did not see this as a personal failing on the part of Williams. "The Williams failure is a failure not of motive or of skill; it is a failure of messianic method" (*Tapia*, 31 January 1971). Referring to the question that was being so frequently asked in Trinidad by those who felt the need for change – "But who we go put?" – Best warned that the issue was not "who we put, but how we change the system". The time had come to "lift our politics above the maneuverings and posturing of the kingmakers and would-be kings. To the extent that we succeed, it will be a matter of "the king is dead, long live the people". Tapia believed that what Trinidad needed most was a radically new and popularly based constitution. To forge this, a constituent assembly consisting of representatives of all recognized groups and institutions must be summoned. The assembly, which would be an informal government, would not only work out a new constitutional settlement, but also define the basic policy alternatives that the country would pursue in the years ahead. As Tapia noted, "For the first time in this country, constitutional change will be initiated from below and not by colonial officials, party conventions, cabinet meetings and rigged Queen's Hall discussions. Who will summon this Constituent Assembly? Not the Government and not Williams. Only the people can do it. When the state breaks down, only the people have the moral authority to set it up again" (*Tapia*, 10 November 1969).

Tapia believed that a great deal of work still had to be done before the group formally became or joined a political party. For the time being, they were content to work at the community level in active cooperation with people. Out of this collaborative effort a new political culture and new policy alternatives might well begin to emerge. In his recommendations for a participatory democracy, Best indeed came very close to what Williams was preaching in the early days of his ministry:

> The time will certainly come when we will need a political party. But if it is to be an authentic political party and not just the electoral apparatus of another Doctor or set of Doctors, it needs to be based on confident, competent membership, well organised in the constituencies. Since we are beginning from a position where people have had little experience of community collaboration and political participation, where the Central Government dominates the lives of the population, and where local leadership is systematically suppressed by social and economic processes, the strategy must be to undertake schemes which will promote grass-roots development. ("Constitutional Reform: Tapia's Proposals", *Tapia Pamphlets* 4–5, 13 June 1971)

Tapia conceded that Williams and the PNM would win the next election. Its strategy, however, was to try to make that victory as pyrrhic as possible by inducing the electorate to boycott the election and by harassing the PNM after its "victory". As Best noted, "There is no sense in which we can 'lose' the election. We will be getting stronger every day and we will be calling the tune for the government. The PNM may reign, but it would not be allowed to rule. The alternatives are not PNM or chaos, but PNM and chaos" (ibid.).

The Democratic Labour Party

One of the most significant political events of the 1971 election was the fact that the main conventional opposition parties, the DLP led by Vernon Jamadar and the ACDC, withdrew from the contest. The two parties had coalesced, had spent a great deal of money advertising their programme, and appeared to many to be gearing themselves for a bitter contest. Three days before nomination day and two weeks before election day (9 May), Robinson declared to a stunned nation that he would not contest any "mock" elections, nor support any party or candidate who did. Some of his party colleagues who were on the rostrum with him at the time of his announcement, and who in their speeches had talked about going to the polls, were dumbfounded. Jamadar complained bitterly and angrily about Robinson's unilateral and autocratic behaviour. Williams, for his part, dismissed Robinson as a "damn fool" and a "half-wit", and ridiculed the ACDC–DLP with the remark that its "marriage" of December had ended in "divorce" by May. He also told the "no" voters that they "could jump in the Gulf of Paria", as far as he was concerned. "Who did they think they were fooling?"

Robinson justified his behaviour in terms of principle. He claimed that there were too many irregularities in the electoral system, and that the use of voting machines and other procedures was intended to legitimize a predetermined result. Robinson insisted on having the voting age reduced to eighteen years, and access for all parties to the state-owned electronic media. His overall demand was that "the country must have unequivocal assurance of the validity of the electoral system". Jamadar, however, felt that the strategy was a mistake. Robinson was putting at risk the integrity of the constitutional order and the rights of citizens. In his view, the issues facing the nation were much too serious for the ACDC–DLP to abstain from voting. These issues should take precedence over electoral reform. Jamadar expressed fear that another system of government could well emerge if the PNM won all thirty-six seats. He was aware that the radicals were talking about "taking revolutionary steps to change the government". Robinson felt otherwise. In his view, a successful election boycott would indicate clearly that the existing political system was no longer legitimate, and that the ensuing crisis would generate new social demands for a redefinition of Trinidad's political economy. Anything short of a fundamental reappraisal of the political and economic system would constitute a "mockery". Robinson's critics felt that an equally powerful explanation was his awareness that the alliance could not win the election. Like most opposition leaders, he did not relish being on the opposition bench, especially since he had himself enjoyed power for fourteen years. He would have Williams's "crown" or nothing at all.

DLP leaders were certain that they would have retained the twelve seats that they previously held, and that there was a good chance that the ACDC could win the extra seats needed to defeat the PNM. They were thus puzzled by Robinson's campaign strategy of concentrating on "sure" DLP constituencies, and there was speculation that having failed to break up the PNM, he was hell-bent on smashing the DLP. Some even believed the unlikely story that there was a racially motivated plot between Robinson and the PNM to destroy the DLP! There was no truth to this collusion thesis, but the DLP strongly believed that Robinson's aim was to "emasculate" the DLP as an organization. Radical groups were elated by the collapse of the merger. Williams, who was certain the PNM would be returned, was dismayed, and invited the DLP to change places with the jackasses in the canefields.

Only two parties challenged the PNM electorally. The more important was Bhadase Maraj's Democratic Liberation Party, which offered no manifesto or programme. Maraj argued that the no-vote strategy would lead to the emergence of a dictatorship, and that Williams would not be the one blamed. The African National Congress, of which few people knew much, presented seven candidates. The PNM was unopposed in eight constituencies. The election campaign was marked by sporadic incidents of violence, including someone throwing homemade bombs into the headquarters of the ruling party and into the homes of the commander in chief of the defence forces and a PNM minister. Attempts were also made to assassinate the commander in chief of the coast guard and the chief state prosecutor in one of the courts martial. Both were seriously injured.

The Democratic Liberation Party made little impact on the electorate and was supported by only 14,921 voters, or 4.22 per cent of those registered. The party did poorly even in areas heavily populated by Indians. It gained the support of no more than 4.88 per cent of the votes cast in areas previously held by the Labour Party. Much to everyone's surprise, Maraj himself lost to a virtually unknown Afro-creole in an area that was more than 90 per cent Hindu. The same pattern held for other DLP areas, even though PNM support actually declined in nine of these constituencies. Although PNM supporters claim that the capture of DLP seats represented a triumph for their party, a more likely explanation was that the hard-core PNM supporters who came out to vote were actively assisted by the DLP, which was less concerned about a PNM victory than about the prospect that the Democratic Liberation Party would become the official opposition. Despite the fact that the DLP endorsed the no-vote campaign, it surreptitiously campaigned for the PNM in Maraj's constituency.

The PNM lived up to its claim of being the premier organized party in Trinidad and Tobago. Despite strong pressures to resign, or at least to introduce pre-electoral reforms, Williams, sensing the political confusion of the opposition, called an election, which the opposition claims caught it by surprise. Using a campaign style that resembled that of the "old world", which it had come to bury in 1956, Williams tried hard to look less "Afro-Saxon" by abandoning his proverbial coat and tie in favour of an open shirt and neckerchief. During the 1971 carnival season, he visited a large number of steelband yards and calypso tents and generally tried to project an image that was "blacker" culturally than had been the case since independence. The popular view was that Williams was "playing mas" (that is, masquerading) for the benefit of the electorate. Similar visits were made to Muslim festivals. In spite of this new "mod" and "Afro" image, the power base of the party had come to rest more and more on old blacks, the fair-skinned and the established. This silent off-white minority made a special effort to turn out to vote for the PNM, which they now saw as the last defendable fortress against chaos and subversion.

The PNM claimed that between June 1969 and June 1971 its membership rose by 6,610 to approximately 60,000. Membership is said to have increased dramatically after April 1970. Many a citizen who had formerly been on the sidelines felt he must record his support for a party that had governed democratically for 15 years. Of the 6,610 new members, 5,787 were adults and only 923 were youths. New membership was heaviest in the middle-class constituency of St Ann's. New recruits were difficult to come by in the inner city – in central Port of Spain there were 52 new recruits, of whom only one was a youth – and in the rural areas (*Trinidad Guardian*, 29 September 1971).

To the great surprise of everyone in Trinidad and Tobago and the wider Caribbean, and much to Williams's embarrassment, the elections gave the PNM complete control of parliament, making Trinidad a de facto one-party state. But the PNM victory was not as unequivocal as appeared initially. As the opposition had hoped, there was massive non-voting: of the 352,802 persons who were registered, only 118,549, or 33.6 per cent, voted. Of these, 99,770, or 28.28 per cent, voted for the PNM. If all thirty-six seats had been contested, however, and if the average turnout in the twenty-eight constituencies is to be taken as a guide, the PNM might well have increased its share of the voting electorate to somewhere in the vicinity of 43 per cent. But this was still the lowest turnout in Trinidad's postwar history. Intimidation and fear of what might happen on polling day discouraged many from turning up at the polls. The absence of meaningful competition had the same effect, even though the issue of voting was the central theme in the election. Many would-be PNM supporters assumed that there was no threat, and that there was therefore no need to be inconvenienced by going to the voting booth.

The details of the election results indicate clearly that the PNM would have retained all the seats it won in 1966 except the one held by Robinson if the ACDC–DLP had contested the election. Surprisingly, the party increased its support in six constituencies, and in all but three others its loss of support was below 10 per cent. The decrease of support over the twenty-eight constituencies was 19,120, while the gain was 2,865, giving a net loss of 16,225 votes. In Williams's constituency, the decrease was 1,126, or 8.09 per cent, and in no constituency did more than 45 per cent of the electorate vote. Sixteen constituencies, including all those formerly controlled by the DLP, were won by less than one-third of the eligible votes, and in ten cases by less than one-quarter. In two cases, seats were won by less than one-eighth of the eligible votes.

While it is true that the erosion of support for the PNM was not as dramatic as expected – only 4.8 per cent over the twenty-eight constituencies contested, if one takes into account the fact that the eligible electorate in 1971 was lower than it was in 1969 by more than one hundred thousand – it is hard to avoid the conclusion that the PNM's victory was a hollow one. Williams was certain, however, that he was still the source of power and authority. As he declared on the eve of polling day, in language reminiscent of Albert Gomes's 1955 statement that "I am the Government of Trinidad and Tobago": "I'm the one who has the power here. When I say 'come', you 'cometh', and when I say 'go', you 'goeth' " (*Newsweek*, 7 June 1971).

Williams pretended that he was not unduly bothered by the fact that there was no legal opposition in parliament, but he did feel it necessary to promise that democratic procedures would be scrupulously respected, and that there would be dialogue with the nation on all major issues. As the government declared via the traditional throne speech,

> In the face of the reality of the political alignment in Parliament, [this] Government will adopt four types of measures to ensure that alternative views are heard and respected. It will seek to elicit the widest possible comment on its proposed legislation before the legislation is passed. Government proposals will be circulated as widely as possible, and will allow for the longest possible period of consultation with the people without interfering with the efficiency of government. . . .
>
> Wherever possible, legislation will first be introduced into the Senate, to the extent that this can be done constitutionally, and without departing too radically from the established parliamentary tradition of the paramountcy of the elected chamber, [this] Government will further enlist the assistance of the Senate in respect of Joint Committees of both Houses of Parliament. The first such Committee to be immediately appointed will consider the question of the reduction of the voting age and the age of the legal majority. (*Trinidad Guardian*, 19 June 1971)

But despite Williams's bland assertion that there was no political or constitutional crisis and that the PNM had won the election, there was a large body of opinion in the country that the PNM was neither a legal nor a legitimate government. The *Express* spoke for many when it declared, "The results of the 1971 General Elections [do] not amount to a victory for the Government. The unprecedented winning by the PNM of all the seats in Parliament simply [makes] obvious the serious crisis which the country has been staring in the eye for a long time now" (*Trinidad Express*, 26 May 1971).

Robinson, who lost a great deal of credibility during and after the campaign, also claimed that the PNM had no moral authority or mandate to govern, and warned that anyone who accepted a position in the regime should expect no respect from the country: "To accept a senatorship would be to sell the country for a mess of pottage. Let us see how the privileged section of the community will behave." He further noted that few people of any political significance contested the election (*Trinidad Express*, 6 June 1971).

Robinson argued that a situation in which a party had the support of only 28 per cent of the electorate and had won all the seats was "subversive" of the constitution. He accused the "grave-yard" government of the PNM of using illegal devices to get around the 1962 constitution, which provided for a leader of the opposition who had the responsibility for nominating four persons to the senate. The reference here is to Williams's gauche and unsuccessful attempt to get the leader of the opposition in the former parliament to nominate four senators on the pretext that until the new parliament met, he still held that post! Robinson criticized the governor general for asking the PNM to form the government. He felt that the governor general should have declared a state of emergency and appointed an interim government, which would arrange within a month for electoral reform including voting by ballot box and the proper conduct of elections (ibid.). This proposal was clearly unrealistic, and received support from no other group. The ACDC, which changed its name to the Democratic Action Congress (DAC), also took the view that there should be no constitutional reform before new elections were held.

Williams ridiculed Robinson's proposals, especially the question of having the governor general declare a state of emergency. As he told the PNM, "Imagine last year this same man opposed the creation of the State of Emergency, and now he wants the Governor General to declare a State of Emergency." Williams also declared that he could not be expected to resign because the opposition did not contest the election. "We got our vote. What do you want us to do? Stop a race because one horse did not go?" The fact that there was no opposition in parliament was not new, Williams stressed, "because for eighteen months the DLP had said nothing and on occasions had walked out and left us to carry on".

Despite opposition, Williams named a sixteen-member cabinet and advised the governor general to name thirteen party and seven independent senators whose names were proposed by some of the major corporate bodies in the society. The four opposition senatorships were simply left vacant after the former leader of the opposition, Vernon Jamadar, refused the governor general's curious and cynical invitation to him to name four persons.

Even though parliament was legally constituted, the spirit of the constitution and its conventions that require consultation between the prime minister and the leader of the opposition were not fulfilled. But constitutions cannot provide for every political "accident", and it is not clear what opposition voices would have said if a party or a coalition with great moral and popular authority had emerged and had won all the seats. The legal problem would have been the same, even though the moral circumstances would have been different. There is really no way to avoid the conclusion that the crisis in Trinidad and Tobago in 1971 was political rather than constitutional, and that the opposition was guilty, perhaps deliberately, of formalism. The real opposition to the PNM after 1962 had always been outside of parliament – the trade unions, the newspapers, and elements in the university community and in the Chamber of Commerce.

Despite Williams's political bravado, he conceded the strength of the opposition campaign by appointing an independent high-powered commission to hear testimony and prepare a draft new constitution. The commission was chaired by the former chief justice, Sir Hugh Wooding.[1] The opposition questioned the legitimacy of a constitutional commission. As Lloyd Best asserted,

> The government's decision to establish a constitutional commission . . . represents the height of executive impertinence. The decision could not be more strictly in the logic of Crown colony government. It maintains the tradition of government from above and therefore misses the whole point of the February Revolution. . . . If Williams had called a constitutional commission . . . between October 1968 and April 1970 . . . it would have been quite feasible for the Commission to initiate meaningful reforms acceptable to the entire population. Now it is too late because it is the bona-fides of the executive which is the issue of the day. . . . If there is to be a constitutional commission, only a constituent assembly or some kind of citizens' conference can have the right to appoint it. (*Tapia*, n.d., 8)

But majority opinion appeared willing to accept Williams's guarantee of an independent commission as an acceptable compromise to Tapia's proposal for a constituent assembly of citizens, provided that the PNM did not insist on having the final say. The DLP agreed to cooperate, and both leading daily newspapers endorsed the idea. Nothing was said about who was to have the final say on the commission's recommendations.

While it could be argued that the PNM and Williams had lost the mandate of heaven, it is clear that the opposition had failed to win it. Although Best, the NJAC and others had articulated a number of brilliant ideas, many of these had not been carefully thought out or related to the contemporary realities of Trinidadian society. It was unreasonable of the opposition to expect Williams to resign after the election when it was evident to everyone in the country, including Williams's strongest critics, that the alternatives offered by the opposition were fragmentation and political irresponsibility. The country was looking for an alternative to Williams and the opposition had allowed itself to be misled into believing that the best strategy for defeating Williams was to boycott the election.

The difficulty with the leaders of the opposition movements was that they all wanted to be the new king. Each believed he was brighter and more legitimate than the other, and no one was willing to defer in the interest of unity. Best and Tapia talked about "new politics" and refused alliances just as the PNM had done at the inception of its career. But the PNM learned that politics involved compromise and alliances and managed to outwit all its rivals. During the post-independence years, the electorate was treated to a parade of new parties all of which had the same goal – overthrowing Williams. But none could muster much popular following, simply because they lacked organizational credibility.

This fear of confusion and extremism was what led many, even the business community, to remain with the PNM when they would have been happier with an alternative. Williams cleverly exploited the weaknesses of the opposition, and was convinced that the worst was over and that the party could hold onto power for another term if not longer. He recognized, however, that he and the "class of 1956" had to give way to younger elites. As he explained when announcing the composition of the new government, "If . . . the Government appears to be unduly large . . . put the cost down to expenditure on training" (*Trinidad Express*, 28 May 1971). Williams appointed a cabinet with five new faces and unburdened himself of a great deal of his vast ministerial responsibilities. He declared that he would concern himself with things such as national awards and public holidays, constitutional matters, information, public relations, training, supervision, coordination and nation-building. This was still a large portfolio, but was considerably smaller than that held previously. It is also worth noting that there were few men in the new cabinet powerful and independent enough to stand up to Williams, who was, in any event, congenitally incapable of any real decentralization of power.

Some hoped that Williams would phase himself out of Trinidad politics before he was forced out rudely, as were Butler, Solomon, Gomes, Maraj and others. A former political colleague of his, Dennis Mahabir, even urged this course upon him. As Mahabir wrote,

> The explosive years arrived. The gap between Eric Williams and the country is not a cliché. Our national heroes are too few. Those we have we do not cherish. Let us then hope that the country will have the co-operation of Eric Williams and that he will go out with grace and dignity. Let him lay down his troubled crown now and write some

more history. The nation will forgive him for his blunders of recent years, his ambivalence and failures. But it will remember him for his courage in 1956. And in the years to come people may even worship his memory as a national hero. (*Trinidad Express*, 25 September 1971)

At the annual convention of the PNM in September 1971, Williams, who was then sixty years old, hinted that he was thinking of retiring soon. "The time approaches," he said, "when, in the words of your popular song, like a bridge over troubled waters, I will lay me down" (ibid.). He was not prepared, however, to anoint an heir apparent. Stung by the behaviour of his "traitorous deputy", A.N.R. Robinson, Williams appointed three deputy political leaders without indicating which of the three, if any, was being groomed as his successor. The three deputies were Kamaluddin Mohammed, Errol Mahabir, and George Chambers. They were made responsible for legislative, party matters, and policy matters respectively. Of the three, Mohammed was senior, having been with the party from the beginning. Tough, durable and resourceful, Mohammed nevertheless had many detractors who believed that he had used his office to amass a fortune. Many Afro-Trinidadians opposed him and Mahabir on racial grounds.

Many of Williams's critics were sceptical about his announced intention, which they viewed as a clever strategy to take the steam out of the campaign against him. It was also claimed that by appointing a troika deputy leadership, he was generating the sort of party intrigue that would provide him with the excuse to hang onto office.

The enterprise of decolonization, begun so hopefully in 1955, had by 1971 reached a major impasse. Government and opposition accused each other of ruling or attempting to rule by the gun and by declarations of states of emergency. Williams believed that there existed in Trinidad "an extremist, anarchist element dedicated to murder, mayhem, kidnaps and violent revolution". The opposition on the other hand claimed that guns, force and official violence had become the order of the day and that the corrupt holy alliance that brutalized the people – the civil service, the church, the police, and the white power structure – had to be completely destroyed before a new edifice could be built.

28   Farewell and Return

One of the strategies that Williams adopted following the 1971 election in order to buy political time was the appointment in June 1971 of the Wooding Constitution Commission, to explore *de novo* the entire question of the appropriateness of the constitutional arrangements under which Trinidad and Tobago was then governed. The strategy had the effect of giving the impression that elections would be held some time shortly after the constitution was revised. In fact, from time to time Williams explicitly linked the holding of new elections to the completion of the reform exercise. It was a clever strategy that helped to take the wind out of the sails of the opposition, because a large part of the attentive public appeared to have faith in the integrity of the commission and its chairman. Only later did it become clear that the constitutional exercise was part of an incremental strategy that Williams designed to help the PNM stay alive politically without having to resort to repression.

The strategy was probably not deliberate *ab initio,* but a combination of circumstances led it to become so. The radical opposition, however, clearly believed that the exercise was from the beginning a patent attempt to sidetrack demands for immediate elections, and that without it, the PNM would have been forced to respond to their demands. Even if the claims of the opposition were correct, it seems clear that other options were available to Williams. Indeed, within a year of the elections and the "political and constitutional crisis", it had become clear to all except those who always believe in imminent cataclysm that there was no unequivocal popular demand for an immediate election. In October 1972, Williams told a cheering party that contrary to what he had said a year before about his willingness to lay down his burdens and step down, he had no intention of quitting political life and would be honoured to lead it to victory in another election. He also indicated that he was prepared to concede to opposition demands for lowering the voting age, for abolishing the voting machines and for electoral reform, because he was confident that the PNM would win, whatever the system used. As he told an enthusiastic party audience,

> I couldn't care less whether we use voting machines, sewing machines, computers, ballot box, Indian ballot box, cardboard box, soap box, show of hands, voice vote or acclamation. As far as I am concerned, "same khaki pants". . . . They ask for constitutional reform, they will get constitutional reform. They want electoral reform, they will get electoral reform. They say they want reduction of the voting age, they will get reduction of the voting age. (*Trinidad Express*, 1 October 1972)

The decision to abandon the machines and to concede the need for electoral reform was a major concession to public opinion that helped to dispel some of the existing political tension.

A number of additional factors helped to abort the demands for fresh elections. One was the question of just what alternative there was to the PNM, a question asked persistently throughout the period. Although many persons considered themselves qualified to inherit "the mandate of heaven", the public remained sceptical and continued to ask "Who we go put?" The Tapia House Group insisted that the proper question was "What we go put?", but for the public, the two questions were closely interwined. Tapia claimed that there was a grave constitutional crisis, that the social contract which bound the community together had come apart, and that it was necessary to summon a constituent assembly that would lay the foundations for a new participatory political community.

At one point, Williams appeared to have solved the problem for those who were scrambling to dislodge him. A little more than a year after he had told the PNM that he would be with them "till death do us part", he told the stunned fifteenth annual convention that he was quitting office. In his farewell address, which sounded like a funeral oration, Williams itemized the various reasons why he was not seeking re-election as political leader of the PNM. The first was what seemed an admission of the impotence of Caribbean states in the face of the powerful multinational corporations:

> Small governments with gross domestic products in most cases far below the assets of a multinational corporation, acting independently, sometimes with the narrowest of national interests in mind, cannot possibly hope to compete against an international conglomerate with a coordinated policy. If a third world country or small Caribbean country finds it hard to keep up with the age of jumbo jets, oil super tankers and massive new electricity generating sets which prove even in developed countries that something can sometimes be too big, they cannot possibly hope to complete with a conglomerate like ITT. (*Trinidad Guardian*, 30 September 1973)

The problem, he said, was rendered far more difficult because of the increasing tendency towards fragmentation in the Caribbean. To quote Williams again,

> After all these years, I get the powerful feeling that the Caribbean has moved back towards colonialism instead of away from it, and that I am a voice in the wilderness in

my campaign for Caribbean integration. . . . It is now clear beyond any possibility of doubt that Caribbean integration will not be achieved in the foreseeable future and that the reality is continued Caribbean disunity and even perhaps the reaffirmation of colonialism. (Ibid.)

Williams also expressed disillusionment with the Caribbean's reliance on tourism which he felt was corrupting and dislocating the economies of the region. "What doth it profit a man if he gains the industrial world and loses his soul and identity" (ibid.).

Another reason given was the lack of national discipline and community consciousness that he once boasted obtained in the society but which continued to prevail after seventeen years of PNM rule. Williams was admitting that the PNM had failed in its ambition to create a disciplined, cohesive society, though his disposition was to blame the society for having betrayed him rather than to accept that his leadership style and strategy were in large part responsible for the paralysing crisis that the nation faced.

On his visit to Cuba in June 1973, Williams had declared that Castro was far more fortunate than he was in that he had a disciplined society. As he told the Cubans, "If we could think that in the next five or six years we could achieve the same general mobilization of the talents of the young people of the country for future service to the country, we would sleep much more easily at night than we do now." Williams was particularly impressed by Cuba's work ethic, and wondered aloud as to what Cuba would have been able to do if it had Trinidad and Tobago's oil resources. Lamented Williams, "Today, 17 years later, the disease of individualism is more pronounced than ever, and such national movement as there is does not go beyond the increased participation in Carnival and the general desire to migrate." Williams was embittered that citizens were not prepared to give up their "freedoms", even in the face of serious crises, whether polio epidemics or outlaws in the hills threatening the peace of the community.

Williams was gravely disturbed by the outbreak of "guerilla" warfare in Trinidad and Tobago in the years after 1970, warfare that had claimed the lives of fifteen persons, most of whom belonged to the National Union of Freedom Fighters, a group that emerged out of the events of 1970. Three of the slain persons were policemen. Many of the "guerillas" were the sons and daughters of middle-class parents who had abandoned conventional careers and comforts in a misguided attempt to remove his regime by force. The report of the Wooding Constitution Commission (see chapter 29) captured the mood of the country when it noted that

the survival of constitutional and parliamentary politics is being challenged as never before in Trinidad and Tobago. Many believe that the institutional channels of constitutional politics no longer respond unless there is some dramatic gesture of confrontation such as a "sick out", a "go slow", a boycott or a march to Whitehall to see the Prime Minister. Some groups have even called on citizens to consider withholding the payment of taxes. Secondary school children have begun to adopt strategies of confrontation and non-negotiable demands. Others have carried this belief into even more extreme action by resorting to armed confrontation. The society has painfully to adjust itself to stories of shootouts, killings and woundings, of early morning searches and of widespread public fear of victimisation by one side or the other. There is danger that we may become insensitive by exposure to the human tragedy in the situation and accept this state of affairs as part of our political culture. Violence breeds violence. Violence or the fear of it invariably tends to make the citizens more receptive to strong police and military procedures. As the process of conflict escalates, traditional civilian, legal and constitutional procedures are short-circuited in favour of more "efficient" methods of law and order. Although all social change involves a measure of conflict, no democracy can long survive in the midst of unrestrained political violence. (1974, 5)

Williams denigrated the "guerilla" movement, which was spearheaded by National Union of Freedom Fighters, by saying that it could not be compared to other movements in Latin America, Asia and Africa in that it lacked a genuine ideological base and a clearly defined external enemy. He blamed the clergy and press for exaggerating and sensationalizing the issue by repeating uncritically charges of repression and brutality when the security forces sought to defend themselves or flush out the guerillas. To quote Williams,

[W]hen we come to talk glibly of "guerillas" in Trinidad and Tobago, one comes up against the basic facts that (a) there is no foreign or colonial aggressor, (b) the mass of the population is not alienated, and (c) to the extent that there is significant and legitimate political dissatisfaction, the population is not satisfied that all the avenues of constitutional political opposition have been exhausted. At the same time, there has been no fundamental ideology associated with the so-called "guerillas", except such vague phrases as power to the people, the people taking over their own communities (whatever that means), or national control of the economy (which would have less meaning in Trinidad than in most other places because of the steady progress in this direction over the years without disrupting the very economy which it sought to control). (*Trinidad Guardian*, 3 April 1974)

As far as he was concerned, the "movement" was nothing more than an "extension of an international movement of crime and violence using 'perhaps' guerilla tactics and techniques as well as hard drugs". It was all mimicry and masquerade.

The National Union of Freedom Fighters was in fact an extremist spin-off from the NJAC that had spearheaded the Black Power movement but which had retreated to cultural nationalism. In one of its various broadsheets, the union declared that "ever since we took up arms in the year 1968 to pursue this goal, our ranks have been reduced by nine deaths; eight in battle and one murdered.

We have seized hundreds of thousands of dollars from enemy banks to finance his destruction, and several weapons to ensure his downfall". Far from lamenting the deaths of their comrades, they declared that their deaths were "as meaningful as the oxygen in our lungs. We define death in our own terms and do not fear it. . . . All people do not have to take up arms to defend themselves, for everybody is not a guerilla. . . . We have no doubt that victory shall be our own whatever the cost" (*Trinidad Guardian*, 23 September 1973; see also Millette 1995b, 625–54). The National Union of Freedom Fighters claimed that the arguments in favour of alternatives to armed revolution had been discredited all over the world.

Williams also lamented his government's inability to secure national consensus on just how far the state should go in attempting to bring the economy under national control. The employers were totally opposed to any intervention, while radical dissidents were making unreasonable demands for nationalization of the oil industry:

> On the one hand there are the dissidents clamouring for nationalization – as if we could ever find the money required for the actual exploitation of what has been discovered so far plus the continued exploration now in progress. On the other hand, there are those who talk as if we should just leave everything to the tender mercies of the foreign companies, notwithstanding the significant developments to the contrary in other oil producing countries. (*Trinidad Guardian*, 2 April 1974)

Williams was also bitter about the breakdown of the economy and the planning process. Not only was there not enough money and human resources to do that which had to be done. More serious was the fact that "[b]udgeting and planning have denigrated into a mad scramble at the public trough by a number of lobbyists, whether individuals or villages or ethnic groups or church groups, on the basis of victory to the strongest or the one with the loudest mouth and the devil take the hindmost – exactly what the PNM laughed at unmercifully and condemned at its birth in 1956, to the plaudits of the population" (ibid., 30 September 1973).

Williams likewise complained about the unhappy relationship that existed between politicians and civil servants whom he would later describe as "an ambitious minority bent on taking over the state", the refusal of his ministers to declare their assets and those of their near relatives as he had required them to, the unwillingness of the PNM members on various legislative units to pay their levies for the upkeep of the party, and the inability of ministers to respect confidences. He also expressed regret about the inability of the party to attract the sort of persons who would make good cabinet material. As he lamented, "The requirements at policy levels do not always coincide with important considerations of party loyalty and party service." Complaints were also made about increasing corruption and the competition for jobs in various public sector projects and the "determination of these on racial grounds". Said Williams, "I do not have it in me to associate with practices of that sort."

Williams told the party that he had spoken without bitterness, without recrimination, without invective, without malice, and as objectively and as unemotionally as could be expected. "If any slight edge of disappointment has showed itself, please attribute it to fatigue. I have decided, with the full support of my daughter (whose only complaint is that it has come three years too late), that I shall not seek reelection as your Political Leader, and that the time has come for me to return to private life and take no further part in political activity."

As if to underline his seriousness, and to convince the many whom he knew would be sceptical about his announcement, the prime minister wrote the queen, renouncing his membership in the privy council. He also renounced all foreign titles and honours, and sought to buy a home that he said was needed to accommodate him in his retirement.

Shortly after the convention, Williams went on vacation, allegedly his first in seventeen years, and handed most of his responsibilities to Francis Prevatt, chairman of the PNM and leader of government business in the senate. He later declared his assets, which were said to be worth TT$234,769, a step that generated some controversy as to whether it was a gesture designed to show that he had not used his office to accumulate great wealth, or one designed to allow him to crack the whip of morality over his colleagues if he reentered the political arena, as some believed he planned to do. As Williams confided to the party, "As I return to private life, I find myself with no place of my own to go, and of equal importance, no place for my collection of books and research documents . . . my daughter and I have decided to proceed jointly to secure an appropriate home and the transaction is now being finalized" (*Trinidad Guardian*, 30 September 1973).

From the party and groups such as the clergy, the business community, and the *Guardian* and the *Express* came entreaties that he reconsider his decision to retire. Williams was urged "to walk that extra mile" until the chaotic political situation in the country had become more settled. There were others, like Tapia leader Lloyd Best, who argued that Williams was responsible for the mess in which the country had found itself and that he was therefore the person least suited to preside over any transition. DAC leader A.N.R. Robinson felt that Williams's planned retirement was a blessing in disguise that would ease the tension in the society. A compromise view came from PNM foundation member and former PNM minister Donald Granado, who felt that an interim government should be set up to handle the transition. To quote Granado (1987), "There can be nothing wrong under the present circumstances with having an interim regime comprising persons from the various groups and organizations (within reason) . . . until such time as the new constitution makes a general election feasible." Granado told Williams that he was still the one man who could preside over the transition, but that Williams "was wanted as the Head of Government on a completely different basis than as head of a single party".

One newspaper that did not endorse the call by the press for Williams to stay was the *Bomb*, the editor of which expressed surprise that the public reaction to the announcement was so cool. Patrick Chokolingo, editor of the *Bomb*, had this to say:

> I must confess that I was among the thousands of people – the hundreds of thousands who felt that "bad luck" for us the day the Doc leaves. I was sure that there would be chaos and confusion, that the black power boys would run rampage in the city, that the NUFF brigade would come down from the hills and so on. Just about nothing was happening, and I could not believe it. Something had gone wrong. It wasn't working out the way I was told it would happen. It is true that last year the Doc promised to lay down his bridge over troubled waters, and it is true for almost a month he refused to sign his nomination papers, and I should have been conditioned to the fact that he was going, but I had come to regard him as a fixture. If he went, who we go put? (*Bomb*, 5 October 1973)

The weekly described Williams's farewell address as a "document of failure, hopelessness and sheer frustration", and said that Williams had suffered "seventeen years of hell, seeing all your hopes and aspirations dashed to smithereens on the rocks of selfishness and greed". It felt that Williams had shot his bolt, and chided the party for trying to persuade him to change his mind. It was a futile call anyway, opined the *Bomb*.

> It would be something shameful if after the Doc had said all those nasty things about the party and the people that he could ever want to stage a comeback. They could recall from now till the twelfth of never, I was sure they could never get Eric Williams in the cockfight. If he could not do it for the last 17 years when he was full of vigor and vitality, when he was rearing to set the world on fire, what makes them believe that he could do it now when he is a tired ageing man. I think that we must praise Caesar for trying hard, but we must not bury him. Maybe that's why the whole country is taking it so well. (Ibid.)

Williams refused to entertain urgent entreaties and requests that he remain in office, agreeing only that he would do nothing until such time as a successor had been elected. He urged the party "to expedite whatever procedures" were needed to bring the matter to a speedy conclusion and suggested that 31 December 1973 would be an appropriate date for him to take his exit, though this was flexible.

Given Williams's apparent refusal to reconsider, the machinery of the party was put into operation to find a replacement. This was done reluctantly, and always with an eye to the fact that there might be a change of heart. Four candidates were mentioned as potential successors, three of whom were deputy leaders of the party – Kamaluddin Mohammed, Errol Mahabir and George Chambers. The fourth was Karl Hudson-Phillips, the former attorney general, who emerged very early as the favourite of the party and the dominant sociological group represented by the party. Of the others, Chambers was not considered sufficiently charismatic. Mahabir, who was then considered "a blue-eyed boy" of the prime minister, discouraged those who sought to advance his candidacy and went off to Brussels. Mohammed was a foundation member of the party and the Indian community saw him as the logical successor, but he was seen by the Afro-creoles in the party as being unelectable, not only because he was Indian, but also because of speculation about how he had come to acquire the wealth he was reputed to have. The latter was the reason most frequently given in public, but the real objection was a racial one; Mohammed was not the only minister about whom there was such gossip. Mohammed himself was aware of the racial nature of the campaign being waged against him. As he said, "I am deeply concerned about the results of a certain propaganda which is currently being spread in the country which can damage the achievements we have made with respect to inter-racial solidarity" (*Trinidad Guardian*, 14 October 1973).

Hudson-Phillips was a controversial figure within the party and in the country because of his activities during the 1970 revolution and in certain highly political court cases that he had handled in his capacity as attorney general. The style of his campaign for the chairmanship of the party in the party elections of 1973 was also viewed by many, both inside and outside the party, with misgivings. In July 1973, he had provoked party stalwarts by calling for a total shakeup and rejuvenation of the party of which he was then vice-chairman. Hudson-Phillips, who was challenging Francis Prevatt, an old "crony" of Williams, was clearly seeking to secure a base among the youth. He told the PNM Youth League that the party was no longer representative of the nation, which was far more youthful in composition than the party.

Hudson-Phillips also complained that the various auxiliaries of the party, such as the Youth League and the Women's League, were no longer in the vanguard of the movement for progressive reform. Instead, the party was being "killed softly" by those whose only claim to position and influence was that they had been foundation members. There was also a tendency to be nostalgic about the past and complacent about the future. Hudson-Phillips felt that there was a cloud "settling upon the party, a cloud . . . of complacency and self-righteousness", blame for which was put on foundation members who monopolized party positions without doing any work and who were not prepared to recognize those who did, whether or not they were foundation members. The vice-chairman called upon the PNM to once more assume the role it had occupied in the 1950s and early 1960s. He also said that it was crucial that the party give guidance to the government, which must listen.

Hudson-Phillips took the opportunity to chide the PNM about its lack of political aggression. In his view, the purpose of politics was the "maintenance of political power and control in every single group in the country. Politics was a game of total warfare, of control of people's minds. . . . If you have power and you do not use it you will lose it", a remark which provoked an angry reaction from Williams. While Hudson-Phillips did not attack Williams directly as he did other ministers, he had clearly thrown down the gauntlet to Williams when he said, perhaps impulsively, "Who vex, vex."

Hudson-Phillips tried to disarm Williams, and party critics who interpreted his speech as a challenge to Williams, by claiming that he was not challenging the prime minister and that his speech was designed to strengthen and re-energize the party, because it was the only one with any semblance of stability and coherence. In his view, the PNM was too much on the defensive and far too apologetic. If it did not answer back the critics, it would lose power by default.

A great deal of what Hudson-Phillips said about the PNM was true, and many shared his views. Younger members and some older ones as well wanted to see a re-energized PNM and felt that the old brigade had to be moved. The *Bomb*, which often functioned as if it were a mouthpiece for Hudson-Phillips, quoted "a PNM top brass" who was backing the attorney general, to the effect that

> A secret but radical move is on in the PNM for a change of the entire constitution and leadership of the party. Since the AG's speech, there have been more calls for change by people who feel that a younger man should be Prime Minister to meet the growing demands of this young nation. If a young man is elected party chairman, then this nation can look forward to a new Prime Minister. That's why our slogan is: Who vex, vex . . . after Eric, Karl is next! The northern and eastern sectors of the PNM are all for Karl. But we are going about our moves constitutionally, and not doing like ANR Robinson did. The move is for change. It is gaining strength and momentum day after day. The Women's League, the Youth League and several party groups with young people are going crazy to establish the change. All of us are thoroughly fed up with the old leadership and its "I have appointed a committee" attitude. The entire country will be eager to see if Eric will abdicate with pomp and vanity, pregnant with steelband music and a holiday for all, or be moved by a PNM coup. (*Bomb*, 10 August 1973)

Williams was obviously "blasted vex" about Hudson-Phillips's challenge, and his first counter came in a letter to the general council in which he complained about the "unorthodox campaign" that Hudson-Phillips was waging to secure the chairmanship of the party and his attempt to indicate that the campaign had his blessing. As he said in the letter,

> The Political Leader remains aloof from these intrigues, avoiding any display of partiality for or against colleagues with whom he necessarily has to work. The best in modern party experience fortifies this. . . . The Attorney-General's election campaign is

being undertaken without my previous knowledge, consent or authorization. I have not sanctioned, do not now sanction and will not sanction the association either of my name or of my picture with the election of any candidate for any office. (Letter to General Council, 9 August 1973)

Williams also made it clear that he regarded Hudson-Phillips's remarks as a challenge, denials to the contrary notwithstanding. The latter's comments were seen as being "insincere, in questionable taste and an obvious attempt to 'mam-aguy' [flatter]". Williams also hinted, though darkly, that the amount of money being spent by Hudson-Phillips on his campaign was evidence of "interference of foreigners in Caribbean affairs". Williams was obviously seeking to discredit Hudson-Phillips, and followed this up by refusing to see the latter, who at the time was still attorney general.

Stung by the prime minister's obvious displeasure, and clearly anticipating that he would be dismissed, Hudson-Phillips chose to resign from the cabinet and to withdraw from the election on the ground that it would do no good to have a party chairman and an attorney general in whose integrity the "undoubted Political Leader" and prime minister had no confidence. In his letter of resignation, he told Williams that he regretted that the efforts which he had been making on behalf of the party and "indeed in your behalf, have been so terribly misunderstood and misconstrued. What has been seen as an attempt to challenge you was intended in fact to boost and bolster you. Sinister motives have been attributed to honest and genuine, you may think misguided, attempts to reactivate the party and to refurbish your image." It was an astonishingly meek statement that showed Hudson-Phillips had lost his political nerve. The statement also reflected the fact that the attorney general knew that he had no real power base in the party, and that he would easily be crushed if he dared to confront the "maximum" leader.

In his reply, Williams rebuked Hudson-Phillips for mixing up party and official affairs in his letter of resignation and of washing the party's dirty linen in public. He also took the opportunity to indicate that there was a fundamental philosophical difference between himself and the former attorney general over the question of the relationship between state and citizen. As he wrote,

You have been publicly credited with such statements as (a) using the power you have unless you wish to lose it, (b) control of people's minds, (c) party control over trade unions, (d) taking a leaf out of other countries' books. I cannot possibly associate my name or my influence with any of these ideas. The responsibility of the PNM, as I see it, is overwhelmingly to assure the country, irrespective of party, that it is competent to rule without making the citizens feel insecure in respect of the abuse of power either by the national executive or the party executive. There is here a much larger issue involved. You will recall the reluctance with which I agreed to your views on the continued responsibility of the Attorney General, a member of the Cabinet, for criminal prosecutions, without interference from any authority. I am now completely convinced that that view is untenable, and that the responsibility for criminal prosecutions should be vested in a public officer, divorced from partisan affiliations and selected by the appropriate constitutional procedures. To the extent that I am able to do so, I intend to advocate this point of view to my party colleagues when appropriate – as an indispensable requirement for the strengthening of our democratic processes. Apart from these fundamental divergences between us, the political reality is that I have come to the end of my term as Political Leader and have taken no steps to seek reelection. Where then does boosting and bolstering me or refurbishing my image – by you or anyone else arise? And why your excessive concern to avoid the impression that you are challenging me? There is no law against this, and it has become conventional, within and outside the party.

. . . I deny your right to dictate to me, the Political Leader of the PNM, what I must or must not say in reply to a newspaper commentary and to the enlightenment of the party rank and file as to political realities in the modern world. . . . If your concern is to "reactivate the party", as you say, by all means feel free to do so. I have never sought to restrain you or anyone else. It is now fairly general knowledge that our appraisal of what is wrong does not coincide, our techniques vary, and my understanding of the larger and ultimate goals is more "philosophical" (as you are wont to say) and less superficial than yours. If the party opts for your ideas, so be it. They will have to lie on the bed they make. (Letter to Hudson-Phillips, 14 September 1973)

Williams was deliberately warning the party and the country that Hudson-Phillips was a hard-liner who would be far more politically repressive than he himself thought necessary. Hudson-Phillips was known in fact to have been in favour of using strong-arm measures during the 1970 disturbances, and was the author of the now notorious Public Order Bill, which public outcry had forced the government to withdraw. Williams later expressed regret that the bill had not been brought to cabinet before it was laid in parliament, but it is difficult to believe that he was not aware of its contents and approved the bill. He had to have sanctioned it. In any event, much of what was contained in the Public Order Bill was later reintroduced on a piecemeal basis – the Summary Offences Act, the Firearms Act and the Sedition Act. One is entitled to speculate as to whether when the chips were down, Williams was any less illiberal than Hudson-Phillips, though he was certainly more sophisticated, "philosophical" and economical in the use of force when he felt that doing so was the lesser evil intended to forestall an unconstitutional overthrow of an elected government.

Hudson-Phillips denied that the legislation which he introduced had not been approved by Williams and his cabinet colleagues, declaring,

I was never so presumptuous as Attorney General and as a member of the Cabinet to take any independent action with respect to any issue whatsoever without the full decision and backing of the Cabinet. I think this is important because many things have been ascribed to me during my term of office as Attorney General. Every single thing as far as I was concerned that I did was done under the umbrella of a collective responsibility. (*Trinidad Express*, 23 May 1976)

Hudson-Phillips, who had offered to resign over the Public Order Bill issue, expressed the belief that any minister who mishandled an issue or did something that was not accepted politically should resign notwithstanding the doctrine of collective responsibility, in order to draw away the criticism and the heat from the remaining members of the cabinet.

Despite the prime minister's expressed reservations about Hudson-Phillips, as the date set for selecting a new political leader to replace Williams drew nearer, it was clear that he was the front runner. As far as Hudson-Phillips was concerned, "man gone, man dey". Of the 250 party groups that made valid nominations, 224 endorsed him as their nominee. Mohammed received the other 26. Mohammed, however, sensed that the question on everybody's mind was whether, despite his statement that he would not interfere in the choice of a successor, Williams would back him rather than allow Hudson-Phillips to be selected as his successor. Would he intervene to "stop Karl"? The party was unlikely to follow his advice and back Mohammed.[1] At the time of his resignation, Williams appeared willing to allow the party to lie on whatever bed it chose to make. As it turned out, however, no election was held, because Williams decided to continue as political leader of the PNM.

The reasons for Williams's decision to continue were a matter for speculation. One school of thought insists that he never intended to withdraw at all, and that the gambit was designed to shock the PNM and nation into the awareness that he was indispensable, and to smoke out Hudson-Phillips and those who were disloyal to him. This view was consistently held by Lloyd Best. To quote him at some length,

On September 30, Williams found himself in a historical situation where three and one half terms of his ministry had brought administration to a standstill, discredited all the institutions, demoralized the nation and created a revolutionary upheaval. The only prospect for succession that he and all conventional eyes could see was a monstrous oligarchy of shallow-minded, empty-headed Jaycees, some inside the party, others outside, but all dressed up, corrupt and incompetent, bent on "total repression" and favoured by "external interference". Faced by the mess that his Doctor Politics had created, Williams declared that he was not seeking re-election. Deprived of political education for 13 years, the country accepted the resignation with relief. This Sunday, December 2, 1973, we will discover that it was only a strategy to win back sympathy and love, a desperate conspiracy to get a mandate. For Williams to stay would undoubtedly be a humiliation, marking him out as one of the most ruthless manipulators ever to have appeared upon the scene of history. But to go would be a much worse fate if only because that would unquestionably be a coward's choice. Men of Williams' arrogance do not meekly withdraw after telling tales about his accomplices and colleagues. Men who have had the rank to change the rules and bend the course of history do not go out like a squib. Men of stature can only die in faith and hope, their gaze transfixed by wide horizons. When it springs a leak, a "traitor deputy" might jump ship – not a captain. Williams simply is not going any place. Every move he has made during and since that last Convention of September 30, has been a calculation aimed at getting room to play. By the attack on the cabinet and the party, on the nation and the region, the Doctor hoped to set himself on a plane apart and clear the way to "Perspectives for a New Society". The declaration of the assets is just the latest double play, superbly timed to raise the ante. To the gullible, it means there is no ace inside the hole. To a practised poker-player, it means that Williams is playing by the golden rule which says that the only card which counts is the last and final one. Stalin, goes the legend, dominated the table because, apart from anything else, he could wait forever. (*Tapia*, 2 December 1973)

Another commentator, C.V. Gocking, was equally convinced that Williams was not retiring but was taking a "calculated risk". Gocking believed that Williams was aware that the PNM had ceased to inspire and that he was seeking to obtain a mandate, not merely from the party but from the country. If the mandate was not forthcoming spontaneously, it would be engineered "through the media in the form of editorials, articles, reports of petitions, memoranda etc. Dr. Williams will be called upon to stay at least to see the constitution through. It will be represented as his moral duty to do so. He will then bow to public demand for this limited purpose." Gocking argued that the tone of Williams's address provided the best clue to his game plan: "Public confession of party failings and inadequacies can furnish a basis for a renewal of its life under a Leader who has frankly proclaimed these weaknesses but can now proceed, with full public and party support, to revitalize and reform it in ways indicated in the Address and to forge a new instrument for guiding the country along the new paths opened up by constitutional reform and the proclamation of a Republic" (*Tapia*, 2 December 1973). Gocking also dismissed the argument that Williams was leaving because of pressure exerted by his daughter. He was of the view that that explanation was psychologically untenable:

> Dr. Williams loves his daughter dearly, but he belongs to a breed of men, found in all fields of human endeavour, who craved distinction – not unworthily, with whom "significance" in the wider world beyond the family is a passion, and whom, nor mother, nor lover, nor wife, nor child can turn from the main bent of their lives. Such men often give love, give their material possessions, but only ill-health, old age or death can quench the flame that gives life meaning and direction. To see, therefore, in his daughter's influence a decisive factor drawing him away from public to private life is psychologically untenable, psychologically all wrong.

This line of argument is difficult to accept, however. It is not easy to understand why Williams would go to the trouble to renounce all the awards that had been made to him by foreign governments, buy a home for himself with so much fanfare, openly criticize his party colleagues and the leaders of Caribbean governments simply to test public reaction and smoke out opposition in the party. That script appears to be much too complicated and again ascribes to Williams a Machiavellian sense that is far too refined. A more probable explanation is that Williams resigned because he was feeling the pressures of office and was in a state of mental despair, both about the party and the state of the country. Perhaps too he was suffering from some sort of mental disorder, and resigned in a fit of depression. This view is firmly held by a number of psychiatrists with whom the author discussed the matter but who do not wish to go on record.

His daughter Erica was indeed concerned about the pressures that were wearying him and was urging him to quit office and live a quiet life. And she firmly believed that he was serious about leaving when he said he would, and cites his letter of resignation to the queen in respect of the privy council as conclusive evidence that he was not faking. Interestingly, close associates of Williams are divided in their view as to whether he was serious or not. One of his trusted ministers, Errol Mahabir, viewed the resignation as a ploy. As he observed at a conference in 1996, "I never in my mind felt that Dr. Williams had any intention of going anywhere. Dr. Williams made that announcement so that crabs could cover their holes. Eric Williams had his reason in 1973 for saying what he said, and it had nothing to do with whether the revenue was going to come and things like that. . . ." (1999, 161). Mahabir conceded that he might have been wrong, but if so, Williams changed his mind very quickly.

Dodderidge Alleyne, Williams's permanent secretary, indicated that he believed Williams and sought to get him to reconsider:

> In 1973 Dr. Williams announced that he was leaving politics, he was giving up. At that time, we were very close. I worked with him, of course he was my Prime Minister. I was his Permanent Secretary. Before that I was Permanent Secretary in the Ministry of Finance. Before that I was Permanent Secretary, Petroleum and Mines, but always whichever Ministry I was at, I worked very closely with him.
>
> And here he was announcing that he was going to leave politics. So one day I said to him, "Why are you leaving now"? He said, "What you mean, why am I leaving now." So I said to him, "What do you think History would say if you left now"? He said, "You do not understand Dod. What you have to understand is what History would say if I do not go now." I don't think I ever got it. So I continued: I said, "These last few years, you didn't have enough money in the Government to do what you wanted to do and you are leaving now when I am sure that by the end of this year, next year, you'll be able to get all the revenues you need to do all those projects you wanted to do." "Who tell you so?" I said, "You sent me to OPEC, you sent me through all of the Middle East,

North Africa, West Africa and now you are arguing who told me that." And by the end of that year 1973 the OPEC countries, Gaddaffi, that great man . . . moved the price of oil up. I don't know what the politicians said to him, but I tried to persuade him not to go. Was I wrong? That is another imponderable of History. I hope you historians will look at it. (1999, 142)

George John, who in those years functioned as Williams's chief public relations officer, also believed that Williams intended to leave but was pressured to change his mind:

Williams never recovered from the events of 1970. In 1973 he told the PNM convention he was retiring, then, faced with national pressure, he changed his mind. I was surprised not by his announcement that he was going but by his decision to stay on as Prime Minister. For he had told me a week or so before the convention that Erica, his daughter, wanted him to go in 1970, but he was pressed to remain in office. "The next time I say I am going no one will be able to stop me," he had declared right there in his untidy barn of an office, sitting in his chair across the desk from me in the visitor's chair. (2002, 224)

Dianne Dupres, Williams's political secretary, also believed he was going. "I think at the time he did want to leave office. I think he did not want renomination in 1973. I don't think it was a ploy. The negative things he was hearing about his faithful servants affected him" (as cited in Mohammed 2000, 5). John Humphrey, an architect and a former member of parliament, was also certain that Williams was intent on taking his exit. As he told a symposium held in 1991, quoted here at some length,

The very first face to face meeting that I had with Dr. Williams was when I had gone to his office at Whitehall with a cheque for $100,000, which was part of my fee for the Convention Centre, to donate it to the country with a suggestion to him that it be used as part of a fund to buy the *Trinidad Guardian*. I had already spoken to a number of very wealthy friends who were prepared to contribute large sums of money for the purpose of Trinidadians owning the *Trinidad Guardian* for at the time it was owned by Lord Thompson. And he asked the question – why not the *Express*. He then asked me to donate $10,000 for the PNM Elections fund, and $5,000 for the PNM Credit Union, and he gave me back the $85,000. That's the first meeting.

As an architect working on the official Prime Minister's residence, I had to communicate very closely with him to get my design brief. I had to spend a lot of time with him. Let me give you some glimpses of Eric's personal life style, and it would help you to understand the simplicity of the man in his personal life style.

His favourite area before we did the job was a little bar adjacent to the kitchen. Now that bar was designed for Lord and Lady Beetham. It was the final residence of a Governor, a colonial Governor and it was a service bar. A service bar is designed for very rapid transmission of drinks, so the bar was extra high to enable the waiters to put the drinks shoulder high to go into the living room to serve. And he had six inches of wrought iron welded to the stool to enable him to reach the bar.

He used to come home from work at 6 o'clock or 6.30 and go into the kitchen just a door away from the bar area take his meal out of the oven, because the domestic staff had left at 4 o'clock or before. It was a rule that no domestic worker should work longer hours than any other worker. So he would go and take his warm food, put it on the bar and climb up on a high stool and eat. But he also took his guests into that room, because one of his hobbies was to mix exotic drinks for anybody who visited him at home. And he did that with great pride.

Now his sleeping quarters: Lord and Lady Beetham had adjoining bedrooms, but they did not share a common bed. He chose Lady Beetham's bedroom and the décor had not been changed – so it had a frilly fancy décor. But he chose Lord Beetham's bedroom for his work area, and it was really a work area – a desk and a credenza where he spread his documents. He had filing cabinets upon filing cabinets with documents. Adjacent to that was a library, and when I checked the library, I found a lot of library books, very valuable books, and when I questioned him about it, he said, "they are much safer with me than they are at the library."

Now, the other favourite area, was a private sitting room. He enjoyed it because that is where his very close friends played . . . cards with him. And that is also where he listened to his classical music. If you visit the house today you will see the designs that were done for Dr. Williams. I converted the bar into a very nice bar-lounge area. I converted the private sitting room with convertible type furniture to enable work sessions and visits from Heads of Governments and the playing of cards and so on, and built in all the musical equipment.

But we had a discussion one day about his future writing. As we were talking about what he had planned for the future of his writing, he told me that he had a series of six documents of West Indian history to produce. He had enough documents to produce six volumes of documents of West Indian history. I volunteered to help him design the covers of these books, and I in fact designed the cover of the first volume, and you will notice that it is a map of the Caribbean. We had agreed that each volume will have a cover on which there will be a map of that historical epoch. He only produced one. Very sadly.

He informed me that he had to rewrite the final chapter of "From Columbus to Castro" because he didn't think that he had done the Cuban Revolution justice. And that was one of the important works that he wanted to do. He said that the major work that he was planning, was a contemporary history of the Caribbean, and that he could not write it while in office, because he would have to say things about living heads of governments and colleagues, and it would be completely unethical while he held office as Prime Minister, that he should do this.

It is these conversations that led me to introduce the idea to him that he should acquire a house, so that when he came out of office, he would have a place to live. And I explained to him, because he hadn't thought of this – Eric Williams never thought about his own personal needs. He only thought about Trinidad and Tobago, and about the Caribbean in the context of the world.

I told him that if he purchased a house he could rent it, and the rent could go to the mortgage company and he wouldn't even feel the amortization, and that in fact was done. A Real Estate Agent was employed, a little house in Goodwood Park, not a grand palace, a humble home, was purchased. Ram Kirpalani rented from him and agreed that when he needed it he would vacate. This is how I know that in 1973, Dr. Williams was trying his best to exit politics. And Erica was pounding him to come out of office and he really wanted to. He wanted quiet retirement to do a tremendous amount of unfinished work.

Ram Kirpalani vacated the house, and they actually started the physical work preparing the house to accommodate his books and to accommodate his needs and that work actually started. So anybody who come along and say that in 1973 he was playing a trick on the country, that is not true. I think the oil boom gave him a new lease on life and stimulated his adrenalin. (Humphrey 1991)

One of the factors that may have strengthened Williams's determination to abandon political life was the deplorable state of the economy in 1973. Gross domestic product growth was in the vicinity of 4.6 per cent in real terms over the period 1960 to 1971. In 1972 it was 4.7 per cent; in 1973, only 0.7 per cent. Foreign reserves had also declined dramatically. Whereas in 1971 there was a surplus of US$21.4 million, in 1972 there was a deficit of US$23.6 million. Many factors were responsible for the sluggishness of the economy, but the most significant of these was the poor performance of the petroleum sector, which suffered a secular decline of some 30 per cent between 1968 and mid-1973 due to a depletion of known reserves. Whereas in 1969, petroleum's contribution to total revenue was 32 per cent, in 1973 it was only 24 per cent.

Central Bank reserves had also fallen by more than one-third during the latter half of 1972 to US$53.1 million. The decline continued during the first half of 1973, reaching a low US$36.2 million in August – less than sufficient to finance a month's imports. As a World Bank report noted, "But for the spectacular increase in oil prices which came about late in 1973 and early in 1974, the foreign exchange position of Trinidad and Tobago might have become critical" (*Economic Position and Prospects of Trinidad and Tobago*, Report No. 4359 TR, July 1974, IBRO/IDA, 1).

As the performance of the economy deteriorated, government revenues declined, giving rise to a major fiscal deficit and extensive borrowing on the local and Euro-dollar market at high rates. To quote a World Bank report,

[F]rom a virtual balance in 1969, the overall deficit . . . increased to TT$49 million in 1970, TT$88 million in 1971 and TT$124 million in 1972. This overall deficit amounted to nearly 6 percent in 1972, indicating a very expansionary budgetary stance which was followed consciously in an effort to maintain economic activity and employment in the face of social disturbances and falling oil production. Heavy reliance was placed on the domestic banking system for financing the increased deficit, and there can be little doubt that this played a part in fostering domestic inflation. ("The Status of the Trinidad Economy", as cited in *Tapia*, 12 August 1973)

Bank borrowing also contributed to a liquidity squeeze that restricted the level of activity in the private sector and had a negative effect on the unemployment situation, which rose from 13 to 14 per cent between 1971 and 1973. By mid-1973, the situation had become worse and there had to be cutbacks in public sector expenditure. Whereas in the three previous years, the rise in current expenditures had averaged 19 per cent annually, this rate of increase was virtually cut in half in 1973. The government imposed strict controls on public expenditure and restrictions on the purchase of consumer durables by imposing sales taxes and a requirement that the commercial banks maintain an additional 2 per cent reserve.

The problem was compounded by the drought of 1973, which affected export food crops as well as the price of imported food. In 1973, the sugar crop was devastated by drought and cane fires, and Trinidad and Tobago was for the first time unable to fill its Commonwealth sugar quota. Only 183,737 tons of sugar were produced, 19.5 per cent below the figure for 1972. Coffee production fell by 5.7 per cent and citrus by 72 per cent. Reduced earnings from agricultural exports aggravated the foreign exchange position. So too, did the completion in 1972 of capital projects in the petroleum sector – the desulphurization plant and the Texaco refinery, the Amoco terminal at Point Galeota, the conversion of the FedChem ammonia plant to hydrogen production and the expansion of the plant at the Shell refinery. Fears about devaluation in 1973 discouraged capital inflows, as did low interest rates.

To make matters worse, prices that had remained stable for many years literally began to gallop in 1973. A great deal of the inflation was imported from countries affected by the energy crisis. Inflation was also caused by the drought and high wage settlements that stimulated demand at a time of declining supplies. Whereas domestic prices had risen by 5.3 per cent between January and November 1972, they rose by 19.3 per cent over the same period in 1973. The increases were particularly high in food. Whereas food prices rose by 24.6 per cent over the period 1968 to 1972, in the first eleven months of 1973 they rose by 29.7 per cent. Rents experienced a similar dramatic increase.

The OPEC revolution which began one month after his farewell address, led Williams to believe that he had made a mistake. The improvement of the economy towards the latter part of 1973 helped to lift the economic gloom and his own spirits. The price of a barrel of oil that was US$2.60 in 1972, went to US$4.60 in the latter part of 1973. The OPEC countries also announced a major increase for January 1974, and the price in Trinidad and Tobago jumped to over US$10, this at a time when Amoco's marine installations were beginning to result in a marked increase in crude oil production. As Williams later said, "It's a new ball game. If the Sheik could play, who is we?" (1973b, 4).

Another factor said to have been of some significance was Williams's failure to get the post of chancellor of the new United Nations University, for which he had reportedly applied. It is believed that when this fell through, there was no place else for him to go. Whatever the reasons, and they may all be of some relevance, Williams's mood changed quickly and he came to regret his decision, proceeding to manipulate a number of willing groups to whip up "the public" (which perhaps to his surprise had begun to show signs of lack of interest) to demand his return. The Inter-Religious Organisation (IRO), a civil society group that brought together some of the country's main religious organizations – Hindus excepted – was one of the groups that, perhaps unwittingly, was crucial to the strategy.

The IRO approached the governor general, Sir Ellis Clarke, who suggested to the group that they should meet the prime minister, which they did. Williams was told that he had a moral obligation to continue in office given the chaos and the uncertainty prevailing in the country, an uncertainty that was generating a flight of capital. The IRO offered itself as an "instrument of peace and reconciliation" in the conflict. The factors giving rise to this state of affairs were said to be

> loss of faith in the operation of the present system to the extent that citizens have committed themselves to affecting change by violent means, polarization of widely differing political, social and economic interests that had bred frustration, discontent and antisocial behaviour leading to violence and excessive use of force; growing lack of awareness of the importance of moral and spiritual values; widespread hostility and denigration aimed at those in public life; an unhealthy tendency in the society to resort to confrontation; an increasing resignation to the fact that the partial reforms that had been achieved in the society had not produced any fundamental reform in the lot of the underprivileged masses whose standards of living remain disturbingly low and whose hopes for the future become dimmer day by day.

The IRO urged Williams to summon a national convention, to be attended by significant political groups, to see whether a reconciliation could be negotiated, a proposal that appeared to interest the prime minister. The IRO, however, denied that it was part of a conscious conspiracy to engineer Williams's return. As Catholic archbishop Anthony Pantin explained, "IRO or no IRO, if Eric Williams did not want to return to office, he would not have done so" (as cited in Boodhoo 2001, 221).

Some opposition groups opposed the IRO's suggestion of a convention on the ground that it was the prime minister himself who was responsible for the crisis. There had in fact been a noticeable lessening of tension following the announcement of his proposed resignation. As Lloyd Best told the IRO, "The Prime Minister has been conspicuously incapable of harnessing our energies for positive and constructive effort. I cannot imagine anybody less competent to lead the country out of these troubled times. While I support the call of IRO leaders for a resolution of the crisis by reconciliation, I believe that the Political Leader of the PNM and his party must be moved to make way for the politics of participation" (*Trinidad Guardian*, 4 November 1973).

It is not clear just what took place behind the scenes, but the fact of the matter is that shortly after the intervention of the IRO, Williams returned to Whitehall from his vacation. Significantly, too, his daughter flew out of Trinidad for the United States, which insiders took as a signal that she had lost the battle to keep her father from changing his mind.

When the PNM convention met on 2 December to elect a successor to Williams, curious things began to happen, things that made it evident that there would in fact be no such election. Instead of proceeding with the election, the convention, by a show of hands, decided by a vote of 348 to 61 (there were 14 abstentions) to send a delegation to the prime minister to plead with him to continue in office "at least until all necessary steps have been taken to implement the proposed new constitution for Trinidad and Tobago". Williams "accepted the invitation" and indicated that he would turn up at the convention at 5 p.m. The need to ensure an orderly constitutional transition was conveniently used by Williams as the cover behind which to mask his bid to hold onto power after he had ceremoniously renounced it.

In his statement to the wildly cheering reconvened convention, Williams said that he had decided to respond positively to the many requests that he had received from various sources, both inside and outside the party. The latter, he said, stressed "the present world economic uncertainties". He also expressed concern that his successor, whoever he was, "would have to seek almost immediately a mandate from the voters, since he would not have owed his position to a general election". Such an election, he seemed to imply, would have had to take place before the constitution reform exercise was completed, something his return would avoid. An immediate election would also mean that the eighteen-year-olds would not be able to vote because they were not yet registered.

Worth pointing out, however, is that Williams must have been aware of these consequential developments when he announced his decision to resign in September. At the time, he appeared to give his personal and family concerns higher priority over those of the public. Once again Williams sought to defuse criticism by indicating that elections were just around the corner and that he was disrupting his personal plans merely to see the constitutional exercise completed. He explained that he had no desire to hold onto what was called "power", nor did he feel any attraction for the "prestige" of the office involved, but he would recognize his obligation and disrupt his personal plans and work. He promised the convention that he would give priority to the holding of elections as soon as possible in order that the people could freely and fairly decide on the party and leader to whom they wish to entrust their mandate:

> The General Election should be held under a new constitution; in other words, the work of the Constitution Commission must not be frustrated. The recommendations of the Commission should be publicly discussed as extensively and as thoroughly as "the public" wishes, based on the widest possible circulation of the Commission's Report, adequate time being allowed for study by the citizens. Such public discussion and any consensus emanating there from should be given full consideration when final decisions are being made. The subsequent legislative and administrative action should be taken as expeditiously as possible. Much time, for example, might be saved by dealing first with the issues of the voting age and the electoral system and procedures on which there already seems to be a large measure of unanimity so that the competent authorities can proceed at once, without awaiting the completion of the published discussion and government's decision on the Commission's entire report, to the registration of new voters and the implementation of any new electoral regulations. As soon as the time element is clearer than it is now, the election date should be announced. (Letter from the prime minister to the convention, 2 December 1973)

The letter, which was carefully drafted, could not have been prepared between the time the delegation arrived to "plead" with the political leader and the time of his return to the convention. Williams had in fact drafted the resolution himself in advance of the arrival of the delegation, who were advised as to what arguments should be adduced to persuade him to return. The draft, which the author obtained from Errol Mahabir, was in Williams's handwriting:

> Whereas:
> achievements over 17 years under leadership;
> bring new constitution into force;
> elections related to new constitution;
> accelerate momentum achieved on Caribbean integration;
> no disruption of economic development and investment;
> defence of national sovereignty against interference economic and political power outside;
> time for party to choose successor for me to groom;
> maintaining overall progress in terms of racial harmony and integration and development of disadvantaged groups;
> Resolved recommends to General Council Convention that Political Leader be asked to continue serving another term.
>
> Re: Dr. Williams withdrawal resignation

The reaction to Williams's "return" was mixed. The bulk of the party was enthusiastic about his change of heart, as was the business community, which saw him as a symbol of "stability". Many of those who had given their support to Hudson-Phillips had done so only because they were convinced that Williams would not change his mind. There were elements in the party, however, who felt that the goodly doctor was not indispensable and that it was immoral and in bad taste for him to have led the party up the garden path and then gone back on his word. The group also felt that the chairman had manipulated the proceedings to ensure that only those in favour of Williams's return would speak, and that the entire scenario had been prearranged. One supporter of Karl Hudson-Phillips, Ferdie Ferreira, who had already begun to behave as if Hudson-Phillips were the new prime minister, declared that the events were "unprecedented and would confuse a lot of people. All we can hope is that Dr. Williams has not won the Convention and lost the party." Most of the dissidents who were supporting Hudson-Phillips either abstained in the voting or swallowed their pride in the interest of maintaining their jobs and perquisites. Three party stalwarts who were known to be close confidants of Williams – Ivan Williams, Ferdie Ferreira and Irwin Merrit – who had begged him to reconsider even before his resignation speech had been made, felt that his behaviour was immoral and refused to make peace with him.

Ferreira's account of what happened before and after Williams's announcement that he would not offer himself for leadership and his decision to return is as follows:

> After 1973, about April 1973, Irwin Merrit, Ivan Williams and I saw Williams twice a week at least, maybe three times [including] after Cabinet on Thursday. We saw him every night. As a matter of fact, we were a sort of Cabinet ourselves. Carl Tull used to be there, and Victor, his brother. When he came to the convention in September and made the statement that he was going, that was the end of our relationship. I saw very definite signs of a man who had began to lose interest in what he was doing. The night he announced his departure, I felt he was going to mash up the Party, because the only people he paid any regard to was the Women's League. He went at everybody else in the Party. He just went wild, and to me, it was the most disgraceful chapter in the history of the PNM. (Ferreira 1991)

Ferreira notes that when the convention took a decision and asked him to stay on, he wrote back saying he would not:

> "I shall not, will not, and cannot reconsider; proceed expeditiously to get a successor before the end of December." And we put the machinery into effect; and then it appeared that he was coming back. In spite of my relationship with Karl, I couldn't conceive the thought of supporting Karl in front of him. I kept asking Boysie Prevatt, Prev you see the old man? Tell him to call me; tell him I want to see him. . . .

We went to the Convention to select a leader, Prevatt came in pretty late, and the Convention started off. From the time we came in, there was a tense atmosphere, and this man, Aldwyn Vidale said – "Who for? Who against? I want Williams, man." The whole atmosphere was tense; who was traitor and who was not. So I say, Ferdi, you are no politician; I am a docker; and I went in a corner and sat down by a window. They called the Convention to order, and Vidale I think it was, took up a mike and started saying, "We want Williams, we want Williams", and with that the crescendo the women jumped up and started this thing, and Prev[att] in his usual immaculate style said, "there seems to be tension here; do we have a motion from the floor?" Because all of this thing was orchestrated already, Daniel Reid got up, supported by Eileen Montenegro [moved a motion].

So they moved the motion, and my good friend from Charlotteville [in Tobago], Big Ben, complete with cow boy hat, dressed up like a circus, was waiting with the car to take the delegation to Williams. They moved the motion, and well everybody was Williams, and they dispatched a delegation consisting of Reid, Montenegro, and about five other people; and they went up.

They came back around 1.00 and spoke to Prev, who got up and announced that they had spoken to the Political Leader and that he was considering. Tension, tension.

That day they said, "Who for Williams return?" "Who against?" "Who abstain stand up." Prevatt called on those who abstained to stand up. I say, they are looking to iden-tify those who must get the whip. Who for? Who against? And then Prevatt say, who abstain stand up. Well people started to tremble. [Laughter] You saw friends abusing each other at the Convention. It was a very disgraceful chapter.

People knew [what was going on] because George Chamber's constituency had something like 22 party groups in St. Ann's East, and none of them had nominated any-body. So they knew what was going on. The whole plan was orchestrated at Salvatori Building with Errol Mahabir and John O'Halloran. (Ibid.)

Notwithstanding what occurred within the PNM to induce Williams to return, there was no widespread popular demand for his return. As one com-mentator noted, "There was no mobilization of public opinion for his recall. The country breathed a sigh of relief; guerilla activities ceased. The scene became cooler. No crisis situation developed which could have been used by him as an excuse for him to say that he was returning to save the country" (*Trinidad Express*, 9 December 1973).

There were indeed massive demonstrations of loyalty and enthusiasm at the convention, which Williams always controlled, but the public as a whole had done nothing really to persuade Williams that he was indispensable. A rally in Woodford Square sponsored by activists was poorly attended. A bus pilgrimage to his home was not very successful. It is clear that Williams wanted to continue in office and orchestrated the strategy to achieve this. One remains firmly convinced, however, that the exercise was not from the very beginning a "plot" to secure legitimacy as some have argued, but a genuine change of mind, the true reasons for which we can only speculate about.

My own view is that in September 1973, Williams resigned because he was a profoundly depressed and disillusioned man who was still suffering from the trauma of 1970. Overwhelmed by a sense of heroic failure and under severe pressure from his beloved daughter, he took his historic exit. Williams was a man of variable moods, however, and his mood quickly changed. OPEC merely provided a life raft by which he could return. He would have returned anyway when his mood changed. As Erica was told when she asked him why he did not get out of politics, "I have got to stay on a little longer and secure the oil money for Trinidad's children" (Boodhoo 2001, 221). What he did not say is that the "sheiks" had provided him with another bite at the cherry, another opportunity to burnish his mythical image and solidify his legacy and his place in Trinidad and Caribbean history.

29 Williams and the Republican Constitution

With the return of Dr Williams, the main focus of political activity shifted to the activities of the Commission on Constitutional Reform, appointed in June 1971 and chaired by former chief justice Sir Hugh Wooding, which submitted its report on 11 January 1974. The three big questions on people's minds were these: What would Williams's reactions to the commission's recommendations be; how long would the exercise of consulting the public take; and in what manner and form would that consultation take place? On the question of the method for resolving the constitutional issue, Williams rejected all the demands that were being made for a constituent assembly or some other kind of national convention. The demand, which was one of the main principles of the Tapia House Group, was also endorsed by some of the members of the commission, who felt that the "illegitimate" parliament was not a fit and proper body to decide an issue of such critical importance.

Telford Georges and Michael de la Bastide, two of the commissioners, were of the view that the members of the constituent assembly should be selected by means of a national election conducted on the basis of proportional representation, which they argued "best mirrored the contending interests in the society". It was also recommended that the assembly should be chaired by someone other than the prime minister or a minister, and that the assembly should be given full power to enact the new constitution and any changes incidental thereto in the electoral laws. The commissioners felt that this device had two advantages: the country would have a preview as to how the system of proportional representation worked in practice, and a constitution hammered out in the proposed assembly would have the imprint of national popular approval.

Tapia also argued that the new constitution had to be legitimated in a popular forum. Tapia's argument was that the country had come to a stage where the "social contract" that bound it into a community was dissolved. The country was facing not merely a political crisis, but a constitutional crisis.

The only way in which the republic could be properly reconstituted again was for the "people" to come together in a "Grand Assembly" to redetermine the rules by which its affairs would be conducted in the future. To quote Tapia:

> All along, the Tapia answer has been that there should be called a Constituent Assembly of the valid parties along with a Conference of Citizens. We participated in the deliberations and meetings of the illegitimately established Wooding Constitution Commission in the vain hope of fashioning the required assembly out of the possibilities present there. We failed because the manipulations of both the ruling party and the conventional opposition, on the left and the right as well, kept significant political confrontation away from the Wooding Convention at Chaguaramas or any of the earlier occasions, because Tapia had not found the key to the people's heart. Now the final non-military option left to our people is to forge the Constituent Assembly out of the illegitimate Parliament itself. ("Illegitimate Parliament or Constituent Assembly of Citizens", *Tapia*, 15 October 1974)

Whatever the theoretical neatness of this argument, Williams was not at all persuaded, and proceeded to use his parliamentary majority to legislate what the new constitution should be. The government did of course make the necessary gestures to legitimate its actions by inviting the public to submit written comments on the report of the commission to an official appointed to receive them, and a draft bill was later published for public comment.[1]

On the question of procedure, the prime minister told parliament that it was not logical to argue that the 1971 parliament was illegitimate and then suggest that that very parliament should be given the power to amend the constitution to create a constituent assembly. Wilfred McKell, the official appointed by Williams to receive public comments on the commission's draft, however, put his finger on one of the real problems that vitiated the demand that there should be a constituent assembly. As he told the prime minister, "Acceptance of this proposal will amount to an admission by the Government that the present Parliament is in fact illegitimate – an admission which no legally elected government can reasonably be expected to make. . . . Its principal defect is that it would involve the creation by Parliament of another constitutional body with competing if not superior legislative power" (as cited in Williams 1974, 12–16).

McKell further noted that the results of the deliberations of the assembly could "hardly be binding either on Cabinet or on Parliament. Should government disagree with a draft constitution, the whole exercise may be rendered abortive". The prime minister agreed with McKell that the demand was politically unacceptable. He argued that his colleagues would "cut his throat" if he conceded that the 1971 parliament had no right to deal with the new constitution. He also made the doubtful claim that the government would not have been able to persuade a sufficient number of the members of the senate to amend the 1962 constitution in order to create the constituent assembly (ibid., 20).

The other genuine objection raised by the prime minister to the proposal was that the public had clearly shown that it was not at all interested in the constitution reform exercise. Attendances at meetings held by the constitution commission were low and very few memoranda were submitted to any of the bodies that had invited them. As Williams noted, "the mass of persons do not feel that there was anything wrong with the constitution at all . . . it is quite clear that your public was not interested in the exercise to the extent that it felt any serious criticism of the Constitution as a whole or major portions thereof [*sic*]" (ibid., 17–22).

A survey carried out by the author in 1974 confirmed the prime minister's opinion that there was no pervasive demand for constitution reform. When respondents were asked whether they thought the country needed a new constitution, only 26 per cent agreed. Twenty per cent said they were satisfied with the old one while 13 per cent were indifferent to the issue. As many as 41 per cent said they had no clear opinion on the issue, though it had been openly agitated for almost six years.

The majority report of the constitution commission proposed a number of changes that were widely expected and these elicited little controversy. The commission's recommendation that eighteen-year-olds be given the vote was acceptable to most persons. Such was also the case with the recommendation to return to the ballot box. The recommendations that generated a great deal of controversy related to the issue of reforming the machinery for demarcating boundaries, and the proposal that the senate be abolished and replaced by a modified form of proportional representation.

With respect to the latter, it was proposed that the conventional first-past-the-post system be used to elect thirty-six members of parliament. A second thirty-six were to be chosen on the basis of party lists, which would be drawn up and made known to the public in advance of the election. There was, however, to be just one election, after which the list seats would be distributed on the basis of the performance of each party. To prevent excessive splintering, it was recommended that no party would be entitled to a share of the thirty-six list seats unless it had won at least one seat, or 5 per cent of the popular vote. In recommending such a hybrid system, the commission felt that their proposal would go a long way towards meeting the complaints of those who believed that the first-past-the-post system discriminated against minority parties, while still making it possible for a majority party to emerge. To quote the commission's report,

> We have so far emphasised the desirability of devising an electoral system which will reflect the political divisions more accurately than does the present system. However, this is not the only purpose of an election. The representative body must be able to produce and sustain a government able to govern the country. A frequent criticism of proportional representation is that it tends to produce coalitions which are inevitably

weak and fail to give the positive leaderships which governments should give, particularly in underdeveloped countries. But, in our view and in the experience of many, coalitions are not inevitably weak. They are often the answer in moments of crisis when national survival requires national solidarity. Further, the fact that a government has an overwhelming majority in parliament does not ensure that it will provide strong government. If it does not in fact enjoy the support of a substantial majority of the people, it may well create crisis conditions if it uses its parliamentary majority to push through policies not basically agreeable to them. Government and people can thus become alienated, and the people may as a result resort to extra-constitutional methods of protest. Having regard to our concern to find a system which would meet the twin needs of representation and efficiency, we recommend an electoral system in which the principles of proportional representation and first-past-the-post system are mixed. (Wooding 1974, 31)

These recommendations were accepted by the opposition DLP and by most of the Indian community. They were also accepted by spokesmen of other minority groups and the white business community. The PNM, the OWTU, the Council of Progressive Trade Unions, the Trinidad and Tobago Labour Congress and the *Trinidad Guardian* all opposed it, though not necessarily for the same reasons. Radical groups such as the CPTU and the OWTU opposed it not only because of their belief that it would foster racialism in voting, but because they felt that it could at some time in the future give the minority elements a veto over certain types of legislation and constitutional changes, assuming of course that this element was dominant in a party that had seats in parliament.

The radical element did not make it clear why this veto would not be just as easy to exercise in a senate, at least with respect to major constitutional amendments that required special majorities in both chambers. Williams argued that the proposals were designed to destroy the PNM and to undermine the centralization and monopolization of power for which it had been responsible. Williams regarded proportional representation, even of the West German mixed variety, as a recipe for instability:

> [T]he experience with proportional representation in other countries establishes that only in very rare circumstances and on very rare occasions does a single party win a majority on its own, that one party, in combination with another smaller one, is liable to govern and maintain stability over the number of years (as in Scandinavia), and that the general rule is a coalition government sometimes embracing many parties which is inherently unstable. There is no reason to believe that Trinidad and Tobago under proportional representation will not find itself saddled with coalition government. (Williams 1974a, 33)

Williams further argued that in a period when Trinidad and Tobago was at the mercy of all sorts of unpredictable international influences that required immediate and firm action, resorting to proportional representation would be distruptive,

> [A] government of Trinidad and Tobago could not hope to survive if it is in the hands of an unstable coalition of proportional representation parties and individuals where a crucial issue might depend on the placation and the vote of some one or other of them. . . . Trinidad and Tobago finds itself rather in the position emphasized by Professor Rupert Emerson, that the prime requirement of the new developing independent states is not for more freedoms but for discipline, and that in any country with tribal, racial or religious hostilities, "the essential need is strong and unified management". (Ibid.)

There was insufficient support for proportional representation among strategic groups in the society, and the recommendations of the Wooding Commission were abandoned. Many of the core recommendations which were linked to proportional representation were also dropped from the new republican constitution which came into effect on 1 August 1976. The new constitution differed in many respects from the independence constitution and from the constitution commission's proposals. There are, however, a number of similarities in the three documents.

The Presidency

In 1976, the strong reservations to republicanism which obtained in 1962 had largely disappeared, thanks in part to the radicalization of opinion and the disenchantment with Eurocentric value systems which prevailed in the late 1960s. The commission shared this pro-republican mood and thus recommended that the president, instead of being appointed on the advice of the prime minister as was the case with the independence constitution, be elected by an electoral college consisting of the members of both houses of the legislature. His election would require only a simple majority. Presidential elections were to take place between ninety and one hundred days after a general election and successful candidates would normally hold office for five years and might be re-elected. While the principle of the electoral college was retained by Williams, he rejected the commission's proposal that local government bodies should be included in the exercise on the ground that such bodies did not have sufficient stature to be given such a role. The commission's argument was that their inclusion in the electoral college would help to upgrade local government, which was its aim. Williams was concerned, however, that the domination of parliament by the ruling party was not normally reflected at the local government level except in the three municipal areas and in one of the eight counties in which the country was divided.

Williams's comments on the commission's proposals were as follows:

[T]hey are so anxious to give the President some status that they make proposals for powers which we had never discussed among ourselves, but I am sure that we will reject it root and branch. And that is, the President is elected by this artificial electoral college, artificial in two senses – that it is an exotic plant in our society, and secondly the membership proposed just does not square with common sense. . . . The State of India is one thing. No local Government body in Trinidad and Tobago approximates the status of a State of India. It therefore cannot approximate the privileges or responsibilities of the representatives of a State of India. By all means, let us upgrade the local bodies. (Williams 1974a, 82)

The question as to how the powers of the executive branch of government should be structured and distributed was of great concern to Williams. He must have recalled it being an issue during the constitutional consultations which took place at Queen's Hall in 1962. Minority ethnic groups and the then political opposition were concerned about the prospect of the prime minister having absolute power to appoint all the key posts in the executive branch as well as the power to appoint the chief justice. To avoid this, the bar council had suggested that the governor general should be given the right to appoint "half a dozen or so of the vital officers of the State, including the Chief Justice, after consultation with the Prime Minister and the Leader of the Opposition". Sir Ellis Clarke, who was the constitutional adviser to the government, opposed this proposal on the ground that it "went halfway or three quarter of the way around towards a republic", which no one wanted at that time. More crucially, it was seen as a recipe for intra-branch conflict. As Clarke told the council spokesman, "By creating a system of dual control, you are setting up a President in the guise of a Governor General, and you are putting him as rival to your Prime minister" (verbatim notes of the Queen's Hall Conference, 1966, 14).

The matter surfaced again during the constitutional discussions that took place when the Independence constitution was being restructured in 1973–74. Interestingly, the Wooding Commission made more or less the same suggestion that had been put forward by the bar council in 1962. Williams was initially hostile to the idea and was suspicious of the commission's aim in doing so, that is, the creation of a rival to the prime minister in the person of the president. He in fact accused the commission of seeking to dilute the power of the prime minister and of inflating that of the president by giving him instrumental roles that would neutralize those of the prime minister in certain contexts. He was correct in his assumptions.

Williams was unwilling to create a situation where the president and prime minister would see themselves as rivals, "two man rats in the same hole", as he put it. This could happen if both wished to claim that they had direct mandates from the electorate. As he explained,

You either elect the man directly by the people, or you have him elected by the assembly, so that in a sort of a way, you will make for a certain opportunity for harmonious relations between your Head of State and your Head of Government which it should be the object of statesmanship to assure in all countries . . . you do not want to depart too much from such continuous traditions as we have here. So that you do not have the conflict between the presidential executive, as in the United States and Latin America, with a congressional majority from a different party. That is an open invitation to tension which could reach the stage, as it has, and will continue to have in many countries, of going outside of the Constitution for the resolution of the conflict. (Williams 1974a, 75)

Williams conceded that it was important to have a president who was not the nominee of the ruling party only. He admitted that the question was a difficult one, but felt that in the public interest, it was better to establish a system in which president and prime minister were not in structural conflict with incentives and opportunities to confront each other. As he told parliament, "It would be far preferable – in the public interest – to have a constitutional system which was based on the possibility of ensuring some sort of harmony between Head of Government and Head of State, than to go all out for a constitutional provision, which I believe is specially entrenched, that invites conflict between the two. You may not have the harmony in practice. You are bound to have tension in fact" (ibid.). Williams, however, hoped that the fact that the two officials belonged to the same political family would serve to discourage confrontation. The commission's formula, in his view, guaranteed that there would be infighting: "The Report of the Commission is aimed at one purpose only – Prime Minister and President fighting. This is only possible in a National Assembly where the President could play ball with members. You will be making of your President – your Head of State – one of the principal politicians in the country, insulating him from the pressures of public opinion in the constituencies. After all, the President would be a man" (ibid., 87).

The commission's proposal to give the president the power to refer a bill to the legislature for reconsideration if he was displeased with it was seen as further evidence of its malintent. As Williams complained,

There is no justification for it. It would lead to total confusion; it would lead to a constant trading of votes, bargaining for this and the other, and you are not going to get legislation that is in the interest of the people which they claim to be their principal motive. A Government with a majority in this House can govern; it can carry its measures. I do not see why the President, whom we think should be elected by a simple majority of the Assembly reflecting the voting patterns in the country, as a whole, should have the power to override the people's representatives and refuse to assent to a bill and send it back to them for their reconsideration. He could not do that as Governor General. Obviously, the Queen could not. And why should the President do that? There are ways and means of doing things without referring back. This is part of the deliberate effort to break down the centralizing tendencies in this country. It has gone too far. (1974a, 83)

We recall here that the independence Marlborough House Conference almost broke down over the issue of consultation with the opposition, and was only prevented from doing so by Williams's last-minute decision to concede the principle, and also to agree to discuss all matters of national importance with the leader of the opposition (see chapter 21). Whatever the intention, the fact is that in practice the principle was only ritualistically honoured. Williams became cynical about what the term meant. As he once said, "People don't seem to understand what consultation means. If I wanted to appoint you Chief Justice and I wrote to the Leader of the Opposition telling him that I was appointing you Chief Justice, then I have consulted you." Williams often consulted by handwritten note or by telephone message. Sometimes he did not bother. He told parliament that the principle of consultation was difficult in practice: "If two people consult, and we have a gentleman's agreement, that automatically calls for two gentlemen. That is the position" (1974a, 87). Williams felt that those with whom he had to deal were not gentlemen and as such he had no choice but to act in the way in which he did.

Leaders of the opposition were justifiably outraged at Williams's condescending behaviour, and bitterly complained to the constitution commission. The commission wrote in its report that "the experience of the past six years indicates that consultation does not really work", and that the concept is impossible to define. "Procedures can be prescribed and followed to the letter while yet the process can be deprived of all meaning. Genuine consultation requires an attitude of mind which political opponents may find difficult to cultivate in the absence of a long tradition" (Wooding 1974, 34).

It is in this context that the commission recommended that some of the power to appoint, which the prime minister enjoyed in the independence constitution, should be reallocated to the president, who would make appointments in his own discretion after consulting with the prime minister, the leader of the opposition and any other persons whose views he might consider it appropriate to seek. The assumption was that the president might bring a different disposition to the consultative process than would a prime minister who might see the need to consult as an unbearable burden.

In making these appointments, the president was required to consult the prime minister and the leader of the opposition. Unlike in the Jamaica constitution, however, no formula was prescribed whereby this consultation would take place, and the constitution was silent on the issue of what happens when the prime minister and the leader of the opposition could not agree on the choice of a candidate.

In Jamaica, the prime minister's choice ultimately prevailed. In Trinidad and Tobago, it was left to the president to act in his own deliberate judgement. The question as to whether he acted after proper consultation was not to be enquired into by any court.

Surprisingly, Williams accepted the commission's proposal on this fundamental issue. As he told parliament, "We are perfectly in agreement with the broad general proposal that certain matters be put in the hands of the president as head of state, and then he decides after consultation with the two people. They are either going to have to work with sufficient sense or they would not work at all, and then you would have some difficulty and that difficulty is going to be resolved . . . in one way" (1974a, 81). It was a magnificent act of prime ministerial self-denial. When asked why Williams had acted thusly, President Ellis Clarke opined that Williams was looking into the future, and was not sure that his successors would be as wise and prudent as he had been in making appointments. Williams may also have assumed that other presidents would not act in the way Clarke did.

Another proposed change in the executive related to the right given to the prime minister to recruit any number of ministers from the senate. Unlike the 1962 constitution, which limited the number of ministers who could be drawn from the senate to two, the proposed constitution imposed no such limit save that the prime minister himself should normally be drawn from the house of representatives. Another novel feature of the proposed constitution was that ministers had the right to attend and participate in debates in any of the two houses of parliament, though they might vote only in the chamber to which they belonged.

Some considered it undemocratic to draw ministers from the senate, seeing that it was not a body elected by the people. They viewed it as a return to the system whereby colonial governors were able to nominate persons to the legislative and executive councils and which most progressive forces had opposed. They also noted that unlike members of the House of Representatives, who retained their seat in parliament if they were relieved of their portfolios in cabinet, senators who were removed from the cabinet by the prime minister could be dismissed from the senate by the president on the prime minister's recommendation. This might well reduce their spirit of independence and their willingness to express their thoughts freely in cabinet and parliament. Others believed that good government required a compromise between representativeness and efficiency with emphasis on the latter. Williams was in fact of the view that the

> electorate, growing daily in sophistication and an affluence as more and more of the younger generation come to maturity will increasingly demand, in so far as they show any interest at all, a superior type and form of representation . . . at the very time when increasing opportunities in the economic sector will draw more and more people away to business and professional activities who two decades ago looked almost instinctively to the political arena. (1974a, 75)

Williams noted that "even larger countries with more talent to draw on, find it difficult to secure sufficient people from among representatives in Parliament to run the ministries of government" (*Trinidad Guardian*, 4 May 1970). Williams also argued that the responsibilities of certain ministries such as finance or education were such that they would perhaps be better performed by people who did not have responsibilities to any specific constituency. The argument was even extended to the prime ministership. To quote Williams, "I believe that the Prime Minister should not be in the elected House at all. The Prime Minister does not represent a single constituency. The Prime Minister represents more than anybody else the entire country. Anybody is free to come to him" (*Trinidad Guardian*, 26 September 1976).

In terms of the legislature, the commission's proposal that standing committees should be appointed for all major functional areas and that they should have the right to examine all bills before they were debated and to call witnesses, was rejected. Williams accused the commission, quite unfairly, of proposing the introduction of the committees in a "cavalier and offhand manner". Standing committees, he noted, constituted

> one of the most difficult, one of the most serious and fundamental issues facing the United States political society in terms of its constitution to-day. The powers of a congressional committee to summon and to be told what is going on, as against the doctrine, always there from the earliest days of the constitution, reaching heights in the last few months that have never before been dreamed of by anybody for or against, of executive privilege. . . . It is not that the Commission is wrong. The Commission has some right on its side, especially if you watch the United States as it has developed – in a way that nobody concerned with the rights of the people's representatives in Parliament and the control of an executive could possibly accept or endorse. But you just don't rush and say that; there are certain things that you just cannot say at a particular time. You would call the Minister of Finance to a committee two or three days before the Budget and say he must come and answer? It depends on what questions you are going to ask. (1974a, 71)

Williams said that he was unsure as to how the institution would work in Trinidad and Tobago. It is worth noting, however, that the constitution commission specifically recommended that committees should not be given unlimited power to hold up legislation referred to it. Legislation had to be reported out of committee after a lapse of thirty days unless parliamentary approval was obtained for an extension. Provision was also made for committees to hold meetings in private if this was felt to be necessary in the interest of security or privacy.

Also rejected was the notion that the auditor general and the ombudsman should be chosen by a three-fifths majority of parliament after an appropriate committee had screened the president's nominees. Williams argued that such a procedure could make it difficult for parliament to agree on a choice of candidate and would encourage parliamentarians "to abuse the Parliamentary immunity given to them as members of Parliament to go and lambaste, and berate and denigrate public figures in the country by saying this, that and the other".

> You have seen it happen in the United States. The idea of the National Assembly approving certain appointments, they just suddenly pull it out; what is the reason for bringing this in from the United States, where it is being challenged as never before, and depositing it here? We couldn't agree to that at all until it has been gone into extremely carefully and it might be possible to have this subject to certain restrictions. I don't know. The idea seems too repugnant in terms of the known characteristics of this society and what it tends to encourage. I don't know that you are enhancing the dignity of our Parliament by giving this legal sanction and constitutional immunity. (Williams 1974a, 73–74).

It might be worthwhile to speculate as to the reasons why Williams took such a hostile view to the recommendations of the constitution commission and why so many of the commission's key recommendations were rejected. One clear reason is the personal animosity that existed between Williams and the chairman and deputy chairman of the commission as well as its other members, whom he described as men who either had failed to gain admission to the PNM (Sir Hugh Wooding) or who had never been on the successful end of election campaigns despite the fact that they had hung on to his shirttails. The latter reference was to Hamilton Maurice, who was a PNM candidate in the federal elections of 1958. Williams also poured scorn on the lawyers and the academics on the commission: "Constitutions are too important a matter to be left to lawyers alone. You must [also] be careful of the political scientist and the professor that you put on the Commission." The references were to the author and Dr Anthony Maingot, both of whom Williams had gone to great lengths to recruit (1974a, 33).[2]

Williams also accused the commissioners of wanting to emasculate the PNM and further other agendas:

> [O]ne tends always somehow to watch these recommendations of the Commission with sometimes very little explanation and they are heading in a certain direction, otherwise. It would be impossible to have written it. It is with a purpose. They have a goal, and that is to destroy the Party and the Party system. There is no party system in Trinidad and Tobago, and only one party that would be recognised anywhere. The others could do what they like, party groupings etc. and with that in mind, one watches everything that is being said here in terms of the political antecedents of some of the personalities. I believe that is a sufficiently decorous way of putting something without necessarily elaborating on it. (1974a, 17)

It is now clear that Williams was at no time interested in fundamental constitutional reform and that the commission was appointed because of the need to buy political time. The "hidden function" of the exercise was to sidetrack the demands of those who were accusing the regime of being both illegal and illegitimate and who were calling upon it to resign.

Williams was genuinely embarrassed by the results of the 1971 election, which had left the PNM with no opposition in parliament. There was also national concern, especially among the Indian and radical black community, that the PNM could and probably would establish an electoral dictatorship that was even more monopolistic than what obtained after 1962. There was thus a strategic need to assuage and pre-empt these anxieties. Thus the decision to establish the "blue ribbon" commission headed by former Chief Justice Wooding, a man whom Williams disliked, but who had enormous credibility. It was a brilliant political stroke.

It is true that Williams was interested in making certain incremental and interstitial changes to the 1962 document to improve its functioning. Williams was concerned about the composition of the senate, the role of the leader of the opposition, the question of the prime minister's obligation to consult with him on certain key appointments and the question of parliamentary committees. He was also interested in the establishment of an ombudsman and a change from monarchy to a republic. He was never interested in any radical systemic reform. Williams denied, however, that his aim was to buy time: "We did not appoint the Commission just to gain time. It was we who started Constitution Reform in this country in 1955 to 1956. . . . It was the party to which all of us minus a couple belong today that first raised the issue of republicanism" (1974a, 23). This did not convince many, including the author, to whom Williams had privately indicated his views as to what the commission should examine.

The commission, misled by Williams's recommendation that the exercise should not be a hurried one, opted to re-explore the essentials of the entire constitutional fabric. It started from scratch and re-evaluated every section and subsection of the 1962 document. The result was an innovative design that, if accepted, might well have meant a fundamental restructuring of the governmental process, probably to the immediate political disadvantage of the ruling party. It is hardly surprising that the DLP supported the commission's recommendations, which it felt would benefit it, while Williams viewed the recommendations as a mortal threat. The 1974 report was seen by many as the "gold standard" by which future reform exercises in the Caribbean would be judged. Dr Maingot correctly prophesied that "the time will come when the country will have to seriously consider the Report of the Wooding Commission" (*Trinidad Guardian*, 24 April 1986).

To discredit the report, Williams adopted the tactic of questioning the bona fides of the commission by imputing foreign linkages to its members. He roundly abused the commissioners and accused them of being politically inexperienced and having malice towards the ruling party. To quote the prime minister,

> It is a little difficult for us to accept as a measure of finality something that comes from a Commission, some of whose members have never been on the successful end of election campaigns. . . . These Constitution babes-in-the-woods seeking to discuss Constitution reform! . . . This party is not going to support something which is written from a point of view, an approach by people who know nothing of the purposes of parliamentary procedure and the operation of government and is written in some places with venom. (Williams 1974a, 74)

The prime minister accused the commission of having an "illogical obsession . . . to reduce the powers of Parliament, to create confusion and to break up the centralization of Parliament, cabinet and the political party" (ibid., 82).

Williams's ad hominem abuse of the commission was as obscene as it was intellectually dishonest – the type of reply one would expect in Woodford Square as opposed to in parliament. The allegation that the recommendations were designed to break up the PNM was peculiar. Surely, the commission was not appointed to preserve the PNM. Its aim was to devise a constitution that would introduce balance in a system that all agreed was too centralized. The prime minister well understood that the proposed constitution was a radical document that was subversive of the neo-Westminster model negotiated in 1962. Thus his enraged response.

The confrontation between Williams and Wooding (who died in July 1974, a few weeks before Williams's vulgar abuse) highlights one of the difficulties posed when experts are called upon to give advice to political actors who have unarticulated reasons for seeking that "advice". Although the commissioners were aware of the need to present a "politically feasible" document that stood some chance of acceptance, they were wrong in their calculations as to what Williams was willing to accept as well as about what the opposition parties and public opinion would force him to concede. By the time the new constitution was being redrafted, the political crisis had more or less passed and Williams had come to believe that there was in fact no critical demand for fundamental constitutional change and little danger that the PNM would lose the forthcoming election. Having appointed the commission, he felt that he had to carry on the exercise to the end. The changes that were made did not justify the expense of that exercise. The ruling party was the only gainer.

It is worth recording that notwithstanding the fact that the government had ample time to process the Wooding Report, the draft constitution bill was rushed through parliament in March 1976. More surprisingly, the bill was hastily prepared and many amendments had to be even more hastily tabled. Given the fact that the opposition had boycotted the 1971 election, there was little opposition in the house of representatives. Most of the opposition came from the independent members of the senate. The exercise was a veritable farce. The *Express* was correct when it observed that the Commission on Constitutional Reform exercise turned out to be a waste of time. The *Express* also observed that the people were not given any opportunity to have their say. "The Government," the paper editorialized, "just cannot push a bill of this importance through Parliament using a steam roller of its majority and call it George" (*Trinidad Express*, 28 March 1976). Yet that was precisely what Williams did.

30 Bloody Tuesday and the "Unmixing" of Oil and Sugar

The years 1971 to 1976 witnessed an intensified effort on the part of radical trade unions to topple the Williams regime. The effort was a continuation of what was attempted in 1966 when the WFP sought to unite "oil and sugar". The organizational expression of this movement was the United Labour Front (ULF), formed in February 1976 following a mammoth rally that brought together the OWTU, led by George Weekes; the All Trinidad Sugar Estates and Factory Workers Trade Union, led by Basdeo Panday; the Transport and Industrial Workers Union, led by Joe Young; and the Trinidad Islandwide Cane Farmers Association, led by Raffique Shah.

The birth of the Front was in part the byproduct of an event that had taken place one year earlier, on 18 March 1975, which came to be known as "Bloody Tuesday", though no blood was shed. The confrontation between the ULF and the police, and by extension the Williams government, took the form of an attempt by oil, sugar and other workers to march from San Fernando to Port of Spain, permission for which had not been sought from the commissioner of police. The marchers claimed that no permission was required because it was a "religious" march for "bread and peace". The police insisted that the march was illegal, and broke it up using rifle butts, truncheons and tear gas. The leaders of the march were manhandled, beaten, arrested and charged under section 118 of the Summary Offences Amendment Act of 1972 for taking part in an illegal march. Twenty-nine others were arrested and charged. When the matter came before the court, the leaders opted to go to jail rather than pay the imposed fines. The obvious aim was to enlist public sympathy. The strategy did not work and the fines were paid by the unions to which these individuals belonged.

Predictably, spokesmen for the marchers accused the Williams government of brutality, "creeping fascism" and attempting to establish a "police state". The repression was condemned by the IRO and several "concerned clergymen", including Catholic archbishop Anthony Pantin. The established print media, the *Express* and the *Guardian*, were also critical of what was seen as overreaction on the part of the police and the army. Williams angrily denied that the march was a genuine religious event, and even threatened to counter-organize a march of his own to show how strong he was.[1] He also denied that the police overreacted. As he declared, "Had it been another third world country, the first thousand would have been shot. No shot was however fired and no one was killed" (Baptiste 1976, 9). Williams was aware, however, that he was faced with a threat that he had to take seriously. A reprise of what had taken place in 1970 and which forced him to declare a state of emergency seemed imminent.

On hearing that George Weekes was arrested, some four hundred union members walked off their jobs at the Port of Spain unit of the Trinidad and Tobago Electricity Commission. The protest spread to the company's other units, and led to an electrical power failure that affected several key areas of the country. The workers were showing that they had resources to fight back, a point that was not lost on Williams. Williams was concerned not only about the incipient coalescing of oil and sugar, as he had been in 1970, but also about the possibility that the radical unions could gain control of the distribution of electricity and petroleum supplies, as well as of public transport, and of the water and telephone companies (Water and Sewerage Authority and TELCO). Thus the passage of a Criminal Law Amendment Bill (1975), which provided for imprisonment for life of anyone found guilty of criminal sabotage.

The events of 18 March 1975 gave rise to an intense debate in radical union circles as to whether the time was ripe to try to seize power. Some radical spokesmen felt that Williams was on the ropes and that power could be seized. The workers, it was said, were now ready. It was also argued that whereas Williams had succeeded in the past in dividing the workers in oil and sugar by co-opting and using Bhadase Sagan Maraj, that strategy had failed. Bhadase, who led the union from 1963 to his death in 1971, was now gone, and the sugar belt was looking for a new messiah. As Raffique Shah, president general for the Trinidad Islandwide Cane Farmers Association and former mutineer, opined, "It was time to take the jump." The solution to the problem had to be political. "Nothing in the world can stop the people now" (Baptiste 1976, 84). Shah argued that "we need state power to bring about a change in the system" (ibid., 220).

There was no consensus, however, as to whether an attempt should be made to seize power by unconventional means. Michael Als, president of the Bank Workers Union, accused Basdeo Panday of holding back the workers just when they were ready to grab power and complete the revolution. Panday was also accused of compromising the movement by holding consultations with the governor general, which in effect meant holding discussions with the prime minister. Panday's reply to the charge was that he "put his trust in God. Men make mistakes; only God does not make mistakes" (Baptiste 1976, 85).

To better understand what was taking place in the trade union movement and the ULF, it is important to focus, if only briefly, on the career of Basdeo Panday, who replaced Maraj as the dominant figure in the sugar belt. In 1965, Panday returned to Trinidad and Tobago from London, where he had studied economics, political science and dramatic arts. He had also qualified as a lawyer. He was drafted into the 1966 general election campaign, and like other every other candidate who fought on behalf of the WFP, failed to get sufficient votes to save his deposit. He thereafter concentrated on his legal practice and served as a legal adviser to the OWTU. In 1973, he was invited to become president general of the All Trinidad Sugar Estates and Factory Workers Trade Union. According to Panday, the general secretary of the union, Rampartap Singh, assumed he would be a figurehead and a tool. Panday had other ideas and ambitions.

Panday's activities in the sugar belt were of deep concern to Williams, who had begun looking around for an alternative to Bhadase Maraj, whom he and Tate and Lyle had seduced and suborned over many years.[2] Bhadase was president general of the sugar union from 1963 to 1971. The events of Bloody Tuesday and the strike activity that Panday had initiated were crippling the sugar industry, and led Williams to alter his strategy. He would seek to drive a wedge between the sugar workers and the oil workers who were also on strike for increased wages. Williams would boast in *Inward Hunger* that keeping these two power bases apart was one of his great achievements.

In January 1974, Panday initiated conversations with Caroni Limited, in which the state had acquired majority ownership from Tate and Lyle, for a 100 per cent wage increase, guaranteed work, worker participation and profit sharing in the industry. Caroni, in which the state had majority ownership, refused to negotiate with Panday on the ground that he was not yet formally recognized as the the president general of the union. The workers, however, remained with Panday, and continued with their strike action. After three months of struggle, the latter sensed that the workers were on the point of capitulation and decided on a change of strategy. He would march to Whitehall. As he later boasted, "I decided to transfer the strike from the industrial stage to the political. The Friday before the march, I received a telephone call from Errol Mahabir [who said], 'Panday, boy, I would like to see you.' 'Well, you cyar come by my house and I ent coming by yours.' Eventually a neutral house was agreed upon. The first thing Errol told me was: 'Boy, the old man say you win. Call Caroni tomorrow and they will agree to see you.' "[3]

Panday said that during that fateful meeting with Mahabir, he was told that the prime minister did not mind the sugar workers having an Indian leader who would carry on as an Indian leader: "We are happy to know that the Indians have found their own George Weekes."

The minute I heard this, I realized that what the Government wanted most was to keep oil and sugar apart. I decided to play a game, and, again it worked like a charm. So shortly after Caroni decided to see me, I called George and told him, "George I don't want to see you for a year. Don't call me. Don't talk to me. Pay no attention to what you read in the Press even if it sounds derogatory. Just trust me." You see, I knew that if Williams thought for a single moment that I was going to align myself with Weekes, my throat would be cut before I could become entrenched. By the end of September 1974, I had won the struggle for guaranteed work and I felt I had the loyalty of the workers. Entrenched now, I went to George and told him that the time had come to continue the job we started in 1966. (Panday interview cited in Baptiste 1976, 285)

The strike, which had crippled both the oil and sugar industries, and which according to Williams cost the country over TT$200 million in lost income, polarized the society and the trade union movement. Much to Williams's anger, the ULF was supported by the West Indies Group of University Teachers, which spoke out publicly. The group argued that the wage and other demands being made by the unions were not unreasonable having regard to prevailing conditions in the world economy and the industries in question. The group also warned Williams against calling for foreign intervention to help prop up the PNM regime.[4]

The established media was also alarmed about what was taking place in the country and the "ominous" official silence that obtained. As the *Express* editorialized,

The industrial relations situation is rapidly approaching crisis level, exemplified by the fact that the country's food – as well as its gasoline – is now affected. With the closing down of Caroni's four factories and Orange Grove's one, the entire sugar milling capacity of Trinidad and Tobago has been brought to a standstill. Texaco's oil refining capacity has virtually ground to a halt and its gas stations have a little, or no petrol available. [And yet] while a national emergency builds up around us, the government appears to be standing majestically aloof from the confusion, as though what is happening in the sugar and oil belts, is not really Whitehall's concern. (Baptiste 1976, 31)

As was his wont, Williams remained silent until he felt that the situation had "matured" sufficiently for him to intervene. By the time he chose to speak on 11 April, the workers had abandoned strike action and the country seemed anxious for a return to "normalcy".

The unions and many others expected Williams to take over Caroni fully. He had signalled this by acquiring an additional 4 per cent of the company's shares. Interestingly, Panday was opposed to the complete state ownership of Caroni that other radicals were demanding. As he declared, "We do not want state capitalism. We want workers to get shares in the Company. That is what we are fighting for." Williams confused everyone by initially refusing to pay the $15 million that

Tate and Lyle wanted for the shares. As he declared, "I am not spending 15 cents on any more shares in that company which is now nothing but idle lands to produce nothing and not give the population the service that that expenditure is designed to produce" (Baptiste 1976, 120). Williams took over the company eventually, much to the surprise of the company directors, who privately conceded that Williams paid more than the company was worth. Williams's decision was clearly driven by patrimonial rather than economic considerations. The state was taking over the plantations on which African slaves and indentured Indians had shed their blood and their sweat. Williams also took over the company to protect the jobs of the workers. Tate and Lyle was aware, however, that King Sugar was dead, and would have settled for less.

Bloody Tuesday was a short-run disaster for the radical unions, and what Lloyd Best said of them was correct: "The ULF was born big and stupid. Against all national advice and without doing a shred of political work, the leaders made their big grandstand play. They huffed and puffed and one windy morning in San Fernando, [commissioner of police] Tony May blew them all away" (Baptiste 1976, 228).

The ULF leadership did not see it that way. They felt that the experience of the workers during and following that event had raised the consciousness of the latter and this had convinced them that it was now time for the ULF to enter the political ring. Initially, both Panday and Weekes had expressed the view that they had no political ambitions and would not enter the political thicket. This was disingenuous, however, particularly on the part of Panday, who at a rally that drew some thirty thousand workers, told his listeners that the time had come to continue the work he had begun in 1966. Power had to be captured from Williams and those who propped him up. As Panday declared,

> We must now consolidate and institutionalize the de facto power which we now have to get control of the State. I believe we ought to learn a lesson from the failure of the black power movement, that we have to go beyond the stage of marching. In 1970, they reached a tremendous height of 'de facto' power, but they didn't know what to do with it. Had they been able to do something with it, our political history would have been different. ULF must not make that same mistake. I will like to see the ULF consolidated into a political movement, but that must not be a decision from the top. It must follow from the wishes of the people. The days of sitting down in the Holiday Inn and declaring a political party are over. For any political movement to be successful, it must burst forth from the bowels of the people. (*Trinidad Express*, 23 February 1976)

Panday was satisfied that the working people of African and Indian descent had made it unequivocally clear that they were ready to capture political power from the PNM in the general elections of 1976:

> The African worker now realizes he has been betrayed by Dr. Williams and has become

more conscious of his economic role and the conflict in his mind between racial affinity and economic reality has been lessened. The economic aspirations of the workers of African descent are now predominant. The situation is the same with the Indian workers – economic aspirations take precedence over racial and political ones. Hence, the two groups can now come together and vote on the basis of class and economic interest for a party that they know will best represent those interest. (*Trinidad Express*, 15 April 1976)

Panday stubbornly opposed those who were insisting that power should be seized by revolutionary means. This position was being taken by the National Union of Freedom Fighters and some of the Marxist and Maoist parties that proliferated at the time, such as the National Movement for the True Independence of Trinago, Students for Change, the National Liberation Movement, and United Revolutionary Organisation. As he declared,

> We must concentrate on the worker achieving political power by conventional means. It is for this reason, in my view, that the United Labour Front is a significant development in the struggle of the working people. Armed revolution in this country is not a feasible idea for two reasons. Firstly our people don't have a history of revolution, so that we are not trained and it's most likely to fail. We can learn from the sprinklings we have had of it, for instance the death of Guy Harewood. We can see the futility there. Secondly, because of the racial composition and the suspicion that has been engendered among the two dominant races, armed revolution is likely to degenerate into a racial conflict. Can you imagine an Indian guerilla killing a Negro child? This is likely to happen, because in such conflicts, many innocent people are likely to be killed. That then is the end of your revolution. (*Trinidad Express*, 5 February 1975)

Panday insisted that although the ULF was a radical working class party it must not become wedded to any obsolete "isms". As he said,

> To call the [ULF programme] this "ism" of that "ism" would be to create confusion in the minds of people, because "isms" have different meanings to different people. The specific mechanism to bring our policies into operation will be determined by the objective realities at any given time and this will change from time to time. We do not wish to import models which are suited to other countries but not suited to our own. We must develop indigenous institutions relevant to our society, our own consciousness and our own state of economic growth. (*Trinidad Express*, 6 April 1976)

Panday denied that he himself was a socialist or that he used the word *socialist* to describe what he stood for. He stressed that his chief goal was not to destroy capitalism but to extend it to the workers. Workers' capitalism would destroy the myth that the interests of workers and managers were irreconcilably opposed.

Williams never really regarded Panday as a serious political threat and was quite prepared to do whatever was necessary to ensure that he was regarded as the replacement for Bhadase Maraj, with whom, as we have seen, he had had a working relationship behind the scenes. Ferdie Ferreira was correct when he noted that "Dr. Williams read Basdeo Panday well, understood him, and played on his ego and ambition. Like Cassius, he was a very ambitious man and Williams was quite happy, recognizing his limitations, to accommodate his limited attributes, once he was able to confine him to the sugar belt. The flamboyant leader had more bark than bite and the party never considered him a serious political threat, as long as the sugar workers got what they assumed was, and what Panday convinced them, was their share of the cake" (*Newsday*, 11 April 2003). Williams was not above inviting Panday to his home for a drink of his "best scotch", when he felt that it was good politics to do so.

31 Williams versus the People's National Movement

The Elections of 1976

I have no desire to hold on to power. But I do not flinch from duty. If it is considered that the nation and the Party require me to continue in office, I shall leave neither nation or Party in the lurch.

– Eric Williams, 1976

The 1976 elections were characterized by a great deal of confusion, uncertainty and despair. There was uncertainty as to how many parties would contest, who would run on which ticket, whether there would be mergers or alliances and even whether there would be any election at all. Lalsingh Harribance, a medium who claimed to have extraordinary powers of ESP, predicted that there would be no elections, and that Eric Williams would be made prime minister for life, after which A.N.R. Robinson would succeed. The opposition groups were also sceptical. Some of the members of the radical ULF believed that if an election were held, and the PNM were to lose to the ULF, attempts would be made to abort the result. Many also felt that there was a distinct possibility that no party would emerge with a clear majority, and that the president would have to play the role of king maker. There was a great deal of anxiety about this, since it was assumed that the president would be partial to the PNM in the event parliament was deadlocked.

At one point, it appeared likely that Williams might opt out of the fray altogether or switch from the Port of Spain South constituency, which he had not visited since 1973 and which contained elements considered to be doubtful in their allegiance. There was speculation that he might go either to the Diego Martin or Point Fortin constituencies, which he had been cultivating for some time. PNM groups in three constituencies had in fact nominated the prime minister.

Williams eventually did contest Port of Spain South, but the constituency was gerrymandered to include the old middle-class district of Woodbrook, which was previously included in the constituency of Port of Spain Central. Working class areas that were previously located in Port of Spain South were attached to the Laventille constituency. Ironically, the new districts added to Port of Spain South were those that had voted against Williams and the PNM in 1956 and for the white-creole dominated POPPG. The "massas" were now firmly in the PNM camp.

A great deal of uncertainty and speculation surrounded what role, if any, race would play in the election. The ULF and its supporters claimed that given the working class struggles that had taken place since 1971, and particularly in 1975, class perceptions would triumph over race, with others claiming the contrary. There was also some curiosity as to how the urban upwardly mobile Indians would react to the socialist-leaning ULF. Would they support it on racial grounds, abstain, or vote PNM? Of interest too was the question of what difference, if any, the eighteen-year-old vote would make on party fortunes.

Williams versus the PNM

All opposition parties campaigned on the theme of "it's time for a change" and "twenty years is enough". Williams emphasized stability, democracy, religious tolerance and personal freedom.

The PNM manifesto also referred to the freedom of the press, of the judiciary, and other freedoms such as the freedom to form political parties, even though their multiplicity was said to have become "a national joke". "We live under no permanent national emergency, our General Elections are not postponed, political dissenters are not in jail, we have been spared political violence, our citizens have a fundamental right to the enjoyment of property, and Trinidad and Tobago is not a one-party state." The manifesto went on to pledge to protect the rights of private property against the "ideological presumptions of our age".

The PNM further boasted that its record of achievement was outstanding, particularly in the fields of education, national ownership and in the quality of life generally. Williams said that notwithstanding its problems, the secondary school system in 1976 represented the most salient achievement of the PNM during its twenty years in power. For every secondary school that existed in 1956, there were now five in 1976, while for every student in the secondary school in 1956, there were eight in 1976. Recurrent expenditure in 1976 – $172 million – was fourteen times that in 1956.

What was interesting, however, was not the PNM's manifesto, but the unorthodox campaign that Williams fought. Williams literally campaigned against the PNM and his cabinet, five members of which he described as "millstones". He told the party in May 1976 that he was grossly dissatisfied with its complacent performance in the selection of candidates, and ordered the entire exercise scrapped and redone. Williams accused the general secretary of the party,

Nicholas Simonette, of "showing a total lack of awareness – or is it perhaps a total contempt for the electoral mood of the country", which he said had "indicated a disdain for traditional electioneering and political parties". Williams also went on to tell the party that

> The electorate wishes no part whatsoever of the majority of the PNM incumbents and nominees, no matter who else is satisfied with them. The public mood accepts that some PNM incumbents have talent, are working reasonably well, are attending to their public duties, are showing initiative, and – whether mistakes are being made or not – are not "passengers". But these are very few indeed. In respect to the vast majority, the public, today, more sophisticated and less untutored than in 1956, would not react today to the slogan of 1956, vote PNM or die, as many did twenty years ago. Who does not understand this in May 1976, understands nothing. (*Trinidad Guardian*, 26 May 1976)

Williams warned that he was not going to pull along on his coat tails anyone with whom he was not satisfied:

> Let it be understood now, once and for all, by all and sundry – the Political Leader has not the slightest intention of encumbering himself, yet again, with these traditional party millstones, unable to speak properly, knowing nothing of the basic issues facing country and world, incompetent for higher responsibilities which ultimately fall on the Political Leader's shoulders, unable – unbelievable though it sounds – even to seek to assist their constituents in difficulty who further turn to the Political Leader and interfere with his attention to his formal, public, national responsibilities.
>
> The Political Leader has not the slightest intention of leading into any election campaign some of the choices of a few party members seeking to arrogate to themselves the right to impose X or Y or Z on an electorate of 15,000.
>
> Either the nominees remain and you get a more appropriate Political Leader, or the Political Leader remains, and you get more appropriate candidates for whom no apology needs to be made. There is no other alternative. (*Trinidad Guardian*, 26 May 1976)

By failing to select more women and youths, the party was also said to be out of touch with the electorate. The emphasis in the new selection exercise, Williams insisted, must be on youth and women around twenty-five years of age or less.

The country was also said to be looking for candidates who could demonstrate their integrity in public affairs. Williams complained that he had sent a memorandum to the party in 1973 (when he indicated he was resigning) dealing with the question of candidate selection and public integrity, but nothing had been done about it. The proposals recommended that cabinet ministers, members of parliament, the tenders board, senior public servants and their wives and children be required to declare their assets and liabilities. It was also recommended then that prospective candidates be required to indicate which companies they held shares in, if any, provide evidence that they were not in arrears with respect to income tax, and make binding arrangements to have 7.5 per cent of their salaries (if elected) paid to the party. Candidates were also required to provide an undated and signed letter of resignation addressed to the Speaker of the House to be held by the political leader to be used in the event that the member defected or was deemed to be undesirable to carry the party's standard. Williams also complained that prospective candidates were soliciting and collecting campaign contributions from businessmen, and that at least "one such contribution constituted a serious impropriety, and called for appropriate action by the Prime Minister". He likewise complained that the refurbishing of the convention centre at Chaguaramas had cost too much, some TT$8 million, and that party members were involved. He opined that the matter should be the subject of a commission of inquiry. To quote Williams,

> The Party's nominations take no account whatsoever of the integrity issue. The Prime Minister can hardly be expected to have to consider X or Y or Z, of whom nothing is known in terms of his assets and liabilities, as persons for higher office and responsibility, who will then, under the Republican Constitution, declare assets and liabilities. In these days of coups and coalitions, the present PNM procedures are an open invitation to crossing the floor after the elections – simply to ensure non-compliance with the Constitution in respect to the law to be passed after the Election setting up the Integrity Commission. More positively, what is required of the Party is an election pledge of constitutional amendments immediately after the election in respect of:
>> crossing the floor – the member must go back to his constituency for a new mandate,
>> widening the scope and requirements of the Integrity Commission,
>> drastic revision of the existing Tenders Board legislation.
>
> This will inevitably call for the selection of appropriate persons as candidates and extracting from them appropriate pledges before they are selected by the Party as candidates. (Ibid.)

Williams ended his address to the general council with what constituted an ultimatum, reproduced here in its entirety:

> I do not seek to return to office. I have no desire to hold on to power. But I do not flinch from duty. If it is considered that the interests of both the nation and the Party require me to continue office, I shall leave neither Nation nor Party in the lurch. But I cannot agree to any compromise of my political principles or any betrayal of conscience. I will not agree to any use of my reputation to confer respectability on any person or group of persons predisposed to corruption or racism or suppression of the fundamental rights of citizens, including their right to their religious beliefs or practices or any imposition of doctrine borrowed from outside on our economic and political patterns.
>
> If I must stay on, I shall do so only as the leader of a team comprising persons of tested competence and loyalty on the one hand and on the other, new recruits both

male and female, both young and old, to be trained in the responsibility of independent nationhood, dedicated to party discipline and morality in public affairs. If these principles I enunciate are not acceptable, then the Party must get a new Political Leader and the country a new Prime Minister more attuned to Party indiscipline and public immorality.

In those circumstances, I shall take no part whatsoever in the election campaign, I would be forced, Mr. Party Chairman, to repeat my request to you, to be relieved of all responsibility for either the draft election manifesto or the screening of Party candidates. Merely for PNM to win another election or give to X or Y or Z a power they do not deserve and might well abuse, I shall not sacrifice the welfare of the Nation or compromise my personal integrity, or break faith with the Party of which I am a foundation member, and which in 20 years has brought Trinidad and Tobago to heights never before dreamed of. (Ibid.)

Members of the party were horrified and embarrassed, and one senior minister said that he was now convinced that the prime minister had "gone off his rocker". So angry were senior party members that they chose to reply openly, going so far as to take to Woodford Square to attack the prime minister – all this on what was assumed to be the eve of the election. Williams was accused of trying to "smash up the party", or looking for an excuse to quit. Either that, or he was trying to get a personal mandate in a manner similar to 1973 when he said he would resign. Allan Harris, who later ran against Williams in Port of Spain South on a Tapia ticket, captured the essence of Williams's strategy when he argued that the latter was affecting a political style of "politics without parties" à la de Gaulle. Williams, he believed, was fearful of the electorate, and sought to put a measure of distance between himself and the PNM. To quote Harris,

> The little King must now stand forth as our guarantee of stability and continuity, as our salvation from the political violence, the racism, the ideological chaos, the suppression of liberties of Jamaica and Guyana. He must again hang out the banner of morality in public affairs, being himself above reproach on that score. In sum, he must now appear as the Great Conservator of values, the Father of the Nation, the Wise Old Patriarch of the Tribe presiding over a time of troubles and transition, guiding our destiny with a firm hand and a secure touch. It is the apotheosis of the Messiah, man made God.
>
> Does not such a transformation require that he shake off the dross of this earth? – those traditional "party millstones". Does not the superior insight of his elevated position require that he dispense with the mundane democratic processes of choosing nominees within the party? Will not the new and elevated perspectives require new and more trustworthy minions and messengers?
>
> In common political language, Williams' strategy for survival is to attempt to sell himself once again, albeit in newly packaged form. To sell himself successfully as a symbol of Stability with Progress, of Order with Integrity, he must have a free hand to choose his running mates. (*Tapia*, 30 May 1976)

In his reply, the general secretary boldly accused Williams of bringing the party and its general secretary into disrepute. To quote Nicholas Simonette,

> This is not the first time that the Political Leader has sought to embarrass, denigrate and distort information relating to the general secretary. But on previous occasions the general secretary allowed these matters to pass in the interest of party discipline and party unity, especially as the general secretary was satisfied that these attempts at castigation and denigration were without foundation. The general secretary was content to let his record of work speak for itself. (*Trinidad Guardian*, 6 June 1976)

Simonette told Williams that he wanted him to understand clearly that this was the last time he would be allowed to do so. In speaking about his own performance, Simonette denied that he was "either complacent or negligent. If those terms described anyone, it was the Prime Minister himself who did nothing to ensure that his proposals were considered and adopted by the General Council in time for them to become part of the party's constitution and regulations for selecting candidates". Simonette also criticized Williams for humiliating the general council by bluntly refusing to give it a copy of his speech and then adding insult to injury by releasing a full statement to the *Guardian*: "The Political Leader displays here political individuality which is repugnant to all that we in the party stand for. I am appalled at his determination to act in defiance of General Council principles of not disseminating information which is the property of the Council without agreement of the Council. This is not the political leader I knew in years gone by and to whom I gave my allegiance in 1956" (ibid.).

Simonette also accused Williams of showing the same "irresponsibility" that he displayed in 1973 by not signalling his consent to nomination after giving cues that he might run in at least three constituencies. He likewise accused him of showing no concern for discipline, and of "doing his own thing" in defiance of the party rules. Simonette said that Williams had given instructions to the party chairman in March 1976 to activate the party for elections, but at that time made no mention of his 1973 memorandum. "If anyone was complacent about his own proposals, it was Dr Williams," said Simonette. He concluded his reply by literally accusing Williams of lying to the party and the country. Williams's words were said to be "utterly misleading".

Some party members felt that the party should repudiate Williams and dare him to resign, but the efforts came to naught as the resumed convention agreed to go through the nomination exercise again. General council member Ferdie Ferreira was vocally angry with Williams. Ferreira explained that any party would have its share of passengers (hangers-on). The PNM picked up a few in 1971 when the elections were boycotted. These twelve represented "traditional opposition seats", and posed no problem in the party because they were likely to lose the election. Of the other twenty-four, fourteen were ministers or parliamentary secretaries and these represented the best the party could get from within its own ranks. Ferreira also warned Williams of his individualistic behaviour; he said it was ruining the party, which he considered to be the country's salvation. Ferreira told Williams that the party is bigger than any individual, and was not the property of any single individual (*Trinidad Guardian*, 7 June 1976).

Simonette, supported by Ferreira, defied Williams by chairing a meeting held on 5 July in Woodford Square, at which Karl Hudson-Phillips spoke. At that meeting, one of the largest held at the square since 1956, the attorney general declared that he would not prostitute himself for the sake of holding office. He would therefore not sign the undated letter as a matter of principle, which in effect meant that he had chosen not to contest the election. In an earlier open letter to the prime minister (dated May 27), Hudson-Phillips had declared that the principle of undated letters could have serious implications for the party and the country: "The principle was not only a threat to democracy as we know it, but could well institutionalize the thin edge of the wedge of dictatorship." It would also be a "severe blow to the integrity and supremacy of Parliament and the freedom of speech and conscience in that august body". "The principle," Hudson-Phillips continued, "could lead to the subjugation of the will of Parliament to a single individual and to a frustration and indeed subjugation of the will of the electorate." Hudson-Phillips accused Williams of seeking to put loyalty above everything and of attempting to grab personal power, something the prime minister had accused others of seeking to do.

Hudson-Phillips refused the suggestion that he should sign the letter and repudiate it after he was elected. He said that such behaviour would be unethical. It was also suicide for a professional man. Hudson-Phillips taunted Williams by noting that the principle of the undated letter had been used by Al Capone in the 1920s. Hudson-Phillips warned Williams that the undated letter not only was prima facie illegal, but would give rise to litigation as candidates disputed whether their undated letters were coerced or subsequently revoked. He hoped the prime minister would abandon an idea that he must have adopted "in a moment of unpardonable weakness" (*Trinidad Express*, 11 June 1976). Hudson-Phillips wondered aloud as to who would hold Dr Williams's undated letter. He suggested that it was preferable to deal with the matter of defecting members of parliament by a constitutional amendment that would require the member to vacate his seat and face the electorate within ninety days of his defection. This is what was eventually done in 1978, when a combination of circumstances, including the defection of one PNM minister and a split in the ULF, provided the two-thirds majority required to amend the constitution. The ULF was also concerned about the problem of members of parliament who crossed the floor.

The controversial undated letter is reproduced here for the sake of historical interest:

The Speaker,
House of Representatives,

Dear Sir,

In accordance with a resolution of a convention of the Peoples National Movement of which I am a member and under whose auspices I was elected to a seat in the House of Representatives for the . . . area, I hereby authorize the Political Leader of the PNM to submit on my behalf to you this my letter of resignation from the House of Representatives in view of the fact that I consider myself no longer a member of the said PNM and I hereby claim no further rights to the seat which I occupy in the said House of Representatives as a result of the elections which I contested under the auspices of the PNM.

The party made attempts to discipline the outspoken three, but these came to naught. The matter became bogged down in procedural and legal technicalities, and it was clear that party sentiment was against any bloodletting on the eve of the election. By voting unanimously to dismiss all disciplinary charges, the general council had indicated that it preferred to close ranks and forget the matter.

The public reaction to this caper ranged all the way from delight to dismay. Those who saw the PNM as the only party that could continue to look after their vested interest or that could provide the stability which they claimed the country needed, were visibly upset, and criticized Williams for seeking to destabilize the party on the eve of a critical election. The opposition could hardly contain itself at what appeared to be the imminent collapse of the PNM juggernaught. Tapia leader Lloyd Best saw the public mud-slinging as the surest sign of a will to self-destruction. He felt that the bottom had fallen out of the "bucket" that Williams had let down in 1956. The PNM had shown that it had no organization or machinery in the local areas and that it was a "Doctor" party. All its structures, such as the party groups, general council and conventions, were mere sham. "The fact of the matter is that few party groups are really functioning and genuine local leaders hardly exist at all." The DAC leader, A.N.R. Robinson, saw the PNM as being "at the end of the road". Williams, he said, was now "making a clean breast of it [and] was admitting what he [Robinson] had been saying for years. His are confessions of absolute defeat" (*Trinidad Guardian*, 16 May 1976). Other commentators felt that the "Party was over", since it was clear that the PNM would not be able to "clean its slate" before the elections.[1]

In a contemporary comment on Williams's speech, this author urged him to retire gracefully from politics, as Harold Wilson had recently done, since he was now the "principal fetter on the continued progress of the nation". Williams was told that "no one takes you seriously any more, not even your closest colleagues. The country needs to take a good hard searching look at itself, one that is not mediated by the distracting prism of your leadership. As an historian, you must recall Oliver Cromwell's rebuke to the Long Parliament as he dismissed it from power: 'You have sat too long here for any good you have been doing. Depart I say and let us have done with you. In the name of God, go!' " (*Trinidad Express*, 30 May 1976).[2]

The bright young men and women whom Williams wanted to lead were not forthcoming, especially since again it had been made clear that his strategy was to use people and then discard them unceremoniously. Many felt that Williams would pull it off, and that out of the "ruins" of the PNM would arise the EWP (Eric Williams Party). Williams, however, chose to bow to the party, which re-endorsed almost all the candidates he had rejected, including the five ministers whom he had publicly identified as "millstones". Efforts to bypass party groups and bring in technocrats proved abortive, because few were willing to stand. As in 1970 when the party sought new blood to put into the senate, few were prepared to offer their services. Although there were fifteen new faces, most of them were in constituencies that the party did not expect to win. Of those, only two were women and they were by no means young. Of the men, only two could be considered to be anywhere near twenty-five years of age.

Williams made no further public comment about his threat to withdraw, however, and led the team in the election and campaigned on behalf of all of them except the "millstone five". He was clearly concerned about the restless mood of the electorate, which was not turning out to election meetings. His research team and Special Branch had informed him that an average of only about 75 persons were turning out to opposition party meetings between March and May of 1976. He feared that the same indifference would greet the PNM: "The only reason why this picture is not true of PNM is that it has held no election meetings."

Williams's campaign must have been one of the most unorthodox ever waged by a political leader. He attacked almost every aspect of his government's administration. He complained about the lack of integrity on the part of parliamentarians, and about the poor performance of the public service and the utilities, in particular the National Housing Authority, the Water and Sewerage Authority and the Telephone Company. Williams went so far as to take the Water and Sewerage Authority from the control of the Ministry of Public Utilities and instead place it under the control of the Ministry of Finance, of which he was head. The minister of public utilities, Sham Mohammed, was one of the named millstones. Viewing Williams's performance, one commentator complained that the prime minister was stealing all the thunder from the opposition. As *Trinidad Express* editor (and former Williams aide) George John wittily observed,

> The most vigorous critic of the government, the most caustic critic of its performance, the strongest and the roughest and the toughest abuser in power is none other than the Prime Minister and party leader himself. Meeting after meeting, he denounces the performances of the public utilities. His ministers have been criticised more by their

leader than by anybody else, to the point where there are four or five ministers, still ministers remember, who he has refused to endorse and on whose campaign platform he will not appear.

What can the other opposition parties do? How in the name of high politics can they oppose a party leader who is publicly opposed to his own ruling party, a Prime Minister who is publicly opposed to his own ministers, a head of government who is publicly opposed to his own government? What in the name of low politics can they say? How can they make their followers believe they will do better than the PNM and the PNM government when the PNM leader says his party is no good and the Prime Minister confesses his government has made too many mistakes? (*Trinidad Express*, 5 September 1976)

Williams's strategy was to affect a presidential style of leadership and set himself up as a paragon of virtue. The strategy required that he distance himself from the PNM and some of his ministerial colleagues. To this end, he declared his assets and called upon others to do the same. During the elections, no meeting of the PNM's strategy committee was called, and it appeared that Williams (aided by Errol Mahabir) was determined to demonstrate to the party that he could win the election without its help. He even let it be known that if the people made it clear that he was not wanted, he was prepared to go. As he told one audience, "I have been hearing it; if you say it loud enough, I will go. But if you feel that I still have a contribution to make, in the words of the popular song, 'if you need me, I will be around' " (*Bomb*, 3 September 1976).

Williams, who at first had not planned to hit the campaign trail but to rely on the media, instead found that he was well received wherever he went. He was not heckled as much as he had feared, thanks in part the security services always in evidence. But the response was good, and Williams expressed himself pleasantly surprised, since he had earlier assumed that the electorate had moved away from street-corner meetings. Williams even became nostalgic about the 1956 campaign. As he said, "PNM's street corner university development, stemming from the original University of Woodford Square, remains our enduring contribution to political thought and practice" (*Trinidad Guardian*, 11 September 1976).

Williams was scornful of the opposition and their call for change. "Change from what to what?" he asked. "You do not change the successful for the unsuccessful; you do not choose winners for losers; you do not change the winners over the past 20 years and put the losers whom we have been beating morning noon and night." He clearly believed that the outcome of the election was not in doubt, and that the PNM would prevail. As he declared, "I don't know which election you are fighting, but I am now fighting the 1981 election." On another occasion Williams put the issue of stability in the following manner: "If one has to guarantee the continuation and extension of that stability . . . which party could be trusted to do that better than the PNM which has had 20 years of bringing you where you are today? We can't guarantee that you'll go with us to heaven, but we're certain that you'll go with them to hell" (*Tapia*, 15 August 1976). "If you do not like the Party, move it in an election; but I would say a little silent prayer. May god bless you when you do" (*Trinidad Guardian*, 13 April 1976).

Williams boasted privately that he could have won the election without campaigning, a claim that is credible. The party bureaucracy, however, claimed that it won the five seats for which the political leader refused to campaign. This is a doubtful claim; voters knew that a victory for the candidates in question would have been a victory for Williams and the PNM. The efforts of the party to get out the vote may, however, have helped to increase the margin of victory. Some of the candidates who were bypassed were anguished when the prime minister hinted at their lack of integrity and they called unsuccessfully on him to clear their names. One, Winston Hinds, ran as an individual – preferring to fight like a man rather than die as a dog.

The United Labour Front

Reflecting on the events prior to and following the 1976 elections, party stalwart Ferdie Ferreira felt that the prime minister had lost his mental balance and had become overly suspicious of the people around him. Much of what he attempted to do was aimed at regaining control of the party, which he felt he had begun to lose. As Ferreira observed, "It was a deliberate strategy to obtain and consolidate political and governmental power/loyalty to our leader who had become, like so many others, insecure in the house he had built and which he assumed belonged to him" (*Sunday Guardian*, 24 July 2005).

The public and even party rank-and-file were very much in the dark as to what the party stood for ideologically, whether or not it was even going to contest the elections, or whether it would go it alone or in alliance with the DAC. In the absence of firm knowledge, rumours spread that the ULF was communist and atheistic. The *Trinidad Guardian* alleged editorially that communist money was entering the country to finance the ULF, and warned that the country must not be allowed to fall into the hands of communists, however well intentioned they might be, since, once in power, communists usually proceed to abolish all rights. To quote the *Guardian*,

> Communists have never come to power anywhere as the government of a country by election. . . . To invite them is to commit virtual suicide, since they would have lost the right to prosperity, the right to think, the right to protest and the right to appeal in one full swoop. . . . We have not had citizens exiled because of their dissent; we have not had them clapped into prison for years without trial. What we have is the freedom of people to write in the Press their most bitter complaints against Ministers and

even the Prime Minister. We have not had people flung into insane asylums for doing this or sent into chain gangs. The communists say they aim at a classless society. This is an elusive dream.

Williams also waged a subtle campaign to denigrate socialism by telling his audiences about some of the experiences that he had had during his state visit to Cuba in 1975. He told audiences that the people of Trinidad and Tobago were freer and far better fed and housed than those in Cuba. What Williams was saying about Cuba, however, was at variance with what he had told the Cubans in 1975 – that he was impressed with Cuba's record in public health, housing, self-reliance and above all in the field of education. "Yesterday at the vocational school I was shown a computer produced by the Faculty of Technology of the University of Havana. In that one computer one could see not only the educational revolution in Cuba, but one could see Cuba's active leadership in the field of education" (*Granma*, July 1975). Williams said that he himself was a pragmatist and not a socialist, and that he would not know what a socialist blueprint was even if he were to see one. Unlike the ULF, the PNM was not planning to take away people's homes or their farms, but was instead planning to give people such things. As he told a rally, "The PNM does not intend to take away anybody's land; it does not intend to take away the cane farmers' land; as far as the PNM is concerned, the cane farmer is the man of the future in the sugar industry, and so long as the PNM is the government, the cane farmers are safe" (*Trinidad Express*, 26 April 1976).

The ULF denied all allegations that its aim was to take away the personal property of the little man, and in fact there was nothing in the statements of the major leaders of the ULF that suggested it was an extreme Marxist movement. The ULF had to deal with yet another persistent charge, namely, that it was the old DLP "writ large". The question of race and voting had come alive following the visit of the Indian cricket team to Trinidad. A majority of Indians appeared to support the Indian team against the West Indian cricketers and there were some ugly incidents between Africans and Indians, whose behaviour was described as being unreasonable. Indian commentators denied this. They saw the response as predictable given the racial patterns of a society that defined Indians as second class. As one put it,

> To ask the Indians to ignore all of this and still be loyal of the country is to ask them to display a quality not possessed by humans at all. This society has alienated Indians. The very values that this society stands for are anathema to Indians. Things may have been different had the Indians and Africans come together at an earlier stage and the way of life of both races been allowed to develop to its fullest potential thereby forging a "national identity." But this development was stunted first by the British and now by those who took over from them. . . . Moreover, the current upsurge of "black-

ness" and attempts to incorporate Indians in the concept can have only disastrous consequences. The first step is for non-Indians in this country to stop thinking of Indians as outsiders and interlopers. Secondly, the inequalities in all spheres of national life must be obliterated. It is significant to note that whereas some black radicals are calling for African-Indian unity, they have neglected to articulate any cause that is peculiar to Indians. They cast their eyes as far as Rhodesia and South Africa and denounce vehemently the apartheid and oppression of their "black brothers" there. But their eyes never fall on Caroni and they breathe not a word about the oppression of their "Indian brothers" there. Basically, the situation in 1976 is the same as it was in 1956 as far as racial unity goes. What exists now is not racial unity but Indian acquiescence in Negro domination. Such a situation does not augur well for the future. There will come a time when the problem will not be able to fit anymore under the carpet. (*Trinidad Guardian*, 25 April 1976)

Indians were particularly upset when James Bain, chairman of the state-owned National Broadcasting Corporation, openly warned the public against the danger of a conjuncture between Indian economic and political power:

The East Indians have increasingly acquired education and have been increasingly invading the fields of the Civil Service, the professions, and the Government. As their numbers must now reach parity with people of African descent, there is a real possibility that in the not too distant future, they will get control of the Government. Should this time come when the East Indian section owns most of the property, business and wealth of the country as well as control of the Government, an imbalance could develop in our society that would cause undesirable stresses and strains that would not be good for the nation. It is an urgent necessity therefore, that all of us give serious thought to these matters, and like sensible people make a conscious effort to counter any undesirable consequences that could develop from such a possible situation. (*Trinidad Express*, 26 April 1976)

Bain was voicing sentiments shared by many non-Indian Trinidadians.

The ULF leadership was concerned about its image in the country, and felt that the only way to escape the trap into which the history and the sociology of the community had forced it was to enter into an alliance with the DAC. It was felt that the country was not yet ready to accept an Indian prime minister. It was this very consideration that had led a former leader of the DLP to offer the leadership first to James Millette and later to A.N.R. Robinson and the ACDC. The problem was compounded for the ULF because it was tarred with the communist brush. It therefore needed an alliance with a party that would help it appeal to African and Indian middle-class voters as well as the African working class whose "false consciousness" might have led them to continue supporting the PNM in spite of what they had gone through since 1970.

Panday had for long been of the view that an alliance with A.N.R. Robinson was necessary if a viable national opposition party were to be created. As he said in an interview with Keith Smith in *People* in 1975,

> We have the sugar workers fully committed, and stage one is over. Soon, if we are lucky, we will have the cane-farmers in the bag plus a certain tenuous liaison with the oil and transport workers, which could complete stage-two, make us more than a sugar worker party, give us most of the sugar belt and a promising image of a more fully working-class base by delivering some of these stubborn oil workers! But that is a big if . . . so we don't dare at this stage to anticipate stage-three; we dare not broach the question of founding a national opposition party. If Jamadar and Lequay were suddenly to patch up their quarrel, then we could end up out in the cold and be left just like George [Weekes], a trades-union leadership incapable of political support. Think what a laugh Williams and Errol Mahabir would have on poor Basdeo Panday. No boy, I must keep my options open. . . . What we can do is open a little window on the possibility of a party by tying down ANR Robinson so that the respectable, well-to-do elements may draw just a little closer and abandon forever any thought of meddling with Jamadar and Lequay. Yes, we must bring Robbie into the game.

Other anti-PNM forces in the country were also for some form of unity between the opposition groups. In the absence of such unity, people felt, the PNM would win by default. Indeed the PNM was aware of its own weakness. As PNM minister Hector McLean had told a party group, "The only thing that was saving the PNM was the inefficiency, bankruptcy and foolishness of the opposition. Do not believe that we have this big, well-run organisation. It is not that. The fact is the other side is too stupid. We are winning by default. It's like a game – the other side ain't turn up." The view of Stephen Maharaj was typical of this persistent belief that a united opposition could beat the PNM:

> The whole electorate is confused about whom to support in this election. The reason for this is because we have a group of selfish leaders, chiefly in the camp of the opposition who refuse to come together and fight the PNM on a common front. . . . The PNM is basically weak throughout the country and is holding on to power only through the lack of a real challenge from the coalition of opposite forces. Any unified front of two or more opposition parties could beat the PNM this time around. An alliance of Panday's United Labour Front and another party could do it. The ULF and the Democratic Action Congress, or the ULF and the DLP, could beat the PNM. The public is thirsting for some sort of alliance; you hear it expressed at every street corner and all over the place. It seems to me the majority of Trinidadians would certainly like to see a change of government and even if opposition does not get together officially, it possible that the opposition parties could win enough seats to be able to form some sort of coalition government.

The ULF coalition was split on the matter of unity with the DAC. Persons like Jack Kelshall, George Weekes and Basdeo Panday supported the attempt to form an alliance. Kelshall noted that it was true the ULF was more progressive than the DAC, but the first objective should be to remove the PNM: "We should not under-estimate the enemy or over-estimate our strength" (*Trinidad Express*, 29 March 1976). Most of the radical elements in the party, groups that had only reluctantly agreed to give the electoral route to power a try, expressed horror at the idea of an alliance with a party that was seen as being basically capitalist .

The DAC was also divided on the merger issue. The pro-capitalist wing of the party did not take kindly to the proposed linkage with a "socialist" party, and that wing controlled a great deal of the party's funds. Many of the Indian professionals in the party were also opposed because they had long been nursing seats that the ULF considered to be "naturally" theirs. The DAC Indians had been named to some of these seats since 1973, and were naturally reluctant to give way. Some members of the party also feared that an alliance with an "Indian" party would alienate the black constituency on which the party was counting to give it control of Whitehall. Yet others felt the ULF should not enter politics but should instead function as the industrial arm of the DAC.

The proposed merger never did materialize, because both parties believed they were stronger than they really were. The ULF claimed that while it wanted the alliance, the DAC leadership did not. "There were too many capitalists in the DAC," asserted Mr Panday (*Trinidad Express*, 13 July 1976). Panday also accused the DAC of being "in collusion with the PNM by deliberately taking the ULF for a ride and then dropping us as they did Vernon Jamadar and the members of the DLP" (ibid.). The allegation was that the DAC wished to maintain the "traditional" pattern of racial voting in the country. It was not a credible allegation, and it indicated the suspiciousness and bitterness that the collapse of the merger had left in its wake.

The evidence suggests that the DAC was principally responsible for the collapse of the merger. For one thing, the DAC had pre-empted the merger arrangements by announcing the names of twenty-four candidates to seats before any firm agreements had been made with the ULF. The DAC claimed that it had to get ready for the elections, and that it could not wait, but they were clearly trying to outmanoeuvre the ULF. In the "final" offer, which was made to the ULF in July 1976, the DAC agreed to stand down only in ten of the thirty-six constituencies, four of which were northern constituencies in which Africans and mixed persons held the balance of power – Barataria, St Ann's, Port of Spain East and Port of Spain North. The ULF quite rightly considered this to be an "insulting and inequitable proposal".

One of the key issues that inhibited agreement was that each party wanted to establish hegemony over the other, so that in the event of victory they would dominate the government. The DAC openly maintained that it was the "premier organisation" in that it was the older of the two parties and the one that had spearheaded the no-vote campaign of 1971 and the struggle against PNM repression between 1971 and 1976. To quote the DAC,

> The DAC remains hopeful that the ULF will recognise the historic continuing and national responsibility of the DAC to be in a state of complete readiness for General Elections, bearing in mind that the DAC spearheaded the historic and victorious no-vote campaign of 1971, has never since recognized the 28 per cent Parliament, has been in the forefront of the struggle for fundamental human rights and freedoms and against repressive laws, has effectively agitated all the major domestic and international issues over the past six years, and has been unswerving in its demand for electoral reform and immediate General Elections. ("The ULF-DAC Alliance: The Truth About Why the Talks Failed", n.d., 5)

The ULF for its part rightly insisted that the situation was a dynamic one, and that things had changed in its favour in the past few months. The ULF wished to contest sixteen to eighteen seats that it felt sure of winning. The DAC insisted it would concede only ten, and on this basis the talks collapsed. It is a moot point as to whether a merger would have made any difference in more than three constituencies – Fyzabad, Princes Town and Nariva. The ULF, however, felt that unity would have resulted in victory. It may well be that the DAC was never interested in a merger at all, but simply went through the exercise to catch the ULF in a state of electoral unpreparedness on the eve of the campaign.

The Campaign

The campaign itself was a lively one, particularly in the two weeks preceding the poll when the square and street corners that had previously stood virtually empty while political speakers addressed pitiably small audiences, gradually began to come alive. As election fever gripped the nation, people shifted from one public meeting to another; one was often reminded of a week before carnival when crowds moved from one pan yard or mas camp to another to see what the various bands were bringing out. As the crowds began to swell and people at last began to pay attention to what the parties were saying, the confidence of the leaders and the headiness of their rhetoric grew. Every party boasted that its crowd was bigger and more committed than the other. Williams for his part bragged about his past achievements, and invited those who did not like his party's policy to "emigrate to Bronx and clean toilets".

The star of the campaign was undoubtedly Basdeo Panday, who appeared to many to be a new charismatic leader. Night after night, he harangued his audience with the gospel of working class unity. "Brothers and Sisters," audiences were told, "the issue is not race but class." All the big Indian capitalists in the country were vilified, as were the Syrians, the Europeans, the multinationals and their defenders in the PNM and the various DLPs. Panday's speeches were brilliant and brought alive the struggle of the African slave and Indian indentured labourer over the centuries with such clarity and pathos that few remained unmoved.

Williams's campaign was a strange one. As indicated above, he spent a great deal of time criticizing his ministers, and admitted that his government had made many critical errors. In response to comments about the unorthodox nature of his campaign, Williams replied that he saw nothing wrong with the prime minister saying that he was not satisfied with the way certain departments were run: "If I had said that I was satisfied, my throat would have been cut. I said I wasn't satisfied, and I'm working to improve it." Williams's strategy was to suggest that the inefficiency was not of his own making, and that if given a new mandate, he would consolidate such gains as had been made over the past twenty years while moving to eliminate those responsible for the poor performance of the government. On more than one occasion, Williams hinted that he would in future rely heavily on nominated members from the senate to staff his cabinet.

The election raised some serious issues, the most significant being the question of who should own the means of production and distribution. On this issue, it was virtually the ULF against the rest. The ULF's position was clear and unequivocal: "Those who labour must hold the reins." The party preached the gospel of nationalism up and down the countryside, telling workers that most of their problems would be solved if the commanding heights of the economy were seized by the state. The problem of unemployment would also be solved in five years. The PNM was depicted as the party that defended the capitalists by introducing harsh and repressive legislation to prevent the workers from getting their just deserts from the capitalists, both local and foreign.

Williams waged a counter-offensive in the countryside, both openly and surreptitiously, against what the PNM manifesto described as the "ideological presumptions of our age". Williams claimed that a vote for the ULF meant a vote against religion and God, and against the private ownership of lands, houses, cars and everything else. Heavy stress was laid on the issue of political freedoms. Williams promised that the PNM under his leadership would never circumscribe anyone's right to worship freely or dissent. Williams conveniently forgot the post-1965 package of repressive laws that had, among other things, restricted the right to strike, to assemble, to read literature of one's choice and to march and demonstrate for political purposes. On the question of nationalizing industry, Williams argued that Trinidad's population of one million was much too small a resource base from which to draw all the expertise that the country needed. Partnership with multinationals was the only meaningful alternative.

Williams was concerned with the problem of managing the existing traditional public sector, and even more so, industries that were now being acquired. As he said, "We come up against the fundamental [problem] that as the country buys more and more into these national industries and owns them, the country less and less has the indigenous talent and expertise to run them. So that when you find somebody that has something, you run the fellow down by the amount of stuff you give him to do" (*Sunday Guardian*, 26 September 1976). The Chamber of Commerce was equally concerned about mismanagement and urged the government to divest its shares and allow indigenous businessmen to manage the industries. Williams promised that a policy divestment would be followed after the election, but he was clearly not prepared to see control of such industries pass into the hands of Chamber of Commerce types in terms of either concentrated shareholding or management responsibility. In Williams's view, the PNM and not the Chamber of Commerce must govern the country. Williams's aim was to expand the role of state in the economy, though not under the banner of socialism as Manley and Burnham had done in Jamaica and Guyana. Not only did this go against his own ideological convictions; putting his policy of state capitalism in a socialist context ran the risk of inviting hostile American reaction as had occurred in Jamaica and Guyana.

In his post-election victory speech Williams returned to the question of socialism. As he said concerning management of the economy,

> It is obvious that some new formula has to be found, and nobody has yet found any formula in any of the countries. I ain't no socialist, so I have nothing to copy. I have to do it by trial and error. . . . The supreme inferiority of these parties in the Caribbean is copying some bloody thing that is more than 30 years old in the outside world, and has been repeatedly disposed of, picked up and now at the end. . . . We are going to go by trial and error, and see what happens physically to give the Cabinet with its decision-making power adequate information on which to take a decision. (*Trinidad Guardian*, 27 September 1976)

Tapia, one of the other two serious parties in the campaign, also joined in the discussion of the issue of foreign domination of the economy. Unlike the ULF, Tapia stressed localization rather than nationalization, arguing that localization was for the population as distinct from the government. Tapia's view was that nationalization was no longer a radical solution. Socialism was described as a "lifeless doctrine which did not require the individual to think or discriminate". The crowds that followed Tapia in the last weeks of the campaign grew larger and larger, and the party was optimistic that it would win a few seats. The same was true of the DAC, though it appeared to have peaked much too early.

Results

The election results came as a shock to most people who had expected a keener contest. The only thing that was not surprising was that the poll was a relatively low one. Only 55.83 per cent of the 565,646 electors turned out to vote compared to 88.11 per cent in 1961 and 65.79 per cent in 1966, the last seriously contested national election. While it was generally expected that the PNM would triumph, few expected it to win so unequivocally. Few persons expected that the leaders of the two DLPs would lose their deposits or that Tapia and the DAC would do so poorly. Tapia, which had declared that it was "the country's last hope", was only able to attract 12,021 of the total of 315,809 votes cast, or 3.81 per cent. The party did not win a single seat and all but one of its 29 candidates lost their deposits, after failing to poll one-eighth of the total votes cast. Only five Tapia candidates obtained more than 10 per cent of the votes cast in their constituencies. One was Lloyd Best, who lost to both the PNM and ULF candidates.

Best's defeat in particular came as a surprise to many who had felt that Tapia would at least win in the constituency that had hosted the party since its founding. One of Tapia's weaknesses was its inability to reach the rural or even the urban masses. It was seen as a reformist party with a heavy intellectual and middle-class bias, and as such never got off the ground. The party drew strong support, however, from the younger white-creole community, from civil servants and the intelligentsia, but this support was too thinly spread to have any electoral impact.

Tapia's problem was in part due to the fact that it was not able to get its message across to the man on the street, who in a sense refused to listen. Tapia's image as a party of impractical people functioned as a sort of screen between the masses and the party communicators, particularly Best, who, try as he might, always managed to hover over the heads of his listeners. The party also suffered the fate of most "third force" movements – it got caught between the two great racial power blocs in the society, which, given all the uncertainties prevailing, relied on the primordial link of race to help decide what to do in the voting booth.

Williams and Tobago

The other party whose performance was puzzling was the DAC, which won the two Tobago seats and the support of only 8.1 per cent of those who voted. The DAC lost every seat in Trinidad, with only seven candidates saving their deposits. Apart from Tobago, the party performed creditably in only four constituencies – Nariva, Toco-Manzanilla, Arima and Fyzabad, where it obtained between 15 and 17 per cent of the votes cast. The party lost constituencies in which it had expected to do well, such as Siparia, to the ULF. Like Tapia, the DAC also got caught between the racial power blocs. Much of DAC's support among Indians melted away as the ULF came on stream. The DAC also failed to break the PNM's stronghold on the black vote, except in Tobago where race was not a major issue.

There was some surprise that the DAC won both Tobago seats. The party had always been strong in Tobago, but no one really expected it to carry Tobago West.

Even so, the victory in that constituency was a narrow one, with the margin being no more than 351 votes. There had always been rivalry between the PNM and the DAC "tribes" in Tobago, and Williams had been anxious to win, if only to embarrass A.N.R. Robinson, whom he had described a "traitorous deputy". The government went so far as to purchase an obsolete ten-year-old boat, the MV *Tobago*, for TT$10 million on the eve of the election. The boat made its maiden trip to Tobago one week before the elections and had to be grounded for several years thereafter due to serious mechanical defects. It was election bribery on a shameful scale. "God fatherism" in the Special Works Programme was also used on an extravagant scale in Tobago (as it was elsewhere) to woo voters, many of whom had come to feel that Tobago was the Cinderella of the country's politics.

Although secessionist sentiment was much weaker than the advocates of secession would have had one believe (all candidates who advocated secession lost their seats), there was a clear feeling that Tobago had to be given more autonomy and control over its affairs as well as a larger slice of the country's resources. Tobagonians resented the fact that almost everything was controlled in Port of Spain, and that they had to undergo the cost and inconvenience of going to Trinidad to get things such as land title deeds, approval for plans, birth and death certificates, or to attend to other official matters. There were also complaints (justified) that the cost of food was much higher in Tobago than it was in Trinidad because of the extra cost of shipping and handling. Tobagonians complained about phones that did not work, poor hospitals, bad roads, an inadequate bus and coastal steamer service and water supply, no tractor services or cold storage facilities at fishing villages, poor sporting facilities and lack of job opportunities for the youth.

Williams denied that the PNM had left Tobago as the most underdeveloped island in the Caribbean, and boasted that between 1958 and 1976, the government had spent about TT$276 million to develop Tobago against a revenue of about $41 million. Tobago's reply was to ask how much was spent on Trinidad by way of comparison. The PNM attributed its defeat in Tobago to the weakness of its election machinery on the island, the fact that nothing had been done to mobilize a party youth corps comparable to that of the DAC, the fact that little political help came from Trinidad during the campaign, the amount of money spent by the DAC, and wild talk about the fact that the offshore oil discovered off the north coast of Trinidad was in Tobago's waters rather than those of Trinidad.

Williams was clearly piqued by the results in Tobago despite his protestations to the contrary, and he told Tobagonians that if they wanted to secede he would not try to stop them. He saw their malaise as being nothing new, part of a "general malaise, a general sickness of people wanting to go off on their own, part of a particular Caribbean madness resulting from all the flotsam and jetsam brought to the Caribbean over a century. If Tobago wanted to go off on their own small island because they have different ways of looking at things, O.K., I am not one to bother. I would take no part in any move designed to keep any part of the Caribbean to some allegiance that that part does not want". Waxing emotional, Williams told Tobagonians,

> If you want to go, go. We are not holding you. I'm not going to send any Coast Guard or ship or army there to hold them back. What for? They want to go, go! Everybody understands today that whatever used to be said in the past, we don't live in any world of true eternal love. The greatest thing today is the divorce celebration. O.K. let's have a divorce celebration! It's a financial matter; what terms do we agree on without bitterness, without any emotion? All they have to tell me is what it is they want and how to do it. I appoint somebody to do it. I have more important things to do. So whenever they are ready, my friends, and they have voted one way, O.K. I for one wasn't too bothered about this. I always suspected that within the ranks of the PNM so-called, there has been a solid section surreptitiously supporting the secession. It is not a crime. There are places that are there already. Others will come. I will be particularly careful not to do anything in my position as the Prime Minister of the country to keep Tobago in line by force. I am against it, and I would advise the population not to do that. I told Tobago a long time ago when this came up: "You all talk about Tobago seceding from Trinidad; no big thing. The thing that you have to worry about is when the movement starts for Trinidad to secede from Tobago – that would be serious". I am for neither. I claim nothing. I propose nothing, except no force. The voters have voted, and I will not use any subterfuge. (*Trinidad Guardian*, 25 September 1976)

But Williams used a great deal of guile and the machinery of state power to whip Tobago back into the official fold and abort the sentiment, such as it was, for secession.

Many Tobagonians denied, however, that their vote was a vote for secession. Some commentators noted that 5,700 persons did not bother to vote at all and that the PNM itself had obtained close to 6,000 of the 13,682 votes cast. There was resentment about the prime minister's statement that Tobago had been "deposited in Trinidad's lap after having been kicked out by its masters", and that Tobago was ungrateful for all that Trinidad had done to develop it. DAC spokesmen argued that Tobago did not have any reason to be grateful to the PNM or the prime minister because funds spent on Tobago were public funds. The fact that Tobago did not contribute more by way of revenues was due to its not being properly developed either in the agricultural sector or with respect to the location of agro-based industries. Most Tobagonians also had to migrate to Trinidad in search of jobs, thus helping to develop Trinidad at the expense of Tobago.

Tobagonians also denied that they had voted DAC because they felt that A.N.R. Robinson stood a good chance of becoming prime minister and that they assumed they were riding a victorious bandwagon. There was, however, some truth in this claim. That the PNM was able to reverse its fortunes in the local government elections that were held in April 1977, winning seven of the eleven seats and 483 more votes than it did in 1976, suggested that many Tobagonians had come to feel that they were wrong in their belief that the DAC was the wave of the future.

Williams and the ULF

In gaining ten seats and 26.85 per cent of the popular vote, the ULF did better than many expected, but not as well as it had hoped. The party elite felt that it would have won nineteen seats, enough to form a government. Some of its candidates wagered heavily on a successful outcome. The party won all the seats that the DLP had formerly controlled except Point-a-Pierre. The party was a victim of a gerrymandering operation that had removed a number of polling stations in which Indians were predominant, from that constituency to Couva South, while others from Tabaquite and Naparima North, which had black majorities, were included. The same type of exercise was carried out in Fyzabad, which the PNM had narrowly won in 1966 but feared they might lose. Pro-PNM polling stations had been taken from Siparia, which the party conceded to the opposition, and relocated in Fyzabad, which the party felt it could carry. As it turned out, even the combined votes of the DAC and the ULF candidates were fewer than those of the PNM candidate – 4,656 compared to 4,877.

The ULF victories in the "Hindu Heartland" were impressive and came as no surprise. Only in Princes Town did the party win by a narrow margin – 290 votes. This was a seat the PNM had counted on winning. The ULF ascribed its overall defeat in the election to irregularities – claiming that polling was deliberately slowed down in areas where the party was expected to do well. It also alleged that many prospective PNM voters whose names were not listed were permitted to vote. Both allegations were correct. Although it was not possible to disenfranchise "ULF" voters in ethnically mixed areas without at the same time also disenfranchising "PNM" voters, there was greater administrative chaos in certain strong ULF constituencies. To determine whether the irregularities were part of a sophisticated strategy to deprive the ULF of seats, particularly in St Patrick, however, is difficult. Panday felt that had there not been what he called "massive electoral fraud", the ULF would have won the election: "I believe that the government deliberately chose officers to man the polling stations who were PNM agents and deliberately slowed down the voting, and who permitted different procedures to apply to different people, depending upon their political views. I do think it was a conspiracy and a massive fraud" (*Trinidad Express*, 21 September 1976). The ULF called for the appointment of a commission of inquiry to probe the irregularities, but there was no official response. There is no disputing that there was a great deal of inefficiency on the part of officials and that there were numerous irregularities, including "polling day registration". But one doubts whether these were on a scale that would have affected the overall results in terms of seats – though it's true that percentages might have been different.

Williams had expected the PNM to win, but given the widespread disenchantment with its performance and the sentiment for change, the party was surprised that it obtained as many as twenty-four seats and as much as 53.57 per cent of the popular votes. The margin of victory was expected to be narrower, particularly in those constituencies where Williams refused to campaign for those whom he deemed to be "millstones". It is clear, however, that pro-PNM voters came out in support of these five candidates knowing that the vote was effectively a vote for Williams and the PNM. The PNM bureaucracy claimed that the five candidates won in spite of Williams. This is doubtful, though the party machine did an impressive job in getting voters to the polls, not only in these five constituencies, but in all except perhaps Tobago.

Two factors seemed to have led to the victory scored by the PNM. One was population fragmentation. Even though time-for-a-change sentiment was strong, there were no alternatives considered viable or legitimate enough to provide a *vehicle* for change. People looked at the PNM devil they knew and at the alternatives they were presented with and opted to remain loyal to the government, or rather to Williams, who miraculously managed to convince a large part of the electorate that he was less politically bankrupt than those seeking to inherit the mandate of heaven.

The other factor that made the resolution of cross-pressure in favour of the PNM easier was the question of race. In the last two weeks before the election, the ULF, which had been building momentum in central and south Trinidad, made a number of successful forays into the north along the east–west corridor. Large numbers of people came to these meetings out of curiosity. Many, however, came from central Trinidad and the garden areas of the north to cheer and support Panday and Shah, who, though they preached the gospel of working class unity, were seen as communal heroes. If professional Indians were cross-pressured, the same was not true of working class Indians for whom both the race and the message of the leaders were satisfactory. The workers understood better than the media that communism and atheism were bogeymen projected to frighten them.

The very factors that made the ULF acceptable to Indians raised questions in the minds of non-Indians. The ULF's decision to make a last-minute drive into the north in general and Port of Spain in particular in a display of strength was counter-productive, as some ULF members had feared it would be. The move gave rise to massive concern on the part of the African population as to what a

ULF victory could mean in terms of race as well as ideology. The election-eve ULF motorcades, accompanied as they were by tassa drumming and candlelight processions, displayed the party's racial bias in a manner that previously had not been fully perceived. A number of ugly incidents frightened non-Indians. It was as if Atilla had appeared at the gates of Rome. The subtle warnings of PNM spokesmen about what would happen if the "PNM" (read African) vote were split suddenly began to take on meaning, and many who had earlier been disposed to flirt with an alternative went into the voting booth and "dropped their X on the balisier".

In his assessment of the election, Lloyd Best assigned great weight to the race factor as an explanation of what happened:

> On election day, and certainly a few days before election day, there was a polarisation in the country in which people settled for the old arrangements, and all the figures make this very clear, whether you take the data by polling divisions within constituencies like my own where the Indian areas voted for ULF and the African areas voted for the PNM. This happened everywhere in the country and the pattern is very clear. The ULF won the traditional DLP seats and the PNM won the traditional PNM seats with some slight changes. And, of course, you have important cases like Point Fortin where a man like Allan Alexander, a former oil worker, national figure, a man born in Point, a considerable man, but he was in the wrong party in the public mind and was rejected. This happened not because they were rejecting Alexander, but oil workers in Point are not going to vote for Panday. (*Sunday Guardian*, 19 September 1976)

Best argued that race was the overriding principle of selection and as such led many to consider parties such as Tapia and DAC as non-starters. The PNM and the ULF were seen as the torchbearers of African and Indian sentiment respectively. In Tobago, however, race was not a variable, and Tobagonians were therefore able to look the issues square in the face and act accordingly. "To be a Tobagonian is to be a different race from either African or Indian, and that is why DAC got their seats in Tobago." That race played such a crucial role in the election was seen to be due to the identity crisis that the electorate faced. The fact that there was so much charlatanry and confusion in terms of parties and issues led voters to fall back on what was certain – their racial identification. Best also blamed the media for the outcome in that they did little to help people make sense of what they saw or heard. The media allegedly starved the electorate of information up until the last minute, and then deluged it with material that was difficult to assimilate. "You got a medical problem which is that if you give people a small dose, it cures them, and if you give them an overdose, it kills them, and that is exactly what happened" (ibid.).

On the specific issue of the motorcade and its impact on voter behaviour, Best had the following to say:

The motorcade was the immediate development that triggered the polarisation. . . . On Saturday morning when the ULF motorcade came through the Eastern Corridor, there were any number of confrontation situations between Indians and Africans. Unfortunately the African population in the North resented the intrusion of all these people from Central and South Trinidad. You could see the passion in the eye, you could hear the exchange of expletive and unseemly comment. You could feel the tension thicken. The sun was hot, the traffic was tangled up, and conditions were ideal for fanning the flames of hate, especially in such constituencies as Tunapuna and Arouca and St. Augustine, where East and West clash most dramatically, at the frontier between the sugar belt and the urban industrialised north. You could imagine how tempers were high, and those who had to gain from it immediately exploited it. Loudspeakers were all over Tunapuna pointing out the perils and risks of voting one way or the other. The battle lines were drawn between ULF and the PNM, and Tapia was out of it altogether. We were ruled out and we didn't have a chance. Our votes reflect our political strength, and this is why everybody is surprised that Tapia did so badly, and even if people say that Tapia is idealistic and therefore could not succeed, how do you explain what happened to Robinson and DAC, a brand of politics everybody claims to understand? (Ibid.)

The *Bomb* (17 September 1976) also agreed that the motorcade swung votes away from the smaller parties:

It was the ULF which forced free-loving citizens of this country to band themselves under the PNM banner for another five years. There is absolutely no doubt that the entire political climate swung the PNM way in those tension-charged 48 hours before election time. Hundreds of people interviewed by the *Bomb* this week, said unashamedly that events during the past two weeks and on the Saturday of that rally, changed their minds considerably. Some who had intended to patronize parties like Lloyd Best's Tapia, ANR Robinson's DAC, and Simbhoonath Capildeo's DLP suddenly realized that their vote was a vital one. And it had to be used to ensure that the ULF did not win. The election tempo was that the ULF must not win, rather than we want the PNM. Basdeo Panday had played right into Eric Williams' hand.

Williams denied that race had the impact that it is alleged to have had:

I was rather surprised . . . when I read that if it hadn't been for – what was it? – particular motorcade, where, whatever it was, wherever it came from or where the hell it went to, if it hadn't been for that motorcade I wouldn't be here tonight. . . . I don't know where the devil you'd be, following the motorcade, wherever the hell it went to. There is no accounting for the views of these commentators. So at once I went and looked at the election results, statistics, and so on; and then I looked at the obvious thing. We are the only party, my dear friends. I keep telling you this, you know this as well as I. Let's say it once more. Some day it's going to get into the hard heads of those commentators. PNM is the only party in the Caribbean which has uniformly controlled the capital city of the country. We controlled it in 1976 as we controlled it on other occasions in our 20-year record. (*Trinidad Guardian*, 26 September 1976)

The editor of the *Trinidad Express*, George John, agreed with the prime minister that the motorcade was a convenient myth invented by the defeated to explain their poor showing:

> If the PNM won, all these parties would have to find some reason, other than their own lack of appeal, their failure to reach the grassroots, the unattractiveness of most of their candidates, the lack of confidence, for one reason or another, which the electorate would have had in their leaders for that result. And as luck would have it, the ULF staged its great motorcade through North Trinidad, a motorcade in which Trinidadians of Indian descent were in the majority and Trinidadians of African descent stood on the sidewalks and watched it drive by. And like Trinidadians, the motorcade did not proceed in funeral silence, but picong floated from the motorcade and mamaguy was wafted back from the sidewalk and into the cars. So according to the losers, this set the stage for a racial confrontation and it caused the PNM voter, who had decided to swing away from the PNM and into the arms of the DAC or Tapia, or was still thinking about it, to say "better the devil we know" kind of thing and remain securely in the Williams fold. All great events have their myths. (16 September 1976)

For Williams to have admitted the salience of race would be, of course, to belittle the PNM's performance. Certainly given the PNM's control over patronage for the past twenty years, it had harnessed a large body of hangers-on and it would have won, motorcade or no motorcade. And the party would have carried the capital city and towns that had been the principal beneficiaries of PNM largesse in terms of amenities, special works employment, and other types of social output. But one wonders just why Tapia and DAC did so poorly. While clearly neither would have won any seats in Trinidad, their percentage of the popular vote might have been higher.

Plate25 Williams with the Women's League. (Eric Williams Memorial Collection, University of the West Indies, St Augustine)

Plate 26 Williams with the first independence cabinet, 1962. (Eric Williams Memorial Collection, University of the West Indies, St Augustine)

Plate 27 Williams with Gerard Montano and Errol Mahabir during 1966 general elections. (Eric Williams Memorial Collection, University of the West Indies, St Augustine)

Plate 28 Williams with daughter Erica and son Alistair at PNM meeting, March 1971. (Trinidad and Tobago Express Ltd)

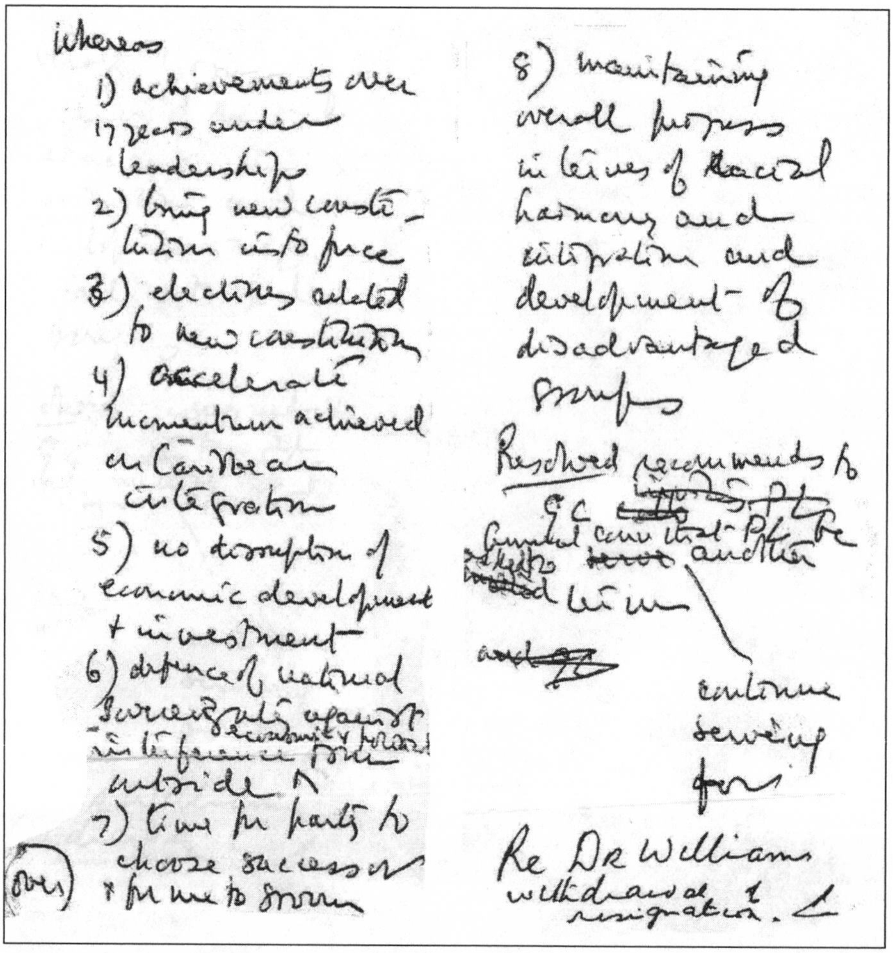

Whereas

1) achievements over 17 years under leadership
2) bring new constitution into force
3) elections related to new constitution
4) accelerate momentum achieved in Caribbean integration
5) no disruption of economic development + investment
6) defence of national sovereignty against interference from outside ^
7) time for party to choose successor + for me to govern
(over)

8) maintaining overall progress in terms of racial harmony and integration and development of disadvantaged groups

Resolved recommends to GC ... *that PM be another* ... *continue serving for*

Re Dr Williams withdrawal & resignation.

Plate 29 Letter in Eric Williams's handwriting, indicating to visiting party delegation why he should be invited to resume political leadership of the PNM. (Eric Williams Memorial Collection, University of the West Indies, St Augustine)

Plate 30 Williams conversing with Senator Francis Prevatt, House of Representatives, December 1974. (Trinidad and Tobago Express Ltd)

PART 6

WILLIAMS AS POLICYMAKER AND POLITICAL MANAGER

32 The Move to the "Left"

Industrial Policy in the
Post-1970 Era

Operation Bootstrap, which inspired Trinidad's Aid to Pioneer Industries, was now a
laughing stock even in Puerto Rico. Our goals in Trinidad and Tobago by contrast,
are the highest level of technological development based on hydrocarbons leading to
petroleum and steel. Our inspiration is the OPEC countries.

   – Eric Williams (1976)

Prior to the Black Power "revolution" of 1970, Williams was pursuing an orthodox
economic strategy that was based on the Puerto Rican "Operation Bootstrap"
model. That model was contemptuously described as "industrialization by invitation" (see chapter 24). In September 1970, the PNM published a new policy statement, "The Chaguaramas Declaration", which it claimed would guide its
activities in the 1970s should it be given another mandate to govern. In a sense,
the document, also referred to as "Perspectives for a New Society", was a fundamental revision of the People's Charter, which it had issued in 1956 and which had
been largely ignored. The new statement was deeply influenced by the protest
movement, and was a calculated attempt by Williams to appropriate what he
considered to be the "constructive" proposals of the Black Power militants. Neo-
colonialism was now recognized as the great danger to be faced by Caribbean
countries. Said Williams, "Too much dependence on metropolitan governments
and metropolitan firms is incompatible with the economic sovereignty of the
people of the Caribbean. Too much domination by the giant international corporations has the same effect in suppressing the potential of the West Indian
people as did the mercantilist links of the plantation economy of the 17th and 18th
centuries" (*Nation*, 25 September 1970).

While admitting the need to strengthen popular participation in the economic
life of the country and to localize decision making over the key sectors of the
economy, "Perspectives" categorically rejected socialism whether of the bureaucratic or the totalitarian variety. "We must definitely avoid the mistake made by

many so-called 'socialist' Third World countries in seeking state domination of the entire economy." On the other hand, "if we adopt the system of liberal capitalism . . . the result will be increased prosperity for a relatively small group of people . . . accompanied by increasing unemployment and the maldistribution of income and wealth. Trinidad's past and present circumstances demand that a middle way be found between the Cuban and Puerto Rican models, a model in which the importance and legitimacy of four sectors of economic activity are recognized: the public sector, the national private sector, the people's sector, and the foreign sector" (ibid.).

The Public Sector

The emphasis to be given to the public sector was in a sense a belated attempt to rationalize and identify as a matter of chosen policy a number of uncoordinated decisions that radicals had pressured the government to take. Even before the demonstrations of February to April 1970, there were strong demands that the banks should be nationalized and that Tate and Lyle and Texaco should be brought under government ownership. Williams zigzagged on the issue. At times, he endorsed greater state ownership of the economy. On other occasions, he strongly opposed this, pointing to the poor economic performance of concerns that had already been taken over, such as BWIA, the Public Transport Service Corporation, and the Trinidad Telephone Company. Williams had even sold 50 and 40 per cent of the state's equity in the telephone company and BWIA respectively, and plans were also being made to dispose of some of the state's holdings in the Hilton Hotel. Williams justified the buy-and-sell policy in terms of national economic need and ideological flexibility. Money, he said, was just not available to meet debt payment schedules, operating costs of public utilities that were not paying their way, and the expansion programmes needed to create jobs. As Williams had remarked, "We must not be side-tracked into empty discussions on dogma regarding the respective roles and the lines of demarcation of the private and public sectors. A pragmatic view is necessary if we are to make a positive assault on the obstacles to our progress. Mixed forms of ownership and management . . . appear to be particularly well suited to our needs and circumstances" (*Trinidad Guardian*, 5 October 1968).

The left claimed that the birthright of the young was being sold for a mess of pottage. As A.N.R. Robinson had complained, "The Caribbean problem is fundamentally an economic one and the ability to run our economic services economically is the real test of independence. If we are not able to run our public enterprises ourselves, it is unlikely that we will be able to run anything else, and we might as well abandon all talk of nationhood and independence" (*Vanguard*, August 1967).

Williams's vote of no confidence in the capacity of Trinidadians to run their economy was dramatically reversed as the chorus of criticism about foreign domination increased. In addition to the industries mentioned above, the public sector now included the following:

- The National Commercial Bank, which was formed out of the assets purchased from the Bank of London and Montreal. The bank was formally launched in July 1970, and it confounded those who predicted failure by doubling its deposits and by making a profit of TT$208,567 (before tax) in its first year of operations.

- The National Petroleum Company, which was to be entrusted with the responsibility for running the chain of twenty-four petrol retail service stations that the government acquired from British Petroleum in May 1971. The government also tried to obtain other outlets from Shell, Texaco and Esso and the ultimate aim was to gain control of at least one-third of total retail outlets.

- The National Sugar Company, which was formed out of properties acquired from Orange Grove Sugar Estates.

- Radio Guardian and Trinidad and Tobago Television Company (TTT), which were acquired from the Thompson chain. The Columbia Broadcasting Service had a 10 per cent equity in TTT and the responsibilities of management.

- The Port Landing Company, in which the state had a 50 per cent equity.

- Trinidad and Tobago External Communications, in which the state held a 51 per cent equity.

- Trinidad–Tesoro Oil Company: the state's 50.1 per cent share in this company was the asset that the PNM acquired from British Petroleum in 1969 largely to save the jobs of 1,400 workers faced with retrenchment.

- Tate and Lyle: 51 per cent of the shares that the government bought under pressure for TT$11 million in 1970. Tate and Lyle continued to manage the company.

The government also announced its intention to participate in Chaguaramas Terminals (a bauxite transshipment operation) to safeguard the interests of Guyana's bauxite industry, the Canadian segment of which had recently been nationalized. Guyana exported bauxite through the deep-water harbour in Chaguaramas.

Williams boasted that Trinidad now had a larger public sector than any other Caribbean territory except Cuba. But, he warned, his government would keep in mind what happened in Ghana and Indonesia and would not "sacrifice the welfare and well being of . . . Trinidad and Tobago on the altar of some intellectual fetish which is now being considerably modified in the countries where it originated" (*Trinidad Guardian*, 2 October 1971).

The People's Sector

The people's sector was the PNM's "revolutionary" answer to the Black Power demands that the dispossessed sons of African slaves and Indian bonded-servants be encouraged and helped to own a piece of their patrimony. The sector was to consist of small-scale agriculture, industry and transport and distribution activities, handicrafts, retail cooperatives, small guest houses and the like. The people's sector differed from the national private sector in that its operations were to be labour-intensive, involve low capitalization and emphasize self-reliance. At the peak of the Black Power movement, a number of cooperative and other self-help schemes mushroomed, and the PNM gave them a measure of assistance with funds and technical assistance. According to Williams, through the people's sector, "We are giving the people . . . a positive role in their economic development as Tanzania did in 1967 with its Arusha declaration of self-reliance." Without ever saying so unequivocally as a matter of public policy, Williams took several initiatives to channel resources and opportunities to black businessmen, particularly in the construction sector. He was known to have been disappointed with what was achieved as a result of these initiatives.

The Foreign Sector

The basic economic policy of the PNM prior to 1970 was that the unemployment problem could only be solved by massive injections of foreign capital into urban infrastructure, tourism and the manufacturing industry. True, strong reservations had always been expressed about the unconscionable demands of foreign investors, but the state mobilized a great deal of the human and material resources to attract and retain their confidence. The new policy statement did not reject foreign capital, but insisted it must now come in on a new self-reliant basis: "Aid and capital must become adjuncts to our internal efforts, not the centre page of our development strategy. Development . . . can be achieved only by the people . . . themselves" (*Nation*, 25 September 1970).

Williams was not reacting solely to the events of 1970 when he sought to shift economic gear. Much of his new thinking on the role of the state in the economy could in fact be detected in the "Third Five-Year Development Plan" (1969–73), which had expressed grave dissatisfaction with the performance of the private sector. The lack of dynamism of that sector was attributed to an "innate inability to seize the numerous investment opportunities available". Given this, the plan, which was largely the work of William Demas, Eugenio Moore and Frank Rampersad, announced that

> The public sector will not hesitate to enter either alone or in partnership with foreign or
> local private capital into the productive fields of industry, tourism and agriculture.

Quite apart from mobilising resources and spending funds on the development of infrastructure, the public sector has an important role to play in building institutions to strengthen the economy, to protect the national interest, and to ensure the development of a truly national economy.

Williams had in fact complained in February 1970 that the general clamour by the demonstrators for national ownership of the economy "suggest[s] that neither the policy of the government nor the measures taken to implement that policy are sufficiently known". And it is a fact that Williams had harboured plans to have the state buy into the banking sector before the events of 1970, which merely gave him the leverage he needed to grab a slice of the banking sector.

The ideas that animated the plan also found expression in the seminal *White Paper on Public Participation in Industrial and Commercial Activities*, issued in 1972. The white paper, which reflected the growing radicalism of the Caribbean intellectual elite, proclaimed that government was now going to "move more positively into transforming the economy by establishing the basis for a greater amount of national self-determination in economic affairs. The private sector could not be relied upon 'alone' to produce the kind of momentum which the country required in order to safeguard the economic independence and provide for additional jobs, economic growth and an equitable distribution of the national income." As Williams himself opined while introducing the third development plan,

> The main barrier to a more autonomous national economy in Trinidad and Tobago is certainly not savings. In any event, our per capita income is very high by the standards of the countries of the Third/world, some $600 (US) per annum; a level approximately that obtaining in the lower income developed countries such as Italy and Japan. The real barrier seems to be lack of self-confidence in our own ability to launch out successfully and operate such enterprises. Thus, we find that those in the country who believe most firmly that we will always depend on foreign capital to an increasing extent are those leading persons in the private sector who are in a position to take the lead in pioneering economic development in the country. (In Sutton 1981, 33)

The authors of the white paper reflected Williams's view that indigenous private entrepreneurs were weak and inexperienced, and lacked the vision necessary to undertake the type of projects necessary to introduce fundamental change in the economy. What was worse, they were still too prone to genuflect to North Atlantic metropoles. Williams's hope – expressed in his budget speech of 1968 – that they would rise to the challenge of becoming significant economic entrepreneurs, had not materialized. The role of prime mover necessarily thus had to fall on the public sector. The white paper was, however, not hostile to private enterprise, whether national or foreign. What was being proposed was a sort of condominium arrangement in which both sectors would make their respective contributions.

Williams's 1972 budget speech made the official position on foreign investment even clearer, declaring that

- We welcome new foreign investment which brings in expertise, new technology and access to export markets to assist and supplement national efforts in our development.
- No new 100 per cent foreign owned enterprises will be allowed in key sectors of the economy, and national participation in joint ventures involving new foreign firms must be of meaningful proportion.
- Alienation of land will not be permitted.
- Existing foreign-owned enterprises must take steps to facilitate national participation, including in particular worker-participation.
- Certain areas of our economy are reserved exclusively for national effort.
- All firms, whatever the structure of their ownership, must in their operations give ample opportunity to transfer to nationals the skill, knowledge and expertise required to run the business.
- Government will take a leading part, including the use of direct participation to expedite national control and ownership.

The government's decision to eschew complete self-reliance and to limit its targets for national involvement was encouraged by its awareness of the "sharp" constraints that the economy would face in the process of becoming "structurally transformed". The most critical constraint was managerial and technical manpower, the use of which had to be optimized. Government was also sensitive to the need for new technology and for overseas markets if its industrialization effort was to succeed. The financial constraint was seen to be critical only in energy-based industries such as oil and petrochemicals. The white paper was aware that state collaboration with foreign corporations often led to an enhanced role for foreign firms in the economy, by providing them with risk-free investment capital, monopoly positions in protected markets, a tamed labour force and freedom to expatriate profits. It therefore indicated that the aim of joint venture operations was to encourage an orderly transfer of both management and equity to nationals in the private sector and to public authorities as well as to encourage the reinvestment of profits in the economy.

The white paper was clearly a nationalist rather than a socialist document. The overriding concern was with employment and national control. As the paper noted: "The participation by public bodies in industrial and commercial enterprises . . . must demonstrate awareness of the fact that the primary problem facing this country is unemployment." The emphasis was therefore to be put on labour-intensive "trigger industries" rather than on capital-intensive projects. To underline the fact that the preoccupation was with nationalism rather than socialism, the white paper further indicated that government considered its shareholding as a "trust", and that its intention was to make any shares that it acquired available to the public as "circumstances permit". The philosophy outlined in these policy statements formed the basis of official thinking and action. In the year following publication of the 1972 white paper, the country's poor financial situation made it impossible for the government to pursue any aggressive strategy of economic nationalism.

The Arab–Israeli war and the dramatic 400 per cent increase in crude oil prices that took place in early 1974 changed all that and precipitated a shift from a policy of cautious economic nationalism towards what one might describe as a posture of arrogant economic nationalism. When the first white paper was written in 1972, the Trinidad government had shareholdings in thirty-two industrial and commercial enterprises valued at just over TT$60 million. When the second white paper was written in 1975, the government's holdings had increased to approximately TT$209 million. Government had by then bought out the remaining shares of Trinidad and Tobago Television, Trinidad and Tobago Telephone Company, and BWIA, and had acquired (in 1974) at a cost of TT$93.6 million, the holdings of Shell Oil Company (Trinidad). It had also taken steps to participate in a number of undertakings in the area of natural gas, fertilizers, insurance and petrochemicals. By the end of 1975, the government's shareholding in industrial and commercial enterprises was in the vicinity of TT$250 million. By December 1977, government holdings had become so swollen that Williams was able to boast that "the Government of Trinidad and Tobago is a billionaire".

Williams went on to indicate that an even greater growth of public enterprises was anticipated, with the imminent establishment of an iron and steel complex, an aluminium smelter, upgrading of the Trinidad and Tobago Oil Company (Trintoc) refinery, an additional ammonia plant, a methanol plant and other energy related enterprises. In addition to these, the government envisaged further investments in hotels as well as an accelerated growth in agro-industries.

Williams and the Radical Left

The left dismissed "Perspectives" with varying degrees of contempt. Some groups accused Williams of stealing their programme, of using the language of the left without any real understanding of what it involved, of follow-fashioning and of making hasty concessions to the "echoes of the People's Parliaments". The Tapia House Group accused Williams of "temporising and faltaying [faltering] on the vital question of our relations with metropolitan business . . . for 13 ominous years". Lloyd Best agreed that majority shareholding was an improvement on the old arrangements that involved total foreign ownership, but argued that

[m]ajority ownership is by no means the same thing as actual control. Real control comes from three things. The first is technological mastery of the intricacies of production, marketing and research. The second is the organisational capacity to translate paper plans into bricks and mortar. And the third is the moral authority to act in concert with the demands of the People's Parliament. The government does not have the technological command required to take hold of petroleum, sugar and banking. The talent and the skill do exist among Trinidadians and Tobagonians, but a climate of intrigue, favouritism and witch-hunting and chronic organizational disorder have completely frustrated the emergence of any solid corps of professional technocrats. Many of our best minds just leave the country. Some stay and rot in the hope for better times. A favoured few become half-arsed politicians, accepting dozens of chairmanships and assignments in which they obviously can do no work save watch the political interest of the Doctor-Czar.

So after 14 years we do not even have a high-powered "techretariat" for petroleum, our very line of life. If the bungling at the National Oil Company is anything like at BWIA and the Transport Corporation, we're in real trouble. At the Hilton and the Telephone Company, we are still dependent on an anonymous who's who of alien experts. At Orange Grove, and now at Caroni, we have had to beg Tate & Lyle to continue management for us. This amounts to allowing them to take their cut even before the profits are computed. Technically incapable of using its legislative, administrative and diplomatic resources to advantage, the government is simply relieving London of putting up capital while we are now taking the risks ourselves. (*Tapia*, 9 August 1970)

Best, who was the leading source of ideas for reforming the political and economic system, believed that what was needed was not simply to assume control, but to imaginatively restructure the strategic institutions of the society to make them more relevant to the circumstances and needs of the common people. The emphasis in Tapia's programme was localization, which was not the same thing as nationalization or appropriation. "It may involve either or both or neither. . . . Economic control . . . is to be achieved through a mixture of individual and co-operative ownership along with a certain amount of central and particularly local government participation in business. . . . The aim is to control not just to own . . . government ownership has very little to do with popular control. . . . Ownership may of course be necessary for securing control. Where it is, localisation will demand ownership" (ibid.).

The radical left also argued that Williams had negotiated poorly in terms of whatever he acquired and that the government had not taken over enough. The radical left argued instead that there could be no political or economic stability until the government decided to face the "multi-national monsters" and make sure that more of the wealth which they take away from the country remained for the benefit of the people. The leader of the OWTU, George Weekes, called on Williams to nationalize Texaco and Amoco, the two major oil companies. Weekes admitted that there would be problems in doing so, but the chance was worth taking: "For any country regardless of its size to nationalize any industry and not to expect problems is to live in a dream world. Only experience will allow us to overcome the problems – even that of finding markets. But if you don't take a chance, you don't have a chance" (*Trinidad Guardian*, 10 January 1976). Weekes said that the takeover of Texaco's service stations was a "small victory for the people, but that was only the crumbs". Texaco should be "entirely" nationalized to ensure that plant and machinery were not run down beyond repair. Some economists at the University of the West Indies also urged nationalization. One of the latter, Dr Trevor Farrell, expressed scorn for the government's "cosmetic nationalization". Farrell argued that Williams had "no coherent petroleum plan or policy", and was throwing the country's money away through its production sharing arrangements and its so-called nationalization policies (see box below).

Williams's Acquisition Style

People talked about the commanding heights in the economy, and Dr. Williams said to me, "Dod, we have to acquire the BP Gas stations." So I negotiated and I bought. We didn't go to Cabinet first. We went to Cabinet after and we created the National Petroleum (NP) Company. Then Esso said they were going to sell their gas stations to Shell, and he said, "Dod, buy half." So we negotiated and we bought half and increased NP.

In 1974, Scotty [Lewis] and I and some others, Harold [Fraser], Lingston [Cumberbatch], I think and others, were in Lagos coming back from the Middle East trip. We had gone to Europe, and all of the Middle East countries, etc. and we were coming back. We got a message: "Dr. Williams says that Scotty and I must start negotiations with Shell in London." I could not for the life of me understand it. I knew that Shell had decided to wind down in a way, not quite [completely] wind down. They saw their production going down to the point where it would be asymptotic with the line approximating the profit line on a horizontal axis.

So we started talking in London, and when we got back to Trinidad, he said, "Dod, you carry on the negotiations from this point." And we concluded the negotiations and we created TRINTOC which they now call PETROTRIN. Incidentally, some people said it was a nonsense to have done it, but we did it at the right time and the first year of operations, TRINTOC made profits greater than the cost of acquiring it.

The same *ad hoc* process was used to purchase the Bank of London and Montreal. The Bank of London and Montreal wrote a letter [saying] that they wanted some change in their ownership, and I went to Dr. Williams at his home with the letter. He read it, he read it, he put it down, he took it up, he read it, and said, "Dod, buy it." I said, "Sir, they are asking for permission to change their ownership." He said, "Dod, I said to buy it." I said, "All right, but I have never bought a Bank

(Continued overleaf)

---

before. I've bought all sorts of things before." He said, "You could buy it, you could buy it." So I went and I negotiated, and I bought it and we created the National Commercial Bank of Trinidad and Tobago. We opened the Bank. I wasn't present at the Opening because I was then negotiating with Texaco for increased revenues. But there was a run on the Bank immediately. So they came to me, and I called Dr. Williams and I said, "Dr. Williams I think we should put a million dollars into the Bank." He said, "Right, let's stabilize it." I put a million dollars. Another week or two [later] there was a further run on the Bank because people were saying this is now a Government Bank which was never the intention. And they were pulling their monies out.

So I put another million in and that stabilized it. Perhaps it needed another million later on. I don't know. But later on it appeared to some people that the Bank was not functioning well. But Dr. Williams said to the Bank: show the flag all over the country of Trinidad and Tobago. And the Bank set up more branches than would normally have been set up. This was a decision from the Prime Minister coming out of 1970 and the Black Power Movement.

And we bought Caroni. First we bought 51 percent. I was with him when we bought 51 percent of Caroni; and then we started buying through London. Every time the price fell below a certain level, we gave instructions to buy. And then I got a message one day; "Dr. Williams says not to buy any more shares of Caroni until and unless he gets a specific Cabinet Minute to that effect." I was sure then that something was happening. I wasn't sure what it was but I was sure that things were not going to be the same again. But even so, the older chaps like Harold Fraser and Hezekiah who was in London consulted me informally and I advised them. And they completed all that we had started to do; and we created Caroni 1975. And I think that Company had great potential for the development of this country. Because we repatriated to Trinidad and Tobago a fantastic acreage, and when later we bought Texaco, we repatriated a greater acreage again which if we handled it properly, could rebound to the benefit of this country. (Testimony of Dodderidge Alleyne to the conference "Capitalism and Slavery 50 Years Later", in *Caribbean Issues* 8, no. 2 [March 1999])

Farrell claimed that the manner in which Shell was purchased was a classic example of "how not to negotiate."[1] He complained that the prime minister did not give the team handling the negotiations clear guidelines as to what the government planned to do, despite repeated written requests for guidelines.[2] Nor did they have the necessary sophistication to deal with the fourth largest oil company in the world. As such, the government was conned into paying three times more for the rundown assets of Shell than should have been paid. Indeed, the state may well have been able to acquire the assets (and the liabilities) for the proverbial US$1. Farrell also complained that Shell was allowed to retain critical areas of its activity, such as licences, patents and the marketing of petrochemicals. Government thus remained dependent on Shell for these as well as for spare parts. Farrell was of the view that if Williams had had a coherent petroleum policy based on Trinidad's own crude reserves, this would not have happened. In his opinion, the optimum strategy for Trinidad was to refine its own crude to produce gasoline and aviation fuel rather than residual fuel oil for export to North America. The aim should have been to meet the needs of the local and Caribbean markets and to use the remainder to provide the basis for industries such as plastics, textiles and fertilizers. One by-product of such a strategy would have been to cut back on Texaco's "excess" refining capacity, which depended on imported crude to meet the needs of the North American market. Farrell's argument was that what was in Texaco's interest was not necessarily in the interest of Trinidad and Tobago: "Little of the Texaco refinery in its present form is of any economic value to the people of Trinidad. What is of economic value is a refinery geared to about 250,000 barrels per day." Given the situation in the industry, Farrell, like Weekes, felt that both Texaco and Amoco should be nationalized: "It is abundantly clear that those companies have to go. It makes no sense for us to have our crude production up to 200,000 barrels per day and have most of this exported by Amoco, while we then have to import from Nigeria, Saudi Arabia and Indonesia. That's clear nonsense. It's fine economics for those companies. It makes sense for them. But it does not make sense for the nation" (*Trindad Express*, 25 June 1975). This policy was recommended in spite of the recognition that Trinidadians did not have the technology and the skill to perform some of the "critical functions" of the industry such as marketing, distribution, exploration, production, research, development and economic planning. Farrell argued, however, that the very fact that Trinidadians could not handle these functions competently after seventy years of involvement in the industry was reason enough for nationalization. Nationals had to be given a chance to learn.

Williams was critical of all such "adventurist" suggestions, although he did indicate that the government was considering participation in both Texaco and Amoco. These plans were dropped, however, and there were reports that Texaco was running down its Trinidad assets. In a number of addresses on the energy problem as it affected Trinidad and Tobago, Williams argued that even though the energy crisis had created a "new ball game", as a small producer, Trinidad was the weakest link in the international chain, and as such was not in a position to follow countries such as Venezuela, Mexico or Indonesia. If Trinidad were to "stick its neck out too far, it would be chopped off". To quote him at length on this point,

> We are a small producer. For every barrel of oil we produce, Abu Dhabi produces 15 at least. So we are, so to speak, at the end of the queue, the bottom of the scale of production. In the second place, whilst we, unlike many of the countries with oil, have developed a substantial refining capacity we, unlike most of these producing countries, depend on imports to the point where Trintoc, which we took over some time ago on behalf of the people of Trinidad and Tobago, depends on imports today, as it depended under the ownership of the multinational corporation for approximately one-third of the crude oil that is processed at Point Fortin. Not more than at best perhaps,

60 to 65,000 barrels of oil processed at Point Fortin is indigenous oil, with another 30,000-odd brought in from outside. (*Trinidad Guardian*, 20 April 1975)

The dependence on outside crude was even greater when the operations of Texaco were considered. To quote Williams further, "In Texaco's refinery, three or four times as large as the Trintoc refinery, we depend for approximately 85 per cent of our requirements on imports. The capacity is approximately 350,000 barrels per day, of which 85 per cent comes from abroad. If you want to take it over, take it over, but you are paying for it" (ibid.). Williams dismissed as irresponsible the suggestion that Trinidad should abandon the international market that Texaco and Amoco now had access to, and concentrate on integrated production for the domestic and Caribbean markets:

> We could not possibly, not with all the cars we have, not with all the buses we have, not with all the other facilities for using petroleum products that we have, utilise this enormous production. . . . What we produce locally today would probably not be sufficient, even taking in the local production on the East Coast by the other company, to sustain more than 50 per cent of the workers now employed in respect of this large oil operations up here. And we are fairly certain, as our advisers have warned us, that the type of oil produced off the East Coast – excellent oil – people pay a lot of money for it, some of the highest priced oil in the world today – is, in the first place not exactly suited to the technology developed in the refinery here that imports so much of the oil. So that if you have to use it, you probably have to make substantial adjustments; and in any case so far, it is not enough. And where we anticipate that it could be enough, to relieve us of the problem of imports, any oil worker present here would know what we mean when we are looking principally for naptha to go for petrochemical developments all down the line; the oil that we have is particularly weak on naptha and is used . . . to get a high price from people who want that oil, and use that to buy the less expensive oil, such as Trintoc is bringing in from Nigeria today, to give us the appropriate by-products – feed stock, I think you all call it, that would diversify production and therefore employ more people. If even you used all you have locally and continue to produce to the extent of your full capacity, unless you and I have decided to discover another national beverage and we drink the damn thing, we could not consume it all. So that you have got to find a market for it. (Ibid.)

Williams was aware, however, that the energy crisis had provided him with the "grand opening" that he needed to reduce dependence on the traditional multinationals. As he told the nation on 20 December 1973,

> The energy crisis through which the world is now passing is not only perhaps one of the worst economic crises the world has faced, it also threatens the very foundation of the economy of a large part of what we call western civilization, which is based on cheap supplies of energy from developing countries. Whether we like it or not, the Arab States have demonstrated dramatically that economic aggression is not a one-way street and

that the so-called developed countries no longer have a monopoly of economic power. They have brought about a dramatic shift in the world balance of power. Whether we like it or not – and most of the world does not like it – the Arab states have converted oil into an enormous political weapon. If the sheik could play, who is we? If we are blessed with the world's greatest resource today, oil, don't blame me, don't blame the people of Trinidad and Tobago. If oil is a weapon, for us it is not a weapon of offence, it is a defensive shield to protect our rights and Caribbean interests. (1973b, 3–4)

And as he explained further:

We work in the context of the new philosophy and practice of government participation with the oil companies which has emerged in the world – the most recent examples being Kuwait's 60–40 agreement with British Petroleum and Gulf Oil which covers production, refining gas liquefaction and transport; Nigeria's current negotiations for a 51 percent participation with Shell and British Petroleum in refining whilst increasing its participation in production from 35 percent to 51 percent; Venezuela's plans to bring forward the original date, 1983, by which concessions to foreign companies will revert to the Government. It is, as they say, a new ball game. For every company that continues to live in the past, there are several knocking at the door which are prepared to accommodate themselves to the future. (Ibid., 4)

In a number of subsequent statements, Williams reiterated his disdain for those who talked about socialism and what they called "genuine nationalization". As far as he was concerned, any talk about socialism or communism was "idiotic" and irrelevant in the context of the Caribbean. Instead of relying on revealed dogma, one had to search continuously for empirically based formulae upon which to base a course of action. Williams emphasized that he would not recognize a socialist blueprint even if he were to see one, since there were so many that made claim to being genuine (*Trinidad Guardian,* October 1976*)*. Williams felt that comprehensive nationalization and state-funded production was much too fiscally risky for a country such as Trinidad. His preference was for production sharing arrangements, which he had seen at work in Indonesia, Venezuela and Peru. In this arrangement, the company took all the risks. One had to do as the Venezuelans and avoid "sterile extremisms".

When you nationalize, you nationalize all the expenses for the production, the dry holes and so on you have to face. Why must we take one million dollars . . . and spend it on what may be a dry hole for oil when I could get that fellow to spend one million dollars, and when he gets production and he reaches a certain figure I say 60 per cent for the people of Trinidad and Tobago; send up the production figure, boy and we get 80 per cent. That is the arrangement. Why don't people come and tell you these things? That is what is involved in national ownership. So that, friends, our policy has been reasonably flexible, allowing us to change emphasis and move in a particular way in accordance with the international situation. (In Sutton 1981, 347)

He noted that the countries of Europe where "genuine" nationalization was in evidence were indebted to what he called the "non-nationalised countries" to the tune of about US$30 billion. Their dependence was not only on funds, but also on the technology produced by the much-abused multinationals. The Soviet Union had found it necessary to import technology from Italy to produce cars, television equipment as well as trucks, computers and baby food. It imported processing equipment and oil-drilling technology from the United States. Williams also observed that much of the agricultural production of the Soviet Union and Eastern European countries such as Poland was the result of either *de jure* or *de facto* private activity. In the latter case, as much as 80 per cent of agricultural farming was in private hands. East Germany was also seen to be dependent on West Germany for shoes (one million pairs were bought in 1976) and on the West for grain. China and the Soviet Union also had to import grain from the West. The same was true of Burma, once the great rice bowl of the world. "Genuine socialism in Burma had genuinely killed Burmese rice production. A poor backward Third World country . . . cutting off its nose in order to spite its face. We are being attacked for not doing it. We like our nose too much" (*Trinidad Guardian*, 18 October 1976).

The point Williams was trying to make was that nationalization did not solve the problems of production and created contradictions that forced such economies to depend on the capitalist world. "If genuine nationalisation was to be defined as . . . an increasing dependence upon the profits and the savings and funds of a non-nationalised country [*sic*], the Government of Trinidad and Tobago had certain apologies to make in respect of its definition of a genuine nationalisation" (ibid.).

Williams's unwillingness to pursue a policy of "genuine nationalization" in the oil industry might well have had something to do with the belief that such a course of action would be both economically unproductive and politically counter-productive in the long run. Williams was aware that European and Caribbean refineries that existed to serve the North American market were experiencing grave difficulties. Texaco Trinidad Inc. was in fact running at 60 per cent of its capacity because there was more profit in refining crude in the United States than in the Caribbean. Oil refined in the United States was now obtaining better prices and tax benefits than oil which was imported already refined. The US government was trying to encourage US-based refineries to operate at full capacity, and to encourage crude oil production in the United States by paying higher prices for "new" crude. The aim was to reduce dependence on OPEC and on offshore refineries that depended on crude from those countries. Radicals saw this as good reason for taking over and rationalizing the oil industry. The prime minister, however, had reason to believe that Texaco would welcome a decision to buy out an industry that in a few years they would find very uneconomical to operate. Williams preferred to enjoy the benefit of the taxes paid by Texaco on refined and transshipped crude while leaving the operation of the refinery to Texaco. Between 1973 and 1976, the oil companies paid TT$3,384.7 million in taxes. Profits, however, were equally high.

Despite his hostility to "genuine nationalization", Williams was equivocal on the issue of the role of the multinationals in Trinidad. At one time he was full of praise for the multinationals; at other times, he attacked them bitterly. In an address he gave in 1975, Williams was sharply critical of the multinationals and called for "concerted international action" to control them. The transnationals were seen as being "the big problem facing the world today". This was said to be particularly true for small countries, because many of the multinationals were more powerful than the countries themselves. The transnationals were accused of being guilty of a variety of sins in Third World countries – paying low wages to workers, ruthlessly overpricing imports that constituted the inputs of branch plant industries, underreporting profits, and evading tax ("The Role of the Multinational Corporations in a Developing Society", *Trinidad Guardian*, 4 May 1975).

In spite of the criticisms, Williams clearly accepted the view that the multi-nationals were necessary for the development of Trinidad and Tobago. His attitude was to some extent schizophrenic. He resented the multinationals for what they did to inhibit national control of the economy, but valued the benefits that he believed the multinationals brought. Williams's strategy was to try to bargain more effectively and creatively with the multinationals rather than to nationalize them as the radicals demanded. The official view was that the benefits of the multinational presence outweighed the costs. The multinationals thus had to be "ritualistically humiliated, while being practically wooed". Even though Williams's regime had nationalized a great deal more than it originally envisaged, its approach to nationalization being essentially defensive, pragmatic and "non-ideological", at least in the Marxist sense. In many instances, the government merely "stumbled" into taking over the branch plant of a multinational in order to protect jobs or to keep the industry from collapsing. Such was the case with the takeover of British Petroleum in 1969. There were, however, some aggressive and emotional takeovers, such as that of the cement industry, a unit of Rugby Portland. When the government took over that industry in 1976, Williams declared, "Oh God! I had to wait 20 years to take control" (*Trinidad Guardian*, 23 August 1976).

Williams's pragmatic approach to nationalization was defended by economist Bernard Primus, one-time chairman of Trinidad–Tesoro Oil Company. To quote Primus, "The conservatism of . . . Government stems from a non-ideological, pragmatic and empirical approach to public policy. Such an approach does not lack merit, as many dangerous pitfalls have been avoided. The ideological visionary with a clear cut road is often unable to turn back or change course on facing reality, because to do so is to forsake the ideological totem pole. The Government's approach has led to nationalism without tears. The Jamaicans are learning how rocky that road can be once they ride the ideological wagon." Primus insisted, however, that "by conviction, word and deed, Williams was a socialist in the generally accepted sense of the word in the Western world, although it would be true to say that he waved no hammer or sickle banners like Burnham" (letter to the author, 14 May 1990). I disagreed firmly with Primus's view about Williams being a socialist. He may be defined more accurately as a populist.

Williams and the National Private Sector

Williams became embroiled in ideological conflict not only with the radical left but with the indigenous private sector. His claim was that the private sector was not sufficiently responsible or conscious of the public interest. Williams set himself and the PNM as the "defensive shield of the little man in his daily battle with the commission agents" who controlled the commercial lifelines of the country. The conflict with the local private sector was a longstanding one that began in 1956 and continued into the 1970s with only brief periods of truce. The conflict was particularly intense in the 1960–61 pre-independence period, when Williams unleashed a venomous attack on the old "massa" complex that he believed had no place in the age of self-government. In one of his 1961 election speeches, Williams promised "to knock down the heads of the massas". As he told them, "This is the age of self-government. . . . Ours is a very simple philosophy. You take from those who have had too much for too long and distribute it among those who have had too little for too long" (Ryan 1972b).

During the period 1963 to 1973, the intensity of the conflict between Williams and local capitalists abated somewhat as both cooperated to contain militant labour. The Industrial Stabilization Act (1965) was the high point of this relationship. Massa in fact seemed to have returned with a vengeance. There were confrontations between the two over the 1966 Finance Act with its new regulations for corporate taxation and withholding taxes, with regulations that required insurance companies to reinvest more of their funds locally, and over price control, but the conflict was somewhat muted. The "prime mover" role that was defined for the state in the mid-1970s, however, generated grave alarm within the indigenous private sector, which believed that the state was becoming far too aggressive and monopolistic. What gave even greater cause for concern was that the state had moved into areas such as food importation – cheese, butter, onions, potatoes, powdered milk – and threatened to move into other areas that were considered the exclusive preserve of the "commission agents". Peak associations representing local importers, local manufacturers, food distributors and other middlemen were shrill in their condemnation of this new departure, as they also were about the government's efforts to control prices on a wide range of essential food items.

The Trinidad Manufacturers' Association was particularly outspoken in its criticism of what it considered the "spectre of state socialism" hovering over Trinidad and Tobago. The association claimed that there was a radical shift in government's thinking with respect to the economy in the past ten years and that a "new ideology" had emerged. This new paternalistic ideology of state socialism was alleged to be suspicious of the market, competition and profit. It also "seems to have abandoned the policy of limiting state control to the 'commanding heights' of the economy, a policy that served, however imprecisely, as a useful guide to private investors, both local and foreign. Apparently abandoned too, was consumer choice, a freedom that one normally associated with liberal and democratic societies" (*Trinidad Express*, 27 February 1977).

The private sector believed that the state sector was grossly inefficient, over-centralized and unresponsive to the changing needs of the society. It also claimed that the state sector was being "over-milked and discouraged by punitive corporation taxes, inflationary conditions that distorted profits, 'endless' red tape and other bureaucratic delays". In the opinion of the Trinidad Manufacturers' Association, "The civil service mandarins and their political bosses . . . who now enjoy undreamt-of power and influence abuse their regulatory power [and refuse] to accept that it is the private sector alone that has been responsible for the great improvements in living standards in Trinidad and Tobago . . . in the last decade, or that it can be responsive enough to satisfy the changing needs and desires of our society" (*Trinidad Express*, 8 November 1978). The private sector believed that Williams's ultimate intention was to set up some sort of state monopoly in food importation such as Guyana and Jamaica had attempted to do, with disastrous consequences. The concern was not only that this would prove to be inefficient and give rise to unintended consequences such as shortages, artificial rationing, black markets and increased pressure and prices on substitutes, but that it would be used as a big stick to show the private sector who was "boss". Any firm that the government wished to drive out of business would have its lines taken over. This was what gave so many businessmen nervous stomachs. As one put it, "We want to know what is government's ultimate policy, not only on the handling of such items as butter and cheese, but on the entire mixed free enterprise system" (*Sunday Guardian*, 30 July 1978).

The private sector also insisted that government allow it to participate in the heavy industries such as steel, aluminium, fertilizers, cement or asphalt through share participation and as members of the boards of those corporations. Unless this was done, the private sector believed that the companies would function as inefficiently as regular government departments, become sources of patronage, and would eventually have to be sustained by heavy hidden state subsidies.

The official responses to these questions and attacks were varied, but they all indicated that the government had embarked on a determined collision course with the private sector, which it believed was ruthlessly exploiting defenceless citizens. On the question of punitive taxation, the government bluntly refused to consider any tax reductions except where it believed it was "getting action along lines we would like". Relief was to be given only where projects were undertaken that generated employment and increased investment. It was noted that tax relief had already been given and that this had cost the government TT$96 million. To reduce corporation tax from 50 and 45 per cent to 40 per cent, as the private sector demanded, would cost the treasury TT$276 million, money that the state preferred to use to subsidize food and education, and to provide food stamps for the aged and poor, and free bus transport for school children and persons on public assistance and pensioners. The government believed that profits would find their way not into new investment, but into "extra yachts and more overseas vacations".

Spokesmen for both the public and the private sectors rationalized their arguments in the name of the public or the national interest. The private sector argued that profit, competition and a minimum of regulation and state interference were in the best interest of the public and the society, both in the short and long run. Far from being a "dirty word", profit was the principal engine of saving and therefore of economic growth. This held whether the economy was organized along capitalist or socialist lines. Given the structural constraints that inhibited efficient and profitable performance in the public sector, one was better advised to rely on private capital to finance growth. Surpluses must thus be permitted the private sector so that there would be sufficient savings to fund growth.

Williams was not convinced that he could or should rely on the private sector and the workings of the market to promote the public interest. The prime minister believed that the private sector wanted a "free-for-all" so that it could make a killing. Williams swore "that that would not be allowed to happen. We are here to protect the society as a whole." He noted that whereas some countries like Jamaica had a gun court, he would like to establish a "prices court", which would not charge a big fine: "I would [simply] confiscate all the materials they are selling above the [permitted] prices." In direct challenge to the Chamber of Commerce, Williams asked party members who attended the PNM's nineteenth annual convention to indicate by a show of hands whether they wished "the Chamber of Commerce to run their affairs". Quite naturally, no hands went up. Williams pledged that his government would continue to try to keep prices down and would seek to negotiate more government-to-government agreements that would eliminate the middleman and make goods directly available to the people (*Trinidad Guardian*, 13 September 1977).

Williams was "opposed to a state controlled economy", but refused to entertain the suggestion that the state should allow the private sector, whether local or foreign, to assume responsibility for the country's industrialization programme on the ground that they had the money and the technological resources to do so. As he had said as early as 1975, "Our basic policy is clear – to put the Government in the driving seat with a view to working out rational plans for development in the national interest" (*Trinidad Guardian*, 14 January 1975). Taking a swipe at the multinationals, Williams poured scorn on the view that the state should depend on "international pick-pockets" to do the job.

Senator Mervyn de Souza, a close ministerial associate of Williams, articulated what had so far been the clearest statement of the official ideology of the ruling party. Government, he said, was not at war with the private sector or the free enterprise system, which he noted was doing extremely well despite its many complaints. What government wished to do was to preserve the essentials of the free enterprise system, which was threatened by unemployment and growing inequality. This required that a considerable measure of income redistribution and welfarism be introduced to defuse the class war potential that existed in the society. The many direct and indirect subsidies provided by the government on food, petroleum, transport and education, which cost TT$144 million between 1973 and 1977 and which was expected to cost TT$181 million in 1978, were part of this strategy. So too were the income tax rebates given to the lower and the lower middle classes. As de Souza told the business community,

> A major programme of redistribution of income could not have been pursued before because it was felt that the economic base may not have been sufficiently strong and such a programme could have slowed down the pace of economic growth. However, because of our present position and the added stimulus which the hydrocarbon industrialisation programme will inject into the economy, we can now attempt a major system of redistribution without affecting the rate of growth in the economy. The business and professional sections must recognise this and accept this as the only way to save our present economic system. It must be considered as it were the price they must pay to ensure the survival of the free enterprise system. (*Trinidad Guardian*, 1 March 1978)

De Souza told businessmen that if there was to be a successful redistribution of income, the better-off groups "must either mark time or even be placed in a slightly worse position for the other sections to catch up" (ibid.). The income gap had, if anything, become worse over the past twenty years, with the lion's share – 48.6 per cent – going to the top 20 per cent of the population, and a marginal share – 1.5 per cent – going to the bottom 20 per cent. The top 10 per cent had, however, lost a bit between 1971 and 1972 – 38.8 per cent – and between 1975 and 1976 – 30.6 per cent.

Williams's aim was to narrow the gap even further by creaming off taxes at the top while placing a welfare cushion on the floor through subsidies or pseudo-work programmes. The question that needed to be determined was the extent to which these programmes had succeeded in limiting the growth of both the super-rich and the super-poor. For our purposes it is sufficient to establish that Williams's intent was there, and that he was trying to pursue a policy of capitalism with a human face. Ironically, other Caribbean countries such as Jamaica and Guyana sought to decorate these very policies with a socialist integument with no evident improvement in mass welfare. Official leadership in Trinidad and Tobago avoided this masquerade, which on the record created more problems than it solved.

Infrastructural Reform

The new development strategy required a Herculean effort to rehabilitate and expand the country's basic infrastructure, which was not keeping pace with what was taking place in the society. The need to rehabilitate and expand was not only occasioned by the growing expectations of the population at large, but also to meet the demands of new industries that were being established. Vast quantities of water and electricity were required for the new energy-based industries, to say nothing of telephones, airport and port facilities, roads, housing, and office accommodation for the growing bureaucracy. In seeking to effect a more dynamic role for the public sector, Williams found that the constraints were "many and complex". How was one to be efficient and economical in implementing projects while at the same time ensuring full public accountability and respect for constitutional and other required processes? Another key constraint was the severe shortage of professional and technical staff in almost all the disciplines related to the project development cycle – engineers, quantity surveyors, lawyers, accountants, architects and draughtsmen. The prime minister noted that the Ministry of Works needed as many as fifty-nine additional engineers. The Ministry of Legal Affairs was equally short of the experienced legal personnel needed in project preparation and vetting. Accountants were in woefully short supply throughout the public sector. And the deficiencies were not restricted to quantity. Also lacking was organizational sophistication and cohesiveness.

In his 1979 budget speech, Williams returned to the problem, which had by then become aggravated by the need to match nationalist rhetoric with performance in time for the 1981 general elections. Williams told parliament that the decisive factor in the development of Trinidad and Tobago was the increased revenues of the country resulting from the rise in oil prices since the end of 1973. He noted that whereas from 1969 to 1973, total current receipts were TT\$1,833 billion, or an average of TT\$366 million a year, during the next five years – 1974 to 1978 – total current receipts were six times as much – TT\$10,661 billion, or an average of

TT$2,132 billion per year. He also noted that by 1978, government had stashed away TT$2,100 billion in thirty-nine special funds. The interest earned on these funds in 1978 alone was TT$100 million.

Because of the construction boom prevailing in the mid-1970s, the government found that many of the projects it had proposed to undertake attracted few tenders of any quality or consequence. Where projects were begun, performance was poor in terms of quality of materials used and workmanship, and subject to costly delays and price overruns. The fees charged by local professionals were also deemed to be extortionate in regard to the service they provided. The prime minister complained that it was "easy to propose that there be greater dependence on local consultants and contractors. What was not easy was to persuade these consultants to remove the rigidity that was basic to their fee structure. What was most difficult was to ensure that price fixing on contracts was not taking place and that performance of local contractors could even approach agreed schedules" (*Hansard*, 1 December 1978, 5).

Given the poor performance of local professionals and the obvious inability of the society to cope with the enormous acceleration of public activity, the options available were to scale down the number of projects to be undertaken or to rely heavily on foreign inputs. The government rejected the former option on the ground that it would be difficult to persuade an expectant and impatient public that its needs for improvement in infrastructural and other long postponed projects should be further deferred. As Williams explained, "It is easy to restrict the number of projects and avoid the more complex and expensive projects. What is difficult to explain to the population, [is] why, with funds readily available, delays must be accepted" (ibid., 6).

Anticipating that reliance on foreign inputs would meet with adverse criticism from indigenous professionals, Williams revealed that many local firms were no more than "front men" for foreign firms. "The Government and the taxpayer must be protected against the growing breed of 'front men' and commission agents who, under the umbrella of going local, provide the front for foreign firms chosen by them without any reference to this Government or any other government." He also complained that some "local firms" bid on projects and proceeded to recruit staff abroad if they were successful. Some of these, being non-nationals, required work permits. As evidence of this growing reliance on foreigners by local contractors, it was revealed that whereas four contractors applied for 47 work permits in 1975, by 1978, some 210 were requested by eight contractors. Of these, 101 were for engineers, 22 for technicians, 55 for managers and 13 for quantity surveyors (ibid.).

Given public expectations and the problems encountered with local professionals in helping the government to respond to these expectations, the decision was taken to experiment with "Government to Government" agreements. As the prime minister put it, "The Government has given consideration to a somewhat novel alternative, *viz.* approaching a government directly and structuring an umbrella arrangement through which the foreign government would sponsor the implementation of a particular project" (ibid., 8).

The new formula, which was recommended by the United Nations Industrial Development Organization, was confidently expected to yield the following advantages:

- Once an overall umbrella agreement has been negotiated between the Governments, the contracting of firms and the mobilization of such firms would take a fraction of the time that is now needed. This may not appear to be significant, but there are instances that now exist where the appointment of a consulting firm using the traditional method of open competition and the Central Tenders board procedure, etc. has taken more than a year, in some cases as much as two years.
- The active lobbying with its undercurrents of corruption would be avoided.
- The particular firm would be subject to pressure, both from the particular agency, as well as its individual government.
- Special arrangements relating to matters such as taxes, duty free importation on equipment, etc. could be more easily handled.
- Attractive financing packages could be negotiated with the individual country.
- Relevant training programs, involving the movement of nationals to the particular foreign country, could be more easily organised.
- Difficulties with a particular firm could be dealt with the attention at the highest level.
- Through careful choice of the country and the firm, specialist skills of the highest calibre can be obtained.
- The country and its citizens could benefit from cross-fertilization of different technologies.
- No one country would dominate the commercial, financial and technological activities of Trinidad and Tobago. For example, this system would avoid the situation that has developed in the motorcar assembly industry, where at this point in time, Trinidad and Tobago is almost completely locked in with a technology from a single country which unfortunately has an appreciating currency which in turn is a major cause for rising costs of vehicles.
- The development of political goodwill on an international check which would hold Trinidad and Tobago in good stead when it moves into the international marketing community.
- The possibility of including reciprocal agreements relating to goods being produced in Trinidad and Tobago for export to these various countries.
- It will inhibit the growth of local commission agents who, for a percentage but

without providing any identifiable services, represent foreign firms of engineers and contractors. (Ibid., 8–9)

It was interesting that with the exception of Japan, all governments who were asked or who were being considered were located in North America or Western Europe. No eastern country was considered, nor were any socialist countries invited. The governments involved were those of Canada, the United Kingdom, Sweden, the Netherlands, Norway, Belgium, Luxembourg, West Germany, France and Austria. The forty-one projects included rehabilitation and additions to the port and the airport, road and bridge construction and repair, rehabilitation of the public transportation system, the building of hospitals, libraries, government offices, abattoirs, public housing and parking complexes, establishment of an official printery, surveying and clearing of wrecks in the harbour, the construction of inter-island ferries, the establishment of cold storage facilities, solutions to local traffic problems, resettlement of agriculture, waste disposal and utilization, dairy production and processing, industrial baking, the establishment of a concrete cement factory, adult education, the reorganization of the system of information storage and retrieval in several government offices, and a school nutrition programme, to name only some.

To coordinate and supervise the negotiations on the various projects, the government established a unit in the Ministry of Finance, the responsibility of which was to

- monitor prices, financial arrangements and schedules;
- ensure meaningful participation by local consultants, contractors and suppliers of support services;
- facilitate the issuing of work permits;
- ensure the provision of materials where these were unavailable in Trinidad and Tobago;
- ensure that prices were internationally competitive;
- advise cabinet where particular firms should be vetoed. (Ibid., 10)

The choice of this strategy provoked a storm of criticism both inside and outside of parliament. It was viewed as a de facto reversion to colonialism with all its assumptions about the incompetence of colonials. Once again, foreigners were being invited to "develop" the country instead of local expertise being asked to do so within their capabilities. To the critics, it was particularly ironic that the strategy was being articulated by someone who had come into politics to prove that indigenous professionals were every whit as competent as their metropolitan counterparts, if not more so. Opposition parliamentarians were extremely critical, as were local professionals, academic analysts and senior civil servants, who warned that none of the advantages envisaged by the prime minister would be achieved.

Williams anticipated these criticisms in his budget speech:

> It is easy to suggest the debarring of foreign expertise with their new and effective systems of construction management and methods of approach which meet the needs of the client based on reward for performance and acceptance of full responsibility for a project as opposed to the traditional limiting of responsibility. What is not so easy to understand is the mentality behind the same lobby that, on the one hand, seeks to flood the market with foreign manufactured goods which local capability can produce, and on the other hand, resists the approach of obtaining needed foreign expertise under the best type of conditions, vetted and sponsored by a friendly government. (Ibid., 5)

Experience with the projects indicated that the critics were right and that Williams had been extremely naive and optimistic in terms of what he hoped to achieve. As it became clear that the strategy was not working, a stream of criticism appeared in the media and in other forums. The critics pointed to the waste and displacement of money and resources involved in many of the projects, the corruption that appeared to be flourishing at several points of the project cycle – both in the metropolitan country involved and in Trinidad and Tobago – and the humiliation and frustrations that local professionals experienced in interfacing with foreign professionals involved in the projects. Relationships between the French and local professionals were particularly bad. In the construction of the Mount Hope Hospital Complex, the French were accused of displaying contempt and a colonialist arrogance of the worst sort. As criticism mounted, the government either defended the strategy or maintained a stony silence, at least in public. No word of comment or criticism of government-to-government contracts appeared in the 1981 budget speech, the last to be delivered by Williams before his death in March 1981. For Williams, the contracts appeared to be "sacred cows", beyond the pale of criticism even by senior civil servants and ministers, some of whom were known to have serious misgivings. Williams did indicate that he believed that the government was attempting to do more than its capabilities permitted. As he told parliament,

> The development programme on which the country has now embarked has increased the government's role as an entrepreneur and a financial intermediary. We must, therefore, consider whether the physical and human resources currently available are sufficient for the continued expansion of this effort and whether the time has come for a comprehensive assessment of the current development strategy. The government must attempt to achieve an adequate and consistent compatibility between the desires and needs of the people, its economic policy goals and its actions to attain those goals. (*Hansard*, 12 December 1980, 16)

The bulk of the criticisms about the performance of the development effort were levelled at public servants, local professionals and workers. Williams bemoaned

- the apparent ease with which highly paid consultants can through error up the tab. In virtually every instance the consultants received payment in full. Miscalculations add to the costs or project with the Government having to pick up the tab for their "services";
- the imprecision of estimates produced by consultants and other professionals which some instance have resulted in the Cabinet taking decisions on very inadequate and wrong information;
- the lack of awareness – one might even say concern – in some Ministries about the importance and significance of the Budget Exercise. There are too many errors of estimates; some Ministries fail to rank their projects in order of priority; many of the reports on the Development Programme have to be re-written or comprehensively edited in the Ministry of Finance. No wonder there are so many demands for supplementary appropriations during the fiscal year. (Ibid., 17)

Shortages of sub-professional skills and materials, and low worker output on construction projects were also identified as factors contributing to the high cost and slow completion rate of public sector projects. "Given all these factors, and with our eyes firmly fixed on developments and problems in other oil producing countries, the time had come for a critical reassessment of the country's development programme" (ibid.). What one needed to do, Williams told parliament, was to review the entire situation and chart out a path that would allow a sustained and manageable growth of the economy while not eroding those priorities identified by government at the start of the decade. The imminence of a general election in 1981, however, made it difficult, if not impossible, for the government to cut back on public sector expenditures. If anything, there had been an increase in public sector activity.

The review and reassessment called for did not come until after the general elections of 1981, which the PNM won for the sixth consecutive time. The 1982 budget speech, delivered by the new prime minister and minister of finance George Chambers, acknowledged that "the objectives of the Government-to-Government arrangements are not being fully met". In the speech the prime minister noted that one project that was expected to be completed in three years at a cost of TT$400 million was significantly behind schedule and that final construction was likely to be completed at a cost some three times the original estimate. Another project, which was expected to cost TT$97.5 million, was also behind schedule and the final estimated cost had doubled. The budget speech noted that "the arrangements have also had their effects on the public service by attracting away from it scarce expertise. This has defeated one of the basic objectives of the arrangements which was to supplement local resources which continue to be in short supply. The position is further aggravated by Government's inability to recruit suitable replacements" (*Hansard*, 4 December 1981, 16).

Alarmed at what was taking place, cabinet, in Minute no. 366 of 1982, appointed a committee under the chairmanship of Lennox Ballah, permanent secretary in the Ministry of External Affairs, to do the following:

- undertake a comprehensive review of the Government-to-Government arrangements, of the projects undertaken to date, and the mechanisms through which the projects are implemented and monitored with a view to assessing the extent to which the aims and objectives of the Government-to-Government arrangements have been fulfilled;
- make recommendations which should specifically include:
- measures to ensure that the institutional arrangements for the monitoring of existing projects are effective;
- whether or not all of the projects contemplated should be proceeded with under Government-to-Government arrangements.

The report to the Ballah committee amply confirmed many of the criticisms that had been made by the critics of the government-to-government strategy. The committee found that few of the anticipated benefits had been achieved and that such benefits as had been achieved were outweighed by the financial and other costs. In terms of the role of the foreign governments, few of them were prepared to guarantee or even supervise effectively the performance of firms from their countries and if anything used their diplomatic staff to obtain the best contractual terms available to foreign firms. As the report complained,

> Foreign missions consult among themselves and have sought to adjust to their particular requirements the best contractual terms offered to a foreign Government by the Government of Trinidad and Tobago. This situation has resulted in a general escalation of terms and benefits for foreign governments and consequently an unnecessary imposition on the limited resources of the country. . . . Foreign governments refused to accept responsibility for the performance of firms even if they were "persuaded" to designate them. The foreign firm consistently gets the support of its foreign government in pressuring government and its agencies for larger concessions for the foreign entity with undesirable consequences for the Government of Trinidad and Tobago. It is true that the contracts are fully commercial endeavours, but it is evident that some foreign contractors and private firms consider Government-to-Government arrangements in more than strictly commercial terms. They see these as providing them with opportunities to exploit situations. (Ballah 1982, 73–74)

Williams had seen government-to-government contracts as a time saver. They were a way of bypassing irritating bureaucratic hurdles and bottlenecks. The foreign governments and the firms were aware, in advance of negotiations, that they were in a monopolistic bargaining situation, and as such, agreements were only concluded expeditiously if the government agreed to all or most of the demands of the foreign enterprise. As the Ballah report observed,

Contract negotiations tended to drag on when the Government of Trinidad and Tobago is unable to accede to some of the demands of the foreign enterprise and in such cases, Letters of Instructions have had to be issued in order that work might be started while negotiations continue. Difficulties in respect of taxation, reimbursibles and other privileges have been important reasons for the delay in concluding negotiations on the contract, for example: for the Golden Grove Prison Complex. In view of the size, complexity and cost of projects involved, commissions and contracts must necessarily take considerable time to negotiate. Time can be saved only by leaving open-ended conditions in respect of price and control over performance. In some cases, the Government-to-Government arrangements have simply succeeded in implanting another layer of bureaucracy (the foreign governments). . . . When pressed to explain the reasons for the delay, the representatives of the Canadian Government have replied that they have their own bureaucratic procedure and regulations to observe. (Ibid., 80–81)

Delays were also occasioned by the need on the part of foreigners to spend time assimilating local standards, regulations, customs, culture and work habits. Some firms took as long as two years to mobilize, leading to scheduling delays. Government-to-government strategy was also expected to eliminate the corruption that had become endemic in public sector projects. The committee found, however, that, if anything, "the lobbying had increased rather than decreased". As the report noted,

The Government-to-Government system eliminates international competitive bidding and places the foreign country in a monopolistic situation. Despite this fact, lobbying has increased rather than decreased as the foreign enterprises, often using local interest groups, push to get contracts for all the projects cited in Memoranda of understanding to which there is party. What is more, foreign government representatives have themselves begun to circumvent the normal channels of communication via the Ministry of External Affairs and to direct to Ministries and Agencies of Government to promote projects (or to get difficulties resolved in their favour). The Committee has no evidence of corruption, but perceives that it cannot be guaranteed that active lobbying with its "undercurrents of corruption" and perhaps actual corruption, will in fact be eliminated since it may exist in the foreign country, and to the extent that foreign firms contract with local firms, it may also take place in Trinidad and Tobago. (81–82)

The evidence available to the committee also indicated that substandard materials that did not meet contract specification were used in many cases despite complaints by local consultants, and that the expected high standard of performance was in many cases not being realized. Also, local contractors made little effort to keep costs down and to meet time schedules. It was also made evident that some of the loan financing arrangements made by some governments on some of the projects that were externally financed in part or fully were not always in the country's favour. After reviewing one particular project, the committee concluded "In actual fact, the government-to-government agreement can result in worse financial packages than would otherwise be available." The committee also charged that there was oligopolistic collusion among contractors to inflate prices and terms and conditions relating to income tax and customs duty exemptions. They even flouted local regulations with impunity.

In terms of the transfer of technology and training that was expected to take place, the evidence suggests that little cross-fertilization took place. In many cases, foreign consultants picked the brains of local professionals, repackaged the information and charged fees that in one case were as much as ten times more than those being charged by their local equivalents. Where training programmes were organized, these had to be paid for separately and not as part of the main contract. In almost every case, the planning and design were done overseas, affording local professionals little opportunity to benefit. On-the-job management was also rigidly controlled by expatriates. On some projects, it also became evident that the personnel who were expected to be in a position to conduct such training sessions were not the most competent available. In some cases, the country chosen to design and construct the project was not the most advanced in the relevant field. In other cases the firms and personnel chosen were selected less with an eye to their competence than to political or other considerations in the countries of origin. The committee claimed that it was repeatedly informed that a number of the foreign "experts" did not have the expertise or the qualifications the job called for and were often learning from experience gained on the job in Trinidad and Tobago. In at least six cases, "experts" were repatriated because they did not possess the required qualifications and expertise.

One of the key weaknesses of the government-to-government strategy in the area of project monitoring was that it made inadequate provision for the inputs of local counterpart groups. As the report noted,

> At the project management level, the failure to benefit is due in part to the lack of qualified Trinidad and Tobago counterpart personnel who could be assigned full-time to co-manage the project. However, the project management functions were almost invariably in the hands of expatriate staff. Local personnel are confined to a peripheral role so that the transfer mechanism is at best very tenuous. Only at the technical level has there been some measure of transfer of know-how obtained on the job. (Ibid., 86)

The absence of competent counterpart staff also meant that there was no group to whom foreign companies could transfer the technology, assuming that they were genuinely pursuing this goal. And the committee found that where competent local professionals were able to detect faults or problems or had discovered that substandard material was being used contrary to contract specifications, some foreign contractors, the French in particular, ignored or disregarded the submissions made.

In making their final assessment of the government-to-government arrangements (the total costs of which were expected to be close to TT$7.5 billion), the Ballah committee agreed that the model was innovative and theoretically desirable, but that in practice, the benefits were illusory rather than real. Far from achieving the stated objectives, the contracts "have engendered an inordinate amount of animosity in the society at large and among the professionals in particular". What was regrettable too was that the foreign countries in question, particularly France, England and West Germany, had done nothing to assist with the negotiation of positive reciprocal arrangements for aviation rights for BWIA, for the export of Trinidad and Tobago–made goods (such as rum and sugar) to Europe, or in stimulating goodwill for Trinidad and Tobago in the international arena. In each case, the net contribution was negative.

In assessing overall responsibility for the failure of the strategy, the committee was nevertheless of the view that the bulk of the blame had to be assigned to the Government of Trinidad and Tobago, which had gone about negotiating the various arrangements in an amateurish manner. The shortcomings were due, they claimed, to the fact that "there was an absence of carefully thought out and well defined development plans for the 1973–81 period and beyond". All sorts of projects were identified by ministry officials, special interest groups and well-placed individuals without any sort of effort having been made by any coordinating agency to establish priorities:

> This resulted in a situation in which different ministers and other agencies of Government, instigated in some cases by foreign governments, their representatives or their companies promoted the initiation of a wide range of projects, not all of which . . . can be said to be high on the list of national priorities. . . . Far too many projects were undertaken at the same time. As a result, Government ministries and departments, given their chronic staff shortages at the professional level were ill equipped to cope with project definition and conceptualization, and project management. These deficiencies were easily and quickly recognized by foreign agencies and appear to have been exploited to the fullest at crucial contract negotiation stage and subsequently. (Ibid., 93)

Given the strictures made on the government-to-government formula, the committee's advice was that projects that were not yet begun should not be undertaken under such an arrangement. If such arrangements were to be contemplated in the future, they should be undertaken only where the expertise or technology was owned by the foreign government itself and the choice made after a competitive selection process was undertaken. In cases where projects had already begun, the committee urged tighter supervision to ensure that time schedules and contract specifications were met and cost overruns minimized.

Government's response to the report was equivocal. It agreed to scrap eighteen of the projects and to review eleven. The remainder were to be continued to completion. In some cases, modifications were proposed to ensure greater involvement on the part of local consultants and professionals as well as more effective control of expenditure and completion schedules. The government rejected the committee recommendation to use the government-to-government formula only where a government owned the technology.

The experiences of the 1970s, coupled with falling oil prices and declining oil production that reduced the country's financial capability, also had the effect of forcing the government to return to comprehensive multi-sectoral planning that Williams, in his anxiety to get things done in a hurry, had deemed unnecessary. In his 1977 budget speech, Williams had taken the view that planning had not enabled the developed industrialized nations to avoid inflation, pollution, shortages, the problem of urban congestion or economic recession. Nor had it enabled developing countries to increase their rate of growth. What was needed, he said, was action in certain key sectors.

The government that came to power following Williams's death and the elections of 1981 felt it necessary to return to the planning that Williams himself had vigorously endorsed in 1969. In his first budget speech, Chambers advised parliament that a national planning commission and a task force would be appointed to reappraise in a comprehensive manner the country's development strategy. The appraisal was to include the following:

- a determination as to whether the government should continue to allocate to the energy-based industrial sector national resources in the same proportion as before;
- a determination of the optimum rate at which to exploit our hydrocarbon reserves;
- a determination of more effective measure to develop the non-oil sector and diversify the export trade of the country;
- a determination of more effective measures to achieve maximum self-sufficiency in food;
- a determination of the proportion of our resources which can prudently be allocated to welfare transfers and subsidies, or put another way, the division of revenues between consumption and investment;
- a determination of priorities within the public sector programmes and of the most appropriate rate of project implementation;
- putting the infrastructure development programme on a more efficient and manageable basis. (*Hansard,* 4 December 1981)

Chambers also told parliament that he was rejecting the forced-pace strategy of development adopted by his predecessor. As he put it, "What emerges with utmost clarity from the experience of the 1970s and the problems arising therefrom is that development is a complex and long-term process involving, among other things, sacrifice, discipline and commitment to the national good. Believe me, there are no shortcuts."

33 Steel versus Brown Sugar

The main thing is to make History, not to write about it.
– Bismarck

Anybody can make History, but only a great man can write about it.
– Oscar Wilde

Here at Point Lisas, sugar gives way to wire rods.
– Eric Williams

Some say one has a responsibility for History. I don't believe it. . . . People like me are not building achievements to leave for future generations.
– Mao Tse-Tung

Having written *Capitalism and Slavery*, one could well understand why, when provided with an opportunity and the requisite resources to follow the path taken by Britain in the age of the industrial revolution, Williams would seek to imitate his former colonial masters. Williams believed that steel symbolized modernity and that the sugar plantation symbolized slavery, indenture and colonialism. The one provided the mechanism for true economic emancipation while the other constituted the basis for persistent poverty and subordination. Frank Barsotti, Williams's permanent secretary from 1975 to his death, tells us that "Williams had an emotional kind of attachment to replacing sugar with steel. This was one of the things operating at the back of his mind. He wanted to wipe out the sugar industry, get it away from him, and the way to do that was through technology, through natural gas as a fuel and as an intermediate product" (Barsolti, 1991).

The start of construction on the iron and steel complex at Point Lisas on 18 October 1977 provided an opportunity for Williams to share his vision of the future economic landscape of Trinidad and Tobago. What was being initiated on that day in October, in Williams's mind, "marked a decisive reversal" of Trinidad and Tobago's economic development strategy from that which obtained in the colonial era. That pattern was characterized by the mercantilist formula, which emphasized the export of primary commodities such as "brown sugar" to the metropole, where value was added downstream and upstream. This strategy employed British ships as well as producers of British refined products and related services. The colonies, those in America included, were thus to "manufacture not a nail, not a horse shoe. They were to produce raw materials only, which were to be sent to England to enable downstream manufacturing operations to provide jobs to expand" (as cited in Sutton 1981, 82).

Williams told Trinidadians that the world economy was witnessing a new strategic conjuncture in which sugar production was no longer a preserve of the non-white colonial world; neither were certain kinds of resources confined to the developed world. The once colonial world had now developed their mineral and energy resources, and one was thus able to reverse the old patterns. "Point Lisas is the symbol of this fundamental reorientation in the national economy. Here at Point Lisas, sugar cane gives way to wire rods" (ibid., 83). Williams went on to do a paen to steel, the production of which, "possibly of all man-made products, has been for many years and will continue to be a bench mark for industrial development and any form of serious industrialization. For many years [steel production] has been monopolized by larger and more developed nations either because of their control of technology, markets or both" (ibid., 83). That era was now over. This view of the role of steel as the yardstick by which development and superpower status was measured, was also shared by Mao Tse-Tung, who set about creating backyard furnaces to produce steel in quantities that would exceed that produced by Great Britain in fifteen years, later shortened to three (Chang and Halliday 2005).

Williams had a clear view as to why steel had to replace sugar, brown or otherwise, and why that monopoly exercised by the north over the periphery had to be broken, difficult as it might be. He noted that attempts had been made to persuade him to take an easier, more conventional and consumerist route to development. He found that option unattractive for all sorts of ideological and other reasons. As he explained,

> Blessed as we are with hydrocarbon resources, we had a choice to make. There have been attempts to persuade us that the simplest and easiest thing to do would be to sit back, export our oil, export our gas, do nothing else and just receive the revenues derived for such exports and, as it were, lead a life of luxury – at least for some limited period. This, the Government has completely rejected, for it amounts to putting the entire nation on the dole. Instead, we have taken what may be the more difficult road and that is – accepting the challenge of entering the world of steel, aluminum, methanol, fertilizer, petrochemicals, in spite of our smallness and in spite of our existing level of technology. We have accepted the challenge of using our hydrocarbon resources in a very definite industrialization process. I am certain that, bearing in mind the skills, the educational level and the ambitions of our people, particularly our young citizens, it was in fact the only choice we could have made.[1] (Sutton 1981, 84)

Trinidad had to take its "rightful place in the international trading community. It is this development that guarantees energy for these various projects not for a mere 10 or 15 years, but at least for 40 years" (*Trinidad Guardian*, 5 October 1978).

The latter route was admittedly strewn with all sorts of minefields and conditionalities in the way of debt-financing agencies, owners of technology, potential equity partners, and their respective brief-holders. There were also problems translating visions into viable projects that could survive sustainably in the hostile world of international trade. Williams knew that problems lay ahead, but he was certain that he had embarked on the correct developmental road. He promised that he would one day provide details of all that was involved in getting the Iron and Steel Company of Trinidad and Tobago Limited (ISCOTT) as well as other energy projects such as Fertilizers of Trinidad and Tobago Limited (FERTRIN) launched, but one is not aware that he ever did so. He openly hinted, however, that among the lessons learned, lessons that would inform the future, was that it was important to diversify sources of funding, technology, management systems, and markets. It was also critical that nationals became involved in marketing.

Ken Julien, the man whom Williams chose to execute the hydrocarbon-based development strategy, the so-called Point Lisas model, agreed that Williams indeed had a vision in respect of the hydrocarbon sector, but chose to go into iron and steel for three principal reasons, that is: the abundance of a cheap energy source in natural gas, a commodity that had previously been flared; the availability of new technologies for steel production, that is, the direct reduction system; and Trinidad and Tobago's strategic location in relation to the world's major steel consumers (North America) and the major exporter of iron ore (Brazil). "These factors," said Julien, "allowed ISCOTT to operate from a very competitive basis in relation to other producers which aimed at the same markets by giving ISCOTT the benefit of cheaper costs" (*People*, September 1981).

Julien noted that many criticized Williams for going into steel at a time when steel plants all over the world were closing. The critics were unaware, however, that those mills were closing as a result of the recession, and because they were producing sheet and plate steel for the ship and motorcar industries. ISCOTT would be producing billets and wire rods, the end products of which were needed in the construction industry, and would be doing so at competitive prices.

Julien was full of praise for Williams's "vision" and also for the political will that the prime minister displayed. This vision, he noted, had previously been articulated in the *White Paper on Natural Gas*, which argued that while oil prices might continue to increase up to 1984, such increases might no longer be able to offset the projected decrease in production. "Trinidad and Tobago therefore, had a reasonable breathing spell of some four or five years over which period it had to develop revenues other than those from oil. This breathing spell called for a definite national strategy and efficient and immediate implementation of any of the policies or decisions which result from the adoption of such a strategy. Natural gas is the only other significant and commercially exploitable natural resource capable of generating revenues of the required magnitude to offset the decline in gross national revenue as forecasted. . . . The future of the national development programme is [thus] inextricably tied to the definition of the country's gas reserves, and the timely production and efficient utilization of these reserves" (Government of Trinidad and Tobago 1981, 5). The government had to reduce dependence on oil, the price of which could be expected to fall. Seventy-five percent of government's revenue then came from oil. Diversification was thus an imperative.

Williams spoke eloquently and with passion about his vision for Trinidad and Tobago to a graduation ceremony for young employees of the Trinidad and Tobago Electricity Commission in 1980. Williams told the awardees that he had much to say and that his decision to say it to them on that particular occasion was "deliberate". He was speaking to them as the youth of the nation who were employed in the field of energy. In his view, the story of Trinidad and Tobago in the 1980s would be the story of youth and energy: "If ever an opportunity was presented to a country to make significant strides in a decade, the decade would be the 80's, and the country would be Trinidad and Tobago."

Williams was angry with critics, both local and foreign, who were trying to discourage him from pursuing this particular dream. As he told the assembled group,

> We are told in no uncertain terms that there is no room for a small third world country in the world of iron and steel. We are told that we should not upset or interfere with the tradition whereby the production of steel, remains dominated by the USA, Japan, the EEC [European Economic Community] countries and Russia. We are told that steel consumption in the world is dropping, and that there is continued depression, and that the difficulties to penetrate even the nearby markets of Latin America and North America are insurmountable. We are told this by the local pundits and their overseas advisers. We are told that our half a million tons would have difficulty in finding a place in the Western World market of almost 500 million tons. It is a challenge, but we will accept it. It is a challenge which you have to meet. We have provided the political will, we have provided the finance, we have provided an environment within the international community which, all things being equal, should be an environment in which most countries will be willing to trade with us. We showed what was possible. No one country now dominates our economy, either in trade, in technology, in finance, or in providing expatriate personnel. But the real challenge still remains; we must make the best steel in the world and at competitive prices. I am told that the plant will be the most modern in the world. Certainly, as Minister of Finance and Corporation Sole, the cost of putting up such a plant should provide us with one of the best. If not, the Board of ISCOTT will be asked pertinent questions by its shareholder.

Williams told his audience that the responsibility for realizing this vision lay with them, the sons and daughters of those who were enslaved or indentured and who toiled on the sugar plantations:

> The eighties must surely belong to you. I urge you to accept that role, that challenge with the same determination, the same sense of discipline, with the same attitude towards productive hard work that your parents and indeed your grandparents had in the 50's, 60's and the decade before that. Where our ancestors toiled in the field producing sugar under conditions of slavery or under conditions of indentured labour, you will have an opportunity to produce steel of the highest quality, to generate electricity. You will have the opportunity in an environment far removed from the conditions experienced by your parents, your grandparents, and their parents. (Press release, Office of the Prime Minister, 4 February 1980)

Not long before his death, Williams again launched an attack on those who were urging him to invest in tourism related projects, including a new airport, instead of steel. He was scornful of those who simply wanted Trinidadians to import consumer durables produced in the metropole. For him, Trinidad had to cease being a nation of consumers. Williams disdained those whom he said were still living in the shadow of the plantation. As he declared in his 1978 budget speech, "Many of our population are still of the mentality of the brown sugar economy asking querulously why do we need steel. . . . We of the PNM have always been the threat to this mentality of the brown sugar economy. . . . We stand today as the only cohesive force in the society against this mentality and in vigorous prosecution of our own nationalist economic identity" (*Trinidad Guardian*, 14 December 1977).

In an address delivered at the Central Bank of Trinidad and Tobago in honour of Williams in May 2005, Julien argued that Williams had a vision of a national energy sector even before the PNM first won political power in 1956.[2] In an earlier address, Julien portrayed Williams as a "modern day Prometheus" who decisively made the critical uphill steps that shaped the future of Trinidad's energy sector (speech at the symposium "Eric Williams in Retrospect", April 1991). Julien made reference to a conference that Williams had organized and chaired at Chaguaramas on "The Best Uses of Our Petroleum Resources" as the place where the model was most clearly outlined for the first time. He also made reference to Williams's statement in *Inward Hunger* that he always paid special attention to oil depletion allowances, and the sale of concessions in Venezuela and Alberta, Canada. Williams's complaint was that "our predecessors had given away our valuable marine areas in the Gulf of Paria; it was freedom on our side of the boundary while in Venezuela, on its side, sold concessions to the highest bidder". Williams also made reference to oil in the People's Charter, in which he complained that from earliest times, "local interest was subordinated to the interests of external capital".

Julien claimed that from 1963 onwards, Williams purposefully laid the ground-work for the emergence of a national energy sector. In 1963, he established the Mostofi Commission to examine the present and future prospects of the oil industry in the context of the economics of the world oil industry. Among the many questions he posed for the commission's study was the extent to which the division of the proceeds of the oil industry was just, and the extent to which "laws which may have been appropriate for the operations of the industry under colonialism was compatible with the aims and aspirations of an independent nation pledged to a democratic form of government". The report of that commission led to a redefinition of the role of the Ministry of Petroleum and Mines, which had been established earlier that year. Julien saw Williams's hand in all of this: "The concept of a national identity for the energy sector [had] begun to develop" (Julien 2005, 13).

Julien saw Williams's acquisition of the interests of British Petroleum Oil Company in 1969 as a defining moment in the emergence of the national energy sector, as a "dramatic move which took courage and a strong political will". The takeover of British Petroleum led inexorably to the decision to acquire that company's marketing outlets and, later on, those of Shell, Esso and Texaco Oil Company, all of which were vested in the Trinidad and Tobago Petroleum Marketing Company. Julien noted that the word *national* appeared for the first time in relation to the energy sector.

The next defining moment was Williams's decision to use natural gas as an energy input in a strategy of industrialization rather than oil as had been suggested in the 1969–73 development plan. Prior to 1975, most of the natural gas generated was burned off. Companies such as Amoco had no interest in it and preferred to depend on oil, which had a ready market. This "free gas", however, had to be monetized with all the challenges that doing so involved. As Julien observed, "The challenge to monetize our natural gas was forbidding and formidable, including a skeptical national community that had not historically identified with the energy sector. The gas was ours, but we had to find the money to bring it on shore" (ibid., 18).

The acquisition of Shell in 1974 and the rebranding of the company as the Trinidad and Tobago Oil Company (Trintoc) was another critical moment in the emergence of a national identity in the energy sector. Williams's speech on the day of the formal takeover indicated clearly that he was aware of the symbolic importance of what was being done, that is, the "lowering of the flag of an external corporation . . . and our flag flying high and riding proud in the breeze symbolizing the ascent of the nation. . . . " (ibid., 19). The other critical defining moment was the decision to enter into joint ventures with W.R. Grace and with Amoco to establish the ammonia and methanol plants, TRINGEN and FERTRIN. These decisions involved a fundamental change in Williams's thinking about the relationship that should exist between the state and large multinationals. Williams had hitherto been of the view that entering into relationships with them inevitably involved the loss of one's "virginity" and of national sovereignty.

The final major decision involved the creation of ISCOTT and the development by the state of the Point Lisas industrial estate and a modern port on the estate, which up to that time was a project developed by the local private sector.[3] Williams died weeks before ISCOTT produced the first billets of steel, but he lived long enough to glimpse the outlines of what he had fought hard to achieve. As he said in his 1981 budget speech, delivered on 5 December 1980, "a use has been found for our national gas, the alternative to which would have been flaring it and burning it, or saving it for export to some large metropolitan country with a thirst for cheap energy". Williams told citizens that they must not behave as though they had just had a windfall. "We must have something to show when the crisis is all over – a new petrochemical complex, the realization of Point Lisas, one or more new planes, [and] a substantial number of additional jobs in new spheres of economic activity."

The question arises as to whether Williams really had a clear and consistent vision of what he wished to do in respect of a national energy sector, as Julien suggests, and whether throughout the years he was carefully laying down the planks that would be needed for this dream to become a reality. Williams indicated that all the things that he did in respect of a national energy policy were not accidents, and had been initiated much earlier. As he told the nation on 1 January 1974 in the third of three speeches on the energy crisis,

> The major step that we have taken here in Trinidad and Tobago is the establishment of co-ordinating machinery embracing all matters relating to petroleum. These matters include relations with other oil producers, prices and revenue, the use of oil revenues, national participation, joint ventures with other governments, emphasis on petroleum-based industries. We are intensifying at home and abroad our discussions with our oil colleagues. Don't get the impression that this is something new or sudden. The cooperation is over ten years old. With Iran we initiated relations through our oil commission of inquiry ten years ago. Eight years ago we were representing Nigeria in international oil discussions and some of their top specialists have served part of their apprenticeship in Trinidad. Our first attempt to increase our oil revenues 15 years ago followed the precedent set in Venezuela. Our contact with Algeria in the field of oil dates from my visit to several African countries nine years ago. (1973b, 6–7)

The visits to which Williams referred were intended to gain entry into OPEC, but were also meant to allow Trinidad and Tobago to learn about what was taking place in the international oil industry (see chapter 38). As we have seen, however (see chapter 32), Williams was often pushed by events and the activities of the radical left and even the orthodox trade unions to adopt nationalist economic policies, and in the case of the acquisition of British Petroleum, for example, the aim was primarily to save jobs, and not to work towards a national energy policy. In much of what he did in this area, the record suggests that he was often a reluctant agent or an opportunist, employing the same characteristics that he displayed on the soccer field. It may be, however, that the vision was always there but that he did not want to get too far ahead of public opinion. This was the view held by C.L.R. James, who observed,

> Nkrumah and his Volta Dam, Nehru and the tremendous strain under which the independent economy is almost cracking and the tension upon the people to establish some steel mills and other premises of a modern existence. Do you know why they do this? Do you think it is purely an economic question? Men who know steel have told me that they question the value in strictly economic terms of some of those steel mills that Nehru is putting up in India. They think he would do better by importing. But I know what those men are after. They are after laying the foundation of a modern community, they are after letting their own population and the rest of the world see that they are making a step from being a hinterland and a backyard of the advanced economies, and taking their place, however humble, however small, as a modern civilized community. (1961, 27)

Williams's industrial policy and management style came in for strong criticism before and after his death. The general complaint was that the focus of the policy was on hydrocarbon-based projects at the expense of agriculture and small and medium-sized enterprises, a policy that led to disinvestment in and neglect of those sections of the economy, a neglect that economists refer to as the "Dutch disease". Typical of this point of view were the comments of Frank Rampersad, one of the architects of Williams's earlier economic strategies, Frank Barsotti, permanent secretary in the Ministry of Finance from 1975 to 1981, and University of the West Indies academics Trevor Farrell, Dennis Pantin and Taimoon Stewart. Williams's ad hoc style of management was also the subject of a great deal of negative comment.

Farrell noted that Williams's pamphlet *The Economic Problems of Trinidad and Tobago* (1955) was harshly critical of the regime that he displaced in 1956. Williams complained then that Albert Gomes had come to power in 1950 and had "found a nation swimming in oil and sucking sugar cane". When he left the nation six years later, it was still swimming in oil and sucking sugar cane. Farrell noted that the same held for Eric Williams: "When he died in 1981, he too left a nation swimming in oil and sucking sugar cane" (1988, 103). Farrell complained that unlike countries such as Sweden, Brazil, Kuwait and Norway, Trinidad and Tobago, like Nigeria and Venezuela, had not been able to "escape the curse of oil. It had not been able to transcend it as a resource and use it to build other downstream industries as Sweden had done with iron ore and their forests. We have not understood in the 25 years how you use oil and gas" (1998, 107).

Rampersad acknowledged that Williams could not depend on the indigenous private sector to drive the economy because the group was small and risk averse. "The indigenous entrepreneurial class is not extensively populated by risk takers in the Schumpeterian sense; by and large, indigenous investors have not demonstrated a willingness to extend the frontiers of production." Moreover, "because of the lumpiness of the capital needs in transforming type investments, the local private sector is often unable to mobilise the required resources to participate meaningfully and sustain these investments through the gestation period" (1988, 15).

Rampersad nevertheless felt that the net effect of the policy was negative:

> Perhaps the most important lesson which the economic experience over the past 25 years teaches us is that durable economic transformation is a relatively slow process, achievable only through step by step progress. Sudden infusions of wealth can be as disruptive as sudden losses of income earning power in the process of promoting beneficial economic change. This is just another way of saying that development is not only for people, it is about people; and sustainable economic and social progress is achievable when the population at large accepts and is prepared to take the action which its posited economic goals realistically demand; in other words, for a nation, there is no "free lunch". (1988, 12)

Rampersad recommended that the state should sell off its investments when they reached the stage of profitability and wind up or dissolve those firms that were chronic loss makers. Future ventures should only be undertaken if they were transformative in nature and had commercial merit, and even then only on a joint-venture basis.

Pantin was even more critical. In his view, Williams's industrial strategy had been a complete failure, and it had failed for a variety of reasons, some economic, others political. At the surface level, failure was due to the dramatic discrepancy between expected and realized prices for the exported commodities. Looking deeper at the cause of failure, Pantin argued that the objectives were unrealistic to begin with: "An investment of some TT$7 billion was expected to yield a revenue and foreign exchange surplus to complement and ultimately replace the oil sector" (1988, 34). The estimated loss on the projects over the period 1981 to 1986 was $1.5 billion, the bulk of which, TT$1 billion, was generated by ISCOTT.

The second factor was the prime minister's obsession with iron and steel. Williams, he said, was trying to replicate the experience of Britain during the industrial revolution. As Williams himself had said in 1978, "Our historical experiences have been dominated by the prohibition of industry and manufacture . . . the slogan was not a nail, not a horseshoe . . . do we instead proceed . . . to create an industrial base, so that when our energy leaves the shores, it carries with it substantial value added and a better marketability, and provide a more secure existence for the future when the oil boom is over?" (as cited in Pantin 1988, 39).

The third factor was political. That rationality and accountability was put on the back burner was explainable by a hidden electoral agenda, that is, to provide jobs in the build-up to the 1981 general elections. To quote Pantin more fully,

> The urgency and certainly from hindsight, indecent haste with which implementation took place suggests that political consideration played a major role in decision-making with regard to the Point Lisas projects. The hidden agenda led to failure to conceptualize the strategy properly and to specify it theoretically. There seemed to be some belief, and it is in fact still widespread today, that natural gas is, by definition, a money tree – simply waiting to be picked, captured in that term "monetizing the gas." There was, and is, little reflection on what should give natural gas this particular innate profitability as opposed to other natural resources – salt for example. (1988, 40)

Pantin argued that it was not obvious that resource-based industrialization was better suited to achieve national development goals than other political strategies. Pantin believed that Trinidad would have been better off putting the petro-dollars into the international banks and using the earnings therefrom to finance needed imports of goods and services.

The fourth factor that conduced to failure was that the country was small, and as such, most of what it produced had to be exported. This was particularly true of steel products, which US firms such as Bethlehem Steel successfully sought to block using non-tariff barriers. The government had not bargained on this development and had not used diplomatic channels to forestall it. Smallness also led to certain human resource limitations, such as a heavy dependence on foreign consultancy and marketing firms that were not really concerned with the interests of the state. They overestimated project prices and marketing costs and underestimated investment costs. There was also inefficiency in project implementation and management. The secrecy and stealth with which the process was attended also made it difficult for the people, or parliament on their behalf, to effect democratic control and monitoring. The "corporation sole" (the minister of finance) controlled everything. The boards reported to him and their activities were beyond the scrutiny of parliament (ibid, 40).

Taimoon Stewart was another severe critic of the development strategies Williams adopted in the 1970s. Stewart's criticism focused on choice of models, on the timing of those choices and on problems in respect of implementation. In her view, the plantation survived:

> There are several reasons why the nationalization thrust was unsustainable. Most important was the inevitability of the debt crisis, given the development path which was followed. Capital goods were acquired at inflated costs with mature technologies that

were proliferating in other semi-peripheral, especially oil exporting countries (and therefore increasing competition and saturating markets). This happened at a time of cyclical global contraction with reduced market capacity and growing protectionism, making the chances of viability very slim. Inexperience and lack of technical knowledge on our part meant that foreign contractors had to be relied on heavily to supply management and technical services at a high cost. Widespread corruption meant that the cost of projects were inflated even further to allow side-payments to those with decision-making power. In the final analysis, the cost of setting up the industries so far exceeded what it would have cost to do the same in the developed countries that unprofitability was practically ensured. (Ryan and Stewart 1995, 739)

Stewart also argued that the new development strategies adopted by Trinidad and Tobago were the same as those adopted in the Middle East and were part of a deliberate strategy metropolitan interests were pursuing to recycle oil revenues:

The logic is simple. With the rise in the price of oil, the high energy cost made these industries in the core decline further in profitability. The solution was the migration of these industries to a low-cost energy area so that production cost would be lower. Money was lent to governments to finance the projects, with the capital goods, materials and technical know-how provided by core industrialists, thus creating employment and profits in the core. Meanwhile, substitutes were developed for those products, as in the case of steel, while protection was provided for struggling home industries. The problems of risks in production and sales were left to the owner, the state, while the firms from the core still reaped more benefits through risk-proof management and services contracts. Sadly, steel, ammonia, urea, methanol were really disguised forms of "brown sugar" and kept the economy "in the shadow of the plantation". (Ibid., 759)

The new industries, Stewart claimed, were designed to take advantage of low-cost energy while still keeping production at the lower value-added level. Most of the value was added in the metropole. "There is no difference in the economic logic between the exploitative use of cheap energy as a factor of production without the benefit of value added processing, and the exploitative use of cheap labour without value added accruing to the country. . . . Once more, the metropole benefited from the development model" (ibid., 751).

Using a Wallersteinian "World Systems" model as her point of departure, Stewart claimed that no sustainable development took place under the Williams regime. What changed was the "form" of penetration. Steel replaced sugar, but the exploitation continued. "Deeper analyses reveal the continuation of the metropole/hinterland or centre-periphery international relations and the retention of the logic of the international division of labour in allocating the highest value added activities to the metropole while the hinterland produces in response to the specific demands of the brain" (ibid., 760).

In sum, notwithstanding what Williams, Julien and others sought to do, the "brain-limb", "prescription-obedience" structure of international economic relations persisted. The North continued to be the source of the high value outputs consumed by the South. The plantation survived in substance, not only in the form of shadows. The environmental costs involved were also serious. Stewart did not say, however, what options ought to have been pursued. What Stewart provided is a determinist model that suggests that countries on the periphery and in the South are caught in traps from which there is no escape.

My own evaluation of Williams's industrial policy following the PNM's loss of power in 1986 was negative, though it was not completely so. As I wrote, "the country is now paying the price for the PNM's economic adventurism. One must however bear in mind that the need on the part of Third World countries to industrialize was part of the orthodoxy of the post-independence age. For Eric Williams, industrial development, was regarded as a *sine qua non* for economic development" (Ryan and Stewart 1988, 155). Fortunately for the society, however, Williams persisted with the energy based industrialization strategy when the signals on the horizon suggested that the strategy needed to be reconsidered. Retreat was politically impossible for him, because to do so would have brought into question the integrity and the "rightness" of his leadership.

From the perspective of those who still endorsed the "small is beautiful" development paradigm and who would have preferred to have the country depend more on services than on agriculture, Williams's industrial strategy was ill conceived and costly for the society in that it led to fiscal profligacy and collapse, and forced the country to genuflect to the International Monetary Fund and the banking consortium known as the Paris Club. While much of this is true, the fact is that if one takes the long rather than the short view, one would have to concede that the industrialization strategy has paid handsome dividends, notwithstanding its negative impact on the surrounding environment. The Point Lisas estate has become one of the most successful industrial showpieces in the Caribbean, one that is now proudly shown to business and official visitors as well as tourists. It is now the country's principal revenue earner and employs directly or indirectly some 7,500 persons and requires no subsidy from the state, except perhaps in the price paid for electricity and gas. Most of the industries established by the state have since been sold to the private sector and the state has recovered its investments many times over. Indeed, the Point Lisas estate has reached its limits and new estates are being created in La Brea and Point Fortin to accommodate other gas-based industries that are due to come on stream soon. It is also worth re-emphasizing that contrary to the claim made by Farrell and Stewart, Williams did succeed in displacing oil and sugar as the country's main exports. These have been replaced by steel, plastics, methanol, liquid ammonia, urea and liquefied natural gas (LNG). Trinidad is now the largest exporter of LNG to the United States and the largest exporter of methanol in the world.

34 Williams and Laventille
The Failure of Black Entrepreneurship

Laventille was always symbolically and otherwise considered to be the political heartland of the PNM, its core "garrison" constituency. The term is also used at times to refer to the black urban underclass generally. Williams was from the beginning regarded by this underclass as their long delayed Messiah. In 1956, the Laventille branch of the party was extremely keen to have Williams represent it instead of city businessman Jang Bahadoorsingh, who was being recommended for the seat. Although Williams eventually chose to fight in Port of Spain South, he nevertheless made a point of identifying with blacks who lived in Laventille, John John and Shanty Town, areas then known as "Desperado" and "Marabunta territory", and which were characterized by a great deal of hooliganism and gang conflict, much of which was related to the steelband.

In commenting on the tendency of the black underclass towards violence, Williams noted that "black on black" violence was a tradition dating back to the period in which human life was "cheap as ticks on cattle". The time had come, however, for the victims of that world to become the authors of their own future. Said Williams, "If Shanty Towners and Laventillians wished to help themselves, they would have to use the vote responsibly." (*Trinidad Guardian*, 16 August 1956). Williams told steel-band men that they had to get involved in politics since "politics determines what you eat, when you eat, how you eat and if you eat" (Goddard 1991, 79).[1]

The people of Laventille took Williams's advice, and the PNM won the Laventille seat convincingly in 1956. It secured 72.7 per cent of the votes cast. The PNM went on to win the Laventille constituency in every succeeding election with substantial majorities. In 1961, it won with 93.4 per cent of the votes cast, the highest percentage the party ever obtained in any constituency in Trinidad and Tobago. In 1966, the PNM secured 79.6 per cent of the votes cast; in 1976 the figure was 80.5 per cent while in 1981 it was 80.1 per cent. In 1971, no elections were held in that constituency because of the "no votes" campaign.

Williams was continually accused of having done little to repay Laventille for the loyalty that it showed to him over the years. The accusation is made that Williams found the blacks in Laventille poor and largely unemployed and left them substantially so. Laventille's only "reward" was said to be the Special Works Programme in all its many incarnations and the patronage made available to community steelbands generally and to Desperadoes in particular. Williams's efforts to develop manufacturing industries through the programme of "industrialization by invitation" failed to alleviate the problem of unemployment. Although the industrialization initiative was concentrated in areas within close proximity to Laventille, it never absorbed any significant amount of labour from that area. In addition, what the economic strategy did was rekindle rural-urban migration as well as migration from other parts of the Caribbean, which served to replenish the reservoir left by those who managed to escape from the culture of poverty that kept many tethered in Laventille.

The 1960s not only witnessed an escalation in the levels of unemployment, but witnessed an increase in industrial, social and political protest, and levels of crime. Within this context the unemployment relief programme, which was introduced in the late 1950s by the PNM as a way of pacifying and rehabilitating the riotous elements in Laventille where gang warfare was endemic, was expanded to include more urban areas, and its budgetary allocation significantly increased.

Expenditure on the programme moved from TT$1.8 million in 1968 to TT$7.6 million in 1970. The county of St George, in which Laventille is situated and which was associated with some of the leading elements in the 1970s protest movement, accounted for more than 80 per cent of the expenditure and between 36 and 47 per cent of the employment that the programme generated.

It is widely believed that the Special Works Programme, which was originally conceived as a way of defanging the riotous urban underclass population, was responsible for destroying the work ethic in Laventille and in the country generally. The "crash programme" or the "depressed areas programme", as the projects were originally termed, were, however, intended to provide skills training for black urban youths in general and persons referred from the prisons and orphanages. These youngsters, it was assumed, would use those skills to become regular members of the workforce or small-scale entrepreneurs. The programmes were also designed to improve the quality of life in depressed rural and urban areas, particularly those areas that were not adequately served by other government agencies. They were geared to provide employment on a labour-intensive basis as well as to develop small contractors.

Publicly at least, Williams was opposed to the policy of requiring individuals to join the PNM to obtain project work. As he told a party convention in 1971, "We have only ourselves to blame for the mess – specifically our morbid obsession with what we sneered at as standpipe politics in 1956. The efforts to rationalize recruitment failed. Everyone jumped in to try and get jobs for the boys and save his own seat." He consoled himself, however, "that all was not lost in the state of special works", and that the laudable and politically necessary aim of providing jobs and improving amenities need not degenerate into a mad scramble.

Over the years, though, project work, by whatever name or acronym it became known – Special Works Programme, Better Village Programme, Development and Environmental Works Division (DEWD), Labour Intensive Development Programme, Unemployment Relief Programme – became integrally linked with PNM party politics. "Work" was given in exchange for votes. Such work was not expected to last for a full day. One signed up for "work", spent an hour or two on the job site, and then retired for the day in some cases to do another job if that option was possible. In many cases, employees either did not show up at all or did not exist. Project supervisors or foremen placed ghost workers on their lists or used the list as a mechanism for extorting a share of the income or sexual favours. Report after report told the same story of abuse and waste of human and material resources. Both the ruling party and the project workers became addicted to the system. Neither liked it, but neither was able to do much to change it.

Several attempts were made over the years to restructure the programme to make it more economically productive and development-oriented, more community based, or to emphasize skills training and entrepreneurship rather than "make work". Failure to achieve success in any of these attempts at reform was ascribed, among other things, to the indiscipline and low productivity of workers who, being temporary, had no incentive to be either disciplined or productive; the use of badjohns and ex-prisoners as supervisors and foremen who intimidated would-be reformers; the inability of project managers to ensure that transport and supplies of material and tools were available on site when workers were recruited; the high proportion of fixed project costs that were due to office supplies, wages and leave benefits – 88 per cent in 1985; lack of coordination among the agencies responsible for planning, financing, auditing and technical execution, as well as politically motivated recruitment, made restructuring difficult.

According to the Errol Mahabir report (1979, 8), "The final selection for the 10 day work period was done usually under intimidating conditions, and in such an *ad hoc*, casual manner that preference and regularity of employment are given to the individual or members on the Master List who can exert the most pressure, or whose representatives have the most influence." Workers with special contacts were able to secure employment for periods that were so frequent as to constitute near "permanent" employment. These were "privileged" casual workers. According to another report, "The DEWD programme, apart from not yielding adequate return for the level of expenditure involved, had also provided a breeding ground for improper and perhaps illegal activities" (Bishop 1985, 12).

Project work thus became associated in the public mind with poor work ethic, idleness and low productivity, and any idle worker was automatically assumed to be a project worker and stigmatized as such. By the end of the 1970s, the "DEWD mentality" had contaminated and corrupted the work ethic in the larger society, to say nothing about the national wage structure. No one would accept jobs with wages lower than that obtained by project workers. Given that a great many of these projects were located in Laventille, that community also became associated with the "DEWD mentality".

Williams sought to exonerate himself from blame for the fact that "special work" had become a feeding trough and a "fake work" mechanism for the party faithful. As he moaned at the 1973 convention, "I have noticed a growing polarization in the country in respect of the scramble for jobs or promotion and the determination of these on racial grounds. . . . I just don't have it in me to associate with practices of that sort." He was also critical of members of parliament and local government representatives who manipulated special works projects to allocate jobs on the basis of patronage, and who used "badjohns" to do dirty political work for the party in its effort to maintain "turf". Williams was seeking to disassociate himself from practices that he had long condoned and even encouraged. He was now finding that it was not easy to reverse a practice that had a momentum of its own. "Special works" had come to define politics at the grassroots level. It was also a policy that disempowered "Laventille", which I use hereafter as a metaphor for the black urban underclass.

Williams paid some attention to the black peasantry, some of whom he sought to settle on lands previously occupied by the Americans at the bases in Wallerfield and Cumuto. The aim was to address the twin issues of increased food production and black alienation from the land. The project failed disastrously. Most of the settlers abandoned the land, which eventually passed to Indian farmers and entrepreneurs (Ryan 1972a, 401–2). In the wake of the 1970 crisis, many voices were heard demanding that blacks must be given a larger piece of the action and that "black power" must involve ownership. The shift of focus from salaried state or private sector employment to ownership of business was encouraged by Williams, who declared himself ready to support a people's sector. He was persuaded that blacks needed a handicap to enable them to catch up with other groups. The people's sector was thus the PNM's "revolutionary" answer to the demand of black radicals that the dispossessed sons of African slaves and Indian bonded-servants should be encouraged and helped to own a piece of their patrimony.

While the concept of the people's sector was not defined in ethnically specific terms, there was an informal understanding that the state, controlled as it was by a party with an Afro-Trinidadian political base, would give special attention to blacks who wished to get involved in business. It was also assumed that the two new national commercial banks that had been established by the state and other local investors in the wake of the 1970 crisis – the Worker's Bank and the National Commercial Bank – would help to provide venture capital to this burgeoning black business elite. Likewise, it was assumed that existing agencies such as the Industrial Development Corporation, the Development Finance Corporation, the Management Development Centre and the Agricultural Development Bank would help by providing financial managerial and other services that would compensate to some extent for the lack of inherited capital, knowledge of the market and business know-how that characterized the black community.

To concretize this commitment to the small man, 1970 was declared "Small Business Year". A Small Business Unit was established in May 1970 as a department of the Industrial Development Corporation in accordance with a cabinet directive and given TT$2.5 million as seed money. Its main goal and function was to promote growth among the nation's small business enterprises. With the formation of the Small Business Unit came a formal definition of a small business, that is, a unit whose capital investment was TT$50,000 and under, represented by land, building, leasehold property, machinery, plant and equipment, stock-in-trade, work in progress, and furniture (in special cases). Enterprises with current investment of over TT$50,000 up to TT$100,000 were also to be included.

Some positive results came of this effort on the part of blacks to break into the business sector. The evidence indicates that quite a few blacks rode the petro-dollar boom and achieved a measure of success in the 1970s. Significant breakthroughs were recorded in the construction industry, in the merchandise retail sector (appliances and other household furnishings, clothing, and so on), in the service sector (taxis, car rentals, bars, clubs, restaurants), in the professions (law, architecture, insurance and accounting firms), janitorial services, valuation, and small supermarkets, to name a few of the niches in which they were to be found. Black businessmen were even able to open stores on Frederick Street, the main commercial street in Port of Spain, and on Henry Street, an equally important business street. The Workers' Bank and the National Commercial Bank also enabled many to secure mortgages to build or buy their own homes. Policies requiring foreign-owned banks and insurance companies to go local also allowed many to acquire shares and jobs in these institutions (Ryan and Stewart, 1995).

Many blacks also achieved success in the construction industry and "suitcase trade".[2] They flew to Panama, Curaçao, Miami and New York and returned with suitcases full of merchandise, which they sold in boutiques, in the "People's Mall" on Queen Street, Port of Spain, or on sidewalks in commercial centres in competition with merchants belonging to other ethnic minority groups, the Syrian–Lebanese in particular, who complained of unfair competition. Many blacks complained that the Syrians, who had themselves started as suitcase traders, were now seeking to deny them use of the route that they had taken to become established. Vendors in the "People's Mall" in midtown Port of Spain claim that the police often raided the mall looking for drugs. The real agenda, in their view, was the ongoing economic war between Syrians and black entrepreneurs.

Some Syrian businessmen chose to cooperate with the new black entrepreneurs rather than seek to destroy them. They either bought goods imported by the suitcase traders or hired blacks as sales agents to whom they provided goods on consignment as their own patrons had done in the past. In some cases, Syrians and blacks worked together as partners. The one had the cash while the other had the licences needed to import the goods. Some blacks simply sold the licences, which they were able to obtain through political connections.

Many blacks also imported food, furniture and other high-demand items during the petroleum-driven boom years of the mid-1970s and early 1980s. Few significant successes were achieved in manufacturing or in the food production sector, despite the state's efforts to promote this type of activity. The manufacturing sector was considered too "volatile", involving too much risk, and too much capital. The time span for earning returns was also deemed to be too long.

In the area of agricultural food production, many blacks who had been allocated lands under the Crown Lands Development Programme during the mid-1960s, the ostensible aim of which was to reduce the country's dependence on imported food and slow down migration to the urban centres that were becoming crowded with job seekers, chose to move into other areas of activity such as driving taxis or working for wages on public or private sector projects. Some also sold the properties that they had obtained cheaply from the state to Indian entrepreneurs who were looking for land on which to grow food or rear livestock. Many of the farms also failed because they could not get credit, technical help, supervision, marketing advice or facilities to store their products. The farmers were also unable to compete with imported food products, all because processors and middlemen, most of whom were Indians, sought to squeeze them out of the market.

Only a few of the companies belonging to the new black entrepreneurial group survived the drastic downturn in economic activity that characterized the 1980s, a downturn triggered by the 1986 drop in production levels and the price of crude petroleum from US$26 to US$9. Most of those who survived were a shadow of their former selves. Many either went into receivership or disappeared completely. Only 119 of the 335 cooperatives that existed in 1984 remained active. The "Drag Brothers", a group of young blacks who went into leather-craft activity, still operated, but few grew beyond mere survival. The creation of this facility on Independence Square was a reaction to the demand of young blacks for space in the centre of town to produce and market their craft. It quickly became a haven for crime, drugs and other forms of dysfunctional activity, and served to disfigure downtown Port of Spain. Williams must certainly have regretted the initiative, which was demolished by a successor PNM administration in the early 1990s.

Parts of Laventille continue to look very much as they did in 1956 when Williams first came to power. On closer examination, however, much has changed. Thanks to the petro-dollar boom, the housing stock has improved considerably. So too have infrastructural services. The offspring of many historically disadvantaged residents also succeeded in getting a secondary education of sorts, and some have done extremely well, thanks to the efforts made by Williams to open up access routes to those who were able to make use of the opportunities provided. Many successful Laventilleans have migrated to other parts of Trinidad and not a few have gone to the United States and Canada. They have been replaced by younger cohorts from the Eastern Caribbean. If parts of Laventille continue to look as dilapidated as they did in the 1950s, and if they remain as crime- and gang-ridden as they did in the days of the Marabuntas, one needs to bear in mind that many of those who occupy the old spaces are new arrivals, and that the drug trade has generated new problems that did not exist in Williams's time.

35   **Williams and His Mandarins**

When I say come, you cometh! When I speak, no dog barks.

When the caravans go through, the dogs bark.
– Eric Williams

The relationship between Williams, his ministers and public servants in Trinidad and Tobago was stormy for a variety of reasons, and almost every senior public servant and minister ended up being a casualty.[1] Between 1956 and 1960, a hybrid constitutional system existed in that there was both a governor and a premier to whom accountability was due. Thus conflict developed between the new political elite, and the old, largely untrained but experienced bureaucratic ruling elite that was mainly "white or near white" ("French creoles"), each wanting to show the other who was boss, both in terms of policy and administrative matters. The old bureaucratic elite was often accused of sabotaging the inexperienced new government and of trying to lobby the governor, who was chairman of the executive council. Conflicts also grew between some of the new ministers and the new technocracy that Williams recruited, many of whom were intellectually superior and better trained than the ministers.

Given the charged political atmosphere that obtained in the decade after independence, both ministers and public servants operated in an environment of uncertainty as to what they should do or not do, and when. Lines of communication were jumbled and many officers were deliberately bypassed, ignored or put on ice. Standing with the prime minister determined whether one was in the loop or not. Many public servants chose to keep a low profile out of fear of rebuke or of being quarantined. As the 1964 *Working Party Report on the Civil Service in the Age of Independence* observed,

> Many civil servants saw their role as skilled assemblers of information to be passed to the top in duly labelled files. The process of decision-making had not become fully geared to cope with either the magnitude or the urgency of the problems which confronted the new nation. Examples were brought to our notice of the difficulty fre-

quently experienced in securing prompt and clear-cut decisions. In many cases, it had not been possible to obtain even an acknowledgement, either in the original communication, or of the several subsequent requests for an early reply. (Lewis 1964, 4)

Williams himself complained of the bureaucratic octopus that was strangling the nation: "In a new country like ours, you'll find that the top men are generally excellent, but the middle level, the junior officers, are frankly inadequate. It's not just a lack of ability. It's also often a lack of sympathy – a kind of indifference bred by the colonial system."

Heated controversies occurred between permanent secretaries and chief technical officers over who had precedence in terms of policy making and access to the minister, and as to whose views should prevail in the preparation of cabinet notes. Allegations were frequent that information was either being spitefully withheld or not made known to the minister by aggrieved officials. There were even serious controversies as to the whether permanent secretaries or chief technical officers who disagreed with their ministers should be permitted to indicate to cabinet that cabinet notes concealed information which if known, might lead to other decisions being taken. Williams dismissed the suggestion that they should be allowed to do so as a "supreme absurdity".

At certain periods, the system was characterized by either excessive centralization, paralysis, or both. As the Working Party report observed, in a veiled criticism of Williams's management style and that of his close advisers, "Practically every decision, no matter how simple, now seems to involve the personal approval of the highest level of officers, and not infrequently of the highest authority itself (i.e. the Prime Minister)." Williams felt that the authors of the report had "exaggerated that aspect of the matter". The result was that most decisions were made by a few key people who worked virtually as personal "slaves" and messengers to the prime minister. Technocrats such as Dodderidge Alleyne, O'Neil Lewis, Eugenio Moore and Frank Rampersad were far more powerful than ministers, who often did not know what was being done in respect of their own ministries.[2]

The personalized relationship between Williams and the group of technocrats whom he had recruited in the years immediately after independence broke down completely in the latter part of 1975. To the surprise and puzzlement of many, Williams chose to make the break with his mandarins a matter of public controversy. In a celebrated television address on 19 September 1975, Williams complained bitterly that he was a victim of inactivity on the part of public servants. He accused public servants of frustrating or slowing down the government's development programme by failing to implement policies agreed to by cabinet, or to release funds that had been approved by that body.

The statements about the public service and the subsequent cabinet reshuffle came amid mounting public disquiet about the chaotic situation in the fields of agriculture, secondary school education and road transportation, as well as uncertainty about the future of the dollar, delays in paying pensions and gratuities, delays in the allocation of houses built with public funds, wastage of public funds on special works projects, and irregularities, losses and possible corruption as revealed in auditor general's reports. The public utilities and the country's infrastructure generally were also in a state of near collapse.

On 3 October 1975, Williams went further and alleged to an astonished seventeenth annual convention of the PNM that a "small and ambitious group of technocrats, one of whom is present with us today, is conspiring to take over responsibility for governing the country from its elected representatives". Williams proceeded to itemize some of the transgressions of his erstwhile blue-eyed mandarins. He complained that agreements had been entered into involving foreign governments or corporations without the knowledge of cabinet or the attorney general involving substantial sums of money. As Williams told the party,

> Under this agreement substantial sums [TT$1,840,000] were paid by Trinidad and Tobago to a French firm [*Enterprise de Researches et D'Activities Petroliers* (Elf/ERAP)] for the construction of a pipeline. The agreement did not have the approval of Cabinet; it was not vetted (as all such agreements are) by the Attorney General; there was no knowledge of it in the Ministry directly concerned; there was no Cabinet approval of the sums paid out. The agreement was signed in a foreign country by a senior civil servant of Trinidad and Tobago. When knowledge of agreement came to cabinet's attention some months later, it was terminated by the Minister concerned and the Prime Minister subsequently reported the matter to the Auditor General and later to the Public Service Commission. (Sutton 1981, 185–86)

Williams went on to quote from letters that he said "underlined the wide gulf separating ministers and civil servants". Some of the other irregular actions included the issuance of invitations for international tenders that completely bypassed the central tenders board as well as violations of financial regulations that he had reported to the auditor general and the Public Service Commission. Williams likewise told the party that he had received a communication from a senior officer that referred to a proposal, made by a consortium in an Arab country, which had the blessings of the country in question in respect of a project that they wished to undertake in Trinidad and Tobago's petroleum industry. Williams said he was urged by the technocrats to "personally examine all the implications of this [proposal] against the background of all our discussions on the EEC, petroleum, natural gas, and future investments". Williams was being encouraged, he said, to accept the proposal. His response was vitriolic. As he told the party, "What was being proposed to the prime minister was a total discarding of all established and prescribed tender procedures, and above all, cabinet's decision on competitive international bidding."

Williams also complained to the party that a senior civil servant brought heavy pressure to bear on him to accept another proposal from an Arab country, which had not yet been considered or approved by the cabinet, because failure to do so might "hamper cooperation and credibility in Arab and Third World Circles", and jeopardize "implementation of plans for [the] economic development of Trinidad and Tobago" (Sutton 1981, 186). Williams complained that "this small group of advisers had formed their own opinions about what should be done with Trinidad's national stake in the oil industry and the National Petroleum Company which they wished to promote". Their advice was that "Trinidad and Tobago should opt for complete national ownership of all oil resources beginning with majority holding and moving rapidly within a period from five to ten years to complete national ownership, with the chosen instrument for the exercise of ownership being the National Petroleum Company" (ibid.). The advisers recommended that the state's interests in Trinidad Tesoro, Shell, Texaco and Amoco (when these were realized) should be vested in the National Petroleum Company, which should also be allocated two or more of the best blocs on the east coast for marine exploitation. They also advised that the National Petroleum Company, which did not then have the in-house capacity or resources to develop these blocs, should initially outsource their exploitation, but should develop a capability within five years that would enable the company to do so themselves.

Williams told the assembly that cabinet rejected the advice given, and chose instead a system of competitive bidding. This was preferred to an arrangement that "suggested that some one company might already have been selected to be NPC's temporary partner. Cabinet preferred a regime of production sharing at no cost to the country to achieve for Trinidad and Tobago our share of the crude oil produced" (Sutton 1981, 188). Another complaint Willliams levelled against the "ambitious technocracy" concerned the advice that they gave about how he should manage the petroleum sector. Williams was told that a new "triple headed animal of oil, politics and foreign policy" had emerged, which required the creation of new structures outside the established public service bureaucracy. Williams, quoting the technocrats, said,

> There is an urgent need to assign active development and management to an agency outside the bureaucracy of the general Civil Service. . . . The Civil Service is simply not geared to swift decision making of the kind required for these very high cost projects and with the political and market situations changing so rapidly. What we will need indeed is a series of multi-disciplinary operating groups embracing the technical, financial, economic and legal angles for each project, all subject to the control of a Cabinet Committee chaired by yourself. These teams, in our view, should be employed by an Energy Authority or Agency working within its own legislative provision, with its own funds and its own procurement system. . . . (Ibid.)

Williams was urged to give personal direction to the petroleum industry. The advice was rejected, as was the recommendation that he should break diplomatic relations with Israel. Williams also disbanded the energy secretariat, which had been formed earlier, and told the party why he chose to do so:

> The setting up of an Energy Secretariat turned out to be a selection by a few persons not authorized to do this, of partisan individuals, transferred from substantive positions in various ministries without the knowledge of the Ministers concerned and without reference to or approval from the Public Service Commission. Cabinet was forced to disband this unconstitutional body and substitute, through the regular constitutional procedures, another Energy Secretariat which was placed within the Ministry of Petroleum and Mines. (Sutton 1981, 188)

Williams was scornful of the suggestion that public servants were too constricted by the existing civil service regulations and bureaucratic procedures that obtained in respect of the Public Service Commission and that they should be allowed to exercise more initiative. Doing that was to invite improprieties of various kinds. As he asked with characteristic acerbity,

> And this initiative of public officers. What of it? Initiative to do what? To violate the financial procedures of which the Auditor general is the Nation's watchdog? To make appointments and transfers within the Civil Service without the approval of the Public Service Commission? To clamour for the Prime Minister arrogating to himself a position in respect of the petroleum industry not consistent with our constitutional procedures? To alter on their own the foreign policy of the country? Must the Prime Minister permit an initiative to subvert the Constitution which he is pledged to uphold? (Ibid., 190)

Williams completed his critique of the "ambitious technocracy" by telling the party faithful that the country had come close to being a victim of a bureaucratic coup d'etat, and that he had heroically rescued the country in the nick of time:

> I wonder how many of you here understand how close we stood in Trinidad and Tobago, thanking the Lord that we are not among those states with their military coups and usurpations, to take over by a technocracy, only wanting someone to convey an aura of respectability by chairing its committee! And I am to be crucified for denying initiative to senior officers! My dear friends, let us call a spade a spade. On the basis of my initiatives over 20 years, the electorate has responded to the PNM. All sorts of people have been brought in or pushed up hanging on to my shirt-tails. My shirt-tails are no longer available to all and sundry, and I am not taking licks any more for anybody. Everyone can talk. As for me, I have only now begun. (Ibid., 191)

Williams returned to the issue on 5 March 1976 in a statement he made to parliament in the middle of discussions relating to the cabinet's draft recommendations on the Report of the Joint Select Committee on the Republican Constitution (1976). (See chapter 29.) He told parliament that he had written to the auditor general on 14 January 1975 advising him of a disturbing number of deviations from authorized financial procedures, including tenders, that had come to his notice. They included, among others, tenders for construction of a gas pipeline, a convention centre at Chaguaramas, pavilion facilities at King George V Park, and dormitory facilities for the coast guard at Teteron Bay. Williams told the auditor general that he was concerned about "these disturbing departures from financial rectitude", and requested that the latter submit any proposals that he might consider appropriate in respect of constitution reform designed to eliminate or control the violations that had been reported to him. (See *Hansard*, 13 June 1975, for a fuller discussion of this issue.)

The prime minister told parliament that the infractions had been brought to his attention almost a year earlier – on 31 January 1974 – but that the document had "disappeared mysteriously".[3] The document brought to his attention that a tender call for the construction of a natural gas pipeline had been issued by the Office of the Prime Minister over the signature of Harold Fraser, commissioner of inland revenue. The call was for a project costing some TT$120 million, which he observed was "possibly the largest single project ever envisaged for Trinidad and Tobago". The tenders board was not involved in the exercise, and the process gave the impression that "the Prime Minister and his Office were above the law".

Williams further advised parliament that a team of international experts assembled by the United Nations had recommended against any of the two bids that were forthcoming in response to the selective tenders call. One of these bids had come from an American group, and the other from a French group. For a variety of reasons that had to do with the prime minister's concern that the amount of available gas might not have been sufficient to supply both the Trinidad and Tobago Electricity Commission and the plants due to come on stream, cabinet abandoned the marine-based pipeline project completely and requested Amoco to design a land-based alternative.

According to Williams, the energy secretariat was unhappy with these developments, and lobbied hard for continued French involvement in the pipeline project. The secretariat believed that the decision to exclude French consultants and contractors conflicted with Trinidad's declared "intention to foster closer relationships with France and the European Economic Community, and that the choice of international organizations based in the United States and dominated by that country seems to conflict with our attempts as an independent nation to control and guide our own destiny". Williams was likewise told that it was "precisely because the French Government was willing to develop relationships with Trinidad and Tobago that we have received a bid from the French firm *Entrepose*. France was sending a message that it was making a political investment in the project, and that there were several other areas which could be affected if this particular project fell through."

Williams had bristled at the implied threat. It was "the first time he had received such a letter from such a source, with such a threat". As he continued, "If we are going to have to deal with tenders on the basis of representations and lobbying of Ministers of Government, life is going to become extremely difficult. . . . Here is a total failure to recognize the fundamental realities of tender procedures in Trinidad and Tobago." Williams was sarcastic as he advised parliament as to what all of this implied: "It is almost as if one was dealing with another government within a government. You make a decision and take some steps, and then they come to tell you, No, we have some advisers of our own; and you go to the UN and then they say, No, No, that interferes with our position as an independent nation" (*Hansard*, 13 June 1975).

Williams was riled by the pressure that the French were bringing to bear on him and on other ministers, and on the technocrats involved who clearly favoured the French company for whatever reason. The French had in fact dangled a number of other projects – aluminium, fertilizer, petrochemical – which they were willing to undertake in Trinidad and Tobago, as well as a sweetener involving the designing, financing and constructing of the pipeline. Williams advised parliament that in the light of all that had happened, cabinet had decided to disband the energy secretariat altogether, and to leave the handling of the matters to the recognized staff of the Ministry of Petroleum and Mines. An angry Williams also decided to break his relationship with the head of the energy secretariat, Dodderidge Alleyne. The break was as violent as it was controversial. Williams brought the alleged infractions of civil service rules to the attention of the Public Service Commission, the body responsible, among other things, for disciplining public servants. Alleyne, who was his permanent secretary and also head of the public service, was interdicted by the Public Service Commission and put on three-quarters salary pending resolution of the matter by a tribunal, under civil servant regulations.

The auditor general's special report dated 6 June 1975 revealed that neither cabinet nor parliament had given approval for the rehabilitation of the Chaguaramas convention centre project, on which a total of TT$6,950,546 had been expended over the period 1969 to 1974, with outstanding commitments amounting to TT$304,982.64. The same held for a pavilion at King George V Park, a dormitory for the coast guard, and several other projects. The officer who was said to be responsible for these infractions was Eugenio Moore, permanent secretary in the Ministry of Planning and a trusted aide to Williams. Moore seemed to have been the sacrificial goat that Williams used to appease the middle-class elements who were protesting the use of King George V Park as a major facility for sporting events.

After regaling parliament with other details of what some of his mandarins had done, Williams surprisingly declared that he was "completely mystified" when he received a letter from the director of personnel administration on 4 March 1976, in which the latter stated that he was forwarding, as requested, copies of Alleyne's replies to the charges proffered against him by the Public Service Commission as well as a copy of the auditor general's reply to one of those replies. Williams indicated to the chairman of the commission, Earl Jones, that he was seeing the charges for the first time, and that he had not laid any charge: "I did not lay any charge; I am not laying any today, and I do not want any laid. It is not my business. . . . I could not believe it."

Williams's letter to Jones continued as follows: "The gravamen of the first charge was the entering into a consultancy agreement with a French company without reference to the Tenders Board. Such charge is fundamentally misconceived as it has not been the practice to refer such agreements to the Tenders Board. . . . The charge is certainly not founded on the question of deviation from financial procedures which I referred to the Auditor General specifying the gas pipeline." Williams went on to make some cryptic remarks suggesting that the core issue was integrity and his loss of confidence in those who once had it. As he declared, "If the Prime Minister does not have confidence in somebody, that's that. That's that."

Williams affected to being annoyed by all that had happened: "The Prime Minister feels very strongly about it because an attempt has been made to associate his office with those violations. I stand for the control of violations, not for the perpetuation of violations. I stand for the objective realization of the fundamentals of public accountability without any dealings with personalities involved, here today, gone tomorrow" (*Hansard*, 12 March 1976).

Williams was clearly inviting the Public Service Commission to drop the matter. As he told the chairman of the commission, "I leave it to you to decide what steps you think it appropriate to take in view of the foregoing." When the chairman of the commission wrote him on 12 March indicating that the matter was being discontinued, Williams claims that he took it as a "mere matter of courtesy and not a matter calling for any intervention by the prime minister except insofar as it might be a reference to improve procedures for control by the Auditor General to stop some of these aberrations and malpractices violating the laws of the country" (ibid., 729).

The Mandarins Strike Back

Williams's version of these events and the developments that followed were challenged by the Public Service Association and the civil servants in question, as well as by others. In his reply to the auditor general, Alleyne claimed that he had signed the agreement with the French consulting agency to which Williams had referred "with the full knowledge of the Prime Minister and in execution of clearly enunciated government policy" (*Trinidad Express,* 18 January 1976). Alleyne produced letters to and from the prime minister to the French president, Georges Pompidou, and to him, which indicated that the prime minister knew of and approved all the arrangements involved in the transaction.[4] According to Alleyne, "The agreement was in fact executed by the Permanent Secretary to the Prime Minister on behalf of the Government with the full knowledge, participation, and approval of the Prime Minister, the Attorney General, the Ministry of Finance and the Finance and Economics Committee of the Cabinet." A representative of the attorney general had signed the documents as witness (ibid.).

Alleyne admitted that the government had initially bypassed the central tenders board when tenders for the pipeline project were called for, but indicated that the secretariat had done this while he was out of the country on government business. The accelerated procedure had been used because of eagerness and an excess of zeal to get the pipeline project completed by November–December 1975 in order to supply energy to the Trinidad and Tobago Electricity Commission. Alleyne later regularized the tendering procedures on his own initiative with the full agreement of the Ministry of Finance and the chairman of the central tenders board.

Alleyne further observed that the gas pipeline was not a project in its own right but part of a larger LNG (liquefied natural gas) project that had been formally approved in April 1972: "Without the pipeline, no other aspect of the plan for the utilization of the gas resources of the East Coast could become a reality." Williams had himself spoken (cf. 1975a) of the need to "accelerate the industrial diversification of Trinidad and Tobago". Ensuring this acceleration required that the pipeline be constructed as speedily as possibly. Alleyne also noted that the government had previously invited Elf–ERAP to be an equity partner in the LNG project and to provide consultancy services in respect of the said plant and other energy based industries. The latter had agreed to provide such services, though not to participate on an equity basis. In Alleyne's view, "There was no need for a separate and new basic agreement to cover their consultancy services in relation to the development of the pipeline."

Alleyne likewise challenged Williams's statements about the energy secretariat, which he noted had been institutionalized by a cabinet directive long before it was formally instituted in February 1974. The secretariat was not an "informal unconstitutional group", as Williams alleged. It had done a great deal of work "negotiating for more tax revenues for Trinidad and Tobago and generally advising Cabinet through the Prime Minister on a host of matters relating to petroleum".

Williams's denial that he ever wanted to have any charge laid by the Public Service Commission (the body responsible for appointing, transferring and dismissing public officers) was also contradicted by the then director of public administration, Wilfred McKell, who confirmed that the attorney general's office had asked him to make available a copy of Alleyne's replies to the charges against him. The call came from the prime minister's office and the Public Service Commission sent the reply. On seeing it, Williams gave instructions that the charges should be withdrawn, claiming that he had come to accept the argument that the conventional practice in awarding consultancies did not require approval of the central tenders board because one was merely seeking to obtain information prior to the possible award of a contract.

A further version of what happened was given by Alleyne at the symposium "Eric Williams in Retrospect", held at the University of the West Indies in 1991. Alleyne indicated then that he still did not know why the prime minister did what he did. We quote his statement at some length:

> I am not sure why he did what he did, and I am not going to try to identify any cause and effect relationship between things and things. Of course a statement was made, and I received some thing from the Auditor General which in other circumstances one would have regarded as the normal kind of letter from the Auditor General asking a head of a Ministry or Department to explain; and in fact I treated it as that. But underlying these questions and the requests for explanations, there was a dagger – in fact there was vitriol. And I showed it to a friend of mine who said, "somebody hates you very much." Why? Have you taken away his girl friend? I said, please, I like Chinese generally, but – [laughter]. I sat down over a relatively long period and researched each question separately; and I responded in the third person, because I was treating it not as something to Dodd Alleyne, but something to the Permanent Secretary to the Prime Minister.
>
> But before I had finished, when I really saw what the thing was coming to, I went to the Ministry of Petroleum and Mines. Boysie Prevatt was then Minister, and I showed him the Auditor General's thing, and when he read it, he said: "Oh, my God, you mean this blasted man is going ahead with this stupidness? I tell him to stop this nonsense." After he had finished, I said to him, "Boysie, I want you to carry this message to Dr. Williams. I have worked very closely with him. I have worked very hard for him. I have achieved a lot under him. If what he is doing is making politics, I will not answer. If however, he is trying to deprive me of my job and my family, I will fight him to the end", and I left.
>
> I submitted my response to the Auditor General and said to him what do you think of it? He said to me – "Dodd, this has answered all possible questions on these matters." I said – thank you very much, and I left the matter there.
>
> This may have been in September; and on December 12th or 15th, someone called and said they had a letter for me from the Public Service Commission. I got a letter saying that I am interdicted. I said, for what? He said, well, you know the Public Service Commission. So I asked the DPA who came across to talk to me. I said – "what is this

all about?" He said, "Dodd, nothing nah man; even if it goes against you, you would-n't lose your pension; we will just give you retirement in the public interest." I said, "but what have I done? What has happened to my response to the Auditor General?" And he said to me: "well I showed it to the Chairman of the Public Service Commission, but told him that it would be better not to show it to the other members of the Public Service Commission because it might prejudice your case in the matter." Now, I know that he wanted the position of Head of the Civil Service. But if he had asked, we could have arranged something; I would just have moved.

In my note to the Auditor General, I did not include certain information. I thought I had put enough, and he [agreed] that I had put enough to answer the questions. But there was one particular matter which I didn't think that as a senior Public Servant, I should make public. I had gone back to Oxford for a year. Dr. Williams had come up; he was going to Italy, Switzerland, France, Germany whatever, and he got one of his sec-retaries to call to find out whether I would accompany him. I said to him that the whole family had been down with the flu, and were now trying to get over it. We had all lost our voices and could he excuse me. The message came back. Dr. Williams says, "Rome is warmer than Oxford, so it is better for you to come with him to recuperate on the trip." I said, okay. I would discuss with my wife. And she said go. I said, all right, I will come to Rome. The next day the message came back – well if you are going to come to Rome, you might as well come with me to Gibraltar. . . .

But one of the important things which is tied in with this whole question of whether or not I had acted improperly concerned a meeting he had had with Pompidou in my presence, where certain things were decided. I didn't think I should tell the Auditor General that. So I did not put it in. But a member of the Public Service Commission had said to a friend of mine that I didn't reply to the Auditor General. I say what you mean? And it was in that context that I found out that the rest of the Public Service Commission thought that I had not responded. . . .

We appeared in the Judges Chambers, the first time in my life, and I am really weary and worried, and angry. And I could tell you in private what I had in mind; but it is a good thing I am a Christian boy. And as we sat there, and I am getting ready to stand up and say something, somebody came in from the Public Service Commission and handed a letter to the Chairman of the panel, who then asked somebody to read it out; and they said, "we have withdrawn all charges." And it was such a tremendous anti-climax. It was decided there and then that they had to give me a letter straight away say-ing that I am re-instated. And I went into office that same afternoon, and I wrote a letter to the Prime Minister:

> Mr. Prime Minister, the Public Service Commission has exonerated . . . me and I am back. There is a meeting of the Central Bank Board. I was going to ask you, but since you are not here, and since I am a member, I propose to attend."

Since that day, he never spoke to me once. He came in, and whenever he passed, if we met, I would say good morning or good afternoon Mr. Prime Minister. If something came to my desk, I wrote whatever I had to, and he would scratch off my name, but would proceed to take the action I recommended but via somebody else. And this went on; and somebody said to me – why don't you stop . . . and I said, I am a slow bowler, I can pitch the ball at the same spot for the rest of the year.

There was considerable curiosity as to why Williams threw in the sponge in the Alleyne affair. The fact that he was going to be called to testify before the tribunal clearly had a great deal to do with his change of mind. Williams wanted to avoid the embarrassment involved in having to give sworn testimony in public that would have forced him to disavow what was claimed in Alleyne's defence statement.

The sequel to the Williams–Alleyne episode was related by Alleyne to the 1991 symposium. According to Alleyne, he received a call from the United Nations in New York asking him to serve as a UN adviser to the Government of Kenya. He was at the time in the "wilderness", but felt that since he was a public servant, the prime minister had to be consulted and his consent given. The prime minister detailed Minister Mervyn de Souza to discuss the matter, because Williams was not speaking directly to Alleyne. Williams supported the request, and indicated that he also wanted Alleyne to go to the International Development Bank to represent Trinidad and Tobago. Alleyne had been "dequarantined".

While in Geneva attending a meeting in March 1981, Alleyne told his wife that he had a strange experience the night before: "It just came in my mind to say – 'Lord, I forgive Eric Williams for everything that he has ever done me.' So she said, 'Did you say it?' I said, 'Yes.' 'Did you mean it?' I said, 'Yes.' She said, 'Good'! Sometime after, at the time I did not know how long, in the middle of the night, Lingston Cumberbatch [Trinidad's ambassador to Geneva] knocked on the door and said to me, 'Dodd, sorry to wake you, but I have had bad news.' I said, 'What happened?' He said, 'We have lost our Prime Minister. . . . They say it is a heart attack.'" Alleyne said he and his wife were relieved that forgiveness had come before Williams's death.

The Moore case took longer to be resolved. Moore, who was also interdicted on three-quarters pay, denied all sixteen charges. In his defence, he told the Public Service Commission that in May 1969, cabinet had decided that the Chaguaramas Development and Implementing Organisation should prepare proposals to develop convention facilities at Chaguaramas and that they should expedite plans so that the said facilities could be used for a meeting of the Commonwealth Parliamentary Association to be held in Trinidad and Tobago in August or September of that year. As chairman of the organization, Moore sought Williams's permission to proceed with the work on a cost-plus basis, because they could not meet the deadline if they followed normal tendering procedures.

Moore claimed that given the time constraint, he suggested that the Hilton be considered as an alternative, but this was not accepted and he was directed to expedite the rehabilitation of the former barracks and subsistence building at Chaguaramas. Williams's insistence on Chaguaramas was linked to his plans to make greater national use of the facilities that included Macqueripe Beach and the golf course, which had been recovered from the Americans in 1967. Politics thus drove the decision. The same obtained in respect of King George V Park. The prime minister wanted the park developed and expanded as a venue for sporting facilities for youth. He saw the project as part of a political strategy designed to re-attract black youth to the PNM following the Black Power events of 1970. Residents of the upscale community surrounding the park were strongly opposed, however, as was the Ministry of Planning and Development. The prime minister overrode objections and insisted on the expansion, which he wanted executed, Moore said, as "speedily as possible even before Cabinet had approved it".

Moore insisted that the other projects that he was accused of undertaking at Teteron without lawful authority were all projects that the prime minister knew about and wanted executed urgently. He also claimed that the consultancy contracts relating to the projects did not fall within the provisions of the central board ordinance. Moore challenged his interdiction in the high court, and argued that the preferment of the charges and the appointment of a tribunal was "unconstitutional, ultra vires and null and void". He also claimed that the prime minister's charges and various public statements constituted an infringement of his "right to a fair hearing".[5]

The high court, presided over by Justice Noor Hassanali, found for the Public Service Commission. The judge ruled on 31 May 1978 that he was not satisfied that the evidence showed that any act on the part of the commission in respect of the plaintiff was "contrary to natural justice". The matter remained in dispute for several years. With Williams's death in 1981, Moore's attorney, Allan Alexander, and the DPA's office struck a deal to have the matter settled. Moore's salary and other benefits were restored, but he did not get the compensation that he sought and thus remained embittered. He was rehabilitated after the National Alliance for Reconstruction came to power in 1986. Moore was appointed permanent secretary to the prime minister and head of the public service – until he fell out with Prime Minister Robinson when he refused to serve unless the prime minister arranged compensation, which Robinson refused to do.

Ministerial Responsibility

The Alleyne and Moore cases raised a number of critical questions. One had to do with whether Williams had behaved appropriately in relation to the Westminster doctrine of ministerial responsibility, which was presumed to obtain in Caribbean constitutional praxis. That doctrine holds that ministers are accountable to parliament for what takes place in their ministries, and that they are also legally responsible for the activities of their administrative subordinates. British ministers had been known to resign rather than cast aspersions on their civil service advisers. Sir Thomas Duglade did this in 1954 in the famous "Crichel Down" affair. The doctrine is of considerable importance in maintaining parliamentary control over the executive, and it was rare for British ministers to name or hint at whom an errant official might be, especially since the latter could not openly reply or defend himself.

The Public Service Association of Trinidad and Tobago, the professional body that represented public sector workers, believed that the doctrine should have held in the Alleyne case, and that "the Prime Minister should have proclaimed to the world, no matter what the consequences, that the official acted under his instructions". Williams chose not to accept responsibility and in fact quoted approvingly an article in the British magazine *The Spectator* that "when bureaucracy is of the size it now is, the doctrine of ministerial responsibility is in practice void" (*Hansard*, 12 March 1976, 683). In a comment on the matter written at the time of the controversy ("The Doctrine of Ministerial Responsibility", *Trinidad Guardian*, 10 October 1976), this author had the following to say, a view that he still holds:

> The Prime Minister was guilty of a grave offence to have gone before a party convention and embarrass senior civil servants even before the Auditor General had taken action on his report. It was also wrong for him to read verbatim to such a gathering confidential advice which was given to him by his advisers. Can the Prime Minister really expect that civil servants would in future give him frank advice on matters which he might be known to oppose? Yet that is what he is urged to do in all the manuals on the Westminster system.

The manner in which the Alleyne and Moore cases were handled sparked a major public controversy about the role of the auditor general, the Public Service Commission and the Public Accounts Committee, and their relationship to the executive and the legislature. There was a widespread view that in their desire to accommodate the prime minister, the auditor general and the head of the Public Service Commission had acted partially and had exceeded their authority. The Public Service Association argued that the two bodies had in fact committed serious breaches of the procedures provided in the constitution and were unnecessarily spreading fear among public servants. The Public Service Association observed that the auditor general, who normally reported to the Public Accounts Committee, had bypassed the entire parliamentary procedure by reporting directly to the Public Service Commission, and had done so with "indecent haste". The commission, which had been instituted in the constitution to protect public servants from the "vengeful and patronistic hand of the politician", had now been used to harass public servants, and in so doing had violated its own regulations.

The Public Service Commission's breach of procedure involved, among other things, charging the head of the public service for "acting unlawfully and bringing the Public Service into disrepute" and also interdicting him with losses of a quarter of his pay at one and the same time *before* he had been given an opportunity to respond to the auditor general's allegations. As the Public Service Association asked, "When the most senior public servant can be suspended from duty by the PSC without any previous communication, what next?" (*Public Service Review*, 30 January 1976).

Interestingly, a member of the Public Service Commission, James Bain, dissented from the decision of the commission to drop the charges. Bain felt that the auditor general's report provided prima facie evidence of indiscipline and should not have been ignored. As Bain argued, "Although the Commission was apparently justified in withdrawing the present charges against Mr. Alleyne, I think it would be a matter for regret if any public officer or officers against whom any charge can properly be preferred are not called upon to answer them" (*Trinidad Guardian*, 19 March 1976). Bain generally felt that civil servants should not violate financial regulations merely because ministers instructed them to do so. If so directed, he said, they should secure confirmation of such instructions in writing.

The response of the Public Service Association to this view was to draw attention to the dilemma in which civil servants often find themselves when ministers instruct them to do things that are unlawful but that may be politically expedient or even in the public interest. If officers continually insist on "confirmation memos", they may be seen as not being cooperative. If they act without written authorization, they run the risk that ministers might refuse to accept responsibility, or worse, disclaim knowledge of their action. Given the absence of clear guidelines, every permanent secretary thus has to play it by ear in an atmosphere of uncertainty.

Williams's handling of the matter raised several other questions. Did he come to believe that some of his trusted public servants had been on the receiving end of improper or other financial inducements offered by the French? If so, why did he not confront them with the allegations and allow them the opportunity to explain and exonerate themselves? It should be noted that Williams was continuously on the receiving end of malevolent gossip and "mauvais langue" from people in the party, members of his cabinet, and the public, and had a seemingly uncurable weakness for believing much of what he was told and acting upon it in a paranoid way. Many close observers believe that this is precisely what happened to Alleyne and Moore and explains Williams's irrational and irascible behaviour towards them.

There are yet other possible explanations. Did Williams fear that his mandarins had discovered something unseemly involving him and some of his ministers relating to Tesoro Oil Company and was attempting to get them out of the power loop? (See chapter 42.) Note that almost the entire upper bureaucracy had been sent abroad in 1974–75 on fact-finding missions relating to options for the oil sector. It is also possible that certain key civil servants had become squeezed in a power play between American and French interests who were bidding to control investments in the oil and natural gas industry, and that, unfortunately for them, they backed the losing French group. In this version, the prime minister is said to have caved in to American pressure and therefore found it difficult to work with advisers who were committed to what he and they once thought was a more genuinely national policy for the hydrocarbon industry.[6]

Yet another likely explanation is that Williams had become disenchanted with overcautious economists who were seeking to restrain him from the economic adventurist path that he seemed bent on pursuing once OPEC-derived petro-dollars began to flow into the country. Williams became a *parvenu* sheik who wanted to be free to spend and build monuments that would form part of his legacy. His public servants urged caution and the need to plan at a time when Williams, under heavy political pressure to deliver needed public amenities, felt he needed room to play.

Many explanations are possible for Williams's behaviour. One cannot discount the possibility, however, that Williams genuinely felt that his trust had been betrayed by some of his officers, and that they had also begun to think of themselves as super-ministers who could fly in his face instead of being mere "servants of the centurion whose role was to save his face or make it look good". They had lost the art of deferential dissent, or so it seemed. Thus the utter violence of his reaction. Possible too is that Williams did not want to be subjected to scrutiny by his mandarins, as Robinson suggests, and that he wanted them out of the way.[7] It is also possible that open "turf" war had broken out between unelected senior public servants and elected ministers, and that the scales had now tipped in favour of the latter.[8] Perhaps none of the above are relevant, and Williams was acting irrationally as a result of the psychiatric condition from which he was said to be suffering.

One minister who worked closely with Williams, and who claimed to have enjoyed his trust, believed that the problem stemmed from the fact that the two public servants had "crossed the line". They had ceased being professionals and had acted arrogantly as political czars who drew their power and authority from being close to Williams. They often abused that power without being aware that Williams's political management style was not to cultivate genuine partners, but to use people to carry out his policies and drop them either when they got too close and thus presumptuous, or when scapegoats were required. The minister further argued that Williams was an insecure, suggestible, paranoid, suspicious, and emotionally unstable individual who had great difficulty handling human relations. He thus found it necessary to identify certain trusted persons – particularly Prevatt, O'Halloran, Moore, Alleyne – to do hatchet jobs and personal errands for him. Some of the hatchet jobs involved his ministerial colleagues, most of whom he disrespected. This invariably involved acting unconstitutionally or without them being informed as to what was happening.

The minister was of the view that one had to understand (as he did) Williams's psychology if one wanted to work sustainably with him. Failure to do so generated a "boomerang" effect. A favourite phrase used by the minister in question and indeed many others to describe what occurred was "getting one's throat cut". The punishment involved being quarantined in the "dog house", and withdrawal of speech and contact with the prime minister for extended periods. Often, the victim was unaware as to why he was being isolated, and many were reduced to tears and to begging for help from intermediaries to effect the needed rapprochement. In the view of this minister, Moore and Alleyne got "their throats cut". They were not only victims of a war between the political and bureaucratic arms of the state. Their cardinal error was to have come too close to Williams.[9]

The Cowering Herd

One disturbing aspect of the prime minister's actions was the effect they had on civil service morale. The public service was traumatized and paralysed until his death. As Reginald Dumas, who replaced Moore as head of the public service, observed,

> When that speech was followed by the sudden fall within days of a number of senior public servants, . . . you will understand that the Public Service had to pull in its horns. From that moment on, a number of things that the Prime Minister had said Ministers could deal with, went to Cabinet, because even ministers took fright. Cabinet notes jumped from 2,346 in 1974 to 3,520 in 1976. By 1981, the number had jumped to 5,159. After what happened in 1975, the Public Service was simply not disposed to take action on its own. It is as simple as that.

Dumas noted that in Jamaica, the total number of notes submitted in 1981 was 676, and in the United Kingdom the figure was 59. In 1983, the number was 36 compared to 3,717 in Trinidad and Tobago ("Eric Williams in Retrospect" symposium, April 1991).

One could not talk about rapid development while at the same time reducing civil servants to a cowering herd, uncertain as to which one would go next, and when. Quite apart from the motives indicated above, the strategy was clearly also part of an overall political tactic of making the bureaucracy in both the regular public service and the statutory bodies, including the utilities, the face-saving scapegoat or smokescreen for the regime's failures over the post-independence years. It was, however, counter-productive. What was more urgently needed than cabinet reshuffles, repostings of permanent secretaries, or "iceboxing" of recalcitrants was a through re-examination and overhaul of the civil service's structures and the assumptions that underpinned those structures.

Permanent secretaries were of the view that some co-ordinating agency drawn from their membership was necessary to assist them in performing their responsibilities, especially since it was not always clear to them just what cabinet had decided. Alleyne established one such board under his chairmanship, but Williams demobilized the caucus, seeing it as a parallel agency to the cabinet and a potential counter-balance to the hegemony and monopoly of information that he wanted to maintain. Many of his ministers were also jealous of the power that the technocrats wielded and their tendency to treat ministers as if they were eunuchs.[10]

This war for turf that had become fully developed by 1975–76 had its antecedents in the events of 1970. According to Moore, "There was a feeling of mutual distrust between public servants and ministers that predated the events that took place in the mid-1970s. Some of the latter were not in agreement with the ideological thrust of the Third Five-Year Plan (1969–73) which signalled a move towards greater state involvement in the economy." The Black Power crisis of 1970 sharpened these feelings of mistrust. According to Moore, "There was concern in 1970 that the Public Service might fall apart, particularly since public servants were embittered by the government's failure to meet their demands. The fear was that public servants might themselves take to the street or not report for work at all." Moore claims that some of the senior men consciously tried to hold things together by acting as a sort of link or bridge to the prime minister:

> We did this not only to keep the Public Service functioning, to keep the machinery of government moving; we did it in an attempt to prevent the Public Service from politicizing itself, as it were, by either taking to the streets, or being absent from the job since it would have been construed that they were in sympathy with what was happening out there in the streets and therefore were not working. It would have been easy for public servants to identify with the demonstrators on the streets. It would have been easy for public servants to sympathise with the cause, because some of the things being said on the streets were identical to the problems which they themselves faced in trying to do their jobs. (Ryan and Stewart 1995, 325)

The effort to serve as a bridge between the upper public service and the prime minister, however, had unanticipated and traumatic consequences. As Moore continued,

> The experience of acting as a link between the Prime Minister and the Public Service,

the experience of working closely with the Prime Minister in this critical period, turned out to be very traumatic because, in the absence of his cabinet (by that time the Cabinet was no longer around him), some of us really perceived that he thought we were the new Cabinet, something that we had been trying to avoid and shun as much as possible. Some of us found ourselves engaged in activities that one would not properly describe as being Public Service in nature. I know for a fact that one of us participated in the negotiations with the military at the risk of his life. I know that one of us was appointed Chairman of a Committee of Inquiry into the Role and Functioning of the Military in a Third World society. I know that two of us were used to recruit new members of his new cabinet." (Ibid., 326)

Moore speculates that the manner in which the top levels of the public service functioned in 1970 and immediately thereafter may well have contributed to the crisis that took place in the public service in the mid-1970s. Williams turned against some of these very officers who had risked their lives and much more. Said Moore,

> We did this in an attempt to look at the ship which we saw was floundering and which we thought we could help steer to a safe harbour without actually taking sides as to who should be the captain of the ship. And I think that the role that we played in this period, and the role which, by extension, the Public Service played in remaining together, and remaining as an institution with some strength, led to the crisis that the Public Service faced a few years later. That strength and that kind of independence that we tried to establish was regarded as a negative political attribute. Therefore, the Public Service had to be destroyed or brought into line. (Ibid.)

Ironically, Williams did not rely on his elected ministers any more after these events than he did previously. In terms of elected ministers, the only one on whom he depended was Errol Mahabir, whom he cultivated and assigned the responsibility for chairing the pivotal finance and economics committee that served as a gatekeeper to the cabinet. Other ministers to whom he turned were drawn from the senate, mainly Mervyn de Souza and John Donaldson. Most of the others were regarded as "millstones". As we shall see, he chose to rely on a new technocracy.

The End of Planning

Williams's answer to the problem of serious public sector reform was to adopt a "bypass" strategy. That strategy involved creating in September 1976 the National Advisory Council (NAC), which brought together representatives of the business community, the trade unions and the public sector, and which proposed the abandonment of long-term planning, and the creation of task forces to implement sectoral strategies to fast-forward the development of the energy sector, the restructure of utilities, and improved management of government business. In an attempt to achieve the latter goal, the NAC recommended creating the post of permanent secretary for administrative improvement. The recommendation was that the post should be assigned to the Office of the Prime Minister. The responsibilities of the proposed post were to be as follows:

- the monitoring and guiding of an integrated programme of administrative improvement;
- to initiate and conduct necessary studies related to the improvement of the management of Government's business;
- to act as a clearing house for the dissemination of management improvement information;
- to consult on a regular basis with Permanent Secretaries and others, individually and collectively to seek new improvements;
- to keep under continuing review the growth of the public service and recommend deployment of resources where considered necessary. (*Annual Report of the National Advisory Committee for the Year 1977*, 27)

This post was never created. Williams was not interested in the creation of any post that resembled that which Alleyne had occupied. Williams in fact refused to fill the post of head of the public service after Alleyne was sent on extended leave. He even advised Barsotti, his new permanent secretary, that he should not expect to be made head of the public service.

In his 1977 budget speech, Williams told parliament that

over the past three years especially, there has been a marked increase in the volume, size, complexity and cost of the capital works being undertaken by the public sector. The pace of these developments has not been matched by the pace of the restructuring of the public service, improvements in staffing in a qualitative sense, and rationalization of the use of existing staff. As a result, the public sector, to a much greater degree than the private sector of the economy, has found itself increasingly unable to cope with the managerial and other requirements for effective implementation of the capital works which it has undertaken or proposes to undertake.

The prime minister indicated that the NAC would be asked to study, as a top priority item, the question as to whether or not planning should be used as a development tool in Trinidad and Tobago. Williams indicated that he himself had come to have reservations about the usefulness of long-term planning and that the government had taken a decision to "hold the line on planning for the time being". Williams went on to accuse the public service of being scandalously inefficient.

In his reply to the prime minister, the president of the Public Service Association, Senator James Manswell, told Williams that public servants were tired of being unfairly criticized, and that the problems of the service had structural causes. Manswell argued that the principal cause of the said inefficiency was to be found in the manner in which cabinet took political decisions and its refusal to put systems and policies in place to address critical problems. The Public Service Association's list of "causes" included the following:

- The lack of clear directions to senior public servants concerning the extent of their authority;
- The existence of important restrictions put upon the management function, stifling initiative regarding budgeting expenditures;
- The lack of co-ordination of work of the various ministries, especially in policy execution;
- Hasty political decisions without fully thinking out all the consequences and the administrative operations which are necessary to give effect to them;
- The refusal or omission to pay greater attention to industrial relations and conditions of work, especially on the work site.

The reason given by the prime minister for his ambivalence was that long-term planning as an activity was difficult, given the environment of uncertainty in which such planning would have to take place. Planning seemed unable to help either developed or developing nations avoid dislocations caused by unpredicted developments in the international economy such as the dramatic rise in the price of petroleum. Planning did not enable industralized nations to avoid the problems of development nor did it enable developing nations to increase their rate of growth.

The NAC, hastily (perhaps) taking its cue from Williams, also came out against "traditional" long-term planning. The council recommended that instead of the conventional five-year plans, specific strategies should be integrated with other ongoing action programmes into a comprehensive document that would then form the basis for budget planning and other major government actions.

The decision to abandon traditional five-year planning caused uneasiness in public service circles. It was felt that without some renewed attempt at planning, a great deal of the newly found oil wealth might vanish without any serious attempt being made to attack some of the underlying social problems of the society, problems that were growing worse because of that wealth. Williams, it should be noted, was not always pessimistic about planning. In a paper presented to a conference on planning at Sussex University in 1969 (and which may have been written for him by his favoured planners), he noted that "discussing planning, [was] like discussing virtue. . . . The purpose of planning in a developing country", Williams told his distinguished audience, was "internally, to impart discipline and enthusiasm to the pursuit of the development effort by both the public and private sectors of the economy. Externally, its purpose is to enable the developing nation to exercise a greater degree of control over its external environment" (*The Purpose of Planning*, cited in Ryan and Bissessar 2002, 324).

Williams then regarded planning as an indispensable tool for national mobilization and manipulation:

> If a politician came into office without intending to plan, he would soon have to invent planning or something very similar. Without a plan, politicians may be tempted to make wild and unrealistic promises which they could not deliver. A realistic plan, which holds out for all to see just what resource constraints exist, helps to discipline the nation and to remind politicians and interested groups that limits exist to what they could demand and expect to receive. Opposition politicians would also be constrained by the datum of the Plan. (Ibid.)

In this way, "planning acts to reduce the hysteria of political debate" and therefore makes dialogue more rational. While planning can never be rid of ideology, it can allow debates on "ideology to be conducted in a slightly cooler atmosphere". Williams also saw planning as a method of helping administrators and ministers fashion programmes that were consistent with those of other departments or agencies. Planning thus helped to restrain the aggrandizing tendencies of ministries that invariably seek to push their programmes at the expense of the wider national effort:

> A plan, by establishing priorities, serves to check the exuberance of individual ministers and to establish a firm scale of priorities among the needs of individual ministries. I can speak there with a certain amount of feeling. Unless the spending ambitions of individual ministries are held firmly in check by constant reference to the Plan, the result in a newly independent country which has just experienced, or is experiencing, an export boom is likely to be financial chaos and the building up a heavy burden of recurrent expenditure. (Ibid.)

The above statement could well have been written in 1977, so prophetic it appeared to be. The same held with respect to Williams's following statement about the civil service: "A national plan can impart a strong sense of collective purpose to the entire civil service and thus infuse the governmental machine with a great deal of enthusiasm."

Williams was aware of course that the mere existence of a national plan was not sufficient in itself to generate enthusiasm among civil servants: "However good a National Plan may be, if the civil service is dissatisfied no sense of purpose will be created. Plan implementation required not only that the plan be a realistic one, which takes into account available financial and manpower resources and displays a sensitivity to political and sociocultural realities; it also required a civil service in which there existed a high degree of managerial competence and coordination as well as high morale."

Note too the prime minister's view that a national plan could provide "a powerful defence of the national sovereignty *vis-à-vis* aid giving institutions and countries. Without such a countervailing shield which sets out national priorities, outsiders often try, both by overt and subtle methods, to dictate what goals the country should pursue." Planning was seen as an indispensable mechanism for containing trade unions. The existence of a plan could help "focus attention on an understanding of politically difficult issues of wages and incomes policies". Without some such point of reference, "no popularly elected politician, pledged to the upliftment of the common man, could lightly decide to impose, or even to request, wage restraint of trade unions" (ibid., 325).

But Williams was not too sanguine that a plan could do much to make multinational firms perform in accordance with national aspirations: "The fact that major decisions about investment, production and employment were made in the head offices of these international giants beyond the jurisdiction of the country" constituted "perhaps the biggest limitation of national planning in the Commonwealth Caribbean countries" (ibid., 326).

It is true that a great deal had happened since 1969, both in Trinidad and elsewhere, to undermine the confidence that the prime minister once had in planning. All over the world, questions were being raised about the tremendous costs involved in producing plans, both in terms of money and manpower, as well as in terms of the cynicism that failure to implement these plans generated among planners and the attentive public alike. Sceptics noted that planners often seemed to go to sleep once the exercise of drawing up the plan was finished, only to be roused a few years later to make preparations for the next plan. The planners themselves blamed the politicians for ignoring and subverting the plan and for giving in too easily to special interests. Politicians, for their part, blamed the planners either for sabotaging the plan or for ignoring the realities of power politics in which the name of the game is survival.

Generally speaking, planning in Third World countries such as Trinidad and Tobago failed because of the inability of the political and administrative institutions of these countries to contain the demands of strategic interest groups. Most of these institutions were fragile and permeable and therefore susceptible to pressures from well-organized groups such as trade unions, chambers of commerce, armies, the white-collar salariat or foreign lobbies. Corruption also helped to distort the implementation process, not only because it led to a wastage of scarce resources, but also because it helped to dissipate energies and generate cynicism among bureaucrats and the public.

Plans also failed because they generally tended to be unrealistic in terms of the goals set, goals that were usually defined without adequate reference to the domestic and external inputs available. As John Maynard Keynes once complained, "Planners often lose sight of the complexities and interdependencies of the real world in a maze of pretentious and unhelpful symbols." The international system was and remained a fickle system, and it was hard to plan in an environment of comprehensive uncertainty. Dramatic events such as coups, secession movements and wars have also been the bane of planning.

Yet, even given all this, it is not certain that conventional comprehensive planning should have been abandoned completely and replaced by incrementalism and adhocracy. A realistic plan still had value in that it could function as a guide and a beacon for national effort. It could still have informed and educated the population and all concerned about the direction in which the nation hoped to move, the steps that had to be taken to get there and the sacrifice that respective groups had to make if national objectives were to be achieved. The solution to the crisis in planning was not to abandon long-term planning, but to plan more realistically and flexibly, making sure that spare resources were left to take care of contingencies. Williams was therefore wiser in 1969 than he appeared to be in 1977. "The Plan," he said then, "must be a symbol of the determination of both the government and the country as a whole to chart a certain course."

The NAC, which virtually replaced the Ministry of Planning, was generally accused of functioning as an executive rather than as an evaluative agency, and of behaving as if it were an alternative to the civil service and the cabinet. The chairman of the NAC, Ken Julien, rejected both of these criticisms. He explained that the NAC was not a "miracle worker", and that its role "must not be overstated, overrated or isolated from other elements in the country". The NAC was neither "a rival institution to ministries or the Cabinet, [n]or a lobby either for private sector interests, trade unions and other specific groups" (*Trinidad Guardian*, 29 April 1977). The NAC was seen as a catalytic agent that could bring together management and technical staffs from various ministries, agencies and statutory boards in an attempt to harmonize and orchestrate these units' development programmes. The NAC observed that agencies had been going about their business without being conscious of what others were doing that might impinge on their own plans.

The need to create advisory bodies that could span the policy universe with greater depth and breadth than the regular civil service and politicians were capable of was a real one, but there was reason to be sceptical about the potential usefulness of the NAC as it was constituted. In the first place, the NAC was not made up of independent-minded men who had the leisure to contemplate public policy. Most of the members of the NAC, including the chairman, were extremely busy men who were only able to give a fraction of their time to the deliberations of that body. None of them were full-time members of the the NAC, and most wore a variety of executive hats. Another basic problem was that certain key members did not have the sort of distance from the day-to-day problems of government that was required if the NAC was to bring fresh ideas to the policy-making process.

The NAC chairman in particular followed prime ministerial cues and initiatives and used the NAC or views expressed by individuals within it to help legitimate those initiatives. This was evident with respect to its recommendation to abandon "traditional" five-year plans. At any rate, given what was known about the decision-making process in Trinidad and Tobago, clearly the NAC would have been quietly ignored if it had not functioned as a handmaiden of the prime minister.

Williams as Public Service Manager

One of the most passionate critics of Williams's bypass strategy was Frank Barsotti, who became his permanent secretary in 1975 after Alleyne was interdicted. Barsotti admitted to being intimidated by the prospect of having to work closely with Williams. He decided that the key to survival was to "ask no favours and carry no news", and also to make sure that all directions given and requests made were clear and unambiguous. Barsotti claims that his strategy worked, and that he and Williams developed a harmonious relationship: "There was some discomfiture on about three or four occasions, but nothing apocalyptic. I often disagreed with what passed for official policy, and wrote and said so. But I survived and benefited intellectually from my association with Dr. Williams" (Barsotti 1991).

Barsotti shared the view that it was a fundamental mistake to abandon economic planning. The OPEC crisis and the economic windfall that followed in its wake led Williams to believe that planning was no longer necessary. But this was precisely the time when planning and the discipline it imposed was most needed. Williams's mind was blown by his good fortune, and he did not fully appreciate the difficulties that would be involved in fast-paced development. He felt that he was truly now the "son of heaven": "Here it is at last; I am a very favoured third world leader with all these financial and physical resources, with people running themselves down to lend me money. So the sky is the limit. It was a kind of emotional thing. . . . Growth versus welfare was out of the window. [It was growth and welfare], and we had the money to pursue both" (Barsotti 1991) Williams in his role as "corporation sole"[12] was of course intellectually aware that there was danger in committing the country to a level of recurrent and overhead expenditures that might not be sustainable, especially if there was a sharp drop in oil prices, and agreed that it was important that reserves be built up. He ignored his own intelligence, however, and the warnings offered by technocrats such as Euric Bobb, governor of the Central Bank, who raised the "red flag" (Report of the Committee to Review Government Expenditure, 1978).

Barsotti endorsed Williams's strategy of creating "special funds", some fifty of which were initiated. There was logic in the strategy in that the funds served as a kind of functional equivalent to planning, and a mechanism for sterilizing some of the petro-dollars. The government placed these with the Central Bank for investment, and in fact earned substantial profits as a result. Said Barsotti, "The strategy made economic sense in that it took money out of the system and in so doing helped to contain if not prevent inflation." The down side of the strategy was that there was no control over expenditure from the funds once parliament had established them. Approval for expenditure was deemed to have been given. This posed accounting problems for the treasury. "So while the policy was good on the one hand, there were problems on the other."

Barsotti believed that planning would have served as an early warning system, identifying some of the problems that later developed: "The 'veil of money' concealed some serious weaknesses in the national economy which would later result in fiscal deficits and spill over to the balance of payments." Barsotti's judgement on Williams was, however, ambivalent:

> Being mortal he was fallible. He made mistakes. His judgement was flawed; he manipulated and was himself manipulated. He had to deal and interface with bright committed and loyal people and with sycophants, charlatans, self-seekers and miscreants. . . . There was a Cabinet and there were senior civil servants and technocrats, [but] there were people outside of the Cabinet and the Public Service who were very influential; even more influential than the insiders. The country's leaders in politics and in other fields – labour, business, religion etc., must all share some of the blame. It cannot all be attributed to . . . the autocratic dominance of Dr. Williams or his charisma. The fact that the country modernized its consumption habits faster than the economy was itself modernized, cannot be blamed on Eric Williams, a man who was austere in his tastes. (Barsotti 1991)

Barsotti was referring to Ken Julien, who had become Williams's technocratic "guru". Some would say, unfairly, his "Rasputin". He agreed, however, that he had to share some of the blame for what happened, because he did not always protest strongly enough. "I should have protested more strongly on occasions, even if it meant more open confrontation with Ministers, but when you are part of the machine, that is not very easily done." Barsotti also noted that many permanent secretaries were treated as second-class clerks, but said that the problem was partly theirs. Too often they washed their hands, saying, "I don't know what government policy is." His advice to them was that they had to help make policy, notwithstanding the attitude of certain ministers who objected to public servants challenging their policies in the finance advisory committee.

Barsotti (1991) conceded that the task forces appointed to bypass the inert public service had tremendous powers, and that the public servants and ministers were afraid to challenge them:

> Certain Ministers were actually afraid of certain people who were in charge of a Task

Force. They were very careful because they did not know what relationship existed between the political leader and the leader of the Task Force. And the leaders of some of those Task Forces even took it upon themselves to write Cabinet Notes. This happened to me, personally. I got a decision one day, a Cabinet decision, and I did not know where the Note had come from. When I enquired, I found that the Note had gone to Cabinet. How did it go to Cabinet? Well, the Task Force leader had written the Note, taken it to the Political Leader. He had initialed it. Nobody challenged the initial, and it went to the Cabinet; it was approved, and a decision came to the permanent secretary in the Ministry of Finance to implement the decision.

Whereupon I went to one of the Ministers in the Ministry of Finance, and I told them that when we get in front of the Public Accounts Committee, I am going to tell them chapter and verse, and we are all going to go down the road together. I put it in writing, and I said, "This is administratively impossible; I am not going to put up with it. I am not going to take responsibility for it, and if it continues, and if it comes as a question from the Public Accounts Committee, we are going down the road together." And strangely, it ceased after that. But that actually took place.

In fact my secretary today has a list of Notes, which she still has in safe keeping because I had three copies made – one I had in a special place, and she had a copy. I can go to her today and get my copy of those Notes that went to Cabinet without going though the permanent secretary. This caused a kind of schism in the whole structure.

Barsotti (1991) also drew attention to another phenomenon that served to emasculate the public service:

People in the Civil Service were wafted out of the Civil Service – people in junior positions – into state enterprises where they got fabulous terms and conditions, much better than permanent secretaries and other senior people got; some of them really did not measure up; they just got moved out; so that all these things had an effect on the administrative structure as a whole.

There were all these stresses and strains in the period between 1973 and 1974, instant wealth and 1981. And in that period, we were in fact trying to do too much. We were trying to take people who were accustomed to just running Ministries in a colonial administration, or just out of a colonial administration, and expecting them to become entrepreneurs and decision makers in an environment which was in some senses, Byzantine.

Whatever talents Williams had, and he had many, managerial capacity was clearly not one of them. The policy-making system over which he presided was much too centralized and personalized. In the Westminster model, delegation of responsibility to civil servants (or committees of civil servants), ministers and cabinet committees was a must if the system was not to break down. In the British system, the cabinet as a whole only considered critical issues, and a minister would be greeted with the sternest displeasure were he to burden his colleagues with matters that should have been resolved at the ministerial or inter-ministerial level. It was often left to the judgement of the minister to determine (with the advice of the cabinet secretary) which issues should be considered by the entire cabinet, which required bilateral consultation with the prime minister, which should be disposed of by his ministry alone and which by an interministerial committee. The system depended on trust, and assumptions of competence and judgement that were clearly lacking in Trinidad and Tobago, where, after nineteen years of party government, little civility existed in the corridors of power.

At the centre of the problem was the archaic way in which the cabinet functioned. Far too many issues of a routine nature were brought to cabinet for settlement. Given the crowded agenda, cabinet did not decide many critical issues until a national crisis made it imperative that action be taken. Indeed, as Williams acknowledged, the traffic jam in the cabinet was much worse than that on the roads. Notes got deferred either because ministers did not read or understand them, or because they desired a postponement for one reason or another, perhaps to consult some vested interest.

The Ministry of Finance also insisted (and properly so) on seeing and commenting on all cabinet notes that had financial implications before they came to cabinet. This requirement was one of the principal bottlenecks in the system, because the permanent secretary in the Ministry of Finance was always heavily burdened with a range of activities, many of which took him abroad. He was therefore often unable to give the requisite attention to urgent matters. The unwillingness to delegate, and the constitutional arrangements that made it difficult for permanent secretaries to delegate responsibilities even when they were willing to do so, imposed additional strains on the decision-making system. The opportunities for delay and sabotage through delay were therefore enormous.

Once decisions were made at cabinet level, they could still be frustrated at the implementation stage. The first source of delay was the primitive way in which decisions were recorded and transformed into authoritative cabinet instructions. At Westminster, there was an effective cabinet secretariat headed by the secretary to the cabinet who was usually the head of the civil service and permanent secretary to the prime minister. Under Williams, there was no cabinet secretariat as such, and the secretary to the cabinet was an administrative officer without any real prestige in the upper civil service hierarchy. Williams had decided that he did not want the head of the public service to be secretary to the cabinet as occurs in the British system and in Barbados. The secretary sat outside the door of cabinet.

One of the responsibilities of the cabinet secretary in the Westminster system was to ensure that cabinet notes reach ministers in sufficient time before cabinet meets. The cabinet secretary must also ensure that cabinet decisions are expeditiously recorded, verified and communicated to ministers and permanent secretaries. Important too is the responsibility to follow through and ensure that decisions are carried out in the spirit in which they were determined by cabinet. An effective secretariat and a cabinet secretary with prestige and standing were therefore essential planks in the machinery of cabinet government. So too were regular meetings of permanent secretaries, chaired by the cabinet secretary. Williams, as we have seen, was fiercely opposed to any attempt on the part of permanent secretaries to meet on a regular basis to co-ordinate policy such as obtains today. The system was clearly ad-hocratic, and the prime minister was largely responsible for the faulty way in which it functioned. He clearly preferred a "guerilla"-like adhocracy even while complaining that he was a victim of inactivity and sabotage.[13]

Chambers and the Technocracy

Following Williams's death and George Chambers assuming office as prime minister, one of the first policy statements made related to the civil service. In a speech to a party convention on 17 May 1981, Chambers announced that he was determined to disestablish the centralized bureaucratic state apparatus that Williams had built up over the years. Excessive centralization was one of the wrongs that had to be put right. Chambers took note of the distrust with which the civil service had come to be regarded by Williams, and the fact that many public servants had themselves ceased to care, and were casting their sympathies elsewhere.

Under the new regime, public servants were no longer required to go to the prime minister or ministers for simple decisions. Ministers were also to be allowed more freedom to manage their portfolios. Delegation of authority was also to become the order of the day and the style of management was to become less personalized and "more relaxed". As Chambers told the convention, in an apparent rebuke to Williams, "Decentralization is the cornerstone of my thinking. I am very concerned to improve and make more effective the management function of the Public Service." Chambers, who appointed a task force to examine the operations of the public service under the chairmanship of Reginald Dumas, told the party that "if people recognize that you really want to have authority decentralized, they will be prepared to break the rules to get things done. Sometimes you will have to do that to get things done".

Chambers knew that this change in attitude would not occur overnight: "Public Servants have not been able to exercise their authority to make decisions for so long now that they must be able to want to do so. It will take time to rearrange the bureaucratic mentality." Chambers likewise opined that "no one, no matter how gifted [he may have been referring to Williams or Julien] should be allowed to establish dominance over state and society". Ministers and civil servants should thus "get back to work". In doing so, "they should feel free to do what they are paid to do, and not fall back on the explanation that they fear crucifixion." (See my "Doctophopia and Decision Making", *Trinidad Express*, 28 March 1982. See also my "New PM Gives Himself Room to Manoeuvre", *Trinidad Express*, 17 May 1981.)

Following independence, the government attempted to streamline and reorient bureaucratic procedures inherited from the colonial era. The structures were patched and extended and some technical surgery was done here and there. Several commissions of inquiry and working parties investigated the operations of the civil service, all of them identifying areas in need of structural reform. For the most part, however, their major recommendations were shelved. In some cases, the commission reports were not even made public. Yet year after year, Williams and other politicians complained about the inefficiency of the public service and the need for reform. One wonders whether Williams was seriously committed to reform or whether he was paying mere lip service in order to deflect attention away from his own failures.

Many civil servants came to believe that Williams did not have any interest in systematic administrative reform out of fear that such reforms would inhibit his penchant for ad hoc incremental strategies for problem-solving. As one permanent secretary observed with some bitterness:

> Increased activity in administrative improvement in Trinidad and Tobago was in part a direct result of the situation which existed prior to 1970 and culminated in the disturbances of that year. Strange as it might seem, it is a fact that increased activities aimed at improving administrative capabilities of a nation's public service seem to be associated always with some form of national disaster, such as war, internal disturbances, etc. and therefore, what took place in Trinidad and Tobago in 1970, to a great extent, led to the appointment of a Working Group under Mr. Cecil Dolly, the appointment of a Committee of Permanent Secretaries and the establishment of the Administrative Improvement Programme, all aimed at improving administration. Regrettably, as 1970 faded in the distance, so too the initial enthusiasm for an improved Public Service tended to disappear. As a consequence, the Permanent Secretaries Committee failed to carry out its functions and a report was not submitted. The recommendations of the Dolly committee, even if they were considered, were not implemented, and the Administrative Improvement Programme floundered on the rocks of complete indifference. (Herrera n.d.)

When problems arose, the tendency was to rely on a selected group of seriously overworked court favourites rather than on established machinery in the relevant ministries. This reliance on task forces inhibited the larger effort to create permanent machinery that could cope with the project implementation.

Like politicians everywhere, Williams became apprehensive whenever administrative changes were proposed that threatened his dominance and ability to exercise patronage. Given his preference for personalized styles of administration, he often saw proposals for administrative reform in conspiratorial terms, even though in other contexts he admitted the need for reform. This then is the paradox. Reforms that were seen as necessary if success was to be achieved in terms of project implementation were often deferred because he felt he stood to lose in the power struggle with bureaucrats. This appears to have been the major problem faced by the team of UN experts who were called in to advise the Trinidad and Tobago government. They continuously complained that qualified and dedicated national staff was not assigned to the improvement project on a full-time basis, that full advantage was not taken of fellowships, and that the government seemed to see no real urgency to provide co-ordination for various aspects of the project. The team concluded that the difficulties they encountered were due to the absence of an unambiguous and positive commitment along the lines which were specifically designed for the creation of permanent machinery for the realization of future administrative improvement plans, programmes and projects.

A rational mind might argue that improved administrative performance that leads to providing services that satisfy the needs and aspirations of the consuming public would redound to the benefit of the responsible politicians; but what appears rational from one perspective is often not viewed as such by others. What is rational given a long-term perspective may not appear to be so when short-term considerations are taken into account. Reformers should always bear in mind that when all is said and done, administrative change involves changing people's motivations. Whether people respond positively or otherwise to demands for change depends in large part on whether they feel they stand to gain or lose when the new administrative arrangements and relationships are put into place. Williams, whose management style was personalistic, clearly wanted to maintain full control of the political and administrative system. Erica Williams believes that this style was consciously chosen and adopted, but was a mask designed to protect her father from being manipulated by those with whom he had to work (cf. chapter 45). The dysfunctional public service in the country today remains one of his abiding legacies.

36 Breaking the "Damn" Circle
The Politics of Education

Long before entering the electoral political arena, Williams had spoken and written passionately about the relationship between education and the political development of a people. Indeed, he had given expression to these thoughts in early versions of his autobiography, which he subtitled "The Education of a Young Colonial". Williams's complaint was that the prevailing educational system in the West Indies totally disregarded its environment. It in fact disparaged that environment: "What the school disparaged, the society despised." Williams was determined that he would do more than understand the psychodynamics of the plantation-driven educational system. He would change it.

His first published contribution to the discourse on the issue came in 1944 when he presented a memorandum containing his views to a committee that the British government established to consider the needs of higher education in the colonies. One year later Williams expanded that memorandum into a book, *Education in the British West Indies*. The basic argument of the book was that Caribbean education not only should develop the personality of the people, but should also concern itself with their economic, social and psychological needs in the context of their aspirations for self-determination and independence. Williams's argument was that the secondary school curriculum should emphasize agriculture and vocational training in the areas of industry and commerce instead of focusing on literary studies. One needed a paradigm shift. The curriculum should also emphasize the reality of the West Indian community. As he put it, "The West Indian school should make a fetish of the West Indian environment."

The corollary of this was that the foreign assumptions that informed the system, including the reliance on external examinations such as he himself had to take at Queen's Royal College, should be abolished and replaced by one that reflected the new emphases in the curriculum. The QRC model had to go.

Education, at least up to secondary school, should also be tuition free, and secondary schools should receive subsidies from the state. Adult education should likewise become a fundamental part and not a subordinate dimension of educational practice, because one was educating a people for development and not merely trying to increase literacy standards. Another key and controversial recommendation was that the state and not the churches should have full and final responsibility for all aspects of education. One had to eliminate the administrative and social dualism that underpinned the current system. As Williams later complained, "I see in the denominational school the breeding ground of disunity . . . recognition of non-Christian denominations which adds a racial difference to religious difference" (*Trinidad Guardian*, 20 May 1955).

On 29 May 1944, Williams told the committee – which was chaired by Sir James Irvine of St Andrew's University in Scotland, and which also included Margery Perham of Oxford and Hugh Springer and Philip Sherlock, both West Indians – during its visit to Washington that the proposed new University of the West Indies should not be affiliated to an English university, but should instead seek to combine the best traditions of both the British and American systems. Williams argued further that the university should be unitary in structure, independent in academic matters and offer a broad curriculum to suit the political, economic and social aspirations of the West Indian people. This new type of education should also train the people to appreciate their democratic privileges and their democratic responsibilities, and must equip them to participate in the practices of democracy. The school should not merely swim with the current. Its duty was to indicate the direction in which the current should be made to flow.

Williams later sought and obtained the advice and support of John Dewey, the distinguished American educationist, who expressed "cordial agreement" with his views. The British educational establishment in London and the colonies were less enthusiastic. In their view, Williams wanted the West Indies to "fly before it could swim". The book in fact failed to find a publisher in the United States or the United Kingdom. Its public outdooring came in 1950 when it was finally published in Trinidad and Tobago by the Teachers' Economic and Cultural Association.

During the 1950s and particularly in the runup to the 1956 general elections, Williams articulated some of the views contained in the book, much to the delight of his secular and nationalist supporters, particularly black anti-clerical teachers. The denominational authorities were, however, apoplectic. As we have seen (chapters 7 and 19), there was undisguised rhetorical warfare between Williams and spokesmen of the denominational boards over the question of the respective roles of the state and church in the delivery of educational products, and the content of those products.

In 1964, the government appointed a working party committee to examine the state of the teaching service in the age of independence. The report of that committee formed the basis of a bill that was debated in parliament on 8 December 1965. The bill sought to make better provision for the establishment of a system of national education in Trinidad and Tobago. In his addresses on the question of the role of the state in the secondary school system, Williams focused, among other aspects, on what the denominational authorities had done with their 20 per cent entitlement. Most, he said, had not used the Common Entrance Examination pass list to recruit students. Williams complained that the principals had claimed the right to admit anyone they wished, which was not what the concordat had intended. The government had had to "put its foot down" on this. The problem had improved, he said, but was still bad.

Williams told parliament that he had identified 166 persons who had been admitted on the basis of the 20 per cent provision, and found that 96 had not qualified on the basis of the list. Some 29 had not even written the examination, while 31 came from preparatory schools controlled by the denominational authorities or from other preparatory schools. "In other words," complained Williams, "the private school at primary level was becoming the chief feeder of the public schools, publicly financed, operated under public prescription" (*Hansard*, 8 December 1965). Williams viewed this as an intolerable public scandal, and swore that "we shall not budge. . . . People must take the examinations and must be on the pass list" (ibid., 260).

Williams also took issue with the view that the state should not undertake the responsibility for education and should instead leave this responsibility to non-governmental agencies. Williams saw this as a "ghastly relic" that took as its point of departure the ideological assumption that education provided by the churches was morally and educationally superior to that provided by the state – a view that had led some to argue that QRC should be given to the Anglican authorities to manage, and that all other state schools should be allocated to these denominational bodies.

Williams was aggressively hostile to this point of view and accused the church of being among the last holdouts of the colonial system: "I unhesitatingly state that one of the principal problems being encountered by the Government of Trinidad and Tobago in this particular stage of our independence, in terms of relations between Church and state is that in the field of the Church, non-nationals rather than nationals are so much in evidence. It is unfortunate that it should appear that the last stronghold of the colonial relationship should be in the ranks of the Church" (ibid., 252). Williams also lamented the fact that the curriculum of the schools had not changed much since 1961, and that the literary bias was still dominant, even in the many neighbourhood schools that had been established by the state following independence. As he complained, "We have noticed an unfortunate tendency in some governmental institutions to reproduce the literary bias which dominates the curriculum in the so-called grammar schools and which has been one of the principal reasons for the enormous weaknesses that the Government of Trinidad and Tobago experience today in particular fields where we have to keep issuing work-permits because we have no qualified nationals" (ibid., 256).

Williams likewise focused on the issue of discipline and expulsion, and insisted that the ultimate sanction of expulsion had to be cabinet and not the principals, whom he feared would exercise the role ascriptively. What was involved here, he opined, was the constitutional rights of the child who had to be protected from the "arrogance of the principal, not to mention the possibility of racial discrimination, always very much in evidence in certain quarters in Trinidad and Tobago". Williams felt that given these possibilities, the best guarantee of the child's welfare was the cabinet of the country: "Cabinet would not hesitate to expel, but this must be the last resort and only Cabinet must be trusted to exercise that power" (ibid., 264). Many regarded this as one of the key decisions that served to undermine discipline in the school system.

Notwithstanding his concern that the curriculum had not been sufficiently modernized, Williams felt that the newly constructed neighbourhood secondary schools had done very well, and he expressed confidence that in future years they would achieve results that were superior to, or at least equal to, the results of the older schools (ibid., 269).

Williams knew that he stood accused of having destroyed his alma mater, QRC, in order to establish the new state schools. To this charge, he pleaded guilty. As he told a vast public audience in Woodford Square on 26 October 1965, QRC was the "mother school" that had "colonized" the newer state schools: "The parents have demanded the neighbourhood school, the school in their area, which we have been trying to build up, using Queen's Royal College as the mother school. It is not that Queen's Royal College has gone down. That is sheer nonsense. It is that Queen's Royal College has sent up the standard in all the daughter schools that have been founded all over the country" (1965b, 92).

Williams also argued that the government could not possibly concentrate on a policy that built up one school to the exclusion of others:

> It is a great pity that some of the denominational schools seem to be doing that, and seem to think that they could talk about an exclusive school in an inclusive state. The thing can't work. You are working for the whole country, and one must recognize – even the most, particularly the most, favoured sections of the community – their responsibility to the less favoured section which is what we have done deliberately and consciously in respect of the teaching staff at Queen's Royal College. This always happens. (Ibid.)

One could not, he insisted, develop an education system based on a few outstanding schools or on the basis of a teacher training programme in which Port of Spain and San Fernando were way above St Patrick. If one did so, one should not be surprised if St Patrick came to San Fernando.

Williams explained that Trinidad and Tobago could not, in the age of independence, continue with the old elite system such as he himself had to endure. The colonial system excluded all those unfortunates who could not pay their way, except for the brilliant and talented few to whom the state made limited concessions. "That's a lot of damned nonsense in 1965. That's how I got my education. . . . That's how I got into the charmed circle. And when you get into the charmed circle, what do you say? I'll break up the damn circle" (Williams 1965b, 93). Williams's vision in 1965, as it had been in 1944, was for a national educational system to sustain a national economy and an integrated society. The nation must come before all its constituent groups and compartments. "Everyone wants an exclusive Church, an exclusive club, an exclusive business. For God's sake, if everyone is going to be exclusive, somebody must be inclusive, the governing party and the Government formed by the governing party [Applause]" (ibid., 93).

Williams thus set himself against the demands on the part of other denominational authorities for the right to establish other schools. As he made clear, he would think twice before getting himself into hot water by encouraging any more schools that would come and say "concordat", though they had never signed the concordat. It is the government schools that were effecting integration. As he continued,

> It is a pity that it should be so, because these schools have a contribution to make. They are making one, but they cannot expect to make it outside of the social perspectives of the country. They cannot expect to be exclusive; they cannot expect that they must pick and choose when they don't have any room for all the people who think highly of them. . . . But for God's sake whatever discrimination you practice, don't make it discrimination on social grounds or because the boy lives in East Dry River or the girl lives up in Gonzales. Not with public funds. Ask me to do a lot, *but don't ask me to negotiate with anybody – I refuse to negotiate with anybody – the rights and privileges of every citizen of Trinidad and Tobago irrespective of religion, race, social status, language, previous conditions of servitude and all the rest.* [Loud applause] (Williams 1965b, 44; emphasis added)

In 1964, Williams invited a UNESCO educational planning mission to outline a strategy for the educational development of Trinidad and Tobago. Arising out of this exercise was a fifteen-year (1968–83) Draft Plan for the Educational Development of Trinidad and Tobago. That plan was informed by a number of assumptions that Williams had enunciated in preceding years in and out of parliament. The introduction to the plan reiterated Williams's view that country could only achieve full national independence on the basis of an educational system that did not rely on foreign assumptions for its existence and growth, and which had as its foundation a relevance to the needs of the people it served (1974).

The foundation principles of the plan were as follows:

- selection of pupils at age 11-plus to be eliminated as soon as resources allowed;
- general education for all children up to age 14 in two stages, that is, primary and junior secondary;
- selection of approximately 35 to 40 per cent of the school population for specialized training at age 15;
- a number of vocational and farm schools to be constructed to train some of those graduating from the 11 to 14 junior secondary schools.

On 18 September 1975, the prime minister submitted to cabinet new and far-reaching proposals calling for a fundamental review of the fifteen-year draft educational plan. Williams told his cabinet that when that plan was put in place ten years earlier, the aim was to provide a "reasonably good education for as many citizens as possible within very limited resources". At that time, Trinidad and Tobago had embarked on an industrial development programme that was "neither dramatic nor revolutionary". The process of economic transformation was expected to be slow and evolutionary, and assumed light-assembly industry. There was no expectation of heavy industry in the fields of petrochemicals and metallurgy. Indeed, the plan was put in place in the shadow of a recession and the "desertion" of British Petroleum.

The economic horizons had changed, he said. "Trinidad and Tobago is now on the threshold of achieving critical mass in the field of high level technology and large-scale development. Any educational plan must recognize this with urgency" (Williams, 1975b, 8). Williams argued that in the new economy, one that was government driven and controlled, citizens of Trinidad and Tobago were expected to play pivotal roles. "Mockery would be made of this policy if having obtained control, one then finds that the people are either not available or trained to occupy challenging positions." Given the resources now available, it was the responsibility of the state to develop the nation's human capital.

What then was to be done? Williams's view was that there was need for a fundamental review of the plan to make five years of post-primary education the norm for *all* students. The curriculum also had to be modified to give technology in all its aspects a "suitable place and priority". This new "national model" required a fundamental modification of what then obtained in the system. Williams noted that the existing plan assumed that only 37 to 40 per cent of the junior secondary school population would go on to full secondary education, and that 60 per cent would either drop out or transfer to separate vocational schools or to farm schools. Williams considered the separate vocational school to be undesirable for a variety of reasons. As he told the cabinet,

> The isolation of a programme in vocational education from the traditional academic programme, or even what is now understood to be a technical education programme, has serious dangers. The obvious one is that, in a short space of time, it will become a place of refuge for the rejects and drop-outs from both the Junior Secondary and Senior Secondary programme. Secondly, it will foster and further develop fragmentation within the society the removal of which, the Education Plan has as a major objective. Thirdly, the staffing of these schools will present enormous difficulties. Regarded as schools at the bottom of the ladder of the educational system, there will be tremendous difficulty in attracting teaching staff of the caliber that is needed for any vocational education programme. The experiences of the John Donaldson Institute when it first began are lessons that should not be easily forgotten. Fourthly, these schools cater for a relatively small number of (400) students, and yet, designed and equipped in an extravagant manner, they cannot represent the best use of limited resources. Additionally, the running of these individual schools with overhead costs of maintenance and staffing being shared by such small numbers will lead either to high per capita unit cost or drastic reduction in current expenses with the consequent deterioration of both facilities and quality of staff. In view of these factors, a programme of vocational education done in isolation in a specific vocational school requires serious review. (1975b, 6)

Williams was merely returning to the strategy that was originally identified in the draft plan before the World Bank and the IDB, agreed to fund the project.

The new "national model" involved the provision of senior grammar, senior composite and senior comprehensive schools. In the latter, five options would be offered – traditional academic, pre-technical, general industrial, commercial and specialized craft. In Williams's view, there were no reasons why these mega-schools could not offer all five options in one location. He agreed, however, that the new schools would present management challenges: "The change from the management of a traditional academic school to one of these comprehensive schools will not be an easy one. Increasing the scope of activities and the numbers of students will in fact compound the problem; but nevertheless, it is one that will have to be faced and should be faced head on at this stage" (ibid., 9).

In retrospect, clearly Williams underestimated the management and other challenges that the change in paradigm involved. Either that, or there were other imperatives driving the change, imperatives that were informed by the fact that a critical election had to be fought and won in 1976, and that parents were demanding that the PNM deliver on its promise of free five-year secondary education. In 1975, Williams was faced by a number of urgent short- and long-term problems. The first was to find places for some ten thousand students who would be graduating from the junior secondary schools in 1976. As we have seen, the initial plan was to construct a number of vocational schools to accommodate some of these students. Difficulties were being encountered, however, with the completion, equipping and staffing of the planned schools. The question was whether efforts should be made to expedite the completion of the schools or effect a dramatic shift that would address the short-term and the long-term problem at one and the same time.

One of the problems that had to be addressed involved funding for the proposed comprehensive schools. Williams's strategy was to abandon the vocational schools altogether and to use the facilities that were already being constructed as the nucleus for the enlarged 14-plus schools. Where construction had not yet begun, the sites earmarked for the vocational school were to be used for the proposed comprehensive schools that were expected to cost some TT$5 million each. Manning, equipping and maintaining the schools would also be expensive. Money was not seen as a critical problem, however, because surplus revenues from the petroleum industry were available if the IDB and the World Bank refused to allow their funds to be used to construct the comprehensive schools.

The other critical issue to be resolved was the role that the denominational schools would play in the new national model. By 1975, Williams's knee-jerk hostility to the denominational schools had abated somewhat, and he had come to view them as "significant" partners in the delivery of educational products. Thus no attempt was made to arbitrarily impose the model on the clerical establishment, an attempt that Williams knew a large section of the populace would reject. As he told cabinet,

> The only question that arises is whether this role should be played in isolation or whether it should conform to a national plan and national policy objectives. . . . It is obvious that serious difficulties can arise in imposing arbitrarily a new model for education on these organizations, particularly when they have established a reputation of developing and maintaining the so-called prestige schools. However, if a national model is firmly established and Government policy objectives clearly stated, it is very likely that, given adequate time, support and advice, these organizations can conform to the national model and play a critical role in the development of the entire educational system. The experience and management available to these organizations are excellent resources, and it can be taken as certain that a request that they play a significant role in meeting the objectives as detailed above and that they undertake programmes oriented towards technology would be entertained. (1975b, 9)

The other key problem was what to do until such time as sufficient space was available to cater to all the graduates of junior secondary schools. The answer was a temporary double-shift system. Williams suspected, however, that the "short-term" nature of the arrangement might not be as short as parents expected.

As he warned, "The population should be made aware that its [i.e., the shift system's] complete removal is tied very much to available financial resources and the continued improvement of these resources" (ibid.).

The new two-tiered policy yielded immediate political benefits for Williams, who was acutely concerned about the malaise that seemed to prevail in the run up to the 1976 elections. Williams knew that there was a general thirst for secondary education, especially among that element that did not expect to get into the prestige schools as a result of their performance in the Common Entrance Examination and could not afford to pay for private secondary education. In 1968, some 5,278 places were being awarded on the basis of this education. As a result of the junior secondary schools that were built after 1968, the number of students entering secondary schools increased to more than 15,390 in 1975. By 1981 when Williams died, there were more than 40,000 places available for students to enter the first level of the secondary school system. The construction of some twenty-one new schools and the use of a double-shift system made this dramatic increase in enrollment possible.

Williams well understood the vote-catching potential of his educational proposals especially among the working and lower middle classes. One of his main policy advisers, Dr Michael Alleyne, argued that the policy was both educationally sound and politically astute. Williams and the PNM thereafter became the darling of those parents and related adults whose offspring benefited by the provision of "free" places at the new schools and who in the past would have been considered "failures". As Alleyne claimed,

> As a political strategy, the Junior Secondary School program was calculated to reap a greater number of votes for the People's National Movement than any other single item in the Party's manifesto. For the people of a society that was just emerging from colonialism, the expansion of secondary education through the creation of Junior Secondary schools promoted the social and economic upward mobility that they were denied during the colonial era. For each child that gained admission into a secondary school, the PNM could count on at least one vote from each parent, in addition to the other adults interested in the child's education. (1996, 89)

The establishment of the junior secondary school and later the senior comprehensives brought aspiring parents long-awaited relief and fulfilment of cherished dreams. It was an election pledge that Williams desperately wanted to fulfil, for on it depended the sustainability of his power base. It is no exaggeration to say that whatever the reasons given for the change of emphasis, it was intense public pressure by parents whose children were about to graduate from the junior secondary school that forced Williams to find more room in the shortest possible time, using innovative pre-fabrication techniques. As Alleyne noted, "Schools had to admit twice the number of students they originally planned to accommodate.

In many cases, students were merely being warehoused in these unfinished structures. The politicians had triumphed over the technicians" (ibid., 90).[1]

The down side of the programme was the shift system, its Achilles' heel. The junior secondary school also suffered from the fact that it was perceived as a place where those who "failed" the Common Entrance Examination were placed. It was a functional equivalent to post-primary schools. As Alleyne noted, "This perception, along with the use of the double shift in the majority of new schools, could be responsible for the negative attitudes that were entertained about these fledgling institutions" (ibid., 101).

Williams's educational reforms of the secondary school system generated a great deal of controversy during the 1970s, and the echo of those controversies continue to be heard. To many who benefited from them, the reforms were his most outstanding contribution to the development of Trinidad and Tobago. He had broken the charmed circle and had let the masses in. Surveys conducted by the author's firm, St Augustine Research Associates, repeatedly indicated that education was the area where people saw Williams's contribution to be most outstanding. In one such survey conducted in 1987, 48 per cent cited education as Williams's greatest contribution (Ryan 1988, 218). There was, however, a decided class dimension to this evaluation. The lower orders were unhappy about the shift system, but to them it was a price they were prepared to pay for the benefits of free secondary education. They saw it as a promissory note that would yield a passport for their progeny to secure white-collar jobs.

The upper social orders were in the main apoplectic about the educational revolution and were thankful that Williams chose not to destroy the denominational schools, as some wanted him to do by introducing a zoning system that would mean that children could not cross zones to access a school of their choice. Those opposed expressed concern that given the fact of segregated residential patterns, zoning might well exacerbate the problem of ethnic concentration in the schools. But the main opposition came from those who did not want the social mixing that zoning would bring.

While the two-tiered system achieved great returns in terms of access to school places, many were severely critical of the problems that it generated: social indiscipline in the schools, problems related to the lack of adult supervision – by both teachers and parents – of children between and after each shift, shortened school hours (by one hour), which made it difficult for students to complete their syllabuses or engage in extra-curricular activity, and the phenomenon of teacher absenteeism that was one of the hallmarks of the system. The latter was encouraged by a system that did not require a commitment from teachers to be on school premises for a full day. Many used the opportunity to attend university or to "moonlight" on second jobs, including operating a taxi-cab, selling insurance and so on. The rate of teacher absenteeism was said to be in the vicinity of 10 per cent. Add to this rules that allowed teachers to be absent for twenty-eight days for private reasons during the school year.

Parents of Indian descent were more critical of the state schools (of whatever type) than their Afro-creole counterparts, even though they too welcomed the opportunity to secure a place in a secondary school, the attendant problems notwithstanding. Some orthodox Hindus opposed the educational plan on precisely the ground that Williams justified it, that is, that it was designed to promote social and cultural integration. As Sat Maharaj, the secretary general of the Sanatan Dharma Maha Sabha, complained, "State directed integration, with the deliberate side-lining of Indian-Hindu cultural retentions, was the subtext of the PNM education project. The PNM schools were located to make ethnic mixing, more than quality education, the main achievement of the junior secondary project" (*Trinidad Guardian*, 7 December 2001). Maharaj charged that Williams turned a blind eye to declining literacy, massive failures in examinations and the sexual victimization of youngsters who were left unsupervised after the first shift or who had to travel long distances to their homes in the near dark after the second shift, because his goal was "vote catching" and not quality education. "Thousands were abandoned because they failed the Common Entrance Education." Maharaj also argued that almost nothing was done to increase skills training, notwithstanding what was said to be the main thrust of the new educational model. Maharaj's conclusion was that "Dr. Williams' educational legacy did not prepare Trinidad and Tobago to function in a globalised 21st century economy" (ibid.).

Many subscribed to Maharaj's ethnic rant, particularly his comments about the social deviance and indiscipline that the schools bred and nurtured, the high failure rate, and the fact that the schools did not produce the technologically trained students that Williams saw as necessary. Many reasons existed for this gap between hoped-for outcomes and what was achieved, not all of which could be ascribed to Williams's political agendas. For one thing, the state schools were disadvantaged from the beginning because, with few exceptions, they received less competent students as determined by the Common Entrance Examination. There were some late developers, but the overall observation holds. The catchment area from which most of the students came was a challenged one. This served to reinforce what was generated *ab initio*.

Even though many principals and teachers were well trained and in many cases were better equipped than some who taught in the so-called prestige schools, the climate and "tone" that prevailed in the comprehensive schools did not encourage them to give of their best. Discipline was often a problem, and many children were virtually left to their own devices. Student toughs and at times their parents often intimidated young teachers, who deemed it more prudent to evade rather than engage students.

Problems were also encountered in finding persons to teach parts of the new curriculum, especially the vocational subjects. In some cases equipment was available but not the teacher. In other cases, neither was available. Many students also continued to prefer grammar-type subjects in the hope of finding white-collar or clerical jobs on graduation. Williams had abandoned the UNESCO-advised strategy of building separate vocational schools because he feared they would be viewed as second-class institutions. Putting both in the same institution, he felt, would avoid such polarization. As Alleyne observed, "Measures were needed to equalize prestige between academic and technical subjects, and that could not be achieved by maintaining separate institutions for the two areas of education" (1996, 99–100). The irony was that the single institution failed to bridge the gap inherited from colonialism and the class system and the vocational aspirations that it nurtured.

Alleyne's conclusions were reinforced by a study undertaken by Rose Osuji, the main findings of which were summarized in "The Academic Achievement of Schools: An Empirical Study" (1995). The study showed that student intake based on results of the Common Entrance Examination and not the administrative styles of principals, teacher behaviour, or student behaviour differentiated a good school, that is, the assisted school, from a poor school, the junior and senior comprehensive school. Type of school attended determined success or failure in public examinations.

- In assisted denominational schools, all the students performed well regardless of social class, race, age and sex characteristics of students, while in Senior Comprehensive Schools, all the students performed poorly. In Government Schools, all students performed moderately.

- Lower class students in assisted schools performed better than middle class students in Government Schools and upper and middle class students in Senior Comprehensive Schools.

- The school was a mirror of the society. The society is stratified along social class, religious, racial and sex lines and these differences are reflected in the presence of different types of school in the society and the ideology they uphold.

- Students from upper and middle social class homes go to good primary schools, assisted denominational schools and perform well. Conversely, students from lower social class homes go to Senior Comprehensive Schools and perform poorly.

- Poor performance in the Senior Comprehensive School is mainly due to the fact that the bottom 20 percent of those who take the Common Entrance Examination are segregated in one type of school.

- Changes in the system will not solve the problem of inequality of access and educational outcome unless the selection mechanism is changed. Otherwise, it is like "digging a hold to fill a hole." In sum, the Concordat is the problem. (Osuji 1995)

Williams was not unaware that there were major problems to be dealt with at the primary school level, where, in his view, the problems began – but choices had to be made. The fact that he chose to give priority to the secondary school reflected his awareness of the critical role that secondary school education played in the social life of colonial societies. It was probably also an emotional reaction to his own experiences as a youngster struggling to win a college exhibition and the coveted Island Scholarship that provided him with the wherewithal to go on to university. While there were deficiencies at both the primary and secondary levels of education, the latter was given priority. By 1975, Williams felt that the time had come to shift the emphasis:

> First priority was given to the secondary school, and secondary education was declared free in 1960. As there were only two Government secondary schools then in existence together with about one dozen denominational schools, mostly Catholic, the first emphasis necessarily had to be placed on the construction of secondary schools and the introduction of the much maligned Common Entrance Examination to provide at least a more objective test of eligibility on grounds of merit rather than on grounds of colour, or race, or parental influence, or religious affiliation. With the diversification of the secondary system now in full swing to include the junior secondary school and the vocational school as well as the comprehensive school, attention is now being given on a fundamental scale . . . to the primary school as the most urgent educational priority in Trinidad and Tobago, repeatedly indicated over the past year by parental protest and demonstrations. (1975b, 11)

There is little evidence, however, that Williams paid a great deal of attention to the needs of the primary school, except to point out that 141 of the 471 were in need of urgent major repairs.

The educational plan assumed that 35 to 40 per cent of the junior secondary school population would go on to senior-level secondary education following a fourteen-plus examination. By the end of the plan period, 63.8 per cent were being provided places. Note too that 85 per cent of the students leaving primary school at age eleven plus were entering secondary school of some type. Much had also been done to provide a new curriculum, and to equip the schools with labs, libraries, computers and other audio-visual equipment. Teachers were also trained to deal with the new elements pouring into the schools that were built, and which were being maintained at great cost.

Despite all of this, the failure rate was as high as 83 per cent in the specialized craft examinations of the National Examinations Council. Performance was also poor in exams administered by the Caribbean Examinations Council. Many professionals claimed the various syllabi were beyond the capacity of most of the students, and that the flaw in the model was to have paid insufficient attention to the primary school, where the deficits were first incurred and accumulated.

Judging by what Williams sought to achieve in the area of education, one would have to conclude that the revolution was a heroic failure, the increase in the number of students attending secondary schools notwithstanding. Many of the schools were little more than warehouses (one education minister even referred to them as "cesspits") that kept underclass youth off the streets, albeit in two shifts. The reasons for failure, as we have seen, were several, but in the final analysis, failure was due to disarticulation among school, home and community, which was most pronounced in the mega junior and senior secondary schools.

For all kinds of reasons, there was a near total breakdown in the homes from which many of the students who attended the junior and senior secondary schools came. In most cases, the students would have been the first members of the family attending secondary schools and their parents or parent surrogates would have been unaware of what was required for success. Students invariably had to compete with the television and the stereo, and would not have been able to enjoy the peace and quiet needed for doing homework, or for reading and study. Some parents and guardians were known to complain that too much "current" (electricity) was being consumed, or that books were too expensive. There were also too few role models, guidance officers and parent–teacher associations available to the students. Then too many parents were young and single and trying to make ends meet. Some were competing with their offspring to be on the party scene. Many were absentees from the home.

The government sought to deal with the problem by ploughing more hardware into the schools when in fact the critical absent resource was the social and cultural capital that could come only from the home and the community. The successes that were achieved in the denominational schools were largely the result of the environment that surrounded students in their homes and their communities. This relationship among home, community, school and performance is supported by studies done in the United States by James Coleman (1988) and others, which indicate that student learning is influenced not only by what happens in school, but also by what happens in the wider home and the community. Coleman's research in Chicago indicated that dropout rates were lower in Catholic and other religious-based high schools than in public high schools, where rates were three times higher. Coleman hypothesized that success in denominational schools was due less to the particular skills of the students than to the environment of the school and the relationship of parents to the school – relationships that are fostered by church membership. As Coleman opined, "We cannot understate the importance of the embeddedness of young persons in the enclaves of adults most proximate to them, first and most prominently the family and second, a surrounding community of adults (exemplified in all these results by the religious community)" (as cited in Putnam 1995, 65).

Several questions need to be asked and answered. Did Williams and the politicians sacrifice quality and excellence on the altar of equality, political expedience and ethnic diversity? Did they deliberately refuse to heed the advice of their professional advisers, both foreign and local, and instead pay more attention to concerns about political survival? Were the programmes implemented on too ambitious a scale and in too compressed a time frame? Were they sustainable? Did the successes in terms of quantity compensate for the failure in terms of quality? Were the failures inevitable given the fact that most of the students who went to the state schools did not bring to the classroom the language, the academic and social skills, the learning styles, the discipline, the teaching styles, the behaviour patterns and the parental support that were traditionally associated with secondary schools in the Caribbean? Did Williams fail the students, or did the students and their parents fail him? In attempting to provide universal free secondary education, did he attempt to do too much too quickly, given all the other things that he sought to do in the economy? My own conclusion is that Williams was ambitious and eager for change, but that the problems were bigger than he was and would have required more human resources than he had at his disposal. Politics and election timetables determined much of what he did.

Dodderidge Alleyne, Williams's permanent secretary, tells the story of how the prime minister came to declare that secondary education should be free. It was done partly to pre-empt the opposition from stealing his thunder. Opposition member of parliament Ashford Sinanan had "committed the error" of saying that it should be introduced forthwith. The minister of education, Patrick Solomon, replied that the government was thinking of it but could not do it now. Williams was not to be upstaged. What followed is as told by Alleyne at the 1991 symposium "Eric Williams in Retrospect":

> Dr. Williams was having a meeting with Pat Rawlins and Scotty Lewis [two of his top public sector aides]. They had torn up his draft Budget Speech, and they had recast it. . . . And then he asked them a very important question, "What do we now tell the people?" So they said, but you have the Budget Speech. He said "No." "What do I tell the people?" And somebody, I think it was Pat, said, "Well, what about free secondary education"? And he slapped his thigh! At the same time, John Donaldson, [Parliamentary Secretary in the Ministry of Education] entered the door, and he [Williams] said, "John, John, come, come, come, we have just decided to have free secondary education."
>
> There was no preparation for the training of teachers. But you see there are some things in history which if they are not done when they are done, are not done at all. So they started building schools. He was turning sod every week or so, and Dr. Williams and Mr. Romain for whom QRC was the alumni, set about to remove all the good

teachers from Queen's Royal College in order to fill these other schools. It was a good thing, although the period when this was being done was very difficult for teachers and for students.

Tranquility, for example, where it was insisted upon that there should be twelve hundred, sixteen hundred, eighteen hundred children. The Principal hid himself in his office, locked in, and when they said, but we can't take any more, they said call Education. Education called the Prime Minister. He said, "You have to take them." And when the Principal asked, "but where do we put them?", he said, "Put them in the corridor, put them anywhere, but don't trouble me." But we got over that period and we now produce more "A" level students than any other country in the Caribbean, some would say more than all of them put together.

Williams and the University of the West Indies

Williams felt strongly that the University of the West Indies should be the centre of Caribbean cultural and political development and should therefore not be apprenticed to a British university. He thus fought to have the University of the West Indies become independent of London University, which occurred in 1962. Williams noted that the university's operational expenses were funded entirely by the governments of the region.

Williams was disappointed with the University of the West Indies and its academic community, to which he was in the main a stranger. He was unhappy with the university for many reasons. In his view, the University was still operating on a "philosophy imposed by a British Commission a quarter of a century ago anticipating large numbers of expatriate staff in the colonial university" (1974b, 13). Its staff–student ratio imitated British universities; its teaching loads of twelve hours per week were also too low. "A contributing government would collapse if that was the responsibility of its senior civil servants." Staff perquisites that had been negotiated when the staff was mainly expatriate – allowances for housing, children, return travel and so on – also came in for criticism.

Williams also charged that the university was too "elitist" and "Mona [Jamaica] centred", and that the appointments system was a "racket which is now becoming the vehicle for rewarding the friends and punishing the enemies of heads who are in no small minority of cases inveterate opponents of the PNM, having for the most part achieved their prominence by nepotism and as a result of discrimination". These were serious charges which upset the university management in general and the principal, Sir Arthur Lewis, who was an old friend (Tignor 2006, 218).

Williams bemoaned the fact that Caribbean scholars at the university had not developed a genuine programme of Caribbean studies: "The sad fact is that, with the unprecedented attention paid to the Caribbean area in the past 15 years, most of the work has come from outside sources, principally the United States and

Britain" (Williams 1974b, 24). Williams felt that not enough work had been done on the minority races of the Caribbean. "The Caribbean universities in the year 2000 would be merely items in the budgets of the next quarter of a century, mere excrescences on the body of universities in affluent countries, unless they take as the goal consciously and deliberately, the production of citizens of an area which is *sui generis*." Williams felt that the basis for such a multilingual programme already existed. He singled out the works of Lamming, Naipaul, Selvon, Salkey Mittelholzer, McKay and C.L.R. James "with his superlative book on cricket". In the non-anglophone Caribbean, he singled out the Martiniquan Aimé Césaire whose works in the fields of history and politics "constitute him one of the greatest literary figures that the Caribbean has ever produced" (ibid., 25). Nicolás Guillén and Fernando Ortiz of Cuba, Jean Price Mars and Jaques Romain of Haiti, and Luis Palés Matos of Puerto Rico also came in for honourable mention. Williams felt that the programme should emphasize, among other aspects, the questions of race, gender, religion, leisure and economics that all students would be required to study as part of their university programme. Whatever their specialization, Williams did not seem to agree with the view of Che Guevara that "there was no purpose to black people studying African history", and that instead, "they need to study Marxist-Leninism" (ibid., 28). One needed to broaden the canon without going to the parochial extremes that seemed to have befallen "black studies" in the United States or the Caribbean, which deemed Shakespeare, the piano and the violin irrelevant. Caribbean universities had a critical role to play in making an enduring contribution to university education the world over. Doing so would require a dialogue between Caribbean universities.

Dissent within the University

One of the critical issues with which Williams had to deal as both a scholar and a politician was freedom of dissent within the academy. Williams observed that academic "involvement" invariably involved a "direct incursion into politics". As a scholar, he knew that this was a feature of university life the world over, and that the Caribbean was not exempt. As he repined, "At the University of the West Indies, political parties have emerged on the campus in open opposition to governments, and faculty members are involved in the organization of trade unions in which they hold office." In the address that he gave on the subject Williams noted that "Caribbean governments had begun to challenge this conception of academic freedom", and that some wanted the Faculty of Social Sciences closed down because they believed that academics were abusing their freedom: As a product himself of a social science faculty, he, however, felt compelled to oppose these proposals. "I could not agree to the throwing out of the baby with the bath water" (1974b, 21).

Williams likewise noted that on grounds of national security, and of their obligations to other states, Caribbean governments had used the device of work permits to debar non-nationals from teaching on campuses in their territories. Jamaica had done so, as had Barbados and Trinidad and Tobago. Williams's intellectual training and instincts as an academic might well have set him apart from Burnham, Barrow, Shearer and Gairy, but his political instincts were much the same as theirs, especially after 1970.

Williams also drew attention to the phenomenon of student dissent on the campus, which had become widespread the world over in the years after 1964 as students sought to change the world, and which recalled the tendency of the Caribbean to imitate whatever was happening in metropolitan countries. He speculated that the unrest would increase, "possibly as the wave receded in metropolitan countries" (ibid., 24). Williams was not opposed to student activism, particularly in matters that affected the management of the university, the delivery of academic programmes, and the content of those programmes as well as community programmes, "subject always to their effect on performance of their primary responsibility which is to study" (ibid., 23).

Williams enunciated his views and intended policies for reshaping UWI in the *White Paper on the National Institute of Higher Education, Research, Science, and Technology*, published in 1977. He was of the view that Trinidad and Tobago in the mid-1970s was involved in a fundamental mini-industrial revolution, and that its educational system had to reflect this shift. One needed to pay more attention to scientific research and technology. The white paper also expressed concern with the complicated and cumbersome process that obtained when new programmes or policies had to be put into effect. Fourteen governments had to be consulted, and horse-trading replaced rationality. Delay was institutionalized. This structure had to be changed drastically to allow for fundamental decentralization. There was also concern about "Mona hegemony", and the white paper's proposal was that any government should be free to establish and fund a national programme without having to seek approval of central university authorities. The latter could advise but not determine. The university's central administration would also retain responsibility for regional programmes and for making appointments above the rank of senior lecturer. The white paper went on to say that local governments should finance all the campus activities in their countries and recover monies from other governments who send students to the particular campus. It also proposed that terms and conditions of service for staff should be a campus responsibility.

This clearly represented a radical break with the idea of a decentralized unitary university to which governments had committed themselves in the past – at least up to 1981 – and it was hardly surprising that the proposals were resisted by those who felt that they would in effect lead to parochialism and to the premature dismantling of the University of the West Indies as a regional institution. It was felt that the proposal would, among other things,

1. have serious consequences for non-campus territories;
2. lead to excessive and expensive duplication of facilities; and that
3. state pressures would make it difficult, if not impossible to maintain uniform standards in matters such as entry requirements, promotions and appointments; and
4. academic quality would decline to the detriment of the reputation of the university and its graduates abroad. (See review of the White Paper in *Caribbean Studies* 7, nos. 3–4 [1978]: 183ff.)

The feeling was that these centrifugal pressures would lead to the balkanization of the university.

Those who considered it important to retain the regional framework of the university readily conceded that modification of the centralized decision-making structure was necessary to make the university more flexible and responsive to the different ideological and political realities of the various states, but they felt that the white paper went too far in the direction of creating what were in fact three separate universities, all flying the faded flag of the University of the West Indies. The fear was that sooner than later, the flag of the university would be hauled down by some state, and that "one from ten" would again "equal nought".

The white paper had a different view of regionalism. It believed that concessions had been made to the idea of a regional university, and that if its proposals were not more or less accepted, and soon, a "complete breakaway of one or other units is inevitable as occurred in the case of Guyana". To quote the white paper, "A Caribbean staff plus the admission of students from all islands would in the final analysis do more to preserve the regional character of the University than structural devices."

Williams was clearly frustrated with what he considered to be the lack of sensitivity on the part of the university's officialdom to Trinidad's concerns, and went as far as rejecting their invitation to him to assume the post of chancellor, lest accepting such a post tied his hands when the time came for going it alone. As he told the country in a broadcast,

> The Minister of Education and Culture has at meeting after meeting sought to emphasize the importance that we as representatives of the Trinidad and Tobago taxpayer attach to the question of indiscriminate expansion without reference to conditions here or without taking into account the priorities we have established. I understand the pressures to which he has been exposed; I have been a part of them too to the extent that when a few weeks ago pressure was brought to bear on me as the Prime Minister to accept the post as Chancellor of the University of the West Indies, I declined. I asked them not to put forward my name, so that in carrying out my duties as Prime

Minister to the taxpayers of the country, I would not in any way be upset emotionally or otherwise by my obligation as Chancellor of the University. It is about time that the Trinidad and Tobago taxpayer be given full account. We have raised this with all of them. We have got nowhere and we are going to do it ourselves. (1975a, 8)

While accepting the need to decentralize the university, many were anxious about the question of its integrity and autonomy. A university must be sensitive to the ideological milieu in which it functions and must be responsive to the needs of the society as defined by those elected by the people. But a university is one of the great estates of the realm, and if it is to be true to its purpose, it cannot be subservient to the state. It is one of the trustees of the people, and a measure of autonomy and political insulation is necessary if it is to fulfil its traditional mission. Those who wished to destroy the freedom of the people first destroy the freedom of the university. That is one of the clearest lessons of modern history. The university is a political resource, and whether one liked it or not, it of necessity has to be in politics. As Williams himself once noted,

[I]t is cliché in some quarters to say the university should be left out of politics, and that in the struggle of modern society, the university should remain as aloof as one of Thomas Hardy's dynasts, holding aloft the torch of learning and maintaining a benevolent neutrality. This conception is quite erroneous. Modern politics, like modern war, is total. Neutrality is untenable. The university is the centre of a perpetual conflict between what it frequently considers, in all sincerity, the needs of education and the pressure of the powerful economic and political groups.

All criticism notwithstanding, the concern then was not with what would happen to the university under the ministry of Williams, who was too steeped in the university tradition to vandalize the campus for narrow political ends. There was always the belief that Williams would not want to go down in history as the man who broke up a university about which he had written so much. He did not disappoint.

37 The Hero as a "Man of Culture"

Williams admired "men of culture", leaders who combined in their heroic essences the roles of king, prophet, poet, priest and man of letters, men such as José Martí, Léopold Senghor and Aimé Césaire. Césaire, whom he considered to be "one of the greatest literary figures that the Caribbean has ever produced", together with Senghor and Léon Damas, were seen as the principal exponents of the concept of *négritude*. Williams was, however, sceptical about the concept of *négritude* and Nkrumah's alternative term, the "African personality", and wondered aloud as to how they would survive the impact of Western technology. Was it not likely that the " 'African robe' would become caught in the machinery of the Western factory?" (EWMC folio 793). Williams understood and agreed with Césaire's view that one could not separate culture and politics, and that "culture should enrich politics as politics enriches culture" (*Trinidad Guardian*, 12 October 1971). He also firmly believed that "in the nationalist struggle, the man of culture had an important role, and that the political leader could only succeed by enlisting culture in the struggle and placing it in the vanguard of the nationalist movement" ("The Political Leader Considered as a Man of Culture", *Présence Africaine* 24–25).

Jawaharlal Nehru was also high on Williams's list of admired leaders, and he paid public tribute to him in 1964 on the occasion of the latter's seventy-fifth birthday. Nehru was described as "a national symbol, a philosopher of anticolonialism and a student of world history". He was also said to be one of the "great figures of our century and one of the greatest champions of freedom of all time" (in Sutton 1981, 233). What Williams admired most about Nehru was the latter's role in stimulating India's cultural "renaissance" and the fact that his concept of India was not that of the Hindu nationalists in the Maha Sabha and the RSS (Rashtra Swayamsevak Sangh), who were advocates of Hindutva. Nehru himself defined his vision in cosmopolitan and internationalist terms: "While we struggle for the freedom of India, we must remember that the great aim is human freedom which includes the freedom of our people as well as other peoples" (ibid., 233). Some would say that both Williams and Nehru misunderstood the reality of India, and appealed only to a restricted occicentric sector of India, which was even then splitting along its religious seams.

Williams also believed that West Indian cultural identity should not be defined in narrow ethnic or geographic terms, saying, "West Indian culture was neither African, Asian, nor European. It was *sui generis*. The West Indian as he has developed over the past four centuries is an African or Asian assimilated to the European." Williams told the Senegalese while on a visit to Dakar in 1964 that "West Indians did not struggle to become more African or Asian, but to become more fully incorporated into the 'European superstructure'". Unlike the African or Asian who still retained most of his ancient values, the West Indian was radically deracinated during slavery and colonialism. As such, his cultural struggle was driven by opposition to "Europe's rejection of him on grounds of colour, race or previous condition of servitude". Likewise, his political struggle sought to achieve "the parliamentary institutions and practices which were limited on purely racial grounds to white people" (ibid., 226).

The existential dilemma of the West Indian was that he had "no indigenous art, social structure, no philosophy of life, no sense of values" to set against the European. Whereas Senghor could talk about *négritude*, the West Indian could not. This vacuum, however, presented opportunities to create something that was uniquely Caribbean (not merely West Indian). Williams thus encouraged Caribbean university elites to develop a programme of Caribbean Studies, which he saw as "a prerequisite to the integration of the Caribbean area". Such a programme would involve, among other aspects, research and dissemination of works on Caribbean religions, Caribbean family structure, Caribbean race relations, and women's liberation. He was also keen that such a programme would involve studies of the societies from which the peoples of the Caribbean came, particularly early India and Africa. He observed, with regret, that the African still suffers from a sense of inferiority and does not want slavery recalled. "As far as I am aware, nothing has been done to study the impact of slavery and the slave trade on African society, meaning by that both the European slave trade and the Arab slave trade" (EWMC folio 793).

Williams showed a keen interest in the cultural renaissance, which had begun to manifest itself in Trinidad and Tobago in the 1950s. He established the Trinidad and Tobago Folklore Society in 1950, and together with other luminaries such as H.O.B. Wooding patronized Beryl McBurnie's Little Carib Dance Company and even wrote some of the company's programme liners. The coming to power of the

PNM in 1956 gave impetus and symbolic status to the folk movement, and Williams's lectures helped to fertilize a latent Caribbean consciousness, not only in Trinidad and Tobago, but elsewhere in the Caribbean. The PNM's victory marked the transition from one era to another. Colonial civilization had come to an end, even if only symbolically. The nation had new official faces. Whereas in the past "culture" was associated with that which was European, it was now redefined to privilege that which was Afro-creole. Williams concretized the change in the *zeitgeist* with his pithy statement that "Massa Day Done", a statement that referred not only to the political system, but to things cultural as well. As the calypsonian the Mighty Power put it in 1965, "Calypso and Steelband is the culture of Trinidad." J.D. Elder, whom Williams appointed director of culture, observed that "The outcome of the new definition of culture was a force transforming the society into a national community with an ideology in which culture was the driving power towards social, political and economic advance. What we are describing as practical material change represents the translation by Williams of the *négritude* and the indigenism which Diop, Césaire and Ortiz were writing about in other Diaspora societies and West Africa" (1996, 4–5).

Williams and the Carnival Development Committee

Following the victory of the PNM in 1956, demands were made that the white domination of pre-carnival shows should be broken. The organizational expression of this mood in the context of carnival was the Carnival Development Committee, which was established in 1957 to break the monopoly of the *Trinidad Guardian,* which sponsored the main carnival competitions. The man chosen to be chairman of the committee was the distinguished attorney Hugh Wooding, who had the historic responsibility to preside over the committee from 1957 to 1958.

The dispute that gave rise to the government's takeover of carnival was a boycott instituted by steelband leaders and calypsonians who protested against the disparity between the quantum of the prize money offered to the carnival queen and that offered to band leaders and calypsonians. Calypsonians demanded a 500 per cent increase in prize money, and bandleaders a 100 per cent increase. The manager of the *Guardian* Neediest Cases Fund, Harry Pitts, refused the request on the ground that the queen contest was the main revenue earner and that revenue from the queen show was used to subsidize the two-day parade. Further subsidies would defeat the purpose for which the contest was instituted. The prize money was eventually increased, but the bandleaders and calypsonians were not satisfied that the demands had been sufficiently met, and they threatened violence against anyone who broke the boycott or attended the queen contest.

It was in this context that Williams appointed Wooding to make recommendations for improving the carnival celebrations. Williams told parliament that the *Guardian* wished to abandon its sponsorship of the carnival parade and asked the government to take it over. Thus the creation of the Carnival Development Committee under Wooding's chairmanship as the organization that would run the competition on a more "national" basis. Williams appealed to the public not to use violence to keep people from attending the queen show. As he told them, "If you do not want to go, don't. But remember there are others with equal privileges who want to go."

Carnival is rarely without confusion, and Wooding and the committee resigned on 20 December 1958. The issue that prompted their resignation was the *Guardian*'s decision to abandon the competition because the government raised objections to some of the things that they were accused of condoning. Feeling that the absence of a queen show in the 1958 carnival had created a void, the Junior Chamber of Commerce decided that it would take up where the *Guardian* left off, a decision that Wooding and the Carnival Development Committee accepted. But Williams was opposed to the Junior Chamber of Commerce–Carnival Development Committee *entente*. The parties met with Patrick Solomon, minister of education and culture, in an effort to resolve the crisis, but the government remained adamant that the show had to reflect the new consciousness stimulated by the coming to power of the PNM in 1956. Solomon was of the view that Wooding himself was too preoccupied with the city-based queen show and not sufficiently with developing carnival in the peripheral towns of the country.

Wooding felt that the intervention of the central government left the committee powerless in the framing of policy relating to carnival because decisions were being taken behind its back. The committee resigned in the midst of preparations for the 1959 carnival season. Williams was enraged and abused Wooding in parliament during a budget debate of 31 December 1958:

> The issue to be decided is: who governs Trinidad? We say it is the Government of Trinidad and Tobago responsible to the Legislative Council, and through the Legislative Council, to the people of Trinidad and Tobago. And those who do not like it could walk out and resign in a body. That was exactly what happened to the Carnival Committee. The Government is going to determine the policy. There is going to be no mistake about that. No body knows better than the Chairman of the Carnival Committee who has resigned, the disgraceful amount of racial discrimination that dominated those Carnival celebrations. It was he who told me about his wife being a judge one year when a dark skinned girl won the prize and was told by a foreign consul who had given the first prize, that if she got that prize, I withdraw the trip for two to my country. I was told that, and we said: no racial discrimination in this Carnival. They will all get out and go. There is going to be no compromise on this issue, and where the Government is responsible, especially through the Ministry of Finance for the proper control of public funds,

everybody is going to be controlled, or otherwise he goes out, and I am responsible to the Legislative Council of Trinidad and Tobago.

Wooding was highly offended by this breach of confidentiality. The *Guardian* called Williams a "Sawdust Caesar", and branded his statement a "downright lie". To quote the *Guardian*,

> We do not know where the lie originated. People who repeat lies may not be the authors of them, but that does not make the lies any less reprehensible. We state categorically than no consul has ever offered a prize trip for a Carnival Queen. To use this alleged consular aberration as an excuse for condemning the Carnival queen competition is irresponsible, petty and foolish. Dr. Williams is fanning the very flames of racialism which he is so anxious to extinguish. (Cited in Ryan 1990, 118)

In terms of other specifics, Williams brought to a conclusion the efforts made by Albert Gomes in 1951 in respect of the Shouters Prohibition Act of 1917, which made the Shouter Baptist religion illegal in Trinidad and Tobago. The Shouter Baptists thereafter remained loyal to Williams and the PNM. Following an exhausting "Meet the People Tour" in 1965, Williams established the Prime Minister's Best Village Trophy Competition, which encouraged far-flung villages and semi-urban communities to compete to produce and exhibit cultural offerings in dance, theatre, craft and indigenous culinary items. The Best Village programme stimulated cultural awareness in the villages and served to unearth the talent that existed in these communities and that hitherto had had no avenues for expression or display. Joyce Wong Sang, who served as co-ordinator of the programme from 1963 to 1986, firmly believes that Best Village rescued Trinidad and Tobago's folk culture from extinction, and that much of what is celebrated today as indigenous culture was fertilized by that competition:

> Calypso was given a big push, drummology (African and Indian) became acceptable; dances such as the bélé and pique, bongo, shango and castillian were given a new lease on life, and village drama brought out the latent talent waiting to be exposed. Local foods, reflecting the rich ethnic diversity of the land, gained a much-needed respectability and the creativity generated by the competition was soon reflected in the national carnival costumes and other portrayals which became exportable items. Village Olympics, environmental awareness and opportunities for employment were additional spin-offs from Best Village. At the end of the day, one can safely conclude that the Prime Minister's Best Village competition breathed new life into a culture which was stagnating and drifting without direction. It energized the national community in general but was particularly influential in renewing our rural communities. Best Village spawned a whole generation of social and cultural creativity, the effects of which are very present in the national community. (1999, 17–18)

Wong Sang also claims that the village movement helped to encourage the formation of several community based steelbands and parang and tassa drum ensembles. In her view, "It is high time that Williams receives the recognition that is due him for having the foresight to institute such a programme which may have been the only one of its kind in the world" (ibid., 30). Williams was also known to have collected money from the private sector to assist steelbandmen and Hindu groups who used the harmonium.

The Best Village programme, however, had several major weaknesses. One was that it encouraged competition and village rivalry rather than cooperation between and among communities. Conflicts over state funding were inevitable. The programme also became associated with the prime minister. It was in fact called the Prime Minister's Best Village Programme and was headquartered in the prime minister's office at Whitehall. One unanticipated by-product of this was the alienation of the Indian community from the programme and the latter's decision to create its own competition, Mastana Bahar, promoted by the East Indian Cultural Association and largely funded by the Indian private sector. Given the weakness of the African private sector, the Best Village Programme and the activities of the black cultural groups were funded largely by the state, which often lacked the resources needed to sustain them.

Insufficient money for research and group sponsorship were not the only problems. The political will to advance the cultural movement also seemed to be missing. No wonder J.D. Elder would complain that "the Ministry of Culture was headed by a number of cultural illiterates from the Minister down to every member of staff" (1996, 10). By 1970, the Better Village Programme (as the Best Village Programme was renamed) was virtually dead. Black artists and the black middle class steered clear of the movement, which was widely seen as an extension of PNM political mobilization at the village level. The wider population also considered it as not worthy of their patronage and were irritated by the fact that it dominated the state-owned television. Villagers, however, many of whom were seeing themselves on television for the first time, appreciated the coverage.

Young urban blacks were profoundly disappointed by what they considered to be the failure of Williams and the PNM to deliver on the promises made in the 1950s and 1960s. Blacks felt that the political kingdom had been won but that the shadow of the plantation was still present everywhere. Inspired by Frantz Fanon's treatise *Black Skin, White Masks*, and by what radical blacks in the United States and elsewhere were saying and doing, alienated blacks began demanding "black power", and the use of more Afrocentric cultural symbols. Jackets and ties and artificially straightened hair gave way to Afro coiffure and dress (dashikis) as blacks sought to "find their identity" in their African heritage.

Williams himself genuflected to the new mood. He exchanged his tie for a cravat, and in response to accusations that local culture had been neglected, made it a point to visit steelband yards and calypso tents to hear first hand what radicalized calypsonians were saying about him and his regime. It was all a political game, however, or so many believed, especially when the state went on to stage concerts headlined by the likes of Mahalia Jackson, whom many regarded as a diva par excellence.

Geddes Granger, a.k.a. Makandal Dagga, who emerged as one of the major figures in the 1970 Black Power revolution, was among those who were disappointed that Williams had not turned out to be the "man of culture" that he had led many to believe he would become. Granger, like many young blacks, was disillusioned and deflated by the aftermath of independence. He felt that independence had meant little more than a big empty party on the Queen's Park Savannah, following which Williams had sent the population to church and home to meditate and pray. Little recognition was being given to the culture of the folk, the fine arts or the nation's culture heroes. To fill this vacuum, Granger and his colleague Roy Mitchell founded Pegasus, a movement whose inspiration and aim was to give greater depth and meaning to the independence that had recently been achieved.

To this end, Pegasus organized several high-profile national activities, among which was a ceremony to present national awards to the country's outstanding artists and national heroes. It was the first such national award function. Pegasus also mobilized human and material resources to construct a National Stadium, as well as a National Arts Centre on the grounds of the Princess Building, and to plan to redesign and reconstruct the city of Port of Spain. Also planned was an elaborate "Project Independence". According to Mitchell, this "was the medium through which all the talented forces in the country were to be brought together to put in place a plan to convert the 'Unity of Spirit' which we had been developing over the years into a new dynamic unity of purpose".

Plans were well afoot to launch the various projects when Williams, fearing that he was being upstaged, struck back. As Mitchell recalled,

> The project was to be launched at the Public Library by the President of the Senate, Mr. J. Hamilton Maurice. The build-up in the media and throughout the citizenry was great. Our membership, now spread all over the country, was keen; the launching was to take place at 6.00 p.m. when, low [*sic*] and behold, microphones appeared throughout the city announcing the staging of a PNM meeting at no less a place than Woodford Square, to commence at about the same time as out proposed launching. Geddes swore to me that he would bring Williams to his knees for this. I could understand why. I too felt the same way, especially when we looked at the faces of our membership. Tears flowed from their eyes, and a now enraged Granger was transformed into a revolutionary politician. (Ryan and Stewart 1995, 109)

In Mitchell's mind, 1970 was a postponement of what had been expected in 1956.

In the wake of the events of 1970, Williams decided to create a new body, the National Cultural Council. In the Speech from the Throne in June 1971, the

PNM government declared that "the country was opening up a whole new vista, the important role envisaged for culture in the development of the nation". Williams insisted, however, that culture must exclude no one; it is a force for the uniting of peoples and the creation of a nation. Williams conceded that little had so far been achieved to enhance understanding of the relationship of culture to the development process, and that what little had been done was ethnically polarized. The expectation was that the NCC would function as a cultural brains trust, which would harness the skills and ideas of the nation's artistic elite. It was expected to conduct research, organize cultural productions, encourage young artists and performers and raise funds from private sources to undertake these and other related activities.

The one-hundred-man-strong NCC proved to be a dismal failure. Its major weakness was that it was a purely advisory and cumbersome body that lacked staff, funding and autonomy. The repressive environment that prevailed in the country was also not conducive to a partnership between the cultural elite and the state. In 1979, the NCC was replaced by a National Foundation for Art and Culture. This too failed to get off the ground during Williams's lifetime, even though money was no longer the problem. Greed replaced culture as the main object of concern.

Williams was savagely criticized by calypsonians, steelbandmen, and supporters of the two art forms for not doing enough to promote their professional activities. The complaints ranged from lack of adequate financial support, to unwillingness to ensure that meaningful and sustained exposure was given to calypso and steelband music on the state-owned media, to not doing enough to ensure that steelband instruments were patented and manufactured in Trinidad and Tobago. George Goddard, president of the National Association of Trinidad and Tobago Steelbandmen, was a consistent critic of Williams for his failure or reluctance to employ pan tuners, construct rehearsal centres, promote the formation of cooperatives, organize summer tours to the United States, or appoint steelbandmen as attachés. Williams pointedly refused ace pan tuner Bertie Marshall's recommendation that the government should invest serious money in the steelband movement. As Williams asked Marshall, "What, you want me to take the people's money and put it in pan?" (*The Bertie Marshall Story*, 24 September 2003; see Keith Smith, *Trinidad Express*, 1 October 2004).

Goddard was openly critical of Williams, but most steelbandmen remained loyal or ambivalent towards the PNM political leader. In response to one of his critical comments made in 1971, Goddard received what he called "a grand response" signed by forty-five steelbandmen. The response, which took the form of a paid advertisement thanking Williams, appeared in the *Sunday Guardian* on 28 February 1971 and read as follows:

> We the members of the following steelbands (sponsored and unsponsored), together with the bandleaders, wish to express our sincerest appreciation and gratitude to our dear Prime Minister, Dr. The Rt. Honourable Eric Williams, who visited our panyard and Mas camps. We cannot find words to truly express what your visits have done for the betterment of the Steelband Movement and the masquerading public, but undoubtedly the interest which you have shown, and continue to show in respect of locating sites, obtaining sponsors, equipping steelbands . . . with instruments . . . has left us all with a feeling, full of hope and inspiration, for the steelbandsman and his music and also the masquerader. We look forward to the continuation of these visits to those bands which you were unable to meet in the short time before Carnival.

Goddard was rebuffed and knew it. As he reflected,

> The list of names of persons who signed the joint statement was indeed impressive with well known names associated with nearly all the major steelbands, perhaps with one or two exceptions. I must say it was a strong message. Who was I to fly in the face of what had to be considered a major view in the steelband movement? Disagree I could with their statement but I could not ignore the force to the significance of 45 signatures of authentic leaders, many of them democratically elected to their positions, as I had been to the presidency of the Association. (1991, 202)

Williams was not above using PNM-affiliated steelbands as political muscle against anti-PNM movements as they emerged, especially during trade union conflicts. Following Williams's death, Goddard had the following to say:

> While it would be true to say that Dr. Williams as Prime Minister of Trinidad and Tobago did not do for panmen half as much as he could or should have done, (and this could have been partly due to the attitude of a great number of panmen), he, in my opinion, still made some contribution under the circumstances which existed for which the steelband movement should have made some tribute as a show of appreciation, and as the old people would say, "be thankful for the little mercies extended by the 'Great One'." (*Trinidad Express*, 28 April 1981)

Goddard was clearly damning Williams with faint praise. Aubrey Adams, who had also been deeply involved in the culture movement as performer, event organizer, and adviser to the government, was equally ambivalent: "The status of the panmen rose considerably and it is no secret that many of the considerations and benefits which they enjoyed through Governmental agencies came about because of the keen personal interest which he himself took in the welfare of the steelband movement. Now, this cannot be truly said of all the [other] art forms" (ibid.). Adams was clearly reflecting the deep disenchantment of the art-loving community that very little, if anything, had been done to encourage or promote national theatre, dance groups or the visual artists, all of whom were flourishing in spite of rather than because of him. Nothing concrete was done to construct the much-talked about performing arts centre where events could be staged or by funding groups involved in creative activity. Petro-dollars could seemingly be found for everything, but not a "petro penny" was being devoted to the arts. As J.D. Elder complained, "While money was being given away to other Caribbean states, the NCC went without qualified staff, adequate equipment, and no audience with Whitehall to insist that the NCC be empowered to do more than advise. The result was disgust and frustration" (1996, 18). Some found it puzzling that Williams the scholar would spend TT$200 million to build a racing track but refuse to allocate TT$10 million to build a national archive.

Williams, however, had a special and close relationship with Rudolph Charles, the cultural hero–cum-leader of Desperados, one of the country's best known steelbands. Williams's political secretary, Dianne Dupres, believes that Williams admired Charles and appreciated his achievements as a pan man and community leader. "He lived vicariously through Rudolph. I think they saw themselves as father figures. Rudolph stood up to him and teased him. He used to say, "I ruling the hill and he ruling down town." Dupres also believes that Charles "brought that freshness to Dr Williams's workday. He took his mind off the cares of the political [world]. So he would take in the Desperadoes panyard too."

Charles believes that it was Williams who made the steelband the success it eventually became. "That's a great man," he said of Williams. "Pan's where it is because of him. But you know our people. Instead of propping him up, they try to bring him down. We don't like anybody to know how great they are."

Williams's endorsement of Desperadoes was said to be the trigger that led corporate Trinidad to support the movement. As Anthony McQuilken, a member of Desperadoes and treasurer of Pan Trinbago, the organization that speaks officially for the steelband movement, recalled, "the big shots came on board because of the band's relationship with the 'Doc'. Leaders before him didn't come to these areas before" (*Trinidad Guardian*, 13 July 2008). The relationship with Charles and "Despers" had important political pay-offs for Williams and the PNM. It assisted greatly in making Laventille the PNM political fortress par excellence: Laventille voted PNM and in return was on the receiving end of PNM patronage. The relationship did not serve Laventille well in the long run, however. Its loyalty was always taken for granted and in return for that loyalty, it received the proverbial crumbs from the rich man's table. (See chapter 34.)

Our firm conclusion is that despite all the promise that was held out in the 1950s, and notwithstanding whatever was achieved in Best Village and the steelband movement, Williams was a failure as a heroic culture-maker. Perhaps he was a "half-hero" in this regard. He was neither an icon in the area of folk culture nor one in the area of the fine arts, the exponents of which deserted him as he had deserted them. The scramble for money and political power, and the effort to build mega structures took precedence over the struggle for cultural excellence and relevance.

38   Small Country in a Big World

In discussing his role in shaping the foreign policy of Trinidad and Tobago, Trinidad's first ambassador to the United Nations and the United States of America, Sir Ellis Clarke, had the following to say:

> A very busy Prime Minister had little time for the Ministry of External Affairs, and the development and elaboration of policy was not entrusted to it. The approach was empirical, and what the policy was, came to be deduced from what was in fact done or said in any given circumstance. Although it may have seemed that extraordinary latitude was accorded to the Permanent Representative in the declaration and application of foreign policy, yet I was so thoroughly attuned to the thinking of the Prime Minister that express communication on a specific topic was hardly ever necessary. (Collymore 2000, 66)

The experience of Trinidad and Tobago in the international arena during its first decade of independence highlights some of the ambiguities of the concept of the "Third World". Even before independence was achieved, there was a widespread expectation that Trinidad and Tobago, with a population consisting mainly of peoples of African and Asian descent, would take its place as an active member of the African-Asian group that was beginning to emerge as a significant factor in international politics. Inspired by Williams, there was a great deal of talk in nationalist circles about the "world of Bandung", a city in Indonesia where an important conference of twenty-one nations of the non-aligned African-Asian group met in 1955. Many Trinidadians followed the anti-imperialist crusades of Nehru, Nkrumah, Nasser and Sukarno with relish and approbation. Their victories were seen to be those of the dispossessed peoples of Trinidad and Tobago, who were themselves involved in an anti-colonial struggle. But though there were many factors that led Trinidadians to identify with the African-Asian bloc, history, geography and economic imperatives linked them to the West. Indeed, the cultural ties with Africa counted for a great deal less than those acquired from Europe and the United States.

Williams and the United States

For Williams, having little Trinidad and Tobago take its place on the world stage was immensely important psychologically. The struggle for Chaguaramas was a significant part of the national struggle. As he said during a speech at Arima in 1959,

> [O]ur little people in Arima and Trinidad will not figure too largely in any history of the world about the middle of the 20th century. They may have a little passage for us, but if we do figure, if we do find ourselves being analyzed by one of the sympathetic analysts of the problems of the world in the middle of the 20th century, let us understand ladies and gentleman, that what we in the PNM have tried to do and succeeded in doing, is to guarantee an enduring place in the history of the Western world in the middle of the 20th century, and that in doing that, we have become the standard bearers in the world, especially in this part of the world, of the principle of nationalism, of the principle of self-determination, of the principle of the emergence of people formerly submerged under colonialism.

Trinidad's struggle was Williams's struggle, his way of making his mark on Caribbean and world history.

During the struggle for Chaguaramas, many feared that following independence, Trinidad's ties to the West would be weakened, if not cut. The threat had been made by Williams and C.L.R. James to expel the Americans from Chaguaramas if they did not heed nationalist aspirations, and the British had been roundly condemned for their pusillanimity with respect to American arrogance in the Caribbean. When the Chaguaramas Agreement was initialled in 1960, however, Williams deliberately went out of his way to declare to the world that Trinidad would not remain neutral. As he said, "Insofar as there is any curtain dividing the world . . . Trinidad, as I have more than once unequivocally stated, is west and not east of it. . . . I am for the West Indies taking their place in the Western Hemisphere" (*Trinidad Guardian*, 11 February 1961). Some felt that in making this statement, Williams had made Trinidad and Tobago ineligible for Third World membership. As Winston Mahabir, then minister of health, lamented, "The West Indies has compromised its independence. . . . What would (it) tell Ghana, India and the Afro-Asian neutralist bloc?"

The Chaguaramas episode illustrated well the dilemmas of small states in the international arena. There was an evident urge on Williams's part, as well as among the general citizenry, to break out of Western colonial and neo-colonial cocoons and identify spiritually and materially with the Third World. But the old colonial tie was powerful in its hold, and was buttressed by what were considered to be important geopolitical and economic realities. It was taken for granted that the Caribbean Sea formed part of the American *mare clausum*.

The Monroe Doctrine had enunciated this for well over a century, and the Johnson Doctrine on the right of the Americans to intervene to prevent communism from establishing itself in the Caribbean, formulated in the midst of the 1965 crisis in Santo Domingo, seemed to confirm it. Cuba had paid the ultimate penalty for defying the Monroe Doctrine, and there was a widespread unwillingness among Trinidadians to run afoul of the American leviathan. Conventional wisdom also had it that Trinidad's economic problems – declining prices and markets for its traditional agricultural products, closed markets for its newer industries, growing unemployment, capital shortages and balance-of-payments problems – could only be solved by greater beneficence and more investment from the West. The West thus had to be sedulously wooed.

Europe

In his autobiography *Inward Hunger*, Williams claimed that the dominant question that faced Trinidad and Tobago after independence was not the ethnic question that was on the agenda at home, nor the east–west question, but the problem posed by Britain's adherence to the European Economic Community (EEC). This was so because of the preferential arrangements that obtained for Trinidad's exports to Britain and the EEC. Williams was concerned about these and wanted assurances from Britain that Trinidad's economic interests in relation to sugar, oil and aid would be safeguarded. Britain was not going to be allowed to abandon its historic responsibilities to the Caribbean, to behave as if the sugar-producing islands of the region had "dropped from the sky". Thus Williams's attendance at the Commonwealth Prime Ministers' 1962 conference, with the leader of the opposition in tow, and his decision to tour Europe following that meeting.

In Brussels, Williams met Frederick Hallstein, the president of the EEC, to whom he presented a memorandum that raised, among other questions, that of "EEC status", which he believed represented certain tangible advantages. "Associated status represented a form of political equality between former colonies and former colonial powers." Williams also believed that what was taking place in respect of Europe could provide a mechanism for integrating the Caribbean. As he told Hallstein, "Europe, which for three and one-half centuries has fought over the Caribbean territories and has been responsible for their present division, now had a unique opportunity, through the European Common Market, of bringing them together economically. Associate Status for Trinidad and Tobago with the European Economic Community will ensure greater integration of the economies of the countries of the Caribbean area" (1969, 290). Williams also claimed that the formal proposal for the establishment of a Commonwealth secretariat came from him, following "hints dropped by Ceylon and Ghana" (ibid., 301).

In the end he was disillusioned and indeed embittered by how little he was able to achieve in his conversations with the British and the "gnomes of Zurich". His expectation that they would willingly assist with the economic reconstruction of Trinidad and Tobago and the rest of the Caribbean was profoundly shaken.

Africa and Asia

In an attempt to foster some measure of economic and cultural cooperation with African countries, Williams went on a celebrated safari in 1964 that took him to Ghana, Senegal, Liberia, Nigeria, Uganda, Kenya, Tanzania, Egypt, Algeria, and Ethiopia. The major aim was to mobilize support for Trinidad's position with respect to a preference regime for sugar. As Williams noted in *Inward Hunger*, "The Geneva Conference (UNCTAD 1) and the future of preference dominated my discussions in Africa" (ibid., 291). Williams also discussed the problems of Trinidad's oil industry with the Algerians. The visit was followed by the establishment of an embassy in Addis Ababa with accreditation of the representative to Senegal, Tanzania and Kenya as well. Subsequently, Williams established ties with Ghana, the United Arab Republic and Nigeria.

During his extended visit, Williams took the opportunity to talk about the role of Africans in the slave trade and the relationship between West Indians and Africans in the past and present. He complained to his listeners at Haile Selassie University in Addis Abbaba that "Africans seem upset by their previous history and seek by the simple formula of forgetting slavery to behave as if it did not occur at all. The African, I believe, still suffers from that sense of inferiority. He does not want slavery recalled." Williams indicated that he was not ashamed of the African connection and they should not be either: "The historical relationship between Africa, principally West Africa, and the West Indies is nothing to be ashamed about, though the Africans don't like it, and I get the feeling that the West Indians like it less."

Williams boasted that West Indians had done a lot for Africa, and that it was time for Africa to reciprocate. He called on African governments to support his campaign to get preferential treatment in the European Common Market for Trinidad's agricultural products – sugar, cocoa and citrus – which he viewed as "a form of reparations, inadequate and belated, for centuries of preferential arrangements imposed by the United Kingdom and in the interest of United Kingdom investors in the West Indies". Williams, however, felt it necessary to clear up a basic misconception held by many in Africa, including those with whom Trinidad diplomats interfaced in the United Nations and in other diplomatic theatres. Trinidad and Tobago was not an African state that would vote automatically with the African bloc (EWMC folios 008 and 162).

Some quarters in Trinidad and Tobago criticized the establishment of a mission with multiple accreditation in Africa on the ground that the number of trading negotiations and consular activities the embassy handled did not justify the heavy expenses involved. But Williams felt that having regard to Trinidad's racial composition, it was important to maintain a symbolic presence in Africa. Moreover, Africa was also a significant power-bloc in the United Nations, and Addis Ababa, as the headquarters of the Organisation of African Unity and the Economic Commission for Africa, was Africa's diplomatic nerve centre. Trinidad in fact on occasion found itself functioning as a broker between the Latin and African groups at the United Nations. Africans not only felt more at ease with Trinidad for cultural reasons, but had a high regard for the competence of its delegates. That Trinidad supported African resolutions on colonialism also helped to generate confidence.

Once a mission had been established in Africa, it was difficult, for internal political reasons, to avoid putting one in India. Moreover, India was an important country in the African-Asian and Non-aligned Movement. In terms of trade possibilities, the Indian mission also had greater justification than the African mission. An ambassador to India was appointed in 1972 and accredited to Ceylon, Singapore, Malaysia and Japan. Trinidad and Tobago maintained a position of neutrality with respect to disputes between India and Pakistan, though it endorsed the admission of Bangladesh to the Commonwealth.

China and the Soviet Bloc

Despite strong American representation and lobbying during the March 1972 debate on China's admission to the United Nations, Trinidad and Tobago voted for the resolution that made it possible for China to take its seat in the United Nations. In the interest of universality, Trinidad would have preferred to see Taiwan retain a seat in the world body, but realizing that the two positions were incompatible, Trinidad was prepared to see Taiwan walk out.

In 1962, the Soviet Union made an offer of "practical aid" to Trinidad and Tobago and in 1965 expressed an interest in establishing diplomatic relations; nothing came of these initiatives. Williams was invited to visit the Soviet Union in 1965, but public opposition forced him to shelve the visit. There was fear that Moscow was seeking to secure another toehold in the Caribbean for "subversive" and mischievous purposes. Williams shared these concerns. He told the Soviets that he did not approve of their support for Cheddi Jagan in Guyana or Castro in Cuba (Basdeo and Mount 2001, 18).

Trinidad established diplomatic relations with the Soviet Union in 1974, though no diplomat was accredited to Moscow. Williams himself visited Moscow in 1975, a move that turned out to be an "absolute diplomatic disaster". J. O'Neil Lewis (1999a) recalls why:

Williams was pontificating about all we are going to do in Trinidad, and he mentioned aluminum, iron, and steel, and plastics. And a rather rough Minister dismissed this little country and dismissed him; and he effectively said, "go back and grow corn and sugar." This was a four-day trip, and this happened the end of the second day; Eric Williams never said a single word to any Russian for the next two days to the embarrassment of everybody concerned; he just shut up. My fear came when Kosygin, the Russian Prime Minister came to the hotel to take the Prime Minister to the Airport, and he proceeded to show, without saying words, the worst bad manners that you could ever think. It was the most frightening two days that I had ever spent. So he came back here with a bitterness, and just one remark, this guy simply said – "Go back to corn and sugar." That incident was the most frightening experience that I ever had. You had to be there to understand – the Prime Minister of this big country comes and sits down next to your Prime Minister, and he opens a book. [Laughter.] And we were sitting there. I was just hoping that the jails had heating. [Laughter.]

OPEC and the Arab World

An important aspect of Trinidad and Tobago's foreign policy under Williams was the move to become a player in the oil business. Williams's quest for inclusion began as early as 1959 when he sent John O' Halloran, the minister of industry, petroleum and mines, to the first Arab Oil Congress in Cairo. Williams was even then convinced that oil was going to be important in international affairs, and that Trinidad and Tobago should establish a presence in whatever was going on. This initiative was followed in the same year when Williams sent J. O'Neil Lewis to the World Petroleum Congress meeting in New York, a meeting that marked the hundredth anniversary of the discovery of petroleum. Lewis recalled that he had written something about oil in his PhD dissertation and had updated it. That updated version was shown to Walter Levy, an international oil consultant whom Williams had invited to Trinidad and Tobago. Levy told Williams that apart from bringing Lewis's paper up to date, there was little he could add to it. " I then became the oil expert [Laughter], and everything [which had] to do with oil, I had to have a say on it" (Oral Reminiscences, 1999a).

In 1963, Williams sent Lewis to an OPEC meeting in Caracas, and Trinidad was represented at an OPEC meeting in Geneva in that year. A team led by Dodderidge Alleyne also visited Saudi Arabia in 1963. Alleyne was sent to see whether Trinidad and Tobago could gain membership, but that meeting was postponed. By then, however, the Arabs had discovered that Trinidad and Tobago was the eighth country to discover oil, and that it was also an important player in the refining of oil, far more so than either Kuwait or Saudi Arabia. The Caracas meeting was also impressed with Trinidad's credentials and thus Trinidad was formally invited to become the seventh member of OPEC, even though it produced only about half of 1 per cent of total world crude output.

Williams chose to be persuaded by Texaco, the US government, and his own petroleum technologist that Trinidad should not become involved with the Arabs and OPEC, which they believed would not last. Williams was also told that Trinidad was already getting the "fifty-fifty" package – 50 per cent of the income from the industry, which was then OPEC's demand – and was persuaded to shun OPEC's invitation. "We never took up membership on OPEC in 1963. Later we were to be reminded of that," recalled Lewis. It would appear that like Mexico, Williams feared that Texaco and the Americans would punish Trinidad and Tobago's oil exports if it joined OPEC. Williams ran away from a fight with Texaco. Given OPEC's then weakness, the price of membership was considered to be too high.

In 1972, Williams sent a mission to the Middle East led by Sir Ellis Clarke. The story of the visit as told by Lewis and Alleyne is an interesting one. According to Lewis, the Trinidad delegation visited a number of Arab countries to discuss, among other issues, Trinidad's relationships with the oil-producing countries of the Middle East and membership in OPEC. The delegation was divided as to whether Trinidad should join OPEC and as to whether the Arabs really wanted them in the grouping. Clarke indicated to an aide that he was not convinced that Trinidad was wanted and chose not to include Iraq on his itinerary; he did not regard the visit to Iraq as necessary. Alleyne, however, strongly urged Clarke to visit Iraq. Clarke claimed that visas would be difficult to secure, and that in any case he another important family obligation, that is, his daughter's graduation. Even after Alleyne indicated that he had accessed the tickets and the visas, which were obtainable in the hotel lobby, Clarke persisted in his view that the Iraq visit was unnecessary and that his schedule did not permit it. Alleyne's offer to lead the delegation to Baghdad in his stead also failed to persuade Clarke to change his mind. Some members of the group strongly believed that even before the group set out to visit the Middle East, Clarke was firmly opposed to Trinidad's membership in OPEC and conveniently used the Iran–Iraq conflict to scuttle Trinidad's prospects for getting in. It is believed that he was acting at the instance of the Americans in general and Texaco in particular.

The failure to visit Iraq was contrary to Williams's instructions that the delegation should visit all countries. As Lewis recalled, "The intention always was that [we] should go to all founding member countries. That was the instruction from the Prime Minister, and it was said that Iraq should not be excluded. If you went to Iran and not Iraq, that would break the thing up. If you excluded both, it would be OK; but to go to one and not the other, given the traditional hostilities between these two countries" would be unacceptable. Alleyne and Lewis concluded that given the omission of Iraq, "we [were] dead".

Iraq did block Trinidad's entry. As Alleyne explained, "We were selected to be a member; we had our seat, but before the meeting broke up in Vienna, the Iraq

Oil Minister made an oracular statement to the effect that 'we have made a number of decisions here today, but the final decision does not rest here. . . . We don't know what is going to happen'." When Lewis and Alleyne got back to the Bristol Hotel, they called Trinidad. "I don't think we got Dr. Williams. I think we got his secretary, Madge Lee Fook, and we said, 'tell him we have been accepted. However, he should not make any statement because from a statement made, we suspect that something may be up in the air'." The ministerial committee's decision was to be confirmed by the founding member governments within thirty days.

Alleyne was not sure whether Williams got the full message, though he felt that they had been as clear as they could be. But Williams went to parliament and declared that Trinidad had become a member of OPEC. "When we heard that he had made a statement, we said, 'Oh God.' And we were shot down by Iraq later." Failure to visit Iraq was diplomatically fatal in the short run, but may have turned out to be a blessing in disguise. As Alleyne would later reflect, "I wonder if . . . Iraq did not do us a favour. I tend to feel that with the confusion [that ensued], and my understanding of it, they probably did us a favour, because there was no real gain to be derived from [being in] OPEC after 1973." Williams would later ask querulously, "Who needs OPEC?"

The story as told by Overand Padmore about Williams's reaction to the call from the Bristol is worth retelling:

> In my first appointment [as a minister], I was in Industry, Commerce, Petroleum and Mines, and I can well remember a particular Cabinet meeting when in rather vague and unclear terms, Dr. Williams was describing and discussing the question of Trinidad and Tobago's application before OPEC. And I remember writing him a little note saying to him – "the Minister of Petroleum and Mines knows nothing of this." I passed the note to him. He looked at it and pushed it in his pocket, but I never got a comment from him.
>
> That Sunday afternoon at about 2.00 o'clock, I was at home, and my telephone rang. As I picked up the "phone", he said, "hello! Bunny we are in"!, and I got the distinct impression of a man dancing a jig. And what came to my mind was Hitler dancing the jig when he heard that Paris had fallen. You know that sense of elation that he had. It tells one thing about the style of the man. Here we are joining OPEC; here I am the Minister responsible, and not involved. ("Eric Williams in Retrospect" symposium, April 1991)

Several countries wanted Trinidad and Tobago to be in OPEC, Kuwait, Nigeria, Saudi Arabia and Venezuela among them, and sought ways to override Iraq's unwillingness to have Trinidad and Tobago become a member. As Lewis tells us, "There was a strong feeling that OPEC would benefit from having Trinidad and Tobago [as a member] because Trinidad and Tobago had an experience that most of them did not have." Lewis recalls that he was in Brussels attending another meeting, and accidentally met several of the oil ministers at the hotel in which OPEC was meeting, and they indicated their wish to have Trinidad join. "So we revived the question of approaching OPEC again. We sent a telegram to Dr. Williams saying that 'there is new interest in Trinidad and Tobago. Should we follow it up?' And he said, 'OK, but channel all things through Dodd and not with the Ministry of External Affairs.'"

At the meeting that followed, Lewis revisited the Iraq encounter, and argued that Iraq had not rejected Trinidad and Tobago. "We argued that all that had happened was that Iraq allowed the 30 days to expire, and that it was possible to reopen the thing, and that Iraq might be willing to do so. They didn't really buy it, but said that [Trinidad] can come in as an Observer; and for the better part of a year, we attended as an Observer."

In 1974, Trinidad was invited to send another mission, and on this occasion, the mission did go to Iraq, with which diplomatic relations had since been established. Trinidad and Tobago was not the only country seeking membership. Colombia, Gabon and Ecuador were also postulants, and it was felt that it would have been difficult to admit Trinidad and Tobago and refuse the other three. The formula proposed was that Trinidad should first become an associate member. Trinidad was assured that within six months, if the invitation was accepted, it would become a full member. Williams refused the invitation. As Lewis (1999a) explained,

> Associate had a derogatory meaning in the Caribbean at the time. We had the Associated States, and it was a sort of second class people; so that Williams could not go to Parliament [having] announced in 1972 that we were full members . . . that we were Associated Members. He could not accept it. And Dodd sent back the word: "Don't accept." So we didn't. But Ecuador and Gabon accepted, and at the next meeting, they became full members.

There is an interesting sequel to the OPEC story, one related by Alleyne. When Williams told him in 1973 that he was retiring from politics, he told Alleyne that funds which he had not had in the past to initiate projects he felt were necessary would become available as a result of the work of OPEC. He reminded Williams that he had sent him and others to the Middle East to get Trinidad into OPEC. Why was Williams leaving when the fruits of the efforts were soon to be realized? "And by the end of that year, Gaddafi, with all his nonsense, that great man had moved the price of oil up. I do not know what the politicians said to him, but I tried to persuade him not to go." Alleyne asked Williams what history would say if he left now. To which Williams replied, " '[Y]ou do not understand. What you have to understand is what History would say if I did not leave now.' Perhaps Williams did not know just how much OPEC would change the world and Trinidad's place in it" (ibid., 142).

The New Ball Game

The oil embargo placed on the United States and Holland and the countries that exported to them – Canada, Puerto Rico and Trinidad and Tobago – was a major page turner in Williams's political life and in Trinidad's foreign policy. Williams now saw that oil was an enormously powerful economic and political weapon, one which, despite Trinidad's overall insignificance as a producer (he once described Trinidad as the "weakest link in the chain of the international oil economy"), he could use to shape the development of the Caribbean. Williams noted that the oil crisis was changing the world economy:

> The oil-producing giants from Iran and Saudi Arabia to Venezuela are making a revolutionary change in the world economy. Instead of the energy going from the developing countries for industries in the developed countries, industries will more and more come from the developed countries to the oil in the developing countries. Herein lies our strength in the Caribbean. If in oil we are the least of the apostles, at least we are an apostle. (1973b, 9)

The regime in oil opened up opportunities for a small country like Trinidad and Tobago. As he said in another of his addresses, "It is as they say, a new ball game. For every company that continues to live in the past, there are several knocking at the door which are prepared to accommodate themselves to the future. Every Japanese corporation that comes to us expresses interest in LNG operations. Trinidad should however not stick its neck out too far, lest it got it chopped off" (11 April 1975).

OPEC and the Caribbean

Williams was aware that Trinidad and Tobago was an economically strategic part of the Caribbean. As such the country must use its advantage, "however temporary, however limited, however unexpected, for Caribbean purposes and the achievement of Caribbean goals, and must take steps to ensure that this goal is not frustrated by the actions of non-Caribbean Governments" (1975a, 7). Williams warned that the fuel shortages and price increases would affect food availability, both in quantity and price. These would also have a negative impact on the tourism industry on which Caribbean islands depended. Williams pledged that BWIA would seek to ensure the viability of the tourist industry, but in return, he expected that BWIA would be declared the regional airline. Much the same was said for the bauxite industries of Jamaica and Guyana, whose refineries needed fuel to operate. Williams pledged to maintain pre-crisis supplies and to replace other non-Trinidad supplies.

In respect of Trinidad and Tobago, Williams told his listeners that at the end of the day, Trinidad should have something to show for the windfall. "We must use the additional revenue to accelerate the restructuring of our economy. We must have something concrete to show when the crisis is all over – a new petrochemical complex, the realization of Point Lisas, one or more new planes, [and] a substantial number of additional jobs in new spheres of economic activity" (1975a, 7). Williams also noted that discussions were ongoing with respect to establishing a steel mill and state participation in a new Texaco refinery, and that negotiations had been completed with respect to establishing a liquid ammonia plant in which government would participate on a fifty–fifty basis.

Williams also believed that oil "would carry sugar along into the European Economic Community" – that is, that the crisis in oil and its availability in Trinidad would help Caribbean sugar producers to increase their leverage in the European market in terms of obtaining quotas and good prices, providing of course that they had sugar to export. "In oil, we have a powerful bargaining weapon; sugar proposes, oil disposes."

The world economic crisis that was precipitated by the Arab oil embargo revealed Williams's ambivalence towards the anglophone Caribbean. In a speech given in 1963, for example, Williams complained about the benign neglect that governed relationships between the United States and the Caribbean. He mused that "If we could get 6 to 7 [independent] states in the Caribbean, I bet they would not be pushing the Caribbean around as we tend to be pushed around now" (as cited in Basdeo and Mount 2001, 26). While he was always firm in his mind that salvation for the region lay in unity and cooperation, he was also fully aware of the insularity and chauvinism that characterized relationships among the islands which he knew had deep historical roots.

Williams's scepticism was manifest. He would have to "see whether centuries of individualism can be buried in one decade of cooperation. . . . All our strength is in our union; all our danger is in our discord." Williams described the Caribbean Community (CARICOM) as a "weak reed" that might not survive. One thus had to look further afield for trading partners to replace that which could well be lost as Britain entered the European Common Market. Two months later, while addressing a PNM convention, Williams was even more pessimistic. As he told the convention, "It is now clear beyond any possibility of doubt that Caribbean integration will not be achieved in the foreseeable future, and that the reality is continued Caribbean disunity, and perhaps even a reaffirmation of colonialism."

Despite his personal antipathy to many of the Caribbean leaders of the time, particularly Barrow and Burnham, the record shows that Williams did not turn his back on the Caribbean completely following independence in 1962, as is commonly believed. A Caribbean[1] Heads of Government conference met in Trinidad in 1963, the first in the series of meetings of "heads". Williams was the prime mover in this meeting. Williams also persisted in his view that there was need for a Caribbean Economic Community comprising the ten member islands of the federation plus Guyana and the other islands in the Caribbean Sea. Even though Trinidad was not a signatory to the Caribbean Free Trade Association (CARIFTA) agreement, which when it was formed in 1965 included only Guyana, Antigua and Barbados, it was well disposed to the initiative and eventually joined in 1968, together with Dominica, Grenada, St Lucia, St Kitts–Nevis and Jamaica.

Williams's commitment to the Caribbean became very clear during the energy crisis, which he saw leading increasingly to a confrontation between oil producers and oil consumers. He was determined to ensure that the economies of the anglophone Caribbean did not collapse as a result of the crisis, and undertook a variety of initiatives to help prop up their economies. These included contribution to a special fund in the Caribbean Development Bank for smaller Caribbean countries, and assistance with their balance-of-payments problems. Williams showed particular concern for the Jamaican economy, which was experiencing a balance-of-payments crunch and which was in a state of near collapse. As he told the House of Representatives following meetings that he had had with the prime ministers of Barbados, Guyana and Jamaica in June 1976, "The major priority for us in the Caribbean was the restoration of the economic health of Jamaica." He continued, "There could be no improvement in the Caribbean when – to put it as crudely as possible – one of Trinidad and Tobago's best economic partners in the Caricom area is in serious difficulty – temporarily I am sure – in which Jamaica finds itself today" (Williams 1976, 1544–45). Williams knew, however, that the Trinidadian population was not sanguine about the policy of funding projects in the Caribbean with their money, and thus felt that he had to make it clear that the loans being made to Jamaica were also in Trinidad's interest:

> If the restoration of the economic health of Jamaica is a major priority for us in the Caribbean, there is the parallel obligation on all of us to recognize that improvement of the health situation in the economic sphere in Jamaica could not possibly be purchased at the cost of any endangering or jeopardizing of the economic health of Trinidad and Tobago which, if that does not mean dollars or dependence on loans, certainly involves the larger question of trade, Caribbean integration and particularly the question of security of jobs and the expansion of job opportunities that would be involved in the agreement that we reached here in Port of Spain. (Ibid.)

Williams was also concerned that if Jamaica was forced to go to the International Monetary Fund for a bail-out, the contraction in the Jamaican economy that would follow upon IMF conditionalities would have implications for Trinidad. "We felt, therefore, that Trinidad and Tobago [had] an extra obligation, not only to Jamaica, but to the entire Caribbean to avoid such an eventuality, if that were possible" (ibid., 1545).

Given all that was happening in the world economy and within the region, Williams felt that Trinidad had an "inescapable obligation to our Caribbean partners". Trinidad, he said, should not seek in any way to profit at their expense. He also mused that Trinidad could well have been in Jamaica's place had it not been for its energy resources. He told the House of Representatives that Trinidad had come "fairly close to [Jamaica's] situation". As Manley was leaving Williams's home in St Ann's, the latter remarked that "there but for the grace of God was Trinidad and Tobago" (ibid., 1548).

The terms of the June 1976 More Developed Country (MDC) Agreement involved Jamaica undertaking to give priority to goods produced in the CARICOM area – assembled motor vehicles, cement, fertilizer, asphalt – to be involved in joint ventures in the production of steel, textiles and food, and to facilitate the rationalization of air services. In return, Trinidad committed itself to providing TT$184.8 million to Jamaica in balance-of-payments support. Barbados promised US$5 million and SDRs (special drawing rights) $3 million, and Guyana SDRs $3 million.[2]

Manley himself wrote of his meetings with Williams in 1976 and about the outcomes of the negotiated agreements:

> Eric Williams, Errol Barrow and Forbes Burnham, the respective prime ministers, had all been extremely helpful within their means. Of course, only oil-rich Trinidad and Tobago was really in a position to offer substantial relief. Williams, a great figure in Caribbean history, was a man of moods. On this occasion he was at the top of his form. We worked out a broad trade agreement in which priority status would be afforded to certain types of goods being produced between us. Meantime, they would lend us US$50 million on normal commercial terms. This was a real help and we both felt that the trade agreement was a genuine step forward in the Caribbean integration process.
>
> The loan was promptly forthcoming and equally promptly serviced as the months passed. At the time when the IMF agreement of 1977 was made, Dr. Williams had agreed to a further loan of US$50 million as part of the foreign exchange package. This was no burden for Trinidad and Tobago whose reserves were then well over a billion TT dollars and rising with the world-wide tide of oil prices. We were a reliable customer with a good repayment record.
>
> The problem was internal politics. A wave of criticism was sweeping Trinidad concerning loans to her Caribbean neighbours while roads needed fixing at home, to say nothing of the telephones which wouldn't work A calypso summed up the mood with the words: "Charity begins at home!" In fact it was a silly argument because the problem was not the loans, a drop in the financial bucket, but the capacity to spend money effectively. Trinidad had oil wealth, but was still a typical developing country. Like the rest of us, she lacked the administrative and technical capacity to spend money effectively. The sudden extra income from the new oil prices could not solve that problem.

But politics is not always about rational things. When the second US$50 million was well overdue and a new foreign exchange crisis upon us with some of the commercial sources lagging as well, a letter arrived. It was handwritten and from Dr. Williams. It spoke of political difficulties. The bottom line, literally and figuratively, was: no second loan! (Manley 1982, 158).

Another difficulty informed Williams's reaction. He expressed regret that Trinidad's expectations that the agreement would lead to an increase in intra-MDC trade did not materialize. Trade figures for 1977 in fact revealed a sharp decline in the value of Trinidad's exports to Jamaica. There was indeed a negative balance of trade of close to TT$20 million. There was a positive balance of TT$10 million in 1978, but if petroleum exports were excluded, there would have been a deficit of TT$33.4 million in 1977 and a similar amount in 1978. Shortages of foreign exchange, the imposition of restrictions on intra-CARICOM trade, and a switch in the sources from which fuel was imported, that is, the Netherlands Antilles, were largely responsible for the fall in the value of Trinidad's exports to Jamaica. The *White Paper on CARICOM 1973–78* estimated that between 1973 and 1978, Trinidad and Tobago had contributed TT$420.8 million to CARICOM institutions and another TT$410.46 million to CARICOM countries under various bilateral arrangements. Direct balance-of-payments supports, the bulk of which went to Jamaica (US$112), amounted to TT$340.8. After reviewing the status of the agreement, the white paper concluded that "the only successfully implemented area of the MDC Agreement has been the financial assistance provided to Jamaica" (Government of Trinidad and Tobago 1979, 34).

The restrictions imposed by Jamaica on goods produced in CARICOM was a source of irritation to Trinidad's manufacturers, who were faced with under-utilization of capacity and increased unit costs, all of which cut into earnings and levels of employment. Williams was also concerned that monies borrowed from Trinidad and Tobago through the Caribbean Aid Council window, a soft loan facility, and other financial instruments, were being used for purposes other than what they were meant to fund. The complaint was that they were being used to meet the costs of missions abroad, prestige projects such as the expansion of national refineries, of national air lines that competed with BWIA, and of several other high-profile institutions that competed with regional equivalents.

Williams's frustration with CARICOM surfaced in an address that he gave at a PNM special convention in Tobago in 1977. As he asked, "What is CARICOM? What is the CARICOM Treaty? The CARICOM Treaty has permitted people to break their obligations to buy things from Trinidad like soup or whatever it is. . . . Our imports from these places are increasing, so it must not be allowed to prevent the legitimate development of the potential of Tobago in respect of industry" (in Sutton 1981, 198).

Williams complained that the leaders of Trinidad's Commonwealth Caribbean neighbours "paid only lip-service to measures for regional or international cooperation for only so long as such measures served their individual purposes or fed the egos of their representatives". Some were also said to be attracted more by the "rhetoric of revolutionary ideologies than by the economic or social needs of the region" (Government of Trinidad and Tobago 1979, 7). There were likewise complaints that certain Caribbean countries not only ignored Trinidad's position on non-interference in the domestic affairs of other states, but went so far as to "instruct Trinidad and Tobago on the subject of which countries it should recognize and with which countries it should cease to have diplomatic intercourse. In this regard, pressures were applied on Trinidad and Tobago to break relations with Israel, and to withhold recognition from Grenada." The white paper also recalled that some Caribbean states sought to deter Trinidad from seeking membership in the Organization of American States (OAS) or from visiting Cuba and countries behind the Iron Curtain.

The white paper likewise bemoaned the fact that some Commonwealth Caribbean countries encouraged "divisive elements from outside the region to involve themselves in the affairs of the region, including efforts to fund development projects which were properly for European Co-operation". The reference was to Venezuela, the complaint being that the initiatives advanced by Trinidad and Tobago to attract development capital had been dissipated by the encouragement being given to a country that seemed overanxious to fill the vacuum resulting from metropolitan countries' abandonment of their responsibilities to countries in the region, as well as Caribbean countries' abandonment of the principles of the regional integration movement (ibid., 9).

Another major enemy of the regional integration movement was said to be eagerness on the part of leaders to go whoring after alien "isms". As the white paper asked mournfully, "Is there any basis for the coordination of foreign policies? Can mutually acceptable strategies be created to project and satisfy the conflicting demands of democratic socialism, cooperative socialism, and the other numerous paths to political, economic and social development that individual CARICOM countries have chosen?" (ibid., 9).

Latin America and the OAS

Williams's relationship with Latin America in general and Venezuela and Cuba in particular went through a number of phases. We deal first with Williams's decision to have Trinidad apply for membership in the OAS. The decision to seek membership in the hemispheric organization was taken to represent an act of greater identification with the Third World. But while most Latin American countries considered themselves to be underdeveloped, the majority, as their reaction to the Cuba revolution showed, were closely identified with and dependent upon the United States.

During the debate preceding the decision to join the OAS, Williams argued that Trinidad and other independent Caribbean states should become members of the OAS by right rather than by grace, because American states were not exclusively Latin. Membership ought to be as automatic as it was with respect to the United Nations. Williams felt that race was one of the factors responsible for the marked lack of enthusiasm shown in Latin America for the entry of the anglophone Caribbean states into the inter-American system

But there were other important reasons for this coolness. Latin Americans feared that English-speaking states would form an introverted group that would be manipulated by the United States and by Britain, which had territorial disputes with several Latin American countries – Argentina and Paraguay – over the Falkland Islands, with Guatemala and Mexico over British Honduras (Belize), and with Venezuela over Guyana. It was feared that the Caribbean Commonwealth countries would vote as a bloc in support of English-speaking countries with which Latin states had disputes. Giving Caribbean countries membership in the OAS, it was said, was tantamount to giving Britain a voice in the councils of the OAS, a view reinforced by remarks made in the Caribbean that the OAS was the only regional organization on which the Commonwealth had no official representation. Latin Americans also had difficulty understanding how an independent country could have as its head of state a sovereign who was at the same time head of state of a former colonial power.

There was also some concern that the entry of the new states would reduce the size of the economic pie available for distribution. It was well known that the desire to participate in Alliance for Progress funds was the main reason for Trinidad's anxiety to enter the OAS. Williams, for example, declared in 1963 that the Alliance for Progress, which the United States had put into place to counter the thrust being made by the Soviets in the Americas, was "one of the best projects in economic aid that had been developed in the modern world. . . . Vast in scope, grandiose in conception, and ambitious in principle" (as cited in Williams 1972c). He noted that Canada, Sweden and other European countries were channelling some of their aid through the alliance, and he felt that before long, it would become one of the major sources of multilateral aid in the world. Williams argued that "Not a single country in Latin America satisfied the criteria for the Alliance for Progress as Trinidad and Tobago satisfied them." Trinidad had an incorrupt and progressive regime and the necessary administrative capacity and will to digest the structural social reforms that the alliance aimed to promote.

But capital and technical help from the Inter-American Development Bank and the Alliance for Progress were not all that attracted Trinidad policymakers to the OAS. Latin America represented a large market right on Trinidad's doorsteps that could not be ignored. As Williams said in 1964, "We are more dependent on trade than most countries. What happens in respect to African unity, the OAS, the Economic Commission for Africa, the Latin American Trade Association or the Central American Common Market is a matter of life and death to us in respect of our export markets and import supplies" (as cited in Ryan 1972b). Membership in the Latin American economic group was seen to be valuable because of the growing hostility to the preferential systems that existed between Britain and France and their former colonies. If, as it was assumed, preferences would soon be abandoned, it was important to secure a share as of right to the inter-American market – particularly with respect to sugar and petroleum.

In view of the fact that Trinidad and Tobago considered itself a Third World country, defence was also an important consideration for joining the OAS. By participating in the collective defence and security arrangements of the OAS, Trinidad would be more secure. Williams was apprehensive about American domination in the hemisphere, but he saw the inter-American system as an attempt on the part of Latin American republics to find a formula that would contain the interventionist impulses of the United States. Since the United States considered Trinidad to be part of the American system and subject to all the "doctrines" enunciated with respect to the hemisphere, whether it subscribed to them or not, Williams thought it advisable to join the OAS and help influence its deliberations from within.

But joining the OAS was not meant to compromise Trinidad and Tobago's neutrality. Indeed, Williams claimed that Trinidad's voice would be heard more respectfully only if it were part of a group. As he noted, "A small state like Trinidad and Tobago can exert little or no influence on major international issues working in isolation. It is only when it was known that Trinidad had the support of a larger grouping that its voice would be listened to at all." In fact, Williams saw Trinidad's role as that of a link or bridge "between the Latin and Anglo-Saxon aspect in Latin affairs . . . and between Africa, Asia and the Western Hemisphere" (Williams 1969, 290).

Some objections were raised within Trinidad and Tobago and in other parts of the anglophone Caribbean as well to membership in the OAS. Fear of the United States was reinforced by America's unilateral interference in the internal affairs of Latin American states. The United States, it was felt, would use the OAS when it could, and act unilaterally when it felt its national interests were at stake. Opponents also feared that the United States would use alliance funds and quota arrangements to force states to toe its line on domestic and foreign policy issues. The fact that Canada showed no real interest in joining led some to advocate caution. There were also reservations about the reality of the economic benefits of membership. Traditional agricultural interests warned that loans from the IDB would never take the place of such tangible trade ties as the Commonwealth Sugar Agreement, which could be neglecting the substance for the shadow.

In the end, the view that prevailed was that the risks of membership had to be taken. Membership in the OAS was not considered incompatible – *de facto* or *de jure*, as Jamaica then argued – with membership in the Commonwealth or with enjoying preferences while they lasted. Nor did it mean abandoning the aim of creating a Caribbean Economic Community. As Williams lamented, "The road towards the latter has been harder perhaps than we anticipated when we first announced the policy." But if and when the CEC did materialize, Williams assumed that there would be no difficulty having it integrated into larger inter-American trading arrangements.

In March 1967, three years after it had acquired observer status, Trinidad, with the active backing of Venezuela, took what was considered then to be its most important foreign policy decision and entered the OAS. Although there was little original enthusiasm within the OAS for having the Commonwealth group join, Trinidad and Tobago eventually succeeded in gaining acceptability. This was in large measure due to the fact that Trinidad's delegates were held in high esteem. Trinidad also played a very active and highly valued part in committee deliberations of the OAS and at United Nations meetings as part of the Latin American group. Williams noted with great pride that Trinidad was the spokesman for the Latin American Group of 24 as well as the spokesman for Africa in the Joint Development Committee of the World Bank and the International Monetary Fund.

The material benefits that Trinidad and Tobago obtained from membership in the OAS were not substantial, however, and there was a feeling that Hispanic solidarity asserted itself in this sphere. Most of the major OAS agencies (and therefore the resultant indirect benefits) were monopolized by Hispanic states, though inexperience with the bureaucratic games that were played in the OAS was partly responsible for Trinidad's performance. In terms of aid projects, not much was achieved.

Williams's early enthusiasm for the Alliance for Progress soon dried up. In *From Columbus to Castro* (1970b), he noted that by 1964–65,

> the Alliance for Progress had already failed, partly because, when the chips were down, the U.S. Government became afraid of genuine social revolution, fearing that all such revolution would be contaminated by "communism", and also partly because any thorough-going social revolution had to affect adversely the interests of the large American corporations operating in Latin America. Thus, we have the supreme paradox of a nation born in revolution taking a consistent counter-revolutionary stand in countries in its backyard.

Relations with Venezuela

One of the significant achievements of Trinidad and Tobago in the early post-independence era was the improvement of relationships with Venezuela. These had been strained because of Venezuela's reluctance to remove the "unjust" 30 per cent surtax on Trinidad goods that had been imposed in 1886 to compel Britain to sign a new commercial treaty with Venezuela. Williams's view was that whatever the historical origins of the conflict, there was no justification for retaining the tax on goods produced in Trinidad and Tobago, but the Venezuelans were reluctant to remove the tax for all sorts of symbolic and strategic reasons. They tactfully indicated that they were "prepared to remove the tax", but dragged their feet in respect of implementing their promise. The government was sympathetic to Trinidad, where President Rómulo Betancourt once lived as an exile, but insisted that it was imperative that the Venezuelan Congress agree to remove the surtax because it was the congress that had imposed it in 1886. Part of the problem was that at the time of Williams's first initiative, Trinidad and Tobago was not yet independent. In their various official reactions to Williams's initiatives, the Venezuelans referred to Trinidad and Tobago not by name but as the "government of that territory".

The Venezuelans had reason to believe that Williams's campaign against the tax was driven by political rather than economic factors, because there was little being produced in Trinidad and Tobago at the time that could be exported to Venezuela. The Venezuelans were in fact right in their belief that Williams's aim was to have Trinidad and Tobago treated as an independent country even though it was not yet formally so. Venezuela, for its part, might well have seen the surtax issue as a bargaining chip in its border dispute with Guyana. When Trinidad and Tobago became independent in August 1962, the surtax had not yet been removed.

In a speech to parliament on 12 January 1962, Williams expressed frustration with Venezuela's foot-dragging on the surtax issue. As he told the House, "There will be no discussions with the Venezuelan Government in which I take part which do not start with the elimination of the surtax: and then we can discuss the question of increased trade" (1969, 303). Williams refused invitations to visit Venezuela or discuss matters with it until 1966 when the tax was unilaterally repealed by Venezuela, a gesture that opened the door to healthy relations between the two countries. Williams met with President Raúl Leoni in Punta del Este in April 1967, following which they discussed matters of mutual concern. They agreed to establish a mixed commission, which met for the first time in Port of Spain in 1967 (ibid.).

Williams later recalled that he had tried to get an agreement on fishing, and had in fact reached certain agreements with the president of Venezuela. Nothing happened, however. Williams saw Venezuela's failure to implement the fishing agreement as an attempt to put pressure on Trinidad and Tobago: "If we can't agree on fish, how can we on oil?" Williams later noted that he had been pressed to hold negotiations with Venezuela, but had been reluctant to do so:

> The pressure on me to hold discussions with Venezuela has been incredible. I have never been able to get any information as to what will be discussed, which Ministers should be present, etc. If, as I think it does, what is involved is that I should join in what has become the Caribbean pilgrimage to Caracas – replacing the pilgrimage to London in which I did not join – then I must say to you, friends and colleagues, in a slight modification of one of the most dynamic statements ever uttered in Trinidad and Tobago:
>
>> Who want to go could go down dey,
>> But me ain't goin' no way
>> – (Sparrow)

Williams declared that he had had his fill of this "fishy business" and that as prime minister, he was washing his hands of it (ibid., 302–3).

Relations improved following the repeal of the surtax, and it may well be that Venezuela had come to realize how important Trinidad was to its own security. When Cuba began providing assistance to elements that were seeking to overthrow the Government of Venezuela, Trinidad responded by forcing the return of a plane that had been hijacked by guerilla elements. Trinidad's chancery in Caracas was machine-gunned in retaliation for this "betrayal". Trinidad's stand on the Venezuela–Cuba crisis was made more explicit in 1967 when a meeting of OAS foreign ministers was told that Trinidad had "extended assurances to the Government of Venezuela that [it] will not permit the soil of Trinidad and Tobago to be used for purposes of subversion against Venezuela. We have also given assurances that we will co-operate with . . . Venezuela . . . to promote our mutual security against overt or covert attacks. In the dispute between the Government of Venezuela and the totalitarian state of Cuba, we wish to state emphatically and unequivocally . . . – we stand by Venezuela."

Trinidad's Ministry of Home Affairs in fact often supplied information to Venezuela about the activities of pro-Castro elements that sought to use Trinidad as a platform for their operations in Venezuela, which on occasion led to their arrest and the seizure of significant caches of arms. Venezuela was grateful for Trinidad's help, and both the minister of home affairs and Williams were given its highest honours. Williams also had dealings with Venezuela in respect to its boundary dispute with Guyana, which he helped to negotiate in 1970, as well as with matters relating to fishing in the waters between the two countries. (The border dispute has not yet been resolved definitively.) He also received help from Venezuela during the Black Power revolution following the 1970 mutiny of the Trinidad and Tobago Regiment and the coast guard. He sought and obtained supplies of arms but subsequently refused to allow the Venezuelan war fleet to enter Trinidad waters or to have its helicopters fly over its airspace.

Relations between Trinidad and Venezuela soured when the latter sought to play a more active role in the Caribbean Sea by offering to use its oil resources to assist Jamaica and other Caribbean islands following the energy crisis of 1973 and thereafter. Williams was irritated not only by what he considered to be Venezuela's challenge to Trinidad's hegemony in the region, but also by the fact that the Commonwealth Caribbean countries that he had pledged to help had negotiated bilateral agreements with Venezuela in respect of fishing and the regional integration of the bauxite industry.

Williams told a PNM convention in 1975 that Venezuela's attitude to the Caribbean was based on two historical arguments. One was that Venezuela was the successor state when Spain renounced its rights to territories that it had "discovered" in the hemisphere, which discoveries had been fortified by the papal bull of 1493. The other was the captaincy general of Venezuela, established in 1777, which fixed the territorial limits of the successor state. Having regard to these historical events, Venezuela claimed Bird Island, 350 miles north of the Venezuelan coastline, the Los Monjes Archipelago, which it disputed with Colombia, the border with Guyana and the islands of Patos, Monos, Chacachaccare and Huevos off the coast of Trinidad. Venezuela also possessed a number of other inhabited islands off its coast, and made claims to the ownership of the continental shelf off that coast.

Given what was taking place in those years in respect to the Law of the Sea, Williams saw Venezuela's various claims as a definite threat to the Caribbean community. While Venezuela and its offshore islands with 1,100 miles of coastline could claim one-fifth of the Caribbean Sea's 750,000 square miles, Trinidad and Tobago (83 miles), Barbados (20 miles), and Jamaica (280 miles) together could claim only 385 miles of coastline and a small share of the Caribbean Sea. Venezuela's exclusive 200-mile economic zone was thus a threat to the entire Caribbean, especially Dominica, Montserrat, St Kitts–Nevis and Trinidad and Tobago. Williams also claimed that Venezuelan publicists were advancing proposals to integrate the region, including creating a "Caribbean Federation . . . based largely on the Caribbean Basin. Venezuelan terminology now forcing its way, with apparently much collusion on the Caribbean side, into the Caribbean vocabulary" (in Sutton 1981, 348–60).

Williams accused Venezuela of using its economic muscle for political ends. Oil was being supplied at pre-1973 prices with the remainder due being treated as a loan. It was a "get oil now pay later policy which tied the Caribbean and Central American beneficiaries to Venezuela's oil tap while also [being] tied to Venezuela as debtors" (ibid., 355). Williams was also chagrined about the agreement being negotiated among Venezuela, Jamaica and Suriname to barter raw materials for oil. The plan was to construct an aluminium smelting plant that was much larger than the one previously negotiated with Jamaica. The proposed plant was to have a capacity of 500,000 tons in 1980 and 1 million tons in subsequent years. In his view, this and other proposals in respect of tourism and trade "represented an attempt on Venezuela's part to become the new financial centre of the World . . . with the indebted Caribbean as its hinterland" (ibid., 357).

Williams clearly felt betrayed by his Caribbean colleagues, whom he tongue-in-cheek considered to be no more honourable than "Brutus". One of them had in fact suggested that the proposed Trinidad–Jamaica–Suriname smelter should be downsized from 200,000 tons to 70,000 tons, when expert advice had indicated that the minimum capacity for a viable smelter was 120,000 tons. Clearly, the aim was to scuttle the smaller project. Williams saw Venezuela's policy as a calculated and open attack on Trinidad. He also felt that his CARICOM colleagues could not have done anything materially worse if their aim was to scuttle CARICOM. Alternatively, there might well have been a plot to bring Venezuela into CARICOM. As Williams told the PNM convention,

> One is forced to wonder, in all this, when will Venezuela be brought in as a member of CARICOM? The Jamaica press has already flown that kite. What will be the effect of this, not only on Venezuela's obligations to the Andean Pact, but on CARICOM, its present industrial and trading patterns? If Venezuela joins CARICOM, the road will be open to it to become a full member of the Caribbean Development Bank. How could that Bank as at present structured and oriented withstand the almighty petrodollar? (Ibid., 359)

Williams accused Venezuela of trying to recolonize the region. He saw its efforts as an attempt to transform the Caribbean Sea into the "Sea of Venezuela". Williams told the convention that Venezuela's maritime ambitions had implications for the economies of all or most of the islands in the Caribbean, especially as it related to fishing:

> Venezuela's Caribbean vision and ambitions, starting off from barren uninhabited rocks to a network of economic arrangements out of which is emerging a Venezuelan oil and industrial metropolis and an indebted Caribbean hinterland, the Caribbean as we know it integrated into Venezuela, the naval power of the future, the oil power of the present, the tourist mecca in the making, its position in its Venezuelan Sea fortified by its 200-mile exclusive economic zone; all to the plaudits of the Caribbean peoples themselves, with Trinidad and Tobago the odd man out. You will understand now why I am pilloried at home and abroad, prodded by Commonwealth colleagues outside of the Caribbean as to why we don't like Venezuela, pestered by Caricom colleagues who want to know what I have against Venezuela, falling one over the other to announce that there is no recolonisation of the Caribbean and attacking me for claiming that there is.
>
> What am I supposed to do or say, friends? All that is going on now, naval bases, protection against outside countries, producing raw materials or semi-finished goods for other centres, our economies integrated into those of outside countries in opposition to

any attempt at vertical integration within – all that was the language of Caribbean colonialism in the 18th century, all that was the price of Caribbean colonialism in the 18th century. But when I say it is exactly that language, that practice which we now face in the 20th century, they have me to hang. What must I – and all historians and political scientists – do, redefine our definition of colonialism?[3] (Ibid., 360)

Williams claimed that his vision of Caribbean integration was inspired by the work of West Indian intellectuals – vertical integration based on bauxite and other Caribbean natural resources. Now, others were seeking to impose their own concept of integration. Said Williams, "Bilateralism is eroding the multilateral emphasis explicit in our Community, and the bilateralism has all the hallmarks of the colonialism implicit in all the statements of Venezuelan publicists – the new Venezuela they preach of in the context of the old colonialism of the Caribbean." Williams was resentful of these efforts: "I have found myself buffeted back and forth when it seemed that the long struggle might end in something tangible." "My friends," he told the Party, "one man can only take so much, and I have had enough. I have decided to take no further part in the matter" (ibid., 357).

Manley did not agree with Williams that the agreements with Mexico and Venezuela would make the Trinidad–Guyana–Jamaica smelter unviable. Manley felt that world demand could absorb all that was likely to be produced by all the plants. He argued that the Trinidad-based smelter would require less than 10 percent of Jamaica's present production, which in any event was scheduled for expansion. He also did not agree that Jamaica would in the process surrender control of its resources and find itself in a neo-colonial relationship (*Trinidad Express*, 3 September 1975; *Trinidad Guardian*, 19 June 1975). Manley, who was personally and ideologically close to Carlos Andrés Pérez, president of Venezuela, as well as to the Non-aligned Movement, did not see the relationship with Venezuela as a threat but as an opportunity for Jamaica to neutralize Canadian and American bauxite producers. He claimed that long before Williams made the offer of the smelter, Jamaica had entered into an agreement in principle with Mexico and Venezuela (Jalumex and Javemex) to establish an aluminium smelter complex and an alumina processing plant that would use Jamaica's bauxite and the energy of Venezuela and Mexico. Plans for this smelter were said to have been enunciated as early as 1973, before the Arab oil embargo (see Lewis 1986, 76–77).

Interestingly, Manley went on record as being of the view that Williams's attack on the Jalumex and Javemex proposals might have been intended to sabotage the Trinidad-based project. He argued that Williams was either "ignorant of the facts" or, "as is more likely, has his own secret reason for not wanting to go through with the smelter after all. [If so], it would be both more frank and more honourable to say so and say why" (*Trinidad Guardian*, 19 June 1975). Manley went on to explain the sequence of who did what and when:

When we heard of the Guyana-Trinidad effort, we already knew of the Venezuela effort and we were very interested. We were quite sure in our minds that there was no connection whatsoever between the two projects. So we got in touch with Dr. Williams and said that Jamaica was very interested. We asked whether it would in any way offend the concept if it were enlarged to include Jamaica. Both he and Mr. Burnham said fine.

Manley noted that the issues were discussed and feasibility studies conducted in the full knowledge that the Venezuela project was on the cards and that production from it would be forthcoming. Notwithstanding that, he felt that by 1979, there would be a world shortage of alumina by as much as 1 million tons. According to Manley, the important thing to note was that before the Trinidad smelter had even been dreamt of, Venezuela's decision to build a 330,000-tonne smelter using Guyana's hydro-electric power had been taken and announced, and was already worldwide information (*Trinidad Express*, 3 September 1975).

In his 1987 book, *Up the Down Escalator*, Manley offers a somewhat different version of what took place. He notes that in June 1974, the prime ministers of Jamaica, Guyana, and Trinidad and Tobago announced the development of a tripartite aluminium smelter. By the end of 1974, however, Trinidad announced that the project would have to be delayed by some three years until the country's electricity and water supply was increased. It was in this context that the crisis between Manley and Williams developed. Manley's statement about what occurred served to put Williams's anger in perspective. As he declared,

> Early in 1975, Jamaica made public plans to enter into a joint venture with Mexico and Venezuela for the purpose of a new bauxite-alumina-aluminum complex. Although this move in no way interfered with previous plans, it seemed to have inflamed latent anti-Venezuelan sentiment in the Trinidadian government. Trinidad made its displeasure clear. In fairness, Trinidad had some cause to object. We did not take steps to explain the Jamaica, Venezuela, Mexico (JAVEMEX) project to them privately ahead of the public announcement. Consequently, they felt that this new venture would only be at the expense of the Jamaica-Guyana-Trinidad plan. In fact, this was not so, because the United States multinational corporations were supplying Mexico with a substantial portion of her annual aluminum needs. The Mexicans intended to replace this with production originating in Mexico. . . . It was some time before the Trinidadians fully appreciated the fact that the Mexico project was completely separate and in no way competitive with their own. In any event, Trinidad seemed to be concerned about the region's ability to market the metal successfully. Granted the flexibility of its natural gas as a source of energy, Trinidad inevitably had other projects competing for the policy go ahead. Consequently, the aluminum plan was seen by them as competing with other possibilities. (Manley 1987, 248–49)

In 1977 the Government of Trinidad and Tobago decided to go it alone in terms of ownership, but left the option open for Jamaica and Guyana to participate as suppliers of alumina. The plant was to be built at Point Lisas, Trinidad.

Williams counter-claimed that he had put the smelter proposal on the table as early as 1970 and that Suriname was included in that proposal. It was again advanced in 1974 and consisted of two projects. The first was an aluminium smelter, collectively owned by three (or four) governments, which would be located in Trinidad. The second project involved the increased production of bauxite and alumina in Jamaica and Suriname, with Trinidad and Tobago participating in the investment: "Our aim is an integrated regional bauxite complex merging Trinidad natural gas and the bauxite of Jamaica, Guyana and I hope Suriname."

Williams was angry with Jamaica and Guyana for refusing to follow his line on Venezuela. He argued that Venezuela never considered itself part of the Caribbean, which he defined in archipelagic terms (though Belize and Guyana were included). Williams's restricted view of what the Caribbean was was informed by his view that the experience of slavery and the plantation were the common denominators of Caribbean civilization, that which gave it its "distinctive cultural identity". As he explained at an Economic Commission for Latin America and the Caribbean (ECLAC) meeting held in Port of Spain in 1975,

> The Caribbean Area, as it is traditionally defined, has a special historical significance and a distinctive cultural identity all its own – a number of islands and a few territories on the mainland, the first areas to be subjected to modern colonialism; plantation economies producing tropical produce and providing markets for the European metropolis, utilizing labour from Asia and Africa working under coercion and in degradation; subjected to the economic laws of the European metropolis; the last of the colonial areas to be totally liberated from the fetters of colonialism; fragmented by differences in languages, religion, and previous political allegiance. (1975c, 10)

Williams felt that hemispheric solidarity was important, particularly since all the states of the region faced similar problems with respect to multinationals and their technology. As he told the sixteenth session of ECLAC, "We would not wish our concern with the separate recognition of the historical and cultural identity of the Caribbean in any way to encourage the fragmentation of hemisphere co-ordination and solidarity" (1975c, 11). Williams nevertheless felt that the special historical, cultural and geographic identity of the Caribbean should be institutionally recognized, and to this end worked for and secured the establishment of a Caribbean Development and Co-operation Committee of ECLAC to deal specifically with Caribbean issues and circumstances. The new sub-regional office of ECLAC was to embrace all Caribbean governmental entities from Belize to Cayenne irrespective of political status (ibid.).

Manley had a different conception of what Caribbean and Caribbean integration meant. As he explained, the Caribbean included all states that had littorals on the Caribbean Sea. This included Venezuela. Manley claimed that he had formulated a theory of "concentric circles" in which the former colonial territories would seek closer and tighter cooperation with their immediate neighbours while simultaneously building platforms for common action through regional associations and international bodies such as the Non-aligned Movement, the Group of 77, and the United Nations. Said Manley (1982, 179): "CARICOM was the necessary step to give the first circle greater coherence."

Manley shared Williams's view that it was important for CARICOM countries to recognize Cuba and China in defiance of the wishes of the United States. He saw this as a declaration of independence from US hegemony. He felt, however, that there was a need to bring Cuba and Venezuela into the Caribbean in order to broaden the Caribbean's economic base. Thus the plan for the aluminium smelter with Guyana and Trinidad and Tobago, as well as that with Venezuela and Mexico. In his mind, "Jamaica was pioneering trading links and other forms of economic cooperation with non-CARICOM states in the Caribbean Basin" (ibid.). Manley believed that economic survival and viability required that "our own transnationals pull together the resources of Jamaica, Trinidad and Tobago, Guyana, Venezuela, Cuba, and all the rest", and that it was "the duty of Caribbean leaders to make it easier for these things to happen" (Manley 1987, 248). Williams's horizons in terms of integrated production arrangements were more regionally limited, and for all kinds of political and diplomatic reasons excluded Cuba and Venezuela.[4]

Others too were highly critical of Trinidad's strategy for regional integration. Among them was Professor Clive Thomas of Guyana, who argued that Williams was the spokesperson for the transnational corporations of the region, which had come to recognize the opportunities that integration would create for them to promote their exports within the region and to rationalize their production arrangements. Thomas also argued that the larger states in the region all had different reasons for buying into the integration movement. Burnham saw Caribbean integration as a long-term solution to the minority racial position of the People's National Congress in Guyana. Jamaica's switch from hostility to support for integration followed its recognition of the scope that integration offered its growing business class. "Similarly, Trinidad and Tobago's cynicism and arrogance towards its regional partners have grown along with its petro-dollars. All this was a class phenomenon rooted in the class character of the ruling regimes of the region" (in Hall 2001, 28–29). It is not clear, however, what connection there was between Williams's arrogance and the class character of the regime. Thomas believed that there was a connection. As he argued, "The ruling petty bourgeoisie of the region have a particular style of politics. The emphasis was on manipulation, opportunism and authoritarianism: There is a marked hostility to mass participation. . . . [The leaders] have a natural distrust of other leaders because they see a reflection of themselves and therefore know the depths of political corruptibility which are possible. They find it hard to work on the basis of consensus politics" (ibid., 30).

Williams's CARICOM colleagues believed him to be paranoid about Venezuela, which was offering them a better deal than that agreed to with Trinidad and Tobago. They believed that he was exaggerating the recolonization threat posed by Venezuela. Williams believed he knew his history better than they did, and was not going to ignore Venezuela's imperial ambitions. As he had said in 1972 while addressing the fourteenth annual PNM convention, "We have to be extremely careful in what we do with the power in our hands and with the destiny which we can in part control" (in Sutton 1981, 351).

Williams and Cuba in the Inter-American System

Williams zigzagged a great deal in his public statements and positions on Castro and the Cuban revolution. In a motion presented to the House of Representatives on 6 December 1963, roughly one year following independence, Williams went out of his way to differentiate Trinidad and Tobago from Cuba in terms of paths to development. He also dealt with the matter in an article in *Le Monde Diplomatique,* published on the first anniversary of independence. In that article, titled "International Perspectives for Trinidad and Tobago", Williams noted that the cases of Cuba and Trinidad and Tobago represented "two dominant points of view that face the world today". The Cuban path involved total state control and direction of the economy and subordination of the trade unions to the state. The Trinidad path rejected this formula, "which has so far not registered any outstanding successes in Cuba". Trinidad's economy was overwhelmingly in private hands and in the hands of large companies, all of which reduced the role of the government in development planning. Williams felt that Trinidad had found a middle way between the outright nationalization of Castro and the old-fashioned capitalist organization backed by the marines and the dollars of the United States of America. The Trinidad path involved the following:

1. active partnership between government and investors in Trinidad and Tobago as against the state direction of the economy in Cuba;
2. a direct democracy superimposed upon a parliamentary tradition in Trinidad and Tobago as against Cuba's one party state dominated by its caudillo;
3. the vision in Trinidad and Tobago of a Caribbean Economic Community with some sort of independent existence as against the submerging of the Cuban personality in the International behind the Iron Curtain. (Williams 1963, 365–67)

In 1969, Williams told Nelson Rockefeller, who had undertaken an exploratory mission to the Caribbean on behalf of President Richard Nixon, that Castro was "erratic, inept, disorganized and wrong on so many issues that he was unlikely to survive". Cuba was in a "total mess", he noted, but was still trying to export his revolution to the rest of the Caribbean. Castro's goals were said to be worthy, but he was going about it the wrong way. "He did not know how to govern" (*Rockefeller Archives: Summary of a Visit to Trinidad and Tobago*, as cited in Basdeo and Mount 2001, 12).

Williams described the Castro government as "a bunch of middle-class misfits who were making a blooming mess of the Cuban economy". He was nevertheless of the view that Cuba was "making a genuine attempt to transform her economic and social structure and achieve a genuine national identity". As such, Cuba should not be ostracized from the American family of nations. In February 1970, Williams told the OAS that adherence to the principle of hemispheric economic solidarity logically impelled him to support the resumption of economic relations with Cuba. He also told the OAS that "economic boycott was not the most realistic nor indeed the most productive attitude to be adopted with a country whose economic and social system we do not share. . . . Within the family of nations of the Hemisphere, reconciliation with the estranged is the ineluctable choice rather than ostracism." Williams noted that a quid pro quo was expected from Cuba:

> A corollary of the economic re-integration of Cuba is of course the strict adherence on the part of that country to a basic tenet of the OAS, namely, non-interference in the internal affairs of any other country. Economic intercourse can never be permitted to degenerate into a medium for attempts at subversion. At all events, within the family of nations of the hemisphere, reconciliation with the estranged is the ineluctable choice, rather than ostracism. (Speech given at the Inter-American Economic and Social Council, 3 February 1970, Caracas, Venezuela; in Sutton 1981, 398)

While continuing to deplore any attempt to export revolution, Trinidad, together with Jamaica, Barbados and Guyana, openly supported proposals for Cuba's re-entry in spite of continuing American and Venezuelan opposition and Cuba's expressed lack of interest in rejoining the organization given its present structure.

One of the indications of Williams's change of attitude to Cuba was the support he gave to Peru's resolution to the General Committee of the Permanent Council of OAS Ambassadors in June 1972. The motion, which was backed by Jamaica and five other OAS states, called for permission to be granted to those member-states that desired to normalize relations with the Cuban government. Williams noted that Cold War politics did not prevent Nixon from opening a window to Peking. It therefore did not come as a surprise when Trinidad and Jamaica established diplomatic ties with Cuba.

Williams's relationship with Castro was ambivalent. At times he welcomed Cuba into the Caribbean family and was full of praise for what Castro was seeking to do to transform the Cuban economy. He even seemed to envy Castro and Cuba, which he saw as the only Caribbean country with a measure of real sovereignty over its economy; Cuba was also cited as the "one bright spot" in the region where genuine racial integration was taking place. As Williams wrote in *From Columbus to Castro*,

> Since the Revolution, Cuba has got rid of the traditional curse of the Caribbean – the sugar plantation – and she has got rid of the twentieth-century bane of the Third World – economic domination by metropolitan companies. She is also the first Caribbean country to have got rid of the legacy of slavery – the obsession with race and colour. Even in this respect she has been ahead of Haiti, where, ever since Independence, the mulatto elite has been in a privileged position vis-à-vis the black masses. In addition, she is the first Caribbean country (leaving aside the very small tourist economies) to have got rid of unemployment. Finally, whatever her economic mistakes, she is the first Caribbean country to have mobilized the entire population in the task of national reconstruction. (1970b, 509)

Williams also observed that Cuba had made significant breakthroughs in expanding the production of poultry, citrus, fish, vegetables and stock feeds, and acknowledged Cuba's achievements in educational development. He noted Cuba's dependence on the Soviet Union, but agreed that unlike its former involvement with the United States, this was a transitional phase through which Cuba had to go until it solved its foreign-exchange difficulties. Williams was not anxious to import the Cuban model into Trinidad: "The real tragedy of Cuba is that she has resorted to a totalitarian framework within which to . . . transform her economy and society. . . . The question arises as to whether there are alternative paths in the Caribbean to economic and social transformation . . . [that are] less revolutionary and more gradualistic . . . less totalitarian and more democratic than the Cuban path, but more autonomous and ultimately self-reliant than the Puerto Rican one" (ibid., 510). Williams believed that his blueprint provided that alternative.

Williams at one time seemed anxious to use Castro, who had visited Trinidad in 1971, and Cuba as a counter to Venezuela in his effort to have the Caribbean defined in a particular way in relation to the Law of the Sea. It is perhaps worth noting that at a meeting in Santo Domingo in 1972, Trinidad's delegates had voted against Cuba's participation in the Law of the Sea meeting, assuming that that was what Williams wanted. Williams had other ideas. He wanted Cuba's support against Venezuela and apologized to Castro for what he described as a "diplomatic blunder" (*Trinidad Express*, 15 July 1972).

It would seem that Castro agreed to support Williams's position, but changed his mind, much to the prime minister's chagrin. According to Dr Anthony Gonzalves of the Institute of International Relations, "When he came back to Trinidad, something happened. No one is clear exactly what happened, but apparently Castro went back on his word: and that virtually turned [Williams] into a beast *vis-à-vis* the Cubans. The Cubans tried to patch up things, but they were unable to . . . he just decided to wash his hands." No one is clear why the Cubans refused. There was speculation that Cuban communists saw Williams's strategy as being essentially colonialist in that he was seeking the cooperation of the Western powers in the region, including the United States, to get the Caribbean Sea defined in a particular way. It was speculated that the Cuban communists were opposed to having Castro sit down with the Americans to discuss the Caribbean Sea. "Whatever it was, it led to a complete breakdown of relations with Cuba, at least for a short while" ("Eric Williams in Retrospect" symposium, April 1991).

Was Williams Isolationist?

Following Williams's death in 1981, there was a great deal of debate as to whether he was a "Caribbean Godfather". There was also debate as to whether he was largely responsible for the collapse of the original federation, and whether having done so, he acted responsibly in terms of what occurred within the region after Trinidad and Jamaica became independent. Anthony Gonzalves argued that in terms of federation, Williams did not get the federal design that he wished and found the British design, and the aid offer that they made, derisive and in other ways unacceptable. As such he was not prepared to bear the cost of federation. Williams complained that Britain had sucked the orange dry and was prepared to do little more than toss away the husk.

Williams denied that he was isolationist, and claimed that it was he who sought to "pick up the pieces" after the collapse of the federation. He also claimed that it was he who cleared the way by private and informal discussions with the prime minister of Jamaica and the premiers of Barbados and British Guiana for the staging of the first Conference of Heads, which was held in Port of Spain in July 1963 and which he hosted. He tells us that in planning the meeting, he took as his model the Organisation of African Unity, and limited participation to the heads of independent or self-governing territories. Williams said that in doing so, he was sensitive to the "propaganda that Trinidad had broken up the old Federation and was seeking to prevent the emergence of a smaller federation" (1965, 381). Williams further tells us that he had wished to invite the Caribbean republics of Cuba, Haiti and Santo Domingo to the meeting of heads, but could not persuade his colleagues to do so. The latter, Jamaica in particular, were unwilling to associate with regimes that did not adhere to the democratic process practised in the Commonwealth countries of the Caribbean.

The second meeting was held in Jamaica in January 1964. The heads did not meet in Barbados in June 1964 as planned. Williams tells us that he had hoped to deal at that meeting with the question of joint diplomatic representation in Africa, Canada–West Indies relationships, and the British Guiana political crisis. Williams felt that the conference idea had received a "mortal blow" when it proved impossible to hold the Barbados meeting. Another meeting was held in British Guiana in 1965, but this was seen as an "anti-climax" that did nothing to restore the conference to its original status and potential.

In these years, Williams also established contacts with the non-English-speaking Caribbean territories and their metropolitan overlords to discuss the question of regionalism in the Caribbean and the promotion of the Caribbean Economic Community. He found the British reaction "inexplicably timid and unfavourable", but continued to urge the British government to promote the economic viability of the smaller territories in the region, and to abandon the policy of making economic assistance dependent on political association in the form of federation (Williams 1973a).

The fractiousness of the relationship between Barrow, Burnham and Bird on the one hand, and Williams on the other, contributed mightily to some of the problems of regional cooperation within the Commonwealth Caribbean. The "Three Bs" resented what they saw as Williams's "arrogance" and his tendency to try to dictate what should be done and to mash up whatever he could not control or dominate. The interpersonal rivalries led in 1965 to the formation of the Caribbean Free Trade Association (CARIFTA) without Trinidad's involvement. Ellis Clarke explains why Trinidad's involvement was long in coming:

> CARIFTA was formed by the "Bs", Burnham, Barrow and Bird. In the process of time the question of Trinidad and Tobago's joining arose. There was a low degree of hostility between both Burnham and Barrow towards Eric Williams. Sonny Ramphal, the Attorney General and Foreign Minister of Guyana, and I met in Washington where I was Ambassador, and we agreed that if any progress was to be made in the region as a whole, some sort of détente had to be made between Williams, Burnham and Barrow. I suggested to Sonny that he talk to Williams, but he didn't think that Williams would see him. I told him I could arrange such a meeting, and this I did.
>
> We met together in Williams' office, and Sonny did all the talking while Williams only listened. Afterwards, he told me that he felt that the meeting had been a failure. Sonny's phrase was that he felt like a stuck gramophone needle when he did all the talking and got no response from Williams. I assured him, however, that all had not been lost, and subsequent events proved me right. (Collymore 2000, 86)

Clarke threw further light on how Trinidad eventually came to join CARIFTA and how the secretariat came to be located in Guyana. He notes that following the meeting between Ramphal and Williams, a decision was taken to have Williams and Burnham meet at Piarco in the VIP room. Burnham was on his way to another country and Piarco was seen by both leaders as a "level playing field". Clarke indicates what was agreed at the clandestine meeting:

> When Bill Williams and Burnham met at Piarco, they achieved the détente that we had been looking for. As a result, a meeting of CARIFTA in Barbados took place, in which Trinidad and Tobago and the other Caribbean territories were being invited to join. It was clearly the intention of Barrow to rub Williams' nose in the dust, but he was unaware of what had occurred between Burnham and Williams at Piarco previously. Barrow attended the meeting to lay down rather harsh conditions for the others to join, but Burnham insisted that all the rest should come in just as the others had done and despite their delay in joining, in no way should any territory be penalized. They should simply be made welcome.
>
> This took Barrow completely by surprise, because he expected Burnham to join with him in embarrassing Williams. However, Barrow yielded reluctantly, and then the question arose as to where the Secretariat should be. Barrow expected it to be in Barbados, but Williams got up and proposed Guyana. The rest of the delegates agreed on Guyana. It was clearly a good bit of horse trading, and so it came about that Guyana was chosen, which, geographically speaking, is the least suitable place for the CARIFTA Secretariat to be. But it was part of the politics in that era. (Collymore 2000, 87–88)

Trinidad eventually joined in 1968.

Despite Williams's pessimism about the status of the heads conferences, these continued to be held annually. The eighth meeting, held in Georgetown in 1972, produced the historic Georgetown Accord and the Caribbean Community Treaty, which was signed in Chaguaramas in 1973. That treaty replaced the expanded CARIFTA agreement. Williams saw the community treaty as a "great step forward, but not too much". It was an effort by the Caribbean to "repudiate its past and take its place in the sun despite earlier frictions, misunderstandings and tensions". He nevertheless wondered aloud whether it would succumb to the high mortality rate associated with other movements of importance in the Caribbean (1973a).

Williams was almost prophetic. In December 1977, the Caribbean Community Treaty was in a state of "near total collapse" (in Sulton 1981, 390). Williams observed that Trinidad and Tobago's export trade to its Caribbean partners had declined catastrophically:

> Clearly our $184m loan to Jamaica in 1976 did nothing to help our principal export maintain its legitimate CARICOM position. By volume, our [fuel] exports to Jamaica were 893,000 barrels in 1973, 3.2m in 1974, 3m in 1975, 756,000 in 1976 (the year of our loan), 693,000 in the first 8 months of 1977. What conclusion must we draw? Is it

that the more we lend, the less we sell? If so, we lend only petrodollars. If we don't sell, where are the dollars to come from? (Ibid.)

After 1976, Williams seems to have turned his back on the Caribbean, leading many to claim that he was now an isolationist. The crisis that followed upon the overthrow of Prime Minister Eric Gairy's regime in Grenada in 1979 by Maurice Bishop and others also gave rise to complaints that Williams had become even more so and that he was responsible in part for the fatal events that took place in 1983 when American troops invaded Grenada to dislodge the People's Revolutionary Government. Williams was also blamed for the fact that notwithstanding the serious crises that the Caribbean had to deal with in the 1970s, there was no Heads of Government meeting between 1975 and 1982. John Donaldson, then minister of external affairs, challenged the view that Williams was isolationist. This, he said, was one of the myths about Williams in respect of the Caribbean that continued to be articulated. He observed that Williams never really cut himself off from other Caribbean leaders, many of whom he invited to Port of Spain during the time when he was said to be isolating himself. As Donaldson noted, "Williams was not present at Caribbean meetings because he was ill. We now realize that between 1976 and 1981, he did not travel because he was ill, terminally ill as it turned out. He did not travel, but he received all the Heads of Caribbean Governments who wanted to speak to him. . . . He couldn't go to the meetings" ("Eric Williams in Retrospect", symposium, April 1991).

Donaldson notes that Milton Cato, premier of St Vincent, came to see Williams; so did Michael Manley of Jamaica and Tom Adams of Barbados. All were met at a prime ministerial level. "The fact that he did not take a plane one way, but that they took a plane to come the other way had nothing to do with him taking up an isolated position. . . . He spoke with everybody, but was still isolated. What you can't say is that he isolated himself from them." Donaldson noted that his meetings with the heads whom he met were cordial, and that some lasted for several days. "Adams spent three days, Manley spent two days on official business and several others as a guest of Dr. Williams" (ibid.).

It was also not true to say that Williams adopted a hands-off attitude towards Bishop and Grenada after they seized power in 1979. Williams sent two trusted friends of Bishop to get him to make a statement as to what he intended to do to legitimize his coup. Bishop was asked to say certain things publicly and quickly so that Trinidad could deal with him seriously. He was also asked to say that he had no intention of establishing a totalitarian regime and that he would call elections early. He was asked to say unequivocally that Grenada would not allow itself to be used as a threat to the other small countries of the Caribbean. Williams also told Bishop that the Westminster model involved more than elections:

"There is more to the Westminster model than just elections. There are the role of law, the multiparty system, the separation of church and state, the traditional liberties and so on. To reject all of them on the ground that the model is inapplicable to Third World conditions, is to throw out the baby with the bath water" (Rose 2002, 302).

Although Williams did not tell Donaldson what he would do if the statement was made, Donaldson implied that Williams, who did not like Gairy or what he stood for, especially his links with Pinochet of Chile, might have endorsed Bishop publicly. Donaldson, who was minister of external affairs, was asked to follow up on the matter. Bishop did not make the statement but instead wrote to Williams. The latter refused to open it unless the suggested statements were openly made. According to Donaldson, the prime minister got tired holding the letter in his hand and subsequently just placed it on the records of the cabinet and refused to open the envelope. It is not known what was in Bishop's letter.

Anthony Gonzalves maintains that Williams did become isolated after 1976, and believes that had he not become so, he might have helped to moderate Cuba's influence on Grenada. This might have averted what subsequently occurred in Grenada:

> He sat back; no action was taken. We did not join with the Venezuelans to compete with the Cubans. . . . It ended up with Williams being a tragic isolationist in the region having few friends. He was not on speaking terms with Mr. Manley, Mr. Castro, with Mr. Burnham or the Venezuelan people; he more or less stood by himself. . . . All the initiatives he took backfired. . . . He ended up being isolated in a sense by consequences. . . . He felt he had no influence. He could not control what Manley did. He could not control lots of things that were happening to him, and justifiably so, because he was an economic power and not a military power. He had economic resources, but economic resources were not enough to compete with the powers that were competing in the area. ("Eric Williams in Retrospect", symposium, April 1991)

Gonzalves was of the view that the problem had to do with Williams's diplomatic style:

> He did not perceive the complexity of the situation, the fact that these countries did not want to isolate Venezuela. He did not perceive how complex the Cuban situation was, the kinds of initiatives one had to take in order to ensure that things would move ahead. All he did was sit and get vexed when he did not get some particular result he wanted. And of course at that particular point in time, he had the resources to get vexed; and he decided he would just stay by himself. . . . The last period seems to be one in which Williams's qualities as a statesman largely diminished. The earlier Williams was to some extent fundamentally different from the later Williams. (Ibid.)

The view that Williams isolated himself from the Caribbean was not unanimous, however. Dr Anselm Francis, also of the Institute of International

Relations, did not agree that Williams had abandoned the Caribbean. He believed that it was more correct to say that Williams was ambivalent. Francis recalled that Williams was instrumental in establishing CARICOM and that the Treaty of Chaguaramas was actually signed in Chaguaramas. He also played an active role in negotiating the Protocol of Port of Spain, which defused the border conflict between Guyana and Venezuela in 1975. He agreed, however, that by the mid-1970s, Williams had become disillusioned with Caribbean leaders, some of whom he felt had betrayed him. This was especially so in respect of Jamaica. Said Francis, "And it would seem that he had that kind of personality that once he feels you betrayed him or didn't do something in the particular way that he wanted, it is the end." This did not mean that he had lost his vision of Caribbean identity. That might explain why he continued to provide generous economic help to alleviate the problems faced by the Caribbean people even though he had little to do with their leaders. "He just became disenchanted as a result of the number of disappointments which he had over the years" (ibid.)

It was in a sense tragic that someone who began by seeing himself as "Mr Caribbean", and who was widely regarded as the "father" and philosopher of Caribbean nationalism, should have ended his career in virtual isolation from what was taking place in the wider Caribbean. Williams felt that the Caribbean had betrayed him rather than the other way around. He noted that despite all they had done or not done, he had made TT$500 million available in 1980 in low-interest loans. to enable them to buy fertilizers, asphalt and petroleum products over the next three years. Notwithstanding that, an "ungrateful" Manley told a People's National Party conference that money was not everything. "Trinidad had a great deal of it, and it was going through the system as if the country had taken a dose of salts." Williams and many Trinidadians understandably felt insulted. Manley later explained that he was misunderstood. His argument was that more than money was needed to effect sustainable development.

Williams denied, if only for the record, that he was responsible for the failures of the Caribbean integration movement. Calypsonian Black Stalin had asked querulously in his 1979 song "Caribbean Man", "How come Mr. West Indian Politician, who went to big institution, can't unite seven million?" Williams was stung by Stalin's angry question, and replied to him in an extended address to a PNM convention on 28 September 1979, saying that "it was not for want of trying on the part of Trinidad and Tobago that disunity prevailed". Williams proceeded to list several things that he had proposed to effect unity, and complained that all his efforts were met with a "monumental silence of the grave. What do we do now?" he sneered. "Call another meeting to discuss whether to bring back the Caribs? What does the calypsonian want? He says that 'morning, noon and night, is just money speech "dem" Prime Minister giving, but that money isn't everything'." True enough, Williams told Stalin, "but Trinidad only gives when asked. Trinidad and Tobago helps where it can, but cannot do all that is expected of it, even if it were willing to subordinate its domestic priorities, which it is not."

Williams told Stalin that he was not to be blamed for the failure to unite the Caribbean. In his view, the question should be put to Manley and Burnham and the politicians of the eastern Caribbean who were prepared to prostitute themselves for a mess of Venezuelan pottage. As he said on another occasion, "I strove hard for West Indian unity, to do something the West Indies could be proud of. What god hath put asunder, let no man join together. That is the law of Caribbean society. That is the history of these disjointed islands populated by persons brought from all parts of Europe, Africa, Asia and latterly, the Americans, a population of transients seeking to go elsewhere" (Williams 1980, 441). He also cynically observed that "there will soon be nothing to integrate in any case; the populations will all have gone." Williams noted the extent to which the people of the Caribbean had migrated to Europe and the Americas, taking with them skills that the Caribbean had paid to develop. His estimate was that between 1946 and 1977, the Caribbean had lost some 1.5 million persons:

> The only possible alternative to this migration pattern in the Caribbean is the one proposed by Trinidad and Tobago – an economic integration of the entire Caribbean irrespective of historical allegiance whether language or nationality. With its greater economic stability and foreign currency reserves Trinidad and Tobago has put forward this proposal. The metropolitan countries are determined not to have it, the Caribbean peoples do not want it. The dependency continues, offered by the developed countries, accepted by the underdeveloped – anything except Trinidad and Tobago, they go a-whoring after false gods. (Ibid., 1980, 445)

Williams, in short, was pleading not guilty to the charges of having failed Trinidad and Tobago and the Caribbean. Much that was hoped for was not achieved; the fault, however, lay not at his doorstep. The world had become more complex than he and many others had understood in 1956, and social and economic change more difficult to engineer than originally thought.

Plate 31 Williams with Errol Mahabir on Budget Day, 1 December 1978. (Trinidad and Tobago Express Ltd)

Plate 32 Signing ceremony with Prime Minister Tom Adams of Barbados at the prime minister's official residence at St Ann's, May 1979. (Trinidad and Tobago Express Ltd)

Plate 33 Erica Williams being introduced to Beverley Manley, wife of Michael Manley, prime minister of Jamaica. (Trinidad and Tobago Express Ltd)

Plate 34 Williams greeting Michael Manley, prime minister of Jamaica. (Eric Williams Memorial Collection, University of the West Indies, St Augustine)

Plate 35 Williams welcomes Dr Cheddi Jagan and Mrs Janet Jagan, heads of government meeting, July 1963. (Eric Williams Memorial Collection, University of the West Indies, St Augustine)

Plate 36 Williams with President Julius Nyerere of Tanzania at Whitehall, 15 September 1974. (Trinidad and Tobago Express Ltd)

Plate Williams with Pierre Trudeau, prime minister of Canada, at Whitehall, 15 April 1971. (Trinidad and Tobago Express Ltd)

PART 7

WILLIAMS
THE MYTH AND THE MAN

39 Liberal Democrat or Sawdust Caesar?

Williams has been characterized variously as a totalitarian, a fascist, a benevolent dictator or a soft authoritarian. Some critics even accused him of having created a police state between 1970 and 1975, or alternatively, claim that he was "saved" from doing so by the OPEC revolution, which allowed him to use money instead of police batons to smother and neutralize dissent. Others counter-claim that Williams was a genuine liberal democrat who never used more state violence than was necessary to deal with threats to the constitutional order, which he was sworn to defend. To determine the extent to which these competing assessments are valid or otherwise, we examine Williams's relationships with the judiciary, the media and the police.

Williams and the Judiciary

The relationship between Williams and the judiciary was in part informed by the relationship that existed between him and Sir Hugh Wooding, the man he invited to become the country's first post-independence chief justice. The two men were rivals for the public's esteem. While Williams was considered by many to be the most outstanding son that the country had produced, Wooding was a strong challenger for that honour. Wooding's achievements were in many fields. In addition to an outstanding career as a student at Queen's Royal College and as a practitioner of the law, he distinguished himself in municipal politics, the world of the university, religion, business and community activity. Wooding felt that he had an obligation to join the nationalist movement and help nurture it as "a backroom boy". His application in 1956 to join the PNM was, however, "summarily" rejected by Williams, who saw him as a potential rival. Wooding was deeply hurt by the rejection, and vowed that he would never again become involved in politics.

Williams and Wooding had their first open clash in 1958, when the latter resigned from the Carnival Development Committee that Williams had asked him to head. The two men had different views about how the committee should be managed and who should have ultimate responsibility for carnival policy. As Williams saw it, "The issue to be decided is: who governs Trinidad? We say it is the Government of Trinidad and Tobago. . . . And those who do not like it could walk and resign in a body."

Notwithstanding this epic clash of the two icons, Williams invited Wooding to become the country's first chief justice. Wooding was not Williams's first choice, however. The job was offered to Ellis Clarke, who had previously served as chief justice in 1961, but only for one session. Clarke subsequently became Williams's constitutional adviser. The parliamentary opposition thus felt that the choice of Clarke as chief justice was inappropriate. Clarke himself agreed that he was perceived as being too aligned to the executive to be considered impartial, and that Wooding would in fact be "more of a gift to the country". Williams's second choice was Justice Hugh McShine, but the parliamentary opposition persuaded Williams that they would prefer Wooding, who had shown his independence of the PNM. Williams's invitation to Wooding and his acceptance were regarded by many as a healing of the breach between the two men.

The relationship between the judiciary and the executive was difficult during the early years of independence. Two areas of controversy were the question of salaries and pensions for judges and the place that the chief justice should occupy in the protocol order. In terms of the latter, Wooding strenuously objected to having the office of chief justice ranked after cabinet ministers, the Speaker, and president of the senate, and refused to attend official functions until such time as the office was placed after that of the governor general and the prime minister, that is, third in precedence. This was eventually conceded when it became clear that the judiciary was firm in its support of the chief justice on this issue.

The question of full pensions for the judiciary was also an issue of great controversy. Before Wooding moved to the bench, it was the practice to recruit judges from the civil service. Judges were thus able to transfer their accumulated pensions from the civil service to the judicial service. Wooding and some of those whom he recruited from the bar would not have been entitled to full pensions under the then rules, because their length of service would have been insufficient (thirty-five years of service was required) to permit them to qualify. Promises were made by the executive, but they were long in being fulfilled. The judges felt that they were being shabbily treated on this and other issues, and protested vigorously. It was noted that in Jamaica, the chief justice was guaranteed a full pension even if he served only one day in office. In a meeting with the governor general called to discuss the issue in 1964, Wooding made it clear that he was prepared to resign if the matter was not satisfactorily resolved, which it eventually was. Resignation would have been disastrous for all concerned. The relationship between the judiciary and the executive improved thereafter, and the Wooding Court was in fact often accused by radical trade unions of being too sympathetic to the new regime and the employer class, and too wedded to British precedent about the role of parliament, which was deemed to be supreme.

Wooding retired from the bench in 1966 and was replaced by Justice Hugh McShine. His relationship with Williams soured in 1970, when he spoke out against the provisions of the Public Order Bill, and again in 1972 when Isaac Hyatali was appointed chief justice instead of Clement Phillips, who was then acting in the post. It was felt that Phillips was not appointed because he was not pliable politically. The overriding factor, however, was not Phillips's health, nor the perception that he was not politically pliable, nor that Wooding had recommended him for the appointment. Hyatali was appointed as part of an ethnic package deal that Williams felt he had to make. Williams wanted to appoint Ellis Clarke to replace the ailing Sir Solomon Hochoy (a Chinese) with a black governor general, and felt that he had to appease the Indian community by appointing Hyatali (who, in any case, was senior to Phillips) chief justice, despite his knowledge that the "creole" legal establishment, Wooding included, was firmly opposed to such an appointment.[1]

Williams's appointment of Hyatali has to be seen against the background of the crisis through which the judiciary was going in 1972. It is clear that Williams did regard Justices Phillips, P.T. Georges and Aubrey Fraser as politically suspect, since they had handed down a number of judgements that went against the state, including the judgement of the military court in the 1970 mutiny trial, which they reversed on the ground that the judge advocate had made a number of legal errors during the court martial. What perhaps galled Williams even more was the fact that the appeal court, consisting of these same three judges, had refused the state's application to appeal the matter to the privy council in February 1972, and that in May 1972, Fraser and Georges were part of a curia that freed another soldier who had been found guilty by the court martial in 1971. The state then sought to bypass the appeal court by going directly to the privy council, which subsequently threw out the state's appeal, forcing an embarrassed government to withdraw charges of treason from all the soldiers, and to advise the mercy committee to free those whose sentences of mutiny had been previously confirmed.

The appointment of Hyatali did not bring to an end the crisis within the judiciary, and between it and the executive. In a sense, the appointment aggravated it, in that it led to the resignations of Justices Telford Georges, Aubrey Fraser and Clement Malone from the bench, and that of Wooding and Justice Algernon (Pope) Wharton, QC, from the Judicial and Legal Services Commission.

Notwithstanding what has been said or implied about Williams's relationship with the judiciary, however, the record suggests that he never openly quarrelled with any judgement given. Nor did he ever seek to intimidate judges such as Burnham did in Guyana, or as others did in several Commonwealth states where judges were fired, detained, executed or made to swear allegiance to the executive. His handling of the judiciary was always constitutionally correct, though he was not above letting judges know, usually through the governor general, when he was displeased with what they did. It may well be that much of what came to be established practice had to do with the prestige of the first chief justice and the status of the court over which he presided, as well as Williams's intellectual Britishness.

Williams and the Media

Williams was not always politically correct in his relationship with the media. He often quarrelled openly with the established print media, which frequently accused him of being a "sawdust Ceasar". The *Trinidad Guardian* often compared him to Hitler and Goebels, and Williams reciprocated by ritualistically consigning the paper to the flames. The media generally were also accused of professional incompetence, obscurantism, resorting to gossip and bacchanal, and deliberate misrepresentation of government's policies and programmes. In the early years, Williams's venom was reserved for the foreign-owned *Trinidad Guardian*. In later years, the *Guardian* became more interested in profits than in politics, leaving the role of effective critic of the government to the *Trinidad Express*, which began publishing in 1969. Williams never missed the opportunity to lampoon both the *Express* and the *Guardian*. As he complained, "We have lived with the hostilities of the media from the day we were conceived. The local press can be no more a respecter of truth or national sovereignty than a press under foreign ownership."

The *Express* was a veritable thorn in Williams's side, particularly in the early 1970s when it functioned as a medium for the publication of radical ideas. Williams was angry with the *Express*, which he once described as "fundamentally, one of the most dishonest newspapers that ever disgraced Trinidad and Tobago" (*Trinidad Express*, 23 May 1971). Williams openly threatened the paper: "When I am ready to deal with the papers, I will deal with them. They are not newspapers. One is an Opposition paper. It does not print anything about the PNM. If it prints it, it distorts it" (ibid.). He was particularly incensed by the hard-hitting columns of "Benedict Wight", the nom de plume of *Express* editor Owen Baptiste, whose pen at times dripped with anti-PNM acid.

Generally, the paper argued that it was doing what it was created to do, that is, give voice to the voiceless. The *Express* also noted that in a real sense it was the creation of the Williams of the 1950s and early 1960s who had taught

"Caliban" how to curse. The views of Ken Gordon, one of the paper's publishers, about Williams's relationship with the print media are worth repeating:

> Dr. Williams was a past master at bringing pressure to bear on the press. He had dealt comprehensively with the *Guardian* on one occasion, publicly tearing up one of its newspapers and consigning it to the flames. Lord Thomson, who later became its owner, [however] had only one ambition for his Caribbean properties, - to make money out of them. He had neither stomach nor desire to fight local issues. And so the *Guardian* hid its impotence under the guise of mirroring the events of the society and leaving the serious issues alone.
>
> The political guns were therefore always trained on the Express. Initially it was expected that we would collapse. When that did not happen, we were singled out for special treatment. But it was always done cleverly. The prime minister could never be faulted for anything he said about press freedom. The letter of the law was strictly observed, but whenever the opportunity presented itself it was "pressure down the line." But this conflict provided us with the opportunity to emerge as the voice of change. We earned a credibility that the *Guardian* could never have and, equally important, learnt how to survive under consistently applied pressure. (1999, 74)

Gordon also tells us that a lot of the pressure that came from Williams was directed through members of the paper's board of directors. Many messages came via Carlton Mack, who was a close friend of Governor General Solomon Hochoy, his co-ethnic. As Gordon recalled,

> We also discovered at the *Express* around that time that pressure against a newspaper is more effective when it is threatened than when it is applied. On more than one occasion, serious differences would occur at board meetings because of messages that had been received either from someone speaking to Dr. Williams or someone who was known to be close to the governor general, Sir Solomon Hochoy. The anticipation of where these implied threats could lead was in itself a nightmare and led to all sorts of dire warnings from the board. On the other hand, when action was taken against us, and an application rejected as in the case of the television licence, or we were deliberately excluded or publicly condemned, this led to a closing of ranks at board level and reinforcing of the independent stance of the newspaper (Ibid., 76).

Williams's relationship with the media is well exemplified by his dealings with Raoul Pantin, a young reporter who was sympathetic to some of the radical movements of the 1970s. His name was in fact on the list of persons to be detained in 1970. Williams, however, felt it might be useful to co-opt him and so delegated William Demas, one of his mandarins, to put an offer on the table. Pantin declined, much to Williams's chagrin. Williams seemed to believe that he could induce Pantin to change his mind and invited the latter to his office for a chat. Pantin was awed by Williams's "aura". As he recalled, "As he talked, shuffling and unshuffling that pipe, for the first time in his life, the reporter understood the meaning of the word, 'aura': it glowed around him like a force field. The reporter thought of the Spider and the fly" (Pantin 1990, 102).

After three meetings, the matter was not pursued. "Throughout it all, the reporter felt he understood their real purpose. . . . He was being probed, assessed, examined like an insect" (ibid., 102–3). Pantin went on to detail the various ways in which Williams's gatekeepers sought to "manage" the media, censor "bad" news, or in some cases in respect of the state-owned electronic media, fire journalists (ibid., 105–6).

The government was also frequently accused of abusing and monopolizing the state-owned radio and television facilities, especially at election time, and seeking to silence or sideline journalists who were not willing to compromise their professional integrity for a mess of pottage. While there were numerous occasions on which the media clashed with the regime generally or with Williams himself, these were no different from what would normally obtain in any mature democracy. Williams never detained a journalist, as occurred routinely in many Commonwealth countries in Africa or Asia. While a number of radical black publications (and some that marketed sex) were banned, no media house was ever shut down or deprived of newsprint, as occurred in Guyana, Grenada and Singapore. Dissent was tolerated (even if denounced) whether in the media, or in the calypso, which was often more critical than the established media. There were, however, a few cases where overzealous authorities sought to second-guess Williams and act in ways that invited the conclusion that he was hostile to media critics.[2]

Williams and State Violence

Between 1972 and 1974 there were numerous manhunts, as well as searches of homes, some belonging to prominent people including two doctors and a permanent secretary. The searches, which were often executed by the dreaded "Flying Squad" under the leadership of the assistant commissioner, Randolph Burroughs, were carried on amid great show of force, and invariably nothing was found to justify the brutality. The public was upset, and there was a general feeling of outrage and anxiety. The clergy, political parties and prominent individuals called angrily for an amnesty to be declared and for the guerillas to be invited to a conference to work out a compromise. The authorities refused to deal with those whom they considered robbers.

There has been much controversy as to how much of this Williams knew and condoned. Khafra Kambon argued that Williams consciously presided over the establishment of a repressive state, though he conceded that Trinidad and Tobago never reached the stage of being a police state such as obtained in much of Latin America. Williams, he also admitted, was not a typical *caudillo*. "But," he insists, "a lot of young people were murdered by Williams. . . . The record indicates that some 29 persons were killed between 1970 and 1973":

> Williams was in power when these people were murdered by the police. There was never any serious effort to try and prevent the kind of outright political murder that was taking place in the 1970s. Not only that; it was Williams himself who was responsible for the appointment of Randolph Burroughs as Police Commissioner, and that was a time when Burroughs had built up a reputation for killing. . . . The only reason he was put there was to give the impression of "dreadness" to the country because he saw the 1970s as "dread times."

Kambon claimed that Williams began to intimidate his challengers as early as 1963, when he was at the height of his popularity:

> Clearly there are times when you will expect a government to react very harshly. In 1970, the Government either had to react very harshly or be overthrown. I have no problem with Williams declaring the State of Emergency and releasing his forces. Whether he called for the Americans or not, I don't have a problem with that. But if we look at a pattern before that, I think the Mbanefo Commission [into Subversive Activity) was very significant because Williams was still at the height of his popularity. The Report was released in 1965, but the Commission was established in 1963. . . . The fact that he would have resorted to a Commission of that kind as early as 1963 tells us something about his personality – maybe a tendency to some kind of paranoia. ("The Black Power Revolution 1970", symposium, April 1990).

Williams's explanation of the appointment of this commission was that he could not ignore the security reports that he was receiving and that suggested communist elements were seeking to penetrate the system. Kambon claims that the belief that Williams was not a repressive leader had to do with his "remarkable intellectual image. He got away with the pretense".

The chief justice, Sir Isaac Hyatali, also expressed concern about the role of the police. The police were said to have a tendency to abuse and exceed their role as keepers of the peace, and assume instead the stance of executioner, as is the rule in some South American republics. In his view, "The illegal or arbitrary act of an agency of the state is an abuse of executive power, however ignorant of it the central executive may be." Hyatali was exonerating Williams, but others rightly felt that he must have been aware of what was being done (*Trinidad Express*, 20 September 1980).

A contradictory view of Williams was offered by Overand Padmore, who was minister of national security for five years under Williams. Padmore claimed that Williams always sought options that eschewed confrontation or the use of state violence. Whenever crises arose, his instructions were to avoid violence whenever possible, and to ensure that no one got hurt. "He was no cowboy and was always slow to respond." This was true in 1970 as well as in 1975 during so-called Bloody Tuesday. Padmore also defended Williams from the allegation that he made Burroughs commissioner of police in order to brutalize those who were challenging the state. Padmore insisted that "he did not put Borroughs there to kill or frighten anybody". According to Padmore, criminals in Trinidad and Tobago did not regard Burroughs as a repressive police officer. "He was a negotiator with them all" ("The Black Power Revolution 1970", symposium, April 1990). Burroughs's principal confrontations with political dissidents took place before he became commissioner, and when he was head of the feared "Flying Squad", which was responsible for a great deal of the repression and the executions that took place in the 1970s. It remains a fact that in the relative quiet of 1980, a paranoid Williams awarded Burroughs the nation's highest honour, the Trinity Cross, presumably for what he had done in the past to contain dissidence and perhaps for what he expected him to continue doing, if necessary, in the turbulent years that might lie ahead.

Williams, however, lacked the ruthlessness of a Burnham or a Gairy. He was critical of Burnham's penchant for de facto one-partyism as well as Michael Manley's seeming willingness to militarize Jamaican society. He also had a great deal to say about the repressive nature of Cuban society, and clearly believed that adopting a socialist strategy of development would have had political consequences that, as a liberal, he abhorred. Socialism, he believed, would lead to "instability, military coups, non-partyism and the castration of political democracy". Williams in fact boasted that Trinidad was "one of the most relaxed democracies in the Third World. No one is locked up for attacking the government".

His record in dealing with labour unrest also compares well with that of most developed countries and was superior to most Third World countries where workers were either shot for demonstrating or detained. As he told workers following the 1975 strike in the oil and sugar industries, which virtually closed down the country: "You keep shouting for all these years about dictatorship and now you find people saying, 'why does the government not do something to make petrol available?' If you want the freedom that we have, this is the price we have to pay. . . . If freedom means irresponsibility, too bad. The police are there to reduce irresponsibility." Williams complimented the police for not shooting anyone. He also noted that the president of Venezuela had dealt ruthlessly with a strike in the oil industry in 1975. He simply told workers that if they did not return to work by a given day, they would be deemed to have lost their jobs. Said Williams, "We did not have to do that. We handled it a bit more (what should I say) diplomatically."

While Trinidad under Williams was a free and open society when compared with most of the world, there is no denying that over the years the statute book became littered with repressive legislation that was used whenever the government felt that the jugular of the system was threatened. One only needs to recall the numerous states of emergency proclaimed between 1965 and 1973, the Industrial Stabilization Bill, the Industrial Relations Bill, the Firearms Ordinance, the Summary Offences Ordinance, the ban on "subversive" literature, and the draconian Public Order Bill (which was only withdrawn after massive public protest). The government also used the army and the police to break strikes in the petroleum and sugar industries and in the postal services. In 1977, all the pilots of the national airline were dismissed after they had gone on what was clearly an illegal strike.

A great deal of the stability and industrial peace that the society enjoyed could be explained in terms of the fact that workers, particularly in the public sector and the essential services, were aware that the government was prepared to incur substantial economic losses in order to make the point that the era of militant collective bargaining was over. As the leader of the All Trinidad Sugar and General Workers Union, Basdeo Panday, noted, "We in sugar have begun to realize that whereas the strike weapon was our effective instrument to improve conditions of work when we were fighting capitalists, we must now devise a new instrument to fight state capitalism since the State has control of the army and the police." Panday claimed that Williams's inability to govern had given rise to a subtle form of fascism: "In its desperate attempts to survive in the teeth of its inability to govern, the PNM has resorted to a subtle form of racism, which, as time progresses, is becoming not so subtle after all. . . . Over the past couple of years, there has been a growing militarization of the state" (address to ULF, 28 October 1979).

The claim that a police state was being created came not only from radical critics of the ruling party. A similar criticism was made by Hector McLean shortly after he resigned as a minister in 1977 and member of the PNM. McLean was critical of the government's decision in December 1977 to declare civil aviation an essential service. "You do not use a sledge hammer to kill a tick. To my mind, this is one of the dangers in what the government is doing." The government, alleged McLean, who was in a position to know, was catapulting the police into more and more areas of national life and was trying to "run the country by police. Government was very quietly building up a police and army presence on an otherwise peaceful and law abiding country." However, McLean was unwilling or unable to say unequivocally whether "this dangerous and insidious trend" was the brainchild of Williams himself or of some of the ministers Williams appointed from the senate after the 1976 elections – ministers McLean claims were not noted for their progressive political tendencies: "I don't think that anyone, even those who have worked closely with him, can successfully pontificate on the things that cause the Prime Minister to tick. But it must either mean that he is in agreement with what has been happening or that he does not wield the power and authority that many people would expect him to wield" (Ryan 1988a, 147).

McLean was hinting that Williams was not as liberal as he appeared. While Williams was clearly a liberal in terms of his intellectual convictions, he often compromised those convictions in the context of practical political action. He believed that no government could permit complete freedom in the exercise of civil rights and that freedom must be exercised with restraint if the society was not to be destroyed when interests tried to maximize every opportunity that existed for profit and advancement. As Thomas Hobbes argued several centuries ago, the leviathan state is the other side of the liberal state. The two are necessary to each other. Hegel would also say that the two representations of the state are dialectically related, and that the hybridized resolution constitutes the synthesis of what is teleological required (see Berlin 2006, 237–48).

Williams's government was, however, economical in the use of force to contain dissidence. Abuses there clearly were, but most would agree that despite them Williams contributed enormously to the creation of a political tradition in which liberal democratic values are still cherished, and that this tradition has made it difficult for successor regimes to set them aside lightly.

Williams's leadership style has been compared with that of Kwame Nkrumah of Ghana, Julius Nyerere of Tanzania and Lee Kuan Yew of Singapore. There is no disputing that Williams was far more reserved in his use of coercion than any of the other three. This is in part due to the fact that the societies were fundamentally different. Ghana, for example, was a more difficult society to manage than Trinidad and Tobago. Its tribally based opposition was more recalcitrant than that of Trinidad and Tobago and far less aware of or committed to the principles of Westminster. Regionalism was also strong in Ghana, as was tribalism, chieftaincy and inter-village rivalry. The same held to a lesser degree in Tanzania. Thus the ease with which their leaderships abandoned the multi-party systems with which they were outfitted at independence. Both Nyerere and Nkrumah also resorted to using systematic preventive detention, outlawing strikes and go-slows, expelling or arresting members of parliament and party members who disagreed with them, silencing newspaper critics, outlawing competitive elections, abolishing chieftaincy (in Tanzania), or, in the case of Ghana, firing and detaining the chief justice.

Williams understood why they felt the need to curtail democratic freedoms, and while he might at times have expressed the wish that he could follow their example in the name of discipline, public order and ease of policy making, he was too committed to being a liberal intellectual of the British stripe to experiment with what he regarded as barbaric political forms. In his view, there was more to the Westminster model than just elections. There was the rule of law, the multiparty system, the separation of church and state, the traditional liberties and so on. To reject all of them on the ground that the model was inapplicable to Third World conditions was to ignore what was foundational about the model (Rose 2002, 302).

Notwithstanding Williams's liberal credentials, he was not above using some of the techniques of political management employed by Nkrumah, Nyerere and Lee, who leaned hard on the media and used the police when necessary to deal with dissidents. He also had C.L.R. James, the distinguished organic intellectual, placed under house arrest, and between 1970 and 1975 had several individuals detained or harassed by the authorities. In sum, like Nyerere, Nkrumah or Lee, Williams was neither a saint nor a Kantian intellectual. The system he established could in some respects be deemed a "dictatorship without the terror". Williams, however, did not call himself the Osagyefo (Redeemer), as Nkrumah did, the Kabaka, as Burnham did, or Joshua, as Michael Manley did. Nor would he have said that the "CPP is Ghana and I am the CPP", as Nkrumah did. But while he never encouraged a personality or loyalty cult, a great deal of cult-like behaviour occurred without him having to actively promote it.

Williams and Lee Kuan Yew

Williams has been compared unfavourably with Lee Kuan Yew in terms of what the latter was able to achieve in creating a disciplined society with high levels of economic development. When Singapore became independent in 1959 as part of the Malaysian Federation, it was a poor struggling economy. Today its per capita GNP is higher than that of Great Britain and five times that of Argentina, Chile and Mexico. While there were several exogenous and geographical factors relating to the Cold War that help to account for Singapore's success, full credit has to be given to Lee and the people of Singapore for what they were able to achieve. Both Lee and Williams understood that success in nation building required discipline and order. But whereas Williams was only prepared to talk about the need for discipline, Lee was prepared to "walk the talk". He was critical of the individualism that obtained in the West, which he felt inevitably led to a breakdown of civil society, and with it the prevalence of alternative family systems, drugs, guns, violent crime, aggressive begging, vagrancy and other forms of public misbehaviour.

While culture helps us to understand the differences between Trinidad and Singapore, the fact is that Lee was more disposed to using an authoritarian political style than was Williams. While Singapore is nominally a democracy, in reality it is an authoritarian state in which an elected ruling elite take key decisions. Lee was sceptical about Western-style democracy, which privileged the inviolable individual. His preference was for an ordered government that was "comfortable because it meets our needs, is not oppressive, and maximizes our opportunities". Singapore, however, was a much more oppressive state than Trinidad was under Eric Williams.

Interestingly, Williams agreed that Trinidad's carnival mentality was a constraint on its development, but he claimed that Singaporeans were beginning to behave like Trinidadians in that they were chafing at the regime of discipline that Lee had forced upon them. Lee had complained that Singaporean workers were becoming "choosy, irresponsible, impatient and money minded", and he once threatened to import foreign skilled and professional workers as a challenge to Singaporeans to improve their own skills. Said Williams, "Were Singaporeans adopting the 'carnival mentality' for which they have criticized Trinidad and Tobago?" (in Sutton 1981, 436).

Williams clearly felt that there were fundamental cultural and social differences between the people of Singapore and those of Trinidad and Tobago, and that any attempt to coerce the latter into disciplined and socially obedient behaviour would be a non-starter. He was correct. The fact that the main group that he led was of African provenance, while that led by Lee was Chinese, made all the difference (Ryan and Stewart 1994). The latter were more family and group based, more stoic and socially obedient, and more future oriented than Trinidadians were and are ever likely to be.

There is abundant evidence that the Chinese worker in Singapore was more hard working and disciplined than his African counterpart in the Caribbean, and that Williams understood what he was up against and opted to flow with the cultural tide – at times even seeming to justify the attitude of the Trinidad worker.

40   Man Talking to Man

Williams and the Calypsonian

Dr Williams came like Moses in biblical history
And he led us like children of Israel to Independency.
  – Mighty Dougla

The calypsonian David Rudder correctly observed that the lyrics of the calypsonian often "make a politician cringe". During the colonial era, the calypso was one of the principal vehicles of political and social protest. The follies and foibles of colonial administrators and those who functioned as agents of the imperial system were lampooned in song by slaves and later by working class poets "*sans humanité*" (without pity or mercy). What it was not possible for the critic to say openly was seditiously articulated during the calypso season, either in the calypso tents or on the streets.

The authorities reacted to this type of "guerilla" protest with a mixture of rage and repression. Officials complained that the names and reputations of "decent" people were sullied in the street and made the subject of vile jests by these "false prophets or grumblers". In 1868, the colonial authorities went so far as to prohibit the singing of any profane song or ballad, and convicted several persons for infringing the law. Another attempt was made to censor calypsos in the politically turbulent 1930s and 1940s. Calypsonians were required to submit the texts of their compositions to the police for scrutiny. This was outright censorship, and calypsonians were angry at this attempt to restrict their poetic licence. This is the tradition of the "calypso war" that informed Williams's relationship with the calypsonians of his day.[1]

In the early years of the PNM, the calypsonian, who was invariably black and of the lower class, saw Eric Williams in much the same way as most blacks of the time. The most successful and influential bard of the time, the Mighty Sparrow, lionized Williams and helped to enhance his aura and legitimacy in the eyes of the black creole community, and also to silence the dissent of those who were not under the PNM's "big tent". He was, in a real sense, the poet laureate of the PNM revolution, and the popular comment was "If Sparrow say so, is so!" Sparrow helped shape the myth that Williams was the messiah, and that to touch him politically was tantamount to committing political "murder", or, at best, apostasy. Gordon Rohlehr is, however, correct when he observes that Sparrow and others "reechoed the politician's tone which was little more than reverberations from the street's rough turbulence".

In one of his classic calypsoes, "William the Conqueror", Sparrow records the outcome of the epic political battle between Williams and Albert Gomes in the 1956 general election (see chapter 9). Williams was the man with the "Big Brains" and Gomes the man with the "Big Belly":

> I am sure you've heard the story
> About Big Brain and Big Belly (*repeat*)
> Well, Sparrow ain't fraid to talk
> Who don't like it can take a walk
> Fight finish, no bruise, no cuts
> But a man fall down on he guts
>
> *Chorus*
> Praise little Eric, rejoice and be glad
> We have a better future here in Trinidad
> PNM, it ain't got nobody like them
> For they have a champion leader,
> William, the Conqueror.
>
> I am no Politician but I could understand
> If it wasn't for Brother Willie
> And his ability
> Trinidad wouldn't go, neither come
> We used to vote for food and rum
> But nowadays, we eating all the feeders and them
> And in the ending, we voting for PNM.

Not surprisingly, Carnival 1957 was a "balisier carnival", and many calypsonians captured the mood in song. People were also urged to drink "balisier" rum, that is, the locally produced Vat 19 rum. The balisier had come to symbolize the new cultural hegemony; it also served as a metaphor for the new state in the making. There was, however, some grumbling about the taxes imposed in Williams's first budget. Sparrow, like many of his listeners, felt that his hero seemed to have taken the people for the proverbial political ride. In the 1957 song "No Doctor No", Sparrow, in the tradition of the griot, issued the first of many warnings to Williams:

Listen, listen carefully
I am a man does never be sorry (*repeat*)
But I went and vote for some council men
They have me now in a pen
After promising to give so much tender care
They forget me as they walk out of Woodford Square

Chorus
They raise up on the taxi fare, No doctor No!
And the blasted milk gone up so dear, No doctor No!
But you must remember we support you in September
You better come good
Because I have a big piece of mango wood

Sparrow had fired a shot across Williams's bow. He nevertheless supported the prime minister's decision to introduce the "pay as you earn" income tax system. As he sang in "You Can't Get Away From the Tax" (1959):[2]

I would like to know, why they blaming the doctor so
Tell me I would like to know, why they blaming the Doctor so
One class of people, while the other class cussing
Running they mouth like they take Brooklax
Only blaming the Doc for they Income Tax

Chorus
But I want them all to know, they can't get away from the tax
Even if you leave and you go, you can't get away from the tax
To New York or Tokyo, you can't get away from the tax
You could jump high or low, you can't get away from the tax
Even quite in Africa, you can't get away from the tax
So you see Doctor or no Doctor, you can't get away from the tax

Sparrow sang another classic song in 1958, "Pay as You Earn", which was also ambivalent towards Williams but which nevertheless supported the PAYE principle:

It's a shame, it's a shame,
But we have weself to blame (repeat)
Because we ask for new government
Now they taking every cent
Cost of living is the same
So it's really a burning shame

Chorus
The Doctor say to pay as you earn
But Sparrow say you paying to learn
And mih father say he sharpening the axe

So when the collector come to pay off the income tax

Plenty people want to cry
They miss the water, the well run dry
But they can't do a thing about it
The money ent going in the Doctor pocket
First of all we want better schools
So we children won't grow up as fools
Then work for you and me
That is what plenty of them cyar see

Everybody is in misery
But this tax ent bothering me
For I ent working no where
And I have no income to share
But Mr. This and Mr. That
Who accustom with they payroll fat
Is to see them shedding tears
Men like De Freitas and Fernandes

When the Doctor went up to England
They bluntly refuse to support his plan
So there is nothing more he could do
Than to get it from me and you
That's the law now in Trinidad
If you doh like it that's too bad
Take your things and clear out today
For all who working must pay
That's the law now in Trinidad

Williams was pleased with Sparrow's calypso, and went so far as to record his appreciation in *Inward Hunger:* "The public reaction to PAYE . . . gave rise to one of the best calypsos in Trinidad's history, the work, as always of Sparrow." Williams also recalled the carnival of 1958, when "all over the place people were singing the song".

Sparrow, it should be noted, went so far as to blame the parliamentary opposition (the DLP) for the ills of the country. As he sang in "Present Government" (1961),

Come on, what is wrong with this Island?
Poor Dr. Williams (repeat)
Everybody doing what they like
Striking when they want to strike
It appears that nobody care
About the Island economy.

Chorus

No gas today, no phone tomorrow
What next I don't know
No drain digging, no rubbish cleaning
Only corbeaux working
The Island as you see, suffering politically
Because the present Government have some stupid opponent
Oh Lord man they ignorant
Because the present Government have some stupid opponent
Not one is intelligent.

Anything at all the Premier say
They always standing in the way
And like they suffering from a mental shock
Talking one set of sewerage talk.
Sometimes you hear over the radio
Big trouble in the Leg. Co.
The premier cannot make a suggestion
Without a big objection
And some of them may want to object
Really should have a rope "round the neck"

Sparrow also pleased Williams with his "Leave the Damn Doctor", which dealt with the prime minister's controversial and secret marriage to Dr Mayleen Mooksang, a dentist of Chinese ancestry (see chapter 1, note 5).

The controversy over the "resignation" of Patrick Solomon from his post as minister of home affairs in 1965 and his reappointment by Williams as minister of external affairs gave rise to "Solomon", one of Sparrow's greatest political calypsos, so well does it capture the essence and contradictions of Williams's political manners. In this calypso, Williams is made to take on the character of the "democratic badjohn", the man who is the "baddest don in town".[3] The calypso is partially reproduced here:

I am going to bring back Solomon
Who doh like it complain to the Commission
None of them going to tell me how to run my Country
I defy any one of you to dictate to me
I am no Dictator
But when I pass an order
Mr. Speaker, this matter must go no further
I have nothing more to say
And it must be done my way
Come on, come on, meeting done for the day

This land is mine
I am the boss
What I say goes
And who vex los
And if I say that Solomon will be Minister of External Affairs
And you ent like it
Get to hell outa here
Who the hell is you to jump and quarrel
PNM is mine lock, stock and barrel
Who give you the privilege to object
Pay yuh taxes, shut up and have respect
I am a tower of strength, yes
I am powerful but modest – unless
I'm forced to be blunt and ruthless
So shut up and don't squawk
This ent no skylark
When I talk no damn dog bark
My word is law
So watch you case
If you slip you slide
This is my place
And if I say that Solomon will be Minister of External Affairs
And you ent like it
Get to hell outa here

Sparrow also endorsed Williams's struggle for Chaguaramas ("The Base"), as well as his stand on federation. Sparrow blamed Jamaica for the breakup of the federation, but chided Williams for not proceeding with the alternative option to establish a new union between Trinidad, Barbados, and the islands of the eastern Caribbean following Jamaica's withdrawal in 1961. As he sang, "I find we should all be together, not separated as we are because of Jamaica. . . . This is no time to say you ain't federating no more." Sparrow complained that the politicians, including Williams, "defeated the whole aim of the federation. They all wanted to be a big fish in a small pond. The people were completely neglected in the entire experiment". As he moaned, "Federation boil down to simply this / Is dog eat dog and survival of the fittest."

Despite his ambivalence to Williams, Sparrow remained in the prime minister's corner, and his advice to his many listeners in the 1961 election was to "wear their balisier on election day". As he told PNM supporters,

Be careful how you voting
Is your own self you hurting (*repeat*)
Well brethren we want a Government

Like the one we have
Don't change the Government
Otherwise you starve.

Chorus

Take out you identification card
And when you voting
Vote for a prosperous Trinidad
Let me tell you, I know you have good intention
Don't forget Sparrow did mention
Wear your balisier on Election Day
The Doctor break away
Wear your balisier on Election Day
Don't mind what Lionel Seukeran say
Wear your balisier on Election Day
Lio go lie till judgement day
Registration, then election
So use your discretion
Don't worry to say you're sorry
Just vote correctly
It's the best ever government
If I lie I die
Don't make no mistake
You sure to miss the water if the well run dry.

Well the People's National Movement
We'll continue showing improvement
Because the Doctor is a born leader
And to us he is like a father
Look we send him quite to Calcutta
Live at Nehru the Indian Messiah
So you see he ain't prejudice
Don't mind Lionel and he stupidness

Over time, however, Sparrow became progressively disillusioned with Williams, and by the late 1970s, emerged as one of his sharpest critics. Williams, in his view, had now become an enemy of the calypsonian, someone whom one crossed at great risk. As he sang in "Prophet of Doom",

If you happen to see and know
When politicians going wrong
With facts and figures prepared to show
It's better to bite your tongue
Them political boss
Consider you a cross

An obstacle to be removed at any cost
A social conscience is really very
Dangerous to your health
The awesome strength of the powers that be
Most certainly will be felt
To tell them that their priorities
And their performance is under par
They will then proceed to describe
To you who you are.

Sparrow was of course not the only calypsonian to celebrate William's struggles and policies in song. Among the many others were the Mighty Striker, Black Stalin, the Mighty Dougla, the Lord Cristo, the Mighty Duke, the Lord Kitchener, the Lord Blakie and the Mighty Wrangler. Striker's "Don't Blame the PNM" (1959) captured the spirit of dependency on Williams that had developed within the black community, and Wrangler was also full of praise for Williams:

Who build the schools in George Street for us?
Nobody but the Doctor
And the north coast road going to Las Cuevas?
Nobody but the Doctor
And the housing scheme we have in Morvant?
Nobody but the Doctor
And who you think build the bridge we call the flyover?
Nobody but the Doctor

The Mighty Duke also came out in support of Williams's campaign to regain the Chaguaramas base. Duke felt that the day on which the people marched with Williams to Chaguaramas was one to remember: "One prayer, one voice, one call, freedom and Independence for all." Also supporting Williams in song was Lord Melody, who dealt, among other subjects, with the race problem as it emerged in the 1950s. As he complained in "We Are the PNM",

They [the Indians] only provoking the old man
I ain't taking no damn nonsense from them
We are the PNM, they too bold face
This ain't politics, they preaching race
They better have respect for the Doctor
Otherwise is straight to Calcutta.

Cristo also viewed the 1961 election in racial terms. His cry in "Election Violence" (1962) was "Whip them PNM. / If the Indians got on 'top', that would be trouble."

Barking Dogs

The dominant role played by Sparrow in the 1950s and 1960s was assumed in the 1970s by a number of calypsonians, but particularly by Chalkdust (Hollis Liverpool). The mood had changed by then, and the calypsonians reflected the widespread disappointment with, and even disdain for, Williams. In a series of hard-hitting calypsos, Chalkdust urged Williams to "Clear His Name" and reply truthfully to the many questions that were being asked about his commitment to the people. Chalkdust told Williams that future generations would want to determine if he was indeed a giant, the man of integrity portrayed in the myth, or simply a "jackass". Chalkdust "put on his guns" to censure and satirize Williams even though "Harribance", a seer, had "warned" him that Williams had occult powers, and that if he were to put his "mouth" on anyone, "dog eat your supper". Chalkdust, who was a teacher, did in fact draw fire from PNM stalwarts for his stinging criticisms of Williams, and was fired by the Ministry of Education in 1969 for breaching the terms of his contract, which prohibited state employees from engaging in remunerative activity without official permission. Chalkdust's "Reply to the Ministry" (1969) listed the many "big pappies", ministers included, who did precisely that without attracting any censure or punishment. Williams, to his credit, chided those who sought to silence Chalkdust. His advice to the PNM Women's League was, "Let the jackass sing."

Some of the songs that Chalkdust sang in the late 1960s and 1970s with great effect were "Massa Day Done" (1971), "Somebody in Whitehall Mad" (1973), "Ah Fraid Karl" (1972) (Karl Hudson-Phillips was the attorney general), "Clear Your Name" (1972), and "Answer to Black Power" (1971). In the latter song, Chalkdust told Williams that he was responsible for the country's massive brain drain since "vital areas like sugar and oil, were not being run by sons of the soil". Chalkdust advised Williams that repression would not extinguish the flames of social discontent. One had to make structural changes in the society – improve the distribution of income, improve technical education and also reduce the expatriate presence. He also called upon Williams to redeem the promise that he had made in 1956 in respect of morality in public affairs:

> Let your ministers now declare
> their financial profits from year to year
> That's the answer to Black Power.

Chalkdust likewise sang about the conflict between Williams and A.N.R. Robinson between 1966 and 1970, but generally supported Williams. Robinson was accused of betraying Williams, a view widely held by PNM stalwarts. Chalkdust "wrote" A.N.R. on Williams's behalf:

Dear ANR, ANR.
The way you speak now I cannot believe
You flattered me just to deceive
You mean you waited until you see me
Cornered with troubles and misery,
Black Power trying to eat my coo coo
And then you throw me in the bamboo?

I put you in charge of Finance
You put me in a monkey pants
I had to transfer you back
Since my friends you attacked
With your stupid old Finance Act.

In "We Blight", Chalkdust told the religious authorities that the ghosts of those whom Williams destroyed were stalking the land, and the country needed prayers to exorcise the demons: "Father, say six masses for Deafy / Like somebody blight this country." Chalkdust, however, supported Williams in his conflict with Jamaica, Barbados and Guyana, the leaders of which, like the Three Blind Mice, showed no gratitude to Williams for the assistance that he had given them to cushion the shocks that the OPEC-generated oil crisis had caused to their economies.

Valentino, the people's calypsonian, was also a thorn in Williams's political flesh. Valentino told Williams that despite the street protests of 1970, the people did not really want any "revolution", at least in an ideological sense. They wanted a more people-centric government:

They talking 'bout power, Doctor, is you who have power
Ah know when you act woulda be a horse of a different colour
You give them a inch, they take a whole yard
And when you had them under yuh clinch people say you bad
Well, when I heard you address the Nation
I knew that was your intention
But some of the powers you exercise
Unfortunately I must criticize

A citizen should withstand the wrong things in his country
Regardless of what happen, that is my ideology
All we meeting with is oppression and a seta strain
Trials and tribulations, sorrows and pain
When we try to shake up the Government
The result was police ill-treatment
But justice must be done, otherwise History
is going to punish you worse than you punish we

We didn't want them trigger happy police
We only wanted to demonstrate in peace
Yet you hold my people and charge them for sedition
We was marching for equality
Black unity, black dignity
Dr. Williams, we didn't want no revolution

Valentino was critical of Williams's reliance on the white creoles and his seeming unwillingness to listen to the cries of the people. In "Barking Dogs", he challenged Williams frontally:

Now this word is me, and I am this word
So let my voice be heard
Fix your hearing aid and hear what I say
Wipe your glasses and see things my way
The song that you hear is an angry one
And I'm sure if you see things clear that all the happiness is gone
But the dogs, the dogs are barking too long
It's a sign that something is wrong

Valentino also sought to destroy the conventional myth that Trinidad is "nice" and a "paradise" ("Dis Place Nice"). Relator likewise complained about Williams's "deafness". "Deaf Panmen" were being led by a deaf conductor.

Stalin and others also raised the theme of social and economic exclusion in 1976. Stalin urged Williams to give the "Blackman a piece of the action". As he sang,

Oil drilling, money making
Mr. Divider, here is a warning
Mih blood in this country
Mih sweat in this country
So when yuh sharing yuh oil bread
Ah say remember me
This ain't no black power talking
This ain't no talk about revolution
Ah say Mr. Divider, listen to me
This is man talking to man
Piece of the Action

Once a oil dollar making here
Black Stalin want a share
Piece of the action, Ah tell you, piece of the action
Ah say, remember that I have family too
Who want food and clothes just like you
Piece of the action, Ah say, piece of the action

> If the Country scrunting, that ent nothing
> But once oil-bread sharing
> Run something

Stalin was upset that Williams was giving money to Barbados, Jamaica and Guyana rather than to people like him, especially since the CARICOM leaders involved had shown no gratitude to Trinidad and Tobago and instead appeared to be laughing at and "bad talking" (ridiculing) Trinidadians.[4] Several other calypsonians felt driven to remind Williams that "Charity Begins at Home". There were those, however, who lauded Williams for his pro-Caribbean stance. The Antiguan calypsonian Swallow deemed Williams "the Caribbean Godfather", and praised Trinidad for being "our big brother" and for sharing the "oil dollar".

Maestro too felt he had to speak truth to power. In to "To Sir with Love", he complained that the professor of the University of Woodford Square had lost his voice. Maestro complained that he and others voted for Williams in 1971, but all he was getting was pressure.

> Mister, mister is me yuh Black brother
> Pressure, pressure, indeed inward hunger
> The people who oppose you endlessly
> They get plenty, but you ent care bout we
> With the 28 high percent I vote
> Now you turn around and stroke a yoke on mih throat
>
> Very slowly
> Yuh killing we softly
> So crude, no food
> Outright ingratitude
> We give you a fighting chance for 18 years
> And all we get in return is blood, sweat and tears
> Now everywhere your rivals have shares
> And under your reign became millionaires
>
> You watch as advantage is being taken
> On your supporters in the land
> We keep supporting and getting nothing
> While millions going from hand to hand
> Tired, retired old timers going from job to job
> Young strong teenagers on corners hustling for bobs
> I do not rap to trap anyone
> Ah just singing a song on what really going on

In "Dread Man" (1977) Maestro told Williams that the working man was being excluded from the economic bonanza:

Plenty money making
Plenty belly aching
Them buy self-loading rifle
To hassle who give trouble
Workman say they want more pay
They send away for the CIA

Maestro was ambivalent about Williams, however, as were black Trinidadians, many of whom had a love-hate relationship with him. Maestro complained in "Mr Trinidadian" (1973), that Trinidadians could not make up their mind "what scene they on", and more importantly, "who we go put" to replace Williams:

Mr. Trinidad, tell me what scene you on
Do you just like political confusion
You criticizing the way you live
Yet you cyar produce an alternative
You say you against the power structure
You ent like the Opposition either
But take care you jump out the hot water
And end up in the centre of the fire
Cause you refuse to vote in election
But then you ent want revolution
You strongly against Communism
You walk out on colonialism
You say Eric Williams have to go
But who to replace him you ent know
So to make a long story short from in front
Trinidadians really ent know what they want.

Lord Kitchener generally supported Williams and the PNM, but he was outraged by the actions of the "Flying Squad", a heavily armed police unit led by Police Commissioner Randolph Burroughs, whose repressive behaviour many assumed was endorsed by Williams:

Oh what a country
Oh what an awful sin
How they jailing people so
Without a hearing
Where is our freedom
Somebody put a hand
Oh Gorm, the Vengeance of Moko
Go surely fall on this land!

Kitchener also sang "Jericho", in which he put the blame on the police and not Williams and the PNM:

Ah hear they looking in town
Leaving houses in such a state
They ransacking all around
Searching doctors and magistrates
Them people so wicked
They even searching the PNM
But if they search Jericho [the guerrilla]
Ah sorry for them

Kitchener's complaints about the repressive nature of the post-1970 regime was echoed by Stalin in "Nothing ent Strange":

Leh we say that when you read your morning newspaper
The headlines say that they hold Stalin for guerrilla
Ah know plenty people may want to shout
But, Brotherman, what is there to shout about
I am living in a yes-man society
Where all the no-men become the enemy
And if you decide to hold tight to your "no"
The system have so much different ways of getting you to go

Nothing, nothing, nothing ent strange
In the life of a man out for change
Once you doh want people talk for you
And won't do the things that they want you to
Your life ent safe whether night or day
Because any number could play
Nothing, nothing, nothing ent strange
In the life of a man out for change

The system have a vicious way of operating
It's like a vulture when it about to attack its victim
Once you say they wrong and feeling you right
It can attack you like a thief in the night
One day you are a hero, next day a traitor
One day you're wealthy, next day a pauper
And just play you smart and too intelligent
You could die in Mayaro in some freak accident

Now I know all 'bout this system and its working
But for a better life for my people I keep fighting
I cannot be destroyed and I'll tell you why
Tell me how many times can a man die
Ah die on the shores of Africa
The Klu Klux Klan lynch me in Alabama

Ah die in '37 striking with Uriah
So charging me for guerrilla you playing with fire.

Kitchener's criticisms of Williams and the PNM were always those of the insider who was disenchanted with his tribal leader, but never so disenchanted that he would consider switching allegiance, as Sparrow eventually did. We thus find Kitchener singing in 1976 that "the Doctor say, PNM / He here to stay, PNM / We have to rule, PNM". After the election of 1981, which followed Williams's death, we also find him echoing George Chambers's prophecy turned fact, that the Organization for National Reconstruction would get "not a damn seat":

Them ONR jump and whine
Making a big show
And they thought they had the crowd behind
Everywhere they go
So they thought that crowd was vote
They say they go cut we throat
Sparrow start to bawl
When he hear not a seat at all
Not a damn seat for them
Sparrow that ingratitude
Trinidadians got a hint
They heard of the plans
The ONR had blueprint
To bring the Cubans
People took it on of course
Say their freedom would be lost
Before this problem
Better put back the PNM
This is what PNM do for we
Not a damn seat for them
They give we freedom and liberty
Not a damn seat for them
Freedom to walk, freedom to protest
Not a damn seat for them
Freedom to talk, freedom of the Press
Not a damn seat for them

The petro-dollar bonanza and the distortions created in the economy and the society as a result of the spiralling inflation of the 1970s were the subject of several calypsos that accused Williams and the PNM of failing to provide needed services for the citizenry, particularly in the areas of health and utility services – water, electricity, telephones and public transport. The Mighty Penguin generated a great deal of laughter with his "Telco Poops", a funny but trenchant critique of the state-owned telephone company. The Mighty Crooner also complained that one had to "ring up today for tomorrow", while the Lord Shorty lamented that one could not even "dial a prayer". BWIA, the Water and Sewerage Authority, the Trinidad and Tobago Electricity Commission, the Roads and Highways Division of the Ministry of Works, and the Public Transport Service Corporation also came in for their share of "picong" (trenchant criticism). Shorty's beautiful and plaintive ballad "Money Ain't No Problem" was perhaps the calypso that best reflected the mood of disenchantment with the weaknesses of the infrastructure and of the politicians and administrators who seemed to be incapable of doing anything about it:

Five to a bed in the hospital
And we can't hear a word
from the Health Minister Kamal
Black, dirty water we have to drink
WASA say it clean, but it smelling stink
And my friends
They shouting
Money ain't no problem
They shouting
Money ain't no problem

Shorty, who was not normally a political commentator, called on the people in "Oh Trinidad" (1976) to get rid of Williams:

Too much of one thing good for nothing
Dig it, dig it
If you have a hernia that can't get better
Cut it, cut it
If yuh man old and falling on he face
Get younger fella to take he place
Put him out
He ent care 'bout you
Put him out
That's the thing to do
Put him out

The judiciary also came in for some harsh commentary from Short Pants and Sugar Stick, both of whom were upset about "the hypocrisy of democracy". Short Pants's complaint was that "The Law Is an Ass" (1979).

This ain't no fun when cases are won
We feel that justice must be done

Don't care how big, don't care how small
The law must be there for all

In response to Williams's statement that "money ain't the problem", Bomber argued that "the problem was no money". Sparrow's "Ripoff" was in the same vein. Sparrow felt that things had come to a pretty pass, and that the devil must certainly "have a hand in running this land":

Rascality and skullduggery
I believe we have reached
Where somebody should be impeached

Where are the politicians in whom we trust
Where are the labour-leaders who leading us
Do they ever hear the people cry
Today I see tears in big man eye
I am asking why
The cost of living so high
Fire in the place
Customs gone to waste
Because of the abject and sad neglect
Now the general expression from all who love this nation,
Is ruination, humiliation,
Like if the devil
Have a hand in running this land

Explainer's highly successful ditty "Dey Kicksin in Parliament" also reflected the mood of public disenchantment with what was taking place in parliament ("the House of Comedy") since the general elections of 1976. Explainer's song also concerned itself with the "war" between the "Flying Squad" and those who had declared themselves to be "guerillas".

Ah say de Government in dis country
Should treat people more seriously
But I want you to get rid of those fellas for me
Dem men who raising dem prices high
Poor man ketchin' his tail to buy
They want him to scrunt until he die
Randy, dem is guerillas
Dem men who make a million in profit
People who work hard to help them get it
And dey carrying home a cent in dey pocket
Dem is guerillas

The Lord Blakie was also disenchanted with Williams and the PNM, whom he felt had been in power "too long". As the calypsonian sang prior to the 1976 general election,

> Too long we leave them there too long
> Now they going wrong, they weak but playing strong
> I won't be deceitful as to say
> They did some good things but in their own way
> But with the good things they did for us we still loss
> You will be shocked when you check back how much it cost
>
> I say any government, they could be past excellent
> They may be the best thing in the world
> They could come from a convent and always sharing present
> And giving paupers their weight in gold
> But any time you leave them in power
> For twenty years, sweet bound to turn sour
> I ent taking sides, I ent talking tough
> Ah just saying twenty years is enough.

Blakie charged that the Carnival Development Committee made efforts to silence him, and interestingly, warned that he would protest to Williams against those who were seeking to prevent him from singing in the tent: "If I was against the Government, I would be a guerilla in the hills. But I am a calypsonian, and until freedom of speech is restricted, I feel that like any other artiste, I should be allowed to deal with any topic within the bounds of the law without victimization or discrimination" (*Trinidad Guardian*, 30 January 1976; as cited in Regis 1999, 125).

The calypsonians of the 1970s were not all critical of the Williams regime, but those who praised the government were clearly overwhelmed by the voices of those who told of corruption, waste, inefficiency, spiralling prices and official rascality. However, many felt and hoped that despite his failures, Williams would emerge politically triumphant in the 1976 general elections – as he in fact did. Crusoe sang in "I Eustace Williams",

> Opposition know they never stood a chance
> Five elections I whip them on their conscience
> In my Party I am absolutely boss
> Who defied me I simply tell them get lost
> With brain, intellect and charisma
> My visions were always superior
> Anyone who attempted to move me from the head
> I just raised mih hand and they politically dead

Caribbean Man

One of the most outstanding calypsos of the 1970s was Stalin's critique of Williams and other Caribbean heads of state in "Caribbean Man" (1979). The words of the calypso, which generated a great deal of controversy among academics, ethnic leaders and politicians, including Williams himself, are as follows:

> You try with a Federation, the whole thing end in confusion
> Caricom and then Carifta, but somehow ah smelling disaster
> Mister West Indian Politician, you went to big institution
> How come you can't unite seven million?
> When a West Indian unity I know is very easy
> If you only rap to you' people and tell them like me.
>
> Dem is one race – De Caribbean Man
> From de same place – De Caribbean Man
> Dat make de same trip – De Caribbean Man
> On the same ship – De Caribbean Man
> So we must push one common intention
> Is for a better life in de region
> For we woman and we children
> Dat must be de ambition of de Caribbean Man
> De Caribbean Man, De Caribbean Man.
>
> A man who don't know his history can't form no unity
> How could a man who don't know his history form his own ideology
> If the rastafari movement spreading and the Carifta dying slow
> Den is something dem rastas know dat dem politicians don't know

Stalin seemed to be arguing that any movement towards Caribbean unity must take as its point of departure the fact that what was being unified were the peoples of the Caribbean and not their economies, and that what most firmly bound these peoples was their common historical experiences – the Middle Passage, life on the slave plantations, and colonialism. These collective experiences had given them a sense of Caribbeaness that was different from that of other groups who had not been forced to abandon their primordial cultures.

Stalin was accused of being "racist and sexist" and generally of being politically incorrect. University of the West Indies sociologist Dr Ramesh Deosaran criticized Stalin for "pushing the view that only people of African descent were entitled to take part in Caribbean unity". Deosaran found the lyrics racist and sexist, and "a gross insult to the vast number of people of other races who have come in different ships and from different places . . . it should be said in no uncertain terms that we – Africans, Indians, Chinese, Syrians, Whites, are all now in the same ship together, and recognition of that fact is the Caribbean spirit". My judgement at the time was that Stalin was using poetic licence to remind Caribbean blacks that they had a great deal in common, which could be used positively for their women and their children. It was seen as a pro-black and not an anti-Indian discourse, as some Indian academics and cultural entrepreneurs claimed. But Stalin subsequently made clear in an interview that his Caribbean Man was of African descent, and that Africans were the ones who had developed the Caribbean and the only ones who were concerned with African unity. In sum, he was unambiguously claiming the Caribbean for the African.[5] (For the exchange of views between Deosaran and the author see *Sunday Express*, 5 and 11 March 1979.)

Williams took issue with this Afrocentric definition of Caribbean Man. He argued, as he had in Dakar, Senegal, in 1964, that Caribbean Man was neither African, Indian, nor European. He was *sui generis*, something new – a new race, if you will. As he told the convention, "Build the nation of Trinidad and Tobago. Bring in all them races; acknowledge all them contributions." He went on to boast that persons of Indian ancestry had done much better in Trinidad and Tobago than anywhere else in the Indian diaspora: "Nowhere in the world is there a country where Indians have achieved higher status and more are accorded genuine recognition than in Trinidad and Tobago, and for most of that, we of the PNM are responsible. No where in the world does the church, speaking collectively of the different sects, feel less threatened, more free, more at home."

While most Afro-Trinidadians agreed with Williams, most Indo-Trinidadians angrily disagreed, and considered his remarks an insult because they seemed to make their achievements dependent on the benevolence of the ruling party. Their view was that they were not a minority and that their successes were achieved in spite of and not because of the PNM. As one attorney argued, "For what prosperity there is in this country, other than the wealth of oil, the Indians are to a great extent responsible. They are still the backbone of our agriculture." This of course conveniently ignores the foundational work done by the enslaved Africans prior to 1845 (*Trinidad Express*, 5 October 1979). Indians were, however, of the view that they would only achieve a status of equality and full recognition when one of their own became prime minister. (See the author's "An Equal Place for Every Race", *Sunday Express*, 30 December 1979.)

Williams returned to Stalin obliquely in an address to the PNM convention in September 1979. The basic issue was whether the Caribbean Sea was an African lake or whether it was really home to several historically dispossessed groups. Williams took the latter view, declaring, "We must come out to play, not perhaps for some time as the Caribbean Man, but the Trinidad and Tobago Man. . . . He must hold forth his model of democratic institutions. . . . He must stand proud in the harmonious environment of a multiracial fully integrated society, free of racial tensions. . . . One race! Let us show the rest of the world" (in Sutton 1981, 454).

In further reply to Stalin, Williams insisted that he put several initiatives on the table to promote discussion of the way forward for Caribbean unity, but that all he got in return was the "silence of the grave" (1994, 67). At the end of his long-winded address, Williams perorated as follows:

> I give you your homework for the next 25 years. Build the Nation of Trinidad and Tobago, bringing in all "them races", acknowledging all their contributions, elevating lowly castes, dignifying despised colours, achieving a syncretism here and a new autonomy there, raising up the poor and the lowly and giving them a positive stake in our society, whether house, land, education, company shares, all under the beneficent government, open to all except the scamps, so that generations yet unborn can repeat the proud boast with which we emblazoned our banners in 1956: "Great is the PNM and it will prevail."

By March 1979, Williams had been in power for twenty-three years, and many of his former supporters and their offspring had come to feel that it was time for him to go. That sentiment was echoed by the calypsonian Lord Relator, who called on Williams to "Take a Rest". Relator's clever calypso was an exercise in deferential dissent, but it was a clear call on Williams to take a long and well-deserved vacation. The song helped Relator to win the coveted title of Carnival Calypso Monarch of 1979 (sung with another critical composition, "High Prices", dealing with the rapid inflation that was eroding the purchasing power of the people). The lyrics were as follows:

> No light, no telephone, and no water
> We in the middle of a big power failure
> I'm sorry but the breakdown is governmental
> And is because of fatigue, physical and mental
> Is useless that we continue to blame
> A horse that is tired and almost lame
> If government can't cope nowadays
> The nation could send them for holidays
>
> *Chorus*
> Now this is not an overthrow
> I eh saying that we must kick them out
> Just so
> So please don't jump to any hasty conclusion
> And cause any confusion
> But they exhausted from working too long
> So before they suffer from a nervous breakdown

As a loving nation we now could all suggest
That Dr. Williams and the PNM take a rest

Since Dr. Williams took over the nation
I can't recall he went on vacation
In the last decade, I heard him repeat
That he willing to take a back seat
So, read between the lines friends and understand
That these are the words of a tired man
So the next sensible thing to do
Is for the nation to say a hearty thank you

Chorus
So you see this is not an overthrow
But if they tired, ah doh see why they can't go
And all who feel that I'm anti-PNM
Well I have some news for them
You see all of them who doh want him to go
They get accustomed to the free co-key-oko
But I suggested a nice rest for the Doc
Before the poor man fall down on the wuk

I say put a next party in power
And give PNM a chance to recover
Let that new party know that they can't be slack
That PNM on holidays and they could tack back
And if they perform, up to satisfaction
We can even give them an extension
Ah doh intend to incite trouble
Ah just suggesting a democratic reshuffle

Remember it was under guidance
That we achieve the independence
Along with free secondary education
And an increase in old people pension
But morality in public affairs
Was replaced by corruption in recent years
And then the word start to spread around
That Dr. Williams know and still encouraging wrong

Relator's suggestion that Williams should be sent on vacation before he fell down on the "wuk" was overtaken by De Lamo's powerful dirge in which he claimed to have "seen" Williams's death and interment in a dream. The song "Apocalypse" (1981) saw four horses taking part in a race at a new racing complex, which was being built amid much controversy and scandal. The horses all represented notorious PNM personalities. The last horse was clearly Williams, whom De Lamo saw heading straight for Lapeyrouse Cemetery:

> Woe unto you, leaders of my Land
> For aiding and abetting the sin of covetousness in this island
> And for lending out my money to build facilities for horse
> When you breaking down my humble shack with your
> Regiment and Police force
> But, behold, what the prophecy say
> That this fourth horse, he was a mangy gray
> So allyuh be careful allyuh don't end up like that unfortunate jockey
> Because the Racing Complex is the Lapeyrouse Cemetery

De Lamo felt that Williams's legacy was bad for the society. As he complained in "Eric Williams' Children" (1984),

> He freed our limbs, but he never freed our minds
> So how come after 27 years
> Freedom from his freedom we cannot find.

De Lamo also felt that the prime minister had failed the children whom he had vowed to emancipate in his Independence Day address and subsequent addresses to them:

> Suffer the little children to come unto Me
> For they shall inherit my Kingdom. . . .
> You see, he left them a legacy of Sodom
> Like sacrificial pawns on a chessboard of politics
> He squandered his children's future with irresponsible antics

Pro-PNM calypsonians did not agree. The Original De Fosto remained loyal to Williams, whom he still saw as the "rising sun". In a moving tribute to him following his death, De Fosto said,

> He was the right and truly Honourable
> A philosopher, author, premier, teacher, the Nation's Father
> He put aside luxury which was of no importance to him
> He was the people's majority, a simple man, a simple king
>
> The time had come for him to go
> Shed no tears, don't prop sorrow
> An illustrious master, that's who he was
> A true born Saviour sent from above
> It was written and so well done
> His number was called, his time had come
> Together we aspire, together we achieve

Interestingly, it was Sparrow who best put in song the stubborn loyalty of the black underclass to Williams. In his post-1981 calypso "We Like It So", Sparrow had PNM loyalists saying the following:

> It ent have a single thing you could say
> Could make me abandon me balisier
> No steel beam go fall down on top me head
> Sparrow, I'se a PNM till ah dead
> And the whole of ONR is only Communist
> They'll take Carnival away
> And make people work each day

There was a great deal of sarcasm here as Sparrow replied to those who taunted him with being a "turncoat". Sparrow, many noted, had openly embraced Williams in 1980 during the PNM's annual convention in September of that year. Sparrow would later admit that he genuinely loved Eric Williams like a "God and a half".

The Mighty Penguin, who sang quite a few songs in the mid-1970s that heckled Williams, later sang the clever "Betty Goaty" (1982), in which he allowed Williams to speak from the grave and express his relief that he was no longer responsible for dealing with the nation's problems and its ungrateful people:

> To build up this Nation I try my best
> End up in mess
> Men I give rank and fame
> Do things to make me shame
> Pillage and rape the land
> And leave me a sad frustrated man
>
> Betty Goaty, Betty Goaty
> I doing well
> Is them in Hell
> Tell all them cross
> Is them who loss
> You know how I was softie
> And 'fraid to give men jail
> Well now I hope somebody
> Lock up some of them tail
> Betty Goaty, Betty Goaty
> Ah just watching and laughing ho-ho-ho
> Betty Goaty tho'

Did Williams ever seek to silence any political calypso or any calypsonian? The evidence suggests that he never did and that, and as Chalkdust contends, he took criticism "as a China Wall". Calypsos were banned from the state media, but most of them "banned themselves", so to speak, because they were lewd and not fit for air play. Regis is correct when he observes that the exercise of authority by the Carnival Development Committee, the body responsible for the state-sponsored calypso competitions during carnival was, if anything, "fitful and arbitrary, rather than oppressive and malicious" (1996, 25). It is likely that they made assumptions as to what he might have wished to have them do. The one seeming exception was the reaction to Relator's "Take a Rest". Relator was excluded from the prime minister's official tour to China, allegedly because the songs that won him the calypso crown were politically inappropriate for such an occasion. Relator was annoyed, and saw the disbarment as being the result of political interference – which it probably was. One could not reasonably expect otherwise.

Having regard to the role he played over the years in commenting on Williams, Chalkdust is given the last word. Despite his many stinging criticisms of Williams, it is clear that the prime minister was Chalkdust's cultural hero and mentor. Chalkdust admits that Williams inspired him to study history. He wrote a calypso called "Dr Williams Loves Me" (1979), in which he expressed puzzlement at some of Williams's antics and political achievements:

> I does often wonder who is Eric's hero
> I does sit and ponder whom does this man follow
> I does stay so and think what it is makes him tick
> To make him do the things he does in public
> For instance, why doesn't he attend a Caricom meeting
> And why in Parliament he does not say a thing
> I've read books in History, Politics of all kind
> Yet his reasons I cannot find
>
> Because when a man could crash George the Fifth Park just so
> Then rebuild it at Mucurapo
> Whom does he follow
> Karl Marx ent say so
> And tell me, what kinda theory
> Could make a MP resign promptly
> Once he leave his Party
> Well that short man does have me thinking
> But now ah size him up by concluding
> Is just calypso he want Chalkie sing
> Ah read all kinda book in History
> No leader ever have three deputy
> You ent see is Calypso they want Chalkie sing

Behind the levity, however, there is evident admiration, so much so that Chalkdust found it difficult to "bury" Williams. As he sang in 1998,

Since 1981 when Eric Williams died,
Ah dress for funeral in mi black suit and tie.
In my mind ah trying to bury his body,
But politicians today they keep stopping me.
Though is 17 years now that Eric met his death,
Ah still dress in black; ah can't bury him as yet.
For where Dr. Williams embrace morality and good taste
Today they replace that good taste with race.

Chorus
Morality that was in Williams' day
Has now changed to giving Ish his backpay.
Is you scratch my back and I will scratch your back
So make your kick back from my contract – so darling
Stop! Stop that funeral.
Government contracts driving me up a wall.
And when ah see they bring back Miss Occah Seepaul,
Ah can't bury Williams at all.[6]

Williams clearly understood the role that the calypso played historically, and accepted that he was not the only "mouthpiece" of the people. He might have been the "only sun in the sky", as the Chinese say, but there were other dragons who were entitled to sing and dance and to "speak truth to power". To be sure, he must have cringed on many an occasion (for example, when Chalkie sang "Nixon's Mistake"), but he did make time to visit the tents in 1971 and 1975, if only to signal that he was not at war with the street poets. He also kept lines open to a few bards – Chalkdust himself and Sparrow, whom he congratulated when he celebrated his twenty-fifth anniversary as a calypso performer in January 1980. Williams reportedly asked his ministerial colleague John Donaldson to indicate to Sparrow that he appreciated the support that he had given him over the years, particularly in the calypsos that dealt with Chaguaramas, "Pay as You Earn", "Leave the Damn Doctor", and "Federation" (see "PM Praises Sparrow's Inspiration", *Trinidad Express*, 6 January 1980). Interestingly, when the PNM celebrated the fiftieth anniversary of the official launching of the party on 24 January 2006, Sparrow and Striker were on hand to mark the event and sing the songs that had helped to make Williams larger than life in the 1950s and early 1960s.

The question has been asked just what the calypso protest activities of the 1970s achieved, if anything, to influence policy. One view is that very little was in fact accomplished. Some calypsonians complained that smutty calypsos sold far better than serious calypsos and that the latter were largely forgotten on Ash Wednesday. Another argument is that the critical calypso functions as an escape valve, as a sort of catharsis for the population that got vicarious satisfaction when they heard their own grievances expressed. They might exclaim "Kaiso" and cheer lustily, but that invariably was the end of the matter. Political calypsos rarely ever resulted in direct political action, and it may well be that Williams came to recognize this and therefore did not feel sufficiently threatened to ban them. As Rohlehr has argued, "Kaiso has never been a substitute for politics."

But this is too narrow a way of viewing the question of social protest. The calypsonian, like the columnist, the cleric or other social critics, helps to shape opinion, to legitimize or undermine values, points of view or modes of action. The result may not be seen immediately or readily, but each tributary helps give form to the stream of public opinion. There is little doubt that these working class philosophers contributed mightily to the shaping of the social consciousness of the society in the Williams years. They built him up in the 1950s and 1960s and they savaged his reputation and unmasked him, even if deferentially, in the late 1960s, 1970s and early 1980s. Consciousness does not always lead to direct or overt political or social action, as Marxists discovered. Social change, more often than not, is a glacial process that happens behind one's back, so to speak, and is never unidirectional. I am convinced, however, that the voice of the calypsonians helped to persuade many that the PNM captain was presiding over a party that was breaking down and a ship that was sinking, and that they contributed to the massive rejection of the party that occurred in 1986.[7]

41   Accounting for My Stewardship

You know how difficult it is to be the Prime Minister of a country where people believe,
that like a conjurer, I can wave a wand and get rid of all their problems?

– Eric Williams

In 1965, Williams took time out to reflect on what independence had meant for
Trinidad and Tobago. Wearied and depressed by the challenges he was then facing, he wrote ten articles that he collectively titled "The Reality of Independence".
Parts of these articles were published as columns in the *Nation*. Some of the material also appeared in the final chapter of his autobiography *Inward Hunger*.

> There is nothing mysterious about Independence. . . . Our independence was achieved
> on August 31st, 1962 as part of a world movement against colonialism – the colonial
> peoples disinclined to tolerate it any longer, the imperialists unable to carry on. The
> British conceded in India after the War. They resisted in Ghana because it was the first
> African colony involved; but when it came to Trinidad a few years later, as I told
> Nkrumah, the difference was that Nkrumah had to conquer an imperialist castle
> whereas the PNM merely took over a worm eaten house. (EWMC folio 1912)

Williams complained that federation was merely a British-inspired move to
provide the basis for Britain's abandonment of the West Indies.

Williams also reflected on the utility of having a defence force that the British
had insisted upon. He advised those who were opposed to it for all kinds of reasons, including cost, that "you can't say you do not want a defence force unless
indeed we are to assume you want subversion". At one point, he said that he took
pride in the army and that he knew what an army meant in the struggle for independence (EWMC folio 1914). Williams was by then obsessed with the question
of communism and threats to national security, and was perhaps anticipating that
the defence force would have a role to play in maintaining law and order. There

was no hint that he anticipated that the defence force would one day regard him as the "enemy". Williams was, however, clearly ambivalent about the role of the army. He told an audience at Oxford University in 1964 that one needs to be careful about army interventions in politics. "We have a mere two or three hundred people in uniform, and if I had my way, I would have thirty to forty and no more than that, a token force to present a guard of honour when a bigshot comes, and we have to trot out the red carpet, and just hope for the best" (EWMC folio 793).

Faced with a growing economic crisis involving a shortage of investment capital and growing unemployment, Williams opined that the country had to tighten its belt and save:

> We can't spend all today and just borrow from foreigners. We must save. We can't price ourselves out of world markets. . . . We can't spend recklessly on foreign produce and jeopardize our balance of payments. We can't have our people hustling for jobs whilst some of us invest profits abroad. We can't have our wages and salaries eaten up by fantastic price increases on imported goods. All of these are the reality of independence. (Ibid.)

Williams remained bitter about Britain's parsimony, and its unwillingness to be generous on the question of the "golden handshake" that countries becoming independent received. He complained that "up to when the Federation died, unannounced, unsung and unwept, we were no nearer any firm decision on the matter of economic aid than we were at the inauguration of the Federation. The United Kingdom made such an unsatisfactory offer to us that we were forced to decline; its principal concern at the Independence Conference was to ensure the heavy entrenchment of the monarchical system. As I said to students at the London School of Economics, Britain had sucked the orange dry and was merely nervous about slipping on the orange peel" (1969, 341). The UK government held its ground for much of 1962 on what monies it was prepared to make available to the Trinidad government by way of a post-independence settlement in respect of outstanding debts, though it was concerned that Trinidad might take retaliatory action against British interests in Trinidad, which were substantial. The British seemed determined to teach Williams that "rudeness does not pay". Williams was equally determined that Trinidad and Tobago had to be respected. As he declared,

> Those discussing with us economic, political or strategic problems will commit gross blunders if they do not realize that, apart from the material questions being discussed, the state of mind of our people must be taken into consideration. It is our right and our duty to ensure that, as we seek to establish the material foundations of our society, we define our spiritual attitude, we reject outworn attitudes, and we substitute new ones suited to our time and place. (EWMC folio 007)

In the end, the settlement was closer to Britain's original offer than what Williams had hoped for; it is clear that he settled for less than expected. Williams would later reflect that the principal beneficiaries of aid were the countries providing the aid. Williams complained that "we get no aid from anybody except some aid that we were able to extract, as the dentist pulls out a tooth, from the US in terms of a military agreement we have with them." "Aid," he said, "was a vulgar form of maintaining influence in one particular country or keeping out somebody's influence." Part of the problem was that the Caribbean was not deemed to be a threat to the economic security of the West. Castro altered the conjuncture. Said Williams, "Until the emergence of Castro and the threat of British Guiana, the strategic significance of the Caribbean was severely limited." Although Williams was unwilling to play the "communist card", he felt that Trinidad should fare better in the calculations of the West.

Williams understood why Trinidad was not securing the benefits of independence, which he felt it deserved and badly needed. The problem was that Trinidad, in terms of where it stood in respect of development, was "neither fish nor fowl", or perhaps it was both fish and fowl. "On the one hand, it has the characteristics of a developed country while on the other, it has all the shortcomings of an undeveloped country" (Williams 1969, 26). Williams indicated that whenever he sought aid, he was told that Trinidad's infrastructure was better than most; that its slums were not as depressed as was the case elsewhere; and that its literacy standard and the percentage of the population in primary and secondary school was higher than obtained elsewhere.

Williams had once been optimistic about how "easy" it would be to transform the colonial economy, which was in reality "an absentee British farm run for the profit of its British owners", to one that was run primarily for the benefit of its citizens. He had since become aware that the industrialization process had many contradictions that he had not anticipated. One was that one had to determine what inputs went into the new industries, and from whence they were sourced. As he observed, "What we have to face is the concrete reality that if we seek to industrialize our very limited economy, the basis must be cheap food. Imported raw materials are cheaper, especially when they are dumped, than our own local production. Which do we prefer, cheap corn or cheap meat?" (ibid., 11). One could import either cheap poultry to satisfy consumer demand, or cheap stock feed to support entrepreneurs who were trying to develop a poultry industry that would help create jobs.

Williams also reminded citizens that nationalization had costs that had to be met, especially if one was paying compensation. Where was the capital for this to come from?

> The reality that we face is that while you hear all sorts of proposals for Government taking over this, that, and the other, the capital for this, that and the other must come from

the outside. Suggest to somebody that we should save more in order to invest in productive enterprises, and we come solidly up against our spendthrift habits and traditions of gluttony which, notorious at Christmas and Carnival time, is as old as West Indian society under modern exploitation. (Ibid., 12)

Williams also returned to the question of size and economic survival. Could genuine independence be achieved by small countries, given the way in which the world economy was currently structured? He had doubts:

> The enduring reality of Independence is that a small country of less than two thousand square miles and less than one million people cannot possibly hope by itself to make its way, economically and politically in a world of more than one hundred Independent nations, the large majority much larger than Trinidad and Tobago, dominated by powerful trading blocs in Europe, in Latin America, in the Communist world, and soon in Africa. (Ibid.)

Given the reality, Williams continued to stress the importance of the Caribbean Economic Community and the markets of Latin America. While markets were important, what was critically absent in the Trinidad and Tobago environment was an "attitude" that sustained independence. Williams agreed that the Trinidadian approach to life was a constraint on development. That approach was inherited from slavery, indenture and colonialism. In the past, for example, praedial larceny and stealing from the government could have been regarded as part of the struggle of the weak against the strong. That justification no longer held:

> We have not yet begun, in the age of independence, to understand that if one takes away Government material on a site, or slacks on the job for which we have had to borrow and pledge the Nation's resources, it is no longer a political response of the weak. . . . It is stealing from one's nation. Here then is the reality of independence – seeking to deal with our problem on a national scale and in an international context with a mentality conceived in slavery, cradled in indenture, and nurtured in colonialism. (Ibid., 24)

Williams was perplexed about the community's relaxed attitude to the grave problems that the nation faced, and came pretty close to accepting the view of Prime Minister Lee Kuan Yew of Singapore that Trinidad's abiding problem was the carnival mentality that prevailed among its population, and which was sowing the seeds of a "cataclysm which threatened to destroy political independence and engulf the entire economy". Said Williams,

> The national community, with a balance of payments problem staring it in the face, living now for now without thought as to what might happen tomorrow, is concerned only with Carnival and calypso, and which band desecrates what. An independent government surrounded by a colonial mentality. All that is left for us now is to have someone appeal to the British government to interfere in our domestic affairs as it did from 1797 to 1962. (Ibid., 45)

Williams had other concerns, among which was the failure of the education system to produce a better quality product. The educational statistics depressed him enormously, although he took comfort in the fact that they could not be blamed on free secondary education since its beneficiaries were not yet part of those figures. Williams was also chagrined by the tendency of all kinds of people to seek audience with him, for reasons that were not always justified: "Every trade union, journalist, diplomat, business organization wishes to see the Prime Minister. Why? In the colonial period, one wrote to the Governor to ask him to attend functions. Today in Independence, you have the mentality unchanged, merely substituted by the Prime Minister. The difference is that the colonial Governor could pass on most of his work to the Colonial Office in England. The Prime Minister cannot" (ibid., 64).

There were at least two positive sides to Trinidad and Tobago's post-independence achievements, as far as Williams was concerned. He boasted, perhaps prematurely, that the new state had not witnessed the kind of ethnic conflict that had developed in the Third World and elsewhere:

> We lack the tribal animosities of Nigeria or the religious passions of India or the economic difficulties of Ceylon or the political difficulties of Israel. By and large we have an interracial harmony, disturbed at election periods, which many will envy. Indians are not repatriated as in Burma, Ceylon, Kenya. We have no "Quebec nation." Our economic and social difficulties are not more formidable than those faced by other emerging countries. Our army is not a Latin American one. We have no Red Guards on the rampage. (Ibid., 342–43)

He also felt that Trinidad and Tobago had indeed shown that liberal democracy could be maintained in tropical post-colonial environments, and that one did not have to resort to one-party states or the excessive use of coercion as a precondition of economic development. As he reflected (the Industrial Stabilization Act and his view about the need for a public order act and greater discipline notwithstanding):

> Other countries have faced these problems and have solved them by undemocratic methods. When the Soviet Union wished to collectivise its agriculture or to allocate a precise percentage of the national product for heavy industry thus subordinating consumer industries, it simply decreed the policy; those who did not like it were sent to Siberia. When the Chinese communists decided that everything was to be subordinated to the steel industry, and that the steel furnaces were to be set up even in the backyards, it simply decreed these policies. One obeyed or else! If a one party state in various parts of the world decides that it should concentrate on status symbols rather than spend the national revenue on education or on agriculture, its rules and its constitutional arrangements permit no opposition whatsoever to its decisions.
>
> We stand out among emerging countries as one of the very few places in which we

seek to arrive at a national consensus by a national discussion in which everyone is free to take part and express himself with placards or by demonstrations or by small day-time meetings in Woodford Square or by Speeches in Parliament. Nothing would be more wonderful than for us to continue this departure from the traditional practice of emerging countries, and to make a success of it. (In Sutton 1981, 420)

In 1973, Eric Williams delivered an evaluative address to the PNM that reeked of unequivocal personal failure and defeat. It was a statement made by a man who had concluded that he had failed, and that others whom he trusted and on whom he depended had also failed and betrayed him. In 1980, the same man addressed the same party. The discourse this time was entirely different. The message was not that everything that was wrong had been put right. In the main, the claim was that he and the party had fulfilled much of what they had set out to achieve in 1956 when the "power and the glory" of leading Trinidad and Tobago out of the desert of colonialism was thrust into his hands.

Williams told the convention that he gave the party five major responsibilities and obligations in 1956: elimination of colonialism, creation of "domestic vistas", national control of Trinidad's economic resources, creation of a spirit of nationhood, and creation of a spirit of Bandung. In respect of the first obligation, he felt that Trinidad and Tobago had done well notwithstanding the fact that colonialism had metastasized into neocolonialism. Williams reviewed the experience of other newly independent countries such as Ghana and Cuba and other quasi-independent states such as Puerto Rico, whose model of development he had sought to imitate in 1956, and concluded that Trinidad had not done badly.

His retrospective evaluation of Puerto Rico was gloomy, and one wonders whether he was frank about what was taking place in Trinidad and Tobago. Williams's conclusion was that the Puerto Rican experiment had failed. Puerto Rico in 1980 was "the quintessence of dependence, the world's greatest welfare state". Puerto Rico, he noted, received over $3 billion a year from the US federal government. Yet the unemployment rate in Puerto Rico was in the vicinity of 20 to 30 per cent and 70 per cent of the population was on food stamps. The much bruited economic growth model produced few jobs since 1965. In sum, concluded Williams, "the bootstrap broke" (ibid.).

Williams noted that the Caribbean had become the American "backyard" or its "Mediterranean", and could expect to become "as polluted as the European Mediterranean". Trinidad, at least so far, seemed to have avoided the worst of what constituted American policy in the Caribbean. One wonders how Williams could so conclude, given what was taking place in respect of the government-to-government programmes (see chapter 32).

The Westminster Model

Lloyd Best argued that Trinidad and Tobago had never adopted the Westminster model, and that what it had in its stead was a modified version of the old crown colony system. Williams disagreed. He argued that the PNM took the Westminster model as its inspiration, but adapted it to suit Trinidad's special conditions. Williams in fact noted that in 1956, "Trinidad and Tobago was a parody and caricature of the Westminster model" (in Sutton 1981, 425–26). The adaptations involved removing the single chamber colonial legislature and introducing the cabinet system and party government.

Williams observed that the Westminster model was said to be irrelevant and unsuitable for Caribbean realities. That could be so, he allowed, but his experience with the model "ran counter to the general historical tradition in the [non-anglophone] Caribbean area. The Westminster model spells democracy and not dictatorship." Williams made sneering references to the "democratic Caesarism" of Pérez Jiménez of Venezuela, the militarism of Cuba where Castro was the commander in chief and gave orders for everything, and to Haiti where military men were ubiquitous. Quoting Réné Depectro, Williams noted that Haiti had produced its own "monsters and barbarities" that had become deeply indigenized and completely internalized.

Williams complained that the English-speaking Caribbean too was becoming progressively militarized, "with civilian heads of government as head of the armed forces sporting military uniforms". He clearly had Guyana in mind. He deplored the trend. "Needless to say, we do not stand for that in Trinidad and Tobago" (ibid., 424–25). Williams felt that the criticisms of it notwithstanding, "the Westminster model had helped Trinidad and Tobago to avoid producing our own barbarities and monsters".

In respect to the role of member of parliament, Williams drew attention to Burke's deliberative member of parliament acting as an individual, but noted that in Trinidad he had been replaced by the PNM member of parliament. In Trinidad, it was now "nonsense to argue . . . that he won his seat as a 'trust from Providence', and that he could cross the floor or publicly disavow his party pledges as he pleases". The Westminster model, however, had other utilities. One of its advantages was that it enabled ruling parties to carry out their legislative programmes without fear of being easily overthrown, as occurs in systems where proportional representation was in place. That is why "We in the PNM have set our face so sternly against proportional representation which enhances the power of the individual, leaves him at the mercy of the lobbyists, foreign and domestic, fragments the party majority, and in Trinidad and Tobago terms, is a dagger pointed at the heart of the PNM" (ibid., 426–27).

Williams noted that the Westminster model had to be further modified to meet some of the complexities and exigencies of governance in Trinidad and Tobago, where management of certain areas of public policy had become so challenging that one had to alter the traditional cabinet system:

> The Ministry of Finance is too large a responsibility for one Minister and it exercises, inevitably, such a control over the general administration and economy that it is preferably headed – almost as if it is a law of a developing country – by the Prime Minister himself as head of what is virtually a committee of Ministers assisting him with various aspects of the Ministry's wide jurisdiction. The Cabinet itself has become steadily a collection of committees, bringing different ministers together and establishing a basis of coordination and teamwork, anathema to those, especially the lobbyists and vested interests, who would prefer an individual to a collective responsibility; the Prime Minister for the most part leaves the committee work to the ministers appointed, their recommendations going straight to the full Cabinet. (Ibid., 430–31)

Interestingly, Williams claimed that he sought to modify the dominance of the ruling party in the interest of increasing accountability, and excluding political interference in the award of contracts by changing the system of tendering for public procurement. He also sought to give a greater role to the National Advisory Council. The aim of the latter innovation was to "extend the area of consultation in the national interest" (ibid., 430). This did not, however, alter the basic character of the Westminster model, "a crucial element of which was disciplined party government with the party being consulted as of right on national issues, but set to deal with crossing of the floor in Parliament or public opposition to the Party's democratic decisions by any of its members" (ibid.).

Socialism and the Private Sector

Williams defended the performance of the state sector and launched a scathing attack on the domestic private sector – "parvenu capitalists", he called them – whom he accused of blaming all the ills of the society on the government, including the prevailing work ethic, which was said to be weak when compared to that of Europe, Australia, the United States and Singapore. Williams complained,

> In the last few months, a ferocious campaign has been launched by the capitalist elements in our society through the organs of public information they own, control or influence, to bulldoze and browbeat the government, and particularly the Prime Minister, into a propaganda gimmick to promote the work ethic. Their basic aim is to push Trinidad and Tobago into a form of undiluted capitalism, as archaic historically as it is precarious economically, with foreign capital and foreign inspiration, seeking to get more out of the workers whom they will throw on the breadline on the flimsiest of provocations. (In Sutton 1981, 437)

The problem with the work ethic, said Williams, was that the nature of that "work" had changed. It was no longer soul satisfying, and workers everywhere were disavowing the gospel of work, replacing it with the gospel of leisure and relaxation. This was true in Germany, Australia and the United States as well as in Singapore. Everywhere, native workers were shunning work and leaving it to poorly paid immigrants and robots. Australia was said to be a "lotus land" in which "leisure is the universal religion and work a detestable heresy".

On the question of socialism, Williams was unequivocally opposed:

> Socialism, no, under whatever guise it may show its head. We are developing something else, genuine partnership between State and its citizens in the ownership of economic activities and our natural resources. Which of you in 1956 or indeed even in 1970 would have dreamed of the possibility of owning shares, equity partnership in a large prosperous bank such as the National Commercial Bank, with the Government, your strong but silent partner – which of you? Which of you would have thought that just around the corner you would have had opportunities to participate with the Government in the ownership of our natural gas, or a large luxury hotel and a brand new steel mill – which of you? I do not know which of the "isms" it is as yet, but we may have to find a new word for it. (Ibid., 455)

The "Enemy" Within

Williams also expressed concern about the growing tendency to squeeze out the small man, the small entrepreneur and even the small trade union. Also criticized was

> the old Massa who is still with us, who attempts to drive a wedge between workers by artificially creating a class called "managers", and who makes a sharp distinction between that class and others. Are they not all workers? The enemy also seeks to project the trade unions and the trade union movement as the source of all evils. What about the enemy who places at the feet of the government all the ills in our society? All evils begin and end with the Government: at least this is what he will have us believe. If there is a shortage of milk, blame the Government. If there is a storm and it floods, it is the Government; if two companies get together and attempt and perhaps succeed in defrauding the Government, it is the Government. (Ibid.)

Williams rebuked those in the society who wanted instant solutions to the problems of development. As he asked plaintively,

> And what about some of our own attitudes? An attitude that wants instant solutions: instant highways throughout the entire nation, instant provision of 20,000 school places, an instant provision of this, that or the other. There is the attitude that Trinidad and Tobago, with less than 20 years in control of its own affairs and little less than six years when our revenue was in excess of our budget expenditure, that this Trinidad

and Tobago must transform its infrastructure to the standards of Toronto, California (I exclude New York), transform its infrastructure to the same level that these countries have enjoyed, the highest standard of living in the world for the past 100 years. These countries that have had tremendous natural resources, large populations and populations based on a large element on migration which have brought money, skills and motivation to develop their new found land; whereas our own brain drain has taken from us some of the expertise and skill particularly needed at this time of development. We cannot be Toronto or Miami or Los Angeles in a matter of years. Indeed we need to debate whether we want to be any of these places. (Ibid.)

Williams indicated that while he expected those responsible for delivering infrastructural services to improve their performance, it was not reasonable to expect "instant transformation". One also had to determine priorities. Should there be a new airport or sixteen thousand school places? Should one build a steel mill, another fertilizer plant, or an airport to cater to the tourist industry? As he told listeners,

> I have heard the criticisms – why build a steel mill? Why build another fertilizer plant? Use that money to build a new airport and put up some new buildings for this or that. And when the money runs out, what will we have. We then have to advertise for tourists to come to our beautiful country and enjoy our facilities etc. and the first real scare, real or otherwise of yellow fever, and that is the end of the tourist. (Ibid., 453)

Williams was also critical of the Trinis who had their feet in two camps – those who enjoyed the free and relaxed life in Trinidad and Tobago but who had a green card in their back pocket. He was likewise critical of those who were unwilling to make sacrifices or meaningful contributions, and who "want us to abandon all our efforts at providing jobs, and open the floodgates to foreign imports, stereos, assembled cars, vegetables etc. He could be our most dangerous enemy" (ibid., 454).

The New Trinidad Man

Like many Third World leaders or activists, Williams was aware of the need to change attitudes as a prerequisite for the development he envisaged. He admitted, however, that he felt a "little nervous talking about a new man. Everyone does it, and has done it." Even Duvalier in Haiti did, advocating a black nation with a black religion and a black Caesar, in which "voodoo is our only originality". Williams recalled that in 1970, the PNM talked about creating a new society, and felt that scepticism notwithstanding, "we must insist that the Trinidad and Tobago man and woman must come alive". He continued,

> We must come out to play, not perhaps for some time the Caribbean Man, but the

Trinidad and Tobago man. He must hold forth his model of democratic institutions, high and clear for the rest of the world to see. He must hold forth his record of human rights, he must stand proud in the harmonious environment of a multiracial fully integrated society, free of the malice of racial tensions, he must begin to show pride – pride in what he has achieved and pride with determination to achieve even more. . . . Let us show the rest of the World. (In Sutton 1981, 454–55).

Williams told the party that Trinidadians must develop their own work ethic and that they couldn't just plead their background of slavery and indenture or say they regret the capitalist work ethic:

> If one does not wish to work for the state, do your own thing. Go downstream, develop services, develop distribution, avoid being agents: the opportunities are there with us, without us. With us, you perhaps have a chance in treating with the conglomerates; without us, the best of luck. We shall try to create the environment where you will have at least a good chance of surviving. Indeed, we are determined to ensure that you survive, but the opportunities are there. What sort of "ism", we do not know yet. (Ibid., 455)

The Succession Question

Williams recalled that he had been asked in 1973 by the Inter-Religious Organisation to delay his departure until a successor was chosen. The IRO had written to him in the following terms:

> While we recognize your right to retire when you so choose, your sudden affirmation to do so has further aggravated the conditions that give rise to the uncertainty of the Nation's future. . . . It is our unanimous opinion even though not one of us is indispensable that you, Sir, have a moral obligation to yourself and moreso to the Nation to fulfill your commitment by piloting our affairs through these stages enumerated previously, so that the will of the people for an orderly and peaceful transition may not be frustrated.

Williams made it clear that he would play no part in helping to choose a successor as some wanted him to do. He thus told the party, "The Political Leader awaits [its] democratic arrangements and decisions for the election of a new leader to lead Party and Nation forward to face the challenges and opportunities that lie ahead. Great is the PNM, I am confident that, with God's grace and your dedication, it will once again prevail" (ibid., 458).

What is one to make of this particular statement? Was Williams in 1980 anticipating that the succession problem would be an agenda item in 1981? Interestingly, Williams made no extended statement about the vexed issue of morality in public affairs, a subject to which we mournfully turn.

42   Sleaze and Immorality in Public Affairs

History ought to be the great propagator of doubt, not an exercise in flag waving or beating of the patriotic drum.
  – Vernon Bogdanor, Professor of Government, Oxford University

. . . morality in Public Affairs
Was replaced by corruption in recent years
And then word start to spread around
That Dr. Williams know and still encouraging wrong
  – Lord Relator, "Take a Rest"

Williams stormed into the political life of Trinidad and Tobago promising to rid the country of the sleaze, rascality and venality associated with the 1950–56 ministerial regime. During these years, Trinidad had earned the unenviable reputation of being the "Sodom and Gomorrah of the Caribbean". Trinidad was also known as the "land of bobol" (corruption), and thus considered by many unfit to serve as the capital city of the new federation being planned. It was thus no surprise that "morality in public affairs" was nailed to the masthead of the PNM, and that Williams committed the party to cleansing the country's "Augean stables". In the years that followed the PNM's victory in 1956, the parliamentary opposition, the Chamber of Commerce, the *Trinidad Guardian*, and the *Clarion* (the radical weekly organ of the TLP) in particular, saw corruption and scandals everywhere. Some of the charges were levelled against Williams himself, while others involved ministers, party officials and their agents.

Williams was accused, among other things, of causing to be concealed or destroyed records of his secret marriage to a Guyanese dentist because he had a change of mind about the "need" for the marriage, one that shocked the party and the country and gave rise to salacious gossip and scandal. He was also accused of not meeting payments that he had been ordered to pay by a Washington, D.C., court for the maintenance of his two children by a previous marriage. It was said that he would be arrested if he ever attempted to enter the United States without a diplomatic visa. A copy of the judgement given by the court was even published. These particular allegations were true, and it is a matter of record that, using various couriers, Williams eventually made good the sums owed to his first wife.

Over the period 1956 to 1961, PNM ministers were also accused of being involved in various sleazy transactions, including a bizarre "car loans" case, a racket relating to the sale of licences to open and operate gas stations, a "Swiss Bank Affair", an islandwide sewerage scheme contracted to a company called Lock Joint, arrangements for the leasing of the *City of Port of Spain*, a ferry that plied the route between Trinidad and Tobago, and the purchase of buses for the Public Service Transport Company from the Leyland Corporation of Great Britain. All of these allegations badly discredited the regime. The Swiss Bank Affair in particular was bothersome to Williams, who decided that he had to take to the University of Woodford Square to deal with the charges. He denied that the bank was brought to Trinidad by the government to finance the sewerage scheme. He noted that the government had consulted the Colonial Office and the Bank of England on the matter, and had also consulted with the British ambassador in Caracas as to the bona fides of Lock Joint.

Williams claimed that the government did not have direct dealings with the Swiss bank itself but with a group of French bankers who had the backing of several financial institutions in the European Common Market. The Swiss bank was said to be the agent of the group, which was negotiating to fund a number of projects, including the provisioning of telephone equipment, buses, the sewerage scheme, electricity, natural gas, shipyards, a graving dock, prefabricated school buildings and so on. The group had offered a loan of TT$96 million over a period of ten years. Williams noted that Ministry of Finance experts had advised against accepting any of the proposals put up by the French consortium and the Swiss bank, whose representatives thereupon submitted additional proposals, which were regarded as extravagant and deceptive, designed to sweeten the deal. Williams titillated the Woodford Square audience by wondering aloud why the financiers had left out "the notorious DLP proposal for the construction of a tunnel to Maracas Bay and the reclamation of the Gulf of Paria? Why, I asked, did they leave out the Red House and the Jail? And so we killed the *mauvais langue* of the Swiss Bank." The suspicions remained, however, especially since two of his senior ministers, Winston Mahabir and Gerard Montano, had accounts in the bank. Interestingly, Williams felt it necessary to quote this speech extensively in his autobiography (1969, 257).

There was also said to be peculation of monies that the private sector contributed to the PNM's donations committee for the purchase and refurbishing of a building to house the PNM's headquarters. Allegations were that the funds were not always deposited in the party treasury or used for the purposes for which they were collected. The regime was also accused of several other fiduciary irregularities, among them deals with Braniff Airways and McDonnell Douglas Corporation to buy and sell aircraft, deals to sell part of the assets of British Petroleum Limited to Tesoro Corporation of Texas, and transactions to construct pipe lines to transport oil and gas in the energy sector. In later years, allegations also flew fast and thick about deals made in the construction of the Iron and Steel Company of Trinidad and Tobago and the Mount Hope hospital, built by the French firm Sodeteg. Corruption was also said to be rampant in the award of import licences, in the sale of scarce foreign exchange by officials of the Central Bank, in the allocation of jobs in the various unemployment relief work programmes, and in the arrangements made to fund and construct a new centralized horse racing complex on the sugar estates once owned by Caroni Limited.

Persistent whispers said that Williams himself was somehow involved in some of these transactions, but the allegations were invariably made *sotto voce*, because no hard evidence supported them. One of the critical exceptions to this "rule" was A.N.R. Robinson, who following his resignation from cabinet in 1970 made public allegations that Williams was personally involved in several of these transactions. In May 1971, Robinson publicly declared that in August 1970, he had received a letter in which it was claimed that the PNM solicited and received a "gift" of US$500,000 from the German-Italian firm Agip-Deminex, following the latter's successful bid for the right to explore for oil in the waters off Trinidad and Tobago's north coast. Robinson said he was told in said letter that it was a "shame" that the political party of which he was the deputy leader was soliciting political gifts from firms whose bids were successful. Robinson was urged to determine where the money had come from, and who received it. The money was said to have been deposited in a local company to camouflage the transaction. Williams, who was accused of having been personally involved in soliciting the gift, brought a libel and slander suit against Robinson, and also the *Trinidad Express*, which published the story.

Robinson claimed that he had three other sources of information about the transaction: Dodderidge Alleyne, permanent secretary to the prime minister, Richard Toby, fiscal adviser to the prime minister, and Charles Heller, a UN consultant. Robinson also claimed that there was a link between that particular transaction and other scandals, all of which were said to have been masterminded by Williams's trusted crony, John O'Halloran. But Toby denied having told Robinson that any corruption was involved in the transaction. Robinson, Toby said, never spoke to him about the matter, "and dragged his name into it for reasons best known to himself". Toby, who handled the negotiations on behalf of the government, claimed that the money in question was a "signature bonus" that all firms whose bids were successful were required to pay to the treasury. Alleyne also denied providing any information to Robinson about the so called "gift".

It was subsequently claimed that the letter, the compromising documents, and the signatures to which Robinson referred were forgeries. Sir Ellis Clarke, then Trinidad and Tobago's ambassador to the United States, was told as much in a letter dated November 1970 and sent to him by Egidio Ortone, the Italian ambassador to the United States. The ambassador claimed that the letter was "evidently intended to undermine the relationship between Agip-Deminex and the Trinidad authorities". According to Agip-Deminex, "We were never influenced in our discussions or into making a decision by the Prime Minister or any member of the government, and Agip-Deminex may have been misunderstood." It was not made clear just what was "misunderstood".

The suit died with Eric Williams in March 1981. Significantly, however, the legal challenge was not actively pursued for close to ten years, giving rise to suspicions that it was merely a "gag writ". Following Williams's death, his successor George Chambers was called upon to investigate the matter. The *Express*, which had openly asked whether Williams was involved in a pay-off scandal, declared that it "deferred judgement about the truth or otherwise of the alleged gift to the party in power", but told Chambers that he must respond positively and comprehensively to the allegations, or, like his predecessor, "stand guilty of participating in a conspiracy of silence" (*Trinidad Express*, 18 October, 4 November 1981; 2 and 22 September 1980). Nothing further came of the matter, and the truth or falsity of the allegation remains undetermined.

In the run-up to the 1976 election, Robinson promised to drop a "bombshell" that would prove conclusively that Williams was personally blemished. He never delivered on that promise. His explanation for not doing so was that people in Trinidad were not yet receptive to the notion that Williams was corrupt. Robinson did make a number of speeches in parliament in which he sought to implicate Williams in the allegations about corruption during the last four years of Williams's life. In a speech delivered in parliament on 1 July 1977, he alleged that the PNM had a secret election fund to which businesses were pressed to contribute. He also referred to the "unbelievable, scandalous corrupt practices" taking place in the Public Transport Service Corporation of Trinidad and Tobago, reports that were sent to the prime minister, who did nothing about them but instead expressed gratitude to the whistle-blower who had supplied the information for "the considerate way in which he had handled the matter". Robinson concluded that the prime minister was not serious about corruption, and that if anything was to be achieved in this regard, one had to start from the "top and go downwards": "covering up a crime is a crime in itself, and high officials of the state are expected to assist in the discovery and prosecution of crimes rather than in the covering up of those crimes. . . . The highest officials, including ministers of government, are being sentenced to jail terms in other countries – not in Trinidad and Tobago, I hasten to emphasize" (1986, 228).

Robinson claimed that corruption was one of the principal reasons why he resigned from the government in 1970. In his letter of resignation, he indicated that he was concerned, among other issues, about

- the abuse of power as a shield to protect political friends guilty of the gravest abuses;
- ministers close to the prime minister who have been guilty of scandalous improprieties;
- party members close to the political leader who have been involved in corruption practices.

The DC-9 Scandal

Williams was badly shaken in August and September 1980 when a story appeared in the *Wall Street Journal* that a "high official" of the Trinidad and Tobago government had been involved in illegal transactions relating to the acquisition of three DC-9 aircraft in 1976 from the McDonnell Douglas Corporation of America. Williams became incandescent on 6 September 1980, when the *Express* published a statement made by Basdeo Panday, leader of the opposition, which suggested that Williams might be involved in yet another pay-off scandal. Panday asked leave of the Speaker of parliament to have the issue debated as a matter of urgent importance, a request that the Speaker predictably denied. The opposition leader told the Speaker that "there was a growing feeling in the country that the government's relative silence so far may be due to the fact that the Prime Minister himself was involved". The matter, he said, "was damaging the image of the nation, nationally and internationally. The country's reputation was subject to ridicule and contempt, and Trinidadians appeared in the eyes of outsiders to be international crooks." On 22 September, Williams sued both the *Trinidad Express* and the *Trinidad Guardian* for libel.

The government engaged itself in a flurry of activity that sought to give the impression that it was pursuing the matter of determining who was the "high official" who had negotiated the deal, and what had happened to the money that was paid by the McDonnell Douglas Corporation to the "businessman" who acted as agent on the agent's behalf. The media called upon Williams to stop pretending that he did not know who the "high official" was, and he was accused by the *Express* of being engaged in a "shallow cover up. What was at issue was not the inability to identify the man, but the refusal to do so."

The issue came to a head on 27 March 1981, when Panday succeeded in bringing a motion to parliament that expressed dissatisfaction with the manner in which the government was handling the McDonnell Douglas issue. During the controversial debate, Panday made reference to a report filed by a special McDonnell Douglas Corporation committee, in which it was revealed that the airline was told by a "high official" in Trinidad and Tobago that it would be favoured in the award of a contract to purchase aircraft if it designated a certain Trinidad businessman as its representative in Trinidad and Tobago. According to the report, the businessman was duly contracted, and it was agreed that the sum of US\$575,000 would be paid to him in installments for his role in facilitating the deal. The ultimate beneficiary was the "high government official".

The government's response was to plead ignorance of the transaction and to demand that McDonnell Douglas provide information as to who the "high government official" and the designated businessman were. To make their determination to contest the claims of the McDonnell Douglas Corporation seem more credible, the government threatened to take legal action if the American firm did not offer an unqualified apology to the members of the government collectively and severally for the imputations contained in the report. The form of the apology was to be approved by the government, and had to be published in a prominent section of the *Wall Street Journal*. Critics argued that the government was bluffing, because it must have known that the report was public information that was the by-product of litigation. "To say the Report was libellous was to accuse the American company of misleading a US Court of Law and therefore charge it with contempt of court and possible perjury" (*Trinidad Express*, 22 September 1980). There were also threats that the government might not take delivery of the last of the three aircraft that were on order (*Hansard*, 17 October 1980 and 27 March 1981).

None of these threats came to anything, because it was clear that McDonnell Douglas was spoiling for a fight and would claim the defence of truth. It was also likely that if any damages were awarded, the amounts would be derisive. The government also failed in its demand that officials of McDonnell Douglas must come Trinidad and Tobago to give testimony as to the identity of the high official and the businessman, as well as other details about the transaction. It likewise failed to get the two officials of the US embassy who had witnessed the signing of the contract to appear in court. The parliamentary opposition felt convinced that the government was only pretending that it wanted the matter ventilated publicly, and that it was creating an elaborate smokescreen to hoodwink and deceive the nation, since it knew, as did other people, who the individuals were. The government was told that the individuals not only were known, but were still conducting business on its behalf, building race tracks for horses and so on. Instead of creating elaborate feints, the government was told that it should resign. The problem, argued Panday, was that the government was terrified that the information they were seeking would become public. As Panday explained, "What the Government is afraid of is 'mouth open, story fall out.' It is obvious that the high official is a conduit to the highest official in this land. That is why he is being hidden. . . . One cannot touch Johnny [because] Johnny knows too much. Johnny is holding secrets for the highest official in the land" (*Hansard*, 27 March 1981, 1987).

This was a direct challenge to Williams. Panday noted that Williams himself had never made a public statement on the matter. Instead, he used the attorney general, Selwyn Richardson, to investigate the various breaches of the exchange control regulations and the tax regime, and junior minister Patrick Manning to speak for him. Panday told Williams that if his concern was about the difficulties involved in getting evidence that would stand up in a court, he should deal with the matter politically. Instead he was making fools and tools of his ministers. Panday was convinced that no further action would be taken on the matter because it was "too close to home". He was correct.

The debate had made clear that John O'Halloran was the person who had effected the deal, and that the monies were not deposited in Trinidad and Tobago. It was also made public that O'Halloran was a close family friend and business crony of the "designated businessman". In an interview given to the *Express*, O'Halloran formally denied that he was in any way involved in the DC-9 transaction. He admitted, however, that the signature on the back of one of the cheques was that of his son, J.E. O'Halloran, who was then living in Toronto, Canada. According to O'Halloran, the designated businessman received the cheque from McDonnell Douglas, and endorsed it to his son, John Junior, who endorsed it before depositing it into an account in Canada.

O'Halloran also admitted that since leaving ministerial office in 1970, he had remained an unofficial adviser of the prime minister, who often called and asked him what he would do "if [he] had to make so-so decision". His advice was never given in an official capacity, however. O'Halloran, who saw Williams every Wednesday, denied that he was a "shadow minister" or "a prodigal son of the Prime Minister", but allowed that he and Williams had "a good relationship. We have had our differences, but 25 years is a long time" (*Trinidad Express*, 17 December 1980). O'Halloran was known, however, to boast that he did not "need" Williams and that it was the latter who needed him. He also admitted that he was the person who raised money for the party.

The Tesoro Scandal

Following the defeat of the PNM in 1986, the new National Alliance for Reconstruction government headed by Prime Minister A.N.R. Robinson appointed a high-powered commission of inquiry to investigate a number of transactions that the PNM had entered into. The work of the commission floundered amid a host of procedural hurdles. Up to July 1990, little had emerged from its deliberations and the commission appeared to have died a natural death, inviting the accusation that in spite of all the allegations about corruption that had been made about Williams and the PNM, it was not able to prove anything. Robinson was accused of being vindictive, spiteful, and obsessed with denigrating the PNM and its founder-leader at all cost. This obsession was seen as prompted by a desire on his part to get even with someone who had humiliated him and his wife.

The "Tesoro affair", one of the matters under examination, was extremely embarrassing for Williams, and he strove mightily to keep it under wraps. In 1968, Williams was facing enormous pressure from the trade unions and the oil companies. The companies were claiming that their drillable assets were drying up, and as such they were forced to cap wells and retrench labour. Between 1963 and 1968, employment in the industry had fallen from 17,800 to 13,500. Important towns such as Fyzabad, Palo Seco, Point Fortin and La Brea were taking on ghostly appearances. More unemployment loomed, and British Petroleum and Shell signalled that they were prepared to sell their assets. Faced with pressure from the OWTU, the government acquired British Petroleum's assets for US$20 million – assets it planned to incorporate in a National Petroleum Company. Williams's initial plan was to enter into a fifty-fifty joint venture with Texaco to manage and operate the assets of British Petroleum, since he was not convinced that Trinidadians could run an oil company and market its products. This was met with strong opposition from the OWTU, however, and Williams was forced to capitulate and to look elsewhere for help to finance and manage the acquired assets of British Petroleum as well as for funds – which the government did not have – to pay the company. It was in this context that Tesoro appeared on the scene, virtually like a thief in the night. But to a desperate Williams, Tesoro was the proverbial "white knight".

The Tesoro Petroleum Corporation, of which little was then known anywhere, was a small oil-producing and marketing company founded in 1964. In 1964, its sales were a mere US$250,000, and it operated at a loss. By 1969, it was producing 3,250 barrels of crude oil per day and its earnings were an unimpressive US$3.6 million. It had not the international experience, nor the markets, nor the financial resources needed by the National Petroleum Company. The company did, however, have good connections in the Continental Bank of Illinois, based in Chicago, which helped it to raise US$25 million to finance the operations of the new joint company, Trinidad–Tesoro Limited.

What was interesting about the deal was that Tesoro paid a mere US$50,000 for the 49.9 per cent equity it acquired. It also only guaranteed US$7.5 million of the loan raised by Continental. It brought nothing else to the table. In return, it was given full control of management, as well as responsibility for finance, marketing, and development of the underdeveloped assets of the company. Within five years, the once struggling company was deemed by *Forbes* (February 1974) to be the "fastest growing energy company in the United States". All was not well in the state of Denmark, however, and there were suspicions that the deal was vitiated by corruption. No proof was forthcoming while Williams was in office. The cover-up was handled expertly.

Secret documents that were made public in Trinidad and Tobago in 1980 indicated that Tesoro and the Government of Trinidad and Tobago, acting through John O'Halloran, then minister of petroleum and mines, entered into a number of agreements on 7 November 1968 that were onerous to Trinidad and Tobago. Under the terms of the agreements, "the workforce was to be reduced from 950 in 1970 to 325 in 1975. In the year beginning 1976 and thereafter, the number of employees was to decline further until the economic depletion of the property is reached." This in a company that was bought to save the jobs of the workers. More startling was that the company that was formed to operate the acquired assets was also given the right to import personnel who could compete with workers unionized by the OWTU. These service workers, who were to be hired by an unaffiliated enterprise selected by Tesoro, enjoyed the right to repatriate their earnings and investments. What was even more astonishing was that the Trinidad government undertook to help the company negotiate labour union agreements with the OWTU.

There were other sweeteners. The government was enjoined to assist the joint company to find opportunities for it to invest its earnings in Tesoro's offshore drilling. Its share in such activities was to be at least 50 per cent. Other provisions involved the payment by Trinidad and Tobago to Tesoro of a management fee of TT$50,000 per annum for the first five years of the contract. In turn, the joint company was to pay to the Trinidad government a consulting fee of $100,000 annually for services rendered to the joint company. These payments were tax deductible. It was also provided that dividends were to be declared after the first five years at the request of either party, and to the extent that cash was available, at 50 per cent of net earnings after tax as certified by auditors.

One of the agreements likewise provided that Tesoro was to be taxed at "arms' length prices". The question as to what constituted "arms' length prices" became a subject of acute controversy in 1974 when the minister of finance, George Chambers, proposed to introduce new petroleum taxes, and Tesoro accused the government of reneging on its 1968 agreement and threatened a law suit. The chairman of the company, Bernard Primus, urged the then minister of petroleum and mines, Errol Mahabir, to try to find a way to resolve the issue in order to save the country "international embarrassment". He was referring to the possibility that the "deals" made in 1968 would be made public. There was also concern that the fact that the CEO of Tesoro had arranged with his investment banker, Peter Detweiller of E.H. Hutton, to procure a prostitute, "preferably blonde", for the finance minister, who was raising a tax matter that threatened to cut into the firm's profits, might also become public. Chambers was due in Ottawa, Canada, to attend meetings of the World Bank and the International Monetary Fund in January 1975. (See "Finance Minister Prefers Blondes", *Trinidad Guardian*, 5 November 1997.)

In June 1975, Mahabir wrote to the prime minister bringing to his attention a letter from Tesoro, which claimed that "the combined effect of tax reference prices, additional tax rates and an increase in profit taxes was placing an unbearable burden on the Company whose cash reserves were dwindling, thus shortening the possible economic life of the company". Mahabir told Williams that "two government directors agreed that the current tax levels were causing a serious drain on the Company which would eventually find itself in an unviable position". Faced with the possibility of "international embarrassment", cabinet, on the advice of the attorney general, agreed that the 1968 agreement was legal and valid, and Tesoro was given TT$30.3 million in tax credits. The company accepted the relief without agreeing to tie it to employment levels. Tesoro clearly felt it held the Trinidad government over a barrel.

Chickens almost came home to roost in 1977 when the US Securities and Exchange Commission began querying Tesoro's accounting practices. In response to the commission's initiatives, Tesoro's board appointed a special committee to "determine the existence of any bribes, kickbacks, rebates, illegal payments, directly or indirectly, for and on behalf of any government official, or any off the book accounting which the company may have obtained". The government, however, managed to ensure that Trinidad and Tobago was not embarrassed by the investigation. To prevent any likelihood of this happening in the future, the government in 1985 even fought off a bid by the Diamond Shamrock Corporation to buy Tesoro. In the end, in 1986 Trinidad and Tobago acquired Tesoro's equity in the joint company for 3.23 million barrels of oil to be paid over an eighteen-month period, and not the US$200 million that Tesoro (Texas) had asked for.

In 1987, the National Alliance for Reconstruction government took Tesoro to court in New York, seeking to recover the bribe that it was certain had been paid to PNM ministers in 1968. More than money was involved. What Robinson wanted most of all was hard evidence that would clearly establish that the late prime minister was privy to the transaction, and that both he and other PNM ministers were beneficiaries. These claims had emerged during the litigation proceedings between Tesoro Corporation and some of its shareholders in the United States in 1977. Among the details was that in 1968, Tesoro was experiencing difficulty persuading civil servants that it had the requisite knowledge and expertise to manage the assets of British Petroleum, and found it necessary to hire agents to overcome the obstacles it faced. It recruited one John Rahr in this capacity. Rahr in turn introduced the directors to John O'Halloran, the minister of petroleum and mines. It was O'Halloran and Francis Prevatt who agreed to sell 49.9 per cent interest in the company for US$50,000 in cash, provided Tesoro made a "political contribution" or a "finder's fee" of approximately US$2 million. The $2 million was a mere 10 per cent of the US$20 million that the Trinidad government had paid for the assets of British Petroleum. Using circuitous routes, the money was deposited in several overseas accounts before finally being stashed in Switzerland. Rahr was the principal courier and O'Halloran the principal beneficiary. Prevatt, chairman of the PNM and a former minister of finance, served as Tesoro's "friend" at court, and was paid US$120,000 per year as a "consulting fee" (Robinson 2004, 146).

While Williams's name was never mentioned in the statement that Robinson made to parliament, one was clearly being invited to connect the dots. The presumption was that Williams was in some material way a beneficiary. Robinson also alleged that Tesoro made several expensive gifts to other government officials, and in so doing had "bought its way into the inner sanctum of the Government. These bribed officials provided information to Tesoro about Williams's moods, and how best to approach him so as to maximize the corporations' profits" (ibid., 148). Tesoro also put its tax problems on the table when Prevatt was acting prime minister in 1975. They calculated that this was an "opportune time to work out all the tax and other problems which they had with the Government of Trinidad and Tobago".

Robinson refers to a "Mr A", a former prime minister, who was in the United States in 1975 on a formal visit: "Tesoro paid to his benefit the sum of US$3,100.00 which was covered up and reported in Tesoro's business records as being for aviation and consulting services rendered. . . . Everyone makes mistakes, but this Tesoro skeleton in Mr. A's closet no doubt had much to do with his refusal thereafter to pursue investigations of Tesoro" (ibid., 146). Robinson was referring to Chambers, who was then finance minister. Chambers, as we have seen, was raising issues about taxes that threatened to cut into Tesoro's income. Tesoro, as noted above, sought to suborn and seduce him with a blonde call girl.

One knowledgeable public servant told the author that he firmly believes that Williams contrived to be out of the country when the tax deals were being negotiated to give himself deniability. Robinson also quoted a Tesoro executive's report about what had been achieved in a particular meeting with a "Mr C" on the internal workings of the Trinidad cabinet: "the Tesoro matter having been resolved in Tesoro's favour, Tesoro has come out stronger rather than weaker, and the Prime Minister has been openly alerted to where the objection to Tesoro came from. 'Mr. C' thought that any further objections to Tesoro would be much more readily identifiable and therefore easier to deal with for the Prime Minister, if he chose to" (ibid., 149). Other documents submitted to parliament (and which seem to have disappeared) indicated that a minister (probably Prevatt) "admitted under examination that he personally kept Dr. Williams fully advised of all that he was doing, and that Dr. Williams personally approved the efforts which were being made to suppress references to Trinidad and Tobago in the United States" (ibid., 152).

Talking about the various anti-corruption campaigns launched by Williams, including the much-touted one led by Attorney General Selwyn Richardson, Robinson claimed that every effort was made to render the latter's efforts futile: "Officials in the former Government who were Tesoro's friends did everything they could to ensure that Minister Richardson could not discover and reveal the extensive web of corruption that took place. In 1980, he was sent on one trip after another to Europe, Africa, North America, South America and even China in an effort to divert his time" (ibid., 152). Robinson claimed that when at "two o'clock that night" he had finished reading the documents that revealed what had gone on, he "went down on his knees and prayed for my country" (ibid., 149).

In the course of investigations into the Tesoro matter, a team of forensic experts hired by the government succeeded in unearthing other information that established conclusively that the US$2 million bribe had been paid to O'Halloran and Prevatt through Rahr, who was the "go between" in the transaction. Rahr, who had previously denied the allegations, was induced to make a sworn death bed deposition detailing how the monies were paid and to whom.[2] Rahr's testimony was corroborated by other evidence and fitted the facts as they were understood. Rahr also supplied clinching documentary evidence of his travels and transactions and had been cross-examined and videotaped in the presence of his lawyer.

Documents that also became available as a result of the investigations revealed that the US$50,000 that was paid in cash for Tesoro's 49.9 per cent share of British Petroleum was recorded as US$2,080,000 in Tesoro's books. What this meant was that the $2 million that was paid in bribes to O'Halloran, plus $30,000 that was paid to or reserved for others, was recorded as being part of the purchase price of the British Petroleum assets. Contrary to what was being said about the fortunes of the company, Tesoro directors boasted about how well it had done since it was founded in 1964. In 1968, the year prior to the acquisition of the Trinidad-based equity, gross income was recorded as being US$24.6 million. In 1969, the year of acquisition, it had tripled to US$70.6 million. In 1974, the company was said to be worth US$534.9 million. The company had shared in the OPEC bonanza. Using company reports as source data, one member of parliament, Eden Shand, estimated that the "shady deal" had cost Trinidad and Tobago over US$1 billion. No wonder Tesoro felt driven to boast in an advertisement in *Time*, 26 August 1974, that "as a result of its pleasant and rewarding association with the [Trinidad] Government, the company hopes to expand its investment in Trinidad and Tobago, and is considering major new projects on the same joint ownership

basis". Robinson claimed (1986, 162) that the government had held secret negotiations with Tesoro for the operation of the "carcass of Shell", which the state had
acquired for TT$93 million in cash. Williams's announcement about the purchase
of Shell and the formation of the Trinidad and Tobago Oil Company was made
on 24 August 1974, two days before the advertisement appeared in *Time*.[3]

The Tesoro matter was settled out of court on the advice of the government's
lawyers, who advised that the government could either lose the case, given that
it could be deemed to be statute barred, or that it would be difficult to get legally
admissible evidence to claim more than Tesoro was offering as a settlement. By the
terms of the settlement, Tesoro Corporation (which had resold its 49.9 per cent
share in Trinidad and Tobago Petroleum Corporation [Trintope] to the
Government of Trinidad and Tobago in 1985 for TT$445 million) agreed to pay
the Trinidad and Tobago government the sum of US$2.8 million to satisfy the lat-
ter's claim for compensation and damages. In turn, the government agreed to
limit Tesoro's liability in an unrelated arbitration matter with another foreign
company, Federation Chemicals. The monies that Tesoro paid the Trinidad government were more than offset by what it saved in the Federation Chemicals
matter, a sum that was said to be more than three times as much. Robinson, however, was less concerned about the economics of the deal. What he wanted was
Williams's scalp. The government boasted that its investigatory efforts had yielded
documentary evidence of ministerial corruption that tangentially implicated
Williams. It was argued that he must have been aware of what his ministers were
doing, and had condoned their tawdry activities. The PNM sought to defend
Williams, but not very successfully.

The government was also accused of attempting to implicate the former head
of state, Sir Ellis Clarke, by alleging that he was "palsy walsy" with Tesoro's corporate executives, who made gifts of various kinds to him. Clarke strenuously
denied that he had taken any monetary gifts from Tesoro or had flown in any
plane paid for by Tesoro. As he insisted, "I dealt with people on a personal basis,
and had no knowledge whatever that Tesoro was in any way involved in anything unseemly." He did admit to having received the gift of a tray from one of
Tesoro's directors whom he and his wife had befriended and whom they had
invited to be a guest at their home. Clarke recalled that when O'Halloran and
Prevatt came through New York on their way to negotiate the deals with Tesoro,
they did not solicit the assistance of the Trinidad and Tobago embassy, which
was then under his leadership. They were tight-lipped about what their mission
was. He was also of the view that a person such as Williams must have been aware
of what they were about. Williams, he opined, was a "lucky man". I presume
that by this he meant that details of the deals only became public after his death,
and that he was saved the embarrassment of having to explain his role.

This narrative indicates that Williams definitely knew and approved of the

Tesoro deal in which public assets were sold at a price considerably lower than what they cost to acquire. The question to be determined is why did he do so? Far from seeing the deal as a sell-out, Williams claimed to be proud of what he had achieved! As he told the country when the formation of the company was being announced in November 1968, "In all the long history of the Commonwealth Caribbean, this is the first time that the people of the country, through their government, have directly participated in the ownership and operation of a mineral enterprise." Williams gave no hint that he believed the agreement was onerous or that he had a weak hand in the negotiations: "People of Trinidad were entering the decade of the seventies better equipped than ever. They had new forms of participation in industry and a cadre of competent nationals in technical and managerial fields, both in government and in industry" (*Trinidad Guardian*, 15 September 1987).

Why did Williams deliberately mislead the nation? Did he, in a fit of desperation, allow himself to be persuaded, on the eve of 1970, that the Tesoro "deal" was better than no deal at all? Several senior public servants were known to have had reservations and concerns about Tesoro, and some asked awkward questions that rattled and irritated Williams. One advised the author that he was puzzled that irritation was expressed when he sought to advise (in writing) the prime minister and the minister of petroleum and mines as to what they were doing in respect of the negotiations for the sale of Shell Oil. The latter remarked that the prime minister wondered whether "a trap was being laid". Why the suspicion? Did someone have "cocoa in the sun" and fear rain?

Public servants also expressed concern that Tesoro was not paying taxes and royalties to the treasury as had British Petroleum, and that the treasury was in fact meeting the cost of Tesoro's share holding. In sum, it was felt that Tesoro was bleeding the treasury in return for the limited management services, and drilling and marketing expertise that it provided. Another concern was that no one was looking after the interest of Trinidad and Tobago in the Trinidad–Tesoro "partnership", even though the chairman of the company was a Trinidad national. The subsequent quarantining of Dodderidge Alleyne and Frank Rampersad, both of whom had openly expressed concern about what was taking place in respect of Tesoro, suggests that they paid a price in terms of their careers for their public spiritedness. William Demas, who also had concerns, "took in front" by decamping for Guyana to become secretary general of CARIFTA.

Developments with respect to the government's claims in Canadian courts that O'Halloran had used his office to secure bribes from companies doing business in Trinidad and Tobago also yielded information that compromised the PNM, and indirectly, Williams.[4] On 4 June 1990, an Ontario court sustained the government's claims and ordered O'Halloran's estate to pay C$8,395,382 (TT$432 million) to the Trinidad and Tobago government and its agencies (BWIA, the Caroni

Racing Complex), even though at the time of his death in 1985 in Canada, only US$10,000 in traveller's cheques were found in O'Halloran's bank account. The government expressed satisfaction with the award. Attorney General Selwyn Richardson, who had pursued the matter, remarked that "right must win out in the end. Justice must prevail." Prime Minister Robinson also saw the award as "a victory, a breakthrough by a developing country seeking to recover money which had been fraudulently spirited away to a developed country". Robert Lindquist of Peat Marwick, who provided forensic services to the government, also expressed satisfaction with the settlement: "It was a risk because we started out with very little. We believe that overall, the investigation and legal action that followed have been of benefit, not only in terms of the money awarded, but in terms of concluding this matter about which there have been rumours for years."[5]

Even as information was being made public about these transactions, many were insisting that Williams was an innocent, or a passive victim at worst. One member of the National Alliance for Reconstruction government, Eden Shand, indicated that he did not think Williams was directly involved in any of the transactions. As he told parliament, "I categorically refuse to believe that Dr. Williams was a thief. He may have been involved in some sort of cover up activity, but I refuse to believe that the Father of the Nation was a thief." Shand told parliament that he had been told by a PNM "insider" that O'Halloran was the PNM's "bagman", and that he "divvied" up the proceeds of his illegal activities to individuals, and not to the party as such. "If he did divvy up a share for Eric Williams, I want to believe that it was without his knowledge, for in his declaration of assets sometime in 1970, there was no sign of wealth" (*Hansard*, 27 July 1990). Several reports are floating around that indicate monies were put into accounts without his "knowledge".

Some of Williams's ministers were embarrassed by his close relationship with O'Halloran. They simply could not understand why he was so tolerant of O'Halloran's misdemeanors, including his open flouting of the law about game cock fighting. Indeed, when Chambers became prime minister following Williams's death, he pledged "to deal with corruption. Wherever the axe falls, the man is going to be chopped". O'Halloran got the message. With Williams's death, he had lost his protector. He discovered that he had needed Williams as much as Williams had needed him. He fled to Canada in 1982, and died there in 1985. Prevatt fled to Costa Rica in 1987, one year after the PNM's electoral defeat. Others fled to Panama (*Trinidad Guardian*, 9 June 1991).

Williams's ghost still hovers over Trinidad and Tobago. Statements continue to be made, especially by those opposed to the PNM, that Williams and the PNM were just as corrupt as Basdeo Panday and the United National Congress were accused of being while they held power between 1994 and 2000. Was Williams a beneficiary, wittingly or unwittingly, of O'Halloran's largesse? Did O'Halloran compromise him by sharing his wealth, as most clever operators do? If so, where did the money go? Was it only the party and its operations that he was concerned about? Was the account that the party reportedly had in Switzerland controlled by O'Halloran alone? If not, who else had access to the account? What about Francis Prevatt, the "heavy hitter" chairman of the party who was widely referred to as "Mr Ten Per Cent"? Prevatt was at the end of almost every financial transaction involving the state. Why did Williams turn a blind eye to his corrupt activities? Why too did Williams retain him as chairman of the party? Was he considered to be invaluable as a political manager and keeper of secrets? Did Williams take the view that every political party needed funds, fundraisers and bagmen who handled things, and that he could trust Prevatt and O'Halloran in this regard?[6] Were there other reasons why Williams trusted O'Halloran and Prevatt? Did they hold dark secrets for him? Why did Williams threaten to "cut the throat" of a minister who complained about the corrupt behaviour of some of his ministers? Why did he choose to use Prevatt to send the message to the puzzled minister? Questions such as these are not easy to answer; most of the principals have either died, or are unwilling to implicate themselves or "insult the memory" of an icon. This holds true even for those who were humiliated or punished by that self-same icon.

Williams's close friend and personal physician, Dr Halsey McShine, has offered a sympathetic explanation for Williams's relationship with O'Halloran. According to McShine, Williams once told him that he was hearing talk about O'Halloran's corrupt activities, and that he ought to remove him as one of the executors of his will. McShine, who himself was one of Williams's executors, later found out that Williams had done nothing about it. Asked why Williams continued the relationship with O'Halloran despite the reports which he was hearing, McShine felt that the answer lay in the prime minister's need for "jovial companionship". "While he was in his [O'Halloran's] company, he is not thinking that he is a crook. He needed his company – jovial companionship." McShine notes that Williams was a lonely man (interview with Bridget Brereton at the University of the West Indies, Oral History and Pictorial Records Programme, February 1991). Other insiders such as Ferdie Ferreira believe that O'Halloran might have endeared himself to Williams in 1956 by helping to raise the funds that he desperately needed to pay off the obligations owed to his wife and children, imposed on him by the courts in Washington, D.C.

It is worth noting that Williams had done a great deal to enhance his reputation as a corruption fighter by coming out passionately in support of the establishment of an Integrity Commission and its insertion in the 1976 republican constitution. There was considerable opposition to setting up such a body from elements within the PNM. The party's chairman, Francis Prevatt, was strongly opposed. Williams insisted that it must be established even if the net result was that "we depopulate the country [and] increase the number of emigrants". As he told parliament,

> Those who believe that this is not suited to this particular country or one can have this country without that, have not got the faintest idea of the sophistication of this electorate which I know better than most of the people because I contributed at least as much as anybody else to developing that sophistication that they have. I am not going to complain about that sophistication. We worked for it. And this is the price you have to pay for it. You are not getting away with it. (*Hansard*, 12 March 1976, 732)

Williams declared his own assets, but little or nothing was done to compel others to do so. The author recalls being told by a PNM senator in 1976 that when she told Prevatt that the prime minister had declared his assets, and that other ministers should do the same, his reply to her was, "You mean he declared his local assets." One wonders whether his stance on the Integrity Commission was one of his celebrated feints made on the eve of an impending election, the outcome of which he was concerned about.

The data suggests that Williams was not what he seemed to be in the myth, and that he operated within and between several boxes. Bernard Primus, who served the government on many public boards, including Trinidad–Tesoro, of which (as we have seen) he was chairman, argued that Williams the person was a man of stature, a Dr Jekyll. As a politician, however, he was quite petty, a Mr Hyde. In the latter guise, he was a disciple of the Machiavelli who wrote *The Prince* as opposed to *The Discourses*. According to Machiavelli,

> the prince cannot observe all those things which are considered good in men, often being obligated, in order to maintain the state, to act against faith, against charity, against humanity, and against religion. He must have a mind disposed to adapt itself according to the wind and as the variations of the future dictate. The experience of our time shows the need for one to have little regard for good faith. One has to be astute enough to confuse men's brains.

According to this perspective, Williams was politically amoral and used men for his various purposes. He had those who looked after his image, the economy and the state, and those who looked after the party and who collected the "customs" dues that were required to finance its operations.[7]

Up to the time he died, however, a majority of Afro-Trinidadians were unwillingly to believe that Williams was tainted by corruption. There were whispers from his critics, but no one asserted with unequivocal confidence that he was crooked. Some were in denial. One senior civil servant who worked closely with Williams told the author that he was reluctant to ask questions that might lead him to think that Williams was a crook. And the fact that Williams lived abstemiously and eschewed show and opulence seemed to convince the doubting Thomases that he was not preoccupied with accumulating material wealth.

It is ironic that the debate on Panday's motion in parliament on the DC-9 transaction took place on 27 March 1981. Seventy-two hours later, Williams was dead. Was that debate the "tipping point"? Did he fear that more details of what went on would emerge, much to his embarrassment? Was he a captive king who had been unwittingly suborned by his money men to the point where he had become so deeply imbricated that he had no choice but to go along? Or was he a willing player, someone who concealed his true essence behind dark glasses and intellectualism that in the final analysis was mere pretense?

Williams's apologia was that he tolerated corruption as an indulgent father, all because he wanted to save the face of his party. As he confessed, "Like the good father, I have forgiven the wrongs of many of my children. I have taken their blame and their shame. All this for the welfare of my party. People are accusing me. I could have done worse, but never did. People whom I have taken from the dump and made men have betrayed me. They have attempted to break me, yet I have been kind to them." Presumably, Williams felt that given all that he had done, History would absolve him and forgive him his trespasses.[8]

One hesitates to libel the dead or to insult his memory, and the brute fact is that we have no justiciable evidence that convicts Williams or proves that he ever asked for or received a bribe. What we do have is evidence that he covered up a great deal of fiscal crookedness on the part of O'Halloran and other persons who were close to him. O'Halloran was clearly the most powerful political personality in the regime apart from Williams himself, and we can only speculate as to the source of his Rasputin-like power.[9] The worst that could be surmised is that O'Halloran might have compromised him in some way, and that he was thereafter unable to blow the whistle without implicating himself and the party. At times, one feels that more was at issue. Perhaps the best way to express this point of view is to quote Chinua Achebe, who in his acerbic little book *The Trouble with Nigeria* had the following to say:

> As we have sunk more and more deeply in the quagmire, we have been "blessed" with a succession of leaders who are said to possess impeccable personal integrity but unfortunately are surrounded by sharks and crooks. I do confess to some personal difficulty in even beginning to visualize genuine integrity in that kind of fix; for it has always seemed to me that the test of integrity is its blunt refusal to be compromised. (1985, 42)[10]

43   **The Last Days of Eric Williams**

The Boss Is Dying

Eric Williams died on 29 March 1981 in circumstances that gave rise to controversy. In some quarters it was believed that he had committed "altruistic suicide"
in the hope that the PNM would not find him too heavy a burden to bear politically. Alternatively, it was believed that his death was "constructive suicide", that
he gave up the will to live because he felt that he had not achieved the political
goals that he set out to achieve in 1956. Others claimed that he felt that his party
and his political colleagues had "betrayed" him and the values of probity for
which he stood. The burden of failure and shame was too much to bear.

There has been a great deal of speculation as to whether Williams knowingly
took his own life. The debate was publicly sparked in 1984 by Dr Anthony
Maingot, a Trinidadian sociologist based at Florida International University, who
claimed that Williams had committed "altruistic suicide" (*Trinidad Guardian*,
25 April 1984). According to Maingot, Williams deliberately chose to die, believing that doing so would be best for the country. Interestingly, Maingot argued
that Williams's aim was to let the curious public have access to his secret files.
He argued that Williams had spent twenty-four years keeping vital matters secret,
and that it was perhaps not surprising in the end that he did what he did. Maingot
hinted that Williams's altruism was provoked by feelings of guilt and shame about
the corruption that he had allowed to flourish. As he wrote, "Why did Williams,
an uncorrupt man, allow corruption to run rampant during the decade or so
before his death?" Suicide may thus have been seen as a way of expiating guilt. His
action may have been designed to let the public know what really went wrong.
Blame would be placed where it properly belonged: on the shoulders of those who
betrayed him and the people (ibid.).

Reactions to Maingot were furious and hostile. They came from Williams's daughter Erica, from his former doctor Halsey McShine, from the *Trinidad Guardian*, and from ardent Williamsphiles. The *Guardian* spoke for many when it argued editorially that Maingot must have known that making such a claim would have "stirred up deep feelings", and that he should not have expressed such views without attempting to justify them by further explanations (ibid.).

McShine, Williams's established friend of fifty years and personal physician, gave two written accounts of what happened in the last month of Williams's life. His first account took the form of a letter dated 1 June, which he wrote to the then prime minister, George Chambers, meant to clear up errors that were said to have been made by the *Trinidad Express*. The second, recorded in February 1991 at the University of the West Indies, was embargoed until his death in October 2006. McShine was extremely sad and embittered about the circumstances that attended Williams's death. He tells us that he was Williams's sole medical adviser following the retirement of Dr David Wyke on grounds of ill health. He examined Williams every two weeks, and during his routine visit on 16 December 1980, he took the PM's blood pressure and tested his urine as he always did. Williams's blood pressure was high, but he refused to take the tablets that McShine wished to prescribe. He felt that the pressure was work related and that it would correct itself. Williams's urine test was normal. Wrote McShine, "He had no sugar that day, and his previous blood sugar had been normal. So I did not suspect diabetes. Nobody suspected that he had diabetes. Every time I tested him he was negative" (interview with Bridget Brereton and Margaret Rouse-Jones at the University of the West Indies, April 1991).

Strangely, or so it seemed to McShine, Williams refused to undergo his next bimonthly medical examination, scheduled for the end of December. For reasons that invite speculation, Williams cancelled his appointment, telling McShine that he would call when he needed him. McShine later denied that he had been dismissed, even though when he subsequently tried to call on the prime minister, Williams refused to answer his doorbell. McShine notes that he last saw his old friend at the PNM's twenty-fifth annual convention on 25 January 1981 and congratulated him on a fine address. He only learned that Williams was ill on 28 March when told so by Dr Courtney Bartholomew, one of Williams's doctors from whom he had become estranged. He did not know that Williams was seriously ill, and indicated to Bartholomew he would only see him if he was summoned by the prime minister himself or someone close to him. Clearly he did not want to be rebuffed. McShine felt Williams might have had an outside chance of survival if he, McShine, had been called in on the morning of Sunday, 29 March. When he was eventually called in at 8 p.m., he was advised by Dr Winston Ince that there was no pulse and that Williams was "beyond recovery". Asked to explain the fact that Williams seemed to have become a diabetic only after his last visit, McShine suggested that the political pressures of his last months in office could have triggered the disease. All that stress, the nurses demonstrating around the Red House. Everybody against him in the last three months. Stress can bring on acute diabetes, of course it can. As if to anticipate the charge that he might have misdiagnosed his celebrated patient's true condition, McShine noted that one could only tell for certain that someone is a diabetic if the test result is positive. As he explained, "Diabetes can come on acutely, we know that. It came on acutely."

McShine did not indicate that he had been told by Dr Johnny Lee, Williams's dentist, sometime in 1979 that his patient was diabetic. Lee had discovered evidence of this on his breath while working on his mouth. McShine denied that this was possible. He would have known if the diagnosis was correct. McShine, who clearly nursed guilty feelings, seems to have believed that Williams may not have known how serious his problem was and was eating foods that he should not have consumed. One wonders whether Williams was that negligent about his health. Interestingly, McShine originally believed that Williams had died from "acute heart failure". As he wrote, "At the time of his death, Dr Ince and I did not know that he was suffering from diabetes. In as much as I had not seen him alive or attended him for three months and Dr Ince had not seen him professionally for a year, we both decided that the presumptive cause of death may have been acute heart failure, but we wished a post-mortem to ascertain the exact cause of death. Dr Ince at this stage strongly suspected uncontrolled diabetes had caused his death." The autopsy confirmed Ince's judgement. The test showed that Williams had concentrations of sugar in his blood in excess of 1600 milligrams and 4+ in his urine, readings that were unusually high. Ince knew, however, that a Japanese doctor, Dr Tayayoshi Takemoto, professor of medicine at the Tokyo Women's Medical College, had examined Williams in December 1974 and found his sugar levels to be quite normal. Williams was diagnosed as suffering from duodenal ulcer and diverticulosis.

Controversy surrounded the question of why the men around Williams did not summon medical help earlier and why his daughter and other members of his family were not informed that he was ill. Several of Williams's ministers and advisers, Errol Mahabir, Kamaluddin Mohammed, John Donaldson, Mervyn de Souza and Ken Julien, were aware on the Thursday and the Friday preceding his death that he was seriously ill. On Thursday, 26 March, Kamaluddin Mohammed noted that the boss "looked distressed and started to perspire. During the short Cabinet meeting, which lasted only forty minutes, he left the room three times. All members of the Cabinet knew that something was not right" (Ghany 1996, 388).

Williams stubbornly refused to listen to their advice to call a doctor. On Friday, 27 January, he slumped in parliament and had to be taken out of the parliamentary chamber and into the office of the attorney general. According to a report about Williams's last days compiled by the *Express,*

That afternoon in Parliament, Mahabir noticed that Williams' condition appeared to have worsened. So rising to speak on the Private Members Bill before the House, he used the occasion to pass Senator Mervyn de Souza a note to take Williams out of the Chamber. De Souza did, leading him to the offices of the Attorney-General under the pretext of wanting to discuss a financial problem. Their action had not escaped Senator John Donaldson who immediately passed Mahabir a note suggesting that Erica Williams-Connell should be told of her father's illness and advised to come home. Mahabir, was however, aware of Williams' continued opposition to bringing Erica home. He had not seen her for two years, but he had the most outrageous reasons to support his feelings that she should stay in Miami. There were reasons that were always irrelevant and sometimes foolish, a friend says, but they showed how paranoid he was in later years. He actually had fears that she would be kidnapped. But he did ask Williams that night whether to send for Erica. "Not yet", he replied. And the matter was dropped.

As soon as he was finished speaking, Mahabir joined Williams and De Souza in the Attorney General's office. Williams had left his black briefcase on the top of his desk. It surprised Mahabir and should have alerted him. He took it with him to Williams and later left it in Donaldson's care.

They were trying to get Williams to go home, but were not being successful. Kamaluddin Mohammed joined them. "Bill", he said, "You'd better go home". Williams became angry. "What are you telling me?" he rebuked. "I know my rights and responsibilities". Mohammed said nothing. As he said, Williams was the master; his job was to obey and follow. But the rest prevailed, and Williams seemed prepared to listen. "But what about the Attorney General's Bill?" he inquired, revealing for the second time that afternoon that he was not in control of the situation.

When Mahabir saw him that evening, he was still in his street clothes: trousers, shirt and balisier tie, and jacket. The housekeeper Claudia informed Mahabir that Williams had had a fever. Mahabir noticed in fact that the fever had not left him and asked whether Williams wanted him to call a doctor. No, Williams said firmly and fretfully. He still did not suspect Williams was seriously ill and left to go to the Hilton to see an Iscott film. There he saw De Souza and Donaldson, and after bringing them up to date on the Prime Minister's condition, he urged them to visit him the next day and to keep in touch with him.

But Williams had been showing other signs of deterioration: his clothes were beginning to appear even more dingy. Wide sweat bands stained the armpits and sleeves of his jackets. Finally, the unhealthy state of his clothes seemed to have offended even Claudia. On the Sunday he died, she had begged Mahabir, when she met him in the morning, to bring in a tailor to make Williams some new clothes. "He has a lot of cloth in his room", she let on. Donaldson and De Souza kept a watch on Williams on Saturday, March 28. They reported that the fever had left Williams during the night and he was in better spirits that day. But he was still too weak to work. Apparently, however, Donaldson urged him to call in a doctor, but Williams was still adamant in his decision to wear out his illness as he was accustomed to wear out his opposition. ("The Last Days of Eric Williams", *Trinidad Express,* 29 March 1991)

When asked why she did not summon medical help when she realized that Williams was gravely ill, his devoted and loyal housekeeper explained that the prime minister had made her pledge that she would not call a doctor, and that she herself was afraid she would lose her job if she did otherwise. When it became evident that Williams was not merely asleep but was becoming comatose and that medical help had to be sought from a local doctor, de Souza, Mahabir and Julien agreed that they would take responsibility jointly and collectively for defying Williams should he decide to "have their skins" following his recovery.

Friends of Williams in general and his family in particular were savagely critical of Williams's ministers for failing to send for help when it was clear that the prime minister was very ill. They felt that the king's men had allowed him to "die like a dog". Williams's family was also angry that even after he was pronounced dead, they were not immediately informed. As Williams's youngest brother, Tony, said, "What manner of men would know a man is dying since he left Parliament the Friday evening and not see it fit to try and get his favourite daughter [Erica] here as quickly as possible or to contact his family here at home? Was it shame? Was it fear of the reception they would receive? Why did the President telephone Erica to ask her about a state funeral for the Prime Minister when he could have walked over to his neighbour's house, which was just twenty-five yards away?" It should be noted here that the prime minister had discontinued the practice of meeting with the president, Ellis Clarke, to advise him about the state of the nation. As Clarke himself tells us, "About two or three years before the death of Eric Williams, appointments for consultation slackened off, and though we were never on bad terms, he became withdrawn" (Collymore 2000, 111).

Tony also revealed that when his brother died, he had on his dark shades, his hearing aid and his balisier tie. He also complained that his brother's body had deteriorated badly because it had been left covered with a thick blanket for thirteen hours. The body, which was clad in an African robe and covered with a blanket, was said to be "puffed to the point of bursting". Asked Tony Williams, "What manner of men would leave a corpse covered with a thick blanket for 13 hours before turning the body over to a mortician?" One might also ask, "What was the significance of the African robe?"

Was Williams aware that he had diabetes? His long-time confidant John O'Halloran told McShine and others that Williams had informed him the Wednesday before he died that he had a "touch of diabetes", and that it was a pity that he (O'Halloran) would be out of the country. Why did Williams consider it unfortunate that O'Halloran was not going to be around? Did he anticipate that something would happen to him? If he knew that he had diabetes, who advised him, and when? If Williams knew that he was hyperglycemic, and not that he was merely suffering from ague or an allergy as he told at least one minister, why did he continue to consume copious quantities of ice cream, cake, syrupy daiquiris, Strepsils – precisely the things he should have avoided? Did he recognize that there was a link between his incontinence and diabetes? Why was he so adamant in his refusal to see a doctor? Was it paranoia, fatalism, mistrust, stubbornness, carelessness or the loss of the will to live? Was it disorientation induced by high levels of sugar in the blood? Or was he, as Chambers believed, severely depressed over missing his daughter, whom he had not seen since 1973 when she flew out of Trinidad following his decision to resume political leadership of the party?

Williams also refused to see his dentists despite the fact that two fillings were troubling him. When he became very ill in 1980 and required a blood transfusion, he refused not only to go to a hospital, but also to have a nurse in attendance while the transfusion was being done in his home by McShine. The latter had to remain with him for over three hours to ensure that there were no complications. One can well understand the prime minister's fear that the *Bomb* or some other tabloid weekly would discover that he was ill and trumpet this to the nation in ways that might embarrass him. But one is at a loss to understand why he refused to see McShine, with whom he had dined regularly for years. (Williams was a lonely man and always needed dining and drinking companions.) What is even more puzzling is that in the end, when he was near death and it was much too late, Williams agreed to see a foreign doctor. Was it disorientation or distrust of things local or a concern for secrecy? Equally curious is the fact that Williams had earlier put his affairs in order. He had paid off most of his house staff, including providing them with terminal benefits, and had kept a few, including his housekeeper, on a month-to-month basis. He had also reportedly made an inventory of his household articles and furniture, indicating which were his and which belonged to the state, and had asked Cuthbert Joseph, his minister of education, to pick up a number of books that were to be donated to schools and libraries. An employee of the library, and not Joseph himself, collected the books. Minister of works Hugh Francis was also called in and given books.

Looking at all these behaviours, it is tempting to conclude that Williams had been planning his death. But did he decide that he would hasten death by deliberately eating the wrong foods, or that he would make death look natural by doing so? Williams must have been bothered by the pervasive social unrest at the time. Though he was disoriented before the sitting began, he must also have been badly stung by some of the things that were said in the media and in parliament on 27 March during debate on a motion introduced by Basdeo Panday, leader of the opposition. Panday pointedly accused him of being a beneficiary of monies illegally collected by O'Halloran from the Tesoro Corporation of Texas and the McDonnell Douglas Corporation for the purchase of three DC-9 aircraft (see chapter 42). Polling data made public by this author on 15 March 1981 had likewise shown that a new party, the Organization for National Reconstruction, which had been publicly launched on 30 November 1980 and which had its inaugural convention on 1 February 1981, was a percentage point ahead of the PNM. Did the poll confirm Williams's worst fears, and did he conclude that electoral defeat and public exposure at the hands of Karl Hudson-Phillips, whom he had rebuffed in 1973, was a fate worse than death? As Owen Baptiste of the *Express* wrote,

> There were signs more and more that Trinidadians were becoming as irritated with his government and rule as Tobagonians had become. The sessions of "accounting to the Taxpayer", his final strategy to deflect blame, criticism, and rage from his government was general. Not just words and heated tempers. Not just rumour, but the survey done by St. Augustine Research Associates produced figures to show that Mr. Hudson Phillips and the Organization for National Reconstruction were gaining ground. ("Last Days of Eric Williams", 29 March 1991)

Mervyn de Souza did not believe that Williams knew he was dying, and said that the prime minister had planned to address a mass rally in South Trinidad immediately following the formal commissioning of the newly constructed Iron and Steel Company, due to take place the following week. But Williams was a master of deception and quite capable of misleading de Souza and others. One will never know for sure whether he made them believe that he would get well again, as he had in January, while secretly resigning himself to death by planned negligence. When de Souza realized on Sunday evening that Williams's condition was critical, he rushed to Ellis Clarke's home to tell him, sobbingly, that "the boss is dying".

My view is that a depressed Williams became suicidal and chose to let nature take its course. Given this determination, one cannot blame the "king's men" for acting the way they did. Williams was a difficult and stubborn person when he wished to be, and it would be unfair to condemn and judge his courtiers without understanding all the circumstances. Even John Donaldson's refusal to telephone Erica in Miami or Williams's family can be understood in the context of his concern as to what could happen if it became publicly known that Williams had died before security arrangements had been put in place. This concern for secrecy and security seems absurd in retrospect, but Trinidad had had no experience, no tradition of what had to be done when a prime minister died in office, especially one who personified the state to the extent that Williams did. Rumours fly fast in Trinidad and Tobago, and no one could have been certain as to what might have been said or done when "town" learned about the circumstances leading to his death. There were rumours that he had planned to expose certain ministers, and that they wanted him out of the way. In a sense everyone was rehearsing and performing at the same time. All that one can say is that Williams lived an extraordinary life, and died as he had lived.

Among other areas of controversy was one having to do with how Williams's close political associates managed his passing. Bitter criticism assailed the wall of silence that followed his death. It was said to be excessive. De Souza, minister in the Ministry of Finance, insists that when he advised Ellis Clarke that the "boss was dying", the president told him to "cap the news" as much as possible to give him time to get things in motion constitutionally. De Souza claims that he went back to the prime minister's house and told Jim Rodriguez, the chief of security, that the "chief is dead" and that the president wanted the news "capped" to give him time to do what had to be done.

De Souza believed he was acting in the public interest, and that this was not an unreasonable request for Clarke to make. The president, however, insisted that he made no such request and suggested that Minister de Souza may have been disoriented. To quote Clarke,

> It is quite possible that because of his close attachment to the Prime Minister, Senator de Souza was disoriented by the sudden shock of seeing the condition of his leader. He came to me tearfully and announced that the Prime Minister was dying. From what he said, I feared that it was only his loyal optimism that led him to this belief. My own fear was that the Prime Minister was dead. I asked him to return and find out the position. Later I had a telephone call from the Prime Minister's House – not from Senator de Souza but from someone else, stating that the Prime Minister was dead. I did not speak to Senator de Souza and certainly gave him no instructions to "cap the news". It was indeed the first time I had heard that expression. (*Trinidad Guardian*, 3 April 1981)

There were also questions as to why it took so long to advise Erica and the Williams family about the illness and death of the patriarch. Williams had been visibly ill since Friday. Was it that friends assumed he was a man apart from his family, a man without a family life? Eric's niece Peggy Gittens diarized what she knew about what took place on Saturday night and Sunday morning. Peggy and her sister Patsy, who both lived in the house with their uncle, returned home on the evening of 29 March as per usual and went upstairs as they were wont to do. They slept the entire night without knowing that their uncle lay dead downstairs. Attempts to alert them by stoning the windows failed to attract their attention. They found out at 5:30 a.m. when they saw a note that had been left for them informing them of their uncle's death. When they sought to enter the room where he lay, it was locked. When they sought the key from the security officer to view the body, they were refused. Only after threatening to break down the door were they given the key. What they found is recorded in their diary: "We saw Uncle Eric lying on the day bed. He was wearing an African robe and covered with a blanket and he looked just like his mother. He looked as though he may have been biting his lip just before he succumbed. There was some dried blood at the side of his nose and his hands were crossed across his body" (Boodhoo 2001, 242).[1]

The Nation in Mourning

The nation mourned Williams's death. It is estimated that close to two hundred thousand persons filed past the casket that contained his body as it lay in the rotunda of the Red House that housed the nation's parliament. That event had almost not occurred. Williams had said at the twentieth PNM convention that he did not want a state funeral when he departed this world: "I wish, and never have wished, no honour, no tribute, no commendation of any sort, no official or public ceremonies when the time comes. I have asked my daughter, who agrees with my decision, to ensure compliance and plead for your goodwill and your respect of what is a deeply personal wish aimed at nobody, critical of no policy" (as cited in Boodhoo 2001, 244). Similar wishes were recorded in his will, in which he asked for a simple cremation ceremony after which his ashes were to be thrown into the sea.

Erica Williams was determined that her father's wishes be kept, and refused all entreaties that they be dishonoured in deference to the public's wishes. As she told those who were interceding, "My father's expressed wish was that there should be no public viewing of his body . . . you had him for 25 years . . . that is enough. . . . It will be a private family affair. That is how he wanted it . . . no awards . . . no ceremony . . . no monuments" ("Last Days of Eric Williams", 29 March 1991). The public was insistent, however, and Erica relented and allowed the body to lie in state so that Trinidad could pay its final respects to their first prime minister. Some female members and supporters of the PNM were not satisfied with this gesture. They wanted to see the face of their departed leader to ensure that his death had not been faked by those he planned to expose as being corrupt: "We want to see the face! No Face, No Votes." At the urging of the PNM elite, Erica addressed those demands, telling the people that her father's wish was that there be no public viewing of his body. As she continued, sobbingly but with great dignity,

> Since I was, to my eternal regret, unable to be with him in his final moment, I consider it not only my duty, but my responsibility as one who loved him perhaps more than life itself, to ensure that his final wishes are carried out to the letter. Permit my beloved father to rest in peace [and] . . . respect his desire for privacy. It was I who made the concession to allow you to pay your last respects, since from the numerous condo-

lences that I have received, I realize that it would have been unfair to deny you your right to make one last private gesture. (Cited in John 1991, 91)

Williams's body was cremated in a hastily imported gas incinerator on Sunday morning, 5 April, after a private "family only" service conducted by Catholic priest Father Garfield Rochard. Notwithstanding Williams's anticlericalism, Erica placed in his hand a rosary that the pope had given her. The cremation lasted for four hours, after which his ashes were scattered in the Gulf of Paria, as per his wishes, by members of the family who had been taken out to sea aboard the MV *Barracuda*.

If one is to go by what was detailed in his will, Williams did not die a wealthy man as so many other Third World leaders did. His estate was valued at some TT$1,614,867. It comprised a home at Goodwood Park, which he had bought in 1973, valued at $625,000; a cash balance in the National Commercial Bank of $37,000; gratuity from the state worth $337,000; a car worth $40,000; belongings (jewellery, crystal and so on) worth $445,000; insurance policies worth $40,000; royalties from books and so on of uncertain value; and a small amount of shares in the Workers' Bank, the PNM Co-operative and the People's Co-operative Bank. The estate was divided in unequal portions among his three children, his nieces and his maids, with Erica getting the largest share. Erica also inherited his book collection and all property (real and personal) to which he might subsequently become entitled. The executors of his will were the National Commercial Bank, assisted by John O'Halloran, Dr Halsey McShine, and his solicitor, Inskip Julien.

The Succession

Eric Williams's death introduced new and dramatic dimensions into the political life of the twin island state. This was particularly so since general elections were due to be held before the end of 1981. Before his death, speculation surrounded whether he would lead the PNM into another election as he had pledged to do on 25 January, when the party celebrated its silver jubilee. Williams seemed aware of the possibility that the PNM either could be defeated outright at the polls, or could find itself in a situation where even though it was the largest single party in the House of Representatives, it could not command an absolute majority and would thus be forced into opposition by a coalition of its rivals. Some believe that rather than face either possibility, Williams would find an excuse to pull out of the race at the last minute. Strategists from the Organization for National Reconstruction (ONR) were seeking to encourage such an outcome by leaking the results of surveys that reportedly showed that the PNM was likely to be defeated in certain key constituencies – including Port of Spain South, which the prime minister represented.

Recall that at the September 1979 PNM convention, Williams had declared that he only had two more years to go. He further indicated that he was leaving centre stage and that he would hereafter be taking a back seat. Curiously, he said he would not wish to compete with the newly elected head of state, who "enjoyed power never entrusted to his predecessor as representative of the Queen". The *Express* (1 October 1979) complained that Williams was now playing the role of umpire, and that Trinidad was without leadership: "No hand was on the steering wheel." The *Express* editorialized that Williams's refusal to agree to choosing a deputy leader might suit the party, but was dysfunctional for the country: "Only someone who does not care particularly what happens to the vehicle will sit comfortably with a back seat driver in charge and who assumes the job of a traffic cop at dangerous intersections." My own view, expressed in 1979, was that Williams was scheming – that the promise of abdication was a ruse to "bamboozle the pretenders", and that the latter would have to fight tooth and nail to dislodge him. "The only way out of political office for Williams was in a casket," I wrote. We now know that Williams was very unwell, and that he may have been genuinely contemplating an exit strategy (*Sunday Express*, 2 October 1979).

No one, not even his closest associates, could say for sure just what Williams would have done in 1981 if he firmly believed that the odds were against him winning a sixth term of office. Party colleagues were convinced that he had every intention of facing the polls and that he was making plans to hit the campaign trail in the near future. In their view, Williams assumed that his "old black magic" was still powerful enough to pull back into the fold those who had either left to join the ONR, which was attracting huge crowds, or those who planned to vote for it on election day in the hope of effecting a change of government. Others were not so certain, suspecting that Williams had grown tired and frustrated about the inefficiency and corruption surrounding him, and that he felt a sense of betrayal that had become difficult to endure.

Those who believed that Williams thought he could win the election, public protests notwithstanding, recalled that it was widely held that the PNM would have been defeated in the 1976 election by the combined efforts of Tapia, the DAC and the ULF, had race not become an important issue in that contest. A great deal of the early support about which Tapia and the DAC had boasted literally evaporated on the eve of the election. The PNM and the ULF, seen by the electorate as the two organizations that best represented Africans and Indians respectively, were the beneficiaries of that vanishing support.

A similar outcome was possible in 1981, yet circumstances were different that year. Anxiety for change had grown between 1976 and 1981 as more people became progressively convinced that the government was unable to govern or manage the society effectively. Inefficiency in the public sector in general and the public utilities in particular was endemic, so much so that the government felt it necessary to organize public meetings at which the boards and managements of the utilities and not ministers themselves were required to account to the taxpayer. It was a palpable attempt to shift the focus of public anger away from the government and onto the utility bosses. It was a way of saying to the public that the government had done its part by making available all the funding necessary to provide systems that were adequate to the demands of the public, but that the utilities themselves had failed to perform as both the government and the public had a right to expect. This author, who was chairman of the Public Utilities Commission, is aware that the reasons for the inefficiency in the public utilities were complex, and that both the government and the utility managements must share the blame. The public, however, was not concerned about locating responsibility. They had become convinced that better had to be done, and there was an organization in the wings – the ONR –that was promising to do just that.

Official corruption had also become more widespread, and reports of one scandal followed others in bewildering succession. As we have seen (chapter 42), reports of deals involving the purchase of planes for the national airline, the award of contracts for the construction of a centralized horse racing complex, or the purchase of boats for the Trinidad-to-Tobago ferry service filled newspaper headlines for well over a year, and the man in the street had become convinced that individuals close to the prime minister were involved and were being protected by him for one dark reason or another. In a poll conducted by this author in January–February 1981, only 6 per cent of those interviewed believed that the government was telling parliament and the public all it knew about a deal negotiated with McDonnell Douglas in 1976 for the purchase of three DC-9 planes. Sixty-nine per cent of the sample was of the view that there was an attempt on the part of the government to stonewall on the issue. Of those who believed that there was indeed a cover-up, 49 per cent said they believed that the prime minister himself was covering up for persons in the party or the cabinet, while 39 per cent felt that he was covering up both for himself and others. Whatever the truth of the matter, the fact remains that on this as well as on other issues, large numbers of people were questioning the credibility of the prime minister, and many had come to believe that nothing the government said or promised could be taken at face value.

The fact that Williams had been losing political ground was further evidenced by the fact that 50 per cent of the sample expressed the view that he should resign as prime minister to make room for a successor. In a similar poll in November 1979, 42 per cent was of that opinion. In terms of race, 54 per cent of the Indians felt he should "take a rest", as the calypsonian Relator declared in song (see chapter 40), compared to 45 per cent of the Africans. It does not of course follow that all those who believed that Williams should resign were hostile to him. But among his supporters were those who nevertheless felt that he had either outlasted

Table 44.1   Do You Think Dr Williams Should Resign as Prime Minister to Make Room for a Successor?

	Percentage	
	1981	1979
Yes	50	52
No	35	46
No opinion	15	12
Total	100	100

his usefulness or deserved a rest. Some were concerned about the humiliation to which he was being exposed. Rather than see the image of their hero tarnished, or see him suffer the ultimate humiliation of an electoral defeat, they preferred that he retire while still on top. This group often made analogy to the fate of the boxer Muhammad Ali. The findings of the poll also provided evidence that the old question of "who we go put?" to replace Williams had been answered for many blacks, who saw Karl Hudson-Phillips, the ONR leader, as a sociologically acceptable alternative. Thirty-three percent of those sampled said he was their choice to be the next prime minister. The support of another 34 per cent was distributed among several others, while the remaining 33 per cent said they did not know whom they preferred. In the 1979 poll, 29 per cent regarded Hudson-Phillips as their choice in the prime ministerial stakes. It is worth nothing that Hudson-Phillips's support in 1981 came from all racial groups. Thirty-eight per cent of the African element chose him, while 31 per cent of the Indians and 29 per cent of the mixed and others did so.

Williams's death dramatically altered the political equation. One widely held view was that his departure was certain to guarantee the defeat of the PNM by the ONR, which was regarded as a PNM clone. Sociologically, the two parties represented the same constituency, though the ONR attracted added support from Indians disillusioned with the ULF and from the white and "off-white" community. This view was based on the assumption that the Hudson-Phillips wing would attract much of the support that the PNM had retained over the years because of personal loyalties to Williams. Voters who could not bring themselves to "betray" Williams while he lived might now feel free to change allegiance, or so it was argued. Polling data collected by the author in January–February 1981 supported this thesis. When asked which party they would vote for if Williams were to resign, only 17 per cent indicated they would vote for the PNM, a drop of 11 per cent. Thirty-three per cent said they would vote for the ONR, a gain of 4 per cent, while 17 per cent said they would vote for "no party", compared to 14 per cent who gave this reply on the previous question.

There was yet another possibility, that is, that Williams could do as much for the PNM in death as he could have were he still alive, and that the party and the new prime minister would benefit from the enormous groundswell of sympathy and affection that Williams's death evoked in the public mind. It was possible that Williams's charisma could become institutionalized in the party itself in the same way the charisma of Christ had become institutionalized in the Catholic Church, allowing any successor, no matter how insignificant, to partake of that charisma.

The outcome of the elections, however, was expected to depend on many other things. In part, it depended on whether the PNM united behind the new prime minister and confirmed him as political leader or whether there was a power struggle in the party. In the end there was no major power struggle, since in critical sections of the public mind, many of the would-be successors had eliminated themselves. Indeed, Clarke's first choice of a successor to Williams was Errol Mahabir. Members of the party elite raised objections to this proposal on the ground that there were too many rumours circulating over Mahabir's dealings with Japanese firms operating in Trinidad. The president's handling of the matter was decisively influenced by the advice given him by the minister of national security, John Donaldson, that he could not guarantee that the security services would accept Mahabir. According to Clarke, he called the three deputy leaders to his residence and urged them to try to reach an accommodation as to who should succeed. George Chambers immediately declared that he was not interested in the succession and left the issue to be resolved between Mahabir and Kamal Mohammed. According to the president, neither was willing to give way. Faced with an impasse, Clarke decided to appoint Chambers as the new prime minister. The agreement was that the appointment would stand until the ruling party met in convention to select its new political leader.

Reflecting on the matter six years later at a symposium organized by the author, Clarke indicated that, ironically, he had written the prime minister earlier in the week telling him that he planned to visit Miami with his wife on a shopping trip and anticipated no problems on the horizon to detain him. He explained his dilemma on the night in question in the following way:

An appointment of the new prime minister had to be made as a matter of urgency. Just think of it for a moment. If there is no Prime Minister, who summons the Cabinet? If there is no Prime Minister, who conveys to the President a decision of the Cabinet; by what authority? Suppose immediately upon the death of a Prime Minister there is an attempted revolution, there is a march, somebody is attempting to seize the radio station and the television station and give orders, who does what? So you will see, I think you will agree, there is the need to have in office at any given time, somebody who can summon a meeting of cabinet, advise the President what to do and have things running satisfactorily. You may therefore consider, ladies and gentlemen, when constitutional amendments are taking place, that this is a matter that should be corrected and that the President ought not to be subjected to the intolerable strain of having to make up his mind in an hour or two about something as important as who shall succeed a deceased prime minister. Although, as I attempted to point out on the morning after the death of the prime minister that what the President does, does not stop the Party from taking such steps as it thinks fit, it would surely be a better procedure for provision to exist for the appointment temporarily of someone while the Party decides who is to be its leader and the President then decides to appoint the leader of the Party, instead of the President appointing someone as prime minister and the Party then determining whether it, so to speak, ratifies the decision of the President, or disagrees with it and appoints someone else and then the complications start. (Ryan 1988c, 170)

The president went on to explain further the predicament in which he found himself that evening:

The view I took academically, and the view I still take, is that an appointment must be made forthwith. Otherwise, you endanger the country. You must do something about it, fill the gap at once. I used to say no President should go to bed at night without knowing whom he would appoint if he is awakened at the middle of the night and told that the Prime Minister is no longer with us. Most of the time I knew whom I would appoint. On the Friday prior to Dr. Williams' death, I thought I knew whom to appoint. It happened that I changed my mind that night.

The events following Dr. Williams' death caused me considerable problems. I had to choose from among the Members of the House of Representative [although] there were three deputy political leaders. But there is no necessity to appoint a deputy political leader. You could have appointed anybody else. But from a practical point of view, those were the three most likely candidates. And in that setting, one sat all three down and one went through a difficult process, a process in which the one who was appointed was first to eliminate himself, whether deliberate or not. . . . I don't know, but he eliminated himself, and the other two did not eliminate themselves. And the result was that there was a deadlock. I had to resort to the one who had eliminated himself to hold the fort.

Clarke made a number of additional statements in response to allegations by Sat Maharaj, secretary general of the Maha Sabha, on Monday, 20 November 1995. Maharaj claimed that the passing over of Mohammed was the "most blatant act of racial discrimination this land has ever seen" (Ghany 1996, 381). Clarke insisted that the race of the leaders was not a factor that moved him. As he explained,

There were very many circumstances that led to the appointment of George Chambers, but certainly I can assure you that race had no part in my decision whatsoever. As a matter of fact, to talk of two Indians is really quite ridiculous. Because I don't know who thinks that Errol Mahabir is an Indian. I certainly never did. And Kamal, I knew as a person very well; certainly I never thought of Kamal as an Indian or George Chambers as non-Indian or anything of the kind. I've already explained over and over the circumstances that led to that appointment. And as I said before, the question of race never entered my mind. (Ibid., 382)

Clarke also went on to repeat his "standoff" version:

> George Chambers declared himself not interested in the post and there was a bit of a standoff between Errol Mahabir and Kamal Mohammed. And in the circumstances, I said very well, I will appoint the man who says he is not interested and leave it to the party to decide who should be its leader. I made it perfectly clear at the time that there was going to be a party convention. That it would be a matter for the party to elect its own leader and that my choosing George Chambers at that particular time did not prevent the party from doing whatever it thought fit. It was up to the party to choose its leader. (Ibid.)

In response to the corruption issue, Clarke confirmed that there was a public perception that the two men were involved in certain irregularities. He stated that he never sought to find out the facts, but could certainly say in respect of Mahabir that he never gave the reports the slightest credence. Maharaj replied that Clarke's assertion that it was up to the party to decide was disingenuous, since he must have known that no party convention would undo what the president had done. Said Maharaj, "So if there was a standoff between Mahabir and Mohammed, then he should have referred this to the party hierarchy and let them make a decision and make a recommendation to him" (ibid.). Ironically, this is precisely what the president did that evening in one way or the other. Whatever the procedure, the outcome was likely to have been much the same.

Mohammed's version is to be found in his biography, *Kamal* (1996). We are told that he was summoned to the president's house by John Donaldson, who told him that the president wished to see him because there was an emergency. Despite his awareness that the prime minister was not well, Mohammed felt that something was wrong with the president, whom he always affectionately called "brother". On arrival, he saw Mervyn de Souza, party chairman Francis Prevatt, Attorney General Selwyn Richardson, Donaldson, Dr Courtenay Bartholomew and the president's son, Peter Clarke.

Mohammed acknowledges that the three deputy leaders met as advised by the party chairman, and that George Chambers expressed no interest in the job. He denies, however, that there was any "standoff" between himself and Mahabir. To quote Mohammed,

> I say categorically (i) there was no question of a standoff between Errol Mahabir and myself; (ii) I have to take the word of Sir Ellis that Chambers was not interested in the post; and, (iii) I am not aware of any irregularities in my case. In fact, I find it puzzling and very troubling that Sir Ellis should be careful enough to exonerate Errol Mahabir in this respect but be silent with respect to me.

The only matter being discussed at that time in relation to any irregularities was the McDonnell Douglas Affair involving the sale of three DC-9 aircraft to BWIA. . . . Other names were involved in that affair, not mine. Since that time, the Tesoro and Sam P. Wallace affairs have become major controversies and my name was never involved in those either. Nor was there ever any perception of corruption against me. (Ghany 1996, 384)

Mohammed raised interesting questions as to why a police escort was sent to accompany George Chambers, while Mohammed had to find his own way to the president's residence:

Such treatment is only reserved for the Prime Minister and the President. Was the decision made before Mahabir and I were called? The way in which our Constitution is drafted, no person, other than Sir Ellis Clarke, will ever be in a position to know.

In fact, I am now of the view that the decision to appoint Chambers was made long before I arrived at President's House. The consultation was purely decorative. Mervyn de Souza told me subsequently that views were expressed by one person in the caucus that if Errol or I were to be appointed as Prime Minister there would be racial riots in the country. I told him that was utter nonsense. Errol Mahabir was a very capable man, and in humility I had a record which would have assured Trinidad and Tobago of stable and settled leadership. (Ibid., 385)

Mohammed was disappointed that he was not given the nod. He regarded himself as being the best qualified by reason of his long and varied experience in office and his longstanding relationship with Williams. It would appear, however, that he was never fully trusted because of allegations that he leaked cabinet decisions to the opposition DLP. One DLP leader had in fact named him as the source of his information about what transpired in the cabinet. Mohammed was also accused of favouring his co-ethnics in the distribution of lands while he served as minister of agriculture, lands and fisheries. It is not true, however, that Chambers was escorted to the president's office by a police detail because he was regarded as the prime minister designate. He was escorted because he could not be reached by phone. The police were told to find him and bring him to the presidential office.

Errol Mahabir also offered his version as to what occurred on that fateful evening. He denied that race was a factor that informed Clarke's choice:

Knowing Sir Ellis Clarke the way I do, I do not think that race was a factor in his deliberations, but I have always wondered what were all the criteria which led to the President's decision. The President was not the only actor in the process. On the night when the decision was taken, our discussions at President's House were more with Mr. Francis Prevatt as chairman of the PNM. It was Mr. Prevatt who advised us that the President intended to select one of us for appointment since we were the three deputy political leaders of the PNM at the time. Mr. [George] Chambers indicated that he was not interested in the post and was prepared to work with either Mr. Mohammed or myself. Mr. Mohammed indicated that he was prepared to work with Mr. Chambers or me and I indicated that I was prepared to work with either Mr. Chambers or Mr. Mohammed. We pointed out that this was really a matter for the President, and we left it entirely to his discretion. There has been some uninformed speculation about how Mr. Mohammed and I responded. I do not know how that decision of ours was conveyed to the President, but we were advised shortly after by Mr. Prevatt that the President had decided to appoint Mr. Chambers as Prime Minister. (Ibid., 386)

Mahabir felt he had a good chance of being appointed, but admitted that given Mr Mohammed's track record and his ten years' ministerial seniority, the latter would have been chosen. Mahabir was clearly disappointed, but felt that the decision was informed by Prevatt's judgement as to which of the three deputy leaders would command the support of a majority in parliament: "It would seem Mr. Chambers was so identified: If I were to guess, I would say that this factor, more than any other, influenced the President's decision" (ibid.).

The versions recounted by Mahabir and Mohammed point to a number of conclusions. The first is that Prevatt was the king-maker while the president was the official messenger, although constitutionally, the decision was his alone to make. One recalls that the president and Prevatt had met socially earlier that day, and while the official story is that they did not discuss the succession, it is difficult to believe that the subject did not come up. Clearly Prevatt had a better sense of what the party and its supporters would accept and advised the president thusly. Prevatt knew that there was an imminent election and that the PNM would find it difficult to defeat the ONR with either Mohammed or Mahabir as its leader. The vote was therefore not so much for Chambers but against either Mohammed or Mahabir, both of whom were widely perceived to be "the twins of bobol", to use the Mighty Sparrow's depiction. Mohammed's view that there never was any perception of corruption against him was simply untrue. There was much gossip about what he did or did not do in the Ministry of Agriculture. Much was also whispered about Mahabir and the sculpted garden allegedly built by Japanese contractors in his home in San Fernando. One also recalls the widespread rumour, more than likely unfounded, that Williams had planned to expose some of his officials in a speech that he was said to be writing for a forthcoming political meeting.

And what of Chambers's "self-denying ordinance"? The story is told that when Chambers first saw the police car, he felt that he was in some sort of trouble because he had no idea why he was being summoned. Chambers may well have been in a state of shock on that particular evening, and his expression of lack of interest may have been genuine, but he was heard to have said at a meeting in Santo Domingo that in any race for the succession to Williams, he was "the darkest of the dark horses", and that he wanted only one term to clear up the mess. That statement explains a lot of what happened when he took office.

Chambers and the 1981 Election

The outcome at the PNM convention that met to address the issues of leadership and the electoral agenda was seen to depend on the extent to which the new prime minister, who had a reputation for hard work, succeeded in cleansing the Augean stables of the party. If he tried and succeeded in purging the party of those who were regarded by the electorate as liabilities, it was believed that many apostates and deviants would return to the PNM church. A move of this sort would have helped to build his image and convince the sceptics that the PNM was being returned to the tradition that Williams had defined for it in 1955–56. The question was whether Chambers felt sufficiently strong politically to undertake this or whether he and his supporters felt that such a strategy could be counter-productive, especially since it might also have involved the demystification and desanctification of Eric Williams. In the end, Chambers was forced to keep most of the old political team, giving rise to disappointment among those who saw him as a reformer.

This author was among those approached by Chambers to join his team. He was asked to run in Port of Spain South, Williams's constituency, but declined. In his discussions with the author, Chambers indicated that Port of Spain South was the Doctor's constituency and he therefore could not put any "jackass" there. He also indicated that he wanted to purge the party of the "old guard" – all except Kamaluddin Mohammed, whom he considered his point man to the Muslim community.

One of the problems facing the newly selected prime minister was that he and the party did not have much time to select and build a winning political combination. Elections had to be held before the end of the year, and the agenda was crowded. A wide assortment of groups was intensely dissatisfied with their lot and was demanding instant redress of grievances. These included doctors, nurses, bus workers, sugar workers, and workers in the fertilizer industry who were demanding that the foreign-owned company be nationalized before they returned to work. The demonstrations that these groups mounted in various parts of the country and around parliament itself in the weeks before the death of Williams, and which in one case forced him to sneak out the back door and into a hastily provided ambulance, were expected to continue once the period of mourning came to a close, as groups sought to press home the advantage that they felt they had in an election year. Chambers was also aware that it would take time for some of the massive public works projects that were underway, and that were expected to propitiate those who had been demanding regular supplies of water, proper roads, and an improvement in the performance of the other utilities, to come on stream.

Chambers was faced, too, with a more determined opposition than was the case in 1976. To confront the PNM, three of the established political parties – the ULF, the DAC and Tapia – formed themselves into a national alliance. The arrangement was that the parties of the alliance would retain their organizational identities but support one another electorally. There was also an agreement that each would not field candidates in areas that others in the alliance were deemed to have a good chance of winning. Thus the DAC alone would face the PNM in Tobago, the ULF in the twelve or fourteen seats which that party had either won in 1976 or in which it performed well, and Tapia in the remainder. The problem was that Tapia did not have any grassroots support and was unlikely to gain much before the election. The party had obtained a mere 3.8 per cent of the popular vote in 1976.

Tapia leader Lloyd Best, however, believed that the formation of the National Alliance would change the chemistry or algebra of the problem. The alliance would represent a qualitatively different formation that would be greater than the sum of its constituent parts. He felt that the planned "party of parties" represented the first real breakaway from the old one-man party, something that would embrace all the elements and the "tribes" in a fundamental way. Said Best, "This coalition party . . . has been organised to give permanent manifestation to the hope for change which the people all over the country see today. The Alliance can make manifest that demand for change and will form the next Government of Trinidad and Tobago." Following Williams's death, Best expressed the view that the prime minister had chosen to make his exit at precisely the moment when it was clear to all the citizens that the political methods of the 1950s and 1960s could no longer guide the country in the 1980s and 1990s: "Dr. Williams in the end has cleared the way so that Trinidad and Tobago can advance."

Polls conducted by the author's firm, St Augustine Research Associates, in March 1981, however, indicated that the alliance would not form the new government. While it was true that many – 48 per cent, according to the poll – were of the view that a union of opposition parties was a desirable goal, and a majority – 51 per cent – believed that such a union could defeat the PNM, for many this assumed that the ONR was part of that alliance. Moreover, it was evident that to many, the alliance was unacceptable. In fact, 36 per cent of those sampled said such an alliance was undesirable. Tapia's agreement to work with parties that its leaders had vehemently criticized in the past was seen as rank opportunism, even though Tapia had indicated as early as 1975 that it was interested in a united front alliance of all the opposition parties against the PNM. But many blacks did not support the notion of an alliance that had the ULF as one of its constituent units because of their assumption that that party would be the dominant group in any such alliance and would in the end assume the parliamentary leadership. For them the issue was not merely a choice of government and prime minister, but which race would control the citadels of power.

The ONR for its part sensed this and refused to participate in any coalition. Instead, it called upon all the other political parties "to clear the coast and let there be a straight fight between the enemy and the ONR". Ferdie Ferreira, a former PNM stalwart and confidant of Williams, who was the party's organization secretary, insisted that the ONR was the only party that had the "political artillery to destroy the enemy". Needless to say, the other opposition parties did not heed this request. The result was many three-cornered contests among the PNM, the ONR and the National Alliance.

Chambers fought the elections as if Williams's ghost were in his corner. He told the PNM convention that the ONR was the product of an anti-Williams conspiracy going back to 1973 when the leader of the "gang" first sought to capture the chairmanship of the party then held by Francis Prevatt. "Williams," he said, "put his foot down firmly on that." Hudson-Phillips and his supporters then sought to capture the leadership of the party. Williams again dealt firmly with that by returning to the political leadership, "robbing the challenger of the opportunity to deliver his 75 page acceptance speech". The next step was to form the ONR to try to capture the government. According to Chambers, Williams frustrated that from the grave, so to speak. As he told the party, "The ONR is not fighting Chambers. They are fighting Williams. Williams, however cannot die and must not die. And it appears that they too are not sure whether Williams is still alive. They can feel his 10 fingers clutching at their throats, bringing them down in the swirling waters of the Dragon's Mouth." Chambers portrayed the "Gang of Five" – Ivan Williams, Ferdie Ferreira, Carlton Gomes, Irwin Merrit and Karl Hudson-Phillips – as wicked ingrates, one of whom had even said of Williams that "he was a man the latchet of whose shoes I am unworthy to unloose. They too wicked. Not a damn seat for them" (*Trinidad Express,* 5 October 1981).

Election Results

To the surprise of many, the PNM won the 1981 election comfortably. The ONR failed to win a single seat. One aspect of the PNM's victory had to do with the deeply seated loyalty that the party retained among the Afro-creole group. For many, membership in the church that Williams built was a way of life. Members may have become disaffected with the pope or with priests, but did not therefore abandon the church. What seems to have happened is that the challenge posed by the ONR helped to refertilize loyalty to the PNM. Many who had come to dislike some of the political sacraments dispensed by the PNM church over the last twenty-five years, or who had become apostates, simply succumbed to the cry that the church was endangered by the machinations of "wicked heretics". Thus the crowds at party meetings and the wild enthusiasm of their responses to the new leader as well as to the parliamentarians whom they were earlier eager to sacrifice. That the party had a new leader who had promised to put right that which was wrong while maintaining intact that which was seen to be right also helped to persuade many that the change of regime, which many felt the country needed, *had already taken place* and within acceptable parameters. A "new" PNM was now in the saddle.

In the weeks following the election, much was said about what the outcome of the elections meant in terms of the nature of the society in Trinidad and what the mandate given to the PNM represented in terms of the potential for change and improvement in the years ahead. One persistent comment was that the voters had given the PNM a mandate to maintain the society as it was, a mandate that reflected a tolerance in the society for mediocrity, corruption, waste, inefficiency, laziness and bacchanal. Patrick Solomon, a former deputy prime minister, shared this pessimistic view: "The philosophy behind the voting presents . . . a depressing picture. . . . We have not only condoned corruption, mismanagement, inefficiency and squandermania; we have given a mandate to have them institutionalized. We might just as well have them enshrined in the Constitution along with the Fundamental Human Rights and Freedoms. It is indeed a dismal picture" (*Trinidad Express*, 15 November 1981).

The deputy political leader of the NJAC, Khafra Kambon, also expressed the view that despite what appeared to be a landslide victory for the PNM, there was "no joy and buoyancy in the society. Everywhere you look, there is a pervasive sense of hopelessness and gloom" (*Trinidad Express*, 18 November 1981). Similar melancholia was also forthcoming from Tapia political guru Lloyd Best. As he bemoaned, "The country has returned into power the party which had governed us to the brink of the revolutionary upheaval in 1970, which had been squandering a gigantic fortune of petro-dollars since the end of 1973, and which by its errors of omission and commission, had converted our country into a virtual slum, into a den of corruption, indiscipline and immorality, into a desert of desperation and despair."

ONR leader Karl Hudson-Phillips also did not accept the results as reflecting the true mood of the people. As far as he was concerned, the ONR like "the majority of the population feels robbed". Hudson-Phillips charged that "the Government is not a properly and fairly elected government and, therefore, does not represent the will of the majority. It is a most dangerous situation for democracy in Trinidad and Tobago. The PNM has brought no change, no hope, no vision to Trinidad and Tobago. The same inefficiencies and corruption will now continue unabated. The PNM will crash under the weight of its own inefficiencies, corruption and dishonesty" (ibid.).

In the opinion of the ONR leader, the PNM used mental violence, fraud and bribery to secure its mandate. The people did not willingly provide it. It can hardly be argued, however, that the vote for the PNM was a vote for political indecency. The claim is highly subjective. If one were to ask PNM voters, the vast majority would have denied that their vote could be interpreted in the way the critics did. There were indeed some persons who had a vested interest in perpetuating some of the negative aspects of PNM rule, but the majority who voted PNM did so because they liked the broad outlines of the system or "way of life" that the PNM had helped to shape and contour over the years, though they nevertheless wished to see improvements within the context of the system. Chambers had promised that these improvements would be forthcoming.

The evidence suggests that a majority of PNM members and supporters did not "like it so", as the opposition suggested, at least not in all its detail. Neither did they endorse everything that had been done by Williams and their party, since it was inconsistent for them to have a positive view towards their party while at the same time disapproving of its negative characteristics and deficiencies. Like the rest of the general citizenry, they wanted a more reliable supply of water and electricity, a better communication system (buses, phones and so on) better roads, a better school system, a better work environment, better entertainment facilities, better paying and more attractive jobs and a host of other facilities. The majority also appreciated that to achieve this output, they themselves had to do better. In a survey carried out by the author in March 1980, close to half the people interviewed (48 per cent) were of the view that it was the people and not the government that was responsible for the state of the country. Thirty-nine per cent disagreed and 13 per cent were unable to decide. The results suggest that many people were aware that they had to share the blame for the problems their society faced, and that Williams and the PNM were not solely responsible.

44　**Apostles, Apostates and Ecumenists**

Nearly all men can stand adversity, but if you want to test a man's character, give him power.

– Abraham Lincoln

Eric Williams is undoubtedly the most controversial political leader that the anglophone Caribbean has produced. He was a leader whom Trinidadians felt, and continue to feel, passionately about. Many venerate, imagine and mythologize him as a genuine charismatic hero; many hate or view him as a failed and flawed anti-hero and a wounded personality. Many feared him; most respect him; few were indifferent to him. Few called him "Bill" to his face. To many, he was the "chief", the "boss", the "old man", "deafy" or "Charlie".

Those who hero-worship Williams, those who vilify him, as well as the attendant ecumenical chorus, all agree that Williams was a scholar and author of international reputation. Even those who have been critical of some of his later scholarly products and even his early classic, *Capitalism and Slavery*, agree that his scholarly output entitles him to a position of prominence in the pan-Caribbean pantheon, alongside icons such as José Martí and Fidel Castro of Cuba, Luis Muñoz Marin of Puerto Rico, Juan Bosch and Joaquin Balaguer of the Dominican Republic, Aimé Césaire of Martinique, V.S. Naipaul, C.L.R. James and George Padmore of Trinidad and Tobago, Derek Walcott and Arthur Lewis of St Lucia, and others.

Williams was a gifted and exemplary teacher and public educator, and his unique creation, the "University of Woodford Square" and its "colleges", has no parallel elsewhere in the Caribbean. What was particularly unique about Williams was the manner in which he combined the roles of scholar, teacher and political leader. He was not merely a diligent researcher and collector of dry historical trivia. He had an encyclopedic mind and a magnificent capacity to integrate and synthesize facts into a compelling narrative that forced readers and audiences to listen and take notice. Few could remain neutral or passive. Williams polarized opinion and in many cases cut straight down the middle.

He was also a master of the art of public speaking. While he lacked the rhetorical skill and soaring oratorical cadences of a Michael Manley or a Martin Luther King, his dry, monotonous delivery kept listeners spellbound. We recall George Lamming's testimony that Williams had the ability to make history whisper and come alive. Others who were part of the generation that came to political maturity in the 1950s and early 1960s share Lamming's assessment. As Muriel Donawa (1991), one of Williams's party and cabinet colleagues, recalled, "He was not graceful, not elegant, not always fluent, yet he came with a power of thought and of expression which moved us from our seats. He spoke with remarkable ability and characteristic earnestness."

Those who got to know Williams up close agree that he was a great conversationalist and raconteur, one who had wit and a great sense of humour whenever he was minded to show that side of his personality. He also had a capacity to use the vernacular, which he employed with telling effect whenever he wished to connect with the man in the street. He was a pugnacious debater who could wipe the floor with his opponents. He did not suffer fools gladly, and even those who were not fools thought twice before crossing swords with him. The debate with Catholic prelate Dom Basil Matthews in 1954 about Aristotle's views on slavery and education established his reputation as a skilled debater, a reputation that was enhanced as he jousted over the years with opposition parliamentarians and radical intellectuals.

Opinions vary, however, as to whether Williams was a "snake charmer" who was easy to relate to, or an abusive, humourless, lonely, austere, socially uncomfortable and bitter man who was all books, papers and historical documents. There are two sharply differing points of view on this subject. One, voiced by a select group of close associates, holds that beneath the frosty bespectacled exterior, Williams was a warm, generous and sympathetic human being, and a genuine "Trini" who enjoyed a good lime, Old Oak rum or "cacapool" (cheap rum), Famous Recipe chicken and chips, Chinese fast food, Anchor cigarettes, as well as cricket, steelband (Invaders was his band), carnival, a good card game, old talk, and female company and flesh (especially Chinese, whose sexual competences he frequently extolled). Muriel Donawa tells us that "what distinguished him most was his cheerfulness, the ease with which he mixed with all, and his utter sincerity. His personal charm was legendary, and the princely grace of being able to make people of humble positions – simple folk – feel at ease and comfortable in his presence" (ibid.). Ferdie Ferreira, another close party associate, remembers him as a "private person who enjoyed all the extra-curricula activities not associated with academic work and or prime ministerial duties, and to my knowledge, he certainly enjoyed them. Please don't ask me what these were." Ferreira (1991) also considered him to be a "people's man":

> In politics, people are the most important investment. Having recognized this, he kept faith with them, even his opponents for whom he had time. His charm, intellect, privacy, and capacity to listen, understand and to analyse the social and economic problems of the society endeared even his enemies to him. Once they came into contact with him, it became extremely difficult not to admire, respect, resist or extricate themselves. Williams respected the masses and kept faith with the Party and the people.

Ferreira also observed that Williams knew how a prime minister was expected to behave and function. "He was almost faultless in this respect. Whenever he was around or expected to arrive, you knew and felt the presence of the general. . . . The atmosphere was always electrifying when he was around."

For Ferreira, there were, however, two leaders, Eric the First and Eric the Second. Eric the First was the beloved master, someone whom we followed "with diligence, respect, and love bordering on devotion. There was no doubt in our minds that the promised land was now within our reach and that our own Caribbean Moses was taking us there." Ferreira (1991) recounts the manner in which the parliamentary opposition, the media and the business elite "bashed" the Afro-based PNM mercilessly, and the manner in which Williams dealt with them:

> The first five years gave Williams his sternest political test which he successfully handled [but] for which he was not prepared. In the face of battle, Williams displayed a courage and capacity during this period that few politicians anywhere in the world would have survived. Having studied his opponents carefully, he recognized their weaknesses and limitations. He always gave them the maximum amount of rope to hang themselves. His patience and tolerance with his opponents, his capacity for entertaining and rewarding them privately and without public ridicule, endeared most of his traditional political enemies to him, including trade union leaders and big business representatives; his tremendous capacity for timing, people and events, confusing and dividing them without their having the slightest intuition were some of his greatest hallmarks.

Errol Mahabir, one of his trusted ministers, agrees with Ferreira and others that Williams was not "the hard task master", or the inscrutable "man of iron who had no feelings" as some make him out to be. He was an ordinary human being with all the foibles, weaknesses, and capacity for tenderness that characterize that species.[1] Mahabir claims that Williams had great concern for the small man, and that "it was very difficult to get any measure through the cabinet unless Dr.

Williams was convinced that it was not going to have too adverse an effect on the small man. [He was] always concerned" (1999, 160). Mahabir averred that Williams understood that the PNM had its basis among the masses, and likewise understood the need to retain contact with the masses and not lose sight of the principles upon which the PNM was founded.

Mahabir also disagrees with the view that Williams was a one-man band in cabinet or the general council, and that he did not brook the opinions of his colleagues: "Let me make it clear as one who worked with Dr. Williams from 1956 to his death in 1981: Dr. Williams was 'primus inter pares.' He was the intellectual superior of most of those people who worked under him, but he listened attentively to what they had to say. Our Cabinet meetings were not meetings of a rubber stamp nature" (ibid., 160). He agreed, however, that Williams knew when to speak and when to use the tactic of silence or the limp handshake: "All my former Cabinet colleagues who are here will agree that Dr. Williams frowned very badly on people speaking out of turn. And many were the persons who found themselves in the dog house because he felt they stepped out of line. Dr. Williams was a master of timing, and always told us in our meetings, 'gentlemen, do not shoot until you see the whites of their eyes' " (ibid., 161–62). Mahabir, incidentally, was among those who were quarantined in Williams's dog house and made to "cry".

Donawa agrees with Mahabir that Williams was always open to persuasion: "The magnificence of his mind never for one moment blinded him to the merits of the opposing point." He had, she argues, "a readiness to listen to all sides of an issue". He was "one of a team while leading it. This is what made him the truly great leader that he was." Donawa also marvelled at Williams's capacity for prudence and timing: "He planned judiciously. Perhaps the strongest feature in him was prudence, never acting until every consideration was maturely weighed, refraining if he saw doubt, but once decided, going through with his purpose whatever obstacles there might be."

Doddridge Alleyne, former head of the public service and former permanent secretary to Williams, endorsed the general view that the prime minister was a "master of timing". As he observed, "He displayed in his tactics and his strategy, great timing, and he knew when to be silent. . . . He had some gestures whenever he heard something that really pleased him. He slapped his thigh, and he would give what one friend whom he later destroyed called the 'long dab', which was really a Freudian thrust. . . . He made his points like that, and it was always telling" (1999, 141).

Another intimate and revealing portrait of Williams was drawn by Dr Halsey McShine, who knew Williams at Queen's Royal College (Williams coached McShine in Spanish when the latter was seeking to win the Island Scholarship) and remembered him as an extremely bright, gifted and ambitious man. In his view, his main weakness was that suffered by most men, "women". His tastes generally were said to be simple. Whenever they ate together, as they often did, Williams microwaved the food that his maid had left in the refrigerator for him. McShine sat on a stool and ate, while Williams ate his meal standing, much to McShine's embarrassment.

His close friends were said to be few. Among them were members of his former wife's family, the Moyous, Kendall Lee, Jackie Chan and a few other Chinese persons with whom he played mahjong, penny poker and other similar games. He also fraternized with a group called the "Liqueur Club", individuals who came to his home for a drink after dinner, which each hosted in turn. Among the members of his group were Alfredo Bermudez, Victor Williams, A.P. Thompson, Wallace Campbell, Carl Tull, Ulric Lee, McShine himself, and a few others. Said McShine, "Eric in this company was relaxed. He did not think of himself as prime minister."

There is a different picture that emerges of Williams and how he managed the men in his cabinet and the public service, and how he related to people generally. In this perspective, Williams was a mean, morose and rude man who struck fear into the minds of his ministers, public service mandarins and party and other associates.[2] This view is perhaps best illustrated by Gerard Montano, whose recollection was given to the author in an extended interview taped in 1990. This section of the interview is recounted in full:

> In 1959 and 1960, Williams was involved with the Chaguaramas issue. At the time, he was ruling his cabinet with a very rough hand and he would hit out at cabinet ministers sharply. I saw him make Kamal cry, and I mean cry. He licked up Winston Mahabir. He licked up Solomon and so forth, and on every occasion I would intervene and say, ". . . but that is not the way to behave." He would stop, scowl at me, but not hit me. But I knew that sooner or later he would turn his attention to me and he would let me have it. Nobody dared reply to him. I was the only one.
>
> So I knew that sooner or later this rebel would have to taste his vengeance, and true enough, he did. One day he lashed out at me. But I was prepared for him. This was before 1958. It must have been in early 1957. I had prepared for him and I knew what he was doing. The party was riding very high. The party had a disciplinary committee, and if you played the fool, you got before the disciplinary committee and you'd be put out. So the disciplinary committee was to keep everybody in order. But not me. But, I knew that if he did that, he could throw me out of the party, though not out of the parliament.
>
> However, three of the fellows began to rally behind me. One was [Donald] Granado, one was Kamal, and the other was Winston, and we were four in there. So, when

Williams turned on me, I bit my tongue like this [demonstrating], but I didn't reply. Everybody could see that I was mad! And I have one hell of a temper! So, after the meeting was over, I said to the fellows, "Boys listen! I'm not taking this if you fellows are. This man must be brought to heel, otherwise we have made a dictator here, and I'm not going to be party of that. This is a lot of nonsense. I've jumped to the defence of every one of you in turn; now I say we call him to order. Let's have a meeting with him." We meet in executive council on Thursday. This is Monday night, I said, "Learie [Constantine], you're the oldest among us and I will appoint you to go to him. . . . If you're afraid to do it, I'd do it myself: but I appoint you to go to him and tell him that unless he sits down and is prepared to meet us and discuss this issue, none of us will go before the executive council on Thursday. You can explain that to the governor how you like."

Learie went and did as he was told. I didn't know at the time how close O'Halloran was with Williams, but I knew that Williams would have got a word for word report, and could assess my anger and my determination, so I said to Learie, "I know that he is not going to want to meet us. You tell him that Gerard said he knows you are not going to want to meet us. But it's all right. You'll face the governor alone and tell him why we're not there." He would have been very embarrassed, so Williams said, "Allright", he'd meet us.

When we met him, he said, "Well, what is it gentlemen?" And each member in his turn said: "Well, Bill [rather timidly], we don't like how you treating us." They were all very mild in the way in which they tried to call him to order. He knew exactly what was happening: he knew I was coming last. So when they were finished, I said, "Bill, let me tell you something, these fellows are all afraid of you. I'm not. And you have been brutalizing every member of this cabinet team here. But I am not putting up with this [expletive deleted]. Either you respect us, or to hell with you. We didn't leave our businesses, our private lives and so to come and follow you here for you to [expletive deleted] all over us. I don't take that [expletive deleted] from you or from anybody. I don't give that [expletive deleted] to anybody else either. Either you respect us and treat us as men or . . . we're finished."

Bill, who was very clever and who realized that he had a real revolt on his hands, smiled, and says, "There is no cabinet in the world that operates without friction and no Cabinet in the world which doesn't fight back. So what's the issue?" I said to him, "As long as you understand that if you abuse me, I'm going to abuse you right back! And let me make it clear to you . . . there is no member of this Board here, or put them altogether, who has the vocabulary for profanity that I could use on you. As long as you understand that, we will respect each other. I never use that profanity until and unless you provoke it." He said, "I have never said that you all cannot disagree." [Laughter]

Now, I gave you that as background because, after that, I was number eight man on the team. I was kept at arm's length. So when the subject of Chaguaramas was being discussed, he would discuss it with his close colleagues and certainly I wasn't close. Winston wasn't close because he supported me. Kamal wasn't close because he supported me, and Granado wasn't close because he supported me. So we were like a team outside. One morning, we were having our executive council meeting in the Red House, and Williams, then looking directly at the four of us, said, "Governor, your Excellency, there are reports emanating from this cabinet or this executive council which are being leaked to the Americans."

When he finished, . . . silence. I said to him, "You finished?" You know me! I'm blunt and ordinary. I said, "You finished?" He said, "Yes." I said, "Well, look, Your Excellency, let me make one thing clear, I'm replying because the prime minister or chief minister is looking at me, together with some of us here. But it is almost as if we're being accused of leaking secrets from the executive council dealing with this Chaguaramas issue. Let me make it clear! I, and some others are not privy at all to what is going on, so we have no secrets. If there is any leak, it must come from those who are privy to the secrets, must come from those who are close to the chief minister, not me. And I can speak for some of my colleagues." The governor was thoroughly embarrassed. Williams was even more so, because he didn't expect this hostile response. Finished with that.

Winston Mahabir, one of the three Island Scholars in Williams's first cabinet, had recollections not fundamentally different from Montano's, though there was some disagreement on details. Mahabir's recollection is that the crisis about which Montano spoke broke over the issue of a radiation scare that Williams claimed had occurred at a tracking station at Chaguaramas. Mahabir was sceptical, but was upset that neither he, Montano, nor Mohammed were taken into confidence on the matter. What was more, O'Halloran and Solomon were sent to England on a secret mission relating to the radiation scare. The "terrible three" members of parliament resolved to confront Williams and give him an ultimatum:

> We were resolved that our position must be clarified before Cabinet Government was instituted. We were not going to continue to share public blame and private guilt over decisions and actions which had eluded our deliberations. We demanded to see Williams. I told Montano and Mohammed beforehand that Williams would seek to divide us as soon as he got an opportunity during our interview. Montano fired the opening salvo – calmly and precisely. What are the facts about radiation? Why have we not been told? Why have Solomon and O'Halloran gone to London? Why were we not told? To our great astonishment, Williams blurted out that he had good reasons not to trust us in certain matters concerning the Americans. Many things that were discussed at ministerial level had found their way back to the American Consul-General. This I could not take! I exploded in inimitable fashion. This was precisely what Williams had hoped for! He proceeded forthwith to condemn me for my temper and to praise Montano for his restraint.
>
> Temper? Heavens above! In retrospect I think I behaved beautifully. Were I given to physical violence, I would have been violent that day. To be told after nearly two years of hard work in the abnormal milieu I have described, that we were touting government secrets to the Americans was tough to take. I let loose my epithets and

subsided. The others carried on in calmer, if equally offended fashion. It was the first and last time that I told Williams what he could do with my ministry. The effect of this combined blasting of Williams was astonishing. Everything was sweetness for months thereafter. (1978, 84–85).

Williams made up with Mahabir by sending him on a secret mission to feel out Ian MacLeod, the colonial secretary, on the issue of independence.

Mahabir described Williams as his "major intellectual godfather", one whom he loved and hated with equal passion. He also noted that Williams was the subject of widespread deification as well as vilification. "Like Christ, he has endured self-immolation and a second coming. He is, however, different from Christ who wrote nothing. It was Christ's apostles who immortalized him. Williams' apostles have a duty to 'mortalize' him, to write about the man they knew" (ibid., 2).

Talking about dynamics in the first cabinet, Mahabir noted that body language was on occasion as important as verbal communication:

> Communication in Cabinet was basically by documents followed by discussions, interspersed with the passage of little notes, sometimes openly, often under the table. But the most interesting modes of communication were non-verbal: Winks, raised eyebrows, grimaces, frowns, hot flushes, head-shaking, head-scratching, head-nodding, finger-tapping, thigh-slapping, (a habit of Williams to give muscle to his point), titters, giggles, guffaws, belly-laughs, contemptuous heh-heh-hehs and haw-haw-haws, twitching, chair-twisting, paper-twirling, under-the-table leg-kicking, going to the washroom, rustling documents, wrestling with pencils, every type of unproductive cough, throat-clearing, nose-blowing, nose-picking, loosening of neck-ties, rolling up of shirt sleeves, and the most powerful signal of all – Williams' adjustment of his hearing-aid, which tripled as a weathervane and a weapon, commanding our united respect. (Ibid., 45)

A sort of hierarchy and role specialization developed in Williams's first cabinet. Learie Constantine was the peacemaker. "His role in Cabinet was characterized by affability, unflappability and a general inability to score. He was the peacemaker, the father-figure, the symbol of loyalty and the good humoured butt of many jokes" (1978, 47). Mahabir considered O'Halloran the *de facto* number two and not Montano:[3]

> From the orbital stand-point, John O'Halloran was closest to Williams. He has a special and highly underrated place in the annals of PNM and its first Cabinet. He probably organized more financial support for the PNM in his time than any other individual. Yet he was more than a collector of customs. In Cabinet, he was the bridge between all of us and Williams whenever the melancholy fit appeared to fall like a weeping cloud upon the latter's head. This important aspect of O'Halloran's role has never been duly recognized. Emotionally he was closer to Williams than any of us. If he appeared swell-

headed, it was because of a brain bursting with secrets. Of course, occupying as he did, such a prominent position in orbit around Williams, he became the object of suspicion. (Ibid., 48)

Montano was independently wealthy, and could speak to Williams without fear of economic strangulation. Mahabir too was a professional, and often stood up to Williams. "Had I been Williams," he said, "I might have resented it." Mahabir was snide in his observations about the other "M", Kamaluddin Mohammed, who was hard to pin down. "Survival politics was his specialty. In Cabinet, he combined passion with patience, defiance with deference, self-preservation with party loyalty" (ibid., 49).

For all his acerbic and humourous criticism of Williams, Mahabir does not go as far as some have in describing him as a *caudillo* or a "doctator" in the vein of Papa Doc of Haiti. However, Williams was not merely *primus inter pares,* but *primus.* Said Mahabir, "He aggrandized the position of premier in a physical, financial and political sense. In building up his office, he used a variety of techniques including the use of smokescreens to conceal his moves. He also had a habit of pretending not to listen to sound propositions advanced by ministers, only to have them resurface later with him as their advertised progenitor. When he wanted to do something, there was no one to stop him." As others have noted, he also used "meet the people", "meet the party", "meet the children" or "meet the manufacturers" tours to enhance his position of *primus.* Important decisions were made on the spot without reference to cabinet.[4] One tactic at which he was a consummate artist was to shift consultation from cabinet to party and vice versa as the situation demanded (ibid., 53). Mahabir agreed, however, that cabinet was not a one-man band. "We had voices in the Cabinet, some more persuasive than others. Some spoke more freely than others. Some were well prepared for Cabinet meetings and Williams as a good teacher, quickly spotted who had or had not done their homework" (ibid., 53).

Mahabir had other things to say about Williams that are worth recalling. He was concerned about and complained to Williams about the prime minister's excessive emphasis on slavery and his parsimonious references to the indentureship phenomenon. Williams promised Mahabir that he would try to redress this imbalance by writing something on the phenomenon of indenture, but invited Mahabir to do so as well. In terms of Williams's "paranoia", Mahabir noted the prime minister's belief that he and his government were threatened by a powerful "Chinese coalition", and that "the head of the whole damned coalition was Solomon Hochoy, the biggest brain of all" (ibid., 74).

Another of Williams's close associates, Patrick Solomon, who was deputy leader of the party, had little positive to say about him as a man and as a power wielder. According to Solomon, Williams came to the political scene because he was not able to fulfil himself elsewhere. The Anglo-American Caribbean Commission refused to appoint him secretary general and declined to even renew or extend his contract. As a result, Williams, "in a cold fury of righteous indignation, took his case and his cause to the people of Trinidad and Tobago and decided to let down his bucket right here at home" (1981, 136).

According to Solomon, no one was left untroubled if he could serve Williams's purpose: "Person after person was used and discarded over the years, even destroyed if he could not be got rid of in any other way, in Williams' triumphant march to the top of the political ladder." He argued that Williams could not imagine anyone performing a disinterested act of kindness; there must be an ulterior motive:

> As Williams climbed up the ladder of success, he grew increasingly suspicious of anyone and everyone of any stature or ability in his vicinity, being convinced that they merely sought an opportunity to either destroy or replace him. Thus, his closest confidants for most of the time were those of little account who, he felt, were sufficiently rewarded by being noticed and merely being in the company of the great man. Such a man would seek – and demand if he could – a full measure of loyalty and support when in difficulties, but could not be counted on to risk anything for a friend or colleague in similar circumstances. (Ibid., 151)

Solomon wrote poignantly about his experiences as a member of the first two Williams cabinets. His recollection was that a measure of unity prevailed in the first few months following the 1956 elections, much to the chagrin of the opposition.[5] Unity and cabinet solidarity were short lived, however, as pressures on the government mounted "I learned, slowly and very painfully, that collective responsibility meant one thing to me and something else to nearly everyone else; that Cabinet loyalty was something I could always count on in fair weather, but likely to wear thin or even vanish when dark clouds loomed on the horizon; that jealousy, envy and Machiavellian intrigue were not the monopoly of the Opposition Front Bench; that friends had sometimes to be feared even more than enemies. In all this, the Chief Minister played of necessity a dominant role" (ibid., 149). In Solomon's view, Williams was no saint. He was no better or worse than other great men of this or any other age: "He is more ruthless perhaps than de Gaulle whom he admired, or Churchill, whom he affected to despise. His abiding fault is his total lack of comprehension of the human animal. To him, all human beings are the same; they either want to buy or have something to sell; and he has a single formula for dealing with them all – if the price is right, he will do business" (ibid., 151).

Solomon had many clashes with Williams. In these encounters, he felt vulnerable because he had virtually given up his medical practice for the second time and had debts relating to house purchase. By 1961, he was weary of fighting Williams's battles, and was finding it difficult to work with him on a sustained basis. Periods of harmony would be followed by periods when relationships were strained. As he explained, "Eric Williams was not the easiest of men to work with, and for all his academic brilliance – or perhaps because of it – he was easy prey to any schemer who chose to fill his ears with poison; and because, as his deputy, I was closest to him, I became the No. 1 target, a situation which by its very monotony was becoming boring" (ibid., 234).

Solomon claims that Williams found his stubbornness and independent spirit too much of a challenge. "I refused to be brow-beaten as so many others were prepared to be, and I tolerated neither malicious sarcasm nor ill-mannered hectoring. On such occasions, I committed the unforgivable sin of answering back – so I had to go sooner or later" (ibid., 234). One incident that led to a clash with Williams involved Solomon's handling of a police matter involving the son of someone whom he eventually married. The man involved was allegedly brutalized by the police, who broke three of his ribs. Solomon, the minister of home affairs, had the man removed from police custody. In this case Solomon clearly abused his office in the interest of someone with whom he had a personal relationship. Williams seized upon the incident to demand Solomon's resignation. In this he was supported by members of the prime minister's inner circle, in particular W.J. Alexander, John O'Halloran, and the attorney general, George Richards. Only Kamaluddin Mohammed and A.N.R. Robinson called to express concern and sympathy. As Solomon recalled, "That was perhaps the most shocking aspect of the whole situation, the grip of fear in which Williams held all those who came close to him. I alone refused to be terrified; therefore I had to go" (ibid., 237).

Solomon's resignation did not sit well with his parliamentary constituency, and other constituencies in the party brought pressure to bear on the prime minister to rescind Solomon's resignation. The matter surfaced at a party convention that was held on the weekend of his resignation, and Williams was given a rough time. Williams and Solomon undertook protracted negotiations to determine whether and under what conditions Solomon would return to the cabinet. Solomon insisted, as part of any reconciliation exercise, on being retained as deputy leader of the party. He would not accept a demotion. He also wanted a guarantee that Williams would not throw him out of the cabinet in future when it suited him. Williams assured him that he would not do so, that he "always wanted [him] in the Cabinet", and that "it was not my decision alone to throw you out". Solomon was not persuaded.

Williams recalled Solomon to the cabinet as minister of external affairs, but chose a curious way to do it. As Solomon wrote,

> Williams was not happy to make the announcement. Smarting under the conviction

that his arm had been twisted by the party and, in particular by the Port of Spain West constituency, and resenting this further affront to his pride and his omnipotence, he fell back, as is usual with him in such cases, on rude blustering and arrogance. He announced to the crowd that he had decided that Solomon was to be brought back into the Cabinet. He had the power under the constitution; Solomon was going to be Minister of External Affairs and anyone who did not like it could "get to hell out". (Ibid., 242)

This particular incident was immortalized by the Mighty Sparrow's calypso, "Get to Hell Outa Here!"[6] The popular view is that Williams was defying public opinion. Instead, he was concealing that he was being forced to rehabilitate his deputy. Solomon was left to vegetate in external affairs.

Williams asked Solomon to give up his Port of Spain West seat and not contest the 1966 election. Solomon himself wanted out, but wished to be assured of a pension and a posting abroad. Members of parliament were not then entitled to a pension and Solomon felt that he could not readily go back to his practice after serving ten long years in parliament as a key minister. He would fight the elections whether Williams wanted him to or not: "It takes almost heroic virtue to carry the weight of Eric Williams for ten long years. . . . Working with Williams was not my idea of heaven, but if he wanted a fight, before or after the [1966] election, he would find me more than willing" (ibid., 245).

Williams, working through the governor general, Sir Solomon Hochoy, accepted Solomon's terms. Solomon then insisted that he and Williams should meet formally to seal the agreement:

My final condition was that the Prime Minister should make a direct approach to me before we could consider the matter finalized. For this I would accept no intermediary. We had been colleagues for 10 years. If we now had to part, it would not be by some back-door arrangement. Besides, there would have to be a firm date fixed for the change over and for the announcements. I had no intention of being left dangling in the air as Williams delights in doing with all those whose lives he may control at one time or another. (Ibid., 246)

Solomon's story is interesting if only because he was one of several who had sacrificed his profession at the insistence of Williams in 1955. He was a hard worker and fought many gruelling battles on behalf of the PNM – more particularly the battles with the Colonial Office on constitution reform, with the Americans on Chaguaramas, with the DLP on constituency delimitation and the Representation of the People Bill and so on. Solomon left the PNM a bitter man. He was equally bitter about Williams. As he averred, "Many who have coveted the No. 2 post in the Trinidad and Tobago hierarchy have yet to learn the dangers of proximity. Those who sup with the devil should use a long spoon" (ibid., 216).

This was a lesson that A.N.R. Robinson learned at great cost. Solomon was deputy leader of the party, but Robinson was Williams's heir apparent. Montano's account of his conversations with Robinson is as follows:

> Now Robinson is a funny fellow. He likes to be thought of as strong, but has to be pushed into the position of being strong . . . . By 1966, Williams was not feeling so close to [Robinson] and when he removed him from the Ministry of Finance, the hostility became open. They would "fall out" and not talk, and I would go to Ray and I'd say, "Ray, what you are doing is wrong. Bill is your leader, and you hope to be leader one day." He said, "You see me, I don't want that at all! Not even if you offered it to me on a platter. I don't want it at all." "But you want it, you deserve it. You are the logical person to inherit leadership. Williams can't carry on too much longer. He will give up, and when he does, you will inherit it. But if you keep being as hostile as you are to him, and fighting him on this, that, and the other, there is no way you will inherit power from him. And again, I'll tell you, if you really want to lead, you must first learn to follow and recognize that if he has the majority, you must fall in line. If you cannot, no problem. You leave the government, you leave the party, you form your own, you go with a group if you like, but this can't work. Don't mix up my hostility or my opposition with yours. You will always find that mine is not tinctured with real hostility. Mine is tinctured with, 'do the right thing', Goddam it! Yours I'm afraid, is a little deeper than that." And he would say to me, "Gerard, coming from you, I understand, I accept. I accept what you say." And I made peace between himself and Williams on three separate occasions, and then on the last occasion, I told Williams, "Look, let's call a halt to this nonsense. Let us be friendly with the man and so forth." And Williams would say to me, "Well, if he is prepared to, I'm prepared to." And Robinson would say the same, and I'd say, "Look, I've spoken to both of you now. Let's show a nice attitude and it would work" . . . . Hostility in cabinet by Robinson led to a closer embrace by him of the element in the university who were in support of activity aimed at the eventual overthrow of Williams, though not yet a violent overthrow. (Interview with author, April 1990)

Robinson insisted that he did not wish to be regarded as Williams's protégé and to be appointed deputy political leader by him, and that he suggested that the post should be offered to either Montano or O'Halloran, both of whom declined. The party constitution was subsequently changed to make the post one that was to be elected by the legislative group. Robinson was elected, receiving more votes than Montano and O'Halloran combined.[7] Williams was not at all happy about this development, but the powerful intervention of Ada Date Camps had served to engender support for Robinson, who reportedly was not even present when the election took place. Robinson eventually resigned from the PNM in 1970 (Williams would claim, incorrectly, that he was expelled) and formed a party of his own, as Montano suggested he should do. One of his complaints was that the party had ceased to function meaningfully, both in private and in public:

I could not be frank at a meeting of the Central Executive or the General Council or the Annual Convention of the PNM. They have all been asphyxiated. I certainly cannot do so at the cocktail parties to which I am not invited even if I wished to go, and which have become the substitute for the constitution of the PNM. For almost four years since the General Election of 1966, the elected government and the ruling party held no public meetings except in the local government elections of 1968 when they had to be suspended as they were a disaster. There were no press conferences by the head of government and hardly any radio broadcasts or television appearances. Even these, however, would be inadequate for a population that aspires to the closest possibly identity between the voter and the elected government. (*Trinidad Express*, 31 August 1970)

Following Williams's death, Robinson was invited by a number of churchmen to give an evaluation of the prime minister. He was not keen to do it, but managed to say the following:

The Trinidad and Tobago and Caribbean situation demanded the highest and most exacting levels of energy, statesmanship, knowledge and experience. Williams recognized that very keenly. It was his personality mainly that brought together on the local scene outstanding patriots such as Pat Solomon and Learie Constantine, economic experts such as Teodoro Moscoso and Arthur Lewis, intellects such as CLR James, George Lamming and Professor Gordon Lewis. The full story has not yet been told, perhaps never will be. But I am convinced that these exacting years consumed more than their fair share of the energies, spiritual resources and intellect of the man.

Whatever the final verdict may be, Eric Eustace Williams has had a unique life, as scholar, statesman and author, and leader of our country to nationhood and independence. He was also a gifted teacher and his life itself will both inspire and teach. Only the future will tell the extent of our own capacity to learn from the life of this remarkable man. (1986, 244–45)

Three other ministers authored, or had authored, accounts of their stewardship in the PNM government: Donald Granado, who was "promoted out" of the cabinet in 1966 to a diplomatic post, Kamaluddin Mohammed, and Overand Padmore. Mohammed told a friend, member of parliament Lionel Seukeran, "Bhai, I keep as far away from Williams as I can. When he calls me, I come. I listen to what he says, do what he says and leave, without talking of trivial things or gossiping about anyone else. He does the talking, I listen and act." Seukeran opined that that servile stance perhaps explains Mohammed's having remained the longest serving PNM minister under Williams (Seukeran 2006, 210). Mohammed's autobiography does not say much about his relationship with Williams while in office. He does tell us, however, that he thinks his survival had to do with his training as a Muslim. "The religion teaches you to be obedient and be respectful, and this I was, even in moments of great disappointment" (as cited in Boodhoo 1986a, 16).

Granado's account is critical of Williams, recalling with understated bitterness that on Independence Day, only Williams and Solomon were allowed to be at the centre of the official activities in Woodford Square. All other ministers had to view the proceedings from the balcony of the Red House. Granado and other ministers, including Montano, objected, arguing that they had all contributed to making the event possible. Williams refused to share centre stage. Said Granado: "We were herded into a room away from the scene of things like unwanted bastards. The decision was made and that was that. There was no opportunity given to anyone to dilute the grandeur and sense of achievement that belonged to Williams alone" (1987, 40).

Granado said little in cabinet. According to him, this did not mean he was afraid to do so. As he explained, even if self-servingly, "There are times when in situations, the best and most important thing that one can say is 'nothing'. Many interpret that philosophy as cowardice and lack of ability to respond. How hopelessly wrong" (ibid., 4). As ambassador to the Court of St James, Granado had opportunities to see how rude Williams could be. He was once summoned by the British prime minister, Sir Alec Douglas-Home, who was angry about the tone of a letter that Williams had sent him. He protested to Granado, asking, "Why does your Prime Minister have to write such strong letters to us?" The letter, which was not copied to Granado ("as usual, I was kept completely in the dark"), concerned the British decision to sell arms to South Africa.

Williams often undermined and humiliated his ministers, deeming many of them millstones and jackasses who were unfit to stand for electoral office or to represent the party and country at the level of the cabinet. Overand Padmore was humiliated on several occasions. He was also often ignored when important decisions affecting his ministry were being discussed or made. As minister of petroleum and mines, he was not advised when Trinidad and Tobago sought admission to OPEC. He also learned from the newspapers that he was being transferred to the Ministry of Agriculture. He was likewise transferred from the Ministry of Finance to the newly created and lowly Ministry of Government Construction and Maintenance as a form of punishment and humiliation. As Padmore himself complained, "Ministers fell afoul of [Williams] for reasons they did not know" ("Eric Williams in Retrospect", symposium, April 1991). According to Padmore, Williams would openly indicate which ministers he wished to see following a meeting: "That was an indication of [which] members of the Cabinet might have been in favour and who might not have been."

Williams was also reluctant to apologize when he offended a minister or mistreated him unjustly. According to Padmore, he would never apologize if he erred. "Don't expect him to come and say to you, 'I made a mistake and I am sorry', but he will let you know by his reaction and his manner and method of dealing that, 'yes, I erred in that particular thing'."

Revealing verbal portraits of Williams are also painted by Ibbit Mosaheb, former chairman of the PNM, by his media adviser George John, by President Ellis Clarke, by his former close associate in founding the PNM, Elton Richardson, by his daughter Erica Williams, by former opposition member of parliament Lionel Seukeran, and by Hindu political fundamentalist H.P. Singh. Ibbit Mosaheb, like the others, complained about Williams's utilitarian approach to friendship and to his colleagues generally. As he observed, "He used people and dropped them all the time. People had functions. When those were completed, he dropped them. That was one of the bad things about Eric – the personality of the man." Mosaheb agreed with Padmore that Williams was not able to apologize: "He was never a man to say 'sorry'. But you will understand by his actions. If he realized he had made a mistake, he compensated by giving you some other responsibility" (interview with Ken Boodhoo, as cited in Mohammed 2001, 179).

Elton Richardson also captured the ambiguity of Williams's political behaviour. As he wrote as early as 1965, "It would be difficult to understand how in any other country, it would be possible to fire a cabinet minister in one week because of injudicious use of power over the police, to praise him the following week, and then tell the public, "those who do not like it can pack up and go". There are many who do not believe he was a dictator, but this much can be said. He will subvert democracy until it is indistinguishable from dictatorship. He does not have the raw courage of a dictator" (*Trinidad and Tobago Index*, no. 2 [Fall 1965]: 28).

One individual who for many years had a ringside seat from which to view the way Williams related to his ministers, his mandarins, representatives of multinational corporations, and colonial and other international officials was Ellis Clarke. Clarke served variously as attorney general, constitutional adviser, ambassador to the United States and the United Nations, governor general and president. Reflecting on how Williams related with him in 1956 and thereafter, Clarke had the following to say:

> The PNM, when it came into power in 1956, was a revolutionary party, and its position was that everything in the past was bad. The war cry then was "heads will roll" and according to the rank and file, one of the heads to roll was mine as I was one of the past regime. Pat Solomon however . . . said to Williams: "He is honest and capable. What more do you want? Benefit from his advice." I then became cautiously acceptable.
>
> On the whole, I got on well with Bill Williams. I was one of the few persons for whom he had some respect and regard. That did not mean that he was easy to get on with. Because of his "political antennae" which he always had out, he knew that I had no political leanings whatsoever, so in no sense was I a rival to him. Among his own Ministers and his own colleagues he was always on the lookout to see that they were all kept in line. He had no such problem with me. On the other hand he felt that I

had been too close to sources of power overseas, so that when I was made Attorney General, he was not very pleased. He once told me that he was not very happy with my appointment, for it should have been his appointment. It wasn't that he had somebody else in mind. He just felt that he should have been consulted. (As cited in Collymore 2000, 43–44)

Williams often benefited from Clarke's negotiating skills and the advice that he gave while ambassador and later head of state, in which capacity Williams was expected to "consult" with him routinely even as the latter was compelled to follow his "advice". Clarke explained how this process worked:

> One had to be extremely flexible with a Prime Minister such as Eric Williams was. He was not a man who followed a consistent policy throughout one's term, and everything had to be very much ad hoc. . . . A matter might arise on which he did not require your view, but if you resurrected the matter three weeks later, he might be prepared to listen. It was very much a question of your trying to determine what was the best way of handling each individual situation. (As cited in Collymore 2000, 43–44, 110–11)

Erica Williams's recollections and observations about her father go a long way in helping us to understand the dynamics of his personality. Erica tells us that after her mother's death in 1953, "Eric Williams the man, to a great extent, gave way to Eric Williams the politician (Boodhoo 1986b, 4)." She said this decision was "consciously" made, with all the consequences. Her belief that had her mother lived, her father would not have gone into politics can certainly be challenged, but there is no telling what sort of politician he might have been had he not been bereaved. Erica tells us that in his later years, her father became an "increasingly solitary and reclusive man who worked more out of his home than in the prime minister's office". She also recalled that he "came alive during election campaigns, and treated each seriously". He also "enjoyed confrontations", and in her view, "knew better than anyone else just when and how to face them".

Erica was not in Trinidad during those critical months of 1970 when the army mutinied, but Williams kept her abreast of what was taking place, writing her frequently. Erica confirms what Montano revealed, that is, that her father did not panic, as some allege, in the face of the mutiny:

> It was potentially a life and death situation. I firmly believe that if the rebel group from the army was able to get out of its base at Teteron, a coup d'etat would have been staged, and my father could possibly have been killed. One of my memories though, is that . . . my father remained calm and generally unruffled unlike many others around him. It was a challenge he met and resolved. He was well equipped to deal with challenges. . . . The army revolt and the attempted revolution . . . in 1970 were surely the most serious challenges he faced during his 25 years in office. But they reckoned without my father who believed he was capable of achieving whatever he set his mind to do. . . . He was strong willed and determined. (Ibid., 10)

She also tells us what we have heard from others, that is, that Williams saw politics as if it were a military undertaking. "My father always viewed most things in life with the precision and strategy worthy of a military campaign. He always enjoyed using a French proverb [*reculer pour mieux sauter*] which translated means, 'retreat in order to [better] advance' " (ibid.).

We know from others that Williams's health began to deteriorate in the early 1970s, and Erica confirms this:

> During the early 1970's, I suspect that my father became increasingly disillusioned about his role as leader, some of his peers, and the society in general. Thus, while he was extremely devoted to the country, he felt that he was not able to achieve all he would have wanted to for it. Possibly, though, because of the kind of person he was – that is, one who always set the highest goals and ideals for himself, and one who believed he controlled his own destiny – he probably would never have been fully satisfied. Great men are doomed to die feeling they have failed. He was disappointed with the mentality of our countrymen. He thought we were much too frivolous, insular, and not interested in a team. Incompetence was a constant thorn in his side. He found that our nationals are overly critical of each other, and especially so of their leaders, although I believe this was so primarily because there was such a myth surrounding him. To that extent, some saw him as a god and not as a man. Thus when he made mistakes, and in the twenty-five-year period that was inevitable, people were extraordinarily vicious. (Ibid., 10)

Erica suggests that Williams's formula for dealing with associates was consciously chosen and was in effect a protective mask:

> His aloof stance was one that was not natural. My father loved to socialize. He enjoyed having people around him. He was not ordinarily a solitary person. Yet there was the political man telling him that he needed to isolate himself, that he should not get too close to people, since doing so could lead to political problems, regardless of whoever such a person was. He did not hesitate to remove himself from anyone if his political image was threatened. Thus the several allegations about his closeness to this or that person or affair are ludicrous for anyone who knew him very well. He would cut himself off from anyone if they had done wrong, if he thought they had done wrong, or if they had disappointed him. His success lay in his willingness to isolate himself; but ultimately it also contributed to his increased alienation from the society.[8] (Ibid.)

Erica speculates that her father must have been in constant emotional turmoil between his disposition as a man and his role as a politician, and that he resolved it by becoming a recluse:

> During the last ten years of my father's life he became a very reclusive, meditative and further disappointed man. Further running the country during that time had become less challenging than in the early years. It had become more routinized. It was somewhat

akin to running an office. By this time, too he was obviously a much older person and his health was not as good as it previously was. This health condition did not contribute to his overall disposition. In the final analysis, however, given the personal choices he had made; the rigid discipline to which he held himself; and the very high goals he had established for both the society and for himself, there could have been no other way. (Ibid.)

Erica says nothing about her father being psychiatrically ill, other than her mention of his growing increasingly reclusive.

Another keen Williams watcher was George John, who functioned for a while as his media adviser. John had the following to say after Williams's passing: "Eric Williams, being human, was not without fault. He was virtually impossible to live with. His ferocious temper was legendary and few of his associates could have escaped a tongue-lashing at one time or another. But his intellectual gifts, his stamina, were beyond question. He was a tremendously hard worker, and he expected those who worked with him to respond in kind" ("Last Days of Eric Williams", *Trinidad Express,* 29 March 1991, 63).

John noted that Williams became more idiosyncratic in the years after 1973: "This was a new Williams, a glum man, more of a recluse than ever before. He seemed to work by fits and starts, though the tongue continued to drip acid. For then, he was over the hill, and the great manipulator increasingly found himself the manipulated by the ruthless about him" (ibid., 34). John nevertheless marvelled at the fact that notwithstanding all Williams's trespasses, so many of the men around him forgave and generally stayed loyal to him:

> The miracle is that a man of Williams' erratic temperament (or perhaps because of it) held sway for so long. Regardless of his open rows with his colleagues, the abominable way he treated his senior civil service advisers (his permanent secretaries acquired the status of an endangered species), his frequent bitter public criticisms of his party, government and ministers, some of whom he described as millstones, and many sections of the community, his people stayed with him, trusted nobody else, and honoured him with their confidence. (Ibid., 33)

Williams did not reciprocate, John noted, and was not loyal to anyone except perhaps John O'Halloran. "He dropped colleagues like a moulting bird dropping feathers." John related a conversation that he had with Learie Constantine, one-time great friend and benefactor of Williams and the first chairman of the PNM. According to John, Constantine told him that "there is only one man in the world, if I were in the room and he walked in, I would walk out. That man is your Prime Minister." Reportedly, the two men had a difference of opinion on a family matter serious enough to have Constantine, who was then high commissioner to London, return home for "clarification". Williams refused to see him. Constantine returned to London and resigned.

During the period 1956 to 1966, the parliamentary opposition bitterly and ferociously criticized Williams. Among the most vocal was Lionel Seukeran, member of parliament for Naparima, at one and the same time an admirer of Williams and a fierce parliamentary critic. He openly confessed that he respected Williams, who he said helped to fertilize his potential as a researcher and a debater. Seukeran shared the conventional view that Williams castrated his cabinet colleagues:

> He would stand no interference with his set plans, would tolerate no disobedience, and no one dared question his authority. He let it be known that while he had got rid of White Massa, he was now the Black Massa, as ruthless, if not more so, and all who conspired to thwart his will had to pay. He awed members of his cabinet into impotency. Some he called millstones around his neck, others not even worthy to have known him, leave alone sitting by his side as equals. He berated them; he scoffed at them. Cunning sycophants, they dared not retaliate. Instead, they flattered his ego, found new methods to flatter him, and quietly bowed to his imperial will. (1991, 11)

Seukeran also knew that Williams was not a one-dimensional man, and that he could behave very differently depending on context. He could be severely critical of the parliamentary opposition and switch off his hearing aid when he felt that they were talking rubbish. He nevertheless respected several members of the parliamentary opposition, though he was not beyond bribing some of them to keep them dependent on him. Among these were Bhadase Maraj, Rudranath Capildeo, and Ashford Sinanan, whom he appointed high commissioner to India. Seukeran conceded that "he had a healthy respect for fearless members of the Opposition, even though he manipulated some by exploiting their weaknesses, either by paying large sums for holdings owned by one, and keeping yet another in full pay and what else I know not in London . . . for these absenteeisms" (Seukeran 2006, 364–66). Seukeran was himself the financial beneficiary of a deal involving the purchase of one of his properties that Williams wished to give Black Power radicals in order to appease them.

Seukeran noted, however, that Williams was gracious and honest enough to recognize that it was the Indians and the whites who had saved him and the country in 1970. According to Seukeran, Williams once said to him, "I want to tell you how grateful I am to the Indian community, and to Bhadase in particular. Were it not for your people, we may not have been sitting here this day, possibly not sitting anywhere. It was their heroic stand that saved the day for us. I have taken cognizance. One thing I cannot understand. How is it the Africans who should be most loyal to me are so ganged up against me?" (ibid., 365)

Williams indicated that he had taken cognizance of what Seukeran had said, and wondered why it was that the Africans, who should have been the most loyal to him, had in fact ganged up against him; whereupon Seukeran replied, "I am happy that you recognize our loyalty and respect for constituted authority. Has it occurred that it took a white man to offset the army mutiny, another to alert and have ready the coast guard, a white commissioner of police, and a half white brigadier to set the seal on peace, and an Indian to confront Black Power?" Seukeran was referring to some of the events that took place in 1970 following the mutiny of the army, and said that he advised Williams that he should appoint more Indians and soldiers to the police service and the defence force (Seukeran 2006, 365).

Seukeran (1991) was loud in his overall praise of Williams and declared himself privileged to have lived in his era and to have known him. He compared him to Julius Caesar, of whom Mark Antony said, "The elements so mixed in him that nature might stand up and say to all the world, 'this was a man'!"

Another critic, H.P. Singh, who had fought in the trenches against Williams in the run-up to independence, paid him a backhanded tribute in his pamphlet *An Indian Enigma*. Singh was prepared to give "Jack his jacket". As he said,

> The writer has been one of the PNM and Eric Williams' severest critics. We have had our misgivings about his competence as well as his bona fides to run the government. We have had our fears about his racial attitudes and prejudices and sentiments. We still have some reservations, justified reservations, on some matters. But we must give Jack his jacket. For although we cannot commend Dr. Williams for anything that he has done, or may have attempted to have done, we are in a position to commend him for what he has not done. Since Marlborough House, no appeal has been made to racial emotionalism, and from then to the present time, Indians are free to walk the streets of the country without fear of being assaulted on the basis of race.
>
> Up to now, the Rule of Law has not been interfered with, and the Judiciary remains independent. . . . Since Marlborough House, his talk is based on national integration and not on miscegenation. The democratic principle of parliamentary government has not been basically infringed. These are achievements, even though they stem from inaction. They could have acted in these matters as some of the new African nations have acted and made things difficult for us and themselves. And so, we congratulate Williams and his government, not for what they have done, but for what they have not done. (1965, 22)

45   The Myth of
Eric Williams

Sons and daughters of Thebes, behold: this was Oedipus,
Greatest of men; he held the key to the deepest mysteries;
Was envied by all his fellow-men for his great prosperity;
Behold, what a full tide of misfortune swept over his head.
Then learn that mortal man must always look to his ending,
and none can be called happy until that day when he carries
his happiness down to the grave in peace.
    – Sophocles

Myth and history are close kin inasmuch as both explain how things got to be the way they are by telling some sort of story. But our common parlance reckons myth to be false while history is, or aspires to be, true. Accordingly, a historian who rejects someone else's conclusions calls them mythical, while claiming that his own view are true. But what seem true to one historian will seem false to another, so one historian's truth becomes another's myth, even at the moment of utterance.
    – H. McNeil

I bid you, kind Sir, as a great intellectual
let your life be an open book to be seen and read by all
in the near future, our children will study in class
they would want to know if you were a giant or simply a jackass
I do hope, Doctor, they would find you a man of integrity.
    – Chalkdust (Hollis Liverpool)

In Greek mythology, Nemesis, the goddess of fate, sometimes punished man by fulfilling his wishes too completely.
    – Henry Kissinger

Williams' apostles have a duty to "mortalize" him.
    – Winston Mahabir

One of the aims of this study was to go behind the mask and the tribal myths to try to answer the perennial question, who was "the real Eric Williams"? Norman Manley once observed that Williams was "more than a man of split personalities; he was many personalities in one . . . the most complicated little man one ever met" (as cited in Sealey 1991, 201). Manley clearly believed that Williams had a paranoid personality. So did his wife Edna, who, in an entry in her diary, wondered how best to "tell the story of Eric Williams". When she first met him in Washington, he was in the midst of divorce proceedings with his first wife Elsie, who was "a nice woman who did not know what she had married when she took on Eric's egotism and drive, and almost his egomania. She [Elsie] did not understand and could not cope with his eternal wars with everyone, his perpetual suspicions and passions, his ceaseless tendency to be over- intense about even the smallest details in life, [and] his total lack of comprehension about a woman's world." Williams's relationship with his second wife was deemed better. "She was a wonderful woman and she loved and understood Eric and was proud of him. He was deeply happy. I was very touched – and a year afterwards she was dead, and he was left alone again, with a baby daughter. It was quite awful, and whenever nowadays the worst of him shows, I remember that bit of tragedy and forgive everything" (Manley 1989, 57–58)

Edna recalled an incident which made them aware just how paranoid Williams really was. One night, while dining at Drumblair, the Manley family home, Williams was full of mirth when suddenly the power failed. "In the half light of the flickering candles, Eric's whole character changed before our very eyes. In the flash of a second, he was literally, as well as figuratively, looking over his shoulder. His voice dropped to a sibilant whisper, and he began to talk of what the English had done to him when he was at Oxford, of how his letters were opened, his messages intercepted, and Washington!! - it simply curdled one's blood" (ibid.).

Eric Williams can be viewed through many lenses. One can employ psychiatric concepts to attempt to plumb the depths of his personality. One can also employ Weber's concept of the charismatic leader who revolutionizes his society. One can also see him in the genre of the Greek hero or Hegelian "great man" in whom triumph and tragedy are dialectically interwined. One can likewise view Williams through Carlylean forms – the hero as king, secular divinity, prophet, poet, man of letters, and as culture maker, whether singly or simultaneously. One can also combine all the concepts in the hope of obtaining a more textured, multi-dimensional, and "unfocused" portrait.

Williams as Greek Hero

The Williams foundational narrative has all the characteristics of a Greek tragedy. One encounters therein themes and plot lines such as the search for glory and excellence, conceit, vanity, arrogance, ambition, historic justice, personal redemption and self-righteous wrath. Also evident are grievings about lack of loyalty, recognition, treachery, betrayal, disobedience, the lust for revenge for wrongs real and imagined, destiny, deliberate overstepping of traditional limits, impious presumption, fear of losing face, retribution, hubris, nemesis, ultimate rejection, heroic failure and the "necessity" of death as the only honourable way out of dishonour.

In our study of his early years we encounter the classic conjuncture: the warrior hero believes that he is favoured by the "gods" of history and the oracle and thus impregnable, forgetting that those whom the "gods" favour either "die" young or fail tragically. We see too where the hero becomes trapped by his belief in the logic and imperative of his mission and the weight of his obligations to his community. He thus seeks to ensure that unlike Kafka's messiah, he would not "arrive too late". Indeed, Williams often wanted to hurry history along, so impatient was he to ensure that he accomplished his assigned tasks.

Classic Greek tragedies reveal that heroes all live with fears, humiliating anxieties and illnesses. They also tell us that the world has cosmic designs that only the gods can see, and that the apparent fortuitous combination of events is part of a decreed design. The dramatic poets also make clear that man is neither unequivocally bad nor good, but that, as Plato noted, "great natures produce great vices as well as great virtues". The Williams myth likewise provides evidence of the poet's adage that the greatness and the fragility of man are inseparable, and that it is their combination and interface that ultimately make up the hero's nature.

Myths are fables or sagas that a folk invent and construct to tell about their past. The Afro-creole tribal narrative has it that Eric Williams is the "founding father" of the nation-state of Trinidad and Tobago, the hero who liberated the twin island from imperial vassalage and economic peonage. According to the primal myth that the man himself consciously, and with the utmost deliberation, did a great deal to create and disseminate, Williams was a poor colonial boy, educated by the taxpayers of Trinidad and Tobago, who enabled him to attend Queen's Royal College and Oxford University. There, after having written a thesis that effectively destroyed the then prevailing *doxa* that enslaved Africans were emancipated by the religiously driven activities of people such as William Wilberforce, Thomas Buxton and the other "saints", he obtained a doctorate.

The myth, as outlined in his autobiography *Inward Hunger* (both the published and unpublished versions) and in his address "My Relations with the Caribbean Commission", further holds that Williams spent seventeen long years in the proverbial wilderness preparing himself for the tasks to which history had assigned him, that is, completing the emancipation project by almost single-handedly leading Trinidad and Tobago and the West Indies to the promised political kingdom, confronting in the process the might of the British empire and America's "manifest destiny" as it expressed itself physically and symbolically in the military bases at Chaguaramas and Wallerfield.

In the unexpurgated version of *Inward Hunger*, Williams tells us of his plan to use his autobiography as a sort of "party programme if he was forced to take a political way out" in his struggle with the Caribbean Commission, which would get a "showdown" if it wanted one. We were also told that "unlike the proverbial prophet, the nationalist historian had his greatest honour among his own people", and that all of the latter's "pent up national pride and West Indian dignity" were caught up in his remark that "they would one day rewrite the history which it was his privilege to teach them". His boast was that he was "the philosopher of West Indian nationalism", the one who would mentally emancipate the Negro in the Caribbean. As he remarked further in his unpublished autobiography,

> Morally, I felt myself obligated to specialize in this neglected field of [Caribbean] research because for fifteen years – from 1922–1937, my education was funded by the people of Trinidad and Tobago. No other West Indian, living or dead, is to such an extent the child of his people. . . I am convinced that the history of my education and my life can point a moral, in one direction in terms of the integration of the Negro in the Western World, and in another, by throwing light on a quite unnecessarily dark cranny in the history of the world, but more important, in terms of the ideological history of the West, its relationship with backward peoples, and its repeated assurances of a better world. (EWMC folio 139)

Additional evidence of Williams's narcissism and vanity is found in the following statement, also in the unpublished version:

> The real derelicts of the Caribbean are the Caribbean people. I am aware of them, I who, paraphrasing St. Paul, by the grace of the people of the Caribbean am what I am and in whom their grace has not been void. The bells toll for me because it tolls for them. It is because I believe and realize this that I present this account of the education and experience of a colonial Negro, of his hopes and fears, his optimism and pessimism, confidence and scepticism, ambition and futility, aspirations and frustration – in the hope not only that it will be relevant to Africa tomorrow, but that it will be of value to the west today. (Ibid.)

The myth also has it that in his long odyssey, the hero encountered several deadly obstacles and faced many challengers, among them the Colonial Office, the American authorities in Washington, the obscurantist white and "black" French-creole "massas" and other recalcitrant minorities, the denominational authorities, especially the Catholics and the Hindus, the prime minister of the federation, Grantley Adams, political leaders of Jamaica and the eastern

Caribbean, including his one-time mentor, Norman Manley, "imps of Satan" such as C.L.R. James and other political denizens of the "Old World", Texaco and the other multinational corporations, the radical trade unions, and above all, the people of Trinidad and Tobago on whose behalf he laboured, but who often betrayed him by their individualism, laziness and backwardness, and their refusal to accept the sacrifices and discipline without which some of his core goals remained unrealized. The people, he felt, had betrayed the patriarchal warrior hero and not the other way around.

One could embellish the myth by listing other enemies and numinous "monstrosities" from the underworld of Trinidad's political life, such as the *Trinidad Guardian,* the *Express* and Albert Gomes, whom Williams believed he had to slay, but the above should suffice to make the point that navigating the channels between the Caribbean versions of Scylla and Charybidis was a challenge that often seemed too onerous to bear. In frustration, the once inwardly hungered hero often longed to be relieved of his burden through resignation, but persisted when orcular signs made it clear that the battle could still be won, and that ultimate relief would come only with death.

All the world loves a hero, and also to anthropomorphize him, and many Afro-Trinidadians bought into the holy scripture. The calypsonians, especially the Mighty Sparrow, played a pivotal role in helping to mythologize Williams. Sparrow told the generation of the 1950s and 1960s that Williams was the "Conqueror" and the "Boss". Whatever he said, went. Those who did not like whatever he said or did were invited to "get to hell outa here" and "go and clean toilets in the Bronx". This study has shown that the reality was often different from what was indicated in the myth, and that the heroic version often lacked verisimilitude, as is the case with all myths. Williams the man was in many respects a caricature of the fabled hero to whom paens should be sung or in whose honour libations should be poured. He was not always the self-sacrificing benevolent patriarch of the myth.

Nor was he in practice always the mortal enemy of the Colonial Office, the US State Department, the US navy, Texaco, Tate and Lyle, W.R. Grace and other multinational corporations, as he often seemed in public; nor did he have to snatch victory from the jaws of a stubborn and recalcitrant Colonial Office that was seeking to preserve the jewels of the empire as "the system of outdoor relief for the British middle classes", which he claims it once was. Britain in fact wanted to close down the Colonial Office; at most, Williams was the expediter of the inevitable; the Americans too had come to believe that Chaguaramas had outlived its usefulness. Their main concern was to avoid precedents that would make it more difficult to hold on to the Panama Canal, Guantánamo, and the base in the Philippines. Despite their apparent intransigence in the early phases of the struggle for Chaguaramas, the US State Department was always at pains to ensure that Williams was treated with "respect and deference". This was a Cold War imperative, especially after the Bay of Pigs fiasco.

In a number of other areas myth and fact do not coincide. This study, and work done by Palmer (2006) and others, reveal that Williams was a late convert to the demand for the return of Chaguaramas and that it was Manley and Adams who had told the Americans that the demand was "irrevocable" at a time when Williams was insisting on the "sanctity of international agreements" and insisting that he was not particularly taken with Chaguaramas as a site. The Williams myth also has him as a staunch supporter of the Westminster model, and he is quoted as saying that "if the British constitution is good enough for Britain it is good enough for Trinidad and Tobago". Yet we find him telling Norman Costar, the British high commissioner to Trinidad and Tobago in 1964, that he was "sympathetic to those African Prime Ministers who after independence tore up the constitutions with which they have been saddled so that they can get on with the real job of governing the country without factious opposition". Costar also claims that Williams told him that "British institutions do not really suit Trinidad and that he has private leanings towards a Presidential system and a one party state" (Palmer 2006, 164–65). The opposition had been accusing Williams of harbouring these sentiments. Williams never gave serious thought to abandoning the Westminster model, however. He in fact dismissed the views of Nyerere and Nkrumah about the virtues of the one-party system which merely resulted in the opposition being driven underground (EWMC folio 793).

The official myth also has it that Williams was an intransigent anti-colonial who was the enemy of the British and the Americans. Yet we encounter him writing to Harold Wilson and inviting himself to visit British universities to discern what could be learned from them – especially Oxford and Cambridge – in trying to restructure the curriculum of the University of the West Indies, its statutes and college system, and also the role British universities could play in reducing reliance on American universities and institutions such as the Ford Foundation. Williams saw the value of calling in the old colonial world to serve as a counterweight to the imperialism of the American new world (ibid., 37).

In much of what he wrote and said in the 1940s and 1950s and in the struggle for the return of Chaguaramas, Williams inveighed against the role played by British and American troops and warships. One is thus a bit surprised to find that as early as 1964, long before the crisis of 1970 presented him with a serious challenge to his authority, Williams was making clear to the British high commissioner that he would not hesitate to call in American marines from the base if he was ever faced with "army trouble". In sum, Williams was ambivalent about the role of the Americans in Chaguaramas because he saw them as guarantors of his regime's stability.

Williams may have come to his "senses" as a result of his visit to Tanzania, where the army had revolted. He reportedly told the British high commissioner to Tanzania and also to Ethiopia that he would not run away as Nyerere had done, and would not have "the slightest hesitation in calling upon US troops based in Trinidad if he was ever faced with a threat, perhaps engineered with the help of the Cubans, to the integrity of Trinidad and Tobago from a determined and unrepresentative minority" (Palmer 2006, 134). This needs to be taken into account in evaluating Williams's decision to call for British and American troops, guns and naval transport in 1970.

Although Williams was primarily responsible for inventing and embellishing the myth for his own political ends, he later debunked some of the self-same myths when they no longer had any instrumental value. Williams himself would tell us that he suspected that the Americans were no longer interested in retaining Chaguaramas. He also admitted that "there was nothing mysterious about Independence, and that it was achieved as part of a world movement against colonialism. . . . When [independence] came to Trinidad, the difference was that [Nkrumah] had to conquer an imperialist castle whereas the PNM merely took over a worm eaten house". This was a point that Norman Manley, Grantley Adams, Rudranath Capildeo and many others had made as early as 1960, when Williams was threatening to declare Trinidad and Tobago independent unilaterally on 22 April 1960 at "11:00 a.m. in the morning".

For all his outward bravado, Williams contrived to avoid direct confrontation with the "enemy", whether it be the US State Department, Texaco, Trinidad Tesoro, W.R. Grace, Tate and Lyle, or the Colonial Office. Invariably, politically influential individuals such as Francis Prevatt, chairman of the party and one-time minister of finance, John O'Halloran, minister of petroleum and mines and party financier, Ellis Clarke, former attorney general, constitutional advisor, governor, and then governor general, the trusted Alan Reece, the last of the white creole senior public servants, and Dodderidge Alleyne, the most influential of the mandarins whom Williams had recruited from Oxford to assist and advise him in the ministry of finance and the prime minister's office, used back- or multi-track channels to negotiate the diplomatic compromises and deals that had to be made to keep the ship of state on an even keel. Some, as we have seen, ran counter to his pledge to inaugurate an era of morality in public affairs.

The back-channel relationships between Williams, the Americans and the British led the late Fitzroy Baptiste to speculate that by 1956 Williams and the PNM had become the party of choice of the Americans in preference to the POPPG, which had failed to excite the urban masses, and the Hindu-dominated PDP of Bhadase Maraj. Baptiste wondered whether "Williams' entry into the political arena in . . . 1956 was at the behest of the United States and Britain in order to foil Maraj and his PDP. We may never know for sure." He believes, however, "that that was the game plan of London and Washington in the context of the Cold War". Baptiste apologized for the speculation and insisted that it was not calculated to dent the iconic image of Eric Williams as a "nationalist leader and Father of Independence of Trinidad and Tobago. . . . My view recognizes the realities of real politik that shaped international relations globally and in the Caribbean in the Cold War era" (2005, 46). My own view is that Williams did not act at the behest of Britain and the United States, though they were quite comfortable with him having regard to the assurances that he had given about where he stood on the ideological issues that mattered.

Williams as Charismatic Leader

Greek tragedy may serve to provide emplotment for the Williams legend, but such an exercise befits a dramatic poet and not a historian or a social scientist. There is still need for a theory or theories that might help to explain the many complex dimensions of the Williams phenomenon. Max Weber's concept of the charismatic hero provides one such theory. Several Caribbean leaders have been analysed using this concept (Allahar, 2001). Weber regards charismatic leadership as one of three ideal types, the patrimonial leader and the legal-rational leader being the other two. Charismatic authority, he tells us, rests on the personal devotion of followers to the lord, who is regarded as being heroic and who is obeyed by his disciples because of who he is and what he stands for. As Weber (1971) tells us, "Charismatic authority rests on the affectual and personal devotion of the follower to the lord and his gifts of grace (charisma). They comprise especially magical abilities, revelations of heroism, power of the mind and of speech. The eternally new, the non-routine, the unheard of and the emotional rapture from it are sources of personal devotion. The purest types are the rule of the prophet, the warrior hero, the great demagogue."

Success in whatever tasks he set himself is critical for the legitimacy and sustainability of charismatic leadership. Failure is almost always fatal. Success is an outward sign that the leader continues to be the "son of heaven". Without such evidence of having a cosmic mandate, the leader loses face. The masses lose faith and begin to entertain suspicions that the gods or History have forsaken him. Caprice also often has its instrumental value, and leaders may deliberately pursue it. It is important that the people see the leader as always "right" in whatever course of action he undertakes, and that no one else is seen to possess gifts, insights and competences that approximate his. Such individuals are potentially traitorous and dangerous rivals who have to be neutralized or ostracized lest they too make counter-claims to charismatic authority. In sum, there can only be one legitimate leader. Charismatic leaders invariably feel or are made to feel by the sycophants that surround them that they are larger than life. Not a few suffer from bouts of "holy madness".

Weber nevertheless sees charismatic authority as one of the great revolutionary and transformative forces of history. The revolutionary hero emerges in those rare moments when societies are experiencing periods of intense stress, disorder, normlessness and institutional collapse. In such times, the messiah's need for a theatre of achievement coincides with the people's collective need for a new order, a new dispensation. The relationship is thus mutual. The leader is the midwife of history who helps to effect the physical and emotional transition from one order to another. His utility declines once this historic task has been completed, and the society is again ready to become routinized and reinstitutionalized. The people, especially those on the periphery, begin to resent the leader's arbitrariness, to be upset by instability, and to place a premium on accountability, and bureaucratic as opposed to personal coordination. It is important to recognize, however, that Weber viewed charismatic authority as a value-neutral "ideal type". He was aware that one could have hybrids such as "hereditary charismatic leaders", or that charisma might inhere in legal rational offices such as that of the prime minister or the papacy. Intellectual prowess publicly displayed can also earn a leader charismatic currency, particularly in situations where skill with the "word" yields increments of status.

Much of what Weber said could be readily applied to Williams. Williams was clearly an authentic charismatic leader who was an object of veneration by the many whose social and psychological needs he fulfilled. Weberian categories could be used to explain his penchant for warrior politics, the personalized and patrimonial nature of his rule, his restlessness and unpredictability, his constant search for gratification, the way he cast aside those whom he once loved and trusted, those whom he cold-bloodedly quarantined, and those whom he deemed traitorous. Like other anti-colonial leaders who became prime ministers, he also inherited some of the charisma and symbolic value that inhered in the office of governor. Further, he was "professor of the word" in a society that venerated those who could manipulate language, whether in the classical idiom of the colonizer or in the vernacular genre of the calypsonian or the carnival.

Williams as an Hegelian "Great Man"

Williams can also be considered "a great man", a "necessary actor" in the Hegelian sense, someone who was conscious of the "spirit of his age" as well as the role that he was required to play in the historical drama being performed on the Caribbean and universal stages. He saw himself as one of the great conductors of the anti-imperial orchestra, the instrument chosen to lead the Caribbean into the post-colonial world. Put differently, his role, as he saw it, was to help dehusk the kernel of the new world, which was struggling to emerge out of its imperial shell. In his view, success in this task would require him to take "revolutionary leaps" and also apply different canons for judging what was politically appropriate or not appropriate, and what was moral or not moral if one was to be heroically effective.

Blame has been ascribed to him for failures in many projects, especially the collapse of the federation. It may be that the outcome of that particular event cannot be properly understood if one focuses only at the level of what various individuals did or did not do. The "objective" as opposed to "empirical" historian might say that the federal idea to which Williams was once wedded was one that was not yet sufficiently matured. The "ideal" was thus "slaughtered on the bench of history", to borrow a phrase from C.L.R. James, where many desirable but as yet unripened ideas are destroyed, seemingly senselessly, by forces incomprehensible to the ordinary mind.

Williams as Wounded Personality

Some analysts have explained Williams's behaviour in terms of his physical characteristics, mainly the fact that he was short in stature, as well as sight- and hearing-impaired. Yet others described him as having a "chip on his shoulder" that they attribute to the social circumstances of his childhood or to the fact that he was a member of a "black" French-creole family which believed that it had been socially and financially disenfranchised by the white side of the family.[1] One American wag, with humour, opined that Williams was quite balanced in that where the Americans were concerned, he had a chip on *each* shoulder.

Others have offered yet other psychohistorical explanations for Williams's political behaviour patterns. In his essay "A Psychological Portrait of Political Power", Ramesh Deosaran (1981) sought to explore the relationship between Williams's personality and his decision to enter the political arena in 1955. Using Laswellian categories (1976), Deosaran argued that Williams's experiences at Queen's Royal College and Oxford and with the Ango-American Caribbean Commission were largely responsible for creating a "wounded personality" for which he sought anodynes by becoming involved in mass politics. Deosaran's thesis is that the early optimism that was generated by his winning the Island Scholarship in 1931, and his early successes at Oxford ("I had come, seen and conquered – at Oxford") did not prepare Williams adequately for the racial humiliations of his later years at Oxford or his experiences at the Caribbean Commission. Thus his resort to aggressive behaviour ("When I could not take it any longer, and could not ignore the racial factor, I blazed out to my principal in a letter"). He also "blazed out" at the *Antigua Star*'s criticisms of *Negro in the Caribbean* and at all those who denied him what he considered his just deserts at the Caribbean Commission. He chose always to retaliate rather than "run", "bow" or "cut cane". The problem, opined Deosaran, was the gap between Williams's estimates of his competence and self-worth and the recognition that was being denied him. He found his self-esteem continuously challenged. Deprivations nurtured his inward hunger. Wrote Deosaran, "By painful humiliations and frustrations, Williams was shaped into an emotionally famished personality – a far cry from the innocent intellectual optimism of his youth. The vehicle used for compensation was entry into politics."

Deosaran recognized of course that many frustrated individuals do not seek to resolve their neuroses by going into popular politics. In Williams's case, however, the timing of events and the social context provided one of those rare conjunctures where the personality's esteem needs and the people's complex needs coincide. Williams, encouraged by his associates, rationalized his motives in terms of the public interest. Deosaran speculated that the nature of the political system helped to encourage Williams's dysfunctional behaviour: "Williams' bipolarities flourished politically within our adversary system of politics. . . . And so he excelled, or was allowed to excel, inflamed by warrior-like and divisive behaviour. In other words, his contradictions became utilitarian" (1981, 18). The dynamics of charismatic leadership and the opportunities offered by his political enemies, both internal and external, to play the role of warrior, also fed his needs. Williams often bragged that his enemies were always giving him opportunities to use his knowledge of Caribbean history to destroy them, and that he "let them have it". Deosaran felt that Williams ought to have attempted to bring harmony into his being as many other people do, either through introspection or by seeking professional help.

Ken Boodhoo explored similar concepts to explain Williams's political behaviour, and he too regarded Williams as having a "narcissistic personality":

> This is a characteristic of many charismatic leaders who believe that they possess great power, physical appeal, and the right to assert their will. In these personalities, two different experiences of the self co-exist. One is the insecure self, characterized by low self-esteem and insecurity, while the other is a grandiose self, driven by the need for achievement and recognition, by fantasies of self-confidence and control. They continually seek public approval and have an authoritarian style that permits them to present their views with more self-confidence than available information warrants. (2001, 132)

Boodhoo argued that the force which drove Williams seemed to be a "yearning for the redress of grievances which represented a narcissistic injury to his self-image. That is, he perceived throughout his life that he was treated as inferior, when he knew he possessed superior intellectual endowments" (ibid.).[2]

Theodore Sealey, former editor of the *Jamaica Gleaner*, quotes a close academic colleague of Williams to make much the same point:

The autobiographical memoir, *Inward Hunger*, is of enormous psychiatrical importance in an understanding of the Williams persona. It reveals at once a profound anguish and a deep rebelliousness: anguish at the historically determined role of the colonial in English society and rebelliousness against that role. It is ambivalent, for it, on the one hand, is full of the natural and necessary anger of a first-class "Black" mind against white mediocrity, on the other, it is full of an eagerness to show the white man that his colonial competitor can play the white man's game even better than the white himself.

There is an aggressive tone which, to the unsympathetic reader, however, can be seen as the mature, nationalist consciousness of a colonial intellectual reacting against the deep psychic wound that all racial prejudice and discrimination leave behind it. It has something of Fanon about it. However, it does not go as far as Fanon in its rejection of European culture. For the book also reveals Dr. Williams as a loyal Oxonian; and few things are more revealing than the confession that his life's dream, while a colonial at Oxford, was to become a permanent member of Oxonian society as an All Souls Fellow. (1991, 196–97)

The Bipolarity Hypothesis

Williams's wildly fluctuating moods, and his chameleon-like and multi-faced behaviour, were the subject of comment by several of his political colleagues and mandarins who had the opportunity to observe him up close. Many medical doctors deemed his behaviour abnormal. Sir Ellis Clarke described him as being paranoidal and as a man of "varying moods"; one had to determine what phase the moon was in before raising certain matters with Williams. Clarke said that Williams had "more sides to him than the Pentagon". He also talked about Williams's "Monday Morning Blues" and his penchant for running to the governor on Mondays to recount all the rumours he had heard over the weekend that he deemed to be fact. A.N.R. Robinson also found Williams's behaviour "aberrant and strange". So too did Solomon Hochoy, Trinidad's first indigenous governor general, who told Norman Costar in 1963 that the British were not dealing with a "rational man" but with a " 'madman' who removed elsewhere anyone who exercised some influence over him" (Palmer 2006, 154). Costar himself told his principals in London that Williams was a man of "unpredictable moods", someone who "rotates his friendships and his enemies" and that "Britain and I in particular could [one day] become the victim of Williams' anger and be put in the dog house for the next six months or so" (ibid., 160). Costar, like Hochoy, considered Williams "not to be a rational man by normal standards, but someone who had a very difficult and notorious temperament which we will have to be prepared to deal with. When he is in these moods, our best policy is to do nothing for him and ask nothing of him and wait for the thaw which would come after several months when he lets it be known that his mood has changed and he is looking for an excuse to bury the hatchet" (ibid., 167–68).

Opposition politician Peter Farquhar also drew attention to Williams's narcissistic behaviour:

> Expert dribblers are apt to fall so deeply in love with themselves and their own expertise that they ignore the objective of scoring goals and amuse themselves and their fans by monopolizing the ball. Williams was such a footballer, and he is such a politician . . . in football, Williams played to the gallery and in politics he does the same . . . in politics he does not care whether his country rises or falls so long as he occupies the centre of the stage. (Ibid., 155)

Williams himself admitted that he did not enjoy being a mere spectator at sporting events.

Gerard Montano, one of Williams's close ministerial colleagues, claimed to have observed on more than one occasion that his "boss" was "depressed". "Williams was a manic depressive. He was right down when Robinson was presenting his 1966 budget, which announced an economic recession. He was slumped in his chair . . . he kept sort of going lower and lower, and I turned to him and said, Bill, you are very depressed." In 1962, Sir Stephen Luke, the federal interim commissioner, had similarly found Williams "depressed and morose" because of what he considered the "niggardliness of Britain's post-independence settlement" (ibid., 149).

Medical practitioners disagree sharply as to whether or not Williams was mentally ill and about the extent and nature of the affliction, if there was any at all. One advised the author that the prime minister was not clinically depressed but that he himself had formed a judgement that Williams became paranoid in later life. Dr Halsey McShine, who attended Williams for many years, also had no knowledge of Williams being clinically depressed. Asked whether he ever considered him paranoid, McShine replied that he was not a psychiatrist and did not know what was in Williams's mind. He did not like using the word *paranoid*, but noted that Williams at times behaved "strangely". For example, he would avoid eating in restaurants out of fear that he might be poisoned. McShine confirmed that Williams believed that the CIA was spying on him, and that his daughter's lover, a white American, was a CIA agent. McShine says that Williams told him "I can't trust the US Security". For this reason, the prime minister refused to attend his daughter's wedding in Miami when she decided to marry the very man whom he suspected of being a spy. McShine surmised that this type of behaviour was an occupational hazard for prime ministers, who might come to suspect that people would plot against or even attempt to kill them. Nevertheless, he believed that Williams began to deteriorate after 1973, and felt that Williams should not have returned to office that year. "It would have been better for him and for Trinidad and Tobago if he had not. He did not however listen." According to McShine, Williams became progressively bitter, suspicious, and reclusive.

Another practitioner, who also knew Williams socially, was of the view that Williams had a mild bipolar problem that was aggravated by the many political crises he had to face, and the corrupt behaviour of the men who formed part of his inner circle. This explanation for Williams's behaviour was offered by several commentators, who saw him as a victim of all that was taking place. Another view held that Williams's mood variability was not an illness, and that his behaviour was merely strange and idiosyncratic at times. Those who were of this opinion conceded that his behaviour was often deliberately ill-mannered, boorish, abrasive and abusive.

The individual who was most open about Williams's illness was Winston Mahabir. In his book *In and Out of Politics* (1978), Mahabir, who trained as a psychiatrist following his break with Williams in 1961 and his return to Canada in 1962, frequently alluded to Williams's emotional immaturity. Mahabir drew attention to the prime minister's capacity to embrace mutually contradictory positions. He was a veritable chameleon:

> Eric Williams (and consequently the PNM) has exhibited curious and sometimes astonishing ambivalence . . . over the past nine years. I use the word ambivalence to mean the coexistence in one person of opposing emotional attitudes towards the same object, person or objective, and the manifestation in both word and deed of these conflicting attitudes. . . . I speak not of flexibility and compromise which are at the core of the art and science of politics. I speak of observable, documentable, recurrent, mutually-contradictory pronouncements and operations. I speak of ambivalence with respect to Indians and whites, ambivalence towards the trappings of colonialism, ambivalence towards West Indianism and to a lesser degree, ambivalence towards the heightened educational needs of an expectant population. (Ibid., 204–6)

One can also add to Mahabir's list Williams's ambivalence towards federation and the extent to which he flip-flopped on the issue of a strong central federal government. Mahabir notes that Williams even failed to mourn the collapse of federation for which he had campaigned with such fervour. "Not a drum was heard, not a funeral note as the Federal corpse was buried. . . . By then, he had good cause to be less excited about Federation as a politician than when he wrote about it as a scholar" (ibid., 217).

Williams also seemed to enjoy making and breaking those with whom he worked. He almost always had to have an enemy, whether it was the Colonial Office, the prime minister of the federation, the *Trinidad Guardian*, the Americans or the multinationals. If there was no enemy, he invented one. As Mahabir put it,

> As Cabinet master and in matters of state, Williams sometimes behaved in the man-

ner of a brilliant military strategist. The general must never be exposed. Send the colonel instead. Emit a smoke-screen. Organise a diversionary movement. Bully the enemy if he is weak. Bluff him or pin-prick him if he is strong. Organise your spy-system. Control the organs of propaganda as far as possible. When embarrassed at home, project an image of international greatness. Always have an enemy, for without one a general would be jobless. He never came unprepared for any Cabinet meeting. He knew before-hand what he wished to achieve and had at his disposal all the ingredients of success – intellectual, emotional, behavioural. (Ibid., 55)

Mahabir observed and commented on Williams's emotional instability, his suspiciousness of others, his tendency to see demons and shadows everywhere, his paranoia, his melancholia, his insistence on loyalty to the party that invariably meant loyalty to him, his inability to accommodate setbacks of any kind, his disposition to trample relentlessly upon the reputations and careers of friends, and his sense of indispensability and irreplaceability that was the party's Achilles' heel as well as the sword of Damocles that he held over the heads of others. The list of those who were casualties over the years of Williams's rule was "terrifyingly long". It included Mahabir himself, Albert Gomes, David Nelson, Patrick Solomon, Ulric Lee, Brinsley Barrow, Carlton Gomes, Elton Richardson, J.H. Steer, his economic adviser J. O'Neil Lewis, Dodderidge Alleyne, Gerry Gordon, Gil Thompson, De Wilton Rogers, and above all his academic and spiritual godfather C.L.R. James, whom he ruthlessly off-loaded when Williams wanted to do a deal with the Americans on Chaguaramas.[3] Williams, it seems, believed, as did Caligula, that it was "much safer to be feared than loved when of the two, either must be dispensed with".

Mahabir claims that the "disturbing aspects of Williams' personality were evident to him in their pre-political association, but that he made allowances for the emotional problems being experienced by a friend". Still, he experienced "a constant mental tug o'war between admiration of the greatness of Williams and wariness of his evil potential" (ibid., 68). Mahabir also noted Williams's "deficient ability to accommodate setbacks of any kind", but he continued to hope that the prime minister's "essential greatness would eventually prevail over his manifest weaknesses".

Mahabir used the term *hypomania* to describe Williams's behaviour, suggesting that his personality disorder was of the "mild" variety, or cyclothymic. He nevertheless felt that while hypomania might be tolerable in the private sphere, it was a concern in a person who held public office. As he put it, "The fate of a country sometimes hinges upon one individual's aberrant impulses, or grossly abnormal interpretations of reality" (ibid., 68).[4] This is especially so when the leader is charismatic and his "vote is the only one that counts", or when the structure of the political order is fragile and unable to constrain dysfunctional behaviour.[5]

Another senior psychiatrist with whom the author discussed the Williams case at length, and who prefers to remain anonymous, emphatically disagreed that Williams's affliction was of the mild variety. He was of the view that too many people who knew the truth were trying to protect Williams, whom they regarded as a tribal icon with a national brand name. He urged the author to "tell the truth about Williams", that is, that he was often a sick man, exhibiting a classic case of bipolar disorder. Williams's high energy and verbose performances, especially during the Chaguaramas episode; his excessive irritability, narcissism, megalomania, grandiosity, paranoia (which was said to have been aggravated by his deafness); his pugnacity, aggression, arrogance, haughtiness, bluster, rudeness, pervasive suspiciousness and distrust of people, especially those who were once close to him; and his tolerance for and encouragement of sycophancy and news carrying – all were seen as symptoms of his illness, which would at times incapacitate him for months. Williams was also known to be an insomniac, to have an inflated sense of his self-importance, and to have delusions about being persecuted, all classic symptoms of the affliction. Correspondingly, when he was down, he was misanthropic, morose, indifferent or pessimistic, gloomy, lethargic, indecisive, impaired in judgement, and given to loss of energy, anger, desire for solitude (or alternatively, a craving for company), secrecy and social withdrawal.

Williams was understandably secretive about his health, and went to great lengths to conceal his illnesses from the public. Once, when he was in need of a blood transfusion, his doctors had to rig up an apparatus at his home to execute the procedure. Pity is deadly to a politician because no one wants to identify with the weak or infirm. Thus he could not let it be known that he was ill, or what is worse, a bit "crazy", especially given the viciousness of a society that has no tolerance for or understanding of "mad" people, whether scientist or politician. Such disclosure could in fact serve as a political death warrant.

While bipolar disorder can afflict persons of any age, it is brought on by age, and by a sense of hopelessness, failure or conflict that gives rise to stress and disorganization. It is also genetically transmitted. When one parent has a bipolar or cyclothymic disorder, the risk to an offspring is estimated to be 15 to 30 per cent. Affected persons are also susceptible to alcoholism and diabetes, afflictions from which Williams's mother reportedly suffered (Boodhoo 2001, 38). Thirty-six per cent of those who suffer from the malady have recurring thoughts of suicide or attempt it, while 15 per cent complete the effort.

There were reports within University of the West Indies medical circles that Williams was being treated by two senior psychiatrists, both of whom have since died. A member of that fraternity told the author that one of the said psychiatrists told him in confidence that he was due to take up a very senior appointment at the St Augustine branch of the university in order to minister to Williams. He recalled being surprised that this information had been shared with him. Close family members of the two doctors were unable to confirm that Williams had ever been a patient of either doctor. One spouse indicated, however, that her husband felt that Williams ought to have been his patient.

Some viewed as evidence of paranoia his installing one-way glass panes in his home in 1970 to prevent people in the Hilton Hotel and the grounds of his residence from peeping into his bedroom, as well as his increasing security measures to ensure his personal safety. His belief that the CIA was seeking to penetrate his household via his daughter or his friends was also seen as evidence of paranoia. Many an irascible outburst, policy reversal, cold shouldering of a former associate, extended silence or even his resignation from office in 1973 and return, and the strange manner of his death in 1981, are explained using this framework.[6]

When the author raised the question of Williams's mental health in June 2006 (*Trinidad Express*, 2 June 2006), Dr Courtenay Bartholomew gave a sharp rebuttal. Bartholomew, who was at one time one of Williams's doctors, insisted that no psychiatrist ever treated the prime minister. He also asserted that the claim that the prime minister was treated not by one, but by two psychiatrists was a "monstrous lie" that it was "ethically indiscreet to print publicly". Bartholomew conceded, however, that Williams "betrayed symptoms of paranoia, trusting no one and suspecting everyone". He also acknowledged that high blood sugars over his last two years or so would also have slowly and progressively altered his mental function (*Trinidad Express*, 4 June 2006).

Another psychiatrist, Dr Edward Moses, agreed with Bartholomew that it was unlikely that Williams ever saw a psychiatrist. He agreed too that Williams's strange behaviour could well be explained by a "developing encephalopathy caused by the underlying metabolic disturbance precipitated by his pathological blood sugars" (*Trinidad Express*, 6 June 2006). Both doctors denied that Williams was a depressive. Moses was emphatic that Williams did not "exhibit any gross evidence of a Manic Depressive Disorder".

The reaction of some of Williams's supporters to assertions that he was psychiatrically ill confirms that there remains a persistent view that Williams is an icon, and that it is *lèse majesté* to "insult" his memory. Some even claim that mortalizing Williams would aggravate the demoralization of the Afro-creole element currently in evidence in the society. Keith Subero, former news editor of the *Trinidad Express*, makes this point plaintively:

> This society needs what I call the fundamentals of Eric Williams's legacy to be institutionalized, for every day, one hears certain sections of our people crying desperately in their quest to find something "to manage this nation's soul". . . . Twenty years after Dr. Williams' death, they possess little knowledge of who he was; they have no understanding of his legacy; and worst, they have no serious frame of reference from which to interpret their present condition, or chart their future. (*Trinidad Express*, 26 June 2006)

Subero's complaint is that the emperor is either "dead" or "near death". If the former, he needs to be resurrected and mythologized. If the latter, he needs to be kept on life support. But those are not the tasks of this biographer.

Post and Robins (1993) remind us that sometimes there is need to seek explanations for seemingly irrational and unexplainable political behaviour in the discipline of abnormal psychiatry. Too often, we overlook the effects of illness and disability on leadership, and seek instead to find answers in terms of rational and impersonal social and structural forces.[7] The two authors identify several political leaders whose mental illness loaded the dice of "history" in particular ways. Among those said to have suffered from bipolar disorder are Lincoln, Viscount Castlereagh, Cromwell, Ludwig of Bararia, George III, Alexander the Great, Fidel Castro, Stalin, Menachem Begin, Hitler and Churchill, to name a few. The authors make the point that mania and depression, especially the latter, are not unusual occurrences and that they can be pharmacologically managed and used to advantage in certain contexts. As they write, "If full blown mania is inconsistent with sustained leadership performances, so called hypomanic behaviour is not. Indeed, many leaders who are seemingly endowed with extra-stores of energy will drive their assistants to the point of exhaustion. *This is usually not recognized as a clinical aberration and may go undetected*" (p. 50; emphasis added).

Williams certainly overworked his key assistants in the senior public service, many of whom were at their desks from 6 a.m. to 10 p.m., often sacrificing their health and families in the process. He may also have been driven by his emotional disturbance to campaign for Chaguaramas, constitutional reform, and independence with honour in the frenzied and dramatic manner in which he did. His behaviour might well have been creative overcompensation, a flight from and defence against depression. Activism replaced apathy. The emotional disorder was externalized. Like Menachem Begin ("I fight, therefore I am!"), he loved a good fight and fought to prove that he was alive, and because "letting them have it" gave him great satisfaction. The US consul general, Walter Orebaugh, an ex–CIA operative, reported to his superiors in Washington in 1959 that Williams was so preoccupied with the Chaguaramas issue that "it border[s] on mania". So concerned was he about the consequences of Williams's behaviour that he advised the secretary of state that "we cannot attack the problem on a piece meal basis. We must . . . decide upon a plan of action and then proceed [with] implementation. . . . We must disengage with Williams and work for his ultimate demise" (as cited in Palmer 2006, 112). Orebaugh sought to get the State Department to put in place a plan to get rid of Williams.

Post and Robins note that psychiatrically ill persons are often unsure about whom to trust, and may even turn against those who were their erstwhile confidants and supporters. Such individuals may become objects of suspicion and may be seen as disloyal. Williams was widely known to be distrustful and suspicious. This provoked many supporters to become sycophants who told him only what they thought he wished to hear for fear of his explosive wrath.[8] Some of the men around Williams were aware of his mood swings in a general way. Some were known to be "sorry" for him, and told the author so. A few others allegedly exploited his weakness and dependence and enriched themselves, knowing that he could not come after them without running the risk of exposure. In sum, he was a "captive king", trapped by his illness.

Winston Churchill's "Black Dog" metaphor provides a window that may help us to understand some of Williams's behaviour. Churchill suffered from depression, which he called his "Black Dog, a faithful companion, sometimes out of sight, but always returning". Churchill was, however, narcissistic and fought off his depression by convincing himself that he was chosen by history for some great role. What Richard Storr says of Churchill is relevant to Williams's "inward hunger", and the instrumental use that he made of this hunger in relation to the great struggles of the 1950s and 1960s:

> The grandiose self-concept and dreams of glory characteristically sail on a sea of insecurity. Indeed, the narcissistic leader, no matter how much success and acclaim he wins, is always vulnerable to setbacks and often prone to depression. No amount of praise can fill the inner void. . . . Old dreams never die. They don't even fade away. Had Churchill died in early 1939, at the age of sixty-five, he would have been considered a failure. As it was, fate and greatness did call him. He was able to say to his doctor and confidant, Lord Moran, near the beginning of World War II, "This cannot be accident, it must be design. I was kept for this job." Perhaps his very exalted self-concept and long and successful personal battle against depression made Churchill an ideal figure to lead Britain in a successful denial of its desperate condition and help his country win through to victory. It is probable that England owed her survival in 1940 to this inner world of make-believe. The kind of inspiration with which Churchill sustained the nation is not based on judgement, but on an irrational conviction independent of actual reality. Only a man convinced that he had a heroic mission, who believed that, in spite of all evidence to the contrary, he could yet triumph, and who could identify himself with a nation's destiny could have conveyed his inspiration to others. (As cited in Post and Robbins, 44)

Like Churchill, Williams was preoccupied with the judgement of "History", with what "History" would say.

It is important to emphasize that bipolar disorder is not a character flaw or a sign of personal weakness, and that many of the "great" men of history, especially artists, have been victims of the affliction. Indeed, some would argue that there is often a link between artistic creativity, dynamic leadership and mental disease, and that "madness is the price some men pay for greatness".[9] The Greeks believed that there was a correlation, if not a causal link, between artistic creativity, heroic or charismatic leadership, and mental illness, and gave currency to the concept of "divine" or "holy" madness. According to Plato, "He who approaches the temple of the muses without inspiration in the belief that crafts-manship alone suffices, will remain a bungler, and his presumptuous poetry will be obscured by the songs of the maniacs." In Plato's view, "craftsmanship" was necessary but not sufficient to achieve artistic excellence. Healthy, harmonious individuals could be creative, but their work is doomed to suffer from a certain "smell of ordinariness". Aristotle also believed that "great artists have all been sub-ject to melancholia". Thomas Mann agreed. "Great artists," he tells us, "are great invalids." Freidrich Nietzche too believed that suffering was necessary to creativ-ity and that disease enhanced "artistic capital". It awakened dormant talents and provided the spur and the surge of energy that incited genius.

If Williams was indeed bipolar, his political style would not have been the only affected activity. We have to assume that his scholarly activity would have been similarly influenced. Williams was known to have a phenomenal memory, rare powers of intellectual conceptualization, concentration and academic imagina-tion. Correspondingly, he was also inordinately vain and given to delusions of intellectual superiority. But few challenge his academic brilliance. Many have indeed adjudged his intellectual work as being that of a "genius" and not merely that of a skilled academic craftsman. The question to be asked and answered is whether this genius was in any way a by-product of his mental condition. As we have seen, in much of what Williams wrote there was a grandiosity of vision and a full-blown sense of historical mission, characteristics known to be associated with bipolar disorder. Williams the "charismatic scholar" envisioned himself as writing for the victims of slavery and colonialism, using his knowledge of the past to excoriate his "enemies" intellectually and emancipate his people politically. The transformative revolution that he envisaged, however, was not to be fought in the streets as had occurred in earlier periods of Caribbean history, but in the intel-lectual trenches of the University of Woodford Square and its constituent colleges. For him, the writing and teaching of history was not an intellectual pastime, but a burden that he felt had been imposed on him.

Williams himself tells us in *Inward Hunger* that he often sought solace in splen-did isolation from the rest of the society, and that, wearied and depressed by the challenges that the society was facing, "he turned off the lights downstairs, took the phone off the hook and repaired to the study upstairs, achieving peace at the price of sunlight, deliberately leaving the files in order to write as a private citizen, maintaining my sanity, and seeing the daily chores and strains in clearer perspec-tive" (1969, 343). Mystery remains as to whether Dr Williams committed "con-structive suicide", in that he stubbornly refused to medicate himself for a diabetic condition of which he had become aware. Notwithstanding the absence of con-clusive evidence, we believe that he was a disillusioned man, and that he had become suicidal and a victim of "Greek necessity", the belief that suicide was an "honourable way out of dishonour".

Plate 38 Williams greeting Indira Gandhi, prime minister of India, during state visit to Trinidad and Tobago. (Trinidad and Tobago Express Ltd)

Plate 39 Williams greeting Dean Rusk, US secretary of state. (Trinidad and Tobago Express Ltd)

Plate 40 Williams greeting Prince Philip and Queen Elizabeth, February 1966. Also pictured: Sir Solomon Hochoy, Lady Hochoy and Erica Williams. (Eric Williams Memorial Collection, University of the West Indies, St Augustine)

Figure 41 Williams welcoming Emperor Haile Selassie of Ethiopia. (Eric Williams Memorial Collection, University of the West Indies, St Augustine)

Figure 42 Williams at press conference with Muhammad Ali, 22 August 1971. (Trinidad and Tobago Express Ltd)

Figure 43 Williams with Andrew Young, US ambassador to the United Nations. (Eric Williams Memorial Collection, University of the West Indies, St Augustine)

Plate 44 Williams with Aldwyn Roberts, a.k.a. Lord Kitchener, and the Honourable Desmond Cartey. (Trinidad and Tobago Express Ltd)

Figure 45 Williams with Slinger Francisco, a.k.a. the Mighty Sparrow. (Trinidad and Tobago Express Ltd)

Plate 46 Williams with caypsonians Chalkdust, Pretender and Lord Blakie. (Eric Williams Memorial Collection, University of the West Indies, St Augustine)

Plate 47 Williams enjoying calypsos with Erica at a tent, January 1971. (Trinidad and Tobago Express Ltd)

46 Williams in the Balance

Universal History . . . is at bottom the History of Great Men. . . . They were the leaders of men; the modelers, patterns and in a wide sense creators, of whatsoever the general mass of men contrived to do or to attain.

— Thomas Carlyle

One only has to penetrate to the essence of any historical event, that is, to the activity of the mass of men who take part in it, to be convinced that the will of the historic hero does not control the actions of the mass but is itself controlled.

— Leo Tolstoy

Because it is apparently intolerable for men to admit the key role of accident, of ignorance, and of unplanned process in their affairs, the leader serves a vital function by personifying and reifying the processes. As an individual, he can be praised and blamed and given "responsibility" in a way that processes cannot. Incumbents of high public office therefore become objects of acclaim for the satisfied, scapegoats for the unsatisfied, and symbols of aspiration or of whatever is opposed.

— Murray Edelman

It remains for the author to offer his own assessment of the Williams legacy and also to try to make sense of the varied and contradictory narratives about the Williams phenomenon. Is there an explanatory key that unlocks and deconstructs these mysteries?

There is no question that Williams's achievements over the twenty-five years of his ministry were of "heroic" proportions. So too were his failures, some of which were tragic. Among his most outstanding achievements was the institutionalizing of two or at most three party politics in Trinidad and Tobago. Williams did not pioneer party politics, but his work gave coherence and order to the party universe where what obtained before was unrestrained individualism. Williams was also the true "father of the nation", notwithstanding that this accolade was challenged by a sizeable cluster of the population, particularly Hindus and whites. He was without challenge the founder of the state of Trinidad and Tobago. More than anyone else, he was responsible for rationalizing the ministerial system and the other bureaucratic structures and policies of the post-colonial state.

Williams also shaped the independence movement that others had inseminated. He gathered all the inchoate forces into one movement that could not be resisted. Williams must also be given a great deal of credit for the manner in which he handled the Colonial Office and the Chaguaramas crisis at a time when the Americans and the British were disinclined to negotiate with a state as insignificant as Trinidad and Tobago. Credit is also due for his mobilization of the population and the Caribbean on the issue without in the process being adventurist.

Of great and paramount importance was Williams's handling of public dissent, the judiciary and the media. In Trinidad and Tobago, unlike what obtained in many newly independent countries, few people were preventively detained outside the context of the events of 1970, and the media was never systematically muzzled. He also helped craft a liberal democratic tradition that has been substantially maintained, even though he was not averse to bending the rules when necessary. Williams also avoided some of the absurdities of Burnham in Guyana, Gairy in Grenada, the Birds in Antigua, Nkrumah in Ghana, and the caudilloism that was evident in Cuba, Haiti, and Latin America generally. He also gave socialism and one-partyism wide berths.

Williams deserves credit too for his pioneering efforts in giving women a central role in the political process at the executive level and his revolutionary efforts in opening up the educational system to all, notwithstanding the incompleteness and downsides of the transformation that he sought to put in place. On the credit side of the ledger one also has to place the heroic achievement of Point Lisas and the national energy sector. His vision and will were largely responsible for the fact that Trinidad and Tobago could boast that brown sugar gave way to iron, steel, urea, methanol and other petrochemicals.

On the negative side, the author's judgement is that Williams mishandled the federal negotiations, even though he was not primarily responsible for the collapse of the experiment. Perhaps everyone underestimated how difficult the task was. He was also not sufficiently inclusive in his handling of independence. On this issue there could and should have been far more consultation with the national community's ethnic minorities. His approach to governance and the parliamentary opposition was also much too unilateral, monopolistic and arrogant. He was the "boss", having won election after election and thus license to govern. There was no need to share power, only to explain to his supporters why he chose this or that option. He expected no dog to bark once he had spoken.

His assimilationist approach to the Indian question was also flawed, even though it was perhaps understandable. Williams did not appreciate that Indians were a people with deeply embedded traditions that they wished to maintain. He saw those traditions as obscurantist and transient, and assumed that they would in time disappear unless they were aggravated by recalcitrant and opportunistic elements within the Indian community. Thus his unfortunate outburst following the federal elections of 1958.

Williams's handling of the non-energy sector of the economy and the labour movement was less than successful, but as we have seen, many systemic factors were beyond his control. One was the nature of Trinidad creole society, which, given its excessive individualism, its rebelliousness and its lackadaisical disposition, was not easy to militarize as was possible in Singapore and South Korea. Williams attempted to impose a measure of discipline in 1965 with the passage of the Industrial Stabilization Act, but that discipline was not sustained. Tired and disillusioned as he eventually became, he never seriously sought to fashion a developmental model with the entrepreneur as cultural hero. Instead, the hero became the person who received rewards by "getting away" with doing little or nothing for a guaranteed wage. By default, the "dewd" (taken from the acronym DEWD used to label the Development and Environmental Works Division, the agency put in place to relieve urban unemployment, and responsible for managing temporary work projects), and the "smartman" became the informal cultural heroes. There was of course a great deal of rhetoric about discipline and the need for saving and production, but no one took the leadership seriously because the leadership itself was not exemplary. Williams followed the people rather than making any serious attempt to lead them. Quite simply, the population was allowed to "play mas".

Part of Williams's dilemma may have been his belief in the need to balance the requirements of discipline, which transformation involves, with the requirements of freedom. The problem was to determine how much compulsion was proper within the basic framework of freedom, and the extent to which post-colonial leadership should give in to the demands for egalitarianism and social welfare that were stimulated during the independence movement but that were beyond the state's economic resources. Lee Kwan Yew of Singapore erred on the side of limiting freedom and postponing consumption and succeeded in transforming Singapore into a productive mini-state that is today the envy of many. Williams chose the other side of freedom. Williams met a society that was dependence-oriented and left that society largely as he found it – as one in which the people looked to the state for rewards and "pay-offs" rather than one in which the pay-off came as a result of individual or family entrepreneurship. In the long run, the Afro-Trinidadian population, which was the most favoured recipient of state patronage, suffered most. The culture of dependence that had developed on the plantation remained deeply entrenched. The society is now feeling the effects.

One must also put on the negative side the fact that Williams's PNM failed to create a society in which morality and probity in public life prevailed. In these areas, there was no positive development. To be sure, compared to Africa, Asia and Latin America, there was not a great deal of corruption, but there was enough of it to indicate that Williams had not succeeded in immunizing his party and government from the virus that consumed society, especially in the 1970s when capitalism, both in the private and the state sector, went mad, and "money was no longer the problem". Williams was, if anything, too relaxed about the problem, preferring to keep his party intact rather than purge delinquents. He knew what was going on, but chose to evade the issue. His explanation was that his supporters had betrayed him but that he would forgive their sins. Many gave him the benefit of the doubt, but a hard core insisted that if one were to connect the dots without blinkers, the evidence that Williams was not a passive victim is too compelling to ignore or overlook.

In terms of his skill as a political manager, Williams was a failure. The government over which he presided for twenty-five years was weak and ineffective. Williams was extremely competent as a protest politician and his skills were well suited to that type of activity. He had the capacity to energize people for the tasks associated with winning self-government and independence. It was, however, more difficult for him to change gears and to manage the society over which he gained control. He could wrest the naval base at Chaguaramas from the Americans, for example, but did little to effect his promised policies to develop the area. He could protest against the colonial orientation of the educational system. Yet he found it difficult to transform the school system along the lines that he had so brilliantly identified. Numerous examples illustrate that while Williams was gifted as a conceptualizer and popularizer of ideas, he was a poor manager of men and institutions. The formal powers were there, but the potential lay untapped. Because of his inability to delegate real responsibility, and an extravagant belief in his own rectitude and competence, decision making was centralized either in his person or in institutions that fettered the hands of subordinates. Regulatory bodies also paralysed initiative at the very top.

Instead of pursuing deregulation and reform, Williams attempted bypass surgery to circumvent government's blocked arteries. He created parallel structures to short-circuit the offending ones. These bodies became in effect a substitute for structural bureaucratic reform. It was a cheap way, in the short run, of avoiding confrontation with the numerous and powerful vested interests that had grown up over the years within the interstices of the bureaucracy and that had come to acquire real power to abort executive will. Yet sabotage was not deliberate or conscious, as Williams seemed to believe in his moments of frustration or pique. The body politic had become comatose, but this was due mainly to institutional inertia. Despite occasional bursts of energy, Williams was rarely able to generate the sustained effort needed to see to it that policy, when decided in cabinet or elsewhere, was pushed through the legislative pipeline and implemented within a reasonable period of time. The system lacked coordination and propulsion, and eventually he seemed to lose interest in energizing it, in part because of illness. The only time things got done was when trade union groups or private sector interests became frustrated after relying on the "usual channels" and adopted unconventional strategies to advertise their grievances in an attempt to jump the queue or derail the policy altogether by changing the arena in which the matter was resolved. They brought other resources to bear on the issue in the hope of forcing it onto the decision makers' agenda. Williams's party thus had to abandon planning and rational decision making as the system lurched from crisis to crisis. Crisis management is the hallmark of a weak, not a strong government.

Though Williams's temperament and skills were unsuited for the tasks of routine management, he ranks high as a crisis manager. And whatever the lens through which we choose to view him – whether straight, prismatic or crooked – he left Trinidad and Tobago better than he found it in 1956, leaving indelible footprints on our landscape. The "hero" had many-splendoured visions, but could not complete all the tasks he assigned himself. And so, Williams was not Plato's mythical, unblemished philosopher king. He was challenged in many ways. On balance, however, his performance was worthy of History's applause.

Notes

Chapter 1

1. In the unpublished pages of his autobiography, Williams tells us that he was not born on 12 October as his birth certificate indicates, but eighteen days earlier. A smallpox epidemic was raging at the time, and stern measures were being taken to enforce vaccination. The midwife and his parents conspired to conceal his birth to avoid having to have him vaccinated, a prophylactic that many parents dreaded. It is to be noted that Williams's birth certificate states that he was born at 16 Dundonald Street and not on Oxford Street as he claims.

   Early drafts of *Inward Hunger* are to be found among Williams's papers in the Eric Williams Memorial Collection, housed at the University of the West Indies, St Augustine, Trinidad and Tobago (EWMC folio 139). These drafts tells us more about Williams's private thoughts and motivations than we learn from *Inward Hunger*, which is more of a manifesto than an autobiography.

2. Williams's family tree is reproduced in *The Book of Trinidad* (Besson and Brereton 1992, 421). The editors describe Williams as "the greatest figure in Trinidad and Tobago's 20th century history . . . the natural inheritor of the best elements of the black and coloured intelligentsia whose traditions date from the Cedula of Population of 1783".

3. In his major study of the Boissière family, Michael Pocock, also a member of that family and thus a relative of Williams, opines that it was not politic for Williams to openly acknowledge kinship with a French-creole family, particularly one that, in conformance with the customs of those days, had ignored the relationship. However, Williams did eventually recognize it. "In his *History of the People of Trinidad and Tobago*, apart from A.A. Cipriani, the champion of the 'barefoot' masses between the two wars, whom he could hardly have excluded, he makes no mention of the considerable role by the white French families in the history of Trinidad. In a work about the island purporting to be a history of its people, this is a major omission and distortion, an illustration of the bias in his writings, referred to above. However, there is one notable exception. In both his *History of the People of Trinidad and Tobago*, and his

monumental history of the Caribbean as a whole, *From Columbus to Castro* . . . he quotes, approvingly, his great-great-uncle, Dr J.V. de Boissière. In 1890, Dr de Boissière spoke in the legislative council against the semi-servitude of the indentured system; in 1897 he opposed the union of Tobago with Trinidad, and in 1893 he spoke against a contribution by Trinidad and Tobago to compensate the latter for the loss of customs revenues. No mention is made of other French [creole] members of the council, particularly Dr L.A.A. de Verteuil. The two doctors served together in the legislative council for nearly thirty years, and there can be no doubt but that Dr de Verteuil overshadowed Dr de Boissière, being the champion of the inhabitants of non-British stock for over half a century. Without detracting from Dr de Boissière's merits, it is tempting to conclude that these approbations of him are yet another of Eric Williams's self-advertisements" (Pocock 1993, 235). One wonders whether Williams would really have wished to advertise his family link to the de Boissières, about which he most certainly would have known. "Williams was ambivalent about the French Creoles. He wanted their political support, but could not ignore the fact that his family had been humiliated by the white members of the Boissière clan who did not acknowledge those who were coloured. As we shall see, this bitterness would become manifest in 1960–1 when Williams declared 'Massa Day Done'. Ironically, Williams would be accused of liking black people in the abstract but not in the flesh. His preference for Chinese women as spouses and of the group in general as social friends is seen as confirming evidence of his alleged Afrophobia."

Williams was also hostile to the "Black French Creoles", those who were not "victims of the Will". As he said in *Negro in the Caribbean*, "This intermediate caste in slave society despised the black side of its ancestry. The mulatto woman preferred to be the mistress of a white man than to marry a black. Like the similar group in New Orleans and Charleston, they occupied a privileged position before emancipation. With the prestige of white blood in their veins, they refused to do laboring work. They despised the 'no-good niggers', and where, as in some cases, they themselves owned slaves, they were as vicious and tyrannical as the poor whites. Some few, educated by an indulgent white father, eventually became owners of land; others, more numerous, settled in the urban areas and became artisans, small clerks, etc. They formed the humble beginnings of the colored and black middle class in the Caribbean" (1942, 58).

4. Williams would later recall his own experience as he reflected on the emotional impact of poverty on young school children. As he told a public meeting dealing with reform of the school system in 1965, "You don't attack the beneficiaries of the secondary education by making it impossible for underprivileged parents, less well-off parents, to dress the child so that it doesn't feel ashamed in respect of the other children in the school. And this uniform is a new thing. In my day they didn't have it. About the only uniform that I used to have as a boy at the secondary school was when the whole family was catching hell, and I didn't have any clothes, all they had to do was take one of my father's old pants, cut it down and put it on me, that is all, and I had to go. (Laughter) What are you laughing at? A lot of you were in the same positions in your day (loud laughter) and you had to run around the place. They called me a lot of names in my school days, but the one which I remember was the time that I used to walk about with a pair of the cut down trousers from my father and as I walked about

the boys just used to say (you know how harsh we can be to our own people), the boys used to say 'homespun'." Eric's sisters, however, claim that as the firstborn, he did not have to wear "hand me downs". They probably forgot that he at times had to wear his father's trousers. Williams himself tells us how the problem arose. "Nature assisted the manipulations of the family budget in my case. As I was small, the long trousers could more easily be postponed. But only for a time. If size did not betray, age did, and age could not long be concealed. Hard calves were in boys' eyes as powerful an argument for long trousers as long legs, and my legs, though short, were well developed."

5. It was also important to Williams's parents whom he and his siblings chose as their friends and potential mates. As he tells us, "My parents showed satisfaction with my first choice of girl friend shortly before leaving for England – the daughter of a prominent coloured professional family with important political status was as great as their disappointment with her substitute – the daughter of a retired school teacher, without education herself or means. They were very old fashioned in their outlook as to parental consent and to approval of a match. My father forbade me to see her. When I refused, they missed no opportunity during my absence to indicate to her how they felt about the match. My father (*patria potestas*) forbade the persona non grata access to the house. They were delighted with my marriage to a woman whose English education, personal means, and family good hair compensated for her humble antecedents."

"My first wife, whose humble antecedents were compensated for by a rich Portugese father, an education in England, and an income of her own, met decidedly with their (my parents')approval. But my father died before our divorce, and I am in no position to say what his attitude would have been to my subsequent marriage to a girl whose sole qualifications were a poor Chinese father, a native intelligence unspoilt by a university education, and a character uncorrupted by a private income. My mother's opinion I never sought" (EWMC folio 139). Williams does not tell us that his first marriage was kept a secret even from one of his boyhood friend, Halsey McShine.

Following Williams death, McShine gave his own account of Williams three marriages. According to him, Williams's first wife was Elsie Ribeiro, whom he married clandestinely in London. The relationship between them became strained, and they were eventually "divorced", though not properly in the eyes of US law. Williams was by all accounts fond of his son by Elsie, but had problems with his first daughter, whose mind was said to have been poisoned by what her mother said about him. Asked to indicate why the marriage failed, McShine opined that Williams was "such an intense academic person that it [the marriage] would have failed with most women". Williams loved his second wife, Soy Moyou, a secretary attached to the Anglo-American Caribbean Commission, but Soy died some three years after their marriage from haemoptysis, an affliction that manifests itself in the coughing up of blood. Erica, Williams's daughter, was two years old when her mother died. Williams became Erica's doting and caring "mother" and loving father.

Williams's third wife was Mayleen Mooksang, a Guyanese dentist with whom he never lived. According to McShine, when Mooksang told Williams that she was pregnant, he felt honour bound to marry her, notwithstanding the urgings of McShine that he should first determine whether she was really pregnant and by whom; missing one's period did not necessarily mean that one was pregnant. But as Williams told McShine,

"I can't take that shame, and I will marry her. After the marriage, I don't want to see her again" (OREP interview with Halsey McShine, February 1991).

Following Williams's death, legal controversy surrounded the question as to whether he was legally married when he died or whether he was a bigamist. His solicitor and one of the executors of his will, Inskip Julien, claimed that he was never properly divorced from Elsie, since he was not a legal resident of the United States when he divorced her in Nevada in 1950 and remarried Soy Moyou. Given this, Julien argued that his gratuity and pension should go to his daughter, Erica, and not to Dr Mooksang. The matter was later settled out of court; the state agreed to pay Dr Mooksang a pension of TT$50,000 per year and TT$637,000 in arrears (Boodhoo 2001, 250).

6. Williams recalled how his father sneered when T.M. Marryshow, his father's friend, asked him what he wanted to do when he grew up. Williams's reply was "a policeman". This provoked "general laughter" and a reprimand from his father, who told him gravely, "Don't be a damn fool."

7. Henry Williams, however, accompanied Eric to Oxford. It was his first vacation outside of Trinidad and Tobago. When he next saw Eric in 1944, the latter had earned a doctorate in philosophy. His father's comment was, "So, you are a doctor after all!" Williams did not see his father after their meeting in 1944. As Halsey McShine tells us, "His father was very ill, and I wrote Eric and told him to please come to see his father. But, Eric said he was so busy, he would not be able to come for three weeks. I tried to keep him alive for those three weeks until Eric could get there. On the day Eric was to come, I told his father, but he died one hour before Eric arrived. He was very sorry he could not come before" (interview with Bridget Brereton and Margaret Rouse-Jones, 22 February 1991).

8. Williams's study habits for the Island Scholarship had served him well at Oxford. As he tells us, "I worked steadily through the entire period . . . and in the excessively long vacations. . . . I made it my practice to spend three weeks at Christmas, three at Easter, six in the summer at Oxford which was at those times almost like a dead city, reading steadily in my rooms and in the college and university libraries" (EWMC folio 139).

9. Williams was a member of the Oxford cricket team and also a "Centaur" in a society for "near soccer blues". James tells us that crowds used to follow him around Oxford to see him play for his college.

10. Told to the author by fellow Oxonian Michael de la Bastide, chief justice of the Caribbean Court of Justice and former chief justice of Trinidad and Tobago, to whom the account of Williams's experience at All Souls was related.

Chapter 2

1. The author visited Howard University in 1960 and met with Frazier and several of Williams's colleagues who were still on the staff of Howard. Frazier, who was dean of the Faculty of Social Sciences, was particularly forthcoming about his regard for Williams's academic accomplishments. He and Williams co-edited *The Economic Future of the Caribbean* (1944), proceedings of a conference held in 1943 that brought together scholars, diplomats and advocates of democracy, self-government, and the

economic development of the Caribbean. This book was republished in 2004. John Hope Franklin was also impressed with Williams's capacity for research and his dedication to his work. He was thus not surprised when the president of the university, Mordecai Johnson, offered Williams a full professorship in 1945 (Williams was then only an assistant professor), "an offer which it is unlikely that he would have offered to any other member of the faculty" (Franklin 1999, 26).

2. Williams was unequivocal, however, about James's book *The Black Jacobins*. As he said in his review of books written on slavery between 1926 and 1942, "This section on Caribbean Slavery can fittingly be closed by consideration of what is undoubtedly the most interesting book in the whole field of slavery" (EWMC folio 129).

3. James was proud of Williams's work on *Capitalism and Slavery*. As he wrote to Constance Webb, his second wife, in 1944, "I have a son, you know. He is thirty years old. I watch over him like a trainer and prize fighter. Of course, he is not my son, really. He is a young West Indian, a scholar of repute who wrote a superb thesis at Oxford for his doctorate — 'The Economic Basis of the Slave Trade and Slavery'. For nearly 12 years now, I have watched him come along. He sometimes is very thoughtless and selfish. But I don't mind. Seeing him develop pleases me" (as cited in Cudjoe 1993, 72).

4. Williams's book has been compared to Charles Beard's *Economic Interpretation of the Constitution of the United States* (1956) in that it recognizes the primacy of the economic factor, but avoids going as far as Marxists do in claiming that the economic struggle between classes can be resolved only by the elimination of classes.

5. Drescher reportedly sent Williams a copy of his book *Econocide* in 1977. To Drescher's regret, Williams chose to ignore the gesture. Drescher had hoped to engage Williams in debate on his version of the facts.

6. For further reading see, among others, Darity (1997), Inikori (2000), Cateau and Carrington (2000), and Solow and Engerman (1987).

7. Williams sent a copy to his "darling daughter" Erica, with the following inscription: "Written in a few days to commemorate the independence of our country. You will like this and appreciate the political effort, associated particularly with me, to give dignity and perspective to a backward colonial country."

8. Williams himself expressed the hope that he would find the time to write the national histories of at least five other Caribbean territories: Barbados, Jamaica, British Guiana and either Martinique or Guadeloupe. "To this assignment, he [the author] proposes to dedicate himself in the next few months; if only as a hobby, if only to get out of his system some of the poison which is perhaps unnecessarily imbibed in political activity in countries which have learned too well the lessons of colonialism" (1962a).

9. Lamming correctly observed that "the Senior Caribbean historian neither had nor encouraged any collaborative contact with the younger generation of Caribbean historians who had been profoundly influenced by his initiatives. The continuity he advocated was in fact made unworkable by his own tendency of sullen withdrawal" (1998, 8).

10. Lamming is more generous in his speculation that *From Columbus to Castro* was part of the five-volume *History of the Caribbean* that Williams had long planned. "The series never got beyond Volume I [1492–1655], and I suspect that the pressures of active politics had now made impossible the meticulous organization of the material that makes

Volume I a work of such compelling fascination. I believe, Williams in these circumstances, decided to collapse all the remaining documents into a different kind of narrative which became *From Columbus to Castro*" (1998, 10).

Williams indicated to John Humphrey, who designed the cover for volume 1, that he was not happy with the final chapter of the book and that he planned to rewrite it. He felt he had not done justice to the Cuban revolution (Humphrey 1991).

11. It was an open secret that Williams used the National Archives as if it were his own library and that much was borrowed and not returned while he lived. When asked by John Humphrey why he had not returned them, Williams replied that the books would be better cared for in his home than in the library (Humphrey 1991).

12. James, who did much to create a personality cult around Williams, described Williams's personality as an "historical accident". "And yet, in the Hegelian dialect, the organic movement proceeds by way of accidents and the sum of accidents constitutes the organic movement" (Cudjoe 1993, 349).

13. Thucydides had the following to say about the difference between the poet, the philosopher and the scientist: "In medicine one must pay attention not to plausible theorizing ('logismos'), but to experience and reason ('logos') together . . . I agree that theorizing is to be approved, provided that it is based on facts, and systematically makes its deductions from what is observed. . . . But conclusions drawn by the unaided reason can hardly be serviceable; only those drawn from observed fact."

14. One must take note of the evidence that Williams's political speeches drew not only on research that he had conducted before entering politics, but also on new material that he consulted while in office. Williams often asked Trinidad ambassadors stationed in Europe and elsewhere to purchase or secure books for him. He also used members of the foreign corps stationed in Trinidad and Tobago to do the same. In a sense, he never gave up being a scholar politician. He worked hard at both.

Chapter 4

1. Williams met Manley when the latter came to Howard to receive an honorary degree circa 1944. According to James, Manley became a member of the Caribbean Commission, and many of the projects introduced into the commission by Williams were discussed in advance with Manley. That Williams was able to stay so long there was because of the support given him by Manley and the Puerto Ricans. And if Manley had won the 1949 elections, either the whole Caribbean Commission would have been reorganized or Williams would have left the commission to go to work with Manley in his planning department (James 1993, 344).

2. It appears that even before Williams was formally dismissed from the commission, he paid a visit to Norman Manley in Jamaica to discuss his political future. Manley had earlier won the general elections in 1955. According to P.J. Patterson (former prime minister of Jamaica), who was then chairman of the External Affairs Commission of the Student Guild of the University of the West Indies, Williams told the students that he planned to found a political party. Patterson's account of Williams's return to Trinidad, which he gave while delivering the Eric Williams Memorial Lecture in 2006, is as follows: "History will attest that it was at a meeting in 1955 when as Guild

Chairman of the External Affairs Commission, I presided over a lecture he delivered in Arts Lecture Room 3 where Dr. Eric Williams announced for the first time on Caribbean soil, his intention to get back to Trinidad, to create the PNM and to embark on his long and illustrious political career. He had resigned one week before from the Anglo-American Caribbean Commission located in Puerto Rico and decided to return home via Jamaica in order to meet with Norman Manley who had won the Elections in Jamaica earlier that year.

"I vividly recall the spellbinding eloquence and erudite analysis from this celebrated Caribbean thinker and visionary to an audience which mesmerized an overflow crowd, consisting virtually of every student and lecturer on the entire Campus. The good Doctor was obviously comfortable – (without the benefit of a single note) – and at his inspirational best. He asserted that the best prospects for the transformation of Caribbean society were to be found in changing the mindset and expanding the mental and psychological horizons of the young. His closing words still resound in my ears. 'I shall return to my homeland for the awakening and upliftment of my people and to rid the country at once and forever of political rascality and corruption.' Ladies and gentlemen, the rest is history." This sequence of events does not square with what Williams and others say, but it does appear that Williams knew he would not be made secretary general and that he had publicly indicated that he would resign if this in fact occurred. This statement was made in Jamaica before anything was said in Trinidad.

3. For details of Williams's divorce and remarriage to Soy Moyou, see Boodhoo 2001, 140–44.

4. Selwyn Cudjoe has made the important point that Williams's sharp tongue and use of language, and especially the local vernacular, was important in terms of how effectively he communicated with his listeners. "In a land where picong was king, Williams, versed in this art form, proved to be one of the reigning monarch; it was his use of metaphorically rich and vividly revealing language that led to the almost mythical status Williams assumed in the society." Williams, he notes, was also good at "gallerying", Trinidad slang for "showing off" (1993, 40–41).

Chapter 7

1. It would appear that Williams had planned to launch the party earlier, but the postponement of the launch allowed him to take part in a 13 October 1955 Conference of the International Confederation of Free Trade Unions in Geneva. Williams attended the conference and held discussions in London with C.L.R. James and George Padmore about plans for the new party. Following his return from London, Williams addressed a University of Woodford Square meeting, held on 5 January 1956. The meeting was told that the programme and the constitution of the party were nearing completion and that an appeal for funds would soon be made. Williams likewise revealed that plans were being made to establish a newspaper. He also told the crowd that he would reject the new constitution that the legislature had approved, and that he was opposed to having the University College of the West Indies run by the University of London, "which discriminated against West Indians in favour of Europeans in the allocation of faculty positions" (Baptiste 2005, 28).

2. The membership of the conference was geographically skewed. One hundred and ten members came from Port of Spain, 18 from Laventille, 18 from St George West, 27 from St Joseph, 7 from Tunapuna, 2 from St George East, 3 from the Eastern Counties, 2 from North Caroni, 2 from South Caroni, 20 from San Fernando, 6 from Pointe-a-Pierre, 1 from St Patrick East, 8 from St Patrick West and 6 from Tobago. No constituency address was given for two delegates.

3. A decision had been made to invite three foreigners, two from Jamaica's People's National Party and one from the Caribbean Area Division of the International Confederation of Free Trade Unions.

4. The other persons elected to office were Ibbit Mosaheb, vice chairman, W.J. Alexander, second vice chairman, Isabel Teshea, lady vice chairman, Donald Granado, general secretary, Kamal Mohammed, assistant general secretary, A.N.R. Robinson, treasurer, D.W. Rogers, education secretary, Sam Worrell, labour relations secretary, and Andrew Carr, public relations secretary and dean of the University of Woodford Square.

   The inaugural general council consisted of twenty-six members: L. Amourer, H. Baptiste, I. Teshea, W.J. Alexander, M. Pierre, S. Worrell, C. Payne, A. Rose, E. Namsoo, A. Carr, H. Maurice, A. Lewis, S. Dolsingh, J. Christopher, J. Antoine, O. Mohammed, K. Mohammed, L. Lovell, H. Dupres, A. St. Hill, E. Pigott, U. Lee, J. Hackshaw, D.W. Rogers, E. Williams, and L. Constantine.

Chapter 9

1. As the manifesto declared explicitly, "We will repel and resist Communism, whether it comes openly or whether it comes, as it often does, with tricks and the deception of high sounding ideals. . . . We do not want any influence by Moscow in our country . . . and we brand as traitors all those who seek to establish that influence."

2. Maraj sought to disguise this reality by inviting several other non-Hindu politicians, Butler included, to join the PDP. The feint was not very successful, though some were bought.

3. Maraj made a great deal of money buying and selling used supplies from the United States Base at Chaguaramas. It would appear that many of these transactions were not above board and involved bribing a US official. The matter was not pursued in order to avoid embarrassment, but the United States did not want Maraj to succeed electorally. (See Baptiste 2005, 17.)

Chapter 10

1. Stollmeyer's co-ethnics were not amused and brought pressure on him to discontinue his relationship with Eric Williams. One of his legal colleagues, Joseph Kelshall, told him in a letter written in July 1955 that he was "horrified to learn that you have associated yourself with that 'drip' Eric Williams. Our clients, Joseph Fernandez and George de Nobriga and Company have very definite views about his activities. Unless you hasten to pull out of that mess, Tim Kelshall and Company are likely to suffer a serious set back. I trust that you will give the matter the most serious consideration and

take prompt steps to let it be known that you are no longer interested in Master Williams' activities."

2. It is not true that the Americans were officially hostile to the PNM. The reverse was in fact the case. There were rumours that Williams had acquired American citizenship while employed at Howard University. The consul inquired of the State Department whether this was so, and was assured that it was not. The State Department was also concerned that Williams might be subject to legal harassment if he sought to enter the United States. Williams had not been paying a court-ordered wife and child maintenance order. The State Department was anxious to ensure that Williams be treated with "respect and deference" since to do otherwise might push him into a position of consistent anti-Americanism. "The Latin American desk of the State Department was thus urged to initiate action to ensure that when Williams had occasion to visit the United States, the Court orders against him would not be operative and that he would be immune from either harassment or arrest therefrom" (as cited in Baptiste 2005, 33).

3. This shout came from the lips of the late Errol Hill, one of Trinidad's most renowned playwrights.

Chapter 12

1. See the recollections of PNM activist Ferdie Ferreira in "The Baptism of a Leader", *Newsday*, 15 November 1998. Ferreira recalled the vicious attacks that were trained on Williams from the media, the Chamber of Commerce, the Christian and non-Christian religions and certain foreign missions. Williams's private business relating to his clandestine marriage to Dr Mayleen Mooksang was relentlessly exposed, as were the problems that he was then having with his first wife in the United States, whom he had divorced in Reno, Nevada, and to whom maintenance payments for her and her children and alimony were legally due.

Chapter 13

1. In the local government elections of 1957, the party won every seat but that of Port of Spain North in which many French creoles lived. Williams was disappointed by this particular loss, but praised the winning candidate, Louis Rostant, for his valiant fight. However, he warned the French creoles, whom he called a "recalcitrant minority", that PNM bulldozers would be coming into the hills to capture that seat.

Chapter 16

1. Some American spokesmen had threatened to "gouge" the base if the Americans were forced out of Chaguaramas. Williams accused the British and the Americans of wanting to deprive him of the political credit of settling the Chaguaramas issue.

Chapter 17

1. Lloyd Best recalled a conversation with Arthur Lewis during a conference in Grenada: "Sir Arthur sat next to me. We began by bad-talking Dr. Eric Williams in copious fashion as the one who had broken up the Federation" (Best 2004). Williams, however,

sought to place blame for the collapse on foreign forces, mainly the British, whom he said saw the federation as a mere vehicle to escape their responsibilities in the region.

Chapter 18

1. Dodderidge Alleyne, a close associate of Williams in these years, suggested that this remark was not entirely original. The exchange at the Institute of Social and Economic Research symposium went as follows:

   Alleyne: I put it to you that while the public utterance would have been Dr. Williams, it may have been like Molière who said, "I take my material wherever I find it. I say no more than that."
   Dr Ryan: Dodd, I was told that that statement, "one from ten leaves nought", somebody else made it and he took it.
   Alleyne: This is what I am telling you. (Laughter)

   Sir Ellis Clarke, whose legal advice to Williams prompted the remark, argued that the federal constitution was the by-product of a British statute and that ten states were involved. Clarke told the Colonial Office that the departure of Jamaica rendered the statute null and void, and that it would either have to be amended, or new legislation enacted. Clarke indicated that he wished he had made the comment himself, but unhesitatingly credited the remark to Williams (interview with Sir Ellis Clarke on 16 November 2005).

2. One recalls that in the document, *The Economics of Nationhood*, it was stated that: "In furtherance of the spirit and objectives of Federation, Trinidad and Tobago has sought by unilateral action to give full effect to the idea of freedom of movement of persons within the Federation even before the period stipulated in the Federal Constitution."

Chapter 19

1. Dr Patrick Solomon also admitted that the PNM had the benefit of being advised by "two qualified land surveyors who were party members. The whole [thing] was as masterly a piece of work as could be expected." Solomon also criticized Maraj for the "slipshod" work that he did, and for his assumption that the PNM would "agree to divide up the spoils" (Solomon 1981, 189). Winston Mahabir was also of the view that "the delimitation of constituency boundaries, endorsed by the Opposition, was a knock out punch, scientifically administered long before election day". The DLP, he averred, "was not robbed by voting machines. By show of hands or voting by satellite, we would have won in 1961" (1978, 142).

2. According to Williams, "They carved [them] up like a fowl. They stole the fowl. They just played ordinary fowl thief" (1969, 254).

Chapter 21

1. Seventeen persons from Trinidad and Tobago went to the Marlborough House Conference: Eric Williams, Ellis Clarke, Wilfred Alexander, George Richards and Owen Mathurin on the PNM side, and on the DLP side, Rudranath Capildeo, Lionel

Seukeran, Peter Farquahar, Mitra and Ashford Sinanan and Tajmool Hosein, the main legal guru of the opposition. The meetings were chaired initially by Ian McLeod, but were concluded with Reginald Maudling in the chair.

Chapter 23

1. Norman Manley had warned Williams about the possible consequences of the party's quick success. As he told him and the party at its second annual convention, "It is very nice to win first time out, but it creates special problems of its own. . . . I have been in politics for 20 years, I know a little about [the problems] of holding a party together." Manley stressed the importance of discipline and loyalty which he said "must be put in front of everything else as a goal that you will never give up, no matter what happens". Manley noted it was impossible to satisfy everyone in a political party. "Grievances galore exist in every relationship, especially in a political party, more so in fact than in any other organization." People often feel ill used. "Politics, after all, has always got to do with what somebody gets out of something." Manley also agreed with Williams that parties in new states had to treat the problem of discipline and loyalty differently from those in more mature democracies in which democratic institutions were more widely and deeply rooted (EWMC folio 644).

2. There has been some controversy as to who was the author of *Perspectives*. Williams claimed it as his work, but James insists that he was the ghost author as he was of so many other papers that we ascribe to Williams. James claims that two months after he returned to Trinidad and Tobago in 1958, he addressed the PNM's general council and used as a basis for his remarks a paper that he had prepared for Williams on the subject of the party's needs. According to James, Williams took notes furiously as was his custom. "Bill should be a permanent secretary! He takes so much notes!" James claims that Williams regurgitated the notes "almost word for word in his address to the third annual convention in October 1958" (see James 1962, 14; James made similar claims in conversation with the author).

Chapter 24

1. Among the leading contributors to the debate as to what options should be pursued by the new Caribbean states were – in addition to Lloyd Best – C.L.R. James, James Millette, Adrian Espinet, Elsa Goveia, Edwin Carrington, George Beckford, Norman Girvan, Orlando Patterson, Havelock Brewster, William Demas, Clive Thomas, Roy Augier, George Lamming, Owen Jefferson, Steve de Castro, Alister McIntyre, Kari Levitt, Syl Lowhar, Archie Singham, and the author. (See Jefferson and Girvan 1971.)

2. The term *doctor politics* was initially used to describe one of Best's New World collaborators, Dr James Millette, and not Dr Williams. (See "Picton to Panday: Doctor Politics in Trinidad and Tobago", in Ryan 2003b; and Ryan 2003a.)

3. The term "cuckoo politics" was coined by Archie Singham (1965) to describe the sort of "ornamental" politics that leaders of Third World societies were forced to engage in because they did not control the real levers of economic and political power. "They thus become more concerned to observe constitutional proprieties than to practice

meaningful politics." The concept was patterned on the behaviour of the cuckoo bird in a clock that merely announced the passage of time without having any other functional use. See Singham (1965)

Chapter 25

1. The author was advised confidentially that Williams went so far as to cause James to be harassed for non-payment of income taxes.

2. For a trenchant reply to James's pamphlet, see Singh 1965.

3. The WFP was preceded by the Political Action Committee, which was formed to fight against the Industrial Stabilization Act, seen as a mechanism to prevent the mixing of oil and sugar.

4. C.L.R. James got 274 votes, George Weekes 471, Jack Kelshall 122, Basdeo Panday 326, Stephen Maharaj 530, Clive Phill 841, George Bowrin 184, Trevor Sudama 148, Khrishna Gowandan 562, Dalip Gopeesingh 327, Eugene Joseph 67, Max Ifill 272, and Lennox Pierre 26.

Chapter 26

1. Kambon believed that many policemen were quietly sympathetic to the Black Power movement and that many of them signalled such by clandestinely putting up pro-NJAC posters in police stations.

2. His attorney general, Karl Hudson-Phillips, challenges this claim. As he opined, "When the Prime Minister on May 24th rationalized his silence by saying he was waiting for the population 'to dip his finger in the wound', that was a lot of nonsense. We had got away with it, as it were, and he was skillfully throwing the blame on the population" (as cited in Ryan 1995, 623). Williams may also have been less than honest when he indicated that there was a plot to overthrow the government that was foiled by developments he did not want to discuss.

3. The main activists were Darcus Howe, Wally Look Lai and Raymond Watts. Look Lai, however, insists that there was no articulated plan to seize the government. They were mainly concerned with preventing the army from repressing the Black Power movement.

4. Ironically, they would also have unknowingly killed the NJAC leadership, many of whom were on the boat being transported into detention at Nelson Island.

5. It was known, for example, that Shah and Lasalle had gone surreptitiously to Cuba.

6. Mohammed was contacted by Special Branch at 10 p.m. on the night preceding his scheduled departure date and told that he was to lead the delegation to the conference. He was not told why Williams was no longer leaving on the scheduled flight. He was, however, advised to offer no explanation but, if pressed, to say that Williams would be attending the conference later. Williams had cancelled two tickets to Jamaica, but did not indicate that it was he who was not travelling. He even went so far as to go to Piarco as if he were in fact travelling.

7. Robinson sued the *Bomb*, the newspaper that made the mischievous claim. According to Robinson, "I was charged with having sat at the Prime Minister's desk while he was

making his way to Jamaica and gone through his papers as part of the design for that coup. A newspaper . . . charged me specifically with that attempted coup . . . I took the newspaper to court, won the case and was awarded damages." (*Sunday Guardian*, 27 November 2005). Robinson's friends in the radical movement wanted him to walk out of the party rather than wait to be pushed. Robinson chose to stay on until 20 September 1970, when the general council attempted to discipline him. On that day, he walked out into the rain without a single other member following him. (See his resignation speech, 1986, 129.)

8. A Venezuelan reconnaissance jet did fly over Trinidad to take pictures of what was going on at Teteron in case there was a need to bomb the ammunition dump at the base, which had been captured by the rebels.

9. Raffique Shah claims that it was his men who told Williams to ask the Venezuelan warships to leave Trinidad's waters. As he wrote, "Two Venezuelan frigates were seen steaming in our direction. Prime Minister Eric Williams was alerted to this new development. Our message to him was clear. This was an internal matter and any attempt by foreign troops would be met with everything we had in our arsenal. Williams was told that if the Venezuelans or other foreign troops intervened in the impasse, they would be confronted by a united Regiment, if not a reunited Defence Force. Williams ordered the coast guard to race to the Venezuelans and ask them to leave our territorial waters. They turned back and averted what might well have been the bloodiest battle this country had ever seen" (*Trinidad Express*, 27 April 2000). For an account of the Chaguaramas negotiations, see Ryan and Stewart 1995.

10. These details were told to the author by officials of the Venezuelan embassy in Port of Spain and by John Humphrey, who saw Williams's handwritten letter requesting help from the Venezuelans.

11. Robinson said that Dennis Healey, the former minister of defence, had told him while he (Robinson) was in Italy discussing the establishment of the International Criminal Court that "Williams was virtually inviting the British to move back into Trinidad and Tobago". According to Healey, the British were appalled and embarrassed and sent telegrams enquiring what was meant and what was required. (See *Trinidad Express*, 25 October 1981.)

12. Dodderidge Alleyne, who was detailed to go down to Chaguaramas to negotiate with the soldiers, believes that there was a plane standing by to evacuate the ministers if his mission had failed. He was asked to phone Prevatt if things went wrong. He believes that he would have been left behind.

13. Williams would later suggest that persons selected to be candidates for elections should show a "balanced temperament" and not panic during crises as some of his colleagues did in April 1970.

Chapter 27

1. The vice chairman was P.T. Georges, former chief justice of Tanzania, and a member of the Appeal Court of Trinidad and Tobago. Other members were Mitra Sinanan, Hamilton Maurice, Gaston Benjamin, Solomon Lutchman, Reginald Dumas, Anthony Maingot, Michael de la Bastide, and Selwyn Ryan.

Chapter 28

1. Mohammed sensed that Williams might not be leaving and therefore did nothing to advance his candidacy, at least in public. He had in fact urged Williams to reconsider, telling him that the consequences of his withdrawal from politics could be fatal to the party, and could cause disintegration in the community. Kamal's position, as articulated in a letter to the secretary of the party, was that he would consider contesting the leadership only if it was certain that Williams was not going to return. Kamal's name was, however, formally advanced at a meeting of a Port of Spain party group and his nomination was seconded by none other than Williams's daughter, Erica.

Chapter 29

1. Curiously and improperly, Williams asked Cecil Dolly, a senior civil servant who had served as the secretary to the commission, to critique the report. Dolly politely declined and was consigned to the proverbial "doghouse".

2. The author was teaching in Uganda when he was summoned home to join the commission. Dr Anthony Maingot was based in the United States. Williams was pleased with a review that he had written of *From Columbus to Castro*. The author well recalls the tense and frigid environment that prevailed when Sir Hugh presented the commission's report to the prime minister. Here were two of the most distinguished and most senior officials of the state, barely able to communicate with each other. A.N.R. Robinson claims that he had tried to warn Sir Hugh and other commissioners (not the author) who privately sought his opinion as to what would happen to their report, but that "he did not foresee the summary manner of their dismissal" (1986, 178).

Chapter 30

1. As Williams complained, "Everything is a blasted prayer. They had better be careful that I don't call a prayer meeting in this country." In his view, which was correct, the definition of the march as a prayer was to circumvent the law (Baptiste 1976, 225).

2. Tate and Lyle was known to be providing Maraj regularly with substantial sums of money. The government also bought three hundred acres of land from Maraj for TT$1,000,000 in 1961, a price deemed excessive at the time. Williams also did whatever he could to make life comfortable for Maraj during his long illness.

3. The person who initially persuaded Panday to cut a deal with Williams and Caroni Limited was Kamaluddin Mohammed, who, on a flight to Toronto, to attend a meeting of the Commonwealth Parliamentary Association, persuaded a by-then "primed" Panday, whom he had invited to the first-class compartment of the aircraft, to sell out the cane farmers. Mahabir was merely the "centre forward" who finalized the deal on Williams's instructions.

4. In 1971, Robinson made the startling announcement that during a cabinet debate on the Industrial Stabilization Act which took place in 1965, there was a proposal to bring in Canadian troops to quell unrest. He claims he fought successfully against this proposal.

Chapter 31

1. Williams's injunction to his party reminded one of that given by Lord Rosebery to the Liberal Party in 1901: "The first advice I have to give to the Party is that it would clean its slate."

2. Williams was also told, "The country is in a terrible state and paralysis has set in; few but the faithful attend public meetings. Few are motivated to do conscientiously the jobs for which they are paid, whether in the private or public sector. . . . No one seems to care anymore what happens to the country, republic or no republic" (Ryan, "The Party Is Over", *Trinidad Express*, 30 May 1976).

Chapter 32

1. It would appear that Williams did not really know what he wanted, but wished to be free to take credit or avoid blame depending on the outcome of the negotiations. Negotiations with Texaco began in 1975, and the negotiators were told to "negotiate hard but accomplish nothing". The impression was created that Williams was playing some game with Texaco and was not really anxious to participate. Texaco was reportedly quite willing to alienate some of its land-based assets that were losing money, but was anxious to retain its refinery and its lubrication and desulphurization plants. It is worth noting that in April 1978, the minister of petroleum and mines admitted to parliament that the government was never interested in "fully acquiring all of Texaco's holdings in the country" (*Trinidad Express*, 22 April 1978).

2. Many of the acquisitions of the commanding heights of the economy that took place were motivated by emotional rather than economic calculations. The takeover of Shell Oil Company and British Petroleum, and of Caroni Limited and Orange Grove Sugar Company, represented attempts on the part of Williams to have the state own a share of the patrimony on behalf of the descendants of the peoples of slavery and indenture. Williams's appetite was whetted by the takeover of Shell and British Petroleum and he wanted to acquire Texaco as well, but was dissuaded from doing so by Prevatt who, advised by Bernard Primus and others, argued that Texaco was too old and too big to chew and swallow.

   Williams accepted the advice and gave instructions to stall the buyout of Texaco. It did not seem to matter much to Williams that he was taking over the carcasses of these oil companies who seemed quite anxious to sell their assets to the state and leave Trinidad and Tobago. The oil companies were concerned about the fact that their workforce was oversized and that their oil fields were drying up. Much the same held for the sugar companies, which had large workforces.

   It was in this context that Trinidad and Tobago became involved with Tesoro. According to Primus, who became chairman of the company, the connection was the result of a chance meeting between Sir Ellis Clarke, who was ambassador to the United States, and Tesoro. Trinidad, he said, was seeking a partner to help keep British Petroleum going. None of the established oil companies were interested in filling the gap left by the departure of British Petroleum. The loss of British Petroleum and Shell, however, meant the loss of jobs. (See chapter 42.)

Chapter 33

1. Williams had been talking about constructing a steel mill in Trinidad long before the OPEC revolution. In a 1965 speech in which he talked about development priorities, he observed that one might have to make a harsh decision. One might have to put emphasis on agriculture before sidewalks or on "encouraging an industry like the steel mill [which] Mr O'Halloran is working on or a huge hotel in Scotland Bay providing regular employment and bringing in foreign exchange. . . . Other things are needed, but they must be subordinated to the steel mill or the Scotland Bay hotel" (Williams 1965b, 129).

2. There was a great deal of curiosity about the relationship between Williams and Julien, who was Williams's energy czar and his dedicated "superman". Julien noted that he and Williams were never social or political friends, and that he always referred to him as "Professor Julien and I to him as Mr. Prime Minister. The truth is we worked well together, but he was extremely close to his then energy minister, Errol Mahabir, and we all worked well together" (*Express Business*, 22 May 2002). Julien noted that he "never really tried to get closer to him than he wanted to. I learnt a lot from him about political and economic history, and similarly, I explained to him the essence of technology. I needed nothing from him and he needed nothing from me. Our relationship remained healthy" (*Sunday Guardian*, 31 August 2003).

3. The original developers of the Point Lisas Development Company were Sydney Knox, Robert Montano, Krishna Narinesingh and Max Marshall.

Chapter 34

1. Williams made the remark at a meeting in response to a statement by Nathaniel Crichlow that the steelbandmen wanted his advice but did not want to get involved in politics. Williams also chastised the steelbandmen for their failure to deliver on tasks that were assigned to them. According to George Goddard, president of the Steelbandmen Association, "Dr. Williams was dressed in white short trousers, blue polo shirt and slippers. He was chain-smoking as he sat on the top of two tiers of steps between his library and another room. Dr. Williams' response to Mr Crichlow went something like this: 'Mr. Crichlow, I am going to be frank. I am afraid that you will not like what I am going to say, but I am going to be frank. You asked me to meet the steelband boys and we met three Sundays ago. We set up a sub-committee to meet here at my home last Sunday. We met, and assignments were given to some of you to report back here today. Where are the members of the sub-committee? Some of them are not here. But you bring a set of irresponsible people to take up two hours and ten minutes of my time talking foolishness, and if I don't put an end to it they will take up another two hours and ten minutes of my time talking more foolishness. I heard it said when I was in England that all Trinidad people like is old talk. I am not against the old talk, but not in my house.'

    "I chimed in: 'I second the motion.' That was the end of that meeting. As we were leaving, Dr. Williams was returning to his library" (Goddard 1991, 80).

2. Williams had made a special effort in the 1960s to encourage black contractors to

break into the construction industry, which was at that time dominated by white firms. A few of them succeeded in the area of housing construction on government projects, but most lacked the capitalization and experience and were disappointments.

Chapter 35

1. The list of one-time favourites who were "wounded in battle" included Dodderidge Alleyne, Eugenio Moore, Frank Rampersad, Cecil Dolly, Patricia Robinson, J. O'Neil Lewis, Luis Barradas, Horatio Nelson, William Demas, Ben Primus, Max Ifill, Carlyle Williams, Lushington Bowen, Harold Fraser, Joseph Herrera and John Buddhu, to name only a few. Only two senior public servants were known to have escaped being quarantined: Isidore Rampersad and Frank Barsotti.

2. According to Lewis, following Jamaica's withdrawal from the federation, he and William Demas sought out Williams, who was in parliament at the time. Williams asked them what they were doing there. Did they not have work to do? Lewis's reply was, "You are our work. We came to find out what you want us to do." "Do about what?" Williams asked. "Jamaica has left the Federation; what are you going to do now?" (Lewis 1991). There were other casualties at the Port Authority and other public utilities that were arbitrary and difficult to understand.

3. There was some doubt as to whether the document did in fact disappear. More than likely, it was "found" when there was a need to use it. It is widely believed that this document was submitted to the prime minister by Frank Rampersad, who was often at odds with Eugenio Moore, the then economic adviser to the prime minister and his chief "expediter".

4. In Paris, Williams had negotiated agreements with President Pompidou that France would assist Trinidad and Tobago in the development of its energy sector, in particular the construction of a gas pipeline and a liquified natural gas plant. In a letter to the French president in July 1973, Williams indicated that he had discussed the oil and gas industries in Trinidad and Tobago with special reference to the possible participation of French capital and expertise in the development of new projects in the marine areas off Trinidad and Tobago. "I had taken this initiative as the result of a conscious cabinet decision to encourage private enterprise from Western Europe, particularly France, so as to counterbalance the preponderance of United Kingdom, United States and Canadian investment in Trinidad and Tobago" (1975a).

5. Williams hinted that some of the individuals involved in the Convention Centre episode were involved in questionable practices. He told a PNM convention on 3 June 1976 that refurbishing of the centre cost over $8 million, which was much too much. He suggested that what occurred should be the subject of a commission of inquiry. He also indicated that members of the party were involved (*Trinidad Express*, 4 June 1976).

6. Alleyne wondered whether an innocent question that he asked at a meeting – "Who is guarding Trinidad and Tobago's interest in negotiation with Tesoro?" – led Williams to believe that he knew about deals being made with Tesoro through John O'Halloran and John Rahr. It is also worth noting that A.N.R. Robinson promised to drop a "bombshell" during the 1976 election campaign. Robinson declared that the "Alleyne affair held the key to the future of politics in Trinidad and Tobago". No exposé was

ever forthcoming. One was, however, led to believe that Alleyne was being scapegoated to save Williams.

A.N.R. Robinson has also speculated that the Alleyne/Moore/Williams crisis had to do with Williams's need to have a free hand to deal with Tesoro without having to look over his shoulder. As he said in his speech to parliament: "Next, it was the oil secretariat set up with much fanfare after much travel abroad in search of membership of OPEC. After our application for membership was turned down on two occasions, we were subsequently queried [by Williams] from a party convention: 'Who wants to get into OPEC anyway?'

"The public castigation and, presumably, disbandment of the oil secretariat and the discrediting of the Permanent Secretary to the Prime Minister and Head of the Civil Service, as well as the Permanent Secretary of the Ministry of Finance, has now effectively left all the top oil secrets in the hands of ministerial transients, one of whom for health purposes, we are told, has taken to travelling to Houston, Texas, on private petroleum corporation jets."

7. One former minister, John Donaldson, told the author that he brought forward a proposal to send Alleyne to Canada as high commissioner, since the latter was languishing in the wilderness. Williams scrawled "Rats arse" over the paper so violently that the paper got torn in the process. He also indicated that he did not want Alleyne anywhere near his home.

8. Errol Mahabir recalls having a confrontation with Moore, who was interfering with a staff member in his ministry without reference to Mahabir as the responsible minister. Incensed, Mahabir told Moore if he wanted to be in charge, he should fight elections. Moore apologized. Thereafter, the relationship between them was said to be cordial. Moore, however, had a reputation of being extremely haughty and arrogant, and of having been openly contemptuous and abusive to ministers. Williams helped to shape this attitude. He often described some of his ministers as "jackasses" and kept them waiting while he had extended discussions with officials, some of whom he regarded as his sons and sources of intellectual stimulation.

9. Williams's favourite methods of punishing those who fell out of his favour (whether minister or public officer) were withdrawal of speech for years on end, locking officers out of their offices and changing the locks, assigning them desks with nothing to do but read newspapers, posting them to Guyana or some other hardship post, removing them from boards, or blocking their reassignment to other posts. When the officer was needed once more, Williams would call him up to the house for drinks and a chat as if nothing had ever happened. No apology or explanation would be forthcoming.

10. One senior public servant, Frank Rampersad, was rude and arrogant enough to openly tell Minister Chambers, in a meeting, to "shut up". This was related to the author by Ben Primus, who was present at the meeting when this exchange took place.

11. Moore was referring to Dodderidge Alleyne, the permanent secretary to the prime minister, and to himself. Both played pivotal roles in relation to the army mutiny of 1970 and its aftermath. (See Ryan and Stewart 1995, ch. 13, 30.)

12. This was the term used to refer to the minister of finance in his capacity as the major shareholder in state-owned enterprise. Prior to the passage of Act No. 5 of 1973, which made the minister of finance "corporation sole", senior civil servants were required to

act on behalf of the state. To meet the legal requirements of the Companies Ordinance, which required such persons to hold at least one share of a company's assets, civil servants were usually required to acquire and hold shares on behalf of the state in their own right – a clumsy and dangerous arrangement. As "corporation sole", the minister of finance "owned and managed" the state sector, both macroscopically and in micro detail.

13. Williams's ad hoc approach to economic management drew posthumous comments from Dodderidge Alleyne. Alleyne did not consider Williams a "superhuman manager". He did, however, describe him as "resourceful" and innovative. "He did not start off by seeing how he could balance the budget in accounting terms, but in terms of what could help to take the country forward, how much would it cost, and how do we find money for that. He took that approach." Alleyne was referring mainly to the period before the OPEC "crisis" when money was a problem. Alleyne noted that many big decisions such as the acquisition of BWIA, the Bank of London and Montreal, and Shell were ad hoc, as was the decision to have free secondary education.

Chapter 36

1. Dr Michael Alleyne notes that whereas only seven of the junior secondary schools were completed by September 1972, eleven of them were actually in use in the academic year 1972/73 (1996, 102).

Chapter 38

1. Forbes Burnham expressed the view that Williams was "courageous" to restart the integration process so soon after the collapse of the federation.

2. Interestingly, Williams blocked the attempt on the part of the *Trinidad Guardian* to export surplus newsprint to the *Jamaica Gleaner*. He also blocked the attempt by a local conglomerate to purchase the *Barbados Advocate*. In his view, the regional media saw itself as part of an American-backed strategy to destabilize the region. "We are unwilling to inflict on a friendly neighbour the abuse to which freedom of the press is exposed in Trinidad and Tobago" (*Hansard*, 14 June 1976, 1544–48).

3. Williams was disdainful of Venezuela's thrust. As he said, "Nowadays so many people want to join the Caribbean that we are not surprised that one day we are going to make love to the señoritas, another day we are going to make love to – I do not know who is come to hug us up!" The eastern Caribbean states were understandably anxious to get as much assistance from Venezuela as they were getting from Williams, or more. It was thus not betrayal, but opportunism.

4. Ironically, some thirty years later, Venezuela is not only discussing production sharing arrangements with Trinidad and Tobago for oil and natural gas but has also forgiven Dominica's debt to it. Venezuela has also given Dominica EC$27 million to be used for various projects and to fund scholarships (*Trinidad Express*, 26 February 2003). (See also "Venezuela Asserts Claim to Bird Island", *Business Guardian*, 20 October 2005, and "Venezuela and Caribbean Energy Matters", *Business Express*, 23 February 2005.)

Chapter 39

1. Williams's written communication to Phillips about his decision was terse:

    Dear Mr. Phillips,

    This is to inform you that the Governor General, acting on my advice, is today appointing Mr. Hyatali Chief Justice, and I am so announcing in the House this afternoon. – Eric Williams

2. The author was often staunchly critical of Williams in his columns in the *Sunday Express*. However, no attempt was ever made to silence him. Williams's strategy was to invite the critic into the official tent.

Chapter 40

1. This chapter drew heavily on the comprehensive works of Gordon Rohlehr (1990, 1998), Louis Regis (1999, 2005), Hollis Liverpool (2003), and the author's previous essays (1979, 1999). Calypso anthologies and essays prepared by Rudy Ottley (1994), Zeno Constance (1996), and Keith Warner (1982) also proved useful.

    Rohlehr's most recent essay, "Change and Prophecy in the Trinidad and Tobago Calypso: Towards the Twenty-first Century" (2000), captures well the various contributions that calypsonians made to the ideological landscape in the twentieth century and which they continue to make. As he observes, "They function as messengers, warners, exhorters and at the same time bring hope and encouragement." Rohlehr opined that Sparrow's "assertive voice" dominated the 1950s and early 1960s and served to "legitimize the Doctor's benevolent dictatorship", while Chalkdust's "calypso essays" and his querulous voice "relentlessly identified the holes in the armour of the PNM" (1998).

2. According to Regis, Sparrow reported that he was called in for "consultations". He did not say who called him in, and one is left to speculate as to whether it was Williams or one of his messengers (1999, 7).

3. Williams often imitated the language of the calypsonian. As one weekly newspaper opined, "He was the best gun talker, picong slinger, opposition crusher of all" ("God Save Our Gracious King", *Tapia* 16, 23 May 1971, as cited in Regis 1999, 250).

4. Manley angered Trinidadians when he declared at a meeting in Kingston that oil money was flowing in Trinidad as if the country had taken a "dose of salts" (that is, a laxative). Manley later apologized, saying that he did not mean to upset Trinidadians. What he was saying was that one needed factors other than money to develop.

5. See his TV interview on TTT on 6 March 1979. Deosaran argued that prior to this "clarification", the calypso had a reasonable chance of being ambiguous enough to imply "inclusion of all races".

6. See Chalkdust's appreciation of Williams in "One Caribbean: Dr. Eric Williams on Carnival, Culture and Development", address given at the University of the Virgin Islands, St. Thomas, USVI, June 2003.

7. The calypso that perhaps best crystallized this desire for "regime change" was Gypsy's

"Captain, the Ship Is Sinking" (1986). Gypsy's calypso, which was absolutely brilliant, captured all the ambiguity and ambivalence with which Williams was regarded. He was a hero, notwithstanding his many flaws. The calypso is reproduced here because it serves as an apt requiem for the Williams regime. The words speak for themselves, except that Williams is misleadingly projected as the one without blame. The old captain was wrong-footed and betrayed by members of his nautical crew. This was clearly not the full story:

The "Trinidad", a luxury liner
Sailing the Caribbean Sea
With an old captain named Eric Williams
For years sailed smooth and free
But sadly Eric Williams passed away
The ship hit rough water that day
Somebody turn the bridge over
To a captain named Chambers
Mih blood crawl
Things start to fall
Hold mih head when a sailor bawl

Captain, the ship is sinking!
Captain, the seas are rough
We gas tanks almost empty
No electricity
We oil pressure reading low
Shall we abandon ship
Or shall we stay on it
And perish slow
We don't know, we don't know
Captain, you tell we what to do

The Trinidad, oh she was a beauty
With wealth that few surpassed
And in her day she sailed majestically
There were few in her class
Faithfully she fulfilled her sailors' needs
Some were overpowered by greed
And so they pilfered slow
Some took by bulk and go
Now she looks dull, she's at a lull
She can barely sit on her hull

The Trinidad, in her days of sailing
She was a friend to one and all
She never once hesitated
To answer all SOS calls
And yes, well she always did her best
To help out those in distress

Now it's so sad to see, she's in difficulty
Some she helped, jeer, some of them cheer
And sarcastically declare

Now there's a lot of fingers pointing
Suspicion is running strong
Who's to be blamed for all her failures
Who's to be blamed for doing her wrong
But please remember I'm warning you
For thirty years she had the same crew
Who hold the keys to her vault, so we know who's at fault
Now it's up to you, it's up to me
To make her worthy to go back to sea

And so I see this Nation
Heading in the wrong direction
The Nation sinking in corruption
Old and young, rich and poor, everyone in confidence there's a leak
Aboard the ship of the mighty and meek
With them attitudes you might get sick
And end up like the Titanic

They have no discipline, little tolerance
So their production can't support their Independence
All they have is this party mentality
From in '56 and the days of Dr. Willie
Since 1970 I and I notice
Oh jah! Trini running last in they consciousness
In partying and feteing they stay the hardest
But Trini gone through in they consciousness

Chapter 42

1. Interestingly, when the first DC-9 aircraft arrived at Piarco, Trinidad, in 1976, Williams went to Piarco in person to receive it. He not only named the plane after Trinidad's 100-metre gold medalist, Halsey Crawford, but gauchely waved the cheque before handing it over to representatives of McDonnell Douglas Corporation. It was at this encounter that he allegedly made the famous comment that "money is no problem". What he actually said, however, was that "money is not the problem". Other things were.

2. In his deposition, Rahr said that he "advised Detwiler [of Tesoro] that the deal would be a good one for Tesoro, and that US$2 million was a trifling amount in relation to the long-term benefits to a small company like Tesoro" (Robinson 2004, 152).

3. In his address on the energy crisis on 15 February 1974, Williams told the country that Tesoro had proposed building a refinery with a capacity of 300,000 barrels a day and a petrochemical complex involving thirteen specific plants, and had also pledged to undertake an aggressive programme of exploration and drilling, both on land and off-

shore. On 28 March 1974, Tesoro was asked for their views of the political climate in Trinidad and Tobago. It replied in a full-page ad published in the *New York Times*. Williams proudly quoted the ad in which Tesoro declared that "it was extremely confident about the stability of the Government of Trinidad and Tobago". Ironically, Tesoro also expressed optimism about its future in the area for a number of reasons, which included "the unquestionable integrity of the Government with whom our relations continue to be excellent" ("Energy Crisis", 8 May 1974).

4. The reporter who covered the investigations into the O'Halloran matter for the Canadian Broadcasting Corporation observed that the authorities in Trinidad seemed to be reluctant to dig up all the dirt on O'Halloran for fear that they might discover that the "George Washington of Trinidad was on the take" (as cited in Pantin 1990, 110–11).

5. There were other scandals that caused suspicion. On 19 September 1980, member of parliament John Humphrey called the names of four persons who were said to have formed a company to act as agents for the purchase of Lockheed 1011 aircraft in 1978. The group allegedly tried to outmanoeuvre another group that wanted to have the state purchase a DC-10 aircraft. Interestingly, the president of the senate ordered the media not to publish the names given. Humphrey threatened to challenge the senate president's ruling, but chose instead to give the initials of the persons involved outside of parliament. No legal action was ever taken against him.

6. Some relativists hold the view that corruption is not all of one type and that it is sometimes necessary to do questionable things to achieve other positive goals. Vittorio Craxi, a former prime minister of Italy, argued that the "Three Patriarchs of Europe" – Helmut Kohl, François Mitterand and Craxi himself – should not be judged by "petty" allegations about illegal slush funds, but by the "huge achievements" in Europe for which they were responsible. As Craxi argued, "There is a huge difference between taking money in exchange for favours and taking money for one's political movement, to build political stability. Kohl, Mitterand and Craxi not only built Europe; they also fought to resolve regional conflicts and bring peace to areas such as the Middle East. They made the world safer for us. . . . The financing of political parties needs to be reviewed. . . . Democratic politics has to be transparent and accountable, but the law can be too severe" (Pope 2001).

7. In his address to the PNM's annual convention in 1980, Williams had a word to say about the party's commitment to morality in public affairs, but only a fleeting and ambiguous word. He did not defend the party's record – perhaps he could not – but took comfort from the fact that Britain and the United States had had their own experiences with corruption and thus had little to say to anyone else about the problem. He in fact quoted one writer to the effect that "nineteenth century Britain and twentieth century Africa are so alike in these matters that Britain cannot speak censoriously to Africa" ("The Party's Stewardship, 1956–1980", in Sutton 1981, 431).

8. Williams on one occasion noted cryptically that "Trinidad and Tobago has been left out of the wave of corruption charges involving Prime Ministers, Presidents and even royalty. That could mean everything and nothing" (*Trinidad Express*, 7 October 1979). He was equally evasive when replying to Raoul Pantin's question as to whether he was "aware that a lot of people are saying your government is absolutely corrupt".

Williams's reply to Pantin was, "The Prime Minister does not know everything that goes on in the Government" (Pantin 1990, 102). He was just as cryptic when he told a PNM convention of Lord Clive of India who, during his trial, remarked that he "stood amazed by his own moderation" (Pantin 1990, 110).

9. O'Halloran's flamboyant lifestyle might well have provided vicarious fascination for Williams. The story is told that when O'Halloran announced in a gathering that a certain "French-creole" lady was made pregnant by him, Williams was happy. O'Halloran, he said, had "crossed the 38th parallel" by impregnating an "enemy of the PNM".

10. Many Afro-Trinidadians, however, continue to believe that Williams was above the sleaze that was so evident in the 1970s in particular, and that what followed later during the UNC regime was qualitatively worse. As calypsonian Chalkdust puts it, "For where Dr. Williams embraced morality and good taste, today they replace that good taste with race." Calypsonian the Mighty Penguin also absolves Williams, who was seen as too much of a softie. As Penguin sang,

> You know how I was a softie
> And fraid to give men jail
> Well I hope somebody
> Lock up some of them tail.

Indo-Trinidadians are more inclined to convict Williams.

Chapter 43

1. The details of what happened on the last weekend of Williams's life are told meticulously by Boodhoo (2001) and need not be fully repeated here.

Chapter 44

1. Mahabir recalls dining with Williams during a visit to Japan. Williams requested that the attendant violinist play the theme from Limelight, "I'll Be Loving You Always". Midway through the rendition, Williams began to sob. On enquiring as to what was wrong, Mahabir was told that that was the song that Williams and his second wife, Soy, had first danced to.

    Another anecdote told by Mahabir reveals Williams's rudeness and sense of humour. He was smoking a pipe in a Japanese restaurant when a clutch of red hot tobacco fell threateningly on his trousers. An attendant geisha rushed to his assistance and sought to extinguish the fire by brushing the offending tobacco off his trousers. To Mahabir's surprise, Williams pushed away the lady. When asked why he had responded so brusquely, Williams explained that "She was close to reaching the point of no return!"

2. Following a meeting in Antigua that went badly, Norman Manley confided to Theodore Sealey, editor of the *Jamaica Gleaner*, that he had just received a letter from Williams, and that "Nobody, nobody, but nobody in my life has been as rude to me as he has been in this letter" (Sealey 1991, 201).

3. Mahabir noted that he was to have been appointed minister of education, but that

Williams was advised that he should not put an Indian in that ministry because it was already infested with too many Indians. He was assigned health, which he preferred. Patrick Solomon was placed in education. One suspects, however, that Williams did so primarily because he wanted to appease the Catholics by placing a church-going Catholic in that ministry. Solomon got on well with Archbishop Finbar Ryan.

4.   Interestingly, Mahabir tells us that in the first administration, Sir Arthur Lewis vetted all ministerial proposals: "Lewis of course had no decision-making ability, but both he and Teodoro Moscoco of Puerto Rico were our consultants on Development Plans. The final decisions rested with Cabinet, although the stamp of Williams was indelibly imprinted on the outcome" (Mahabir 1978, 51).

5.   There was, however, one particular incident involving Solomon that Mahabir recalls. Shortly after the election campaign of 1956, a doctor advised Williams to take four weeks' leave. Williams exploded when he saw Solomon sitting in his chair as deputy prime minister. "'Sick leave! Sick leave! What the hell do you take me for? A blasted civil servant? Besides, I suspect your concern about me!' said Williams, spitting out his words with vicious emphasis. We were all astounded" (Mahabir 1978, 72–73).

Interestingly, Williams did trust Solomon's loyalty. According to Mahabir, Williams at one time had plans to go to the federal level. He told him that he (Mahabir) and Williams "will go Federal. Pat can look after things here" (Mahabir 1978, 77). Williams also relied on Solomon to negotiate with the Colonial Office on constitutional reform and on radiation at a time when he was suspicious of the loyalty of Montano and Mahabir on these issues. Mahabir smirked that Williams was seeking to transform Trinidad into a "clown colony". He considered the radiation "scare" a smoke screen and a "red herring".

6.   A.N.R. Robinson advised the author that Solomon was not brought back not because of pressure from the party but because Robinson did not accept Williams's invitation to act as prime minister in his absence.

7.   Robinson blamed James for creating a personality cult around Williams. He also denied that his relationship with Williams had anything to do with his wife being put in cold storage by Williams. He also has a somewhat different version as to why Solomon was recalled to office. Williams, he said, had to leave the country, and asked him to act as prime minister. He duly considered the offer but declined (in writing), giving as his reason the problems he was experiencing in the Ministry of Finance with respect to the finance bill. Solomon was not aware of this aspect of the matter and ascribed his recall to pressure brought by his constituency (interview with A.N.R. Robinson, December 2005).

8.   Williams himself admitted that he was ill (he suffered from diverticulosis and diabetes, among other things), and expressed "happiness that he was able to address Parliament during the debate on constitutional reform" (*Hansard*, 5 March 1976, 660).

Chapter 45

1.   Williams makes a cryptic observation about his father's "three great expectations". One was that his wife's father, Jules Boissière, would be a beneficiary of the will of his father, Monsieur Jean Nicholas de Boissière, the French-creole baron of Champs

Elysées, Maraval. Jules was the mulatto son of Jean Nicholas and a black Trinidadian woman. Eliza, Jules's second child, brought up her eleven brothers and sisters while still a teenager, and considered herself a member of the Boissière family. The story, as told by Gèrard Besson (1988) and Michael Pocock (1993), is that Eliza and Henry were "victims of the will", in that her father was not given the bequest ($4,000) that was left him by his father. Besson argues that his family experiences help to explain the "chip" on Williams's shoulder and his political hostility to the white French-creole "massas". Besson may well be exaggerating the impact of the "will" on Williams's posture towards the French creoles. Williams was always careful to point out that "massa" was not a racial term and that there were black massas and Indian ones (sahibs) as well.

2. Interestingly, Boodhoo (2001, 132) compared Williams's political behaviour to that of Fidel Castro, whose energy level was legendary and who made heavy demands on his subordinates for efficiency and discipline. Boodhoo suggests, but does not assert unequivocally, that Williams was a "manic-depressive". As he writes, "This type of personality oscillates through a cycle from mania to depression. Of such leaders, it has been noted that when manic, they overwhelm those around them with their massive energy and a flood of instructions about all the things that must be done at once. Everything is a crisis." Boodhoo advised the author that although he gleaned from some of his interviews that Williams was bipolar, he did not have firm evidence or the requisite training to make an unequivocal claim to that effect.

3. Mahabir drew particular attention to Williams's treatment of C.L.R. James, Williams's "spiritual father"; he believed that treatment must have led many to wonder what Williams would do to them when their turn came: "To retain power, would Williams not continue to be completely ruthless to the point of being unresponsive to the chords of 30 years of friendship? These are some of the questions that caused a shudder in some who, even while they were objects of current favours, feared the unpredictable day of doom" (1978, 69–72).

4. In our discussions about my book *Race and Nationalism in Trinidad and Tobago*, Mahabir once chided me for always trying to find rational explanations for whatever Williams did. In his view, Williams was a clever actor who understood the need for strategic *coups de théâtre*. Like Deosaran, Mahabir explains much of Williams's behaviour in Lasswellian terms. Williams was described as a "power wielder who sought and used power as a means of compensation for feelings of deprivation" (1978, 67–68). In this view, Williams was the brilliant but psychiatrically flawed genius hero for whom the exercise of power was a form of self-medication for the poisoned wounds that deformed his personality. Politics was a way of letting his enemies, both shadowy and real, "have it" (a famous and much-used Williams phrase), no matter who or what else was hurt collaterally in the process.

5. One of the medical practitioners interviewed recalled a discussion that he had with a number of professional colleagues, including Mahabir and Elton Richardson, during a luncheon meeting of the medical association in 1962. The discussion centred on the question of whether Williams should be certified as mentally ill and warded.

6. The reasons put forward for Williams's resignation from office in 1973 are varied, but there is little doubt that he was deeply depressed when he stepped down. His "Farewell Address" to the party is an extremely weepy document in which Williams complains

about being the "lone voice in the wilderness" on key matters such as Caribbean integration, corruption, social discipline and other pathologies. It might be pertinent here to quote the statement of Ferdie Ferreira, who was a close associate of Williams prior to the events of 1973, which Ferreira considered the "most disgraceful in the life of the party". As Ferreira recalled, "My personal view is that after 1973, Dr. Williams began to deteriorate. He isolated himself; there are no two ways about it. He had not been in his constituency for the whole period of 1976 to 1981. He wasn't going anywhere. He never even went to South Port of Spain. He started putting distance between himself [and the party] and he put up this big tall wall saying that people were peeping at him from the Hilton. He was a major case of paranoia. And he was certainly not the same person that we knew prior to 1973.

"He would come to the Parliament, and he would sit and he would say nothing. He would come to Party meetings, stay for some time and leave. So he instilled a certain amount of fear in the Party. It was not only the Parliament, or Caribbean leaders, but the Party, and Party members knew it. . . . The architect of his protection and to me one of the strongest human beings I ever met in my life (I don't know who God made him with) is this guy you call Prevatt. . . . In the last days I spent in the Party, Boysie Prevatt was certainly more articulate than Williams in the General Council and the Central Executive. I cannot speak about the Cabinet, because I was never in it. . . . He was the person that kept the Party together. Williams was isolating himself; nobody could see him except a few members of the Cabinet; but the Party people could not" ("Eric Williams in Retrospect", symposium, April 1991).

7. What Post and Robbins say of paranoia, "the most political of all mental illnesses", seems to have application in this case: "Paranoids tend to be rigid and unwilling to compromise. In a new situation, they tend to lose sight of the context as they conduct a narrowly focused search for confirmation of their biases and disregard contrary evidence. Trying to breach the rigidity of the paranoid can produce unfortunate consequences. Well-meaning attempts to reassure or reason with them will usually provoke anger, and the helpful person can even become the object of suspicions and be seen as disloyal. The paranoid's hyper vigilance and readiness to retaliate often generate fear and uneasiness in others. People tread lightly and carefully around a paranoid, walking on eggshells lest they provoke anger.

"The paranoid leader's view of his adversary is strong and central. He sees the world as full of conflict and the adversary as evil, an immutable threat to his and the national interest. Thus, in a crisis situation, the paranoid leader will not see his adversary as eager to avoid conflict, but rather will attribute malevolent motivations, will construct a worst-case scenario. This conviction that persuasion and compromise are impossible in turn pushes the paranoid to pre-emptive action" (Post and Robbins 1993, 51–52).

8. Ministers were known to enquire of senior public servants who were close to Williams what his mood was if they had to interact with him. Some jokingly said they checked to see on what side of his mouth his cigarette was lodged in order to assess his disposition.

9. It is of course obvious that those who suffer from bipolar disorders do not all achieve greatness. Among the "immortals" who suffered from diseases that enhanced their creativity were Dante, Michelangelo, Byron, T.S. Eliot, Dickens, Walter Scott, Blake,

Flaubert, Poe, D.H. Lawrence, Emerson, Faulkner, Hemingway, Virginia Woolf, Ibsen, Cézanne, Matisse, Picasso, van Gogh, Jackson Pollock, Goya, Tennessee Williams, Joyce, Styron, Conrad, Kafka, Schumann, Chopin, Handel, Mahler, Rachmaninoff, Mozart, Charlie Mingus, Berlin, Cole Porter, Nietzsche, Einstein, to name but a few. Opinions, however, differ among psychiatrists and artists themselves as to which comes first, mental disorder or artistic and intellectual creativity. Are people with mental illness drawn to certain callings that incline them to seek to express themselves in particular ways, or is it that certain professions, such as politics, magnify latent symptoms of mental illness? Is excess creativity brought on by disease or is disease transformed by creativity? (For discussion of these issues, see Sandblom 1992.)

References

Achebe, Chinua. 1985. *The Trouble with Nigeria*. London: Heinemann.

Allahar, Anton, ed. 2001. *Caribbean Charisma*. Kingston: Ian Randle.

Alleyne, Doddridge. 1999. "Oral Reminiscences". *Caribbean Issues* 3, no. 2.

Alleyne, Michael. 1996. *Nationhood from the School Bag: A Historical Analysis of the Development of Secondary Education in Trinidad and Tobago*. New York: OAS.

Ballah, Lennox. 1982. "Report of the Committee Appointed by Cabinet to Review the Entire Programme of Government Arrangements" [typescript].

Baptiste, Fitzroy. 1999. "The Federal Process in the West Indies as Seen by the United States 1947–1962". *Social and Economic Studies* 48, no. 4.

———. 2005. "The Emergence of Eric Williams and the PNM in Trinidad and Tobago Politics as Gleaned from US State Department Records, 1952–1956". Paper presented to 39th Annual Conference of the Association of Caribbean Historians, Cartagena, Colombia, 9–16 May 2005.

Baptiste, Owen, ed. 1976. *Crisis*. Trinidad: Inprint Caribbean.

Barsotti, Frank. 1991. "Williams in Retrospect" [typescript]. Paper presented to the symposium "Eric Williams in Retrospect: The Williams Legacy Ten Years Later". Institute for Social and Economic Research, University of the West Indies, St Augustine, Trinidad and Tobago, April 1991.

Barrow, R.H. 1967. *Plutarch and His Times*. London: Chatto and Windus.

Basdeo, Sahadeo, and Graeham Mount. 2001. *The Foreign Relations of Trinidad and Tobago*. Port of Spain: Lexicon.

Baudrillard, Jean. 1997. "The Illusion of the End". In *The Postmodern History Reader,* edited by Kenneth Jenkins. London: Routledge.

Bauer, P.T. 1981. *Equality, the Third World and Economic Delusion*. London: Weidenfeld and Nicholson.

Beard, Charles. 1956. *An Economic Interpretation of the Constitution*. Princeton, NJ: Princeton University Press.

Berlin, Isaiah. 2006. *Political Ideas in the Romantic Age*. Princeton, NJ: Princeton University Press.

Besson, Gèrard. 1988. "The Adjustment of a French Creole Family to the Post Emancipation Period" [typescript].

Besson, Gèrard, and Bridget Brereton. 1992. *The Book of Trinidad*. Port of Spain: Paria Publications.

Best, Lloyd. 1965. "From Chaguaramas to Slavery?". *New World Quarterly* 2, no. 1 (Dead Season).

———. 1970. *Black Power and National Reconstruction*. Tunapuna: Tapia House Group.

———. 2004. "Economic Theory and Economic Policy in the 20th Century West Indies". *Integrationist* 2, no. 1 (June).

Bishop, C. 1985. Report of the Joint Ministry /Union DEWD Monitoring Committee, Ministry of Planning, Trinidad and Tobago.

Boodhoo, Ken, ed. 1986a. *Eric Williams: The Man and the Leader*. Lanham, MD: University Press of America.

———, ed. 1986b. *My Father: Interviews with Erica Williams-Connell*. New York: University Press of America.

———. 1998. "The Caribbean Vision of Dr. Eric Williams". *Caribbean Issues* 8, no. 1.

———. 1999. "Eric Williams: The Myth and the Man". *Caribbean Issues* 8, no. 2.

———. 2001. *The Elusive Eric Williams*. Kingston: Ian Randle.

Boyke, Roy, ed. 1972. *Patterns of Progress*. Port of Spain: Key Publications.

Braveboy, Jacqueline. 1973. "The Venezuela–Guyana Boundary Dispute: A Study in Conflict Resolution" [MSc thesis, typescript]. St Augustine, Trinidad and Tobago: Institute of International Relations, University of the West Indies.

Brereton, Bridget. 1999. "Eric Williams: Anti-Colonial Historian". In *Enterprise of the Indies*, edited by George Lamming. Port of Spain: The Trinidad and Tobago Institute of the West Indies.

Brewster, Havelock. 1967. "The Sugar Industry, Our Life and Death". *New World Pamphlet*, no. 4.

Brown, Andrew. 1983. *A New Companion to Greek Tragedy*. Bekenha, UK: Croom Helm.

Buhle, Paul. 1988. *CLR James: The Artist as Revolutionary*. London: Verso Books.

Campbell, Carl. 1996. "Williams versus Hammond 1946: The Nationalist Agenda in Education". Paper presented to the Conference on Capitalism and Slavery: Fifty Years Later. University of the West Indies, St Augustine, Trinidad and Tobago, 24–28 September 1996.

Carrington, Selwyn. 1991. "Capitalism and Slavery: The West Indian Response to Abolition and Its Place in the Historiographical Literature" [typescript]. Paper presented to the symposium "Eric Williams in Retrospect: The Williams Legacy Ten Years Later". Institute for Social and Economic Research, University of the West Indies, St Augustine, Trinidad and Tobago, April 1991.

Cateau, Heather, and Selwyn Carrington, eds. 2000. *Capitalism and Slavery Fifty Years Later: Eric Eustace Williams – An Assessment of the Man and His Work*. New York: Peter Lang.

Chang, Jung, and John Halliday. 2005. *Mao*. New York: Knopf.

Clarke, Charles Arden. 1958. "Eight Years of Transition in Ghana". *African Affairs* 57 (January).

Coleman, James. 1988. "Social Capital in the Creation of Human Capital". American Journal of Sociology 94, supp.

Collymore, George. 2000. *In the Fires of Hope: A Biography of Ellis Clarke*. Port of Spain: J. Hernandez.

Constance, Zeno. 1996. *De Roaring Seventies: Introduction to the Politics of the Seventies*. Self-published. Jordan's Printing Service.

Cudjoe, Selwyn. 1983. *Movement of the People*. New York: Calaloux Publications.

———. 1993. *Eric Williams Speaks*. Wellesley, Mass.: Calaloux Publications.

———. 1995. *CLR James: His Intellectual Legacies*. Amherst: University of Massachusetts Press.

Dalley, F.W. 1947. *Trade Union Organisation and Industrial Relations in Trinidad*. Port of Spain: Government Printery.

Darity, William. 1997. "Eric Williams and Slavery: A West Indian Viewpoint?" *Callaloo* 20, no. 4.

Demas, William. 1965. *The Economics of Development in Small Countries with Special Reference to the Caribbean*. Montreal: McGill University Press.

Deosaran, Ramesh. 1981. *Eric Williams: The Man, His Ideas and His Politics*. Port of Spain: Signum Publishing Company.

———. 1986. "A Psychological Portrait of Power". In *Eric Williams: The Man and the Leader*, ed. Ken Boodhoo. Lanham, MD: University Press of America.

Donawa, Muriel. 1991. "The Williams Legacy: Ten Years Later" [typescript]. Paper presented to the symposium "Eric Williams in Retrospect: The Williams Legacy Ten Years Later". Institute for Social and Economic Research, University of the West Indies, St Augustine, Trinidad and Tobago, April 1991.

Drescher, Seymour. 1977. *Econocide: British Slavery in the Era of Abolition*. Pittsburgh: University of Pittsburgh Press.

———. 2000. "Capitalism and Slavery after Fifty Years". In *Capitalism and Slavery Fifty Years Later*, edited by Heather Cateau and Selwyn Carrington. New York: Peter Lang.

Elder, J.D. 1996. "Eric Williams and the Management of Culture Change, 1956–81" [typescript]. Paper presented to Conference on Capitalism and Slavery: Fifty Years Later. University of the West Indies, St Augustine, Trinidad and Tobago, 24–28 September 1996.

Farrell, Trevor. 1988. "The Development Experience". In *Trinidad and Tobago: The Independence Experience 1962–1987*, edited by Selwyn Ryan. St Augustine, Trinidad and Tobago: Institute of Social and Economic Research.

Ferreira Ferdie 1991. "Williams in Retrospect" [typescript]. Paper presented to the symposium "Eric Williams in Retrospect: The Williams Legacy Ten Years Later". Institute for Social and Economic Research, University of the West Indies, St Augustine, Trinidad and Tobago, April 1991.

Figueira, Daurius. 2003. *Simbhoonath Capildeo: Father of Hindu Nationalism in Trinidad and Tobago*. New York: Universe, Inc.

Franklyn, John Hope. 2000. "Williams at Howard University". In *Capitalism and Slavery: Fifty Years Later: An Assessment of the Man and His Work*, edited by Heather Cateau and Selwyn Carrington. New York: Peter Lang.

Ghany, Hamid. 1996. *Kamal: A Lifetime of Politics, Religion and Culture*. St Augustine, Trinidad and Tobago: Multimedia Production Centre, School of Education, University of the West Indies.

———. 1999. "Eric Williams and Bi-Cameralism in Trinidad and Tobago". *Caribbean Issues* 8, no. 2.

Goddard, George. 1991. *Forty Years in the Steelband*. London: Karia Press.

Gomes, Albert. 1974. *Through a Maze of Colour*. Trinidad and Tobago: Key Publications.

Girvan, Norman, and Owen Jefferson. 1971. *Readings in the Political Economy of the Caribbean.* Kingston: New World.

Gordon, Ken. 1999. *Getting it Write: Winning Caribbean Press Freedom.* Kingston: Ian Randle.

Gordon, Marilyn. 1999. "Oral Reminiscences". *Caribbean Issues* 8, no. 2.

Goveia, Elsa. 1964. "New Shibboleths for Old: Review of Eric Williams' *British Historians and the West Indies*". *Caribbean Quarterly* 10, no. 2 (June).

Government of Trinidad and Tobago. 1981. *White Paper on Natural Gas.* Port of Spain: Government Printery.

———. 1979. *White Paper on Caricom 1973–78.* Port of Spain: Government Printery.

Gramsci, Antonio. 1971. *Selections from a Prison Notebook.* London: Lawrence and Wishart.

Granado, Donald. 1987. Autobiography. Typescript.

Green, William. 1976. *British Slave Emancipation: The Sugar Colonies and the Great Experiment 1830–1865.* Oxford: Clarendon Press.

Hall, Kenneth, ed. 2001. *The CARICOM Community: Beyond Survival.* Kingston: Ian Randle.

Haraksingh, K. 1999. "Image and Icon: Indians in the Intellectual Perspective of Eric Williams". *Caribbean Issues* 8, no. 2.

Harris, Abram. 1936. *The Negro as Capitalist: A Study of Banking and Business Among American Negroes.* Philadelphia: Rumford Press.

Hart, Richard. 1989. *The Abolition of Slavery.* London: Community Education Trust.

Hempton, David. 1996. *The Religion of the People: Methodism and Popular Religion 1750–1900.* London: Routledge.

Henke, Holger. 2000. *Jamaica's Foreign Policy 1972–1989.* Kingston: University of the West Indies Press.

Hennessy, Alistair, ed. 1992. *Intellectuals in the Twentieth Century Caribbean.* Warwick University Caribbean Studies. London: Macmillan Press.

Herrera, J.H. N.d. "The Need for a New Administration". Typescript.

Heywood, Linda. 1998. "Eric Williams: The Howard Years". *Caribbean Issues* 8, no. 1.

Holt, Thomas. 1992. *The Problem of Freedom, Race, Labour and Politics in Jamaica and Britain, 1832–1938.* Baltimore: Johns Hopkins University Press.

Hudson-Phillips, Karl. 1995. "The Betrayal of the Spirit of 1956". In *The Black Power Revolution 1970: A Retrospective,* edited by Selwyn Ryan and Taimoon Stewart. St Augustine, Trinidad and Tobago: Institute of Social and Economic Research.

Humphrey, John. 1991. Statement made at the symposium "Eric Williams in Retrospect: The Williams Legacy Ten Years Later". Institute for Social and Economic Research, University of the West Indies, St Augustine, Trinidad and Tobago, April 1991.

Ifill, Max. 1986. *The Politics of Dr. Eric Williams and the PNM* [occasional paper no. 1]. San Fernando: People's Democratic Society.

Indian Association of Trinidad and Tobago. 1962. Memorandum on Draft Trinidad and Tobago Constitution.

Inikori, Joseph. 2000. "Capitalism and Slavery Fifty Years After: Eric Williams and the Changing Explanations of the Industrial Revolution". In *Capitalism and Slavery Fifty Years Later,* edited by Heather Cateau and Selwyn Carrington. New York: Peter Lang.

James, C.L.R. (a.k.a. W.F. Carlton). 1943. "The West Indies in Review: Recent Developments in the Caribbean". In *The New International.* June 1943. Reprinted as

"Eric Williams and the Negro Question" in *C.L.R. James and the Negro Question*. Jackson, Miss.: University Press of Mississippi.

———. 1961. *Federation: We Failed Miserably: How and Why?* [pamphlet]. Port of Spain.

———. 1962. *Party Politics in the West Indies* [pamphlet]. Port of Spain.

———. 1980 [1963]. *Black Jacobins*. New York: Allison and Busby.

———. 1964. "Parties, Politics and Economics in the Caribbean". *Freedom Ways* 4, no. 3 (Summer): 318.

———. 1965. *West Indians of East Indian Descent* [pamphlet]. Port of Spain.

———. 1993. "A Convention Appraisal". In *Eric Williams Speaks,* edited by Selwyn Cudjoe. Wellesley, Mass.: Calaloux Publications.

John, George, ed. 1991. *Williams: His Life and His Politics*. Port of Spain: Trinidad Express.

———. 2002. *Beyond the Front Page, Memoirs of a Caribbean Journalist*. St Augustine, Trinidad and Tobago: School for Continuing Education.

Joseph, Cuthbert. 1982. "Eric Williams and Education in Trinidad and Tobago". *Journal of Caribbean Studies* 3, no. 1 and 2.

Julien, Ken. 2005. "The Emergence of the National Energy Sector". Address to the Central Bank of Trinidad and Tobago. 10 June.

Kambon, Khafra. 1988. *For Bread, Justice and Freedom: A Political Biography of George Weekes*. London: New Beacon.

Kellner, Hans. 1997. "Language and Historical Presentation". In *The Post Modern Reader*, edited by Keith Jenkins. London: Routledge.

Kelshall, Candace. 1995. "Mutiny or Revolution". In *The Black Power Revolution 1970: A Retrospective*, edited by Selwyn Ryan and Taimoon Stewart. St Augustine, Trinidad and Tobago: Institute of Social and Economic Research.

Klass, Morton. 1961. *East Indians in Trinidad*. New York: Columbia University Press.

Kuan Yew, Lee. 1994. "A Conversation with Lee Kuan Yew". *Foreign Affairs*, March–April.

———. 2000. *Third World to First: The Singapore Story, 1965–2000*. New York: HarperCollins.

La Guerre, John. 1993. *Dilemmas of a Cultural Policy in Trinidad and Tobago* [typescript]. St Augustine, Trinidad and Tobago: University of the West Indies.

———. 1995. "The Indian Response to Black Power: A Continuing Dilemma". In *The Black Power Revolution 1970: A Retrospective,* edited by Selwyn Ryan and Taimoon Stewart. St Augustine, Trinidad and Tobago: Institute of Social and Economic Research.

———. 2000. *Basdeo Panday: A Political Biography*. Trinidad: Chakra Publishing House.

Lamming, George. 1998. "The Legacy of Eric Williams". *Caribbean Issues* 8, no. 1.

Lasswell, Harold. 1960. *Psychopathology and Politics*. Chicago: University of Chicago Press.

———. 1976. *Power and Personality*. New York: Norton.

Levitt, Kari. 2005. *Reclaiming Development: Independent Thought and Caribbean Community*. Kingston: Ian Randle.

Lewis, Gordon. 1963. "History of the People of Trinidad and Tobago: A Review". *Caribbean Studies* 3, no. 1.

Lewis, J. O'Neil. 1991. "The Williams Legacy: Ten Years Later" [typescript]. Paper presented to the symposium "Eric Williams in Retrospect: The Williams Legacy Ten Years Later". Institute for Social and Economic Research, University of the West Indies, St Augustine, Trinidad and Tobago, April 1991.

———. 1999a. "Oral Reminiscences". *Caribbean Issues* 8, no. 2.

———. 1999b. "From West Indian Federation to the Caribbean Economic Community". *Social and Economic Studies* 48, no. 4.

Lewis, Vaughn. 1986. "Issues and Trends in January in Jamaican Foreign Policy". In *Jamaica in the Seventies*, edited by Carl Stone and Aggrey Brown. Kingston: Ian Randle.

Lewis, W. Arthur. 1965. *The Agony of the Eight*. Bridgetown: Advocate Commercial Printery.

Liverpool, Hollis. 2003. "One Caribbean: Dr. Eric Williams on Carnival, Culture and Development 1986." [typescript]. Lecture delivered at University of the Virgin Islands, St Thomas, US Virgin Islands.

Mahabir, Errol. 1999. "Oral Reminiscences". *Caribbean Issues* 8, no. 2.

Mahabir, Winston. 1978. *In and Out of Politics*. Port of Spain: Inprint Caribbean.

Maingot, Anthony. 1994 *The United States and the Caribbean*. London: Macmillan Caribbean.

Manderson-Jones, R.B. 1990. *Jamaican Foreign Policy in the Caribbean 1962–1988*. Kingston: Caricom Publishers.

Manley, Edna. 1989. *The Diaries*. Kingston: Heinemann.

Manley, Michael. 1982. *Struggle in the Periphery*. London: Writers & Readers Publishing Cooperative.

———. 1987. *Up the Down Escalator*. London: Andre Deutsch.

Maurice, Hamilton. 1960. "Education Report of the Committee on General Education" [typescript]. Port of Spain.

Millette, James. 1995a. "C.L.R. James and the Politics of Trinidad and Tobago, 1938–1970". In *CLR James: His Intellectual Legacies*, edited by Selwyn Cudjoe. Amherst: University of Massachusetts Press.

———. 1995b. "Towards the Black Power Revolt of 1970". In *The Black Power Revolution of 1970*, ed. Selwyn Ryan and Taimoon Stewart. St Augustine, Trinidad and Tobago: Institute of Social and Economic Research.

———. 1998. "The Party of 1956: Eric Williams and Party Politics in Trinidad and Tobago". *Caribbean Issues* 8, no. 1.

Mitchell, Roy. 1995. "The Making of Makandal Daaga". In *The Black Power Revolution 1970: A Retrospective*, edited by Selwyn Ryan and Taimoon Stewart. St Augustine, Trinidad and Tobago: Institute of Social and Economic Research.

Mohammed, Kamaluddin. 1999. "Oral Reminiscences". *Caribbean Issues* 8, no. 2.

Mohammed, Patricia. 1996. "Midnight's Children and the Legacy of Nationalism in Trinidad" [typescript]. Paper presented to Conference on Capitalism and Slavery: Fifty Years Later. University of the West Indies, St Augustine, Trinidad and Tobago, 24–28 September 1996.

———. 2001. "A Very Public Private Man: Sketches in a Biography of Eric Eustace Williams", in *Caribbean Charisma*, edited by Anton Allahar. Kingston: Ian Randle.

Montano, Gerard (a.k.a. Mr. Q). 1995. "A Politician Recalls 1970". In *The Black Power Revolution 1970: A Retrospective*, edited by Selwyn Ryan and Taimoon Stewart. St Augustine, Trinidad and Tobago: Institute of Social and Economic Research.

Moore, Eugenio. 1995. "Reflections of a Public Servant". In *The Black Power Revolution 1970: A Retrospective*, edited by Selwyn Ryan and Taimoon Stewart. St Augustine, Trinidad and Tobago: Institute of Social and Economic Research.

Mordecai, Sir John. 1968. *The West Indies: The Federal Negotiations*. London: Allen and Unwin.

Naipaul, V.S. 1962. *The Middle Passage*. London: Penguin.

National Joint Action Committee (NJAC). 1970. "Slavery to Slavery". Typescript.

———. 1972. *Conventional Politics or Revolution*. San Fernando: Vanguard.

———. 1981. *An Analysis of the Economic System* [publication no. 2].

———. n.d. *People's Declaration of Policy for the Development of a New Trinidad and Tobago* [pamphlet]. Port of Spain: NJAC.

Neptune, Harvey. 2007. *Caliban and the Yankees: Trinidad and the United States Occupation*. Chapel Hill: University of North Carolina Press.

O'Shaughnessy, Andrew. 2000. "Williams as Historian". In *Capitalism and Slavery Fifty Years Later*, edited by Heather Cateau and Selwyn Carrington. New York: Peter Lang.

Osuji, Rose. 1995. "The Academic Achievement of Schools: An Empirical Study". *Caribbean Dialogue* 2, no. 2.

Ottley, Rudy. 1994. *Williams and Calypso in Trinidad and Tobago* [typescript]. Self-published, Arima Publishing.

Oxaal, Ivar. 1968. "'Chaguaramas to Slavery?' Review of Lloyd Best's 'Chaguaramas to Slavery'". *Trinidad and Tobago Index*, no. 3 (Winter).

———. 1968. *Black Intellectuals Come to Power: The Rise of Creole Nationalism in Trinidad and Tobago*. Cambridge, Mass.: Schenkman.

Padmore, Overand. 1999. "Federation: The Demise of an Idea". *Social and Economic Studies* 48, no. 4.

Palmer, Colin. 2006. *Eric Williams and the Making of the Modern Caribbean*. Kingston: Ian Randle.

Pantin, Dennis. 1988. "Whither Point Lisas? Lessons for the Future". In *Trinidad and Tobago: The Independence Experience, 1962–1987*, edited by Selwyn Ryan. St Augustine, Trinidad and Tobago: Institute of Social and Economic Research.

Pantin, Raoul. 1990. *Black Power Day*. Santa Cruz, Port of Spain: Hatuey Publications.

Parmasad, Kenneth. 1999. "Among a Recalcitrant People". *Caribbean Issues* 8, no. 2.

People's National Movement (PNM). 1966. *Major Party Documents*. Port of Spain.

Pocock, Michael. 1993. *Out of the Shadows of the Past*. Port of Spain: Paria.

Pope, Jeremy. 2001. "Funding Political Parties: Why? Who? How?" Paper presented to Commonwealth Parliamentary Association, Wilton Park, June 2001.

Post, Jerrold, and Robert Robbins. 1993. *When Illness Strikes the Leader: The Dilemma of the Captive King*. New Haven, CT: Yale University Press.

Pratt, Cranford. 2000. "Julius Nyerere: The Ethical Foundations of His Legacy". *The Round Table* 355: 365–74.

Primus, Bernard. 1976. "The Petroleum Industry in Trinidad". *Industrial and Commercial Report* 5, no. 2.

Putnam, Robert. 1995. "Bowling Alone: America's Declining Social Capital". *Journal of Democracy*.

———. 2000. *Bowling Alone*. New York: Simon and Schuster.

Queen's Hall. 1962. "Verbatim Notes of the Proceedings of the Meeting on the Draft Constitution". 25–27 April 1962.

Rampersad, Frank. 1988. "The Development Experience: Reflection". In *Trinidad and Tobago: The Independence Experience, 1962–1987*, edited by Selwyn Ryan. St Augustine, Trinidad and Tobago: Institute of Social and Economic Research.

Reddock, Rhoda. 1998. "Women, the Creole Nationalist Movement and the Rise of Eric

Williams and the PNM in Mid 20th Century Trinidad and Tobago". *Caribbean Issues* 8, no. 1.

Regis, Louis. 1996. "Williams and the Management of Cultural Change 1956–1981" [typescript]. Paper presented at the Conference on Capitalism and Slavery: Fifty Years Later. University of the West Indies, St Augustine, Trinidad and Tobago, 24–28 September 1996.

———. 1999. *The Political Calypso: True Opposition in Trinidad and Tobago 1962–1987*. Kingston: University of the West Indies Press.

———. 2005. "Reflections on a Legend". *Trinidad and Tobago Review* (4 April).

Richardson, Elton. 1984. *Revolution or Evolution: The Scholarship of Eric Williams*. San Juan, Trinidad and Tobago: Inprint Caribbean.

Robinson, A.N.R. 1986. "Selected Speeches from a Political Career 1960–86". In *Caribbean Man*, edited by Gregory Shaw. Port of Spain: Inprint Publications.

———. 2001. *The Mechanics of Independence*. Kingston: University of the West Indies Press.

———. 2004. *Presidential Papers and Other Essays*. St Augustine, Trinidad and Tobago: School of Continuing Studies, University of the West Indies.

Rodney, Walter. 1974. *How Europe Underdeveloped Africa*. Washington, D.C.: Howard University Press.

Rogers, D.W. 1975. *The Rise of the People's National Movement, Volume I*. Port of Spain: Ideal Printery.

Rohlehr, Gordon. 1970. "History as Absurdity, Review of Columbus to Castro". *Tapia* 1, nos. 11–12. (Reprinted in *Is Massa Day Dead?*, edited by Orde Coombs. New York: Anchor Books, 1974, 69–108.)

———. 1990. "Man Talking to Man, Calypso and Social Confrontation in Trinidad 1970–84". In *My Strangled City and other Essays*. Port of Spain: Longman Caribbean.

———. 1998. "The Culture of Williams: Context, Performance, Legacy". *Trinidad and Tobago Review* (March).

———. 2000. "Change and Prophecy in the Trinidad and Tobago Calypso Towards the Twenty-First Century". *Trinidad and Tobago Review* (April).

Rose, Euclid. 2002. *Dependency and Socialism in the Modern Caribbean: Superpower Intervention in Guyana, Jamaica and Grenada*. Boston: Lexington Books.

Ryan, Count Finbar. 1960. *Pastoral on the Roman Catholic Education of Youth*. Port of Spain: N.p.

Ryan, Selwyn. 1966. "The Struggle for Afro-Indian Solidarity in Trinidad and Tobago". *Index* no. 4 (September). St Augustine, Trinidad and Tobago: University of the West Indies.

———. 1971. "Restructuring the Trinidad Economy". In *Readings in the Political Economy of the Caribbean*, edited by Norman Girvan and Owen Jefferson. Kingston: New World.

———. 1972a. *Race and Nationalism in Trinidad and Tobago*. Toronto: University of Toronto Press.

———. 1972b. "Third World Unit". In *Patterns of Progress: Ten Years of Independence*, edited by Roy Boyke. Port of Spain: Key Publications.

———. 1977. "The Transition from Monarchy to Republic". *The Parliamentarian: A Journal of the Parliaments of the Commonwealth* 58, no. 3.

———. 1978. "Ideology and Leadership in Trinidad and Tobago". *Caribbean Issues* 4, no. 2.

———. 1979. "Voices of Protest". In *Trinidad Carnival*. Port of Spain: Key Caribbean Publishers.

———. 1986. "The Limits of Executive Power". In *Eric Williams: The Man and the Leader*, edited by Ken Boodhoo. New York: University Press of America.

———. 1988a. "Dr. Eric Williams, The People's National Movement, and the Independence Experience: A Retrospective". In *Trinidad and Tobago: The Independence Experience, 1962–1987*, edited by Selwyn Ryan. St Augustine, Trinidad and Tobago: Institute of Social and Economic Research.

———. 1988b. "Popular Attitudes Towards Independence, Race Relations and the People's National Movement". In *Trinidad and Tobago: The Independence Experience, 1962–1987*, edited by Selwyn Ryan. St Augustine, Trinidad and Tobago: Institute of Social and Economic Research.

———, ed. 1988c. *Trinidad and Tobago: The Independence Experience, 1962–1987*. St Augustine, Trinidad and Tobago: Institute of Social and Economic Research.

———. 1989. *Revolution and Reaction: Parties and Politics in Trinidad and Tobago*. St Augustine, Trinidad and Tobago: Institute of Social and Economic Research.

———. 1990. *The Pursuit of Honour: The Life and Times of H.O.B. Wooding*. St Augustine, Trinidad and Tobago: Institute of Social and Economic Research.

———. 1995. "The Chacacabana Negotiations". In *The Black Power Revolution 1970: A Retrospective*, edited by Selwyn Ryan and Taimoon Stewart. St Augustine, Trinidad and Tobago: Institute of Social and Economic Research.

———. 1997a. *Behind the Bridge, Poverty, Politics and Patronage in Laventille*. St Augustine, Trinidad and Tobago: Institute of Social and Economic Research.

———1997b. Calypso and Politics in Trinidad and Tobago 1996–1998. *Caribbean Dialogue* 3, no. 4 (October–December).

———. 1998. "Eric Williams and Party Politics in Trinidad and Tobago". *Caribbean Issues* 8, no. 1.

———. 1999. "East Indians, West Indians and the Quest for Caribbean Political Unity". *Social and Economic Studies* 48, no. 4.

———. 2003a. *Deadlock, Ethnicity and Electoral Competition in Trinidad and Tobago 1995–2002*. St Augustine, Trinidad and Tobago: Sir Arthur Lewis Institute of Social and Economic Studies.

———, ed. 2003b. *Independent Thought and Caribbean Perspectives*. St Augustine, Trinidad and Tobago: Sir Arthur Lewis Institute of Social and Economic Studies.

Ryan, Selwyn, and Anne Marie Bissessar, eds. 2002. *Governance in the Caribbean*. St Augustine, Trinidad and Tobago: Sir Arthur Lewis Institute of Social and Economic Studies.

Ryan, Selwyn, and Taimoon Stewart. 1995. *The Black Power Revolution 1970: A Retrospective*. St Augustine, Trinidad and Tobago: Institute of Social and Economic Research.

Samaroo, Brinsley. 1998. "The Race Factor in the Independence Discussions at Marlborough House, 1962". *Caribbean Issues* 8, no. 1.

———. 2000. "Preparing for Politics: The Pre-PNM Years of Eric Williams". Paper presented at Conference on Eric Williams, Wellesley College, April 2000.

Sandblom, Phillip. 1992. *Creativity and Disease: How Illness Affects Literature, Art and Music*. New York: Marion Boyars Publishers.

Sealey, Theodore. 1991. *Caribbean Leaders*. Kingston: Kingston Publishers.

Seecheran, Clem. 2005. *Sweetening Bitter Sugar: Jock Campbell, The Booker Reformer in Guyana 1934–1966*. Kingston: Ian Randle.

Seukeran, Lionel. 1991. "Eric Williams in Retrospect". Paper presented to the symposium
Eric Williams in Retrospect: The Williams Legacy Ten Years Later. Institute for Social
and Economic Research, University of the West Indies, St Augustine, Trinidad and
Tobago, April 1991.

———. 2006. *Mr. Speaker Sir.* Port of Spain: Chandabose Publications.

Shah, Raffique. 1995a. "Reflections on the Mutiny and Trial". In *The Black Power Revolution
1970: A Retrospective,* edited by Selwyn Ryan and Taimoon Stewart. St Augustine,
Trinidad and Tobago: Institute of Social and Economic Research.

———. 1995b. "The People Have Absolved Me". In *The Black Power Revolution 1970: A
Retrospective,* edited by Selwyn Ryan and Taimoon Stewart. St Augustine, Trinidad and
Tobago: Institute of Social and Economic Research.

Siewah, Samaroo, ed. 1994. *Lotus and the Dagger: The Capildeo Speeches.* Tunapuna, Trinidad
and Tobago: Chakra Publications.

Singh, H.P. 1962a. *Hour of Decision* [pamphlet]. Port of Spain.

———.1962b. *That Unitary State* [pamphlet]. Port of Spain.

———. 1965. *An Indian Enigma* [pamphlet]. Port of Spain.

Singham, Archie. 1965. "Three Cases of Constitutionalism and Cuckoo Politics: Ceylon,
British Guiana and Grenada", *New World Quarterly,* no. 1 (Dead Season).

Solomon, Patrick. 1981. *Solomon: An Autobiography.* Trinidad: Inprint Caribbean
Publications.

Solow, Barbara, and Stanley Engerman, eds. 1987. *British Capitalism and Caribbean Slavery:
The Legacy of Eric Williams.* Cambridge: Cambridge University Press.

Springer, H.W. 1962. *Reflections on the Failure of the First West Indian Federation.* Cambridge,
Mass.: Harvard University Press.

Stephens, John, and Evelyn Stephens. 1986. *Democratic Socialism in Jamaica.* Princeton, New
Jersey: Princeton University Press.

Stewart, Taimoon. 1995. "The Aftermath of 1970: Transformation, Reversal or Continuity".
In *The Black Power Revolution 1970: A Retrospective,* edited by Selwyn Ryan and Taimoon
Stewart. St Augustine, Trinidad and Tobago: Institute of Social and Economic
Research.

Sutton, Paul, ed. 1981. *Forged from the Love of Liberty: Selected Speeches of Dr. Eric Williams.*
Trinidad and Tobago: Longman Caribbean.

Tapia. 1973. *Power to the People: Proposals for a New Constitution.* Tunapuna: Tapia House
Group.

———. 1974. *Tapia's New World: Proposals for Trinidad and Tobago.* Tunapuna: Tapia House
Group.

———. N.d. *Black Power and National Reconstruction: Proposals Following the February
Revolution* [pamphlet]. Tunapuna: Tapia House Group.

Thomas, C.Y. 2001. "The Community Is a Big Paper Tiger". In *The CARICOM Community:
Beyond Survival,* edited by Kenneth Hall. Kingston: Ian Randle.

Tignor, Robert. 2006. *W. Arthur Lewis and the Birth of Development Economics.* Princeton:
Princeton University Press.

Warner, Keith. 1982. *Kaiso! The Trinidad Calypso: A Study of the Calypso as Oral Literature.*
Washington, D.C.: Three Continents Press.

Weber, Max. 1971. "The Three Types of Legitimate Rule". In *The Classic Statements,* edited
by Marello Truzzi. New York: Random House.

Williams, Eric. 1942. *The Negro in the Caribbean*. Washington, D.C.: The Associates in Negro Folk Education.

———. 1955a. *My Relations with the Caribbean Commission*. Port of Spain: Teachers' Economic and Cultural Association.

———. 1955b. *The Case for Party Politics in Trinidad and Tobago*. Port of Spain: Teachers' Economic and Cultural Association.

———. 1955c. *Constitution Reform in Trinidad and Tobago*. Port of Spain: Teachers' Economic and Cultural Association.

———. 1955d. *Economic Problems of Trinidad and Tobago*. Port of Spain: Teachers' Economic and Cultural Association.

———. 1955e. *The Historical Background of Race Relations in the Caribbean* [Public Affairs pamphlet no. 3]. People's Education Movement.

———. 1956. *The People's Charter: A Statement of Fundamental Principles*. Port of Spain: PNM Publishing Company.

———. 1957. "Race Relations in Caribbean Society". In *Caribbean Studies: A Symposium*, edited by Vera Rubin. Kingston: Institute of Social and Economic Research.

———. 1959. *From Slavery to Chaguaramas*. Port of Spain: PNM Publishing Company.

———. 1960a. *Responsibilities of the Party Member*. Port of Spain: PNM Publishing Company.

———. 1960b. *The Approach of Independence*. Port of Spain: PNM Publishing Company.

———. 1961a. *Massa Day Done*. Port of Spain: PNM Publishing Company.

———. 1961b. *Report on the Inter-Governmental Conference*. Port of Spain: Office of the Prime Minister, Trinidad and Tobago.

———. 1962a. *A History of the People of Trinidad and Tobago*. Port of Spain: PNM Publishing Company.

———. 1962b. *Speech on Independence*. Port of Spain: PNM Publishing Company.

———. 1963a. "International Perspectives for Trinidad and Tobago". *Le Monde Diplomatique*. Paris (August).

———. 1963b. *Documents in West Indian History 1492–1655*. Port of Spain: PNM Publishing Company.

———. 1964. *British Historians and the West Indies*. Port of Spain: PNM Publishing Company.

———. 1965a. *Two Lectures on Federation*. Port of Spain: PNM Publishing Company.

———. 1965b. *Three Speeches on the Public Service, the National Economy and the National Community*. Port of Spain: PNM Publishing Company.

———. 1966. *Capitalism and Slavery*. New York: Capricorn Edition.

———. 1969. *Inward Hunger: The Education of a Prime Minister*. London: Andre Deutsch.

———. 1970a. *The Chaguaramas Declaration: Perspectives for a New Society*. The People's Charter 1956 Revised. Port of Spain: PNM Publishing Company.

———. 1970b. *From Columbus to Castro: The History of the Caribbean 1492–1969*. London: Andre Deutsch.

———. 1972a. *Address to the 14th Annual Convention*. Port of Spain: PNM Publishing Company.

———. 1972b. "Patterns of Progress". In *Trinidad and Tobago: Ten Years of Independence*, edited by Roy Boyke. Port of Spain: Key Caribbean Publications.

———. 1972c. "The Purpose of Planning". In *The Crisis in Planning*, edited by M. Faber and D. Seers. Vol. 1. London: Chatto and Windus.

———. 1973a. "The Caribbean Community Treaty". Speech to the House of Representatives, July.

———. 1973b. "The Energy Crisis 1973–1974: Three Addresses by Dr Eric Williams". Public Relations Division, Office of the Prime Minister.

———. 1974a. "Speech on Constitution Reform". *Hansard* (13 and 17 December).

———. 1974b. "The University in the Caribbean in the Late 20th Century, 1980–1999". *Caribbean Educational Bulletin* 2, no. 1.

———. 1975a. *The Energy Crisis 1975: An Address to the Nation by Dr. Eric Williams, Prime Minister of Trinidad and Tobago at Point Fortin*. 11 April, 1975. Port of Spain: Government Printery.

———. 1975b. "Prime Minister's Proposals to Cabinet on Education". 18 September 1975.

———. 1975c. Statement by the Prime Minister of Trinidad and Tobago to 16th Session of ECLAC, Port of Spain, 6–14 May 1975.

———. 1975d. "The Threat to the Caribbean Community". Speech to a Special Convention of the People's National Movement, Chaguaramas, 15 June 1975.

———. 1976. "The Caribbean Community". Speech to Parliament on Prime Minister's Agreement. *Hansard* (14 June).

———. 1977a. "Speech to the House of Representatives on Caribbean Integration, December 1977". In *Forged from the Love of Liberty*, edited by Paul Sutton. Trinidad: Longman Caribbean.

———. 1977b. Speech at Formal Opening of Tunapuna Branch of the National Insurance Board. Trinidad and Tobago: Government Printery.

———. 1980. "The Party's Stewardship 1956 to 1980". In *Forged from the Love of Liberty*, edited by Paul Sutton. Trinidad: Longman Caribbean.

———. 1994. "The Making of Caribbean Man". Speech to PNM Convention 1979, edited by J. O'Neil Lewis. San Juan, Trinidad.

Williams, Eric, with Franklyn Frazier, eds. 1944. *The Economic Future of the Caribbean*. Washington, D.C.: Howard University Press.

Wong Sang, Joyce. 1999. "The Prime Minister's Best Village Competition". *Caribbean Issues* 8, no. 2.

Wood, E.F.L. 1921. *Report on His Visit to the West Indies and British Guiana*. London: CMD.

Wooding, H.O.B. 1974. *Report of the Constitution Commission*. Trinidad and Tobago: Arima Publishing.

Worcester, Kent. 1996. *CLR James: A Political Biography*. Albany: State University of New York.

Index

Hunt, Onemia, 11
Hyatali, Isaac, 649, 653

Ifill, Max, 374
Incas, 29
Ince, Dr Winston, 716–17
Independence, 299–316, 317, 446;
 Independence Day, 313–16; Marlborough
 House Conference, 306–13; Queen's Hall
 Constitutional Convention, 300–306;
Independent Labour Party, 70, 109
India, 27, 41, 178, 266, 369, 531, 594–95, 606,
 609
Indian immigration, 47
Indian community (in Trinidad), 47, 89, 114,
 122–29, 251, 303, 319, 343, 381, 444, 463,
 783–84
Indian National Association, 306, 307, 308, 320
Indonesia, 255, 495, 503, 505
Industrial court, 352
Industrial Development Corporation, 299,
 397, 540
Industrial policy, 113, 345, 493–523
Industrial Relations Bill, 655
Industrial Revolution, 39, 40
Industrial Stabilization Act, 351, 352, 353, 354,
 356, 372, 375, 508, 690
Industrial Stabilization Bill, 352, 655
Industrialization by Invitation, 340, 341, 345,
 537. *See also* Operation Bootstrap; Puerto
 Rican model
Industrialization strategy, 524–35
Infrastructural reform strategy, 512–23, 695
Inikori, Joseph, 38
Inniss, Clifford, 147
Insurance Act, 353
Integrity Commission, 465, 712–13
Inter-American Development Bank, 580, 620,
 621
International Monetary Fund (IMF), 535, 616,
 617, 622
Inter-Religious Organisation (IRO), 435–36,
 455, 696
Invaders (steelband), 739
Inward Hunger (Williams), 11, 46, 63, 70, 128,
 229, 264, 314, 357, 528, 686, 761
Iran, 530
Irois Bay, 190, 218
Iron and Steel Company of Trinidad and
 Tobago (ISCOTT), 499, 424, 526, 530, 532,
 699

Irrazabal, Carlos, 395
Israel, 547, 619
Irvine, James, 575
Italy, 497, 506

Jacobites, 11
Jagan, Cheddi, 51, 348
Jamadar, Vernon, 409, 414, 475, 476
Jamaica, 42, 43, 69, 79, 80, 81, 115, 118, 121,
 142, 186, 201, 209, 216, 221, 251, 253, 255, 301,
 313, 317, 362, 378, 384, 392, 394, 398, 448–49,
 466, 479, 508, 509, 510, 512, 559, 591, 616,
 618, 625, 629, 634, 637, 648, 654, 664, 668,
 670, 762; and the collapse of the West
 Indies federation, 232–38, 240–42; Jamaica
 referendum, 236, 240–42, 299
Jamaica Labour Party, 233, 238
James, C.L.R., 24, 28, 33–35, 43, 44, 55–57,
 66–67, 194, 196, 197, 198, 199, 204–5, 208,
 226, 228, 238, 265, 270, 294, 301, 305, 315,
 319, 329, 338, 345, 353, 359–80, 531, 590, 606,
 657, 738, 763, 768, 773; *West Indians of East
 Indian Descent*, 372–73
James, Selma, 44
Japan, 27, 497, 515, 609
Jenkins, Douglas, 152
Jiménez, Pérez, 692
John, George, 416, 431, 470–71, 487, 753,
 756
John John, 536
Johnson, Gerald, 36
Johnson Doctrine, 607
Jones, Earl, 550
Jones, Hugh, 23
Joseph, Cuthbert, 720
Joseph, Eugene, 374
Joseph, Roy, 76, 175,
Judicial and Legal Services Commission, 649
Julien, Inskip, 724
Julien, Ken, 526–27, 528–29, 530, 534, 566,
 568, 571, 717
Junior Chamber of Commerce, 597

Kamal (Mohammed), 98
Kambon, Khafra, 374, 375, 384, 652–53, 736
Kelshall, Jack, 374, 475–76
Kennedy, John, F., 223, 348–49
Kent House, 70
Kenya, 608,
Keynes, John Maynard, 565–66
King, Charlie, 121

King, Martin Luther, 739
King George V Park pavilion facilities, 548, 549–50, 555
Kirpalani, Ram, 433
Kitchener, Lord, 666, 671–73
Kuwait, 505, 531

La Brea, 704
Lamming, George, 54, 116, 590, 739
Lancaster House Conference, 236, 250
Land reform, 341–42
Lange, Ray, 300
Lasalle, Rex, 391
Laski, Harold, 23
Latin America, 348–49, 783, 785
Latin American Trade Association, 621
Laventille, 18, 264, 463, 536–42
Law of the Sea, 625, 633
Lee, Edward, 94
Lee, Dr Johnny, 717
Lee, Kendal, 742
Lee, Ulric, 98, 331, 742, 773
Leeward Islands, 79, 246, 255
Lennox-Boyd, Alan, 148
Leoni, Raúl, 623
Lequay, Alloy, 475
Levitt, Kari, 358
Lewis, Gordon, 47–48, 137
Lewis, J. O'Neil, 223, 237, 299, 544, 773
Lewis, Scotty, 588
Lewis, W. Arthur 21, 86, 111, 113, 238–39, 240, 242–43, 245, 253, 255, 589, 738
Liberal Party, 355, 377
Liberia, 608
Lindquist, Robert, 711
Liquefied natural gas (LNG). *See* natural gas
Little Carib Dance Company, 595
Little Eight, 246, 252
Liverpool, Hollis. *See* Chalkdust
Lock Joint, 698
Locke, Alain, 28, 30, 31, 80
Logan, Rayford, 30
London School of Economics, 23, 329, 687
London University, 589
Los Monjes Archipelago: Venezuela's claim to, 625
Lovelace, Earl, 403
Luke, Sir Stephen, 771
Luxembourg, 515

Macaulay, Lord, 40

Mack, Carlton, 651
Macmillan, Harold, 225, 240, 369
Macqueripe Beach, 555
Maestro, 670–71
Maha Sabha, 123, 124, 128, 129, 172, 304, 307, 317, 386, 584, 594
Mahabir, Dennis, 94, 95, 292, 415–16
Mahabir, Errol, 416, 423–24, 430, 437, 457, 471, 475, 538, 561, 705–6, 717, 718, 728–32, 740–41
Mahabir, Winston, 73–74, 77, 94, 95, 96, 97, 172, 180–82, 196, 215, 226, 229, 318, 330, 606, 698, 742–43, 744–46, 772–73; *In and Out of Politics*, 20; *The Real Eric Williams*, 330
Maharaj, Sat, 584, 729, 730
Maharaj, Stephen, 211, 374, 375, 475
Maingot, Anthony, 451, 452, 715–16
Malaysia, 352, 609, 657
Malaya, 206
Malone, Clement, 649
Management Development Centre, 540
Manley, Edna, 70, 760
Manley, Michael, 479, 617–18, 627–28, 629–30, 637, 654, 657, 739
Manley, Norman, 22, 51, 54, 66, 69–70, 72–73, 76, 86, 118, 121, 198, 216, 220, 233, 234–35, 237, 238, 348, 362, 760, 763, 764, 765
Manning, Patrick, 703
Manswell, James, 562–63
Mao Tse-Tung, 525
Maraj, Badhase, 119, 122, 129, 142, 146, 152, 172–73, 175, 183, 209, 268–69, 303, 315, 317, 380, 386, 410, 415, 456, 457, 461, 757
Marlborough House Conference, 306–13, 315, 320, 448
Marryshow, T.A., 51, 198
Mars, Jean Price, 590
Marshall, Bertie, 601
Martí, José, 594, 738
Martinique, 12, 590, 738
Marxists, 37, 39, 329, 370, 376, 379, 381, 391, 405
"Massa Day Done" campaign strategy, 272, 287–95, 368, 596
Mastana Bahar, 599
Matthews, Dom Basil, 90–91, 95, 739
Maudling, Reginald, 242, 245, 307, 309, 310, 313
Maurice, Hamilton, 250, 276, 451, 600

National Liberation Movement, 460
National Movement for the True
  Independence of Trinbago, 460
National Petroleum Company, 495, 500, 546,
  704
National Stadium, 600
National Sugar Company, 495
National Union of Freedom Fighters, 405,
  419–21, 460
Nationalization, 344, 494–95, 497, 498–99,
  507–8
Natural gas, 526–27, 529; pipeline project,
  548, 549, 550, 551, 803n4
Negro in the Caribbean, The (Williams), 31–34,
  63, 64
Nehru, Jawaharlal, 78, 121, 123, 124, 227, 531,
  594–95, 605; *Discovery of India*, 123;
  Glimpses of World History, 125
Nelson, David, 71–72, 330, 773
Neptune, Harvey, 48, 199
Netherlands, the, 515
Netherlands Antilles, 618
New World Group, 345, 374, 407
New World Quarterly, 370
New Zealand, 352
Newtown, 16
Nigeria, 255, 266, 369, 393–94, 504, 505, 530,
  531, 608
Nkrumah, Kwame, 78, 83, 121, 134, 200, 227,
  308, 347, 531, 594, 605, 656, 657, 686, 764,
  765, 783
"No Vote" campaign, 536
Northern Ireland, 255
Norway, 515, 531
Nunez, Clive, 374
Nyerere, Julius, 394, 395, 656, 657, 764, 765

Obeah, 18
O'Connor, Quintin, 106
O'Halloran, John, 289, 355, 360, 384, 559, 699,
  703, 705, 706–14, 720, 721, 724, 743, 744,
  745, 748, 750, 765
Oil industry, 110–11, 121, 340, 370, 372–73,
  382, 387, 433–35, 455, 458, 500–507, 529,
  531–32, 546, 558
Oilfield Workers Trade Union (OWTU), 106,
  151, 352, 353, 370, 375, 376, 381, 444, 455, 456,
  457, 500, 704, 705
Ombudsman, 450, 452
Operation Bootstrap, 30, 52, 493, 691. *See also*
  Industrialization by Invitation

Orange Grove Sugar Estates, 495, 500
Orebaugh, Walter, 776
Organisation of African Unity, 609, 634
Organization of American States (OAS), 361,
  619–22, 632
Organization for National Reconstruction
  (ONR), 721, 724, 725, 726, 727, 732, 734–37
Organization of Petroleum Exporting
  Countries (OPEC), 57, 430–31, 434–35, 440,
  506, 530, 558, 567, 647, 668, 708, 752
Organized labour. *See* trade unions
Ortiz, Fernando, 590, 596
Ortone, Egidio, 700
Osuji, Rose, 585
Oxaal, Ivar 91, 146, 284, 315, 367
Oxford University, 20, 23–27, 30, 40, 47, 68,
  69, 80, 329, 687, 760, 761, 764, 765, 768

Padmore, George, 64, 738
Padmore, Overand, 752
Pakistan, 125, 128, 266, 369, 609
Palés Matos, Luis, 590
Palo Seco, 704
Pan-Africanism, 247
Pan Trinbago, 603
Panama, 540, 711; Panama Canal, 763
Panday, Basdeo, 375, 455, 456–61, 474–75,
  476, 477–78, 483, 484, 486, 655, 701–3, 711,
  714, 720–21
Pantin, Anthony, 455
Pantin, Dennis, 531, 532–33
Pantin, Raoul, 651–52
Papal Donation (1493), 247
Paraguay, 620
Paris Club, 535
Parliament, 453, 468
Parliamentary Opposition Group, 139
Party of Political Progress Groups (POPPG),
  117–19, 122, 144, 149, 151, 269, 463, 765
Party Politics in the West Indies (James), 362
PAYE, introduction of, 167–68
Peasant proprietorship, 32, 111–12
Peat Marwick, 711
Pegasus movement, 600
Pemberton, 55
Penguin, 673–74, 682
People (weekly newspaper), 370
People's Charter, 493, 528
People's Cooperative Bank, 724
People's Democratic Party (PDP), 118, 122–29,
  146, 147, 149, 151, 319, 380, 765

Quan Yew, Lee, 656, 657–58, 689, 784
Quandros, Janio, 348
Queen's Hall, 299, 408
Queen's Hall Conference 1962 (constitutional convention), 300–306, 311, 446
Queen's Park Savannah, 282, 284, 600
Queen's Royal College (QRC), 18, 19, 22, 23, 24, 75, 94, 574, 576, 577, 588–89, 647, 741, 761, 768; Literary Society, 65

Race issues, 49, 84, 171, 176, 177–84, 204–5, 251–52, 262, 266, 271–72, 272–73, 274–75, 278–85, 288–93, 298, 302, 308, 317–21, 343, 349, 367, 375, 382, 391–92, 402–4, 424, 463, 473–74, 484–87, 595, 597, 649, 666, 677–78, 729
Radio Guardian, 494
Ragatz, Lowell, 30, 35, 36
Rahr, John, 706–7, 708
Rampersad, Frank, 496, 531, 532, 544, 710
Ramphal, Shridath, 635
Ramsay, James, 40
Rashtra Swayamsevak Sangh, 94
Rawlins, Pat, 588
Reality of Independence (Williams), 351, 686
Reece, Alan, 765
Regional Economic Committee, 69
Reid, Daniel, 439
Relator, 669, 679–80, 683, 726
Representation of the People Bill, 264, 749
Republican constitution, 441–54, 465
Rhodesia, 402, 474
Richards, Alfred, 75
Richards, George, 748
Richardson, Elton, 73–74, 93, 94, 95, 98, 753, 773
Richardson, Selwyn, 703, 708, 711, 730
Robinson, A.N.R., 98, 353, 354, 356, 385, 390, 392–93, 396–97, 398, 399, 405–7, 409–10, 413, 422, 462, 469, 474–75, 481, 482, 486, 494, 555, 667–68, 699–701, 703–4, 706–9, 711, 748, 750–51, 770, 771
Robinson, Patricia, 237–38, 355
Rochard, Father Garfield, 724
Rodney riots, 394
Rodney, Walter, 381
Rogers, De Wilton, 73, 89, 90, 92–93, 94, 98, 101, 330–32, 773
Rohlehr, Gordon, 50–51, 368, 660, 685
Rojas, John, 106, 151
Romain, Jacques, 590

Roman Catholic Church, 95, 130–35, 150–51, 176, 272–77, 289, 338, 400, 435, 762
Roosevelt, President, 186
Rose, Andrew, 98, 250, 251
Rosenwald Foundation, 30
Royal Bank of Canada, 383
Rudder, David, 659
Ryan, Archbishop Finbar, 274

St Andrew's University, 575
St Augustine Research Associates, 583, 734
St Catherine Society at Oxford, 23, 30
St George County, 263
St George County Council, 254
St Kitts–Nevis, 71, 252, 616, 625
St Lucia, 253, 616, 738
St Mary's College
St Patrick, 578
St Vincent, 18, 637
Salkey, Andrew, 590
Samaroo, Brinsley, 55, 125, 127
Sampath, Martin, 181
Sampson, Valda, 89
San Fernando, 77, 263, 296, 380, 407, 578
Sanatan Dharma Maha Sabha. *See* Maha Sabha
Santo Domingo, 348, 607, 634
Schiff, Stanley, 152
Schools, 574–89; shift system, 581–83
Scotland, 575
Sealey, Theodore, 769–70
Seamen and Waterfront Workers Trade Union, 270
Second World War, 78, 198, 222
Sedition Act, 427
Seigler, Timothy, 215
Seignoret, Eustace, 94
Selvon, Samuel, 590
Senegal, 608
Senghor, Léopold, 594, 595
Seukeran, Lionel, 142, 190, 201, 203, 211, 273, 284, 295, 386, 397, 751, 753, 757–58
Shah, Raffique, 390–91, 455, 456, 484
Shand, Eden, 708, 711
Shanty Town, 384, 536
Shearer, Hugh, 394, 591
Shell Oil Company, 495, 499, 502, 505, 529, 546, 704, 709, 710
Sherlock, Philip, 575
Short Pants, 674–75
Shorty, 674